Less managing. More teaching. Greater learning.

INSTRUCTORS...

Would you like your **students** to show up for class **more prepared**?
(Let's face it, class is much more fun if everyone is engaged and prepared...)

Want an **easy way to assign** homework online and track student **progress**?
(Less time grading means more time teaching...)

Want an **instant view** of student or class performance?
(No more wondering if students understand...)

Need to **collect data and generate reports** required for administration or accreditation?
(Say goodbye to manually tracking student learning outcomes...)

Want to **record and post your lectures** for students to view online?
(The more students can see, hear, and experience class resources, the better they learn...)

With **McGraw-Hill's** *Connect,*™

INSTRUCTORS GET:

- Simple **assignment management**, allowing you to spend more time teaching.

- **Auto-graded** assignments, quizzes, and tests.

- **Detailed visual reporting** where student and section results can be viewed and analyzed.

- Sophisticated **online testing** capability.

- A **filtering and reporting** function that allows you to easily assign and report on materials that are correlated to learning objectives and Bloom's taxonomy.

- An easy-to-use **lecture capture** tool.

- The option to **upload course documents** for student access.

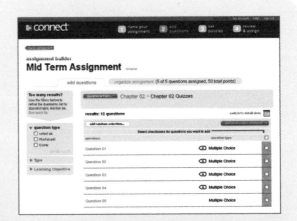

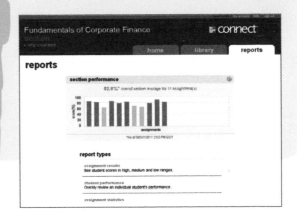

Eighth Canadian Edition

Fundamentals of
Corporate Finance

STEPHEN A. ROSS
Massachusetts Institute of Technology

RANDOLPH W. WESTERFIELD
University of Southern California

BRADFORD D. JORDAN
University of Kentucky

GORDON S. ROBERTS
Schulich School of Business, York University

McGraw-Hill
Ryerson
Connect. Learn. Succeed.

ISBN-13: 978-0-07-105160-6
ISBN-10: 0-07-105160-0

1 2 3 4 5 6 7 8 9 0 QGV 1 9 8 7 6 5 4 3

Printed and bound in the United States of America.

Care has been taken to trace ownership of copyright material contained in this text; however, the publisher will welcome any information that enables it to rectify any reference or credit for subsequent editions.

Director of Product Management: *Rhondda McNabb*
Senior Product Manager: *Kimberley Veevers*
Marketing Manager: *Jeremy Guimond*
Senior Manager, Development: *Kelly Dickson*
Senior Product Developer: *Maria Chu*
Senior Product Team Associate: *Christine Lomas*
Photo/Permissions Research: *Maria Chu*
Supervising Editor: *Joanne Limebeer*
Copy Editors: *Armour Robert Templeton, Bradley T. Smith/First Folio Resource Group Inc.*
Production Coordinator: *Tammy Mavroudi*
Cover Design: *Word & Image*
Cover Images: *Modern architecture (Vetta archives), columns (Philip and Karen Smith)*
Interior Design: *Word & Image*
Page Layout: *Tom Dart/First Folio Resource Group Inc.*
Printer: *Quad/Graphics Versailles*

Library and Archives Canada Cataloguing in Publication

Fundamentals of corporate finance / Stephen A. Ross ... [et al.].—8th Canadian ed.
Includes bibliographical references and indexes.

ISBN 978-0-07-105160-6

1. Corporations—Finance—Textbooks. I. Ross,
Stephen A

HG4026.F86 2013   658.15   C2012-906997-3

ABOUT THE AUTHORS

Stephen A. Ross

Sloan School of Management, Franco Modigliani Professor of Finance and Economics, Massachusetts Institute of Technology

Stephen A. Ross is the Franco Modigliani Professor of Finance and Economics at the Sloan School of Management, Massachusetts Institute of Technology. One of the most widely published authors in finance and economics, Professor Ross is recognized for his work in developing the Arbitrage Pricing Theory and his substantial contributions to the discipline through his research in signalling, agency theory, option pricing, and the theory of the term structure of interest rates, among other topics. A past president of the American Finance Association, he currently serves as an associate editor of several academic and practitioner journals. He is a trustee of CalTech.

Randolph W. Westerfield

Marshall School of Business, University of Southern California

Randolph W. Westerfield is Dean Emeritus of the University of Southern California's Marshall School of Business and is the Charles B. Thornton Professor of Finance.

He came to USC from the Wharton School, University of Pennsylvania, where he was the chairman of the finance department and a member of the finance faculty for 20 years. He is a member of several public company boards of directors, including Health Management Associates, Inc., William Lyons Homes, and the Nicholas Applegate growth fund. His areas of expertise include corporate financial policy, investment management, and stock market price behaviour.

Bradford D. Jordan

Gatton College of Business and Economics, Professor of Finance and holder of the Richard W. and Janis H. Furst Endowed Chair in Finance, University of Kentucky

Bradford D. Jordan is Professor of Finance and holder of the Richard W. and Janis H. Furst Endowed Chair in Finance at the University of Kentucky. He has a long-standing interest in both applied and theoretical issues in corporate finance and has extensive experience teaching all levels of corporate finance and financial management policy. Professor Jordan has published numerous articles on issues such as cost of capital, capital structure, and the behaviour of security prices. He is a past president of the Southern Finance Association, and he is co-author (with Thomas W. Miller, Jr.) of *Fundamentals of Investments: Valuation and Management*, 4e, a leading investments text, published by McGraw-Hill/Irwin.

Gordon S. Roberts

Schulich School of Business, York University, Canadian Imperial Bank of Commerce Professor of Financial Services

Gordon S. Roberts is Canadian Imperial Bank of Commerce Professor of Financial Services at the Schulich School of Business, York University. His extensive teaching experience includes finance classes for undergraduate and MBA students, executives, and bankers in Canada and internationally. Professor Roberts conducts research on the pricing of bank loans and the regulation of financial institutions. He has served on the editorial boards of several Canadian and international academic journals. Professor Roberts has been a consultant to a number of regulatory bodies responsible for the oversight of financial institutions and utilities.

BRIEF CONTENTS

CONTENTS

CHAPTER 26

BEHAVIOURAL FINANCE: IMPLICATIONS
FOR FINANCIAL MANAGEMENT   **750**

PREFACE

Fundamentals of Corporate Finance continues on its tradition of excellence that has earned it its status as market leader. The rapid and extensive changes in financial markets and instruments has placed new burdens on the teaching of Corporate Finance in Canada. As a result, every chapter has been updated to provide the most current examples that reflect Corporate Finance in today's world. This best-selling text is written with one strongly held principle—that Corporate Finance should be developed and taught in terms of a few integrated powerful ideas: Emphasis on Intuition, Unified Valuation Approach, and Managerial Focus.

An Emphasis on Intuition We are always careful to separate and explain the principles at work on an intuitive level before launching into any specifics. The underlying ideas are discussed first in very general terms and then by way of examples that illustrate in more concrete terms how a financial manager might proceed in a given situation.

A Unified Valuation Approach We treat net present value (NPV) as the basic concept underlying corporate finance. Many texts stop well short of consistently integrating this important principle. The most basic notion—that NPV represents the excess of market value over cost—tends to get lost in an overly mechanical approach to NPV that emphasizes computation at the expense of understanding. Every subject covered in *Fundamentals of Corporate Finance* is firmly rooted in valuation, and care is taken throughout the text to explain how particular decisions have valuation effects.

A Managerial Focus Students will not lose sight of the fact that financial management concerns *management*. Throughout the text, the role of the financial manager as decision maker is emphasized, and the need for managerial input and judgement is stressed. "Black box" approaches to finance are consciously avoided.

These three themes work together to provide a sound foundation, and a practical and workable understanding of how to evaluate and make financial decisions.

New to This Edition In addition to retaining the coverage that has characterized *Fundamentals of Corporate Finance* from the beginning, the Eighth Canadian Edition features enhanced Canadian content on current issues such as:

- **Perspective on the financial crisis of 2007–2009 and its aftermath, in particular, the European government debt credit crisis (Chapters 1, 12, and 24, among others).**
- **Updated and expanded coverage of corporate governance, social responsibility, ethical investing, and shareholder activism (Chapters 1, 8, and 23).**
- **Addition of a new chapter on Behavioural Finance (Chapter 26).**
- **Refocusing of the derivatives coverage on Enterprise Risk Management (Chapter 24).**

This book was designed and developed explicitly for a first course in business or corporate finance, for both finance majors and non-majors alike. In terms of background or prerequisites, the book is nearly self-contained, assuming some familiarity with basic algebra and accounting concepts, while still reviewing important accounting principles very early on. The organization of this text has been developed to give instructors the flexibility they need.

Just to give an idea of the breadth of coverage in the Eighth Canadian Edition, the following grid presents, for each chapter, some of the most significant features, as well as a few selected chapter highlights. Of course, in every chapter, opening vignettes, boxed features, in-chapter illustrated examples using real companies, and end-of-chapter materials have been thoroughly updated as well.

Chapters	Selected Topics of Interest	Benefits to You
PART ONE OVERVIEW OF CORPORATE FINANCE		
Chapter 1 Introduction to Corporate Finance	• *New material:* Perspective on the financial crisis of 2007–2009 and its aftermath, in particular, the European government debt credit crisis	• Links to headlines on financial crisis.
	• Goal of the firm and agency problems	• Stresses value creation as the most fundamental aspect of management and describes agency issues that can arise.
	• Ethics, financial management, and executive compensation	• Brings in real-world issues concerning conflicts of interest and current controversies surrounding ethical conduct and management pay.
Chapter 2 Financial Statements, Cash Flow, and Taxes	• *New material:* Financial statements conforming to IFRS	• Links to current practice.
	• Cash flow vs. earnings	• Defines cash flow and the differences between cash flow and earnings.
	• Market values vs. book values	• Emphasizes the relevance of market values over book values.
PART TWO FINANCIAL STATEMENTS AND LONG-TERM FINANCIAL PLANNING		
Chapter 3 Working with Financial Statements	• Using financial statement information	• Discusses the advantages and disadvantages of using financial statements.
Chapter 4 Long-Term Financial Planning and Corporate Growth	• Explanation of alternative formulas for sustainable and internal growth rates	• Explanation of growth rate formulas clears up a common misunderstanding about these formulas and the circumstances under which alternative formulas are correct.
	• Thorough coverage of sustainable growth as a planning tool	• Provides a vehicle for examining the interrelationships among operations, financing, and growth.
PART THREE VALUATION OF FUTURE CASH FLOWS		
Chapter 5 Introduction to Valuation: The Time Value of Money	• First of two chapters on time value of money	• Relatively short chapter introduces the basic ideas on time value of money to get students started on this traditionally difficult topic.
Chapter 6 Discounted Cash Flow Valuation	• Second of two chapters on time value of money	• Covers more advanced time value topics with numerous examples, calculator tips, and Excel spreadsheet exhibits. Contains many real-world examples.
Chapter 7 Interest Rates and Bond Valuation	• *New material:* Discussion of bond fund strategies at time of European government debt crisis	• Links chapter material to current events.
	• "Clean" vs. "dirty" bond prices and accrued interest	• Clears up the pricing of bonds between coupon payment dates and also bond market quoting conventions.
	• Bond ratings	• Up-to-date discussion of bond rating agencies and ratings given to debt. Includes the latest descriptions of ratings used by DBRS.
Chapter 8 Stock Valuation	• *New material:* Stock valuation using multiples	• Broadens coverage of valuation techniques.
	• *New material:* Examples of shareholder activism at Canadian Pacific and Magna International	• Expands governance coverage and links chapter material to current events.

Chapters	Selected Topics of Interest	Benefits to You
PART FOUR CAPITAL BUDGETING		
Chapter 9 Net Present Value and Other Investment Criteria	• *New material:* Enhanced discussion of multiple IRRs and modified IRR	• Clarifies properties of IRR.
	• *New material:* Practice of capital budgeting in Canada	• Current Canadian material demonstrates relevance of techniques presented.
	• First of three chapters on capital budgeting	• Relatively short chapter introduces key ideas on an intuitive level to help students with this traditionally difficult topic.
	• NPV, IRR, payback, discounted payback, and accounting rate of return	• Consistent, balanced examination of advantages and disadvantages of various criteria.
Chapter 10 Making Capital Investment Decisions	• Project cash flow	• Thorough coverage of project cash flows and the relevant numbers for a project analysis.
	• Alternative cash flow definitions	• Emphasizes the equivalence of various formulas, thereby removing common misunderstandings.
	• Special cases of DCF analysis	• Considers important applications of chapter tools.
Chapter 11 Project Analysis and Evaluation	• *New material:* Detailed examples added of scenario analysis in gold mining and managerial options in zoo management	• Brings technique to life in real-world example.
	• Sources of value	• Stresses the need to understand the economic basis for value creation in a project.
	• Scenario and sensitivity "what if" analyses	• Illustrates how to apply and interpret these tools in a project analysis.
	• Break-even analysis	• Covers cash, accounting, and financial break-even levels.
PART FIVE RISK AND RETURN		
Chapter 12 Lessons from Capital Market History	• *New material:* Capital market history updated through 2011, new section on market volatility in 2008, In Their Own Words box on the crash of 2008 and the efficient markets hypothesis	• Extensively covers historical returns, volatilities, and risk premiums.
	• Geometric vs. arithmetic returns	• Discusses calculation and interpretation of geometric returns. Clarifies common misconceptions regarding appropriate use of arithmetic vs. geometric average returns.
	• Market efficiency	• Discusses efficient markets hypothesis along with common misconceptions.
Chapter 13 Return, Risk, and the Security Market Line	• *New material:* Correlations in the financial crisis	• Explains instability in correlations with a current example.
	• Diversification, systematic and unsystematic risk	• Illustrates basics of risk and return in straightforward fashion.
	• Beta and the security market line	• Develops the security market line with an intuitive approach that bypasses much of the usual portfolio theory and statistics.
PART SIX COST OF CAPITAL AND LONG-TERM FINANCIAL POLICY		
Chapter 14 Cost of Capital	• Cost of capital estimation	• Contains a complete step-by-step illustration of cost of capital for publicly traded Loblaw Companies.
Chapter 15 Raising Capital	• Dutch auction IPOs	• Explains uniform price auctions using Google IPO as an example.
	• IPO "quiet periods"	• Explains the OSC's and SEC's quiet period rules.
	• Lockup agreements	• Briefly discusses the importance of lockup agreements.
	• IPOs in practice	• Takes in-depth look at IPOs of Facebook and Athabasca Oil Sands.
Chapter 16 Financial Leverage and Capital Structure Policy	• *New material:* Pecking order theory	• Expands coverage of capital structure.
	• Basics of financial leverage	• Illustrates the effect of leverage on risk and return.
	• Optimal capital structure	• Describes the basic trade-offs leading to an optimal capital structure.
	• Financial distress and bankruptcy	• Briefly surveys the bankruptcy process.
Chapter 17 Dividends and Dividend Policy	• *New material:* Recent Canadian survey evidence on dividend policy	• Survey results show the most important (and least important) factors that financial managers consider when setting dividend policy.
	• Dividends and dividend policy	• Describes dividend payments and the factors favouring higher and lower payout policies.

Chapters	Selected Topics of Interest	Benefits to You
PART SEVEN SHORT-TERM FINANCIAL PLANNING AND MANAGEMENT		
Chapter 18 Short-Term Finance and Planning	• Operating and cash cycles • Short-term financial planning	• Stresses the importance of cash flow timing. • Illustrates creation of cash budgets and potential need for financing.
Chapter 19 Cash and Liquidity Management	• Float management • Cash collection and disbursement	• Covers float management thoroughly. • Examines systems that firms use to handle cash inflows and outflows.
Chapter 20 Credit and Inventory Management	• Credit management • Inventory management	• Analysis of credit policy and implementation. • Briefly surveys important inventory concepts.
PART EIGHT TOPICS IN CORPORATE FINANCE		
Chapter 21 International Corporate Finance	• Exchange rate, political, and governance risks • Foreign exchange • International capital budgeting	• Discusses hedging and issues surrounding sovereign and governance risks. • Covers essentials of exchange rates and their determination. • Shows how to adapt basic DCF approach to handle exchange rates.
Chapter 22 Leasing	• Synthetic leases • Leases and lease valuation	• Discusses controversial practice of financing off the statement of financial position (also referred to as off-balance sheet financing). • Discusses essentials of leasing.
Chapter 23 Mergers and Acquisitions	• *New material:* Expanded discussion of dual class stock, investor activism, and ownership and control • Alternatives to mergers and acquisitions • Divestitures and restructurings • Mergers and acquisitions	• Presents topical issues with Canadian examples. • Covers strategic alliances and joint ventures and explains why they are important alternatives. • Examines important actions such as equity carve-outs, spins-offs, and split-ups. • Develops essentials of M&A analysis, including financial, tax, and accounting issues.
PART NINE DERIVATIVE SECURITIES AND CORPORATE FINANCE		
Chapter 24 Enterprise Risk Management	• *New material:* Enterprise risk management framework and insurance • *New material:* Recent survey results on derivatives use • Hedging with forwards, futures, swaps, and options	• Illustrates need to manage risk and some of the most important types of risk. • Relates material to practice by financial executives. • Shows how many risks can be managed with financial derivatives.
Chapter 25 Options and Corporate Securities	• Put-call parity and Black–Scholes • Options and corporate finance	• Develops modern option valuation and factors influencing option values. • Applies option valuation to a variety of corporate issues, including mergers and capital budgeting.
Chapter 26 (New Chapter) Behavioural Finance: Implications for Financial Management	• Introduction to Behavioural Finance • Behavioural Finance and market efficiency • Market efficiency and the performance of professional money managers	• Introduces biases, framing effects, and heuristics. • Explains limits to arbitrage and discusses bubbles and crashes, including the Crash of 2008. • Expands on efficient markets discussion in Chapter 12 and relates it to Behavioural Finance.

In addition to illustrating pertinent concepts and presenting up-to-date coverage, the authors strive to present the material in a way that makes it logical and easy to understand. To meet the varied needs of the intended audience, our text is rich in valuable learning tools and support.

Each feature can be categorized by the benefit to the student:
- Real Financial Decisions
- Application Tools
- Study Aids

Real Financial Decisions

We have included key features that help students connect chapter concepts to how decision makers use this material in the real world.

In Their Own Words Boxes A unique series of brief essays are written by distinguished scholars and by Canadian practitioners on key topics in the text. To name just a few, these include essays by Jeremy Siegel on efficient market theory and the financial crisis, Eric Lie on option backdating, and Heather Pelant on investment risk.

IN THEIR OWN WORDS...

Jeremy Siegel on Efficient Market Theory and the Crisis

Financial journalist and best-selling author Roger Lowenstein didn't mince words in a piece for the *Washington Post* this summer: "The upside of the current Great Recession is that it could drive a stake through the heart of the academic nostrum known as the efficient-market hypothesis." In a similar vein, the highly respected money manager and financial analyst Jeremy Grantham wrote in his quarterly letter last January: "The incredibly inaccurate efficient market theory [caused] a lethally dangerous combination of asset bubbles, lax controls

thought that underlying collateral—the home—could always cover the principal in the event the homeowner defaulted. These models led credit agencies to rate these subprime mortgages as "investment grade."

But this assessment was faulty. From 2000 through 2006, national home prices rose by 88.7%, far more than the 17.5% gain in the consumer price index or the paltry 1% rise in median household income. Never before have home prices jumped that far ahead of prices and incomes.

This should have sent up red flags and cast doubts on using

Enhanced Real-World Examples There are many current examples integrated throughout the text, tying chapter concepts to real life through illustration and reinforcing the relevance of the material. For added reinforcement, some examples tie into the chapter-opening vignettes.

Web Links We have added and updated website references, a key research tool directing students to websites that tie into the chapter material.

Integrative Mini Cases These longer problems seek to integrate a number of topics from within the chapter. The Mini Cases allow students to test and challenge their abilities to solve real-life situations for each of the key sections of the text material.

Internet Application Questions Questions relevant to the topic discussed in each chapter, are presented for the students to explore using the Internet. Students will find direct links to the websites included in these questions on the Ross Connect site and linked out directly from the eBook.

Application Tools

Realizing that there is more than one way to solve problems in Corporate Finance, we include sections that will not only encourage students to learn different problem-solving methods, but will also help them learn or brush up on their financial calculator and Excel® spreadsheet skills.

Calculator Hints   This feature introduces students to problem solving with the assistance of a financial calculator. Sample keystrokes are provided for illustrative purposes, although individual calculators will vary.

CALCULATOR HINTS	**Annuity Payments**

Finding annuity payments is easy with a financial calculator. In our example just above, the PV is $100,000, the interest rate is 18 percent, and there are five years. We find the payment as follows:

Enter	5	18	100,000		
	N	**I/Y**	**PV**	**PMT**	**FV**
Solve for				−31,978	

Here we get a negative sign on the payment because the payment is an outflow for us.

Spreadsheet Strategies   This feature either introduces students to Excel® or helps them brush up on their Excel® spreadsheet skills, particularly as they relate to Corporate Finance. This feature appears in self-contained sections and shows students how to set up spreadsheets to analyze common financial problems—a vital part of every business student's education.

SPREADSHEET STRATEGIES	**How to Calculate Bond Prices and Yields Using a Spreadsheet**

Most spreadsheets have fairly elaborate routines available for calculating bond values and yields; many of these routines involve details that we have not discussed. However, setting up a simple spreadsheet to calculate prices or yields is straightforward, as our next two spreadsheets show:

	A	B	C	D	E	F	G	H
1								
2			Using a spreadsheet to calculate bond values					
3								
4	Suppose we have a bond with 22 years to maturity, a coupon rate of 8 percent, and a yield to							

Excel® Spreadsheet Templates   Selected questions within the end-of-chapter material, identified by the following icon: ⬈, can be solved using the Excel® Spreadsheet Templates available on this text's Connect. These Excel® templates are a valuable extension of the Spreadsheet Strategies feature.

Study Aids

We want students to get the most from this resource and their course, and we realize that students have different learning styles and study needs. We therefore present a number of study features to appeal to a wide range of students.

Chapter Learning Objectives   This feature maps out the topics and learning goals in each chapter. Each end-of-chapter problem is linked to a learning objective to help students organize their study time appropriately.

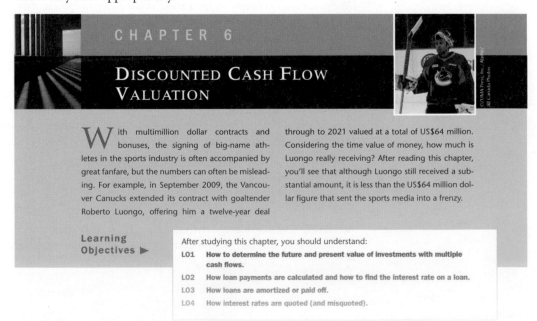

CHAPTER 6

DISCOUNTED CASH FLOW VALUATION

With multimillion dollar contracts and bonuses, the signing of big-name athletes in the sports industry is often accompanied by great fanfare, but the numbers can often be misleading. For example, in September 2009, the Vancouver Canucks extended its contract with goaltender Roberto Luongo, offering him a twelve-year deal through to 2021 valued at a total of US$64 million. Considering the time value of money, how much is Luongo really receiving? After reading this chapter, you'll see that although Luongo still received a substantial amount, it is less than the US$64 million dollar figure that sent the sports media into a frenzy.

Learning Objectives ▶

After studying this chapter, you should understand:

LO1   How to determine the future and present value of investments with multiple cash flows.

LO2   How loan payments are calculated and how to find the interest rate on a loan.

LO3   How loans are amortized or paid off.

LO4   How interest rates are quoted (and misquoted).

Concept Building   Chapter sections are intentionally kept short to promote a step-by-step, building block approach to learning. Each section is then followed by a series of short concept questions that highlight the key ideas just presented. Students use these questions to make sure they can identify and understand the most important concepts as they read.

Numbered Examples   Separate numbered and titled examples are extensively integrated into the chapters. These examples provide detailed applications and illustrations of the text material in a step-by-step format. Each example is completely self-contained so students don't have to search for additional information. Based on our classroom testing, these examples are among the most useful learning aids because they provide both detail and explanation.

Key Terms   Within each chapter, key terms are highlighted in **boldface** type the first time they appear. Key terms are defined in the text, and also in a running glossary in the margins of the text for quick reminders. For reference, there is a list of key terms at the end of each chapter and a full glossary with page references for each term at the back of the textbook.

Summary Tables   These tables succinctly restate key principles, results, and equations. They appear whenever it is useful to emphasize and summarize a group of related concepts.

Key Equations   These are called out in the text and identified by equation number. An Equation Index is available at the end of the book and a Formula Sheet can be found on the text's Connect site.

Chapter Summary and Conclusion   These paragraphs review the chapter's key points and provide closure to the chapter.

Chapter Review Problems and Self-Test   Appearing after the Summary and Conclusions and Key Terms, each chapter includes Chapter Review Problems and a Self-Test section. These questions and answers allow students to test their abilities in solving key problems related to the chapter content and provide instant reinforcement.

Concepts Review and Critical Thinking Questions   This section facilitates students' knowledge of key principles, and their intuitive understanding of chapter concepts. A number of the questions relate to the chapter-opening vignette—reinforcing students' critical-thinking skills and the learning of chapter material.

Concepts Review and Critical Thinking Questions

1. (LO3) What effect would the following actions have on a firm's current ratio? Assume that net working capital is positive.
    a.   Inventory is purchased.
    b.   A supplier is paid.
    c.   A short-term bank loan is repaid.
    d.   A long-term debt is paid off early.
    e.   A customer pays off a credit account.
    f.   Inventory is sold at cost.
    g.   Inventory is sold for a profit.
2. (LO3) In recent years, Cheticamp Co. has greatly increased its current ratio. At the same time, the quick ratio has fallen. What has happened? Has the liquidity of the company

closely watched for semiconductor manufacturers. A ratio of 0.93 indicates that for every $100 worth of chips shipped over some period, only $93 worth of new orders is received. In February 2006, the semiconductor equipment industry's book-to-bill reached 1.01, compared to 0.98 during the month of January 2006. The book-to-bill ratio reached a low of 0.78 during October 2006. The three-month average of worldwide bookings in January 2006 was $1.30 billion, an increase of 6 percent over January 2005, while the three-month average of billings in February 2006 was $1.29 billion, a 2 percent increase from February 2005. What is this ratio intended to measure? Why do you think it is so closely watched?

9.   (LO5) So-called "same-store sales" are a very important mea-

Questions and Problems   We have found that many students learn better when they have plenty of opportunity to practise; therefore, we provide extensive end-of-chapter questions and problems. These are labelled by topic and separated into three learning levels: Basic, Intermediate, and Challenge. Throughout the text, we have worked to supply interesting problems that illustrate real-world applications of chapter material. Answers to selected end-of-chapter material appear in Appendix B (now available on Connect).

As described earlier in this Preface, students' learning and understanding of the chapter content is further supported by the following end-of-chapter materials:

- **Internet Application Questions**
- **Mini Cases**
- **Suggested Readings** (now available on Connect)

McGraw-Hill Connect™ is a web-based assignment and assessment platform that gives students the means to better connect with their coursework, with their instructors, and with the important concepts that they will need to know for success now and in the future.

With Connect, instructors can deliver assignments, quizzes, and tests online. Nearly all the questions from the text are presented in an auto-gradeable format and tied to the text's learning objectives. Instructors can edit existing questions and write entirely new problems. Instructors can track individual student performance—by question, assignment, or in relation to the class overall—with detailed grade reports. Integrate grade reports easily with Learning Management Systems (LMS) such as WebCT and Blackboard.

By choosing Connect, instructors are providing their students with a powerful tool for improving academic performance and truly mastering course material. Connect allows students to practise important skills at their own pace and on their own schedule. Importantly, students' assessment results and instructors' feedback are all saved online—so students can continually review their progress and plot their course to success.

Connect also provides 24/7 online access to an eBook—an online edition of the text—to aid them in successfully completing their work, wherever and whenever they choose.

Key Features

Simple Assignment Management

With Connect, creating assignments is easier than ever, so you can spend more time teaching and less time managing.

- Create and deliver assignments easily with selectable end-of-chapter questions and testbank material to assign online.
- Streamline lesson planning, student progress reporting, and assignment grading to make classroom management more efficient than ever.
- Go paperless with the eBook and online submission and grading of student assignments.

Smart Grading

When it comes to studying, time is precious. Connect helps students learn more efficiently by providing feedback and practice material when they need it, where they need it.

- Automatically score assignments, giving students immediate feedback on their work and side-by-side comparisons with correct answers.
- Access and review each response; manually change grades or leave comments for students to review.
- Reinforce classroom concepts with practice tests and instant quizzes.

Instructor Library

The Connect Instructor Library is your course creation hub. It provides all the critical resources you'll need to build your course, just how you want to teach it.

- Assign eBook readings and draw from a rich collection of textbook-specific assignments.
- Access to all instructor resources:

  Connect content   Prepared by Merlyn Foo, Athabasca University.

  Instructor's Manual   Prepared by Lewis Stevenson, Brock University. The Instructor's Manual contains two main sections. The first section contains a chapter outline with lecture tips, real-world tips, and ethics notes. The second section includes detailed solutions for all end-of-chapter problems.

Computerized Test Bank   Prepared by Sepand Jazzi, Kwantlen Polytechnic University. The computerized test bank is available through EZ Test Online—a flexible and easy-to-use electronic testing program—that allows instructors to create tests from book-specific items. EZ Test accommodates a wide range of question types and allows instructors to add their own questions. Test items are also available in Word format (Rich text format). For secure online testing, exams created in EZ Test can be exported to WebCT and Blackboard. EZ Test Online is supported at mhhe.com/eztest where users can download a Quick Start Guide, access FAQs, or log a ticket for help with specific issues.

PowerPoint® Presentation   Prepared by Anne Inglis. The Microsoft® PowerPoint® Presentation slides have been enhanced to better illustrate chapter concepts.

Image Bank   All figures and tables are available in digital format on the McGraw-Hill Connect™ site associated with this text, which can be found at mcgrawhillconnect.ca.

Excel® Templates (with Solutions)   Prepared by Brent Matheson, University of Waterloo. Excel® templates are included with solutions for end-of-chapter problems indicated by an Excel® icon in the margin of the text.

- View assignments and resources created for past sections.
- Post your own resources for students to use.

eBook

Connect reinvents the textbook learning experience for the modern student. Every Connect subject area is seamlessly integrated with Connect eBooks, which are designed to keep students focused on the concepts key to their success.

- Provide students with a Connect eBook, allowing for anytime, anywhere access to the textbook.
- Merge media, animation and assessments with the text's narrative to engage students and improve learning and retention.
- Pinpoint and connect key concepts in a snap using the powerful eBook search engine.
- Manage notes, highlights, and bookmarks in one place for simple, comprehensive review.

No two students are alike. McGraw-Hill LearnSmart™ is an intelligent learning system that uses a series of adaptive questions to pinpoint each student's knowledge gaps. LearnSmart then provides an optimal learning path for each student, so that they spend less time in areas they already know and more time in areas they don't. The result is LearnSmart's adaptive learning path helps students retain more knowledge, learn faster, and study more efficiently.

Lyryx for Corporate Finance

Lyryx Assessment for Finance is a leading-edge online assessment system, designed to support both students and instructors. The assessment takes the form of a homework assignment called a Lab. The assessments are algorithmically generated and automatically graded so that students get instant grades and feedback. New Labs are randomly generated each time, providing the student with unlimited opportunities to try a type of question. After they submit a Lab for marking, students receive extensive feedback on their work, thus promoting their learning experience.

Please contact your *i*Learning Sales Specialist for additional information on the Lyryx Assessment Finance system. Visit <u>lyryx.com</u>.

Superior Learning Solutions and Support

The McGraw-Hill Ryerson team is ready to help you assess and integrate any of our products, technology, and services into your course for optimal teaching and learning performance. Whether it's helping your students improve their grades, or putting your entire course online, the McGraw-Hill Ryerson team is here to help you do it. Contact your *i*Learning Sales Specialist today to learn how to maximize all of McGraw-Hill Ryerson's resources!

For more information on the latest technology and Learning Solutions offered by McGraw-Hill Ryerson and its partners, please visit us online: **mcgrawhill.ca/he/solutions**.

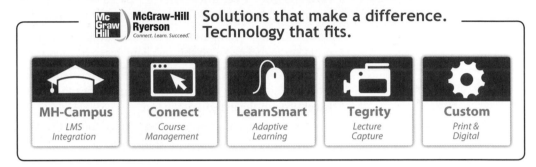

Course Management

CourseSmart brings together thousands of textbooks across hundreds of courses in an e-textbook format, providing unique benefits to students and faculty. By purchasing an e-textbook, students can save up to 50 percent off the cost of a print textbook, reduce their impact on the environment, and gain access to powerful Web tools for learning, including full-text search, notes and highlighting, and e-mail tools for sharing notes between classmates. For faculty, CourseSmart provides instant access to review and compare textbooks and course materials in their discipline area without the time, cost, and environmental impact of mailing print examination copies. For further details contact your McGraw-Hill Ryerson *i*Learning Sales Specialist or go to **coursesmart.com**.

McGraw-Hill Ryerson offers a range of flexible integration solutions for Blackboard, WebCT, Desire2Learn, Moodle, and other leading learning management platforms. Please contact your local McGraw-Hill Ryerson *i*Learning Sales Specialist for details.

McGraw-Hill's **Create Online** gives you access to the most abundant resource at your fingertips—literally. With a few mouse clicks, you can create customized learning tools simply and affordably. McGraw-Hill Ryerson has included many of our market-leading textbooks within Create Online for ebook and print customization as well as many licensed readings and cases. For more information, go to **mcgrawhillcreate.ca**.

ACKNOWLEDGEMENTS

We never would have completed this book without the incredible amount of help and support we received from colleagues, editors, family members, and friends. We would like to thank, without implicating, all of you.

For starters, a great many of our colleagues read the drafts of our first and current editions. Our reviewers continued to keep us working on improving the content, organization, exposition, and Canadian content of our text. To the following reviewers, we are grateful for their many contributions to the Eighth Canadian Edition:

Mohamed Ayadi, *Brock University*
Larry Bauer, *Memorial University*
Jaime Morales Burgos, *Trent University*
Bill Dawson, *University of Western Ontario*
Chris Duff, *Royal Roads University*
Shantanu Dutta, *University of Ontario Institute of Technology*
Larbi Hammami, *McGill University*
Andras Marosi, *University of Alberta*
Brent Matheson, *University of Waterloo*
Judy Palm, *Vancouver Island University*
William Rentz, *University of Ottawa*
David Roberts, *Southern Alberta Institute of Technology*
Jun Yang, *Acadia University*
Yuriy Zabolotnyuk, *Carleton University*

A special thank you must be given to Hamdi Driss, Schulich School of Business, and VijayShree Vethantham for their vigilant effort of technical proofreading and, in particular, careful checking of the solutions in the *Instructor's Manual*. Their keen eyes and attention to detail have contributed greatly to the quality of the final product.

Several of our most respected colleagues and journalists contributed essays, entitled "In Their Own Words," that appear in selected chapters. To these individuals we extend a special thanks:

Edward Altman, *New York University*
James Darroch, *York University*
Christine Dobby, *Financial Post*
Robert C. Higgins, *University of Washington*
Ken Hitzig, *Accord Financial Corp.*
Erik Lie, *University of Iowa*
Robert C. Merton, *Harvard University*
Merton H. Miller, *University of Chicago*
Heather Pelant, *Barclays Global Investors Canada*
Jay R. Ritter, *University of Florida*
Robert J. Schiller, *Yale University*
Hersh Shefrin, *Santa Clara University*
Jeremy Siegel, *University of Pennsylvania*
Bennett Stewart, *Stern Stewart & Co.*
Jamie Sturgeon, *Financial Post*
Samuel Weaver, *The Hershey Company*
David Weitzner, *York University*

Ganesh Kannan, recent Schulich MBA graduate, deserves special mention for his role in producing the Eighth Canadian Edition. He capably researched updates, drafted revisions, and responded to editorial queries; and his excellent input was essential to this edition.

Much credit goes to a "AAA-rated" group of people at McGraw-Hill Ryerson who worked on the Eighth Canadian Edition. Leading the team was Kimberley Veevers, Senior Product Manager, who continued her role as champion of this project by arranging unparalleled support for the development of the text and support package for this edition. Maria Chu, Senior Product Developer, efficiently and cheerfully supervised the reviews and revision as she has done for many prior editions. Production and copy-editing were handled ably by Joanne Limebeer, Supervising Editor, and Robert Templeton and Bradley T. Smith, First Folio Resource Group Inc., Copy Editors.

Through the development of this edition, we have taken great care to discover and eliminate errors. Our goal is to provide the best Canadian textbook available in Corporate Finance.

Please forward your comments to:
Professor Gordon S. Roberts
Schulich School of Business, York University
4700 Keele Street,
Toronto, Ontario
M3J IP3

Or, email your comments to **groberts@schulich.yorku.ca**.

Stephen A. Ross
Randolph W. Westerfield
Bradford D. Jordan
Gordon S. Roberts

C H A P T E R   1

INTRODUCTION TO CORPORATE FINANCE

Tim Hortons Inc. has come a long way since its 1964 inception in Hamilton, Ontario under the title "Tim Horton Donuts." Today, the company is the largest quick-service restaurant chain in Canada, and is among the well-recognized brands in the country. Founded as a sole proprietorship by Tim Horton, and later run as a partnership with Ron Joyce, the company began with a specialized focus on coffee and donuts. Following Horton's death in 1974, Joyce continued to run the business under an aggressive expansion strategy. By February 1987, Tim Hortons had opened 300 stores across Canada. In 1995, Tim Hortons was acquired by Wendy's International Inc., which gave new impetus to the expansion of the brand in the United States. Eleven years later in March of 2006, Tim Hortons held its initial public offering (IPO) and was fully spun off by Wendy's International in September of the same year. With more than 4,000 locations in Canada, the United States, and the Gulf Cooperation Council, the majority of which are franchisee owned, the Tim Hortons story touches on different business forms, corporate goals, and corporate control, all topics that are discussed in this chapter. Tim Hortons is a registered trademark of The TDL Marks Corporation. Used with permission.

Learning Objectives ▶

After studying this chapter, you should understand:

LO1   The basic types of financial management decisions and the role of the financial manager.

LO2   The financial implications of the different forms of business organization.

LO3   The goal of financial management.

LO4   The conflicts of interest that can arise between managers and owners.

LO5   The roles of financial institutions and markets.

To begin our study of modern corporate finance and financial management, we need to address two central issues: First, what is corporate finance, and what is the role of the financial manager in the corporation? Second, what is the goal of financial management? To describe the financial management environment, we look at the corporate form of organization and discuss some conflicts that can arise within the corporation. We also take a brief look at financial institutions and financial markets in Canada.

1.1 | Corporate Finance and the Financial Manager

In this section, we discuss where the financial manager fits in the corporation. We start by looking at what corporate finance is and what the financial manager does.

What Is Corporate Finance?

Imagine that you were to start your own business. No matter what type you started, you would have to answer the following three questions in some form or another:

1. What long-term investments should you take on? That is, what lines of business will you be in and what sorts of buildings, machinery, equipment, and research and development facilities will you need?
2. Where will you get the long-term financing to pay for your investment? Will you bring in other owners or will you borrow the money?
3. How will you manage your everyday financial activities, such as collecting from customers and paying suppliers?

These are not the only questions by any means, but they are among the most important. Corporate finance, broadly speaking, is the study of ways to answer these three questions.

Accordingly, we'll be looking at each of them in the chapters ahead. Though our discussion focuses on the role of the financial manager, these three questions are important to managers in all areas of the corporation. For example, selecting the firm's lines of business (Question 1) shapes the jobs of managers in production, marketing, and management information systems. As a result, most large corporations centralize their finance function and use it to measure performance in other areas. Most CEOs have significant financial management experience.

The Financial Manager

For current issues facing CFOs, see cfo.com

A striking feature of large corporations is that the owners (the shareholders) are usually not directly involved in making business decisions, particularly on a day-to-day basis. Instead, the corporation employs managers to represent the owners' interests and make decisions on their behalf. In a large corporation, the financial manager is in charge of answering the three questions we raised earlier.

It is a challenging task because changes in the firm's operations and shifts in Canadian and global financial markets mean that the best answers for each firm are changing, sometimes quite rapidly. Globalization of markets and advanced communications and computer technology, as well as increased volatility of interest rates and foreign exchange rates, have raised the stakes in financial management decisions. We discuss these major trends and how they are changing the financial manager's job after we introduce you to some of the basics of corporate financial decisions.

The financial management function is usually associated with a top officer of the firm, such as a vice president of finance or some other chief financial officer (CFO). Figure 1.1 is a simplified organization chart that highlights the finance activity in a large firm. The CFO reports to the president, who is the chief operating officer (COO) in charge of day-to-day operations. The COO reports to the chairman, who is usually chief executive officer (CEO). However, as businesses become more complex, there is a growing pattern among large companies to separate the roles of Chairman and CEO. The CEO has overall responsibility to the board. As shown, the vice president of finance coordinates the activities of the treasurer and the controller. The controller's office handles cost and financial accounting, tax payments, and management information systems. The treasurer's office is responsible for managing the firm's cash, its financial planning, and its capital expenditures. These treasury activities are all related to the three general questions raised earlier, and the chapters ahead deal primarily with these issues. Our study thus bears mostly on activities usually associated with the treasurer's office.

Financial Management Decisions

As our discussion suggests, the financial manager must be concerned with three basic types of questions. We consider these in greater detail next.

capital budgeting
The process of planning and managing a firm's investment in long-term assets.

CAPITAL BUDGETING   The first question concerns the firm's long-term investments. The process of planning and managing a firm's long-term investments is called **capital budgeting**. In capital budgeting, the financial manager tries to identify investment opportunities that are worth more to the firm than they will cost to acquire. Loosely speaking, this means that the value of the cash flow generated by an asset exceeds the cost of that asset. The types of investment opportunities that would typically be considered depend in part on the nature of the firm's business. For example, for a restaurant chain like Tim Hortons, deciding whether or not to open stores would be a major capital budgeting decision. Some decisions, such as what type of computer system to purchase, might not depend so much on a particular line of business.

Financial managers must be concerned not only with how much cash they expect to receive, but also with when they expect to receive it and how likely they are to receive it. Evaluating the size, timing, and risk of future cash flows is the essence of capital budgeting. We discuss how to do this in detail in the chapters ahead.

FIGURE 1.1

A simplified organization chart. The exact titles and organization differ from company to company.

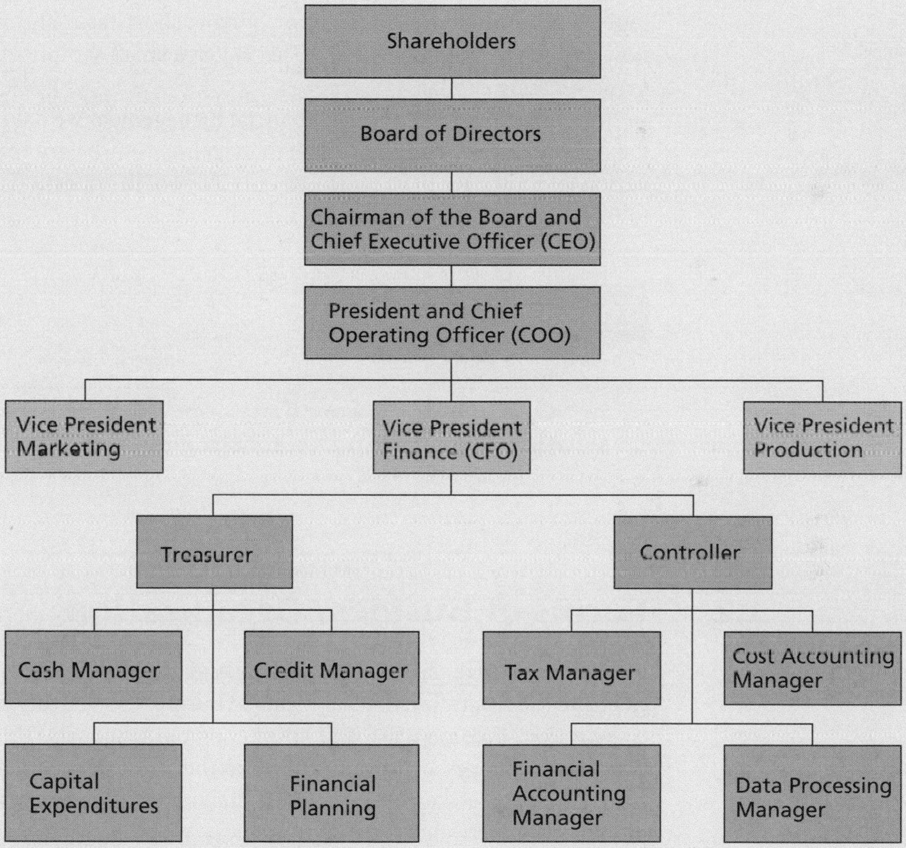

CAPITAL STRUCTURE The second major question for the financial manager concerns how the firm should obtain and manage the long-term financing it needs to support its long-term investments. A firm's **capital structure** (or financial structure) refers to the specific mixture of short-term debt, long-term debt, and equity the firm uses to finance its operations. The financial manager has two concerns in this area. First, how much should the firm borrow; that is, what mixture is best? The mixture chosen affects both the risk and value of the firm. Second, what are the least expensive sources of funds for the firm?

capital structure
The mix of debt and equity maintained by a firm.

If we picture the firm as a pie, then the firm's capital structure determines how that pie is sliced. In other words, what percentage of the firm's cash flow goes to creditors and what percentage goes to shareholders? Management has a great deal of flexibility in choosing a firm's financial structure. Whether one structure is better than any other for a particular firm is the heart of the capital structure issue.

In addition to deciding on the financing mix, the financial manager has to decide exactly how and where to raise the money. The expenses associated with raising long-term financing can be considerable, so different possibilities must be carefully evaluated. Also, corporations borrow money from a variety of lenders, tapping into both Canadian and international debt markets, in a number of different—and sometimes exotic—ways. Choosing among lenders and among loan types is another of the jobs handled by the financial manager.

working capital management
Planning and managing the firm's current assets and liabilities.

WORKING CAPITAL MANAGEMENT   The third major question concerns **working capital management**. The phrase *working capital* refers to the difference between a firm's short-term assets, such as inventory, and its short-term liabilities, such as money owed to suppliers. Managing the firm's working capital is a day-to-day activity that ensures the firm has sufficient resources to continue its operations and avoid costly interruptions. This involves a number of activities, all related to the firm's receipt and disbursement of cash.

Some of the questions about working capital that must be answered are: (1) How much cash and inventory should we keep on hand? (2) Should we sell on credit? If so, what terms should we offer, and to whom should we extend them? (3) How do we obtain any needed short-term financing? Will we purchase on credit or borrow short-term and pay cash? If we borrow short-term, how and when should we do it? This is just a small sample of the issues that arise in managing a firm's working capital.

The three areas of corporate financial management we have described—capital budgeting, capital structure, and working capital management—are very broad categories. Each includes a rich variety of topics; we have indicated only a few of the questions that arise in the different areas. The following chapters contain greater detail.

Concept Questions

1. What is the capital budgeting decision?
2. Into what category of financial management does cash management fall?
3. What do you call the specific mixture of short-term debt, long-term debt, and equity that a firm chooses to use?

1.2 | Forms of Business Organization

Large firms in Canada, such as CIBC and BCE, are almost all organized as corporations. We examine the five different legal forms of business organization—sole proprietorship, partnership, corporation, income trust, and co-operative—to see why this is so. Each of the three forms has distinct advantages and disadvantages in the life of the business, the ability of the business to raise cash, and taxes. A key observation is that, as a firm grows, the advantages of the corporate form may come to outweigh the disadvantages.

Sole Proprietorship

sole proprietorship
A business owned by a single individual.

A **sole proprietorship** is a business owned by one person. This is the simplest type of business to start and is the least regulated form of organization. Depending on where you live, you can start up a proprietorship by doing little more than getting a business licence and opening your doors. For this reason, many businesses that later become large corporations start out as sole proprietorships. There are more proprietorships than any other type of business.

As the owner of a sole proprietorship, you keep all the profits. That's the good news. The bad news is that the owner has *unlimited liability* for business debts. This means that creditors can look beyond assets to the proprietor's personal assets for payment. Similarly, there is no distinction between personal and business income, so all business income is taxed as personal income.

For more information on forms of business organization, see the "Starting a Business" section at canadianlawsite.ca; also see canadabusiness.ca

The life of a sole proprietorship is limited to the owner's life span, and, importantly, the amount of equity that can be raised is limited to the proprietor's personal wealth. This limitation often means that the business cannot exploit new opportunities because of insufficient capital. Ownership of a sole proprietorship may be difficult to transfer, since this requires the sale of the entire business to a new owner.

Partnership

partnership
A business formed by two or more co-owners.

A **partnership** is similar to a proprietorship, except that there are two or more owners (partners). In a *general partnership*, all the partners share in gains or losses, and all have unlimited liability for all partnership debts, not just some particular share. The way partnership gains (and losses) are divided is described in the *partnership agreement*. This agreement can be an informal oral agreement, or a lengthy, formal written document.

In a *limited partnership*, one or more *general partners* has unlimited liability and runs the business for one or more *limited partners* who do not actively participate in the business. A limited partner's liability for business debts is limited to the amount contributed to the partnership. This form of organization is common in real estate ventures, for example.

The advantages and disadvantages of a partnership are basically the same as those for a proprietorship. Partnerships based on a relatively informal agreement are easy and inexpensive to form. General partners have unlimited liability for partnership debts, and the partnership terminates when a general partner wishes to sell out or dies. All income is taxed as personal income to the partners, and the amount of equity that can be raised is limited to the partners' combined wealth. Ownership by a general partner is not easily transferred because a new partnership must be formed. A limited partner's interest can be sold without dissolving the partnership. But finding a buyer may be difficult, because there is no organized market in limited partnerships.

Based on our discussion, the primary disadvantages of sole proprietorship and partnership as forms of business organization are (1) unlimited liability for business debts on the part of the owners, (2) limited life of the business, and (3) difficulty of transferring ownership. These three disadvantages add up to a single, central problem: the ability of such businesses to grow can be seriously limited by an inability to raise cash for investment.

Corporation

corporation
A business created as a distinct legal entity owned by one or more individuals or entities.

In terms of size, the **corporation** is the most important form of business organization in Canada. A corporation is a legal entity separate and distinct from its owners; it has many of the rights, duties, and privileges of an actual person. Corporations can borrow money and own property, can sue and be sued, and can enter into contracts. A corporation can even be a general partner or a limited partner in a partnership, and a corporation can own stock in another corporation.

Not surprisingly, starting a corporation is somewhat more complicated than starting the other forms of business organization, but not greatly so for a small business. Forming a corporation involves preparing *articles of incorporation* (or a charter) and a set of *bylaws*. The articles of incorporation must contain a number of things, including the corporation's name, its intended life (which can be forever), its business purpose, and the number of shares that can be issued. This information must be supplied to regulators in the jurisdiction where the firm is incorporated. Canadian firms can be incorporated under either the federal *Canada Business Corporation Act* or provincial law.[1]

The bylaws are rules describing how the corporation regulates its own existence. For example, the bylaws describe how directors are elected. These bylaws may be a very simple statement of a few rules and procedures, or they may be quite extensive for a large corporation. The bylaws may be amended or extended from time to time by the shareholders.

In a large corporation, the shareholders and the management are usually separate groups. The shareholders elect the board of directors, which then selects the managers. Management is charged with running the corporation's affairs in the shareholders' interest. In principle, shareholders control the corporation because they elect the directors.

As a result of the separation of ownership and management, the corporate form has several advantages. Ownership (represented by shares of stock) can be readily transferred, and the life of the corporation is therefore not limited. The corporation borrows money in its own name. As a result, the shareholders in a corporation have limited liability for corporate debts. The most they can lose is what they have invested.[2]

---

[1] In some provinces, the legal documents of incorporation are called letters patent or a memorandum of association.

[2] An important exception is negligence by a corporate director. If this can be proven, for example in a case of environmental damage, the director may be liable for more than the original investment.

While limited liability makes the corporate form attractive to equity investors, lenders sometimes view the limited liability feature as a disadvantage. If the borrower experiences financial distress and is unable to repay its debt, limited liability blocks lenders' access to the owners' personal assets. For this reason, chartered banks often circumvent limited liability by requiring that owners of small businesses provide personal guarantees for company debt.

The relative ease of transferring ownership, the limited liability for business debts, and the unlimited life of the business are the reasons why the corporate form is superior when it comes to raising cash. If a corporation needs new equity, for example, it can sell new shares of stock and attract new investors. The number of owners can be huge; larger corporations have many thousands or even millions of shareholders.

The corporate form has a significant disadvantage. Because a corporation is a legal entity, it must pay taxes. Moreover, money paid out to shareholders in dividends is taxed again as income to those shareholders. This is *double taxation*, meaning that corporate profits are taxed twice—at the corporate level when they are earned, and again at the personal level when they are paid out.[3]

As the discussion in this section illustrates, the need of large businesses for outside investors and creditors is such that the corporate form generally is best for such firms. We focus on corporations in the chapters ahead because of the importance of the corporate form in the Canadian and world economies. Also, a few important financial management issues, such as dividend policy, are unique to corporations. However, businesses of all types and sizes need financial management, so the majority of the subjects we discuss bear on all forms of business.

A CORPORATION BY ANOTHER NAME   The corporate form of organization has many variations around the world. The exact laws and regulations differ from country to country, of course, but the essential features of public ownership and limited liability remain. These firms are often designated as joint stock companies, public limited companies, or limited liability companies, depending on the specific nature of the firm and the country of origin.

In addition to international variations, there are specialized forms of corporations in Canada and the U.S. One increasingly common example is the professional corporation set up by architects, accountants, lawyers, dentists and others who are licensed by a professional governing body. A professional corporation has limited liability but each professional is still open to being sued for malpractice.

Income Trust

Starting in 2001, the income trust, a non-corporate form of business organization, grew in importance in Canada.[4] In response to the growing importance of this sector, provincial legislation extended limited liability protection, previously limited to corporate shareholders, to trust unit holders. Along the same lines, at the end of 2005, the TSX began to include income trusts in its benchmark S&P / TSX composite index.

Business income trusts (also called income funds) hold the debt and equity of an underlying business and distribute the income generated to unit holders. Because income trusts are not corporations, they are not subject to corporate income tax and their income is typically taxed only in the hands of unit holders. As a result, investors viewed trusts as tax-efficient and were generally willing to pay more for a company after it converted from a corporation to a trust. However, this tax advantage largely disappeared on Halloween 2006 when the government announced plans to tax income trusts at the same rate as corporations starting in 2011. As a result, most income trusts converted to corporations. The number of income trusts reduced from 179 (with a market capitalization of $112.1 billion) in 2009 to 65 (with a market capitalization of $51.5 billion) in mid-2011.

---

[3] The dividend tax credit for individual shareholders and a corporate dividend exclusion reduce the bite of double taxation for Canadian corporations. These tax provisions are discussed in Chapter 2. Trusts and limited partnerships are designed to avoid double taxation.

[4] For more on income trusts see J. Fenwick and B. Kalymon, "A Note on Income Trusts," Ivey Publishing, 2004 and Department of Finance, "Tax and Other Issues Related to Publicly Listed Flow-Through Entities (Income Trusts and Limited Partnerships)," September 8, 2005. Data for TSX: Jan S. Koyanagi, "Income Trusts on Toronto Stock Exchange," TSX, January 2007. Chapter 2 covers income trust income and taxation in more detail.

Co-operative (Co-op)

A co-operative is an enterprise that is equally owned by its members who share the benefits of co-operation, based on how much they use the co-operative's services.[5] The co-ops are generally classified into four types:

- Consumer Co-op: This provides products or services to its members (such as a retail co-op, housing, health-care or child-care co-op)
- Producer Co-op: This processes and markets the goods or services produced by its members, and supplies products or services necessary to the members' professional activities (such as independent entrepreneurs, artisans, or farmers)
- Worker Co-op: This provides employment for its members. In this co-op, the employees are members and owners of the enterprise.
- Multi-Stakeholder Co-op: This serves the needs of different stakeholder groups—such as employees, clients, and other interested individuals and organizations (examples include health, home care and other social enterprises)

There are more than 18 million members in Canada, which means every four out of ten Canadians are members of a co-op. There are various key benefits of co-op such as to help producers compete effectively in the marketplace, to server rural and remote communities, to develop community leadership, to build social capital and to promote local ownership and control.

Table 1.1 reviews the key features of Sole Proprietorship, Partnership and Corporation in Canada.

TABLE 1.1   Forms of business organization

	Sole Proprietorship	**Partnership**	**Corporation**
Definition	A business owned by a single individual.	A business formed by two or more co-owners.	A business created as a distinct legal entity owned by one or more individuals or entities.
Pros	• Simplest form of business to start and is the least regulated. • Owner keeps all profits.	• Simplest form of business to start with little regulation. • Owners keep all profits. • Access to more human and financial capital. • Limited partner(s) have limited liability.	• Ownership can be easily transferred. • Life of corporation not limited to lives of owners or managers. • Corporation has limited liability. • Ability to raise and access large sums of capital in both debt and equity markets.
Cons	• Owner has unlimited liability for business debts. • Business income taxed as personal income. • Life of sole-proprietorship limited to life of owner. • Limited ability to raise financing. • Difficulty in transferring ownership of a sole proprietorship.	• General partner(s) have unlimited liability for business debts. • Business income taxed as personal income. • Life of partnership limited to lives of owners. • Difficulty in transferring ownership. • Possible disagreements over partnership.	• Double taxation. • Lenders sometimes view the limited liability as a disadvantage and require the owners of small corporations to make personal guarantees. • More complex and expensive form of organization to establish.

Concept Questions

1. What are the three forms of business organization?
2. What are the primary advantages and disadvantages of a sole proprietorship or partnership?
3. What is the difference between a general and a limited partnership?
4. Why is the corporate form superior when it comes to raising cash?

---

[5] For more on Co-operatives in Canada visit the website of the Co-operatives Secretariat at coop.gc.ca/

1.3 | The Goal of Financial Management

Assuming that we restrict ourselves to for-profit businesses, the goal of financial management is to make money or add value for the owners. This goal is a little vague, of course, so we examine some different ways of formulating it to come up with a more precise definition. Such a definition is important because it leads to an objective basis for making and evaluating financial decisions.

Possible Goals

If we were to consider possible financial goals, we might come up with some ideas like the following:
- Survive in business.
- Avoid financial distress and bankruptcy.
- Beat the competition.
- Maximize sales or market share.
- Minimize costs.
- Maximize profits.
- Maintain steady earnings growth.

These are only a few of the goals we could list. Furthermore, each of these possibilities presents problems as a goal for a financial manager.

For example, it's easy to increase market share or unit sales; all we have to do is lower our prices or relax our credit terms. Similarly, we can always cut costs simply by doing away with things such as research and development. We can avoid bankruptcy by never borrowing any money or taking any risks, and so on. It's not clear that any of these actions would be in the shareholders' best interests.

Profit maximization would probably be the most commonly cited goal, but even this is not a very precise objective. Do we mean profits this year? If so, then actions such as deferring maintenance, letting inventories run down, and other short-run cost-cutting measures tend to increase profits now, but these activities aren't necessarily desirable.

The goal of maximizing profits may refer to some sort of long-run or average profits, but it's still unclear exactly what this means. First, do we mean something like accounting net income or earnings per share? As we see in more detail in the next chapter, these accounting numbers may have little to do with what is good or bad for the firm. Second, what do we mean by the long run? What is the appropriate trade-off between current and future profits?

Although the goals we've just listed are all different, they fall into two classes. The first of these relates to profitability. The goals involving sales, market share, and cost control all relate, at least potentially, to different ways of earning or increasing profits. The second group, involving bankruptcy avoidance, stability, and safety, relate in some way to controlling risk. Unfortunately, these two types of goals are somewhat contradictory. The pursuit of profit normally involves some element of risk, so it isn't really possible to maximize both safety and profit. What we need, therefore, is a goal that encompasses both these factors.

The Goal of Financial Management

The financial manager in a corporation makes decisions for the shareholders of the firm. Given this, instead of listing possible goals for the financial manager, we really need to answer a more fundamental question: From the shareholders' point of view, what is a good financial management decision?

If we assume that shareholders buy stock because they seek to gain financially, the answer is obvious: Good decisions increase the value of the stock, and poor decisions decrease it.

Given our observation, it follows that the financial manager acts in the shareholders' best interests by making decisions that increase the value of the stock. The appropriate goal for the financial manager can thus be stated quite easily:

> The goal of financial management is to maximize the current value per share of existing stock.

The goal of maximizing the value of the stock avoids the problems associated with the different goals we listed earlier. There is no ambiguity in the criterion, and there is no short-run versus long-run issue. We explicitly mean that our goal is to maximize the current stock value. If this goal seems a little strong or one-dimensional to you, keep in mind that the shareholders in a firm are residual owners. By this we mean that they are only entitled to what is left after employees, suppliers, and creditors (and anyone else with a legitimate claim) are paid their due. If any of these groups go unpaid, the shareholders get nothing. So, if the shareholders are winning in the sense that the leftover, residual, portion is growing, it must be true that everyone else is winning also. For example, following its stock split in 2005 to mid 2012, technology giant Apple Inc. has increased value to its shareholders with a 1400 percent rise in its share price.[6] Apple attributes this financial success to major improvements in its bottom line and market share through the development and introduction of innovative products such as the iPod, iPhone, iPad, and MacBooks series.

Because the goal of financial management is to maximize the value of the stock, we need to learn how to identify those investments and financing arrangements that favourably impact the value of the stock. This is precisely what we are studying. In fact, we could have defined corporate finance as the study of the relationship between business decisions and the value of the stock in the business.

To make the market value of the stock a valid measure of financial decisions requires an *efficient capital market*. In an efficient capital market, security prices fully reflect available information. The market sets the stock price to give the firm an accurate report card on its decisions. We return to capital market efficiency in Part Five.

A More General Goal

Given our goal of maximizing the value of the stock, an obvious question comes up: What is the appropriate goal when the firm is privately owned and has no traded stock? Corporations are certainly not the only type of business, and the stock in many corporations rarely changes hands, so it's difficult to say what the value per share is at any given time.

To complicate things further, some large Canadian companies such as Irving are privately owned. Many large firms in Canada are subsidiaries of foreign multinationals, while others are controlled by a single domestic shareholder.

Recognizing these complications, as long as we are dealing with for-profit businesses, only a slight modification is needed. The total value of the stock in a corporation is simply equal to the value of the owners' equity. Therefore, a more general way of stating our goal is to maximize the market value of the owners' equity. This market value can be measured by a business appraiser or by investment bankers if the firm eventually goes public.

With this in mind, it doesn't matter whether the business is a proprietorship, a partnership, or a corporation. For each of these, good financial decisions increase the market value of the owners' equity and poor financial decisions decrease it. In fact, although we choose to focus on corporations in the chapters ahead, the principles we develop apply to all forms of business. Many of them even apply to the not-for-profit sector.

Finally, our goal does not imply that the financial manager should take illegal or unethical actions in the hope of increasing the value of the equity in the firm. What we mean is that the financial manager best serves the owners of the business by identifying opportunities that add to the firm because they are desired and valued in the free marketplace.

In fact, truthful financial reporting is incredibly important to the long run viability of capital markets. The collapse of companies like Enron and Worldcom has illustrated what a dramatic impact unethical behaviour can have on public trust and confidence in our financial institutions. The ability of companies to raise capital and of our economies to function efficiently is based on this trust and confidence. If investors cannot assume that the information they receive is honest and truthful, many of the models and theories we learn through this textbook no longer apply.[7]

Concept Questions

1. What is the goal of financial management?
2. What are some shortcomings of the goal of profit maximization?
3. How would you define corporate finance?

---

[6] A current stock price quote for Apple Inc. can be found at google.com/finance.

[7] For more on ethics and financial reporting visit the website of the Canadian Centre for Ethics and Corporate Policy at ethicscentre.ca

1.4 | The Agency Problem and Control of the Corporation

We've seen that the financial manager acts in the best interest of the shareholders by taking actions that increase the value of the stock. However, we've also seen that in large corporations ownership can be spread over a huge number of shareholders. Or a large shareholder may control a block of shares. In these cases, will management necessarily act in the best interests of the shareholders? Put another way, might not management pursue its own goals (or those of a small group of shareholders) at the shareholders' expense? We briefly consider some of the arguments next.

Agency Relationships

The relationship between shareholders and management is called an *agency relationship*. Such a relationship exists whenever someone (the principal) hires another (the agent) to represent his or her interests. For example, you might hire someone (an agent) to sell a car that you own. In all such relationships, there is a possibility of conflict of interest between the principal and the agent. Such conflict is called an **agency problem**.

agency problem
The possibility of conflicts of interest between the shareholders and management of a firm.

In hiring someone to sell your car, you agree to pay a flat fee when the car sells. The agent's incentive is to make the sale, not necessarily to get you the best price. If you paid a commission of, say, 10 percent of the sale price instead of a flat fee, this problem might not exist. This example illustrates that the way an agent is compensated is one factor that affects agency problems.

Management Goals

To see how management and shareholders' interests might differ, imagine that the firm has a new investment under consideration. The new investment favourably impacts the share value, but it is a relatively risky venture. The owners of the firm may wish to take the investment because the stock value will rise, but management may not because of the possibility that things will turn out badly and management jobs will be lost. If management does not take the investment, the shareholders may have lost a valuable opportunity. This is one example of an *agency cost*.

More generally, agency costs refer to the costs of the conflict of interests between shareholders and management. These costs can be indirect or direct. An indirect agency cost is a lost opportunity such as the one we have just described.

Direct agency costs come in two forms: The first is a corporate expenditure that benefits management but costs the shareholders. Perhaps the purchase of a luxurious and unneeded corporate jet would fall under this heading. The second direct agency cost is an expense that arises from the need to monitor management actions. Paying outside auditors to assess the accuracy of financial statement information is one example.

Some argue that if left to themselves, managers would maximize the amount of resources they have control over or, more generally, corporate power or wealth. This goal could lead to an overemphasis on corporate size or growth. For example, cases where management is accused of overpaying to buy up another company just to increase the size of the business or to demonstrate corporate power are not uncommon. Obviously, if overpayment does take place, such a purchase does not benefit the shareholders.

Our discussion indicates that management may tend to overemphasize organizational survival to protect job security. Also, management may dislike outside interference, so independence and corporate self-sufficiency may be important goals.

Do Managers Act in the Shareholders' Interests?

Whether managers do, in fact, act in the best interest of shareholders depends on two factors. First, how closely are management goals aligned with shareholder goals? This question relates to the way managers are compensated. Second, can managers be replaced if they do not pursue shareholder goals? This issue relates to control of the firm. As we discuss, there are a number of reasons to think that, even in the largest firms, management has a significant incentive to act in the interest of shareholders.[8]

---

[8] The legal system is another important factor in restraining managers and controlling shareholders. The common law system in place in Canada, the U.S., and U.K. offers the greatest protection of shareholder rights according to R. La Porta, F. Lopez-de-Silanes, A. Schliefer, and R. W. Vishny, "Law and Finance," *Journal of Political Economy*, December 1998.

MANAGERIAL COMPENSATION   Management frequently has a significant economic incentive to increase share value for two reasons: First, managerial compensation, particularly at the top, is usually tied to financial performance in general and often to the share value in particular. For example, managers are frequently given the option to buy stock at current prices. The more the stock is worth, the more valuable this option becomes.[9] The second incentive managers have relates to job prospects. Better performers within the firm get promoted. More generally, those managers who are successful in pursuing shareholder goals are in greater demand in the labour market and thus command higher salaries.

Of course, in management compensation, as with other areas of business, matters sometimes get off track. Many observers believe that top executives are overpaid. For example, shareholders of Novartis criticized the company for excessively compensating its chairman, Daniel Vasella, when he was paid over $21 million in 2011.[10] One control on compensation is the 'say on pay' initiative whereby a firm's shareholders have the right to vote on the remuneration of executives. Going further, creative forms of excessive corporate compensation at U.S. companies like Worldcom, Tyco, and Adelphia led to the passage of the *Sarbanes-Oxley Act* in 2002. The act is intended to protect investors from corporate abuses. For example, one section prohibits personal loans from a company to its officers, such as the ones that were received by former Worldcom CEO Bernie Ebbers.

Excessive management pay and unauthorized management consumption are examples of agency costs.[11]

CONTROL OF THE FIRM   Control of the firm ultimately rests with shareholders. They elect the board of directors, who, in turn, hire and fire management. In 2007, frustrated with his management tactics and overly generous compensation package, shareholders of Home Depot pressured the board of directors into ousting CEO Robert Nardelli.[12] From replacing CEOs to entire boards to demanding changes in a firm's articles of incorporation, shareholder activism is becoming increasingly prominent worldwide. For example, shareholders of HudBay Minerals Inc. halted a proposed acquisition of Lundin Mining Corp. in 2008 over objections to issuing the 153 million shares that would be needed to fund the purchase.[13] Poorly managed firms are more attractive as acquisitions than well-managed firms because a greater turnaround potential exists. Thus, avoiding a takeover by another firm gives management another incentive to act in the shareholders' interest.

The available theory and evidence substantiate that shareholders control the firm and that shareholder wealth maximization is the relevant goal of the corporation. Even so, at times management goals are undoubtedly pursued at the expense of the shareholders, at least temporarily. For example, management may try to avoid the discipline of a potential takeover by instituting "poison pill" provisions to make the stock unattractive. Or the firm may issue non-voting stock to thwart a takeover attempt. Canadian shareholders, particularly pension funds and other institutional investors, are becoming increasingly active in campaigning against such management actions.[14]

corporate governance
Rules for corporate organization and conduct.

Large funds like the Ontario Teachers' Pension Plan Board have set up detailed **corporate governance** and proxy voting guidelines for the companies in which they invest. Smaller funds may employ the services of firms like Institutional Shareholder Services (ISS) to advise them on how to vote on proposed governance changes.

STAKEHOLDERS   Our discussion thus far implies that management and shareholders are the only parties with an interest in the firm's decisions. This is an oversimplification, of course.

---

[9] Employee stock options allow the manager to purchase a certain number of shares at a fixed price over a specified period of time. By providing the manager an ownership stake in the company, the options are meant to align the manager's goals and actions with the shareholders' interests. For more on employee stock options, see Chapter 25.

[10] 2011 Dow Jones & Company, Inc.

[11] Because it requires management to pay out almost all of the cash flow to unit holders, the income trust form of organization can help to control these agency costs.

[12] *The New York Times*, January 4, 2007.

[13] financialpost.com/news/Shareholders+step+forefront/5433163/story.html

[14] We discuss takeovers and pension managers' activism in monitoring management activities in Chapter 23.

Employees, customers, suppliers, and various levels of government all have financial interests in the firm.

Taken together, these various groups are called **stakeholders** in the firm. In general, a **stakeholder** is a shareholder, creditor, or other individual (or group) that potentially has a claim on the cash flows of the firm. Such groups also attempt to exert control over the firm by introducing alternate, socially oriented goals such as preserving the environment or creating employment equity. Even though stakeholder pressures may create additional costs for owners, almost all major corporations pay close attention to stakeholders because stakeholder satisfaction is consistent with shareholder wealth maximization. Table 1.2 summarizes concerns of various stakeholders.

stakeholder
Anyone who potentially has a claim on a firm.

sustainalytics.com

TABLE 1.2   Inventory of typical stakeholders and issues

Company	Employees		Shareholders	Customers	Suppliers	Public Stakeholders	Competitors
Company history	General policy Compensation and rewards	Benefits Training and development	General policy Shareholder communications and complaints	General policy Customer communications	General policy Relative power	Public health, safety, and protection	General policy
Industry background	Career planning	Employee assistance program	Product safety	Other supplier issues	Environmental issues
Organization structure	Health promotion	Shareholder advocacy	Customer complaints		Public policy involvement
Economic performance	Leaves of absence	Absenteeism and turnover	Shareholder rights	Special customer services		Community relations
Competitive environment	Dismissal and appeal	Relationships with unions	Other shareholder issues	Other customer issues		Social investment and donations
Mission or purpose	Retirement and termination counselling	Termination, layoff, and redundancy				
Corporate codes	Women in management and on the board	Employment equity and discrimination				
Stakeholder and social issues	Employee communication	Day care and family accommodation				
Management	Part-time temporary, or contract employees	Occupational health and safety				
		Other employee or human resource issues				

Source: M. B. E. Clarkson, "Analyzing Corporate Performance: A New Approach," *Canadian Investment Review*, Fall 1991, p. 70. (Reprinted with permission from Canadian Investment Review, Rogers Media Publishing.)

Corporate Social Responsibility and Ethical Investing

Well-managed large corporations seek to maintain a reputation as good corporate citizens with detailed policies on important social issues. Investors are becoming increasingly concerned with corporate social responsibility (CSR) and may turn to firms like Sustainalytics, founded by Michael Jantzi in Canada, for information. Sustainalytics provides a social responsibility rating for corporations based on over 200 indicators of responsible behaviour with respect to stakeholder issues that dovetail with those in Figure 1.2: community and society, customers, corporate governance, employees, environment, and human rights. Jantzi ratings also assess controversial business activities; these include, alcohol, gaming, genetic engineering, nuclear power, pornography, tobacco, and weapons. An example Jantzi rating for Nexen Inc. is shown in Figure 1.2.

More than sixty companies that avoid controversial business activities and score well on Jantzi's other criteria are included in its Jantzi Social Index. Ethical investment mutual funds such as Ethical Growth and Investors Summa offer an opportunity to buy a portfolio of Canadian companies that meet criteria similar to Jantzi's. Similar funds exist in the U.S. and Europe.

You might wonder about the performance of such funds: Can investors "do well by doing good"? The results to date are mixed. A Canadian study suggests that socially responsible investing during the 1990s produced returns similar to those of the overall market after adjusting for risk and concludes that "investing for the soul may not hurt the bottom line." However, because ethical funds tend to invest more heavily in "clean" tech companies, it remains an open question whether this finding applies in other periods. A more recent U.S. study argues that socially responsible investing imposes a heavy penalty on return.[15] Given the mixed evidence, major Canadian institutional investors like the Ontario Teachers' Pension Plan and the Ontario Municipal Employees Retirement System pay careful attention to corporate social responsibility in selecting investments but do not eliminate companies from their portfolios based solely on environmental and other social issues.[16] To address controversy over their corporate social responsibility Canadian mining companies like Barrick Gold and Sherritt International provide detailed information on their CSR activities in Latin America where they are the third largest source of foreign investment after the United States and Spain.[17]

FIGURE 1.2

Sustainalytics Global Platform–Nexen Inc.

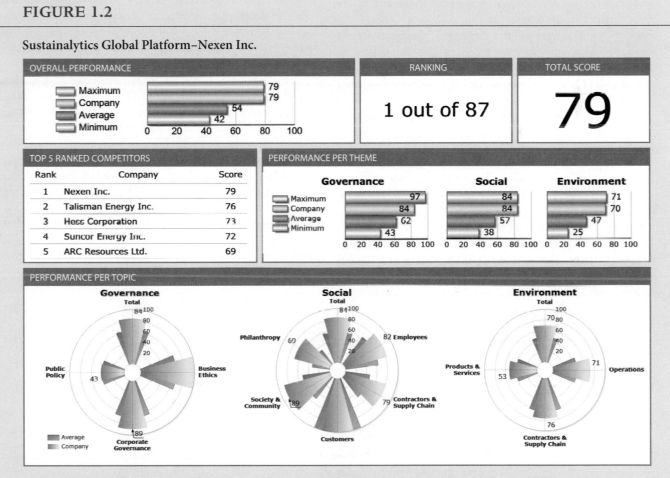

Source: Sustainalytics. Used with permission.

[15] P. Amundson and S.R. Foerster, "Socially Responsible Investing: Better for Your Soul or Your Bottom Line?" *Canadian Investment Review*, Winter 2001, pp. 26–34 and C. Geczy, R. F. Stambaugh and D. Levin, "Investing in Socially Responsible Mutual Funds," October 2005, available at SSRN: ssrn.com/sol3/papers.cfm?abstract_id=416380.

[16] For a detailed summary of arguments in favour of socially responsible investing by pension funds, see "A legal framework for the integration of environmental, social and governance issues into institutional investment," by Freshfields Bruckhaus Deringer and the UNEP Finance Initiative, October 2005, available at www.unepfi.org/publications/investment/?&0=

[17] J. Sagebien et al., "The Corporate Social Responsibility of Canadian Mining Companies in Latin America: A Systems Perspective," *Canadian Foreign Policy*, 14, 3 (2008), 103–128

IN THEIR OWN WORDS...

David Weitzner and James Darroch on Why Moral Failures Precede Financial Crises

Innovation and crises are endemic to the financial system and while every failure leads to significant regulatory improvement, it has never been enough to prevent the next financial crisis. Yet, each crisis has unique elements and the current crisis cannot be understood without seeing how financial innovation fundamentally changed the financial system of the USA and consequently for those financial systems connected to the USA—essentially the globe. To this end, it is important to note that the drivers of the problems—structured finance products—were essentially creatures of the unregulated or lightly regulated side of the US financial system, where greed was unchecked. While there was clearly a failure of regulation, it should be first seen as a failure in scope of regulation. But it is equally important to understand how hubris united with greed was instrumental in players working to create an unregulated market. What is stunning about the current crisis is that it is the result of governance failures of both the boards of financial institutions and markets despite significant regulatory reforms in the banking world—Basel II—and corporate governance in the USA—Sarbanes-Oxley (SOX). The lesson to be learned is that regulatory reform without ethical reform will never be enough. The faith that public policymakers had resolved the major economic issues associated with business cycles and volatility combined with the private sector's faith in hyper-rational modern finance and unregulated markets created an environment conducive to the growth of greed. The arrogant faith in the new financial order led to a lack of attention to governance and ethics despite famous ethical failures and heightened regulatory concerns. While it is often said that success breeds success, long bull markets and excess liquidity breed over-confidence and an over-commitment to revenue-generating activities as opposed to control activities. In this environment of weak governance, unethical behavior flourishes. Management scholars have already faced tough questions about the ethical implications of their theoretical suppositions (Ghoshal, 2005), but the current financial woes have led to renewed calls for a more central place for ethical considerations in mainstream management theories along with new questions about the significant role greed and hubris tend to play in the practice of management. We believe that the time has come for researchers concerned with the financial system and the question of ethics to address explicitly the problem of greed.

The immediate challenge is to restore trust not only among financial institutions to restore the inter-bank markets, but also trust from the public. This is a tall order. Greed led to the governance failures at both the market and individual institutional level. Financial players who should have been committed to the good of the system in order to ensure that they could create wealth for themselves while improving the lot of others failed to recognize this obligation. Rather, greed and hubris led to the enrichment of the few to the cost of the many. It would be naive to believe that a moral renaissance is at hand and will solve all ills, so until that time we must enforce rules to promote the virtue of transparency to prevent shadow worlds in the financial system.

Source: *From the authors* Used with permission.

David Weitzner is an Instructor (Strategy/Policy) and James Darroch is an Associate Professor (Policy) at Schulich School of Business, York University.

Concept Questions

1. What is an agency relationship?
2. What are agency problems and how do they come about? What are agency costs?
3. What incentives do managers in large corporations have to maximize share value?
4. What role do stakeholders play in determining corporate goals?

1.5 | Financial Markets and the Corporation

We've seen that the primary advantages of the corporate form of organization are that ownership can be transferred more quickly and easily than with other forms and that money can be raised more readily. Both of these advantages are significantly enhanced by the existence of financial institutions and markets. Financial markets play an extremely important role in corporate finance.

FIGURE 1.3

Cash flows between the firm and the financial markets

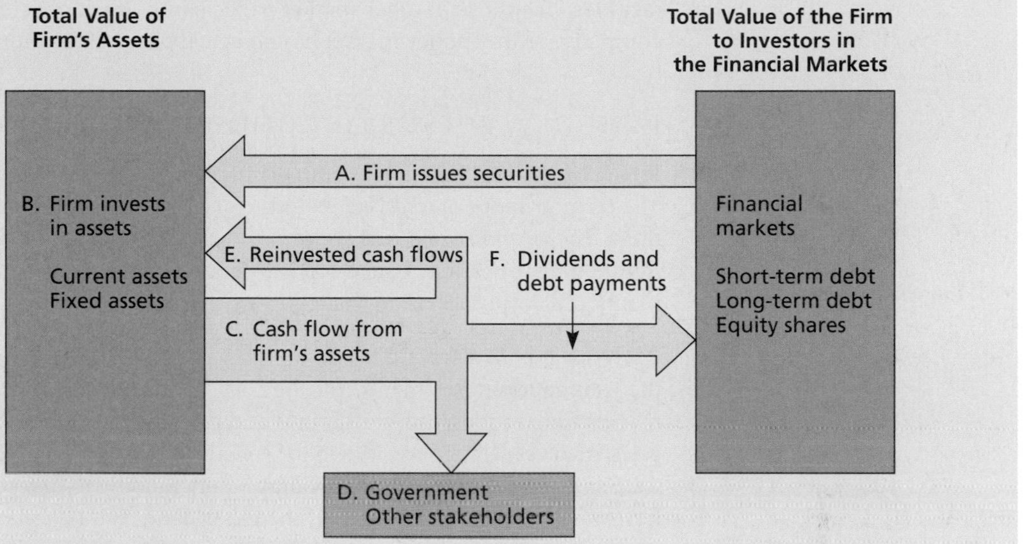

A. Firm issues securities to raise cash.
B. Firm invests in assets.
C. Firm's operations generate cash flow.
D. Cash is paid to government as taxes. Other stakeholders may receive cash.
E. Reinvested cash flows are plowed back into firm.
F. Cash is paid out to investors in the form of interest and dividends.

Cash Flows to and from the Firm

The interplay between the corporation and the financial markets is illustrated in Figure 1.3. The arrows in Figure 1.3 trace the passage of cash from the financial markets to the firm and from the firm back to the financial markets.

Suppose we start with the firm selling shares of stock and borrowing money to raise cash. Cash flows to the firm from the financial market (A). The firm invests the cash in current and fixed assets (B). These assets generate some cash (C), some of which goes to pay corporate taxes (D). After taxes are paid, some of this cash flow is reinvested in the firm (E). The rest goes back to the financial markets as cash paid to creditors and shareholders (F).

Companies like Tim Hortons routinely make decisions that create such cash flows to and from the firm. For example, in 2010 the company used increased cash flow from operations to fund its growth requirements.

A financial market, like any market, is just a way of bringing buyers and sellers together. In financial markets, it is debt and equity securities that are bought and sold. Financial markets differ in detail, however. The most important differences concern the types of securities that are traded, how trading is conducted, and who the buyers and sellers are. Some of these differences are discussed next.

Money versus Capital Markets

money markets
Financial markets where short-term debt securities are bought and sold.

capital markets
Financial markets where long-term debt and equity securities are bought and sold.

Financial markets can be classified as either **money markets** or **capital markets**. Short-term debt securities of many varieties are bought and sold in money markets. These short-term debt securities are often called money market instruments and are essentially IOUs. For example, a bankers acceptance represents short-term borrowing by large corporations and is a money-market instrument. Treasury bills are an IOU of the government of Canada. Capital markets are the markets for long-term debt and shares of stock, so the Toronto Stock Exchange, for example, is a capital market.

The money market is a dealer market. Generally, dealers buy and sell something for themselves, at their own risk. A car dealer, for example, buys and sells automobiles. In contrast, brokers and agents match buyers and sellers, but they do not actually own the commodity. A real estate agent or broker, for example, does not normally buy and sell houses.

The largest money-market dealers are chartered banks and investment dealers. Their trading facilities, like those of other market participants, are connected electronically via telephone and computer, so the money market has no actual physical location.

Primary versus Secondary Markets

Financial markets function as both primary and secondary markets for debt and equity securities. The term *primary markets* refers to the original sale of securities by governments and corporations. The *secondary markets* are where these securities are bought and sold after the original sale. Equities are, of course, issued solely by corporations. Debt securities are issued by both governments and corporations. In the following discussion, we focus only on corporate securities.

PRIMARY MARKETS   In a primary market transaction, the corporation is the seller, and the transaction raises money for the corporation. Corporations engage in two types of primary market transactions: public offerings and private placements. A public offering, as the name suggests, involves selling securities to the general public. For example, in 1999 and early 2000, investors were snapping up new issues providing equity funding to untested dot-com IPOs (initial public offerings). A private placement, on the other hand, is a negotiated sale involving a specific buyer. These topics are covered in some detail in Part 6, so we only introduce the bare essentials here.

Most publicly offered debt and equity securities are underwritten. In Canada, underwriting is conducted by *investment dealers* specialized in marketing securities. Examples are RBC Capital Markets, Scotia Capital, BMO Capital Markets, and CIBC World Markets.

When a public offering is underwritten, an investment dealer or a group of investment dealers (called a *syndicate*) typically purchase the securities from the firm and market them to the public. The underwriters hope to profit by reselling the securities to investors at a higher price than they pay the firm.

By law, public offerings of debt and equity must be registered with provincial authorities, of which the most important is the Ontario Securities Commission (OSC). Registration requires the firm to disclose a great deal of information before selling any securities. The accounting, legal, and underwriting costs of public offerings can be considerable.

Partly to avoid the various regulatory requirements and the expense of public offerings, debt and equity are often sold privately to large financial institutions such as life insurance companies or mutual funds. Such private placements do not have to be registered with the OSC and do not require the involvement of underwriters.

SECONDARY MARKETS   A secondary market transaction involves one owner or creditor selling to another. Therefore, the secondary markets provide the means for transferring ownership of corporate securities. There are two kinds of secondary markets: *auction markets* and *dealer markets*.

Dealer markets in stocks and long-term debt are called *over-the-counter* (OTC) markets. Trading in debt securities takes place over the counter, with much of the trading now conducted electronically. The expression *over-the-counter* refers to days of old when securities were literally bought and sold at counters in offices around the country. Today, like the money market, a significant fraction of the market for stocks and all of the market for long-term debt have no central location; the many dealers are connected electronically.

THIRD AND FOURTH MARKETS   A third market involves trading exchange-listed securities in OTC markets. This allows investors to trade large volume of securities directly without an exchange. Fourth Market trading involves institution-to-institution trading without using the services of brokers or dealers.

TRADING IN CORPORATE SECURITIES   The equity shares of most of the large firms in Canada trade in organized auction and dealer markets. The largest stock market in Canada is the Toronto Stock Exchange (TSX). It is owned and operated as a subsidiary of the TMX Group for the trading of senior securities. Table 1.3 shows the top ten stock markets in the world in 2011, Toronto ranked number eight based on market value. The TMX Group also runs the

TSX Venture Exchange for listing smaller, emerging companies. The four main industries represented on the Venture Exchange are biotechnology, information technology, mining, and oil and gas.

Auction markets differ from dealer markets in two ways: First, an auction market or exchange, unlike a dealer market, has a physical location (like Wall Street). Second, in a dealer market, most of the buying and selling is done by the dealer. The primary purpose of an auction market, on the other hand, is to match those who wish to sell with those who wish to buy. Dealers play a limited role.

In addition to the stock exchanges, there is a large OTC market for stocks. In 1971, the U.S. National Association of Securities Dealers (NASD) made available to dealers and brokers an electronic quotation system called NASDAQ (NASD Automated Quotation system, pronounced "naz-dak" and now spelled "Nasdaq"). In January 2006, Nasdaq took the next step forward when its application to be registered as a national stock exchange was accepted by the U.S. Securities and Exchange Commission. There are roughly three times as many companies on Nasdaq as there are on NYSE, but they tend to be much smaller in size and trade less actively. There are exceptions, of course. For example, tech giants Microsoft and Intel trade on Nasdaq. Nonetheless, the total value of Nasdaq stocks is considerably less than the total value of the NYSE stocks.

TABLE 1.3

Largest stock markets in the world by market capitalization in 2011	Rank in 2011	Stock Exchanges	Market Capitalization (in U.S. $ billions)
	1	NYSE Euronext (US)	$11,796
	2	NASDAQ OMX (US)	3,845
	3	Tokyo Stock Exchange Group	3,325
	4	London Stock Exchange Group	3,266
	5	NYSE Euronext (Europe)	2,447
	6	Shanghai Stock Exchange	2,357
	7	Hong Kong Exchanges	2,258
	8	TMX Group	1,912
Source: World Federation of Stock Exchanges at <u>world-exchanges.org</u>	9	BM&FBOVESPA	1,229
	10	Australian Securities Exchange	1,198

LISTING Stocks that trade on an organized exchange are said to be listed on that exchange. To be listed, firms must meet certain minimum criteria concerning, for example, asset size and number of shareholders. These criteria differ for various exchanges.

The requirements for listing on the TSX Venture are not as strict as those for listing on the TSX, although the listing process is quite similar. The TSX Venture, however, has two different tiers that companies can register under. Companies can list shares on the second tier with as little as $500,000 in net tangible assets and $50,000 in pre-tax earnings. Both tiers require that there exist 300 public shareholders, holding one board lot or more; Tier 1 also requires that there be 1 million free trading shares with a market value of $1 million or more, and Tier 2 requires at least 500,000 free trading shares with a market value of $500,000 or more. These requirements make it possible for smaller companies that would not normally be able to obtain listing on the TSX to acquire equity financing.

The TSX has the most stringent requirements of the exchanges in Canada. For example, to be listed on the TSX, a company is expected to have at least 1,000,000 freely tradable shares with a market value of at least $4 million and a total of at least 300 shareholders with at least 100 shares each.[18] There are additional minimums on earnings, assets, and number of shares outstanding. Research suggests that listing on exchanges adds valuable liquidity to a company's shares.[19] In

---

[18] tmx.com/en/pdf/InternationalGuidetoListing.pdf

[19] Relevant studies include S. R. Foerster and G. A. Karolyi, "The Effects of Market Segmentation and Investor Recognition on Asset Prices: Evidence from Foreign Stocks Listings in the U.S.," *Journal of Finance,* 54: 3, 1999, 981–1013 and U.R. Mittoo, "The Winners and Losers of Listings in the U.S.," *Canadian Investment Review,* Fall 1998, 13–17.

November 2002, the TSX itself went public and listed its shares for the first time. With an offering of just under 19 million shares at an initial offering price of $18, the TSX easily exceeded its own listing requirements.

1.6 | Financial Institutions

Financial institutions act as *intermediaries* between investors (funds suppliers) and firms raising funds. (Federal and provincial governments and individuals also raise funds in financial markets, but our examples focus on firms.) Financial institutions justify their existence by providing a variety of services that promote the efficient allocation of funds. These institutions also serve as intermediaries for households and individuals—providing a medium where individuals can save and borrow money. Individuals and households may choose to save not only in the traditional savings and chequing accounts, but also in savings plans such as a Registered Retirement Savings Plan (RRSP), Registered Education Savings Plan (RESP), or Tax-Free Savings Account (TFSA). Canadian financial institutions include *chartered banks and other depository institutions—trust companies, credit unions, investment dealers, insurance companies, pension funds, and mutual funds.*

Table 1.4 ranks the top eleven publicly traded financial institutions in Canada by market capitalization in 2011. They include the Big Six chartered banks, three life insurance companies, one financial holding company, and a diversified financial services company. Because they are allowed to diversify by operating in all provinces, Canada's chartered banks are of a reasonable size on an international scale.

Chartered banks operate under federal regulation, accepting deposits from suppliers of funds and making commercial loans to mid-sized businesses, corporate loans to large companies, and personal loans and mortgages to individuals.[20] Banks make the majority of their income from the *spread* between the interest paid on deposits and the higher rate earned on loans. This is *indirect finance.*

Chartered banks also provide other services that generate fees instead of spread income. For example, a large corporate customer seeking short-term debt funding can borrow *directly* from another large corporation with funds supplied through a *bankers acceptance.* This is an interest-bearing IOU stamped by a bank guaranteeing the borrower's credit. Instead of spread income, the bank receives a *stamping fee.* Bankers acceptances are an example of *direct finance.* Notice that the key difference between direct finance and indirect finance is that in direct finance funds do not pass through the bank's balance sheet in the form of a deposit and loan. Often called *securitization* because a security (the bankers acceptance) is created, direct finance is growing rapidly.

TABLE 1.4

Largest financial institutions in Canada, by market capitalization, December 2011	Rank	Company	Market Capitalization ($ billion)
	1	Royal Bank of Canada	$79.9
	2	Toronto Dominion	72.5
	3	Bank of Nova Scotia	59.7
	4	Bank of Montreal	38.7
	5	Canadian Imperial Bank of Commerce	32.5
	6	Manulife Financial Corp.	21.6
	7	Great-West Lifeco	21.2
	8	Power Financial	20.1
	9	Sun Life Financial Inc.	13.3
	10	National Bank of Canada	12.3
Source: tmx.com/en/pdf/mig/ TSX_TSXV_Issuers.xls	11	IGM Financial	11.5

Trust companies also accept deposits and make loans. In addition, trust companies engage in fiduciary activities—managing assets for estates, registered retirement savings plans, and so on.

---

[20] Loan and mortgage calculations are discussed in Chapter 6.

Like trust companies, credit unions also accept deposits and make loans. Caisses Desjardins du Quebec is a major Quebec credit union, but does not appear in Table 1.4 because it is member-owned and not publicly traded.

Investment dealers are non-depository institutions that assist firms in issuing new securities in exchange for fee income. Investment dealers also aid investors in buying and selling securities. Chartered banks own majority stakes in five of Canada's top 15 investment dealers.

Insurance companies include property and casualty insurance and health and life insurance companies. Life insurance companies engage in indirect finance by accepting funds in a form similar to deposits and making loans. Manulife Financial and Sun Life Financial are major life insurance companies that have expanded aggressively to become rivals of the chartered banks.

Fuelled by the aging of the Canadian population and the longest bull market in history, assets in pension and mutual funds grew rapidly in the 1990s. Pension funds invest contributions from employers and employees in securities offered by financial markets. Mutual funds pool individual investments to purchase diversified portfolios of securities. There are many different types of mutual funds. Table 1.5 shows the totals of mutual fund assets by fund type. In June 2011, the two largest categories were Canadian and foreign equity. However, the Canadian mutual fund market is small on a global scale. Table 1.6 shows the percentage of global mutual fund market by geography.

TABLE 1.5

Total net assets by fund type in June 2011

	Net Assets ($ billions)
Canadian Equity	$137.4
Global and International Equity	61.4
U.S. Equity	21.3
Sector Equity	18.2
Domestic Balanced	163.6
Global Balanced	129.5
Canadian Fixed Income	71.1
Global and High Yield Fixed Income	16.1
Specialty Funds	5.2
Money Market Funds	32.5
Total	$656.3

Source: Data drawn from Investment Funds Institute of Canada, Monthly statistics, June 2011. ific.ca.

TABLE 1.6

Global mutual fund industry by geography (*Percentage of total net assets, year-end 2011*)

Total worldwide mutual fund assets	$23.8 trillion
	Percentage of total net assets
United States	49
Europe	30
Africa and Asia/Pacific	13
Other Americas (includes Canada)	8

Source: Investment Company Institute, European Fund and Asset Management Association, and other national mutual fund associations

Hedge funds are another growing group of financial institutions. According to the 2011 Hedge Fund Asset Flows & Trends report published by HedgeFund.net, the industry had approximately US$2.561 trillion under management worldwide in the second quarter of 2011. Hedge funds are largely unregulated and privately managed investment funds catering to sophisticated investors, which look to earn high returns using aggressive financial strategies prohibited by mutual funds. These strategies may include arbitrage,[21] high levels of leverage,[22] and active involvement in the derivatives market. However, hedge funds are not restricted to investing in financial instruments—some hedge fund strategies involve acquiring stakes in public or private companies and pressuring the board to sell the business. In January 2011, the Canadian hedge fund industry was worth between $35 billion and $40 billion.[23] There is a high risk associated with hedge funds as these are highly unregulated and subject to fraud. In 2011, Raj Rajaratnam, hedge-fund tycoon and founder of Galleon Group was sentenced to 11 years in prison for insider trading. He amassed over $72 million by using illegal tips to trade in stocks of companies including Goldman Sachs Group Inc., Intel Corp., Google Inc., ATI Technologies Inc., and Clearwire Corp.[24]

We base this survey of the principal activities of financial institutions on their main activities today. Recent deregulation now allows chartered banks, trust companies, insurance companies, and investment dealers to engage in most of the activities of the others with one exception: Chartered banks are not allowed to sell life insurance through their branch networks. Although not every institution plans to become a one-stop financial supermarket, the different types of institutions are likely to continue to become more alike.

Concept Questions

1. What are the principal financial institutions in Canada? What is the principal role of each?
2. What are direct and indirect finance? How do they differ?
3. How are money and capital markets different?
4. What is a dealer market? How do dealer and auction markets differ?
5. What is the largest auction market in Canada?

1.7 | Trends in Financial Markets and Financial Management

Like all markets, financial markets are experiencing rapid globalization. Globalization also makes it harder for investors to shelter their portfolios from financial shocks in other countries. In the summer of 1998, the Asian financial crisis shook financial markets around the world. With increasing globalization, interest rates, foreign exchange rates, and other macroeconomic variables have become more volatile. The toolkit of available financial management techniques has expanded rapidly in response to a need to control increased risk from volatility and to track complexities arising from dealings in many countries. Computer technology improvements are making new **financial engineering** applications practical.

financial engineering
Creation of new securities or financial processes.

When financial managers or investment dealers design new securities or financial processes, their efforts are referred to as financial engineering. Successful financial engineering reduces and controls risk and minimizes taxes. Financial engineering creates a variety of debt and equity securities and reinforces the trend toward securitization of credit introduced earlier. A controversial example is the invention and rapid growth of trading in options, futures, and other **derivative securities**. Derivative securities are very useful in controlling risk, but they have also produced large losses when mishandled. For example, in 2008 during the financial crisis, American International Group (AIG) owed hefty Credit Default Swaps Settlement payments to various banks. When AIG was about to go bankrupt, the U.S. government intervened and bailed out the company by providing $182 billion.[25]

derivative securities
Options, futures, and other securities whose value derives from the price of another, underlying, asset.

Financial engineering also seeks to reduce financing costs of issuing securities as well as the

---

[21] The practice of taking advantage of a price differential between two or more markets.

[22] The use of debt to increase the potential return of an investment.

[23] Source: cbc.ca/news/business/taxseason/story/2011/01/17/f-hedge-funds-industry-canada.html. To learn more about hedge fund developments, visit hedgefund.net.

[24] articles.economictimes.indiatimes.com/2012-09-08/news/33696695_1_raj-rajaratnam-roomy-khan-oral-arguments

[25] theglobeandmail.com/globe-investor/aig-profit-lifted-by-aia-stake-tax-benefit/article2119948/

costs of complying with rules laid down by regulatory authorities. An example is the Short Form Prospectus Distribution (SFPD) allowing firms that frequently issue new equity to bypass most of the OSC registration requirements.

In addition to financial engineering, advances in technology have created e-business, bringing new challenges for the financial manager. For example, consumers ordering products on a company's website expect rapid delivery and failure to meet these expectations can damage a company's image. This means that companies doing e-business with consumers must invest in supply chain management as well as in additional inventory.

rbcroyalbank.com

Technological advances have also created opportunities to combine different types of financial institutions to take advantage of economies of scale and scope. For example, Royal Bank, Canada's largest chartered bank, owns Royal Trust and RBC Dominion Securities. Such large institutions operate in all provinces and internationally and enjoy more lax regulations in some jurisdictions than in others. Financial institutions pressure authorities to deregulate in a push-pull process called the **regulatory dialectic.**

regulatory dialectic
The pressures financial institutions and regulatory bodies exert on each other.

For example, in 1998 and again in 2002, banks planned mergers in an effort to pressure the federal government to grant approval. Although the federal government turned down the mergers, we believe this issue is dormant, not dead, and will reemerge in the not too distant future.

Not all trends are driven by technology. In the aftermath of the technology bubble of the late 1990s, stakeholders and regulators have become very interested in corporate governance reform, a topic we introduced earlier in the chapter. For example, proponents of such reform argue that a stronger, independent board of directors can prevent management excesses.

Another trend underlying the global financial crisis starting in 2007 was excessive financial leverage. Following the technology bubble and September 11, the United States Federal Reserve looked to aggressively lower interest rates in order to restore confidence in the economy. In the U.S., individuals with bad credit ratings, sub-prime borrowers, looked to banks to provide loans at historically low interest rates for home purchases. Investors also reacted to these low rates by seeking higher returns. The financial industry responded by manufacturing sub-prime mortgages and asset-backed securities. However, once housing prices began to cool and interest rates rose, sub-prime borrowers started defaulting on their loans and the collapse of the sub-prime market ensued. With mortgages serving as the underlying asset supporting most of the financial instruments that investment banks, institutions, and retail buyers had acquired, these assets lost much of their value and hundreds of billions of dollars of write-downs followed.

Canada faced much the same external environments in the leadup to the crisis as the US did. But despite its financial and economic integration with the US, Canada did not experience a single bank failure or bailout., The difference was that a highly stable branch banking system dominated by six large institutions forms the heart of Canada's financial system. Banks dominate lending and credit creation nationally and account for over 60% of total financial assets in Canada.[26]

These trends have made financial management a much more complex and technical activity. For this reason, many students of business find introductory finance one of their most challenging subjects. The trends we reviewed have also increased the stakes. In the face of increased global competition, the payoff for good financial management is great. The finance function is also becoming important in corporate strategic planning. The good news is that career opportunities (and compensation) in financial positions are quite attractive.

1.8 | Outline of the Text

Now that we've completed a quick tour of the concerns of corporate finance, we can take a closer look at the organization of this book. The text is organized into the following nine parts:

Part 1: Overview of Corporate Finance

Part 2: Financial Statements and Long-Term Financial Planning

Part 3: Valuation of Future Cash Flows

Part 4: Capital Budgeting

---

[26] Donald J.S. Brean, Lawrence Kryzanowski & Gordon S. Roberts (2011): Canada and the United States: Different roots, different routes to financial sector regulation, Business History, 53:2, 249–269

Part 5:   Risk and Return
Part 6:   Cost of Capital and Long-Term Financial Policy
Part 7:   Short-Term Financial Planning and Management
Part 8:   Topics in Corporate Finance
Part 9:   Derivative Securities and Corporate Finance

Part 1 of the text contains some introductory material and goes on to explain the relationship between accounting and cash flow. Part 2 explores financial statements and how they are used in finance in greater depth.

Parts 3 and 4 contain our core discussion on valuation. In Part 3, we develop the basic procedures for valuing future cash flows with particular emphasis on stocks and bonds. Part 4 draws on this material and deals with capital budgeting and the effect of long-term investment decisions on the firm.

In Part 5, we develop some tools for evaluating risk. We then discuss how to evaluate the risks associated with long-term investments by the firm. The emphasis in this section is on coming up with a benchmark for making investment decisions.

Part 6 deals with the related issues of long-term financing, dividend policy, and capital structure. We discuss corporate securities in some detail and describe the procedures used to raise capital and sell securities to the public. We also introduce and describe the important concept of the cost of capital. We go on to examine dividends and dividend policy and important considerations in determining a capital structure.

The working capital question is addressed in Part 7. The subjects of short-term financial planning, cash management, and credit management are covered.

Part 8 contains the important special topic of international corporate finance. Part 9 covers risk management and derivative securities.

1.9 | SUMMARY AND CONCLUSIONS

This chapter has introduced you to some of the basic ideas in corporate finance. In it, we saw that:

1. Corporate finance has three main areas of concern:
   a. What long-term investments should the firm take? This is the capital budgeting decision.
   b. Where will the firm get the long-term financing to pay for its investment? In other words, what mixture of debt and equity should we use to fund our operations? This is the capital structure decision.
   c. How should the firm manage its everyday financial activities? This is the working capital decision.
2. The goal of financial management in a for-profit business is to make decisions that increase the value of the stock or, more generally, increase the market value of the equity.
3. The corporate form of organization is superior to other forms when it comes to raising money and transferring ownership interest, but it has the disadvantage of double taxation.
4. There is the possibility of conflicts between shareholders and management in a large corporation. We called these conflicts agency problems and discussed how they might be controlled and reduced.
5. The advantages of the corporate form are enhanced by the existence of financial markets. Financial institutions function to promote the efficiency of financial markets. Financial markets function as both primary and secondary markets for corporate securities and can be organized as either dealer or auction markets. Globalization, deregulation, and financial engineering are important forces shaping financial markets and the practice of financial management.

Of the topics we've discussed thus far, the most important is the goal of financial management: Maximizing the value of the stock. Throughout the text, as we analyze financial decisions, we always ask the same question: How does the decision under consideration affect the value of the shares?

Key Terms

agency problem (page 10)
capital budgeting (page 2)
capital markets (page 15)
capital structure (page 3)
corporate governance (page 11)
corporation (page 5)
derivative securities (page 20)

financial engineering (page 20)
money markets (page 15)
partnership (page 5)
regulatory dialectic (page 21)
sole proprietorship (page 4)
stakeholder (page 12)
working capital management (page 4)

Chapter Review Problems and Self-Test

1. **The Financial Management Decision Process (LO1)** What are the three types of financial management decisions? For each type of decision, give an example of a business transaction that would be relevant.

2. **Sole Proprietorships and Partnerships (LO2)** What are the three primary disadvantages to the sole proprietorship and partnership forms of business organization? What benefits are there to these types of business organization as opposed to the corporate form?

3. **Corporate Organization (LO2)** What is the primary disadvantage of the corporate form of organization? Name at least two advantages of corporate organization.

4. **Corporate Finance Organizational Structure (LO4)** In a large corporation, what are the two distinct groups that report to the chief financial officer? Which group is the focus of corporate finance?

5. **The Goal of Financial Management (LO3)** What goal should always motivate the actions of the firm's financial manager?

6. **Corporate Agency Issues (LO4)** Who owns a corporation? Describe the process whereby the owners control the firm's management. What is the main reason that an agency relationship exists in the corporate form of organization? In this context, what kind of problems can arise?

7. **Financial Markets (LO5)** An initial public offering (IPO) of a company's securities is a term you've probably noticed in the financial press. Is an IPO a primary market transaction or a secondary market transaction?

8. **Financial Markets (LO5)** What does it mean when we say the Toronto Stock Exchange is both an auction market and a dealer market? How are auction markets different from dealer markets? What kind of market is Nasdaq?

9. **Not-for-Profit Firm Goals (LO3)** Suppose you were the financial manager of a not-for-profit business (a not-for-profit hospital, perhaps). What kinds of goals do you think would be appropriate?

10. **Firm Goals and Stock Value (LO3)** Evaluate the following statement: "Managers should not focus on the current stock value because doing so will lead to an overemphasis on short-term profits at the expense of long-term profits."

11. **Firm Goals and Ethics (LO3)** Can our goal of maximizing the value of the stock conflict with other goals, such as avoiding unethical or illegal behaviour? In particular, do you think subjects like customer and employee safety, the environment, and the general good of society fit in this framework, or are they essentially ignored? Try to think of some specific scenarios to illustrate your answer.

12. **Firm Goals and Multinational Firms (LO3)** Would our goal of maximizing the value of the stock be different if we were thinking about financial management in a foreign country? Why or why not?

13. **Agency Issues and Corporate Control (LO4)** Suppose you own shares in a company. The current price per share is $25. Another company has just announced that it wants to buy your company and will pay $35 per share to acquire all the outstanding shares. Your company's management immediately begins fighting off this hostile bid. Is management acting in the shareholders' best interests? Why or why not?

14. **Agency Issues and International Finance (LO4)** Corporate ownership varies around the world. Historically, individuals have owned the majority of shares in public corporations in the United States. In Canada this is also the case, but ownership is more often concentrated in the hands of a majority shareholder. In Germany and Japan, banks, other financial institutions, and large companies own most of the shares in public corporations. How do you think these ownership differences affect the severity of agency costs in different countries?

15. **Major Institutions and Markets (LO5)** What are the major types of financial institutions and financial markets in Canada?

16. **Direct versus Indirect Finance (LO5)** What is the difference between direct and indirect finance? Give an example of each.

17. **Current Major Trends (LO5)** What are some of the major trends in Canadian financial markets? Explain how these trends affect the practice of financial management in Canada.

Internet Application Questions

1. Equity markets are an important source of capital for private firms in Canada. Take a tour of the Toronto Stock Exchange at tmx.com. What is the TSX Composite Index? Check out Index Lists/Information under Investor Information. What does a change in the TSX Composite Index tell you?

2. Canadian banks are actively involved in financing home mortgages. Describe the role played by the Canada Mortgage and Housing Corporation in home mortgages (cmhc.ca). What is the *National Housing Act*? Can an investor participate in the mortgage "pool" represented by housing loans insured by the CMHC? Click on the Investment Opportunities menu on the CMHC homepage and describe Mortgage Backed Securities offered by the CMHC.

3. The choice of business organization form depends on many factors. The following website from British Columbia outlines the pros and cons of a sole proprietorship, partnership, and corporation: www.smallbusinessbc.ca/starting-a-business/legal-requirements.

   Can you suggest a few reasons why some firms that were organized as partnerships decided to incorporate (e.g., Goldman Sachs (goldmansachs.com) with shares traded on the NYSE (nyse.com)?

4. Ethical investing following socially responsible principles is gaining popularity. The Social Investment Organization website provides information about these principles and on Canadian ethical mutual funds at socialinvestment.ca. Sustainalytics offers research services to support socially responsible investing at sustainalytics.com/. How does investing in ethical funds differ from investing in general? What has been the performance record of Canadian ethical funds?

5. Ontario Securities Commission (OSC) administers and enforces securities law in the province of Ontario. The OSC website (osc.gov.on.ca) outlines various security laws and instruments. Visit the 'Securities Law and Instruments' section and check out the latest instruments, rules and policies. What are *Securities Act* (Ontario) and *Commodity Futures Act*?

FINANCIAL STATEMENTS, CASH FLOW, AND TAXES

I n 2011, the Ontario Securities Commission (OSC) began investigating Sino-Forest Corp., one of the leading commercial plant operators in People's Republic of China. The OSC found the company to have misrepresented some of its revenue and/or exaggerated some of its timber holdings. In August 2011, Allen Chan, the CEO of Sino-Forest Corp., had resigned amid allegations of fraud and misconduct.

The story of Sino-Forest Corp. highlights the issue of reliability of financial statements and the importance of understanding the financial reporting of companies. Financial statements are discussed in this chapter.

Learning Objectives ▶

After studying this chapter, you should understand:

LO1 The difference between accounting value (or "book" value) and market value.

LO2 The difference between accounting income and cash flow.

LO3 How to determine a firm's cash flow from its financial statements.

LO4 The difference between average and marginal tax rates.

LO5 The basics of Capital Cost Allowance (CCA) and Undepreciated Capital Cost (UCC).

In this chapter, we examine financial statements, cash flow, and taxes. Our emphasis is not on preparing financial statements. Instead, we recognize that financial statements are frequently a key source of information for financial decisions, so our goal is to briefly examine such statements and point out some of their more relevant features along with a few limitations. We pay special attention to some of the practical details of cash flow. By cash flow, we simply mean the difference between the number of dollars that come in and the number that go out. A crucial input to sound financial management, cash flow analysis is used throughout the book. For example, bankers lending to businesses are looking increasingly at borrowers' cash flows as the most reliable measures of each company's ability to repay its loans. In another example, most large companies base their capital budgets for investments in plant and equipment on analysis of cash flow. As a result, there is an excellent payoff in later chapters for knowledge of cash flow.

One very important topic is taxes because cash flows are measured after taxes. Our discussion looks at how corporate and individual taxes are computed and at how investors are taxed on different types of income. A basic understanding of the Canadian tax system is essential for success in applying the tools of financial management.

2.1 | Statement of Financial Position

statement of financial position
Financial statement showing a firm's accounting value on a particular date. Also known as a balance sheet.

The **statement of financial position**, also referred to as the balance sheet, is a snapshot of the firm. It is a convenient means of organizing and summarizing what a firm owns (its *assets*), what a firm owes (its *liabilities*), and the difference between the two (the firm's *equity*) at a given time. Figure 2.1 illustrates how the traditional statement of financial position is constructed. As shown, the left-hand side lists the assets of the firm, and the right-hand side lists the liabilities and equity. However, most publicly accountable enterprises in Canada choose a vertical format for the statement of financial position.

In 2011, publicly traded firms in Canada switched to **International Financial Reporting Standards (IFRS)**.[1] Under IFRS, a company enjoys flexibility over how to present its statement

---

[1] cica.ca/ifrs//index.aspx

of financial position. For example, in applications of IFRS in Europe, many companies list fixed assets at the top of the left-hand side of their balance sheets. In Canada, the practice is to retain the order used under GAAP.

FIGURE 2.1

The statement of financial position model of the firm. Left side lists total value of assets. Right side, or total value of the firm to investors, determines how the value is distributed.

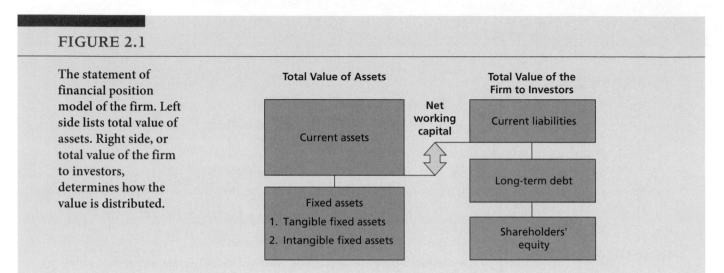

Assets

Assets are classified as either *current* or *fixed*. A fixed asset is one that has a relatively long life. Fixed assets can either be *tangible*, such as a truck or a computer, or *intangible*, such as a trademark or patent. Accountants refer to these assets as *capital assets*. A current asset has a life of less than one year. This means that the asset will convert to cash within 12 months. For example, inventory would normally be purchased and sold within a year and is thus classified as a current asset. Obviously, cash itself is a current asset. Accounts receivable (money owed to the firm by its customers) is also a current asset.

Liabilities and Owners' Equity

The firm's liabilities are the first thing listed on the right-hand side of the statement of financial position. These are classified as either *current* or *long-term*. Current liabilities, like current assets, have a life of less than one year (meaning they must be paid within the year) and are listed before long-term liabilities. Accounts payable (money the firm owes to its suppliers) is one example of a current liability.

A debt that is not due in the coming year is a long-term liability. A loan that the firm will pay off in five years is one such long-term debt. Firms borrow long-term from a variety of sources. We use the terms *bond* and *bondholders* generically to refer to long-term debt and long-term creditors, respectively.

Finally, by definition, the difference between the total value of the assets (current and fixed) and the total value of the liabilities (current and long-term) is the *shareholders' equity*, also called *common equity* or *owners' equity*. This feature of the statement of financial position is intended to reflect the fact that, if the firm were to sell all of its assets and use the money to pay off its debts, whatever residual value remained would belong to the shareholders. So, the statement of financial position balances because the value of the left-hand side always equals the value of the right-hand side. That is, the value of the firm's assets is equal to the sum of liabilities and shareholders' equity:[2]

$$\text{Assets} = \text{Liabilities} + \text{Shareholders' equity} \qquad [2.1]$$

This is the statement of financial position identity or equation, and it always holds because shareholders' equity is defined as the difference between assets and liabilities.

---

[2] The terms *owners' equity* and *shareholders' equity* are used interchangeably to refer to the equity in a corporation. The term *net worth* is also used. Variations exist in addition to these.

Net Working Capital

As shown in Figure 2.1, the difference between a firm's current assets and its current liabilities is called *net working capital*. Net working capital is positive when current assets exceed current liabilities. Based on the definitions of current assets and current liabilities, this means that the cash available over the next 12 months exceeds the cash that must be paid over that same period. For this reason, net working capital is usually positive in a healthy firm.[3]

EXAMPLE 2.1: Building the Statement of Financial Position

A firm has current assets of $100, fixed assets of $500, short-term debt of $70, and long-term debt of $200. What does the statement of financial position look like? What is shareholders' equity? What is net working capital?

In this case, total assets are $100 + 500 = $600 and total liabilities are $70 + 200 = $270, so shareholders' equity is the difference: $600 − 270 = $330. The statement of financial position would thus look like:

Assets		Liabilities	
Current assets	$100	Current liabilities	$ 70
Fixed assets	500	Long-term debt	200
		Shareholders' equity	330
Total assets	$600	Total liabilities and shareholders' equity	$600

Net working capital is the difference between current assets and current liabilities, or $100 − 70 = $30.

Table 2.1 shows a simplified statement of financial position for Canadian Enterprises Limited. The assets in the statement of financial position are listed in order of the length of time it takes for them to convert to cash in the normal course of business. Similarly, the liabilities are listed in the order in which they would normally be paid.

TABLE 2.1

Canadian Enterprises Limited
Statement of Financial Position as of December 31, 2011 and 2012
($ millions)

Assets	2011	2012	Liabilities and Owners' Equity	2011	2012
Current assets			Current liabilities		
Cash	$ 114	$ 160	Accounts payable	$ 232	$ 266
Accounts receivable	445	688	Notes payable	196	123
Inventory	553	555	Total	$ 428	$ 389
Total	$ 1,112	$ 1,403			
			Long-term debt	$ 408	$ 454
Fixed assets			Owners' equity		
Net, plant and equipment	$ 1,644	$ 1,709	Common shares	600	640
			Retained earnings	1,320	1,629
			Total	$ 1,920	$ 2,269
Total assets	$ 2,756	$ 3,112	Total liabilities and owners' equity	$ 2,756	$ 3,112

The structure of the assets for a particular firm reflects the line of business that the firm is in and also managerial decisions about how much cash and inventory to maintain and about credit policy, fixed asset acquisition, and so on.

---

[3] Chapter 18 discusses net working capital in detail.

The liabilities side of the statement of financial position primarily reflects managerial decisions about capital structure and the use of short-term debt. For example, in 2012, total long-term debt for Canadian Enterprises Limited was $454 and total equity was $640 + 1,629 = $2,269, so total long-term financing was $454 + 2,269 = $2,723. Of this amount, $454/2,723 = 16.67% was long-term debt. This percentage reflects capital structure decisions made in the past by the management of Canadian Enterprises.

Three particularly important things to keep in mind when examining a statement of financial position are liquidity, debt versus equity, and market value versus book value.[4]

Liquidity

Liquidity refers to the speed and ease with which an asset can be converted to cash. Gold is a relatively liquid asset; a custom manufacturing facility is not. Liquidity really has two dimensions: ease of conversion versus loss of value. Any asset can be converted to cash quickly if we cut the price enough. A highly liquid asset is therefore one that can be quickly sold without significant loss of value. An illiquid asset is one that cannot be quickly converted to cash without a substantial price reduction.

Assets are normally listed on the statement of financial position in order of decreasing liquidity, meaning that the most liquid assets are listed first. Current assets are relatively liquid and include cash and those assets that we expect to convert to cash over the next 12 months. Accounts receivable, for example, represents amounts not yet collected from customers on sales already made. Naturally, we hope these will convert to cash in the near future. Inventory is probably the least liquid of the current assets, at least for many businesses.

Fixed assets are, for the most part, relatively illiquid. These consist of tangible things such as buildings and equipment. Intangible assets, such as a trademark, have no physical existence but can be very valuable. Like tangible fixed assets, they won't ordinarily convert to cash and are generally considered illiquid.

Liquidity is valuable. The more liquid a business is, the less likely it is to experience financial distress (that is, difficulty in paying debts or buying needed assets). Unfortunately, liquid assets are generally less profitable to hold. For example, cash holdings are the most liquid of all investments, but they sometimes earn no return at all—they just sit there. Therefore, the trade-off is between the advantages of liquidity and forgone potential profits. We discuss this trade-off further in the rest of the book.

Debt versus Equity

To the extent that a firm borrows money, it usually gives creditors first claim to the firm's cash flow. Equity holders are only entitled to the residual value, the portion left after creditors are paid. The value of this residual portion is the shareholders' equity in the firm and is simply the asset value less the value of the firm's liabilities:

Shareholders' equity = Assets − Liabilities

This is true in an accounting sense because shareholders' equity is defined as this residual portion. More importantly, it is true in an economic sense: If the firm sells its assets and pays its debts, whatever cash is left belongs to the shareholders.

The use of debt in a firm's capital structure is called *financial leverage*. The more debt a firm has (as a percentage of assets), the greater is its degree of financial leverage. As we discuss in later chapters, debt acts like a lever in the sense that using it can greatly magnify both gains and losses. So financial leverage increases the potential reward to shareholders, but it also increases the potential for financial distress and business failure.

Value versus Cost

The accounting value of a firm's assets is frequently referred to as the *carrying value* or the *book value* of the assets. IFRS allows companies to use the historical cost method; it also allows use of

---

[4]Chapters 3 and 4 expand on financial statement analysis.

the revaluation (fair value) method. When a company adopts the revaluation method, all items in a class of assets should be revalued simultaneously, and the revaluation should be performed with enough regularity to ensure that, at the statement of financial position date, the carrying amount is not materially different from the fair value amount. Thus a class of property, plant, and equipment with significant unpredictable changes in fair value will require more frequent revaluations (every one or two years) than will another class of asset that has insignificant changes in fair value (e. g., a building may only require revaluation every three to five years).

Market value is the price at which willing buyers and sellers trade the assets. Management's job is to create a value for the firm that is higher than its cost. When market values are considerably below book values, it is customary accounting practice to write down assets. For example, in 2011, Suncor Energy Inc., took a massive $514 million write-down of Libyan assets as a result of instability in the war torn country.[5] Sometimes, huge write-offs are also indicative of overstated profits in previous years, as assets were not expensed properly.

There are many users of a firm's statement of financial position and each may seek different information from it. A banker may look at a balance sheet for evidence of liquidity and working capital. A supplier may also note the size of accounts payable, which reflects the general promptness of payments. Many users of financial statements, including managers and investors, want to know the value of the firm, not its cost. This is not found on the statement of financial position. In fact, many of a firm's true resources (good management, proprietary assets, and so on) do not appear on the statement of financial position. Henceforth, whenever we speak of the value of an asset or the value of the firm, we will normally mean its market value. So, for example, when we say the goal of the financial manager is to increase the value of the stock, we mean the market value of the stock.

EXAMPLE 2.2: Market versus Book Value

The Quebec Corporation has fixed assets with a book value of $700 and an appraised market value of about $1,000. Net working capital is $400 on the books, but approximately $600 would be realized if all the current accounts were liquidated. Quebec Corporation has $500 in long-term debt, both book value and market value. What is the book value of the equity? What is the market value?

We can construct two simplified statements of financial position, one in accounting (book value) terms and one in economic (market value) terms:

QUEBEC CORPORATION
Statement of Financial Position
Market Value versus Book Value

	Book	Market		Book	Market
Assets			*Liabilities*		
Net working capital	$ 400	$ 600	Long-term debt	$ 500	$ 500
Net fixed assets	700	1,000	Shareholders' equity	600	1,100
	$1,100	$1,600		$1,100	$1,600

Concept Questions

1. What does the statement of financial position identity?
2. What is liquidity? Why is it important?
3. What do we mean by financial leverage?
4. Explain the difference between accounting value and market value. Which is more important to the financial manager? Why?

---

[5] Scott Haggett and Jeffrey Jones, "Canadian oil profits marred by production woes" financialpost.com, July 28, 2011. business.financialpost.com/2011/07/28/canadian-oil-profits-marred-by-production-woes/.

2.2 | Statement of Comprehensive Income

statement of comprehensive income
Financial statement summarizing a firm's performance over a period of time. Formerly called the income statement.

The **statement of comprehensive income** measures performance over some period of time, usually a year. The statement of comprehensive income equation is:

$$\text{Revenues} - \text{Expenses} = \text{Income} \qquad [2.2]$$

If you think of the statement of financial position as a snapshot, then you can think of statement of comprehensive income as a video recording covering the period between, before, and after pictures. Table 2.2 gives a simplified statement of comprehensive income for Canadian Enterprises.

The initial thing reported on the statement of comprehensive income would usually be revenue and expenses from the firm's principal operations. Subsequent parts include, among other things, financing expenses such as interest paid. Taxes paid are reported separately. The last item is *net income* (the so-called bottom line). Net income is often expressed on a per-share basis and called *earnings per share (EPS)*.

TABLE 2.2

CANADIAN ENTERPRISES
2012 Statement of Comprehensive Income
($ millions)

Net sales		$ 1,509
Cost of goods sold		750
Depreciation		65
Earnings before interest and taxes		$ 694
Interest paid		70
Income before taxes		$ 624
Taxes		250
Net income		$ 374
Addition to retained earnings	$309	
Dividends	65	

As indicated, Canadian Enterprises paid cash dividends of $65. The difference between net income and cash dividends, $309, is the addition to retained earnings for the year. This amount is added to the cumulative retained earnings account on the statement of financial position. If you'll look back at the two statements of financial position for Canadian Enterprises in Table 2.1, you'll see that retained earnings did go up by this amount, $1,320 + 309 = $1,629.

EXAMPLE 2.3: Calculating Earnings and Dividends per Share

Suppose that Canadian had 200 million shares outstanding at the end of 2012. Based on the preceding statement of comprehensive income, what was Canadian's EPS? What were the dividends per share?

From the statement of comprehensive income in Table 2.2 Canadian had a net income of $374 million for the year. Since 200 million shares were outstanding, EPS was $374/200 = $1.87 per share. Similarly, dividends per share were $65/200 = $.325 per share.

When looking at the statement of comprehensive income, the financial manager needs to keep three things in mind: IFRS, cash versus non-cash items, and time and costs.

International Financial Reporting Standards (IFRS)

As pointed out earlier, the focus in financial decisions is on market value, which depends on cash flow. However, like the statement of financial position, the statement of comprehensive income has many different users and the accounting profession has developed IFRS to provide information for a broad audience not necessarily concerned with cash flow. For this reason, it is necessary to make adjustments to information on statements of comprehensive income to obtain cash flow.

For example, revenue is recognized on the statement of comprehensive income when the earnings process is virtually completed and an exchange of goods or services has occurred. Therefore, the unrealized appreciation in owning property will not be recognized as income. This provides a device for smoothing income by selling appreciated property at convenient times. For example, if the firm owns a tree farm that has doubled in value, then in a year when its earnings from other businesses are down, it can raise overall earnings by selling some trees. The matching principle of IFRS dictates that revenues be matched with expenses. Thus, income is reported when it is earned or accrued, even though no cash flow has necessarily occurred. (For example, when goods are sold for credit, sales and profits are reported.)

Non-Cash Items

non-cash items
Expenses charged against revenues that do not directly affect cash flow, such as depreciation.

A primary reason that accounting income differs from cash flow is that a statement of comprehensive income contains **non-cash items.** The most important of these is *depreciation*. Suppose a firm purchases an asset for $5,000 and pays in cash. Obviously, the firm has a $5,000 cash outflow at the time of purchase. However, instead of deducting the $5,000 as an expense, an accountant might depreciate the asset over a five-year period.

If the depreciation is straight-line and the asset is written down to zero over that period, $5,000/5 = $1,000 would be deducted each year as an expense.[6] The important thing to recognize is that this $1,000 deduction isn't cash—it's an accounting number. The actual cash outflow occurred when the asset was purchased.

The depreciation deduction is an application of the representational faithfulness principle in accounting. The revenues associated with an asset would generally occur over some length of time. So the accountant seeks to expense the purchase of the asset with the benefits produced from owning it as a way of representing the use of the asset over time.

As we shall see, for the financial manager, the actual timing of cash inflows and outflows is critical in coming up with a reasonable estimate of market value, so we need to learn how to separate the cash flows from the non-cash accounting entries.

Time and Costs

It is often useful to think of the future as having two distinct parts: the short run and the long run. These are not precise time periods. The distinction has to do with whether costs are fixed or variable. In the long run, all business costs are variable. Given sufficient time, assets can be sold, debts can be paid, and so on.

If our time horizon is relatively short, however, some costs are effectively fixed—they must be paid no matter what (property taxes, for example). Other costs, such as wages to workers and payments to suppliers, are still variable. As a result, even in the short run, the firm can vary its output level by varying expenditures in these areas.

The distinction between fixed and variable costs is important, at times, to the financial manager, but the way costs are reported on the statement of comprehensive income is not a good guide as to which costs are which. The reason is that, in practice, accountants tend to classify costs as either product costs or period costs.

Product costs include such things as raw materials, direct labour expense, and manufacturing overhead. These are reported on the statement of comprehensive income as costs of goods sold, but they include both fixed and variable costs. Similarly, period costs are incurred during a particular time period and are reported as selling, general, and administrative expenses. Once again, some of these period costs may be fixed and others may be variable. The company president's salary, for example, is a period cost and is probably fixed, at least in the short run.

---

[6]By *straight-line*, we mean that the depreciation deduction is the same every year. By *written down to zero*, we mean that the asset is assumed to have no value at the end of five years. Tax depreciation is discussed in more detail later in the chapter.

2.3 | Cash Flow

At this point, we are ready to discuss one of the most important pieces of financial information that can be gleaned from financial statements: cash flow. There is no standard financial statement for presenting this information in the way that we wish. Therefore, we discuss how to calculate cash flow for Canadian Enterprises and point out how the result differs from standard financial statement calculations. There is a standard accounting statement called the statement of cash flows, but it is concerned with a somewhat different issue and should not be confused with what is discussed in this section. The accounting statement of cash flows is discussed in Chapter 3.

From the statement of financial position identity, we know that the value of a firm's assets is equal to the value of its liabilities plus the value of its equity. Similarly, the cash flow from assets must equal the sum of the cash flow to bondholders (or creditors) plus the cash flow to shareholders (or owners):

$$\text{Cash flow from assets} = \text{Cash flow to bondholders} + \text{Cash flow to shareholders} \qquad [2.3]$$

This is the cash flow identity. It says that the cash flow from the firm's assets is equal to the cash flow paid to suppliers of capital to the firm. A firm generates cash through its various activities; that cash is either used to pay creditors or paid out to the owners of the firm.

Cash Flow from Assets

cash flow from assets
The total of cash flow to bondholders and cash flow to shareholders, consisting of: operating cash flow, capital spending, and additions to net working capital.

Cash flow from assets involves three components: operating cash flow, capital spending, and additions to net working capital. *Operating cash flow* refers to the cash flow that results from the firm's day-to-day activities of producing and selling. Expenses associated with the firm's financing of its assets are not included because they are not operating expenses.

As we discussed in Chapter 1, some portion of the firm's cash flow is reinvested in the firm. *Capital spending* refers to the net spending on fixed assets (purchases of fixed assets less sales of fixed assets). Finally, *additions to net working capital* is the amount spent on net working capital. It is measured as the change in net working capital over the period being examined and represents the net increase in current assets over current liabilities. The three components of cash flow are examined in more detail next.

operating cash flow
Cash generated from a firm's normal business activities.

OPERATING CASH FLOW   To calculate **operating cash flow,** we want to calculate revenues minus costs, but we don't want to include depreciation since it's not a cash outflow, and we don't want to include interest because it's a financing expense. We do want to include taxes, because taxes are, unfortunately, paid in cash.

If we look at the statement of comprehensive income in Table 2.2, Canadian Enterprises had earnings before interest and taxes (EBIT) of $694. This is almost what we want since it doesn't include interest paid. We need to make two adjustments: First, recall that depreciation is a non-cash expense. To get cash flow, we first add back the $65 in depreciation since it wasn't a cash deduction. The second adjustment is to subtract the $250 in taxes since these were paid in cash. The result is operating cash flow:

Canadian Enterprises thus had a 2012 operating cash flow of $509 as shown in Table 2.3.

There is an unpleasant possibility for confusion when we speak of operating cash flow. In accounting practice, operating cash flow is often defined as net income plus depreciation. For Canadian Enterprises in Table 2.2, this would amount to $374 + 65 = $439.

The accounting definition of operating cash flow differs from ours in one important way: Interest is deducted when net income is computed. Notice that the difference between the $509 operating cash flow we calculated and this $439 is $70, the amount of interest paid for the year.

TABLE 2.3

CANADIAN ENTERPRISES 2012 Operating Cash Flow	
Earnings before interest and taxes	$694
+ Depreciation	65
− Taxes	250
Operating cash flow	$509

This definition of cash flow thus considers interest paid to be an operating expense. Our definition treats it properly as a financing expense. If there were no interest expense, the two definitions would be the same.

To finish our calculations of cash flow from assets for Canadian Enterprises, we need to consider how much of the $509 operating cash flow was reinvested in the firm. We consider spending on fixed assets first.

CAPITAL SPENDING   Net capital spending is just money spent on fixed assets less money received from the sale of fixed assets. At the end of 2011, net fixed assets were $1,644. During the year, we wrote off (depreciated) $65 worth of fixed assets on the statement of comprehensive income. So, if we did not purchase any new fixed assets, we would have had $1,644 − 65 = $1,579 at year's end. The 2012 statement of financial position shows $1,709 in net fixed assets, so we must have spent a total of $1,709 − 1,579 = $130 on fixed assets during the year:

Ending fixed assets	$ 1,709
− Beginning fixed assets	1,644
+ Depreciation	65
Net investment in fixed assets	$ 130

This $130 is our net capital spending for 2012.

Could net capital spending be negative? The answer is yes. This would happen if the firm sold more assets than it purchased. The net here refers to purchases of fixed assets net of any sales.

CHANGE IN NET WORKING CAPITAL   In addition to investing in fixed assets, a firm also invests in current assets. For example, going back to the statement of financial position in Table 2.1, we see that, at the end of 2012, Canadian Enterprises had current assets of $1,403. At the end of 2011, current assets were $1,112, so, during the year, Canadian Enterprises invested $1,403 − 1,112 = $291 in current assets.

As the firm changes its investment in current assets, its current liabilities usually change as well. To determine the changes to net working capital, the easiest approach is just to take the difference between the beginning and ending net working capital (NWC) figures. Net working capital at the end of 2012 was $1,403 − 389 = $1,014. Similarly, at the end of 2011, net working capital was $1,112 − 428 = $684. So, given these figures, we have:

Ending NWC	$ 1,014
− Beginning NWC	684
Change in NWC	$ 330

Net working capital thus increased by $330. Put another way, Canadian Enterprises had a net investment of $330 in NWC for the year.

CONCLUSION   Given the figures we've come up with, we're ready to calculate cash flow from assets. The total cash flow from assets is given by operating cash flow less the amounts invested in fixed assets and net working capital. So, for Canadian Enterprises we have:

CANADIAN ENTERPRISES
2012 Cash Flow from Assets

Operating cash flow	$ 509
— Net capital spending	130
— Changes in NWC	330
Cash flow from assets	$ 49

free cash flow
Another name for cash flow from assets.

A NOTE ON "FREE" CASH FLOW   Cash flow from assets sometimes goes by a different name, **free cash flow.** Of course, there is no such thing as "free" cash. Instead, the name refers to cash that the firm is free to distribute to creditors and shareholders because it is not needed for working capital or fixed asset investment. Free cash flow is the cash flow minus any reinvestment required to maintain the firm's competitive advantage. We will stick with "cash flow from assets" as our label for this important concept because, in practice, there is some variation in exactly how free cash flow is computed; different users calculate it in different ways. Nonetheless, whenever you hear the phrase "free cash flow," you should understand that what is being discussed is cash flow from assets or something quite similar.

Cash Flow to Creditors and Shareholders

The cash flows to creditors and shareholders represent the net payments to creditors and owners during the year. They are calculated in a similar way. **Cash flow to creditors** is interest paid less net new borrowing; **cash flow to shareholders** is dividends less net new equity raised.

cash flow to creditors
A firm's interest payments to creditors less net new borrowings.

cash flow to shareholders
Dividends paid out by a firm less net new equity raised.

CASH FLOW TO CREDITORS   Looking at the statement of comprehensive income in Table 2.2, Canadian paid $70 in interest to creditors. From the statement of financial position in Table 2.1, long-term debt rose by $454 − 408 = $46. So, Canadian Enterprises paid out $70 in interest, but it borrowed an additional $46. Net cash flow to creditors is thus:

CANADIAN ENTERPRISES
2012 Cash Flow to Creditors

Interest paid	$70
— Net new borrowing	46
Cash flow to creditors	$24

Cash flow to creditors is sometimes called cash flow to bondholders; we use these interchangeably.

CASH FLOW TO SHAREHOLDERS   From the statement of comprehensive income, we see that dividends paid to shareholders amount to $65. To calculate net new equity raised, we need to look at the common share account. This account tells us how many shares the company has sold. During the year, this account rose by $40, so $40 in net new equity was raised. Given this, we have:

CANADIAN ENTERPRISES
2012 Cash Flow to Shareholders

Dividends paid	$65
— Net new equity	40
Cash flow to shareholders	$25

The cash flow to shareholders for 2012 was thus $25.

The last thing that we need to do is to check that the cash flow identity holds to be sure that we didn't make any mistakes. Cash flow from assets adds up the sources of cash flow while cash flow to creditors and shareholders measures how the firm uses its cash flow. Since all cash flow has to be accounted for, total sources (cash flow from assets) must equal total uses (cash flow to creditors and shareholders). Earlier we found the cash flow from assets is $49. Cash flow to creditors and shareholders is $24 + 25 = $49, so everything checks out. Table 2.4 contains a summary of the various cash flow calculations for future reference.

Two important observations can be drawn from our discussion of cash flow: First, several types of cash flow are relevant to understanding the financial situation of the firm. *Operating cash flow,* defined as earnings before interest and depreciation minus taxes, measures the cash generated from operations not counting capital spending or working capital requirements. It should usually be positive; a firm is in trouble if operating cash flow is negative for a long time because the firm is not generating enough cash to pay operating costs. *Total cash flow* of the firm includes capital spending and additions to net working capital. It will frequently be negative. When a firm is growing at a rapid rate, the spending on inventory and fixed assets can be higher than cash flow from sales.

Second, net income is not cash flow. The net income of Canadian Enterprises in 2012 was $374 million, whereas total cash flow from assets was $49 million. The two numbers are not usually the same. In determining the economic and financial condition of a firm, cash flow is more revealing.

EXAMPLE 2.4: Cash Flows for Dole Cola

During the year, Dole Cola Ltd. had sales and costs of $600 and $300, respectively. Depreciation was $150 and interest paid was $30. Taxes were calculated at a straight 40 percent. Dividends were $30. All figures are in millions of dollars. What was the operating cash flow for Dole? Why is this different from net income?

The easiest thing to do here is to create an statement of comprehensive income. We can then fill in the numbers we need. Dole Cola's statement of comprehensive income follows:

DOLE COLA 2012 Statement of Comprehensive Income ($ millions)

Net sales	$600
Cost of goods sold	300
Depreciation	150
Earnings before interest and taxes	$150
Interest paid	30
Taxable income	$120
Taxes	48
Net income	$ 72
Retained earnings	$42
Dividends	30

Net income for Dole is thus $72. We now have all the numbers we need; so referring back to the Canadian Enterprises example, we have:

DOLE COLA 2012 Operating Cash Flow ($ millions)

Earnings before interest and taxes	$ 150
+ Depreciation	150
− Taxes	48
Operating cash flow	$ 252

As this example illustrates, operating cash flow is not the same as net income, because depreciation and interest are subtracted out when net income is calculated. If you recall our earlier discussion, we don't subtract these out in computing operating cash flow because depreciation is not a cash expense and interest paid is a financing expense, not an operating expense.

TABLE 2.4   Cash flow summary

The cash flow identity

Cash flow from assets = Cash flow to creditors (or bondholders) + Cash flow to shareholders (or owners)

Cash flow from assets

Cash flow from assets = Operating cash flow − Net capital spending − Changes in net working capital (NWC)
where:

a. Operating cash flow = Earnings before interest and taxes (EBIT)
               + Depreciation
               − Taxes

b. Net capital spending = Ending net fixed assets
                  − Beginning net fixed assets
                  + Depreciation

c. Changes in NWC = Ending NWC
              − Beginning NWC

Cash flow to creditors (bondholders)

Cash flow to creditors = Interest paid − Net new borrowing

Cash flow to shareholders (owners)

Cash flow to shareholders = Dividends paid − Net new equity raised

Net Capital Spending

Suppose that beginning net fixed assets were $500 and ending net fixed assets were $750. What was the net capital spending for the year?

From the statement of comprehensive income for Dole, depreciation for the year was $150. Net fixed assets rose by $250. We thus spent $150 to cover the depreciation and an additional $250 as well, for a total of $400.

Change in NWC and Cash Flow from Assets

Suppose that Dole Cola started the year with $2,130 in current assets and $1,620 in current liabilities. The corresponding ending figures were $2,260 and $1,710. What was the change in NWC during the year? What was cash flow from assets? How does this compare to net income?

Net working capital started out as $2,130 − 1,620 = $510 and ended up at $2,260 − 1,710 = $550. The change in NWC was thus $550 − 510 = $40. Putting together all the information for Dole we have:

DOLE COLA 2012 Cash Flow from Assets

Operating cash flow	$252
− Net capital spending	400
− Changes in NWC	40
Cash flow from assets	−$188

Dole had a cash flow from assets of negative $188. Net income was positive at $72. Is the fact that cash flow from assets is negative a cause for alarm? Not necessarily. The cash flow here is negative primarily because of a large investment in fixed assets. If these are good investments, the resulting negative cash flow is not a worry.

CASH FLOW TO CREDITORS AND SHAREHOLDERS   We saw that Dole Cola had cash flow from assets of −$188. The fact that this is negative means that Dole raised more money in the form of new debt and equity than it paid out for the year. For example, suppose we know that Dole didn't sell any new equity for the year. What was cash flow to shareholders? To bondholders?

Because it didn't raise any new equity, Dole's cash flow to shareholders is just equal to the cash dividend paid:

DOLE COLA 2012 Cash Flow to Shareholders

Dividends paid	$30
− Net new equity	0
Cash flow to shareholders	$30

Now, from the cash flow identity the total cash paid to bondholders and shareholders was −$188. Cash flow to shareholders is $30, so cash flow to bondholders must be equal to −$188 − $30 = −$218:

$$\text{Cash flow to bondholders} + \text{Cash flow to shareholders} = -\$188$$
$$\text{Cash flow to bondholders} + \$30 = -\$188$$
$$\text{Cash flow to bondholders} = -\$218$$

From the statement of comprehensive income, interest paid is $30. We can determine net new borrowing as follows:

DOLE COLA 2012 Cash Flow to Bondholders

Interest paid	$ 30
− Net new borrowing	−248
Cash flow to bondholders	−$218

As indicated, since cash flow to bondholders is −$218 and interest paid is $30, Dole must have borrowed $248 during the year to help finance the fixed asset expansion.

Concept Questions

1. What is the cash flow identity? Explain what it says.
2. What are the components of operating cash flow?
3. Why is interest paid not a component of operating cash flow?

2.4 | Taxes

Taxes are very important because, as we just saw, cash flows are measured after taxes. In this section, we examine corporate and personal tax rates and how taxes are calculated. We apply this knowledge to see how different types of income are taxed in the hands of individuals and corporations.

The size of the tax bill is determined through tax laws and regulations in the annual budgets of the federal government (administered by Canada Revenue Agency (CRA)) and provincial governments. If the various rules of taxation seem a little bizarre or convoluted to you, keep in mind that tax law is the result of political, as well as economic, forces. According to economic theory, an ideal tax system has three features. First, it should distribute the tax burden equitably, with each taxpayer shouldering a "fair share." Second, the tax system should not change the efficient allocation of resources by markets. If this happened, such distortions would reduce economic welfare. Third, the system should be easy to administer.

The tax law is continually evolving so our discussion cannot make you a tax expert. Rather it gives you an understanding of the tax principles important for financial management along with the ability to ask the right questions when consulting a tax expert. The Canada Revenue Agency allows students in Canada to claim an education tax credit. The credit reduces income tax based on the number of months that a student is enrolled in a qualifying educational program at a designated educational institution.

Individual Tax Rates

Individual tax rates in effect for federal taxes for 2012 are shown in Table 2.5. These rates apply to income from employment (wages and salary) and from unincorporated businesses. Investment income is also taxable. Interest income is taxed at the same rates as employment income, but special provisions reduce the taxes payable on dividends and capital gains. We discuss these in detail later in the chapter. Table 2.5 also provides information on provincial taxes for selected provinces. Other provinces and territories follow similar approaches, although they use different rates and brackets.

To illustrate, suppose you live in British Columbia and have a taxable income over $75,042. Your tax on the next dollar is:[7]

32.50% = federal tax rate + provincial tax rate = 22% + 10.50%

Average versus Marginal Tax Rates

average tax rate
Total taxes paid divided by total taxable income.

marginal tax rate
Amount of tax payable on the next dollar earned.

In making financial decisions, it is frequently important to distinguish between average and marginal tax rates. Your **average tax rate** is your tax bill divided by your taxable income; in other words, the percentage of your income that goes to pay taxes. Your **marginal tax rate** is the extra tax you would pay if you earned one more dollar. The percentage tax rates shown in Table 2.5 are all marginal rates. To put it another way, the tax rates in Table 2.5 apply to the part of income in the indicated range only, not all income.

Following the equity principle, individual taxes are designed to be progressive with higher incomes taxed at a higher rate. In contrast, with a flat rate tax, there is only one tax rate, and this rate is the same for all income levels. With such a tax, the marginal tax rate is always the same as the average tax rate. As it stands now, individual taxation in Canada is progressive but approaches a flat rate for the highest incomes. Alberta has introduced a flat tax.

---

[7] Actual rates are somewhat higher, as we ignore surtaxes that apply in higher brackets.

TABLE 2.5

Individual income tax rates—2012 (current as of December 31, 2011)

	Tax Rates	Tax Brackets	Rates	Surtax Thresholds
Federal	15.00%	Up to $42,707		
	22.00	42,708–85,414		
	26.00	85,415–132,406		
	29.00	132,407 and over		
British Columbia	5.06%	Up to $37,013		
	7.70	37,014–74,028		
	10.50	74,029–84,993		
	12.29	84,994–103,205		
	14.70	103,206 and over		
Alberta	10.00%	All income		
Saskatchewan	11.00%	Up to $42,065		
	13.00	42,066–120,185		
	15.00	120,186 and over		
Manitoba	10.80%	Up to $31,000		
	12.75	31,001–67,000		
	17.40	67,001 and over		
Ontario	5.05%	Up to $39,020		
	9.15	39,021–78,043	20%	$4,213
	11.16	78,044 and over	36	5,392
Quebec	16.00%	Up to $40,100		
	20.00	40,101–80,200		
	24.00	80,201 and over		
New Brunswick	9.10%	Up to $38,190		
	12.10	38,191–76,380		
	12.40	76,381–124,178		
	14.30	124,179 and over		
Nova Scotia	8.79%	Up to $29,590		
	14.95	29,591–59,180		
	16.67	59,181–93,000		
	17.50	93,001–150,000		
	21.00	150,001 and over		
Prince Edward Island	9.80%	Up to $31,984		
	13.80	31,985–63,969		
	16.70	63,970 and over	10%	$12,500
Newfoundland	7.70%	Up to $32,893		
	12.50	32,894–65,785		
	13.30	65,786 and over		

Source: © 2011 KPMG LLP, a Canadian limited liability partnership and a member firm of the KPMG network of independent member firms affiliated with KPMG International Cooperative ("KPMG International"), a Swiss entity. All rights reserved. The information contained herein is of a general nature and is not intended to address the circumstances of any particular individual or entity. Although we endeavour to provide accurate and timely information, there can be no guarantee that such information is accurate as of the date it is received or that it will continue to be accurate in the future. No one should act on such information without appropriate professional advice after a thorough examination of the particular situation.

TABLE 2.6

Combined marginal tax rates for individuals in top federal tax bracket (over $132,407)—2012 (current as of December 31, 2011)

Provinces/ Territories	Interest and Regular Income (%)	Capital Gains (%)	Eligible Dividends (%)	Non-eligible Dividends (%)
British Columbia	43.70	21.85	26.11	33.71
Alberta	39.00	19.50	19.29	27.71
Saskatchewan	44.00	22.00	24.81	33.33
Manitoba	46.40	23.20	28.13	39.15
Ontario	46.41	23.21	29.54	32.57
Quebec	48.22	24.11	32.81	36.35
New Brunswick	43.30	21.65	24.33	30.83
Nova Scotia	50.00	25.00	36.06	36.21
Prince Edward Island	47.37	23.69	30.50	41.17
Newfoundland	42.30	21.15	22.47	29.96

Source: © 2011 KPMG LLP, a Canadian limited liability partnership and a member firm of the KPMG network of independent member firms affiliated with KPMG International Cooperative ("KPMG International"), a Swiss entity. All rights reserved. The information contained herein is of a general nature and is not intended to address the circumstances of any particular individual or entity. Although we endeavour to provide accurate and timely information, there can be no guarantee that such information is accurate as of the date it is received or that it will continue to be accurate in the future. No one should act on such information without appropriate professional advice after a thorough examination of the particular situation.

Normally, the marginal tax rate is relevant for decision making. Any new cash flows are taxed at that marginal rate. Since financial decisions usually involve new cash flows or changes in existing ones, this rate tells us the marginal effect on our tax bill.

Taxes on Investment Income

When introducing the topic of taxes, we warned that tax laws are not always logical. The treatment of dividends in Canada is at least a partial exception because there are two clear goals: First, corporations pay dividends from after-tax income so tax laws shelter dividends from full tax in the hands of shareholders. This diminishes double taxation, which would violate the principle of equitable taxation. Second, the **dividend tax credit** applies only to dividends paid by Canadian corporations. The result is to encourage Canadian investors to invest in Canadian firms as opposed to foreign companies.[8]

With these goals in mind, to see how dividends are taxed, we start with common shares held by individual investors. Table 2.6 shows the combined marginal tax rates for individuals in top federal tax bracket. For example, an individual in top federal tax bracket in Manitoba will pay $232 as taxes on a capital gain of $1,000.

The dividends are taxed far more lightly than regular income. Dividend taxation became lighter under recent changes with the stated goal of making dividend-paying stocks more attractive in comparison to income trusts. The federal government announced an increase in the gross-up of the federal dividend tax credit to the levels shown in Table 2.6.

Individual Canadian investors also benefit from a tax reduction for **capital gains.** Capital gains arise when an investment increases in value above its purchase price. For capital gains, taxes apply at 50 percent of the applicable marginal rate. For example, individuals in Newfoundland in the highest bracket in Table 2.6 would pay taxes on capital gains at a nominal rate of 21.15 percent = 42.30% × 0.50.

Table 2.6 shows that, for an individual in the top bracket, salary and interest are taxed far more heavily than capital gains and dividend income.

In practice, capital gains are lightly taxed because individuals pay taxes on **realized capital gains** only when stock is sold. Because many individuals hold shares for a long time (have unrealized capital gains), the time value of money dramatically reduces the effective tax rate on capital gains.[9] Also, investors can manage capital gain realization to offset with losses in many cases.

Corporate Taxes

Canadian corporations, like individuals, are subject to taxes levied by the federal and provincial governments. Corporate taxes are passed on to consumers through higher prices, to workers through lower wages, or to investors through lower returns.

Table 2.7 shows corporate tax rates using Alberta as an example. You can see from the table that small corporations (income less than $400,000) and, to a lesser degree, manufacturing and processing companies, receive a tax break in the form of lower rates.

Comparing the rates in Table 2.7 with the personal tax rates in Table 2.5 appears to reveal a tax advantage for small businesses and professionals that form corporations. The tax rate on corporate income of, say, $150,000 is less than the personal tax rate assessed on the income of unincorporated businesses. But this is oversimplified because dividends paid to the owners are also taxed, as we saw earlier.

Taxable Income

In Section 2.2 we discussed the statement of comprehensive income for Canadian Enterprises (Table 2.2); it includes both dividends and interest paid. An important difference is that interest paid is deducted from EBIT in calculating income but dividends paid are not. Because interest is

---

dividend tax credit
Tax formula that reduces the effective tax rate on dividends.

capital gains
The increase in value of an investment over its purchase price.

realized capital gains
The increase in value of an investment, when converted to cash.

---

[8] Evidence that the dividend tax credit causes investors to favour Canadian stocks is provided in L. Booth, "The Dividend Tax Credit and Canadian Ownership Objectives," *Canadian Journal of Economics* 20 (May 1987).

[9] L. Booth and D. J. Johnston, "The Ex-Dividend Day Behavior of Canadian Stock Prices: Tax Changes and Clientele Effects," *Journal of Finance* 39 (June 1984). Booth and Johnston find a "very low effective tax rate on capital gains" in the 1970s. They compare their results with a U.S. study that found an effective tax rate on capital gains under 7 percent.

a tax-deductible expense, debt financing has a tax advantage over financing with common shares. To illustrate, Table 2.2 shows that Canadian Enterprises paid $250 million in taxes on taxable income of $624 million. The firm's tax rate is $250/624 = 40\%$. This means that to pay another $1 in dividends, Canadian Enterprises must increase EBIT by $1.67. Of the marginal $1.67 EBIT, 40 percent, or 67 cents, goes in taxes, leaving $1 to increase dividends. In general, a taxable firm must earn $1/(1 - $ Tax rate) in additional EBIT for each extra dollar of dividends. Because interest is tax deductible, Canadian Enterprises needs to earn only $1 more in EBIT to be able to pay $1 in added interest.

The tables are turned when we contrast interest and dividends earned by the firm. Interest earned is fully taxable just like any other form of ordinary income. Dividends on common shares received from other Canadian corporations qualify for a 100 percent exemption and are received tax free.[10]

TABLE 2.7   **Corporate tax rates in percentages in 2012 (current as of December 31, 2011)**

	Federal (%)	Alberta (%)	Combined (%)
Basic corporations	15	10	25
All small corporations with a taxable income less than $400,000	11	3	14

Source: © 2011 KPMG LLP, a Canadian limited liability partnership and a member firm of the KPMG network of independent member firms affiliated with KPMG International Cooperative ("KPMG International"), a Swiss entity. All rights reserved. The information contained herein is of a general nature and is not intended to address the circumstances of any particular individual or entity. Although we endeavour to provide accurate and timely information, there can be no guarantee that such information is accurate as of the date it is received or that it will continue to be accurate in the future. No one should act on such information without appropriate professional advice after a thorough examination of the particular situation.

Global Tax Rates

Corporate and individual tax rates vary around the world. Corporate rates range from 10 percent in Bulgaria to 40 percent in India. Wealthy individuals in countries such as Canada, France, U.K., Sweden, and other high-taxing nations look for opportunities and tax laws that allow them to move their wealth to countries such as Monaco and Hong Kong where they can enjoy individual tax rates as low as 0 percent.[11]

How taxable income gains are calculated also varies. For instance, the U.S. tax regime distinguishes between short-term capital gains (one year or less) taxed at ordinary income rates and long-term capital gains (more than one year), which receive preferential tax rates ranging between 0 and 15 percent depending on one's marginal tax rate. Canada does not have a tiered capital gains tax system. Unlike the U.S. where long-term capital gains are taxed at lower rates than dividends, individuals in Canada have an incentive to hold dividend-paying stocks as dividends are taxed only marginally more than capital gains.

Capital Gains and Carry-forward and Carry-back

When a firm disposes of an asset for more than it paid originally, the difference is a capital gain. As with individuals, firms receive favourable tax treatment on capital gains. At the time of writing, capital gains received by corporations are taxed at 50 percent of the marginal tax rate.

loss carry-forward, carry-back
Using a year's capital losses to offset capital gains in past or future years.

When calculating capital gains for tax purposes, a firm nets out all capital losses in the same year. If capital losses exceed capital gains, the net capital loss may be carried back to reduce taxable capital gains in the three prior years. Under the **carry-back** feature, a firm files a revised tax return and receives a refund of prior years' taxes. For example, suppose Canadian Enterprises

---

[10] The situation is more complicated for preferred stock dividends, as we discuss in Chapter 7.

[11] William Perez, "Capital Gains Tax Rates," *Tax Planning: U.S.*

experienced a net capital loss of $1 million in 2012 and net capital gains of $300,000 in 2011, $200,000 in 2010, and $150,000 in 2009. Canadian could carry back a total of $650,000 to get a refund on its taxes. The remaining $350,000 can be carried forward indefinitely to reduce future taxes on capital gains.

A similar **carry-forward** provision applies to operating losses. The carry-back period is three years and carry-forward is allowed up to seven years.

Income Trust Income and Taxation

As stated in Chapter 1, a revised tax regime was introduced for Income Trusts in 2011. Under this regime their tax treatment is like that of corporations, and their investors are treated like shareholders.

Income trust structure has worked well for trusts in stable businesses with strong cash-flow-generating abilities; examples are AltaGas Income Fund or Boston Pizza Royalty Fund. As cash flows fluctuate in riskier industries, trusts have had to reduce or suspend distributions. When this happened to Halterm—a trust based on the container port business in Halifax—in 2003, the unit price dropped by 59 percent.

As we explained in Chapter 1, at the end of October 2006, the federal government announced plans to tax income trusts as corporations. Applicable to trusts in existence in October 2006 starting in 2011 and immediately to new trusts, these plans put an end to new trust conversions.[12] In the meantime, the tax changes to income trusts include increased dividend tax credits (illustrated in Table 2.8) to remove the advantage of income trust distribution. Under the new system, the tax exempt investor (income trusts in this case) will be taxed at the same rate of large corporations.

TABLE 2.8   Taxation of Income Trust Distributions vs. Dividends

Investor	Previous System		New System	
	Income Trust (Income)	Large Corporation (Dividend)	Income Trust (Non-Portfolio Earnings)	Large Corporation (Dividend)
Taxable Canadian (*)	46%	46%	45.5%	45.5%
Canadian tax-exempt	0%	32%	31.5%	31.5%
Taxable U.S. investor (**)	15%	42%	41.5%	41.5%

(*) All rates in the table are as of 2011, include both entity- and investor-level tax (as applicable) and reflect already-announced rate reductions and the additional 0.5% corporate rate reduction described below. Rates for "Taxable Canadian" assume that top personal income tax rates apply and that provincial governments increase their dividend tax credit for dividends of large corporations.
(**) Canadian taxes only. U.S. tax will in most cases also apply.

Source: fin.gc.ca/n06/06-061-eng.asp

Market reaction to news of the modified income trust taxation rule illustrates the efficient market hypothesis (EMH). As will be discussed in Chapter 11, the EMH holds that prices reflect all available information. On November 1, 2006, the day following the announcement of the new taxes, share prices of Yellow Pages Income Trust, AltaGas Income Fund, and Boston Pizza Royalties Income Fund all fell by more than 10 percent. In addition, income trust prices fell by lesser amounts in the days prior to the announcement, suggesting that rumours surrounding the new taxes were leaked at that time.[13]

---

[12] ScotiaMcLeod, "Federal Government to Implement New Tax Fairness Plan," November 1, 2006.

[13] L. Kryzanowski and Y. Lu, "In Government We Trust: Rise and Fall of Canadian Business Income Trust Conversion," *Managerial Finance* 35, pp. 789–802.

2.5 | Capital Cost Allowance

**capital cost allowance
(CCA)**
Depreciation for tax
purposes, not necessarily the
same as depreciation under
IFRS.

Capital cost allowance (CCA) is depreciation for tax purposes in Canada. Capital cost allowance is deducted in determining income. Because the tax law reflects various political compromises, CCA is not the same as depreciation under IFRS so there is no reason calculation of a firm's income under tax rules has to be the same as under IFRS. For example, taxable corporate income may often be lower than accounting income because the company is allowed to use accelerated capital cost allowance rules in computing depreciation for tax purposes while using straight-line depreciation for IFRS reporting.[14]

CCA calculation begins by assigning every capital asset to a particular class. An asset's class establishes its maximum CCA rate for tax purposes. Intangible assets like leasehold improvements in Table 2.9 follow straight-line depreciation for CCA. For all other assets, CCA follows the declining balance method. The CCA for each year is computed by multiplying the asset's book value for tax purposes, called undepreciated capital cost (UCC), by the appropriate rate.

The CCA system is unique to Canada and differs in many respects from the ACRS depreciation method used in the United States. One key difference is that in the Canadian system, the expected salvage value (what we think the asset will be worth when we dispose of it) and the actual expected economic life (how long we expect the asset to be in service) are not explicitly considered in the calculation of capital cost allowance. Some typical CCA classes and their respective CCA rates are described in Table 2.9.

half-year rule
CRA's requirement to figure
CCA on only one-half of an
asset's installed cost for its
first year of use.

To illustrate how capital cost allowance is calculated, suppose your firm is considering buying a van costing $30,000, including any setup costs that must (by law) be capitalized. (No rational, profitable business would capitalize, for tax purposes, anything that could legally be expensed.) Table 2.9 shows that vans fall in Class 10 with a 30 percent CCA rate. To calculate the CCA, we follow CRA's **half-year rule** that allows us to figure CCA on only half of the asset's installed cost in the first year it is put in use. Table 2.10 shows the CCA for our van for the first five years.

TABLE 2.9

**Common capital cost
allowance classes**

Class	Rate	Assets
1	4%	Buildings acquired after 1987
8	20	Furniture, photocopiers
10	30	Vans, trucks, tractors, and equipment
13	Straight-line	Leasehold improvements
16	40	Taxicabs and rental cars
43	30	Manufacturing equipment

TABLE 2.10

**Capital cost allowance
for a van**

Year	Beginning UCC	CCA	Ending UCC
1	$15,000[*]	$4,500	$10,500
2	25,500[†]	7,650	17,850
3	17,850	5,355	12,495
4	12,495	3,748	8,747
5	8,747	2,624	6,123

[*]One-half of $30,000.
[†]Year 1 ending balance 1 + Remaining half of $30,000.

---

[14] Where taxable income is less than accounting income, the difference goes into a long-term liability account on the statement of financial position labelled deferred taxes.

As we pointed out, in calculating CCA under current tax law, the economic life and future market value of the asset are not an issue. As a result, the UCC of an asset can differ substantially from its actual market value. With our $30,000 van, UCC after the first year is $15,000 less the first year's CCA of $4,500, or $10,500. The remaining UCC values are summarized in Table 2.10. After five years, the undepreciated capital cost of the van is $6,123.

Asset Purchases and Sales

When an asset is sold, the UCC in its asset class (or pool) is reduced by what is realized on the asset or by its original cost, whichever is less. This amount is called the adjusted cost of disposal. Suppose we wanted to sell the van in our earlier example after five years. Based on historical averages of resale prices, it will be worth, say, 25 percent of the purchase price or .25 × $30,000 = $7,500. Since the price of $7,500 is less than the original cost, the adjusted cost of disposal is $7,500 and the UCC in Class 10 is reduced by this amount.

Table 2.10 shows that the van has a UCC after five years of $6,123. The $7,500 removed from the pool is $1,377 more than the undepreciated capital cost of the van we are selling, and future CCA deductions will be reduced as the pool continues. On the other hand, if we had sold the van for, say, $4,000, the UCC in Class 10 would be reduced by $4,000 and the $2,123 excess of UCC over the sale price would remain in the pool. Then, future CCA increases as the declining balance calculations depreciate the $2,123 excess UCC to infinity.

EXAMPLE 2.5: Capital Cost Allowance Incentives in Practice

Since capital cost allowance is deducted in computing income, larger CCA rates reduce taxes and increase cash flows. As we pointed out earlier, finance ministers sometimes tinker with the CCA rates to create incentives. For example, in a federal budget a few years ago, the minister announced an increase in CCA rates from 20 to 30 percent for manufacturing and processing assets. The combined federal/provincial corporate tax rate for this sector is 36.1 percent in Ontario.

Mississauga Manufacturing was planning to acquire new processing equipment to enhance efficiency and its ability to compete with U.S. firms. The equipment had an installed cost of $1 million. How much additional tax will the new measure save Mississauga in the first year the equipment is put into use?

Under the half-year rule, UCC for the first year is 1/2 × $1 million = $500,000. The CCA deductions under the old and new rates are:

Old rate: CCA = .20 × $500,000 = $100,000
New rate: CCA = .30 × $500,000 = $150,000

Because the firm deducts CCA in figuring taxable income, taxable income will be reduced by the incremental CCA of $50,000. With $50,000 less in taxable income, Mississauga Manufacturing's combined tax bill would drop by $50,000 × .361 = $18,050.

---

net acquisitions
Total installed cost of capital acquisitions minus adjusted cost of any disposals within an asset pool.

So far we focused on CCA calculations for one asset. In practice, firms often buy and sell assets from a given class in the course of a year. In this case, we apply the **net acquisitions** rule. From the total installed cost of all acquisitions, we subtract the adjusted cost of disposal of all assets in the pool. The result is net acquisitions for the asset class. If net acquisitions are positive, we apply the half-year rule and calculate CCA as we did earlier. If net acquisitions is negative, there is no adjustment for the half-year rule.

WHEN AN ASSET POOL IS TERMINATED   Suppose your firm decides to contract out all transport and to sell all company vehicles. If the company owns no other Class 10 assets, the asset pool in this class is terminated. As before, the adjusted cost of disposal is the net sales proceeds or the total installed cost of all the pool assets, whichever is less. This adjusted cost of disposal is subtracted from the total UCC in the pool. So far, the steps are exactly the same as in our van example where the pool continued. What happens next is different. Unless the adjusted cost of disposal just happens to equal the UCC exactly, a positive or negative UCC balance remains and this has tax implications.

terminal loss
The difference between UCC and adjusted cost of disposal when the UCC is greater.

A positive UCC balance remains when the adjusted cost of disposal is less than UCC before the sale. In this case, the firm has a **terminal loss** equal to the remaining UCC. This loss is deductible from income for the year. For example, if we sell the van after two years for $10,000, the UCC of

$17,850 in Table 2.10 exceeds the market value by $7,850 as Table 2.12 shows. The terminal loss of $7,850 gives rise to a tax saving of .40 × $7,850 = $3,140. (We assume the tax rate is 40 percent.)

A negative UCC balance occurs when the adjusted cost of disposal exceeds UCC, in the pool. To illustrate, return to our van example and suppose that this van is the only Class 10 asset our company owns when it sells the pool for $7,500 after five years. There is a $1,377 excess of adjusted cost of disposal (7,500 − 6,123) over UCC, so the final UCC credit balance is $1,377.

recaptured depreciation
The taxable difference between adjusted cost of disposal and UCC when UCC is smaller.

The company must pay tax at its ordinary tax rate on this balance. The reason that taxes must be paid is that the difference in adjusted cost of disposal and UCC is excess CCA **recaptured** when the asset is sold. We over depreciated the asset by $7,500 − $6,123 = $1,377. Because we deducted $1,377 too much in CCA, we paid $551 too little in taxes (at 40 percent), and we simply have to make up the difference.

EXAMPLE 2.6: CCA Calculations

Staple Supply Ltd. has just purchased a new computerized information system with an installed cost of $160,000. The computer qualifies for a CCA rate of 45 percent. What are the yearly capital cost allowances? Based on historical experience, we think that the system will be worth only $10,000 when we get rid of it in four years. What will be the tax consequences of the sale if the company has several other computers still in use in four years? Now suppose that Staple Supply will sell all its assets and wind up the company in four years.

In Table 2.11, at the end of Year 4, the remaining balance for the specific computer system mentioned would be $20,630.[15] The pool is reduced by $10,000, but it will continue to be depreciated. There are no tax consequences in Year 4. This is only the case when the pool is active. If this were the only computer system, we would have been closing the pool and would have been able to claim a terminal loss of $20,630 − $10,000 = $10,630.

TABLE 2.11

CCA for computer system

Year	Beginning UCC	CCA	Ending UCC
1	$ 80,000*	$36,000	$44,000
2	124,000†	55,800	68,200
3	68,200	30,690	37,510
4	37,510	16,880	20,630

*One-half of $160,000.
†Year 1 ending balance 1 + Remaining half of $160,000.

Notice that this is *not* a tax on a capital gain. As a general rule, a capital gain only occurs if the market price exceeds the original cost. To illustrate a capital gain, suppose that instead of buying the van, our firm purchased a classic car for $50,000. After five years, the classic car will be sold for $75,000. The sale price would exceed the purchase price, so the adjusted cost of disposal is $50,000 and UCC pool is reduced by this amount. The total negative balance left in the UCC pool is $50,000 − $6,123 = $43,877 and this is recaptured CCA. In addition, the firm has a capital gain of $75,000 − $50,000 = $25,000, the difference between the sale price and the original cost.[16]

TABLE 2.12

UCC and terminal loss

UCC	Market value	Terminal loss	Tax Savings
17,850	10,000	7850	3140
6123	7500	−1377	−551

---

[15] In actuality, the capital cost allowance for the entire pool will be calculated at once, without specific identification of each computer system.

[16] This example shows that it is possible to have a recapture of CCA without closing out a pool if the UCC balance goes negative.

EXAMPLE 2.7: Capital Loss, CCA Recapture, and Terminal Loss

T-Grill is a manufacturer and distributor of high-end commercial barbeques. In 2010, the company purchased $900,000 worth of manufacturing equipment, subject to Class 43 for CCA purposes. Class 43 assets depreciate at an annual rate of 30 percent. In 2012, T-Grill's CEO decided to sell the existing manufacturing equipment for $500,000 and outsource production to India. As a result, it no longer holds class 43 assets. Does this transaction result in a capital gain, CCA recapture, or terminal loss?

A capital gain occurs when the selling price exceeds the original cost of the asset. In T-Grill's case, the selling price of $500,000 is below the original cost of $900,000 so there is no capital gain.

CCA recapture occurs when the selling price is greater than the ending UCC. According to Table 2.13, at the end of 2012, T-Grill had an ending UCC of $374,850.

$$CCA \text{ recapture} = \text{Lower of selling price and the} \\ \text{original cost} - \text{Ending UCC}$$
$$= \$500,000 - \$374,850$$
$$= \$125,150$$

T-Grill must pay tax on the $125,150.

However, what if due to economic turmoil, T-Grill could only sell its manufacturing equipment for $300,000. Would it continue to have a CCA recapture, or will it now experience a terminal loss?

$$CCA \text{ terminal loss} = \$300,000 - \$374,850$$
$$= -\$74,850.$$

T-Grill now has a terminal loss of $74,850 and this amount is considered as a tax-deductible expense.

TABLE 2.13

CCA for manufacturing equipment

Year	Beginning UCC	CCA	Ending UCC
2010	$450,000	$135,000	$315,000
2011	765,000	229,500	535,500
2012	535,500	160,650	374,850

Concept Questions

1. What is the difference between capital cost allowance and IFRS depreciation?
2. Why do governments sometimes increase CCA rates?
3. Reconsider the CCA increase discussed in Example 2.5. How effective do you think it was in stimulating investment? Why?

2.6 | SUMMARY AND CONCLUSIONS

This chapter has introduced you to some of the basics of financial statements, cash flow, and taxes. The Sino-Forest example that was introduced at the start of the chapter shows just how important these issues can be for shareholders. In this chapter, we saw that:

1. The book values on an accounting statement of financial position can be very different from market values. The goal of financial management is to maximize the market value of the stock, not its book value.

2. Net income as it is computed on the statement of comprehensive income is not cash flow. A primary reason is that depreciation, a non-cash expense, is deducted when net income is computed.

3. Marginal and average tax rates can be different; the marginal tax rate is relevant for most financial decisions.

4. There is a cash flow identity much like the statement of financial position identity. It says that cash flow from assets equals cash flow to bondholders and shareholders. The calculation

of cash flow from financial statements isn't difficult. Care must be taken in handling non-cash expenses, such as depreciation, and in not confusing operating costs with financial costs. Most of all, it is important not to confuse book values with market values and accounting income with cash flow.

5. Different types of Canadian investment income, dividends, interest, and capital gains are taxed differently.

6. Corporate income taxes create a tax advantage for debt financing (paying tax-deductible interest) over equity financing (paying dividends). Chapter 15 discusses this in depth.

7. Capital cost allowance (CCA) is depreciation for tax purposes in Canada. CCA calculations are important for determining cash flows.

Key Terms

average tax rate (page 37)
capital cost allowance (CCA) (page 42)
capital gains (page 39)
cash flow from assets (page 32)
cash flow to creditors (page 34)
cash flow to shareholders (page 34)
dividend tax credit (page 39)
free cash flow (page 34)
half-year rule (page 42)
loss carry-forward, carry-back (page 40)

marginal tax rate (page 37)
net acquisitions (page 43)
non-cash items (page 31)
operating cash flow (page 32)
realized capital gains (page 39)
recaptured depreciation (page 44)
statement of comprehensive income (page 30)
statement of financial position (page 25)
terminal loss (page 43)

Chapter Review Problems and Self-Test

2.1 **Cash Flow for B.C. Resources Ltd.** This problem will give you some practice working with financial statements and calculating cash flow. Based on the following information for B.C. Resources Ltd., prepare an statement of comprehensive income for 2012 and statement of financial positions for 2011and 2012. Next, following our Canadian Enterprises examples in the chapter, calculate cash flow for B.C. Resources, cash flow to bondholders, and cash flow to shareholders for 2012. Use a 40-percent tax rate throughout. You can check your answers in the next section.

	2011	2012
Sales	$4,203	$4,507
Cost of goods sold	2,422	2,633
Depreciation	785	952
Interest	180	196
Dividends	225	250
Current assets	2,205	2,429
Net fixed assets	7,344	7,650
Current liabilities	1,003	1,255
Long-term debt	3,106	2,085

Answers to Self-Test Problems

2.1 In preparing the statement of financial positions, remember that shareholders' equity is the residual and can be found using the equation:

Total assets = Total liabilities + Total equity

With this in mind, B.C. Resources' statement of financial positions are as follows:

B.C. RESOURCES LTD.
Statement of Financial Position as of December 31, 2011 and 2012

	2011	2012		2011	2012
Current assets	$2,205	$ 2,429	Current liabilities	$1,003	$ 1,255
Net fixed assets	7,344	7,650	Long-term debt	3,106	2,085
			Equity	5,440	6,739
Total assets	$9,549	$10,079	Total liabilities and shareholders' equity	$9,549	$10,079

The statement of comprehensive income is straightforward:

B.C. RESOURCES LTD.
2012 Statement of Comprehensive Income

Sales	$ 4,507
Costs of goods sold	2,633
Depreciation	952
Earnings before interest and taxes	$ 922
Interest paid	196
Taxable income	$ 726
Taxes (40%)	290
Net income	$ 436

Dividends	$250	
Addition to retained earnings	186	

Notice that we've used a flat 40 percent tax rate. Also notice that retained earnings are just net income less cash dividends. We can now pick up the figures we need to get operating cash flow:

B.C. RESOURCES LTD.
2012 Operating Cash Flow

Earnings before interest and taxes	$ 922
+ Depreciation	952
− Taxes	290
Operating cash flow	$ 1,584

Next, we get the capital spending for the year by looking at the change in fixed assets, remembering to account for the depreciation:

Ending net fixed assets	$ 7,650
− Beginning net fixed assets	7,344
+ Depreciation	952
Net capital spending	$ 1,258

After calculating beginning and ending NWC, we take the difference to get the change in NWC:

Ending NWC	$ 1,174
− Beginning NWC	1,202
Change in NWC	−$ 28

We now combine operating cash flow, net capital spending, and the change in net working capital to get the total cash flow from assets:

B.C. RESOURCES LTD.
2012 Cash Flow from Assets

Operating cash flow	$ 1,584
− Net capital spending	1,258
− Change in NWC	28
Cash flow from assets	$ 354

To get cash flow to creditors, notice that long-term borrowing decreased by $1,021 during the year and that interest paid was $196:

B.C. RESOURCES LTD.
2012 Cash Flow to Creditors

Interest paid	$ 196
− Net new borrowing	1,021
Cash flow to creditors	$1,217

Finally, dividends paid were $250. To get net new equity, we have to do some extra calculating. Total equity was found by balancing the statement of financial position. During 2012, equity increased by $6,739 − 5,440 = $1,299. Of this increase, $186 was from additions to retained earnings, so $1,113 in new equity was raised during the year. Cash flow to shareholders was thus:

B.C. RESOURCES LTD.
2012 Cash Flow to Shareholders

Dividends paid	$ 250
− Net new equity	1,113
Cash flow to shareholders	−$ 863

As a check, notice that cash flow from assets, $354, does equal cash flow to creditors plus cash flow to shareholders ($1,217 − 863 = $354).

Concepts Review and Critical Thinking Questions

1. **Liquidity (LO1)** What does liquidity measure? Explain the trade-off a firm faces between high liquidity and low liquidity levels.

2. **Accounting and Cash Flows (LO2)** Why might the revenue and cost of figures shown on a standard statement of comprehensive income not be representative of the actual inflows and outflows that occurred during a period?

3. **Book Values versus Market Values (LO1)** In preparing a statement of financial position, why do you think standard accounting practice focuses on historical cost rather than market value?

4. **Operating Cash Flow (LO3)** In comparing accounting net income and operating cash flow, name two items you typically find in the net income that are not in operating cash flow. Explain what each is and why it is excluded on operating cash flow.

5. **Book Values versus Market Values (LO1)** Under standard accounting rules, it is possible for a company's liabilities to exceed its assets. When this occurs, the owners' equity is negative. Can this happen with market values? Why or why not?

6. **Cash Flow for Assets (LO3)** Suppose a company's cash flow from assets is negative for a particular period. Is this necessarily a good sign or a bad sign?

7. **Operating Cash Flow (LO3)** Suppose a company's operating cash flow has been negative for several years running. Is this necessarily a good sign or a bad sign?

8. **Net Working Capital and Capital Spending (LO3)** Could a company's change in NWC be negative in a given year? Explain how this might come about. What about net capital spending?

9. **Cash Flow to Shareholders and Creditors (LO3)** Could a company's cash flow to shareholders be negative in a given year? Explain how this might come about. What about cash flow to creditors?

10. **Enterprise Value (LO1)** A firm's *enterprise value* is equal to the market value of its debt and equity, less the firm's holdings of cash and cash equivalents. This figure is particularly relevant to potential purchasers of the firm. Why?

Questions and Problems

Basic
(Questions 1–12)

1. **Building a Statement of Financial Position (LO1)** Oakville Pucks Inc. has current assets of $5,100, net fixed assets of $23,800, current liabilities of $4,300, and long-term debt of 7,400. What is the value of the shareholders' equity account for this firm? How much is net working capital?

2. **Building an Statement of Comprehensive Income (LO1)** Burlington Exterminators Inc. has sales of $586,000, cost of $247,000, depreciation expense of $43,000, interest expense of $32,000, and a tax rate of 35 percent. What is the net income for this firm?

3. **Dividends and Retained Earnings (LO1)** Suppose the firm in Problem 2 paid out $73,000 in cash dividends. What is the addition to retained earnings?

4. **Per-Share Earnings and Dividends (LO1)** Suppose the firm in Problem 3 had 85,000 shares of common stock outstanding. What is the earnings per share, or EPS, figure? What is the dividends per share figure?

5. **Market Values and Book Values (LO1)** Kimbo Widgets Inc. purchased new cloaking machinery three years ago for $7 million. The machinery can be sold to the Rimalons today for $4.9 million. Kimbo's current statement of financial position shows net fixed assets of $3.7 million, current liabilities of $1.1 million, and net working capital of $380,000. If all the current assets were liquidated today, the company would receive $1.6 million cash. What is the book value of Kimbo's assets today? What is the market value?

6. **Calculating Taxes (LO4)** The Grimsby Co. in Alberta had $236,000 in 2012 taxable income. Using the rates from Table 2.7 in the chapter, calculate the company's 2012 income taxes.

7. **Tax rates (LO4)** In Problem 6 what is the average tax rate? What is the marginal tax rate?

8. **Calculating OCF (LO3)** Fergus Inc. has sales of $27,500, costs of $13,280, depreciation expense of $2,300, and interest expense of $1,105. If the tax rate is 35 percent, what is the operating cash flow, or OCF?

9. **Calculating Net Capital Spending (LO3)** Yale Driving School's 2011 statement of financial position showed net fixed assets of $3.4 million, and the 2012 statement of financial position showed net fixed assets of $4.2 million. The company's 2012 statement of comprehensive income showed a depreciation expense of $385,000. What was net capital spending in 2012?

10. **Calculating Changes in NWC (LO3)** The 2011 statement of financial position of Owosso Inc. showed current assets of $2,100 and current liabilities of $1,380. The 2012 statement of financial position showed current assets of $2,250 and current liabilities of $1,710. What was the company's 2012 change in net working capital or NWC?

11. **Cash Flow to Creditors (LO3)** The 2011 statement of financial position of Roger's Tennis Shop Inc. showed long-term debt of $2.6 million, and the 2012 statement of financial position showed long term debt of $2.9 million. The 2012 Statement of Comprehensive Income showed an interest expense of $170,000. What was the firm's cash flow to creditors during 2012?

12. **Cash Flow to Shareholders (LO3)** The 2011 statement of financial position of Roger's Tennis Shop Inc. showed $740,000 in the common stock account and $5.2 million in the additional retained earnings account. The 2012 statement of financial position showed $815,000 and $5.5 million in the same two accounts, respectively. If the company paid out $490,000 in cash dividends during 2012, what was the cash flow to shareholders for the year?

Intermediate
(Questions 13–24)

13. **Calculating Total Cash Flows (LO3)** Given the information for Roger's Tennis Shop Inc. in Problem 11 and 12, suppose you also know the firm's net capital spending for 2011 was $940,000, and that the firm reduced its net working capital investment by $85,000. What was the firm's 2012 operating cash flow, or OCF?

14. **Calculating Total Cash Flows (LO3)** Teeswater Corp. shows the following information on its 2012 statement of comprehensive income: sales = $196,000; costs = $104,000; other expenses = $6,800; depreciation expense = $9,100; interest expense = $14,800; taxes = $21,455; dividends = $10,400. In addition, you're told that the firm issued $5,700 in new equity during 2012 and redeemed $7,300 in outstanding long-term debt.

    a. What is the 2012 operating cash flow?

    b. What is the 2012 cash flow to creditors?

    c. What is the 2012 cash flow to shareholders?

    d. If net fixed assets increased by $27,000 during the year, what was the addition to NWC?

15. **Using Statement of Comprehensive Income (LO1)** Given the following information for Lucan Pizza Co., calculate the depreciation expense: sales = $41,000; costs = $19,500; addition to retained earnings = $5,100; dividends paid = $1,500; interest expense = $4,500; tax rate = 35 percent.

16. **Preparing a Statement of Financial Position (LO1)** Prepare a 2012 statement of financial position for Listowel Corp. based on the following information: cash = $195,000; patents and copyrights = $780,000; accounts payable = $405,000; accounts receivable = $137,000; tangible net fixed assets = $2,800,000; inventory = $264,000; notes payable = $160,000; accumulated retained earnings = $1,934,000; long-term debt = $1,195,000.

17. **Residual Claims (LO1)** Pelham Inc. is obligated to pay its creditors $7,300 during the year.

    a. What is the market value of the shareholder's equity if assets have a market value of $8,400?

    b. What if assets equal $6,700?

18. **Marginal versus Average Tax Rates (LO4)** (Refer to Table 2.7) Corporation Growth has $88,000 in taxable income, and Corporation Income has $8,800,000 in taxable income.

    a. What is the tax bill for each?

    b. Suppose both firms have identified a new project that will increase taxable income by $10,000. How much additional taxes will each firm pay? Is this amount the same? if not, why?

19. **Net Income and OCF (LO2)** During 2012, Thorold Umbrella Corp. had sales of $730,000. Cost of goods sold, administrative and selling expenses, and depreciation expenses were $580,000, $105,000, and $135,000, respectively. In addition, the company had an interest expense of $75,000 and a tax rate of 35 percent. (Ignore any tax loss carry-back or carry-forward provisions.)

    a. What is Thorold's net income for 2012?

    b. What is its operating cash flow?

    c. Explain your results in (a) and (b).

20. **Accounting Values versus Cash Flows (LO3)** In Problem 19, suppose Thorold Umbrella Corp. paid out $25,000 in cash dividends. Is this possible? If spending on net fixed assets and net working capital was zero, and if no new stock was issued during the year, what do you know about the firm's long-term debt account?

21. **Calculating Cash Flows (LO2)** Nanticoke Industries had the following operating results for 2012: sales $22,800; cost of goods sold = $16,050; depreciation expense = $4,050; interest expense = $1,830; dividends paid = $1,300. At the beginning of the year, net assets were $13,650, current assets were $4,800, and current liabilities were $2,700. At the end of the year, net fixed assets were $16,800, current assets were $5,930, and current liabilities were $3,150. The tax rate for 2012 was 34 percent.

    a. What is net income for 2012?

    b. What is the operating cash flow for 2012?

    c. What is the cash flow from assets for 2012? Is this possible? Explain.

    d. If no new debt was issued during the year, what is the cash flow to creditors? What is the cash flow to shareholders? Explain and interpret the positive and negative signs of your answers in (a) through (d).

22. **Calculating Cash Flows (LO3)** Consider the following abbreviated financial statements for Barrie Enterprises:

BARRIE Enterprises
2011 and 2012 Partial Statement of Financial Position

Assets			Liabilities and Owner's Equity		
	2011	2012		2011	2012
Current Assets	$ 653	$ 707	Current liabilities	$ 261	$ 293
Net fixed Assets	2,691	3,240	Long-term debt	1,422	1,512

BARRIE Enterprises
2012 Statement of Comprehensive Income

Sales	$8,280
Costs	3,861
Depreciation	738
Interest Paid	211

    a. What is owner's equity for 2011 and 2012?

    b. What is the change in net working capital for 2012?

    c.   In 2012, Barrie Enterprises purchased $1,350 in new fixed assets. How much in fixed assets did Barrie Enterprises sell? What is the cash flow from assets for the year? (The tax rate is 35 percent.)

    d.   During 2012, Barrie Enterprises raised $270 in new long-term debt. How much long-term debt must Barrie Enterprises have paid off during the year? What is the cash flow to creditors?

23. **Income Trust Distributions vs. Corporate Dividends (LO4)** The Bancroft Company is currently structured as an income trust. It is considering restructuring the company to become a corporation, but is unsure if this would benefit shareholders. Company executives have asked for your advice. They tell you that the corporate tax rate is 35 percent, last year's net income before tax was $500,000 and there are 10,000 outstanding shares. If the company decides to restructure into a corporation, one income trust unit will become one share. From your experience doing your own tax returns, you know that dividends are taxed at 23 percent and income and interest income are taxed at 48 percent. Is it worth it for the Bancroft Company to restructure into a corporation? If so, how much more would an investor gain if that investor owned 2000 shares?

Challenge **24.** **Net Fixed Assets and Depreciation (LO3)** On the statement of financial position, the net fixed assets (NFA) account is equal to
(Questions the gross fixed assets (FA) account (which records the acquisition cost of fixed assets) minus the accumulated depreciation (AD)
24–36) account (which records the total depreciation taken by the firm against its fixed assets). Using the fact that NFA = FA − AD, show that the expression given in the chapter for net capital spending, $NFA_{end} - NFA_{beg} + D$ (where D is the depreciation expense during the year), is equivalent to $FA_{end} - FA_{beg}$.

Use the following information for Clarington Inc. for Problems 25 and 26 (assume the tax rate is 34 percent):

	2011	2012
Sales	$7,233	$8,085
Depreciation	1,038	1,085
Cost of goods sold	2,487	2,942
Other expenses	591	515
Interest	485	579
Cash	3,972	4,041
Accounts receivable	5,021	5,892
Short-term notes payable	732	717
Long-term debt	12,700	15,435
Net fixed assets	31,805	33,291
Accounts payable	3,984	4,025
Inventory	8,927	9,555
Dividends	882	1,011

25. **Financial Statements (LO1)** Draw up an statement of comprehensive income and statement of financial position for this company for 2011 and 2012.

26. **Calculating Cash Flow (LO3)** For 2012, calculate the cash flow from assets, cash flow to creditors, and cash flow to shareholders.

27. **Taxes on Investment Income (LO4)** Linda Milner, an Alberta investor, receives $40,000 in dividends from Okotoks Forest Products shares, $20,000 in interest from a deposit in a chartered bank, and a $20,000 capital gain from Cremona Mines shares. Use the information in Tables 2.5 and 2.6 to calculate the after-tax cash flow from each investment. Ms. Milner's federal tax rate is 29 percent.

28. **Investment Income (LO4)** Assuming that Ms. Milner's cash flows in Problem 27 came from equal investments of $75,000 each, find her after-tax rate of return on each investment.

29. **CCA (LO5)** Scugog Manufacturing Ltd. just invested in some new processing machinery to take advantage of more favourable CCA rates in a new federal budget. The machinery qualifies for 25 percent CCA rate and has an installed cost of $500,000. Calculate the CCA and UCC for the first five years.

30. **UCC (LO5)** A piece of newly purchased industrial equipment costs $1,000,000. It is Class 8 property with a CCA rate of 20 percent. Calculate the annual depreciation allowances and end-of-year book values (UCC) for the first five years.

31. **CCA and UCC (LO5)** Our new computer system cost us $100,000. We will outgrow it in five years. When we sell it, we will probably get only 20 percent of the purchase price. CCA on the computer will be calculated at a 30 percent rate (Class 10). Calculate the CCA and UCC values for five years. What will be the after-tax proceeds from the sale assuming the asset class is continued? Assume a 40 percent tax rate.

32. **CCA (LO5)** Havelock Industries bought new manufacturing equipment (Class 8) with a CCA rate of 20 percent for $4,125,000 in 2011 and then paid $75,000 for installation it capitalized in Class 8. The firm also invested $4 million in a new brick building (Class 3) with a CCA rate of 5 percent. During 2011 Havelock finished the project and put it in use. Find the total CCA for Havelock for 2011 and 2012.

33. **UCC (LO5)** Kanata Construction specializes in large projects in Edmonton and Saskatoon. In 2011, Kanata invested $1.5 million in new excavating equipment, which qualifies for a CCA rate of 50 percent. At the same time the firm sold some older equipment on the secondhand market for $145,000. When it was purchased in 2008, the older equipment cost $340,000. Calculate the UCC for the asset pool in each year from 2008 through 2012.

34. **Income Tax (LO4)** A resident of Alberta has taxable income from employment of $170,000. This individual is considering three investments of equal risk and wishes to determine the after-tax income for each:

    a. $57,000 worth of bonds with a coupon rate of 5 percent.

    b. 250 shares of stock that will pay a dividend at the end of the year of $25 per share.

    c. 500 shares of another stock that is expected to increase in value by $15 per share during the year.

35. **Tax Loss Carry-back and Carry-forward (LO4)** The Stayner Company experienced an operating loss of $4,100,000 in 2009. Taxable income figures for recent years are given below. Show how the firm can maximize its tax refunds.

	2006	2007	2008	2009	2010	2011	2012
Taxable income ($000)	$116	$140	$168	($600)	$40	$40	$40

36. **UCC (LO5)** A proposed cost-saving device has an installed cost of $99,200. It is in Class 43 (30 percent rate) for CCA purposes. It will actually function for five years, at which time it will have no value.

    a. Calculate UCC at the end of five years.

    b. What are the tax implications when the asset is sold?

MINI CASE

Nepean Boards is a small company that manufactures and sells snowboards in Ottawa. Scott Redknapp, the founder of the company, is in charge of the design and sale of the snowboards, but he is not from a business background. As a result, the company's financial records are not well maintained.

The initial investment in Nepean Boards was provided by Scott and his friends and family. Because the initial investment was relatively small, and the company has made snowboards only for its own store, the investors haven't required detailed financial statements from Scott. But thanks to word of mouth among professional boarders, sales have picked up recently, and Scott is considering a major expansion. His plans include opening another snowboard store in Calgary, as well as supplying his "sticks" (boarder lingo for boards) to other sellers.

Scott's expansion plans require a significant investment, which he plans to finance with a combination of additional funds from outsiders plus some money borrowed from the banks. Naturally, the new investors and creditors require more organized and detailed financial statements than Scott previously prepared. At the urging of his investors, Scott has hired financial analyst Jennifer Bradshaw to evaluate the performance of the company over the past year.

After rooting through old bank statements, sales receipts, tax returns, and other records, Jennifer has assembled the following information:

	2011	2012
Cost of goods sold	$126,038	$159,143
Cash	18,187	27,478
Depreciation	35,581	40,217
Interest expense	7,735	8,866
Selling and administrative expenses	24,787	32,352
Accounts payable	32,143	36,404
Fixed assets	156,975	191,250
Sales	247,259	301,392
Accounts receivable	12,887	16,717
Notes payable	14,651	15,997
Long-term debt	79,235	91,195
Inventory	27,119	37,216
New equity	0	15,600

Nepean Boards currently pays out 50 percent of net income as dividends to Scott and the other original investors, and has a 20 percent tax rate. You are Jennifer's assistant, and she has asked you to prepare the following:

1. A statement of comprehensive income for 2011 and 2012.

2. A statement of financial position for 2011 and 2012.

3. Operating cash flow for the year.

4. Cash flow from assets for 2012.

5. Cash flow to creditors for 2012.

6. Cash flow to shareholders for 2012.

Questions

1. How would you describe Nepean Boards' cash flows for 2012? Write a brief discussion.

2. In light of your discussions in the previous question, what do you think about Scott's expansion plans?

Internet Application Questions

1. The distinction between capital investment and current expenditure is somewhat arbitrary. Nevertheless, from the tax viewpoint, a distinction must be made to calculate depreciation and its associated tax shield. The following link at Canada Revenue Agency provides a set of pointers to distinguish whether an expenditure is considered capital in nature, or whether it is a current expense.

   cra-arc.gc.ca/E/pub/tp/it128r/it128r-e.html

   Use the guidelines in the link above to classify the following expenses as capital or current:

   a. Your company buys a fleet of trucks for material delivery

   b. The local barbershop buys a new chair

   c. The local barbershop buys a new pair of scissors

   What assumptions did you need to make to answer the above questions?

2. Capital cost allowance is not the only tax shelter available to Canadian firms. In some cases, notably cultural industries, there are both federal and provincial tax credits to offset a portion of the production costs involved in content development. The following website at Canada Revenue Agency describes the Film or Video Production Tax Credit (FTC), which is available to qualified producers.

   cra-arc.gc.ca/tx/nnrsdnts/flm/ftc-cip/menu-eng.html

   For a company with $1 million in production costs, what is the size of the federal FTC?

3. The Canadian Institute of Chartered Accountants (cica.ca/index.aspx) provides standards and guidance for new issues, and solicits comments for new policies. Click on What's New and pick one item from Guidance and one item from Comments. Summarize the new guidelines and critique the comments article. Note that items on this site change from time to time.

4. The home page for Air Canada can be found at aircanada.ca. Locate the most recent annual report, which contains a statement of financial position for the company. What is the book value of equity for Air Canada? The market value of a company is the number of shares of stock outstanding times the price per share. This information can be found at ca.finance.yahoo.com using the ticker symbol for Air Canada (AC). What is the market value of equity? Which number is more relevant for shareholders?

CHAPTER 3

WORKING WITH FINANCIAL STATEMENTS

Courtesy of Suncor Energy

On November 17, 2011, common shares of Canadian energy company, Suncor Energy Inc., traded at $33.15 on the Toronto Stock Exchange (TSX). At that price, Bloomberg reported that the company had a price–earnings (P/E) ratio of 11.30. In other words, investors were willing to pay $11.30 for every dollar of income earned by Suncor Energy. At the same time, investors were willing to pay $18.01 for every dollar earned by TransCanada Corporation. At the other extreme was RIM, which, at that time, had a P/E ratio of 3.32. However, the company was still trading at $19.25. At that time, the typical stock on the S&P/TSX Composite Index was trading at a P/E of 15.23, or roughly 15 times earnings, as they say on Bay Street.

Price–earnings comparisons are examples of financial ratios. As we will see in this chapter, there is a wide variety of financial ratios, all designed to summarize specific aspects of a firm's financial position. In addition to discussing how to analyze financial statements and compute financial ratios, we will have quite a bit to say about who uses this information and why.

Learning Objectives ▶

After studying this chapter, you should understand:

LO1   The sources and uses of a firm's cash flows.

LO2   How to standardize financial statements for comparison purposes.

LO3   How to compute and, more importantly, interpret some common ratios.

LO4   The determinants of a firm's profitability.

LO5   Some of the problems and pitfalls in financial statement analysis.

In Chapter 2, we discussed some of the essential concepts of financial statements and cash flows. Part 2, this chapter and the next, continues where our earlier discussion left off. Our goal here is to expand your understanding of the uses (and abuses) of financial statement information.

Financial statement information crops up in various places in the remainder of our book. Part 2 is not essential for understanding this material, but it helps give you an overall perspective on the role of financial statement information in corporate finance.

A good working knowledge of financial statements is desirable simply because such statements, and numbers derived from those statements, are the primary means of communicating financial information both within the firm and outside the firm. In short, much of the language of corporate finance is rooted in the ideas we discuss in this chapter.

Furthermore, as we shall see, there are many different ways of using financial statement information and many different types of users. This diversity reflects the fact that financial statement information plays an important part in many types of decisions.

In the best of all worlds, the financial manager has full market value information about all the firm's assets. This rarely (if ever) happens. So the reason we rely on accounting figures for much of our financial information is that we almost always cannot obtain all (or even part) of the market information that we want. The only meaningful benchmark for evaluating business decisions is whether or not they create economic value (see Chapter 1). However, in many important situations, it is not possible to make this judgement directly because we can't see the market value effects of decisions.

We recognize that accounting numbers are often just pale reflections of economic reality, but they frequently are the best available information. For privately held corporations, not-for-profit businesses, and smaller firms, for example, very little direct market value information exists. The accountant's reporting function is crucial in these circumstances.

Clearly, one important goal of the accountant is to report financial information to the user in a form useful for decision making. Ironically, the information frequently does not come to the user in such a form. In other words, financial statements don't come with a user's guide. This chapter and the next are first steps in filling this gap.

3.1 | Cash Flow and Financial Statements: A Closer Look

At the most fundamental level, firms do two different things: They generate cash and they spend it. Cash is generated by selling a product, an asset, or a security. Selling a security involves either borrowing or selling an equity interest (i.e., shares of stock) in the firm. Cash is spent by paying for materials and labour to produce a product and by purchasing assets. Payments to creditors and owners also require spending cash.

In Chapter 2, we saw that the cash activities of a firm could be summarized by a simple identity:

Cash flow from assets = Cash flow to creditors + Cash flow to owners

This cash flow identity summarizes the total cash result of all the transactions the firm engaged in during the year. In this section, we return to the subject of cash flows by taking a closer look at the cash events during the year that lead to these total figures.

Sources and Uses of Cash

sources of cash
A firm's activities that generate cash.

uses of cash
A firm's activities in which cash is spent.

Those activities that bring in cash are called **sources of cash.** Those activities that involve spending cash are called **uses of cash** (or applications of cash). What we need to do is to trace the changes in the firm's statement of financial position to see how the firm obtained its cash and how the firm spent its cash during some time period.

To get started, consider the statement of financial position for the Prufrock Corporation in Table 3.1. Notice that we have calculated the changes in each of the items on the statement of financial position over the year from the end of 2011 to the end of 2012.

Looking over the statement of financial position for Prufrock, we see that quite a few things changed during the year. For example, Prufrock increased its net fixed assets by $149,000 and its inventory by $29,000. Where did the money come from? To answer this and related questions, we must identify those changes that used up cash (uses) and those that brought cash in (sources). A little common sense is useful here. A firm uses cash by either buying assets or making payments. So, loosely speaking, an increase in an asset account means the firm bought some net assets, a use of cash. If an asset account went down, then, on a net basis, the firm sold some assets. This would be a net source. Similarly, if a liability account goes down, then the firm has made a net payment, a use of cash.

Given this reasoning, there is a simple, albeit mechanical, definition that you may find useful. An increase in a left-hand side (asset) account or a decrease in a right-hand side (liability or equity) account is a use of cash. Likewise, a decrease in an asset account or an increase in a liability (or equity) account is a source of cash.

Looking back at Prufrock, we see that inventory rose by $29. This is a net use since Prufrock effectively paid out $29 to increase inventories. Accounts payable rose by $32. This is a source of cash since Prufrock effectively has borrowed an additional $32 by the end of the year. Notes payable, on the other hand, went down by $35, so Prufrock effectively paid off $35 worth of short-term debt—a use of cash.

TABLE 3.1

PRUFROCK CORPORATION
Statement of Financial Position as of December 31, 2011 and 2012
($ thousands)

	2011	2012	Change
Assets			
Current assets			
Cash	$ 84	$ 98	+$ 14
Accounts receivable	165	188	+ 23
Inventory	393	422	+ 29
Total	$ 642	$ 708	+$ 66
Fixed assets			
Net plant and equipment	2,731	2,880	+ 149
Total assets	$ 3,373	$ 3,588	+$ 215
Liabilities and Owners' Equity			
Current liabilities			
Accounts payable	$ 312	$ 344	+$ 32
Notes payable	231	196	− 35
Total	$ 543	$ 540	−$ 3
Long-term debt	$ 531	$ 457	−$ 74
Owners' equity			
Common stock	500	550	+ 50
Retained earnings	1,799	2,041	+ 242
Total	$ 2,299	$ 2,591	+$ 292
Total liabilities and owners' equity	$ 3,373	$ 3,588	+$ 215

Based on our discussion, we can summarize the sources and uses from the statement of financial position as follows:

Sources of cash:	
Increase in accounts payable	$ 32
Increase in common stock	50
Increase in retained earnings	242
Total sources	$ 324
Uses of cash:	
Increase in accounts receivable	$ 23
Increase in inventory	29
Decrease in notes payable	35
Decrease in long-term debt	74
Net fixed asset acquisitions	149
Total uses	$ 310
Net addition to cash	$ 14

The net addition to cash is just the difference between sources and uses, and our $14 result here agrees with the $14 change shown on the statement of financial position.

This simple statement tells us much of what happened during the year, but it doesn't tell the whole story. For example, the increase in retained earnings is net income (a source of funds) less dividends (a use of funds). It would be more enlightening to have these reported separately so we could see the breakdown. Also, we have only considered net fixed asset acquisitions. Total or gross spending would be more interesting to know.

To further trace the flow of cash through the firm during the year, we need an income statement. For Prufrock, the results are shown in Table 3.2. Because we are looking at cash flow during calendar year 2012, we focus on the 2012 statement of comprehensive income.

TABLE 3.2

PRUFROCK CORPORATION
Statement of Comprehensive Income
($ thousands)

	2012
Sales	$ 2,311
Cost of goods sold	1,344
Depreciation	276
Earnings before interest and taxes	$ 691
Interest paid	141
Taxable income	$ 550
Taxes	187
Net income	$ 363
Addition to retained earnings	$ 242
Dividends	121

Notice here that the $242 addition to retained earnings we calculated from the statement of financial position is just the difference between the 2012 net income of $363 and that year's dividend of $121.

The Statement of Cash Flows

statement of cash flows
A firm's financial statement that summarizes its sources and uses of cash over a specified period.

There is some flexibility in summarizing the sources and uses of cash in the form of a financial statement. However, when it is presented, the result is called the **statement of cash flows**.

We present a particular format in Table 3.3 for this statement. The basic idea is to group all the changes into one of three categories: operating activities, financing activities, and investment activities. The exact form differs in detail from one preparer to the next.

TABLE 3.3

PRUFROCK CORPORATION
2012 Statement of Cash Flows

Operating activities	
Net income	$ 363
Plus:	
Depreciation	276
Increase in accounts payable	32
Less:	
Increase in accounts receivable	−23
Increase in inventory	−29
Net cash from operating activity	$ 619
Investment activities:	
Fixed asset acquisitions	−$425
Net cash from investment activity	−$425
Financing activities:	
Decrease in notes payable	−$ 35
Decrease in long-term debt	−74
Dividends paid	−121
Increase in common stock	50
Net cash from financing activity	−$180
Net increase in cash	$ 14

Don't be surprised if you come across different arrangements. The types of information presented may be very similar, but the exact order can differ. The key thing to remember is that we started out with $84 in cash and ended up with $98, for a net increase of $14. We're just trying to see what events led to this change.

Going back to Chapter 2, there is a slight conceptual problem here. Interest paid should really go under financing activities, but, unfortunately, that's not the way the accounting is handled. The reason, you may recall, is that interest is deducted as an expense when net income is computed. Also, notice that our net purchase of fixed assets was $149. Since we wrote off $276 worth (the depreciation), we must have actually spent a total of $149 + 276 = $425 on fixed assets.

Once we have this statement, it might seem appropriate to express the change in cash on a per-share basis, much as we did for net income. Although standard accounting practice does not report this information, it is often calculated by financial analysts. The reason is that accountants believe that cash flow (or some component of cash flow) is not an alternative to accounting income, so only earnings per share are to be reported.

Now that we have the various cash pieces in place, we can get a good idea of what happened during the year. Prufrock's major cash outlays were fixed asset acquisitions and cash dividends. The firm paid for these activities primarily with cash generated from operations.

Prufrock also retired some long-term debt and increased current assets. Finally, current liabilities were virtually unchanged, and a relatively small amount of new equity was sold. Altogether, this short sketch captures Prufrock's major sources and uses of cash for the year.

Concept Questions

1. What is a source of cash? Give three examples.
2. What is a use or application of cash? Give three examples.

3.2 | Standardized Financial Statements

The next thing we might want to do with Prufrock's financial statements is to compare them to those of other, similar companies. We would immediately have a problem, however. It's almost impossible to directly compare the financial statements for two companies because of differences in size. In Canada, this problem is compounded because some companies are one of a kind. BCE is an example. Further, large Canadian companies usually span two, three, or more industries, making comparisons extremely difficult.

To start making comparisons, one obvious thing we might try to do is to somehow standardize the financial statements. One very common and useful way of doing this is to work with percentages instead of total dollars. In this section, we describe two different ways of standardizing financial statements along these lines.

Common-Size Statements

common-size statement
A standardized financial statement presenting all items in percentage terms. Statement of financial position is shown as a percentage of assets and income statements as a percentage of sales.

To get started, a useful way of standardizing financial statements is to express the statement of financial position as a percentage of total assets and to express the statement of comprehensive income as a percentage of sales. Such a financial statement is called a **common-size statement**. We consider these statements next.

COMMON-SIZE STATEMENT OF FINANCIAL POSITION   One way, but not the only way, to construct a common-size statement of financial position is to express each item as a percentage of total assets. Prufrock's 2011 and 2012 common-size statement of financial position are shown in Table 3.4.

Notice that some of the totals don't check exactly because of rounding errors. Also, notice that the total change has to be zero, since the beginning and ending numbers must add up to 100 percent.

TABLE 3.4

PRUFROCK CORPORATION
Common-Size Statement of Financial Position
December 31, 2011 and 2012

	2011	2012	Change
Assets			
Current Assets			
Cash	2.5%	2.7%	+0.2%
Accounts receivable	4.9	5.2	+0.3
Inventory	11.7	11.8	+0.1
Total	19.0	19.7	+0.7
Fixed assets			
Net plant and equipment	81.0	80.3	−0.7
Total assets	100.0%	100.0%	0.0%
Liabilities and Owners' Equity			
Current liabilities			
Accounts payable	9.2%	9.6%	+0.4%
Notes payable	6.8	5.5	−1.3
Total	16.1	15.1	−1.0
Long-term debt	15.7	12.7	−3.0
Owners' equity			
Common stock	14.8	15.3	+0.5
Retained earnings	53.3	56.9	+3.6
Total	68.2	72.2	+4.0
Total liabilities and owners' equity	100.0%	100.0%	0.0%

In this form, financial statements are relatively easy to read and compare. For example, just looking at the two statement of financial position for Prufrock, we see that current assets were 19.7 percent of total assets in 2012, up from 19 percent in 2011. Current liabilities declined from 16.1 percent to 15.1 percent of total liabilities and owners' equity over that same time. Similarly, total equities rose from 68.2 percent of total liabilities and owners' equity to 72.2 percent.

Overall, Prufrock's liquidity, as measured by current assets compared to current liabilities, increased over the year. Simultaneously, Prufrock's indebtedness diminished as a percentage of total assets. We might be tempted to conclude that the statement of financial position has grown stronger. We say more about this later.

COMMON-SIZE INCOME STATEMENTS   A useful way of standardizing statements of comprehensive income is to express each item as a percentage of total sales, as illustrated for Prufrock in Table 3.5.

Common-size statements of comprehensive income tell us what happens to each dollar in sales. For Prufrock in 2012 for example, interest expense eats up $.061 out of every sales dollar and taxes take another $.081. When all is said and done, $.157 of each dollar flows through to the bottom line (net income), and that amount is split into $.105 retained in the business and $.052 paid out in dividends.

These percentages are very useful in comparisons. For example, a very relevant figure is the cost of goods sold percentage. For Prufrock, $.582 of each $1 in sales goes to pay for goods sold in 2012 as compared to $.624 in 2011. The reduction likely signals improved cost controls in 2012. To pursue this point, it would be interesting to compute the same percentage for Prufrock's main competitors to see how Prufrock's improved cost control in 2012 stacks up.

COMMON-SIZE STATEMENTS OF CASH FLOW   Although we have not presented it here, it is also possible and useful to prepare a common-size statement of cash flows. Unfortunately, with the current statement of cash flows, there is no obvious denominator such as total assets or total sales. However, when the information is arranged similarly to Table 3.5, each item can be expressed as a percentage of total sources or total uses. The results can then be interpreted as the percentage of total sources of cash supplied or as the percentage of total uses of cash for a particular item.

TABLE 3.5

PRUFROCK CORPORATION
Common-Size Statement of Comprehensive Income

	2011	2012
Sales	100.0%	100.0%
Cost of goods sold	62.4	58.2
Depreciation	12.0	11.9
Earnings before interest and taxes	25.6	29.9
Interest paid	6.2	6.1
Taxable income	19.4	23.8
Taxes	7.8	8.1
Net income	11.6%	15.7%
Addition to retained earnings	5.8%	10.5%
Dividends	5.8%	5.2%

Common-Base-Year Financial Statements: Trend Analysis

Imagine that we were given statement of financial position for the last 10 years for some company and we were trying to investigate trends in the firm's pattern of operations. Does the firm use more or less debt? Has the firm grown more or less liquid? A useful way of standardizing financial statements is to choose a base year and then express each item relative to the base amount. We call such a statement a **common-base-year statement.**

common-base-year statement
A standardized financial statement presenting all items relative to a certain base year amount.

For example, Prufrock's inventory rose from $393 to $422. If we pick 2011 as our base year, then we would set inventory equal to 1 for that year. For the next year, we would calculate inventory relative to the base year as $422/$393 = 1.07. We could say that inventory grew by about 7 percent during the year. If we had multiple years, we would just divide each one by $393. The resulting series is very easy to plot, and it is then very easy to compare two or more different companies. Table 3.6 summarizes these calculations for the asset side of the statement of financial position.

COMBINED COMMON-SIZE AND BASE-YEAR ANALYSIS   The trend analysis we have been discussing can be combined with the common-size analysis discussed earlier. The reason for doing this is that as total assets grow, most of the other accounts must grow as well. By first forming the common-size statements, we eliminate the effect of this overall growth.

For example, Prufrock's accounts receivable were $165, or 4.9 percent of total assets in 2011. In 2012, they had risen to $188, which is 5.2 percent of total assets. If we do our trend analysis in terms of dollars, the 2012 figure would be $188/$165 = 1.14, a 14 percent increase in receivables. However, if we work with the common-size statements, the 2012 figure would be 5.2%/4.9% = 1.06. This tells us that accounts receivable, as a percentage of total assets, grew by 6 percent. Roughly speaking, what we see is that of the 14 percent total increase, about 8 percent (14% − 6%) is attributable simply to growth in total assets. Table 3.6 summarizes this discussion for Prufrock's assets.

Concept Questions

1. Why is it often necessary to standardize financial statements?
2. Name two types of standardized statements and describe how each is formed.

TABLE 3.6

PRUFROCK CORPORATION
Summary of Standardized Statement of Financial Position (Asset side only)
($ thousands)

	Assets		Common-Size		Common Base-Year	Combined Common-Size and Base-Year
	2011	2012	2011	2012	2011	2012
Current Assets						
Cash	$ 84	$ 98	2.5%	2.7%	1.17	1.08
Accounts receivable	165	188	4.9	5.2	1.14	1.06
Inventory	393	422	11.7	11.8	1.07	1.01
Total current assets	$ 642	$ 708	19.0	19.7	1.10	1.04
Fixed assets						
Net plant and equipment	2,731	2,880	81.0	80.3	1.05	0.99
Total assets	$ 3,373	$ 3,588	100.0%	100.0%	1.06	1.00

The common-size numbers are calculated by dividing each item by total assets for that year. For example, the 2011 common-size cash amount is $84/$3,373 = 2.5%. The common–base-year numbers are calculated by dividing each 2012 item by the base-year dollar (2011) amount. The common-base cash is thus $98/$84 = 1.17, representing a 17 percent increase. The combined common-size and base-year figures are calculated by dividing each common-size amount by the base-year (2011) common-size amount. The cash figure is therefore 2.7%/2.5% = 1.08, representing an 8 percent increase in cash holdings as a percentage of total assets.

3.3 | Ratio Analysis

financial ratios
Relationships determined from a firm's financial information and used for comparison purposes.

Another way of avoiding the problem of comparing companies of different sizes is to calculate and compare **financial ratios.** Such ratios are ways of comparing and investigating the relationships between different pieces of financial information. Using ratios eliminates the size problem since the size effectively divides out. We're then left with percentages, multiples, or time periods.

There is a problem in discussing financial ratios. Since a ratio is simply one number divided by another, and since there is a substantial quantity of accounting numbers out there, there are a huge number of possible ratios we could examine. Everybody has a favourite, so we've restricted ourselves to a representative sampling. We chose the sample to be consistent with the practice of experienced financial analysts. Another way to see which ratios are used most often in practice is to look at the output of commercially available software that generates ratios.

Once you have gained experience in ratio analysis, you will find that 20 ratios do not tell you twice as much as 10. You are looking for problem areas, not an exhaustive list of ratios, so you don't have to worry about including every possible ratio.

What you do need to worry about is the fact that different people and different sources frequently don't compute these ratios in exactly the same way, and this leads to much confusion. The specific definitions we use here may or may not be the same as ones you have seen or will see elsewhere.[1] When you are using ratios as a tool for analysis, you should be careful to document how you calculate each one.

We defer much of our discussion of how ratios are used and some problems that come up with using them to the next section. For now, for each of the ratios we discuss, several questions come to mind:

1. How is it computed?
2. What is it intended to measure, and why might we be interested?
3. What might a high or low value be telling us? How might such values be misleading?
4. How could this measure be improved?

Financial ratios are traditionally grouped into the following categories:

---

[1] For example, we compute ratios using year-end statement of financial position values in the denominators, while many other sources use average ending values from last year and the current year.

1. Short-term solvency or liquidity ratios.
2. Long-term solvency or financial leverage ratios.
3. Asset management or turnover ratios.
4. Profitability ratios.
5. Market value ratios.

We consider each of these in turn. To illustrate ratio calculations for Prufrock, we use the ending statement of financial position (2012) figures unless we explicitly say otherwise. After calculating the 2012 ratios, we illustrate the inferences you can make from them by making two comparisons for each ratio. The comparisons draw on numbers in Table 3.7 that summarize each ratio's 2012 value and also present corresponding values for Prufrock in 2011 and for the industry average.[2]

Short-Term Solvency or Liquidity Measures

As the name suggests, short-term solvency ratios as a group are intended to provide information about a firm's liquidity, and these ratios are sometimes called liquidity measures. The primary concern is the firm's ability to pay its bills over the short run without undue stress. Consequently, these ratios focus on current assets and current liabilities.

For obvious reasons, liquidity ratios are particularly interesting to short-term creditors. Since financial managers are constantly working with banks and other short-term lenders, an understanding of these ratios is essential.

One advantage of looking at current assets and liabilities is that their book values and market values are likely to be similar. Often (but not always), these assets and liabilities just don't live long enough for the two to get seriously out of step. This is true for a going concern that has no problems in selling inventory (turning it into receivables) and then collecting the receivables, all at book values. Even in a going concern, all inventory may not be liquid, since some may be held permanently as a buffer against unforeseen delays.

On the other hand, like any type of near-cash, current assets and liabilities can and do change fairly rapidly, so today's amounts may not be a reliable guide to the future. For example, when a firm experiences financial distress and undergoes a loan workout or liquidation, obsolete inventory and overdue receivables often have market values well below their book values.

CURRENT RATIO   One of the best known and most widely used ratios is the current ratio. As you might guess, the current ratio is defined as:

$$\text{Current ratio} = \text{Current assets/Current liabilities} \qquad [3.1]$$

For Prufrock, the 2012 current ratio is:

$$\text{Current ratio} = \$708/540 = 1.31$$

Because current assets and liabilities are, in principle, converted to cash over the following 12 months, the current ratio is a measure of short-term liquidity. The unit of measurement is either dollars or times. So, we could say that Prufrock has $1.31 in current assets for every $1 in current liabilities, or we could say that Prufrock has its current liabilities covered 1.31 times over. To a creditor, particularly a short-term creditor such as a supplier, the higher the current ratio, the better. To the firm, a high current ratio indicates liquidity, but it also may indicate an inefficient use of cash and other short-term assets. Absent some extraordinary circumstances, we would expect to see a current ratio of at least 1, because a current ratio of less than 1 would mean that net working capital (current assets less current liabilities) is negative. This would be unusual in a healthy firm, at least for most types of business. Some analysts use a rule of thumb that the current ratio should be at least 2.0 but this can be misleading for many industries.

Applying this to Prufrock, we see from Table 3.7 that the current ratio of 1.31 for 2012 is higher than the 1.18 recorded for 2011 and slightly above the industry average. For this reason, the analyst has recorded an OK rating for this ratio.

[2]In this case the industry average figures are hypothetical. We will discuss industry average ratios in some detail later.

TABLE 3.7   Selected financial ratios for Prufrock

Short-Term Solvency (Liquidity)	2011	2012	Industry	Rating
Current ratio	1.18	1.31	1.25	OK
Quick ratio	0.46	0.53	0.60	—
Cash ratio	0.15	0.18	0.20	OK
Net working capital to Total assets	2.9%	4.7%	5.2%	OK
Interval measure (days)	182	192	202	OK
Turnover				
Inventory turnover	3.3	3.2	4.0	—
Days' sales in inventory	111	114	91	—
Receivables turnover	12.5	12.3	11.5	OK
Days' sales in receivables	29	30	32	OK
NWC turnover	20.9	13.8	14.6	—
Fixed asset turnover	0.76	0.80	0.90	OK
Total asset turnover	0.61	0.64	0.71	OK
Financial Leverage				
Total debt ratio	0.32	0.28	0.42	++
Debt/equity	0.47	0.39	0.72	++
Equity multiplier	1.47	1.39	1.72	+
Long-term debt ratio	0.16	0.15	0.16	+
Times interest earned	4.2	4.9	2.8	++
Cash coverage ratio	6.2	6.9	4.2	++
Profitability				
Profit margin	11.6%	15.7%	10.7%	++
Return on assets (ROA)	7.1%	10.1%	7.6%	+
Return on equity (ROE)	10.5%	14.0%	13.1%	+
Market Value Ratios				
Price-earnings ratio (P/E)	12.0	14.27	12.0	+
Market-to-book ratio	2.4	2.0	1.92	+
EV/EBITDA	6.5	5.93	5.5	+

Comments: Company shows strength relative to industry in avoiding increased leverage. Profitability is above average. Company carries more inventory than the industry average, causing weakness in related ratios. Market value ratios are strong.

EXAMPLE 3.1: Current Events

Suppose a firm were to pay off some of its suppliers and short-term creditors. What would happen to the current ratio? Suppose a firm buys some inventory for cash. What happens in this case? What happens if a firm sells some merchandise?

The first case is a trick question. What happens is that the current ratio moves away from 1. If it is greater than 1 (the usual case), it gets bigger; but if it is less than 1, it gets smaller. To see this, suppose the firm has $4 in current assets and $2 in current liabilities for a current ratio of 2. If we use $1 in cash to reduce current liabilities, then the new current ratio is ($4 − $1)/($2 − $1) = 3. If we reverse this

to $2 in current assets and $4 in current liabilities, the current ratio would fall to 1/3 from 1/2.

The second case is not quite as tricky. Nothing happens to the current ratio because cash goes down while inventory goes up—total current assets are unaffected.

In the third case, the current ratio would usually rise because inventory is normally shown at cost and the sale would normally be at something greater than cost (the difference is the mark-up). The increase in either cash or receivables is therefore greater than the decrease in inventory. This increases current assets, and the current ratio rises.

In general, the current ratio, like any ratio, is affected by various types of transactions. For example, suppose the firm borrows long term to raise money. The short-run effect would be an increase in cash from the issue proceeds and an increase in long-term debt. Current liabilities would not be affected, so the current ratio would rise.

Finally, note that an apparently low current ratio may not be a bad sign for a company with a large reserve of untapped borrowing power.

THE QUICK (OR ACID-TEST) RATIO   Inventory is often the least liquid current asset. It's also the one for which the book values are least reliable as measures of market value, since the quality of the inventory isn't considered. Some of it may be damaged, obsolete, or lost.

More to the point, relatively large inventories are often a sign of short-term trouble. The firm may have overestimated sales and overbought or overproduced as a result. In this case, the firm may have a substantial portion of its liquidity tied up in slow-moving inventory.

To further evaluate liquidity, the *quick* or *acid-test ratio* is computed just like the current ratio, except inventory is omitted:

$$\text{Quick ratio} = \frac{\text{Current assets} - \text{Inventory}}{\text{Current liabilities}} \qquad [3.2]$$

Notice that using cash to buy inventory does not affect the current ratio, but it reduces the quick ratio. Again, the idea is that inventory is relatively illiquid compared to cash.

For Prufrock, this ratio in 2012 was:

$$\text{Quick ratio} = [\$708 - 422]/\$540 = .53$$

The quick ratio here tells a somewhat different story from the current ratio, because inventory accounts for more than half of Prufrock's current assets. To exaggerate the point, if this inventory consisted of, say, unsold nuclear power plants, this is a cause for concern.

Table 3.7 provides more information. The quick ratio has improved from 2011 to 2012, but it is still less than the industry average. At a minimum, this suggests Prufrock still is carrying relatively more inventory than its competitors. We need more information to know if this is a problem.

Other Liquidity Ratios

We briefly mention three other measures of liquidity. A very short term creditor might be interested in the *cash ratio:*

$$\text{Cash ratio} = (\text{Cash} + \text{Cash equivalents})/\text{Current liabilities} \qquad [3.3]$$

You can verify that this works out to be .18 for Prufrock in 2012. According to Table 3.7, this is a slight improvement over 2011 and around the industry average. Cash adequacy does not seem to be a problem for Prufrock.

Because net working capital (NWC) is frequently viewed as the amount of short-term liquidity a firm has, we can measure the ratio of *NWC to total assets:*

$$\text{Net working capital to total assets} = \text{Net working capital}/\text{Total assets} \qquad [3.4]$$

A relatively low value might indicate relatively low levels of liquidity. For Prufrock in 2012, this ratio works out to be ($708 − 540)/$3,588 = 4.7%. As with the cash ratio, comparisons with 2011 and the industry average indicate no problems.

Finally, imagine that Prufrock is facing a strike and cash inflows are beginning to dry up. How long could the business keep running? One answer is given by the *interval measure:*

$$\text{Interval measure} = \text{Current assets}/\text{Average daily operating costs} \qquad [3.5]$$

Costs for the year 2012, excluding depreciation and interest, were $1,344. The average daily cost was $1,344/365 = $3.68 per day. The interval measure is thus $708/$3.68 = 192 days. Based on this, Prufrock could hang on for six months or so, about in line with its competitors.[3]

---

[3]Sometimes depreciation and/or interest is included in calculating average daily costs. Depreciation isn't a cash expense, so this doesn't make a lot of sense. Interest is a financing cost, so we excluded it by definition (we only looked at operating costs). We could, of course, define a different ratio that included interest expense.

Long-Term Solvency Measures

Long-term solvency ratios are intended to address the firm's long-run ability to meet its obligations or, more generally, its financial leverage. These are sometimes called *financial leverage ratios* or just *leverage ratios*. We consider three commonly used measures and some variations. These ratios all measure debt, equity, and assets at book values. As we stressed at the beginning, market values would be far better, but these are often not available.

TOTAL DEBT RATIO   The *total debt ratio* takes into account all debts of all maturities to all creditors. It can be defined in several ways, the easiest of which is:

$$\text{Total debt ratio} = [\text{Total assets} - \text{Total equity}]/\text{Total assets} \qquad [3.6]$$
$$= [\$3,588 - 2,592]/\$3,588 = .28$$

In this case, an analyst might say that Prufrock uses 28 percent debt.[4] There has been a large volume of theoretical research on how much debt is optimal, and we discuss this in Part 6. Taking a more pragmatic view here, most financial analysts would note that Prufrock's use of debt has declined slightly from 2011 and is considerably less than the industry average. To find out if this is good or bad, we would look for more information on the financial health of Prufrock's competitors. The rating and comment in Table 3.7 suggest that competitors are overleveraged and that Prufrock's more moderate use of debt is a strength.

Regardless of the interpretation, the total debt ratio shows that Prufrock has $.28 in debt for every $1 in assets in 2012. Therefore, there is $.72 in equity ($1 − $.28) for every $.28 in debt. With this in mind, we can define two useful variations on the total debt ratio, the *debt/equity ratio* and the *equity multiplier*. We illustrate each for Prufrock for 2012:

$$\text{Debt/equity ratio} = \text{Total debt}/\text{Total equity} \qquad [3.7]$$
$$= \$.28/\$.72 = .39$$

$$\text{Equity multiplier} = \text{Total assets}/\text{Total equity} \qquad [3.8]$$
$$= \$1/\$.72 = 1.39$$

The fact that the equity multiplier is 1 plus the debt/equity ratio is not a coincidence:

$$\text{Equity multiplier} = \text{Total assets}/\text{Total equity} = \$1/\$.72 = 1.39$$
$$= (\text{Total equity} + \text{Total debt})/\text{Total equity}$$
$$= 1 + \text{Debt/Equity ratio} = 1.39$$

The thing to notice here is that given any one of these three ratios, you can immediately calculate the other two, so they all say exactly the same thing. You can verify this by looking at the comparisons in Table 3.7.

A BRIEF DIGRESSION: TOTAL CAPITALIZATION VERSUS TOTAL ASSETS
Frequently, financial analysts are more concerned with the firm's long-term debt than its short-term debt because the short-term debt is constantly changing. Also, a firm's accounts payable may be more a reflection of trade practice than debt management policy. For these reasons, the long-term debt ratio is often calculated as:

$$\text{Long-term debt ratio} = \frac{\text{Long-term debt}}{\text{Long-term debt} + \text{Total equity}} \qquad [3.9]$$
$$= \$457/[\$457 + 2,591] = \$457/\$3,048 = .15$$

The $3,048 in total long-term debt and equity is sometimes called the firm's *total capitalization,* and the financial manager frequently focuses on this quantity rather than total assets. As you can see from Table 3.7, the long-term debt ratio follows the same trend as the other financial leverage ratios.

To complicate matters, different people (and different books) mean different things by the term *debt ratio.* Some mean total debt, and some mean long-term debt only, and, unfortunately, a substantial number are simply vague about which one they mean.

This is a source of confusion, so we choose to give two separate names to the two measures. The same problem comes up in discussing the debt/equity ratio. Financial analysts frequently

---

[4]Total equity here includes preferred stock (discussed in Chapter 14 and elsewhere), if there is any. An equivalent numerator in this ratio would be (Current liabilities + Long-term debt).

calculate this ratio using only long-term debt.

TIMES INTEREST EARNED   Another common measure of long-term solvency is the times interest earned (TIE) ratio. Once again, there are several possible (and common) definitions, but we'll stick with the most traditional:

$$\text{Times interest earned ratio} = \text{EBIT/Interest} \qquad [3.10]$$
$$= \$691/\$141 = 4.9 \text{ times}$$

As the name suggests, this ratio measures how well a company has its interest obligations covered. For Prufrock, the interest bill is covered 4.9 times over in 2012. Table 3.7 shows that TIE increased slightly over 2011 and exceeds the industry average. This reinforces the signal of the other debt ratios.

CASH COVERAGE   A problem with the TIE ratio is that it is based on EBIT, which is not really a measure of cash available to pay interest. The reason is that depreciation, a non-cash expense, has been deducted out. Since interest is most definitely a cash outflow (to creditors), one way to define the cash coverage ratio is:

$$\text{Cash coverage ratio} = [\text{EBIT} + \text{Depreciation}]/\text{Interest} \qquad [3.11]$$
$$= [\$691 + 276]/\$141 = \$967/\$141 = 6.9 \text{ times}$$

The numerator here, EBIT plus depreciation, is often abbreviated EBITDA (earnings before interest, taxes, depreciation, and amortization). It is a basic measure of the firm's ability to generate cash from operations, and it is frequently used as a measure of cash flow available to meet financial obligations. If depreciation changed dramatically from one year to the next, cash coverage could give a different signal than TIE. In the case of Prufrock, the signals are reinforcing as you can see in Table 3.7.[5]

Asset Management, or Turnover, Measures

We next turn our attention to the efficiency with which Prufrock uses its assets. The measures in this section are sometimes called *asset utilization ratios*. The specific ratios we discuss can all be interpreted as measures of turnover. What they are intended to describe is how efficiently or intensively a firm uses its assets to generate sales. We first look at two important current assets, inventory and receivables.

INVENTORY TURNOVER AND DAYS' SALES IN INVENTORY   During 2012, Prufrock had a cost of goods sold of $1,344. Inventory at the end of the year was $422. With these numbers, *inventory turnover* can be calculated as:

$$\text{Inventory turnover} = \text{Cost of goods sold/Inventory} \qquad [3.12]$$
$$= \$1,344/\$422 = 3.2 \text{ times}$$

In a sense, the company sold or turned over the entire inventory 3.2 times.[6] As long as Prufrock is not running out of stock and thereby forgoing sales, the higher this ratio is, the more efficiently it is managing inventory.

If we turned our inventory over 3.2 times during the year, then we can immediately figure out how long it took us to turn it over on average. The result is the average *days' sales in inventory* (also known as the "inventory period"):

$$\text{Days' sales in inventory} = 365 \text{ days/Inventory turnover} \qquad [3.13]$$
$$= 365/3.2 = 114 \text{ days}$$

This tells us that, roughly speaking, inventory sits 114 days on average in 2012 before it is sold. Alternatively, assuming we used the most recent inventory and cost figures, it should take about 114 days to work off our current inventory.

---

[5] Any one-time transactions, such as capital gains or losses, should be netted out of EBIT before calculating cash coverage.

[6] Notice that we used cost of goods sold in the top of this ratio. For some purposes, it might be more useful to use sales instead of costs. For example, if we wanted to know the amount of sales generated per dollar of inventory, then we could just replace the cost of goods sold with sales.

Looking at Table 3.7, it would be fair to state that Prufrock has a 114 days' supply of inventory. Ninety-one days is considered normal. This means that, at current daily sales, it would take 114 days to deplete the available inventory. We could also say that we have 114 days of sales in inventory. Table 3.7 registers a negative rating for inventory because Prufrock is carrying more than the industry average. This could be a sign of poor financial management in overinvesting in inventory that will eventually be sold at a normal markup. Worse, it could be that some of Prufrock's inventory is obsolete and should be marked down. Or it could be that Prufrock is simply selling a different product mix than its competitors and nothing is wrong. What the ratio tells us is that we should investigate further.

Returning to ratio calculation, it might make more sense to use the average inventory in calculating turnover. Inventory turnover would then be $1,344/[($393 + $422)/2] = 3.3$ times.[7] It really depends on the purpose of the calculation. If we are interested in how long it will take us to sell our current inventory, then using the ending figure (as we did initially) is probably better.

In many of the ratios we discuss next, average figures could just as well be used. Again, it really depends on whether we are worried about the past when averages are appropriate, or the future, when ending figures might be better. Also, using ending figures is very common in reporting industry averages; so, for comparison purposes, ending figures should be used. In any event, using ending figures is definitely less work, so we'll continue to use them.

RECEIVABLES TURNOVER AND DAYS' SALES IN RECEIVABLES   Our inventory measures give some indications of how fast we can sell products. We now look at how fast we collect on those sales. The receivables turnover is defined in the same way as inventory turnover:

$$\text{Receivables turnover} = \text{Sales/Accounts receivable} \qquad [3.14]$$
$$= \$2,311/\$188 = 12.3 \text{ times}$$

Loosely speaking, we collected our outstanding credit accounts and reloaned the money 12.3 times during 2012.[8]

This ratio makes more sense if we convert it to days, so the *days' sales in receivables* is:

$$\text{Days' sales in receivables} = 365 \text{ days/Receivables turnover} \qquad [3.15]$$
$$= 365/12.3 = 30 \text{ days}$$

Therefore, on average, we collected on our credit sales in 30 days in 2012. For this reason, this ratio is very frequently called the *average collection period (ACP) or days sales outstanding (DSO)*.

EXAMPLE 3.2: Payables Turnover

Here is a variation on the receivables collection period. How long, on average, does it take for Prufrock Corporation to pay its bills in 2012? To answer, we need to calculate the accounts payable turnover rate using cost of goods sold.[7] We assume that Prufrock purchases everything on credit.

The cost of goods sold is $1,344, and accounts payable are $344. The turnover is therefore $1,344/\$344 = 3.9$ times. So payables turned over about every $365/3.9 = 94$ days. On average then, Prufrock takes 94 days to pay. As a potential creditor, we might take note of this fact.

Also, note that if we are using the most recent figures, we could also say that we have 30 days' worth of sales that are currently uncollected. Turning to Table 3.7, we see that Prufrock's average collection period is holding steady on the industry average, so no problem is indicated. You will learn more about this subject when we discuss credit policy in Chapter 20.

ASSET TURNOVER RATIOS   Moving away from specific accounts like inventory or receivables, we can consider several "big picture" ratios. For example, NWC *turnover* is:

---

[7] Notice we have calculated the average as (Beginning value + Ending value)/2.

[8] Here we have implicitly assumed that all sales are credit sales. If they are not, then we would simply use total credit sales in these calculations, not total sales.

[9] This calculation could be refined by changing the numerator from cost of goods sold to purchases.

$$\text{NWC turnover} = \text{Sales/NWC}$$ [3.16]
$$= \$2,311/(\$708 - \$540) = 13.8 \text{ times}$$

Looking at Table 3.7, you can see that NWC turnover is smaller than the industry average. Is this good or bad? This ratio measures how much work we get out of our working capital. Once again, assuming that we aren't missing out on sales, a high value is preferred. Likely, sluggish inventory turnover causes the lower value for Prufrock.

Similarly, *fixed asset turnover* is:

$$\text{Fixed asset turnover} = \text{Sales/Net fixed assets}$$ [3.17]
$$= \$2,311/\$2,880 = .80 \text{ times}$$

With this ratio, we see that, for every dollar in fixed assets, we generated $.80 in sales.

Our final asset management ratio, the *total asset turnover,* comes up quite a bit. We see it later in this chapter and in the next chapter. As the name suggests, the total asset turnover is:

$$\text{Total asset turnover} = \text{Sales/Total assets}$$ [3.18]
$$= \$2,311/\$3,588 = .64 \text{ times}$$

In other words, for every dollar in assets, we generate $.64 in sales in 2012. Comparisons with 2011 and with the industry norm reveal no problem with fixed asset turnover. Because the total asset turnover is slower than the industry average, this points to current assets—and in this case, inventory—as the source of a possible problem.

Profitability Measures

The measures we discuss in this section are probably the best known and most widely used of all financial ratios. In one form or another, they are intended to measure how efficiently the firm uses its assets and how efficiently the firm manages its operations. The focus in this group is on the bottom line, net income.

PROFIT MARGIN   Companies pay a great deal of attention to their *profit margins*:

$$\text{Profit margin} = \text{Net income/Sales}$$ [3.19]
$$= \$363/\$2,311 = 15.7\%$$

EXAMPLE 3.3: More Turnover

Suppose you find that a particular company generates $.40 in sales for every dollar in total assets. How often does this company turn over its total assets?

The total asset turnover here is .40 times per year. It takes $1/.40 = 2.5$ years to turn them over completely.

This tells us that Prufrock, in an accounting sense, generates a little less than 16 cents in profit for every dollar in sales in 2012. This is an improvement over 2011 and exceeds the industry average.

All other things being equal, a relatively high profit margin is obviously desirable. This situation corresponds to low expense ratios relative to sales. However, we hasten to add that other things are often not equal.

For example, lowering our sales price normally increases unit volume, but profit margins normally shrink. Total profit (or more importantly, operating cash flow) may go up or down; so the fact that margins are smaller isn't necessarily bad. After all, isn't it possible that, as the saying goes, "Our prices are so low that we lose money on everything we sell, but we make it up in volume!"?[10]

Two other forms of profit margin are sometimes analyzed. The simplest is gross profit margin, which considers a company's performance in making profits above the cost of goods sold (COGS). The next stage is to consider how well the company does at making money once general and administrative costs (SGA) are considered.

---

[10]No, it's not.

$$\text{Gross profit margin} = (\text{Sales} - \text{COGS})/\text{Sales}$$
$$\text{Operating profit margin} = (\text{Sales} - \text{COGS} - \text{SGA})/\text{Sales}$$

RETURN ON ASSETS   *Return on assets* (ROA) is a measure of profit per dollar of assets. It can be defined several ways, but the most common is:[11]

$$\text{Return on assets} = \text{Net income}/\text{Total assets} \qquad\qquad [3.20]$$
$$= \$363/\$3,588 = 10.12\%$$

RETURN ON EQUITY   *Return on equity* (ROE) is a measure of how the shareholders fared during the year. Since benefiting shareholders is our goal, ROE is, in an accounting sense, the true bottom-line measure of performance. ROE is usually measured as:[12]

$$\text{Return on equity} = \text{Net income}/\text{Total equity} \qquad\qquad [3.21]$$
$$= \$363/\$2,591 = 14\%$$

For every dollar in equity, therefore, Prufrock generated 14 cents in profit, but, again, this is only correct in accounting terms.

Because ROA and ROE are such commonly cited numbers, we stress that they are accounting rates of return. For this reason, these measures should properly be called return on *book* assets and return on *book* equity. In fact, ROE is sometimes called return on net worth. Whatever it's called, it would be inappropriate to compare the result to, for example, an interest rate observed in the financial markets. We have more to say about accounting rates of return in later chapters.

From Table 3.7, you can see that both ROA and ROE are more than the industry average. The fact that ROE exceeds ROA reflects Prufrock's use of financial leverage. We examine the relationship between these two measures in more detail next.

Market Value Measures

Our final group of measures is based, in part, on information that is not necessarily contained in financial statements—the market price per share of the stock. Obviously, these measures can only be calculated directly for publicly traded companies.

EXAMPLE 3.4: ROE and ROA

Because ROE and ROA are usually intended to measure performance over a prior period, it makes a certain amount of sense to base them on average equity and average assets, respectively. For Prufrock, how would you calculate these for 2012?

We begin by calculating average assets and average equity:

$$\text{Average assets} = (\$3,373 + \$3,588)/2 = \$3,481$$
$$\text{Average equity} = (\$2,299 + \$2,591)/2 = \$2,445$$

With these averages, we can recalculate ROA and ROE as follows:

$$\text{ROA} = \$363/\$3,481 = 10.43\%$$
$$\text{ROE} = \$363/\$2,445 = 14.85\%$$

These are slightly higher than our previous calculations because assets grew during the year, with the result that the average is less than the ending value.

We assume that Prufrock has 33,000 shares outstanding at the end of 2012 and the stock sold for $157 per share at the end of the year.[13] If we recall that Prufrock's net income was $363,000, its earnings per share (EPS) are:

---

[11] An alternate definition abstracting from financing costs of debt and preferred shares is in R. H. Garrison, G. R. Chesley, and R. F. Carroll, *Managerial Accounting*, 5th Canadian ed. (Whitby, Ontario: McGraw-Hill Ryerson, 2001), chap. 17.

[12] Alternative methods for calculating some financial ratios have also been developed. For example, the Canadian Securities Institute defines ROE as the return on common equity, which is calculated as the ratio of net income less preferred dividends to common equity.

[13] In this example, basic shares outstanding was used to compute EPS. However, one may also calculate diluted EPS by adding all outstanding options and warrants to shares outstanding. P/E ratios (as will be discussed next) rely on diluted EPS figures.

$$\text{EPS} = \frac{\text{Net Income}}{\text{Shares Outstanding}} = \$363/33 = \$11$$

PRICE/EARNINGS RATIO   The first of our market value measures, the *price/earnings (P/E) ratio* (or multiple) is defined as:

$$\text{P/E ratio} = \text{Price per share/Earnings per share} \qquad\qquad [3.22]$$
$$= \$157/\$11 = 14.27 \text{ times}$$

In the vernacular, we would say that Prufrock shares sell for 14.27 times earnings, or we might say that Prufrock shares have or carry a P/E multiple of 14.27. In 2011, the P/E ratio was 12 times, the same as the industry average.

Because the P/E ratio measures how much investors are willing to pay per dollar of current earnings, higher P/Es are often taken to mean that the firm has significant prospects for future growth. Such expectations of higher growth likely go a long way toward explaining why Suncor Energy had a much higher price-earnings ratio than RIM in the example we used to open the chapter. If a firm had no or almost no earnings, its P/E would probably be quite large; so, as always, care is needed in interpreting this ratio.

Sometimes analysts divide PE ratios by expected future earnings growth rates (after multiplying the growth rate by 100). The result is the PEG ratio. Suppose Prufrock's anticipated growth rate in EPS was 6 percent. Its PEG ratio would then be 14.27/6 = 2.38. The idea behind the PEG ratio is that whether a PE ratio is high or low depends on expected future growth. High PEG ratios suggest that the PE may be too high relative to growth, and vice versa.

MARKET-TO-BOOK RATIO   A second commonly quoted measure is the *market-to-book ratio:*

$$\text{Market-to-book ratio} = \text{Market value per share/Book value per share} \qquad [3.23]$$
$$= \$157/(\$2,591/33) = \$157/\$78.5 = 2 \text{ times}$$

Notice that book value per share is total equity (not just common stock) divided by the number of shares outstanding. Table 3.7 shows that the market-to-book ratio was 2.4 in 2011.

Since book value per share is an accounting number, it reflects historical costs. In a loose sense, the market-to-book ratio therefore compares the market value of the firm's investments to their cost. A value less than 1 could mean that the firm has not been successful overall in creating value for its shareholders. Prufrock's market-to-book ratio exceeds 1 and this is a positive indication.

ENTERPRISE VALUE/EARNINGS BEFORE INTEREST, TAX, DEPRECIATION, AND AMORTIZATION   Perhaps the most commonly cited market value measure used by practitioners is the Enterprise Value/Earnings Before Interest, Tax, Depreciation, and Amortization (EV/EBITDA) multiple.

$$\text{EV/EBITDA multiple} = [\text{Market value of equity} + \text{market value of interest-bearing debt}^{14}$$
$$+ \text{ preferred shares} + \text{minority interest} - \text{Cash (and cash}$$
$$\text{equivalents)}]/\text{EBITDA}$$
$$= [(33,000 \times \$157) + (\$196,000 + \$457,000) - \$98,000]/(\$691,000$$
$$+ \$276,000)$$
$$= 5.93 \text{ times}$$

Notice how unlike the P/E or market-to-book ratios, the EV/EBITDA multiple values the company as a whole and not just the equity portion of the company. Minority interest is added back so that the EV also becomes "consolidated," and the numerator and denominator of the ratio are consistent. EBITDA is used as a rough proxy for a firm's cash flows. Therefore, the EV/EBITDA looks to examine how many times more a firm's capital holders value the company relative to the cash flow the company generates.

The appeal of the EV/EBITDA ratio is two-fold: (1) EBITA seems to be replacing EBITDA in common parlance. It is less susceptible to accounting manipulation. The more one moves down the income statement, the more leeway financial statement preparers have in presenting their

---

[14] In this example, we assume that the debt of the company is not traded and hence, the market value of debt is equal to the book value of debt.

company. Given that EBITDA is higher on the income statement than earnings, it is a more trustworthy figure and more comparable between companies. (2) It can be used to value companies with negative cash flows. Some companies have negative earnings, especially start-ups, and thus they cannot be valued using a P/E ratio.

TABLE 3.8   **Common financial ratios**

I. Short-Term Solvency or Liquidity Ratios

$$\text{Current ratio} = \frac{\text{Current assets}}{\text{Current liabilities}}$$

$$\text{Quick ratio} = \frac{\text{Current assets} - \text{Inventory}}{\text{Current liabilities}}$$

$$\text{Cash ratio} = \frac{\text{Cash}}{\text{Current liabilities}}$$

$$\text{Net working capital} = \frac{\text{Net working capital}}{\text{Total assets}}$$

$$\text{Interval measure} = \frac{\text{Current assets}}{\text{Average daily operating costs}}$$

II. Long-Term Solvency or Financial Leverage Ratios

$$\text{Total debt ratio} = \frac{\text{Total assets} - \text{Total equity}}{\text{Total assets}}$$

$$\text{Debt/equity ratio} = \frac{\text{Total debt}}{\text{Total equity}}$$

$$\text{Equity multiplier} = \frac{\text{Total assets}}{\text{Total equity}}$$

$$\text{Long-term debt ratio} = \frac{\text{Long-term debt}}{\text{Long-term debt} + \text{Total equity}}$$

$$\text{Times interest earned} = \frac{\text{EBIT}}{\text{Interest}}$$

$$\text{Cash coverage ratio} = \frac{\text{EBIT} + \text{Depreciation}}{\text{Interest}}$$

III. Asset Utilization Turnover Ratios

$$\text{Inventory turnover} = \frac{\text{Cost of goods sold}}{\text{Inventory}}$$

$$\text{Days' sales in inventory} = \frac{365 \text{ days}}{\text{Inventory turnover}}$$

$$\text{Receivables turnover} = \frac{\text{Sales}}{\text{Accounts receivable}}$$

$$\text{Days' sales in receivables} = \frac{365 \text{ days}}{\text{Receivables turnover}}$$

$$\text{NWC turnover} = \frac{\text{Sales}}{\text{NWC}}$$

$$\text{Fixed asset turnover} = \frac{\text{Sales}}{\text{Net fixed assets}}$$

$$\text{Total asset turnover} = \frac{\text{Sales}}{\text{Total assets}}$$

IV. Profitability Ratios

$$\text{Profit margin} = \frac{\text{Net income}}{\text{Sales}}$$

$$\text{Return on assets (ROA)} = \frac{\text{Net income}}{\text{Total assets}}$$

$$\text{Return on equity (ROE)} = \frac{\text{Net income}}{\text{Total equity}}$$

$$\text{ROE} = \frac{\text{Net income}}{\text{Sales}} \times \frac{\text{Sales}}{\text{Assets}} \times \frac{\text{Assets}}{\text{Equity}}$$

V. Market Value Ratios

$$\text{Price-earning ratio} = \frac{\text{Price per share}}{\text{Earnings per share}}$$

$$\text{Market-to-book ratio} = \frac{\text{Market value per share}}{\text{Book value per share}}$$

$$\text{EV/EBITDA} = [\text{Market value of equity} \\ + \text{Market value of interest-bearing debt} \\ + \text{Preferred shares} + \text{Minority interest} \\ - \text{Cash (and cash equivalent)}]/\text{EBITDA}$$

It is entirely possible for start-ups to have a negative EBITDA, but very rare for the mature companies, making EV/EBITDA a good metric to evaluate performance of mature companies unlike the start-up ones.

This completes our definitions of some common ratios. We could tell you about more of them, but these are enough for now. We'll leave it here and go on to discuss in detail some ways of using these ratios in practice. Table 3.8 summarizes the formulas for the ratios that we discussed.

Concept Questions

1. What are the five groups of ratios? Give two or three examples of each kind.
2. Turnover ratios all have one of two figures as numerators. What are they? What do these ratios measure? How do you interpret the results?
3. Profitability ratios all have the same figure in the numerator. What is it? What do these ratios measure? How do you interpret the results?

3.4 | The Du Pont Identity

As we mentioned in discussing ROA and ROE, the difference between these two profitability measures is a reflection of the use of debt financing or financial leverage. We illustrate the relationship between these measures in this section by investigating a famous way of decomposing ROE into its component parts.

To begin, let's recall the definition of ROE:

$$\text{Return on equity} = \text{Net income/Total equity}$$

If we were so inclined, we could multiply this ratio by Assets/Assets without changing anything:

$$\text{Return of equity} = \text{Net Income/Total equity} \times \text{Assests/Assets}$$
$$= \text{Net Income/Assets} \times \text{Assets/Equity}$$

Notice that we have expressed the return on equity as the product of two other ratios—return on assets and the equity multiplier:

$$\text{ROE} = \text{ROA} \times \text{Equity multiplier} = \text{ROA} \times (1 + \text{Debt/Equity ratio})$$

Looking back at Prufrock in 2012, for example, the debt/equity ratio was .39 and ROA was 10.12 percent. Our work here implies that Prufrock's return on equity, as we previously calculated, is:

$$\text{ROE} = 10.12\% \times 1.39 = 14\%$$

The difference between ROE and ROA can be substantial, particularly for certain businesses. For example, Royal Bank of Canada had an ROA of only 0.70 percent in 2011, which might be attributed to the financial crisis. The banks tend to borrow a lot of money, and, as a result, have relatively large equity multipliers. For Royal Bank, ROE was around 18 percent in that year, implying an equity multiplier of 25.71.

We can further decompose ROE by multiplying the top and bottom by total sales:

$$\text{ROE} = \text{Net income/Sales} \times \text{Sales/Assets} \times \text{Assets/Equity}$$
$$= \text{Profit margin} \times \text{Total asset turnover} \times \text{Equity multiplier}$$

What we have now done is to partition the return on assets into its two component parts, profit margin and total asset turnover. This last expression is called the **Du Pont identity**, after E. I. Du Pont de Nemours & Company, which popularized its use.

Du Pont identity
Popular expression breaking ROE into three parts: profit margin, total asset turnover, and financial leverage.

We can check this relationship for Prufrock by noting that in 2012 the profit margin was 15.7 percent and the total asset turnover was .64. ROE should thus be:

$$\text{ROE} = \text{Profit margin} \times \text{Total asset turnover} \times \text{Equity multiplier}$$
$$= 15.5\% \times .64 \times 1.39$$
$$= 14\%$$

This 14 percent ROE is exactly what we had before.

The Du Pont identity tells us that ROE is affected by three things:

1. Operating efficiency (as measured by profit margin).
2. Asset use efficiency (as measured by total asset turnover).
3. Financial leverage (as measured by the equity multiplier).

Weakness in either operating or asset use efficiency (or both) shows up in a diminished return on assets, which translates into a lower ROE.

Considering the Du Pont identity, it appears that the ROE could be leveraged up by increasing the amount of debt in the firm. It turns out that this only happens when the firm's ROA exceeds the interest rate on the debt. More importantly, the use of debt financing has a number of other effects, and, as we discuss at some length in Part 6, the amount of leverage a firm uses is governed by its capital structure policy.

The decomposition of ROE we've discussed in this section is a convenient way of systematically approaching financial statement analysis. If ROE improves, then the Du Pont identity tells you where to start looking for the reasons. To illustrate, we know from Table 3.7, that ROE for Prufrock increased from 10.4 percent in 2011 to 14 percent in 2012. The Du Pont identity can tell us why. After decomposing ROE for 2011, we can compare the parts with what we found earlier for 2012. For 2011:

$$\text{ROE} = 10.4\% = \text{Profit margin} \times \text{Total asset turnover} \times \text{Equity multiplier}$$
$$= 11.6\% \times .61 \times 1.47$$

For 2012:

$$\text{ROE} = 14\% = 15.7\% \times .64 \times 1.39$$

This comparison shows that the improvement in ROE for Prufrock was caused mainly by the higher profit margin.

A higher ROE is not always a sign of financial strength, however, as the example of General Motors illustrates. In 1989, GM had an ROE of 12.1 percent. By 1993, its ROE had improved to 44.1 percent, a dramatic improvement. On closer inspection, however, we find that, over the same period, GM's profit margin had declined from 3.4 to 1.8 percent, and ROA had declined from 2.4 to 1.3 percent. The decline in ROA was moderated only slightly by an increase in total asset turnover from .71 to .73 over the period.

Given this information, how is it possible for GM's ROE to have climbed so sharply? From our understanding of the Du Pont identity, it must be the case that GM's equity multiplier increased substantially. In fact, what happened was that GM's book equity value was almost wiped out overnight in 1992 by changes in the accounting treatment of pension liabilities. If a company's equity value declines sharply, its equity multiplier rises. In GM's case, the multiplier went from 4.95 in 1989 to 33.62 in 1993. In sum, the dramatic "improvement" in GM's ROE was almost entirely due to an accounting change that affected the equity multiplier and doesn't really represent an improvement in financial performance at all.

Concept Questions

1. Return on assets (ROA) can be expressed as the product of two ratios. Which two?
2. Return on equity (ROE) can be expressed as the product of three ratios. Which three?

EXAMPLE 3.5: Food versus Variety Stores

Table 3.9 shows the ratios of the Du Pont identity for food and variety stores. The return on equity ratios (ROEs) for the two industries are roughly comparable. This is despite the higher profit margin achieved by variety stores. To overcome their lower profit margin, food stores turn over their assets faster and use more financial leverage. Du Pont analysis allows us to go further by asking why food stores have higher total asset turnover. The reason is higher inventory turnover—15.4 times for food stores versus 4.9 times for variety stores. Figure 3.1 shows the interaction of statement of financial position and income statement items through the Du Pont analysis.

TABLE 3.9

Du Pont identity ratios for food and variety stores	Industry	Profit Margin	Total Asset Turnover	Equity Multiplier	Return on Equity
	Food stores	1.0%	3.56	3.04	10.8%
	Variety stores	1.8	2.60	2.58	12.1

FIGURE 3.1

The Du Pont analysis

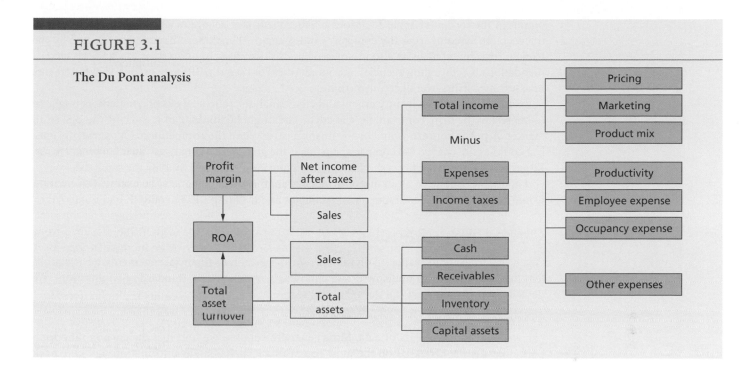

3.5 | Using Financial Statement Information

Our last task in this chapter is to discuss in more detail some practical aspects of financial statement analysis. In particular, we look at reasons for doing financial statement analysis, how to get benchmark information, and some of the problems that come up in the process.

Why Evaluate Financial Statements?

As we have discussed, the primary reason for looking at accounting information is that we don't have, and can't reasonably expect to get, market value information. Remember that whenever we have market information, we would use it instead of accounting data. Also, when accounting and market data conflict, market data should be given precedence.

Financial statement analysis is essentially an application of management by exception. In many cases, as we illustrated with our hypothetical company, Prufrock, such analysis boils down to comparing ratios for one business with some kind of average or representative ratios. Those ratios that differ the most from the averages are tagged for further study.

INTERNAL USES   Financial information has a variety of uses within a firm. Among the most important of these is performance evaluation. For example, managers are frequently evaluated and compensated on the basis of accounting measures of performances such as profit margin and return on equity. Also, firms with multiple divisions frequently compare the performance of those divisions using financial statement information.

Another important internal use that we explore in the next chapter is planning for the future. As we see, historical financial statement information is very useful for generating projections about the future and for checking the realism of assumptions made in those projections.

EXTERNAL USES   Financial statements are useful to parties outside the firm, including short-term and long-term creditors and potential investors. For example, we would find such information quite useful in deciding whether or not to grant credit to a new customer. Chapter 20 shows how statistical models based on ratios are used in credit analysis in predicting insolvency.

If your firm borrows from a chartered bank, you can expect your loan agreement to require you to submit financial statements periodically. Most bankers use computer software to prepare common-size statements and to calculate ratios for their accounts. Standard software produces output in the format of Table 3.7. More advanced software generates a preliminary diagnosis of the account by comparing the company's ratios against benchmark parameters selected by the banker. Investment analysts also use ratio analysis software as input to their buy and sell recommendations. Credit rating agencies like Standard & Poor's and DBRS rely on financial statements in assessing a firm's overall creditworthiness.

In addition to its use by investment and credit analysts, ratio analysis of competitors might be of interest to the firm. For example, Canadian Tire might be thinking of reentering the U.S. retail market. A prime concern would be the financial strength of the competition. Of course, the analyst could easily change the comparison firms if the goal were to analyze Canadian competitors. Either way, comparison firms should be in the same industries and roughly the same size.

Finally, we might be thinking of acquiring another firm. Financial statement information would be essential in identifying potential targets and deciding what to offer.

Choosing a Benchmark

Given that we want to evaluate a division or a firm based on its financial statements, a basic problem immediately comes up. How do we choose a benchmark or a standard of comparison? We describe some ways of getting started in this section.

TIME-TREND ANALYSIS   One standard we could use is history. In our Prufrock example, we looked at two years of data. More generally, suppose we find that the current ratio for a particular firm is 2.4 based on the most recent financial statement information. Looking back over the last 10 years, we might find that this ratio has declined fairly steadily.

Based on this, we might wonder if the liquidity position of the firm has deteriorated. It could be, of course, that the firm has made changes to use its current assets more efficiently, that the nature of the firm's business has changed, or that business practices have changed. If we investigate, these are all possible explanations. This is an example of what we mean by management by exception—a deteriorating time trend may not be bad, but it does merit investigation.

PEER GROUP ANALYSIS   The second means of establishing a benchmark is to identify firms that are similar in the sense that they compete in the same markets, have similar assets, and operate in similar ways. In other words, we need to identify a *peer group*. This approach is often used together with time-trend analysis and the two approaches are complementary.

In our analysis of Prufrock, we used an industry average without worrying about where it came from. In practice, matters are not so simple because no two companies are identical. Ultimately, the choice of which companies to use as a basis for comparison involves judgement on the part of the analyst. One common way of identifying peers is based on the North American Industry Classification System (NAICS) codes. These are five-digit codes established by the statistical agencies of Canada, Mexico, and the United States for statistical reporting purposes. Firms with the same NAICS code are frequently assumed to be similar.

Various other benchmarks are available.[15] You can turn to Statistics Canada publications and website that include typical statements of financial position, statements of comprehensive income, and selected ratios for firms in about 180 industries. Other sources of benchmarks for Canadian companies include financial data bases available from The Financial Post Datagroup and Dun & Bradstreet Canada.[16] Several financial institutions gather their own financial ratio data bases by compiling information on their loan customers. In this way, they seek to obtain more up-to-date information than is available from services like Statistics Canada and Dun & Bradstreet.

Obtaining current information is not the only challenge facing the financial analyst. Most large Canadian corporations do business in several industries so the analyst must often compare the company against several industry averages. Also keep in mind that the industry average is not necessarily where firms would like to be. For example, agricultural analysts know that farmers are suffering with painfully low average profitability coupled with excessive debt. Despite these shortcomings, the industry average is a useful benchmark for the management by exception approach we advocate for ratio analysis.

---

[15] This discussion draws on L. Kryzanowski, M.C. To and R. Seguin, *Business Solvency Risk Analysis,* Institute of Canadian Bankers, 1990, chap. 3.

[16] Analysts examining U.S. companies will find comparable information available from Robert Morris Associates.

Problems with Financial Statement Analysis

We close our chapter on financial statements by discussing some additional problems that can arise in using financial statements. In one way or another, the basic problem with financial statement analysis is that there is no underlying theory to help us identify which quantities to look at and to guide us in establishing benchmarks.

As we discuss in other chapters, there are many cases where financial theory and economic logic provide guidance to making judgements about value and risk. Very little such help exists with financial statements. This is why we can't say which ratios matter the most and what a high or low value might be.

One particularly severe problem is that many firms are conglomerates, owning more-or-less unrelated lines of business. The consolidated financial statements for such firms as Sears Canada don't really fit any neat industry category. More generally, the kind of peer group analysis we have been describing is going to work best when the firms are strictly in the same line of business, the industry is competitive, and there is only one way of operating.

Another problem that is becoming increasingly common is having major competitors and natural peer group members in an industry scattered around the globe. As we discussed in Chapter 2, the trend toward adopting IFRS improves comparability across many countries but the U.S. remains on GAAP. This complicates interpretation of financial statements for companies like Manulife Financial that operate in both the U.S. and Canada as well as internationally.

Even companies that are clearly in the same line of business may not be comparable. For example, electric utilities engaged primarily in power generation are all classified in the same group. This group is often thought to be relatively homogeneous. However, utilities generally operate as regulated monopolies, so they don't compete with each other. Many have shareholders, and many are organized as cooperatives with no shareholders. There are several different ways of generating power, ranging from hydroelectric to nuclear, so their operating activities can differ quite a bit. Finally, profitability is strongly affected by regulatory environment, so utilities in different locations can be very similar but show very different profits.

Several other general problems frequently crop up. First, different firms use different accounting procedures for inventory, for example. This makes it difficult to compare statements. Second, different firms end their fiscal years at different times. For firms in seasonal businesses (such as a retailer with a large Christmas season), this can lead to difficulties in comparing statements of financial position because of fluctuations in accounts during the year. Finally, for any particular firm, unusual or transient events, such as a onetime profit from an asset sale, may affect financial performance. In comparing firms, such events can give misleading signals.

Concept Questions

1. What are some uses for financial statement analysis?
2. Where do industry average ratios come from and how might they be useful?
3. Why do we say that financial statement analysis is management by exception?
4. What are some problems that can come up with financial statement analysis?

3.6 | SUMMARY AND CONCLUSIONS

This chapter has discussed aspects of financial statement analysis:

1. Sources and uses of cash. We discussed how to identify the ways that businesses obtain and use cash, and we described how to trace the flow of cash through the business over the course of the year. We briefly looked at the statement of cash flows.

2. Standardized financial statements. We explained that differences in size make it difficult to compare financial statements, and we discussed how to form common-size and common-base-period statements to make comparisons easier.

3. Ratio analysis. Evaluating ratios of accounting numbers is another way of comparing financial statement information. We therefore defined and discussed a number of the most commonly reported and used financial ratios. We also developed the famous Du Pont identity as a way of analyzing financial performance.

4. Using financial statements. We described how to establish benchmarks for comparison purposes and discussed some of the types of available information. We then examined some of the problems that can arise.

After you study this chapter, we hope that you will have some perspective on the uses and abuses of financial statements. You should also find that your vocabulary of business and financial terms has grown substantially.

Key Terms

common-base-year statement (page 59)
common-size statement (page 57)
Du Pont identity (page 71)
financial ratios (page 60; Table 3.8, p. 70)

sources of cash (page 54)
statement of cash flows (page 56)
uses of cash (page 54)

Chapter Review Problems and Self-Test

3.1 **Sources and Uses of Cash** Consider the following statement of financial position for the Philippe Corporation. Calculate the changes in the various accounts and, where applicable, identify the change as a source or use of cash. What were the major sources and uses of cash? Did the company become more or less liquid during the year? What happened to cash during the year?

PHILIPPE CORPORATION
tatement of Financial Position as of December 31, 2011 and 2012 ($ millions)

	2011	2012
Assets		
Current assets		
Cash	$ 210	$ 215
Accounts receivable	355	310
Inventory	507	328
Total	$ 1,072	$ 853
Fixed assets		
Net plant and equipment	$ 6,085	$ 6,527
Total assets	$ 7,157	$ 7,380
Liabilities and Owners' Equity		
Current liabilities		
Accounts payable	$ 207	$ 298
Notes payable	1,715	1,427
Total	$ 1,922	$ 1,725
Long-term debt	$ 1,987	$ 2,308
Owners' equity		
Common stock and paid-in surplus	$ 1,000	$ 1,000
Retained earnings	2,248	2,347
Total	$ 3,248	$ 3,347
Total liabilities and owners' equity	$ 7,157	$ 7,380

3.2 **Common-Size Statements** Below is the most recent income statement for Philippe. Prepare a common-size statement of comprehensive income based on this information. How do you interpret the standardized net income? What percentage of sales goes to cost of goods sold?

PHILIPPE CORPORATION
2012 Statement of Comprehensive Income ($ millions)

Sales	$ 4,053
Cost of goods sold	2,780
Depreciation	550
Earnings before interest and taxes	$ 723
Interest paid	502
Taxable income	$ 221
Taxes (34%)	75
Net income	$ 146
Dividends	$47
Addition to retained earnings	99

3.3 **Financial Ratios** Based on the statement of financial position and income statement in the previous two problems, calculate the following ratios for 2012:

Current ratio	_____
Quick ratio	_____
Cash ratio	_____
Inventory turnover	_____
Receivables turnover	_____
Days' sales in inventory	_____
Days' sales in receivables	_____
Total debt ratio	_____
Long-term debt ratio	_____
Times interest earned ratio	_____
Cash coverage ratio	_____

3.4 **ROE and the Du Pont Identity** Calculate the 2012 ROE for the Philippe Corporation and then break down your answer into its component parts using the Du Pont identity.

Answers to Self-Test Problems

3.1   We've filled in the answers in the following table. Remember, increases in assets and decreases in liabilities indicate that we spent some cash. Decreases in assets and increases in liabilities are ways of getting cash.

PHILIPPE CORPORATION
Statement of Financial Position as of December 31, 2011 and 2012
($ millions)

	2011	2012	Change	Source or Use of Cash
Assets				
Current assets				
Cash	$ 210	$ 215	+$ 5	
Accounts receivable	355	310	− 45	Source
Inventory	507	328	− 179	Source
Total	$1,072	$ 853	−$ 219	
Fixed assets				
Net plant and equipment	$6,085	$6,527	+$ 442	Use
Total assets	$7,157	$7,380	+$ 223	
Liabilities and Owners' Equity				
Current liabilities				
Accounts payable	$ 207	$ 298	+$ 91	Source
Notes payable	1,715	1,427	− 288	Use
Total	$1,922	$1,725	−$ 197	
Long-term debt	$1,987	$2,308	+$ 321	Source

	2011	2012	Change	Source or Use of Cash
Owners' equity				
Common stock and paid-in surplus	$1,000	$1,000	+$ 0	—
Retained earnings	2,248	2,347	+ 99	Source
Total	$3,248	$3,347	+$ 99	
Total liabilities and owners' equity	$7,157	$7,380	+$ 223	

Philippe used its cash primarily to purchase fixed assets and to pay off short-term debt. The major sources of cash to do this were additional long-term borrowing and, to a larger extent, reductions in current assets and additions to retained earnings.

The current ratio went from $1,072/1,922 = .56 to $853/1,725 = .49, so the firm's liquidity appears to have declined somewhat. Overall, however, the amount of cash on hand increased by $5.

3.2   We've calculated the common-size income statement below. Remember that we simply divide each item by total sales.

PHILIPPE CORPORATION
2012 Common-Size Statement of Comprehensive Income

Sales	100.0%
Cost of goods sold	68.6
Depreciation	13.6
Earnings before interest and taxes	17.8
Interest paid	12.3
Taxable income	5.5
Taxes (34%)	1.9
Net income	3.6%
Dividends	1.2%
Addition to retained earnings	2.4%

Net income is 3.6 percent of sales. Because this is the percentage of each sales dollar that makes its way to the bottom line, the standardized net income is the firm's profit margin. Cost of goods sold is 68.6 percent of sales.

3.3   We've calculated the following ratios based on the ending figures. If you don't remember a definition, refer back to Table 3.8.

Current ratio	$853/$1,725 = .49 times
Quick ratio	$525/$1,725 = .30 times
Cash ratio	$215/$1,725 = .12 times
Inventory turnover	$2,780/$328 = 8.48 times

Receivables turnover	$4,053/$310 = 13.07 times
Days' sales in inventory	365/8.48 = 43.06 days
Days' sales in receivables	365/13.07 = 27.92 days
Total debt ratio	$4,033/$7,380 = 54.6%
Long-term debt ratio	$2,308/$5,655 = 40.8%
Times interest earned ratio	$723/$502 = 1.44 times
Cash coverage ratio	$1,273/$502 = 2.54 times

3.4   The return on equity is the ratio of net income to total equity. For Philippe, this is $146/$3,347 = 4.4%, which is not outstanding. Given the Du Pont identity, ROE can be written as:

$$\text{ROE} = \text{Profit margin} \times \text{Total asset turnover} \times \text{Equity multiplier}$$
$$= \$146/\$4,053 \times \$4,053/\$7,380 \times \$7,380/\$3,347$$
$$= 3.6\% \times 0.549 \times 2.20$$
$$= 4.4\%$$

Notice that return on assets, ROA, is 3.6% × 0.549 = 1.98%.

Concepts Review and Critical Thinking Questions

1.   **(LO3)** What effect would the following actions have on a firm's current ratio? Assume that net working capital is positive.
   a.   Inventory is purchased.
   b.   A supplier is paid.
   c.   A short-term bank loan is repaid.
   d.   A long-term debt is paid off early.
   e.   A customer pays off a credit account.
   f.   Inventory is sold at cost.
   g.   Inventory is sold for a profit.

2.   **(LO3)** In recent years, Cheticamp Co. has greatly increased its current ratio. At the same time, the quick ratio has fallen. What has happened? Has the liquidity of the company improved?

3.   **(LO3)** Explain what it means for a firm to have a current ratio equal to .50. Would the firm be better off if the current ratio were 1.50? What if it were 15.0? Explain your answers.

4.   **(LO3)** Fully explain the kind of information the following financial ratios provide about a firm:
   a.   Quick ratio
   b.   Cash ratio
   c.   Interval measure
   d.   Total asset turnover
   e.   Equity multiplier
   f.   Long-term debt ratio
   g.   Times interest earned ratio
   h.   Profit margin
   i.   Return on assets
   j.   Return on equity
   k.   Price-earnings ratio

5.   **(LO2)** What types of information do common-size financial statements reveal about the firm? What is the best use for these common-size statements? What purpose do common-base year statements have? When would you use them?

6.   **(LO3)** Explain what peer group analysis means. As a financial manager, how could you use the results of peer group analysis to evaluate the performance of your firm?

7.   **(LO4)** Why is the Du Pont identity a valuable tool for analyzing the performance of a firm? Discuss the types of information it reveals as compared to ROE considered by itself.

8.   **(LO3)** Specialized ratios are sometimes used in specific industries. For example, the so-called book-to-bill ratio is closely watched for semiconductor manufacturers. A ratio of 0.93 indicates that for every $100 worth of chips shipped over some period, only $93 worth of new orders is received. In February 2006, the semiconductor equipment industry's book-to-bill reached 1.01, compared to 0.98 during the month of January 2006. The book-to-bill ratio reached a low of 0.78 during October 2006. The three-month average of worldwide bookings in January 2006 was $1.30 billion, an increase of 6 percent over January 2005, while the three-month average of billings in February 2006 was $1.29 billion, a 2 percent increase from February 2005. What is this ratio intended to measure? Why do you think it is so closely watched?

9.   **(LO5)** So-called "same-store sales" are a very important measure for companies as diverse as Canadian Tire and Tim Hortons. As the name suggests, examining same-store sales means comparing revenues from the same stores or restaurants at two different points in time. Why might companies focus on same-store sales rather than total sales?

10.   **(LO2)** There are many ways of using standardized financial information beyond those discussed in this chapter. The usual goal is to put firms on an equal footing for comparison purposes. For example, for auto manufacturers, it is common to express sales, costs, and profits on a per-car basis. For each of the following industries, give an example of an actual company and discuss one or more potentially useful means of standardizing financial information:
   a.   Public utilities
   b.   Large retailers
   c.   Airlines
   d.   Online services
   e.   Hospitals
   f.   University textbook publishers

11.   **(LO5)** In recent years, several manufacturing companies have reported the cash flow from the sale of Treasury securities in the cash from operations section of the statement of cash flows. What is in the problem with this practice? Is there any situation in which this practice would be acceptable?

12.   **(LO1)** Suppose a company lengthens the time it takes to pay suppliers. How would this affect the statement of cash flows? How sustainable is the change in cash flows from this practice?

Questions and Problems

Basic
(Questions 1–17)

1. **Calculating Liquidity Ratios (LO3)** Carman Inc. has net working capital of $1,370, current liabilities of $3,720 and inventory of $1,950. What is the current ratio? What is the quick ratio?

2. **Calculating Profitability Ratios (LO3)** Teulon Inc. has sales of $29 million, total assets of $17.5 million, and total debt of $6.3 million. If the profit margin is 8 percent, what is net income? What is ROA? What is ROE?

3. **Calculating the Average Collection Period (LO3)** Grunthal Lumber Yard has a current accounts receivable balance of $431,287. Credit sales for the year ended were $3,943,709. What is the receivables turnover? The days' sales in receivables? How long did it take on average for credit customers to pay off their accounts during the past year?

4. **Calculating Inventory Turnover (LO3)** The Morden Corporation has ending inventory of $407,534, and cost of goods sold for the year just ended was $4,105,612. What is the inventory turnover? The days' sales in inventory? How long on average did a unit of inventory sit on the shelf before it was sold?

5. **Calculating Leverage Ratios (LO3)** Plumas Inc. has a total debt ratio of 0.63. What is its debt–equity ratio? What is its equity multiplier?

6. **Calculating Market Value Ratios (LO3)** Manitou Corp. had additions to retained earnings for the year just ended of $430,000. The firm paid out $175,000 in cash dividends, and it has ending total equity of $5.3 million. If Bellanue currently has 210,000 shares of common stock outstanding, what are the earnings per share? Dividends per share? Book value per share? If the stock currently sells for $63 per share, what is the market-to-book ratio? The price–earnings ratio? If the company had sales of $4.5 million, what is the price–sales ratio?

7. **Du Pont Identity (LO4)** If Garson Rooters Inc. has an equity multiplier of 2.80, total asset turnover of 1.15, and a profit margin of 5.5 percent, what is its ROE?

8. **Du Pont Identity (LO4)** Glenboro Fire Prevention Corp. has a profit margin of 6.80 percent, total asset turnover of 1.95, and ROE of 18.27 percent. What is this firm's debt–equity ratio?

9. **Source and Uses of Cash (LO1)** Based on the following information for Dauphin Corp., did cash go up or down? By how much? Classify each event as a source or use of cash.

Decrease in inventory	$375
Decrease in accounts payable	190
Increase in notes payable	210
Increase in accounts receivable	105

10. **Calculating Average Payables Period (LO3)** For 2012, Hartney Inc. had a cost of goods sold of $28,834. At the end of the year, the account payable balance was $6,105. How long on average did it take the company to pay off its suppliers during the year? What might a large value for this ratio imply?

11. **Cash Flow and Capital Spending (LO1)** For the year just ended, Winkler Frozen Yogurt showed an increase in its net fixed assets account of $835. The company took $148 in depreciation expense for the year. How much did Winkler spend on new fixed assets? Is this a source or use of cash?

12. **Equity Multiplier and Return on Equity (LO4)** Bowsman Fried Chicken Company has a debt–equity ratio of 0.65. Return on assets is 8.5 percent, and total equity is $540,000. What is the equity multiplier? Net income? Return on equity?

Birtle Corporation reports the following statement of financial position information for 2011 and 2012. Use this information to work on Problems 13 through 17.

Birtle CORPORATION
2011 and 2012 Statement of Financial Position

Assets			Liabilities and Owners' Equity		
	2011	**2012**		**2011**	**2012**
Current assets			Current liabilities		
Cash	$ 8,436	$ 10,157	Accounts payable	$ 43,050	$ 46,821
Accounts receivable	21,530	23,406	Notes payable	18,384	17,382
Inventory	38,760	42,650	Total	$ 61,434	$ 64,203
Total	$ 68,726	$ 76,213	Long-term debt	$ 25,000	$ 32,000
Fixed assets			Owners' equity		
Net plant and equipment	226,706	248,306	Common stock and paid-in surplus	$ 40,000	$ 40,000
			Retained earnings	168,998	188,316
			Total	$208,998	$228,316
Total assets	$295,432	$324,519	Total liabilities and owners' equity	$295,432	$324,519

13. **Preparing Standardized Financial Statements (LO2)** Prepare the 2011 and 2012 common size statement of financial position for Birtle.

14. **Preparing Standardized Financial Statements (LO2)** Prepare the 2012 common-base-year statement of financial position for Birtle.

15. **Preparing Standardized Financial Statements (LO2)** Prepare the 2012 combined common-size, common-base-year statement of financial position for Birtle.

16. **Sources and Uses of Cash (LO1)** For each account on Birtle Corporation's statement of financial position, show the change in the account during 2012 and note whether this change was a source or use of cash. Do your numbers add up and make sense? Explain your answer for total assets as compared to your answer for total liabilities and owners' equity.

17. **Calculating Financial Ratios (LO3)** Based on the statement of financial position given for Birtle, calculate the following financial ratios for each year:

    a. Current ratio

    b. Quick ratio

    c. Cash ratio

    d. NWC to total assets ratio

    e. Debt–equity ratio and equity multiplier

    f. Total debt ratio and long-term debt ratio

Intermediate
(Questions 18–30)

18. **Using the Du Pont Identity (LO4)** Ethelbert Inc. has sales of $5,276, total assets of $3,105, and a debt–equity ratio of 1.40. If its return on equity is 15 percent, what is its net income?

19. **Days' Sales in Receivables (LO3)** Gunton Corp. has net income of $218,000, a profit margin of 8.70 percent, and an accounts receivable balance of $132,850. Assuming 70 percent of sales are on credit, what are the Gunton's days' sales in receivables?

20. **Ratios and Fixed Assets (LO3)** The Fortier Company has a long-term debt ratio of 0.45 and a current ratio of 1.25. Current liabilities are $875, sales are $5,780, profit margin is 9.5 percent, and ROE is 18.5 percent. What is the amount of the firm's net fixed assets?

21. **Profit Margin (LO5)** In response to complaints about high prices, a grocery chain runs the following advertising campaign: "If you pay your child $3 to go buy $50 worth of groceries, then your child makes twice as much on the trip as we do." You've collected the following information from the grocery chain's financial statements:

(millions)	
Sales	$750
Net income	$22.5
Total assets	$420
Total debt	$280

    Evaluate the grocery chain's claim. What is the basis for the statement? Is this claim misleading? Why or why not?

22. **Return on Equity (LO3)** Firm A and Firm B have total debt ratios of 35 percent and 30 percent and return on assets of 12 percent and 11 percent, respectively. Which firm has a greater return on equity?

23. **Calculating the Cash Coverage Ratio (LO3)** Brunkild Inc.'s net income for the most recent year was $13,168. The tax rate was 34 percent. The firm paid $3,605 in total interest expense and deducted $2,382 in depreciation expense. What was Giant's cash coverage ratio for the year?

24. **Cost of Goods Sold (LO3)** Montcalm Corp. has current liabilities of $365,000, a quick ratio of 0.85, inventory turnover of 5.8, and a current ratio of 1.4. What is the cost of goods sold for the company?

25. **Ratios and Foreign Companies (LO3)** Wolseley PLC has a net loss of £13,482 on sales of £138,793 (both in thousands of pounds). Does the fact that these figures are quoted in a foreign currency make any difference? Why? What was the company's profit margin? In dollars, sales were $274,213,000. What was the net loss in dollars?

Some recent financial statements for Earl Grey Golf Corp. follow. Use this information to work on problems 26 through 30.

EARL GREY GOLF CORP.
2011 and 2012 Statement of Financial Position

Assets	2011	2012	Liabilities and Owners' Equity	2011	2012
Current assets			Current liabilities		
Cash	$ 21,860	$ 22,050	Accounts payable	$ 19,320	$ 22,850
Accounts receivable	11,316	13,850	Notes payable	10,000	9,000
Inventory	23,084	24,650	Other	9,643	11,385
Total	$ 56,260	$ 60,550	Total	$ 38,963	$ 43,235
Fixed assets			Long-term debt	$ 75,000	$ 85,000
Net plant and equipment	$234,068	$260,525	Owners' equity Common stock and paid-in surplus	$ 25,000	$ 25,000
			Retained earnings	151,365	167,840
			Total	$176,365	$192,840
Total assets	$290,328	$321,075	Total liabilities and owners' equity	$290,328	$321,075

EARL GREY GOLF CORP.
2012 Statement of Comprehensive Income

Sales		$305,830
Cost of goods sold		210,935
Depreciation		26,850
Earnings before interest and tax		$ 68,045
Interest paid		11,930
Taxable income		$ 56,115
Taxes (35%)		19,640
Net Income		$ 36,475
Dividends	$ 20,000	
Additions to retained earnings	16,475	

26. **Calculating Financial Ratios (LO3)** Find the following financial ratios for Earl Grey Golf Corp. (use year-end figures rather than average values where appropriate):

Short-term solvency ratios
a. Current ratio _____
b. Quick ratio _____
c. Cash ratio _____

Asset utilization ratios
d. Total asset turnover _____
e. Inventory turnover _____
f. Receivables turnover _____

Long-term solvency ratios
g. Total debt ratio _____
h. Debt-equity ratio _____
i. Equity multiplier _____
j. Times interest earned ratio _____
k. Cash coverage ratio _____

Profitability ratios
l. Profit margin _____
m. Return on assets _____
n. Return on equity _____

27. **Du Pont Identity (LO4)** Construct the Du Pont identity for Earl Grey Golf Corp.

28. **Calculating the Interval Measure (LO3)** For how many days could Earl Grey Golf Corp. continue to operate if its cash inflows were suddenly suspended?

29. **Statement of Cash Flows (LO1)** Prepare the 2012 statement of cash flows for Earl Grey Golf Corp.

30. **Market Value Ratios (LO3)** Earl Grey Golf Corp. has 25,000 shares of common stock outstanding, and the market price for a share of stock at the end of 2012 was $43. What is the price-earnings ratio? What are the dividends per share? What is the market-to-book ratio at the end of 2012? If the company's growth rate is 9 percent, what is the PEG ratio?

MINI CASE

Ed Cowan was recently hired by Tuxedo Air Inc. to assist the organization with its financial planning and to evaluate the organization's performance. Ed graduated from university six years ago with a finance degree. He has been employed in the finance department of a TSX100 company since then.

Tuxedo Air was founded 12 years ago by friends Mark Taylor and Jack Rodwell. The organization manufactured and sold light airplanes over this period, and its products have received high reviews for safety and reliability. The organization has a niche market in that it sells primarily to individuals who own and fly their own airplanes. The company has two models; the Sparrow, which sells for $53,000, and the Vulture, which sells for $78,000.

Although the company manufactures aircraft, its operations are different from commercial aircraft companies. Tuxedo Air builds aircraft to order. By using prefabricated parts, the organization can complete the manufacture of an airplane in only five weeks. The organization also receives a deposit on each order, as well as another partial payment before the order is complete. In contrast, a commercial airplane may take one and one-half to two years to manufacture once the order is placed.

Mark and Jack have provided the following financial statements. Ed has gathered the industry ratios for the light airplane manufacturing industry.

Tuxedo Air Inc.
2012 Statement of Comprehensive Income

Sales	$30,499,420
Cost of goods sold	22,224,580
Other expenses	3,867,500
Depreciation	1,366,680
EBIT	$ 3,040,660
Interest	478,240
Taxable income	$ 2,562,420
Taxes (40%)	1,024,968
Net income	$ 1,537,452
Dividends	$560,000
Add to retained earnings	977,452

Tuxedo Air Inc.
2012 Statement of Financial Position

Assets			Liabilities and Equity		
Current Assets			Current liabilities		
Cash	$	441,000	Accounts payable	$	889,000
Accounts receivable		708,400	Notes payable		2,030,000
			Total current liabilities		2,919,000
Inventory		1,037,120			
Total current assets	$	2,186,520	Long-term debt	$	5,320,000
Fixed assets			Owners' equity		
Net plant and equipment	$16,122,400		Common stock	$	350,000
			Retained earnings		9,719,920
			Total equity		$10,069,920
Total assets	$18,308,920		Total liabilities and owners' equity	$18,308,920	

Light Airplane Industry Ratios

	Lower Quartile	Median	Upper Quartile
Current ratio	0.50	1.43	1.89
Quick ratio	0.21	0.38	0.62
Cash ratio	0.08	0.21	0.39
Total asset turnover	0.68	0.85	1.38
Inventory turnover	4.89	6.15	10.89
Receivables turnover	6.27	9.82	14.11
Total debt ratio	0.44	0.52	0.61
Debt-equity ratio	0.79	1.08	1.56
Equity multiplier	1.79	2.08	2.56
Times interest earned	5.18	8.06	9.83
Cash coverage ratio	5.84	8.43	10.27
Profit margin	4.05%	6.98%	9.87%
Return on assets	6.05%	10.53%	13.21%
Return on equity	9.93%	16.54%	26.15%

Questions

1. Using the financial statements provided for Tuxedo Air, calculate each of the ratios listed in the table for the light aircraft industry.

2. Mark and Jack agree that a ratio analysis can provide a measure of the company's performance. They have chosen Bombardier as an aspirant company. Would you choose Bombardier as an aspirant company? Why or why not? There are other aircraft manufacturers Tuxedo Air could use as aspirant companies. Discuss whether it is appropriate to use any of the following companies: Boeing, XOJET, Piper Aircraft, and AeroCentury.

3. Compare the performance of Tuxedo Air to the industry. For each ratio, comment on why it might be viewed as positive or negative relative to the industry. Suppose you create an inventory ratio calculated as inventory divided by current liabilities. How do you think Tuxedo Air would compare to the industry average?

Internet Application Questions

1. Ratio analysis is a powerful tool in determining the quality of a firm's liabilities. For example, bond rating agencies employ ratio analysis in combination with other risk assessment tools to sort companies' debt into risk categories. Higher risk debt typically carries higher yields. Go to Standard & Poor's Canada (standardandpoors.com) and click on Ratings Action Press Release. How do financial ratios impact ratings?

2. DBRS (dbrs.com) employs a different rating scale for short-term and long-term debt. Which ratios do you think are important for rating short-term and long-term debt? Is it possible for a firm to get a high rating for short-term debt and a lower rating for long-term debt?

3. Many Canadian companies now provide online links to their financial statements. Try the following link to Shaw Communications (shaw.ca/en-ca/InvestorRelations/FinancialReports/AnnualReports). How would you rate Shaw's long-term debt based on the criteria employed by DBRS?

4. Find the most recent financial statements for Loblaws at loblaw.com and for Husky Energy at huskyenergy.com. Calculate the asset utilization ratio for these two companies. What does this ratio measure? Is the ratio similar for both companies? Why or why not?

5. Find the most recent financial statements for Metro Inc. at metro.ca.

   a) Identify three of Metro's competitors and obtain the most recent financial statements from their company website. Briefly mention the reason for choosing these competitors.

   b) Refer to Table 3.8 and calculate the ratio for these companies.

   c) Analyze how Metro Inc. is faring against these competitors after calculating these ratios.

   d) Calculate two non-standard ratios—Number of stores per square foot and number of sales per store. Analyze how each company is faring against each other in these ratios. (Refer to Management Discussion & Analysis part of the Annual Report for answering this question)

CHAPTER 4

LONG-TERM FINANCIAL PLANNING AND CORPORATE GROWTH

In 2011, Bank of Nova Scotia, Canada's third largest bank by assets, acquired an almost 20% stake in Bank of Guangzhou for about C$719 million, expanding its presence in China. Bank of Guangzhou is the 29th largest bank in China by assets and has 84 branches around Guangzhou, the country's third richest city behind Shanghai and Beijing.

Scotiabank has a long history of acquiring small stakes in foreign banks that usually increase over time. This is a key part of Scotiabank's long term strategy for growth. "These are all consumers that are going to want to buy houses and buy cars, and that's good for banking generally. It fits in the same footprint and same basis that we made investments in Central America and Latin America," Brian Porter, Scotiabank's group head of international banking, said in an interview. Acquisitions and the issuance of securities are both components of long-term financial planning and growth, which will be discussed in this chapter.

Learning Objectives ▶

After studying this chapter, you should understand:

LO1 The objectives and goals of financial planning.

LO2 How to compute the external financing needed to fund a firm's growth.

LO3 How to apply the percentage of sales method.

LO4 The factors determining the growth of the firm.

LO5 How to compute the sustainable and internal growth rates.

LO6 Some of the problems in planning for growth.

gm.ca

A lack of effective long-range planning is a commonly cited reason for financial distress and failure. This is especially true for small businesses—a sector vital to the creation of future jobs in Canada. As we develop in this chapter, long-range planning is a means of systematically thinking about the future and anticipating possible problems before they arrive. There are no magic mirrors, of course, so the best we can hope for is a logical and organized procedure for exploring the unknown. As one member of General Motors Corporation's board was heard to say, "Planning is a process that at best helps the firm avoid stumbling into the future backwards."

Financial planning establishes guidelines for change and growth in a firm. It normally focuses on the "big picture." This means it is concerned with the major elements of a firm's financial and investment policies without examining the individual components of those policies in detail.

Our primary goals in this chapter are to discuss financial planning and to illustrate the interrelatedness of the various investment and financing decisions that a firm makes. In the chapters ahead, we examine in much more detail how these decisions are made.

We begin by describing what is usually meant by financial planning. For the most part, we talk about long-term planning. Short-term financial planning is discussed in Chapter 18. We examine what the firm can accomplish by developing a long-term financial plan. To do this, we develop a simple, but very useful, long-range planning technique: the percentage of sales approach. We describe how to apply this approach in some simple cases, and we discuss some extensions.

To develop an explicit financial plan, management must establish certain elements of the firm's financial policy. These basic policy elements of financial planning are:

1. The firm's needed investment in new assets. This arises from the investment opportunities that the firm chooses to undertake, and it is the result of the firm's capital budgeting decisions.
2. The degree of financial leverage the firm chooses to employ. This determines the amount of borrowing the firm uses to finance its investments in real assets. This is the firm's capital structure policy.
3. The amount of cash the firm thinks is necessary and appropriate to pay shareholders. This is the firm's dividend policy.
4. The amount of liquidity and working capital the firm needs on an ongoing basis. This is the firm's net working capital decision.

As we shall see, the decisions that a firm makes in these four areas directly affect its future profitability, its need for external financing, and its opportunities for growth.

A key lesson from this chapter is that the firm's investment and financing policies interact and thus cannot truly be considered in isolation from one another. The types and amounts of assets that the firm plans on purchasing must be considered along with the firm's ability to raise the necessary capital to fund those investments.

bmo.com

Financial planning forces the corporation to think about goals. A goal frequently espoused by corporations is growth, and almost all firms use an explicit, company-wide growth rate as a major component of their long-run financial planning. In January 2011, Bank of Montreal acquired a Hong Kong based wealth management firm, Lloyd George Management. By increasing its presence in China's fast growing financial sector, BMO sought to expand the bank's wealth management division through tapping attractive growth opportunities in China's emerging market. This strategy shows that growth is an important goal for most large companies.

There are direct connections between the growth that a company can achieve and its financial policy. In the following sections, we show that financial planning models can help you better understand how growth is achieved. We also show how such models can be used to establish limits on possible growth. This analysis can help companies avoid the sometimes fatal mistake of growing too fast.

4.1 | What Is Financial Planning?

Financial planning formulates the way financial goals are to be achieved. A financial plan is thus a statement of what is to be done in the future. Most decisions have long lead times, which means they take a long time to implement. In an uncertain world, this requires that decisions be made far in advance of their implementation. A firm that wants to build a factory in 2014, for example, might have to begin lining up contractors and financing in 2012, or even earlier.

Growth as a Financial Management Goal

cott.com

Because we discuss the subject of growth in various places in this chapter, we start out with an important warning: Growth, by itself, is *not* an appropriate goal for the financial manager. In fact, as we have seen, rapid growth isn't always good for a firm. Cott Corp., a Toronto-based bottler of private-label soft drinks, is another example of what happens when a firm grows too fast. The company aggressively marketed its soft drinks in the early 1990s, and sales exploded. However, despite its growth in sales, the company lost $29.4 million for the fiscal year ended January 27, 1996.

Cott's pains included the following: (1) aluminum prices rose; (2) the firm faced price competition; (3) costs surged as Cott built corporate infrastructure in anticipation of becoming a much bigger company; and (4) the firm botched expansion into the United Kingdom. Cott quickly grabbed a 25 percent market share by undercutting the big brands, but then had to hire an outside bottler at a cost much higher than the cost of bottling in its own plants to meet the demand. Half the cases sold in the United Kingdom in 1995 were sold below cost, bringing a loss to the company as a whole. Cott is now focusing on slower growth while keeping a line on operating costs.

As we discussed in Chapter 1, the appropriate goal is increasing the market value of the owners' equity. Of course, if a firm is successful in doing this, growth usually results. Growth may thus be a desirable consequence of good decision making, but it is not an end unto itself. We discuss growth simply because growth rates are so commonly used in the planning process. As we see, growth is a convenient means of summarizing various aspects of a firm's financial and investment policies. Also, if we think of growth as growth in the market value of the equity in the firm, then the goals of growth and increasing the market value of the equity in the firm are not all that different.

Dimensions of Financial Planning

It is often useful for planning purposes to think of the future as having a short run and a long run. The short run, in practice, is usually the coming 12 months. We focus our attention on financial planning over the long run, which is usually taken to be the coming two to five years. This is called the **planning horizon,** and it is the first dimension of the planning process that must be established.[1]

In drawing up a financial plan, all of the individual projects and investments that the firm undertakes are combined to determine the total needed investment. In effect, the smaller investment proposals of each operational unit are added up and treated as one big project. This process is called **aggregation.** This is the second dimension of the planning process.

Once the planning horizon and level of aggregation are established, a financial plan would need inputs in the form of alternative sets of assumptions about important variables. For example, suppose a company has two separate divisions: one for consumer products and one for gas turbine engines. The financial planning process might require each division to prepare three alternative business plans for the next three years.

1. A worst case. This plan would require making relatively pessimistic assumptions about the company's products and the state of the economy. This kind of disaster planning would emphasize a division's ability to withstand significant economic adversity, and it would require details concerning cost cutting, and even divestiture and liquidation. For example, the bottom was dropping out of the PC market in 2001. That left big manufacturers like Compaq, Dell, and Gateway locked in a price war, fighting for market share at a time when sales were stagnant.

2. A normal case. This plan would require making the most likely assumptions about the company and the economy.

3. A best case. Each division would be required to work out a case based on optimistic assumptions. It could involve new products and expansion and would then detail the financing needed to fund the expansion.

In this example, business activities are aggregated along divisional lines and the planning horizon is three years. This type of planning, which considers all possible events, is particularly important for cyclical businesses (businesses with sales that are strongly affected by the overall state of the economy or business cycles). For example, in 2006 New York-based investment bank, Lehman Brothers predicted corporate earnings growth of 7% in the next year. Even though the company posted record earnings in 2007, the next year turned out completely different. Just to show you how hard it is to predict the future, Lehman Brothers filed for bankruptcy in 2008 as the financial crisis took hold. The company's investment banking and trading division in North America was acquired by Barclays and the company's franchise in the Asia-Pacific region was acquired by Nomura Holdings. In March 2012, Lehman emerged from bankruptcy and will operate as a liquidating company for a few years to pay back around $65 billion to creditors and investors.

What Can Planning Accomplish?

Because the company is likely to spend a lot of time examining the different scenarios that could become the basis for the company's financial plan, it seems reasonable to ask what the planning process will accomplish.

EXAMINING INTERACTIONS   As we discuss in greater detail later, the financial plan must make explicit the linkages between investment proposals for the different operating activities of the firm and the financing choices available to the firm. In other words, if the firm is planning on expanding and undertaking new investments and projects, where will the financing be obtained to pay for this activity?

planning horizon
The long-range time period the financial planning process focuses on, usually the next two to five years.

aggregation
The process by which smaller investment proposals of each of a firm's operational units are added up and treated as one big project.

---

[1] The techniques we present can also be used for short-term financial planning.

EXPLORING OPTIONS   The financial plan provides the opportunity for the firm to develop, analyze, and compare many different scenarios in a consistent way. Various investment and financing options can be explored, and their impact on the firm's shareholders can be evaluated. Questions concerning the firm's future lines of business and questions of what financing arrangements are optimal are addressed. Options such as marketing new products or closing plants might be evaluated. As Research in Motion (RIM) shares plunged in 2012, the company explored several options including shifting its focus from smart phones to tablets and possibly selling some divisions.

AVOIDING SURPRISES   Financial planning should identify what may happen to the firm if different events take place. In particular, it should address what actions the firm would take if things go seriously wrong or, more generally, if assumptions made today about the future are seriously in error. Thus, one of the purposes of financial planning is to avoid surprises and develop contingency plans. For example, at the end of June 2011, quarterly net income of Toyota fell to $14 million from $2.5 billion due to the massive earthquake and tsunami in Japan.[2] The quake disrupted production and came on top of Toyota's problems in recovering from massive recalls in 2010. Thus, a lack of planning for sales growth can be a problem for even the biggest companies.

ENSURING FEASIBILITY AND INTERNAL CONSISTENCY   Beyond a specific goal of creating value, a firm normally has many specific goals. Such goals might be couched in market share, return on equity, financial leverage, and so on. At times, the linkages between different goals and different aspects of a firm's business are difficult to see. Not only does a financial plan make explicit these linkages, but it also imposes a unified structure for reconciling differing goals and objectives. In other words, financial planning is a way of checking that the goals and plans made with regard to specific areas of a firm's operations are feasible and internally consistent. Conflicting goals often exist. To generate a coherent plan, goals and objectives have to be modified therefore, and priorities have to be established.

For example, one goal a firm might have is 12 percent growth in unit sales per year. Another goal might be to reduce the firm's total debt ratio from 40 percent to 20 percent. Are these two goals compatible? Can they be accomplished simultaneously? Maybe yes, maybe no. As we discuss later, financial planning is a way of finding out just what is possible, and, by implication, what is not possible.

The fact that planning forces management to think about goals and to establish priorities is probably the most important result of the process. In fact, conventional business wisdom says that plans can't work, but planning does. The future is inherently unknown. What we can do is establish the direction that we want to travel in and take some educated guesses about what we will find along the way. If we do a good job, we won't be caught off guard when the future rolls around.

COMMUNICATION WITH INVESTORS AND LENDERS   Our discussion to this point has tried to convince you that financial planning is essential to good management. Because good management controls the riskiness of a firm, equity investors and lenders are very interested in studying a firm's financial plan. As discussed in Chapter 15, securities regulators require that firms issuing new shares or debt file a detailed financial plan as part of the *prospectus* describing the new issue. For example, Aureus Mining Inc. filed a prospectus[3] on April 20, 2011, providing a detailed financial plan for the use of proceeds to be raised through its initial public offer. Chartered banks and other financial institutions that make loans to businesses almost always require prospective borrowers to provide a financial plan. In small businesses with limited resources for planning, pressure from lenders is often the main motivator for engaging in financial planning.

Concept Questions

1. What are the two dimensions of the financial planning process?
2. Why should firms draw up financial plans?

---

[2] money.cnn.com/2011/08/02/news/international/toyota/index.htm

[3] The Company's prospectus can be accessed from the website sedar.com.

4.2 | Financial Planning Models: A First Look

Just as companies differ in size and products, the financial planning process differs from firm to firm. In this section, we discuss some common elements in financial plans and develop a basic model to illustrate these elements.

A Financial Planning Model: The Ingredients

Most financial planning models require the user to specify some assumptions about the future. Based on those assumptions, the model generates predicted values for a large number of variables. Models can vary quite a bit in their complexity, but almost all would have the following elements:

SALES FORECAST   Almost all financial plans require an externally supplied sales forecast. In the models that follow, for example, the sales forecast is the driver, meaning that the user of the planning model supplies this value and all other values are calculated based on it. This arrangement would be common for many types of business; planning focuses on projected future sales and the assets and financing needed to support those sales.

Frequently, the sales forecast is given as a growth rate in sales rather than as an explicit sales figure. These two approaches are essentially the same because we can calculate projected sales once we know the growth rate. Perfect sales forecasts are not possible, of course, because sales depend on the uncertain future state of the economy and on industry conditions.

For example, at the time of writing in winter 2012, Canadian commodity producers are revisiting their sales forecasts in light of the European debt crisis and possible slowdown in China. To help firms come up with such projections, some economic consulting firms specialize in macroeconomic and industry projections. Economic and industry forecasts are also available on databases such as IHS Global Insight.

As we discussed earlier, we are frequently interested in evaluating alternative scenarios even though the sales forecast may not be accurate due to unforeseen events. Our goal is to examine the interplay between investment and financing needs at different possible sales levels, not to pinpoint what we expect to happen.

PRO FORMA STATEMENTS   A financial plan has forecasted statements of comprehensive income and financial position, and a statement of cash flows. These are called pro forma statements, or pro formas for short. The phrase *pro forma* literally means "as a matter of form." This means that the financial statements are the forms we use to summarize the different events projected for the future. At a minimum, a financial planning model generates these statements based on projections of key items such as sales.

Spreadsheets to use for pro forma statements can be obtained at jaxworks.com

In the planning models we describe later, the pro formas are the output from the financial planning model. The user supplies a sales figure, and the model generates the resulting statements of comprehensive income and financial position.

ASSET REQUIREMENTS   The plan describes projected capital spending. At a minimum, the projected statements of financial position contain changes in total fixed assets and net working capital. These changes are effectively the firm's total capital budget. Proposed capital spending in different areas must thus be reconciled with the overall increases contained in the long-range plan.

FINANCIAL REQUIREMENTS   The plan includes a section on the financial arrangements that are necessary. This part of the plan should discuss dividend policy and debt policy. Sometimes firms expect to raise cash by selling new shares of stock or by borrowing. Then, the plan has to spell out what kinds of securities have to be sold and what methods of issuance are most appropriate. These are subjects we consider in Part 6 when we discuss long-term financing, capital structure, and dividend policy.

CASH SURPLUS OR SHORTFALL   After the firm has a sales forecast and an estimate of the required spending on assets, some amount of new financing is often necessary because projected total assets exceed projected total liabilities and equity. In other words, the statement of financial position no longer balances.

Because new financing may be necessary to cover all the projected capital spending, a financial "plug" variable must be designated. The cash surplus or shortfall (also called the "plug") is the designated source or sources of external financing needed to deal with any shortfall (or surplus) in financing and thereby to bring the statement of financial position into balance.

For example, a firm with a great number of investment opportunities and limited cash flow may have to raise new equity. Other firms with few growth opportunities and ample cash flow have a surplus and thus might pay an extra dividend. In the first case, external equity is the plug variable. In the second, the dividend is used.

ECONOMIC ASSUMPTIONS   The plan has to explicitly describe the economic environment in which the firm expects to reside over the life of the plan. Among the more important economic assumptions that have to be made are the level of interest rates and the firm's tax rate, as well as sales forecasts, as discussed earlier.

A Simple Financial Planning Model

We begin our discussion of long-term planning models with a relatively simple example.[4] The Computerfield Corporation's financial statements from the most recent year are as follows:

COMPUTERFIELD CORPORATION
Financial Statements

Statement of Comprehensive Income		Statement of Financial Position			
Sales	$1,000	Assets	$500	Debt	$250
Costs	800			Equity	250
Net Income	$ 200	Total	$500	Total	$500

Unless otherwise stated, the financial planners at Computerfield assume that all variables are tied directly to sales and that current relationships are optimal. This means that all items grow at exactly the same rate as sales. This is obviously oversimplified; we use this assumption only to make a point.

Suppose that sales increase by 20 percent, rising from $1,000 to $1,200. Then planners would also forecast a 20 percent increase in costs, from $800 to $800 × 1.2 = $960. The pro forma statement of comprehensive income would thus be:

PRO FORMA
Statement of Comprehensive Income

Sales	$1,200
Costs	960
Net income	$ 240

The assumption that all variables would grow by 20 percent enables us to easily construct the pro forma statement of financial position as well:

PRO FORMA STATEMENT OF FINANCIAL POSITION

Assets	$600 (+100)	Debt	$300 (+50)
		Equity	300 (+50)
Total	$600 (+100)	Total	$600 (+100)

Notice that we have simply increased every item by 20 percent. The numbers in parentheses are the dollar changes for the different items.

Now we have to reconcile these two pro formas. How, for example, can net income be equal to $240 and equity increase by only $50? The answer is that Computerfield must have paid out the difference of $240 − 50 = $190, possibly as a cash dividend. In this case, dividends are the plug variable.

Suppose Computerfield does not pay out the $190. Here, the addition to retained earnings is the full $240. Computerfield's equity thus grows to $250 (the starting amount) + 240 (net income) = $490, and debt must be retired to keep total assets equal to $600.

With $600 in total assets and $490 in equity, debt has to be $600 − 490 = $110. Since we started with $250 in debt, Computerfield has to retire $250 − 110 = $140 in debt. The resulting pro forma statement of financial position would look like this:

---

[4]Computer spreadsheets are the standard way to execute this and the other examples we present. Appendix 10B gives an overview of spreadsheets and how they are used in planning with capital budgeting as the application.

PRO FORMA STATEMENT OF FINANCIAL POSITION

Assets	$600 (+100)	Debt	$110 (−140)
		Equity	490 (+240)
Total	$600 (+100)	Total	$600 (+100)

In this case, debt is the plug variable used to balance out projected total assets and liabilities.

This example shows the interaction between sales growth and financial policy. As sales increase, so do total assets. This occurs because the firm must invest in net working capital and fixed assets to support higher sales levels. Since assets are growing, total liabilities and equity, the right-hand side of the statement of financial position, grow as well.

The thing to notice from our simple example is that the way the liabilities and owners' equity change depends on the firm's financing policy and its dividend policy. The growth in assets requires that the firm decide on how to finance that growth. This is strictly a managerial decision. Also, in our example the firm needed no outside funds. As this isn't usually the case, we explore a more detailed situation in the next section.

Concept Questions

1. What are the basic concepts of a financial plan?

2. Why is it necessary to designate a plug in a financial planning model?

4.3 | The Percentage of Sales Approach

In the previous section, we described a simple planning model in which every item increased at the same rate as sales. This may be a reasonable assumption for some elements. For others, such as long-term borrowing, it probably is not, because the amount of long-term borrowing is something set by management, and it does not necessarily relate directly to the level of sales.

In this section, we describe an extended version of our simple model. The basic idea is to separate the items on the statements of comprehensive income and financial position into two groups, those that do vary directly with sales and those that do not. Given a sales forecast, we are able to calculate how much financing the firm needs to support the predicted sales level.

An Illustration of the Percentage of Sales Approach

percentage of sales approach
Financial planning method in which accounts are projected depending on a firm's predicted sales level.

The financial planning model we describe next is based on the **percentage of sales approach.** Our goal here is to develop a quick and practical way of generating pro forma statements. We defer discussion of some bells and whistles to a later section.

THE STATEMENT OF COMPREHENSIVE INCOME   We start with the most recent statement of comprehensive income for the Rosengarten Corporation, as shown in Table 4.1. Notice that we have still simplified things by including costs, depreciation, and interest in a single cost figure.

Rosengarten has projected a 25 percent increase in sales for the coming year, so we are anticipating sales of $1,000 × 1.25 = $1,250. To generate a pro forma statement of comprehensive income, we assume that total costs continue to run at $800/$1,000 = 80% of sales. With this assumption, Rosengarten's pro forma statement is as shown in Table 4.2. The effect here of assuming that costs are a constant percentage of sales is to assume that the profit margin is constant. To check this, notice that the profit margin was $132/$1,000 = 13.2%. In our pro forma, the profit margin is $165/$1,250 = 13.2%; so it is unchanged.

Next, we need to project the dividend payment. This amount is up to Rosengarten's management. We assume that Rosengarten has a policy of paying out a constant fraction of net income in the form of a cash dividend. From the most recent year, the **dividend payout ratio** was:

dividend payout ratio
Amount of cash paid out to shareholders divided by net income.

$$\text{Dividend payout ratio} = \text{Cash dividends/Net income} \qquad [4.1]$$
$$= \$44/\$132$$
$$= 33\ 1/3\%$$

TABLE 4.1	
ROSENGARTEN CORPORATION Statement of Comprehensive Income	
Sales	$ 1,000
Costs	800
Taxable income	$ 200
Taxes	68
Net income	$ 132
Addition to retained earnings	$88
Dividends	$44

TABLE 4.2	
ROSENGARTEN CORPORATION Pro Forma Statement of Comprehensive Income	
Sales (projected)	$ 1,250
Costs (80% of sales)	1,000
Taxable income	$ 250
Taxes	85
Net income	$ 165

We can also calculate the ratio of the addition to retained earnings to net income as:

Retained earnings/Net income = $88/$132 = 66 2/3%

retention ratio or plowback ratio
Retained earnings divided by net income.

This ratio is called the **retention ratio** or **plowback ratio,** and it is equal to 1 minus the dividend payout ratio because everything not paid out is retained. Assuming that the payout and retention ratios are constant, the projected dividends and addition to retained earnings would be:

Projected addition to retained earnings = $165 × 2/3 = $110
Projected dividends paid to shareholders = $165 × 1/3 = 55
Net income $165

THE STATEMENT OF FINANCIAL POSITION To generate a pro forma statement of financial position, we start with the most recent statement in Table 4.3. On our statement, we assume that some of the items vary directly with sales, while others do not. For those items that do vary with sales, we express each as a percentage of sales for the year just completed. When an item does not vary directly with sales, we write "n/a" for "not applicable."

For example, on the asset side, inventory is equal to 60 percent of sales ($600/$1,000) for the year just ended. We assume that this percentage applies to the coming year, so for each $1 increase in sales, inventory rises by $.60. More generally, the ratio of total assets to sales for the year just ended is $3,000/$1,000 = 3, or 300%.

capital intensity ratio
A firm's total assets divided by its sales, or the amount of assets needed to generate $1 in sales.

This ratio of total assets to sales is sometimes called the **capital intensity ratio.** It tells us the assets needed to generate $1 in sales; so the higher the ratio is, the more capital intensive is the firm. Notice also that this ratio is just the reciprocal of the total asset turnover ratio we defined in the last chapter. For Rosengarten, assuming this ratio is constant, it takes $3 in total assets to generate $1 in sales (apparently Rosengarten is in a relatively capital intensive business). Therefore, if sales are to increase by $100, Rosengarten has to increase total assets by three times this amount, or $300.

On the liability side of the statement of financial position, we show accounts payable varying with sales. The reason is that we expect to place more orders with our suppliers as sales volume increases, so payables should change spontaneously with sales. Notes payable, on the other hand, represent short-term debt such as bank borrowing. These would not vary unless we take specific actions to change the amount, so we mark them as n/a.

Similarly, we use n/a for long-term debt because it won't automatically change with sales. The same is true for common stock. The last item on the right-hand side, retained earnings, varies with sales, but it won't be a simple percentage of sales. Instead, we explicitly calculate the change in retained earnings based on our projected net income and dividends.

We can now construct a partial pro forma statement of financial position for Rosengarten. We do this by using the percentages we calculated earlier wherever possible to calculate the projected amounts. For example, fixed assets are 180 percent of sales; so, with a new sales level of $1,250, the fixed asset amount is 1.80 × $1,250 = $2,250, an increase of $2,250 − 1,800 = $450 in plant and equipment. Importantly, for those items that don't vary directly with sales, we initially assume no change and simply write in the original amounts. The result is the pro forma statement of financial position in Table 4.4. Notice that the change in retained earnings is equal to the $110 addition to retained earnings that we calculated earlier.

TABLE 4.3

ROSENGARTEN CORPORATION
Partial Pro Forma Statement of Financial Position

	($)	(%)		($)	(%)
	Assets			*Liabilities and Owners' Equity*	
Current assets			Current liabilities		
Cash	$ 160	16%	Accounts payable	$ 300	30%
Accounts receivable	440	44	Notes payable	100	n/a
Inventory	600	60	Total	$ 400	n/a
Total	$1,200	120%			
			Long-term debt	$ 800	n/a
Fixed assets			Owners' equity		
Net plant and equipment	$1,800	180%	Common stock	$ 800	n/a
			Retained earnings	1,000	n/a
			Total	$1,800	n/a
Total assets	$3,000	300%	Total liabilities and owners' equity	$3,000	n/a

external financing needed (EFN)

The amount of financing required to balance both sides of the statement of financial position.

Inspecting our pro forma statement of financial position, we notice that assets are projected to increase by $750. However, without additional financing, liabilities and equity only increase by $185, leaving a shortfall of $750 − 185 = $565. We label this amount **external financing needed (EFN)**.

FULL-CAPACITY SCENARIO   Our financial planning model now reminds us of one of those good news/bad news jokes. The good news is that we're projecting a 25 percent increase in sales. The bad news is that this isn't going to happen unless we can somehow raise $565 in new financing.

This is a good example of how the planning process can point out problems and potential conflicts. If, for example, Rosengarten has a goal of not borrowing any additional funds and not selling any new equity, a 25 percent increase in sales is probably not feasible.

When we take the need for $565 in new financing as a given, Rosengarten has three possible sources: short-term borrowing, long-term borrowing, and new equity. The choice of a combination among these three is up to management; we illustrate only one of the many possibilities.

TABLE 4.4

ROSENGARTEN CORPORATION
Partial Pro Forma Statement of Financial Position

	Present Year	Change from Previous Year		Present Year	Change from Previous Year
	Assets			*Liabilities and Owners' Equity*	
Current assets			Current liabilities		
Cash	$ 200	$ 40	Accounts payable	$ 375	$ 75
Accounts receivable	550	110	Notes payable	100	0
			Total	$ 475	$ 75
Inventory	750	150			
Total	$1,500	$300	Long-term debt	$ 800	$ 0
Fixed assets			Owners' equity		
Net plant and equipment	$2,250	$450	Common stock	$ 800	$ 0
			Retained earnings	1,110	110
			Total	$1,910	$110
Total assets	$3,750	$750	Total liabilities and owners' equity	$3,185	$185
			External financing needed	$ 565	

TABLE 4.5

ROSENGARTEN CORPORATION
Pro Forma Statement of Financial Position

	Present Year	Change from Previous Year		Present Year	Change from Previous Year
Assets			*Liabilities and Owners' Equity*		
Current assets			Current liabilities		
Cash	$ 200	$ 40	Accounts payable	$ 375	$ 75
Accounts receivable	550	110	Notes payable	325	225
			Total	$ 700	$ 300
Inventory	750	150	Long-term debt	$ 1,140	$ 340
Total	$ 1,500	$ 300	Owners' equity		
Fixed assets			Common stock	$ 800	$ 0
Net plant and equipment	$ 2,250	$ 450	Retained earnings	1,110	110
			Total	$ 1,910	$ 110
Total assets	$ 3,750	$ 750	Total liabilities and owners' equity	$ 3,750	$ 750

Suppose that Rosengarten decides to borrow the needed funds. The firm might choose to borrow some short-term and some long-term. For example, current assets increased by $300 while current liabilities rose by only $75. Rosengarten could borrow $300 − 75 = $225 in short-term notes payable in the form of a loan from a chartered bank. This would leave total net working capital unchanged. With $565 needed, the remaining $565 − 225 = $340 would have to come from long-term debt. Two examples of long-term debt discussed in Chapter 15 are a bond issue and a term loan from a chartered bank or insurance company. Table 4.5 shows the completed pro forma statement of financial position for Rosengarten.

Even though we used a combination of short- and long-term debt as the plug here, we emphasize that this is just one possible strategy; it is not necessarily the best one by any means. There are many other scenarios that we could (and should) investigate. The various ratios we discussed in Chapter 3 come in very handy here. For example, with the scenario we have just examined, we would surely want to examine the current ratio and the total debt ratio to see if we were comfortable with the new projected debt levels.

Now that we have finished our statement of financial position, we have all of the projected sources and uses of cash. We could finish off our pro formas by drawing up the projected statement of changes in financial position along the lines discussed in Chapter 3. We leave this as an exercise and instead investigate an important alternative scenario.

EXCESS CAPACITY SCENARIO The assumption that assets are a fixed percentage of sales is convenient, but it may not be suitable in many cases. For example, we effectively assumed that Rosengarten was using its fixed assets at 100 percent of capacity because any increase in sales led to an increase in fixed assets. For most businesses, there would be some slack or excess capacity, and production could be increased by, perhaps, running an extra shift. For example, Bombardier's wheelset operation centre began in operation in 2011 at Siegen in Germany. The company plans to use the excess capacity of the centre to serve wider markets in Europe.

If we assume that Rosengarten is only operating at 70 percent of capacity, the need for external funds would be quite different. By 70 percent of capacity, we mean that the current sales level is 70 percent of the full capacity sales level:

Current sales = $1,000 = .70 × Full capacity sales
Full capacity sales = $1,000/.70 = $1,429

This tells us that sales could increase by almost 43 percent—from $1,000 to $1,429—before any new fixed assets were needed.

In our previous scenario, we assumed it would be necessary to add $450 in net fixed assets. In the current scenario, no spending on net fixed assets is needed, because sales are projected to rise to $1,250, which is substantially less than the $1,429 full capacity level.

As a result, our original estimate of $565 in external funds needed is too high. We estimated that $450 in net new fixed assets would be needed. Instead, no spending on new net fixed assets is necessary. Thus, if we are currently operating at 70 percent capacity, we only need $565 − 450 = $115 in external funds. The excess capacity thus makes a considerable difference in our projections.

These alternative scenarios illustrate that it is inappropriate to manipulate financial statement information blindly in the planning process. The output of any model is only as good as the input assumptions or, as is said in the computer field, GIGO: garbage in, garbage out. Results depend critically on the assumptions made about the relationships between sales and asset needs. We return to this point later.

EXAMPLE 4.1: EFN and Capacity Usage

Suppose Rosengarten were operating at 90 percent capacity. What would be sales at full capacity? What is the capital intensity ratio at full capacity? What is EFN in this case?

Full capacity sales would be $1,000/.90 = $1,111. From Table 4.3, fixed assets are $1,800. At full capacity, the ratio of fixed assets to sales is thus:

Fixed assets/Full capacity sales = $1,800/$1,111 = 1.62

This tells us that we need $1.62 in fixed assets for every $1 in sales once we reach full capacity. At the projected sales level of $1,250, we need $1,250 × 1.62 = $2,025 in fixed assets. Compared to the $2,250 we originally projected, this is $225 less, so EFN is $565 − 225 = $340.

Current assets would still be $1,500, so total assets would be $1,500 + 2,025 = $3,525. The capital intensity ratio would thus be $3,525/$1,250 = 2.82, less than our original value of 3 because of the excess capacity. See Table 4.6 for a partial pro forma statement of financial position. Total pro forma assets exceed the sum of total liabilities and owners' equity by EFN = $340.

TABLE 4.6

ROSENGARTEN CORPORATION
partial pro forma Statement of Financial Position

	Present Year	Change from Previous Year		Present Year	Change from Previous Year
Current Assets			Current liabilities		
Cash	$ 200	$ 40	Accounts payable	$ 375	$ 75
Accounts			Notes payable	100	0
receivable	550	110	Total	475	75
Inventory	750	150			
Total	$ 1,500	$ 300	Long-term debt	$ 800	$ 0
Fixed assets			Owners' equity		
Net plant and equipment	$ 2,025	$ 225	Common stock	$ 800	$ 0
			Retained earnings	1,110	110
			Total	$ 1,910	$ 110
Total Assets	$ 3,525	$ 525	Total liabilities and owners' equity	$ 3,185	$ 185
			External financing needed	$ 340	

Concept Questions

1. What is the basic idea behind the percentage of sales approach?
2. Unless it is modified, what does the percentage of sales approach assume about fixed asset capacity usage?

4.4 | External Financing and Growth

External financing needed and growth are obviously related. All other things being the same, the higher the rate of growth in sales or assets, the greater will be the need for external financing. In the previous section, we took a growth rate as a given, and then we determined the amount of external financing needed to support the growth. In this section, we turn things around a bit. We take the firm's financial policy as a given and then examine the relationship between that financial policy and the firm's ability to finance new investments and thereby grow.

This approach can be very useful because, as you have already seen, growth in sales requires financing, so it follows that rapid growth can cause a company to grow broke.[5] Companies that neglect to plan for financing growth can fail even when production and marketing are on track. From a positive perspective, planning growth that is financially sustainable can help an excellent company achieve its potential. This is why managers, along with their bankers and other suppliers of funds, need to look at sustainable growth.

External Financing Needed and Growth

To begin, we must establish the relationship between EFN and growth. To do this, we introduce Table 4.7, simplified statements of comprehensive income and financial position for the Hoffman Company. Notice that we have simplified the statement of financial position by combining short-term and long-term debt into a single total debt figure. Effectively, we are assuming that none of the current liabilities varies spontaneously with sales. This assumption isn't as restrictive as it sounds. If any current liabilities (such as accounts payable) vary with sales, we can assume they have been netted out in current assets.[6] Also, we continue to combine depreciation, interest, and costs on the statement of comprehensive income.

TABLE 4.7

HOFFMAN COMPANY
Statements of Comprehensive Income and Financial Position

Statement of Comprehensive Income

Sales	$500
Costs	400
Taxable income	$100
Taxes	34
Net income	$ 66
Addition to retained earnings	$44
Dividends	$22

Statement of Financial Position

Assets	$	% of Sales	Liabilities	$	% of Sales
Current assets	$ 200	40%	Total debt	$250	n/a
Net fixed assets	300	60	Owners' equity	250	n/a
Total assets	$ 500	100%	Total liabilities and owners' equity	$500	n/a

The following symbols are useful:

S = Previous year's sales = $500
A = Total assets = $500
D = Total debt = $250
E = Total equity = $250

[5] This phrase and the following discussion draws heavily on R. C. Higgins, "How Much Growth Can a Firm Afford?" *Financial Management* 6, Fall 1977, pp. 7–16.

[6] This assumption makes our use of EFN here consistent with how we defined it earlier in the chapter.

In addition, based on our earlier discussions of financial ratios, we can calculate the following:

$$p = \text{Profit margin} = \$66/\$500 = 13.2\%$$
$$R = \text{Retention ratio} = \$44/\$66 = 2/3$$
$$ROA = \text{Return on assets} = \$66/\$500 = 13.2\%$$
$$ROE = \text{Return on equity} = \$66/\$250 = 26.4\%$$
$$D/E = \text{Debt/equity ratio} = \$250/\$250 = 1.0$$

Suppose the Hoffman Company is forecasting next year's sales level at $600, a $100 increase. The capital intensity ratio is $500/$500 = 1, so assets need to rise by 1 × $100 = $100 (assuming full capacity usage). Notice that the percentage increase in sales is $100/$500 = 20%. The percentage increase in assets is also 20 percent: 100/$500 = 20%. As this illustrates, assuming a constant capital intensity ratio, the increase in total assets is simply $A \times g$, where g is growth rate in sales:

$$\text{Increase in total assets} = A \times g$$
$$= \$500 \times 20\%$$
$$= \$100$$

In other words, the growth rate in sales can also be interpreted as the rate of increase in the firm's total assets.

Some of the financing necessary to cover the increase in total assets comes from internally generated funds and shows up in the form of the addition to retained earnings. This amount is equal to net income multiplied by the plowback or retention ratio, R. Projected net income is equal to the profit margin, p, multiplied by projected sales, $S \times (1 + g)$. The projected addition to retained earnings for Hoffman can thus be written as:

$$\text{Addition to retained earnings} = p(S)R \times (1 + g)$$
$$= .132(\$500)(2/3) \times 1.20$$
$$= \$44 \times 1.20$$
$$= \$52.80$$

Notice that this is equal to last year's addition to retained earnings, $44, multiplied by $(1 + g)$.

Putting this information together, we need $A \times g = \$100$ in new financing. We generate $p(S)R \times (1 + g) = \$52.80$ internally, so the difference is what we need to raise. In other words, we find that EFN can be written as:

$$\text{EFN} = \text{Increase in total assets} - \text{Addition to retained earnings} \qquad [4.2]$$
$$= A(g) - p(S)R \times (1 + g)$$

For Hoffman, this works out to be

$$\text{EFN} = \$500(.20) - .132(\$500)(2/3) \times 1.20$$
$$= \$100 - \$52.80$$
$$= \$47.20$$

We can check that this is correct by filling in pro forma statements of comprehensive income and financial position, as in Table 4.8. As we calculated, Hoffman needs to raise $47.20.

Looking at our equation for EFN, we see that EFN depends directly on g. Rearranging things to highlight this relationship, we get:

$$\text{EFN} = -p(S)R + [A - p(S)R] \times g \qquad [4.3]$$

Plugging in the numbers for Hoffman, the relationship between EFN and g is:

$$\text{EFN} = -.132(\$500)(2/3) + [\$500 - .132(\$500)(2/3)] \times g$$
$$= -44 + 456 \times g$$

Notice that this is the equation of a straight line with a vertical intercept of −$44 and a slope of $456.

The relationship between growth and EFN is illustrated in Figure 4.1. The y-axis intercept of our line, −$44, is equal to last year's addition to retained earnings. This makes sense because, if the growth in sales is zero, then retained earnings are $44, the same as last year. Furthermore, with no growth, no net investment in assets is needed, so we run a surplus equal to the addition to retained earnings, which is why we have a negative sign.

The slope of the line in Figure 4.1 tells us that for every .01 (1 percent) in sales growth, we need an additional $456 × .01 = $4.56 in external financing to support that growth.

TABLE 4.8

HOFFMAN COMPANY Pro Forma Statements of Comprehensive Income and Financial Position

Statement of Comprehensive Income

Sales	$600.0
Costs (80% of sales)	480.0
Taxable income	$120.0
Taxes	40.8
Net income	$ 79.2

Addition to retained earnings	$52.8
Dividends	$26.4

Statement of Financial Position

	$	% of Sales		$	% of Sales
Assets			Liabilities		
Current assets	$240.0	40%	Total debt	$ 250.0	n/a
Net fixed assets	360.0	60	Owners' equity	302.8	n/a
Total assets	$600.0	100%	Total liabilities	$ 552.8	n/a
			External funds needed	$ 47.2	

FIGURE 4.1

External financing needed and growth in sales for the Hoffman Company

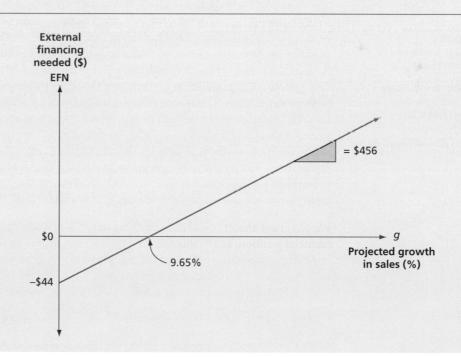

Internal Growth Rate

Looking at Figure 4.1, there is one growth rate of obvious interest. What growth rate can we achieve with no external financing? We call this the **internal growth rate** because it is the rate the firm can maintain with only internal financing. This growth rate corresponds to the point where our line crosses the horizontal axis, that is, the point where EFN is zero. At this point, the required increase in assets is exactly equal to the addition to retained earnings, and EFN is therefore zero.

Figure 4.1 shows that this rate is just under 10 percent.

We can easily calculate this rate by setting EFN equal to zero:

$$EFN = -p(S)R + [A - p(S)R] \times g \qquad\qquad [4.4]$$
$$g = p(S)R/[A - p(S)R]$$
$$= .132(\$500)(2/3)/[\$500 - .132(\$500)(2/3)]$$
$$= 44/[500 - 44]$$
$$= 44/456 = 9.65\%$$

Hoffman can therefore grow at a 9.65 percent rate before any external financing is required. With a little algebra, we can restate the expression for the internal growth rate (Equation 4.4) as:[7]

$$\text{Internal growth rate} = \frac{ROA \times R}{1 - ROA \times R} \qquad\qquad [4.5]$$

For Hoffman, we can check this by recomputing the 9.65 percent internal growth rate

$$= \frac{.132 \times 2/3}{1 - .132 \times 2/3}$$

Financial Policy and Growth

Suppose Hoffman, for whatever reason, does not wish to sell any new equity. As we discuss in Chapter 15, one possible reason is simply that new equity sales can be very expensive. Alternatively, the current owners may not wish to bring in new owners or contribute additional equity themselves. For a small business or a start-up, the reason may be even more compelling: All sources of new equity have likely already been tapped and the only way to increase equity is through additions to retained earnings.

In addition, we assume that Hoffman wishes to maintain its current debt/equity ratio. To be more specific, Hoffman (and its lenders) regard its current debt policy as optimal. We discuss why a particular mixture of debt and equity might be better than any other in Chapters 14 and 15. For now, we say that Hoffman has a fixed **debt capacity** relative to total equity. If the debt/equity ratio declines, Hoffman has excess debt capacity and can comfortably borrow additional funds.

Assuming that Hoffman does borrow to its debt capacity, what growth rate can be achieved? The answer is the **sustainable growth rate (SGR),** the maximum growth rate a firm can achieve with no external *equity* financing while it maintains a constant debt/equity ratio. To find the sustainable growth rate, we go back to Equation 4.2 and add another term for new borrowings (up to debt capacity). One way to see where the amount of new borrowings comes from is to relate it to the addition to retained earnings. Because this addition increases equity, it reduces the debt/equity ratio. Since sustainable growth is based on a constant debt/equity ratio, we use new borrowings to top up debt. Because we are now allowing new borrowings, EFN* refers to outside equity only. Because no new outside equity is available, EFN* = 0 as the D/E ratio is constant,

$$\therefore D/E = \frac{\text{New borrowing}}{\text{Addition to retained earnings}}$$

$$\text{New borrowing} = D/E[p(S)R(1 + g)]$$

$$EFN^* = \text{Increase in total assets} - \text{Addition to retained earnings} - \text{New borrowing} \qquad [4.6]$$
$$= A(g) - p(S)R \times (1 + g) - p(S)R \times (1 + g)[D/E]$$
$$EFN^* = 0$$

With some algebra we can solve for the sustainable growth rate.

$$g^* = ROE \times R/[1 - ROE \times R] \qquad\qquad [4.7]$$

This growth rate is called the firm's sustainable growth rate (SGR).

For example, for the Hoffman Company, we already know that the ROE is 26.4 percent and the retention ratio, R, is 2/3. The sustainable growth rate is thus:

debt capacity
The ability to borrow to increase firm value.

sustainable growth rate (SGR)
The growth rate a firm can maintain given its debt capacity, ROE, and retention ratio.

---

[7]To derive Equation 4.5 from (4.4) divide through by A and recognize that ROA = $p(S)/A$.

$$g^* = (ROE \times R)/(1 - ROE \times R)$$
$$= .176 \,/\, .824$$
$$= 21.4\%$$

This tells us that Hoffman can increase its sales and assets at a rate of 21.4 percent per year without selling any additional equity and without changing its debt ratio or payout ratio. If a growth rate in excess of this is desired or predicted, something has to give.

To better see that the SGR is 21.4 percent (and to check our answer), we can fill out the pro forma financial statements assuming that Hoffman's sales increase at exactly the SGR. We do this to verify that if Hoffman's sales do grow at 21.4 percent, all needed financing can be obtained without the need to sell new equity, and, at the same time, the debt/equity ratio can be maintained at its current level of 1.

To get started, sales increase from $500 to $500 × (1 + .214) = $607. Assuming, as before, that costs are proportional to sales, the statement of comprehensive income would be:

HOFFMAN COMPANY
Pro Forma Statement of Comprehensive Income

Sales	$607
Costs (80% of sales)	486
Taxable income	$121
Taxes	41
Net income	$ 80

Given that the retention ratio, R, stays at 2/3, the addition to retained earnings is $80 × (2/3) = $53, and the dividend paid is $80 − 53 = $27.

We fill out the pro forma statement of financial position (Table 4.9) just as we did earlier. Note that the owners' equity rises from $250 to $303 because the addition to retained earnings is $53. As illustrated, EFN is $53. If Hoffman borrows this amount, its total debt rises to $250 + 53 = $303. The debt/equity ratio therefore is $303/$303 − 1 as desired, thereby verifying our earlier calculations. At any other growth rate, something would have to change.

TABLE 4.9

HOFFMAN COMPANY
Pro Forma Statement of Financial Position

	$	% of Sales		$	% of Sales
Current assets	$242	40	Total debt	$250	n/a
Net fixed assets	364	60	Owners' equity	303	n/a
Total assets	$606	100	Total liabilities	$553	n/a
			External funds needed	$ 53	

To maintain the debt/equity ratio at 1, Hoffman can increase debt to $338, an increase of $88. This leaves $412 − $88 = $324 to be raised by external equity. If this is not available, Hoffman could try to raise the full $412 in additional debt. This would rocket the debt/equity ratio to ($250 + $412)/$338 = 1.96, basically doubling the target amount.

Given that the firm's bankers and other external lenders likely had considerable say over the target D/E in the first place, it is highly unlikely that Hoffman could obtain this much additional debt. The most likely outcome is that if Hoffman insists on doubling sales, the firm would grow bankrupt.

EXAMPLE 4.2: Growing Bankrupt

Suppose the management of Hoffman Company is not satisfied with a growth rate of 21 percent. Instead, the company wants to expand rapidly and double its sales to $1,000 next year. What will happen? To answer this question we go back to the starting point of our previous example.

We know that the sustainable growth rate for Hoffman is 21.3 percent, so doubling sales (100 percent growth) is not possible unless the company obtains outside equity financing or allows its debt/equity ratio to balloon beyond 1. We can prove this with simple pro forma statements.

Pro Forma Statement of Comprehensive Income

Sales		$ 1,000
Costs (80% of sales)		800
Taxable income		$ 200
Taxes		68
Net income		$ 132
Dividends (1/3)	$ 44	
Addition to retained earnings	88	

Pro Forma Statement of Financial Position

Current assets	$ 400	Total debt	$250
Fixed assets	600	Owners' equity	338
Total assets	$ 1,000	Total liabilities	$588
		External funds needed	$412

Determinants of Growth

In the last chapter, we saw that the return on equity could be decomposed into its various components using the Du Pont identity. Because ROE appears prominently in the determination of the SGR, the important factors in determining ROE are also important determinants of growth. To see this, recall that from the Du Pont identity, ROE can be written as:

$$\text{ROE} = \text{Profit margin} \times \text{Total asset turnover} \times \text{Equity multiplier}\,[8]$$

Using our current symbols for these ratios,

$$\text{ROE} = p(S/A)(1 + D/E)$$

If we substitute this into our expression for g^* (SGR), we see that the sustainable growth rate can be written in greater detail as:

$$g^* = \frac{p(S/A)(1 + D/E) \times R}{1 - p(S/A)(1 + D/E) \times R} \qquad [4.8]$$

Writing the SGR out in this way makes it look a little complicated, but it does highlight the various important factors determining the ability of a firm to grow.

Examining our expression for the SGR, we see that growth depends on the following four factors:

1. **Profit margin.** An increase in profit margin, p, increases the firm's ability to generate funds internally and thereby increase its sustainable growth.

2. **Dividend policy.** A decrease in the percentage of net income paid out as dividends increases the retention ratio, R. This increases internally generated equity and thus increases sustainable growth.

3. **Financial policy.** An increase in the debt/equity ratio, D/E, increases the firm's financial leverage. Since this makes additional debt financing available, it increases the sustainable growth rate.

---

[8] Remember that the equity multiplier is the same as 1 plus the debt/equity ratio.

4. Total asset turnover. An increase in the firm's total asset turnover, S/A, increases the sales generated for each dollar in assets. This decreases the firm's need for new assets as sales grow and thereby increases the sustainable growth rate. Notice that increasing total asset turnover is the same thing as the decreasing capital intensity.

The sustainable growth rate is a very useful planning number. What it illustrates is the explicit relationship between the firm's four major areas of concern: its operating efficiency as measured by p, its asset use efficiency as measured by S/A, its dividend policy as measured by R, and its financial policy as measured by D/E.

Given values for all four of these, only one growth rate can be achieved. This is an important point, so it bears restating:

> If a firm does not wish to sell new equity and its profit margin, dividend policy, financial policy, and total asset turnover (or capital intensity) are all fixed, there is only one possible maximum growth rate.

As we described early in this chapter, one of the primary benefits to financial planning is to ensure internal consistency among the firm's various goals. The sustainable growth rate captures this element nicely. For this reason, sustainable growth is included in the software used by commercial lenders at several Canadian chartered banks in analyzing their accounts.

Also, we now see how to use a financial planning model to test the feasibility of a planned growth rate. If sales are to grow at a rate higher than the sustainable growth rate, the firm must increase profit margins, increase total asset turnover, increase financial leverage, increase earnings retention, or sell new shares.

At the other extreme, suppose the firm is losing money (has a negative profit margin) or is paying out more than 100 percent of earnings in dividends so that R is negative. In each of these cases, the negative SGR signals the rate at which sales and assets must shrink. Firms can achieve negative growth by selling assets and closing divisions. The cash generated by selling assets is often used to pay down excessive debt taken on earlier to fund rapid expansion. For example, in 2011, Lionsgate Entertainment, the Vancouver based mini-studio, sold its non-core assets to pay down its debt. This was done primarily to address investor worries and to strengthen its statement of financial position.

A Note on Sustainable Growth Rate Calculations

Very commonly, the sustainable growth rate is calculated using just the numerator in our expression, ROE × R. This causes some confusion, which we can clear up here. The issue has to do with how ROE is computed. Recall that ROE is calculated as net income divided by total equity. If total equity is taken from an ending statement of financial position (as we have done consistently, and is commonly done in practice), then our formula is the right one. However, if total equity is from the beginning of the period, then the simpler formula is the correct one.

EXAMPLE 4.3: Sustainable Growth

The Sandar Company has a debt/equity ratio of .5, a profit margin of 3 percent, a dividend payout of 40 percent, and a capital intensity ratio of 1. What is its sustainable growth rate? If Sandar desires a 10 percent SGR and plans to achieve this goal by improving profit margins, what would you think?

The sustainable growth rate is:

$g^* = .03(1)(1 + .5)(1 − .40)/[1 − .03(1)(1 + .5)(1 − .40)]$
$\qquad = 2.77\%$

To achieve a 10 percent growth rate, the profit margin has to rise. To see this, assume that g^* is equal to 10 percent and then solve for p:

$.10 = p(1.5)(.6)/[1 − p(1.5)(.5)]$
$\qquad p = .1/.99 = 10.1\%$

For the plan to succeed, the necessary increase in profit margin is substantial, from 3 percent to about 10 percent. This may not be feasible.

In principle, you'll get exactly the same sustainable growth rate regardless of which way you calculate it (as long you match up the ROE calculation with the right formula). In reality, you may see some differences because of accounting-related complications. By the way, if you use the average of beginning and ending equity (as some advocate), yet another formula is needed. Note: all of our comments here apply to the internal growth rate as well.

One more point that is important to note is that for the sustainable growth calculations to work, assets must increase at the same rate as sales as shown in [4.6]. If any items do not change at the same rate, the formulas will not work properly.

Concept Questions

1. What are the determinants of growth?
2. How is a firm's sustainable growth related to its accounting return on equity (ROE)?
3. What does it mean if a firm's sustainable growth rate is negative?

IN THEIR OWN WORDS...

Robert C. Higgins on Sustainable Growth

MOST FINANCIAL OFFICERS know intuitively that it takes money to make money. Rapid sales growth requires increased assets in the form of accounts receivable, inventory, and fixed plant, which, in turn, require money to pay for assets. They also know that if their company does not have the money when needed, it can literally "grow broke." The sustainable growth equation states these intuitive truths explicitly.

Sustainable growth is often used by bankers and other external analysts to assess a company's creditworthiness. They are aided in this exercise by several sophisticated computer software packages that provide detailed analyses of the company's past financial performance, including its annual sustainable growth rate.

Bankers use this information in several ways. Quick comparison of a company's actual growth rate to its sustainable rate tells the banker what issues will be at the top of management's financial agenda. If actual growth consistently exceeds sustainable growth, management's problem will be where to get the cash to finance growth. The banker thus can anticipate interest in loan products. Conversely, if sustainable growth consistently exceeds actual, the banker had best be prepared to talk about investment products, because management's problem will be what to do with all the cash that keeps piling up in the till.

Bankers also find the sustainable growth equation useful for explaining to financially inexperienced small business owners and overly optimistic entrepreneurs that, for the long-run

viability of their business, it is necessary to keep growth and profitability in proper balance.

Finally, comparison of actual to sustainable growth rates helps a banker understand why a loan applicant needs money and for how long the need might continue. In one instance, a loan applicant requested $100,000 to pay off several insistent suppliers and promised to repay in a few months when he collected some accounts receivable that were coming due. A sustainable growth analysis revealed that the firm had been growing at four to six times its sustainable growth rate and that this pattern was likely to continue in the foreseeable future. This alerted the banker that impatient suppliers were only a symptom of the much more fundamental disease of overly rapid growth, and that a $100,000 loan would likely prove to be only the down payment on a much larger, multiyear commitment.

Robert C. Higgins is Professor Emeritus of Finance and Marguerite Reimers Endowed Faculty Fellow at the University of Washington Michael G. Foster School of Business. He pioneered the use of sustainable growth as a tool for financial analysis.

4.5 | Some Caveats on Financial Planning Models

Financial planning models do not always ask the right questions. A primary reason is that they tend to rely on accounting relationships and not financial relationships. In particular, the three basic elements of firm value tend to get left out, namely, cash flow size, risk, and timing.

Because of this, financial planning models sometimes do not produce output that gives the user many meaningful clues about what strategies would lead to increases in value. Instead, they divert the user's attention to questions concerning the association of, say, the debt/equity ratio and firm growth.

The financial model we used for the Hoffman Company was simple, in fact, too simple. Our model, like many in use today, is really an accounting statement generator at heart. Such models are useful for pointing out inconsistencies and reminding us of financial needs, but they offer very little guidance concerning what to do about these problems.

In closing our discussion, we should add that financial planning is an iterative process. Plans are created, examined, and modified over and over. The final plan is a negotiated result between all the different parties to the process. In practice, long-term financial planning in some corporations relies too much on a top-down approach. Senior management has a growth target in mind and it is up to the planning staff to rework and ultimately deliver a plan to meet that target. Such plans are often made feasible (on paper or a computer screen) by unrealistically optimistic assumptions on sales growth and target debt/equity ratios. The plans collapse when lower sales make it impossible to service debt. This is what happened to Campeau's takeover of Federated Department Stores, as we discuss in Chapter 23.

As a negotiated result, the final plan implicitly contains different goals in different areas and also satisfies many constraints. For this reason, such a plan need not be a dispassionate assessment of what we think the future will bring; it may instead be a means of reconciling the planned activities of different groups and a way of setting common goals for the future.

Concept Questions

1. What are some important elements often missing in financial planning models?
2. Why do we say that planning is an iterative process?

4.6 | SUMMARY AND CONCLUSIONS

Financial planning forces the firm to think about the future. We have examined a number of features of the planning process. We describe what financial planning can accomplish and the components of a financial model. We go on to develop the relationship between growth and financing needs. Two growth rates, internal and sustainable, are summarized in Table 4.10. The table recaps the key difference between the two growth rates. The internal growth rate is the maximum growth rate that can be achieved with no external financing of any kind. The sustainable growth rate is the maximum growth rate that can be achieved with no external equity financing while maintaining a constant debt/equity ratio. For Hoffman, the internal growth rate is 9.65 percent and the sustainable growth rate is 21.3 percent. The sustainable growth rate is higher because the calculation allows for debt financing up to a limit set by the target debt/equity ratio. We discuss how a financial planning model is useful in exploring that relationship.

Corporate financial planning should not become a purely mechanical activity. When it does, it probably focuses on the wrong things. In particular, plans all too often are formulated in terms of a growth target with no explicit linkage to value creation, and they frequently are overly concerned with accounting statements. Nevertheless, the alternative to financial planning is stumbling into the future backwards.

TABLE 4.10   Summary of internal and sustainable growth rates from Hoffman Company example

I. INTERNAL GROWTH RATE

Internal growth rate $= \dfrac{ROA \times R}{1 - ROA \times R} = \dfrac{.132 \times 2/3}{1 - 0.132 \times 2/3} = 9.65\%$

where

$\quad$ ROA = Return on assets = Net income/Total assets = 13.2%

$\quad\quad$ R = Plowback (retention) ratio = 2/3

$\quad\quad\quad$ = Addition to retained earnings/Net income

The internal growth rate is the maximum growth rate that can be achieved with no external financing of any kind.

II. SUSTAINABLE GROWTH RATE

Sustainable growth rate $= \dfrac{ROE \times R}{1 - ROE \times R} = \dfrac{0.264 \times (2/3)}{1 - 0.264 \times (2/3)} = 21.3\%$

where

$\quad$ ROE = Return on equity = Net income/Total equity = 26.4%

$\quad\quad$ R = Plowback (retention) ratio = 2/3

$\quad\quad\quad$ = Addition to retained earnings/Net income

The sustainable growth rate is the maximum growth rate that can be achieved with no external equity financing while maintaining a constant debt/equity ratio.

Key Terms

aggregation (page 86)

capital intensity ratio (page 91)

debt capacity (page 98)

dividend payout ratio (page 90)

external financing needed (EFN) (page 92)

internal growth rate (page 97)

percentage of sales approach (page 90)

planning horizon (page 86)

retention ratio or plowback ratio (page 91)

sustainable growth rate (SGR) (page 98)

Chapter Review Problems and Self-Test

4.1   **Calculating EFN** Based on the following information for the Skandia Mining Company, what is EFN if sales are predicted to grow by 10 percent? Use the percentage of sales approach and assume the company is operating at full capacity. The payout ratio is constant.

SKANDIA MINING COMPANY
Financial Statements

Statement of Comprehensive Income		
Sales		$ 4,250.0
Costs		3,876.0
Taxable income		$ 374.0
Taxes (34%)		127.2
Net income		$ 246.8
Dividends	$ 82.4	
Addition to retained earnings	164.4	

Statement of Financial Position			
Assets		*Liabilities and Owners' Equity*	
Current assets	$ 900	Current liabilities	$ 500
Net fixed assets	2,200	Long-term debt	$ 1,800
Total	$ 3,100	Owners' equity	800
		Total liabilities and owners' equity	$3,100

4.2   **EFN and Capacity Use** Based on the information in Problem 4.1, what is EFN, assuming 60 percent capacity usage for net fixed assets? Assuming 95 percent capacity?

4.3   **Sustainable Growth** Based on the information in Problem 4.1, what growth rate can Skandia maintain if no external financing is used? What is the sustainable growth rate?

Answers to Self-Test Problems

4.1   We can calculate EFN by preparing the pro forma statements using the percentage of sales approach. Note that sales are forecasted to be $4,250 × 1.10 = $4,675.

SKANDIA MINING COMPANY
Pro Forma Financial Statements
Statement of Comprehensive Income

Sales	$ 4,675.0	Forecast
Costs	4,263.6	91.2% of sales
Taxable income	$ 411.4	
Taxes (34%)	$ 139.9	
Net income	$ 271.5	
Dividends	$ 90.6	33.37% of net
Addition to retained earnings	180.9	income

Statement of Financial Position

Assets			Liabilities and Owners' Equity		
Current assets	$ 990.0	21.18%	Current liabilities	$ 550	11.76%
Net fixed assets	2,420.0	51.76%	Long-term debt	$ 1,800.0	n/a
Total assets	$ 3,410.0	72.94%	Owners' equity	980.9	n/a
			Total liabilities and owners' equity	3,330.9	n/a
			EFN	$ 79.1	n/a

Also applying the formula for EFN in Equation 4.2, we get

$$EFN = A(g) - p(S)R \times (1 + g)$$
$$= 3100\,(0.1) - [.05807588 \times 4250 \times .666126418 \times 1.1]$$
$$= 310 - 180.84$$
$$= 129.16$$

Why is the answer different using two methods? Because, in the percentage of sales approach it was assumed that current liabilities were accounts payable (or a similar account) that spontaneously increases with sales. Hence this amount needs to be deducted from the total assets of $3,100 to get $2,600. If we use this number in the EFN formula, the value is 79.16 which is closer to the answer obtained in sales approach.

4.2　Full-capacity sales are equal to current sales divided by the capacity utilization. At 60 percent of capacity:

$$\$4,250 = .60 \times \text{Full-capacity sales}$$
$$\$7,083 = \text{Full-capacity sales}$$

With a sales level of $4,675, no net new fixed assets will be needed, so our earlier estimate is too high. We estimated an increase in fixed assets of $2,420 - 2,200 = $220. The new EFN will thus be $79.1 - 220 = -$140.9, a surplus. No external financing is needed in this case. At 95 percent capacity, full-capacity sales are $4,474. The ratio of fixed assets to full-capacity sales is thus $2,200/4,474 = 49.17%. At a sales level of $4,675, we will thus need $4,675 × .4917 = $2,298.7 in net fixed assets, an increase of $98.7. This is $220 - 98.7 = $121.3 less than we originally predicted, so the EFN is now $79.1 - 121.3 = $42.2, a surplus. No additional financing is needed.

4.3　Skandia retains R = 1 − .3337 = 66.63% of net income. Return on assets is $246.8/3,100 = 7.96%. The internal growth rate is:

$$\frac{\text{ROA} \times R}{1 - \text{ROA} \times R} = \frac{.0796 \times .6663}{1 - .0796 \times .6663}$$
$$= 5.60\%$$

Return on equity for Skandia is $246.8/800 = 30.85%, so we can calculate the sustainable growth rate as:

$$\frac{\text{ROE} \times R}{1 - \text{ROE} \times R} = \frac{.3085 \times .6663}{1 - .3085 \times .6663}$$
$$R = 25.87\%$$

Concepts Review and Critical Thinking Questions

1.　(LO1) Why do you think most long-term financial planning begins with sales forecasts? Put differently, why are future sales the key input?

2.　(LO1) Would long-range financial planning be more important for a capital intensive company, such as a heavy equipment manufacturer, or an import-export business? Why?

3.　(LO2) Testaburger, Ltd., uses no external financing and maintains a positive retention ratio. When sales grow by 15 percent, the firm has a negative projected EFN. What does this tell you about the firm's internal growth rate? How about the sustainable growth rate? At this same level of sales growth, what will happen to the projected EFN if the retention ratio is increased? What if the retention ratio is decreased? What hap-

pens to the projected EFN if the firm pays out all of its earnings in the form of dividends?

4.　(LO2, 3) Broslofski Co. maintains a positive retention ratio and keeps its debt-equity ratio constant every year. When sales grow by 20 percent, the firm has a negative projected EFN. What does this tell you about the firm's sustainable growth rate? Do you know, with certainty, if the internal growth rate is greater than or less than 20 percent? Why? What happens to the projected EFN if the retention ratio is increased? What if the retention ratio is decreased? What if the retention ratio is zero?

Use the following information to answer the next six questions: A small business called The Grandmother Calendar

Company began selling personalized photo calendar kits. The kits were a hit, and sales soon sharply exceeded forecasts. The rush of orders created a huge backlog, so the company leased more space and expanded capacity, but it still could not keep up with demand. Equipment failed from overuse and quality suffered. Working capital was drained to expand production, and, at the same time, payments from customers were often delayed until the product was shipped. Unable to deliver on orders, the company became so strapped for cash that employee pay cheques began to bounce. Finally, out of cash, the company ceased operations entirely three years later.

5. **(LO6)** Do you think the company would have suffered the same fate if its product had been less popular? Why or why not?

6. **(LO6)** The Grandmother Calendar Company clearly had a cash flow problem. In the context of the cash flow analysis we developed in Chapter 2, what was the impact of customers not paying until orders were shipped?

7. **(LO6)** The firm actually priced its product to be about 20 percent less than that of competitors, even though the Grandmother calendar was more detailed. In retrospect, was this a wise choice?

8. **(LO6)** If the firm was so successful at selling, why wouldn't a bank or some other lender step in and provide it with the cash it needed to continue?

9. **(LO6)** Which is the biggest culprit here: too many orders, too little cash, or too little production capacity?

10. **(LO6)** What are some of the actions that a small company like The Grandmother Calendar Company can take if it finds itself in a situation in which growth in sales outstrips production capacity and available financial resources? What other options (besides expansion of capacity) are available to a company when orders exceed capacity?

Questions and Problems

Basic
(Questions 1–15)

1. **Pro Forma Statements (LO3)** Consider the following simplified financial statements for the Steveston Corporation (assuming no income taxes):

Statement of Comprehensive Income		Statement of Financial Position			
Sales	$ 23,000	Assets	$15,800	Debt	$ 5,200
Costs	16,700			Equity	10,600
Net income	$ 6,300	Total	$15,800	Total	$15,800

Steveston has predicted a sales increase of 15 percent. It has predicted that every item on the statement of financial position will increase by 15 percent as well. Create the pro forma statements and reconcile them. What is the plug variable here?

2. **Pro Forma Statements and EFN (LO2, 3)** In the previous question, assume Steveston pays out half of net income in the form of a cash dividend. Costs and assets vary with sales, but debt and equity do not. Prepare the pro forma statements and determine the external financing needed.

3. **Calculating EFN (LO2)** The most recent financial statements for Marpole Inc. are shown here (assuming no income taxes):

Statement of Comprehensive Income		Statement of Financial Position			
Sales	$ 6,300	Assets	$18,300	Debt	$12,400
Costs	3,890			Equity	5,900
Net income	$ 2,410	Total	$18,300	Total	$18,300

Assets and costs are proportional to sales. Debt and equity are not. No dividends are paid. Next year's sales are projected to be $7,434. What is the external financing needed?

4. **EFN (LO2)** The most recent financial statements for Suncrest Inc. are shown here:

Statement of Comprehensive Income		Statement of Financial Position			
Sales	$19,500	Assets	$98,000	Debt	$ 52,500
Costs	15,000			Equity	45,500
Taxable income	$ 4,500	Total	$98,000	Total	$98,000
Taxes (40%)	1,800				
Net income	$ 2,700				

Assets and costs are proportional to sales. Debt and equity are not. A dividend of $1,400 was paid, and Suncrest wishes to maintain a constant payout ratio. Next year's sales are projected to be $21,840. What is the external financing needed?

5. **EFN (LO2)** The most recent financial statements for Kitsilano Inc. are shown here:

Statement of Comprehensive Income		Statement of Financial Position			
Sales	$ 4,200	Current Assets	$ 3,600	Current Liabilities	$ 2,100
Costs	3,300	Fixed Assets	7,900	Long-term debt	3,650
Taxable income	$ 900			Equity	$ 5,750
Taxes (34%)	306	Total	$11,500	Total	$11,500
Net income	$ 594				

Assets, costs, and current liabilities are proportional to sales. Long-term debt and equity are not. Kitsilano maintains a constant 40 percent dividend payout ratio. Like every other firm in its industry, next year's sales are projected to increase by exactly 15 percent. What is the external financing needed?

6. **Calculating Internal Growth (LO5)** The most recent financial statements for Burnaby Co. are shown here:

Statement of Comprehensive Income		Statement of Financial Position			
Sales	$13,250	Current Assets	$10,400	Debt	$17,500
Costs	9,480	Fixed Assets	28,750	Equity	21,650
Taxable income	$ 3,770	Total	$39,150	Total	$ 39,150
Taxes (40%)	1,508				
Net income	$ 2,262				

Assets and costs are proportional to sales. Debt and equity are not. Burnaby maintains a constant 30 percent dividend payout ratio. No external equity financing is possible. What is the internal growth rate?

7. **Calculating Sustainable Growth (LO5)** For the company in the previous problem, what is the sustainable growth rate?

8. **Sales and Growth (LO2)** The most recent financial statements for Cariboo Co. are shown here:

Statement of Comprehensive Income		Statement of Financial Position			
Sales	$ 42,000	Current Assets	$ 21,000	Long-term Debt	$ 51,000
Costs	28,500	Fixed Assets	86,000	Equity	56,000
Taxable income	$ 13,500	Total	$107,000	Total	$107,000
Taxes (34%)	4,590				
Net income	$ 8,910				

Assets and costs are proportional to sales. The company maintains a constant 30 percent dividend payout ratio and a constant debt-equity ratio. What is the maximum increase in sales that can be sustained, assuming no new equity is issued?

9. **Calculating Retained Earnings from Pro Forma Income (LO3)** Consider the following statement of comprehensive income for the Dartmoor Corporation:

DARTMOOR CORPORATION
Statement of Comprehensive Income

Sales	$ 38,000
Costs	18,400
Taxable income	$ 19,600
Taxes (34%)	6,664
Net income	$ 12,936
Dividends	$5,200
Addition to retained earnings	7,736

A 20 percent growth rate in sales is projected. Prepare a pro forma statement of comprehensive income assuming costs vary with sales and the dividend payout ratio is constant. What is the projected addition to retained earnings?

10. **Applying Percentage of Sales (LO3)** The statement of financial position for the Dartmoor Corporation follows. Based on this information and the statement of comprehensive income in the previous problem, supply the missing information using the percentage of sales approach. Assume that accounts payable vary with sales, whereas notes payable do not. Put "n/a" where needed.

DARTMOOR CORPORATION
Statement of Financial Position

Assets	$	Percentage of Sales	Liabilities and Owners' Equity	$	Percentage of Sales
Current assets			Current liabilities		
Cash	$ 3,050	_____	Accounts payable	$ 1,300	_____
Accounts receivable	6,900	_____	Notes payable	6,800	_____
Inventory	7,600	_____	Total	$ 8,100	_____
Total	$17,550	_____	Long-term debt	$ 25,000	_____
Fixed assets			Owners' equity		
Net plant and			Common stock and paid-in surplus	$15,000	_____
equipment	$ 34,500	_____	Retained earnings	3,950	_____
Total assets	$ 52,050	_____	Total	$ 18,950	_____
			Total liabilities and owners' equity	$ 52,050	_____

11. **EFN and Sales (LO2, 3)** From the previous two questions, prepare a pro forma statement of financial position showing EFN, assuming a 15 percent increase in sales, no new external debt or equity financing, and a constant payout ratio.

12. **Internal Growth (LO5)** If Sunbury Hobby Shop has a 8 percent ROA and a 20 percent payout ratio, what is its internal growth rate?

13. **Sustainable Growth (LO5)** If the Whalley Corp. has a 15 percent ROE and a 25 percent payout ratio, what is its sustainable growth rate?

14. **Sustainable Growth (LO5)** Based on the following information, calculate the sustainable growth rate for Lesner's Kickboxing:

> Profit margin = 8.2%
> Capital intensity ratio = .75
> Debt-equity ratio = .40
> Net income = $43,000
> Dividends = $12,000

What is the ROE here?

15. **Sustainable Growth (LO5)** Assuming the following ratios are constant, what is the sustainable growth rate?

> Total asset turnover = 2.50
> Profit margin = 7.8%
> Equity multiplier = 1.80
> Payout ratio = 60%

Intermediate
(Questions
16–29)

16. **Full-Capacity Sales (LO3)** Mud Bay Services Inc. is currently operating at only 95 percent of fixed asset capacity. Current sales are $550,000. How fast can sales grow before any new fixed assets are needed?

17. **Fixed Assets and Capacity Usage (LO3)** For the company in the previous problem, suppose fixed assets are $440,000 and sales are projected to grow to $630,000. How much in new fixed assets are required to support this growth in sales?

18. **Full-Capacity Sales (LO3)** If a company is operating at 60 percent of fixed asset capacity and current sales are $350,000, how fast can that company grow before any new fixed assets are needed?

19. **Full-Capacity Sales (LO4)** Elgin Brick Manufacturing sold $200,000 of red bricks in the last year. They were operating at 94 percent of fixed asset capacity. How fast can Elgin Brick grow before they need to purchase new fixed assets?

20. **Growth and Profit Margin (LO4)** Hazelmere Co. wishes to maintain a growth rate of 12 percent a year, a debt-equity ratio of 1.20, and a dividend payout ratio of 30 percent. The ratio of total assets to sales is constant at 0.75. What profit margin must the firm achieve?

21. **Growth and Debt-Equity Ratio (LO4)** A firm wishes to maintain a growth rate of 11.5 percent and a dividend payout ratio of 30 percent. The ratio of total assets to sales is constant at 0.60, and profit margin is 6.2 percent. If the firm also wishes to maintain a constant debt-equity ratio, what must it be?

22. **Growth and Assets (LO4)** A firm wishes to maintain an internal growth rate of 7 percent and a dividend payout ratio of 25 percent. The current profit margin is 5 percent and the firm uses no external financing sources. What must total asset turnover be?

 23. **Sustainable Growth (LO5)** Based on the following information, calculate the sustainable growth rate for Zeppelin Guitars Inc.:

> Profit margin = 4.8%
> Total asset turnover = 1.25
> Total debt ratio = 0.65
> Payout ratio = 30%

What is the ROA here?

24. **Sustainable Growth and Outside Financing (LO2, 5)** You've collected the following information about Grandview Toy Company Inc.:

> Sales = $195,000
> Net income = $17,500
> Dividends = $9,300
> Total debt = $86,000
> Total equity = $58,000

What is the sustainable growth rate for Grandview Toy Company Inc.? If it does grow at this rate, how much new borrowing will take place in the coming year, assuming a constant debt-equity ratio? What growth rate could be supported with no outside financing at all?

 25. **Sustainable Growth Rate (LO5)** Langley County Inc. had equity of $135,000 at the beginning of the year. At the end of the year, the company had total assets of $250,000. During the year the company sold no new equity. Net income for the year was $19,000 and dividends were $2,500. What is the sustainable growth rate for the company? What is the sustainable growth rate if you use the formula ROE × R and beginning of period equity? What is the sustainable growth rate if you use end of period equity in this formula? Is this number too high or too low? Why?

26. **Internal Growth Rates (LO5)** Calculate the internal growth rate for the company in the previous problem. Now calculate the internal growth rate using ROA × R for both beginning of period and end of period total assets. What do you observe?

27. **Calculating EFN (LO2)** The most recent financial statements for Hopington Tours Inc. follow. Sales for 2013 are projected to grow by 20 percent. Interest expense will remain constant; the tax rate and the dividend payout rate will also remain constant. Costs, other expenses, current assets, and accounts payable increase spontaneously with sales. If the firm is operating at full capacity and no new debt or equity is issued, what is the external financing needed to support the 20 percent growth rate in sales?

HOPINGTON TOURS INC.
2012 Statement of Comprehensive Income

Sales	$ 929,000
Costs	723,000
Other expenses	19,000
Earnings before interest and taxes	$ 187,000
Interest paid	14,000
Taxable income	$ 173,000
Taxes (35%)	60,550
Net income	$ 112,450
Dividends	$33,735
Addition to retained earnings	78,715

HOPINGTON TOURS INC.
Statement of Financial Position as of December 31, 2012

Assets		Liabilities and Owners' Equity	
Current assets		Current liabilities	
Cash	$ 25,300	Accounts payable	$ 68,000
Accounts receivable	40,700	Notes payable	17,000
Inventory	86,900	Total	$ 85,000
Total	$152,900	Long-term debt	$158,000
Fixed assets		Owners' equity	
Net plant and		Common stock and paid-in surplus	$140,000
equipment	$413,000	Retained earnings	182,900
		Total	$322,900
Total assets	$565,900	Total liabilities and owners' equity	$565,900

28. **Capacity Usage and Growth (LO2)** In the previous problem, suppose the firm was operating at only 80 percent capacity in 2012. What is EFN now?

29. **Calculating EFN (LO2)** In Problem 27, suppose the firm wishes to keep its debt-equity ratio constant. What is EFN now?

Challenge 30. **EFN and Internal Growth (LO2, 5)** Redo Problem 27 using sales growth rates of 15 and 25 percent in addition to 20 percent. (Questions 30–32) Illustrate graphically the relationship between EFN and the growth rate, and use this graph to determine the relationship between them. At what growth rate is the EFN equal to zero? Why is this internal growth rate different from that found by using the equation in the text?

31. **EFN and Sustainable Growth (LO2, 5)** Redo Problem 29 using sales growth rates of 30 and 35 percent in addition to 20 percent. Illustrate graphically the relationship between EFN and the growth rate, and use this graph to determine the relationship between them. At what growth rate is the EFN equal to zero? Why is this sustainable growth rate different from that found by using the equation in the text?

32. **Constraints on Growth (LO4)** Aberdeen Records Inc. wishes to maintain a growth rate of 12 percent per year and a debt-equity ratio of .30. Profit margin is 6.70 percent, and the ratio of total assets to sales is constant at 1.35. Is this growth rate possible? To answer, determine what the dividend payout ratio must be. How do you interpret the result?

33. **EFN (LO2)** Define the following:

S = Previous year's sales
A = Total assets
E = Total equity
g = Projected growth in sales
PM = Profit margin
b = Retention (plowback) ratio

Assuming all debt is constant, show that EFN can be written as follows:

EFN = −PM(S)b + (A − PM(S)b) × g

Hint: Asset needs will equal $A \times g$. The addition to retained earnings will equal PM(S) $b \times (1 + g)$.

34. **Growth Rates (LO3)** Based on the result in Problem 33, show that the internal and sustainable growth rates are as given in the chapter. *Hint:* For the internal growth rate, set EFN equal to zero and solve for g.

35. **Sustainable Growth Rate (LO3)** In the chapter, we discussed the two versions of the sustainable growth rate formula. Derive the formula ROE × b from the formula given in the chapter, where ROE is based on beginning of period equity. Also, derive the formula ROA × b from the internal growth rate formula.

MINI CASE

After Ed completed the ratio analysis for Tuxedo Air (see Chapter 3), Mark and Jack approached him about planning for next year's sales. The company had historically used little planning for investment needs. As a result, the company experienced some challenging times because of cash flow problems. The lack of planning resulted in missed sales, as well as periods where Mark and Jack were unable to draw salaries. To this end, they would like Ed to prepare a financial plan for the next year so the company can begin to address any outside investment requirements. The statements of comprehensive income and financial position are shown here:

Questions

1. Calculate the internal growth rate and sustainable growth rate for Tuxedo Air. What do these numbers mean?

2. Tuxedo Air is planning for a growth rate of 12 percent next year. Calculate the EFN for the company assuming the company is operating at full capacity. Can the company's sales increase at this growth rate?

3. Most assets can be increased as a percentage of sales. For instance, cash can be increased by any amount. However, fixed assets must be increased in specific amounts because it is impossible, as a practical matter, to buy part of a new plant or machine. In this case, a company has a "staircase" or "lumpy" fixed cost structure. Assume Tuxedo Air is currently producing at 100 percent capacity. As a result, to increase production, the company must set up an entirely new line at a cost of $5,000,000. Calculate the new EFN with this assumption. What does this imply about capacity utilization for the company next year?

Tuxedo Air Inc.
2012 Statement of Comprehensive Income

Sales	$ 30,499,420
Cost of goods sold	22,224,580
Other expenses	3,867,500
Depreciation	1,366,680
EBIT	$ 3,040,660
Interest	478,240
Taxable income	$ 2,562,420
Taxes (40%)	1,024,968
Net income	1,537,452

Dividends	$560,000	
Addition to retained earnings	977,452	

Tuxedo Air Inc.
2012 Statement of Financial Position

Assets			Liabilities and Owners' Equity		
Current Assets			Current liabilities		
Cash	$	441,000	Accounts payable	$	889,000
Accounts receivable		708,400	Notes payable		2,030,000
Inventory		1,037,120	Total		2,919,000
Total	$	2,186,520	Long-term debt	$	5,320,000
Fixed assets			Owners' equity		
Net plant and equipment	$	16,122,400	Common stock	$	350,000
			Retained earnings		9,719,920
			Total equity		10,069,920
Total assets	$	18,308,920	Total liabilities and owners' equity	$	18,308,920

Internet Application Questions

1. Go to theglobeandmail.com/globe-investor/ and enter the ticker symbol "TRP-T" for TransCanada Corp. When you get the quote, follow the "Analysts" link. What is projected earnings growth for next year? For the next five years? How do these earnings growth projections compare to the industry and to the TSX-S&P index?

2. You can find the homepage for Barrick at barrick.com. Go to the "Annual & Quarterly Report" under "Investors" menu. Using the growth in sales for the most recent year as the projected sales growth rate for next year, construct a pro forma statements of comprehensive income and financial position.

3. Locate the most recent annual financial statements for Canadian Tire at corp.canadiantire.ca by clicking on "Investors" and then on "Annual Reports." Using the information from the financial statements, what is the internal growth rate for Canadian Tire? What is the sustainable growth rate?

PART 3

CHAPTER 5

INTRODUCTION TO VALUATION: THE TIME VALUE OF MONEY

Courtesy of Canadian Tire

In 1922, two brothers from Toronto, John W. Billes and Alfred J. Billes, with a combined savings of $1,800, bought the Hamilton Tire and Garage Limited at the corner of Gerrard and Hamilton streets in Toronto. In 1923, this company was sold and the brothers set up a new company under the name Canadian Tire Corp. at the corner of Yonge and Isabella streets. Canadian Tire is now one of Canada's top 60 publicly traded companies and is listed in the Toronto Stock Exchange. The market capitalization of Canadian Tire in January 2012 was $5.3 billion.

Assuming that the owners were still alive and sold the company in 2012 for $5.3 billion, is giving up $1,800 in exchange for $5.3 billion in 90 years a good deal? On the plus side the owners get back around three million times the money they had invested. That probably sounds excellent, but on the down side, they had to wait 90 long years to get it. What you need to know is how to analyze this trade-off; this chapter gives you the tools you need.

Learning Objectives ▶

After studying this chapter, you should understand:

LO1 How to determine the future value of an investment made today.

LO2 How to determine the present value of cash to be received at a future date.

LO3 How to find the return on an investment.

LO4 How long it takes for an investment to reach a desired value.

One of the basic problems that financial managers face is how to determine the value today of cash flows that are expected in the future. For example, suppose your province's finance minister asked your advice on overhauling the provincial lottery with a view toward increasing revenues to help balance the budget. One attractive idea is to increase the size of the prizes while easing the strain on the treasury by spreading out the payments over time. Instead of offering $1 million paid immediately, the new lottery would pay $1 million in 10 annual payments of $100,000. How much money would this idea save the province? The answer depends on the time value of money, the subject of this chapter.

In the most general sense, the phrase *time value of money* refers to the fact that a dollar in hand today is worth more than a dollar promised at some time in the future. On a practical level, one reason for this is that you could earn interest while you waited; so a dollar today would grow to more than a dollar later. The trade-off between money now and money later thus depends on, among other things, the rate you can earn by investing. Our goal in this chapter is to explicitly evaluate this trade-off between dollars today and dollars at some future time.

A thorough understanding of the material in this chapter is critical to understanding material in subsequent chapters, so you should study it with particular care. We will present a number of examples in this chapter. In many problems, your answer may differ from ours slightly. This can happen because of rounding and is not a cause for concern.

5.1 | Future Value and Compounding

future value (FV)
The amount an investment is worth after one or more periods. Also compound value.

We begin by studying future value. **Future value (FV)** refers to the amount of money to which an investment would grow over some length of time at some given interest rate. Put another way, future value is the cash value of an investment sometime in the future. We start out by considering the simplest case, a single-period investment.

Investing for a Single Period

Suppose you were to invest $100 in a savings account that pays 10 percent interest per year. How much will you have in one year? You would have $110. This $110 is equal to your original *principal* of $100 plus $10 in interest that you earn. We say that $110 is the future value (FV) of $100 invested for one year at 10 percent, and we simply mean that $100 today is worth $110 in one year, given that 10 percent is the interest rate.

In general, if you invest for one period at an interest rate of *r*, your investment grows to $(1 + r)$ per dollar invested. In our example, *r* is 10 percent, so your investment grows to $(1 + .10) = 1.1$ dollars per dollar invested. You invested $100 in this case, so you ended up with $100 \times (1.10) = \$110$.

You might wonder if the single period in this example has to be a year. The answer is no. For example, if the interest rate were 2 percent per quarter, your $100 would grow to $100 \times (1 + .02) = \$102$ by the end of the quarter. You might also wonder if 2 percent every quarter is the same as 8 percent per year. The answer is again no, and we'll explain why a little later.

Investing for More than One Period

Going back to your $100 investment, what will you have after two years, assuming the interest rate doesn't change? If you leave the entire $110 in the bank, you will earn $110 \times .10 = \$11$ in interest during the second year, so you will have a total of $110 + 11 = \$121$. This $121 is the future value of $100 in two years at 10 percent. Another way of looking at it is that one year from now you are effectively investing $110 at 10 percent for a year. This is a single-period problem, so you'll end up with $1.1 for every dollar invested or $110 \times 1.1 = \$121$ total.

This $121 has four parts. The first part is the $100 original principal. The second part is the $10 in interest you earned in the first year along with another $10 (the third part) you earn in the second year, for a total of $120. The last $1 you end up with (the fourth part) is interest you earn in the second year on the interest paid in the first year: $10 \times .10 = \$1$.

compounding
The process of accumulating interest in an investment over time to earn more interest.

This process of leaving your money and any accumulated interest in an investment for more than one period, thereby *reinvesting* the interest, is called **compounding**. Compounding the interest means earning **interest on interest**, so we call the result **compound interest**. With **simple interest**, the interest is not reinvested, so interest is earned each period only on the original principal. We now take a closer look at how we calculated the $121 future value. We multiplied $110 by 1.1 to get $121. The $110, however, was $100 also multiplied by 1.1. In other words:

interest on interest
Interest earned on the reinvestment of previous interest payments.

$$\begin{aligned} \$121 &= \$110 \times 1.1 \\ &= (\$100 \times 1.1) \times 1.1 \\ &= \$100 \times (1.1 \times 1.1) \\ &= \$100 \times 1.1^2 \\ &= \$100 \times 1.21 \end{aligned}$$

compound interest
Interest earned on both the initial principal and the interest reinvested from prior periods.

simple interest
Interest earned only on the original principal amount invested.

As our example suggests, the future value of $1 invested for *t* periods at a rate of *r* per period is:

$$\text{Future value} = \$1 \times (1 + r)^t \tag{5.1}$$

The expression $(1 + r)^t$ is sometimes called the *future value interest factor* (or just *future value factor*) for $1 invested at *r* percent for *t* periods and can be abbreviated as FVIF (r, t).

In our example, what would your $100 be worth after five years? We can first compute the relevant future value factor as:

$$(1 + r)^t = (1 + .10)^5 = 1.1^5 = 1.6105$$

Your $100 would thus grow to:

$$\$100 \times 1.6105 = \$161.05$$

EXAMPLE 5.1: Interest on Interest

Suppose you locate a two-year investment that pays 4 percent per year. If you invest $325, how much will you have at the end of the two years? How much of this is simple interest? How much is compound interest?

At the end of the first year, you would have $325 × (1 + .04) = $338. If you reinvest this entire amount and thereby compound the interest, you would have $338 × 1.04 = $351.52 at the end of the second year. The total interest you earn is thus $351.52 − 325 = $26.52. Your $325 original principal earns $325 × .04 = $13 in interest each year, for a two-year total of $26 in simple interest. The remaining $26.52 − 26 = $0.52 results from compounding. You can check this by noting that the interest earned in the first year is $13. The interest on interest earned in the second year thus amounts to $13 × .04 = $0.52, as we calculated.

The growth of your $100 each year is illustrated in Table 5.1. As shown, the interest earned in each year is equal to the beginning amount multiplied by the interest rate of 10 percent.

In Table 5.1, notice that the total interest you earn is $61.05. Over the five-year span of this investment, the simple interest is $100 × .10 = $10 per year, so you accumulate $50 this way. The other $11.05 is from compounding.

TABLE 5.1   Future values of $100 at 10 percent

Year	Beginning Amount	Simple Interest		Interest on Interest		Total Interest Earned	Ending Amount
1	$100.00	10		0.00		$10.00	$110.00
2	110.00	10		1.00		11.00	121.00
3	121.00	10		2.10		12.10	133.10
4	133.10	10		3.31		13.31	146.41
5	146.41	10		4.64		14.64	161.05
		Total simple interest	50	Total interest on interest	$11.05	Total interest	$61.05

Figure 5.1 illustrates the growth of the compound interest in Table 5.1. Notice how the simple interest is constant each year, but the compound interest you earn gets bigger every year. The size of the compound interest keeps increasing because more and more interest builds up and there is thus more to compound.

Future values depend critically on the assumed interest rate, particularly for long-lived investments. Figure 5.2 illustrates this relationship by plotting the growth of $1 for different rates and lengths of time. Notice that the future value of $1 after 10 years is about $6.20 at a 20 percent rate, but it is only about $2.60 at 10 percent. In this case, doubling the interest rate more than doubles the future value.

To solve future value problems, we need to come up with the relevant future value factors. There are several different ways of doing this. In our example, we could have multiplied 1.1 by itself five times. This will work just fine, but it would get to be very tedious for, say, a 30-year investment.

For a discussion of time value concepts (and more) see financeprofessor.com or teachmefinance.com

Fortunately, there are several easier ways to get future value factors. Most calculators have a key labelled y^x . You can usually just enter 1.1, press this key, enter 5, and press the = key to get the answer. This is an easy way to calculate future value factors because it's quick and accurate.

Alternatively, you can use a table that contains future value factors for some common interest rates and time periods. Table 5.2 contains some of these factors. Table A.1 on the book's website contains a much larger set. To use the table, find the column that corresponds to 10 percent. Then look down the rows until you come to five periods. You should find the factor that we calculated, 1.6105.

FIGURE 5.1

Future value, simple interest, and compound interest

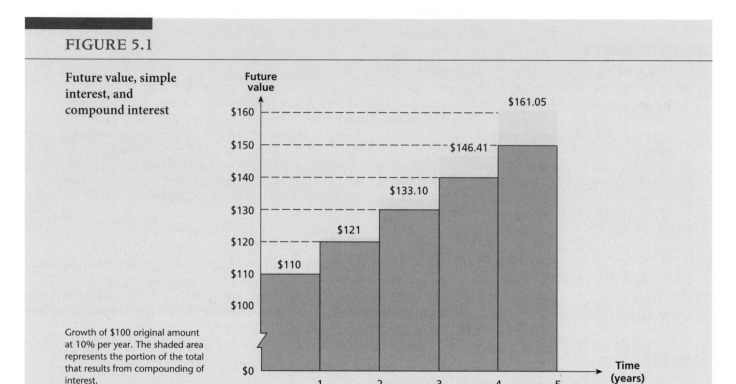

Growth of $100 original amount at 10% per year. The shaded area represents the portion of the total that results from compounding of interest.

FIGURE 5.2

Future value of $1 for different periods and rates

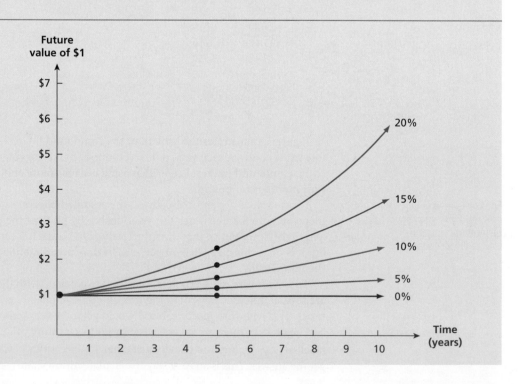

TABLE 5.2

Future value interest factors		Interest Rate			
	Periods	5%	10%	15%	20%
	1	1.0500	1.1000	1.1500	1.2000
	2	1.1025	1.2100	1.3225	1.4400
	3	1.1576	1.3310	1.5209	1.7280
	4	1.2155	1.4641	1.7490	2.0736
	5	1.2763	1.6105	2.0114	2.4883

Tables similar to Table 5.2 are not as common as they once were because they predate inexpensive calculators and are only available for a relatively small number of rates. Interest rates are often quoted to three or four decimal points, so the number of tables needed to deal with these accurately would be quite large. As a result, business people rarely use them. We illustrate the use of a calculator in this chapter.

EXAMPLE 5.2: Compound Interest

You've located an investment that pays 4 percent. That rate sounds good to you, so you invest $400. How much will you have in three years? How much will you have in seven years? At the end of seven years, how much interest have you earned? How much of that interest results from compounding?

Based on our discussion, we can calculate the future value factor for 4 percent and three years as:

$$(1 + r)^t = 1.04^3 = 1.1249$$

Your $400 thus grows to:

$$\$400 \times 1.1249 = \$449.96$$

After seven years, you would have:

$$\$400 \times 1.04^7 = \$400 \times 1.3159 = \$526.36$$

Since you invested $400, the interest in the $526.36 future value is $526.36 − 400 = $126.36. At 4 percent, your $400 investment earns $400 × .04 = $16 in simple interest every year. Over seven years, the simple interest thus totals 7 × $16 = $112. The other $126.36 − 112 = $14.36 is from compounding.

EXAMPLE 5.3: How Much for that Cup?

To further illustrate the effect of compounding for long horizons, consider the case of the Stanley Cup. The cup, the oldest team trophy in North America, was originally purchased by the governor general of Canada, Frederick Arthur Stanley, in 1893. Lord Stanley paid $48.67 for the cup 120 years ago. The Hockey Hall of Fame in Toronto has the cup insured for $1.5 million, although to millions of fans across Canada, it is priceless.[1] What would the sum Lord Stanley paid for the cup be worth today if he had invested it at 10 percent rather than purchasing the cup?

120 years, at 10 percent, $48.67 grows quite a bit. How much? The future value factor is approximately:

$$(1 + r)^t = (1.10)^{120} = 92,709.07$$
$$FV = \$48.67 \times 92,709.07 = \$4,512,150.38$$

Well, $4,512,150.38 is a lot of money, considerably more than $1.5 million—of course, no hockey fan would recommend that Lord Stanley should have invested the money rather than buy the cup!

This example is something of an exaggeration, of course. In 1893, it would not have been easy to locate an investment that would pay 10 percent every year without fail for the next 120 years.

---

[1] When this value for the Stanley Cup was reported in 2012, the practice of compounding interest was already more than 600 years old.

These tables still serve a useful purpose. To make sure that you are doing the calculations correctly, pick a factor from the table and then calculate it yourself to see that you get the same answer. There are plenty of numbers to choose from.

The effect of compounding is not great over short time periods, but it really starts to add up as the horizon grows. To take an extreme case, suppose one of your more frugal ancestors had invested $5 for you at a 6 percent interest 200 years ago, how much would you have today? The future value factor is a substantial $(1.06)^{200} = 115,125.90$ (you won't find this one in a table), so you would have $\$5 \times 115,125.90 = \$575,629.52$. Notice that the simple interest is just $\$5 \times 0.06 = \$.30$ per year. After 200 years, this amounts to $60. The rest is from reinvesting. Such is the power of compound interest!

CALCULATOR HINTS	**Using a Financial Calculator**

Although there are the various ways of calculating future values, as we have described so far, many of you will decide that a financial calculator is the way to go. If so, you should read this extended hint; otherwise, you can skip it.

A financial calculator is simply an ordinary calculator with a few extra features. In particular, it knows some of the most commonly used financial formulas, so it can directly compute things like future values.

Financial calculators have the advantage that they handle a lot of the computation, but that is really all. In other words, you still have to understand the problem; the calculator just does some of the arithmetic. We therefore have two goals for this section. First, we'll discuss how to compute future values. After that, we'll show you how to avoid the most common mistakes people make when they start using financial calculators. Note that the actual keystrokes vary from calculator to calculator, so the following examples are for illustrative purposes only.

How to Calculate Future Values with a Financial Calculator

Examining a typical financial calculator, you will find five keys of particular interest. They usually look like this:

$$\boxed{\text{N}} \quad \boxed{\text{I/Y}} \quad \boxed{\text{PV}} \quad \boxed{\text{PMT}} \quad \boxed{\text{FV}}$$

For now, we need to focus on four of these. The keys labelled $\boxed{\text{PV}}$ and $\boxed{\text{FV}}$ are just what you would guess, present value and future value. The key labelled $\boxed{\text{N}}$ refers to the number of periods, which is what we have been calling t. Finally, $\boxed{\text{I/Y}}$ stands for the interest rate, which we have called r.*

If we have the financial calculator set up right (see our next section), then calculating a future value is very simple. Take a look back at our question involving the future value of $100 at 10 percent for five years. We have seen that the answer is $161.05. The exact keystrokes will differ depending on what type of calculator you use, but here is basically all you do:

1. Enter 100 followed by the +/− key. Press the $\boxed{\text{PV}}$ key. (The negative sign is explained below.)

2. Enter 10. Press the $\boxed{\text{I/Y}}$ key. (Notice that we entered 10, not .10; see below.)

3. Enter 5. Press the $\boxed{\text{N}}$ key.

Now we have entered all of the relevant information. To solve for the future value, we need to ask the calculator what the FV is. Depending on your calculator, you either press the button labelled "CPT" (for compute) and then press $\boxed{\text{FV}}$, or else you just press $\boxed{\text{FV}}$

---

*The reason financial calculators use N and I/Y is that the most common use for these calculators is determining loan payments. In this context, N is the number of payments and I/Y is the interest rate on the loan. But, as we will see, there are many other uses of financial calculators that don't involve loan payments and interest rates.

Either way, you should get 161.05. If you don't (and you probably won't if this is the first time you have used a financial calculator!), we will offer some help in our next section.

Before we explain the kinds of problems that you are likely to run into, we want to establish a standard format for showing you how to use a financial calculator. Using the example we just looked at, in the future, we will illustrate such problems like this:

Enter	5	10	−100		
	N	**I/Y**	**PV**	**PMT**	**FV**
Solve for					161.05

If all else fails, you can read the manual that came with the calculator.

How to Get the Wrong Answer Using a Financial Calculator

There are a couple of common (and frustrating) problems that cause a lot of trouble with financial calculators. In this section, we provide some important *dos* and *don'ts*. If you just can't seem to get a problem to work out, you should refer back to this section.

There are two categories we examine: three things you need to do only once and three things you need to do every time you work a problem. The things you need to do just once deal with the following calculator settings:

1. *Make sure your calculator is set to display a large number of decimal places.* Most financial calculators only display two decimal places; this causes problems because we frequently work with numbers—like interest rates—that are very small.
2. *Make sure your calculator is set to assume only one payment per period or per year.* Most financial calculators assume monthly payments (12 per year) unless you say otherwise.
3. *Make sure your calculator is in "end" mode.* This is usually the default, but you can accidently change to "begin" mode.

If you don't know how to set these three things, see your calculator's operating manual. There are also three things you need to do every time you work a problem:

1. *Before you start, completely clear out the calculator.* This is very important. Failure to do this is the number one reason for wrong answers; you simply must get in the habit of clearing the calculator every time you start a problem. How you do this depends on the calculator, but you must do more than just clear the display. For example, on a Texas Instruments BA II Plus you must press **2nd** then **CLR** **TVM** for *clear time value of money*. There is a similar command on your calculator. Learn it!

   Note that turning the calculator off and back on won't do it. Most financial calculators remember everything you enter, even after you turn them off. In other words, they remember all your mistakes unless you explicitly clear them out. Also, if you are in the middle of a problem and make a mistake, *clear it out and start over*. Better to be safe than sorry.
2. *Put a negative sign on cash outflows.* Most financial calculators require you to put a negative sign on cash outflows and a positive sign on cash inflows. As a practical matter, this usually just means that you should enter the present value amount with a negative sign (because normally the present value represents the amount you give up today in exchange for cash inflows later). By the same token, when you solve for a present value, you shouldn't be surprised to see a negative sign.
3. *Enter the rate correctly.* Financial calculators assume that rates are quoted in percent, so if the rate is .08 (or 8 percent), you should enter 8, not .08.

One way to determine if you may have made a mistake while using your financial calculator is to complete a check for reasonableness. This means that you should think about the problem logically, and consider whether your answer seems like a reasonable or even possible one. For example, if you are determining the future value of $100 invested for three years at 5 percent, an answer of $90 is clearly wrong. Future value has to be greater than the original amount invested.

If you follow these guidelines (especially the one about clearing the calculator), you should have no problem using a financial calculator to work almost all of the problems in this and the next few chapters. We'll provide additional examples and guidance where appropriate.

A Note on Compound Growth

If you are considering depositing money in an interest-bearing account, the interest rate on that account is just the rate at which your money grows, assuming you don't remove any of it. If that rate is 10 percent, each year you simply have 10 percent more money than you had the year before. In this case, the interest rate is just an example of a compound growth rate.

The way we calculated future values is actually quite general and lets you answer some other types of questions related to growth. For example, your company currently has 10,000 employees. You've estimated that the number of employees grows by 3 percent per year. How many employees will there be in five years? Here, we start with 10,000 people instead of dollars, and we don't think of the growth rate as an interest rate, but the calculation is exactly the same:

$$10,000 \times (1.03)^5 = 10,000 \times 1.1593 = 11,593 \text{ employees}$$

There will be about 1593 net new hires over the coming five years.

EXAMPLE 5.4: Dividend Growth

Over the 16 years ending in 2011, the Royal Bank of Canada's dividend grew from $0.29 to $2.08, an average annual growth rate of 13.10 percent.[2] Assuming this growth continues, what will the dividend be in 2014?

Here we have a cash dividend growing because it is being increased by management, but, once again, the calculation is the same:

$$
\begin{aligned}
\text{Future value} &= \$2.08 \times (1.1310)^3 \\
&= \$2.08 \, (1.4467) \\
&= \$3.01
\end{aligned}
$$

The dividend will grow by $0.93 over that period. Dividend growth is a subject we return to in a later chapter.

Concept Questions

1. What do we mean by the future value of an investment?
2. What does it mean to compound interest? How does compound interest differ from simple interest?
3. In general, what is the future value of $1 invested at r per period for t periods?

5.2 | Present Value and Discounting

When we discuss future value, we are thinking of questions such as: What will my $2,000 investment grow to if it earns a 6.5 percent return every year for the next six years? The answer to this question is what we call the future value of $2,000 invested at 6.5 percent for six years (check that the answer is about $2,918).

Another type of question that comes up even more often in financial management is obviously related to future value. Suppose you need to have $10,000 in 10 years, and you can earn 6.5 percent on your money. How much do you have to invest today to reach your goal? You can verify that the answer is $5,327.26. How do we know this? Read on.

---

[2]
$$
\begin{aligned}
\$2.08 &= \$0.29 \times (1 + g)^{16} \\
7.1724 &= (1 + g)^{16} \\
(7.1724)^{1/16} &= 1 + g \\
1.1310 &= 1 + g \\
g &= 13.10\%
\end{aligned}
$$

The Single-Period Case

present value (PV)
The current value of future cash flows discounted at the appropriate discount rate.

We've seen that the future value of $1 invested for one year at 10 percent is $1.10. We now ask a slightly different question: How much do we have to invest today at 10 percent to get $1 in one year? In other words, we know the future value here is $1, but what is the **present value (PV)**? The answer isn't too hard to figure out. Whatever we invest today will be 1.1 times bigger at the end of the year. Since we need $1 at the end of the year:

$$\text{Present value} \times 1.1 = \$1$$

Or:

$$\text{Present value} = \$1/1.1 = \$.909$$

discount
To calculate the present value of some future amount.

This present value is the answer to the following question: What amount, invested today, will grow to $1 in one year if the interest rate is 10 percent? Present value is thus just the reverse of future value. Instead of compounding the money forward into the future, we **discount** it back to the present.

EXAMPLE 5.5: Single Period PV

Suppose you need $400 to buy textbooks next year. You can earn 4 percent on your money. How much do you have to put up today?

We need to know the PV of $400 in one year at 4 percent. Proceeding as we just did:

$$\text{Present value} \times 1.04 = \$400$$

We can now solve for the present value:

$$\text{Present value} = \$400 \times (1/1.04) = \$384.62$$

Thus, $384.62 is the present value. Again, this just means that investing this amount for one year at 4 percent results in your having a future value of $400.

From our examples, the present value of $1 to be received in one period is generally given as:

$$\text{PV} - \$1 \times [1/(1 + r)] = \$1/(1 + r)$$

We next examine how to get the present value of an amount to be paid in two or more periods into the future.

Present Values for Multiple Periods

Suppose you need to have $1,000 in two years. If you can earn 7 percent, how much do you have to invest to make sure that you have the $1,000 when you need it? In other words, what is the present value of $1,000 in two years if the relevant rate is 7 percent?

Based on your knowledge of future values, we know that the amount invested must grow to $1,000 over the two years. In other words, it must be the case that:

$$\$1,000 = \text{PV} \times 1.07^2$$
$$= \text{PV} \times 1.1449$$

Given this, we can solve for the present value as:

$$\text{Present value} = \$1,000/1.1449 = \$873.44$$

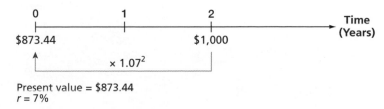

Present value = $873.44
$r = 7\%$

Therefore, you must invest $873.44 to achieve your goal.

As you have probably recognized by now, calculating present values is quite similar to calculating future values, and the general result looks much the same. The present value of $1 to be received t periods in the future at a discount rate of r is:

$$PV = \$1 \times [1/(1 + r)^t] = \$1/(1 + r)^t \tag{5.2}$$

The quantity in brackets, $1/(1 + r)^t$, goes by several different names. Since it's used to discount a future cash flow, it is often called a *discount factor*. With this name, it is not surprising that the rate used in the calculation is often called the **discount rate**. We tend to call it this in talking about present values. The discount rate is also sometimes referred to as the interest rate or rate of return. Regardless of what it is called, the discount rate is related to the risk of the cash flows. The higher the risk, the larger the discount rate and the lower the present value.

discount rate
The rate used to calculate the present value of future cash flows.

The quantity in brackets is also called the *present value interest factor* for $1 at r percent for t periods and is sometimes abbreviated as PVIF(r,t). Finally, calculating the present value of a future cash flow to determine its worth today is commonly called *discounted cash flow (DCF)* valuation.

To illustrate, suppose you need $1,000 in three years. You can earn 5 percent on your money. How much do you have to invest today? To find out, we have to determine the present value of $1,000 in three years at 5 percent. We do this by discounting $1,000 back three periods at 5 percent. With these numbers, the discount factor is:

$$1/(1 + .05)^3 = 1/1.1576 = .8638$$

The amount you must invest is thus:

$$\$1,000 \times .8638 = \$863.80$$

We say that $863.80 is the present or discounted value of $1,000 to be received in three years at 5 percent.

EXAMPLE 5.6: Saving up for a Ferrari

You would like to buy the latest model Ferrari 458 Spider. You have about $230,000 or so, but the car costs $274,000. If you can earn 4 percent, how much do you have to invest today to buy the car in two years? Do you have enough? Assume the price will stay the same.

What we need to know is the present value of $274,000 to be paid in two years, assuming a 4 percent rate. Based on our discussion, this is:

$$PV = \$274,000/1.04^2 = \$274,000/1.0816 = \$253,328.40$$

You're still about $23,328.40 short, even if you're willing to wait two years.

There are tables for present value factors just as there are tables for future value factors, and you use them in the same way (if you use them at all). Table 5.3 contains a small set. A much larger set can be found in Table A.2 on the book's website.

TABLE 5.3

Present value interest factors

Periods	Interest Rate			
	5%	10%	15%	20%
1	.9524	.9091	.8696	.8333
2	.9070	.8264	.7561	.6944
3	.8638	.7513	.6575	.5787
4	.8227	.6830	.5718	.4823
5	.7835	.6209	.4972	.4019

In Table 5.3, the discount factor we just calculated (.8638) can be found by looking down the column labelled 5% until you come to the third row.

CALCULATOR
HINTS

You solve present value problems on a financial calculator just as you do future value problems. For the example we just examined (the present value of $1,000 to be received in three years at 5 percent), you would do the following:

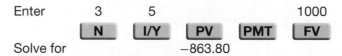

Enter   3   5   1000

[N] [I/Y] [PV] [PMT] [FV]

Solve for   −863.80

Notice that the answer has a negative sign; as we discussed above, that's because it represents an outflow today in exchange for the $1,000 inflow later.

As the length of time until payment grows, present values decline. As Example 5.7 illustrates, present values tend to become small as the time horizon grows. If you look out far enough, they will always get close to zero. Also, for a given length of time, the higher the discount rate is, the lower is the present value. Put another way, present values and discount rates are inversely related. Increasing the discount rate decreases the PV and vice versa.

EXAMPLE 5.7: The 'Thriller' jacket

In June 2011, Michael Jackson's zombie-ridden 'Thriller' jacket was sold in an auction for $1.8 million. Assuming that the original value of the jacket was $20,000 in 1983, what rate of return did his jacket earn?

Rate of return earned by his jacket is:

$$\$20,000 = \$1,800,000/(1 + r)^{28}$$
$$(1 + r)^{28} = 90.00$$
$$1 + r = 1.1743$$
$$r = 17.43\%$$

The discount rate, r, is found to be 17.43 percent.

Concept Questions

1. What do we mean by the present value of an investment?
2. The process of discounting a future amount back to the present is the opposite of doing what?
3. What do we mean by the discounted cash flow or DCF approach?

5.3 | More on Present and Future Values

Look back at the expressions that we came up with for present and future values, and you will see a very simple relationship between the two. We explore this relationship and some related issues in this section.

Present versus Future Value

What we called the present value factor is just the reciprocal of (that is, 1 divided by) the future value factor:

Future value factor $= (1 + r)^t$
Present value factor $= 1/(1 + r)^t$

In fact, the easy way to calculate a present value factor on many calculators is to first calculate the future value factor and then press the [1/x] key to flip it over.

If we let FV_t stand for the future value after t periods, the relationship between future value and present value can be written very simply as one of the following:

$$PV \times (1 + r)^t = FV_t \tag{5.3}$$
$$PV = FV_t/(1 + r)^t = FV_t \times [1/(1 + r)^t]$$

This last result we call the *basic present value equation*. We use it throughout the text. There are a

number of variations that come up, but this simple equation underlies many of the most important ideas in corporate finance.[3]

EXAMPLE 5.8: Evaluating Investments

To give you an idea of how we use present and future values, consider the following simple investment. Your company proposes to buy an asset of $335,000. This investment
is very safe. You will sell the asset in three years for
$400,000. You know that you could invest the $335,000
elsewhere at 3 percent with very little risk. What do you
think of the proposed investment?

This is a good investment. Why? Because If you can invest the $335,000 elsewhere at 3 percent, after three years
it would grow to:

$$\$335{,}000 \times (1 + r)^t = \$335{,}000 \times 1.03^3$$
$$= \$335{,}000 \times 1.0927$$
$$= \$366{,}054.50$$

Because the proposed investment pays out $400,000, it is
better than other alternative that we have. Another way of
saying the same thing is to notice that the present value of
$400,000 in three years at 3 percent is:

$$\$400{,}000 \times [1/(1 + r)^t] = \$400{,}000/1.03^3 =$$
$$\$400{,}000/1.0927 = \$366{,}065.71$$

This tells us that we have to invest about $366,000 to get
$400,000 in three years, not $335,000. We return to this
type of analysis later.

Determining the Discount Rate

For a downloadable Windows-
based financial calculator, go to
calculator.org

Frequently, we need to determine what discount rate is implicit in an investment. We can do this
by looking at the basic present value equation:

$$PV = FV_t/(1 + r)^t$$

There are only four parts to this equation: the present value (PV), the future value (FV_t), the
discount rate (r), and the life of the investment (t). Given any three of these, we can always find
the fourth part.

To illustrate what happens with multiple periods, let's say that we are offered an investment
that costs us $100 and doubles our money in eight years. To compare this to other investments,
we would like to know what discount rate is implicit in these numbers. This discount rate is called
the *rate of return* or sometimes just return for the investment. In this case, we have a present value
of $100, a future value of $200 (double our money), and an eight-year life. To calculate the return,
we can write the basic present value equation as:

$$PV = FV_t/(1 + r)^t$$
$$\$100 = \$200/(1 + r)^8$$

It could also be written as:

$$(1 + r)^8 = 200/100 = 2$$

We now need to solve for r. There are three ways we could do it:

1. Use a financial calculator.
2. Solve the equation for $1 + r$ by taking the eighth root of both sides. Since this is the same
   thing as raising both sides to the power of 1/8 or .125, this is actually easy to do with the y^x
   key on a calculator. Just enter 2, then press y^x , enter .125, and press the = key. The
   eighth root should be about 1.09, which implies that r is 9 percent.
3. Use a future value table. The future value factor after eight years is equal to 2. Look across
   the row corresponding to eight periods in Table A.1 to see that a future value factor of 2 corresponds to the 9 percent column, again implying that the return here is 9 percent.[4]

---

[3] The process of applying the present value equation is known as discounting. If you apply the future value equation,
you are compounding.

[4] There is a useful "back-of-the-envelope" means of solving for r—the Rule of 72. For reasonable rates of return, the
time it takes to double your money is given approximately by 72/r%. In our example, this is 72/r% = 8 years, implying
that r is 9 percent as we calculated. This rule is fairly accurate for discount rates in the 5 percent to 20 percent range.

| CALCULATOR HINTS | We can illustrate how to calculate unknown rates using a financial calculator using these numbers. For our example, you would do the following: |

Enter   8   −100   200

| N | I/Y | PV | PMT | FV |

Solve for   9.05

As in our previous examples, notice the minus sign on the present value.

EXAMPLE 5.9: Finding r for a Single Period Investment

You are considering a one-year investment. If you put up $1,250, you would get back $1,350. What rate is this investment paying?

First, in this single-period case, the answer is fairly obvious. You are getting a total of $100 in addition to your $1,250. The rate of return on this investment is thus $100/1,250 = 8$ percent.

More formally, from the basic present value equation, the present value (the amount you must put up today) is $1,250. The future value (what the present value grows to) is $1,350. The time involved is one period, so we have:

$$\$1,250 = \$1,350/(1 + r)^1$$
$$(1 + r) = \$1,350/\$1,250 = 1.08$$
$$r = 8\%$$

In this simple case, of course, there was no need to go through this calculation, but, as we describe later, it gets a little harder when there is more than one period.

Not taking the time value of money into account when computing growth rates or rates of return often leads to some misleading numbers in the real world. For example, in 1997, Nissan announced plans to restore 56 vintage Datsun 240Zs and sell them to consumers. The price tag of a restored Z? About $38,000, which was at least 700 percent greater than the cost of a 240Z when it sold new 27 years earlier. As expected, many viewed the restored Zs as potential investments because they are a virtual carbon copy of the classic original.

EXAMPLE 5.10: Saving for University

Many Canadian universities are increasing their tuition and fees. You estimate that you will need about $100,000 to send your child to a university in eight years. You have about $45,000 now. If you can earn 4 percent, will you make it? At what rate will you just reach your goal?

If you can earn 4 percent, the future value of your $45,000 in eight years would be:

$$FV = \$45,000 \times (1.04)^8 = \$45,000 \times 1.3686 = \$61,587$$

So you will not make it easily. The minimum rate is the unknown r in the following:

$$FV = \$45,000 \times (1 + r)^8 = \$100,000$$
$$(1 + r)^8 = \$100,000/\$45,000 = 2.2222$$

To get the exact answer, we could use a financial calculator or we can solve for r:

$$(1 + r) = 2.2222^{(1/8)} = 2.2222^{.125} = 1.1050$$
$$r = 10.50\%$$

EXAMPLE 5.11: Only 10,956 Days to Retirement

You would like to retire in 30 years as a millionaire. If you have $10,000 today, what rate of return do you need to earn to achieve your goal?

The future value is $1 million. The present value is $10,000, and there are 30 years until payment. We need to calculate the unknown discount rate in the following:

$$\$10,000 = \$1,000,000/(1 + r)^{30}$$
$$(1 + r)^{30} = 100$$

The future value factor is thus 100. You can verify that the implicit rate is about 16.59 percent.

If history is any guide, we can get a rough idea of how well you might expect such an investment to perform. According to the numbers quoted above, a Z that originally sold for about $5,289 twenty-seven years earlier would sell for about $38,000 in 1997. See if you don't agree that this represents a return of 7.58 percent per year, far less than the gaudy 700 percent difference in the values when the time value of money is ignored.

Our example shows it's easy to be misled when returns are quoted without considering the time value of money. However, it's not just the uninitiated who are guilty of this slight form of deception. The title of a recent feature article in a leading business magazine predicted the Dow-Jones Industrial Average would soar to a 70 percent gain over the coming five years. Do you think it meant a 70 percent return per year on your money? Think again!

Finding the Number of Periods

Why does the Rule of 72 work? See moneychimp.com

Suppose we were interested in purchasing an asset that costs $50,000. We currently have $25,000. If we can earn 12 percent on this $25,000, how long until we have the $50,000? The answer involves solving for the last variable in the basic present value equation, the number of periods. You already know how to get an approximate answer to this particular problem. Notice that we need to double our money. From the Rule of 72, this would take $72/12 = 6$ years at 12 percent.

EXAMPLE 5.12: Waiting for Godot

You've been saving to buy the Godot Company. The total cost will be $10 million. You currently have about $2.3 million. If you can earn 5 percent on your money, how long will you have to wait? At 16 percent, how long must you wait?

At 5 percent, you'll have to wait a long time. From the basic present value equation:

$$\$2.3 = 10/(1.05)^t$$
$$1.05^t = 4.35$$
$$t = 30 \text{ years}$$

At 16 percent, things are a little better. Check for yourself that it would take about 10 years.

To come up with the exact answer, we can again manipulate the basic present value equation. The present value is $25,000, and the future value is $50,000. With a 12 percent discount rate, the basic equation takes one of the following forms:

$$\$25,000 = \$50,000/(1.12)^t$$
$$\$50,000/25,000 = (1.12)^t = 2$$

We thus have a future value factor of 2 for a 12 percent rate. To get the exact answer, we have to explicitly solve for t (or use a financial calculator)[5].

Stripped coupons are a widely held investment. You purchase them for a fraction of their face value. For example, suppose you buy a Government of Canada stripped coupon for $50 on July 1, 2012. The coupon will mature after 12 years on July 1, 2024 and pay its face value of $100. You invest $50 and receive double your money after 12 years, what rate do you earn?

Learn more about using Excel™ for time value and other calculations at studyfinance.com

Because this investment is doubling in value in 12 years, the Rule of 72 tells you the answer right away: $72/12 = 6$ percent. You can check this using the basic time value equation.

This example completes our introduction to basic time value concepts. Table 5.4 summarizes present and future value calculations for your reference.

---

[5]To solve for t, we have to take the logarithm of both sides of the equation:
$$1.12^t = 2$$
$$\log 1.12^t = \log 2$$
$$t \log 1.12 = \log 2$$
We can then solve for t explicitly:
$$t = \log 2/\log 1.12$$
$$= 6.1163$$
Almost all calculators can determine a logarithm; look for a key labelled *log* or *ln*. If both are present, use either one.

SPREADSHEET STRATEGIES

Using a Spreadsheet for Time Value of Money Calculations

More and more business people from many different areas (and not just finance and accounting) rely on spreadsheets to do all the different types of calculations that come up in the real world. As a result, in this section, we will show you how to use a spreadsheet to handle the various time value of money problems we presented in this chapter. We will use Microsoft Excel™, but the commands are similar for other types of software. We assume you are already familiar with basic spreadsheet operations.

As we have seen, you can solve for any one of the following four potential unknowns: future value, present value, the discount rate, or the number of periods. With a spreadsheet, there is a separate formula for each. In Excel, these are as follows:

To Find	Enter This Formula
Future value	= FV (rate,nper,pmt,pv)
Present value	= PV (rate,nper,pmt,fv)
Discount rate	= RATE (nper,pmt,pv,fv)
Number of periods	= NPER (rate,pmt,pv,fv)

In these formulas, pv is the present value, fv is the future value, nper is the number of periods, and rate is the discount, or interest, rate.

There are two things that are a little tricky here. First, unlike a financial calculator, you have to enter the rate into the spreadsheet as a decimal. Second, as with most financial calculators, you have to put a negative sign on either the present value or the future value to solve for the rate or the number of periods. For the same reason, if you solve for a present value, the answer will have a negative sign unless you input a negative future value. The same is true when you compute a future value.

To illustrate how you might use these formulas, we will go back to an example in the chapter. If you invest $25,000 at 12 percent per year, how long until you have $50,000? You might set up a spreadsheet like this:

	A	B	C	D	E	F	G	H
1								
2		Using a spreadsheet for time value of money calculations						
3								
4	If we invest $25,000 at 12 percent, how long until we have $50,000? We need to solve							
5	for the unknown number of periods, so we use the formula NPER(rate, pmt, pv, fv).							
6								
7	Present value (pv):	$25,000						
8	Future value (fv):	$50,000						
9	Rate (rate):	0.12						
10								
11	Periods:	6.1162554						
12								
13	The formula entered in cell B11 is = NPER(B9, 0, –B7, B8); notice that pmt is zero and that pv							
14	has a negative sign on it. Also notice that rate is entered as a decimal, not a percentage.							

TABLE 5.4   Summary of time-value calculations

I. Symbols:

PV = Present value, what future cash flows are worth today

FV_t = Future value, what cash flows are worth in the future

r = Interest rate, rate of return, or discount rate per period—typically, but not always, one year

t = Number of periods—typically, but not always, the number of years

C = Cash amount

II. Future value of C invested at r percent for t periods:

$$FV_t = C \times (1 + r)^t$$

The term $(1 + r)^t$ is called the *future value factor*.

III. Present value of C to be received in t periods at r percent per period:

$$PV = C/(1 + r)^t$$

The term $1/(1 + r)^t$ is called the *present value factor*.

IV. The basic present value equation giving the relationship between present and future value is:

$$PV = FV_t/(1 + r)^t$$

Concept Questions

1. What is the basic present value equation?
2. In general, what is the present value of $1 to be received in t periods, assuming a discount rate of r per period?
3. What is the Rule of 72?

5.4 | SUMMARY AND CONCLUSIONS

This chapter has introduced you to the basic principles of present value and discounted cash flow valuation. In it, we explained a number of things about the time value of money, including:

1. For a given rate of return, the value at some point in the future of an investment made today can be determined by calculating the future value of that investment.
2. The current worth of a future cash flow or a series of cash flows can be determined for a given rate of return by calculating the present value of the cash flow(s) involved.
3. The relationship between present value (PV) and future value (FV) for a given rate r and time t is given by the basic present value equation:

$$PV = FV_t/(1 + r)^t$$

As we have shown, it is possible to find any one of the four components (PV, FV_t, r, or t) given the other three components.

The principles developed in this chapter will figure prominently in the chapters to come. The reason for this is that most investments, whether they involve real assets or financial assets, can be analyzed using the discounted cash flow (DCF) approach. As a result, the DCF approach is broadly applicable and widely used in practice. Before going on, you might want to do some of the problems that follow.

Key Terms

compound interest (page 112)
compounding (page 112)
discount (page 119)
discount rate (page 120)

future value (FV) (page 112)
interest on interest (page 112)
present value (PV) (page 119)
simple interest (page 112)

Chapter Review Problems and Self-Test

5.1 **Calculating Future Values** Assume you deposit $10,000 today in an account that pays 6 percent interest. How much will you have in five years?

5.2 **Calculating Present Values** Suppose you have just celebrated your 19th birthday. A rich uncle has set up a trust fund for you that will pay you $150,000 when you turn 30. If the relevant discount rate is 9 percent, how much is this fund worth today?

5.3 **Calculating Rates of Return** You've been offered an investment that will double your money in 10 years. What rate of return are you being offered? Check your answer using the Rule of 72.

5.4 **Calculating the Number of Periods** You've been offered an investment that will pay you 9 percent per year. If you invest $15,000, how long until you have $30,000? How long until you have $45,000?

5.5 **Compound Interest** In 1867, George Edward Lee found on his property in Ontario an astrolabe (a 17th-century navigating device) originally lost by Samuel de Champlain. Lee sold the astrolabe to a stranger for $10. In 1989, the Canadian Museum of Civilization purchased the astrolabe for $250,000 from the New York Historical Society. (How it got there is a long story.) It appears that Lee had been swindled; however, suppose he had invested the $10 at 10 percent. How much was it worth 140 years later in 2007?

Answers to Self-Test Problems

5.1 We need to calculate the future value of $10,000 at 6 percent for five years. The future value factor is:

$$1.06^5 = 1.3382$$

The future value is thus $10,000 × 1.3382 = $13,382.26.

5.2 We need the present value of $150,000 to be paid in 11 years at 9 percent. The discount factor is:

$$1/1.09^{11} = 1/2.5804 = .3875$$

The present value is thus about $58,130.

5.3 Suppose you invest, say, $1,000. You will have $2,000 in 10 years with this investment. So, $1,000 is the amount you have today, or the present value, and $2,000 is the amount you will have in 10 years, or the future value. From the basic present value equation, we have:

$$\$2,000 = \$1,000 \times (1 + r)^{10}$$
$$2 = (1 + r)^{10}$$

From here, we need to solve for r, the unknown rate. As shown in the chapter, there are several different ways to do this. We will take the 10th root of 2 (by raising 2 to the power of 1/10):

$$2^{(1/10)} = 1 + r$$
$$1.0718 = 1 + r$$
$$r = 7.18\%$$

Using the Rule of 72, we have $72/t = r\%$, or $72/10 = 7.2\%$, so our answer looks good (remember that the Rule of 72 is only an approximation).

5.4 The basic equation is:

$$\$30,000 = \$15,000 \times (1 + .09)^t$$
$$2 = (1 + .09)^t$$

If we solve for t, we get that $t = 8.04$ years. Using the Rule of 72, we get $72/9 = 8$ years, so, once again, our answer looks good. To get $45,000, verify for yourself that you will have to wait 12.75 years.

5.5 At 10 percent, the $10 would have grown quite a bit over 140 years. The future value factor is:

$$(1 + r)^t = 1.1^{140} = 623,700.26$$

The future value is thus on the order of:

$$\$10 \times 623,700.26 = \$6,237,003.$$

Concepts Review and Critical Thinking Questions

1. **(LO2)** The basic present value equation has four parts. What are they?
2. **(LO1, 2)** What is compounding? What is discounting?
3. **(LO1, 2)** As you increase the length of time involved, what happens to future values? What happens to present values?
4. **(LO1, 2)** What happens to a future value if you increase the rate r? What happens to a present value?

The next four questions refer to a stripped coupon issued by the Province of Ontario.

5. **(LO2)** Why would an investor be willing to pay $76.04 today in exchange for a promise to receive $100 in the future?
6. **(LO2)** Would you be willing to pay $500 today in exchange for $10,000 in 30 years? What would be the key considerations in answering yes or no? Would your answer depend on who is making the promise to repay?
7. **(LO2)** Suppose that when the Province of Ontario offered the bond for $76.04, the Province of Alberta had offered an essentially identical security. Do you think it would have a higher or lower price? Why?
8. **(LO2)** The Province of Ontario bonds are actively bought and sold by investment dealers. If you obtained a price today, do you think the price would exceed the $76.04 original price? Why? If you looked in the year 2010, do you think the price would be higher or lower than today's price? Why?

Questions and Problems

Basic
(Questions 1–15)

1. **Simple Interest versus Compound Interest (LO1)** Bank of Vancouver pays 8 percent simple interest on its savings account balances, whereas Bank of Calgary pays 8 percent interest compounded annually. If you made a $5,000 deposit in each bank, how much more money would you earn from your Bank of Calgary account at the end of 10 years?

2. **Calculating Future Values (LO1)** For each of the following, compute the future value:

Present Value	Years	Interest Rate	Future Value
$2,250	11	10%	
8,752	7	8	
76,355	14	17	
183,796	8	7	

3. **Calculating Present Values (LO2)** For each of the following, compute the present value:

Present Value	Years	Interest Rate	Future Value
	6	7%	$15,451
	7	13	51,557
	23	14	886,073
	18	9	550,164

4. Calculating Interest Rates (LO3) Solve for the unknown interest rate in each of the following:

Present Value	Years	Interest Rate	Future Value
$240	2		$297
360	10		1,080
39,000	15		185,382
38,261	30		531,618

5. Calculating the Number of Periods (LO4) Solve for the unknown number of years in each of the following:

Present Value	Years	Interest Rate	Future Value
$560		9%	$1,284
810		10	4,341
18,400		17	364,518
21,500		15	173,439

6. Calculating Interest Rates (LO3) Assume the total cost of a university education will be $290,000 when your child enters university in 18 years. You currently have $55,000 to invest. What annual rate of interest must you earn on your investment to cover the cost of your child's university education?

7. Calculating the Number of Periods (LO4) At 7 percent interest, how long does it take to double your money? To quadruple it?

8. Calculating Interest Rates (LO3) In 2013, the automobile industry announced the average vehicle selling price was $34,958. Five years earlier, the average price was $27,641. What was the annual percentage increase in vehicle selling price?

9. Calculating the Number of Periods (LO4) You're trying to save to buy a new $170,000 BMW 3 series sedan. You have $40,000 today that can be invested at your bank. The bank pays 5.3 percent annual interest on its accounts. How long will it be before you have enough to buy the car?

10. Calculating Present Values (LO2) Normandin Inc. has an unfunded pension liability of $650 million that must be paid in 20 years. To assess the value of the firm's stock, financial analysts want to discount this liability back to the present. If the relevant discount rate is 7.4 percent, what is the present value of this liability?

11. Calculating Present Values (LO2) You have just received notification that you have won the $1 million first prize in Lamarche lottery. However, the prize will be awarded on your 100th birthday (assuming you're around to collect), 80 years from now. What is the present value of your windfall if the appropriate discount rate is 10 percent?

12. Calculating Future Values (LO1) Your coin collection contains fifty 1952 silver dollars. If your grandparents purchased them for their face value when they were new, how much will your collection be worth when you retire in 2057, assuming they appreciate at a 4.5 percent annual rate?

13. Calculating Interest Rates and Future Values (LO1, 3) In 1970, the prize money of the Canadian Open Tennis tournament was $15,000. In 2012, the prize money was $2,648,700. What was the percentage increase in the prize money over this period? If the winner's prize continues to increase at the same rate, what will it be in 2040?

14. Calculating Present Values (LO2) The first comic book featuring Superman was sold in 1938. In 2005, the estimated price for this comic book in good condition was about $485,000. This represented a return of 25.90 percent per year. For this to be true, what must the comic book have sold for when new?

15. Calculating Rates of Return (LO3) Although appealing to more refined tastes, art as a collectible has not always performed so profitably. During 2003, Sothebys sold the Edgar Degas bronze sculpture *Petit Danseuse de Quartorze Ans* at auction for a price of $10,311,500. Unfortunately for the previous owner, he had purchased it in 1999 at a price of $12,377,500. What was his annual rate of return on this sculpture?

Intermediate (Questions 16–20)

16. Calculating Rates of Return (LO3) On February 2, 2013, an investor held some Province of Ontario stripped coupons in a self-administered RRSP at ScotiaMcLeod, an investment dealer. Each coupon represented a promise to pay $100 at the maturity date on January 13, 2019 but the investor would receive nothing until then. The value of the coupon showed as $76.04 on the investor's screen. This means that the investor was giving up $76.04 on February 2, 2013 in exchange for $100 to be received just less than six years later.

a. Based upon the $76.04 price, what rate was the yield on the Province of Ontario bond?

b. Suppose that on February 2, 2014, the security's price was $81.00. If an investor had purchased it for $76.04 a year earlier and sold it on this day, what annual rate of return would she have earned?

c. If an investor had purchased the security at market on February 2, 2014, and held it until it matured, what annual rate of return would she have earned?

17. Calculating Present Values (LO2) Suppose you are still committed to owning a $170,000 BMW (see Question 9). If you believe your mutual fund can achieve an 11 percent annual rate of return and you want to buy the car in 10 years on the day you turn 30, how much must you invest today?

18. Calculating Future Values (LO1) You have just made your first $4,000 contribution to your registered retirement saving plan (RRSP). Assuming you earn a 11 percent rate of return and make no additional contributions, what will your account be worth when you retire in 45 years? What if you wait 10 years before contributing? (Does this suggest an investment strategy?)

19. Calculating Future Values (LO1) You are scheduled to receive $20,000 in two years. When you receive it, you will invest it for six more years at 8.4 percent per year. How much will you have in eight years?

20. Calculating the Number of Periods (LO4) You expect to receive $10,000 at graduation in two years. You plan on investing it at 11 percent until you have $75,000. How long will you wait from now?

CHAPTER 6

DISCOUNTED CASH FLOW VALUATION

©ZUMA Press, Inc./Alamy/ All Canada Photos

With multimillion dollar contracts and bonuses, the signing of big-name athletes in the sports industry is often accompanied by great fanfare, but the numbers can often be misleading. For example, in September 2009, the Vancouver Canucks extended its contract with goaltender Roberto Luongo, offering him a twelve-year deal through to 2021 valued at a total of US$64 million. Considering the time value of money, how much is Luongo really receiving? After reading this chapter, you'll see that although Luongo still received a substantial amount, it is less than the US$64 million dollar figure that sent the sports media into a frenzy.

Learning Objectives ▶

After studying this chapter, you should understand:

LO1   **How to determine the future and present value of investments with multiple cash flows.**

LO2   **How loan payments are calculated and how to find the interest rate on a loan.**

LO3   **How loans are amortized or paid off.**

LO4   **How interest rates are quoted (and misquoted).**

In our previous chapter, we covered the basics of discounted cash flow valuation. However, so far, we have only dealt with single cash flows. In reality, most investments have multiple cash flows. For example, if Tim Hortons or Second Cup is thinking of opening a new outlet, there will be a large cash outlay in the beginning and then cash inflows for many years. In this chapter, we begin to explore how to value such investments.

When you finish this chapter, you should have some very practical skills. For example, you will know how to calculate your own car payments or student loan payments. You will also be able to determine how long it will take to pay off a credit card if you make the minimum payment each month (a practice we do not recommend). We will show you how to compare interest rates to determine which are the highest and which are the lowest, and we will also show you how interest rates can be quoted in different, and at times deceptive, ways.

6.1 | Future and Present Values of Multiple Cash Flows

Thus far, we have restricted our attention to either the future value of a lump-sum present amount or the present value of some single future cash flow. In this section, we begin to study ways to value multiple cash flows. We start with future value.

Future Value with Multiple Cash Flows

Suppose you deposit $100 today in an account paying 8 percent. In one year, you will deposit another $100. How much will you have in two years? This particular problem is relatively easy. At the end of the first year, you will have $108 plus the second $100 you deposit, for a total of $208. You leave this $208 on deposit at 8 percent for another year. At the end of this second year, it is worth:

$$\$208 \times 1.08 = \$224.64$$

Figure 6.1 is a *time line* that illustrates the process of calculating the future value of these two $100 deposits. Figures such as this one are very useful for solving complicated problems. Almost any time you are having trouble with a present or future value problem, drawing a time line will help you to see what is happening.

In the first part of Figure 6.1, we show the cash flows on the time line. The most important thing is that we write them down where they actually occur. Here, the first cash flow occurs today, which we label as Time 0. We therefore put $100 at Time 0 on the time line. The second $100 cash flow occurs one year from today, so we write it down at the point labelled as Time 1. In the second part of Figure 6.1, we calculate the future values one period at a time to come up with the final $224.64.

When we calculated the future value of the two $100 deposits, we simply calculated the balance as of the beginning of each year and then rolled that amount forward to the next year. We could have done it another, quicker way. The first $100 is on deposit for two years at 8 percent, so its future value is:

$$\$100 \times 1.08^2 = \$100 \times 1.1664 = \$116.64$$

The second $100 is on deposit for one year at 8 percent, and its future value is thus:

$$\$100 \times 1.08 = \$108$$

The total future value, as we previously calculated, is equal to the sum of these two future values:

$$\$116.64 + 108 = \$224.64$$

Based on this example, there are two ways to calculate future values for multiple cash flows: (1) compound the accumulated balance forward one year at a time or (2) calculate the future value of each cash flow first and then add them up. Both give the same answer, so you can do it either way.

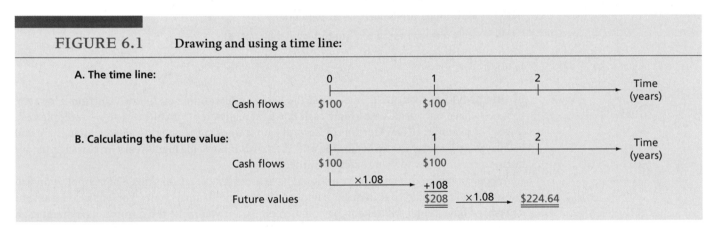

FIGURE 6.1   Drawing and using a time line:

A. The time line:

B. Calculating the future value:

EXAMPLE 6.1: Saving up Revisited

You think you will be able to deposit $4,000 at the end of each of the next three years in a bank account paying 3 percent interest. You currently have $7,000 in the account. How much will you have in three years? In four years?

At the end of the first year, you will have:

$$\$7,000 \times 1.03 + 4,000 = \$11,210$$

At the end of the second year, you will have:

$$\$11,210 \times 1.03 + 4,000 = \$15,546.30$$

Repeating this for the third year gives:

$$\$15,546.30 \times 1.03 + 4,000 = \$20,012.69$$

Therefore, you will have $20,012.69 in three years. If you leave this on deposit for one more year (and don't add to it), at the end of the fourth year, you'll have:

$$\$20,012.69 \times 1.03 = \$20,613.07$$

To illustrate the two different ways of calculating future values, consider the future value of $2,000 invested at the end of each of the next five years. The current balance is zero, and the rate is 10 percent. We first draw a time line, as shown in Figure 6.2.

On the time line, notice that nothing happens until the end of the first year, when we make the first $2,000 investment. This first $2,000 earns interest for the next four (not five) years. Also notice that the last $2,000 is invested at the end of the fifth year, so it earns no interest at all.

Figure 6.3 illustrates the calculations involved if we compound the investment one period at a time. As illustrated, the future value is $12,210.20.

Figure 6.4 goes through the same calculations, but the second technique is used. Naturally, the answer is the same.

FIGURE 6.2

Time line for $2,000 per year for five years

FIGURE 6.3   Future value calculated by compounding forward one period at a time:

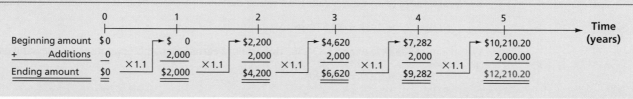

FIGURE 6.4

Future value calculated by compounding each cash flow separately:

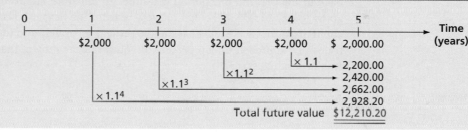

EXAMPLE 6.2: Saving up Once Again

If you deposit $100 in one year, $200 in two years, and $300 in three years, how much will you have in three years? How much of this is interest? How much will you have in five years if you don't add additional amounts? Assume a 4 percent interest rate throughout.

We will calculate the future value of each amount in three years. Notice that the $100 earns interest for two years, and the $200 earns interest for one year. The final $300 earns no interest. The future values are thus:

$$\begin{aligned}
\$100 \times 1.04^2 &= \quad \$108.16 \\
\$200 \times 1.04 &= \quad 208.00 \\
+ \$300 &= \quad \underline{300.00} \\
\text{Total future value} &= \quad \$616.16
\end{aligned}$$

The total future value is thus $616.16. The total interest is:

$$\$616.16 - (100 + 200 + 300) = \$16.16$$

How much will you have in five years? We know that you will have $616.16 in three years. If you leave that in for two more years, it will grow to:

$$\$616.16 \times 1.04^2 = \$616.16 \times 1.0816 = \$666.44$$

Notice that we could have calculated the future value of each amount separately. Once again, be careful about the lengths of time. As we previously calculated, the first $100 earns interest for only four years, the second deposit earns three years' interest, and the last earns two years' interest:

$$\begin{aligned}
\$100 \times 1.04^4 &= \$100 \times 1.1699 = \$116.99 \\
\$200 \times 1.04^3 &= \$200 \times 1.1249 = \quad 224.98 \\
\$300 \times 1.04^2 &= \$300 \times 1.0816 = \quad \underline{324.48} \\
\text{Total future value} &= \$666.45
\end{aligned}$$

Present Value with Multiple Cash Flows

It will turn out that we will very often need to determine the present value of a series of future cash flows. As with future values, there are two ways we can do it. We can either discount back one period at a time, or we can just calculate the present values individually and add them up.

Suppose you need $1,000 in one year and $2,000 more in two years. If you can earn 9 percent on your money, how much do you have to put up today to exactly cover these amounts in the future? In other words, what is the present value of the two cash flows at 9 percent?

The present value of $2,000 in two years at 9 percent is:

$$\$2,000/1.09^2 = \$1,683.36$$

The present value of $1,000 in one year is:

$$\$1,000/1.09 = \$917.43$$

Therefore, the total present value is:

$$\$1,683.36 + 917.43 = \$2,600.79$$

To see why $2,600.79 is the right answer, we can check to see that after the $2,000 is paid out in two years, there is no money left. If we invest $2,600.79 for one year at 9 percent, we will have:

$$\$2,600.79 \times 1.09 = \$2,834.86$$

We take out $1,000, leaving $1,834.86. This amount earns 9 percent for another year, leaving us with:

$$\$1,834.86 \times 1.09 = \$2,000$$

This is just as we planned. As this example illustrates, the present value of a series of future cash flows is simply the amount that you would need today in order to exactly duplicate those future cash flows (for a given discount rate).

An alternative way of calculating present values for multiple future cash flows is to discount back to the present, one period at a time. To illustrate, suppose we had an investment that was going to pay $1,000 at the end of every year for the next five years. To find the present value, we could discount each $1,000 back to the present separately and then add them up. Figure 6.5 illustrates this approach for a 6 percent discount rate; as shown, the answer is $4,212.37 (ignoring a small rounding error).

FIGURE 6.5

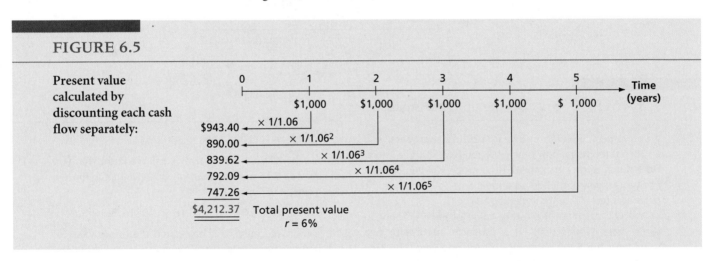

Present value calculated by discounting each cash flow separately:

Alternatively, we could discount the last cash flow back one period and add it to the next-to-the-last cash flow:

$$(\$1,000/1.06) + 1,000 = \$943.40 + 1,000 = \$1,943.40$$

We could then discount this amount back one period and add it to the Year 3 cash flow:

$$(\$1,943.40/1.06) + 1,000 = \$1,833.40 + 1,000 = \$2,833.40$$

This process could be repeated as necessary. Figure 6.6 illustrates this approach and the remaining calculations.

FIGURE 6.6

Present value calculated by discounting back one period at a time

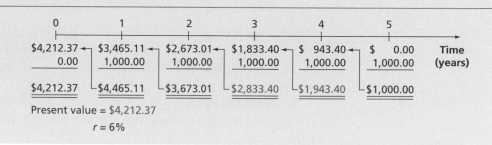

Present value = $4,212.37

$r = 6\%$

If we consider Roberto Luongo's twelve-year contract introduced at the start of the chapter, and use a 5 percent discount rate, what is the present value of his agreement? In 2009, the remaining amount to be paid to him was US$64 million over twelve years. Assuming he is paid US$5.33 million annually starting in 2010, the actual payout is:

$5.33 million/$1.05 = 5.08$ million
$5.33 million/$1.05^2 = 4.83$ million
$5.33 million/$1.05^3 = 4.60$ million
$5.33 million/$1.05^4 = 4.39$ million
$5.33 million/$1.05^5 = 4.18$ million
$5.33 million/$1.05^6 = 3.98$ million
$5.33 million/$1.05^7 = 3.79$ million
$5.33 million/$1.05^8 = 3.61$ million
$5.33 million/$1.05^9 = 3.44$ million
$5.33 million/$1.05^{10} = 3.27$ million
$5.33 million/$1.05^{11} = 3.12$ million
$5.33 million/$1.05^{12} = 2.97$ million

Therefore, in 2009, his contract is actually only worth US$52.59 (summing the present values above and adding the US$5.33 million paid in 2009), not the publicized US$64 million.

EXAMPLE 6.3: How Much is it Worth?

You are offered an investment that will pay you $200 in one year, $400 the next year, $600 the next year, and $800 at the end of the next year. You can earn 3 percent on very similar investments. What is the most you should pay for this one?

We need to calculate the present value of these cash flows at 3 percent. Taking them one at a time gives:

$200 \times 1/1.03^1 = \$200/1.0300 = \$ \ 194.17$
$400 \times 1/1.03^2 = \$400/1.0609 = \ \ \ \ 377.04$
$600 \times 1/1.03^3 = \$600/1.0927 = \ \ \ \ 549.10$
$800 \times 1/1.03^4 = \$800/1.1255 = \ \ \ \ 710.80$
Total present value = $1,831.11

If you can earn 3 percent on your money, then you can duplicate this investment's cash flows for $1,831.11, so this is the most you should be willing to pay.

CALCULATOR HINTS

How to Calculate Present Values with Multiple Future Cash Flows Using a Financial Calculator

To calculate the present value of multiple cash flows with a financial calculator, we will simply discount the individual cash flows one at a time using the same technique we used in our previous chapter, so this is not really new. There is a shortcut, however, that we can show you. We will use the numbers in Example 6.3 to illustrate.

To begin, of course we first remember to clear out the calculator! Next, from Example 6.3, the first cash flow is $200 to be received in one year and the discount rate is 3 percent, so we do the following:

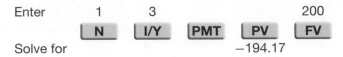

Enter   1   3   200

| N | I/Y | PMT | PV | FV |

Solve for   −194.17

Now, you can write down this answer to save it, but that's inefficient. All calculators have a memory where you can store numbers. Why not just save it there? Doing so cuts way down on mistakes because you don't have to write down and/or rekey numbers, and it's much faster.

Next we value the second cash flow. We need to change N to 2 and FV to 400. As long as we haven't changed anything else, we don't have to reenter I/Y or clear out the calculator, so we have:

Enter   2   400

| N | I/Y | PMT | PV | FV |

Solve for   −377.04

You save this number by adding it to the one you saved in our first calculation, and so on for the remaining two calculations.

As we will see in a later chapter, some financial calculators will let you enter all of the future cash flows at once, but we'll discuss that subject when we get to it.

EXAMPLE 6.4: How Much is it Worth? Part 2

You are offered an investment that will make three $5,000 payments. The first payment will occur four years from today. The second will occur in five years, and the third will follow in six years. If you can earn 4 percent, what is the most this investment is worth today? What is the future value of the cash flows?

We will answer the questions in reverse order to illustrate a point. The future value of the cash flows in six years is:

$$(\$5,000 \times 1.04^2) + (5,000 \times 1.04) + 5,000$$
$$= \$5,408 + 5,200 + 5,000 = \$15,608$$

The present value must be:

$$\$15,608/1.04^6 = \$12,335.23$$

Let's check this. Taking them one at a time, the PVs of the cash flows are:

$$\$5,000 \times 1/1.04^6 = \$5,000/1.2653 = \$\ 3,951.57$$
$$\$5,000 \times 1/1.04^5 = \$5,000/1.2167 = \ \ \ 4,109.64$$
$$\$5,000 \times 1/1.04^4 = \$5,000/1.1699 = \ \underline{\ \ \ 4,274.02}$$
$$\text{Total present value} = \$12,335.23$$

This is as we previously calculated. The point we want to make is that we can calculate present and future values in any order and convert between them using whatever way seems most convenient. The answers will always be the same as long as we stick with the same discount rate and are careful to keep track of the right number of periods.

A Note on Cash Flow Timing

In working present and future value problems, cash flow timing is critically important. In almost all such calculations, it is implicitly assumed that the cash flows occur at the *end* of each period. In fact, all the formulas we have discussed, all the numbers in a standard present value or future value table, and, very importantly, all the preset (or default) settings on a financial calculator assume that cash flows occur at the end of each period. Unless you are very explicitly told otherwise, you should always assume that this is what is meant.

As a quick illustration of this point, suppose you are told that a three-year investment has a first-year cash flow of $100, a second-year cash flow of $200, and a third-year cash flow of $300. You are asked to draw a time line. Without further information, you should always assume that the time line looks like this:

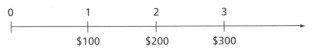

On our time line, notice how the first cash flow occurs at the end of the first period, the second at the end of the second period, and the third at the end of the third period.

How to Calculate Present Values with Multiple Future Cash Flows Using a Spreadsheet

Just as we did in our previous chapter, we can set up a basic spreadsheet to calculate the present values of the individual cash flows as follows. Notice that we have simply calculated the present values one at a time and added them up:

	A	B	C	D	E
1					
2			Using a spreadsheet to value multiple future cash flows		
3					
4	What is the present value of $200 in one year, $400 the next year, $600 the next year, and				
5	$800 the last year if the discount rate is 12 percent?				
6					
7	Rate:	0.12			
8					
9	Year	Cash flows	Present values	Formula used	
10	1	$200	$178.57	=PV($B$7, A10, 0, −B10)	
11	2	$400	$318.88	=PV($B$7, A11, 0, −B11)	
12	3	$600	$427.07	=PV($B$7, A12, 0, −B12)	
13	4	$800	$508.41	=PV($B$7, A13, 0, −B13)	
14					
15		Total PV:	**$1,432.93**	=SUM(C10:C13)	
16					
17	Notice the negative signs inserted in the PV formulas. These just make the present values have				
18	positive signs. Also, the discount rate in cell B7 is entered as $B$7 (an "absolute" reference) because				
19	it is used over and over. We could have just entered ".12" instead, but our approach is more flexible.				
20					

Concept Questions

1. Describe how to calculate the future value of a series of cash flows.
2. Describe how to calculate the present value of a series of cash flows.
3. Unless we are explicitly told otherwise, what do we always assume about the timing of cash flows in present and future value problems?

6.2 | Valuing Level Cash Flows: Annuities and Perpetuities

We will frequently encounter situations in which we have multiple cash flows that are all the same amount. For example, a very common type of loan repayment plan calls for the borrower to repay the loan by making a series of equal payments over some length of time. Almost all consumer loans (such as car loans and student loans) and home mortgages feature equal payments, usually made each month.

annuity
A level stream of cash flows for a fixed period of time.

More generally, a series of constant or level cash flows that occur at the end of each period for some fixed number of periods is called an ordinary **annuity**; or, more correctly, the cash flows are said to be in ordinary annuity form. Annuities appear frequently in financial arrangements, and there are some useful shortcuts for determining their values. We consider these next.

Present Value for Annuity Cash Flows

Suppose we were examining an asset that promised to pay $500 at the end of each of the next three years. The cash flows from this asset are in the form of a three-year, $500 annuity. If we wanted to earn 10 percent on our money, how much would we offer for this annuity?

From the previous section, we know that we can discount each of these $500 payments back to the present at 10 percent to determine the total present value:

$$\text{Present value} = (\$500/1.1^1) + (500/1.1^2) + (500/1.1^3)$$
$$= (\$500/1.1) + (500/1.21) + (500/1.331)$$
$$= \$454.55 + 413.22 + 375.66$$
$$= \$1,243.43$$

This approach works just fine. However, we will often encounter situations in which the number of cash flows is quite large. For example, a typical home mortgage calls for monthly payments over 25 years, for a total of 300 payments. If we were trying to determine the present value of those payments, it would be useful to have a shortcut.

Because the cash flows of an annuity are all the same, we can come up with a very useful variation on the basic present value equation. It turns out that the present value of an annuity of C dollars per period for t periods when the rate of return or interest rate is r is given by:

$$\text{Annuity present value} = C \times \left(\frac{1 - \text{Present value factor}}{r} \right) \qquad [6.1]$$
$$= C \times \left\{ \frac{1 - 1/(1 + r)^t}{r} \right\}$$

The term in parentheses on the first line is sometimes called the present value interest factor for annuities and abbreviated PVIFA(r,t).

The expression for the annuity present value may look a little complicated, but it isn't difficult to use. Notice that the term on the second line, $1/(1 + r)^t$, is the same present value factor we've been calculating. In our example from the beginning of this section, the interest rate is 10 percent and there are three years involved. The usual present value factor is thus:

$$\text{Present value factor} = 1/1.1^3 = 1/1.331 = .75131$$

To calculate the annuity present value factor, we just plug this in:

$$\text{Annuity present value factor} = (1 - \text{Present value factor})/r$$
$$= (1 - .75131)/.10$$
$$= .248685/.10 = 2.48685$$

Just as we calculated before, the present value of our $500 annuity is then:

$$\text{Annuity present value} = \$500 \times 2.48685 = \$1,243.43$$

ANNUITY TABLES   Just as there are tables for ordinary present value factors, there are tables for annuity factors as well. Table 6.1 contains a few such factors; Table A.3 on the book's website contains a larger set. To find the annuity present value factor, look for the row corresponding to three periods and then find the column for 10 percent. The number you see at that intersection should be 2.4869 (rounded to four decimal places), as we calculated. Once again, try calculating a few of these factors yourself and compare your answers to the ones in the table to make sure you know how to do it. If you are using a financial calculator, just enter $1 as the payment and calculate the present value; the result should be the annuity present value factor.

SPREADSHEET STRATEGIES

Annuity Present Values

Using a spreadsheet to find annuity present values goes like this:

	A	B	C	D	E	F	G
1							
2		Using a spreadsheet to find annuity present values					
3							
4	What is the present value of $500 per year for 3 years if the discount rate is 10 percent?						
5	We need to solve for the unknown present value, so we use the formula PV(rate, nper, pmt, fv).						
6							
7	Payment amount per period:	$500					
8	Number of payments:	3					
9	Discount rate:	0.1					
10							
11	Annuity present value:	$1,243.43					
12							
13	The formula entered in cell B11 is =PV(B9, B8, −B7, 0); notice that fv is zero and that						
14	pmt has a negative sign on it. Also notice that rate is entered as a decimal, not a percentage.						
15							
16							
17							

Annuity Present Values

To find annuity present values with a financial calculator, we need to use the **PMT** key (you were probably wondering what it was for). Compared to finding the present value of a single amount, there are two important differences. First, we enter the annuity cash flow using the **PMT** key, and, second, we don't enter anything for the future value, FV. So, for example, the problem we have been examining is a three-year, $500 annuity. If the discount rate is 10 percent, we need to do the following (after clearing out the calculator!):

Enter   3   10   500

    N   **I/Y**   **PMT**   **PV**   **FV**

Solve for   −1,243.43

As usual, we get a negative sign on the PV.

FINDING THE PAYMENT   Suppose you wish to start up a new business that specializes in the latest of health food trends, frozen yak milk. To produce and market your product, you need to borrow $100,000. Because it strikes you as unlikely that this particular fad will be long-lived, you propose to pay off the loan quickly by making five equal annual payments. If the interest rate is 18 percent, what will the payment be?

TABLE 6.1

Annuity present value interest factors

Periods	Interest Rate			
	5%	10%	15%	20%
1	.9524	.9091	.8696	.8333
2	1.8594	1.7355	1.6257	1.5278
3	2.7232	2.4869	2.2832	2.1065
4	3.5460	3.1699	2.8550	2.5887
5	4.3295	3.7908	3.3522	2.9906

In this case, we know the present value is $100,000. The interest rate is 18 percent, and there are five years. The payments are all equal, so we need to use the annuity formula and find the relevant annuity factor and solve for the unknown cash flow:

$$\text{Annuity present value} = \$100,000 = C \times [(1 - \text{Present value factor})/r]$$
$$= C \times \{[1 - (1/1.18^5)]/.18\}$$
$$= C \times [(1 - .4371)/.18]$$
$$= C \times 3.1272$$
$$C = \$100,000/3.1272 = \$31,977$$

Therefore, you'll make five payments of just under $32,000 each.

Annuity Payments

Finding annuity payments is easy with a financial calculator. In our example just above, the PV is $100,000, the interest rate is 18 percent, and there are five years. We find the payment as follows:

Enter   5   18   100,000

    N   **I/Y**   **PV**   **PMT**   **FV**

Solve for   −31,978

Here we get a negative sign on the payment because the payment is an outflow for us.

SPREADSHEET STRATEGIES

Annuity Payments

Using a spreadsheet to work annuity payments for the new business example goes like this:

	A	B	C	D	E	F	G
1							
2		Using a spreadsheet to find annuity payments					
3							
4	What is the annuity payment if the present value is $100,000, the interest rate is 18 percent, and						
5	there are 5 periods? We need to solve for the unknown payment in an annuity, so we use the						
6	formula PMT(rate, nper, pv, fv).						
7							
8	Annuity present value:	$100,000					
9	Number of payments:	5					
10	Discount rate:	0.18					
11							
12	Annuity payment:	$31,977.78					
13							
14	The formula entered in cell B12 is =PMT(B10, B9, −B8, 0); notice that fv is zero and that the payment						
15	has a negative sign because it is an outflow to us.						
16							

EXAMPLE 6.5: How Much Can You Afford?

After carefully going over your budget, you have determined you can afford to pay $632 per month towards a new Honda Civic. You visit your bank's website and find that the going rate is 1 percent per month for 48 months. How much can you borrow?

To determine how much you can borrow, we need to calculate the present value of $632 per month for 48 months at 1 percent per month. The loan payments are in ordinary annuity form, so the annuity present value factor is:

$$\text{Annuity PV factor} = (1 - \text{Present value factor})/r$$
$$= [1 - (1/1.01^{48})]/.01$$
$$= (1 - .6203)/.01 = 37.9740$$

With this factor, we can calculate the present value of the 48 payments of $632 each as:

$$\text{Present value} = \$632 \times 37.9740 = \$24,000$$

Therefore, $24,000 is what you can afford to borrow and repay.

EXAMPLE 6.6: Finding the Number of Payments

You ran a little short on your February vacation, so you put $1,000 on your credit card. You can only afford to make the minimum payment of $20 per month. The interest rate on the credit card is 1.5 percent per month. How long will you need to pay off the $1,000?

What we have here is an annuity of $20 per month at 1.5 percent per month for some unknown length of time. The present value is $1,000 (the amount you owe today). We need to do a little algebra (or else use a financial calculator):

$$\$1,000 = \$20 \times [(1 - \text{Present value factor})/.015]$$
$$(\$1,000/20) \times .015 = 1 - \text{Present value factor}$$
$$\text{Present value factor} = .25 = 1/(1 + r)^t$$
$$1.015^t = 1/.25 = 4$$

At this point, the problem boils down to asking the question, how long does it take for your money to quadruple at 1.5 percent per month? The answer is about 93 months:

$$1.015^{93} = 3.99 \approx 4$$

It will take you about 93/12 = 7.75 years to pay off the $1,000 at this rate. If you use a financial calculator for problems like this one, you should be aware that some automatically round up to the next whole period.

CALCULATOR HINTS

Finding the Number of Payments

To solve this one on a financial calculator, do the following:

Enter		1.5	−20	1,000	
	N	I/Y	PMT	PV	FV
Solve for	93.11				

Notice that we put a negative sign on the payment you must make, and we have solved for the number of months. You still have to divide by 12 to get our answer. Also, some financial calculators won't report a fractional value for N; they automatically (without telling you) round up to the next whole period (not to the nearest value). With a spreadsheet, use the function =NPER(rate,pmt,pv,fv); be sure to put in a zero for fv and to enter −20 as the payment.

FINDING THE RATE   The last question we might want to ask concerns the interest rate implicit in an annuity. For example, an insurance company offers to pay you $1,000 per year for 10 years if you will pay $6,710 up front. What rate is implicit in this 10-year annuity?

In this case, we know the present value ($6,710), we know the cash flows ($1,000 per year), and we know the life of the investment (10 years). What we don't know is the discount rate:

$$\$6{,}710 = \$1{,}000 \times [(1 - \text{Present value factor})/r]$$
$$\$6{,}710/1{,}000 = 6.71 = \{1 - [1/(1 + r)^{10}]\}/r$$

So, the annuity factor for 10 periods is equal to 6.71, and we need to solve this equation for the unknown value of r. Unfortunately, this is mathematically impossible to do directly. The only way to find a value for r is to use a calculator, a table, or trial and error.

To illustrate how to find the answer by trial and error[1], suppose a relative of yours wants to borrow $3,000. She offers to repay you $1,000 every year for four years. What interest rate are you being offered?

The cash flows here have the form of a four-year, $1,000 annuity. The present value is $3,000. We need to find the discount rate, r. Our goal in doing so is primarily to give you a feel for the relationship between annuity values and discount rates.

We need to start somewhere, and 10 percent is probably as good a place as any to begin. At 10 percent, the annuity factor is:

Annuity present value factor $= [1 - (1/1.10^4)]/.10 = 3.1699$

The present value of the cash flows at 10 percent is thus:

Present value $= \$1{,}000 \times 3.1699 = \$3{,}169.90$

You can see that we're already in the right ballpark.

Is 10 percent too high or too low? Recall that present values and discount rates move in opposite directions: increasing the discount rate lowers the PV and vice versa. Our present value here is too high, so the discount rate is too low. If we try 12 percent:

Present value $= \$1{,}000 \times \{[1 - (1/1.12^4)]/.12\} = \$3{,}037.35$

Now we're almost there. We are still a little low on the discount rate (because the PV is a little high), so we'll try 13 percent:

Present value $= \$1{,}000 \times \{[1 - (1/1.13^4)]/.13\} = \$2{,}974.47$

This is less than $3,000, so we now know that the answer is between 12 percent and 13 percent, and it looks to be about 12.5 percent. For practice, work at it for a while longer and see if you find that the answer is about 12.59 percent.

---

[1] Financial calculators rely on trial and error to find the answer. That's why they sometimes appear to be "thinking" before coming up with the answer. Actually, it is possible to directly solve for r if there are fewer than five periods, but it's usually not worth the trouble.

Finding the Rate

Alternatively, you could use a financial calculator to do the following:

Enter   4   1,000   −3,000

  $\boxed{\text{N}}$ $\boxed{\text{I/Y}}$ $\boxed{\text{PMT}}$ $\boxed{\text{PV}}$ $\boxed{\text{FV}}$

Solve for   12.59

Notice that we put a negative sign on the present value (why?). With a spreadsheet, use the function =RATE(nper,pmt,pv,fv); be sure to put in a zero for fv and to enter 1,000 as the payment and −3,000 as the pv.

To illustrate a situation in which finding the unknown rate can be very useful, let us consider provincial lotteries, which often offer you a choice of how to take your winnings. In a recent drawing, participants were offered the option of receiving a lump-sum payment of $400,000 or an annuity of $800,000 to be received in equal installments over a 20-year period. (At the time, the lump-sum payment was always half the annuity option.) Which option was better?

To answer, suppose you were to compare $400,000 today to an annuity of $800,000/20 = $40,000 per year for 20 years. At what rate do these have the same value? This is the same problem we've been looking at; we need to find the unknown rate, r, for a present value of $400,000, a $40,000 payment, and a 20-year period. If you grind through the calculations (or get a little machine assistance), you should find that the unknown rate is about 7.75 percent. You should take the annuity option if that rate is attractive relative to other investments available to you.

To see why, suppose that you could find a low risk investment with a rate of return of 6 percent. Your lump sum of $400,000 would generate annual payments of only $34,874 as opposed to the $40,000 offered by the lottery. The payments are lower because they are calculated assuming a return of 6 percent while the lottery offer is based on a higher rate of 7.75 percent. This example shows why it makes sense to think of the discount rate as an opportunity cost—the return one could earn on an alternative investment of equal risk. We will have a lot more to say on this later in the text.

Future Value for Annuities

On occasion, it's also handy to know a shortcut for calculating the future value of an annuity. For example, suppose you plan to contribute $2,000 every year into a Registered Retirement Savings Plan (RRSP) paying 8 percent. If you retire in 30 years, how much will you have?

One way to answer this particular problem is to calculate the present value of a $2,000, 30-year annuity at 8 percent to convert it to a lump sum, and then calculate the future value of that lump sum:

$$\text{Annuity present value} = \$2,000 \times (1 - 1/1.08^{30})/.08$$
$$= \$2,000 \times 11.2578$$
$$= \$22,515.57$$

The future value of this amount in 30 years is:

$$\text{Future value} = \$22,515.57 \times 1.08^{30} = \$22,515.57 \times 10.0627 = \$226,566.42$$

We could have done this calculation in one step:

$$\text{Annuity future value} = \text{Annuity present value} \times (1.08^{30})$$
$$= \$2,000 \times (1 - 1/1.08^{30})/.08 \times (1.08)^{30}$$
$$= \$2,000 \times (1.08^{30} - 1)/.08$$
$$= \$2,000 \times (10.0627 - 1)/.08$$
$$= \$2,000 \times 113.2832 = \$226,566.4$$

As this example illustrates, there are future value factors for annuities as well as present value factors. In general, the future value factor for an annuity is given by:

$$\text{Annuity FV factor} = (\text{Future value factor} - 1)/r \qquad [6.2]$$
$$= ((1 + r)^t - 1)/r$$

CALCULATOR HINTS

Future Values of Annuities

Of course, you could solve this problem using a financial calculator by doing the following:

Enter   30   8   −2,000

| N | I/Y | PMT | PV | FV |

Solve for   226,566.42

Notice that we put a negative sign on the payment (why?). With a spreadsheet, use the function = FV(rate,nper,pmt,pv); be sure to put in a zero for pv and to enter −2,000 as the payment.

For example, True North Distillers has just placed a shipment of Canadian whiskey in a bonded warehouse where it will age for the next eight years. An exporter plans to buy $1 million worth of whiskey in eight years. If the exporter annually deposits $95,000 at year-end in a bank account paying 8 percent interest, would there be enough to pay for the whiskey?

In this case, the annuity future value factor is given by:

$$\text{Annuity FV factor} = (\text{Future value factor} - 1)/r$$
$$= (1.08^8 - 1)/.08$$
$$= (1.8509 - 1)/.08$$
$$= 10.6366$$

The future value of this eight-year, $95,000 annuity is thus:

$$\text{Annuity future value} = \$95,000 \times 10.6366$$
$$= \$1,010,480$$

Thus, the exporter would make it with $10,480 to spare.

In our example, notice that the first deposit occurs in one year and the last in eight years. As we discussed earlier, the first deposit earns seven years' interest; the last deposit earns none.

A Note on Annuities Due

So far, we have only discussed ordinary annuities. These are the most important, but there is a fairly common variation. Remember that with an ordinary annuity, the cash flows occur at the end of each period. When you take out a loan with monthly payments, for example, the first loan payment normally occurs one month after you get the loan. However, when you lease an apartment, the first lease payment is usually due immediately. The second payment is due at the beginning of the second month, and so on. A lease is an example of an **annuity due**. An annuity due is an annuity for which the cash flows occur at the beginning of each period. Almost any type of arrangement in which we have to prepay the same amount each period is an annuity due.

annuity due
An annuity for which the cash flows occur at the beginning of the period.

There are several different ways to calculate the value of an annuity due. With a financial calculator, you simply switch it into "due" or "beginning" mode. It is very important to remember to switch it back when you are done! Another way to calculate the present value of an annuity due can be illustrated with a time line. Suppose an annuity due has five payments of $400 each, and the relevant discount rate is 10 percent. The time line looks like this:

Notice how the cash flows here are the same as those for a *four*-year ordinary annuity, except that there is an extra $400 at Time 0. For practice, check to see that the value of a four-year ordinary annuity at 10 percent is $1,267.95. If we add on the extra $400, we get $1,667.95, which is the present value of this annuity due.

There is an even easier way to calculate the present or future value of an annuity due. If we assume cash flows occur at the end of each period when they really occur at the beginning, then we discount each one by one period too many. We could fix this by simply multiplying our answer by $(1 + r)$, where r is the discount rate. In fact, the relationship between the value of an annuity due and an ordinary annuity is just:

$$\text{Annuity due value} = \text{Ordinary annuity value} \times (1 + r) \qquad [6.3]$$

This works for both present and future values, so calculating the value of an annuity due involves two steps: (1) calculate the present or future value as though it were an ordinary annuity, and (2) multiply your answer by $(1 + r)$.

Perpetuities

perpetuity
An annuity in which the cash flows continue forever.

consol
A type of perpetuity.

We've seen that a series of level cash flows can be valued by treating those cash flows as an annuity. An important special case of an annuity arises when the level stream of cash flows continues forever. Such an asset is called a **perpetuity** because the cash flows are perpetual. One type of perpetuities is called a **consol**.

Since a perpetuity has an infinite number of cash flows, we obviously can't compute its value by discounting each one. Fortunately, evaluating a perpetuity turns out to be the easiest possible case. Consider a perpetuity that costs $1,000 and offers a 12 percent rate of return with payments at the end of each period. The cash flow each year must be $1,000 \times .12 = $120. More generally, the present value of a perpetuity ($PV = $1,000) multiplied by the rate ($r = 12\%$) must equal the cash flow ($C = $120):

$$\text{Perpetuity present value} \times \text{Rate} = \text{Cash flow} \qquad [6.4]$$
$$PV \times r = C$$

Therefore, given a cash flow and a rate of return, we can compute the present value very easily:

$$PV \text{ for a perpetuity} = C/r = C \times (1/r)$$

For example, an investment offers a perpetual cash flow of $500 every year. The return you require on such an investment is 8 percent. What is the value of this investment? The value of this perpetuity is:

$$\text{Perpetuity } PV = C \times (1/r) = \$500/.08 = \$6{,}250$$

Another way of seeing why a perpetuity's value is so easy to determine is to take a look at the expression for an annuity present value factor:

$$\text{Annuity present value factor} = (1 - \text{Present value factor})/r \qquad [6.5]$$
$$= (1/r) \times (1 - \text{Present value factor})$$

As we have seen, when the number of periods involved gets very large, the present value factor gets very small. As a result, the annuity factor gets closer and closer to $1/r$. At 10 percent, for example, the annuity present value factor for 100 years is:

$$\text{Annuity present value factor} = (1/.10) \times (1 - 1/1.10^{100})$$
$$= (1/.10) \times (1 - .000073)$$
$$\approx (1/.10)$$

Table 6.2 summarizes the formulas for annuities and perpetuities.

EXAMPLE 6.7: Early Bird RRSPs

Every February, financial institutions advertise their various RRSP products. While most people contribute just before the deadline, RRSP sellers point out the advantages of contributing early—greater returns because of compounding. In our example of the future value of annuities, we found that contributing $2,000 each year at the end of the year would compound to $226,566 in 30 years at 8 percent. Suppose you made the contribution at the beginning of each year. How much more would you have after 30 years?

Annuity due future value
$= \text{Payment} \times \text{Annuity FV factor} \times (1 + r)$
$= \$2{,}000 \times (1.08^{30} - 1)/.08 \times (1.08) = \$244{,}692$

Alternatively, you could simply estimate the value as $226,566 \times 1.08 = $244,691 since you are effectively earning one extra year worth of interest.[2]

You would have $244,692 − $226,566 = $18,126 more.

---

[2]The answers vary slightly due to rounding.

TABLE 6.2   **Summary of annuity and perpetuity calculations**

I. Symbols:

PV = Present value, what future cash flows are worth today

FV_t = Future value, what cash flows are worth in the future

r = Interest rate, rate of return, or discount rate per period—typically, but not always, one year

t = Number of periods—typically, but not always, the number of years

C = Cash amount

II. Future value of C per period for t periods at r percent per period:

$FV_t = C \times \{[1 + r)^t - 1]/r\}$

A series of identical cash flows is called an annuity, and the term $[(1 + r)^t - 1]/r$ is called the *annuity future value factor*.

III. Present value of C per period for t periods at r percent per period:

$PV = C \times \{1 - [1/(1 + r)^t]\}/r$

The term $\{1 - [1/(1 + r)^t]\}/r$ is called the *annuity present value factor*.

IV. Present value of a perpetuity of C per period:

$PV = C/r$

A *perpetuity* has the same cash flow every year forever.

EXAMPLE 6.8: Preferred Stock

Fixed-rate preferred stock is an important example of a perpetuity.[3] When a corporation sells fixed rate preferred, the buyer is promised a fixed cash dividend every period (usually every quarter) forever. This dividend must be paid before any dividend can be paid to regular shareholders, hence the term *preferred*.

Suppose the Home Bank of Canada wants to sell preferred stock at $100 per share. A very similar issue of preferred stock already outstanding has a price of $40 per share and offers a dividend of $1 every quarter. What dividend would the Home Bank have to offer if the preferred stock is going to sell?

The issue that is already out has a present value of $40 and a cash flow of $1 every quarter forever. Since this is a perpetuity:

$$\text{Present value} = \$40 = \$1 \times (1/r)$$
$$r = 2.5\%$$

To be competitive, the new Home Bank issue would also have to offer 2.5 percent per quarter; so, if the present value is to be $100, the dividend must be such that:

$$\text{Present value} = \$100 = C \times (1/.025)$$
$$C = \$2.50 \text{ (per quarter)}$$

Growing Perpetuities

growing perpetuity
A constant stream of cash flows without end that is expected to rise indefinitely.

The perpetuities we have discussed so far are annuities with constant payments. In practice, it is common to find perpetuities with growing payments. For example, imagine an apartment building in which cash flows to the landlord after expenses will be $100,000 next year. These cash flows are expected to rise at 5 percent per year. If we assume that this rise will continue indefinitely, the cash flow stream is termed a **growing perpetuity**. With an 11 percent discount rate, the present value of the cash flows can be represented as

$$PV = \frac{\$100,000}{1.11} + \frac{100,000(1.05)}{(1.11)^2} + \frac{\$100,000(1.05)^2}{(1.11)^3} + \cdots + \frac{100,000(1.05)^{N-1}}{(1.11)^N} + \cdots$$

Algebraically, we can write the formula as

$$PV = \frac{C}{(1 + r)} + \frac{C \times (1 + g)}{(1 + r)^2} + \frac{C \times (1 + g)^2}{(1 + r)^3} + \cdots \frac{C \times (1 + g)^{N-1}}{(1 + r)^N} + \cdots$$

---

[3]Corporations also issue floating rate preferred stock, as we discuss in Chapter 8.

where C is the cash flow to be received one period hence, g is the rate of growth per period, expressed as a percentage, and r is the interest rate. This formula is an example of the geometric series formula taught in high school.

Fortunately, the formula reduces to the following simplification:[4]

Formula for Present Value of Growing Perpetuity:

$$PV = \frac{C}{r - g}$$

[6.6]

Using this equation, the present value of the cash flows from the apartment building is

$$\frac{\$100,000}{0.11 - 0.05} = \$1,666,667$$

There are three important points concerning the growing perpetuity formula:

1. *The Numerator.* The numerator is the cash flow one period hence, not at date 0. Consider the following example:

EXAMPLE 6.9

Hoffstein Corporation is just about to pay a dividend of $3.00 per share. Investors anticipate that the annual dividend will rise by 6 percent a year forever. The applicable interest rate is 11 percent. What is the price of the stock today?

The numerator in the formula is the cash flow to be received next period. Since the growth rate is 6 percent, the dividend next year is $3.18 (or $3.00 × 1.06). The price of the stock today is

$$\$66.60 = \underset{\substack{\text{Imminent} \\ \text{dividend}}}{\$3.00} + \underset{\substack{\text{Present value of dividend all} \\ \text{dividends beginning a year} \\ \text{from now}}}{\frac{\$3.18}{0.11 - 0.06}}$$

The price of $66.60 includes both the dividend to be received immediately and the present value of all dividends beginning a year from now. The formula only makes it possible to calculate the present value of all dividends beginning a year from now. Be sure you understand this example; test questions on this subject always seem to confuse a few of our students.

---

2. *The Interest Rate and the Growth Rate.* The interest rate r must be greater than the growth rate g for the growing perpetuity formula to work. Consider the case in which the growth rate approaches the interest rate in magnitude. Then the denominator in the growing perpetuity formula gets infinitesimally small and the present value grows infinitely large. The present value is in fact undefined when r is less than g.

3. *The Timing Assumption.* Cash generally flows into and out of real-world firms both randomly and nearly continuously. However, our growing perpetuity formula assumes that cash flows are received and disbursed at regular and discrete points in time. In the example of the apartment, we assumed that the net cash flows only occurred once a year. In reality, rent cheques are commonly received every month. Payments for maintenance and other expenses may occur at any time within the year.

The growing perpetuity formula can be applied only by assuming a regular and discrete pattern of cash flow. Although this assumption is sensible because the formula saves so much time, the user should never forget that it is an assumption. This point will be mentioned again in the chapters ahead.

---

[4]PV is the sum of an infinite geometric series:

$$PV = a(1 + x + x^2 + \ldots)$$

where $a = C/(1 + r)$ and $x = (1 + g)/(1 + r)$. Previously we showed that the sum of an infinite geometric series is $a/(1 - x)$. Using this result and substituting for a and x, we find

$$PV = C/(r - g)$$

Note that this geometric series converges to a finite sum only when x is less than 1. This implies that the growth rate, g, must be less than the interest rate, r.

Growing Annuity

Cash flows in business are very likely to grow over time, either due to real growth or inflation. The growing perpetuity, which assumes an infinite number of cash flows, provides one formula to handle this growth. We now introduce a **growing annuity**, which is a *finite* number of growing cash flows. Because perpetuities of any kind are rare, a formula for a growing annuity often comes in handy. The formula is[5]

growing annuity
A finite number of growing annual cash flows.

Formula for Present Value of Growing Annuity:

$$PV = \frac{C}{r-g}\left[1 - \left(\frac{1+g}{1+r}\right)^t\right]$$

[6.7]

where, as before, C is the payment to occur at the end of the first period, r is the interest rate, g is the rate of growth per period, expressed as a percentage, and t is the number of periods for the annuity.

EXAMPLE 6.10

Gilles Lebouder, a second-year MBA student, has just been offered a job at $90,000 a year. He anticipates his salary increasing by 2 percent a year until his retirement in 40 years. Given an interest rate of 5 percent, what is the present value of his lifetime salary?

We simplify by assuming he will be paid his $90,000 salary exactly one year from now, and that his salary will continue to be paid in annual installments. From the growing annuity formula, the calculation is

Present value of Gilles's lifetime salary
= $90,000 × [1/(0.05 − 0.02)] × [1 − {(1 + 0.02)/(1 + 0.05)}⁴⁰]
= $2,059,072.50

Though the growing annuity is quite useful, it is more tedious than the other simplifying formulas.

Concept Questions

1. In general, what is the present value of an annuity of C dollars per period at a discount rate of r per period? The future value?
2. In general, what is the present value of a perpetuity?
3. In general, what is the present value of a growing perpetuity?
4. In general, what is the present value of a growing annuity?

6.3 | Comparing Rates: The Effect of Compounding

The last issue we need to discuss has to do with the way interest rates are quoted. This subject causes a fair amount of confusion because rates are quoted in many different ways. Sometimes the way a rate is quoted is the result of tradition, and sometimes it's the result of legislation. Unfortunately, at times, rates are quoted in deliberately deceptive ways to mislead borrowers and investors. We will discuss these topics in this section.

---

[5]This can be proved as follows. A growing annuity can be viewed as the difference between two growing perpetuities. Consider a growing perpetuity A, where the first payment of C occurs at date 1. Next, consider growing perpetuity B, where the first payment of $C(1 + g)^T$ is made at date $T + 1$. Both perpetuities grow at rate g. The growing annuity over T periods is the difference between annuity A and annuity B. This can be represented as:

Date	0	1	2	3	⋯	T	T+1	T+2	T+3
Perpetuity A		C	$C×(1+g)$	$C×(1+g)^2$	⋯	$C×(1+g)^{T-1}$	$C×(1+g)^T$	$C×(1+g)^{T+1}$	$C×(1+g)^{T+2}⋯$
Perpetuity B							$C×(1+g)^T$	$C×(1+g)^{T+1}$	$C×(1+g)^{T+2}⋯$
Annuity		C	$C×(1+g)$	$C×(1+g)^2$	⋯	$C×(1+g)^{T-1}$			

The value of perpetuity A is $\frac{C}{r-g}$.

The value of perpetuity B is $\frac{C×(1+g)^T}{r-g} × \frac{1}{(1+r)^T}$.

The difference between the two perpetuities is given by the formula for the present value of a growing annuity.

Effective Annual Rates and Compounding

If a rate is quoted as 10 percent compounded semiannually, then what this means is that the investment actually pays 5 percent every six months. A natural question then arises: Is 5 percent every six months the same thing as 10 percent per year? It's easy to see that it is not. If you invest $1 at 10 percent per year, you will have $1.10 at the end of the year. If you invest at 5 percent every six months, then you'll have the future value of $1 at 5 percent for two periods, or:

$$\$1 \times 1.05^2 = \$1.1025$$

This is $.0025 more. The reason is very simple. What has occurred is that your account was credited with $1 × .05 = 5 cents in interest after 6 months. In the following six months, you earned 5 percent on that nickel, for an extra 5 × .05 = .25 cents.

As our example illustrates, 10 percent compounded semiannually is actually equivalent to 10.25 percent per year. Put another way, we would be indifferent between 10 percent compounded semiannually and 10.25 percent compounded annually. Anytime we have compounding during the year, we need to be concerned about what the rate really is.

In our example, the 10 percent is called a **stated interest rate**, or **quoted interest rate**. As you will see later in the chapter, other terms are used to describe this rate as well. It is simply the interest rate charged per period multiplied by the number of periods per year. The 10.25 percent, which is actually the rate that you will earn, is called the **effective annual rate (EAR)**. To compare different investments or interest rates, we will always need to convert to effective rates. Some general procedures for doing this are discussed next.

Calculating and Comparing Effective Annual Rates

To see why it is important to work only with effective rates, suppose you've shopped around and come up with the following three rates:

Bank A: 15 percent compounded daily
Bank B: 15.5 percent compounded quarterly
Bank C: 16 percent compounded annually

Which of these is the best if you are thinking of opening a savings account? Which of these is best if they represent loan rates?

To begin, Bank C is offering 16 percent per year. Because there is no compounding during the year, this is the effective rate. Bank B is actually paying .155/4 = .03875 or 3.875 percent per quarter. At this rate, an investment of $1 for four quarters would grow to:

$$\$1 \times 1.03875^4 = \$1.1642$$

The EAR, therefore, is 16.42 percent. For a saver, this is much better than the 16 percent rate Bank C is offering; for a borrower, it's worse.

Bank A is compounding every day. This may seem a little extreme, but it is very common to calculate interest daily. In this case, the daily interest rate is actually:

$$.15/365 = .000411$$

This is .0411 percent per day. At this rate, an investment of $1 for 365 periods would grow to:

$$\$1 \times 1.000411^{365} = \$1.1618$$

The EAR is 16.18 percent. This is not as good as Bank B's 16.42 percent for a saver, and not as good as Bank C's 16 percent for a borrower.

This example illustrates two things. First, the highest quoted rate is not necessarily the best. Second, the compounding during the year can lead to a significant difference between the quoted rate and the effective rate. Remember that the effective rate is what you get or what you pay.

If you look at our examples, you see that we computed the EARs in three steps. We first divided the quoted rate by the number of times that the interest is compounded. We then added 1 to the result and raised it to the power of the number of times the interest is compounded. Finally, we subtracted the 1. If we let m be the number of times the interest is compounded during the year, these steps can be summarized simply as:

$$\text{EAR} = [1 + (\text{Quoted rate}/m)]^m - 1 \qquad [6.8]$$

stated interest rate or quoted interest rate
The interest rate expressed in terms of the interest payment made each period. Also, quoted interest rate.

effective annual rate (EAR)
The interest rate expressed as if it were compounded once per year.

For example, suppose you are offered 7 percent compounded monthly. In this case, the interest is compounded 12 times a year; so m is 12. You can calculate the effective rate as:

$$\begin{aligned}
\text{EAR} &= [1 + (\text{Quoted rate}/m)]^m - 1 \\
&= [1 + (.07/12)]^{12} - 1 \\
&= 1.0058^{12} - 1 \\
&= 1.0723 - 1 \\
&= 7.23\%
\end{aligned}$$

EXAMPLE 6.11: What's the EAR?

A bank is offering 12 percent compounded quarterly. If you put $100 in an account, how much will you have at the end of one year? What's the EAR? How much will you have at the end of two years?

The bank is effectively offering 12%/4 = 3% every quarter. If you invest $100 for four periods at 3 percent per period, the future value is:

$$\begin{aligned}
\text{Future value} &= \$100 \times 1.03^4 \\
&= \$100 \times 1.1255 \\
&= \$112.55
\end{aligned}$$

The EAR is 12.55 percent: $100 × (1 + .1255) = $112.55.

We can determine what you would have at the end of two years in two different ways. One way is to recognize that two years is the same as eight quarters. At 3 percent per quarter, after eight quarters, you would have:

$100 × 1.03^8 = $100 × 1.2668 = $126.68

Alternatively, we could determine the value after two years by using an EAR of 12.55 percent; so after two years you would have:

$100 × 1.1255^2 = $100 × 1.2688 = $126.68

Thus, the two calculations produce the same answer. This illustrates an important point. Anytime we do a present or future value calculation, the rate we use must be an actual or effective rate. In this case, the actual rate is 3 percent per quarter. The effective annual rate is 12.55 percent. It doesn't matter which one we use once we know the EAR.

EXAMPLE 6.12: Quoting a Rate

Now that you know how to convert a quoted rate to an EAR, consider going the other way. As a lender, you know you want to actually earn 18 percent on a particular loan. You want to quote a rate that features monthly compounding. What rate do you quote?

In this case, we know the EAR is 18 percent and we know this is the result of monthly compounding. Let q stand for the quoted rate. We thus have:

$$\begin{aligned}
\text{EAR} &= [1 + (\text{Quoted rate}/m)]^m - 1 \\
.18 &= [1 + (q/12)]^{12} - 1 \\
1.18 &= [1 + (q/12)]^{12}
\end{aligned}$$

We need to solve this equation for the quoted rate. This calculation is the same as the ones we did to find an unknown interest rate in Chapter 5:

$$\begin{aligned}
1.18^{(1/12)} &= 1 + (q/12) \\
1.18^{.08333} &= 1 + (q/12) \\
1.0139 &= 1 + (q/12) \\
q &= .0139 \times 12 \\
&= 16.68\%
\end{aligned}$$

Therefore, the rate you would quote is 16.68 percent, compounded monthly.

Mortgages

Mortgages are a very common example of an annuity with monthly payments. All major financial institutions have websites providing mortgage information. For example, CIBC's website has a mortgage calculator on the mortgages menu. To understand mortgage calculations, keep in mind two institutional arrangements: First, although payments are monthly, regulations for Canadian financial institutions require that mortgage rates be quoted with semi-annual compounding. Thus, the compounding frequency differs from the payment frequency. Second, financial institutions offer mortgages with interest rates fixed for various periods ranging from 6 months to 25 years. As the borrower, you must choose the period for which the rate is fixed. (We offer some guidance in Example 6.14.) In any case, payments on conventional mortgages are calculated to maturity (usually after 25 years).

EXAMPLE 6.13: What Are Your Payments?

A financial institution is offering a $100,000 mortgage at a quoted semiannual rate of 6 percent. Assume the mortgage is amortized over 25 years. To find the payments, we need to find the quoted monthly rate. To do this, we convert the quoted semiannual rate to an EAR:

$$\text{EAR} = [1 + \text{Quoted rate}/m]^m - 1$$
$$= [1 + .06/2]^2 - 1$$
$$= 1.03^2 - 1$$
$$= 6.09\%$$

Then we find the quoted monthly rate used to calculate the payments:

$$\text{Quoted rate}/m = (\text{EAR} + 1)^{1/m} - 1$$
$$\text{Quoted rate}/12 = (1.0609)^{1/12} - 1$$
$$= 1.004939 - 1$$
$$= 0.4939\%$$

Annuity present value = $100,000
$$= C \times (1 - \text{Present value factor})/r$$

$$\$100,000 = C \times (1 - 1/1.004939^{300})/.004939$$
$$= C \times (1 - .22808)/.004939$$
$$= C \times 156.2907$$
$$C = \$639.83$$

Your monthly payments will be $639.83.

EXAMPLE 6.14: Choosing the Mortgage Term

Earlier we pointed out that while mortgages are amortized over 300 months, the rate is fixed for a shorter period, usually no longer than five years. Suppose the rate of 6 percent in Example 6.13 is fixed for five years and you are wondering whether to lock in this rate or to take a lower rate of 4 percent fixed for only one year. If you chose the one-year rate, how much lower would your payments be for the first year?

The payments at 4 percent are $525.63, a reduction of $111.40 per month. If you choose to take the shorter-term mortgage with lower payments, you are betting that rates will not take a big jump over the next year, leaving you with a new rate after one year much higher than 6 percent. While the mortgage formula cannot make this decision for you (it depends on risk and return discussed in Chapter 12), it does give you the risk you are facing in higher monthly payments. In 1981, mortgage rates were around 20 percent!

EARs and APRs

annual percentage rate (APR)
The interest rate charged per period multiplied by the number of periods per year.

Sometimes it's not clear whether a rate is an effective annual rate. A case in point concerns what is called the **annual percentage rate (APR)** on a loan. Cost of borrowing disclosure regulations (part of the *Bank Act*) in Canada require that lenders disclose an APR on virtually all consumer loans. This rate must be displayed on a loan document in a prominent and unambiguous way.

EXAMPLE 6.15: What Rate Are You Paying?

Depending on the issuer, a typical credit card agreement quotes an interest rate of 10 percent APR. Monthly payments are required. What is the actual interest rate you pay on such a credit card?

Based on our discussion, an APR of 10 percent with monthly payments is really .10/12 = .0083 or 0.83 percent per month. The EAR is thus:

$$\text{EAR} = [1 + (.10/12)]^{12} - 1$$
$$= 1.0083^{12} - 1$$
$$= 1.1043 - 1$$
$$= 10.43\%$$

This is the rate you actually pay.

Given that an APR must be calculated and displayed, an obvious question arises: Is an APR an effective annual rate? Put another way, if a bank quotes a car loan at 12 percent APR, is the consumer actually paying 12 percent interest? Surprisingly, the answer is no. There is some confusion over this point, which we discuss next.

The confusion over APRs arises because the law requires lenders to compute the APR in a particular way. By law, the APR is simply equal to the interest rate per period multiplied by the number of periods in a year.[6] For example, if a bank is charging 1.2 percent per month on car loans, then the APR that must be reported is 1.2% × 12 = 14.4%. So, an APR is, in fact, a quoted or stated rate in the sense we've been discussing. For example, an APR of 12 percent on a loan calling for monthly payments is really 1 percent per month. The EAR on such a loan is thus:

$$\text{EAR} = [1 + \text{APR}/12]^{12} - 1$$
$$= 1.01^{12} - 1 = 12.6825\%$$

The difference between an APR and an EAR probably won't be all that great, but it is somewhat ironic that truth-in-lending laws sometimes require lenders to be *un*truthful about the actual rate on a loan.

Taking It to the Limit: A Note on Continuous Compounding

If you made a deposit in a savings account, how often could your money be compounded during the year? If you think about it, there isn't really any upper limit. We've seen that daily compounding, for example, isn't a problem. There is no reason to stop here, however. We could compound every hour or minute or second. How high would the EAR get in this case? Table 6.3 illustrates the EARs that result as 10 percent is compounded at shorter and shorter intervals. Notice that the EARs do keep getting larger, but the differences get very small.

TABLE 6.3

Compounding frequency and effective annual rates

Compounding Period	Number of Times Compounded	Effective Annual Rate
Year	1	10.00000%
Quarter	4	10.38129
Month	12	10.47131
Week	52	10.50648
Day	365	10.51558
Hour	8,760	10.51703
Minute	525,600	10.51709

As the numbers in Table 6.3 seem to suggest, there is an upper limit to the EAR. If we let q stand for the quoted rate, then, as the number of times the interest is compounded gets extremely large, the EAR approaches:

$$\text{EAR} = e^q - 1 \qquad [6.9]$$

where e is the number 2.71828 (look for a key labelled "e^x" on your calculator). For example, with our 10 percent rate, the highest possible EAR is:

$$\text{EAR} = e^q - 1$$
$$= 2.71828^{.10} - 1$$
$$= 1.1051709 - 1$$
$$= 10.51709\%$$

In this case, we say that the money is compounded continuously, or instantaneously. What is happening is that interest is being credited the instant it is earned, so the amount of interest grows continuously.

---

[6]Note that we have simplified the discussion somewhat, as the *Bank Act* requires that the APR include costs such as up-front fees associated with borrowing the funds.

Concept Questions

1. If an interest rate is given as 12 percent compounded daily, what do we call this rate?
2. What is an APR? What is an EAR? Are they the same thing?
3. In general, what is the relationship between a stated interest rate and an effective interest rate? Which is more relevant for financial decisions?
4. What does continuous compounding mean?

6.4 | Loan Types and Loan Amortization

Whenever a lender extends a loan, some provision will be made for repayment of the principal (the original loan amount). A loan might be repaid in equal installments, for example, or it might be repaid in a single lump sum. Because the way that the principal and interest are paid is up to the parties involved, there is actually an unlimited number of possibilities.

In this section, we describe a few forms of repayment that come up quite often, and more complicated forms can usually be built up from these. The three basic types of loans are pure discount loans, interest-only loans, and amortized loans. Working with these loans is a very straightforward application of the present value principles that we have already developed.

Pure Discount Loans

The *pure discount loan* is the simplest form of loan. With such a loan, the borrower receives money today and repays a single lump sum at some time in the future. A one-year, 10 percent pure discount loan, for example, would require the borrower to repay $1.10 in one year for every dollar borrowed today.

Because a pure discount loan is so simple, we already know how to value one. Suppose a borrower was able to repay $25,000 in five years. If we, acting as the lender, wanted a 12 percent interest rate on the loan, how much would we be willing to lend? Put another way, what value would we assign today to that $25,000 to be repaid in five years? Based on our work in Chapter 5, we know the answer is just the present value of $25,000 at 12 percent for five years:

$$
\begin{aligned}
\text{Present value} &= \$25,000/1.12^5 \\
&= \$25,000/1.7623 \\
&= \$14,186
\end{aligned}
$$

Pure discount loans are very common when the loan term is short, say, a year or less. In recent years, they have become increasingly common for much longer periods.

EXAMPLE 6.16: Treasury Bills

When the Government of Canada borrows money on a short-term basis (a year or less), it does so by selling what are called Treasury bills or T-bills for short. A T-bill is a promise by the government to repay a fixed amount at some future time, for example, in 3 or 12 months.

Treasury bills are pure discount loans. If a T-bill promises to repay $10,000 in 12 months, and the market interest rate is 4 percent, how much does the bill sell for in the market?

Since the going rate is 4 percent, the T-bill sells for the present value of $10,000 to be paid in one year at 4 percent, or:

$$\text{Present value} = \$10,000/1.04 = \$9,615.38$$

In recent years, the Government of Canada has emphasized T-bills over Canada Savings Bonds when seeking short-term financing. T-bills are originally issued in denominations of $1 million. Investment dealers buy T-bills and break them up into smaller denominations, some as small as $1,000, for resale to individual investors.

Interest-Only Loans

A second type of loan repayment plan calls for the borrower to pay interest each period and to repay the entire principal (the original loan amount) at some point in the future. Loans with such a repayment plan are called *interest-only loans*. Notice that if there is just one period, a pure discount loan and an interest-only loan are the same thing.

For example, with a three-year, 10 percent, interest-only loan of $1,000, the borrower would pay $1,000 × .10 = $100 in interest at the end of the first and second years. At the end of the third year, the borrower would return the $1,000 along with another $100 in interest for that year. Similarly, a 50-year interest-only loan would call for the borrower to pay interest every year for the next 50 years and then repay the principal. In the extreme, the borrower pays the interest every period forever and never repays any principal. As we discussed earlier in the chapter, the result is a perpetuity.

Most bonds issued by the Government of Canada, the provinces, and corporations have the general form of an interest-only loan. Because we consider bonds in some detail in the next chapter, we defer a further discussion of them for now.

Amortized Loans

With a pure discount or interest-only loan, the principal is repaid all at once. An alternative is an *amortized loan*, with which the lender may require the borrower to repay parts of the loan amount over time. The process of providing for a loan to be paid off by making regular principal reductions is called *amortizing* the loan.

A simple way of amortizing a loan is to have the borrower pay the interest each period plus some fixed amount. This approach is common with medium-term business loans. For example, suppose a student takes out a $5,000, five-year loan at 9 percent for covering a part of her tuition fees. The loan agreement calls for the borrower to pay the interest on the loan balance each year and to reduce the loan balance each year by $1,000. Because the loan amount declines by $1,000 each year, it is fully paid in five years.

In the case we are considering, notice that the total payment will decline each year. The reason is that the loan balance goes down, resulting in a lower interest charge each year, whereas the $1,000 principal reduction is constant. For example, the interest in the first year will be $5,000 × .09 = $450. The total payment will be $1,000 + 450 = $1,450. In the second year, the loan balance is $4,000, so the interest is $4,000 × .09 = $360, and the total payment is $1,360. We can calculate the total payment in each of the remaining years by preparing a simple amortization schedule as follows:

Year	Beginning Balance	Total Payment	Interest Paid	Principal Paid	Ending Balance
1	$5,000	$1,450	$ 450	$1,000	$4,000
2	4,000	1,360	360	1,000	3,000
3	3,000	1,270	270	1,000	2,000
4	2,000	1,180	180	1,000	1,000
5	1,000	1,090	90	1,000	0
Totals		$6,350	$1,350	$5,000	

Notice that in each year, the interest paid is given by the beginning balance multiplied by the interest rate. Also notice that the beginning balance is given by the ending balance from the previous year.

Probably the most common way of amortizing a loan is to have the borrower make a single, fixed payment every period. Almost all consumer loans (such as car loans) and mortgages work this way. For example, suppose our five-year, 9 percent, $5,000 loan was amortized this way. How would the amortization schedule look?

We first need to determine the payment. From our discussion earlier in the chapter, we know that this loan's cash flows are in the form of an ordinary annuity. In this case, we can solve for the payment as follows:

$$\$5,000 = C \times \{[1 - (1/1.09^5)]/.09\}$$
$$= C \times [(1 - .6499)/.09]$$

This gives us:

$$C = \$5,000/3.8897$$
$$= \$1,285.46$$

The borrower will therefore make five equal payments of $1,285.46. Will this pay off the loan? We will check by filling in an amortization schedule.

In our previous example, we knew the principal reduction each year. We then calculated the interest owed to get the total payment. In this example, we know the total payment. We will thus calculate the interest and then subtract it from the total payment to calculate the principal portion in each payment.

In the first year, the interest is $450, as we calculated before. Because the total payment is $1,285.46, the principal paid in the first year must be:

Principal paid = $1,285.46 − 450 = $835.46

The ending loan balance is thus:

Ending balance = $5,000 − 835.46 = $4,164.54

The interest in the second year is $4,164.54 × .09 = $374.81, and the loan balance declines by $1,285.46 − 374.81 = $910.65. We can summarize all of the relevant calculations in the following schedule:

Year	Beginning Balance	Total Payment	Interest Paid	Principal Paid	Ending Balance
1	$5,000.00	$1,285.46	$ 450.00	$ 835.46	$4,164.54
2	4,164.54	1,285.46	374.81	910.65	3,253.89
3	3,253.89	1,285.46	292.85	992.61	2,261.28
4	2,261.28	1,285.46	203.52	1,081.94	1,179.34
5	1,179.34	1,285.46	106.14	1,179.32	0.02
Total		$6,427.30	$1,427.31	$5,000.00	

The ending balance at Year 5 is 0.02 and not 0 due to rounding error using the financial calculator in finding the payment. In practice, the 2 cents would be added to the final payment.

Because the loan balance declines to zero, the five equal payments do pay off the loan. Notice that the interest paid declines each period. This isn't surprising because the loan balance is going down. Given that the total payment is fixed, the principal paid must be rising each period.

If you compare the two loan amortizations in this section, you will see that the total interest is greater for the equal total payment case, $1,427.31 versus $1,350. The reason for this is that the loan is repaid more slowly early on, so the interest is somewhat higher. This doesn't mean that one loan is better than the other; it simply means that one is effectively paid off faster than the other. For example, the principal reduction in the first year is $835.46 in the equal total payment case as compared to $1,000 in the first case.

CALCULATOR HINTS

How to Calculate the Amortization of Loan Payments Using a Financial Calculator

The amortization of loan payments may be determined using your calculator once you have mastered the calculation of a loan payment. Once you have completed the four-step procedure to find the loan payment, you can find the amortization of any payment.

To begin, of course, we must remember to clear the calculator!

Enter	5	9	5,000		
	N	I/Y	PV	PMT	FV
Solve for				−1285.46	

To use the amortization worksheet, press [2nd] [AMORT].

At payment number, P1 = 1.00, press the down arrow key to view the ending balance after the payment is made as well as the interest and principal portions of the second payment. This gives you a balance of $4,164.54 and the principal returned equal to $835.46. To view the ending balance after the next payment press [CPT] at P1. This changes P1 from 1.00 to 2.00. Then, press down arrow key again to view ending balance, principal and interest portions and repeat these steps for P1 = 3.00, 4.00, and 5.00. The ending balance of $0.02 at P1 = 5.00 is due to rounding error in the financial calculator.

SPREADSHEET STRATEGIES

Loan Amortization Using a Spreadsheet

Loan amortization is a very common spreadsheet application. To illustrate, we will set up the problem that we have just examined, a five-year, $5,000, 9 percent loan with constant payments. Our spreadsheet looks like this:

	A	B	C	D	E	F	G	H
1								
2			Using a spreadsheet to amortize a loan					
3								
4			Loan amount:	$5,000				
5			Interest rate:	0.09				
6			Loan term:	5				
7			Loan payment:	$1,285.46				
8				Note: payment is calculated using PMT(rate, nper, –pv, fv)				
9			Amortization table:					
10								
11			Year	Beginning	Total	Interest	Principal	Ending
12				Balance	Payment	Paid	Paid	Balance
13			1	$5,000.00	$1,285.46	$450.00	$835.46	$4,164.54
14			2	4,164.54	1,285.46	374.81	910.65	3,253.88
15			3	3,253.88	1,285.46	292.85	992.61	2,261.27
16			4	2,261.27	1,285.46	203.51	1,081.95	1,179.32
17			5	1,179.32	1,285.46	106.14	1,170.32	0.00
18			Totals		6,427.31	1,427.31	5,000.00	
19								
20			Formulas in the amortization table:					
21								
22			Year	Beginning	Total	Interest	Principal	Ending
23				Balance	Payment	Paid	Paid	Balance
24			1	=+D4	=$D$7	=+$D$5*C13	=+D13–E13	=+C13–F13
25			2	=+G13	=$D$7	=+$D$5*C14	=+D14–E14	=+C14–F14
26			3	=+G14	=$D$7	=+$D$5*C15	=+D15–E15	=+C15–F15
27			4	=+G15	=$D$7	=+$D$5*C16	=+D16–E16	=+C16–F16
28			5	=+G16	=$D$7	=+$D$5*C17	=+D17–E17	=+C17–F17
29								
30			Note: totals in the amortization table are calculated using the SUM formula.					
31								

The ending balance using MS Excel is rounded to zero.

EXAMPLE 6.17: Student Loan Amortization

An increasing number of Canadian university and college students are financing their education via government and bank loans, student lines of credits, credit cards, and/or loans from family members. Suppose you owe $20,000 in government loans upon graduation. The interest rate is 6 percent, compounded monthly (for the sake of simplicity, assume this rate is fixed), and you estimate that you can make monthly payments of $250. What will be the remaining balance of your loan after one year? How long will it take for you to pay off your debt?

The interest paid each month is simply 0.5 percent (6 percent ÷ 12 months) multiplied by the beginning balance. The principal paid is the total payment less the monthly interest amount.

Month	Beginning Balance	Total Payment	Interest Paid	Principal Paid	Ending Balance
1	$20,000.00	$250.00	$100.00	$150.00	$19,850.00
2	19,850.00	250.00	99.25	150.75	19,699.25
3	19,699.25	250.00	98.50	151.50	19,547.75
.	.	.	.	.	.
12	18,308.13	250.00	91.54	158.46	18,149.67

Using an amortization schedule as the one above, you can see that at the end of one year, your remaining balance is $18,149.67.

To calculate the number of months it will take to pay off the $20,000 you can follow the calculations below (or use a financial calculator).

$20,000 = $250 × [(1 – Present value factor)/0.005]
0.6 = Present value factor
Present value factor = 0.6 = $1/(1 + 0.005)^t$
= $1.005^t = 1/0.6 = 1.67$
= $1.005^{102} \approx 1.66$

Thus, it will take you approximately 102 months or a bit over eight and a half years to pay off your student loan.

EXAMPLE 6.18: Partial Amortization, or the "Bullet" Loan

As we explained earlier, real estate lending usually involves mortgages with a loan period far shorter than the mortgage life. A common example might call for a five-year loan with, say, a 15-year amortization. This means the borrower makes a payment every month of a fixed amount based on a 15-year amortization. However, after 60 months, the borrower either negotiates a new five-year loan or makes a single, much larger payment called a *balloon* or *bullet* to pay off the loan. Balloon payments are common in both commercial and residential mortgages. In either case, because the monthly payments don't fully pay off the loan, the loan is said to be partially amortized.

Suppose we have a $100,000 commercial mortgage with a 5 percent rate compounded semiannually and a 20-year (240-month) amortization. Further suppose that the mortgage has a five-year balloon. What will the monthly payment be? How big will the balloon payment be?

The monthly payment can be calculated based on an ordinary annuity with a present value of $100,000. To find the monthly rate, we first have to find the EAR and then convert it to a quoted monthly rate. To do this, we convert the quoted semiannual rate to an EAR.

$$
\begin{aligned}
EAR &= [1 + \text{Quoted rate}/m]^m - 1 \\
&= [1 + .05/2]^2 - 1 \\
&= 1.0250^2 - 1 \\
&= 5.06\%
\end{aligned}
$$

Then, we find the quoted monthly rate used to calculate the payments:

$$
\begin{aligned}
\text{Quoted rate}/m &= (EAR + 1)^{1/m} - 1 \\
\text{Quoted rate}/12 &= (1.0506)^{1/12} - 1 \\
&= 1.0041 - 1 = 0.41\%
\end{aligned}
$$

The quoted monthly rate is 0.41 percent and there are $12 \times 20 = 240$ payments. To find the payment amount, we use the annuity present value formula.

$$
\begin{aligned}
\text{Annuity present value} &= \$100,000 \\
&= C \times (1 - \text{Present value factor})/r \\
\$100,000 &= C \times (1 - 1/1.0041^{240})/.0041 \\
&= C \times (1 - .3746)/.0041 \\
&= C \times 152.5366 \\
C &= \$655.58
\end{aligned}
$$

Your monthly payments will be $655.58

Now, there is an easy way and a hard way to determine the balloon payment. The hard way is to actually amortize the loan for 60 months to see what the balance is at that time. The easy way is to recognize that after 60 months, we have a $240 - 60 = 180$-month loan. The payment is still $655.58 per month, and the interest rate is still .41 percent per month. The loan balance is thus the present value of the remaining payments:

$$
\begin{aligned}
\text{Loan balance} &= \$655.58 \times (1 - 1/1.0041^{180})/.0041 \\
&= \$655.58 \times 127.1220 \\
&= \$83,338.64
\end{aligned}
$$

The balloon payment is a substantial $83,339. Why is it so large? To get an idea, consider the first payment on the mortgage. The interest in the first month is $100,000 \times .0041 = $410. Your payment is $655.58, so the loan balance declines by only $245.58. Since the loan balance declines so slowly, the cumulative pay down over five years is not great.[7]

Concept Questions

1. What is a pure discount loan? An interest-only loan?

2. What does it mean to amortize a loan?

3. What is a balloon payment? How do you determine its value?

---

[7] To get the precise payment of $657.13 you need to carry 6 decimal places in the interest rate using 0.412392 percent.

6.5 | SUMMARY AND CONCLUSIONS

This chapter rounds out your understanding of fundamental concepts related to the time value of money and discounted cash flow valuation. Several important topics were covered, including:

1. There are two ways of calculating present and future values when there are multiple cash flows. Both approaches are straightforward extensions of our earlier analysis of single cash flows.

2. A series of constant cash flows that arrive or are paid at the end of each period is called an ordinary annuity, and we described some useful shortcuts for determining the present and future values of annuities.

3. Interest rates can be quoted in a variety of ways. For financial decisions, it is important that any rates being compared be first converted to effective rates. The relationship between a quoted rate, such as an annual percentage rate (APR), and an effective annual rate (EAR) is given by:

$$EAR = [1 + (\text{Quoted rate}/m]^m - 1$$

where m is the number of times during the year the money is compounded.

4. Many loans are annuities. The process of providing for a loan to be paid off gradually is called amortizing the loan, and we discussed how amortization schedules are prepared and interpreted.

The principles developed in this chapter will figure prominently in the chapters to come. The reason for this is that most investments, whether they involve real assets or financial assets, can be analyzed using the discounted cash flow (DCF) approach. As a result, the DCF approach is broadly applicable and widely used in practice. For example, the next two chapters show how to value bonds and stocks using an extension of the techniques presented in this chapter. Before going on, therefore, you might want to do some of the problems that follow.

Key Terms

annual percentage rate (APR) (page 148)
annuity (page 135)
annuity due (page 141)
consol (page 142)
effective annual rate (EAR) (page 146)

growing annuity (page 145)
growing perpetuity (page 143)
perpetuity (page 142)
stated interest rate or quoted interest rate (page 146)

Chapter Review Problems and Self-Test

6.1   **Present Values with Multiple Cash Flows** A first-round draft choice quarterback has been signed to a three-year, $25 million contract. The details provide for an immediate cash bonus of $2 million. The player is to receive $5 million in salary at the end of the first year, $8 million the next, and $10 million at the end of the last year. Assuming a 15 percent discount rate, is this package worth $25 million? How much is it worth?

6.2   **Future Value with Multiple Cash Flows** You plan to make a series of deposits in an individual retirement account. You will deposit $1,000 today, $2,000 in two years, and $2,000 in five years. If you withdraw $1,500 in three years and $1,000 in seven years, assuming no withdrawal penalties, how much will you have after eight years if the interest rate is 7 percent? What is the present value of these cash flows?

6.3   **Annuity Present Value** You are looking into an investment that will pay you $12,000 per year for the next 10 years. If you require a 15 percent return, what is the most you would pay for this investment?

6.4   **APR versus EAR** The going rate on student loans is quoted as 8 percent APR. The terms of the loans call for monthly payments. What is the effective annual rate (EAR) on such a student loan?

6.5   **It's the Principal that Matters** Suppose you borrow $10,000. You are going to repay the loan by making equal annual payments for five years. The interest rate on the loan is 14 percent per year. Prepare an amortization schedule for the loan. How much interest will you pay over the life of the loan?

6.6   **Just a Little Bit Each Month** You've recently finished your MBA at the Darnit School. Naturally, you must purchase a new Lexus ES 350 immediately. The car costs about $42,000. The bank quotes an interest rate of 15 percent APR for a 72-month loan with a 10 percent down payment. You plan on trading the car in for a new one in two years. What will your monthly payment be? What is the effective interest rate on the loan? What will the loan balance be when you trade the car in?

Answers to Self-Test Problems

6.1   Obviously, the package is not worth $25 million because the payments are spread out over three years. The bonus is paid today, so it's worth $2 million. The present values for the three subsequent salary payments are:

$$(\$5/1.15) + (8/1.15^2) + (10/1.15^3) = (\$5/1.15) + (8/1.132) + (10/1.152)$$
$$= \$16.9721 \text{ million}$$

The package is worth a total of $16.9721 million.

6.2   We will calculate the future values for each of the cash flows separately and then add them up. Notice that we treat the withdrawals as negative cash flows:

$$
\begin{array}{rll}
\$1,000 \times 1.07^8 = & \$1,000 \times 1.7182 = & \$1,718.19 \\
\$2,000 \times 1.07^6 = & \$2,000 \times 1.5007 = & 3,001.46 \\
-\$1,500 \times 1.07^5 = & -\$1,500 \times 1.4026 = & -2,103.83 \\
\$2,000 \times 1.07^3 = & \$2,000 \times 1.2250 = & 2,450.09 \\
-\$1,000 \times 1.07^1 = & -\$1,000 \times 1.0700 = & -1,070.00 \\
& \text{Total future value} = & \$3,995.91 \\
\end{array}
$$

This value includes a small rounding error.

To calculate the present value, we could discount each cash flow back to the present or we could discount back a single year at a time. However, because we already know that the future value in eight years is $3,995.91, the easy way to get the PV is just to discount this amount back eight years:

$$
\begin{aligned}
\text{Present value} &= \$3,995.91/1.07^8 \\
&= \$3,995.91/1.7182 \\
&= \$2,325.65
\end{aligned}
$$

We again ignore a small rounding error. For practice, you can verify that this is what you get if you discount each cash flow back separately.

6.3   The most you would be willing to pay is the present value of $12,000 per year for 10 years at a 15 percent discount rate. The cash flows here are in ordinary annuity form, so the relevant present value factor is:

$$
\begin{aligned}
\text{Annuity present value factor} &= (1 - \text{Present value factor})/r \\
&= [1 - (1/1.15^{10})]/.15 \\
&= (1 - .2472)/.15 \\
&= 5.0188
\end{aligned}
$$

The present value of the 10 cash flows is thus:

$$
\begin{aligned}
\text{Present value} &= \$12,000 \times 5.0188 \\
&= \$60,225
\end{aligned}
$$

This is the most you would pay.

6.4   A rate of 8 percent APR with monthly payments is actually $8\%/12 = .67\%$ per month. The EAR is thus:

$$\text{EAR} = [1 + (.08/12)]^{12} - 1 = 8.30\%$$

6.5   We first need to calculate the annual payment. With a present value of $10,000, an interest rate of 14 percent, and a term of five years, the payment can be determined from:

$$
\begin{aligned}
\$10,000 &= \text{Payment} \times \{[1 - (1/1.14^5)]/.14\} \\
&= \text{Payment} \times 3.4331
\end{aligned}
$$

Therefore, the payment is $10,000/3.4331 = $2,912.84 (actually, it's $2,912.8355; this will create some small rounding errors in the following schedule). We can now prepare the amortization schedule as follows:

Year	Beginning Balance	Total Payment	Interest Paid	Principal Paid	Ending Balance
1	$10,000.00	$ 2,912.84	$1,400.00	$ 1,512.84	$8,487.16
2	8,487.16	2,912.84	1,188.20	1,724.63	6,762.53
3	6,762.53	2,912.84	946.75	1,966.08	4,796.45
4	4,796.45	2,912.84	671.50	2,241.33	2,555.12
5	2,555.12	2,912.84	357.72	2,555.12	0.00
Totals		$14,564.17	$4,564.17	$10,000.00	

6.6   The cash flows on the car loan are in annuity form, so we only need to find the payment. The interest rate is $15\%/12 = 1.25\%$ per month, and there are 72 months. The first thing we need is the annuity factor for 72 periods at 1.25 percent per period:

$$
\begin{aligned}
\text{Annuity present value factor} &= (1 - \text{Present value factor})/r \\
&= [1 - (1/1.0125^{72})]/.0125 \\
&= [1 - (1/2.4459)]/.0125 \\
&= (1 - .4088)/.0125 \\
&= 47.2925
\end{aligned}
$$

The present value is the amount we finance. With a 10 percent down payment, we will be borrowing 90 percent of $42,000, or $37,800.

So, to find the payment, we need to solve for C in the following:

$37,800 = C \times$ Annuity present value factor

$= C \times 47.2925$

Rearranging things a bit, we have:

$C = \$37,800 \times (1/47.2925)$

$= \$37,800 \times .02115$

$= \$799.28$

Your payment is just under $800 per month.

The actual interest rate on this loan is 1.25 percent per month. Based on our work in the chapter, we can calculate the effective annual rate as:

$$\text{EAR} = (1.0125)^{12} - 1 = 16.08\%$$

The effective rate is about one point higher than the quoted rate.

To determine the loan balance in two years, we could amortize the loan to see what the balance is at that time. This would be fairly tedious to do by hand. Using the information already determined in this problem, we can instead simply calculate the present value of the remaining payments. After two years, we have made 24 payments, so there are $72 - 24 = 48$ payments left. What is the present value of 48 monthly payments of $799.28 at 1.25 percent per month? The relevant annuity factor is:

Annuity present value factor $= (1 - \text{Present value factor})/r$

$= [1 - (1/1.0125^{48})]/.0125$

$= [1 - (1/1.8154)]/.0125$

$= (1 - .5509)/.0125$

$= 35.9315$

The present value is thus:

Present value $= \$799.28 \times 35.9315 = \$28,719.37$

You will owe about $28,726 on the loan in two years.

Concepts Review and Critical Thinking Questions

1. **(LO1)** In evaluating an annuity present value, there are four pieces. What are they?

2. **(LO1)** As you increase the length of time involved, what happens to the present value of an annuity? What happens to the future value?

3. **(LO1)** What happens to the future value of an annuity if you increase the rate r? What happens to the present value?

4. **(LO1)** What do you think about a lottery advertising a $500,000 prize when the lump-sum option is $250,000? Is it deceptive advertising?

5. **(LO1)** If you were an athlete negotiating a contract, would you want a big signing bonus payable immediately and smaller payments in the future, or vice versa? How about from the team's perspective?

6. **(LO1)** Suppose two athletes sign 10-year contracts for $90 million. In one case, we're told that the $90 million will be paid in 10 equal installments. In the other case, we're told that the $90 million will be paid in 10 installments, but the installments will increase by 6 percent per year. Who got the better deal?

Questions and Problems

Basic
(Questions 1–29)

1. **Present Value and Multiple Cash Flows (LO1)** Buena Vista Co. has identified an investment project with the following cash flows. If the discount rate is 10 percent, what is the present value of these cash flows? What is the present value at 18 percent? At 24 percent?

Year	Cash Flow
1	$950
2	1,040
3	1,130
4	1,075

2. **Present Value and Multiple Cash Flows (LO1)** Investment X offers to pay you $6,000 per year for nine years, whereas Investment Y offers to pay you $8,000 per year for six years. Which of these cash flow streams has the higher present value if the discount rate is 5 percent? If the discount rate is 22 percent?

3. **Future Value and Multiple Cash Flows (LO1)** Dundonald Inc. has identified an investment project with the following cash flows. If the discount rate is 8 percent, what is the future value of these cash flows in year 4? What is the future value at a discount rate of 11 percent? At 24 percent?

Year	Cash Flow
1	$ 940
2	1,090
3	1,340
4	1,405

4. **Calculating Annuity Present Value (LO1)** An investment offers $5,300 per year for 15 years, with the first payment occurring one year from now. If the required return is 7 percent, what is the value of the investment? What would the value be if the payments occurred for 40 years? For 75 years? Forever?

5. **Calculating Annuity Cash Flows (LO1)** If you put up $34,000 today in exchange for a 7.65 percent, 15-year annuity, what will the annual cash flow be?

6. **Calculating Annuity Values (LO1)** Your company will generate $73,000 in annual revenue each year for the next eight years from a new information database. If the appropriate interest rate is 8.5 percent, what is the present value of the savings?

7. **Calculating Annuity Values (LO1)** If you deposit $4,000 at the end of each of the next 20 years into an account paying 11.2 percent interest, how much money will you have in the account in 20 years? How much will you have if you make deposits for 40 years?

8. **Calculating Annuity Values (LO1)** You want to have $90,000 in your savings account 10 years from now, and you're prepared to make equal annual deposits into the account at the end of each year. If the account pays 6.8 percent interest, what amount must you deposit each year?

9. **Calculating Annuity Values (LO2)** Erindale Bank offers you a $50,000, seven-year term loan at 7.5 percent annual interest. What will your annual loan payment be?

10. **Calculating Annuity Values (LO1)** A six-year lease requires payment of $1,059.00 at the beginning of every three months. If money is worth 5 percent compounded monthly, what is the cash value of the lease?

11. **Calculating Perpetuity Values (LO1)** The Sutherland Life Insurance Co. is trying to sell you an investment policy that will pay you and your heirs $25,000 per year forever. If the required return on this investment is 7.2 percent, how much will you pay for the policy?

12. **Calculating Perpetuity Values (LO1)** In the previous problem, suppose a sales associate told you the policy costs $375,000. At what interest rate would this be a fair deal?

13. **Calculating EAR (LO4)** Find the EAR in each of the following cases:

Stated Rate (APR)	Number of Times Compounded	Effective Rate (EAR)
8%	Quarterly	
16	Monthly	
12	Daily	
15	Infinite	

14. **Calculating APR (LO4)** Find the APR, or stated rate, in each of the following cases:

Stated Rate (APR)	Number of Times Compounded	Effective Rate (EAR)
	Semiannually	8.6%
	Monthly	19.8
	Weekly	9.4
	Infinite	16.5

15. **Calculating EAR (LO4)** Royal Grandora Bank charges 14.2 percent compounded monthly on its business loans. First United Bank charges 14.5 percent compounded semiannually. As a potential borrower, which bank would you go to for a new loan?

16. **Calculating APR (LO4)** Dunfermline Credit Corp. wants to earn an effective annual return on its consumer loans of 16 percent per year. The bank uses daily compounding on its loans. What interest rate is the bank required by law to report to potential borrowers? Explain why this rate is misleading to an uninformed borrower.

17. **Calculating Future Values (LO1)** What is the future value of $2,100 in 17 years assuming an interest rate of 8.4 percent compounded semiannually?

18. **Calculating Future Values (LO1)** Edzeil Credit Bank is offering 9.3 percent compounded daily on its savings accounts. If you deposit $4,500 today, how much will you have in the account in 5 years? In 10 years? In 20 years?

19. **Calculating Present Values (LO1)** An investment will pay you $58,000 in seven years. If the appropriate discount rate is 10 percent compounded daily, what is the present value?

20. **EAR versus APR (LO4)** Big Show's Pawn Shop charges an interest rate of 30 percent per month on loans to its customers. Like all lenders, Big Show must report an APR to consumers. What rate should the shop report? What is the effective annual rate?

21. **Calculating Loan Payments (LO2, 4)** You want to buy a new sports coupe for $68,500, and the finance office at the dealership has quoted you a 6.9 percent APR loan for 60 months to buy the car. What will your monthly payments be? What is the effective annual rate on this loan? Assume that the APR is compounded monthly.

22. **Calculating Number of Periods (LO3)** One of your customers is delinquent on his accounts payable balance. You've mutually agreed to a repayment schedule of $500 per month. You will charge 1.3 percent per month interest on the overdue balance. If the current balance is $18,000, how long will it take for the account to be paid off?

23. **Calculating EAR (LO4)** Bergheim's Quick Loans Inc. offers you "three for four or I knock on your door." This means you get $3 today and repay $4 when you get your pay cheque in one week (or else). What's the effective annual return Bergheim's earns on this lending business? If you were brave enough to ask, what APR would Bergheim's say you were paying?

24. **Valuing Perpetuities (LO1)** Gledhow Life Insurance Co. is selling a perpetuity contract that pays $1,800 monthly. The contract currently sells for $95,000. What is the monthly return on this investment vehicle? What is the APR? The effective annual return?

25. **Calculating Annuity Future Values (LO1)** You are planning to make monthly deposits of $300 into a retirement account that pays 10 percent interest compounded monthly. If your first deposit will be made one month from now, how large will your retirement account be in 30 years?

26. **Calculating Annuity Future Values (LO1)** In the previous problem, suppose you make $3,600 annual deposits into the same retirement account. How large will your account balance be in 30 years?

27. **Calculating Annuity Present Values (LO1)** Beginning three months from now, you want to be able to withdraw $2,300 each quarter from your bank account to cover tuition expenses over the next four years. If the account pays .65 percent interest per quarter, how much do you need to have in your bank account today to meet your expense needs over the next four years?

28. **Discounted Cash Flow Analysis (LO1)** If the appropriate discount rate for the following cash flows is 11 percent compounded quarterly, what is the present value of the cash flows?

Year	Cash Flow
1	$ 725
2	980
3	0
4	1,360

29. **Discounted Cash Flow Analysis (LO1)** If the appropriate discount rate for the following cash flows is 8.45 percent per year, what is the present value of the cash flows?

Year	Cash Flow
1	$1,650
2	0
3	4,200
4	2,430

Intermediate
(Questions 30–58)

30. **Simple Interest versus Compound Interest (LO4)** Vanscoy Bank pays 7 percent simple interest on its investment accounts. If Vade Bank pays interest on its accounts compounded annually, what rate should the bank set if it wants to match Vanscoy Bank over an investment horizon of 10 years?

31. **Calculating EAR (LO4)** You are looking at an investment that has an effective annual rate of 17 percent. What is the effective semiannual return? The effective quarterly return? The effective monthly return?

32. **Calculating Interest Expense (LO2)** You receive a credit card application from Thode Bank offering an introductory rate of 1.5 percent per year, compounded monthly for the first six months, increasing thereafter to 18 percent compounded monthly. Assuming you transfer the $5,000 balance from your existing credit card and make no subsequent payments, how much interest will you owe at the end of the first year?

33. **Calculating Annuities (LO1)** You are planning to save for retirement over the next 30 years. To do this, you will invest $700 a month in a stock account and $300 a month in a bond account. The return of the stock account is expected to be 11 percent, and the bond account will pay 6 percent. When you retire, you will combine your money into an account with a 9 percent return. How much can you withdraw each month from your account assuming a 25-year withdrawal period? Assume that the APR is compounded monthly.

34. **Calculating Future Values (LO1)** You have an investment that will pay you 1.07 percent per month. How much will you have per dollar invested in one year? In two years?

35. **Calculating Annuity Payments (LO1)** You want to be a millionaire when you retire in 40 years. How much do you have to save each month if you can earn 12 percent annual return? How much do you have to save if you wait 10 years before you begin your deposits? 20 years? Assume that the APR is compounded monthly.

36. **Calculating Rates of Return (LO2)** Suppose an investment offers to quadruple your money in 12 months (don't believe it). What rate of return per quarter are you being offered?

 37. **Comparing Cash Flow Streams (LO1)** You've just joined the investment banking firm of Dewey, Cheatum, and Howe. They've offered you two different salary arrangements. You can have $95,000 per year for the next two years, or you can have $70,000 per year for the next two years, along with a $45,000 signing bonus today. The bonus is paid immediately, and the salary is paid at the end of each year. If the interest rate is 10 percent compounded monthly, which do you prefer?

38. **Growing Annuity (LO1)** You have just won the lottery and will receive $1,000,000 every year. You will receive payments for 30 years, which will increase 5 percent per year. If the appropriate discount rate is 9 percent, what is the present value of your winnings?

39. **Growing Annuity (LO1)** Your job pays you only once a year for all the work you did over the previous 12 months. Today, December 31, you just received your salary of $50,000 and you plan to spend all of it. However, you want to start saving for retirement beginning next year. You have decided that one year from today you will begin depositing 5 percent of your annual salary in an account that will earn 11 percent per year. Your salary will increase at 4 percent per year throughout your career. How much money will you have on the date of your retirement 40 years from today?

40. **Present Value and Interest Rates (LO1)** What is the relationship between the value of an annuity and the level of interest rates? Suppose you just bought a 10-year annuity of $6,000 per year at the current interest rate of 10 percent per year. What happens to the value of your investment if interest rates suddenly drop to 5 percent? What if interest rates suddenly rise to 15 percent?

41. **Calculating the Number of Payments (LO2)** You're prepared to make monthly payments of $340, beginning at the end of this month, into an account that pays 6 percent interest compounded monthly. How many payments will you have made when your account balance reaches $20,000?

42. **Calculating Annuity Present Values (LO2)** You want to borrow $73,000 from your local bank to buy a new sailboat. You can afford to make monthly payments of $1,450, but no more. Assuming monthly compounding, what is the highest rate you can afford on a 60-month APR loan?

43. **Calculating Annuity Present Values (LO2)** Maddy Christiansen received $2,900 today July 1, 2012 from her annuity. Ms. Christiansen has been receiving similar payments on the first of each month for several years from an annuity that will expire on

September 1, 2015. If she discounts the future cash flows at an annual rate of 8 percent, what is the present value of her annuity including the July 1 payment? Assume that the APR is compounded monthly.

44. **Calculating Loan Payments (LO2)** You need a 30-year, fixed-rate mortgage to buy a new home for $240,000. Your mortgage bank will lend you the money at a 6.35 percent APR (semi-annual) for this 360-month loan. However, you can afford monthly payments of only $1,150, so you offer to pay off any remaining loan balance at the end of the loan in the form of a single balloon payment. How large will this balloon payment have to be for you to keep your monthly payments at $1,150?

45. **Present and Future Values (LO1)** The present value of the following cash flow stream is $6,550 when discounted at 10 percent annually. What is the value of the missing cash flow?

Year	Cash Flow
1	$1,700
2	?
3	2,100
4	2,800

46. **Calculating Present Values (LO1)** You just won the Luck o' Luck Lottery. You will receive $1 million today plus another 10 annual payments that increase by $500,000 per year. Thus, in one year, you receive $1.5 million. In two years you get $2 million, and so on. If the appropriate interest rate is 9 percent, what is the present value of your winnings?

47. **EAR versus APR (LO4)** You have just purchased a new warehouse. To finance the purchase, you've arranged for a 30-year mortgage loan for 80 percent of the $2,900,000 purchase price. The monthly payment on this loan will be $15,000. What is the APR on this loan? The EAR?

48. **Present Value and Break-Even Interest (LO1)** Consider a firm with a contract to sell an asset for $165,000 three years from now. The asset costs $94,000 to produce today. Given a relevant discount rate on this asset of 13 percent per year, will the firm make a profit on this asset? At what rate does the firm just break even?

49. **Present Value and Multiple Cash Flows (LO1)** What is the present value of $4,000 per year, at a discount rate of 10 percent, if the first payment is received 8 years from now and the last payment is received 25 years from now?

50. **Variable Interest Rates (LO1)** A 15-year annuity pays $1,500 per month, and payments are made at the end of each month. If the interest rate is 11 percent compounded monthly for the first seven years, and 7 percent compounded monthly thereafter, what is the present value of the annuity?

51. **Comparing Cash Flow Streams (LO1)** You have your choice of two investment accounts. Investment A is a 15-year annuity that features end-of-month $1,200 payments and has an interest rate of 8.5 percent compounded monthly. Investment B is a 8 percent continuously compounded lump sum investment, also good for 15 years. How much money would you need to invest in B today for it to be worth as much as investment A 15 years from now?

52. **Calculating Present Value of a Perpetuity (LO1)** Given an interest rate of 6.2 percent per year, what is the value at date $t = 7$ of a perpetual stream of $3,500 payments that begins at date $t = 15$?

53. **Calculating EAR (LO4)** A local finance company quotes a 16 percent interest rate on one-year loans. So, if you borrow $25,000, the interest for the year will be $4,000. Because you must repay a total of $29,000 in one year, the finance company requires you to pay $29,000/12, or $2,416.67, per month over the next 12 months. Is this a 16 percent loan? What rate would legally have to be quoted? What is the effective annual rate?

54. **Calculating Present Values (LO1)** A 5-year annuity of ten $7,000 semiannual payments will begin 8 years from now, with the first payment coming 8.5 years from now. If the discount rate is 10 percent compounded monthly, what is the value of this annuity five years from now? What is the value three years from now? What is the current value of the annuity?

55. **Calculating Annuities Due (LO1)** As discussed in the text, an ordinary annuity assumes equal payments at the end of each period over the life of the annuity. An *annuity due* is the same thing except the payments occur at the beginning of each period instead. Thus, a three-year annual annuity due would have periodic payment cash flows occurring at years 0, 1, and 2, whereas a three-year annual ordinary annuity would have periodic payment cash flows occurring at years 1, 2 and 3.

    a. At a 9.5 percent annual discount rate, find the present value of an eight-year ordinary annuity contract of $950 payments.

    b. Find the present value of the same contract if it is an annuity due.

56. **Calculating Annuities Due (LO1)** You want to buy a new Ducati Monster 696 for $68,000. The contract is in the form of a 60-month annuity due at an 7.85 percent APR. What will your monthly payment be? Assume that the APR is compounded monthly.

57. **Amortization with Equal Payments (LO3)** Prepare an amortization schedule for a five-year loan of $42,000. The interest rate is 8 percent per year, and the loan calls for equal annual payments. How much interest is paid in the third year? How much total interest is paid over the life of the loan?

58. **Amortization with Equal Principal Payments (LO3)** Rework Problem 57 assuming that the loan agreement calls for a principal reduction of $8,400 every year instead of equal annual payments.

Challenge 59. **Calculating Annuity Values (LO1)** Bilbo Baggins wants to save money to meet three objectives. First, he would like to be able
(Questions   to retire 30 years from now with retirement income of $20,000 per month for 25 years, with the first payment received 30 years
59–81)   and 1 month from now. Second, he would like to purchase a cabin in Rivendell in 10 years at an estimated cost of $380,000.
                Third, after he passes on at the end of the 25 years of withdrawals, he would like to leave an inheritance of $900,000 to his
                nephew Mitchell. He can afford to save $2,500 per month for the next 10 years. If he can earn a 10 percent EAR before he retires
                and an 7 percent EAR after he retires, how much will he have to save each month in years 11 through 30?

60. **Calculating Annuity Values (LO1)** After deciding to buy a new Mercedes-Benz C Class sedan, you can either lease the car or purchase it on a three-year loan. The car you wish to buy costs $32,000. The dealer has a special leasing arrangement where you pay $99 today and $450 per month for the next three years. If you purchase the car, you will pay it off in monthly payments over the next three years at an 7 percent APR compounded monthly. You believe you will be able to sell the car for $23,000 in three years. Should you buy or lease the car? What break-even resale price in three years would make you indifferent between buying and leasing?

61. **Calculating Annuity Values (LO1)** An All-Pro defensive lineman is in contract negotiations. The team has offered the following salary structure:

Time	Salary
0	$7,000,000
1	$4,500,000
2	$5,600,000
3	$6,000,000
4	$6,800,000
5	$7,900,000
6	$8,800,000

All salaries are to be paid in lump sums. The player has asked you as his agent to renegotiate the terms. He wants a $9 million signing bonus payable today and a contract value increase of $1,400,000. He also wants an equal salary paid every three months, with the first pay cheque three months from now. If the interest rate is 5.5 percent compounded daily, what is the amount of his quarterly cheque? Assume 365 days in a year.

62. **Calculating Annuity Values (LO1)** You are buying a new Porsche Boxter, priced at $65,200. You will pay $4,700 now and the rest monthly, in a four year loan. All rates are APRs. The automobile dealership is offering a sales promotion where either:

   a. You will receive a $2,000 discount cheque now and the annual interest rate on the loan is 6.1 percent, or

   b. The annual interest rate on the loan will be 1.2 percent but there is no discount.

   Compare the two options by calculating the present value of each option, assuming the discount rate is 8 percent. Which option is a better deal?

63. **Discount Interest Loans (LO4)** This question illustrates what is known as *discount interest*. Imagine you are discussing a loan with a somewhat unscrupulous lender. You want to borrow $25,000 for one year. The interest rate is 15 percent. You and the lender agree that the interest on the loan will be .15 × $25,000 = $3,750. So the lender deducts this interest amount from the loan up front and gives you $21,250. In this case, we say that the discount is $3,750. What's wrong here?

64. **Calculating Annuity Values (LO1)** You are serving on a jury. A plaintiff is suing the city for injuries sustained after a freak street sweeper accident. In the trial, doctors testified that it will be five years before the plaintiff is able to return to work. The jury has already decided in favour of the plaintiff. You are the foreperson of the jury and propose that the jury give the plaintiff an award to cover the following: (a) The present value of two years' back pay. The plaintiff's annual salary for the last two years would have been $47,000 and $50,000, respectively. (b) The present value of five years' future salary. You assume the salary will be $55,000 per year. (c) $100,000 for pain and suffering. (d) $20,000 for court costs. Assume that the salary payments are equal amounts paid at the end of each month. If the interest rate you choose is a 8 percent EAR, what is the size of the settlement? If you were the plaintiff, would you like to see a higher or lower interest rate?

65. **EAR versus APR (LO4)** Two banks in the area offer 30-year, $240,000 mortgages at 6.8 percent and charge a $2,300 loan application fee. However, the application fee charged by Insecurity Bank and Trust is refundable if the loan application is denied, whereas that charged by I.M. Greedy and Sons Mortgage Bank is not. The current disclosure law requires that any fees that will be refunded if the applicant is rejected be included in calculating the APR, but this is not required with nonrefundable fees (presumably because refundable fees are part of the loan rather than a fee). What are the EARs on these two loans? What are the APRs? Assume that the APR is compounded monthly.

66. **Calculating EAR with Add-On Interest (LO4)** This problem illustrates a deceptive way of quoting interest rates called *add-on interest*. Imagine that you see an advertisement for Crazy Judy's Stereo City that reads something like this: "$1,000 Instant Credit! 14% Simple Interest! Three Years to Pay! Low, Low Monthly Payments!" You're not exactly sure what all this means and somebody has spilled ink over the APR on the loan contract, so you ask the manager for clarification.

   Judy explains that if you borrow $1,000 for three years at 14 percent interest, in three years you will owe:

   $1,000 × 1.14³ = $1,000 × 1.48154 = $1,481.54

   Now, Judy recognizes that coming up with $1,481.54 all at once might be a strain, so she lets you make "low, low monthly payments" of $1,481.54/36 = $41.15 per month, even though this is extra bookkeeping work for her.

   Is this a 14 percent loan? Why or why not? What is the APR on this loan? What is the EAR? Why do you think this is called add-on interest?

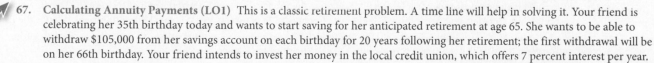

67. **Calculating Annuity Payments (LO1)** This is a classic retirement problem. A time line will help in solving it. Your friend is celebrating her 35th birthday today and wants to start saving for her anticipated retirement at age 65. She wants to be able to withdraw $105,000 from her savings account on each birthday for 20 years following her retirement; the first withdrawal will be on her 66th birthday. Your friend intends to invest her money in the local credit union, which offers 7 percent interest per year.

She wants to make equal annual payments on each birthday into the account established at the credit union for her retirement fund.

a. If she starts making these deposits on her 36th birthday and continues to make deposits until she is 65 (the last deposit will be on her 65th birthday), what amount must she deposit annually to be able to make the desired withdrawals at retirement?

b. Suppose your friend has just inherited a large sum of money. Rather than making equal annual payments, she has decided to make one lump sum payment on her 35th birthday to cover her retirement needs. What amount does she have to deposit?

c. Suppose your friend's employer will contribute $1,500 to the account every year as part of the company's profit-sharing plan. In addition, your friend expects a $150,000 distribution from a family trust fund on her 55th birthday, which she will also put into the retirement account. What amount must she deposit annually now to be able to make the desired withdrawals at retirement?

68. **Calculating the Number of Periods (LO2)** Your Christmas ski vacation was great, but it unfortunately ran a bit over budget. All is not lost: You just received an offer in the mail to transfer your $10,000 balance from your current credit card, which charges an annual rate of 19.8 percent, to a new credit card charging a rate of 6.2 percent. How much faster could you pay the loan off by making your planned monthly payments of $200 with the new card? What if there was a 2 percent fee charged on any balances transferred?

69. **Future Value and Multiple Cash Flows (LO1)** An insurance company is offering a new policy to its customers. Typically, the policy is bought by a parent or grandparent for a child at the child's birth. The details of the policy are as follows: The purchaser (say, the parent) makes the following six payments to the insurance company:

First birthday: $900
Second birthday: $900
Third birthday: $1,000
Fourth birthday: $1,000
Fifth birthday: $1,100
Sixth birthday: $1,100

After the child's sixth birthday, no more payments are made. When the child reaches age 65, he or she receives $500,000. If the relevant interest rate is 12 percent for the first six years and 8 percent for all subsequent years, is the policy worth buying?

70. **Calculating a Balloon Payment (LO2)** You have just arranged for a $750,000 mortgage to finance the purchase of a large tract of land. The mortgage has an 8.1 percent APR (semi-annual), and it calls for monthly payments over the next 30 years. However, the loan has an eight-year balloon payment, meaning that the loan must be paid off then. How big will the balloon payment be?

71. **Calculating Interest Rates (LO4)** A financial planning service offers a university savings program. The plan calls for you to make six annual payments of $9,000 each, with the first payment occurring today, your child's 12th birthday. Beginning on your child's 18th birthday, the plan will provide $20,000 per year for four years. What return is this investment offering?

72. **Break-Even Investment Returns (LO4)** Your financial planner offers you two different investment plans. Plan X is a $20,000 annual perpetuity. Plan Y is a 10-year, $28,000 annual annuity. Both plans will make their first payment one year from today. At what discount rate would you be indifferent between these two plans?

73. **Perpetual Cash Flows (LO1)** What is the value of an investment that pays $15,000 every *other* year forever, if the first payment occurs one year from today and the discount rate is 10 percent compounded daily? What is the value today if the first payment occurs four years from today?

74. **Ordinary Annuities and Annuities Due (LO1)** As discussed in the text, an annuity due is identical to an ordinary annuity except that the periodic payments occur at the beginning of each period and not at the end of the period. Show that the relationship between the value of an ordinary annuity and the value of an otherwise equivalent annuity due is:

Annuity due value = Ordinary annuity value × $(1 + r)$

Show this for both present and future values.

75. **Calculating Growing Annuities (LO1)** You have 40 years left until retirement and want to retire with $2 million. Your salary is paid annually, and you will receive $40,000 at the end of the current year. Your salary will increase at 3 percent per year, and you can earn an 11 percent return on the money you invest. If you save a constant percentage of your salary, what percentage of your salary must you save each year?

76. **Calculating EAR (LO4)** A cheque-cashing store is in the business of making personal loans to walk-up customers. The store makes only one-week loans at 7 percent interest per week.

a. What APR must the store report to its customers? What EAR are customers actually paying?

b. Now suppose the store makes one-week loans at 7 percent discount interest per week (see Problem 63). What's the APR now? The EAR?

c. The cheque-cashing store also makes one-month add-on interest loans at 7 percent discount interest per week. Thus if you borrow $100 for one month (four weeks), the interest will be ($100 × 1.07⁴) − 100 = $31.08. Because this is discount interest, your net loan proceeds today will be $68.92. You must then repay the store $100 at the end of the month. To help you out, though, the store lets you pay off this $100 in installments of $25 per week. What is the APR of this loan? What is the EAR?

77. **Present Value of a Growing Perpetuity (LO1)** What is the equation for the present value of a growing perpetuity with a payment of *C* one period from today if the payments grow by *C* each period?

78. **Rule of 72 (LO4)** Earlier, we discussed the Rule of 72, a useful approximation for many interest rates and periods for the time it takes a lump sum to double in value. For a 10 percent interest rate, show that the "Rule of 73" is slightly better. For what rate is the Rule of 72 exact? *(Hint: Use the Solver function in Excel.)*

79. **Rule of 69.3 (LO4)** A corollary to the Rule of 72 is the Rule of 69.3. The Rule of 69.3 is exactly correct except for rounding when interest rates are compounded continuously. Prove the Rule of 69.3 for continuously compounded interest.

MINI CASE

The MBA Decision

Raj Danielson graduated from university six years ago with a finance undergraduate degree. Although he is satisfied with his current job, his goal is to become an investment banker. He feels that an MBA degree would allow him to achieve this goal. After examining schools, he has narrowed his choice to either Assiniboine University or the University of Passy. Both schools encourage internships, but to get class credit for the internship, no salary can be accepted. Other than internships, neither school allows its students to work while enrolled in its MBA program.

Raj currently works at the money management firm of Prash and Sid. His annual salary at the firm is $55,000 and his salary is expected to increase at 3 percent per year until retirement. He is currently 28 years old and expects to work for 38 more years. His current job includes a fully paid health insurance plan, and his current average tax rate is 26 percent. Raj has a savings account with enough money to cover the entire cost of his MBA program.

The Sentinel School of Business at Assiniboine University is one of the top MBA programs in the country. The MBA degree requires two years of full-time enrollment at the university. The annual tuition is $63,000, payable at the beginning of each school year. Books and other supplies are estimated to cost $2,500 per year. Raj expects that after graduation from Assiniboine, he will receive a job offer for about $98,000 per year, with a $15,000 signing bonus. The salary at this job will increase at 4 percent per year. Because of the higher salary, his average income tax rate will increase to 31 percent.

The Pond School of Business at the University of Passy began its MBA program 16 years ago. The Pond School is smaller and less well known than the Sentinel School. It offers an accelerated one-year program, with a tuition cost of $80,000 to be paid upon matriculation. Books and other supplies for the program are expected to cost $3,500. Raj thinks that he will receive an offer of $81,000 per year upon graduation, with a $10,000 signing bonus. The salary at this job will increase at 3.5 percent per year. His average tax rate at this level of income will be 29 percent.

Both schools offer a health insurance plan that will cost $300 per year, payable at the beginning of the year. Raj also estimates that room and board expenses will cost $20,000 per year at both schools. The appropriate discount rate is 6.5 percent.

Questions

1. How does Raj's age affect his decision to get an MBA?

2. What other, perhaps nonquantifiable, factors affect Raj's decision to get an MBA?

3. Assuming all salaries are paid at the end of each year, what is the best option for Raj from a strictly financial standpoint?

4. Raj believes that the appropriate analysis is to calculate the future value of each option. How would you evaluate this statement?

5. What initial salary would Raj need to receive to make him indifferent between attending Assiniboine University and staying in his current position?

6. Suppose, instead of being able to pay cash for his MBA, Raj must borrow the money. The current borrowing rate is 5.4 percent. How would this affect his decision?

Internet Application Questions

1. Buying a house frequently involves borrowing a significant portion of the house price from a lending institution such as a bank. Often times, the bank provides repayment of the loan based on long amortization periods. The following site maintained by Royal LePage shows the effect of increasing your monthly payment on the amortization period.

   royallepage.ca/en/realestateguide/buying/preparing/index.aspx

   Note that increasing the monthly payment has a disproportionate impact on reducing the amortization period. Can you explain why this happens?

2. Alberta Treasury Branch (atb.com) offers a variation of GIC called a Springboard® GIC. Click on their homepage and estimate the effective annual yield on a five-year Springboard® GIC. How does this compare to the yield on a five-year standard GIC offered by CIBC (cibc.com)?

3. Toyota of Canada (toyota.ca) offers its own financing plans that may sometimes compare favourably to bank financing. Pick a vehicle from this website, and use Toyota's pricing calculator to estimate your monthly financing payment for this car. Assume zero down payment. How does Toyota's financing compare with the lending rates at CIBC? What is the present value of your savings if you choose to finance through Toyota?

APPENDIX 6A

PROOF OF ANNUITY PRESENT VALUE FORMULA

An *annuity* is a level stream of regular payments that lasts for a fixed number of periods. Not surprisingly, annuities are among the most common kinds of financial instruments. The pensions that people receive when they retire are often in the form of an annuity. Leases, mortgages, and pension plans are also annuities.

To figure out the present value of an annuity, we need to evaluate the following equation:

$$\frac{C}{1+r} + \frac{C}{(1+r)^2} + \frac{C}{(1+r)^3} + \cdots + \frac{C}{(1+r)^T}$$

The present value of only receiving the coupons for T periods must be less than the present value of a consol, but how much less? To answer this, we have to look at consols a bit more closely.

Consider the following time chart:

Date (or end of year)	0	1	2	3...T	T + 1	T + 2
Consol 1		C	C	C...C	C	C...
Consol 2					C	C...
Annuity		C	C	C...C		

Consol 1 is a normal consol with its first payment at date 1. The first payment of consol 2 occurs at date $T+1$.

The present value of having cash flow of C at each of T dates is equal to the present value of consol 1 minus the present value of consol 2. The present value of consol 1 is given by

$$PV = \frac{C}{r}$$

Consol 2 is just a consol with its first payment at date $T + 1$. From the perpetuity formula, this consol will be worth C/r at date T.[8] However, we do not want the value at date T. We want the value now; in other words, the present value at date 0. We must discount C/r back by T periods. Therefore, the present value of consol 2 is

$$PV = \frac{C}{r}\left[\frac{1}{(1+r)^T}\right]$$

The present value of having cash flows for T years is the present value of a consol with its first payment at date 1 minus the present value of a consol with its first payment at date $T + 1$. Thus, the present value of an annuity is the first formula minus the second formula. This can be written as

$$\frac{C}{r} - \frac{C}{r}\left[\frac{1}{(1+r)^T}\right]$$

This simplifies to the formula for the present value of an annuity:

$$PV = C\left[\frac{1}{r} - \frac{1}{r(1+r)^T}\right]$$
$$= C[1 - \{1/(1+r)^T\}]/r$$

---

[8] Students frequently think that C/r is the present value at date $T + 1$ because the consol's first payment is at date $T + 1$. However, the formula values the annuity as of one period before the first payment.

CHAPTER 7

INTEREST RATES AND BOND VALUATION

On July 11, 2012, the Government of Canada conducted an auction worth $3.4 billion of 1.5% bonds due September 1, 2017. The proceeds from the bond issue were used for general government purposes. DBRS, formerly known as the Dominion Bond Rating Service, gave the Government of Canada bond its highest possible rating, AAA, which puts the bond in the league of the safest in the world. Despite the uncertainty surrounding European debt troubles, Canada has the flexibility to withstand these hurdles without compromising its strong credit profile. Bonds issued by such safe institutions carry lower yields. In this chapter, we will learn more about bonds and what makes them risky or safe.

Learning Objectives ▶

After studying this chapter, you should understand:

LO1	**Important bond features and types of bonds.**
LO2	**Bond values and yields and why they fluctuate.**
LO3	**Bond ratings and what they mean.**
LO4	**How bond prices are quoted.**
LO5	**The impact of inflation on interest rates.**
LO6	**The term structure of interest rates and the determinants of bond yields.**

Our goal in this chapter is to introduce you to bonds. We begin by showing how the techniques we developed in Chapters 5 and 6 can be applied to bond valuation. From there, we go on to discuss bond features and how bonds are bought and sold. One important thing we learn is that bond values depend, in large part, on interest rates. We therefore close out the chapter with an examination of interest rates and their behaviour.

7.1 | Bonds and Bond Valuation

When a corporation or government wishes to borrow money from the public on a long-term basis, it usually does so by issuing or selling debt securities that are generically called bonds. In this section, we describe the various features of corporate bonds and some of the terminology associated with bonds. We then discuss the cash flows associated with a bond and how bonds can be valued using our discounted cash flow procedure.

Bond Features and Prices

A bond is normally an interest-only loan, meaning the borrower pays the interest every period, but none of the principal is repaid until the end of the loan. For example, suppose Alcan wants to borrow $1,000 for 30 years and that the interest rate on similar debt issued by similar corporations is 12 percent. Alcan thus pays $.12 \times \$1,000 = \$120$ in interest every year for 30 years. At the end of 30 years, Alcan repays the $1,000. As this example suggests, a bond is a fairly simple financing arrangement. There is, however, a rich jargon associated with bonds, so we use this example to define some of the more important terms.

In our example, the $120 regular interest payments that Alcan promises to make are called the bond's **coupons**. Because the coupon is constant and paid every year, the type of bond we are describing is sometimes called a *level coupon bond*. The amount repaid at the end of the loan

coupon
The stated interest payment made on a bond.

face value or par value
The principal amount of a bond that is repaid at the end of the term. Also par value.

coupon rate
The annual coupon divided by the face value of a bond.

maturity date
Specified date at which the principal amount of a bond is paid.

is called the bond's **face value** or **par value**. As in our example, this par value is usually $1,000 for corporate bonds, and a bond that sells for its par value is called a par bond. Government of Canada and provincial bonds frequently have much larger face or par values. Finally, the annual coupon divided by the face value is called the **coupon rate** on the bond, which is $120/1,000 = 12%; so the bond has a 12 percent coupon rate.

The number of years until the face value is paid is called the bond's time to **maturity**. A corporate bond would frequently have a maturity of 30 years when it is originally issued, but this varies. Once the bond has been issued, the number of years to maturity declines as time goes by.

Bond Values and Yields

As time passes, interest rates change in the market place. The cash flows from a bond, however, stay the same because the coupon rate and maturity date are specified when it is issued. As a result, the value of the bond fluctuates. When interest rates rise, the present value of the bond's remaining cash flows declines, and the bond is worth less. When interest rates fall, the bond is worth more.

yield to maturity (YTM)
The market interest rate that equates a bond's present value of interest payments and principal repayment with its price.

To determine the value of a bond on a particular date, we need to know the number of periods remaining until maturity, the face value, the coupon, and the market interest rate for bonds with similar features. This interest rate required in the market on a bond is called the bond's **yield to maturity (YTM)**. This rate is sometimes called the bond's *yield* for short. Given this information, we can calculate the present value of the cash flows as an estimate of the bond's current market value.

Figure 7.1 shows a bond certificate for a Government of Canada bond maturing on November 1, 1980. The right hand side of the figure shows the individual coupons that could be clipped off for redemption. Today, most bonds are traded online and do not have physical certificates but investors still use the same terminology.

FIGURE 7.1

The Government of Canada Bonds with coupons

Source: Dave Rogers
(whathesaid.ca)

For example, suppose Royal Bank were to issue a bond with 10 years to maturity. The Royal Bank bond has an annual coupon of $56. Suppose similar bonds have a yield to maturity of 5.6 percent. Based on our previous discussion, the Royal Bank bond pays $56 per year for the next 10 years in coupon interest. In 10 years, Royal Bank pays $1,000 to the owner of the bond. The cash flows from the bond are shown in Figure 7.2. What would this bond sell for?

FIGURE 7.2

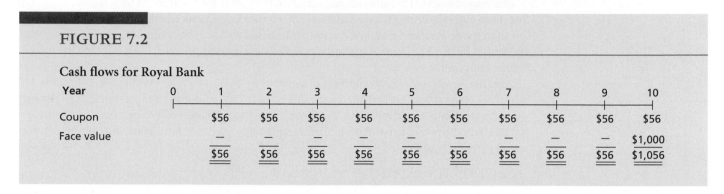

Cash flows for Royal Bank

Year	0	1	2	3	4	5	6	7	8	9	10
Coupon		$56	$56	$56	$56	$56	$56	$56	$56	$56	$56
Face value		—	—	—	—	—	—	—	—	—	$1,000
		$56	$56	$56	$56	$56	$56	$56	$56	$56	$1,056

rbcroyalbank.com

As illustrated in Figure 7.2, the Royal Bank bond's cash flows have an annuity component (the coupons) and a lump sum (the face value paid at maturity). We thus estimate the market value of the bond by calculating the present value of these two components separately and adding the results together. First, at the going rate of 5.6 percent, the present value of the $1,000 paid in 10 years is:

$$\text{Present value} = \$1,000/1.056^{10} = \$1,000/1.7244 = \$579.91$$

Second, the bond offers $56 per year for 10 years, so the present value of this annuity stream is:

$$\begin{aligned}\text{Annuity present value} &= \$56 \times (1 - 1/1.056^{10})/.056 \\ &= \$56 \times (1 - 1/1.7244)/.056 \\ &= \$56 \times 7.5016 \\ &= \$420.09\end{aligned}$$

We can now add the values for the two parts together to get the bond's value:

$$\text{Total bond value} = \$579.91 + 420.09 = \$1,000.00$$

A good bond site to visit is pfin. ca/canadianfixedincome/ Default.aspx

This bond sells for its exact face value. This is not a coincidence. The going interest rate in the market is 5.6 percent. Considered as an interest-only loan, what interest rate does this bond have? With a $56 coupon, this bond pays exactly 5.6 percent interest only when it sells for $1,000.

To illustrate what happens as interest rates change, suppose a year has gone by. The Royal Bank bond now has nine years to maturity. If the interest rate in the market had risen to 7.6 percent, what would the bond be worth? To find out, we repeat the present value calculations with nine years instead of 10, and a 7.6 percent yield instead of a 5.6 percent yield. First, the present value of the $1,000 paid in nine years at 7.6 percent is:

$$\text{Present value} = \$1,000/1.076^{9} = \$1,000/1.9333 = \$517.25$$

Second, the bond now offers $56 per year for nine years, so the present value of this annuity stream at 7.6 percent is:

$$\begin{aligned}\text{Annuity present value} &= \$56 \times (1 - 1/1.076^{9})/.076 \\ &= \$56 \times (1 - 1/1.9333)/.076 \\ &= \$56 \times 6.3520 \\ &= \$355.71\end{aligned}$$

We can now add the values for the two parts together to get the bond's value:

$$\text{Total bond value} = \$517.25 + 355.71 = \$872.96$$

Online bond calculators are available at personal.fidelity.com

Therefore, the bond should sell for about $873. In the vernacular, we say this bond, with its 5.6 percent coupon, is priced to yield 7.6 percent at $873.

The Royal Bank bond now sells for less than its $1,000 face value. Why? The market interest rate is 7.6 percent. Considered as an interest-only loan of $1,000, this bond pays only 5.6 percent, its coupon rate. Because this bond pays less than the going rate, investors are only willing to lend something less than the $1,000 promised repayment. A bond that sells for less than face value, or at a discount, is called a *discount bond.*

The only way to get the interest rate up to 7.6 percent is for the price to be less than $1,000 so that the purchaser, in effect, has a built-in gain. For the Royal Bank bond, the price of $873 is $127 less than the face value, so an investor who purchased and kept the bond would get $56 per year and would have a $127 gain at maturity as well. This gain compensates the lender for the below-market coupon rate.

Another way to see why the bond is discounted by $127 is to note that the $56 coupon is $20 below the coupon on a newly issued par value bond, based on current market conditions. By this we mean the bond would be worth $1,000 only if it had a coupon of $76 per year. In a sense, an investor who buys and keeps the bond gives up $20 per year for nine years. At 7.6 percent, this annuity stream is worth:

$$\text{Annuity present value} = \$20 \times (1 - 1/1.076^9)/.076$$
$$= \$20 \times 6.3520$$
$$= \$127.04$$

This is just the amount of the discount.

What would the Royal Bank bond sell for if interest rates had dropped by 2 percent instead of rising by 2 percent? As you might guess, the bond would sell for more than $1,000. Such a bond is said to sell at a *premium* and is called a *premium bond.*

This case is just the opposite of a discount bond. The Royal Bank bond still has a coupon rate of 5.6 percent when the market rate is only 3.6 percent. Investors are willing to pay a premium to get this extra coupon. The relevant discount rate is 3.6 percent, and there are nine years remaining. The present value of the $1,000 face amount is:

$$\text{Present value} = \$1,000/1.036^9 = \$1,000/1.3748 = \$727.38$$

The present value of the coupon stream is:

$$\text{Annuity present value} = \$56 \times (1 - 1/1.036^9)/.036$$
$$= \$56 \times (1 - 1/1.3748)/.036$$
$$= \$56 \times 7.5728$$
$$= \$424.08$$

We can now add the values for the two parts together to get the bond's value:

$$\text{Total bond value} = \$727.38 + 424.08 = \$1,151.46$$

Total bond value is, therefore, about $151 in excess of par value. Once again, we can verify this amount by noting that the coupon is now $20 too high. The present value of $20 per year for nine years at 3.6 percent is:

$$\text{Annuity present value} = \$20 \times (1 - 1/1.036^9)/.036$$
$$= \$20 \times 7.5728$$
$$= \$151.46$$

This is just as we calculated.

Based on our examples, we can now write the general expression for the value of a bond. If a bond has (1) a face value of F paid at maturity, (2) a coupon of C paid per period, (3) t periods to maturity, and (4) a yield of r per period, its value is:

$$\text{Bond value} = C \times (1 - 1/(1 + r)^t)/r + F/(1 + r)^t \qquad [7.1]$$

$$\text{Bond value} = \text{Present value of the coupons} + \text{Present value of the face amount}$$

As we have illustrated in this section, bond prices and interest rates (or market yields) always move in opposite directions like the ends of a seesaw. Most bonds are issued at par, with the coupon rate set equal to the prevailing market yield or interest rate. This coupon rate does not change over time. The coupon yield, however, does change and reflects the return the coupon represents based on current market prices for the bond. Finally, the yield to maturity is the interest rate that equates the present value of the bond's coupons and principal repayments with the current market price (i.e., the total annual return the purchaser would receive if the bond were held to maturity).

When interest rates rise, a bond's value, like any other present value, declines. When interest rates are above the bond's coupon rate, the bond sells at a discount. Similarly, when interest rates fall, bond values rise. Interest rates below the bond's coupon rate cause the bond to sell at a premium. Even if we are considering a bond that is riskless in the sense that the borrower is certain to make all the payments, there is still risk in owning the bond. We discuss this next.

EXAMPLE 7.1: Semiannual Coupons

In practice, bonds issued in Canada usually make coupon payments twice a year. So, if an ordinary bond has a coupon rate of 8 percent, the owner gets a total of $80 per year, but this $80 comes in two payments of $40 each. Suppose we were examining such a bond. The yield to maturity is quoted at 10 percent.

Bond yields are quoted like APRs; the quoted rate is equal to the actual rate per period multiplied by the number of periods. With a 10 percent quoted yield and semiannual payments, the true yield is 5 percent per six months. The bond matures in seven years. What is the bond's price? What is the effective annual yield on this bond?

Based on our discussion, we know the bond would sell at a discount because it has a coupon rate of 4 percent every six months when the market requires 5 percent every six months. So, if our answer exceeds $1,000, we know that we made a mistake.

To get the exact price, we first calculate the present value of the bond's face value of $1,000 paid in seven years. This seven years has 14 periods of six months each. At 5 percent per period, the value is:

Present value = $1,000/1.05^{14} = $1,000/1.9799 = $505.08

The coupons can be viewed as a 14-period annuity of $40 per period. At a 5 percent discount rate, the present value of such an annuity is:

$$\text{Annuity present value} = \$40 \times (1 - 1/1.05^{14})/.05$$
$$= \$40 \times (1 - .5051)/.05$$
$$= \$40 \times 9.8980$$
$$= \$395.92$$

The total present value gives us what the bond should sell for:

Total present value = $505.08 + 395.92 = $901.00

To calculate the effective yield on this bond, note that 5 percent every six months is equivalent to:

Effective annual rate = $(1 + .05)^2 - 1 = 10.25\%$

The effective yield, therefore, is 10.25 percent.

Interest Rate Risk

The risk that arises for bond owners from fluctuating interest rates (market yields) is called *interest rate risk*. How much interest risk a bond has depends on how sensitive its price is to interest rate changes. This sensitivity directly depends on two things: the time to maturity and the coupon rate. Keep the following in mind when looking at a bond:

1. All other things being equal, the longer the time to maturity, the greater the interest rate risk.
2. All other things being equal, the lower the coupon rate, the greater the interest rate risk.

We illustrate the first of these two points in Figure 7.3. As shown, we compute and plot prices under different interest rate scenarios for 10 percent coupon bonds with maturities of one year and 30 years. Notice how the slope of the line connecting the prices is much steeper for the 30-year maturity than it is for the one-year maturity.[1] This tells us that a relatively small change in interest rates could lead to a substantial change in the bond's value. In comparison, the one-year bond's price is relatively insensitive to interest rate changes.

Intuitively, the reason longer-term bonds have greater interest rate sensitivity is that a large portion of a bond's value comes from the $1,000 face amount. The present value of this amount isn't greatly affected by a small change in interest rates if it is to be received in one year. If it is to be received in 30 years, however, even a small change in the interest rate can have a significant effect once it is compounded for 30 years. The present value of the face amount becomes much more volatile with a longer-term bond as a result.

---

[1] We explain a more precise measure of this slope, called duration, in Appendix 7A. Our example assumes that yields of one-year and 30-year bonds are the same.

FIGURE 7.3

Interest rate risk and time to maturity

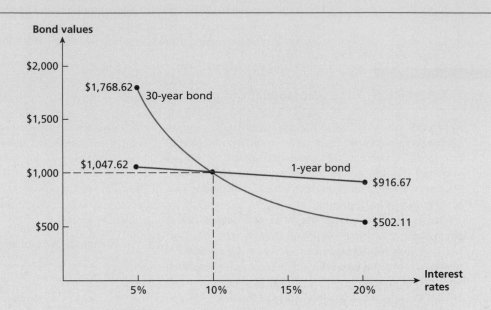

Value of a Bond with a 10% Coupon Rate for Different Interest Rates and Maturities

	Time to Maturity	
Interest Rate	1 Year	30 Years
5%	$1,047.62	$1,768.62
10%	1,000.00	1,000.00
15%	956.52	671.70
20%	916.67	502.11

The reason that bonds with lower coupons have greater interest rate risk is essentially the same. As we just discussed, the value of a bond depends on the present value of its coupons and the present value of the face amount. If two bonds with different coupon rates have the same maturity, the value of the one with the lower coupon is proportionately more dependent on the face amount to be received at maturity. As a result, all other things being equal, its value fluctuates more as interest rates change. Put another way, the bond with the higher coupon has a larger cash flow early in its life, so its value is less sensitive to changes in the discount rate.

Finding the Yield to Maturity

Frequently, we know a bond's price, coupon rate, and maturity date, but not its yield to maturity. For example, suppose we were interested in a six-year, 8 percent coupon bond. A broker quotes a price of $955.14. What is the yield on this bond?

We've seen that the price of a bond can be written as the sum of its annuity and lump-sum components. With an $80 coupon for six years and a $1,000 face value, this price is:

$$\$955.14 = \$80 \times (1 - 1/(1 + r)^6)/r + \$1,000/(1 + r)^6$$

where r is the unknown discount rate or yield to maturity. We have one equation here and one unknown, but we cannot solve it for r explicitly. The only way to find the answer exactly is to use trial and error.

This problem is essentially identical to the one we examined in the last chapter when we tried to find the unknown interest rate on an annuity. However, finding the rate (or yield) on a bond is even more complicated, because of the $1,000 face amount.

We can speed up the trial-and-error process by using what we know about bond prices and yields: The bond has an $80 coupon and is selling at a discount. We thus know that the yield is greater than 8 percent. If we compute the price at 10 percent:

$$\text{Bond value} = \$80 \times (1 - 1/1.10^6)/.10 + \$1,000/1.10^6$$
$$= \$80 \times (4.3553) + \$1,000/1.7716$$
$$= \$912.89$$

At 10 percent, the value we calculate is lower than the actual price, so 10 percent is too high. The true yield must be somewhere between 8 percent and 10 percent. At this point, it's "plug and chug" to find the answer. You would probably want to try 9 percent next. If you do, you will see that this is, in fact, the bond's yield to maturity. As the trial-and-error process can be very time consuming, a more common method of calculating a bond's yield is to use a financial calculator or financial spreadsheet software. Our discussion of bond valuation is summarized in Table 7.1.

TABLE 7.1   **Summary of bond valuation**

I. FINDING THE VALUE OF A BOND:

Bond value = $C \times (1 - 1/(1 + r)^t)/r + F/(1 + r)^t$ where:

    C = the coupon paid each period
    r = the rate per period
    t = the number of periods
    F = the bond's face value

II. FINDING THE YIELD ON A BOND:

Given a bond value, coupon, time to maturity, and face value, it is possible to find the implicit discount rate or yield to maturity by trial and error only. To do this, try different discount rates until the calculated bond value equals the given value. Remember that increasing the rate decreases the bond value.

EXAMPLE 7.2: Bond Yields

You're looking at two bonds identical in every way except for their coupons and, of course, their prices. Both have 12 years to maturity. The first bond has a 5 percent coupon rate and sells for $932.16. The second has a 6 percent coupon rate. What do you think it would sell for?

Because the two bonds are very similar, they must be priced to yield about the same rate. We begin by calculating the yield on the 5 percent coupon bond. A little trial and error reveals that the yield is actually 5.8 percent:

$$\text{Bond value} = \$50 \times (1 - 1/1.058^{12})/.058 +$$
$$\$1,000/1.058^{12}$$
$$= \$50 \times 8.4759 + \$1,000/1.9671$$
$$= \$423.80 + 508.36$$
$$= \$932.16$$

With an 5.8 percent yield, the second bond sells at a premium because of its $60 coupon. Its value is:

$$\text{Bond value} = \$60 \times (1 - 1/1.058^{12})/.058 + \$1,000/1.058^{12}$$
$$= \$60 \times 8.4765 + \$1,000/1.9671$$
$$= \$508.59 + 508.36$$
$$= \$1,016.95$$

What we did in pricing the second bond is what bond traders do. Bonds trade over the counter in a secondary market made by investment dealers and banks. Suppose a bond trader at, say, BMO Nesbitt Burns receives a request for a selling price on the second bond from another trader at, say, ScotiaCapital. Suppose further that the second bond has not traded recently. The trader prices it off the first actively traded bond.

CALCULATOR HINTS

How to Calculate Bond Prices and Yields Using a Financial Calculator

Many financial calculators have fairly sophisticated built-in bond valuation routines. However, these vary quite a lot in implementation, and not all financial calculators have them. As a result, we will illustrate a simple way to handle bond problems that will work on just about any financial calculator.

To begin, of course, we first remember to clear out the calculator! Next, for Example 7.2, we have two bonds to consider, both with 12 years to maturity. The first one sells for $932.16 and has a 5 percent coupon rate. To find its yield, we can do the following:

Enter	12		50	−932.16	1,000
	N	**I/Y**	**PMT**	**PV**	**FV**
Solve for		5.8			

Notice that we entered both a future value of $1,000, representing the bond's face value, and a payment of $50 per year ($1,000 × 5 percent), representing the bond's annual coupon. Since the face value and annual coupon are cash inflows to the investor they are entered as positive values. On the contrary, the bond's price, which we entered as the present value, has a negative sign as it is a cash outflow.

For the second bond, we now know that the relevant yield is 5.8 percent. It has a 6 percent coupon and 12 years to maturity, so what's the price? To answer, we just enter the relevant values and solve for the present value of the bond's cash flows:

Enter	12	5.8	60		1,000
	N	**%i**	**PMT**	**PV**	**FV**
Solve for				−1,016.95	

There is an important detail that comes up here. Suppose we have a bond with a price of $902.29, 10 years to maturity, and a coupon rate of 6 percent. As we mentioned earlier, most bonds actually make semiannual payments. Assuming that this is the case for the bond here, what's the bond's yield? To answer, we need to enter the relevant numbers like this:

Enter	20		30	−902.29	1,000
	N	**I/Y**	**PMT**	**PV**	**FV**
Solve for		3.7			

Notice that we entered $30 as the payment because the bond actually makes payments of $30 every six months. Similarly, we entered 20 for N because there are actually 20 six-month periods. When we solve for the yield, we get 3.7 percent, but the tricky thing to remember is that this is the yield *per six months*, so we have to double it to get the right answer: 2 × 3.7 = 7.4 percent, which would be the bond's reported yield.

SPREADSHEET STRATEGIES

How to Calculate Bond Prices and Yields Using a Spreadsheet

Most spreadsheets have fairly elaborate routines available for calculating bond values and yields; many of these routines involve details that we have not discussed. However, setting up a simple spreadsheet to calculate prices or yields is straightforward, as our next two spreadsheets show:

	A	B	C	D	E	F	G	H
1								
2			**Using a spreadsheet to calculate bond values**					
3								
4	Suppose we have a bond with 22 years to maturity, a coupon rate of 8 percent, and a yield to							
5	maturity of 9 percent. If the bond makes semiannual payments, what is its price today?							
6								
7	Settlement date:	1/1/13						
8	Maturity date:	1/1/35						
9	Annual coupon rate:	0.08						
10	Yield to maturity:	.09						
11	Face value (% of par):	100						
12	Coupons per year:	2						
13	Bond price (% of par):	**90.49**						
14								
15	The formula entered in cell B13 is = PRICE(B7, B8, B9, B10, B11, B12); notice that face value and bond							
16	price are given as a percentage of face value.							

In our spreadsheets, notice that we had to enter two dates: a settlement date and a maturity date. The settlement date is just the date you actually pay for the bond, and the maturity date is the day the bond actually matures. In most of our problems, we don't explicitly have these dates, so we have to make them up. For example, since our bond has 22 years to maturity, we just picked 1/1/2013 (January 1, 2013) as the settlement date and 1/1/2035 (January 1, 2035) as the maturity date. Any two dates would do as long as they are exactly 22 years apart, but these are particularly easy to work with. Finally, notice that we had to enter the coupon rate and yield to maturity in annual terms and then explicitly provide the number of coupon payments per year.

	A	B	C	D	E	F	G	H
1								
2			**Using a spreadsheet to calculate bond yields**					
3								
4	Suppose we have a bond with 22 years to maturity, a coupon rate of 8 percent, and a price of							
5	$960.17. If the bond makes semiannual payments, what is its yield to maturity?							
6								
7	Settlement date:	1/1/13						
8	Maturity date:	1/1/35						
9	Annual coupon rate:	0.08						
10	Bond price (% of par):	96.017						
11	Face value (% of par):	100						
12	Coupons per year:	2						
13	Yield to maturity:	**0.084**						
14								
15	The formula entered in cell B13 is = YIELD(B7, B8, B9, B10, B11, B12); notice that face value and bond							
16	price are entered as a percentage of face value.							

7.2 | More on Bond Features

In this section, we continue our discussion of corporate debt by describing in some detail the basic terms and features that make up a typical long-term corporate bond. We discuss additional issues associated with long-term debt in subsequent sections.

Securities issued by corporations may be classified roughly as *equity securities* and *debt securities*. At the crudest level, a debt represents something that must be repaid; it is the result of borrowing money. When corporations borrow, they generally promise to make regularly scheduled interest payments and to repay the original amount borrowed (that is, the principal). The person or firm making the loan is called the *creditor*, or *lender*. The corporation borrowing the money is called the *debtor*, or *borrower*.

From a financial point of view, the main differences between debt and equity are the following:

1. Debt is not an ownership interest in the firm. Creditors generally do not have voting power.
2. The corporation's payment of interest on debt is considered a cost of doing business and is fully tax deductible. Dividends paid to shareholders are *not* tax deductible.
3. Unpaid debt is a liability of the firm. If it is not paid, the creditors can legally claim the assets of the firm. This action can result in liquidation or reorganization, two of the possible consequences of bankruptcy. Thus, one of the costs of issuing debt is the possibility of financial failure. This possibility does not arise when equity is issued. In 2010, Canwest, a major Canadian media company, failed to make an interest payment on its debt, and as a result had to file for bankruptcy protection.

Is It Debt or Equity?

Sometimes it is not clear if a particular security is debt or equity. For example, suppose a corporation issues a perpetual bond with interest payable solely from corporate income if and only if earned. Whether or not this is really a debt is hard to say and is primarily a legal and semantic issue. Courts and taxing authorities would have the final say.

Corporations are very adept at creating exotic, hybrid securities that have many features of equity but are treated as debt. Obviously, the distinction between debt and equity is very important for tax purposes. So one reason that corporations try to create a debt security that is really equity is to obtain the tax benefits of debt and the bankruptcy benefits of equity.

As a general rule, equity represents an ownership interest, and it is a residual claim. This means that equity holders are paid after debt holders. As a result of this, the risks and benefits associated with owning debt and equity are different. To give just one example, note that the maximum reward for owning a debt security is ultimately fixed by the amount of the loan, whereas there is no upper limit to the potential reward from owning an equity interest.

Long-Term Debt: The Basics

Ultimately, all long-term debt securities are promises by the issuing firm to pay the principal when due and to make timely interest payments on the unpaid balance. Beyond this, a number of features distinguish these securities from one another. We discuss some of these features next.

The maturity of a long-term debt instrument refers to the length of time the debt remains outstanding with some unpaid balance. Debt securities can be short-term (maturities of one year or less) or long-term (maturities of more than one year).[2]

Debt securities are typically called *notes*, *debentures*, or *bonds*. Strictly speaking, a bond is a secured debt, but, in common usage, the word *bond* refers to all kinds of secured and unsecured debt. We use the term generically to refer to long-term debt.

The two major forms of long-term debt are public-issue and privately placed. We concentrate on public-issue bonds. Most of what we say about them holds true for private-issue, long-term debt as well. The main difference between public-issue and privately placed debt is that the latter is directly placed with a lender and not offered to the public. Since this is a private transaction, the specific terms are up to the parties involved.

There are many other dimensions to long-term debt, including such things as security, call features, sinking funds, ratings, and protective covenants. The following table illustrates these features for a Manitoba Telecom Services Inc. medium-term note issued in September 2011. If some of these terms are unfamiliar, have no fear. We discuss them all next.

Features of Manitoba Telecom Services Inc.—Medium-Term Notes (unsecured) issue

Terms		Explanation
Amount of Issue	$200 million	The company will issue $200 million of bonds.
Issue Date	09/30/11	The bonds will be sold on September 30, 2011.
Maturity Date	10/01/18	The bonds will be paid in 7 years.
Annual Coupon	4.59	Each bondholder will receive $45.90 per bond per year.
Face Value	$1,000	The denomination of the bonds is $1,000.
Issue Price	99.988	The issue price will be 99.988% of the $1,000 face value per bond.
Yield to Maturity	4.59	If the bond is held to maturity, bondholders will receive a stated annual rate of return equal to 4.59 percent.
Coupon Payment	04/01 and 10/01	Coupons of $45.90/2 = $22.95 will be paid semi-annually on these dates.
Security	Unsecured	The bonds are debentures.
Rating	DBRS BBB	The bond is of satisfactory credit quality, but is not as high as A or AA.

Source: sedar.com

Many of these features are detailed in the bond indenture, so we discuss this now.

The Indenture

indenture
Written agreement between the corporation and the lender detailing the terms of the debt issue.

The **indenture** is the written agreement between the corporation (the borrower) and its creditors. It is sometimes referred to as the deed of trust.[3] Usually, a trustee (a trust company) is appointed by the corporation to represent the bondholders. The trust company must (1) make sure the terms of the indenture are obeyed, (2) manage the sinking fund (described later), and (3) represent the bondholders in default, that is, if the company defaults on its payments to them.

The bond indenture is a legal document. It can run several hundred pages and generally makes for very tedious reading. It is an important document, however, because it generally includes the

---

[2] There is no universally agreed-upon distinction between short-term and long-term debt. In addition, people often refer to medium-term debt, which has a maturity of more than 1 year and less than 3 to 5, or even 10, years.

[3] The words *loan agreement* or *loan contract* are usually used for privately placed debt and term loans.

following provisions:

1. The basic terms of the bonds.
2. The amount of the bonds issued.
3. A description of property used as security if the bonds are secured.
4. The repayment arrangements.
5. The call provisions.
6. Details of the protective covenants.

We discuss these features next.

TERMS OF A BOND   Corporate bonds usually have a face value (that is, a denomination) of $1,000. This is called the *principal value*, and it is stated on the bond certificate. So, if a corporation wanted to borrow $1 million, it would have to sell 1,000 bonds. The par value (that is, the initial accounting value) of a bond is almost always the same as the face value.

Corporate bonds are usually in **registered form**. For example, the indenture might read as follows: Interest is payable semiannually on July 1 and January 1 of each year to the person in whose name the bond is registered at the close of business on June 15 or December 15, respectively.

This means the company has a registrar who records the ownership of each bond and records any changes in ownership. The company pays the interest and principal by cheque mailed directly to the address of the owner of record. A corporate bond may be registered and may have attached coupons. To obtain an interest payment, the owner must separate a coupon from the bond certificate and send it to the company registrar (the paying agent).

Alternatively, the bond could be in **bearer form**. This means the certificate is the basic evidence of ownership, and the corporation pays the bearer. Ownership is not otherwise recorded, and, as with a registered bond with attached coupons, the holder of the bond certificate detaches the coupons and sends them to the company to receive payment.

There are two drawbacks to bearer bonds: First, they are difficult to recover if they are lost or stolen. Second, because the company does not know who owns its bonds, it cannot notify bondholders of important events. The bearer form of ownership does have the advantage of easing transactions for investors who trade their bonds frequently.

SECURITY   Debt securities are classified according to the collateral and mortgages used to protect the bondholder.

Collateral is a general term that, strictly speaking, means securities (for example, bonds and stocks) pledged as security for payment of debt. For example, collateral trust bonds often involve a pledge of common stock held by the corporation. This pledge is usually backed by marketable securities. However, the term *collateral* often is used much more loosely to refer to any form of security.

Mortgage securities are secured by a mortgage on the real property of the borrower. The property involved may be real estate, transportation equipment, or other property. The legal document that describes a mortgage on real estate is called a mortgage trust indenture or trust deed.

Sometimes mortgages are on specific property, for example, a railroad car. This is called a chattel mortgage. More often, blanket mortgages are used. A blanket mortgage pledges all the real property owned by the company.[4]

Bonds frequently represent unsecured obligations of the company. A **debenture** is an unsecured bond, where no specific pledge of property is made. The term **note** is generally used for such instruments if the maturity of the unsecured bond is less than 10 or so years when it is originally issued. Debenture holders only have a claim on property not otherwise pledged; in other words, the property that remains after mortgages and collateral trusts are taken into account.

At the current time, most public bonds issued by industrial and finance companies are debentures. However, most utility and railroad bonds are secured by a pledge of assets.

SENIORITY   In general terms, *seniority* indicates preference in position over other lenders, and debts are sometimes labelled as "senior" or "junior" to indicate seniority. Some debt is *subordinated*, as in, for example, a subordinated debenture.

In the event of default, holders of subordinated debt must give preference to other specified

---

registered form
Registrar of company records ownership of each bond; payment is made directly to the owner of record.

bearer form
Bond issued without record of the owner's name; payment is made to whoever holds the bond.

debenture
Unsecured debt, usually with a maturity of 10 years or more.

note
Unsecured debt, usually with a maturity under 10 years.

---

[4] Real property includes land and things "affixed thereto." It does not include cash or inventories.

creditors. Usually, this means the subordinated lenders are paid off from cash flow and asset sales only after the specified creditors have been compensated. However, debt cannot be subordinated to equity.

sinking fund
Account managed by the bond trustee for early bond redemption.

REPAYMENT   Bonds can be repaid at maturity, at which time the bondholder receives the stated or face value of the bonds, or they may be repaid in part or in entirety before maturity. Early repayment in some form is more typical and is often handled through a sinking fund.

A **sinking fund** is an account managed by the bond trustee for the purpose of repaying the bonds. The company makes annual payments to the trustee, who then uses the funds to retire a portion of the debt. The trustee does this by either buying up some of the bonds in the market or calling in a fraction of the outstanding bonds. We discuss this second option in the next section.

There are many different kinds of sinking fund arrangements. The fund may start immediately or be delayed for 10 years after the bond is issued. The provision may require the company to redeem all or only a portion of the outstanding issue before maturity. From an investor's viewpoint, a sinking fund reduces the risk that the company will be unable to repay the principal at maturity. Since it involves regular purchases, a sinking fund improves the marketability of the bonds.

call provision
Agreement giving the corporation the option to repurchase the bond at a specified price before maturity.

call premium
Amount by which the call price exceeds the par value of the bond.

deferred call
Call provision prohibiting the company from redeeming the bond before a certain date.

call protected
Bond during period in which it cannot be redeemed by the issuer.

Canada plus call
Call provision that compensates bond investors for interest differential, making it unattractive for an issuer to call a bond.

THE CALL PROVISION   A **call provision** allows the company to repurchase or "call" part or all of the bond issue at stated prices over a specified period. Corporate bonds are usually callable.

Generally, the call price is more than the bond's stated value (that is, the par value). The difference between the call price and the stated value is the **call premium**. The call premium may also be expressed as a percentage of the bond's face value. The amount of the call premium usually becomes smaller over time. One arrangement is to initially set the call premium equal to the annual coupon payment and then make it decline to zero the closer the call date is to maturity.

Call provisions are not usually operative during the first part of a bond's life. This makes the call provision less of a worry for bondholders in the bond's early years. For example, a company might be prohibited from calling its bonds for the first 10 years. This is a **deferred call**. During this period, the bond is said to be **call protected**.

Many long-term corporate bonds outstanding in Canada have call provisions as we just described. New corporate debt features a different call provision referred to as a **Canada plus call**. This new approach is designed to replace the traditional call feature by making it unattractive for the issuer ever to call the bonds. Unlike the standard call, with the Canada call the exact amount of the call premium is not set at the time of issuance. Instead, the Canada plus call stipulates that, in the event of a call, the issuer must provide a call premium which will compensate investors for the difference in interest between the original bond and new debt issued to replace it. This compensation cancels the borrower's benefit from calling the debt and the result is that the call will not occur.

The Canada plus call takes its name from the formula used to calculate the difference in the interest; to determine the new, lower interest rate, the formula adds a premium to the yield on Canadas (Government of Canada bonds).

protective covenant
Part of the indenture limiting certain transactions that can be taken during the term of the loan, usually to protect the lender's interest.

PROTECTIVE COVENANTS   A **protective covenant** is that part of the indenture or loan agreement that limits certain actions a company might otherwise wish to take during the term of the loan. Covenants are designed to reduce the agency costs faced by bondholders. By controlling company activities, they reduce the risk of the bonds.

For example, common covenants limit the dividends the firm can pay and require bondholder approval for any sale of major assets. This means that, if the firm is headed for bankruptcy, it cannot sell all the assets and pay a liquidating dividend to stockholders, leaving the bondholders with only a corporate shell. Protective covenants can be classified into two types: negative covenants and positive (or affirmative) covenants.

A *negative covenant* is a "thou shalt not." It limits or prohibits actions that the company may take. Here are some typical examples:

1. The firm must limit the amount of dividends it pays according to some formula.
2. The firm cannot pledge any assets to other lenders.
3. The firm cannot merge with another firm.
4. The firm cannot sell or lease any major assets without approval by the lender.
5. The firm cannot issue additional long-term debt.

A *positive covenant* is a "thou shalt." It specifies an action that the company agrees to take or a condition the company must abide by. Here are some examples:

1. The company must maintain its working capital at or above some specified minimum level.
2. The company must periodically furnish audited financial statements to the lender.
3. The firm must maintain any collateral or security in good condition.

This is only a partial list of covenants; a particular indenture may feature many different ones.

> ### Concept Questions
>
> 1. What are the distinguishing features of debt as compared to equity?
> 2. What is the indenture? What are protective covenants? Give some examples.
> 3. What is a sinking fund?

7.3 | Bond Ratings

Firms frequently pay to have their debt rated. The two leading bond rating firms in Canada are Standard & Poor's (S&P) and DBRS. Moody's and Standard & Poor's are the largest U.S. bond raters and they often rate Canadian companies that raise funds in U.S. bond markets.[5] The debt ratings are an assessment of the creditworthiness of the corporate issuer. The definitions of creditworthiness used by bond rating agencies are based on how likely the firm is to default and what protection creditors have in the event of a default.

Remember that bond ratings only concern the possibility of default. Earlier in this chapter, we discussed interest rate risk, which we defined as the risk of a change in the value of a bond from a change in interest rates. Bond ratings do not address this issue. As a result, the price of a highly rated bond can still be quite volatile.

Bond ratings are constructed from information supplied by the corporation. The rating classes and information concerning them are shown in Table 7.2. Table 7.2 shows ratings by DBRS. Standard & Poor's follows a similar system.

TABLE 7.2

Descriptions of ratings used by DBRS

AAA	Highest credit quality. The capacity for the payment of financial obligations is exceptionally high and unlikely to be adversely affected by future events.
AA	Superior credit quality. The capacity for the payment of financial obligations is considered high. Credit quality differs from AAA only to a small degree. Unlikely to be significantly vulnerable to future events.
A	Good credit quality. The capacity for the payment of financial obligations is substantial, but of lesser credit quality than AA. May be vulnerable to future events, but qualifying negative factors are considered manageable.
BBB	Adequate credit quality. The capacity for the payment of financial obligations is considered acceptable. May be vulnerable to future events.
BB	Speculative, non-investment-grade credit quality. The capacity for the payment of financial obligations is uncertain. Vulnerable to future events.
B	Highly speculative credit quality. There is a high level of uncertainty as to the capacity to meet financial obligations.
CCC/ CC/ C	Very highly speculative credit quality. In danger of defaulting on financial obligations. There is little difference between these three categories, although CC and C ratings are normally applied to obligations that are seen as highly likely to default, or subordinated to obligations rated in the CCC to B range. Obligations in respect of which default has not technically taken place but is considered inevitable may be rated in the C category.
D	A financial obligation has not been met or it is clear that a financial obligation will not be met in the near future or a debt instrument has been subject to a distressed exchange. A downgrade to D may not immediately follow an insolvency or restructuring filing as grace periods or extenuating circumstances may exist.

Source: © 2012 DBRS, dbrs.com. Used with permission.

---

[5] They also rate bonds issued by the individual provinces.

The highest rating a firm can have is AAA and such debt is judged to be the best quality and to have the lowest degree of risk. This rating is not awarded very often; AA ratings indicate very good quality debt and are much more common. Investment grade bonds are bonds rated at least BBB. The lowest ratings are for debt that is in default.

In the 1980s, a growing part of corporate borrowing took the form of low-grade, or junk, bonds, particularly in the United States. If they are rated at all, such low-grade bonds are rated below investment grade by the major rating agencies. Junk bonds are also called *high-yield* bonds, as they yield an interest rate 3 to 5 percentage points (300 to 500 basis points) higher than that of AAA-rated debt. Original issue junk bonds have never been a major source of funds in Canadian capital markets. Their niche has been filled in part by preferred shares and to a lesser extent, income bonds. In recent years, some Canadian corporations with large debt financing needs have issued bonds below investment grade (in 2011 Armtec Holdings Ltd. had a Standard & Poor's corporate credit rating of B) while others had their bonds downgraded after issue. For example, in August 2011, S&P downgraded U.S Treasury bonds for the first time in history from AAA to AA+.

Concept Questions

1. What is a junk bond?
2. What does a bond rating say about the risk of fluctuations in a bond's value from interest rate changes?

7.4 | Some Different Types of Bonds

Thus far, we have considered "plain vanilla" bonds. In this section, we look at some more unusual types, the products of financial engineering: stripped bonds, floating-rate bonds, and others.

Financial Engineering

When financial managers or their investment bankers design new securities or financial processes, their efforts are referred to as financial engineering.[6] Successful financial engineering reduces and controls risk and minimizes taxes. It also seeks to reduce financing costs of issuing and servicing debt as well as costs of complying with rules laid down by regulatory authorities. Financial engineering is a response to the trends we discussed in Chapter 1, globalization, deregulation, and greater competition in financial markets.

When applied to debt securities, financial engineering creates exotic, hybrid securities that have many features of equity but are treated as debt. The most common example of a hybrid security is a convertible bond, which gives the bondholder the option to exchange the bond for company shares. Another example, as we noted earlier, is a perpetual bond that pays interest solely from corporate income *only* when it is earned and at no other time. Whether these bonds are actually debt is difficult to determine and in many cases, the final verdict is left to legal and taxing authorities.

Distinguishing between debt and equity is particularly important for taxation purposes. Interest paid on corporate debt is tax deductible, while dividends paid to shareholders are not.

As a general rule, equity represents an ownership interest and it is a residual claim (shareholders are paid after debt holders). Compared with debt, equity also carries greater risks and rewards. Thus, from an investor's perspective the risks and benefits of owning the two types of securities are quite different.

Financial engineers can alter this division of claims by selling bonds with *warrants* attached giving bondholders options to buy stock in the firm. These warrants allow holders to participate in future rewards beyond the face value of the debt. We discuss other examples of financial engineering throughout this chapter.

---

[6]For more on financial engineering, see John Finnerty, "Financial Engineering in Corporate Finance: An Overview," in *The Handbook of Financial Engineering*, eds. C. W. Smith and C. W. Smithson (New York: Harper Business, 1990).

IN THEIR OWN WORDS...

Edward I. Altman on Junk Bonds

ONE OF THE most important developments in corporate finance over the last 20 years has been the reemergence of publicly owned and traded low-rated corporate debt. Originally offered to the public in the early 1900s to help finance some of our emerging growth industries, these high-yield, high-risk bonds virtually disappeared after the rash of bond defaults during the Depression. Recently, however, the junk bond market has been catapulted from being an insignificant element in the corporate fixed-income market to being one of the fastest-growing and most controversial types of financing mechanisms.

The term *junk* emanates from the dominant type of low-rated bond issues outstanding prior to 1977 when the "market" consisted almost exclusively of original-issue investment-grade bonds that fell from their lofty status to a higher-default risk, speculative-grade level. These so-called fallen angels amounted to about $8.5 billion in 1977. At the end of 1998, fallen angels comprised about 10 percent of the $450 billion publicly owned junk bond market.

Beginning in 1977, issuers began to go directly to the public to raise capital for growth purposes. Early users of junk bonds were energy-related firms, cable TV companies, airlines, and assorted other industrial companies. The emerging growth company rationale coupled with relatively high returns to early investors helped legitimize this sector.

By far the most important and controversial aspect of junk bond financing was its role in the corporate restructuring movement from 1985 to 1989. High-leverage transactions and acquisitions, such as leveraged buyouts (LBOs), which occur when a firm is taken private, and leveraged recapitalizations (debt-for-equity swaps), transformed the face of corporate America, leading to a heated debate as to the economic and social consequences of firms' being transformed with debt-equity ratios of at least 6:1.

These transactions involved increasingly large companies, and the multibillion-dollar takeover became fairly common, finally capped by the huge $25+ billion RJR Nabisco LBO in 1989. LBOs were typically financed with about 60 percent senior bank and insurance company debt, about 25–30 percent subordinated public debt (junk bonds), and 10–15 percent equity. The junk bond segment is sometimes referred to as "mezzanine" financing because it lies between the "balcony" senior debt and the "basement" equity.

These restructurings resulted in huge fees to advisors and underwriters and huge premiums to the old shareholders who were bought out, and they continued as long as the market was willing to buy these new debt offerings at what appeared to be a favourable risk-return trade-off. The bottom fell out of the market in the last six months of 1989 due to a number of factors including a marked increase in defaults, government regulation against S&Ls' holding junk bonds, and a recession.

The default rate rose dramatically to 4 percent in 1989 and then skyrocketed in 1990 and 1991 to 10.1 percent and 10.3 percent, respectively, with about $19 billion of defaults in 1991. By the end of 1990, the pendulum of growth in new junk bond issues and returns to investors swung dramatically downward as prices plummeted and the new-issue market all but dried up. The year 1991 was a pivotal year in that, despite record defaults, bond prices and new issues rebounded strongly as the prospects for the future brightened.

In the early 1990s, the financial market was questioning the very survival of the junk bond market. The answer was a resounding "yes," as the amount of new issues soared to record annual levels of $40 billion in 1992 and almost $60 billion in 1993, and in 1997 reached an impressive $119 billion. Coupled with plummeting default rates (under 2.0 percent each year in the 1993–97 period) and attractive returns in these years, the risk-return characteristics have been extremely favourable.

The junk bond market today is a quieter one compared to that of the 1980s, but, in terms of growth and returns, it is healthier than ever before. While the low default rates in 1992–98 helped to fuel new investment funds and new issues, the market will experience its ups and downs in the future. It will continue, however, to be a major source of corporate debt financing and a legitimate asset class for investors.

Edward I. Altman is Max L. Heine Professor of Finance and vice director of the Salomon Center at the Stern School of Business of New York University. He is widely recognized as one of the world's experts on bankruptcy and credit analysis as well as on the high-yield, or junk bond, market. Updates on his research are at stern.nyu.edu/~ealtman.

---

stripped bond or zero-coupon bond
A bond that makes no coupon payments, thus initially priced at a deep discount.

Stripped Bonds

A bond that pays no coupons must be offered at a price that is much lower that its stated value. Such a bond is called a **stripped bond** or **zero-coupon bond**.[7] Stripped bonds start life as normal

---

[7] A bond issued with a very low coupon rate (as opposed to a zero coupon rate) is an original issue, discount (OID) bond.

coupon bonds. Investment dealers engage in bond stripping when they sell the principal and coupons separately.

Suppose the DDB Company issues a $1,000 face value five-year stripped bond. The initial price is set at $497. It is straightforward to check that, at this price, the bonds yield 15 percent to maturity. The total interest paid over the life of the bond is $1,000 − 497 = $503.

For tax purposes, the issuer of a stripped bond deducts interest every year even though no interest is actually paid. Similarly, the owner must pay taxes on interest accrued every year as well, even though no interest is actually received.[8] This second tax feature makes taxable stripped bonds less attractive to taxable investors. However, they are still a very attractive investment for tax-exempt investors with long-term dollar-denominated liabilities, such as pension funds, because the future dollar value is known with relative certainty. Stripped coupons are attractive to individual investors for tax-sheltered registered retirement savings plans (RRSPs).

Floating-Rate Bonds

The conventional bonds we have talked about in this chapter have fixed-dollar obligations because the coupon rate is set as a fixed percentage of the par value. Similarly, the principal is set equal to the par value. Under these circumstances, the coupon payment and principal are fixed.

With *floating-rate bonds (floaters)*, the coupon payments are adjustable. The adjustments are tied to the Treasury bill rate or another short-term interest rate. For example, the Royal Bank has outstanding $250 million of floating-rate notes maturing in 2083. The coupon rate is set at 0.40 percent more than the bankers acceptance rate.

Floating rate bonds were introduced to control the risk of price fluctuations as interest rates change. A bond with a coupon equal to the market yield is priced at par. In practice, the value of a floating-rate bond depends on exactly how the coupon payment adjustments are defined. In most cases, the coupon adjusts with a lag to some base rate, and so the price can deviate from par within some range. For example, suppose a coupon-rate adjustment is made on June 1. The adjustment might be based on the simple average of Treasury bill yields during the previous three months. In addition, the majority of floaters have the following features:

1. The holder has the right to redeem his or her note at par on the coupon payment date after some specified amount of time. This is called a put provision, and it is discussed later.
2. The coupon rate has a floor and a ceiling, meaning the coupon is subject to a minimum and a maximum.

Other Types of Bonds

Many bonds have unusual or exotic features, such as the so-called catastrophe, or cat, bonds. To give an example of an unusual cat bond, the Fédération Internationale de Football Association (FIFA) issued $260 million worth of cat bonds to protect against the cancellation of the 2006 FIFA World Cup soccer tournament due to terrorism. Under the terms of the offer, the bondholders would lose up to 75 percent of their investment if the World Cup were to be cancelled.

Most cat bonds, however, cover natural disasters. For example, in 2011, Muteki Limited issued catastrophe bonds valued at $1.7 billion for Japanese carrier Zenkyoren and it experienced a major loss due to earthquakes and the tsunami in Japan.

As these examples illustrate, bond features are really only limited by the imaginations of the parties involved. Unfortunately, there are far too many variations for us to cover in detail here. We therefore close out this discussion by mentioning only a few of the more common types.

Income bonds are similar to conventional bonds, except that coupon payments depend on company income. Specifically, coupons are paid to bondholders only if the firm's income is sufficient. In Canada, income bonds are usually issued by firms in the process of reorganizing to try to overcome financial distress. The firm can skip the interest payment on an income bond without being in default. Purchasers of income bonds receive favourable tax treatment on interest received. *Real return bonds* have coupons and principal indexed to inflation to provide a stated

---

[8] The way the yearly interest on a stripped bond is calculated is governed by tax law and is not necessarily the true compound interest.

real return. In 1993, the federal government issued a *stripped real return bond* packaging inflation protection in the form of a zero coupon bond.

A *convertible bond* can be swapped for a fixed number of shares of stock anytime before maturity at the holder's option. Convertibles are debt/equity hybrids that allow the holder to profit if the issuer's stock price rises.

Asset-backed bonds are backed by a diverse pool of illiquid assets such as accounts receivable collections, credit card debt, or mortgages. If an issuing company defaults on its bond debt repayments, bondholders become legally entitled to cash flows generated from these illiquid pools of assets. Asset backing or securitization reduces risk provided that the assets are of high quality. In the credit crisis of 2007–2008, bonds backed by sub-prime mortgages to risky borrowers lost most of their value.

retractable bond
Bond that may be sold back to the issuer at a prespecified price before maturity.

A **retractable bond** or *put bond* allows the holder to force the issuer to buy the bond back at a stated price. As long as the issuer remains solvent, the put feature sets a floor price for the bond. It is, therefore, just the reverse of the call provision and is a relatively new development. We discuss convertible bonds, call provisions, and put provisions in more detail in Chapter 25.

A given bond may have many unusual features. Two fairly recent exotic bonds are CoCo bonds, which have a coupon payment, and NoNo bonds, which are zero coupon bonds. CoCo and NoNo bonds are contingent convertible, putable, callable, subordinated bonds. The contingent convertible clause is similar to the normal conversion feature, except the contingent feature must be met. For example, a contingent feature may require that the company stock trade at 110 percent of the conversion price for 20 out of the most recent 30 days. Valuing a bond of this sort can be quite complex, and the yield to maturity calculation is often meaningless. For example, in 2011, Credit Suisse issued CoCo bonds worth 6 billion Swiss francs at a coupon rate of 9% to 9.5%. Coco bonds are gaining popularity after the recession of 2008, as the bonds can be converted into equity once the stock price recovers and a threshold is reached.

Concept Questions

1. Why might an income bond be attractive to a corporation with volatile cash flows? Can you think of a reason why income bonds are not more popular?

2. What do you think the effect of a put feature on a bond's coupon would be? How about a convertibility feature? Why?

7.5 | Bond Markets

Bonds are bought and sold in enormous quantities every day. You may be surprised to learn that the trading volume in bonds on a typical day is many, many times larger than the trading volume in stocks (by trading volume, we simply mean the amount of money that changes hands). Here is a finance trivia question: What is the largest securities market in the world? Most people would guess the New York Stock Exchange. In fact, the largest securities market in the world in terms of trading volume is the U.S. Treasury market.

How Bonds Are Bought and Sold

As we mentioned all the way back in Chapter 1, most trading in bonds takes place OTC: over the counter. Recall that this means that there is no particular place where buying and selling occur. Instead, dealers around the country (and around the world) stand ready to buy and sell. The various dealers are connected electronically.

One reason the bond markets are so big is that the number of bond issues far exceeds the number of stock issues. A corporation would typically have only one common stock issue outstanding (there are exceptions to this that we discuss in our next chapter). However, a single large corporation could easily have a dozen or more note and bond issues outstanding.

Because the bond market is almost entirely OTC, it has little or no *transparency*. A financial market is transparent if it is possible to easily observe its prices and trading volume. On the Toronto Stock Exchange, for example, it is possible to see the price and quantity for every single transaction.

In contrast, in the bond market, it is usually not possible to observe either. Transactions are privately negotiated between parties, and there is little or no centralized reporting of transactions.

Although the total volume of trading in bonds far exceeds that in stocks, only a very small fraction of the total bond issues that exist actually trade on a given day. This fact, combined with the lack of transparency in the bond market, means that getting up-to-date prices on individual bonds is often difficult or impossible, particularly for smaller corporate or municipal issues. Instead, a variety of sources of estimated prices exist and are very commonly used.

Bond Price Reporting

If you were to visit the website for the *National Post*, you would see information on various bonds issued by the Government of Canada, the provinces and provincial crown corporations, and large corporations. Figure 7.4 reproduces excerpts from the bond quotations on January 5, 2012. If you look down the list under "Corporate," you come to an entry marked "Loblaw 6.05 Jun 09/34." This tells us the bond was issued by Loblaw Companies Ltd. and it will mature on June 09, 2034. The 6.05 is the bond's coupon rate, so the coupon is 6.05 percent of the face value. Assuming the face value is $1,000, the annual coupon on this bond is 0.0605 × $1,000 = $60.50.

The column marked Bid $ gives us the last available bid price on the bond at close of business the day before. The bid price is the price a buyer is willing to pay for a security. This price was supplied by the *National Post*. As with the coupon, the price is quoted as a percentage of face value; so, again assuming a face value of $1,000, this bond last sold for 106.08 percent of $1,000 or $1,060.80. Quoting bond prices as percentages of face value is common practice. Because this bond is selling for about 106.08 percent of its par value, it is trading at a premium. The last column marked Yield % gives the going market yield to maturity on the Loblaw bond as 5.57 percent. This yield is lower than the coupon rate of 6.05 percent, which explains why the bond is selling above its par value. The market yield is below the coupon rate by 0.48 percent, or 48 basis points. (In bond trader's jargon, one basis point equals 1/100 of 1 percent.) This causes the price premium to be above par.

EXAMPLE 7.3: Bond Pricing in Action

Investment managers who specialize in bonds use bond pricing principles to try to make money for their clients by buying bonds whose prices they expect to rise. An interest rate anticipation strategy starts with a forecast for the level of interest rates. Such forecasts are extremely difficult to make consistently. In Chapter 12, we discuss in detail how difficult it is to beat the market.

Suppose a manager had predicted a significant drop in interest rates in 2013. How should such a manager have invested?

This manager would have invested heavily in bonds with the greatest price sensitivity; that is, in bonds whose prices would rise the most as rates fell. Based on the earlier discussion, you should recall that such price-sensitive bonds have longer times to maturity and low coupons.

Suppose you wanted to bet on the expectation that interest rates were going to fall significantly using the bond quotations in Figure 7.4. Suppose further that your client wanted to invest only in Government of Canada bonds. Which would you buy?

A Note on Bond Price Quotes

clean price
The price of a bond net of accrued interest; this is the price that is typically quoted.

dirty price
The price of a bond including accrued interest, also known as the full or invoice price. This is the price the buyer actually pays.

If you buy a bond between coupon payment dates, the price you pay is usually more than the price you are quoted. The reason is that standard convention in the bond market is to quote prices "net of accrued interest," meaning that accrued interest is deducted to arrive at the quoted price. This quoted price is called the **clean price**. The price you actually pay, however, includes the accrued interest. This price is the **dirty price**, also known as the "full" or "invoice" price.

An example is the easiest way to understand these issues. Suppose you buy a bond with a 6 percent annual coupon, payable semiannually. You actually pay $1,080 for this bond, so $1,080 is the dirty, or invoice, price. Further, on the day you buy it, the next coupon is due in four months, so you are between coupon dates. Notice that the next coupon will be $30.

The accrued interest on a bond is calculated by taking the fraction of the coupon period that has passed, in this case two months out of six, and multiplying this fraction by the next coupon, $30. So, the accrued interest in this example is 2/6 × $30 = $10. The bond's quoted price (i.e., its clean price) would be $1,080 − $10 = $1,070.[9]

FIGURE 7.4   Sample bond quotations

PC Bond Indices on 2012.01.05
Data provided by: National Post

Bond Index	Index Level	Average Yield	Daily Total Return	Daily Price Return	MTD Total Return
Universe	861.18	2.35	0.16	0.15	−0.21
Short	628.24	1.55	0.04	0.03	0.01
Mid	916.27	2.60	0.13	0.12	−0.08
Long	1,281.73	3.44	0.37	0.36	−0.68
Canada	194.85	1.54	0.14	0.13	−0.23
All Govt.	846.54	2.03	0.16	0.15	−0.25
Federal	784.90	1.54	0.12	0.11	−0.17
Provincial	978.32	2.75	0.23	0.22	−0.37
Municipal	1,019.67	2.71	0.15	0.14	−0.24
All Corp	925.45	3.25	0.14	0.13	−0.10
Maple	126.41	4.10	0.09	0.07	−0.04
RRB	523.46	0.28	0.52	0.51	−0.24
91 day Tbill	387.01	0.82	0	n. a.	0.02

Source: financialpost.com/markets/data/bonds-pc.html, Jan 05, 2012; Used with permission.

Canadian Bonds on 2012.01.05
Data provided by: National Post

Federal

	Coupon	Maturity Date	Bid $	Yield %
Canada	2	Mar 01/14	102.18	0.97
Canada	10.25	Mar 15/14	119.98	0.97
Canada	5	Jun 01/14	109.49	0.98
Canada	11.25	Jun 01/15	133.70	1.10
Canada	4.5	Jun 01/15	111.23	1.12
Canada	3	Dec 01/15	106.86	1.19
Canada	4	Jun 01/16	111.67	1.26
Canada	2.75	Sep 01/16	106.54	1.29
Canada	4	Jun 01/17	113.48	1.40
Canada	4.25	Jun 01/18	116.54	1.52
Canada	3.75	Jun 01/19	114.21	1.70
Canada	3.5	Jun 01/20	112.62	1.87
Canada	9.75	Jun 01/21	167.09	1.91
Canada	5.75	Jun 01/29	146.60	2.45
Canada	5.75	Jun 01/33	152.50	2.55
CHT	2.2	Mar 15/14	102.36	1.10
CHT	2.75	Jun 15/16	105.24	1.52
CHT	3.8	Jun 15/21	105.24	1.52

Provincial

	Coupon	Maturity Date	Bid $	Yield %
B C	4.7	Jun 18/37	120.78	3.46
HydQue	6.5	Feb 15/35	145.12	3.61
HydQue	6.0	Feb 15/40	142.15	3.60
NovaSc	6.6	Jun 01/27	139.23	3.32
Ontario	5	Mar 08/14	108.04	1.22
Ontario	4.3	Mar 08/17	111.86	1.88
Quebec	5.5	Dec 01/14	111.78	1.33
Quebec	5	Dec 01/15	112.89	1.57

Corporate

	Coupon	Maturity Date	Bid $	Yield %
Bell	4.85	Jun 30/14	106.18	2.27
Bell	6.10	Mar 16/35	112.25	5.19
BMO	5.10	Apr 21/16	110.07	2.60
BMO	6.17	Jul 16/14	104.01	1.80
BNS	3.43	Oct 30/13	105.28	1.58
BNS	3.34	Mar 25/15	104.04	2.03
CIBC	3.15	Nov 02/15	100.67	2.96
Enbridge	4.53	Mar 09/20	108.70	3.31
GE CAP	5.68	Sep 10/19	110.80	4.03
GWLife	4.65	Aug 13/20	104.89	3.97
HSBC	4.8	Apr 10/17	106.46	3.44
HydOne	4.64	Mar 03/16	109.87	2.14
HydOne	5.36	May 20/36	120.07	4.06
Loblaw	6.05	Jun 09/34	106.08	5.57
MLI	7.768	Apr 08/19	118.74	4.69
MLI	5.059	Dec 15/36	80.91	6.64
RoyBnk	3.18	Mar 16/15	103.75	1.96
RoyBnk	3.18	Nov 02/15	100.87	2.94
SunLife	5.59	Jan 30/18	106.03	4.44
TD Bnk	5.763	Dec 18/17	112.17	3.48

Source: financialpost.com/markets/data/bonds-canadian.html, Jan 05, 2012; Used with permission.

[9] The way accrued interest is calculated actually depends on the type of bond being quoted: for example, Government of Canada or corporate. The difference has to do with exactly how the fractional period is calculated. In our example above, we implicitly treated the months as having exactly the same length (i.e., 30 days each, 360 days in a year), which is the way corporate bonds are quoted in the U.S. In Canada, the calculation assumes 365 days in a year. In contrast, Government of Canada and U.S. treasury bonds use actual day counts in quoting prices.

Bond Funds

A bond fund is a mutual fund that invests in bonds and other debt securities. In addition to Canada bonds, these include mortgages and provincial, corporate and municipal debt. A example of a bond fund that is very prominent in North America is the Pacific Investment Management Company (PIMCO), one of the world's largest bond management companies with assets of around $250 billion U.S., run by the well-known U.S. money manager, Bill Gross. In June 2012, Gross' PIMCO Total Return attracted $1.4 billion as the firm shied away from securities in Spain and Portugal in favour of U.S. Treasuries and Mortgage Securities. As the European crisis worsened in 2012, investors continued to avoid Europe Securities. Four of the region's main countries—Portugal, Italy, Greece, and Spain (also referred to as PIGS) failed to generate enough economic growth and were in immediate danger of possible default. As a result, Moody's Investors Service downgraded several of the countries' ratings. By avoiding bonds issued by such countries, PIMCO was able to improve its return.

Concept Questions

1. What are the cash flows associated with a bond?
2. What is the general expression for the value of a bond?
3. Is it true that the only risk associated with owning a bond is that the issuer will not make all the payments? Explain.
4. Figure 7.4 shows two Canada bonds, both maturing on June 1, 2015. These bonds are both issued by the Government of Canada and they have identical maturities. Why do they have different yields?

7.6 | Inflation and Interest Rates

So far, we haven't considered the role of inflation in our various discussions of interest rates, yields, and returns. Because this is an important consideration, we consider the impact of inflation next.

Real versus Nominal Rates

real rates
Interest rates or rates of return that have been adjusted for inflation.

nominal rates
Interest rates or rates of return that have not been adjusted for inflation.

In examining interest rates, or any other financial market rates such as discount rates, bond yields, rates of return, and required returns, it is often necessary to distinguish between **real rates** and **nominal rates**. Nominal rates are called "nominal" because they have not been adjusted for inflation. Real rates are rates that have been adjusted for inflation.

To see the effect of inflation, suppose prices are currently rising by 5 percent per year. In other words, the rate of inflation is 5 percent. An investment is available that will be worth $115.50 in one year. It costs $100 today. Notice that with a present value of $100 and a future value in one year of $115.50, this investment has a 15.5 percent rate of return. In calculating this 15.5 percent return, we did not consider the effect of inflation, however, so this is the nominal return.

What is the impact of inflation here? To answer, suppose pizzas cost $5 apiece at the beginning of the year. With $100, we can buy 20 pizzas. Because the inflation rate is 5 percent, pizzas will cost 5 percent more, or $5.25, at the end of the year. If we take the investment, how many pizzas can we buy at the end of the year? Measured in pizzas, what is the rate of return on this investment?

Our $115.50 from the investment will buy us $115.50/5.25 = 22 pizzas. This is up from 20 pizzas, so our pizza rate of return is 10 percent. What this illustrates is that even though the nominal return on our investment is 15.5 percent, our buying power goes up by only 10 percent because of inflation. Put another way, we are really only 10 percent richer. In this case, we say that the real return is 10 percent.

Alternatively, we can say that with 5 percent inflation, each of the $115.50 nominal dollars we get is worth 5 percent less in real terms, so the real dollar value of our investment in a year is:

$$\$115.50/1.05 = \$110$$

Current and historical Treasury yield information is available at bankofcanada.ca

What we have done is to *deflate* the $115.50 by 5 percent. Because we give up $100 in current buying power to get the equivalent of $110, our real return is again 10 percent. Because we have removed the effect of future inflation here, this $110 is said to be measured in current dollars.

The difference between nominal and real rates is important and bears repeating:

> The nominal rate on an investment is the percentage change in the number of dollars you have.

The real rate on an investment is the percentage change in how much you can buy with your dollars, in other words, the percentage change in your buying power.

The Fisher Effect

Fisher effect
The relationship between nominal returns, real returns, and inflation.

Our discussion of real and nominal returns illustrates a relationship often called the **Fisher effect** (after the great economist Irving Fisher). Because investors are ultimately concerned with what they can buy with their money, they require compensation for inflation.[10] Let R stand for the nominal rate and r stand for the real rate. The Fisher effect tells us that the relationship between nominal rates, real rates, and inflation can be written as:

$$1 + R = (1 + r) \times (1 + h) \qquad [7.2]$$

where h is the inflation rate.

In the preceding example, the nominal rate was 15.50 percent and the inflation rate was 5 percent. What was the real rate? We can determine it by plugging in these numbers:

$$1 + .1550 = (1 + r) \times (1 + .05)$$
$$1 + r = 1.1550/1.05 = 1.10$$
$$r = 10\%$$

This real rate is the same as we had before. If we take another look at the Fisher effect, we can rearrange things a little as follows:

$$1 + R = (1 + r) \times (1 + h) \qquad [7.3]$$
$$R = r + h + r \times h$$

What this tells us is that the nominal rate has three components. First, there is the real rate on the investment, r. Next, there is the compensation for the decrease in the value of the money originally invested because of inflation, h. The third component represents compensation for the fact that the dollars earned on the investment are also worth less because of the inflation.

This third component is usually small, so it is often dropped. The nominal rate is then approximately equal to the real rate plus the inflation rate:

$$R \approx r + h \qquad [7.4]$$

A good example of the Fisher effect in practice comes from the history of interest rates in Canada.[11] In 1980, the average T-bill rate over the year was around 13 percent. In contrast, in 2011, the average rate was much lower, at under 1 percent. The inflation rates for the same two years were approximately 10 percent for 1980 and about 2.9 percent for 2011. Lower expected inflation goes a long way toward explaining why interest rates were lower in 2011 than in 1980.

EXAMPLE 7.4: The Fisher Effect

If investors require a 10 percent real rate of return, and the inflation rate is 8 percent, what must be the approximate nominal rate? The exact nominal rate?

First of all, the nominal rate is approximately equal to the sum of the real rate and the inflation rate: 10% + 8% = 18%. From the Fisher effect, we have:

$$1 + R = (1 + r) \times (1 + h)$$
$$= 1.10 \times 1.08$$
$$= 1.1880$$

Therefore, the nominal rate will actually be closer to 19 percent.

---

[10] Here we are referring to the *expected* inflation rate, rather than the actual inflation rate. Buyers and sellers of investments must use their best estimate of future inflation rates at the time of a transaction. Actual rates of inflation are not known until a considerable period after the purchase or sale, when all the cash flows from the investment instrument have taken place.

[11] You can find historical and international data on interest rates and inflation at economist.com, and bankofcanada.ca

The Fisher effect also holds on an international scale. While 2011interest rates were low in Canada compared to 1980, they were considerably higher than for the same year in Japan. In that country, the 2011 average inflation rate was −0.5 percent, while the Bank of Japan's short-term rates were 0 percent.

It is important to note that financial rates, such as interest rates, discount rates, and rates of return, are almost always quoted in nominal terms.

Inflation And Present Values

One question that often comes up is the effect of inflation on present value calculations. The basic principle is simple: Either discount nominal cash flows at a nominal rate or discount real cash flows at a real rate. As long as you are consistent, you will get the same answer.

To illustrate, suppose you want to withdraw money each year for the next three years, and you want each withdrawal to have $25,000 worth of purchasing power as measured in current dollars. If the inflation rate is 4 percent per year, then the withdrawals will simply have to increase by 4 percent each year to compensate. The withdrawals each year will thus be:

$$C_1 = \$25,000(1.04) = \$26,000$$
$$C_2 = \$25,000(1.04)^2 = \$27,040$$
$$C_3 = \$25,000(1.04)^3 = \$28,121.60$$

What is the present value of these cash flows if the appropriate nominal discount rate is 10 percent? This is a standard calculation, and the answer is:

$$PV = \$26,000/1.10 + \$27,040/1.10^2 + \$28,121.60/1.10^3 = \$67,111.75$$

Notice that we discounted the nominal cash flows at a nominal rate.

To calculate the present value using real cash flows, we need the real discount rate. Using the Fisher equation, the real discount rate is:

$$(1 + R) = (1 + r)(1 + h)$$
$$(1 + .10) = (1 + r)(1 + .04)$$
$$r = .0577$$

By design, the real cash flows are an annuity of $25,000 per year. So, the present value in real terms is:

$$PV = \$25,000[1 - (1/1.0577^3)]/.0577 = \$67,111.65$$

Thus, we get exactly the same answer (after allowing for a small rounding error in the real rate). Of course, you could also use the growing annuity equation we discussed in the previous chapter. The withdrawals are increasing at 4 percent per year; so using the growing annuity formula, the present value is:

$$PV = \$26,000 \left[\frac{1 - \left(\frac{1 + .04}{1 + .10}\right)^3}{.10 - .04} \right] = \$26,000(2.58122) = \$67,111.75$$

This is exactly the same present value we calculated before.

Concept Questions

1. What is the difference between a nominal and a real return? Which is more important to a typical investor?

2. What is the Fisher effect?

7.7 | Determinants of Bond Yields

We are now in a position to discuss the determinants of a bond's yield. As we will see, the yield on any particular bond is a reflection of a variety of factors, some common to all bonds and some specific to the issue under consideration.

The Term Structure of Interest Rates

At any point in time, short-term and long-term interest rates will generally be different. Sometimes short-term rates are higher, sometimes lower. Through time, the difference between short- and long-term rates has ranged from essentially zero to up to several percentage points, both positive and negative.

term structure of interest rates
The relationship between nominal interest rates on default-free, pure discount securities and time to maturity; that is, the pure time value of money.

The relationship between short- and long-term interest rates is known as the **term structure of interest rates**. To be a little more precise, the term structure of interest rates tells us what *nominal* interest rates are on *default-free, pure discount* bonds of all maturities. These rates are, in essence, "pure" interest rates because they involve no risk of default and a single, lump-sum future payment. In other words, the term structure tells us the pure time value of money for different lengths of time.

When long-term rates are higher than short-term rates, we say that the term structure is upward sloping, and, when short-term rates are higher, we say it is downward sloping. The term structure can also be "humped." When this occurs, it is usually because rates increase at first, but then begin to decline as we look at longer- and longer-term rates. The most common shape of the term structure, particularly in modern times, is upward sloping, but the degree of steepness has varied quite a bit.

What determines the shape of the term structure? There are three basic components. The first two are the ones we discussed in our previous section, the real rate of interest and the rate of inflation. The real rate of interest is the compensation investors demand for forgoing the use of their money. You can think of it as the pure time value of money after adjusting for the effects of inflation.

The real rate of interest is the basic component underlying every interest rate, regardless of the time to maturity. When the real rate is high, all interest rates will tend to be higher, and vice versa. Thus, the real rate doesn't really determine the shape of the term structure; instead, it mostly influences the overall level of interest rates.

In contrast, the prospect of future inflation very strongly influences the shape of the term structure. Investors thinking about lending money for various lengths of time recognize that future inflation erodes the value of the dollars that will be returned. As a result, investors demand compensation for this loss in the form of higher nominal rates. This extra compensation is called the **inflation premium**.

inflation premium
The portion of a nominal interest rate that represents compensation for expected future inflation.

If investors believe that the rate of inflation will be higher in future, then long-term nominal interest rates will tend to be higher than short-term rates. Thus, an upward-sloping term structure may be a reflection of anticipated increases in inflation. Similarly, a downward-sloping term structure probably reflects the belief that inflation will be falling in the future.

The third, and last, component of the term structure has to do with interest rate risk. As we discussed earlier in the chapter, longer-term bonds have much greater risk of loss resulting from changes in interest rates than do shorter-term bonds. Investors recognize this risk, and they demand extra compensation in the form of higher rates for bearing it. This extra compensation is called the **interest rate risk premium**. The longer the term to maturity, the greater the interest rate risk, so the interest rate risk premium increases with maturity. However, as we discussed earlier, interest rate risk increases at a decreasing rate, so the interest rate risk premium does as well.[12]

interest rate risk premium
The compensation investors demand for bearing interest rate risk.

Putting the pieces together, we see that the term structure reflects the combined effect of the real rate of interest, the inflation premium, and the interest rate risk premium. Figure 7.5 shows how these can interact to produce an upward-sloping term structure (in the top part of Figure 7.5) or a downward-sloping term structure (in the bottom part).

In the top part of Figure 7.5, notice how the rate of inflation is expected to rise gradually. At the same time, the interest rate risk premium increases at a decreasing rate, so the combined effect is to produce a pronounced upward-sloping term structure. In the bottom part of Figure 7.5, the rate of inflation is expected to fall in the future, and the expected decline is enough to offset the interest rate risk premium and produce a downward-sloping term structure. Notice that if the rate of inflation was expected to decline by only a small amount, we could still get an upward-sloping term structure because of the interest rate risk premium.

---

[12]In days of old, the interest rate risk premium was called a "liquidity" premium. Today, the term *liquidity premium* has an altogether different meaning, which we explore in our next section. Also, the interest rate risk premium is sometimes called a maturity risk premium. Our terminology is consistent with the modern view of the term structure.

We assumed in drawing Figure 7.5 that the real rate would remain the same. Actually, expected future real rates could be larger or smaller than the current real rate. Also, for simplicity, we used straight lines to show expected future inflation rates as rising or declining, but they do not necessarily have to look like this. They could, for example, rise and then fall, leading to a humped yield curve.

FIGURE 7.5

The term structure of interest rates

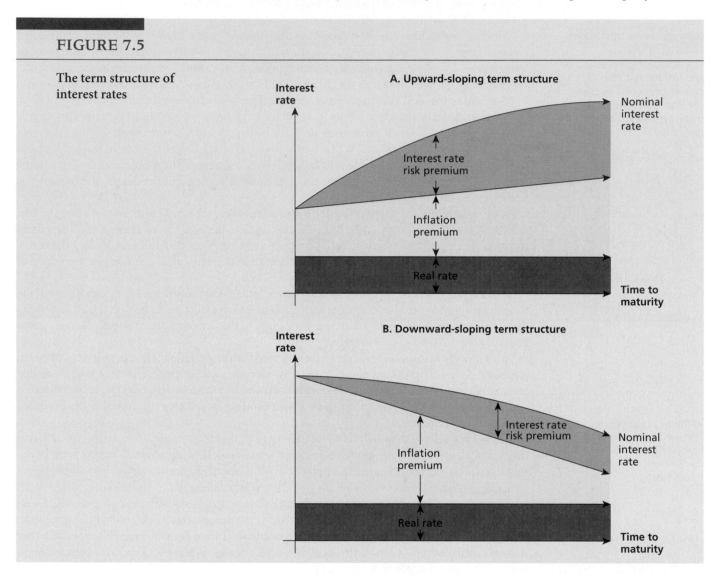

Bond Yields and the Yield Curve: Putting It All Together

Going back to Figure 7.4, recall that we saw that the yields on Government of Canada bonds of different maturities are not the same. Each day, we can plot the Canada bond prices and yields shown in Figure 7.4, relative to maturity. This plot is called the **Canada yield curve** (or just the yield curve). Figure 7.6 shows the yield curve drawn from the yields in Figure 7.4.

As you probably now suspect, the shape of the yield curve is a reflection of the term structure of interest rates. In fact, the Canada yield curve and the term structure of interest rates are almost the same thing. The only difference is that the term structure is based on pure discount bonds, whereas the yield curve is based on coupon bond yields. As a result, Canada yields depend on the three components that underlie the term structure—the real rate, expected future inflation, and the interest rate risk premium.

Canada bonds have three important features that we need to remind you of: they are default-free, they are taxable, and they are highly liquid. This is not true of bonds in general, so we need to examine what additional factors come into play when we look at bonds issued by corporations or municipalities.

Canada yield curve
A plot of the yields on Government of Canada notes and bonds relative to maturity.

The first thing to consider is credit risk, that is, the possibility of default. Investors recognize that issuers other than the Government of Canada may or may not make all the promised payments on a bond, so they demand a higher yield as compensation for this risk. This extra compensation is called the **default risk premium**. Earlier in the chapter, we saw how bonds were rated based on their credit risk. What you will find if you start looking at bonds of different ratings is that lower-rated bonds have higher yields.

default risk premium
The portion of a nominal interest rate or bond yield that represents compensation for the possibility of default.

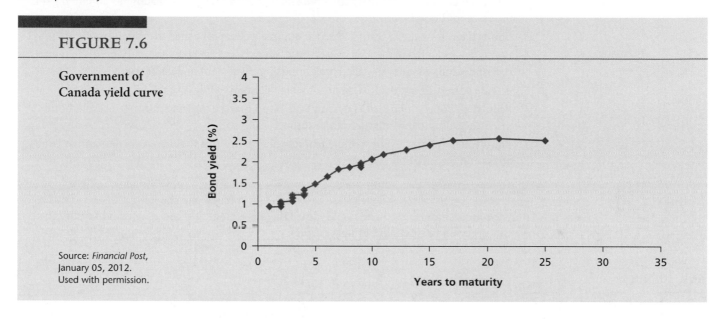

FIGURE 7.6

Government of Canada yield curve

Source: *Financial Post*, January 05, 2012. Used with permission.

An important thing to recognize about a bond's yield is that it is calculated assuming that all the promised payments will be made. As a result, it is really a promised yield, and it may or may not be what you will earn. In particular, if the issuer defaults, your actual yield will be lower, probably much lower. This fact is particularly important when it comes to junk bonds. Thanks to a clever bit of marketing, such bonds are now commonly called high-yield bonds, which has a much nicer ring to it; but now you recognize that these are really high-*promised* yield bonds. Taxability also affects the bond yields as bondholders have to pay income tax on the interest income they receive from privately issued bonds.

Finally, bonds have varying degrees of liquidity. As we discussed earlier, there are an enormous number of bond issues, most of which do not trade on a regular basis. As a result, if you wanted to sell quickly, you would probably not get as good a price as you could otherwise. Investors prefer liquid assets to illiquid ones, so they demand a **liquidity premium** on top of all the other premiums we have discussed. As a result, all else being the same, less liquid bonds will have higher yields than more liquid bonds.

liquidity premium
The portion of a nominal interest rate or bond yield that represents compensation for lack of liquidity.

Conclusion

If we combine all of the things we have discussed regarding bond yields, we find that bond yields represent the combined effect of no fewer than six things. The first is the real rate of interest. On top of the real rate are five premiums representing compensation for (1) expected future inflation, (2) interest rate risk, (3) default risk, (4) tax status, and (5) lack of liquidity. As a result, determining the appropriate yield on a bond requires careful analysis of each of these effects.

Concept Questions

1. What is the term structure of interest rates? What determines its shape?
2. What is the Canada yield curve?
3. What are the six components that make up a bond's yield?

7.8 | Summary and Conclusions

This chapter has explored bonds, bond yields, and interest rates. We saw that:

1. Determining bond prices and yields is an application of basic discounted cash flow principles.
2. Bond values move in the direction opposite that of interest rates, leading to potential gains or losses for bond investors.
3. Bonds have a variety of features spelled out in a document called the indenture.
4. Bonds are rated based on their default risk. Some bonds, such as Treasury bonds, have no risk of default, whereas so-called junk bonds have substantial default risk.
5. A wide variety of bonds exist, many of which contain exotic or unusual features.
6. Almost all bond trading is OTC, with little or no market transparency. As a result, bond price and volume information can be difficult to find.
7. Bond yields reflect the effect of the real rate and premiums that investors demand as compensation for inflation and interest rate risk.

In closing, we note that bonds are a vital source of financing to governments and corporations of all types. Bond prices and yields are a rich subject, and our one chapter necessarily touches on only the most important concepts and ideas. There is a great deal more we could say, but instead we will move on to stocks in our next chapter.

Key Terms

bearer form (page 175)
call premium (page 176)
call protected (page 176)
call provision (page 176)
Canada plus call (page 176)
Canada yield curve (page 188)
clean price (page 182)
coupon (page 165)
coupon rate (page 165)
debenture (page 175)
default risk premium (page 189)
deferred call (page 176)
dirty price (page 182)
face value or par value (page 165)
Fisher effect (page 185)

indenture (page 174)
inflation premium (page 187)
interest rate risk premium (page 187)
liquidity premium (page 189)
maturity date (page 165)
nominal rates (page 184)
note (page 175)
protective covenant (page 176)
real rates (page 184)
registered form (page 175)
retractable bond (page 181)
sinking fund (page 176)
stripped bond or zero-coupon bond (page 179)
term structure of interest rates (page 187)
yield to maturity (YTM) (page 166)

Chapter Review Problems and Self-Test

7.1   Bond Values A Microgates Industries bond has a 10 percent coupon rate and a $1,000 face value. Interest is paid semiannually, and the bond has 20 years to maturity. If investors require a 12 percent yield, what is the bond's value? What is the effective annual yield on the bond?

7.2   Bond Yields A Macrohard Corp. bond carries an 8 percent coupon, paid semiannually. The par value is $1,000 and the bond matures in six years. If the bond currently sells for $911.37, what is its yield to maturity? What is the effective annual yield?

Answers to Self-Test Problems

7.1   Because the bond has a 10 percent coupon yield and investors require a 12 percent return, we know that the bond must sell at a discount. Notice that, because the bond pays interest semiannually, the coupons amount to $100/2 = $50 every six months. The required yield is 12%/2 = 6% every six months. Finally, the bond matures in 20 years, so there are a total of 40 six-month periods.

The bond's value is thus equal to the present value of $50 every six months for the next 40 six-month periods plus the present value of the $1,000 face amount:

$$\text{Bond value} = \$50 \times (1 - 1/1.06^{40})/.06 + 1,000/1.06^{40}$$
$$= \$50 \times 15.04630 + 1,000/10.2857$$
$$= \$849.54$$

Notice that we discounted the $1,000 back 40 periods at 6 percent per period, rather than 20 years at 12 percent. The reason is that the effective annual yield on the bond is $1.06^2 - 1 = 12.36\%$, not 12 percent. We thus could have used 12.36 percent per year for 20 years when we calculated the present value of the $1,000 face amount, and the answer would have been the same.

7.2   The present value of the bond's cash flows is its current price, $911.37. The coupon is $40 every six months for 12 periods. The face value is $1,000. So the bond's yield is the unknown discount rate in the following:

$$\$911.37 = \$40 \times [1 - 1/(1 + r)^{12}]/r + 1,000/(1 + r)^{12}$$

The bond sells at a discount. Because the coupon rate is 8 percent, the yield must be something in excess of that.

If we were to solve this by trial and error, we might try 12 percent (or 6 percent per six months):

$$\text{Bond value} = \$40 \times (1 - 1/1.06^{12})/.06 + 1,000/1.06^{12}$$
$$= \$832.32$$

This is less than the actual value, so our discount rate is too high. We now know that the yield is somewhere between 8 and 12 percent. With further trial and error (or a little machine assistance), the yield works out to be 10 percent, or 5 percent every six months.

By convention, the bond's yield to maturity would be quoted as $2 \times 5\% = 10\%$. The effective yield is thus $1.05^2 - 1 = 10.25\%$.

Concepts Review and Critical Thinking Questions

1.   (LO1) Is it true that a Government of Canada security is risk-free?

2.   (LO2) Which has greater interest rate risk, a 30-year Canada bond or a 30-year BB corporate bond?

3.   (LO4) With regard to bid and ask prices on a Canada bond, is it possible for the bid price to be higher? Why or why not?

4.   (LO4) Canada bid and ask quotes are sometimes given in terms of yields, so there would be a bid yield and an ask yield. Which do you think would be larger? Explain.

5.   (LO1) A company is contemplating a long-term bond issue. It is debating whether or not to include a call provision. What are the benefits to the company from including a call provision? What are the costs? How do these answers change for a put provision?

6.   (LO1) How does a bond issuer decide on the appropriate coupon rate to set on its bonds? Explain the difference between the coupon rate and the required return on a bond.

7.   (LO5) Are there any circumstances under which an investor might be more concerned about the nominal return on an investment than the real return?

8.   (LO3) Companies pay rating agencies such as DBRS to rate their bonds, and the costs can be substantial. However, companies are not required to have their bonds rated in the first place; doing so is strictly voluntary. Why do you think they do it?

9.   (LO3) Canada bonds are not rated. Why? Often, junk bonds are not rated. Why?

10.   (LO6) What is the difference between the term structure of interest rates and the yield curve?

Questions and Problems

Basic
(Questions 1–14)

1.   **Interpreting Bond Yields (LO2)** Is the yield to maturity on a bond the same thing as the required return? Is YTM the same thing as the coupon rate? Suppose today a 10 percent coupon bond sells at par. Two years from now, the required return on the same bond is 8 percent. What is the coupon rate on the bond then? The YTM?

2.   **Interpreting Bond Yields (LO2)** Suppose you buy a 7 percent coupon, 20-year bond today when it's first issued. If interest rates suddenly rise to 15 percent, what happens to the value of your bond? Why?

3.   **Bond Prices (LO2)** Malahat Inc. has 7.5 percent coupon bonds on the market that have 10 years left to maturity. The bonds make annual payments. If the YTM on these bonds is 8.75 percent, what is the current bond price?

4.   **Bond Yields (LO2)** Leechtown Co. has 9 percent coupon bonds on the market with nine years left to maturity. The bonds make annual payments. If the bond currently sells for $934, what is its YTM?

5.   **Coupon Rates (LO2)** Goldstream Enterprises has bonds on the market making annual payments, with 13 years to maturity, and selling for $1,045. At this price, the bonds yield 7.5 percent. What must the coupon rate be on the bonds?

6.   **Bond Prices (LO2)** Langford Co. issued 11-year bonds a year ago at a coupon rate of 6.9 percent. The bonds make semiannual payments. If the YTM on these bonds is 7.4 percent, what is the current bond price?

7.   **Bond Yields (LO2)** Braemar Corp. issued 12-year bonds 2 years ago at a coupon rate of 8.4 percent. The bonds make semiannual payments. If these bonds currently sell for 105 percent of par value, what is the YTM?

8.   **Coupon Rates (LO2)** Happy Valley Corporation has bonds on the market with 14.5 years to maturity, a YTM of 6.8 percent, and a current price of $924. The bonds make semiannual payments. What must the coupon rate be on these bonds?

9.   **Calculating Real Rates of Return (LO5)** If Treasury bills are currently paying 7 percent and the inflation rate is 3.8 percent, what is the approximate real rate of interest? The exact real rate?

10.   **Inflation and Nominal Returns (LO5)** Suppose the real rate is 3 percent and the inflation rate is 4.7 percent. What rate would you expect to see on a Treasury bill?

11.   **Nominal and Real Returns (LO5)** An investment offers a 14 percent total return over the coming year. Jim Flaherty thinks the total real return on this investment will be only 9 percent. What does Jim believe the inflation rate will be over the next year?

12. **Nominal versus Real Returns (LO5)** Say you own an asset that had a total return last year of 11.4 percent. If the inflation rate last year was 4.8 percent, what was your real return?

13. **Bond Pricing (LO2)** This problem refers to bond quotes in Figure 7.4. Calculate the price of the Canada Jun 01/15 to prove that it is 111.23 as shown. Assume that today is January 05, 2012.

14. **Bond Value (LO2)** At the time of the last referendum, Quebec provincial bonds carried a higher yield than comparable Ontario bonds because of investors' uncertainty about the political future of Quebec. Suppose you were an investment manager who thought the market was overplaying these fears. In particular, suppose you thought that yields on Quebec bonds would fall by 50 basis points. Which bonds would you buy or sell? Explain in words.

Intermediate 15. **Bond Price Movements (LO2)** Bond X is a premium bond making annual payments. The bond pays a 8 percent coupon, has a
(Questions   YTM of 6 percent, and has 13 years to maturity. Bond Y is a discount bond making annual payments. This bond pays a 6 percent
15–28)   coupon, has a YTM of 8 percent, and also has 13 years to maturity. If interest rates remain unchanged, what do you expect the price of these bonds to be one year from now? In three years? In eight years? In 12 years? In 13 years? What's going on here? Illustrate your answers by graphing bond prices versus time to maturity.

16. **Interest Rate Risk (LO2)** Both Bond Sam and Bond Dave have 9 percent coupons, make semiannual payments and are priced at par value. Bond Sam has 3 years to maturity, whereas Bond Dave has 20 years to maturity. If interest rates suddenly rise by 2 percent, what is the percentage change in the price of Bond Sam? Of Bond Dave? If rates were to suddenly fall by 2 percent instead, what would the percentage change in the price of Bond Sam be then? Of Bond Dave? Illustrate your answers by graphing bond prices versus YTM. What does this problem tell you about the interest rate risk of longer-term bonds?

17. **Interest Rate Risk (LO2)** Bond J is a 4 percent coupon bond. Bond K is a 12 percent coupon bond. Both bonds have nine years to maturity, make semiannual payments and have a YTM of 8 percent. If interest rates suddenly rise by 2 percent, what is the percentage price change of these bonds? What if rates suddenly fall by 2 percent instead? What does this problem tell you about the interest rate risk of lower coupon bonds?

 18. **Bond Yields (LO2)** Oak Bay Software has 9.2 percent coupon bonds on the market with nine years to maturity. The bonds make semiannual payments and currently sell for 106.8 percent of par. What is the current yield on the bonds? The YTM? The effective annual yield?

19. **Bond Yields (LO2)** Airbutus Co. wants to issue new 20-year bonds for some much-needed expansion projects. The company currently has 8 percent coupon bonds on the market that sell for $930, make semiannual payments, and mature in 20 years. What coupon rate should the company set on its new bonds if it wants them to sell at par?

20. **Accrued Interest (LO2)** You purchase a bond with an invoice price of $968. The bond has a coupon rate of 7.4 percent, and there are five months to the next semiannual coupon date. What is the clean price of the bond?

21. **Accrued Interest (LO2)** You purchase a bond with a coupon rate of 6.8 percent and a clean price of $1,073. If the next semiannual coupon payment is due in three months, what is the invoice price?

22. **Finding the Bond Maturity (LO2)** Colwood Corp. has 8 percent coupon bonds making annual payments with a current yield of 7.5 percent. How many years do these bonds have left until they mature?

23. **Using Bond Quotes (LO4)** Suppose the following bond quotes for IOU Corporation appear in the financial page of today's newspaper. Assume the bond has a face value of $1,000 and the current date is April 15, 2013. What is the yield to maturity of the bond? What is the yield to maturity on a comparable Bank of Canada issue?

Company (Ticker)	Coupon	Maturity	Last Price	Last Yield	EST Spread	UST	EST Vol (000s)
IOU (IOU)	7.2	Apr 15, 2023	108.96	??	468	10	1,827

24. **Bond Prices versus Yields (LO2)**

   a. What is the relationship between the price of a bond and its YTM?

   b. Explain why some bonds sell at a premium over par value while other bonds sell at a discount. What do you know about the relationship between the coupon rate and the YTM for premium bonds? What about for discount bonds? For bonds selling at par value?

   c. What is the relationship between the current yield and YTM for premium bonds? For discount bonds? For bonds selling at par value?

25. **Interest on Zeroes (LO2)** Tillicum Corporation needs to raise funds to finance a plant expansion, and it has decided to issue 25-year zero coupon bonds to raise the money. The required return on the bonds will be 9 percent.

   a. What will these bonds sell for at issuance?

   b. What interest deduction can Tillicum Corporation take on these bonds in the first year? In the last year?

   c. Based on your answers in (b), which interest deduction method would Tillicum Corporation prefer? Why?

26. **Zero Coupon Bonds (LO2)** Suppose your company needs to raise $30 million and you want to issue 30-year bonds for this purpose. Assume the required return on your bond issue will be 8 percent, and you're evaluating two issue alternatives: an 8 percent annual coupon bond and a zero coupon bond. Your company's tax rate is 35 percent.

   a. How many of the coupon bonds would you need to issue to raise the $30 million? How many of the zeroes would you need to issue?

   b. In 30 years, what will your company's repayment be if you issue the coupon bonds? What if you issue the zeroes?

c. Based on your answers in (a) and (b), why would you ever want to issue the zeroes? To answer, calculate the firm's after-tax cash outflows for the first year under the two different scenarios.

27. **Finding the Maturity (LO2)** You've just found a 10 percent coupon bond on the market that sells for par value. What is the maturity on this bond?

28. **Real Cash Flows (LO5)** You want to have $1.5 million in real dollars in an account when you retire in 40 years. The nominal return on your investment is 11 percent and the inflation rate is 3.8 percent. What real amount must you deposit each year to achieve your goal?

Challenge 29. (Questions 29–31)

29. **Components of Bond Returns (LO2)** Bond P is a premium bond with a 12 percent coupon. Bond D is a 6 percent coupon bond currently selling at a discount. Both bonds make annual payments, have a YTM of 9 percent, and have five years to maturity. What is the current yield for bond P? For bond D? If interest rates remain unchanged, what is the expected capital gains yield over the next year for bond P? For bond D? Explain your answers and the interrelationships among the YTM, coupon rate, and capital gains yield.

30. **Holding Period Yield (LO2)** The YTM on a bond is the interest rate you earn on your investment if interest rates don't change. If you actually sell the bond before it matures, your realized return is known as the *holding period yield* (HPY).

a. Suppose that today you buy an 7 percent annual coupon bond for $1,060. The bond has 10 years to maturity. What rate of return do you expect to earn on your investment?

b. Two years from now, the YTM on your bond has declined by 1 percent, and you decide to sell. What price will your bond sell for? What is the HPY on your investment? Compare this yield to the YTM when you first bought the bond. Why are they different?

31. **Valuing Bonds (LO2)** The Metchosin Corporation has two different bonds currently outstanding. Bond M has a face value of $20,000 and matures in 20 years. The bond makes no payments for the first six years, then pays $1,100 every six months over the subsequent eight years, and finally pays $1,400 every six months over the last six years. Bond N also has a face value of $20,000 and a maturity of 20 years; it makes no coupon payments over the life of the bond. If the required return on both these bonds is 7 percent compounded semiannually, what is the current price of bond M? Of bond N?

MINI CASE

Financing Tuxedo Air's Expansion Plans with a Bond Issue

Mark Taylor and Jack Rodwell, the owners of Tuxedo Air, have decided to expand their operations. They instructed their newly hired financial analyst, Ed Cowan, to enlist an underwriter to help sell $35 million in new 10-year bonds to finance construction. Chris has entered into discussions with Suzanne Lenglen, an underwriter from the firm of Raines and Warren, about which bond features Tuxedo Air should consider and what coupon rate the issue will likely have.

Although Ed is aware of the bond features, he is uncertain about the costs and benefits of some features, so he isn't sure how each feature would affect the coupon rate of the bond issue. You are Suzanne's assistant, and she has asked you to prepare a memo to Ed describing the effect of each of the following bond features on the coupon rate of the bond. She would also like you to list any advantages or disadvantages of each feature:

1. The security of the bond—that is, whether the bond has collateral.
2. The seniority of the bond.
3. The presence of a sinking fund.
4. A call provision with specified call dates and call prices.
5. A deferred call accompanying the call provision.
6. A Canada plus call provision.
7. Any positive covenants. Also, discuss several possible positive covenants Tuxedo Air might consider.
8. Any negative covenants. Also, discuss several possible negative covenants Tuxedo Air might consider.
9. A conversion feature (note that Tuxedo Air is not a publicly traded company).
10. A floating-rate coupon.

Internet Application Questions

1. The Bank of Canada maintains a site containing historical bond yields. Pick a short-term bond and a real return bond and compare their yields. What is your expectation of inflation for the coming year? bankofcanada.ca/rates/interest-rates/canadian-bonds/

2. Barclays Global Investors has two exchange traded bond funds, iG5 and iG10. Explain the advantage of investing in exchange traded bond funds relative to buying the bonds outright. group.barclays.com

3. Go to the website of DBRS at dbrs.com. Use Quick Search and Ticker Lookup to find Manufacturers Life Insurance Company and look up its rating. Do the same for Loblaw Companies Limited and Rogers Communications Inc. Which companies are investment grade? Are any junk? Now click on Rating and Methodologies. Which are the key factors in determining ratings?

APPENDIX 7A

ON DURATION

Our discussion of interest rate risk and applications explains how bond managers can select bonds to enhance price volatility when interest rates are falling. In this case, we recommended buying long-term, low-coupon bonds. When they apply this advice, Canadian bond managers use *duration*—a measure of a bond's effective maturity incorporating both time to maturity and coupon rate. This Appendix explains how duration is calculated and how it is used by bond managers.

Consider a portfolio consisting of two pure discount (zero coupon) bonds. The first bond matures in one year and the second after five years. As pure discount bonds, each provides a cash flow of $100 at maturity and nothing before maturity. Assuming the interest rate is 10 percent across all maturities, the bond prices are:

$$\text{Value of the one-year discount bond: } \frac{\$100}{1.10} = \$90.91$$

$$\text{Value of the five-year discount bond: } \frac{\$100}{(1.10)^5} = \$62.09$$

Which of these bonds would produce the greater percentage capital gain if rates drop to 8 percent across all maturities? From the text discussion, we know that price volatility increases with maturity and decreases with the coupon rate. Both bonds have the same coupon rate (namely zero), so the five-year bond should produce the larger percentage gain.

To prove this, we calculate the new prices and percentage changes. The one-year bond is now priced at $92.59 and has increased in price by 1.85%.[13] The five-year bond is now priced at $68.06 for a price rise of 9.61 percent. You should be able to prove that the effect works the other way. If interest rates rise to 12 percent across maturities, the five-year bond will have the greater percentage loss.

If all bonds were pure discount bonds, time to maturity would be a precise measure of price volatility. In reality, most bonds bear coupon payments. Duration provides a measure of effective maturity that incorporates the impact of differing coupon rates.

Duration

We begin by noticing that any coupon bond is actually a combination of pure discount bonds. For example, a five-year, 10 percent coupon bond, with a face value of $100, is made up of five pure discount bonds:

1. A pure discount bond paying $10 at the end of Year 1.
2. A pure discount bond paying $10 at the end of Year 2.
3. A pure discount bond paying $10 at the end of Year 3.
4. A pure discount bond paying $10 at the end of Year 4.
5. A pure discount bond paying $110 at the end of Year 5.

Because the price volatility of a pure discount bond is determined only by its maturity, we would like to determine the average maturity of the five pure discount bonds that make up a five-year coupon bond. This leads us to the concept of duration.

We calculate average maturity in three steps for the 10 percent coupon bond:

1. Calculate present value of each payment using the bond's yield to maturity. We do this as

Year	Payment	Present Value of Payment by Discounting at 10%
1	$ 10	$ 9.091
2	10	8.264
3	10	7.513
4	10	6.830
5	110	68.302
Total		$100.000

2. Express the present value of each payment in relative terms. We calculate the relative value of a single payment as the ratio of the present value of the payment to the value of the bond. The value of the bond is $100. We have

---

[13] The percentage price increase is: ($92.59 − $90.91)/$90.91 = 1.85%.

Year	Payment	Present Value of Payment	Relative value = Present Value of Payment ÷ Value of Bond
1	$ 10	$ 9.091	$9.091/$100 = 0.09091
2	10	8.264	0.08264
3	10	7.513	0.07513
4	10	6.830	0.0683
5	110	68.302	0.68302
Total		$100.000	1.00000

The bulk of the relative value, 68.302 percent, occurs at Year 5 because the principal is paid back at that time.

3. Weight the maturity of each payment by its relative value. We have
4.1699 years = 1 year × 0.09091 + 2 years × 0.08264 + 3 years × 0.07513 + 4 years × 0.06830 + 5 years × 0.68302

There are many ways to calculate the average maturity of a bond. We have calculated it by weighting the maturity of each payment by the payment's present value. We find that the effective maturity of the bond is 4.1699 years. *Duration* is a commonly used word for effective maturity. Thus, the bond's duration is 4.1699 years. Note that duration is expressed in units of time.[14]

Because the five-year, 10 percent coupon bond has a duration of 4.1699 years, its percentage price fluctuations should be the same as those of a zero coupon bond with a duration of 4.1699 years.[15] It turns out that a five-year, 1 percent coupon bond has a duration of 4.9020 years. Because the 1 percent coupon bond has a higher duration than the 10 percent bond, the 1 percent coupon bond should be subject to greater price fluctuations. This is exactly what we expected.

Why does the 1 percent bond have a greater duration than the 10 percent bond, even though they both have the same five-year maturity? As mentioned earlier, duration is an average of the maturity of the bond's cash flows, weighted by the present value of each cash flow. The 1 percent coupon bond receives only $1 in each of the first four years. Thus, the weights applied to Years 1 through 4 in the duration formula will be low. Conversely, the 10 percent coupon bond receives $10 in each of the first four years. The weights applied to Years 1 through 4 in the duration formula will be higher.

In general, the percentage price changes of a bond with high duration are greater than the percentage price changes for a bond with low duration. This property is useful to investment managers who seek superior performance. These managers extend portfolio duration when rates are expected to fall and reduce duration in the face of rising rates.

Because forecasting rates consistently is almost impossible, other managers hedge their returns by setting the duration of their assets equal to the duration of liabilities. In this way, market values on both sides of the balance sheet adjust in the same direction keeping the market value of net worth constant. Duration hedging is often called portfolio immunization.

Current research on Government of Canada bond returns shows that duration is a practical way of measuring bond price volatility and an effective tool for hedging interest rate risk.

Appendix Questions and Problems

A.1 Why do portfolio managers use duration instead of term to maturity as a measure of a bond's price volatility?

A.2 Calculate the duration of a seven-year Canada bond with a 8 percent coupon and a yield of 4 percent.

A.3 You are managing a bond portfolio following a policy of interest-rate anticipation. You think that rates have bottomed and are likely to rise. The average duration of your portfolio is 5.5 years. Which bonds are more attractive for new purchases, those with a 10-year duration or three-year duration? Explain.

---

[14] Also note that we discounted each payment by the interest rate of 10 percent. This was done because we wanted to calculate the duration of the bond before a change in the interest rate occurred. After a change in the rate to say 8 or 12 percent, all three of our steps would need to reflect the new interest rate. In other words, the duration of a bond is a function of the current interest rate.

[15] Actually, the relationship only exactly holds true in the case of a one-time shift in the flat yield curve, where the change in the spot rate is identical for all different maturities. But duration research finds that the error is small.

CHAPTER 8

STOCK VALUATION

WestJet Airlines Ltd. is a Canadian low-cost carrier headquartered in Calgary. Effective January 2012, WestJet's dividend was $0.05 per share quarterly, or $0.20 per share annually. In contrast, Air Canada, Canada's largest airline headquartered in Montreal, has never paid a dividend. In January 2012, a share of Air Canada traded on the TSX for $1, while a share of WestJet was worth $12. How might investors decide on these valuations? While there are many factors that drive share prices, dividends are one of the most frequently analyzed. This chapter explores dividends, stock values, and the connection between them.

Learning Objectives ▶

After studying this chapter, you should understand:

LO1 How stock prices depend on future dividends and dividend growth.

LO2 The characteristics of common and preferred stocks.

LO3 The different ways corporate directors are elected to office.

LO4 The stock market quotations and the basics of stock market reporting.

aircanada.com
westjet.com

In our previous chapter, we introduced you to bonds and bond valuation. In this chapter, we turn to the other major source of financing for corporations, common and preferred stock. We first describe the cash flows associated with a share of stock and then go on to develop a very famous result, the dividend growth model. From there, we move on to examine various important features of common and preferred stock, focusing on shareholder rights. We close out the chapter with a discussion of how shares of stock are traded and how stock prices and other important information are reported in the financial press.

8.1 | Common Stock Valuation

In practice, it is more difficult to value a share of common stock than a bond for at least three reasons. First, not even the promised cash flows are known in advance. Second, the life of the investment is essentially forever because common stock has no maturity. Third, there is no way to easily observe the rate of return that the market requires. Nonetheless, there are cases under which we can come up with the present value of the future cash flows for a share of stock and thus determine its value.

Common Stock Cash Flows

Imagine that you are buying a share of stock today. You plan to sell the stock in one year. You somehow know that the stock will be worth $70 at that time. You predict that the stock will also pay a $10 per share dividend at the end of the year. If you require a 25 percent return on your investment, what is the most you would pay for the stock? In other words, what is the present value of the $10 dividend along with the $70 ending value at 25 percent?

If you buy the stock today and sell it at the end of the year, you will have a total of $80 in cash. At 25 percent:

Present value = ($10 + 70)/1.25 = $64

Therefore, $64 is the value you would assign to the stock today.

More generally, let P_0 be the current price of the stock, and define P_1 to be the price in one period. If D_1 is the cash dividend paid at the end of the period, then:

$$P_0 = (D_1 + P_1)/(1 + r) \qquad [8.1]$$

where r is the required return in the market on this investment.

Notice that we really haven't said much so far. If we wanted to determine the value of a share of stock today (P_0), we would have to come up with its value in one year (P_1). This is even harder to do in the first place, so we've only made the problem more complicated.[1]

What is the price in one period, P_1? We don't know in general. Instead, suppose that we somehow knew the price in two periods, P_2. Given a predicted dividend in two periods, D_2, the stock price in one period would be:

$$P_1 = (D_2 + P_2)/(1 + r)$$

If we were to substitute this expression for P_1 into our expression for P_0, we would have:

$$P_0 = \frac{D_1 + P_1}{(1 + r)} = \frac{D_1 + \dfrac{D_2 + P_2}{1 + r}}{(1 + r)}$$

$$= \frac{D_1}{(1 + r)^1} + \frac{D_2}{(1 + r)^2} + \frac{P_2}{(1 + r)^2}$$

Now we need to get a price in two periods. We don't know this either, so we can procrastinate again and write:

$$P_2 = (D_3 + P_3)/(1 + r)$$

If we substitute this back in for P_2, we would have:

$$P_0 = \frac{D_1}{(1 + r)^1} + \frac{D_2}{(1 + r)^2} + \frac{P_2}{(1 + r)^2}$$

$$= \frac{D_1}{(1 + r)^1} + \frac{D_2}{(1 + r)^2} + \frac{\dfrac{D_3 + P_3}{1 + r}}{(1 + r)^2}$$

$$= \frac{D_1}{(1 + r)^1} + \frac{D_2}{(1 + r)^2} + \frac{D_3}{(1 + r)^3} + \frac{P_3}{(1 + r)^3}$$

Notice that we can push the problem of coming up with the stock price off into the future forever. Importantly, no matter what the stock price is, the present value is essentially zero if we push it far enough away.[2] What we would be left with is the result that the current price of the stock can be written as the present value of the dividends beginning in one period and extending out forever:

$$P_0 = \frac{D_1}{(1 + r)^1} + \frac{D_2}{(1 + r)^2} + \frac{D_3}{(1 + r)^3} + \frac{D_4}{(1 + r)^4} + \frac{D_5}{(1 + r)^5} + \dots$$

We have illustrated here that the price of the stock today is equal to the present value of all the future dividends. How many future dividends are there? In principle, there can be an infinite number. This means we still can't compute a value for the stock because we would have to forecast an infinite number of dividends and then discount them all. In the next section, we consider some special cases where we can get around this problem.

---

[1] The only assumption we make about the stock price is that it is a finite number no matter how far away we push it. It can be extremely large, just not infinitely so. Since no one has ever observed an infinite stock price, this assumption is plausible.

[2] One way of solving this problem is the "bigger fool" approach, which asks how much a bigger fool (than you) would pay for the stock. This approach has considerable appeal in explaining speculative bubbles that occur when prices rise to irrational levels and then fall when the bubble bursts. Our discussion focuses on more ordinary times when prices are based on rational factors.

EXAMPLE 8.1: Growth Stock

You might be wondering about shares of stock in companies that currently pay no dividends. Small, growing companies frequently plow back everything and thus pay no dividends. Many such companies are in mining, oil and gas, and high tech. For example, at the time of writing, CGI Group Inc., an IT services company headquartered in Montreal, was trading at $18 per share and paid no dividends. Are such shares actually worth nothing? When we say that the value of the stock is equal to the present value of the future dividends, we don't rule out the possibility that some number of those dividends are zero. They just can't all be zero.

Imagine a hypothetical company that had a provision in its corporate charter prohibiting the payment of dividends now or ever. The corporation never borrows any money,

never pays out any money to shareholders in any form whatsoever, and never sells any assets. Such a corporation couldn't really exist because the shareholders wouldn't stand for it. However, the shareholders could always vote to amend the charter if they wanted to. If it did exist, however, what would the stock be worth?

The stock is worth absolutely nothing. Such a company is a financial black hole. Money goes in, but nothing valuable ever comes out. Because nobody would ever get any return on this investment, the investment has no value. This example is a little absurd, but it illustrates that when we speak of companies that don't pay dividends, what we really mean is that they are not currently paying dividends.

Common Stock Valuation: Some Special Cases

There are a few very useful special circumstances where we can come up with a value for the stock. What we have to do is make some simplifying assumptions about the pattern of future dividends. The three cases we consider are (1) the dividend has a zero growth rate, (2) the dividend grows at a constant rate, and (3) the dividend grows at a constant rate after some length of time. We consider each of these separately.[3]

ZERO GROWTH   The case of zero growth is one we've already seen. A share of common stock in a company with a constant dividend is much like a share of preferred stock. From Example 6.8 in Chapter 6, we know that the dividend on a share of fixed-rate preferred stock has zero growth and thus is constant through time. For a zero growth share of common stock, this implies that:

$$D_1 = D_2 = D_3 = D = \text{constant}$$

So, the value of the stock is:

$$P_0 = \frac{D}{(1+r)^1} + \frac{D}{(1+r)^2} + \frac{D}{(1+r)^3} + \frac{D}{(1+r)^4} + \frac{D}{(1+r)^5} +$$

Since the dividend is always the same, the stock can be viewed as an ordinary perpetuity with a cash flow equal to D every period. The per-share value is thus given by:

$$P_0 = D/r \qquad\qquad [8.2]$$

where r is the required return.

For example, suppose the Eastcoast Energy Company has a policy of paying a $10 per share dividend every year. If this policy is to be continued indefinitely, what is the value of a share of stock if the required return is 20 percent? As it amounts to an ordinary perpetuity, the stock is worth $10/.20 = $50 per share.

CONSTANT GROWTH   Suppose we knew that the dividend for some company always grows at a steady rate. Call this growth rate g. If we let D_0 be the dividend just paid, then the next dividend, D_1 is:

$$D_1 = D_0 \times (1+g)$$

---

[3] Growth simply compares dollar dividends over time. In Chapter 12 we examine inflation and growth.

The dividend in two periods is:

$$D_2 = D_1 \times (1 + g)$$
$$= [D_0 \times (1 + g)] \times (1 + g)$$
$$= D_0 \times (1 + g)^2$$

We could repeat this process to come up with the dividend at any point in the future. In general, from our discussion of compound growth in previous chapters, we know that the dividend t periods in the future, D_t, is given by:

$$D_t = D_0 \times (1 + g)^t$$

As we showed in Chapter 6, a stock with dividends that grow at a constant rate forever is an example of a growing perpetuity. This will come in handy shortly when we are ready to find the present value of this dividend stream.

The assumption of steady dividend growth might strike you as peculiar. Why would the dividend grow at a constant rate? The reason is that, for many companies—chartered banks, for example—steady growth in dividends is an explicit goal. For example, in 2011, Fortis Inc., a St. John's, Newfoundland and Labrador based international diversified electric utility holding company, increased its dividend by 3.6% to $1.16 per share; this increase was notable because it was the 40th in a row. Such companies with a policy of consistently increasing dividends every year for a specific period of time are known as "dividend aristocrats". In Canada, the time frame to attain dividend aristocrat status is five consecutive years of dividend increases. These companies are monitored by the S&P/TSX Canadian Dividend Aristocrats Index. In the United States, it takes at least 25 consecutive years of increasing dividends for a company to qualify for the S&P 500 Dividend Aristocrats Index. Note also that by using a constant growth rate, we are simply trying to estimate the expected average growth rate over a long period of time. While we use this expected average value in our model, the actual growth rate does not have to be the same every year. This subject falls under the general heading of dividend policy, so we defer further discussion of it to Chapter 17.

EXAMPLE 8.2: Dividend Growth Revisited

The Bank of Manitoba has just paid a dividend of $3 per share. The dividend grows at a steady rate of 8 percent per year. Based on this information, what would the dividend be in five years?

Here we have a $3 current amount that grows at 8 percent per year for five years. The future amount is thus:

$$\$3 \times (1.08)^5 = \$3 \times 1.4693 = \$4.41$$

The dividend, therefore, increases by $1.41 over the coming five years.

If the dividend grows at a steady rate, we have replaced the problem of forecasting an infinite number of future dividends with the problem of coming up with a single growth rate, a considerable simplification. Taking D_0 to be the dividend just paid and g to be the constant growth rate, the value of a share of stock can be written as:

$$P_0 = \frac{D_1}{(1 + r)^1} + \frac{D_2}{(1 + r)^2} + \frac{D_3}{(1 + r)^3} + \cdots$$
$$= \frac{D_0(1 + g)^1}{(1 + r)^1} + \frac{D_0(1 + g)^2}{(1 + r)^2} + \frac{D_0(1 + g)^3}{(1 + r)^3} + \cdots$$

As long as the growth rate, g, is less than the discount rate, r, the present value of this series of cash flows can be written very simply using the growing perpetuity formula from Chapter 6.

$$P_0 = \frac{D_0 \times (1 + g)}{r - g} = \frac{D_1}{r - g} \qquad [8.3]$$

dividend growth model
A model that determines the current price of a stock as its dividend next period, divided by the discount rate less the dividend growth rate.

This elegant result goes by a lot of different names. We call it the **dividend growth model**.[4] By any

_____

[4] It is often called the Gordon Model in honour of the late Professor Myron Gordon, University of Toronto, its best-known developer.

name, it is very easy to use. To illustrate, suppose D_0 is $2.30, r is 13 percent, and g is 5 percent. The price per share is:

$$
\begin{aligned}
P_0 &= D_0 \times (1 + g)/(r - g) \\
&= \$2.30 \times (1.05)/(.13 - .05) \\
&= \$2.415/(.08) \\
&= \$30.19
\end{aligned}
$$

We can actually use the dividend growth model to get the stock price at any point in time, not just today. In general, the price of the stock as of time t is:

$$
P_t = \frac{D_t \times (1 + g)}{r - g} = \frac{D_{t+1}}{r - g} \tag{8.4}
$$

In our example, suppose we were interested in the price of the stock in five years, P_5. We first need the dividend at time 5, D_5. Since the dividend just paid is $2.30 and the growth rate is 5 percent per year, D_5 is:

$$
D_5 = \$2.30 \times (1.05)^5 = \$2.30 \times 1.2763 = \$2.935
$$

From the dividend growth model, the price of stock in five years is:

$$
P_5 = \frac{D_5 \times (1 + g)}{r - g} = \frac{\$2.935 \times (1.05)}{.13 - .05} = \frac{\$3.0822}{.08} = \$38.53
$$

EXAMPLE 8.3: Bank of Prince Edward Island

The next dividend for the Bank of Prince Edward Island (BPEI) will be $4.00 per share. Investors require a 16 percent return on companies such as BPEI. The bank's dividend increases by 6 percent every year. Based on the dividend growth model, what is the value of BPEI stock today? What is the value in four years?

The only tricky thing here is that the next dividend, D_1, is given as $4.00, so we won't multiply this by $(1 + g)$. With this in mind, the price per share is given by:

$$
\begin{aligned}
P_0 &= D_1/(r - g) \\
&= \$4.00/(.16 - .06) \\
&= \$4.00/(.10) \\
&= \$40.00
\end{aligned}
$$

Because we already have the dividend in one year, the dividend in four years is equal to $D_1 \times (1 + g)^3 = \$4.00 \times (1.06)^3 = \$4.764$. The price in four years is therefore:

$$
\begin{aligned}
P_4 &= [D_4 \times (1 + g)]/(r - g) \\
&= [\$4.764 \times 1.06]/(.16 - .06) \\
&= \$5.05/(.10) \\
&= \$50.50
\end{aligned}
$$

Notice in this example that P_4 is equal to $P_0 \times (1 + g)^4$:

$$
P_4 = \$50.50 = \$40.00 \times (1.06)^4 = P_0 \times (1 + g)^4
$$

To see why this is so, notice that:

$$
P_4 = D_5/(r - g)
$$

However, D_5 is just equal to $D_1 \times (1 + g)^4$, so we can write P_4 as:

$$
\begin{aligned}
P_4 &= D_1 \times (1 + g)^4/(r - g) \\
&= \{D_1/(r - g)\} \times (1 + g)^4 \\
&= P_0 \times (1 + g)^4
\end{aligned}
$$

This last example illustrates that the dividend growth model has the implicit assumption that the stock price will grow at the same constant rate as the dividend. This really isn't too surprising. What it tells us is that if the cash flows on an investment grow at a constant rate through time, so does the value of that investment.

You might wonder what would happen with the dividend growth model if the growth rate, g, were greater than the discount rate, r. It looks like we would get a negative stock price because $r - g$ would be less than zero. But this is not what would happen.

Instead, if the constant growth rate exceeds the discount rate, the stock price is infinitely large. Why? When the growth rate is bigger than the discount rate, the present value of the dividends keeps on getting bigger and bigger. Essentially, the same is true if the growth rate and the discount rate are equal. In both cases, the simplification that allows us to replace the infinite stream of dividends with the dividend growth model is "illegal," so the answers we get from the dividend growth model are nonsense unless the growth rate is less than the discount rate.

NON-CONSTANT GROWTH The last case we consider is non-constant growth. The main reason to consider this is to allow for supernormal growth rates over some finite length of time. As we discussed earlier, the growth rate cannot exceed the required return indefinitely, but it certainly could do so for some number of years. To avoid the problem of having to forecast and discount an infinite number of dividends, we require that the dividends start growing at a constant rate sometime in the future.[5]

To give a simple example of non-constant growth, consider a company that is not currently paying dividends. You predict that in five years, the company will pay a dividend for the first time. The dividend will be \$.50 per share. You expect this dividend to grow at 10 percent indefinitely. The required return on companies such as this one is 20 percent. What is the price of the stock today?

To see what the stock is worth today, we find out what it will be worth once dividends are paid. We can then calculate the present value of that future price to get today's price. The first dividend will be paid in five years, and the dividend will grow steadily from then on. Using the dividend growth model, the price in four years will be:

$$P_4 = D_5/(r - g)$$
$$= \$.50/(.20 - .10)$$
$$= \$5.00$$

If the stock will be worth \$5.00 in four years, we can get the current value by discounting this back four years at 20 percent:

$$P_0 = \$5.00/(1.20)^4 = \$5.00/2.0736 = \$2.41$$

The stock is therefore worth \$2.41 today.

The problem of non-constant growth is only slightly more complicated if the dividends are not zero for the first several years. For example, suppose you have come up with the following dividend forecasts for the next three years:

Year	Expected Dividend
1	\$1.00
2	2.00
3	2.50

After the third year, the dividend will grow at a constant rate of 5 percent per year. The required return is 10 percent. What is the value of the stock today?

As always, the value of the stock is the present value of all the future dividends. To calculate this present value, we begin by computing the present value of the stock price three years down the road just as we did previously. We then add in the present value of the dividends paid between now and then. So, the price in three years is:

$$P_3 = D_3 \times (1 + g)/(r - g)$$
$$= \$2.50 \times (1.05)/(.10 - .05)$$
$$= \$52.50$$

We can now calculate the total value of the stock as the present value of the first three dividends plus the present value of the price at time 3, P_3:

$$P_0 = D_1/(1 + r)^1 + D_2/(1 + r)^2 + D_3/(1 + r)^3 + P_3/(1 + r)^3$$
$$= \$1.00/1.10 + \$2.00/1.10^2 + \$2.50/1.10^3 + \$52.50/1.10^3$$
$$= \$0.91 + 1.65 + 1.88 + 39.44$$
$$= \$43.88$$

Thus, the value of the stock today is \$43.88.

The case of Apple Inc. illustrates the importance of growth in the pricing of a stock. When Apple finally declared dividends in 2012, it was enjoying super-normal growth.

---

[5] This type of analysis can also be done to take into account negative growth rates, which are really just a special case of supernormal growth.

EXAMPLE 8.4: Supernormal Growth

Genetic Engineering Ltd. has been growing at a phenomenal rate of 30 percent per year because of its rapid expansion and explosive sales. You believe that this growth rate will last for three more years and then drop to 10 percent per year. If the growth rate remains at 10 percent indefinitely, what is the total value of the stock? Total dividends just paid were $5 million, and the required return is 20 percent.

Genetic Engineering is an example of supernormal growth. It is unlikely that 30 percent growth can be sustained for any extended time. To value the equity in this company, we calculate the total dividends over the supernormal growth period:

Year	Total Dividends (in $ millions)	
1	$5.00 × (1.3) = $	6.500
2	6.50 × (1.3) =	8.450
3	8.45 × (1.3) =	10.985

The price at year 3 can be calculated as:

$$P_3 = D_3 \times (1 + g)/(r - g)$$

where g is the long-run growth rate. So we have:

$$P_3 = \$10.985 \times (1.10)/(.20 - .10) = \$120.835$$

To determine the value today, we need the present value of this amount plus the present value of the total dividends:

$$\begin{aligned} P_0 &= D_1/(1 + r)^1 + D_2/(1 + r)^2 + D_3/(1 + r)^3 + P_3/(1 + r)^3 \\ &= \$6.50/1.20 + \$8.45/1.20^2 + \$10.985/1.20^3 + \\ &\quad \$120.835/1.20^3 \\ &= \$5.42 + 5.87 + 6.36 + 69.93 \\ &= \$87.58 \end{aligned}$$

The total value of the stock today is thus $87.58 million. If there were, for example, 20 million shares, the stock would be worth $87.58/20 = $4.38 per share.

Changing the Growth Rate

When investment analysts use the dividend valuation model, they generally consider a range of growth scenarios. The way to do this is to set up the model on a spreadsheet and vary the inputs. For example, in our original analysis of Genetic Engineering Ltd. we chose numbers for the inputs as shown in the baseline scenario in the following table. The model calculated the price per share as $4.38. The table shows two other possible scenarios. In the best case, the super-normal growth rate is 40 percent and continues for five instead of three years. Starting in Year 6, the normal growth rate is higher at 13 percent. In the worst case, normal growth starts immediately and there is no supernormal growth spurt. The required rate of return is 20 percent in all three cases.

The table shows that the model-calculated price is very sensitive to the inputs. In the worst case, the model price drops to $2.50; in the best case, it climbs to $8.14. Of course, there are many other scenarios we could consider with our spreadsheet. For example, many investment analysts use a three-stage scenario with two supernormal and one normal growth rate. To illustrate, we could input a supernormal growth rate of 40 percent for three years, a second supernormal growth rate of 20 percent for two years, and then a normal growth rate of 10 percent indefinitely.

	Baseline	Best Case	Worst Case
Supernormal growth rate	30%	40%	n/a
Supernormal growth period	3 years	5 years	0 years
Normal growth rate	10%	13%	10%
Required rate of return	20%	20%	20%
Model calculated price	$4.38	$8.14	$2.50

The number of possible scenarios is infinite but we have done enough to show that the value of a stock depends greatly on expected growth rates and how long they last. Our examples also show that valuing stocks with the dividend growth model is far from an exact science. In fact, the model has come under criticism based on a hindsight exercise comparing the present value of dividends against market prices for broad stock indexes. Critics raise two points. First, in the late 1990s, the level of the market, and especially tech stocks, was far higher than the present value of expected dividends. Second, market prices are far more volatile than the present value of dividends.

These criticisms suggest that, while it is a useful analytical tool, the dividend growth model is not the last word on stock valuation. We look at alternative valuation techniques later in the chapter.

Components of the Required Return

Thus far, we have taken the required return or discount rate, r, as given. We have quite a bit to say on this subject in Chapters 12 and 13. For now, we want to examine the implications of the dividend growth model for this required return. Earlier, we calculated P_0 as:

$$P_0 = D_1/(r - g)$$

If we rearrange this to solve for r, we get:

$$(r - g) = D_1/P_0$$
$$r = D_1/P_0 + g \qquad [8.5]$$

This tells us that the total return, r, has two components: The first of these, D_1/P_0, is called the **dividend yield**. The second part of the total return is the growth rate, g. We know that the dividend growth rate is also the rate at which the stock price grows (see Example 8.3). Thus, this growth rate can be interpreted as the **capital gains yield**, that is, the rate at which the value of the investment grows.

To illustrate the components of the required return, suppose we observe a stock selling for $20 per share. The next dividend will be $1 per share. You think that the dividend will grow by 10 percent more or less indefinitely. What return does this stock offer you if this is correct? The dividend growth model calculates total return as:

$$r = \text{Dividend yield} + \text{Capital gains yield}$$
$$r = D_1/P_0 + g$$

The total return works out to be:

$$r = \$1/\$20 + 10\%$$
$$= 5\% + 10\%$$
$$= 15\%$$

This stock, therefore, has a return of 15 percent.

We can verify this answer by calculating the price in one year, P_1, using 15 percent as the required return. Based on the dividend growth model, this price is:

$$P_1 = D_1 \times (1 + g)/(r - g)$$
$$= \$1 \times (1.10)/(.15 - .10)$$
$$= \$1.1/.05$$
$$= \$22$$

Notice that this $22 is $20 × (1.1), so the stock price has grown by 10 percent as it should. If you pay $20 for the stock today, you would get a $1 dividend at the end of the year and have a $22 − 20 = $2 gain. Your dividend yield is thus $1/$20 = 5%. Your capital gains yield is $2/$20 = 10%, so your total return would be 5% + 10% = 15%. Our discussion of stock valuation is summarized in Table 8.1.

It is important to note that dividends and dividend growth, although commonly used to estimate share value, are not the only factors that drive share prices. Factors like industry life cycle, the business cycle, supply or demand shocks (e.g., oil price spikes), liquidation value of the firm, replacement cost of the firm's assets, and investor psychology are examples of other potentially important price drivers.[6]

To get a feel for actual numbers in this context, consider that, according to the 2010 Value Line Investment Survey, Proctor & Gamble's dividends were expected to grow by 6 percent over the next 5 years, compared to a historical growth rate of 12 percent over the preceding 5 years and 11 percent over the preceding 10 years. In 2010, the projected dividend for the coming year was given at US $1.95. The stock price at that time was US$67 per share. What is the return investors require on P&G? Here, the dividend yield is 2.9 percent and the capital gains yield is 6 percent, giving a total required return of 8.9 percent.

---

[6]A readable article on behavioural finance is: Robert J. Shiller, "From Efficient Markets Theory to Behavioral Finance," *Journal of Economic Perspectives*, American Economic Association, vol. 17(1), pages 83–104, Winter 2003.

---

dividend yield
A stock's cash dividend divided by its current price.

capital gains yield
The dividend growth rate or the rate at which the value of an investment grows.

STOCK VALUATION USING MULTIPLES   An obvious problem with our dividend-based approach to stock valuation is that many companies don't pay dividends. What do we do in such cases? A common approach is to make use of the PE ratio, which we defined in Chapter 3 as the ratio of a stock's price per share to its earnings per share (EPS) over the previous year. The idea here is to have some sort of benchmark or reference PE ratio, which we then multiply by earnings to come up with a price:

$$\text{Price at time } t = P_t = \text{Benchmark PE ratio} \times \text{EPS}_t$$

The benchmark PE ratio could come from one of several possible sources. It could be based on similar companies (perhaps an industry average or median), or it could be based on a company's own historical values. For example, suppose we are trying to value Rovio Entertainment Limited, the creator of the video game *Angry Birds* used in various smartphones. Rovio does not pay dividends, but, after studying the industry, you feel that a PE ratio of 20 is appropriate for a company like this one. Total earnings over the four most recent quarters combined are $2 per share, so you think the stock should sell for 20 × $2 = $40. If it is going for less than $40, you might view it an attractive purchase and vice versa if it sells for more than $40.

Security analysts spend a lot of time forecasting future earnings, particularly for the coming year. A PE ratio that is based on estimated future earnings is called a "forward" PE ratio. For example, suppose you felt that Rovio's earnings for the coming year were going to be $2.50, reflecting the growing popularity of *Angry Birds*. In this case, if the current stock price is $40, the forward PE ratio is $40/$2.50 = 16.

Finally, notice that your benchmark PE ratio of 20 applies to earnings over the previous year. If earnings over the coming year turn out to be $2.50, then the stock price one year from today should be 20 × $2.50 = $50. Forecast prices such as this one are often called "target" prices.

Often we will be interested in valuing newer companies that both don't pay dividends and are not yet profitable, meaning that earnings are negative. What do we do now? One answer is to use the Price-sales ratio, which we also introduced in Chapter 3. As the name suggests, this ratio is the price per share on the stock divided by sales per share. You use this ratio just as you use the PE ratio, except you use sales per share instead of earnings per share. As with PE ratios, Price-to-sales ratios vary depending on company age and industry. Typical values are in the 0.8–2.0 range, but they can be much higher for younger, faster growing companies such as Rovio.

TABLE 8.1   Summary of stock valuation

The General Case

In general, the price today of a share of stock, P_0, is the present value of all of its future dividends, $D_1, D_2, D_3, \ldots$

$$P_0 = \frac{D_1}{(1+r)^1} + \frac{D_2}{(1+r)^2} + \frac{D_3}{(1+r)^3} + \cdots$$

where r is the required return.

Zero Growth Case

If there is no growth in dividends, the price can be written as

$$P_0 = \frac{D_1}{r}$$

Constant Growth Case

If the dividend grows at a steady rate, g, the price can be written as:

$$P_0 = \frac{D_1}{(r-g)}$$

This result is called the *dividend growth model*.

Supernormal Growth Case

If the dividend grows steadily after t periods, the price can be written as:

$$P_0 = \frac{D_1}{(1+r)^1} + \frac{D_2}{(1+r)^2} + \cdots + \frac{D_t}{(1+r)^t} + \frac{P_t}{(1+r)^t}$$

where

$$P_t = \frac{D_t \times (1+g)}{(r-g)}$$

Valuation using Multiples

For stocks that don't pay dividends (or have erratic dividend growth rates), we can value them using the PE ratio and/or the Price-sales ratio:

$$P_t = \text{Benchmark PE ratio} \times \text{EPS}_t$$
$$P_t = \text{Benchmark Price-sales ratio} \times \text{Sales per share}$$

The Required Return

The required return, r, can be written as the sum of two things:

$$r = D_1/P_0 + g$$

where D_1/P_0 is the dividend yield and g is the *capital gains yield* (which is the same thing as the growth rate in the dividends for the steady growth case).

8.2 | Common Stock Features

common stock
Equity without priority for dividends or in bankruptcy.

The term **common stock** means different things to different people, but it is usually applied to stock that has no special preference either in dividends or in bankruptcy.

Shareholders' Rights

The conceptual structure of the corporation assumes that shareholders elect directors who, in turn, hire management to carry out their directives. Shareholders, therefore, control the corporation through their right to elect the directors. Generally, only shareholders have this right.

Directors are elected each year at an annual meeting. Despite the exceptions we discuss later, the general idea is "one share, one vote" (not one shareholder, one vote). Corporate democracy is thus very different from our political democracy. With corporate democracy, the "golden rule" prevails absolutely.[7] Large institutional investors, like the Caisse de dépôt and Ontario Teachers' Pension Plan Board, take an active interest in exercising their votes to influence the corporate governance practices of the companies in their portfolios. For example, they are concerned that the elections for directors allow large investors to have an independent voice on the board.[8]

The introduction of new exchange listing rules and the *Sarbanes-Oxley Act* (SOX) in the United States, after the fallout of corporations such as Enron, legally enforces many aspects of U.S. corporate governance. Such practices, however, remain largely voluntary in Canada. Canadian firms are legally required to disclose whether or not they wish to comply with a recommendation of best practices put forth in the Dey Report published in 1994, but they are not legally mandated to follow the recommendations. Large Canadian firms often cross-list in the U.S. seeking increased liquidity, lower cost of capital, and access to foreign investors. When they do so, Canadian firms must comply with SOX.

Recent concern over company performance, including issues like managerial compensation and option packages, has renewed focus on shareholder activism. While shareholders often vote for the recommendations of management and/or the board of directors, concerned shareholders could also enter into a proxy contest. A proxy contest is essentially a fight for shareholder votes between parties attempting to control the corporation. For example, in 2012, one of Canadian Pacific Railway Ltd.'s largest shareholders, activist investor, William Ackman, waged a successful proxy battle to oust the existing CEO, Fred Green. While the board of directors backed the existing CEO, Ackman was in favour of Hunter Harrison, who was credited with successfully turning around Canadian Pacific's rival Canadian National Railway Company. After Ackman's group gathered a large number of proxy votes, the board backed down and installed Harrison.

After the global collapse of financial markets, shareholder activists increased their criticism of executive compensation packages. In early 2009, in response to these concerns, Canada's six largest banks adopted measures giving their shareholders a voice in determining executive pay packages. Beginning in 2010, these "say on pay" policies, give shareholders an advisory and non-binding vote on executive compensation.

Directors are elected at an annual shareholders' meeting by a vote of the holders of a majority of shares present and entitled to vote. However, the exact mechanism for electing directors differs across companies. The two most important methods are cumulative voting and straight voting; we discuss these in Appendix 8A.

OTHER RIGHTS The value of a share of common stock in a corporation is directly related to the general rights of shareholders. In addition to the right to vote for directors, shareholders usually have the following rights under the *Canadian Business Corporations Act*:

1. The right to share proportionally in dividends paid.
2. The right to share proportionally in assets remaining after liabilities have been paid in a liquidation.
3. The right to vote on shareholder matters of great importance, such as a merger, usually done at the annual meeting or a special meeting.

---

[7] The golden rule: Whosoever has the gold makes the rules.

[8] A good shareholder resource is the Canadian Coalition for Good Governance (www.ccgg.ca). You can find current examples of governance policies at lacaisse.com.en and otpp.com.

In addition, shareholders sometimes have the right to share proportionally in any new stock sold. This is called the *preemptive right*. Essentially, a preemptive right means that a company wishing to sell stock must first offer it to the existing shareholders before offering it to the general public. The purpose is to give a shareholder the opportunity to protect his or her proportionate ownership in the corporation.

Dividends

dividends
Return on capital of corporation paid by company to shareholders in either cash or stock.

A distinctive feature of corporations is that they have shares of stock on which they are authorized by their bylaws to pay dividends to their shareholders. **Dividends** paid to shareholders represent a return on the capital directly or indirectly contributed to the corporation by the shareholders. The payment of dividends is at the discretion of the board of directors.

Some important characteristics of dividends include the following:

1. Unless a dividend is declared by the board of directors of a corporation, it is not a liability of the corporation. A corporation cannot default on an undeclared dividend. As a consequence, corporations cannot become bankrupt because of nonpayment of dividends. The amount of the dividend and even whether it is paid are decisions based on the business judgement of the board of directors.

2. The payment of dividends by the corporation is not a business expense. Dividends are not deductible for corporate tax purposes. In short, dividends are paid out of after-tax profits of the corporation.

3. Dividends received by individual shareholders are partially sheltered by a dividend tax credit discussed in detail in Chapter 2. Corporations that own stock in other corporations are permitted to exclude 100 percent of the dividend amounts they receive from taxable Canadian corporations. The purpose of this provision is to avoid the double taxation of dividends.

Classes of Stock

Some firms have more than one class of common stock.[9] Often, the classes are created with unequal voting rights. Canadian Tire Corporation, for example, has two classes of common stock both publicly traded. The voting common stock was distributed as follows in 1990: 61 percent to three offspring of the company founder and the rest divided among Canadian Tire dealers, pension funds, and the general public. The non-voting, Canadian Tire A stock was more widely held.

canadiantire.ca

There are many other Canadian corporations with restricted (non-voting) stock. Such stock made up around 15 percent of the market values of TSX listed shares at the end of 1989. Non-voting shares must receive dividends no lower than dividends on voting shares. Some companies pay a higher dividend on the non-voting shares. In 2011, Canadian Tire paid $1.10 per share on both classes of stock.

A primary reason for creating dual classes of stock has to do with control of the firm. If such stock exists, management of a firm can raise equity capital by issuing non-voting or limited-voting stock while maintaining control.

Because it is only necessary to own 51 percent of the voting stock to control a company, non-voting shareholders could be left out in the cold in the event of a takeover bid for the company. To protect the non-voting shareholders, most companies have a "coattail" provision giving non-voting shareholders either the right to vote or to convert their shares into voting shares that can be tendered to the takeover bid. In the Canadian Tire case, all Class A shareholders become entitled to vote and the coattail provision is triggered if a bid is made for "all or substantially all" of the voting shares.

The effectiveness of the coattail provision was tested in 1986 when the Canadian Tire Dealers Association offered to buy 49 percent of the voting shares from the founding Billes family. In the absence of protection, the non-voting shareholders stood to lose substantially. The dealers bid at a large premium for the voting shares that were trading at $40 before the bid. The non-voting shares were priced at $14. Further, since the dealers were the principal buyers of Canadian Tire products, control of the company would have allowed them to adjust prices to benefit themselves over the non-voting shareholders.

---

[9] Our discussion of Canadian Tire draws heavily on Elizabeth Maynes, Chris Robinson, and Alan White, "How Much Is a Share Vote Worth?" *Canadian Investment Review,* Spring 1990, pp. 49–56.

The key question was whether the bid triggered the coattail. The dealers and the Billes family argued that the offer was for 49 percent of the stock not for "all or substantially all" of the voting shares. In the end, the Ontario Securities Commission ruled that the offer was unfair to the holders of the A shares and its view was upheld in two court appeals.

As a result, investors believe that coattails have protective value but remain skeptical that they afford complete protection. In January 2012, Canadian Tire voting stock traded at a substantial premium over non-voting stock.

Sometimes there is a huge gap between different classes of voting shares. For example, Magna International Inc., the Canadian auto parts manufacturer, established its dual class structure in 1978 with around 112 million Class A subordinate voting shares, each carrying one vote and around 726,000 Class B shares, each carrying 300 votes per share. The Class A shares were publicly traded on both the TSX and NYSE, while the Class B shares were fully owned by a trust controlled by the company founder, Frank Stronach. In 2010, Magna agreed to eliminate its dual class structure through a shareholder and court-approved plan of agreement. Magna made this change due to investor pressure for a more straightforward voting structure. More generally, institutional investors tend to hold smaller positions in dual class firms.[10]

Concept Questions

1. What rights do shareholders have?
2. Why do some companies have two classes of stock?

8.3 | Preferred Stock Features

preferred stock
Stock with dividend priority over common stock, normally with a fixed dividend rate, often without voting rights.

Preferred stock differs from common stock because it has preference over common stock in the payment of dividends and in the distribution of corporation assets in the event of liquidation. Preference means the holders of the preferred shares must receive a dividend (in the case of an ongoing firm) before holders of common shares are entitled to anything. If the firm is liquidated, preferred shareholders rank behind all creditors but ahead of common shareholders.

Preferred stock is a form of equity from a legal, tax, and regulatory standpoint. In the last decade, chartered banks were important issuers of preferred stock as they moved to meet higher capital requirements. Importantly, however, holders of preferred stock generally have no voting privileges.

Stated Value

bmo.com

Preferred shares have a stated liquidating value. The cash dividend is described in dollars per share or as a percentage of the stated value. For example, Bank of Montreal's "$1.625" translates easily into a dividend yield of 6.5 percent of $25 stated value.

Cumulative and Non-Cumulative Dividends

A preferred dividend is not like interest on a bond. The board of directors may decide not to pay the dividends on preferred shares, and their decision may have nothing to do with the current net income of the corporation.

Dividends payable on preferred stock are either cumulative or non-cumulative; most are cumulative. If preferred dividends are cumulative and are not paid in a particular year, they are carried forward as an *arrearage*. Usually both the cumulated (past) preferred dividends plus the current preferred dividends must be paid before the common shareholders can receive anything.

Unpaid preferred dividends are not debts of the firm. Directors elected by the common shareholders can defer preferred dividends indefinitely. However, in such cases:

1. Common shareholders must also forgo dividends.
2. Holders of preferred shares are often granted voting and other rights if preferred dividends have not been paid for some time.

---

[10]Ortiz-Molina, H., & Zhao, X. (2008). Do voting rights affect institutional investment decisions? evidence from dual-class firms. *Financial Management, 37*(4), 713–745

Because preferred shareholders receive no interest on the cumulated dividends, some have argued that firms have an incentive to delay paying preferred dividends.

EXAMPLE 8.5: Preferred Stock Price

A preferred stock is an example of a share with a constant, zero-growth dividend. At the close of the trading day on January 12, 2012, CIBC's class D preferred shares Series 26 showed the following information on the TSX:

The price of the share can be derived using the zero-growth formula. If the rate of return demanded by investors for preferred shares with similar risk is 5.51 percent, the price of CM.PR.D is calculated as:

$$P_0 = D/r$$
$$P_0 = 1.44/0.0551$$
$$P_0 = \$26.13$$

Why did we assume a discount rate of 5.51 percent? We simply rearranged the zero-growth formula and calculated r as:

$$r = D/P_0$$
$$r = 1.44/26.14$$
$$r = 0.0551$$

Other than a difference due to rounding, the price we calculated and the one reported on the TSX are the same! This should not surprise you as investors would be unwilling to invest in a security that did not offer their required rate of return.

Company	Ticker	Volume	High	Low	Close	Net Chg	52 Wk High	52 Wk Low	Div	Yield
CIBC	CM.PR.D	1,250	26.14	26.05	26.14	−0.08	26.22	24.80	1.44	5.50

Is Preferred Stock Really Debt?

A good case can be made that preferred stock is really debt in disguise, a kind of equity bond. Preferred shareholders receive a stated dividend only, and, if the corporation is liquidated. Often, preferreds carry credit ratings much like bonds. Furthermore, preferred stock is sometimes convertible into common stock. Preferred stocks are often callable by the issuer and the holder often has the right to sell the preferred stock back to the issuer at a set price.

In addition, in recent years, many new issues of preferred stock have had obligatory sinking funds. Such a sinking fund effectively creates a final maturity since the entire issue is ultimately retired. For example, if a sinking fund required that 2 percent of the original issue be retired each year, the issue would be completely retired in 50 years.

On top of all of this, preferred stocks with adjustable dividends have been offered in recent years. For example, a CARP is a cumulative, adjustable rate, preferred stock. There are various types of floating-rate preferreds, some of which are quite innovative in the way the dividend is determined. For example, Royal Bank of Canada used to have First Preferred Shares Series C where dividends were set at 2/3 of the bank's average Canadian prime rate with a floor dividend of 6.67 percent per year.

For all these reasons, preferred stock seems to be a lot like debt. In comparison to debt yields, the yields on preferred stock can appear very competitive. For example, the Royal Bank has another preferred stock with a $1.225 stated dividend. In January 2012, the market price of the $1.225 Royal Bank preferred was $25.56. This is a $1.225/$25.56 = 4.79% yield, similar to the yield on Royal Bank long-term debt. Also at that time, long-term Government of Canada bonds were yielding around 3 percent due to continuing easy monetary policy due to continued unsettled conditions in Europe.

In addition to the competitive yields, corporate investors have a further incentive to hold the preferred stock issued by other corporations rather than holding their debt because 100 percent of the dividends they receive are exempt from income taxes. Similarly, individual investors receive a dividend tax credit for preferred dividends, although it is much smaller than the corporate tax break. Overall, from the time of the financial crisis in 2008 to the time of writing in the winter of 2012, preferred stock was highly attractive.

Preferred Stock and Taxes

Turning to the issuers' point of view, a tax loophole encourages corporations that are lightly taxed or not taxable due to losses or tax shelters to issue preferred stock. Such low-tax companies can make little use of the tax deduction on interest. However, they can issue preferred stock and enjoy lower financing costs because preferred dividends are significantly lower than interest payments.

In 1987, the federal government attempted to close this tax loophole by introducing a tax of 40 percent of the preferred dividends to be paid by the issuer of preferred stock. The tax is refunded (through a deduction) to taxable issuers only. The effect of this (and associated) tax changes was to narrow but not close the loophole.

Table 8.2 shows how Zero Tax Ltd., a corporation not paying any income taxes, can issue preferred shares attractive to Full Tax Ltd., a second corporation taxable at a combined federal and provincial rate of 45 percent. The example assumes that Zero Tax is seeking $1,000 in financing through either debt or preferred stock and that Zero Tax can issue either debt with a 10 percent coupon or preferred stock with a 6.7 percent dividend.[11]

Table 8.2 shows that with preferred stock financing, Zero Tax pays out 6.7% × $1,000 = $67.00 in dividends and 40% × $67.00 = $26.80 in tax on the dividends for a total after-tax outlay of $93.80. This represents an after-tax cost of $93.80/$1,000 = 9.38%. Debt financing is more expensive with an outlay of $100 and an after-tax yield of 10 percent. So Zero Tax is better off issuing preferred stock.

From the point of view of the purchaser, Full Tax Ltd., the preferred dividend is received tax free for an after-tax yield of 6.7 percent. If it bought debt issued by Zero Tax instead, Full Tax would pay income tax of $45 for a net after-tax receipt of $55 or 5.5 percent. So again, preferred stock is better than debt.

Of course, if we change the example to make the issuer fully taxable, the after-tax cost of debt drops to 5.5 percent making debt financing more attractive. This reinforces our point that the tax motivation for issuing preferred stock is limited to lightly taxed companies.

TABLE 8.2

Tax loophole on preferred stock

	Preferred	Debt
Issuer: Zero Tax Ltd.		
Preferred dividend/interest paid	$ 67.00	$100.00
Dividend tax at 40%	26.80	0.00
Tax deduction on interest	0.00	0.00
Total financing cost	$ 93.80	$100.00
After-tax cost	9.38%	10.00%
Purchaser: Full Tax Ltd.		
Before-tax income	$ 67.00	$100.00
Tax	0.00	45.00
After-tax income	$ 67.00	$ 55.00
After-tax yield	6.70%	5.50%

Beyond Taxes

For fully taxed firms, the fact that dividends are not an allowable deduction from taxable corporate income is the most serious obstacle to issuing preferred stock, but there are a couple of reasons beyond taxes why preferred stock is issued.

First, firms issuing preferred stock can avoid the threat of bankruptcy that might otherwise exist if debt were relied on. Unpaid preferred dividends are not debts of a corporation, and preferred shareholders cannot force a corporation into bankruptcy because of unpaid dividends.

[11] We set the preferred dividend at around two-thirds of the debt yield to reflect market practice as exemplified by the Royal Bank issue discussed earlier. Further discussion of preferred stock and taxes is in I. Fooladi, P. A. McGraw, and G. S. Roberts, "Preferred Share Rules Freeze Out the Individual Investor," *CA Magazine*, April 11, 1988, pp. 38–41.

A second reason for issuing preferred stock concerns control of the firm. Since preferred shareholders often cannot vote, preferred stock may be a means of raising equity without surrendering control.

On the demand side, most preferred stock is owned by corporations. Corporate income from preferred stock dividends enjoys a tax exemption, which can substantially reduce the tax disadvantage of preferred stock. Some of the new types of adjustable-rate preferred stocks are highly suited for corporations needing short-term investments for temporarily idle cash.

Concept Questions

1. What is preferred stock?
2. Why is it arguably more like debt than equity?
3. Why is it attractive for firms that are not paying taxes to issue preferred stock?
4. What are two reasons unrelated to taxes why preferred stock is issued?

8.4 | Stock Market Reporting

If you look through the pages of the *National Post*, in another financial newspaper, or at theglobeandmail.com/globe-investor/, you find information on a large number of stocks in several different markets.[12] Figure 8.1 reproduces "The TSX Top 100" from the *National Post* on January 13, 2012. For a more detailed listing of all stocks on the TSX, you can visit financialpost.com or the website of a similar financial newspaper. In Figure 8.1, locate the line for Lundin Mining Corp. The Close, as you might have guessed, is the closing, price during the day. The Net Change of −0.15 tells us the closing price of $4.53 per share is $0.15 lower than the closing price the day before.

FIGURE 8.1

TSX—Daily Most Active Stocks on January 13, 2012— *Financial Post*

Company	Symbol	Volume	Close	Net Change
Bombardier Inc	BBD.B	16,575,251	4.41	−0.09
iShares S&P/TSX 60 Index	XIU	7,378,897	17.54	−0.06
Connacher Oil & Gas Ltd	CLL	4,157,009	1.09	+0.07
Lake Shore Gold Corp	LSG	4,145,020	1.39	−0.13
Manulife Financial Corp	MFC	3,911,353	11.92	+0.03
Nexen Inc	NXY	3,783,411	18.07	−0.14
Talisman Energy Inc	TLM	3,765,932	11.74	−0.41
Suncor Energy Inc	SU	3,651,347	32.63	−0.02
Horizons BetaPro Gas Bull	HNU	3,597,822	5.39	−0.37
AuRico Gold Inc	AUQ	3,534,807	8.77	−0.14
Royal Bank of Canada	RY	3,295,669	52.09	−0.68
Orbite Aluminae Inc	ORT	3,005,032	2.99	+0.16
Yamana Gold Inc	YRI	2,980,941	16.05	−0.04
Poseidon Concepts Corp	PSN	2,707,659	13.80	+0.01
Lundin Mining Corp	LUN	2,636,242	4.53	−0.15
Horizons BetaPro Oil Bull	HOU	2,461,270	6.33	+0.02
Horizons BetaPro Oil Bear	HOD	2,356,799	5.37	−0.03
Thomson Reuters Corp	TRI	2,255,529	28.56	−0.14
Uranium One Inc	UUU	2,225,826	2.37	−0.11
Encana Corp	ECA	2,206,800	17.89	−0.31

Source: Reprinted with permission of the *Financial Post*, January 13, 2012.

Volume tells us how many shares traded during the day. For example, the 2,636,242 for Lundin Mining Corp. tells us that 2,636,242 shares changed hands. If the average price during the day was $4.5 or so, the dollar volume of transactions was on the order of $4.5 × 2,636,242 = $11,863,089 worth of Lundin stock.

---

[12]To look up detailed stock information on line, any one of the following Web pages can provide excellent data: canada.com/business, theglobeandmail.com/globe-investor/, ca.finance.yahoo.com, or money.ca.msn.com/.

Growth Opportunities

We previously spoke of the growth rate of dividends. We now want to address the related concept of growth opportunities. Imagine a company with a level stream of earnings per share in perpetuity. The company pays all these earnings out to shareholders as dividends. Hence,

$$EPS = Div$$

where EPS is *earnings per share* and Div is dividends per share. A company of this type is frequently called a *cash cow*.

From the perpetuity formula of the previous chapter, the value of a share of stock is:

Value of a share of stock when firm acts as a cash cow: $\dfrac{EPS}{r} = \dfrac{Div}{r}$

where r is the discount rate on the firm's stock.

The preceding policy of paying out all earnings as dividends may not be the optimal one. Many firms have growth opportunities, that is, opportunities to invest in profitable projects. Because these projects can represent a significant fraction of the firm's value, it would be foolish to forgo them to pay out all earnings as dividends.

Although management frequently thinks of a set of growth opportunities, let's focus on only one opportunity; that is, the opportunity to invest in a single project. Suppose the firm retains the entire dividend at Date 1 to invest in a particular capital budgeting project. The net present value per share of the project as of Date 0 is NPVGO, which stands for the *net present value (per share) of the growth opportunity.*

What is the price of a share of stock at Date 0 if the firm decides to take on the project at Date 1? Because the per-share value of the project is added to the original stock price, the stock price must now be:

Stock price after firm commits to new project: $\dfrac{EPS}{r} + NPVGO$

This equation indicates that the price of a share of stock can be viewed as the sum of two different items: The first term (EPS/r) is the value of the firm if it rested on its laurels, that is, if it simply distributed all earnings to the shareholders. The second term is the additional value if the firm retains earnings to fund new projects.

Application: The Price-Earnings Ratio

Even though our stock valuation formulas focused on dividends, not earnings, financial analysts often rely on price earnings ratios (P/Es). Financial newspapers and websites also report P/Es.

We showed in the previous section that

Price per share $= \dfrac{EPS}{r} + NPVGO$

Dividing by EPS yields

$$\frac{\text{Price per share}}{\text{EPS}} = \frac{1}{r} + \frac{\text{NPVGO}}{\text{EPS}}$$

The left-hand side is the formula for the price-earnings ratio. The equation shows that the P/E ratio is related to the net present value of growth opportunities. As an example, consider two firms each having just reported earnings per share of $1. However, one firm has many valuable growth opportunities while the other firm has no growth opportunities at all. The firm with growth opportunities should sell at a higher price because an investor is buying both current income of $1 and growth opportunities. Suppose the firm with growth opportunities sells for $16 and the other firm sells for $8. The $1 earnings per share appears in the denominator of the P/E ratio for both firms. Thus, the P/E ratio is 16 for the firm with growth opportunities, but only 8 for the firm without the opportunities.

Because P/E ratios are based on earnings and not cash flows, investors should follow up with cash flow analysis using the dividend valuation model. Using a spreadsheet to look at different growth scenarios lets investors quantify projected growth in cash flows.

salesforce.com/   In January 2012, stocks like Salesforce.com were trading at P/Es over 5000! This was mainly due to the sudden surge in cloud computing services. Clearly the P/E analysis we present could never explain these prices in terms of growth opportunities. Some analysts who recommended buying these stocks developed a new measure called the PEG ratio to justify their recommendation. Although it is not based on any theory, the PEG ratio became popular among proponents of Internet stocks. On the other side, many analysts believed that the market had lost touch with reality. To these analysts, Internet stock prices were the result of speculative fever. Subsequent events support the second group of analysts.

Concept Questions

1. What are the relevant cash flows for valuing a share of common stock?
2. Does the value of a share of stock depend on how long you expect to keep it?
3. How does expected dividend growth impact on the stock price in the dividend valuation model? Is this consistent with the NPVGO approach?

IN THEIR OWN WORDS...

Robert J. Shiller on How a Bubble Stayed Under the Radar

ONE great puzzle about the recent housing bubble is why even most experts didn't recognize the bubble as it was forming.

Alan Greenspan, a very serious student of the markets, didn't see it, and, moreover, he didn't see the stock market bubble of the 1990s, either. In his 2007 autobiography, *The Age of Turbulence: Adventures in a New World*, he talks at some length about his suspicions in the 1990s that there was irrational exuberance in the stock market. But in the end, he says, he just couldn't figure it out: "I'd come to realize that we'd never be able to identify irrational exuberance with certainty, much less act on it, until after the fact."

With the housing bubble, Mr. Greenspan didn't seem to have any doubt: "I would tell audiences that we were facing not a bubble but a froth—lots of small local bubbles that never grew to a scale that could threaten the health of the overall economy."

The failure to recognize the housing bubble is the core reason for the collapsing house of cards we are seeing in financial markets in the United States and around the world. If people do not see any risk, and see only the prospect of outsized investment returns, they will pursue those returns with disregard for the risks.

Were all these people stupid? It can't be. We have to consider the possibility that perfectly rational people can get caught up in a bubble. In this connection, it is helpful to refer to an important bit of economic theory about herd behavior.

Three economists, Sushil Bikhchandani, David Hirshleifer, and Ivo Welch, in a classic 1992 article, defined what they call "information cascades" that can lead people into serious error. They found that these cascades can affect even perfectly rational people and cause bubblelike phenomena. Why? Ultimately, people sometimes need to rely on the judgment of others, and therein lies the problem. The theory provides a framework for understanding the real estate turbulence we are now observing.

Mr. Bikhchandani and his co-authors present this example: Suppose that a group of individuals must make an important decision, based on useful but incomplete information. Each one of them has received some information relevant to the decision, but the information is incomplete and "noisy" and does not always point to the right conclusion.

Let's update the example to apply it to the recent bubble: The individuals in the group must each decide whether real estate is a terrific investment and whether to buy some property. Suppose that there is a 60 percent probability that any one person's information will lead to the right decision.

In other words, that person's information is useful but not definitive—and not clear enough to make a firm judgment about something as momentous as a market bubble. Perhaps that is how Mr. Greenspan assessed the probability that he could make an accurate judgment about the stock market bubble.

The theory helps explain why he—or anyone trying to verify the existence of a market bubble—may have squelched his own judgment.

The fundamental problem is that the information obtained by any individual—even one as well-placed as the chairman of the Federal Reserve—is bound to be incomplete. If people could somehow hold a national town meeting and share their independent information, they would have the opportunity to see the full weight of the evidence. Any individual errors would be averaged out, and the participants would collectively reach the correct decision.

Of course, such a national town meeting is impossible. Each person makes decisions individually, sequentially, and reveals his decisions through actions—in this case, by entering the housing market and bidding up home prices.

Suppose houses are really of low investment value, but the first person to make a decision reaches the wrong conclusion (which happens, as we have assumed, 40 percent of the time). The first person, A, pays a high price for a home, thus signaling to others that houses are a good investment.

The second person, B, has no problem if his own data seem to confirm the information provided by A's willingness to pay a high price. But B faces a quandary if his own information seems to contradict A's judgment. In that case, B would conclude that he has no worthwhile information, and so he must make an arbitrary decision—say, by flipping a coin to decide whether to buy a house.

The result is that even if houses are of low investment value, we may now have two people who make purchasing decisions that reveal their conclusion that houses are a good investment.

As others make purchases at rising prices, more and more people will conclude that these buyers' information about the market outweighs their own.

Mr. Bikhchandani and his co-authors worked out this rational herding story carefully, and their results show that the probability of the cascade leading to an incorrect assumption is 37 percent. In other words, more than one-third of the time, rational individuals, all given information that is 60 percent accurate, will reach the wrong collective conclusion.

Thus, we should expect to see cascades driving our thinking from time to time, even when everyone is absolutely rational and calculating.

This theory poses a major challenge to the "efficient markets" view of the world, which assumes that investors are like independent-minded voters, relying only on their own information to make decisions. The efficient-markets view holds that the market is wiser than any individual: in aggregate, the market will come to the correct decision. But the theory is flawed because it does not recognize that people must rely on the judgments of others.

Now, let's modify the Bikhehandani-Hirshleifer-Welch example again, so that the individuals are no longer purely rational beings. Instead, they are real people, subject to emotional reactions.

Furthermore, these people are being influenced by agencies like the National Association of Realtors, which is conducting a public-relations campaign intended to show that putting money into housing is a reliable way to build wealth. Under these circumstances, it's easy to understand how even experts could come to believe that housing is a spectacular investment.

It is clear that just such an information cascade helped to create the housing bubble. And it is now possible that a downward cascade will develop—in which rational individuals become excessively pessimistic as they see others bidding down home prices to abnormally low levels.

Robert J. Shiller is Arthur M. Okun Professor of Economics at Yale and co-founder and chief economist of MacroMarkets LLC. He also writes for The New York Times. His comments are reproduced with permission from the March 2, 2008 edition.

8.5 | SUMMARY AND CONCLUSIONS

This chapter has covered the basics of stocks and stock valuation. The key points include:

1. The cash flows from owning a share of stock come in the form of future dividends. We saw that in certain special cases it is possible to calculate the present value of all the future dividends and thus come up with a value for the stock.

2. As the owner of shares of common stock in a corporation, you have various rights, including the right to vote to elect corporate directors. Voting in corporate elections can be either cumulative or straight. Most voting is actually done by proxy, and a proxy battle breaks out when competing sides try to gain enough votes to have their candidates for the board elected.

3. In addition to common stock, some corporations have issued preferred stock. The name stems from the fact that preferred shareholders must be paid first, before common shareholders can receive anything. Preferred stock has a fixed dividend.

This chapter completes Part 3 of our book. By now, you should have a good grasp of what we mean by present value. You should also be familiar with how to calculate present values, loan payments, and so on. In Part 4, we cover capital budgeting decisions. As you will see, the techniques you learned in Chapters 5—8 form the basis for our approach to evaluating business investment decisions.

Key Terms

capital gains yield (page 203)
common stock (page 205)
cumulative voting (page 218)
dividend growth model (page 199)
dividend yield (page 203)

dividends (page 206)
preferred stock (page 207)
proxy (page 218)
straight voting (page 218)

Chapter Review Problems and Self-Test

8.1   Dividend Growth and Stock Valuation The Brigapenski Co. has just paid a cash dividend of $2 per share. Investors require a 16 percent return from investments such as this. If the dividend is expected to grow at a steady 8 percent per year, what is the current value of the stock? What will the stock be worth in five years?

8.2   More Dividend Growth and Stock Valuation In Self-Test Problem 8.1, what would the stock sell for today if the dividend was expected to grow at 20 percent per year for the next three years and then settle down to 8 percent per year, indefinitely?

Answers to Self-Test Problems

8.1   The last dividend, D_0, was $2. The dividend is expected to grow steadily at 8 percent. The required return is 16 percent. Based on the dividend growth model, we can say that the current price is:

$$P_0 = D_1/(r - g) = D_0 \times (1 + g)/(r - g)$$
$$= \$2 \times 1.08/(.16 - .08)$$
$$= \$2.16/.08 = \$27$$

We could calculate the price in five years by calculating the dividend in five years and then using the growth model again. Alternatively, we could recognize that the stock price will increase by 8 percent per year and calculate the future price directly. We'll do both. First, the dividend in five years will be:

$$D_5 = D_0 \times (1 + g)^5$$
$$= \$2 \times 1.4693$$
$$= 2.9387$$

The price in five years would therefore be:

$$P_5 = D_5 \times (1 + g)/(r - g)$$
$$= \$2.9387 \times 1.08/.08$$
$$= \$3.1738/.08$$
$$= \$39.67$$

Once we understand the dividend model, however, it's easier to notice that:

$$P_5 = P_0 \times (1 + g)^5$$
$$= \$27 \times (1.08)^5$$
$$= \$27 \times 1.4693$$
$$= \$39.67$$

Notice that both approaches yield the same price in five years.

8.2   In this scenario, we have supernormal growth for the next three years. We'll need to calculate the dividends during the rapid-growth period and the stock price in three years. The dividends are:

$$D_1 = \$2.00 \times 1.20 = \$2.400$$
$$D_2 = \$2.40 \times 1.20 = \$2.880$$
$$D_3 = \$2.88 \times 1.20 = \$3.456$$

After three years, the growth rate falls to 8 percent indefinitely. The price at that time, P_3, is thus:

$$P_3 = D_3 \times (1 + g)/(r - g)$$
$$= \$3.456 \times 1.08/(.16 - .08)$$
$$= \$3.7325/.08$$
$$= \$46.656$$

To complete the calculation of the stock's present value, we have to determine the present value of the three dividends and the future price:

$$P_0 = \frac{D_1}{(1 + r)^1} + \frac{D_2}{(1 + r)^2} + \frac{D_3}{(1 + r)^3} + \frac{P_3}{(1 + r)^3}$$
$$= \frac{\$2.40}{1.16} + \frac{2.88}{1.16^2} + \frac{3.456}{1.16^3} + \frac{46.656}{1.16^3}$$
$$= \$2.07 + 2.14 + 2.21 + 29.89$$
$$= \$36.31$$

Concepts Review and Critical Thinking Questions

1. **(LO1)** Why does the value of a share of stock depend on dividends?

2. **(LO1)** A substantial percentage of the companies listed on the TSX and the Nasdaq don't pay dividends, but investors are nonetheless willing to buy shares in them. How is this possible given your answer to the previous question?

3. **(LO1)** Referring to the previous question, under what circumstances might a company choose not to pay dividends?

4. **(LO1)** Under what two assumptions can we use the dividend growth formula presented in the chapter to determine the value of a share of stock? Comment on the reasonableness of these assumptions.

5. **(LO2)** Suppose a company has a preferred stock issue and a common stock issue. Both have just paid a $2 dividend. Which do you think will have a higher price, a share of the preferred or a share of the common?

6. **(LO1)** Based on the dividend growth model, what are the two components of the total return on a share of stock? Which do you think is typically larger?

7. **(LO1)** In the context of the dividend growth model, is it true that the growth rate in dividends and the growth rate in the price of the stock are identical?

8. **(LO3)** When it comes to voting in elections, what are the differences between political democracy and corporate democracy?

9. **(LO3)** Is it unfair or unethical for corporations to create classes of stock with unequal voting rights?

10. **(LO2)** Some companies, such as Canadian Tire, have created classes of stock with no voting rights at all. Why would investors buy such stock?

Questions and Problems

Basic
(Questions 1–8)

1. **Stock Values (LO1)** The Stopperside Wardrobe Co. just paid a dividend of $1.95 per share on its stock. The dividends are expected to grow at a constant rate of 6 percent per year indefinitely. If investors require a 11 percent return on The Stopperside Wardrobe Co. stock, what is the current price? What will the price be in three years? In 15 years?

2. **Stock Values (LO1)** The next dividend payment by Kilbride Inc. will be $2.10 per share. The dividends are anticipated to maintain a 5 percent growth rate forever. If the stock currently sells for $48.00 per share, what is the required return?

3. **Stock Values (LO1)** For the company in the previous problem, what is the dividend yield? What is the expected capital gains yield?

4. **Stock Values (LO1)** Torbay Corporation will pay a $3.04 per share dividend next year. The company pledges to increase its dividend by 3.8 percent per year indefinitely. If you require an 11 percent return on your investment, how much will you pay for the company's stock today?

5. **Stock Valuation (LO1)** Glenhill Co. is expected to maintain a constant 5.2 percent growth rate in its dividends indefinitely. If the company has a dividend yield of 6.3 percent, what is the required return on the company's stock?

6. **Stock Valuation (LO1)** Suppose you know that a company's stock currently sells for $47 per share and the required return on the stock is 11 percent. You also know that the total return on the stock is evenly divided between a capital gains yield and a dividend yield. If it's the company's policy to always maintain a constant growth rate in its dividends, what is the current dividend per share?

7. **Stock Valuation (LO1)** Goulds Corp. pays a constant $9.75 dividend on its stock. The company will maintain this dividend for the next 11 years and will then cease paying dividends forever. If the required return on this stock is 10 percent, what is the current share price?

8. **Valuing Preferred Stock (LO1)** Big Pond Inc. has an issue of preferred stock outstanding that pays a $5.50 dividend every year in perpetuity. If this issue currently sells for $108 per share, what is the required return?

Intermediate
(Questions 9–20)

9. **Stock Valuation (LO1)** Talcville Farms just paid a dividend of $3.50 on its stock. The growth rate in dividends is expected to be a constant 5 percent per year indefinitely. Investors require a 14 percent return on the stock for the first three years, a 12 percent return for the next three years, and an 10 percent return thereafter. What is the current share price?

10. **Nonconstant Growth (LO1)** Foxtrap Bearings Inc. is a young start-up company. No dividends will be paid on the stock over the next nine years because the firm needs to plow back its earnings to fuel growth. The company will pay a $10 per share dividend in 10 years and will increase the dividend by 5 percent per year thereafter. If the required return on this stock is 14 percent, what is the current share price?

11. **Non-constant Dividends (LO1)** Kelligrews Inc. has an odd dividend policy. The company has just paid a dividend of $6 per share and has announced that it will increase the dividend by $4 per share for each of the next 5 years, and then never pay another dividend. If you require an 11 percent return on the company's stock, how much will you pay for a share today?

12. **Non-constant Dividends (LO1)** Chamberlain Corporation is expected to pay the following dividends over the next four years: $11, $8, $5, and $2. Afterward, the company pledges to maintain a constant 5 percent growth rate in dividends forever. If the required return on the stock is 12 percent, what is the current share price?

13. **Supernormal Growth (LO1)** Duffs Co. is growing quickly. Dividends are expected to grow at a 30 percent rate for the next three years, with the growth rate falling off to a constant 6 percent thereafter. If the required return is 13 percent and the company just paid a $1.80 dividend, what is the current share price?

14. **Supernormal Growth (LO1)** Rabbit Town Corp. is experiencing rapid growth. Dividends are expected to grow at 25 percent per year during the next three years, 15 percent over the following year, and then 8 percent per year indefinitely. The required return on this stock is 13 percent, and the stock currently sells for $76 per share. What is the projected dividend for the coming year?

15. **Negative Growth (LO1)** Foxtrap Inc. is a mature manufacturing firm. The company just paid a $10.46 dividend, but management expects to reduce the payout by 4 percent per year indefinitely. If you require an 11.5 percent return on this stock, what will you pay for a share today?

16. **Finding the Dividend (LO1)** Codner Corporation stock currently sells for $64 per share. The market requires a 10 percent return on the firm's stock. If the company maintains a constant 4.5 percent growth rate in dividends, what was the most recent dividend per share paid on the stock?

17. **Valuing Preferred Stock (LO1)** Peachytown Bank just issued some new preferred stock. The issue will pay a $20 annual dividend in perpetuity, beginning 20 years from now. If the market requires a 6.4 percent return on this investment, how much does a share of preferred stock cost today?

18. **Using Stock Quotes (LO4)** You have found the following stock quote for Enerplus Corp. in the Globe Investor on January 19, 2012. What was the closing price for this stock that appeared in *yesterday's* paper? If the company currently has 232,455 shares of stock outstanding, what was net income for the most recent four quarters?

52-WEEK		STOCK	YLD		VOL		NET
HI	LO	(DIV)	%	PE	100s	CLOSE	CHG
32.83	23.00	ERF 2.16	9.20	10.21	179	??	0.03

19. **Two-Stage Dividend Growth Model (LO1)** Upper Gullies Corp. just paid a dividend of $1.25 per share. The dividends are expected to grow at 28 percent for the next eight years and then level off to a 6 percent growth rate indefinitely. If the required return is 13 percent, what is the price of the stock today?

20. **Two-Stage Dividend Growth Model (LO1)** Lance Cove Choppers Inc. is experiencing rapid growth. The company expects dividends to grow at 25 percent per year for the next 11 years before leveling off at 6 percent into perpetuity. The required return on the company's stock is 12 percent. If the dividend per share just paid was $1.74, what is the stock price?

Challenge 21. **Capital Gains versus Income (LO1)** Consider four different stocks, all of which have a required return of 19 percent and a (Questions most recent dividend of $4.50 per share. Stocks W, X, and Y are expected to maintain constant growth rates in dividends for the 21–25) foreseeable future of 10 percent, 0 percent, and −5 percent per year, respectively. Stock Z is a growth stock that will increase its dividend by 20 percent for the next two years and then maintain a constant 12 percent growth rate thereafter. What is the dividend yield for each of these four stocks? What is the expected capital gains yield? Discuss the relationship among the various returns that you find for each of these stocks.

22. **Stock Valuation (LO1)** Most corporations pay quarterly dividends on their common stock rather than annual dividends. Barring any unusual circumstances during the year, the board raises, lowers, or maintains the current dividend once a year and then pays this dividend out in equal quarterly installments to its shareholders.

    a. Suppose a company currently pays a $3.20 annual dividend on its common stock in a single annual installment, and management plans on raising this dividend by 6 percent per year indefinitely. If the required return on this stock is 12 percent, what is the current share price?

    b. Now suppose the company in (a) actually pays its annual dividend in equal quarterly installments; thus, the company has just paid a $.80 dividend per share, as it has for the previous three quarters. What is your value for the current share price now? (*Hint:* Find the equivalent annual end-of-year dividend for each year.) Comment on whether you think this model of stock valuation is appropriate.

23. **Non-constant Growth (LO1)** Holyrood Co. just paid a dividend of $2.45 per share. The company will increase its dividend by 20 percent next year and will then reduce its dividend growth rate by 5 percentage points per year until it reaches the industry average of 5 percent dividend growth, after which the company will keep a constant growth rate forever. If the required return on Holyrood stock is 11 percent, what will a share of stock sell for today?

24. **Non-constant Growth (LO1)** This one's a little harder. Suppose the current share price for the firm in the previous problem is $63.82 and all the dividend information remains the same. What required return must investors be demanding on Holyrood stock? (*Hint:* Set up the valuation formula with all the relevant cash flows, and use trial and error to find the unknown rate of return.)

25. **Constant Dividend Growth Model (LO1)** Assume a stock has dividends that grow at a constant rate forever. If you value the stock using the constant dividend growth model, how many years worth of dividends constitute one-half of the stock's current price?

MINI CASE

Stock Valuation at Siddle Inc.

Siddle Inc. was founded nine years ago by brother and sister Wendy and Peter Siddle. The company manufactures and installs commercial heating, ventilation, and cooling (HVAC) units. Siddle Inc. has experienced rapid growth because of a proprietary technology that increases the energy efficiency of its units. The company is equally owned by Wendy and Peter. The original partnership agreement between the siblings gave each 50,000 shares of stock. In the event either wished to sell stock, the shares first had to be offered to the other at a discounted price.

Although neither sibling wants to sell, they have decided they should value their holdings in the company. To get started, they have gathered information about their main competitors, summarized in the table below.

In addition, they found that Expert HVAC Corporation's negative earnings per share were the result of an accounting write-off last year. Without the write-off, earnings per share for the company would have been $1.06.

Last year, Siddle Inc. had an EPS of $4.54 and paid a dividend to Wendy and Peter of $63,000 each. The company also had a return on equity of 25 percent. The siblings believe that 20 percent is an appropriate required return for the company.

Questions

1. Assuming the company continues its current growth rate, what is the value per share of the company's stock?

2. To verify their calculations, Wendy and Peter have hired David Boon as a consultant. David was previously an equity analyst and covered the HVAC industry. David has examined the company's financial statements, as well as its competitors. Although Siddle Inc. currently has a technological advantage, his research indicates that other companies are investigating methods to improve efficiency. Given this, David believes that the company's technological advantage will last only for the next five years. After that period, the company's growth will likely slow to the industry growth average. Additionally, David believes that the required return used by the company is too high. He believes the industry average required return is more appropriate. Under this growth rate assumption, what is your estimate of the stock price?

3. What is the industry average price-earnings ratio? What is the price-earnings ratio for Siddle Inc.? Is this the relationship you would expect between the two ratios? Why?

4. Wendy and Peter are unsure how to interpret the price-earnings ratio. After some head scratching, they've come up with the following expression for the price-earnings ratio:

$$\frac{P_0}{E_1} = \frac{1 - b}{R - (ROE \times b)}$$

Beginning with the constant dividend growth model, verify this result. What does this expression imply about the relationship between the dividend payout ratio, the required return on the stock, and the company's ROE?

5. Assume the company's growth rate slows to the industry average in five years. What future return on equity does this imply, assuming a constant payout ratio?

6. After discussing the stock value with David, Wendy and Peter agree that they would like to increase the value of the company stock. Like many small business owners, they want to retain control of the company, but they do not want to sell stock to outside investors. They also feel that the company's debt is at a manageable level and do not want to borrow more money. How can they increase the price of the stock? Are there any conditions under which this strategy would not increase the stock price?

Siddle Inc. Competitors

	EPS	DPS	Stock Price	ROE	R
Arctic Cooling Inc.	$0.79	$0.20	$14.18	10%	10%
National Heating & Cooling	1.38	0.62	11.87	13	13
Expert HVAC Corp.	−0.48	0.38	13.21	14	12
Industry Average	$0.56	$0.40	$13.09	12.33%	11.67%

Internet Application Questions

1. What are the latest corporate governance policies of institutional investors? Go to <u>lacaisse.com/en</u> and <u>otpp.com</u> to see. How do these large Canadian institutions seek to ensure the practice of corporate governance?

2. Stock valuation is difficult because dividends are difficult to forecast. Go to Suncor's website (<u>suncor.com</u>) and click on "Investor Centre". Use the information provided and the dividend growth model to estimate the implied growth for Suncor's dividends. Is this reasonable? Can you form a similar conclusion by looking at Suncor's P/E ratio?

3. Barclays Global Investors (<u>group.barclays.com</u>) has an exchange traded equity fund, i60 (<u>ca.ishares.com/product_info/fund/overview/XIU.htm?fundSearch=true&qt=XIU</u>). The i60 trades on the Toronto Stock Exchange (<u>tmx.com</u>) and invests in 60 firms that comprise the S&P/TSX 60 Index. Explain the advantage of investing in exchange traded funds relative to buying the stocks outright, and relative to buying index funds from banks.

4. Explore the wealth of online materials about stocks by going to <u>theglobeandmail.com/globe-investor/</u>. Enter the ticker symbol, BCE-T and view the summary of BCE Inc.

APPENDIX 8A

CORPORATE VOTING

To illustrate the two different voting procedures, imagine that a corporation has two shareholders: Smith with 20 shares and Jones with 80 shares. Both want to be directors. Jones, however, does not want Smith to be a director. We assume that four directors are to be elected.

cumulative voting
Procedure where a shareholder may cast all votes for one member of the board of directors.

CUMULATIVE VOTING   The effect of **cumulative voting** is to permit minority participation.[13] If cumulative voting is permitted, the total number of votes that each shareholder may cast is determined first. This is usually calculated as the number of shares (owned or controlled) multiplied by the number of directors to be elected.

With cumulative voting, the directors are elected all at once. In our example, this means that the top four vote getters will be the new directors. A shareholder can distribute votes however he or she wishes.

Will Smith get a seat on the board? If we ignore the possibility of a five-way tie, the answer is yes. Smith casts $20 \times 4 = 80$ votes, and Jones casts $80 \times 4 = 320$ votes. If Smith gives all his votes to himself, he is assured of a directorship. The reason is that Jones can't divide 320 votes among four candidates in such a way as to give all of them more than 80 votes, so Smith would finish fourth at worst.

In general, if there are N directors up for election, $1/(N + 1)$ percent of the stock (plus one share) would guarantee you a seat. In our current example, this is $1/(4 + 1) = 20\%$. So the more seats that are up for election at one time, the easier (and cheaper) it is to win one.

straight voting
Procedure where a shareholder may cast all votes for each member of the board of directors.

proxy
Grant of authority by shareholder allowing for another individual to vote his or her shares.

STRAIGHT VOTING   With **straight voting**, the directors are elected one at a time. Each time, Smith can cast 20 votes and Jones can cast 80. As a consequence, Jones elects all the candidates. The only way to guarantee a seat is to own 50 percent plus one share. This also guarantees that you would win every seat, so it's really all or nothing. For example, as of February 2012, the Bombardier family controlled 79.23 percent of the firm's outstanding Class A common shares and 54.39 percent of all voting rights related to all issued and outstanding voting shares.[14] Consequently, if the company were to use the straight voting procedure, the Bombardier family would successfully influence all outcomes.

PROXY VOTING   A **proxy** is the grant of authority by a shareholder to someone else to vote his or her shares. For convenience, much of the voting in large public corporations is actually done by proxy.

EXAMPLE 8A.1: Buying the Election

Stock in JRJ Corporation sells for $20 per share and features cumulative voting. There are 10,000 shares outstanding. If three directors are up for election, how much does it cost to ensure yourself a seat on the board?

The question here is how many shares of stock it will take to get a seat. The answer is 2,501, so the cost is 2,501 × $20 = $50,020. Why 2,501? Because there is no way the remaining 7,499 votes can be divided among three people to give all of them more than 2,501 votes. For example, suppose two people receive 2,502 votes and the first two seats. A third person can receive at most 10,000 − 2,502 − 2,502 − 2,501 = 2,495, so the third seat is yours.

As we've illustrated, straight voting can "freeze out" minority shareholders; that is the rationale for cumulative voting. But devices have been worked out to minimize its impact.

One such device is to stagger the voting for the board of directors. With staggered elections, only a fraction of the directorships are up for election at a particular time. Thus, if only two directors are up for election at any one time, it takes $1/(2 + 1) = 33.33\%$ of the stock to guarantee a seat. Overall, staggering has two basic effects:

1. Staggering makes it more difficult for a minority to elect a director when there is cumulative voting because there are fewer to be elected at one time.
2. Staggering makes takeover attempts less likely to be successful because it is more difficult to vote in a majority of new directors.

We should note that staggering may serve a beneficial purpose. It provides "institutional memory," that is, continuity on the board of directors. This may be important for corporations with significant long-range plans and projects.

---

[13] By minority participation, we mean participation by shareholders with relatively small amounts of stock.

[14] bombardier.com/en

As we have seen, with straight voting, each share of stock has one vote. The owner of 10,000 shares has 10,000 votes. Many companies have hundreds of thousands or even millions of shareholders. Shareholders can come to the annual meeting and vote in person, or they can transfer their right to vote to another party.

Obviously, management always tries to get as many proxies transferred to it as possible. However, if the shareholders are not satisfied with management, an outside group of shareholders can try to obtain votes via proxy. They can vote by proxy to replace management by adding enough directors. Or they can vote to oppose certain specific measures proposed by management. For example, proxyholders can vote against granting generous stock options to management. This activity is called a proxy battle and we come back to it in more detail in Chapter 23.

In Canada, large pension fund managers have increasingly used proxy voting to establish social responsibility in the firms in which they invest. Such organizations have also developed their own proxy voting guidelines to ensure voting is conducted using principles of good corporate governance.

Appendix Review Problem and Self-Test

A.1 Cumulative versus Straight Voting The Krishnamurti Corporation has 500,000 shares outstanding. There are four directors up for election. How many shares would you need to own to guarantee that you will win a seat if straight voting is used? If cumulative voting is used? Ignore possible ties.

Answer to Appendix Self-Test Problem

A.1 If there is straight voting, you need to own half the shares, or 250,000. In this case, you could also elect the other three directors. With cumulative voting, you need $1/(N + 1)$ percent of the shares, where N is the number of directors up for election. With four directors, this is 20 percent, or 100,000 shares.

Appendix Question and Problem

A.1 Voting for Directors The shareholders of Vycom, Inc., need to elect six new directors to the board. There are 2 million shares of common stock outstanding. How many shares do you need to own to guarantee yourself a seat on the board if:

a. The company uses cumulative voting procedures?

b. The company uses straight voting procedures?

CHAPTER 9

NET PRESENT VALUE AND OTHER INVESTMENT CRITERIA

AuRico Gold

Courtesy of AuRico Gold

A uRico Gold Inc. is a leading intermediate gold and silver mining and exploration company headquartered in Halifax. It has a diversified portfolio of mines in Canada, Mexico, and Australia. In August 2011, the company announced that it would acquire NorthGate Minerals. For the 12-month period ending on December 31, 2010, NorthGate Minerals' total revenue was valued at around $485 million. At the time of the announcement, AuRico Gold Inc. noted that not only would the purchase increase its total revenue, but also would establish the company as a leading intermediate, low cost producer with a substantial growth platform and a compelling valuation opportunity.

The acquisition by AuRico Gold is an example of a capital budgeting decision. When the deal was closed in October 2011, NorthGate Minerals was purchased for around $1.5 billion. Investing millions of dollars to acquire a company is a major undertaking that requires serious evaluation of the potential risks and rewards. In this chapter, we will discuss the basic tools in making such decisions.

Learning Objectives ▶

After studying this chapter, you should understand:

LO1 **How to compute the net present value and why it is the best decision criterion.**

LO2 **The payback rule and some of its shortcomings.**

LO3 **The discounted payback rule and some of its shortcomings.**

LO4 **Accounting rates of return and some of the problems with them.**

LO5 **The internal rate of return criterion and its strengths and weaknesses.**

LO6 **The modified internal rate of return.**

LO7 **The profitability index and its relation to net present value.**

auricogold.com

In Chapter 1, we identified the three key areas of concern to the financial manager. The first of these was deciding which fixed assets to buy. We called this the capital budgeting decision. In this chapter, we begin to deal with the issues that arise in answering this question.

The process of allocating or budgeting capital is usually more involved than just deciding whether to buy a particular fixed asset. We frequently face broader issues such as whether to launch a new product or enter a new market. Decisions such as these determine the nature of a firm's operations and products for years to come, primarily because fixed asset investments are generally long-lived and not easily reversed once they are made.

The most fundamental decision that a business must make concerns its product line. What services will we offer or what will we sell? In what markets will we compete? What new products will we introduce? The answer to any of these questions requires that the firm commit its scarce and valuable capital to certain types of assets. As a result, all these strategic issues fall under the general heading of capital budgeting. The process of capital budgeting could thus be given a more descriptive (not to mention impressive) name: strategic asset allocation.

For the reasons we have discussed, the capital budgeting question is probably the most important issue in corporate finance. How a firm chooses to finance its operations (the capital structure question) and how a firm manages its short-term operating activities (the working capital question) are certainly issues of concern; however, fixed assets define the business of the firm. Airlines, for example, are airlines because they operate airplanes, regardless of how they finance them.

Any firm possesses a huge number of possible investments. Each of these possible investments is an option available to the firm. Some of these options are valuable and some are not. The essence of successful financial management, of course, is learning to identify which are which. With this in mind, our goal in this chapter is to introduce you to the techniques used to analyze potential business ventures to decide which are worth undertaking.

We present and compare a number of different procedures used in practice. Our primary goal is to acquaint you with the advantages and disadvantages of the various approaches. As we shall see, the most important concept is the idea of net present value. When evaluating each method and determining which to use, it is important to look at three very important criteria and ask yourself the following questions:

- Does the decision rule adjust for the time value of money?
- Does the decision rule adjust for risk?
- Does the decision rule provide information on whether we are creating value for the firm?

A good decision rule will adjust for both the time value of money and risk, and will determine whether value has been created for the firm, and thus its shareholders.

9.1 | Net Present Value

The Basic Idea

An investment is worth undertaking if it creates value for its owners. In the most general sense, we create value by identifying an investment that is worth more in the marketplace than it costs us to acquire. How can something be worth more than it costs? It's a case of the whole being worth more than the cost of the parts.

For example, suppose you buy a run-down house for $65,000 and spend another $25,000 on painters, plumbers, and so on to get it fixed. Your total investment is $90,000. When the work is completed, you place the house back on the market and find that it's worth $100,000. The market value ($100,000) exceeds the cost ($90,000) by $10,000. What you have done here is to act as a manager and bring together some fixed assets (a house), some labour (plumbers, carpenters, and others), and some materials (carpeting, paint, and so on). The net result is that you have created $10,000 in value by employing business skills like human resources (hiring labour), project management, and marketing. Put another way, this $10,000 is the *value added* by management.

With our house example, it turned out after the fact that $10,000 in value was created. Things thus worked out very nicely. The real challenge, of course, was to somehow identify ahead of time whether or not investing the necessary $90,000 was a good idea. This is what capital budgeting is all about, namely, trying to determine whether a proposed investment or project will be worth more than it costs once it is in place.

net present value (NPV)
The difference between an investment's market value and its cost.

For reasons that will be obvious in a moment, the difference between an investment's market value and its cost is called the **net present value (NPV)** of the investment. In other words, net present value is a measure of how much value is created or added today by undertaking an investment. Given our goal of creating value for the shareholders, the capital budgeting process can be viewed as a search for investments with positive net present values.

With our run-down house, you can probably imagine how we would make the capital budgeting decision. We would first look at what comparable, fixed-up properties were selling for in the market. We would then get estimates of the cost of buying a particular property and bringing it up to market. At this point, we have an estimated total cost and an estimated market value. If the difference is positive, this investment is worth undertaking because it has a positive estimated net present value. There is risk, of course, because there is no guarantee that our estimates will turn out to be correct.

As our example illustrates, investment decisions are greatly simplified when there is a market for assets similar to the investment we are considering. Capital budgeting becomes much more difficult when we cannot observe the market price for at least roughly comparable investments. We are then faced with the problem of estimating the value of an investment using only indirect market information. Unfortunately, this is precisely the situation the financial manager usually encounters. We examine this issue next.

Estimating Net Present Value

Imagine that we are thinking of starting a business to produce and sell a new product, say, organic fertilizer. We can estimate the start-up costs with reasonable accuracy because we know what we need to buy to begin production. Would this be a good investment? Based on our discussion, you know that the answer depends on whether the value of the new business exceeds the cost of starting it. In other words, does this investment have a positive NPV?

This problem is much more difficult than our fixer-upper house example because entire fertilizer companies are not routinely bought and sold in the marketplace, so it is essentially impossible to observe the market value of a similar investment. As a result, we must somehow estimate this value by other means.

discounted cash flow (DCF) valuation
The process of valuing an investment by discounting its future cash flows.

Based on our work in Chapters 5 and 6, you may be able to guess how we estimate the value of our fertilizer business. We begin by trying to estimate the future cash flows that we expect the new business to produce. We then apply our basic discounted cash flow procedure to estimate the present value of those cash flows. Once we have this number, we estimate NPV as the difference between the present value of the future cash flows and the cost of the investment. As we mentioned in Chapter 6, this procedure is often called **discounted cash flow (DCF) valuation**.

To see how we might estimate NPV, suppose we believe that the cash revenues from our fertilizer business will be $20,000 per year, assuming everything goes as expected. Cash costs (including taxes) will be $14,000 per year. We will wind down the business in eight years. The plant, property, and equipment will be worth $2,000 as salvage at that time. The project costs $30,000 to launch. We use a 15 percent discount rate[1] on new projects such as this one. Is this a good investment? If there are 1000 shares of stock outstanding, what will be the effect on the price per share from taking it?

From a purely mechanical perspective, we need to calculate the present value of the future cash flows at 15 percent. The net cash flow inflow will be $20,000 cash income less $14,000 in costs per year for eight years. These cash flows are illustrated in Figure 9.1. As Figure 9.1 suggests, we effectively have an eight-year annuity of $20,000 − 14,000 = $6,000 per year along with a single lump-sum inflow of $2,000 in eight years. Calculating the present value of the future cash flows thus comes down to the same type of problem we considered in Chapter 6. The total present value is:

$$\text{Present value} = \$6,000 \times (1 - 1/1.15^8)/.15 + 2,000/1.15^8$$
$$= \$6,000 \times 4.4873 + 2,000/3.0590$$
$$= \$26,924 + 654$$
$$= \$27,578$$

FIGURE 9.1

Project cash flows ($000s)

Time (years)	0	1	2	3	4	5	6	7	8
Initial cost	−$30								
Inflows		$20	$20	$20	$20	$20	$20	$20	$20
Outflows		− 14	− 14	− 14	− 14	− 14	− 14	− 14	− 14
Net inflow		$ 6	$ 6	$ 6	$ 6	$ 6	$ 6	$ 6	$ 6
Salvage									2
Net cash flow	−$30	$ 6	$ 6	$ 6	$ 6	$ 6	$ 6	$ 6	$ 8

---

[1] The discount rate reflects the risk associated with the project. Here it is assumed that all new projects have the same risk.

When we compare this to the $30,000 estimated cost, the NPV is:

$$NPV = -\$30,000 + 27,578 = -\$2,422$$

Therefore, this is not a good investment. Based on our estimates, taking it would decrease the total value of the stock by $2,422. With 1000 shares outstanding, our best estimate of the impact of taking this project is a loss of value of $2,422/1000 = $2.422 per share.

Our fertilizer example illustrates how NPV estimates can help determine whether or not an investment is desirable. From our example, notice that, if the NPV is negative, the effect on share value would be unfavourable. If the NPV is positive, the effect would be favourable. As a consequence, all we need to know about a particular proposal for the purpose of making an accept/reject decision is whether the NPV is positive or negative.

Given that the goal of financial management is to increase share value, our discussion in this section leads us to the *net present value rule:*

> An investment should be accepted if the net present value is positive and rejected if it is negative.

In the unlikely event that the net present value turned out to be zero, we would be indifferent to taking the investment or not taking it.

Two comments about our example are in order: First, it is not the rather mechanical process of discounting the cash flows that is important. Once we have the cash flows and the appropriate discount rate, the required calculations are fairly straightforward. The task of coming up with the cash flows and the discount rate in the first place is much more challenging. We have much more to say about this in the next several chapters. For the remainder of this chapter, we take it as given that we have estimates of the cash revenues and costs and, where needed, an appropriate discount rate.

The second thing to keep in mind about our example is that the −$2,422 NPV is an estimate. Like any estimate, it can be high or low. The only way to find out the true NPV would be to place the investment up for sale and see what we could get for it. We generally won't be doing this, so it is important that our estimates be reliable. Once again, we have more to say about this later. For the rest of this chapter, we assume the estimates are accurate.

Going back to the decision criteria set out at the beginning of the chapter, we can see that the NPV method of valuation meets all three conditions. It adjusts cash flows for both the time value of money and risk through the choice of discount rate (discussed in detail in Chapter 14), and the NPV figure itself tells us how much value will be created with the investment.

As we have seen in this section, estimating NPV is one way of assessing the merits of a proposed investment. It is certainly not the only way that profitability is assessed, and we now turn to some alternatives. As we shall see, when compared to NPV, each of the ways of assessing profitability that we examine is flawed in some key way; so NPV is the preferred approach in principle, if not always in practice.

EXAMPLE 9.1: Using the NPV Rule

Suppose we are asked to decide whether or not a new consumer product should be launched. Based on projected sales and costs, we expect that the cash flows over the five-year life of the project will be $2,000 in the first two years, $4,000 in the next two, and $5,000 in the last year. It will cost about $10,000 to begin production. We use a 10 percent discount rate to evaluate new products. What should we do here?

Given the cash flows and discount rate, we can calculate the total value of the product by discounting the cash flows back to the present:

Present value = $2,000/1.1 + 2,000/1.1^2 + 4,000/1.1^3 +
$\qquad$ 4,000/1.1^4 + 5,000/1.1^5
$\qquad$ = $1,818 + 1,653 + 3,005 + 2,732 + 3,105
$\qquad$ = $12,313

The present value of the expected cash flows is $12,313, but the cost of getting those cash flows is only $10,000, so the NPV is $12,313 − 10,000 = $2,313. This is positive; so, based on the net present value rule, we should take on the project.

SPREADSHEET STRATEGIES

Calculating NPVs with a Spreadsheet

Spreadsheets are commonly used to calculate NPVs. Examining the use of spreadsheets in this context also allows us to issue an important warning. Let's rework Example 9.1:

	A	B	C	D	E	F	G	H
1								
2				Using a spreadsheet to calculate net present values				
3								
4	From Example 9.1, the project's cost is $10,000. The cash flows are $2,000 per year for the first							
5	two years, $4,000 per year for the next two, and $5,000 in the last year. The discount rate is							
6	10 percent; what's the NPV?							
7								
8		Year	Cash flow					
9		0	-$10,000	Discount rate =		10%		
10		1	2,000					
11		2	2,000		NPV =	$2,102.72	(*wrong* answer)	
12		3	4,000		NPV =	$2,312.99	(*right* answer)	
13		4	4,000					
14		5	5,000					
15	The formula entered in cell F11 is =NPV(F9, C9:C14). This gives the wrong answer because the NPV function							
16	calculates the sum of the present value of each number in the series, assuming that the first number occurs at							
17	the end of the first period. Therefore, in this example the year 0 value is discounted by 1 year or 10 percent							
18	(we clearly don't want this number to be discounted at all).							
19	The formula entered in cell F12 is =NPV(F9, C10:C14) + C9. This gives the right answer because the							
20	NPV function is used to calculate the present value of the cash flows for future years and then the initial cost is							
21	subtracted to calculate the answer. Notice that we added cell C9 because it is already negative.							

In our spreadsheet example just above, notice that we have provided two answers. By comparing the answers to that found in Example 9.1, we see that the first answer is wrong even though we used the spreadsheet's NPV formula. What happened is that the "NPV" function in our spreadsheet is actually a PV function; unfortunately, one of the original spreadsheet programs many years ago got the definition wrong, and subsequent spreadsheets have copied it! Our second answer shows how to use the formula properly.

The example here illustrates the danger of blindly using calculators or computers without understanding what is going on; we shudder to think of how many capital budgeting decisions in the real world are based on incorrect use of this particular function. We will see another example of something that can go wrong with a spreadsheet later in the chapter.

CALCULATOR HINTS

Finding NPV

You can solve this problem using a financial calculator by doing the following:

CF

CFo = −$10,000
C01 = $2,000
F01 = 2
C02 = $4,000
F02 = 2   I = 10%
C03 = $5,000   **I/Y**
F03 = 1   NPV = CPT
                           NPV

The answer to the problem is: $2,312.99

NOTE: To toggle between the different cash flow and NPV options, use the [SET] **↓** **↑** arrows found on the calculator.

Concept Questions

1. What is the net present value rule?
2. If we say that an investment has an NPV of $1,000, what exactly do we mean?

9.2 | The Payback Rule

It is very common in practice to talk of the payback on a proposed investment. Loosely, the payback is the length of time it takes to recover our initial investment. Because this idea is widely understood and used, we examine and critique it in some detail.

Defining the Rule

We can illustrate how to calculate a payback with an example. Figure 9.2 shows the cash flows from a proposed investment. How many years do we have to wait until the accumulated cash flows from this investment equal or exceed the cost of the investment? As Figure 9.2 indicates, the initial investment is $50,000. After the first year, the firm has recovered $30,000, leaving $20,000. The cash flow in the second year is exactly $20,000, so this investment pays for itself in exactly two years. Put another way, the **payback period** is two years. If we require a payback of, say, three years or less, then this investment is acceptable. This illustrates the *payback period rule:*

payback period
The amount of time required for an investment to generate cash flows to recover its initial cost.

> Based on the payback rule, an investment is acceptable if its calculated payback is less than some prespecified number of years.

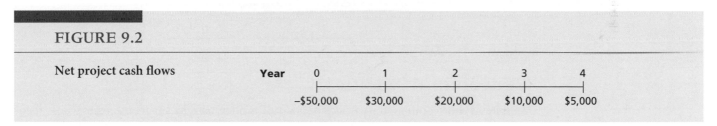

FIGURE 9.2

Net project cash flows

In our example, the payback works out to be exactly two years. This won't usually happen, of course. When the numbers don't work out exactly, it is customary to work with fractional years. For example, suppose the initial investment is $60,000, and the cash flows are $20,000 in the first year and $90,000 in the second. The cash flows over the first two years are $110,000, so the project obviously pays back sometime in the second year. After the first year, the project has paid back $20,000, leaving $40,000 to be recovered. To figure out the fractional year, note that this $40,000 is $40,000/$90,000 = 4/9 of the second year's cash flow. Assuming that the $90,000 cash flow is paid uniformly throughout the year, the payback would thus be 1 4/9 years.

Analyzing the Payback Period Rule

When compared to the NPV rule, the payback period rule has some rather severe shortcomings. Perhaps the biggest problem with the payback period rule is coming up with the right cutoff period because we don't really have an objective basis for choosing a particular number. Put another way, there is no economic rationale for looking at payback in the first place, so we have no guide as to how to pick the cutoff. As a result, we end up using a number that is arbitrarily chosen.

Another critical disadvantage is that the payback period is calculated by simply adding the future cash flows. There is no discounting involved, so the time value of money is ignored. Finally, a payback rule does not consider risk differences. The payback rule would be calculated the same way for both very risky and very safe projects.

Suppose we have somehow decided on an appropriate payback period, say two years or less. As we have seen, the payback period rule ignores the time value of money for the first two years. More seriously, cash flows after the second year are ignored. To see this, consider the two investments, Long and Short, in Table 9.1. Both projects cost $250. Based on our discussion, the payback on Long is 2 + $50/100 = 2.5 years, and the payback on Short is 1 + $150/200 = 1.75 years. With a cutoff of two years, Short is acceptable and Long is not.

Is the payback period rule giving us the right decisions? Maybe not. Suppose again that we require a 15 percent return on this type of investment. We can calculate the NPV for these two investments as:

$$\text{NPV(Short)} = -\$250 + 100/1.15 + 200/1.15^2 \quad = -\$11.81$$
$$\text{NPV(Long)} = -\$250 + 100 \times (1 - 1/1.15^4)/.15 \quad = \$35.50$$

Now we have a problem. The NPV of the shorter-term investment is actually negative, meaning that taking it diminishes the value of the shareholders' equity. The opposite is true for the longer-term investment—it increases share value.

Our example illustrates two primary shortcomings of the payback period rule. First, by ignoring time value, we may be led to take investments (like Short) that actually are worth less than they cost. Second, by ignoring cash flows beyond the cutoff, we may be led to reject profitable long-term investments (like Long). More generally, using a payback period rule tends to bias us toward shorter-term investments.

TABLE 9.1

Investment projected cash flows	Year	Long	Short
	1	$100	$100
	2	100	200
	3	100	0
	4	100	0

Redeeming Qualities

Despite its shortcomings, the payback period rule is often used by small businesses whose managers lack financial skills. It is also used by large and sophisticated companies when making relatively small decisions. There are several reasons for this. The primary reason is that many decisions simply do not warrant detailed analysis because the cost of the analysis would exceed the possible loss from a mistake. As a practical matter, an investment that pays back rapidly and has benefits extending beyond the cutoff period probably has a positive NPV.

Small investment decisions are made by the hundreds every day in large organizations. Moreover, they are made at all levels. As a result, it would not be uncommon for a corporation to require, for example, a two-year payback on all investments of less than $10,000. Investments larger than this are subjected to greater scrutiny. The requirement of a two-year payback is not perfect for reasons we have seen, but it does exercise some control over expenditures and thus limits possible losses.

In addition to its simplicity, the payback rule has several other features to recommend it. First, because it is biased toward short-term projects, it is biased toward liquidity. In other words, a payback rule favours investments that free up cash for other uses more quickly. This could be very important for a small business; it would be less so for a large corporation. Second, the cash flows that are expected to occur later in a project's life are probably more uncertain. Arguably, a payback period rule takes into account the extra riskiness of later cash flows, but it does so in a rather draconian fashion—by ignoring them altogether.

We should note here that some of the apparent simplicity of the payback rule is an illusion. We still must come up with the cash flows first, and, as we discussed previously, this is not easy to do. Thus, it would probably be more accurate to say that the concept of a payback period is both intuitive and easy to understand.

Summary of the Rule

To summarize, the payback period is a kind of "break-even" measure. Because time value is ignored, you can think of the payback period as the length of time it takes to break even in an accounting sense, but not in an economic sense. The biggest drawback to the payback period rule is that it doesn't ask the right question. The relevant issue is the impact an investment will have on the value of our stock, not how long it takes to recover the initial investment. Thus, the payback period rule fails to meet all three decision criteria.

Nevertheless, because it is so simple, companies often use it as a screen for dealing with the myriad of minor investment decisions they have to make. There is certainly nothing wrong with this practice. As with any simple rule of thumb, there will be some errors in using it, but it would not have survived all this time if it weren't useful. Now that you understand the rule, you can be on the alert for those circumstances under which it might lead to problems. To help you remember, the following table lists the pros and cons of the payback period rule.

Advantages and Disadvantages of the Payback Period Rule

Advantages	Disadvantages
1. Easy to understand.	1. Ignores the time value of money.
2. Adjusts for uncertainty of later cash flows.	2. Requires an arbitrary cutoff point.
3. Biased towards liquidity.	3. Ignores cash flows beyond the cutoff point.
	4. Biased against long-term projects, such as research and development, and new projects.
	5. Ignores any risks associated with projects.

The Discounted Payback Rule

discounted payback period
The length of time required for an investment's discounted cash flows to equal its initial cost.

We saw that one of the shortcomings of the payback period rule was that it ignored time value. There is a variation of the payback period, the **discounted payback period**, that fixes this particular problem. The discounted payback period is the length of time until the sum of the discounted cash flows equals the initial investment. The *discounted payback rule* is:

> An investment is acceptable if its discounted payback is less than some prescribed number of years.

To see how we might calculate the discounted payback period, suppose we require a 12.5 percent return on new investments. We have an investment that costs $300 and has cash flows of $100 per year for five years. To get the discounted payback, we have to discount each cash flow at 12.5 percent and then start adding them. We do this in Table 9.2. We have both the discounted and the undiscounted cash flows in Table 9.2. Looking at the accumulated cash flows, the regular payback is exactly three years (look for the arrow in Year 3). The discounted cash flows total $300 only after four years, so the discounted payback is four years as shown.[2]

TABLE 9.2

Ordinary and discounted payback

Year	Cash Flow Undiscounted	Cash Flow Discounted	Accumulated Cash Flow Undiscounted	Accumulated Cash Flow Discounted
1	$100	$89	$100	$ 89
2	100	79	200	168
3	100	70	→300	238
4	100	62	400	→300
5	100	55	500	355

How do we interpret the discounted payback? Recall that the ordinary payback is the time it takes to break even in an accounting sense. Since it includes the time value of money, the discounted payback is the time it takes to break even in an economic or financial sense. Loosely speaking, in our example, we get our money back along with the interest we could have earned elsewhere in four years.

Based on our example, the discounted payback would seem to have much to recommend it. You may be surprised to find out that it is rarely used. Why? Probably because it really isn't any simpler than NPV. To calculate a discounted payback, you have to discount cash flows, add them up, and compare them to the cost, just as you do with NPV. So, unlike an ordinary payback, the discounted payback is not especially simple to calculate.

---

[2] In this case, the discounted payback is an even number of years. This won't ordinarily happen, of course. However, calculating a fractional year for the discounted payback period is more involved than for the ordinary payback, and it is not commonly done.

A discounted payback period rule still has a couple of significant drawbacks. The biggest one is that the cutoff still has to be arbitrarily set and cash flows beyond that point are ignored.[3] As a result, a project with a positive NPV may not be acceptable because the cutoff is too short. Also, just because one project has a shorter discounted payback period than another does not mean it has a larger NPV.

All things considered, the discounted payback is a compromise between a regular payback and NPV that lacks the simplicity of the first and the conceptual rigour of the second. Nonetheless, if we need to assess the time it takes to recover the investment required by a project, the discounted payback is better than the ordinary payback because it considers time value. In other words, the discounted payback recognizes that we could have invested the money elsewhere and earned a return on it. The ordinary payback does not take this into account.

The advantages and disadvantages of the discounted payback are summarized in the following table:

Discounted Payback Period Rule

Advantages	*Disadvantages*
1. Includes time value of money.	1. May reject positive NPV investments.
2. Easy to understand.	2. Requires an arbitrary cutoff point.
3. Does not accept negative estimated NPV investments.	3. Ignores cash flows beyond the cutoff date.
4. Biased towards liquidity.	4. Biased against long-term projects, such as research and development, and new projects.

Concept Questions

1. What is the payback period? The payback period rule?
2. Why do we say that the payback period is, in a sense, an accounting break-even?

9.3 | The Average Accounting Return

average accounting return (AAR)
An investment's average net income divided by its average book value.

Another attractive, but flawed, approach to making capital budgeting decisions is the **average accounting return (AAR)**. There are many different definitions of the AAR. However, in one form or another, the AAR is always defined as:

$$\frac{\text{some measure of average accounting profit}}{\text{some measure of average accounting value}}$$

The specific definition we use is:

$$\frac{\text{Average net income}}{\text{Average book value}}$$

To see how we might calculate this number, suppose we are deciding whether to open a store in a new shopping mall. The required investment in improvements is $500,000. The store would have a five-year life because everything reverts to the mall owners after that time. The required investment would be 100 percent depreciated (straight-line) over five years, so the depreciation would be $500,000/5 = $100,000 per year. The tax rate for this small business is 25 percent.[4] Table 9.3 contains the projected revenues and expenses. Based on these figures, net income in each year is also shown.

To calculate the average book value for this investment, we note that we started out with a book value of $500,000 (the initial cost) and ended up at $0. The average book value during the life of the investment is thus ($500,000 + 0)/2 = $250,000. As long as we use straight-line depreciation, the average investment is always 1/2 of the initial investment.[5]

---

[3] If the cutoff were forever, then the discounted payback rule would be the same as the NPV rule. It would also be the same as the profitability index rule considered in a later section.

[4] These depreciation and tax rates are chosen for simplicity. Chapter 10 discusses depreciation and taxes.

[5] We could, of course, calculate the average of the six book values directly. In thousands, we would have ($500 + 400 + 300 + 200 + 100 + 0)/6 = $250.

TABLE 9.3

Projected yearly revenue and costs for average accounting return

	Year 1	Year 2	Year 3	Year 4	Year 5
Revenue	$433,333	$450,000	$266,667	$200,000	$133,333
Expenses	200,000	150,000	100,000	100,000	100,000
Earnings before depreciation	$233,333	$300,000	$166,667	$100,000	$ 33,333
Depreciation	100,000	100,000	100,000	100,000	100,000
Earnings before taxes	$133,333	$200,000	$ 66,667	$ 0	−$ 66,667
Taxes ($T_c = 0.25$)	33,333	50,000	16,667	0	−16,667
Net income	$100,000	$150,000	$ 50,000	$ 0	−$ 50,000

$$\text{Average net income} = \frac{(\$100,000 + 150,000 + 50,000 + 0 - 50,000)}{5} = \$50,000$$

$$\text{Average investment} = \frac{\$500,000 + 0}{2} = \$250,000$$

Looking at Table 9.3, net income is $100,000 in the first year, $150,000 in the second year, $50,000 in the third year, $0 in Year 4, and −$50,000 in Year 5. The average net income, then, is:

$$[\$100,000 + 150,000 + 50,000 + 0 + (-\$50,000)]/5 = \$50,000$$

The average accounting return is:

$$\text{AAR} = \text{Average net income/Average book value} = \$50,000/\$250,000$$
$$= 20\%$$

If the firm has a target AAR less than 20 percent, this investment is acceptable; otherwise it is not. The *average accounting return rule* is thus:

> Based on the average accounting return rule, a project is acceptable if its average accounting return exceeds a target average accounting return.

As we see in the next section, this rule has a number of problems.

Analyzing the Average Accounting Return Method

You recognize the first drawback to the AAR immediately. Above all else, the AAR is not a rate of return in any meaningful economic sense. Instead, it is the ratio of two accounting numbers, and it is not comparable to the returns offered, for example, in financial markets.[6]

One of the reasons the AAR is not a true rate of return is that it ignores time value. When we average figures that occur at different times, we are treating the near future and the more distant future the same way. There was no discounting involved when we computed the average net income, for example.

The second problem with the AAR is similar to the problem we had with the payback period rule concerning the lack of an objective cutoff period. Since a calculated AAR is really not comparable to a market return, the target AAR must somehow be specified. There is no generally agreed-on way to do this. One way of doing it is to calculate the AAR for the firm as a whole and use this for a benchmark, but there are lots of other ways as well.

The third, and perhaps worst, flaw in the AAR is that it doesn't even look at the right things. Instead of cash flow and market value, it uses net income and book value. These are both poor substitutes because the value of the firm is the present value of future cash flows. As a result, an AAR doesn't tell us what the effect on share price will be from taking an investment, so it does not tell us what we really want to know.

---

[6] The AAR is closely related to the return on assets (ROA) discussed in Chapter 3. In practice, the AAR is sometimes computed by first calculating the ROA for each year and then averaging the results. This produces a number that is similar, but not identical, to the one we computed.

Does the AAR have any redeeming features? About the only one is that it almost always can be computed. The reason is that accounting information is almost always available, both for the project under consideration and for the firm as a whole. We hasten to add that once the accounting information is available, we can always convert it to cash flows, so even this is not a particularly important fact. The AAR is summarized in the following table:

Average Accounting Return Rule

Advantages	Disadvantages
1. Easy to calculate.	1. Not a true rate of return; time value of money is ignored.
2. Needed information is usually available.	2. Uses an arbitrary benchmark cutoff rate.
	3. Based on accounting (book) values, not cash flows and market values.

Concept Questions

1. What is an accounting rate of return (AAR)?

2. What are the weaknesses of the AAR rule?

9.4 | The Internal Rate of Return

internal rate of return (IRR)
The discount rate that makes the NPV of an investment zero.

We now come to the most important alternative to NPV, the **internal rate of return**, universally known as the IRR. As you will see, the IRR is closely related to NPV. With the IRR, we try to find a single rate of return that summarizes the merits of a project. Furthermore, we want this rate to be an internal rate in the sense that it depends only on the cash flows of a particular investment, not on rates offered elsewhere.

To illustrate the idea behind the IRR, consider a project that costs $100 today and pays $110 in one year. Suppose you were asked, "What is the return on this investment?" What would you say? It seems both natural and obvious to say that the return is 10 percent because, for every dollar we put in, we get $1.10 back. In fact, as we see in a moment, 10 percent is the internal rate of return or IRR on this investment.

Is this project with its 10 percent IRR a good investment? Once again, it would seem apparent that this is a good investment only if our required return is less than 10 percent. This intuition is also correct and illustrates the *IRR rule:*

> Based on the IRR rule, an investment is acceptable if the IRR exceeds the required return. It should be rejected otherwise.

If you understand the IRR rule, you should see that we used the IRR (without defining it) when we calculated the yield to maturity of a bond in Chapter 7. In fact, the yield to maturity is the bond's IRR.[7] More generally, many returns for different types of assets are calculated the same way.

Imagine that we wanted to calculate the NPV for our simple investment. At a discount rate of *r*, the NPV is:

$$NPV = -\$100 + 110/(1 + r)$$

Suppose we didn't know the discount rate. This presents a problem, but we could still ask how high the discount rate would have to be before this project was unacceptable. We know that we are indifferent to taking or not taking this investment when its NPV is just equal to zero. In other words, this investment is economically a break-even proposition when the NPV is zero because value is neither created nor destroyed. To find the break-even discount rate, we set NPV equal to zero and solve for *r*:

$$NPV = 0 = -\$100 + 110/(1 + r)$$
$$\$100 = \$110/(1 + r)$$
$$1 + r = \$110/100 = 1.10$$
$$r = 10\%$$

---

[7] Strictly speaking, this is true for bonds with annual coupons. Typically, bonds carry semiannual coupons so yield to maturity is the six-month IRR expressed as a stated rate per year. Further, the yield to maturity is based on cash flows promised by the bond issuer as opposed to cash flows expected by a firm.

FIGURE 9.3

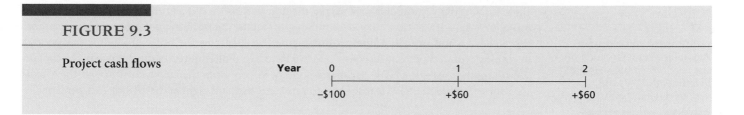

Project cash flows

By now, you have probably noticed that the IRR rule and the NPV rule appear to be quite similar. In fact, the IRR is sometimes simply called the discounted cash flow or DCF return. The easiest way to illustrate the relationship between NPV and IRR is to plot the numbers we calculated in

This 10 percent is what we already have called the return on this investment. What we have now illustrated is that the internal rate of return on an investment (or just return for short) is the discount rate that makes the NPV equal to zero. This is an important observation, so it bears repeating:

> The IRR on an investment is the return that results in a zero NPV when it is used as the discount rate.

The fact that the IRR is simply the discount rate that makes the NPV equal to zero is important because it tells us how to calculate the returns on more complicated investments. As we have seen, finding the IRR turns out to be relatively easy for a single period investment. However, suppose you were now looking at an investment with the cash flows shown in Figure 9.3. As illustrated, this investment costs $100 and has a cash flow of $60 per year for two years, so it's only slightly more complicated than our single period example. If you were asked for the return on this investment, what would you say? There doesn't seem to be any obvious answer (at least to us). Based on what we now know, we can set the NPV equal to zero and solve for the discount rate:

$$NPV = 0 = -\$100 + 60/(1 + IRR) + 60/(1 + IRR)^2$$

Unfortunately, the only way to find the IRR in general is by trial and error, either by hand or by calculator. This is precisely the same problem that came up in Chapter 5 when we found the unknown rate for an annuity and in Chapter 7 when we found the yield to maturity on a bond. In fact, we now see that, in both of those cases, we were finding an IRR.

In this particular case, the cash flows form a two-period, $60 annuity. To find the unknown rate, we can try various different rates until we get the answer. If we were to start with a 0 percent rate, the NPV would obviously be $120 − 100 = $20. At a 10 percent discount rate, we would have:

$$NPV = -\$100 + 60/1.1 + 60/(1.1)^2 = \$4.13$$

Now, we're getting close. We can summarize these and some other possibilities as shown in Table 9.4. From our calculations, the NPV appears to be zero between 10 and 15 percent, so the IRR is somewhere in that range. With a little more effort, we can find that the IRR is about 13.1 percent.[8] So, if our required return is less than 13.1 percent, we would take this investment. If our required return exceeds 13.1 percent, we would reject it.

TABLE 9.4

NPV at different discount rates

Discount Rate	NPV
0%	$20.00
5	11.56
10	4.13
15	−2.46
20	−8.33

By now, you have probably noticed that the IRR rule and the NPV rule appear to be quite similar. In fact, the IRR is sometimes simply called the discounted cash flow or DCF return. The easiest way to illustrate the relationship between NPV and IRR is to plot the numbers we calculated in

[8] With a lot more effort (or a calculator or personal computer), we can find that the IRR is approximately (to 15 decimal points) 13.0662386291808 percent, not that anybody would ever want this many decimal points.

net present value profile
A graphical representation of the relationship between an investment's NPVs and various discount rates.

Table 9.4. On the vertical or *y*-axis we put the different NPVs. We put discount rates on the horizontal or *x*-axis. If we had a very large number of points, the resulting picture would be a smooth curve called a **net present value profile**. Figure 9.4 illustrates the NPV profile for this project. Beginning with a 0 percent discount rate, we have $20 plotted directly on the *y*-axis. As the discount rate increases, the NPV declines smoothly. Where does the curve cut through the *x*-axis? This occurs where the NPV is just equal to zero, so it happens right at the IRR of 13.1 percent.

FIGURE 9.4

An NPV profile

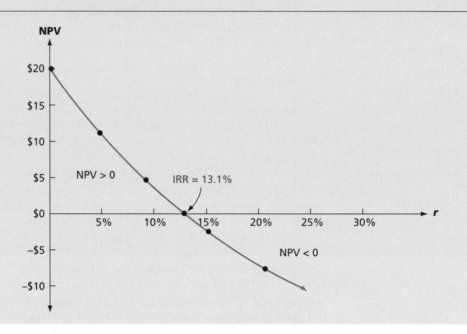

In our example, the NPV rule and the IRR rule lead to identical accept/reject decisions. We accept an investment using the IRR rule if the required return is less than 13.1 percent. As Figure 9.4 illustrates, however, the NPV is positive at any discount rate less than 13.1 percent, so we would accept the investment using the NPV rule as well. The two rules are equivalent in this case.

At this point, you may be wondering whether the IRR and the NPV rules always lead to identical decisions. The answer is yes as long as two very important conditions are met: First, the project's cash flows must be conventional, meaning that the first cash flow (the initial investment) is negative and all the rest are positive. Second, the project must be independent, meaning the decision to accept or reject this project does not affect the decision to accept or reject any other. The first of these conditions is typically met, but the second often is not. In any case, when one or both of these conditions is not met, problems can arise. We discuss some of these next.

EXAMPLE 9.2: Calculating the IRR

A project has a total up-front cost of $435.44. The cash flows are $100 in the first year, $200 in the second year, and $300 in the third year. What's the IRR? If we require an 18 percent return, should we take this investment?

We'll describe the NPV profile and find the IRR by calculating some NPVs at different discount rates. You should check our answers for practice. Beginning with 0 percent, we have:

Discount Rate	NPV
0%	$164.56
5	100.36
10	46.15
15	0.00
20	−39.61

The NPV is zero at 15 percent, so 15 percent is the IRR. If we require an 18 percent return, we should not take the investment. The reason is that the NPV is negative at 18 percent (check that it is −$24.47). The IRR rule tells us the same thing in this case. We shouldn't take this investment because its 15 percent return is less than our required 18 percent return.

Problems with the IRR

Problems with the IRR come about when the cash flows are not conventional or when we are trying to compare two or more investments to see which is best. In the first case, surprisingly, the simple question—What's the return?—can become very difficult to answer. In the second case, the IRR can be a misleading guide.

NON-CONVENTIONAL CASH FLOWS   Suppose we have an oil sands project that requires a $60 investment. Our cash flow in the first year will be $155. In the second year, the mine is depleted, but we have to spend $100 to restore the terrain. As Figure 9.5 illustrates, both the first and third cash flows are negative.

FIGURE 9.5

Project cash flows

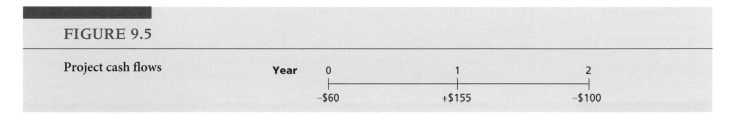

SPREADSHEET STRATEGIES

Calculating IRRs with a Spreadsheet

Because IRRs are so tedious to calculate by hand, financial calculators and, especially, spreadsheets are generally used. The procedures used by various financial calculators are too different for us to illustrate here, so we will focus on using a spreadsheet. As the following example illustrates, using a spreadsheet is very easy.

	A	B	C	D	E	F	G	H
1								
2			Using a spreadsheet to calculate internal rates of return					
3								
4	Suppose we have a four-year project that costs $500. The cash flows over the four-year life will be							
5	$100, $200, $300, and $400. What is the IRR?							
6								
7		Year	Cash flow					
8		0	-$500					
9		1	100		IRR =	27.3%		
10		2	200					
11		3	300					
12		4	400					
13								
14								
15	The formula entered in cell F9 is =IRR(C8:C12). Notice that the Year 0 cash flow has a negative							
16	sign representing the initial cost of the project.							
17								

CALCULATOR HINTS

Finding IRR

You can solve this problem using a financial calculator by doing the following:

CF

CFo = −$500

C01 = $100

F01 = 1

C02 = $200

F02 = 1

C03 = $300

F03 = 1   IRR = CPT

C04 = $400   **IRR**

F04 = 1

The answer to the problem is: 27.2732%

NOTE: To toggle between the different cash flow options, use the ↓ ↑ arrows found on the calculator.

To find the IRR on this project, we can calculate the NPV at various rates:

Discount Rate %	NPV
0	−$5.00
10	−1.74
20	−0.28
30	0.06
40	−0.31

The NPV appears to be behaving in a very peculiar fashion here. As the discount rate increases from 0 percent to 30 percent, the NPV starts out negative and becomes positive. This seems backward because the NPV is rising as the discount rate rises. It then starts getting smaller and becomes negative again. What's the IRR? To find out, we draw the NPV profile in Figure 9.6.

In Figure 9.6, notice that the NPV is zero when the discount rate is 25 percent, so this is the IRR. Or is it? The NPV is also zero at 33⅓ percent. Which of these is correct? The answer is both or neither; more precisely, there is no unambiguously correct answer. This is the **multiple rates of return** problem. Many financial computer packages (including the best seller for personal computers) aren't aware of this problem and just report the first IRR that is found. Others report only the smallest positive IRR, even though this answer is no better than any other.

multiple rates of return
One potential problem in using the IRR method if more than one discount rate makes the NPV of an investment zero.

FIGURE 9.6

NPV and the multiple IRR problem

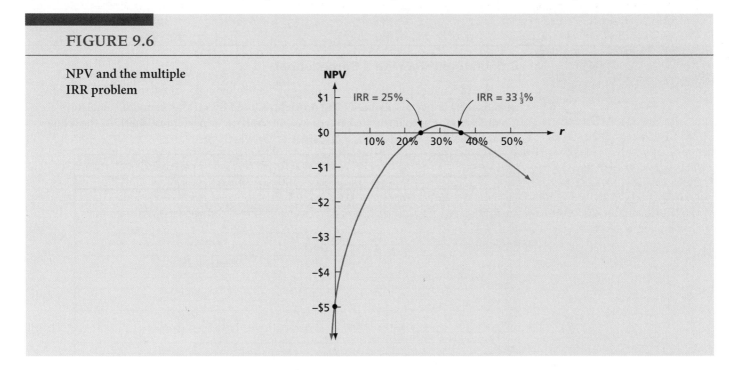

In our current example, the IRR rule breaks down completely. Suppose our required return were 10 percent. Should we take this investment? Both IRRs are greater than 10 percent, so, by the IRR rule, maybe we should. However, as Figure 9.6 shows, the NPV is negative at any discount rate less than 25 percent, so this is not a good investment. When should we take it? Looking at Figure 9.6 one last time, the NPV is positive only if our required return is between 25 and 33⅓ percent.

Non-conventional cash flows occur when a project has an outlay (negative cash flow) at the end (or in some intermediate period in the life of a project) as well as the beginning. Earlier, we gave the example of a strip mine with its major environmental cleanup costs at the end of the project life. Another common example is hotels which must renovate their properties periodically to keep up with competitors' new buildings. This creates a major expense gives hotel projects a non-conventional cash flow pattern.

The moral of the story is that when the cash flows aren't conventional, strange things can start to happen to the IRR. This is not anything to get upset about, however, because the NPV rule, as always, works just fine. This illustrates that, oddly enough, the obvious question—What's the rate of return?—may not always have a good answer.

mutually exclusive investment decisions
One potential problem in using the IRR method is the acceptance of one project excludes that of another.

MUTUALLY EXCLUSIVE INVESTMENTS   Even if there is a single IRR, another problem can arise concerning **mutually exclusive investment decisions**. If two investments, X and Y, are mutually exclusive, then taking one of them means we cannot take the other. For example, if we own one corner lot, we can build a gas station or an apartment building, but not both. These are mutually exclusive alternatives.

Thus far, we have asked whether or not a given investment is worth undertaking. A related question, however, comes up very often: Given two or more mutually exclusive investments, which one is the best? The answer is simple enough: The best one is the one with the largest NPV. Can we also say that the best one has the highest return? As we show, the answer is no.

To illustrate the problem with the IRR rule and mutually exclusive investments, consider the cash flows from the following two mutually exclusive investments:

EXAMPLE 9.3: What's the IRR?

You are looking at an investment that requires you to invest $51 today. You'll get $100 in one year, but you must pay out $50 in two years. What is the IRR on this investment?

You're on the alert now to the non-conventional cash flow problem, so you probably wouldn't be surprised to see more than one IRR. However, if you start looking for an IRR by trial and error, it will take you a long time. The reason is that there is no IRR. The NPV is negative at every discount rate, so we shouldn't take this investment under any circumstances. What's the return of this investment? Your guess is as good as ours.

EXAMPLE 9.4: "I Think, Therefore I Know How Many IRRs There Can Be."

We've seen that it's possible to get more than one IRR. If you wanted to make sure that you had found all of the possible IRRs, how could you tell? The answer comes from the great mathematician, philosopher, and financial analyst Descartes (of "I think; therefore I am" fame). Descartes's rule of signs says that the maximum number of IRRs is equal to the number of times that the cash flows change sign from positive to negative and/or negative to positive.[9]

In our example with the 25 and 33⅓ percent IRRs, could there be yet another IRR? The cash flows flip from negative to positive, then back to negative, for a total of two sign changes. As a result, the maximum number of IRRs is two, and, from Descartes's rule, we don't need to look for any more. Note that the actual number of IRRs can be less than the maximum (see Example 9.3).

Year	Investment A	Investment B
0	−$100	−$100
1	50	20
2	40	40
3	40	50
4	30	60
IRR	24%	21%

Since these investments are mutually exclusive, we can take only one of them. Simple intuition suggests that Investment A is better because of its higher return. Unfortunately, simple intuition is not always correct.

To see why investment A is not necessarily the better of the two investments, we've calculated the NPV of these investments for different required returns:

Discount Rate %	NPV(A)	NPV(B)
0	$60.00	$70.00
5	43.13	47.88
10	29.06	29.79
15	17.18	14.82
20	7.06	2.31
25	−1.63	−8.22

[9]To be more precise, the number of IRRs that are bigger than −100 percent is generally equal to the number of sign changes, or it differs from the number of sign changes by an even number. Thus, for example, if there are five sign changes, there are either five, three, or one IRRs. If there are two sign changes, there are either two IRRs or no IRRs.

SPREADSHEET STRATEGIES

Calculating IRRs with a Spreadsheet for non-conventional cash flows

The spreadsheet shows the IRR calculation of the oil sands project.

	A	B	C	D	E	F	G	H
1								
2		**Using a spreadsheet to calculate internal rates of return for non-conventional cash flows**						
3								
4	Suppose we have an oil sands project that requires a $60 investment.							
5	The cash flows over the 2 year life are $155 and –$100. What is the IRR							
6								
7		Year	Cash flow					
8		0	($60)					
9		1	$155		IRR =	25%		
10		2	($100)					
11								
12	The formula entered in cell E9 is =IRR(C8:C10). Notice that the Year 0 and Year 2 cash flow is negative.							

The spreadsheet calculates only the smaller value of IRR. The MIRR (modified IRR) function in MS Excel addresses the multiple IRR problem. Further, it allows the user to override an unrealistic assumption implicit in the IRR method that the positive cash flows are reinvested at the IRR instead of the cost of capital. MIRR fixes both the issues by taking the cash, flows, finance rate (interest rates to be paid for negative cash flows) and reinvestment rate (interest rates that would be earned on the cash during the investment period) as input and returning a single value. Refer to Appendix 9A to know more about MIRR.

The IRR for A (24 percent) is larger than the IRR for B (21 percent). However, if you compare the NPVs, you'll see that which investment has the higher NPV depends on our required return. B has greater total cash flow, but it pays back more slowly than A. As a result, it has a higher NPV at lower discount rates.

In our example, the NPV and IRR rankings conflict for some discount rates. If our required return is 10 percent, for instance, B has the higher NPV and is thus the better of the two even though A has the higher return. If our required return is 15 percent, there is no ranking conflict: A is better.

The conflict between the IRR and NPV for mutually exclusive investments can be illustrated as we have done in Figure 9.7 by plotting their NPV profiles. In Figure 9.7, notice that the NPV profiles cross at about 11 percent. This discount rate is referred to as the cross-over point. Notice also that at any discount rate less than 11 percent, the NPV for B is higher. In this range, taking B benefits us more than taking A, even though A's IRR is higher. At any rate greater than 11 percent, project A has the greater NPV.

FIGURE 9.7

NPV and the IRR ranking problem

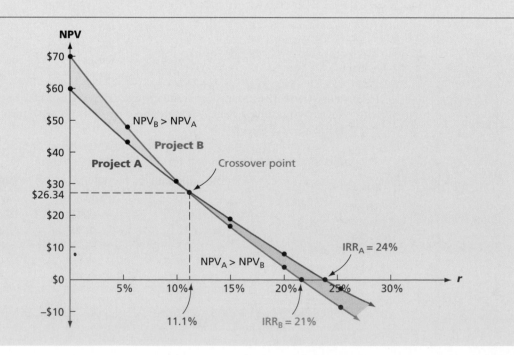

What this example illustrates is that whenever we have mutually exclusive projects, we shouldn't rank them based on their returns. More generally, anytime we are comparing investments to determine which is best, IRRs can be misleading. Instead, we need to look at the relative NPVs to avoid the possibility of choosing incorrectly. Remember, we're ultimately interested in creating value for the shareholders, so the option with the higher NPV is preferred, regardless of the relative returns.

If this seems counterintuitive, think of it this way. Suppose you have two investments. One has a 10 percent return and makes you $100 richer immediately. The other has a 20 percent return and makes you $50 richer immediately. Which one do you like better? We would rather have $100 than $50, regardless of the returns, so we like the first one better.

A final, important consideration in choosing between investment options is the actual amount of funds to be invested. In our example above, the options involve different amounts of money ($70,000 versus $60,000). In this case, we must consider whether we have sufficient funds to undertake a particular option, and if we choose the smaller investment, what to do with the excess funds. Some important tools to handle this situation, like the profitability index and capital rationing, will be discussed further in this section of the text.

There are often challenges while evaluating mutually exclusive projects in real life. For example, when the World Trade Center (twin towers) was destroyed in a terrorist attack on September 11, 2011, there was a lot of debate about the usage of the site. There were many conflicting parties suggesting mutually exclusive projects for the site. The Port Authority of New York and New Jersey could have built another twin towers or it could have used the site for community purposes. In such scenarios, evaluating mutually exclusive projects based on NPV and IRR becomes difficult as there are lots of external stakeholders involved. Finally, the Port Authority of New York and New Jersey decided on five new office towers—One WTC, Memorial and Museum, Transportation Hub, WTC Retail and a Performing Arts Center slated for completion in 2013.

Redeeming Qualities of the IRR

Despite its flaws, the IRR is very popular in practice, more so than even the NPV. It probably survives because it fills a need that the NPV does not. In analyzing investments, people in general and financial analysts in particular seem to prefer talking about rates of return rather than dollar values.

EXAMPLE 9.5: Calculating the Crossover Rate

In Figure 9.7, the NPV profiles cross at about 11 percent. How can we determine just what this crossover point is? The crossover rate, by definition, is the discount rate that makes the NPVs of two projects equal. To illustrate, suppose we have the following two mutually exclusive investments:

Year	Investment A	Investment B
0	−$400	−$500
1	250	320
2	280	340

What's the crossover rate?

To find the crossover, consider moving out of Investment A and into Investment B. If you make the move, you'll have to invest an extra $100 = ($500 − 400). For this $100 investment, you'll get an extra $70 = ($320 − 250) in the first year and an extra $60 = ($340 − 280) in the second year. Is this a good move? In other words, is it worth investing the extra $100?

Based on our discussion, the NPV of the switch, NPV (B − A) is:

$$NPV(B - A) = -\$100 + \$70/(1 + r) + \$60/(1 + r)^2$$

We can calculate the return on this investment by setting the NPV equal to zero and solving for the IRR;

$$NPV(B - A) = 0 = -\$100 + \$70/(1 + r) + \$60/(1 + r)^2$$

If you go through this calculation, you will find the IRR is exactly 20 percent. What this tells us is that at a 20 percent discount rate, we are indifferent between the two investments because the NPV of the difference in their cash flows is zero. As a consequence, the two investments have the same value, so this 20 percent is the crossover rate. Check that the NPV at 20 percent is $2.78 for both.

In general, you can find the crossover rate by taking the difference in the cash flows and calculating the IRR using the differences. It doesn't make any difference which one you subtract from which. To see this, find the IRR for (A − B); you'll see it's the same number. Also, for practice, you might want to find the exact crossover in Figure 9.7. (Hint: It's 11.0704 percent.)

In a similar vein, the IRR also appears to provide a simple way of communicating information about a proposal. One manager might say to another: "Remodelling the clerical wing has a 20 percent return." This may somehow be simpler than saying: "At a 10 percent discount rate, the net present value is $4,000."

Finally, under certain circumstances, the IRR may have a practical advantage over NPV. We can't estimate the NPV unless we know the appropriate discount rate, but we can still estimate the IRR. Suppose we only had a rough estimate of the required return on an investment, but we found, for example, that it had a 40 percent return. We would probably be inclined to take it since it is very unlikely that the required return is that high. The advantages and disadvantages of the IRR follow:

Internal Rate of Return Rule

Advantages	*Disadvantages*
1. Closely related to NPV, generally leading to identical decisions.	1. May result in multiple answers or no answer with non-conventional cash flows.
2. Easy to understand and communicate.	2. May lead to incorrect decisions in comparisons of mutually exclusive investments.

To address some of the problems that can crop up with the standard IRR, it is often proposed that a modified version be used. As we will see, there are several different ways of calculating a modified IRR, or MIRR, but the basic idea is to modify the cash flows first and then calculate an IRR using the modified cash flows. Appendix 9A discusses MIRR.

Concept Questions

1. Under what circumstances will the IRR and NPV rules lead to the same accept/reject decisions? When might they conflict?
2. Is it generally true that an advantage of the IRR rule over the NPV rule is that we don't need to know the required return to use the IRR rule?

9.5 | The Profitability Index

profitability index (PI)
The present value of an investment's future cash flows divided by its initial cost. Also benefit/cost ratio.

benefit/cost ratio
The profitability index of an investment project.

Another method used to evaluate projects is called the **profitability index (PI)** or **benefit/cost ratio**. This index is defined as the present value of the future cash flows divided by the initial investment. So, if a project costs $200 and the present value of its future cash flows is $220, the profitability index value would be $220/200 = 1.10. Notice that the NPV for this investment is $20, so it is a desirable investment.

More generally, if a project has a positive NPV, the present value of the future cash flows must be bigger than the initial investment. The profitability index would thus be bigger than 1.00 for a positive NPV investment and less than 1.00 for a negative NPV investment.

How do we interpret the profitability index? In our example, the PI was 1.10. This tells us that, per dollar invested, $1.10 in value or $.10 in NPV results. The profitability index thus measures "bang for the buck," that is, the value created per dollar invested. For this reason, it is often proposed as a measure of performance for government or other not-for-profit investments. They can use the index by attempting to quantify both tangible and intangible costs and benefits of a particular program. For example, the cost of a tree planting program might be simply the value of the trees and the labour to plant them. The benefits might be improvement to the environment and public enjoyment (the dollar value of which would have to be estimated). Also, when capital is scarce, it may make sense to allocate it to those projects with the highest PIs. We return to this issue in a later chapter.

The PI is obviously very similar to the NPV. However, consider an investment that costs $5 and has a $10 present value and an investment that costs $100 with a $150 present value. The first of these investments has an NPV of $5 and a PI of 2. The second has an NPV of $50 and a PI of 1.50. If these were mutually exclusive investments, the second one is preferred even though it has a lower PI.[10] This ranking problem is very similar to the IRR ranking problem we saw in the previous section. In all, there seems to be little reason to rely on the PI instead of the NPV. Our discussion of the PI is summarized in the following table:

---

[10] Both IRR and PI are affected by the scale issue when projects are of different size.

Profitability Index Rule

Advantages	Disadvantages
1. Closely related to NPV, generally leading to identical decisions.	1. May lead to incorrect decisions in comparisons of mutually exclusive investments.
2. Easy to understand and communicate.	
3. May be useful when available investment funds are limited.	

Concept Questions

1. What does the profitability index measure?
2. How would you state the profitability index rule?

9.6 | The Practice of Capital Budgeting

So far, this chapter has asked the question: Which capital budgeting methods should companies be using? An equally important question is: Which methods are companies using? Table 9.5 goes a long way toward answering this question. As can be seen from the table, three-quarters of Canadian companies use the NPV method and two-thirds use IRR.[11] This is not surprising, given the theoretical advantages of these approaches.

TABLE 9.5

Capital Budgeting Techniques used by Canadian firms

Source: Table 3 from Baker, H. K., Dutta, S., & Saadi, S. (2011). Corporate finance practices in Canada: Where do we stand? Multinational Finance Journal, 15(3–4), 157.

	% of Often or Always
Net present value	74.6
Internal rate of return	68.4
Payback period	67.2
Accounting rate of return	39.7
Discounted payback	24.8
Adjusted present value	17.2
Profitability index	11.2
Modified internal rate of return	12.0
Real options	10.4

Over half of these companies use the payback method, a rather surprising result given the conceptual problems with this approach. And while discounted payback represents a theoretical improvement over regular payback, the usage here is far less. Perhaps companies are attracted to the user-friendly nature of payback.

You might expect the capital budgeting methods of large firms to be more sophisticated than the methods of small firms. After all, large firms have the financial resources to hire more sophisticated employees. Table 9.6 provides some support for this idea. Here, the managers of Canadian firms indicate frequency of use of the various capital budgeting methods on a scale of 0 (never) to 4 (always). Both the IRR and payback methods are used more frequently in large firms than in small firms. The use of the NPV method is similar for large and the small firms. Capital budgeting for not-for-profit organizations such as hospitals must balance the hospital mission with financial resource availability. Managers of hospitals maximize value by accepting projects that fulfill the hospital mission while maintaining liquidity and solvency. These managers may accept some projects with the least negative NPVs[12] because they contribute to the fulfillment of the hospital mission.

---

[11] Baker, H. K., Dutta, S., & Saadi, S. (2011). Corporate finance practices in Canada: Where do we stand? Multinational Finance Journal, 15(3–4), 157.

[12] Negative NPV projects have costs greater than the benefits generated.

The use of quantitative techniques in capital budgeting varies with the industry. As you would imagine, firms that are better able to estimate cash flows precisely are more likely to use NPV. For example, estimation of cash flow in certain aspects of the oil business is quite feasible. Because of this, energy-related firms were among the first to use NPV analysis. Conversely, the flows in the motion picture business are very hard to project. The grosses of great hits like *Avatar*, *The Dark Knight Rises*, and *The Avengers* were far, far greater than anyone imagined. The big failures like *Waterworld* were unexpected as well. Consequently, NPV analysis is frowned upon in the movie business.

TABLE 9.6

Frequency of use of various capital budgeting methods for Canadian firms

Source: Table 3 from Baker, H. K., Dutta, S., & Saadi, S. (2011). Corporate finance practices in Canada: Where do we stand? Multinational Finance Journal, 15(3–4), 157.

	Large Firms	Small Firms
Net present value	2.92	2.95
Internal rate of return	3.40	2.52
Payback period	3.04	2.73
Accounting rate of return	2.04	1.67
Discounted payback	0.61	1.34
Adjusted present value	1.04	0.88
Profitability index	0.32	0.60
Modified internal rate of return	0.40	0.53
Real options	0.68	0.35

TABLE 9.7   Summary of investment criteria

I. DISCOUNTED CASH FLOW CRITERIA Net Present Value (Npv)

Definition: The difference between a project's market value and cost.
  Rule: Invest in projects with positive NPVs.
Advantages: No serious flaws; preferred decision criteria.

Internal Rate of Return (IRR)

Definition: The discount rate that makes the estimated NPV equal to zero.
  Rule: Invest in projects when their IRR exceeds the required return.
Advantages: Closely related to NPV; leads to the exact same decision as NPV for conventional, independent projects.
Disadvantages: Cannot use to rank mutually exclusive projects or when project cash flows are unconventional.

Profitability Index (PI)

Definition: Ratio of present value to cost. Also known as the benefit/cost ratio.
  Rule: Invest in projects when the index exceeds one.
Advantages: Similar to NPV.
Disadvantages: Cannot use to rank mutually exclusive projects.

ii. Payback Criteria Payback Period

Definition: The length of time until the sum of an investment's cash flows equals its cost.
  Rule: Invest in projects with payback periods less than the cutoff point.
Advantages: Easy to use and understand.
Disadvantages: Ignores risk, the time value of money and cash flows beyond the cutoff point.

Discounted Payback Period

Definition: The length of time until the sum of an investment's discounted cash flows equals its cost.
  Rule: Invest in projects if the discounted payback period is less than the cutoff point.
Advantages: Includes time value of money, easy to understand. Ignores cash flows after the cutoff point.
Disadvantages: Ignores cash flows after the cutoff point.

III. Accounting Criteria Average Accounting Return (AAR)

Definition: A measure of accounting profit relative to book value.
  Rule: Invest in projects if their AAR exceeds a benchmark AAR.
Advantages: Easy to calculate, information is readily available.
Disadvantages: Not a true rate of return; ignores time value of money, cash flows, and market values.

In Chapter 11 we discuss what types of capital budgeting techniques firms with less predictable cash flows can use.

Table 9.7 provides a summary of investment criteria for capital budgeting. The table discusses the benefits and flaws of each approach.

Concept Questions

1. What are the most commonly used capital budgeting procedures?
2. Since NPV is conceptually the best procedure for capital budgeting, why do you think that multiple measures are used in practice?

9.7 | SUMMARY AND CONCLUSIONS

This chapter has covered the different criteria used to evaluate proposed investments. The six criteria, in the order we discussed them, are:

1. Net present value (NPV)
2. Payback period
3. Discounted payback period
4. Average accounting return (AAR)
5. Internal rate of return (IRR)
6. Profitability index (PI)

Before making a proposed investment, the above criteria need to be evaluated on the basis of the following decision rules:

a. Does the decision rule adjust for the time value of money?
b. Does the decision rule adjust for risk?
c. Does the decision rule provide information on whether we are creating value for the firm?

We illustrated how to calculate each of these and discussed the interpretation of the results. We also described the advantages and disadvantages of each of them. Ultimately, a good capital budgeting criterion must tell us two things. First, is a particular project a good investment? Second, if we have more than one good project, but we can only take one of them, which one should we take? The main point of this chapter is that only the NPV criterion can always provide the correct answer to both questions.

For this reason, NPV is one of the two or three most important concepts in finance, and we will refer to it many times in the chapters ahead. When we do, keep two things in mind: (1) NPV is always just the difference between the market value of an asset or project and its cost, and (2) the financial manager acts in the shareholders' best interests by identifying and taking positive NPV projects.

Finally, we noted that NPVs can't normally be observed in the market; instead, they must be estimated. Because there is always the possibility of a poor estimate, financial managers use multiple criteria for examining projects. These other criteria provide additional information about whether a project truly has a positive NPV.

Key Terms

average accounting return (AAR) (page 228)
benefit/cost ratio (page 238)
discounted cash flow (DCF) valuation (page 222)
discounted payback period (page 227)
internal rate of return (IRR) (page 230)
multiple rates of return (page 234)

mutually exclusive investment decisions (page 234)
net present value (NPV) (page 221)
net present value profile (page 232)
payback period (page 225)
profitability index (PI) (page 238)

Chapter Review Problems and Self-Test

9.1   **Investment Criteria** This problem will give you some practice calculating NPVs and paybacks. A proposed overseas expansion has the following cash flows

Year	Cash Flow
0	−$200
1	50
2	60
3	70
4	200

Calculate the payback, the discounted payback, and the NPV at a required return of 10 percent.

9.2   **Mutually Exclusive Investments** Consider the following two mutually exclusive investments. Calculate the IRR for each and the crossover rate. Under what circumstances will the IRR and NPV criteria rank the two projects differently?

Year	Investment A	Investment B
0	−$75	−$75
1	20	60
2	40	50
3	70	15

9.3   **Average Accounting Return** You are looking at a three-year project with a projected net income of $2,000 in Year 1, $4,000 in Year 2, and $6,000 in Year 3. The cost is $12,000, which will be depreciated straight-line to zero over the three-year life of the project. What is the average accounting return (AAR)?

Answers to Self-Test Problems

9.1   In the following table, we have listed the cash flow, cumulative cash flow, discounted cash flow (at 10 percent), and cumulative discounted cash flow for the proposed project.

Year	Cash Flow Undiscounted	Cash Flow Discounted	Accumulated Cash Flow Undiscounted	Accumulated Cash Flow Discounted
1	$ 50	$ 45.45	$ 50	$ 45.45
2	60	49.59	110	95.04
3	70	52.59	180	147.63
4	200	136.60	380	284.23

Recall that the initial investment was $200. When we compare this to accumulated undiscounted cash flows, we see that payback occurs between Years 3 and 4. The cash flows for the first three years are $180 total, so, going into the fourth year, we are short by $20. The total cash flow in Year 4 is $200, so the payback is 3 + ($20/200) = 3.10 years.

Looking at the accumulated discounted cash flows, we see that the discounted payback occurs between Years 3 and 4. The discounted cash flows for the first three years are $147.63 in total, so, going into the fourth year, we are short by $52.37. The total discounted cash flow in Year 4 is $136.60, so the payback is 3 + ($52.37/136.60) = 3.38 years. The sum of the discounted cash flows is $284.23, so the NPV is $84.23. Notice that this is the present value of the cash flows that occur after the discounted payback.

9.2   To calculate the IRR, we might try some guesses, as in the following table:

Discount Rate	NPV(A)	NPV(B)
0%	$55.00	$50.00
10	28.83	32.14
20	9.95	18.40
30	−4.09	7.57
40	−14.80	−1.17

Several things are immediately apparent from our guesses. First, the IRR on A must be between 20 percent and 30 percent (why?). With some more effort, we find that it's 26.79 percent. For B, the IRR must be a little less than 40 percent (again, why?); it works out to be 38.54 percent. Also, notice that at rates between 0 percent and 10 percent, the NPVs are very close, indicating that the crossover is in that vicinity.

To find the crossover exactly, we can compute the IRR on the difference in the cash flows. If we take the cash flows from A minus the cash flows from B, the resulting cash flows are:

Year	A − B
0	$ 0
1	−40
2	−10
3	55

These cash flows look a little odd, but the sign only changes once, so we can find an IRR. With some trial and error, you'll see that the NPV is zero at a discount rate of 5.42 percent, so this is the crossover rate.

The IRR for B is higher. However, as we've seen, A has the larger NPV for any discount rate less than 5.42 percent, so the NPV and IRR rankings will conflict in that range. Remember, if there's a conflict, we will go with the higher NPV. Our decision rule is thus very simple: take A if the required return is less than 5.42 percent, take B if the required return is between 5.42 percent and 38.54 percent (the IRR on B), and take neither if the required return is more than 38.54 percent.

9.3   Here we need to calculate the ratio of average net income to average book value to get the AAR. Average net income is:

Average net income = ($2,000 + 4,000 + 6,000)/3 = $4,000

Average book value is:

Average book value = $12,000/2 = $6,000

So the average accounting return is:

AAR = $4,000/$6,000 = 66.67%

This is an impressive return. Remember, however, that it isn't really a rate of return like an interest rate or an IRR, so the size doesn't tell us a lot. In particular, our money is probably not going to grow at a rate of 66.67 percent per year, sorry to say.

Concepts Review and Critical Thinking Questions

1. **(LO2, 3)** If a project with conventional cash flows has a payback period less than the project's life, can you definitively state the algebraic sign of the NPV? Why or why not? If you know that the discounted payback period is less than the project's life, what can you say about the NPV? Explain.

2. **(LO2, 3, 6, 7)** Suppose a project has conventional cash flows and a positive NPV. What do you know about its payback? Its discounted payback? Its profitability index? Its IRR? Explain.

3. **(LO2)** Concerning payback:
   a. Describe how the payback period is calculated and describe the information this measure provides about a sequence of cash flows. What is the payback criterion decision rule?
   b. What are the problems associated with using the payback period as a means of evaluating cash flows?
   c. What are the advantages of using the payback period to evaluate cash flows? Are there any circumstances under which using payback might be appropriate? Explain.

4. **(LO3)** Concerning discounted payback:
   a. Describe how the discounted payback period is calculated and describe the information this measure provides about a sequence of cash flows. What is the discounted payback criterion decision rule?
   b. What are the problems associated with using the discounted payback period as a means of evaluating cash flows?
   c. What conceptual advantage does the discounted payback method have over the regular payback method? Can the discounted payback ever be longer than the regular payback? Explain.

5. **(LO4)** Concerning AAR:
   a. Describe how the average accounting return is usually calculated and describe the information this measure provides about a sequence of cash flows. What is the AAR criterion decision rule?
   b. What are the problems associated with using the AAR as a means of evaluating a project's cash flows? What underlying feature of AAR is most troubling to you from a financial perspective? Does the AAR have any redeeming qualities?

6. **(LO1)** Concerning NPV:
   a. Describe how NPV is calculated and describe the information this measure provides about a sequence of cash flows. What is the NPV criterion decision rule?
   b. Why is NPV considered to be a superior method of evaluating the cash flows from a project? Suppose the NPV for a project's cash flows is computed to be $2,500. What does this number represent with respect to the firm's shareholders?

7. **(LO5)** Concerning IRR:
   a. Describe how the IRR is calculated and describe the information this measure provides about a sequence of cash flows. What is the IRR criterion decision rule?
   b. What is the relationship between IRR and NPV? Are there any situations in which you might prefer one method over the other? Explain.
   c. Despite its shortcomings in some situations, why do most financial managers use IRR along with NPV when evaluating projects? Can you think of a situation in which IRR might be a more appropriate measure to use than NPV? Explain.

8. **(LO7)** Concerning the profitability index:
   a. Describe how the profitability index is calculated and describe the information this measure provides about a sequence of cash flows. What is the profitability index decision rule?
   b. What is the relationship between the profitability index and NPV? Are there any situations in which you might prefer one method over the other? Explain.

9. **(LO2, 5)** A project has perpetual cash flows of C per period, a cost of I, and a required return of R. What is the relationship between the project's payback and its IRR? What implications does your answer have for long-lived projects with relatively constant cash flows?

10. **(LO1)** In early 2013, U.S retailer Target planned to open more than 100 stores in Canada. Also, in March 2011, Tata Steel, 10th largest steel maker in the world, announced its intention to invest around $5 billion in Quebec's iron ore. What are some of the reasons that foreign manufacturers of products as diverse as retail and steel are opening up their facilities in Canada?

11. **(LO1)** What are some of the difficulties that might come up in actual applications of the various criteria we discussed in this chapter? Which one would be the easiest to implement in actual applications? The most difficult?

12. **(LO1, 7)** Are the capital budgeting criteria we discussed applicable to not-for-profit corporations? How should such entities make capital budgeting decisions? What about different levels of government, i.e., federal, provincial, and municipal? Should they evaluate spending proposals using these techniques?

13. **(LO5)** One of the less flattering interpretations of the acronym MIRR is "meaningless internal rate of return." Why do you think this term is applied to MIRR?

14. **(LO1, 6)** It is sometimes stated that "the net present value approach assumes reinvestment of the intermediate cash flows at the required return." Is this claim correct? To answer, suppose you calculate the NPV of a project in the usual way. Next, suppose you do the following:

a. Calculate the future value (as of the end of the project) of all the cash flows other than the initial outlay assuming they are reinvested at the required return, producing a single future value figure for the project.

b. Calculate the NPV of the project using the single future value calculated in the previous step and the initial outlay. It is easy to verify that you will get the same NPV as in your original calculation only if you use the required return as the reinvestment rate in the previous step.

15. (LO5) It is sometimes stated that "the internal rate of return approach assumes reinvestment of the intermediate cash flows at the internal rate of return." Is this claim correct? To answer, suppose you calculate the IRR of a project in the usual way. Next, suppose you do the following:

a. Calculate the future value (as of the end of the project) of all the cash flows other than the initial outlay assuming they are reinvested at the IRR, producing a single future value figure for the project.

b. Calculate the IRR of the project using the single future value calculated in the previous step and the initial outlay. It is easy to verify that you will get the same IRR as in your original calculation only if you use the IRR as the reinvestment rate in the previous step.

Questions and Problems

Basic
(Questions 1–19)

1. Calculating Payback (LO2) What is the payback period for the following set of cash flows?

Year	Cash Flow
0	−$6,400
1	1,600
2	1,900
3	2,300
4	1,400

2. Calculating Payback (LO2) An investment project provides cash inflows of $765 per year for eight years. What is the project payback period if the initial cost is $2,400? What if the initial cost is $3,600? What if it is $6,500?

3. Calculating Payback (LO2) McKernan Inc. imposes a payback cutoff of three years for its international investment projects. If the company has the following two projects available, should they accept either of them?

Year	Cash Flow (A)	Cash Flow (B)
0	−$40,000	−$60,000
1	19,000	14,000
2	25,000	17,000
3	18,000	24,000
4	6,000	270,000

4. Calculating Discounted Payback (LO3) An investment project has annual cash inflows of $4,200, $5,300, $6,100, and $7,400, and a discount rate of 14 percent. What is the discounted payback period for these cash flows if the initial cost is $7,000? What if the initial cost is $10,000? What if it is $13,000?

5. Calculating Discounted Payback (LO3) An investment project costs $15,000 and has annual cash flows of $4,300 for six years. What is the discounted payback period if the discount rate is zero percent? What if the discount rate is 5 percent? If it is 19 percent?

6. Calculating AAR (LO4) You're trying to determine whether to expand your business by building a new manufacturing plant. The plant has an installation cost of $15 million, which will be depreciated straight-line to zero over its four-year life. If the plant has projected net income of $1,938,200, $2,201,600, $1,876,000 and $1,329,500 over these four years, what is the project's average accounting return (AAR)?

7. Calculating IRR (LO5) A firm evaluates all of its projects by applying the IRR rule. If the required return is 16 percent, should the firm accept the following project?

Year	Cash Flow
0	−$34,000
1	16,000
2	18,000
3	15,000

8. Calculating NPV (LO1) For the cash flows in the previous problem, suppose the firm uses the NPV decision rule. At a required return of 12 percent, should the firm accept this project? What if the required return was 35 percent?

9. Calculating NPV and IRR (LO1, 5) A project that provides annual cash flows of $28,500 for nine years costs $138,000 today. Is this a good project if the required return is 8 percent? What if it's 20 percent? At what discount rate would you be indifferent between accepting the project and rejecting it?

10. **Calculating IRR (LO5)** What is the IRR of the following set of cash flows?

Year	Cash Flow
0	−$19,500
1	9,800
2	10,300
3	8,600

11. **Calculating NPV(LO1)** For the cash flows in the previous problem, what is the NPV at a discount rate of zero percent? What if the discount rate is 10 percent? If it is 20 percent? If it is 30 percent?

12. **NPV versus IRR (LO1, 5)** Parkallen Inc. has identified the following two mutually exclusive projects:

Year	Cash Flow (A)	Cash Flow (B)
0	−$43,000	−$43,000
1	23,000	7,000
2	17,900	13,800
3	12,400	24,000
4	9,400	26,000

    a.   What is the IRR for each of these projects? Using the IRR decision rule, which project should the company accept? Is this decision necessarily correct?

    b.   If the required return is 11 percent, what is the NPV for each of these projects? Which project will the company choose if it applies the NPV decision rule?

    c.   Over what range of discount rates would the company choose Project A? Project B? At what discount rate would the company be indifferent between these two projects? Explain.

13. **NPV versus IRR (LO1, 5)** Consider the following two mutually exclusive projects:

Year	Cash Flow (X)	Cash Flow (Y)
0	−$15,000	−$15,000
1	8,150	7,700
2	5,050	5,150
3	6,800	7,250

Sketch the NPV profiles for X and Y over a range of discount rates from zero to 25 percent. What is the crossover rate for these two projects?

14. **Problems with IRR (LO5)** Belgravia Petroleum Inc. is trying to evaluate a generation project with the following cash flows:

Year	Cash Flow
0	−$45,000,000
1	78,000,000
2	−14,000,000

    a.   If the company requires a 12 percent return on its investments, should it accept this project? Why?

    b.   Compute the IRR for this project. How many IRRs are there? Using the IRR decision rule, should the company accept the project? What's going on here?

15. **Calculating Profitability Index (LO7)** What is the profitability index for the following set of cash flows if the relevant discount rate is 10 percent? What if the discount rate is 15 percent? If it is 22 percent?

Year	Cash Flow
0	−$14,000
1	7,300
2	6,900
3	5,700

16. **Problems with Profitability Index (LO1, 7)** The Hazeldean Computer Corporation is trying to choose between the following two mutually exclusive design projects:

Year	Cash Flow (I)	Cash Flow (II)
0	−$53,000	−$16,000
1	27,000	9,100
2	27,000	9,100
3	27,000	9,100

    a.   If the required return is 10 percent and the company applies the profitability index decision rule, which project should the firm accept?

    b.   If the company applies the NPV decision rule, which project should it take?

    c.   Explain why your answers in (a) and (b) are different.

17. **Comparing Investment Criteria (LO1, 2, 3, 5, 7)** Consider the following two mutually exclusive projects:

Year	Cash Flow (A)	Cash Flow (B)
0	−$300,000	−$40,000
1	20,000	19,000
2	50,000	12,000
3	50,000	18,000
4	390,000	10,500

Whichever project you choose, if any, you require a 15 percent return on your investment.

   a.   If you apply the payback criterion, which investment will you choose? Why?

   b.   If you apply the discounted payback criterion, which investment will you choose? Why?

   c.   If you apply the NPV criterion, which investment will you choose? Why?

   d.   If you apply the IRR criterion, which investment will you choose? Why?

   e.   If you apply the profitability index criterion, which investment will you choose? Why?

   f.   Based on your answers in (a) through (e), which project will you finally choose? Why?

 18. **NPV and Discount Rates (LO1)** An investment has an installed cost of $684,680. The cash flows over the four-year life of the investment are projected to be $263,279, $294,060, $227,604, and $174,356. If the discount rate is zero, what is the NPV? If the discount rate is infinite, what is the NPV? At what discount rate is the NPV just equal to zero? Sketch the NPV profile for this investment based on these three points.

19. **MIRR (LO6)** Ritchie Ride Corp. is evaluating a project with the following cash flows:

Year	Cash Flow
0	−$16,000
1	6,100
2	7,800
3	8,400
4	6,500
5	−5,100

The company uses a 10 percent interest rate on all of its projects. Calculate the MIRR of the project using all three methods.

Intermediate 20. **NPV and the Profitability Index (LO6)** If we define the NPV index as the ratio of NPV to cost, what is the relationship
(Questions between this index and the profitability index?
20–22)

21. **Cash Flow Intuition (LO1, 7)** A project has an initial cost of I, has a required return of R, and pays C annually for N years.

   a.   Find C in terms of I and N such that the project has a payback period just equal to its life.

   b.   Find C in terms of I, N, and R such that this is a profitable project according to the NPV decision rule.

   c.   Find C in terms of I, N, and R such that the project has a benefit-cost ratio of 2.

22. **MIRR (LO 6)** Suppose the company in Problem 19 uses an 11 percent discount rate and an 8 percent reinvestment rate on all of its projects. Calculate the MIRR of the project using all three methods using these interest rates.

Challenge 23. **Payback and NPV (LO2, 5)** An investment under consideration has a payback of seven years and a cost of $724,000. If the
(Questions required return is 12 percent, what is the worst-case NPV? The best-case NPV? Explain. Assume the cash flows are conventional.
23–28)
24. **Multiple IRRs (LO5)** This problem is useful for testing the ability of financial calculators and computer software. Consider the following cash flows. How many different IRRs are there (*Hint:* search between 20 percent and 70 percent)? When should we take this project?

Year	Cash Flow
0	−$ 1,512
1	8,586
2	−18,210
3	17,100
4	−6,000

25. **NPV Valuation (LO1)** The Argyll Corporation wants to set up a private cemetery business. According to the CFO, Kepler Wessels, business is "looking up." As a result, the cemetery project will provide a net cash inflow of $85,000 for the firm during the first year, and the cash flows are projected to grow at a rate of 6 percent per year forever. The project requires an initial investment of $1,400,000.

   a.   If Argyll requires a 13 percent return on such undertakings, should the cemetery business be started?

   b.   The company is somewhat unsure about the assumption of a 6 percent growth rate in its cash flows. At what constant growth rate would the company just break even if it still required a 13 percent return on investment?

26. **Problems with IRR (LO1, 5)** A project has the following cash flows:

Year	Cash Flow
0	$58,000
1	−34,000
2	−45,000

What is the IRR for this project? If the required return is 12 percent, should the firm accept the project? What is the NPV of this project? What is the NPV of the project if the required return is 0 percent? 24 percent? What is going on here? Sketch the NPV profile to help you with your answer.

27. **Problems with IRR (LO5)** Avonmore Corp. has a project with the following cash flows:

Year	Cash Flow
0	$20,000
1	−26,000
2	13,000

What is the IRR of the project? What is happening here?

28. **NPV and IRR (LO1, 5)** Garneau International Limited is evaluating a project in Erewhon. The project will create the following cash flows:

Year	Cash Flow
0	−$750,000
1	205,000
2	265,000
3	346,000
4	220,000

All cash flows will occur in Erewhon and are expressed in dollars. In an attempt to improve its economy, the Erewhon government has declared that all cash flows created by a foreign company are "blocked" and must be reinvested with the government for one year. The reinvestment rate for these funds is 4 percent. If Garneau uses an 11 percent required return on this project, what are the NPV and IRR of the project? Is the IRR you calculated the MIRR of the project? Why or why not?

MINI CASE

Ferdinand Gold Mining

Rio Ferdinand, the owner of Ferdinand Gold Mining, is evaluating a new gold mine in Fort McMurray. Paul Pogba, the company's geologist, has just finished his analysis of the mine site. He has estimated that the mine would be productive for eight years, after which the gold would be completely mined. Paul has taken an estimate of the gold deposits to Julia Davids, the company's financial officer. Julia has been asked by Rio to perform an analysis of the new mine and present her recommendation on whether the company should open the new mine.

Julia has used the estimates provided by Paul to determine the revenues that could be expected from the mine. She has also projected the expense of opening the mine and the annual operating expenses. If the company opens the mine, it will cost $600 million today, and it will have a cash outflow of $95 million nine years from today in costs associated with closing the mine and reclaiming the area surrounding it. The expected cash flows each year from the mine are shown in the table. Ferdinand Mining has a 12 percent required return on all of its gold mines.

Year	Cash Flow
0	−$600,000,000
1	75,000,000
2	120,000,000
3	160,000,000
4	210,000,000
5	240,000,000
6	160,000,000
7	130,000,000
8	90,000,000
9	−95,000,000

1. Construct a spreadsheet to calculate the payback period, internal rate of return, modified internal rate of return, and net present value of the proposed mine.

2. Based on your analysis, should the company open the mine?

Internet Application Questions

1. Net Present Value analysis assumes market efficiency. In fact, we can back out whether a particular investment had positive NPV by observing the market reaction to its announcement. These are typically made over the wire to news agencies, and are also reported on the company's website. For example, go to the homepage of Enbridge Inc. (enbridge.com/) and click on Media Center. On November 16, 2011, Enbridge announced that it would acquire 50 % stake in Seaway Crude Pipeline Company. Go to the Enbridge Investor Relations site (enbridge.com/InvestorRelations.aspx) and get the company's stock price chart surrounding this date. Assuming that all of the price movement was due to the announcement, discuss whether the Seaway bid was a positive NPV investment for Enbridge.

2. NPV analysis assumes that managers' objective is to maximize shareholders' value. Directors on the boards of Canadian firms are required to look after the best interests of the corporation. Traditionally, this has meant the best interests of shareholders. The law firm of Osler, Hoskin and Harcourt maintains a public website providing detailed descriptions of the duties and responsibilities of Canadian directors (osler.com/NewsResources/Publications/Guides/). What are some of the difficulties in broadening the definition of corporate stakeholders? Do you think shareholders' interests alone should be considered by directors? Why or why not?

3. The Ontario Teachers' Pension Plan has the responsibility to manage the retirement investments of teachers in the Province of Ontario. The plan presents its views and policies on corporate governance under the Governance link at the site otpp.com. From the shareholders' perspective, what role should social responsibility and ethical considerations play in a firm's investment analysis? Can these non-financial factors actually enhance shareholder value in the long term? How should companies take this into account in NPV decisions?

4. Here's a concept most finance classes tiptoe around: a captive capital provider. Can a conglomerate successfully grow around its own capital-providing corporation? Or will internal capital ruin all NPV calculations? For GE Corp (ge.com), the answer is a big affirmative in favour of GE Capital (gecapital.com).

   Do you think this is a successful strategy to imitate by other conglomerates? Do you see parallels with the Main Bank system of financing within Japanese keiretsu firms?

5. You have a project that has an initial cash outflow of −$20,000 and cash inflows of $6,000; $5,000; $4,000; and $3,000, respectively, for the next four years. Go to datadynamica.com/FinCalc/, and select the "On-line NPV IRR Calculator" link. Enter the cash flows. If the required return is 12 percent, what is the NPV of the project? The IRR?

APPENDIX 9A

THE MODIFIED INTERNAL RATE OF RETURN

This appendix presents the MIRR. To illustrate, let's go back to the cash flows in Figure 9.5: −$60, +$155, and −$100. As we saw, there are two IRRs, 25 percent and 33⅓ percent. We next illustrate three different MIRRs, all of which have the property that only one answer will result, thereby eliminating the multiple IRR problem.

METHOD #1: THE DISCOUNTING APPROACH With the discounting approach, the idea is to discount all negative cash flows back to the present at the required return and add them to the initial cost. Then, calculate the IRR. Because only the first modified cash flow is negative, there will be only one IRR. The discount rate used might be the required return, or it might be some other externally supplied rate. We will use the project's required return.

If the required return on the project is 20 percent, then the modified cash flows look like this:

$$\text{Time 0: } -\$60 + \frac{\$100}{1.20^2} = -\$129.44$$

Time 1: + $155

Time 2: + $0

If you calculate the MIRR now, you should get 19.74 percent.

METHOD #2: THE REINVESTMENT APPROACH With the reinvestment approach, we compound all cash flows (positive and negative) except the first out to the end of the project's life and then calculate the IRR. In a sense, we are "reinvesting" the cash flows and not taking them out of the project until the very end. The rate we use could be the required return on the project, or it could be a separately specified "reinvestment rate." We will use the project's required return. When we do, here are the modified cash flows:

Time 0: − $60
Time 1: + 0
Time 2: − $100 + ($155 × 1.2) = $86

The MIRR on this set of cash flows is 19.72 percent, or a little lower than we got using the discounting approach.

METHOD #3: THE COMBINATION APPROACH   As the name suggests, the combination approach blends our first two methods. Negative cash flows are discounted back to the present, and positive cash flows are compounded to the end of the project. In practice, different discount or compounding rates might be used, but we will again stick with the project's required return.

With the combination approach, the modified cash flows are as follows:

Time 0: $-\$60 + \dfrac{\$100}{1.20^2} = -\$129.44$

Time 1: + 0
Time 2: $\$155 \times 1.2 = \$186$

See if you don't agree that the MIRR is 19.87 percent, the highest of the three.

MIRR OR IRR: WHICH IS BETTER?   MIRRs are controversial. At one extreme are those who claim that MIRRs are superior to IRRs, period. For example, by design, they clearly don't suffer from the multiple rate of return problem.

At the other end, detractors say that MIRR should stand for "meaningless internal rate of return." As our example makes clear, one problem with MIRRs is that there are different ways of calculating them, and there is no clear reason to say one of our three methods is better than any other. The differences are small with our simple cash flows, but they could be much larger for a more complex project. Further, it's not clear how to interpret an MIRR. It may look like a rate of return; but it's a rate of return on a modified set of cash flows, not the project's actual cash flows.

We're not going to take sides. However, notice that calculating an MIRR requires discounting, compounding, or both, which leads to two obvious observations. First, if we have the relevant discount rate, why not calculate the NPV and be done with it? Second, because an MIRR depends on an externally supplied discount (or compounding) rate, the answer you get is not truly an "internal" rate of return, which, by definition, depends on only the project's cash flows.

We *will* take a stand on one issue that frequently comes up in this context. The value of a project does not depend on what the firm does with the cash flows generated by that project. A firm might use a project's cash flows to fund other projects, to pay dividends, or to buy an executive jet. It doesn't matter: How the cash flows are spent in the future does not affect their value today. As a result, there is generally no need to consider reinvestment of interim cash flows.

MAKING CAPITAL INVESTMENT DECISIONS

In August 2011, Rogers Communications launched Smart Home Monitoring. This service offers complete home monitoring and an automated solution that lets homeowners control appliances and thermostats remotely using a smartphone. Rogers offered this new technology initially in Ontario and expects to release this service soon in other areas.

The expenditures associated with the launch of Smart Home Monitoring represent a capital budgeting decision. In this chapter, we will investigate, in detail, capital budgeting decisions, how they are made, and how to look at them objectively.

This chapter follows up on the previous one by delving more deeply into capital budgeting. In the last chapter, we saw that cash flow estimates are a critical input into a net present value analysis, but we didn't say much about where these cash flows come from; so we will now examine this question in some detail.

Learning Objectives ▶

After studying this chapter, you should understand:

LO1 How to determine relevant cash flows for a proposed project.

LO2 How to project cash flows and determine if a project is acceptable.

LO3 How to calculate operating cash flow using alternative methods.

LO4 How to calculate the present value of a tax shield on CCA.

LO5 How to evaluate cost-cutting proposals.

LO6 How to analyze replacement decisions.

LO7 How to evaluate the equivalent annual cost of a project.

LO8 How to set a bid price for a project.

So far, we've covered various parts of the capital budgeting decision. Our task in this chapter is to start bringing these pieces together. In particular, we show you how to "spread the numbers" for a proposed investment or project and, based on those numbers, make an initial assessment about whether or not the project should be undertaken.

In the discussion that follows, we focus on setting up a discounted cash flow analysis. From the last chapter, we know that the projected future cash flows are the key element in such an evaluation. Accordingly, we emphasize working with financial and accounting information to come up with these figures.

rogers.com/smarthome/

In evaluating a proposed investment, we pay special attention to deciding what information is relevant to the decision at hand and what information is not. As we shall see, it is easy to overlook important pieces of the capital budgeting puzzle.

We wait until the next chapter to describe in detail how to evaluate the results of our discounted cash flow analysis. Also, where needed, we assume that we know the relevant required return or discount rate reflecting the risk of the project. We continue to defer discussion of this subject to Part 5.

10.1 | Project Cash Flows: A First Look

The effect of undertaking a project is to change the firm's overall cash flows today and in the future. To evaluate a proposed investment, we must consider these changes in the firm's cash flows and then decide whether they add value to the firm. The most important step, therefore, is to decide which cash flows are relevant and which are not.

Relevant Cash Flows

incremental cash flows
The difference between a firm's future cash flows with a project and without the project.

What is a relevant cash flow for a project? The general principle is simple enough: A relevant cash flow for a project is a change in the firm's overall future cash flow that comes about as a direct consequence of the decision to take that project. Because the relevant cash flows are defined in terms of changes in or increments to the firm's existing cash flow, they are called the **incremental cash flows** associated with the project.

The concept of incremental cash flow is central to our analysis, so we state a general definition and refer back to it as needed:

> The incremental cash flows for project evaluation consist of any and all changes in the firm's future cash flows that are a direct consequence of taking the project.

This definition of incremental cash flows has an obvious and important corollary: Any cash flow that exists regardless of whether or not a project is undertaken is not relevant.

The Stand-Alone Principle

stand-alone principle
Evaluation of a project based on the project's incremental cash flows.

In practice, it would be very cumbersome to actually calculate the future total cash flows to the firm with and without a project, especially for a large firm. Fortunately, it is not really necessary to do so. Once we identify the effect of undertaking the proposed project on the firm's cash flows, we need focus only on the resulting project's incremental cash flows. This is called the **stand-alone principle.**

What the stand-alone principle says is that, once we have determined the incremental cash flows from undertaking a project, we can view that project as a kind of minifirm with its own future revenues and costs, its own assets, and, of course, its own cash flows. We are then primarily interested in comparing the cash flows from this minifirm to the cost of acquiring it. An important consequence of this approach is that we evaluate the proposed project purely on its own merits, in isolation from any other activities or projects.

Concept Questions

1. What are the relevant incremental cash flows for project evaluation?
2. What is the stand-alone principle?

10.2 | Incremental Cash Flows

We are concerned here only with those cash flows that are incremental to a project. Looking back at our general definition, it seems easy enough to decide whether a cash flow is incremental or not. Even so, there are a few situations when mistakes are easy to make. In this section, we describe some of these common pitfalls and how to avoid them.

Sunk Costs

sunk cost
A cost that has already been incurred and cannot be removed and therefore should not be considered in an investment decision.

A **sunk cost,** by definition, is a cost we have already paid or have already incurred the liability to pay. Such a cost cannot be changed by the decision today to accept or reject a project. Put another way, the firm has to pay this cost no matter what. Based on our general definition of incremental cash flow, such a cost is clearly not relevant to the decision at hand. So, we are always careful to exclude sunk costs from our analysis.

That a sunk cost is not relevant seems obvious given our discussion. Nonetheless, it's easy to fall prey to the sunk cost fallacy. For example, suppose True North Distillery Ltd. hires a financial consultant to help evaluate whether or not a line of maple sugar liqueur should be launched. When the consultant turns in the report, True North objects to the analysis because the consultant did not include the hefty consulting fee as a cost to the liqueur project.

Who is correct? By now, we know that the consulting fee is a sunk cost, because the consulting fee must be paid whether or not the liqueur line is launched (this is an attractive feature of the consulting business).

A more subtle example of a cost that can sometimes be sunk is overhead. To illustrate, suppose True North Distillery is now considering building a new warehouse to age the maple sugar liqueur. Should a portion of overhead costs be allocated to the proposed warehouse project? If the overhead costs are truly sunk and independent of the project, the answer is no. An example of such an overhead cost is the cost of maintaining a corporate jet for senior executives. But if the new warehouse requires additional reporting, supervision, or legal input, these overheads should be part of the project analysis.

Opportunity Costs

opportunity cost
The most valuable alternative that is given up if a particular investment is undertaken.

When we think of costs, we normally think of out-of-pocket costs, namely, those that require us to actually spend some amount of cash. An **opportunity cost** is slightly different; it requires us to give up a benefit. A common situation arises where another division of a firm already owns some of the assets that a proposed project will be using. For example, we might be thinking of converting an old rustic water-powered mill that we bought years ago for $100,000 into upscale condominiums.

If we undertake this project, there will be no direct cash outflow associated with buying the old mill since we already own it. For purposes of evaluating the condo project, should we then treat the mill as free? The answer is no. The mill is a valuable resource used by the project. If we didn't use it here, we could do something else with it. Like what? The obvious answer is that, at a minimum, we could sell it. Using the mill for the condo complex thus has an opportunity cost: We give up the valuable opportunity to do something else with it.

There is another issue here. Once we agree that the use of the mill has an opportunity cost, how much should the condo project be charged? Given that we paid $100,000, it might seem we should charge this amount to the condo project. Is this correct? The answer is no, and the reason is based on our discussion concerning sunk costs.

The fact that we paid $100,000 some years ago is irrelevant. It's sunk. At a minimum, the opportunity cost that we charge the project is what it would sell for today (net of any selling costs) because this is the amount that we give up by using it instead of selling it.[1]

Side Effects

erosion
The portion of cash flows of a new project that come at the expense of a firm's existing operations.

Remember that the incremental cash flows for a project include all the resulting changes in the *firm's* future cash flows. It would not be unusual for a project to have side, or spillover, effects, both good and bad. For example, when Air Canada began operations of Tango, its first discount airline, in late 2001, it had to recognize the possibility that sales from Tango would come at the expense of sales from its main fleet. The negative impact on cash flows is called **erosion,** and the same general problem anticipated by Air Canada could occur for any multiline consumer product producer or seller.[2] In this case, the cash flows from the new line should be adjusted downwards to reflect lost profits on other lines.

In accounting for erosion, it is important to recognize that any sales lost as a result of launching a new product might be lost anyway because of future competition. Erosion is only relevant when the sales would not otherwise be lost.

---

[1] Economists sometimes use the acronym TANSTAAFL, which is short for "there ain't no such thing as a free lunch", to describe the fact that only very rarely is something truly free. Further, if the asset in question is unique, the opportunity cost might be higher because there might be other valuable projects we could undertake that would use it. However, if the asset in question is of a type that is routinely bought and sold (a used car, perhaps), the opportunity cost is always the going price in the market because that is the cost of buying another one.

[2] More colourfully, erosion is sometimes called *piracy* or *cannibalism*.

disneyworld.disney.go.com
hp.com

Side effects show up in a lot of different ways. For example, one of Walt Disney's concerns when it built Euro Disney was that the new park would drain visitors from the Florida park, a popular vacation destination for Europeans.

There are beneficial side effects, of course. For example, you might think that Hewlett-Packard would have been concerned when the price of a printer that sold for $500 to $600 in 2003 declined to below $100 by 2007, but they weren't. What HP realized was that the big money is in the consumables that printer owners buy to keep their printers going, such as ink-jet cartridges, laser toner cartridges, and special paper. The profit margins for these products are astounding, reaching as high as 70 percent.

Net Working Capital

Normally, a project requires that the firm invest in net working capital in addition to long-term assets. For example, a project generally needs some amount of cash on hand to pay any expenses that arise. In addition, a project needs an initial investment in inventories and accounts receivable (to cover credit sales). Some of this financing would be in the form of amounts owed to suppliers (accounts payable), but the firm has to supply the balance. This balance represents the investment in net working capital.

It's easy to overlook an important feature of net working capital in capital budgeting. As a project winds down, inventories are sold, receivables are collected, bills are paid, and cash balances can be drawn down. These activities free up the net working capital originally invested. So, the firm's investment in project net working capital closely resembles a loan. The firm supplies working capital at the beginning and recovers it toward the end.

Financing Costs

In analyzing a proposed investment, we do not include interest paid or any other financing costs such as dividends or principal repaid, because we are interested in the cash flow generated by the assets from the project. As we mentioned in Chapter 2, interest paid, for example, is a component of cash flow to creditors, not cash flow from assets.

More generally, our goal in project evaluation is to compare the cash flow from a project to the cost of acquiring that project to estimate NPV. The particular mixture of debt and equity that a firm actually chooses to use in financing a project is a managerial variable and primarily determines how project cash flow is divided between owners and creditors. This is not to say that financing costs are unimportant. They are just something to be analyzed separately, and are included as a component of the discount rate. We cover this in later chapters.

Inflation

Because capital investment projects generally have long lives, price inflation or deflation is likely to occur during the project's life. It is possible that the impact of inflation will cancel out—changes in the price level will impact all cash flows equally—and that the required rate of return will also shift exactly with inflation. But this is unlikely, so we need to add a brief discussion of how to handle inflation.

As we explained in more detail in Chapter 7, investors form expectations of future inflation. These are included in the discount rate as investors wish to protect themselves against inflation. Rates including inflation premiums are called nominal rates. In Brazil, for example, where the inflation rate is very high, discount rates are much higher than in Canada.

Given that nominal rates include an adjustment for expected inflation, cash flow estimates must also be adjusted for inflation.[3] Ignoring inflation in estimating the cash inflows would lead to a bias against accepting capital budgeting projects. As we go through detailed examples of capital budgeting, we comment on making these inflation adjustments. Appendix 10A discusses inflation effects further.

---

[3] In Chapter 7, we explained how to calculate real discount rates. The term, *real,* in finance and economics means adjusted for inflation, that is, net of the inflation premium. A less common alternative approach uses real discount rates to discount real cash flows.

Capital Budgeting and Business Taxes in Canada

capital cost allowance (CCA)
Depreciation method under Canadian tax law allowing for the accelerated write-off of property under various classifications.

In Canada, various levels of government commonly offer incentives to promote certain types of capital investment. These include grants, investment tax credits, more favourable rates for **capital cost allowance (CCA),** and subsidized loans. Since these change a project's cash flows, they must be factored into capital budgeting analysis.

Other Issues

There are other things to watch for. First, we are interested only in measuring cash flow. Moreover, we are interested in measuring it when it actually occurs, not when it arises in an accounting sense. Second, we are always interested in after-tax cash flow since tax payments are definitely a cash outflow. In fact, whenever we write incremental cash flows, we mean after-tax incremental cash flows. Remember, however, that after-tax cash flow and accounting profit or net income are different things.

Concept Questions

1. What is a sunk cost? An opportunity cost? Provide examples of each.
2. Explain what erosion is and why it is relevant.
3. Explain why interest paid is not a relevant cash flow for project valuation.
4. Explain how consideration of inflation comes into capital budgeting.

10.3 | Pro Forma Financial Statements and Project Cash Flows

When we begin evaluating a proposed investment, we need a set of pro forma or projected financial statements. Given these, we can develop the projected cash flows from the project. Once we have the cash flows, we can estimate the value of the project using the techniques we described in the previous chapter.

In calculating the cash flows, we make several simplifying assumptions to avoid bogging down in technical details at the outset. We use straight-line depreciation as opposed to capital cost allowance. We also assume that a full year's depreciation can be taken in the first year. In addition, we construct the example so the project's market value equals its book cost when it is scrapped. Later, we address the real-life complexities of capital cost allowance and salvage values introduced in Chapter 2.

Getting Started: Pro Forma Financial Statements

pro forma financial statements
Financial statements projecting future years' operations.

Pro forma financial statements introduced in Chapter 4 are a convenient and easily understood means of summarizing much of the relevant information for a project. To prepare these statements, we need estimates of quantities such as unit sales, the selling price per unit, the variable cost per unit, and total fixed costs. We also need to know the total investment required, including any investment in net working capital.

To illustrate, suppose we think we can sell 50,000 cans of shark attractant per year at a price of $4.30 per can. It costs us about $2.50 per can to make the attractant, and a new product such as this one typically has only a three-year life (perhaps because the customer base dwindles rapidly). We require a 20 percent return on new products.

Fixed operating costs for the project, including such things as rent on the production facility, would run $12,000 per year.[4] Further, we need to invest $90,000 in manufacturing equipment. For simplicity, we assume this $90,000 will be 100 percent depreciated over the three-year life of

---

[4] By fixed cost, we literally mean a cash outflow that occurs regardless of the level of sales. This should not be confused with some sort of accounting period charge.

the project in equal annual amounts.[5] Furthermore, the cost of removing the equipment roughly equals its actual value in three years, so it would be essentially worthless on a market value basis as well. Finally, the project requires a $20,000 investment in net working capital. This amount remains constant over the life of the project. In Table 10.1, we organize these initial projections by first preparing the pro forma statements of comprehensive income.

TABLE 10.1

Projected statement of comprehensive income, shark attractant project

Sales (50,000 units at $4.30/unit)	$215,000
Variable costs ($2.50/unit)	125,000
Gross profit	$ 90,000
Fixed costs	$ 12,000
Depreciation ($90,000/3)	30,000
EBIT	$ 48,000
Taxes (40%)	19,200
Net income	$ 28,800

Once again, notice that we have not deducted any interest expense. This is always so. As we described earlier, interest paid is a financing expense, not a component of operating cash flow.

We can also prepare a series of abbreviated statements of financial position that show the capital requirements for the project as we've done in Table 10.2. Here we have net working capital of $20,000 in each year. Fixed assets are $90,000 at the start of the project's life (Year 0), and they decline by the $30,000 in depreciation each year, ending at zero. Notice that the total investment given here for future years is the total book or accounting value, not market value.

TABLE 10.2

Projected capital requirements, shark attractant project

	Year			
	0	1	2	3
Net working capital	$ 20,000	$20,000	$20,000	$0
Net fixed assets	90,000	60,000	30,000	0
Total investment	$110,000	$80,000	$50,000	$0

At this point, we need to start converting this accounting information into cash flows. We consider how to do this next.

Project Cash Flows

To develop the cash flows from a project, we need to recall (from Chapter 2) that cash flow from assets has three components: operating cash flow, capital spending, and additions to net working capital. To evaluate a project or minifirm, we need to arrive at estimates for each of these.
Once we have estimates of the components of cash flow, we can calculate cash flow for our minifirm just as we did in Chapter 2 for an entire firm:

Project cash flow = Project operating cash flow
 — Project additions to net working capital
 — Project capital spending

We consider these components next.

[5] We also assume that a full year's depreciation can be taken in the first year. Together with the use of straight-line depreciation, this unrealistic assumption smooths the exposition. We bring in real-life complications of capital cost allowance and taxes (introduced in Chapter 2) later in the chapter.

PROJECT OPERATING CASH FLOW   To determine the operating cash flow associated with a project, recall the definition of operating cash flow:

$$\text{Operating cash flow} = \text{Earnings before interest and taxes (EBIT)}$$
$$+ \text{Depreciation}$$
$$- \text{Taxes}$$

As before, taxes in our equation are taxes assuming that there is no interest expense. To illustrate the calculation of operating cash flow, we use the projected information from the shark attractant project. For ease of reference, Table 10.1 contains the statement of comprehensive income.

Given this statement in Table 10.1, calculating the operating cash flow is very straightforward. As we see in Table 10.3, projected operating cash flow for the shark attractant project is $58,800.

TABLE 10.3

Projected operating cash flow, shark attractant project

EBIT	$48,000
Depreciation	30,000
Taxes	–19,200
Operating cash flow	$58,800

PROJECT NET WORKING CAPITAL AND CAPITAL SPENDING   We next need to take care of the fixed asset and net working capital requirements. Based on our preceding statements of financial position, the firm must spend $90,000 up front for fixed assets and invest an additional $20,000 in net working capital. The immediate outflow is thus $110,000. At the end of the project's life, the fixed assets are worthless, but the firm recovers the $20,000 tied up in working capital.[6] This leads to a $20,000 inflow in the last year.

On a purely mechanical level, notice that whenever we have an investment in net working capital, that investment has to be recovered; in other words, the same number needs to appear with the opposite sign.

Project Total Cash Flow and Value

Given the information we've accumulated, we can finish the preliminary cash flow analysis as illustrated in Table 10.4.

Now that we have cash flow projections, we are ready to apply the various criteria we discussed in the last chapter. The NPV at the 20 percent required return is:

$$\text{NPV} = -\$110,000 + \$58,800/1.2 + \$58,800/1.2^2 + 78,800/1.2^3$$
$$= \$25,435$$

TABLE 10.4

Projected total cash flows, shark attractant project

	Year			
	0	1	2	3
Operating cash flow	0	$58,800	$58,800	$58,800
Additions to NWC	–$ 20,000	0	0	20,000
Capital spending	–90,000	0	0	0
Total cash flow	–$110,000	$58,800	$58,800	$78,800
DCF	–$110,000	$49,000	$40,833	$45,602
NPV	$ 25,435			

---

[6] In reality, the firm would probably recover something less than 100 percent of this amount because of bad debts, inventory loss, and so on. If we wanted to, we could just assume that, for example, only 90 percent was recovered and proceed from there.

So, based on these projections, the project creates more than $25,000 in value and should be accepted. Also, the return on this investment obviously exceeds 20 percent (since the NPV is positive at 20 percent). After some trial and error, we find that the IRR works out to be about 34 percent.

In addition, if required, we could go ahead and calculate the payback and the average accounting return (AAR). Inspection of the cash flows shows that the payback on this project is just a little under two years (check that it's about 1.85 years).[7]

From the last chapter, the AAR is average net income divided by average book value. The net income each year is $28,800. The average (in thousands) of the four book values (from Table 10.2) for total investment is ($110 + 80 + 50 + 20)/4 = $65, so the AAR is $28,800/65,000 = 44.31 percent.[8] We've already seen that the return on this investment (the IRR) is about 34 percent. The fact that the AAR is larger illustrates again why the AAR cannot be meaningfully interpreted as the return on a project.

Concept Questions

1. What is the definition of project operating cash flow? How does this differ from net income?
2. In the shark attractant project, why did we add back the firm's net working capital investment in the final year?

10.4 | More on Project Cash Flow

In this section, we take a closer look at some aspects of project cash flow. In particular, we discuss project net working capital in more detail. We then examine current tax laws regarding depreciation. Finally, we work through a more involved example of the capital investment decision.

A Closer Look at Net Working Capital

In calculating operating cash flow, we did not explicitly consider the fact that some of our sales might be on credit. Also, we may not have actually paid some of the costs shown. In either case, the cash flow has not yet occurred. We show here that these possibilities are not a problem as long as we don't forget to include additions to net working capital in our analysis. This discussion thus emphasizes the importance and the effect of doing so.

Suppose that during a particular year of a project we have the following simplified statement of comprehensive income:

Sales	$500
Costs	310
Net income	$190

Depreciation and taxes are zero. No fixed assets are purchased during the year. Also, to illustrate a point, we assume the only components of net working capital are accounts receivable and payable. The beginning and ending amounts for these accounts are:

	Beginning of Year	End of Year	Change
Accounts receivable	$880	$910	+$30
Accounts payable	550	605	+ 55
Net working capital	$330	$305	−$25

Based on this information, what is total cash flow for the year? We can begin by mechanically applying what we have been discussing to come up with the answer. Operating cash flow in this particular case is the same as EBIT since there are no taxes or depreciation; thus, it equals $190.

---

[7] We're guilty of a minor inconsistency here. When we calculated the NPV and the IRR, we assumed all the cash flows occurred at end of year. When we calculated the payback, we assumed the cash flow occurred uniformly through the year.

[8] Notice that the average total book value is not the initial total of $110,000 divided by 2. The reason is that the $20,000 in working capital doesn't depreciate. Notice that the average book value could be calculated as (beginning book value + ending book value)/2 = ($110,000 + 20,000)/2 = $65,000. Also, the ending book value is taken as $20,000 instead of zero as the NWC is returned an instant after the project ends, i.e. after 3 years.

Also, notice that net working capital actually *declined* by $25, so the addition to net working capital is negative. This just means that $25 was freed up during the year. There was no capital spending, so the total cash flow for the year is:

$$\text{Total cash flow} = \text{Operating cash flow} - \text{Additions to NWC} - \text{Capital spending}$$
$$= \$190 - (-\$25) - \$0$$
$$= \$215$$

Now, we know that this $215 total cash flow has to be "dollars in" less "dollars out" for the year. We could, therefore, ask a different question: What were cash revenues for the year? Also, what were cash costs?

To determine cash revenues, we need to look more closely at net working capital. During the year, we had sales of $500. However, accounts receivable rose by $30 over the same time period. What does this mean? The $30 increase tells us that sales exceeded collections by $30. In other words, we haven't yet received the cash from $30 of the $500 in sales. As a result, our cash inflow is $500 − 30 = $470. In general, cash income is sales minus the increase in accounts receivable.

Cash outflows can be similarly determined. We show costs of $310 on the statement of comprehensive income, but accounts payable increased by $55 during the year. This means we have not yet paid $55 of the $310, so cash costs for the period are just $310 − 55 = $255. In other words, in this case, cash costs equal costs less the increase in accounts payable.[9]

Putting this information together, cash inflows less cash outflows is $470 − 255 = $215, just as we had before. Notice that:

$$\text{Cash flow} = \text{Cash inflow} - \text{Cash outflow}$$
$$= (\$500 - 30) - (\$310 - 55)$$
$$= (\$500 - \$310) - (30 - 55)$$
$$= \text{Operating cash flow} - \text{Change in NWC}$$
$$= \$190 - (-25) = \$215$$

More generally, this example illustrates that including net working capital changes in our calculations has the effect of adjusting for the discrepancy between accounting sales and costs and actual cash receipts and payments.

EXAMPLE 10.1: Cash Collections and Costs

For the year just completed, Combat Wombat Telestat Ltd. (CWT) reports sales of $998 and costs of $734. You have collected the following beginning and ending statement of financial position information:

	Beginning	Ending
Accounts receivable	$100	$110
Inventory	100	80
Accounts payable	100	70
Net working capital	$100	$120

Based on these figures, what are cash inflows? Cash outflows? What happened to each? What is net cash flow?

Sales were $998, but receivables rose by $10. So cash collections were $10 less than sales, or $988. Costs were $734, but inventories fell by $20. This means we didn't replace $20 worth of inventory, so cash costs are actually overstated by this amount. Also, payables fell by $30. This means that, on a net basis, we actually paid our suppliers $30 more than the value of what we received from them, resulting in a $30 understatement of cash costs. Adjusting for these events, cash costs are $734 − 20 + 30 = $744. Net cash flow is $988 − 744 = $244.

Finally, notice that net working capital increased by $20 overall. We can check our answer by noting that the original accounting sales less costs of $998 − 734 is $264. In addition, CWT spent $20 on net working capital, so the net result is a cash flow of $264 − 20 = $244, as we calculated.

Depreciation and Capital Cost Allowance

As we note elsewhere, accounting depreciation is a noncash deduction. As a result, depreciation has cash flow consequences only because it influences the tax bill. The way that depreciation is computed for tax purposes is thus the relevant method for capital investment decisions. Chapter

---

[9] If there were other accounts, we might have to make some further adjustments. For example, a net increase in inventory would be a cash outflow.

2 introduced the capital cost allowance (CCA) system—Canada Revenue Agency's version of depreciation. We use CCA in the example that follows.

An Example: The Majestic Mulch and Compost Company (MMCC)

At this point, we want to go through a somewhat more involved capital budgeting analysis. Keep in mind as you read that the basic approach here is exactly the same as that in the earlier shark attractant example. We have only added more real-world detail (and a lot more numbers).
MMCC is investigating the feasibility of a new line of power mulching tools aimed at the growing number of home composters. Based on exploratory conversations with buyers for large garden shops, we project unit sales as follows:

Year	Unit Sales
1	3000
2	5000
3	6000
4	6500
5	6000
6	5000
7	4000
8	3000

The new power mulcher would be priced to sell at $120 per unit to start. When the competition catches up after three years, however, we anticipate that the price would drop to $110.[10]

The power mulcher project requires $20,000 in net working capital at the start. Subsequently, total net working capital at the end of each year would be about 15 percent of sales for that year. The variable cost per unit is $60, and total fixed costs are $25,000 per year.

It costs about $800,000 to buy the equipment necessary to begin production. This investment is primarily in industrial equipment and thus falls in Class 8 with a CCA rate of 20 percent.[11] The equipment will actually be worth about $150,000 in eight years. The relevant tax rate is 40 percent, and the required return is 15 percent. Based on this information, should MMCC proceed?

OPERATING CASH FLOWS   There is a lot of information here that we need to organize. The first thing we can do is calculate projected sales. Sales in the first year are projected at 3000 units at $120 apiece, or $360,000 total. The remaining figures are shown in Table 10.5.

TABLE 10.5

Projected revenues,
power mulcher project

Year	Unit Price	Unit Sales	Revenues
1	$120	3000	$360,000
2	120	5000	600,000
3	120	6000	720,000
4	110	6500	715,000
5	110	6000	660,000
6	110	5000	550,000
7	110	4000	440,000
8	110	3000	330,000

Next, we compute the CCA on the $800,000 investment in Table 10.6. Notice how, under the half-year rule (Chapter 2), UCC is only $400,000 in Year 1.[12]

---

[10] To be consistent, these prices include an inflation estimate.

[11] Chapter 2 explains CCA classes.

[12] Companies may purchase a capital item any time within the year, so it is assumed that they purchase it halfway through the year.

TABLE 10.6

	Year	Beginning UCC	CCA	Ending UCC
Annual CCA, power mulcher project (Class 8, 20% rate)	1	$400,000	$ 80,000	$320,000
	2	720,000	144,000	576,000
	3	576,000	115,200	460,800
	4	460,800	92,160	368,640
	5	368,640	73,728	294,912
	6	294,912	58,982	235,930
	7	235,930	47,186	188,744
	8	188,744	37,749	150,995

With this information, we can prepare the pro forma statements of comprehensive income, as shown in Table 10.7.

TABLE 10.7

Projected statements of comprehensive income, power mulcher project

	Year							
	1	2	3	4	5	6	7	8
Unit price	$ 120	$ 120	$ 120	$ 110	$ 110	$ 110	$ 110	$ 110
Unit sales	3,000	5,000	6,000	6,500	6,000	5,000	4,000	3,000
Revenues	$360,000	$600,000	$720,000	$715,000	$660,000	$550,000	$440,000	$330,000
Variable costs	180,000	300,000	360,000	390,000	360,000	300,000	240,000	180,000
Fixed costs	25,000	25,000	25,000	25,000	25,000	25,000	25,000	25,000
CCA	80,000	144,000	115,200	92,160	73,728	58,982	47,186	37,749
EBIT	75,000	131,000	219,800	207,840	201,272	166,018	127,814	87,251
Taxes	30,000	52,400	87,920	83,136	80,509	66,407	51,126	34,901
Net income	$ 45,000	$ 78,600	$131,880	$124,704	$120,763	$ 99,611	$ 76,688	$ 52,350

From here, computing the operating cash flows is straightforward. The results are illustrated in the first part of Table 10.8.

ADDITIONS TO NWC   Now that we have the operating cash flows, we need to determine the additions to NWC. By assumption, net working capital requirements change as sales change. In each year, we generally either add to or recover some of our project net working capital. Recalling that NWC starts at $20,000 and then rises to 15 percent of sales, we can calculate the amount of NWC for each year as illustrated in Table 10.9.

As illustrated in Table 10.9, during the first year, net working capital grows from $20,000 to .15 × 360,000 = $54,000. The increase in net working capital for the year is thus $54,000 − 20,000 = $34,000. The remaining figures are calculated the same way.

Remember that an increase in net working capital is a cash outflow and a decrease in net working capital is a cash inflow. This means that a negative sign in this table represents net working capital returning to the firm. Thus, for example, $16,500 in NWC flows back to the firm in Year 6. Over the project's life, net working capital builds to a peak of $108,000 and declines from there as sales begin to drop.

We show the result for additions to net working capital in the second part of Table 10.8. Notice that at the end of the project's life there is $49,500 in net working capital still to be recovered. Therefore, in the last year, the project returns $16,500 of NWC during the year and then returns the remaining $49,500 for a total of $66,000 (the addition to NWC is −$66,000).

TABLE 10.8

Projected cash flows, power mulcher project

	0	1	2	3	4	5	6	7	8
					Year				

I. Operating Cash Flow

	0	1	2	3	4	5	6	7	8
EBIT		$ 75,000	$131,000	$219,800	$207,840	$201,272	$166,018	$127,814	$ 87,251
CCA		80,000	144,000	115,200	92,160	73,728	58,982	47,186	37,749
Taxes		30,000	52,400	87,920	83,136	80,509	66,407	51,126	34,901
Operating cash flow		$125,000	$222,600	$247,080	$216,864	$194,491	$158,593	$123,874	$ 90,099

II. Net Working Capital

	0	1	2	3	4	5	6	7	8
Initial NWC	$ 20,000								
NWC increases		$ 34,000	$ 36,000	$ 18,000	−$ 750	−$ 8,250	−$ 16,500	−$ 16,500	−$ 16,500
NWC recovery									−$ 49,500
Additions to NWC	$ 20,000	$ 34,000	$ 36,000	$ 18,000	−$ 750	−$ 8,250	−$ 16,500	−$ 16,500	−$ 66,000

III. Capital Spending

	0	1	2	3	4	5	6	7	8
Initial outlay	$800,000								
After-tax salvage									−$150,000
Capital spending	$800,000								−$150,000

TABLE 10.9

Additions to net working capital, power mulcher project

Year	Revenues	Net Working Capital	Increase
0		$ 20,000	
1	$360,000	54,000	$ 34,000
2	600,000	90,000	36,000
3	720,000	108,000	18,000
4	715,000	107,250	−750
5	660,000	99,000	−8,250
6	550,000	82,500	−16,500
7	440,000	66,000	−16,500
8	330,000	49,500	−16,500

Finally, we have to account for the long-term capital invested in the project. In this case, we invest $800,000 at Time 0. By assumption, this equipment would be worth $150,000 at the end of the project. It will have an undepreciated capital cost of $150,995 at that time as shown in Table 10.6. As we discussed in Chapter 2, this $995 shortfall of market value below UCC creates a tax refund ($995 × 40 percent tax rate = $398) only if MMCC has no continuing Class 8 assets. However, we assume the company would continue in this line of manufacturing so there is no tax refund. Making this assumption is standard practice unless we have specific information about plans to close an asset class. Given our assumption, the difference of $995 stays in the asset pool, creating future tax shields.[13] The investment and salvage are shown in the third part of Table 10.8.

---

[13] We show the detailed calculations in Section 10.6.

TABLE 10.10

Projected total cash flow, power mulcher project

	Year								
	0	1	2	3	4	5	6	7	8
Operating cash flow		$125,000	$222,600	$247,080	$216,864	$194,491	$158,593	$123,874	$ 90,099
Additions to NWC	−$ 20,000	− 34,000	− 36,000	− 18,000	750	8,250	16,500	16,500	66,000
Capital spending	− 800,000	0	0	0	0	0	0	0	150,000
Total project cash flow	−$820,000	$ 91,000	$186,600	$229,080	$217,614	$202,741	$175,093	$140,374	$306,099
Cumulative cash flow	−$820,000	−$729,000	−$542,400	−$313,320	−$ 95,706	$107,035	$282,128	$422,503	$728,602
Discounted cash flow @ 15%	−$820,000	$ 79,130	$141,096	$150,624	$124,422	$100,798	$ 75,698	$ 52,772	$100,064
NPV	$ 4,604								
IRR	15.15%								
PB	4.47								

TOTAL CASH FLOW AND VALUE   We now have all the cash flow pieces, and we put them together in Table 10.10. Note that an increase in net working capital is a cash outflow and a decrease in net working capital is a cash inflow and that a negative sign shows working capital returning to the firm. In addition to the total project cash flows, we have calculated the cumulative cash flows and the discounted cash flows. At this point, it's essentially "plug and chug" to calculate the net present value, internal rate of return, and payback.

If we sum the discounted flows and the initial investment, the net present value (at 15 percent) works out to be $4,604. This is positive, so, based on these preliminary projections, the power mulcher project is acceptable. The internal or DCF rate of return is slightly greater than 15 percent since the NPV is positive. It works out to be 15.15, again indicating that the project is acceptable.[14]

Looking at the cumulative cash flows, we see that the project has almost paid back after four years since the cumulative cash flow is almost zero at that time. As indicated, the fractional year works out to be 95,706/202,741 = .47, so the payback is 4.47 years. We can't say whether or not this is good since we don't have a benchmark for MMCC. This is the usual problem with payback periods.

CONCLUSION   This completes our preliminary DCF analysis. Where do we go from here? If we have a great deal of confidence in our projections, there is no further analysis to be done. We should begin production and marketing immediately. It is unlikely that this would be the case. For one thing, NPV is not that far above zero and IRR is only marginally more than the 15 percent required rate of return. Remember that the result of our analysis is an estimate of NPV, and we usually have less than complete confidence in our projections. This means we have more work to do. In particular, we almost surely want to evaluate the quality of our estimates. We take up this subject in the next chapter. For now, we look at alternative definitions of operating cash flow, and we illustrate some different cases that arise in capital budgeting.

Concept Questions

1. Why is it important to consider additions to net working capital in developing cash flows? What is the effect of doing so?
2. How is depreciation calculated for fixed assets under current tax law? What effect do expected salvage value and estimated economic life have on the calculated capital cost allowance?

---

[14] Appendix 10B shows how to analyze Majestic Mulch using a spreadsheet.

10.5 | Alternative Definitions of Operating Cash Flow

The analysis we have been through in the previous section is quite general and can be adapted to almost any capital investment problem. In the next section, we illustrate some particularly useful variations. Before we do so, we need to discuss the fact that different definitions of project operating cash flow are commonly used, both in practice and in finance texts.

As we see, the different definitions of operating cash flow all measure the same thing. If they are used correctly, they all produce the same answer, and one is not necessarily any better or more useful than another. Unfortunately, the fact that alternative definitions are used sometimes leads to confusion. For this reason, we examine several of these variations next to see how they are related.

In the following discussion, keep in mind that when we speak of cash flow, we literally mean dollars in less dollars out. This is all that we are concerned with. Different definitions of operating cash flow simply amount to different ways of manipulating basic information about sales, costs, depreciation, and taxes to get at cash flow.

To begin, it will be helpful to define the following:

$$OCF = \text{Project operating cash flow}$$
$$S = \text{Sales}$$
$$C = \text{Operating costs}$$
$$D = \text{Depreciation for tax purposes, i.e., CCA}^{15}$$
$$T_C = \text{Corporate tax rate}$$

For a particular project and year under consideration, suppose we have the following estimates:

$$S = \$1,500$$
$$C = \$700$$
$$D = \$600$$
$$T_C = 40\%$$

With these definitions, notice that EBIT is:

$$
\begin{aligned}
EBIT &= S - C - D \\
&= \$1,500 - 700 - 600 \\
&= \$200
\end{aligned}
$$

Once again, we assume no interest is paid, so the tax bill is:

$$
\begin{aligned}
\text{Taxes} &= EBIT \times T_C = (S - C - D) \times T_C \\
&= \$200 \times .40 = \$80
\end{aligned}
$$

When we put all of this together, project operating cash flow (OCF) is:

$$
\begin{aligned}
OCF &= EBIT + D - \text{Taxes} \\
&= (S - C - D) + D - (S - C - D) \times T_C \\
&= \$200 + 600 - 80 = \$720
\end{aligned}
\qquad [10.1]
$$

If we take a closer look at this definition of OCF, we see that there are other definitions that could be used. We consider these next.

The Bottom-Up Approach

Since we are ignoring any financing expenses such as interest in our calculations of project OCF, we can write project net income as:

$$
\begin{aligned}
\text{Project net income} &= EBIT - \text{Taxes} \\
&= (S - C - D) - (S - C - D) \times T_C \\
&= (S - C - D) \times (1 - T_C) \\
&= (\$1,500 - 700 - 600) \times (1 - .40) \\
&= \$200 \times .60 \\
&= \$120
\end{aligned}
$$

---

[15] In this discussion, we use the terms *depreciation* and *CCA* interchangeably.

With this in mind, we can develop a slightly different and very common approach to the cash flow question by restating Equation (10.1) as follows:

$$
\begin{aligned}
\text{OCF} &= (S - C - D) + D - (S - C - D) \times T_C \\
&= (S - C - D) \times (1 - T_C) + D \\
&= \text{Project net income} + \text{Depreciation} \qquad \text{[10.2]} \\
&= \$120 + 600 \\
&= \$720
\end{aligned}
$$

This is the bottom-up approach. Here we start with the accountant's bottom line (net income) and add back any non-cash deductions such as depreciation. It is important to remember that this definition of operating cash flow as net income plus depreciation is only equivalent to our definition, and thus correct, when there is no interest expense subtracted in the calculation of net income.

For the shark attractant project, net income was $28,800 and depreciation was $30,000, so the bottom-up calculation is:

$$
\text{OCF} = \$28,800 + 30,000 = \$58,800
$$

This again is the correct answer.

The Top-Down Approach

A closely related, and perhaps more obvious, manipulation of our definition is to cancel the depreciation expense where possible:

$$
\begin{aligned}
\text{OCF} &= (S - C - D) + D - (S - C - D) \times T_C \\
&= (S - C) - (S - C - D) \times T_C \\
&= \text{Sales} - \text{Costs} - \text{Taxes} \qquad \text{[10.3]} \\
&= \$1,500 - 700 - 80 = \$720
\end{aligned}
$$

This is the top-down approach. Here we start at the top of the statement of comprehensive income with sales and work our way down to net cash flow by subtracting costs, taxes, and other expenses. Along the way, we simply leave out any strictly non-cash items such as depreciation.

For the shark attractant project, the top-down cash flow can be readily calculated. With sales of $215,000, total costs (fixed plus variable) of $137,000, and a tax bill of $19,200, the OCF is:

$$
\text{OCF} = \$215,000 - 137,000 - 19,200 = \$58,800
$$

This is just as we had before.

The Tax Shield Approach

The final variation on our basic definition of OCF is the tax shield approach. This approach will be very useful for some problems we consider in the next section. The tax shield definition of OCF is:

$$
\begin{aligned}
\text{OCF} &= (S - C - D) + D - (S - C - D) \times T_C \qquad \text{[10.4]} \\
&= (S - C) \times (1 - T_C) + D \times T_C
\end{aligned}
$$

With our numbers, this works out to be:

$$
\begin{aligned}
&= (S - C) \times (1 - T_C) + D \times T_C \\
&= \$800 \times .60 + \$600 \times .40 \\
&= \$480 + 240 \\
&= \$720
\end{aligned}
$$

This is just as we had before.

This approach views OCF as having two components: The first part, $(S - C) \times (1 - T_C)$, is what the project's cash flow would be if there were no depreciation expense. In this case, this would-have-been cash flow is $480.

depreciation (CCA) tax shield
Tax saving that results from the CCA deduction, calculated as depreciation multiplied by the corporate tax rate.

The second part of OCF in this expression, $D \times T_C$, is called the **depreciation (CCA) tax shield.** We know that depreciation is a non-cash expense. The only cash flow effect from deducting depreciation is to reduce our taxes, a benefit to us. At the current 40 percent corporate tax rate, every dollar in CCA expense saves us 40 cents in taxes. So, in our example, the $600 in depreciation saves us $600 \times .40 = $240 in taxes.

TABLE 10.11

Alternative definitions of operating cash flow

Approach	Formula
Basic	OCF = EBIT + Depreciation − Taxes
Bottom-up	OCF = Net income + Depreciation
Top-down	OCF = Sales − Costs − Taxes
Tax shield	OCF = (Sales − Costs) $(1 - T_c)$ + Depreciation × T_c

For the shark attractant project we considered earlier in the chapter, the CCA tax shield would be $30,000 × .40 = $12,000. The after-tax value for sales less costs would be ($240,000 − 162,000) × (1 − .40) = $46,800. Adding these together yields the right answer:

OCF = $46,800 + 12,000 = $58,800

This verifies this approach.

Conclusion

Table 10.11 summarizes the four approaches to computing OCF. Now that we've seen that all these definitions are the same, you're probably wondering why everybody doesn't just agree on one of them. One reason, as we see in the next section, is that different definitions are useful in different circumstances. The best one to use is whichever happens to be the most convenient for the problem at hand.

10.6 | Applying the Tax Shield Approach to the Majestic Mulch and Compost Company Project

If you look back over our analysis of MMCC, you'll see that most of the number crunching involved finding CCA, EBIT, and net income figures. The tax shield approach has the potential to save us considerable time.[16] To realize on that potential, we do the calculations in a different order from Table 10.10. Instead of adding the cash flow components down the columns for each year and finding the present value of the total cash flows, we find the present values of each source of cash flows and add the present values.

The first source of cash flow is $(S − C)(1 − T_C)$ as shown for each year on the first line of Table 10.12. The figure for the first year, $93,000, is the first part of the OCF equation.

TABLE 10.12

Tax shield solution, power mulcher project

		Year							
	0	1	2	3	4	5	6	7	8
$(S − C)(1 − T_c)$		$93,000	$165,000	$201,000	$180,000	$165,000	$135,000	$105,000	$ 75,000
Additions to NWC	−$20,000	−34,000	−36,000	−18,000	750	8,250	16,500	16,500	66,000
Capital spending	−800,000								150,000

Totals	
PV of $(S − C)(1 − T_c)$	$645,099
PV of additions to NWC	−49,179
PV of capital spending	−750,965
PV of CCA tax shield	159,649
NPV	$ 4,604

---

[16] This is particularly true if we set it up using a spreadsheet. See Appendix 10B.

TABLE 10.13

PV of tax shield on CCA

Year	Tax Shield		
	CCA	.40 × CCA	PV at 15%
1	$ 80,000	$32,000	$27,826
2	144,000	57,600	43,554
3	115,200	46,080	30,298
4	92,160	36,864	21,077
5	73,728	29,491	14,662
6	58,982	23,593	10,200
7	47,186	18,874	7,096
8	37,749	15,100	4,936
		PV of tax shield on CCA	$159,649

$$OCF = (S - C)(1 - T_C) + DT_C$$
$$= (360,000 - 180,000 - 25,000)(1 - .40) + 80,000(.40)$$
$$= 93,000 + 32,000 = \$125,000$$

Calculating the present value of the $93,000 for the first year and adding the present values of the other $(S - C)(1 - T_C)$ figures in Table 10.12 gives a total present value for this source of $645,099 as seen in the lower part of Table 10.12.

The second term is the tax shield on CCA for the first year. Table 10.13 reproduces the first year's tax shield of $32,000 along with the corresponding tax shields for each year. The total present value of the CCA tax shield is shown as $159,649.

The additions to net working capital and capital expenditure are essentially the same as in Table 10.10. Their present values are shown in the lower part of Table 10.12. The NPV is the sum of the present value of the four sources of cash flow. The answer, $4,604 is identical to what we found earlier in Table 10.10.

Present Value of the Tax Shield on CCA

Further time savings are possible by using a formula that replaces the detailed calculation of yearly CCA. The formula is based on the idea that tax shields from CCA continue in perpetuity as long as there are assets remaining in the CCA class.[17] This idea is important because it gives us insight into when we can apply the formula in solving a problem in practice. The formula applies when the CCA asset class (or pool) will remain open when the project is completed. As we explained earlier, it is standard practice to assume that the asset class remains open unless we have specific information to the contrary. If, however, in a special case, we find that the pool will be closed out at the end of the project's life, we should not use this formula. The pool will only close if there are no remaining assets in the class. If this happens, the annual CCA values should be calculated to determine the UCC at the end of the project. If there is a terminal loss (i.e., the salvage value is less than this UCC), then there is a further tax shield when the asset is sold. If there is a gain (i.e., the salvage value is greater than this UCC), then there will be a recapture of a portion of the tax savings.[18] To calculate the present value of the tax shield on CCA, we find the present value of an infinite stream of tax shields abstracting from two practical implications—the half-year rule for CCA and disposal of the asset. We then adjust the formula.

Our derivation uses the following terms:

I = Total capital investment in the asset which is added to the pool
d = CCA rate for the asset class
T_C = Company's marginal tax rate

---

[17] Strictly speaking, the UCC for a class remains positive as long as there are physical assets in the class and the proceeds from disposal of assets is less than total UCC for the class.

[18] Alternatively, the formula could be applied and the end-of-project effects calculated and discounted appropriately.

$$k = \text{Discount rate}$$
$$S_n = \text{Salvage or disposal value of the asset in year } n$$
$$M_n = \text{Asset life in years}$$

We can use the dividend valuation formula from Chapter 8 to derive the present value of the CCA tax shield. Recall that when dividends grow at a constant rate, g, the stock price is

$$P_0 = \frac{D_1}{k + g}$$

To apply this to the tax shield problem, we recognize that the formula can be generalized for any growing perpetuity where for example, Payment 3 = (Payment 2) $\times$ (1 + g)

$$PV = \frac{\text{1st payment}}{(\text{Discount rate}) + (\text{Growth rate})}$$

Since we are temporarily ignoring the half-year rule, the growth rate in CCA payments is equal to $(-d)$. The declining UCC value implies negative growth. Thus, to account for the decline, the growth rate equals $(-d)$. For example, in Table 10.13:

$$CCA_3 = CCA_2 (1 + (-d))$$
$$CCA_3 = 144,000 (1 + (-.20))$$
$$CCA_3 = 144,000 (.8) = 115,200$$

Given the growth rate as $(-d)$, we need the 1st payment to complete the formula. This is the first year's tax shield IdT_C. We can now complete the formula:

$$PV(\text{CCA tax shield}) = \frac{\text{1st payment}}{(\text{Discount rate}) - (\text{Growth rate})}$$

$$= \frac{IdT_C}{k - (-d)}$$

$$= \frac{IdT_C}{k + d}$$

The next step is to extend the formula to adjust for CRA's half-year rule. This rule implies that a firm adds one-half of the incremental capital cost of a new project in Year 1 and the other half in Year 2. The result is that we now calculate the present value of the tax shield in two parts: The present value of the stream starting the first year is simply one-half of the original value:

$$PV \text{ of 1st half} = 1/2 \frac{IdT_C}{k + d}$$

The PV of the second half (deferred one year) is the same quantity (bracketed term) discounted back to time zero. The total present value of the tax shield on CCA under the half-year rule is the sum of the two present values.

$$PV \text{ tax shield on CCA} = \frac{1/2 \, IdT_C}{k + d} + \left[\frac{1/2 \, IdT_C}{k + d} \right] / (1 + k)$$

With a little algebra we can simplify the formula:

$$PV = \frac{1/2 \, IdT_C}{k + d} [1 + 1/(1 + k)] = \frac{1/2 \, IdT_C}{k + d} \left[\frac{1 + k + 1}{1 + k} \right]$$

$$PV = \frac{IdT_C}{k + d} \left[\frac{1 + .5k}{1 + k} \right]$$

The final adjustment for salvage-value begins with the present value in the salvage year, n of future tax shields beginning in Year $n + 1$:

$$\frac{S_n dT_c}{d + k}$$

We discount this figure back to today and subtract it to get the complete formula:[19]

$$PV \text{ tax shield on CCA} = \frac{[IdT_c]}{d + k} \times \frac{[1 + .5k]}{1 + k} - \frac{S_n dT_c}{d + k} \times \frac{1}{(1 + k)^n} \qquad [10.5]$$

---

[19] By not adjusting the salvage value for the half-year rule, we assume there will be no new investment in year n.

Using the first part of the formula, the present value of the tax shield on MMCC's project is $170,932 assuming the tax shield goes on in perpetuity:

$$= \frac{800,000(.20)(.40)}{.20 + .15} \times \frac{1 + .5 \times (.15)}{1 + .15}$$
$$= 182,857 \times 1.08/1.15 = \$170,932$$

The adjustment for the salvage value is

$$\frac{-150,000(.20)(.40)}{.20 + .15} \times \frac{1}{(1 + .15)^8}$$

$$= -34,286 \times 1/(1.15)^8 = -\$11,208$$

The present value of the tax shield on CCA is the sum of the two present values:

$$\text{Present value of tax shield from CCA} = \$170,932 - \$11,208$$
$$= \$159,724$$

Salvage Value versus UCC

There is a slight difference between this calculation for the present value of the tax shield on CCA and what we got in Table 10.13 by adding the tax shields over the project life. The difference arises whenever the salvage value of the asset differs from its UCC. The formula solution is more accurate as it takes into account the future CCA on this difference. In this case, the asset was sold for $150,000 and had UCC of $150,995. The $995 left in the pool after eight years creates an infinite stream of CCA tax shields. At Time 8, this stream has a present value of [$995(.20)(.40)]/[.20 + .15] = $227.43. At Time 0, the present value of this stream at 15 percent is about $75. To get the precise estimate of the present value of the CCA tax shield, we need to add this to the approximation in Table 10.13: $159,649 + $75 = $159,724.

EXAMPLE 10.2: The Ogopogo Paddler

Harvey Bligh, of Kelowna, British Columbia, is contemplating purchasing a paddle-wheel boat that he will use to give tours of Okanagan Lake in search of the elusive Ogopogo. Bligh has estimated cash flows from the tours and discounted them back over the eight-year expected life of the boat at his 20 percent required rate of return. The summary of his calculations follows:

Investment	−$250,000.00
Working capital	−50,000.00
PV of salvage	11,628.40
PV of NWC recovery	11,628.40
PV of after-tax operating income	251,548.33
PV of CCATS	?
NPV	?

He is struggling with the CCA tax shield calculation and is about to dump the project as it appears to be unprofitable. Is the project as unprofitable as Bligh believes?

The salvage value of the boat is $50,000, the combined federal and provincial corporate tax rate in British Columbia is 43 percent, and the CCA rate is 15 percent on boats.

$$\text{PV tax shield on CCA} = \frac{[IdT_c]}{d + k} \times \frac{[1 + .5k]}{1 + k}$$
$$- \frac{S_n dT_C}{d + k} \times \frac{1}{(1 + k)^n}$$

1st term = [($250,000 × .15 × .43)/(.15 + .20)]
  × [(1 + .50 × .20)/(1 + .20)]
  = $42,232.14

2nd term = [($50,000 × .15 × .43)/(.15 + .20)]
  × 1/(1 + .20)^8
  = $2,142.95

PV of CCATS = $42,232.14 − 2,142.95 = $40,089.19

The NPV of the investment is $14,894.32. Bligh should pursue this venture.

Concept Questions

1. What is meant by the term depreciation (CCA) tax shield?
2. What are the top-down and bottom-up definitions of operating cash flow?

10.7 | Some Special Cases of Discounted Cash Flow Analysis

To finish our chapter, we look at four common cases involving discounted cash flow analysis. The first case involves investments that are primarily aimed at improving efficiency and thereby cutting costs. The second case demonstrates analysis of a replacement decision. The third case arises in choosing between equipment with different economic lives. The fourth and final case we consider comes up when a firm is involved in submitting competitive bids.

There are many other special cases that we should consider, but these four are particularly important because problems similar to these are so common. Also, they illustrate some very diverse applications of cash flow analysis and DCF valuation.

Evaluating Cost-Cutting Proposals

One decision we frequently face is whether to upgrade existing facilities to make them more cost-effective. The issue is whether the cost savings are large enough to justify the necessary capital expenditure. For example, in 2012, Caterpillar Inc., the American industrial giant, decided to cut the wages of its London, Ontario employees by 50 percent. When the union rebelled, Caterpillar closed its London plant, Electro-Motive Canada.

Suppose we are considering automating some part of an existing production process presently performed manually in one of our plants. The necessary equipment costs $80,000 to buy and install. It will save $35,000 per year (pre-tax) by reducing labour and material costs. The equipment has a five-year life and is in Class 8 with a CCA rate of 20 percent. Due to rapid obsolescence, it will actually be worth nothing in five years. Should we do it? The tax rate is 40 percent, and the discount rate is 10 percent.

As always, the initial step in making this decision is to identify the relevant incremental cash flows. We keep track of these in the following table. First, determining the relevant capital spending is easy enough. The initial cost is $80,000 and the salvage value after five years is zero. Second, there are no working capital consequences here, so we don't need to worry about additions to net working capital.

Operating cash flows are the third component. Buying the new equipment affects our operating cash flows in two ways. First, we save $35,000 pretax every year. In other words, the firm's operating income increases by $35,000, so this is the relevant incremental project operating income. After taxes, this represents an annual cash flow of $21,000 as shown in the following table:

				Year		
	0	**1**	**2**	**3**	**4**	**5**
Investment	−$80,000					
NWC	0					
Subtotal	−80,000					
Op. income		$35,000	$35,000	$35,000	$35,000	$35,000
Taxes		14,000	14,000	14,000	14,000	14,000
Subtotal		21,000	21,000	21,000	21,000	21,000
Salvage						0
Total	−$80,000	$21,000	$21,000	$21,000	$21,000	$21,000

Present value of the tax shield on the CCA:

$$PV = \frac{80,000(.20)(.40)}{.20 + .10} \times \frac{1 + .5(.10)}{1 + .10}$$
$$= \$20,364$$

Present value of the after-tax operating savings:

$$PV = \$21,000 \times (1 - (1/1.10^5))/.10$$
$$= \$21,000 \times 3.7908$$
$$= \$79,607$$

NPV	
Investment	−$ 80,000
Operating cash flows	79,607
PV of salvage	0
CCATS	20,364
NPV	$ 19,971

Second, we have a tax shield on the incremental CCA created by the new equipment. This equipment has zero salvage so the formula is simplified as shown. CCA goes on forever and the present value of the tax shield is the sum of an infinite series. The present value is $20,364.

We can now finish our analysis by finding the present value of the $21,000 after-tax operating savings and adding the present values. At 10 percent, it's straightforward to verify that the NPV here is $19,971, so we should go ahead and automate.

EXAMPLE 10.3: To Buy or Not to Buy

We are considering the purchase of a $200,000 computer-based inventory management system. It is in Class 10 with a CCA rate of 30 percent. The computer has a four-year life. It will be worth $30,000 at that time. The system would save us $60,000 pretax in inventory-related costs. The relevant tax rate is 43.5 percent. Because the new set-up is more efficient than our existing one, we would be able to carry less total inventory and thus free $45,000 in net working capital. What is the NPV at 16 percent? What is the DCF return (the IRR) on this investment?

We begin by calculating the operating cash flow. The after-tax cost savings are $60,000 × (1 − .435) = $33,900. The present value of the tax shield on the CCA is found using the formula we first used in the Majestic Mulch and Compost Company problem.

$$PV = \frac{200{,}000(.30)(.435)}{.30 + .16} \times \frac{1 + .5(.16)}{1 + .16}$$
$$- \frac{30{,}000(.30)(.435)}{.30 + .16} \times \frac{1}{(1 + .16)^4}$$
$$= \$48{,}126$$

The capital spending involves $200,000 up front to buy the system. The salvage is $30,000. Finally, and this is the somewhat tricky part, the initial investment in net working capital is a $45,000 inflow because the system frees working capital. Furthermore, we have to put this back in at the end of the project's life. What this really means is simple:

While the system is in operation, we have $45,000 to use elsewhere.

To finish our analysis, we can compute the total cash flows:

	Year				
	0	1	2	3	4
Investment	−$200,000				
NWC	45,000				
Subtotal	−155,000				
Operating income		$60,000	$60,000	$60,000	$60,000
Taxes		26,100	26,100	26,100	26,100
After-tax operating income		33,900	33,900	33,900	33,900
NWC returned					−45,000

NPV	
Investment	−$200,000
NWC recovered now	45,000
Operating income	94,858
PV of salvage	16,569
PV of NWC returned	−24,853
CCATS	48,126
NPV	−$ 20,300

At 16 percent, the NPV is −$20,300, so the investment is not attractive. After some trial and error, we find that the NPV is zero when the discount rate is 9.36 percent, so the IRR on this investment is about 9.36 percent.[20]

Replacing an Asset

Instead of cutting costs by automating a manual production process, companies often need to decide whether it is worthwhile to enhance productivity by replacing existing equipment with newer models or more advanced technology. Suppose the promising numbers we calculated for the automation proposal encourage you to look into buying three more sets of equipment to replace older technology on your company's other production lines. Three new sets of equipment

---

[20] This IRR is tricky to compute without a spreadsheet because the asset is sold for $30,000, which is less than its undepreciated capital cost (after four years) of $48,000. Capital cost allowance on the difference remains in the pool and goes on to infinity. For this reason, we need to solve for the CCATS by trial and error.

cost $200,000 to buy and install. (Your projected cost is less than the earlier $80,000 per machine because you receive a quantity discount from the manufacturer.)

This time, the analysis is more complex because you are going to replace existing equipment. You bought it four years ago for $150,000 and expect it to last for six more years. Due to rapid technological advances, the existing equipment is only worth $50,000 if you sell it today. The more efficient newer technology would save you $75,000 per year in production costs over its projected six-year life.[21] These savings could be realized through reduced wastage and downtime on the shop floor.

If you retain the current equipment for the rest of its working life, you can expect to realize $10,000 in scrap value after six years. The new equipment, on the other hand, is saleable in the second-hand market and is expected to have a salvage value of $30,000 after six years.

With regard to working capital, the new equipment requires a greater stock of specialized spare parts but offers an offsetting reduction in wastage of work in process. On balance, no change in net working capital is predicted.

You determine that both the existing and new equipment are Class 8 assets with a CCA rate of 20 percent. Your firm requires a return of 15 percent on replacement investments and faces a tax rate of 44 percent. Should you recommend purchase of the new technology?

There is a lot of information here and we organize it in Table 10.14. The first cash flow is the capital outlay—and the difference between the cost of the new and the sale realization on the old equipment. To address CCA, we draw on the discussion in Chapter 2. There will still be undepreciated capital cost in the Class 8 pool because the amount we are adding to the pool (purchase price of new equipment) is greater than the amount we are subtracting (salvage on old equipment). Because we are not creating a negative balance of undepreciated capital cost (recapturing CCA) or selling all the pool's assets, there are no tax adjustments to the net outlay. The incremental salvage in six years is treated in the same way.[22]

TABLE 10.14

Replacement of existing asset ($000s)

	Year							NPV	
	0	**1**	**2**	**3**	**4**	**5**	**6**	Investment	−$200,000
Investment	−$200							Salvage recovered now	50,000
Salvage on old	50							Operating cash flows	158,948
NWC additions	0							PV of salvage forgone	−4,323
Subtotal	−150							PV of salvage recovered	12,970
Op. savings		$75	$75	$75	$75	$75	$75	CCATS	33,081
Taxes		33	33	33	33	33	33	NPV	$ 50,676
Subtotal		42	42	42	42	42	42		
Salvage forgone							−10		
Salvage							30		

The fact that we are making a net addition to the asset pool in Class 8 simplifies calculation of the tax shield on CCA. In this common case, Canada Revenue Agency's half-year rule applies to the net addition to the asset class. So, we simply substitute the incremental outlay for C in the present value of tax shield formula. Finally, we substitute the incremental salvage for S and crank the formula.[23]

---

[21] For simplicity, we assume that both the old and new equipment have six-year remaining lives. Later, we discuss how to analyze cases in which lives differ.

[22] Here we are making an implicit assumption that at the end of six years the deduction of salvage will not exhaust the Class 8 pool. If this were not the case, the excess, recaptured depreciation (i.e., the amount by which salvage value exceeds the undepreciated cost of the pool to which the asset belongs), would be taxable at the firm's tax rate of 44 percent.

[23] The present value of tax shield formula does not adjust the salvage for the half-year rule. This means we are assuming that, while the asset class will continue beyond Year 6, no new assets will be added in that year. We make this and the other tax assumptions to illustrate common situations without bogging down in the fine points of taxes.

$$PV = \frac{150,000(.20)(.44)}{.20 + .15} \times \frac{1 + .5(.15)}{1 + .15} - \frac{20,000(.20)(.44)}{.20 + .15} \times \frac{1}{(1 + .15)^6}$$
$$= \$33,081$$

Additions to net working capital are not relevant here. After-tax operating savings are calculated in the same way as in our prior examples. Table 10.14 shows that the replacement proposal has a substantial positive NPV and seems attractive. Another example on replacement is provided in Example 10.4 below.

EXAMPLE 10.4: Replacement

Theatreplex Oleum is considering replacing a projector system in one of its cinemas. The new projector has super-holographic sound and is able to project laser-sharp images. These features would increase the attendance at the theatre; and the new projector could cut repair costs dramatically. The new projector costs $250,000 and has a useful life of 15 years, at which time it could be sold for $20,000. The projector currently being used was purchased for $150,000 five years ago and can be sold now for $50,000. In 15 years the old projector would be scrapped for $5,000. The new projector would increase operating income by $50,000 annually; it belongs to Class 9 for CCA calculations with a rate of 25 percent. Theatreplex requires a 15 percent return on replacement assets and the corporate tax rate is 43.5 percent. Should Theatreplex replace the projector?

We begin calculating the profitability of such an investment by finding the present value of the increased operating income:

$$\text{After-tax flow} = \$50,000 \times (1 - .435)$$
$$= \$28,250$$

$$PV = \$28,250 \times (1 - 1/(1.15)^{15})/.15$$
$$= \$28,250 \times 5.84737$$
$$= \$165,188$$

The next step is to calculate the present value of the net salvage value of the new projector:

$$PV = (\$20,000 - 5,000) \times 1/(1.15)^{15}$$
$$= \$1,843$$

The last step is to calculate the present value tax shield on the CCA:

$$PV = \frac{200,000(.25)(.435)}{.25 + .15} \times \frac{1 + .5(.15)}{1 + .15}$$
$$- \frac{15,000(.25)(.435)}{.25 + .15} \times \frac{1}{(1 + .15)^{15}}$$
$$= 54,375 \times 1.075/1.15 - 4,078 \times 1/(1.15)^{15}$$
$$= \$50,829 - \$501$$
$$= \$50,328$$

The NPV is found by adding these present values to the original investment:

Net investment	−$200,000
Increased operating income	165,188
Net salvage	1,843
CCATS	50,328
NPV	$ 17,359

The investment surpasses the required return on investments for Theatreplex Oleum and should be pursued.

Evaluating Equipment with Different Lives

Our previous examples assumed, a bit unrealistically, that competing systems had the same life. The next problem we consider involves choosing among different possible systems, equipment, or procedures with different lives. For example, hospital managers need to decide which type of infusion pump to order for use in operating rooms to deliver anesthesia to patients undergoing surgery. Some pumps are single use while other, more expensive models last for 5 or 7 years and carry different types of delivery tubing and maintenance costs. As always, our goal is to maximize net present value. To do this, we place the projects on a common horizon for comparison. Equivalent annual cost (EAC) is often used as a decision-making tool in capital budgeting when comparing projects of unequal life spans.

The approach we consider here is only necessary when two special circumstances exist: First, the possibilities under evaluation have different economic lives. Second, and just as important, we need whatever we buy more or less indefinitely. As a result, when it wears out, we buy another one.

We can illustrate this problem with a simple example that holds the benefits constant across different alternatives. This way we can focus on finding the least-cost alternative.[24] Imagine that

---

[24] Alternatively, in another case, the costs could be constant and the benefits differ. Then we would maximize the equivalent annual benefit.

we are in the business of manufacturing stamped metal subassemblies. Whenever a stamping mechanism wears out, we have to replace it with a new one to stay in business. We are considering which of two stamping mechanisms to buy.

Machine A costs $100 to buy and $10 per year to operate. It wears out and must be replaced every two years. Machine B costs $140 to buy and $8 per year to operate. It lasts for three years and must then be replaced. Ignoring taxes, which one should we go with if we use a 10 percent discount rate?

In comparing the two machines, we notice that the first is cheaper to buy, but it costs more to operate and it wears out more quickly. How can we evaluate these trade-offs? We can start by computing the present value of the costs for each:

$$\text{Machine A: PV} = -\$100 + -\$10/1.1 + -10/1.1^2 = -\$117.36$$
$$\text{Machine B: PV} = -\$140 + -\$8/1.1 + -\$8/1.1^2 + -\$8/1.1^3 = -\$159.89$$

Notice that all the numbers here are costs, so they all have negative signs. If we stopped here, it might appear that A is the more attractive since the PV of the costs is less. However, all we have really discovered so far is that A effectively provides two years' worth of stamping service for $117.36, while B effectively provides three years' worth for $159.89. These are not directly comparable because of the difference in service periods.

We need to somehow work out a cost per year for these two alternatives. To do this, we ask the question: What amount, paid each year over the life of the machine, has the same PV of costs? This amount is called the **equivalent annual cost (EAC).**

equivalent annual cost (EAC)

The present value of a project's costs calculated on an annual basis.

Calculating the EAC involves finding an unknown payment amount. For example, for Machine A, we need to find a two-year ordinary annuity with a PV of −$117.36 at 10 percent. Going back to Chapter 6, the two-year annuity factor is:

$$\text{Annuity factor} = [1 - 1/1.10^2]/.10 = 1.7355$$

For Machine A, then, we have:

$$\text{PV of costs} = -\$117.36 = \text{EAC} \times 1.7355$$

$$\text{EAC} = -\$117.36/1.7355$$
$$= -\$67.62$$

For Machine B, the life is three years, so we first need the three-year annuity factor:

$$\text{Annuity factor} = [1 - 1/1.10^3]/.10 = 2.4869$$

We calculate the EAC for B just as we did for A:

$$\text{PV of costs} = \$159.89 = \text{EAC} \times 2.4869$$

$$\text{EAC} = -\$159.89/2.4869$$
$$= -\$64.29$$

Based on this analysis, we should purchase B because it effectively costs $64.29 per year versus $67.62 for A. In other words, all things considered, B is cheaper. Its longer life and lower operating cost are more than enough to offset the higher initial purchase price. Using the EAC approach, hospitals make cost-effective decisions regarding similar devices using common capital investment formulas.[25]

Setting the Bid Price

Early on, we used discounted cash flow to evaluate a proposed new product. A somewhat different (and very common) scenario arises when we must submit a competitive bid to win a job. Under such circumstances, the winner is whoever submits the lowest bid.

There is an old saw concerning this process: the low bidder is whoever makes the biggest mistake. This is called the winner's curse. In other words, if you win, there is a good chance that you underbid. In this section, we look at how to set the bid price to avoid the winner's curse. The procedure we describe is useful anytime we have to set a price on a product or service.

---

[25] Sinclair, D. R. (2010), Equivalent annual cost: a method for comparing the cost of multi-use medical devices, Canadian Anesthesiologists Society, Vol. 57, pp. 521–522.

EXAMPLE 10.5: Equivalent Annual Costs

This extended example illustrates what happens to the EAC when we consider taxes. You are evaluating two different pollution control options. A filtration system costs $1.1 million to install and $60,000 pre-tax annually to operate. It would have to be replaced every five years. A precipitation system costs $1.9 million to install, but only $10,000 per year to operate. The precipitation equipment has an effective operating life of eight years. The company rents its factory and both systems are considered leasehold improvements so straight-line capital cost allowance is used throughout, and neither system has any salvage value. Which method should we select if we use a 12 percent discount rate? The tax rate is 40 percent.

We need to consider the EACs for the two approaches because they have different service lives, and they will be replaced as they wear out. The relevant information is summarized in Table 10.15.

Notice that the operating cash flow is actually positive in both cases because of the large CCA tax shields.[26] This can occur whenever the operating cost is small relative to the purchase price.

To decide which system to purchase, we compute the EACs for both using the appropriate annuity factors:

Filtration system: $-\$912,550 = \text{EAC} \times 3.6048$
$$\text{EAC} = -\$253,149 \text{ per year}$$

Precipitation system: $-\$1,457,884 = \text{EAC} \times 4.9676$
$$\text{EAC} = -\$293,479 \text{ per year}$$

The filtration system is the cheaper of the two, so we select it. The longer life and smaller operating cost of the precipitation system are not sufficient to offset its higher initial cost.

TABLE 10.15

Equivalent annual cost

	Filtration System	Precipitation System
After-tax operating cost	−$ 36,000	−$ 6,000
Annual CCATS	88,000	95,000
Operating cash flow	$ 52,000	$ 89,000
Economic life	5 years	8 years
Annuity factor (12%)	3.6048	4.9676
Present value of operating cash flow	$ 187,450	$ 442,116
Capital spending	−$1,100,000	−$1,900,000
Total PV of costs	−$ 912,550	−$1,457,884

To illustrate how to set a bid price, imagine that we are in the business of buying stripped-down truck platforms and then modifying them to customer specifications for resale. A local distributor has requested bids for five specially modified trucks each year for the next four years, for a total of 20 trucks.

We need to decide what price per truck to bid. The goal of our analysis is to determine the lowest price we can profitably charge. This maximizes our chances of being awarded the contract while guarding against the winner's curse.

Suppose we can buy the truck platforms for $10,000 each. The facilities we need can be leased for $24,000 per year. The labour and material cost to do the modification works out to be about $4,000 per truck. Total cost per year would thus be

$$\$24,000 + 5 \times (\$10,000 + 4,000) = \$94,000$$

---

[26] We ignore the half-year rule for simplicity here. Also note that it is possible to rework Example 10.5 (and reach the same answer) treating the EAC as equivalent annual cash flows. In this case, the inflows have minus signs and the EAC is positive.

We need to invest $60,000 in new equipment. This equipment falls in Class 8 with a CCA rate of 20 percent. It would be worth about $5,000 at the end of the four years. We also need to invest $40,000 in raw materials inventory and other working capital items. The relevant tax rate is 43.5 percent. What price per truck should we bid if we require a 20 percent return on our investment?

TABLE 10.16

Setting the bid price

	Cash Flow	Year	PV at 20%
Capital spending	−$60,000	0	−$60,000
Salvage	5,000	4	2,411
Additions to NWC	−40,000	0	−40,000
	40,000	4	19,290
After-tax operating income	$(S - 94,000)(1 - .435)$	1–4	?
Tax shield on CCA			$11,438
NPV			$0

$$PV = \frac{60,000(.20)(.435)}{.20 + .20} \times \frac{1 + .5(.20)}{1 + .20} - \frac{5,000(.20)(.435)}{.20 + .20} \times \frac{1}{(1 + .20)^4}$$
$$= \$11,438$$

We start by looking at the capital spending and net working capital investment. We have to spend $60,000 today for new equipment. The after-tax salvage value is simply $5,000 assuming as usual that at the end of four years, other assets remain in Class 8. Furthermore, we have to invest $40,000 today in working capital. We get this back in four years.

We can't determine the after-tax operating income just yet because we don't know the sales price. The present value of the tax shield on CCA works out to be $11,438. The calculations are in Table 10.16 along with the other data. With this in mind, here is the key observation: The lowest possible price we can profitably charge results in a zero NPV at 20 percent. The reason is, at that price we earn exactly the required 20 percent on our investment.

Given this observation, we first need to determine what the after-tax operating income must be for the NPV to be equal to zero. To do this, we calculate the present values of the salvage and return of net working capital in Table 10.16 and set up the NPV equation.

$$NPV = 0 = -\$60,000 + 2,411 - 40,000 + 19,290 + PV(\text{annual after-tax incremental})$$
$$\text{operating income}) + 11,438$$
$$PV \text{ (annual after-tax incremental operating income)} = \$66,861$$

Since this represents the present value of an annuity, we can find the annual "payments,"

$$PV \text{ (annuity)} = \$66,861 = P[1 - 1/1.20^4]/.20$$
$$P = \$25,828$$

The annual incremental after-tax operating income is $25,828. Using a little algebra we can solve for the necessary sales proceeds, S.

$$\$25,828 = (S - 94,000)(1 - .435)$$
$$\$45,713 = S - 94,000$$
$$S = \$139,713$$

Since the contract is for five trucks, this represents $27,943 per truck. If we round this up a bit, it looks like we need to bid about $28,000 per truck. At this price, were we to get the contract, our return would be a bit more than 20 percent.

Concept Questions

1. Under which circumstances do we have to worry about unequal economic lives? How do you interpret the EAC?
2. In setting a bid price, we used a zero NPV as our benchmark. Explain why this is appropriate.

10.8 | Summary and Conclusions

This chapter describes how to put together a discounted cash flow analysis. In it, we covered:

1. The identification of relevant project cash flows. We discussed project cash flows and described how to handle some issues that often come up, including sunk costs, opportunity costs, financing costs, net working capital, and erosion.

2. Preparing and using pro forma or projected financial statements. We showed how such financial statement information is useful in coming up with projected cash flows, and we also looked at some alternative definitions of operating cash flow.

3. The role of net working capital and depreciation in project cash flows. We saw that including the additions to net working capital was important because it adjusted for the discrepancy between accounting revenues and costs and cash revenues and costs. We also went over the calculation of capital cost allowance under current tax law.

4. Some special cases in using discounted cash flow analysis. Here we looked at four special issues: cost-cutting investments, replacement decisions, the unequal lives problem, and how to set a bid price.

The discounted cash flow analysis we've covered here is a standard tool in the business world. It is a very powerful tool, so care should be taken in its use. The most important thing is to get the cash flows identified in a way that makes economic sense. This chapter gives you a good start on learning to do this.

Key Terms

capital cost allowance (CCA) (page 254)
depreciation (CCA) tax shield (page 264)
equivalent annual cost (EAC) (page 273)
erosion (page 252)
incremental cash flows (page 251)

opportunity cost (page 252)
pro forma financial statements (page 254)
stand-alone principle (page 251)
sunk cost (page 251)

Chapter Review Problems and Self-Test

These problems give you some practice with discounted cash flow analysis. The answers follow.

10.1   Capital Budgeting for Project X   Based on the following information for Project X, should we undertake the venture? To answer, first prepare a pro forma statement of comprehensive income for each year. Second, calculate the operating cash flow. Finish the problem by determining total cash flow and then calculating NPV assuming a 20 percent required return. Use a 40 percent tax rate through-out. For help, look back at our shark attractant and power mulcher examples.

Project X is a new type of audiophile-grade stereo amplifier. We think we can sell 500 units per year at a price of $10,000 each. Variable costs per amplifier run about $5,000 per unit, and the product should have a four-year life. We require a 20 percent return on new products such as this one.

Fixed costs for the project run $610,000 per year. Further, we need to invest $1,100,000 in manufacturing equipment. This equipment belongs to class 8 for CCA purposes. In four years, the equipment can be sold for its UCC value. We would have to invest $900,000 in working capital at the start. After that, net working capital requirements would be 30 percent of sales.

10.2   Calculating Operating Cash Flow   Mater Pasta Ltd. has projected a sales volume of $1,432 for the second year of a proposed expansion project. Costs normally run 70 percent of sales, or about $1,002 in this case. The capital cost allowance will be $80, and the tax rate is 40 percent. What is the operating cash flow? Calculate your answer using the top-down, bottom-up, and tax shield approaches described in the chapter.

10.3   Spending Money to Save Money   For help on this one, refer back to the computerized inventory management system in Example 10.3. Here, we're contemplating a new, mechanized welding system to replace our current manual system. It costs $600,000 to get the new system. The cost will be depreciated at a 30 percent CCA rate. Its expected life is four years. The system would actually be worth $100,000 at the end of four years.

We think the new system could save us $180,000 per year pre-tax in labour costs. The tax rate is 44 percent. What is the NPV of buying the new system? The required return is 15 percent.

Answers to Self-Test Problems

10.1   To develop the pro forma statements of comprehensive income, we need to calculate the depreciation for each of the four years. The relevant CCA percentages, allowances, and UCC values for the first four years are:

Year	CCA rate	Eligible UCC	Allowance	Ending UCC
1	20.0%	$550,000	$110,000	$990,000
2	20.0	990,000	198,000	792,000
3	20.0	792,000	158,400	633,600
4	20.0	633,600	126,720	506,880

The projected statements of comprehensive income, therefore, are as follows:

	Year			
	1	2	3	4
Sales	$5,000,000	$5,000,000	$5,000,000	$5,000,000
Variable costs	2,500,000	2,500,000	2,500,000	2,500,000
Fixed costs	610,000	610,000	610,000	610,000
CCA deduction	110,000	198,000	158,400	126,720
EBIT	$1,780,000	$1,692,000	$1,731,600	$1,763,280
Taxes (40%)	712,000	676,800	692,640	705,312
Net income	$1,068,000	$1,015,200	$1,038,960	$1,057,968

Based on this information, the operating cash flows are:

	Year			
	1	2	3	4
EBIT	$1,780,000	$1,692,000	$1,731,600	$1,763,280
CCA deduction	110,000	198,000	158,400	126,720
Taxes	712,000	−676,800	−692,640	−705,312
Operating cash flow	$1,178,000	$1,213,200	$1,197,360	$1,184,688

We now have to worry about the non-operating cash flows. Net working capital starts at $900,000 and then rises to 30 percent of sales, or $1,500,000. This is a $600,000 addition to net working capital.

Finally, we have to invest $1,100,000 to get started. In four years, the market and book value of this investment would be identical, $506,880. Under our usual going-concern assumption, other Class 8 assets remain in the pool. There are no tax adjustments needed to the salvage value.

When we combine all this information, the projected cash flows for Project X are:

	Year				
	0	1	2	3	4
Operating cash flow		$1,178,000	$1,213,200	$1,197,360	$1,184,688
Additions to NWC	−$ 900,000	−600,000			1,500,000
Capital spending	−1,100,000				506,880
Total cash flow	−$2,000,000	$ 578,000	$1,213,200	$1,197,360	$3,191,568

With these cash flows, the NPV at 20 percent is:

$$\text{NPV} = -\$2,000,000 + 578,000/1.2 + 1,213,200/1.2^2 + 1,197,360/1.2^3 + 3,191,568/1.2^4$$
$$= \$1,556,227$$

So this project appears quite profitable.

10.2   We begin by calculating the project's EBIT, its tax bill, and its net income.

EBIT = $1,432 − 1,002 − 80 = $350
Taxes = $350 × .40 = $140
Net income = $350 − 140 = $210

With these numbers, operating cash flow is:

OCF = EBIT + D − Taxes
    = $350 + 80 − 140
    = $290

Using the other OCF definitions, we have:

Tax shield OCF = $(S − C) × (1 − .40) + D × .40$
    = ($1,432 − $1,002) × .60 + 80 × .40
    = $290

Bottom-up OCF = Net income + D
    = $210 + 80
    = $290

$$\text{Top-down OCF} = S - C - \text{Taxes}$$
$$= \$1,432 - 1,002 - 140$$
$$= \$290$$

As expected, all of these definitions produce exactly the same answer.

10.3   The $180,000 pre-tax saving gives an after-tax amount of:

$$(1 - .44) \times \$180,000 = \$100,800$$

The present value of this four-year annuity amounts to:

$$PV = \$100,800 \times \left(1 - \frac{1}{1.15^4}\right)/.15$$
$$= \$100,800 \times 2.8550$$
$$= \$287,782$$

The present value of the tax shield on the CCA is:

$$PV = \frac{600,000(.30)(.44)}{.15 + .30} \times \frac{(1 + .5(.15))}{1 + .15} - \frac{100,000(.30)(.44)}{.15 + .30} \times \frac{1}{(1.15)^4}$$
$$= 164,522 - 16,771$$
$$= \$147,750$$

The only flow left undiscounted is the salvage value of the equipment. The present value of this flow is:

$$PV = \$100,000 \times 1/1.15^4$$
$$= \$100,000 \times .5718$$
$$= \$57,175$$

There are no working capital consequences, so the NPV is found by adding these three flows and the initial investment.

Investment	−$600,000
PV of labour savings	287,782
PV of salvage	57,175
CCATS	147,750
NPV	−$107,293

You can verify that the NPV is −$107,293, and the return on the new welding system is only about 5.4 percent. The project does not appear to be profitable.

Concepts Review and Critical Thinking Questions

1.   **(LO1)** In the context of capital budgeting, what is an opportunity cost?

2.   **(LO1)** In our capital budgeting examples, we assumed that a firm would recover all of the working capital it invested in a project. Is this a reasonable assumption? When might it not be valid?

3.   **(LO7)** When is EAC analysis appropriate for comparing two or more projects? Why is this method used? Are there any implicit assumptions required by this method that you find troubling? Explain.

4.   **(LO1)** "When evaluating projects, we're only concerned with the relevant incremental after-tax cash flows. Therefore, because depreciation is a non-cash expense, we should ignore its effects when evaluating projects." Critically evaluate this statement.

5.   **(LO1)** A major textbook publisher has an existing finance textbook. The publisher is debating whether or not to produce an "essentialized" version, meaning a shorter (and lower-priced) book. What are some of the considerations that should come into play?

In 2008, Indigo Books & Music Inc. launched a new chain called Pistachio selling stationery, gifts, home decor and organic apothecary items.

6.   **(LO1)** In evaluating the decision to start Pistachio, under what circumstances might Indigo Books & Music have concluded that erosion was irrelevant?

7.   **(LO1)** In evaluating Pistachio, what do you think Indigo needs to assume regarding the profit margins that exist in this market? Is it likely they will be maintained when others enter this market?

Questions and Problems

Basic
(Questions 1–34)

1.   **Relevant Cash Flows (LO1)** White Oak Garden Inc. is looking at setting up a new manufacturing plant in London, Ontario to produce garden tools. The company bought some land six years ago for $6 million in anticipation of using it as a warehouse and distribution site, but the company has since decided to rent these facilities from a competitor instead. If the land were sold today, the company would net $6.4 million. The company wants to build its new manufacturing plant on this land; the plant will cost $14.2 million to build, and the site requires $890,000 worth of grading before it is suitable for construction. What is the proper cash-flow amount to use as the initial investment in fixed assets when evaluating this project? Why?

2.   **Relevant Cash Flows (LO1)** Nilestown Corp. currently sells 30,000 motor homes per year at $53,000 each, and 12,000 luxury motor coaches per year at $91,000 each. The company wants to introduce a new portable camper to fill out its product line; it hopes to sell 19,000 of these campers per year at $13,000 each. An independent consultant has determined that if Nilestown

introduces the new campers, it should boost the sales of its existing motor homes by 4500 units per year, and reduce the sales of its motor coaches by 900 units per year. What is the amount to use as the annual sales figure when evaluating this project? Why?

3. **Calculating Projected Net Income (LO1)** A proposed new investment has projected sales of $830,000. Variable costs are 60 percent of sales, and fixed costs are $181,000; depreciation is $77,000. Prepare a pro forma statement of comprehensive income assuming a tax rate of 35 percent. What is the projected net income?

4. **Calculating OCF (LO3)** Consider the following statement of comprehensive income:

Sales	$824,500
Costs	538,900
Depreciation	126,500
EBIT	?
Taxes (34%)	?
Net income	?

Fill in the missing numbers and then calculate the OCF. What is the CCA tax shield?

5. **OCF from Several Approaches (LO3)** A proposed new project has projected sales of $108,000, costs of $51,000, and CCA of $6,800. The tax rate is 35 percent. Calculate operating cash flow using the four different approaches described in the chapter and verify that the answer is the same in each case.

6. **Calculating Net Income (LO1)** A proposed new investment has projected sales in Year 5 of $940,000. Variable costs are 41 percent of sales and fixed costs are $147,000. CCA for the year will be $104,000. Prepare a projected statement of comprehensive income, assuming a 35 percent tax rate.

7. **Calculating Depreciation (LO1, 2)** A new electronic process monitor costs $990,000. This cost could be depreciated at 30 percent per year (Class 10). The monitor would actually be worthless in five years. The new monitor would save $460,000 per year before taxes and operating costs. If we require a 15 percent return, what is the NPV of the purchase? Assume a tax rate of 40 percent.

8. **NPV and NWC Requirements (LO2)** In the previous question, suppose the new monitor also requires us to increase net working capital by $47,200 when we buy it. Further suppose that the monitor could actually be worth $100,000 in five years. What is the new NPV?

9. **NPV and CCA (LO2)** In the previous question, suppose the monitor was assigned a 25 percent CCA rate. All the other facts are the same. Will the NPV be larger or smaller? Why? Calculate the new NPV to verify your answer.

10. **Identifying Relevant Costs (LO1)** Rick Bardles and Ed James are considering building a new bottling plant to meet expected future demand for their new line of tropical coolers. They are considering putting it on a plot of land they have owned for three years. They are analyzing the idea and comparing it to some others. Bardles says, "Ed, when we do this analysis, we should put in an amount for the cost of the land equal to what we paid for it. After all, it did cost us a pretty penny." James retorts, "No, I don't care how much it cost—we have already paid for it. It is what they call a sunk cost. The cost of the land shouldn't be considered." What would you say to Bardles and James?

11. **Calculating Salvage Value**[27] **(LO4)** Consider an asset that costs $548,000 and can be depreciated at 20 percent per year (Class 8) over its eight-year life. The asset is to be used in a five-year project; at the end of the project, the asset can be sold for $105,000. If the relevant tax rate is 35 percent, what is the after-tax cash flow from the sale of the asset? You can assume that there will be no assets left in the class in six years.

12. **Identifying Cash Flows (LO2)** Last year, Lambeth Pizza Corporation reported sales of $102,000 and costs of $43,500. The following information was also reported for the same period:

	Beginning	Ending
Accounts receivable	$45,120	$38,980
Inventory	53,500	59,140
Accounts payable	68,320	75,250

Based on this information, what was Lambeth' change in net working capital for last year? What was the net cash flow?

13. **Calculating Project OCF (LO3)** Hubrey Home Inc. is considering a new three-year expansion project that requires an initial fixed asset investment of $3.9 million. The fixed asset falls into Class 10 for tax purposes (CCA rate of 30 percent per year), and at the end of the three years can be sold for a salvage value equal to its UCC. The project is estimated to generate $2,650,000 in annual sales, with costs of $840,000. If the tax rate is 35 percent, what is the OCF for each year of this project?

14. **Calculating Project NPV (LO2)** In the previous problem, supposed the required return on the project is 12 percent. What is the project's NPV?

15. **Calculating Project Cash Flow from Assets (LO1, 2)** In the previous problem, suppose the project requires an initial investment in net working capital of $300,000 and the fixed asset will have a market value of $210,000 at the end of the project. What is the project's Year 0 net cash flow? Year 1? Year 2? Year 3? What is the new NPV?

16. **NPV Applications (LO1, 2)** We believe we can sell 90,000 home security devices per year at $150 a piece. They cost $130 to manufacture (variable cost). Fixed production costs run $215,000 per year. The necessary equipment costs $785,000 to buy and would be depreciated at a 25 percent CCA rate. The equipment would have a zero salvage value after the five-year life of the

---

[27] Recall that terminal losses and recapture in CCA calculations were covered in Chapter 2.

project. We need to invest $140,000 in net working capital up front; no additional net working capital investment is necessary. The discount rate is 19 percent, and the tax rate is 35 percent. What do you think of the proposal?

17. **Identifying Cash Flows (LO2)** Suppose a company has $15,200 in sales during a quarter. Over the quarter, accounts receivable increased by $9,500. What were cash collections?

18. **Stand-Alone Principle (LO1)** Suppose a financial manager is quoted as saying: "Our firm uses the stand-alone principle. Since we treat projects like mini firms in our evaluation process, we include financing costs, because financing costs are relevant at the firm level." Critically evaluate this statement.

19. **Relevant Cash Flows (LO1)** Kilworth Plexiglass Inc. is looking to set up a new manufacturing plant to produce surfboards. The company bought some land seven years ago for $7.2 million in anticipation of using it as a warehouse and distribution site, but the company decided to rent the facilities from a competitor instead. The land was appraised last week for $962,000. The company wants to build its new manufacturing plant on this land; the plant will cost $25 million to build, and the site requires an additional $586,000 in grading before it will be suitable for construction. What is the proper cash flow amount to use as the initial investment in fixed assets when evaluating this project? Why?

20. **Relevant Cash Flows (LO1)** Melrose Motorworks Corp. currently sells 23,000 compact cars per year at $14,690 each, and 38,600 luxury sedans at $43,700 each. The company wants to introduce a new mid-sized sedan to fill out its product line; it hopes to sell 28,500 of the cars per year at $33,600 each. An independent consultant has determined that if Melrose introduces the new cars, it should boost the sales of its existing compacts by 12,500 units per year, while reducing the unit sales of its luxury sedans by 8200 units per year. What is the annual cash flow amount to use as the sales figure when evaluating this project? Why?

21. **Project Evaluation (LO1, 2)** Fox Hollow Franks is looking at a new system with an installed cost of $560,000. This equipment is depreciated at a rate of 20 percent per year (Class 8) over the project's five-year life, at the end of which the sausage system can be sold for $85,000. The sausage system will save the firm $165,000 per year in pre-tax operating costs, and the system requires an initial investment in net working capital of $29,000. If the tax rate is 34 percent and the discount rate is 10 percent, what is the NPV of this project?

22. **Project Evaluation (LO1, 2)** Your firm is contemplating the purchase of a new $720,000 million computer-based order entry system. The PVCCATS is $260,000, and the machine will be worth $280,000 at the end of the five-year life of the system. You will save $350,000 before taxes per year in order processing costs and you will be able to reduce working capital by $110,000 (this is a one-time reduction). If the tax rate is 35 percent, what is the IRR for this project?

23. **Project Evaluation (LO1, 2)** In the previous problem, suppose your required return on the project is 20 percent, your pre-tax cost savings are now $300,000 per year, and the machine can be depreciated at 30 percent (Class 10). Will you accept the project? What if the pre-tax savings are only $240,000 per year? At what level of pre-tax cost savings would you be indifferent between accepting the project and not accepting it?

24. **Calculating a Bid Price (LO8)** We have been requested by a large retailer to submit a bid for a new point-of-sale credit checking system. The system would be installed, by us, in 89 stores per year for three years. We would need to purchase $1,300,000 worth of specialized equipment. This will be depreciated at a 20 percent CCA rate. We will sell it in three years, at which time it will be worth about half of what we paid for it. Labour and material cost to install the system is about $96,000 per site. Finally, we need to invest $340,000 in working capital items. The relevant tax rate is 36 percent. What price per system should we bid if we require a 20 percent return on our investment? Try to avoid the winner's curse.

25. **Alternative OCF Definitions (LO3)** Next year, Byron Corporation estimates that they will have $425,000 in sales, $96,000 in operating costs, and their corporate tax rate will be 35 percent. Undepreciated capital costs (UCC) will be $375,000 and the CCA rate will be 20 percent.

   a.   What is estimated EBIT for next year?

   b.   Using the bottom-up approach, what is the operating cash flow?

   c.   Using the tax shield method, what is the operating cash flow?

26. **Alternating OCF Definitions (LO3)** The Arva Logging Company is considering a new logging project in Ontario, requiring new equipment with a cost of $280,000. For the upcoming year, they estimate that the project will produce sales of $650,000 and $490,000 in operating costs. The CCA rate will be 25 percent and their net profits will be taxed at a corporate rate of 38 percent. Use the top-down approach and the tax shield approach to calculate the operating cash flow for the first year of the project for the Arva Logging Company.

27. **EAC (LO7)** Lobo is a leading manufacturer of positronic brains, a key component in robots. The company is considering two alternative production methods. The costs and lives associated with each are:

Year	Method 1	Method 2
0	$6,700	$9,900
1	400	620
2	400	620
3	400	620
4		620

Assuming that Lobo will not replace the equipment when it wears out, which should it buy? If Lobo is going to replace the equipment, which should it buy ($r = 13\%$)? Ignore depreciation and taxes in answering.

28. **Calculating Cash Flows and EAC (LO7)** In the previous question, suppose all the costs are before taxes and the tax rate is 39 percent. Both types of equipment would be depreciated at a CCA rate of 25 percent (Class 9), and would have no value after the project. What are the EACs in this case? Which is the preferred method?

29. **Calculating EAC (LO7)** A five-year project has an initial fixed asset investment of $270,000, an initial NWC investment of $25,000, and an annual OCF of −$42,000. The fixed asset is fully depreciated over the life of the project and has no salvage value. If the required return is 11 percent, what is this project's equivalent annual cost, or EAC?

30. **Calculating EAC (LO7)** You are evaluating two different silicon wafer milling machines. The Techron I costs $290,000, has a three-year life, and has pre-tax operating costs of $67,000 per year. The Techron II costs $510,000, has a five-year life, and has pre-tax operating costs of $35,000 per year. Both milling machines are in Class 8 (CCA rate of 20 percent per year). Assume a salvage value of $40,000. If your tax rate is 35 percent and your discount rate is 10 percent, compute the EAC for both machines. Which do you prefer? Why?

31. **Calculating EAC (LO7)** You are considering two different methods for constructing a new warehouse site. The first method would use prefabricated building segments, would have an initial cost of $6.5 million, would have annual maintenance costs of $150,000, and would last for 25 years. The second alternative would employ a new carbon-fibre panel technology, would have an initial cost of $8.2 million, would have maintenance costs of $650,000 every 10 years, and is expected to last for 40 years. Both buildings would be in CCA Class 1 (at a rate of 4 percent) and it is expected that each would have a salvage value equivalent to 25 percent of its construction cost at the end of its useful life. The discount rate the firm uses in evaluating projects is 11 percent. The tax rate is 35 percent. What is the annual cost for each option, and which would you pick?

32. **Calculating EAC (LO7)** A seven-year project has an initial investment of $550,000 and an annual operating cost of $32,000 in the first year. The operating costs are expected to increase at the rate of inflation, which is projected at 2 percent for the life of the project. The investment is in Class 7 for CCA purposes, and will therefore be depreciated at 15 percent annually. The salvage value at the end of the project will be $98,000. The firm's discount rate is 11 percent, and the company falls in the 35 percent tax bracket. What is the EAC for the investment?

33. **Calculating a Bid Price (LO8)** Komoka Enterprises needs someone to supply it with 185,000 cartons of machine screws per year to support its manufacturing needs over the next five years, and you've decided to bid on the contract. It will cost you $940,000 to install the equipment necessary to start production. The equipment will be depreciated at 30 percent (Class 10), and you estimate that it can be salvaged for $70,000 at the end of the five-year contract. Your fixed production costs will be $305,000 per year, and your variable production costs should be $9.25 per carton. You also need an initial net working capital of $75,000. If your tax rate is 35 percent and you require a 12 percent return on your investment, what bid price should you submit?

34. **Cost-cutting Proposals (LO5)** Caradoc Machine Shop is considering a four-year project to improve its production efficiency. Buying a new machine press for $560,000 is estimated to result in $210,000 in annual pre-tax cost savings. The press falls into Class 8 for CCA purposes (CCA rate of 20 percent per year), and it will have a salvage value at the end of the project of $80,000. The press also requires an initial investment in spare parts inventory of $20,000, along with an additional $3,000 in inventory for each succeeding year of the project. If the shop's tax rate is 35 percent and its discount rate is 9 percent, should Caradoc buy and install the machine press?

Intermediate 35. **Cash Flows and NPV (LO2)** We project unit sales for a new household-use laser-guided cockroach search and destroy system
(Questions as follows:
35–45)

Year	Unit Sales
1	93,000
2	105,000
3	128,000
4	134,000
5	87,000

The new system will be priced to sell at $380 each.

The cockroach eradicator project will require $1,800,000 in net working capital to start, and total net working capital will rise to 15 percent of the change in sales. The variable cost per unit is $265, and total fixed costs are $1,200,000 per year. The equipment necessary to begin production will cost a total of $24 million. This equipment is mostly industrial machinery and thus qualifies for CCA at a rate of 20 percent. In five years, this equipment will actually be worth about 20 percent of its cost.

The relevant tax rate is 35 percent, and the required return is 18 percent. Based on these preliminary estimates, what is the NPV of the project?

36. **Replacement Decisions (LO6)** An officer for a large construction company is feeling nervous. The anxiety is caused by a new excavator just released onto the market. The new excavator makes the one purchased by the company a year ago obsolete. As a result, the market value for the company's excavator has dropped significantly, from $600,000 a year ago to $50,000 now. In 10 years, it would be worth only $3,000. The new excavator costs only $950,000 and would increase operating revenues by $90,000 annually. The new equipment has a 10-year life and expected salvage value of $175,000. What should the officer do? The tax rate is 35 percent, the CCA rate, 25 percent for both excavators, and the required rate of return for the company is 14 percent.

37. **Replacement Decisions (LO6)** A university student painter is considering the purchase of a new air compressor and paint gun to replace an old paint sprayer. (Both items belong to Class 9 and have a 25 percent CCA rate.) These two new items cost $12,000 and have a useful life of four years, at which time they can be sold for $1,600. The old paint sprayer can be sold now for $500 and

could be scrapped for $250 in four years. The entrepreneurial student believes that operating revenues will increase annually by $8,000. Should the purchase be made? The tax rate is 22 percent and the required rate of return is 15 percent.

38. **Different Lives (LO7)** The Tempo Golf and Country Club in London, Ontario is evaluating two different irrigation system options. An underground automatic irrigation system will cost $9.2 million to install and $80,000 pre-tax annually to operate. It will not have to be replaced for 20 years. An aboveground system will cost $6.8 million to install, but $190,000 per year to operate. The aboveground equipment has an effective operating life of nine years. The country club leases its land from the city and both systems are considered leasehold improvements; as a result, straight-line capital cost allowance is used throughout, and neither system has any salvage value. Which method should we select if we use a 13 percent discount rate? The tax rate is 39 percent.

39. **Comparing Mutually Exclusive Projects (LO1, 2)** Mapleton Enterprises Inc. is evaluating alternative uses for a three-story manufacturing and warehousing building that it has purchased for $975,000. The company could continue to rent the building to the present occupants for $75,000 per year. These tenants have indicated an interest in staying in the building for at least another 15 years. Alternatively, the company could make leasehold improvements to modify the existing structure to use for its own manufacturing and warehousing needs. Mapleton's production engineer feels the building could be adapted to handle one of two new product lines. The cost and revenue data for the two product alternatives follow.

	Product A	Product B
Initial cash outlay for building modifications	$102,000	$192,250
Initial cash outlay for equipment	382,000	456,000
Annual pre-tax cash revenues (generated for 15 years)	323,100	396,000
Annual pre-tax cash expenditures (generated for 15 years)	174,700	235,700

The building will be used for only 15 years for either product A or product B. After 15 years, the building will be too small for efficient production of either product line. At that time, Mapleton plans to rent the building to firms similar to the current occupants. To rent the building again, Mapleton will need to restore the building to its present layout. The estimated cash cost of restoring the building if product A has been undertaken is $19,200; if product B has been produced, the cash cost will be $129,250. These cash costs can be deducted for tax purposes in the year the expenditures occur.

Mapleton will depreciate the original building shell (purchased for $975,000) at a CCA rate of 5 percent, regardless of which alternative it chooses. The building modifications fall into CCA Class 13 and are depreciated using the straight-line method over a 15-year life. Equipment purchases for either product are in Class 8 and have a CCA rate of 20 percent. The firm's tax rate is 36 percent, and its required rate of return on such investments is 16 percent.

For simplicity, assume all cash flows for a given year occur at the end of the year. The initial outlays for modifications and equipment will occur at $t = 0$, and the restoration outlays will occur at the end of year 15. Also, Mapleton has other profitable ongoing operations that are sufficient to cover any losses.

Which use of the building would you recommend to management?

40. **Valuation of the Firm (LO1, 2)** The Mosley Wheat Company (MWC) has wheat fields that currently produce annual profits of $1,100,000. These fields are expected to produce average annual profits of $820,000 in real terms forever. MWC has no depreciable assets, so the annual cash flow is also $820,000. MWC is an all-equity firm with 385,000 shares outstanding. The appropriate discount rate for its stock is 16 percent. MWC has an investment opportunity with a gross present value of $1,900,000. The investment requires a $1,400,000 outlay now. MWC has no other investment opportunities. Assume all cash flows are received at the end of each year. What is the price per share of MWC?

41. **Comparing Mutually Exclusive Projects (LO4)** Kingsmill Industrial Systems Company (KISC) is trying to decide between two different conveyor belt systems. System A costs $360,000, has a four-year life, and requires $135,000 in pre-tax annual operating costs. System B costs $430,000, has a six-year life, and requires $98,000 in pre-tax annual operating costs. Both systems are to be depreciated at 30 percent per year (Class 10) and will have no salvage value. Whichever project is chosen, it will *not* be replaced when it wears out. If the tax rate is 34 percent and the discount rate is 12 percent, which project should the firm choose?

42. **Comparing Mutually Exclusive Projects (LO4)** Suppose in the previous problem that KISC always needs a conveyor belt system; when one wears out, it must be replaced. Which project should the firm choose now?

43. **Calculating a Bid Price (LO8)** Consider a project to supply 140 million postage stamps per year to Canada Post for the next five years. You have an idle parcel of land available that cost $1,300,000 five years ago; if you sold the land today, it would net you $1,800,000, after tax. If you sold the land five years from now, the land can be sold again for a net $1,800,000 after tax. You will need to install $4.6 million in new manufacturing plant and equipment to actually produce the stamps. The equipment qualifies for a CCA rate of 30 percent and can be sold for $756,000 at the end of the project. You will also need $569,000 in initial net working capital for the project, and an additional investment of $68,000 every year thereafter. Your production costs are 0.9 cents per stamp, and you have fixed costs of $961,000 per year. If your tax rate is 34 percent and your required return on this project is 11 percent, what bid price should you submit on the contract?

44. **Replacement with Unequal Lives (LO7)** BIG Industries needs computers. Management has narrowed the choices to the SAL 5000 and the DET 1000. It would need 12 SALs. Each SAL costs $15,900 and requires $1,850 of maintenance each year. At the end of the computer's six-year life, BIG expects to be able to sell each one for $1,300. On the other hand, BIG could buy 10 DETs. DETs cost $19,000 each and each machine requires $1,700 maintenance every year. They last for four years and have no resale

value. Whichever model BIG chooses, it will buy that model forever. Ignore tax effects, and assume that maintenance costs occur at year-end. Which model should BIG buy if the cost of capital is 15 percent?

45. **Replacement with Unequal Lives (LO7)** Kiss 92.5 is considering the replacement of its old, fully depreciated sound mixer. Two new models are available. Mixer X has a cost of $743,000, a six-year expected life, and after-tax cash flow savings of $296,000 per year. Mixer Y has a cost of $989,000, a 10-year life, and after-tax cash flow of $279,000 per year. No new technological developments are expected. The cost of capital is 12 percent. Should Kiss 92.5 replace the old mixer with X or Y?

Challenge 46.
(Questions
46–53)

46. **Abandonment Decisions (LO1, 2)** For some projects, it may be advantageous to terminate the project early. For example, if a project is losing money, you might be able to reduce your losses by scrapping out the assets and terminating the project, rather than continuing to lose money all the way through to the project's completion. Consider the following project of Norman Clapper Inc. The company is considering a four-year project to manufacture clap-command garage door openers. This project requires an initial investment of $7 million with a CCA of 40 percent over the project's life. An initial investment in net working capital of $2 million is required to support spare parts inventory; this cost is fully recoverable whenever the project ends. The company believes it can generate $5 million in pre-tax revenues with $2.5 million in total pre-tax operating costs. The tax rate is 39 percent and the discount rate is 13 percent. The market value of the equipment over the life of the project is as follows:

Year	Market Value (Millions)
1	$5.00
2	4.74
3	2.60
4	0.00

a. Assuming Norman Clapper operates this project for four years, what is the NPV?

b. Now compute the project NPV assuming the project is abandoned after only one year, after two years, and after three years. What economic life for this project maximizes its value to the firm? What does this problem tell you about not considering abandonment possibilities when evaluating projects?

47. **Capital Budgeting Renovations (LO1, 2)** Suppose we are thinking about renovating a leased office. The renovations would cost $364,000. The renovations will be depreciated straight-line to zero over the five-year remainder of the lease.

The new office would save us $36,000 per year in heating and cooling costs. Also, absenteeism should be reduced and the new image should increase revenues. These last two items would result in increased operating revenues of $43,000 annually. The tax rate is 36 percent, and the discount rate is 13 percent. Strictly from a financial perspective, should the renovations take place?

48. **Calculating Required Savings (LO5, 8)** A proposed cost-saving device has an installed cost of $620,000. It is in Class 8 (CCA rate = 20%) for CCA purposes. It will actually function for five years, at which time it will have no value. There are no working capital consequences from the investment, and the tax rate is 35 percent.

a. What must the pre-tax cost savings be for us to favour the investment? We require a 11 percent return. (*Hint*: This one is a variation on the problem of setting a bid price.)

b. Suppose the device will be worth $90,000 in salvage (before taxes). How does this change your answer?

49. **Cash Flows and Capital Budgeting Choices (LO1, 2)** Dexter Company has recently completed a $1.3 million, two-year marketing study. Based on the results, Dexter has estimated that 19,600 of its new RUR-class robots could be sold annually over the next eight years at a price of $45,900 each. Variable costs per robot are $35,000 and fixed costs total $39.1 million.

Start-up costs include $96.5 million to build production facilities, $7.2 million in land, and $19.2 million in net working capital. The $96.5 million facility is made up of a building valued at $16 million that will belong to CCA Class 3 and $80.5 million of manufacturing equipment (belonging to CCA Class 8). Class 3 has a CCA rate of 5 percent, while Class 8 has a rate of 20 percent. At the end of the project's life, the facilities (including the land) will be sold for an estimated $27.9 million; assume the building's value will be $8.7 million. The value of the land is not expected to change.

Finally, start-up would also entail fully deductible expenses of $4.6 million at Year 0. Dexter is an ongoing, profitable business and pays taxes at a 39 percent rate. Dexter uses a 17 percent discount rate on projects such as this one. Should Dexter produce the RUR-class robots?

50. **Project Evaluation (LO2)** Aylmer-in-You (AIY) Inc. projects unit sales for a new opera tenor emulation implant as follows:

Year	Unit Sales
1	107,000
2	123,000
3	134,000
4	156,000
5	95,500

Production of the implants will require $800,000 in net working capital to start and additional net working capital investments each year equal to 40 percent of the projected sales increase for the following year. (Because sales are expected to fall in Year 5, there is no NWC cash flow occurring for Year 4.) Total fixed costs are $192,000 per year, variable production costs are $295 per unit, and the units are priced at $395 each. The equipment needed to begin production has an installed cost of $19.5 million. Because the implants are intended for professional singers, this equipment is considered industrial machinery and thus falls into Class 8 for tax purposes (20 percent). In five years, this equipment can be sold for about 30 percent of its acquisition cost. AIY is in the 40 percent marginal tax bracket and has a required return on all its projects of 23 percent. Based on these preliminary project estimates, what is the NPV of the project? What is the IRR?

51. **Calculating Required Savings (LO5)** A proposed cost-saving device has an installed cost of $865,000. The device will be used in a six-year project, but is classified as manufacturing and processing equipment for tax purposes. The required initial net working capital investment is $58,000, the marginal tax rate is 36 percent, and the project discount rate is 13.5 percent. The device has an estimated Year 6 salvage value of $138,000. What level of pre-tax cost savings do we require for this project to be profitable? The CCA rate is 20 percent.

52. **Replacement Decisions (LO6)** Suppose we are thinking about replacing an old computer with a new one. The old one cost us $420,000 one year ago; the new one will cost $368,000. The new machine will be in CCA Class 10 (30 percent). It will probably be worth about $198,000 after five years.

The old computer is being depreciated at a rate of $140,000 per year. It will be completely written off in three years. If we don't replace it now, we will have to replace it in two years. We can sell it now for $190,000; in two years, it will probably be worth half that. The new machine will save us $130,000 per year in maintenance costs. The tax rate is 38 percent and the discount rate is 13 percent.

   a. Suppose we only consider whether or not we should replace the old computer now without worrying about what's going to happen in two years. What are the relevant cash flows? Should we replace it or not? (*Hint*: Consider the net change in the firm's after-tax cash flows if we do the replacement.)

   b. Suppose we recognize that if we don't replace the computer now, we will be replacing it in two years. Should we replace now or should we wait? (*Hint*: What we effectively have here is a decision either to "invest" in the old computer (by not selling it) or to invest in the new one.) Notice that the two investments have unequal lives.

53. **Financial Break-Even Analysis (LO8)** To solve the bid price problem presented in the text, we set the project NPV equal to zero and found the required price using the definition of OCF. Thus the bid price represents a financial break-even level for the project. This type of analysis can be extended to many other types of problems.

   a. In Problem 33, assume that the price per carton is $15 and find the project NPV. What does your answer tell you about your bid price? What do you know about the number of cartons you can sell and still break even? How about your level of costs?

   b. Solve Problem 33 again with the price still at $15 but find the quantity of cartons per year that you can supply and still break even.

   c. Repeat (b) with a price of $15 and a quantity of 185,000 cartons per year, and find the highest level of fixed costs you could afford and still break even.

MINI CASE

As a financial analyst at Glencolin International (GI) you have been asked to evaluate two capital investment alternatives submitted by the production department of the firm. Before beginning your analysis, you note that company policy has set the cost of capital at 15 percent for all proposed projects. As a small business, GI pays corporate taxes at the rate of 35 percent.

The proposed capital project calls for developing new computer software to facilitate partial automation of production in GI's plant. Alternative A has initial software development costs projected at $185,000, while Alternative B would cost $320,000. Software development costs would be capitalized and qualify for a capital cost allowance (CCA) rate of 30 percent. In addition, IT would hire a software consultant under either alternative to assist in making the decision whether to invest in the project for a fee of $16,000 and this cost would be expensed when it is incurred.

To recover its costs, GI's IT department would charge the production department for the use of computer time at the rate of $375 per hour and estimates that it would take 182 hours of computer time per year to run the new software under either alternative. GI owns all its computers and does not currently operate them at capacity. The information technology (IT) plan calls for this excess capacity to continue in the future. For security reasons, it is company policy not to rent excess computing capacity to outside users.

If the new partial automation of production is put in place, expected savings in production cost (before tax) are projected as follows:

Year	Alternative A	Alternative B
1	$82,000	$112,000
2	82,000	124,000
3	64,000	101,000
4	53,000	93,000
5	37,000	56,000

As the capital budgeting analyst, you are required to answer the following in your memo to the production department:

a) Calculate the net present value of each of the alternatives. Which would you recommend?

b) The CFO suspects that there is a high risk that new technology will render the production equipment and this automation software obsolete after only three years. Which alternative would you now recommend? (Cost savings for Years 1 to 3 would remain the same.)

c) GI could use excess resources in its Engineering department to develop a way to eliminate this step of the manufacturing process by the end of year 3. The salvage value of the equipment (including any CCA and tax impact) would be $50,000 at the end of Year 3, $35,000 at the end of Year 4, and zero after five years. Should Engineering develop the solution and remove the equipment before the five years are up? Which alternative? When?

Internet Application Questions

1. From time to time, governments at various levels provide tax incentives to promote capital investments in key industries. The Province of Manitoba introduced the Mining & Exploration Tax Incentives program in the form of bonus tax credits (on top of normal deductions). Information on this program is found in the following release: gov.mb.ca/ctt/invest/busfacts/govt/min_taxc.html

Explain how this incentive will affect new exploration activity. Is it possible that such tax incentives alter the NPV of a project?

2. In addition to NPV and IRR, Economic Value Added (EVA®) analysis (sternstewart.com/?content=proprietary&p=eva) has emerged as a popular tool for capital budgeting and valuation. EVA was developed and is patented by Stern Stewart & Co (sternstewart.com). Explain the mechanics of EVA and show its equivalence to NPV. Provide at least two reasons why EVA and NPV may differ in implementation.

3. Toyota Canada expected the capital expansion of its Cambridge, Ontario facility to total $680 million (CDN). The plant began production of 60,000 Lexus RX300 (which have since been renamed RX330 and RX350) luxury SUVs annually in September 2003. Information on Toyota Canada's plans for further expansion of Lexus production can be found at media.toyota.ca/pr/tci/en/lexus/toyota-to-expand-lexus-production-236830.aspx. Assuming profit of $5,000 on the Lexus, a 15-year production horizon, and a 15 percent discount rate, do you think Toyota made a good investment decision? What other factors need to be considered? Why?

APPENDIX 10A

MORE ON INFLATION AND CAPITAL BUDGETING

This text states that interest rates can be expressed in either nominal or real terms. For example, suppose the nominal interest rate is 12 percent and inflation is expected to be 8 percent next year. Then the real interest rate is approximately

$$\text{Real rate} = \text{Nominal rate} - \text{Expected inflation rate}$$
$$= 12\% - 8\% = 4\%.$$

Similarly, cash flows can be expressed in either nominal or real terms. Given these choices, how should one express interest rates and cash flows when performing capital budgeting?

Financial practitioners correctly stress the need to maintain consistency between cash flows and discount rates. That is, nominal cash flows must be discounted at the nominal rate. Real cash flows must be discounted at the real rate. The NPV is the same when cash flows are expressed in real quantities. The NPV is always the same under the two different approaches.

Because both approaches always yield the same result, which one should be used? Students will be happy to learn the following rule: Use the approach that is simpler. In the Shields Electric case, nominal quantities produce a simpler calculation. That is because the problem gave us nominal cash flows to begin with.

However, firms often forecast unit sales per year. They can easily convert these forecasts to real quantities by multiplying expected unit sales each year by the product price at Date 0. (This assumes the price of the product rises at exactly the rate of inflation.) Once a real discount rate is selected, NPV can easily be calculated from real quantities. Conversely, nominal quantities complicate the example, because the extra step of converting all real cash flows to nominal cash flows must be taken.

EXAMPLE 10A.1: Real or Nominal?

Shields Electric forecasts the following nominal cash flows on a particular project:

	Date		
	0	1	2
Cash Flow	−$1,000	$600	$650

The nominal interest rate is 14 percent, and the inflation rate is forecast to be 5 percent. What is the value of the project?

Using Nominal Quantities   The NPV can be calculated as:

$$\$26.47 = -\$1,000 + \frac{\$600}{1.14} + \frac{\$650}{(1.14)^2}$$

The project should be accepted.

Using Real Quantities The real cash flows are:

	Date		
	0	1	2
Cash Flow	−$1,000	$571.43	$589.57
		$\frac{\$600}{1.05}$	$\frac{\$650}{(1.05)^2}$

The real interest rate is approximately 9 percent (14 percent − 5 percent); precisely it is 8.57143 percent.[27]

The NPV can be calculated as

$$\$26.47 = -\$1,000 + \frac{\$571.32}{1.0857143} + \frac{\$589.57}{(1.0857143)^2}$$

---

[28] The exact calculation is 8.57143% = (1.14/1.05) − 1. It is explained in Chapter 12.

Appendix Questions and Problems

A.1 Repeat Question 27, assuming that all cash flows and discount rates provided are nominal rates, and that the inflation rate is 3 percent. What are the real cash flows and the real rate of return? What is the new EAC for the production methods if inflation is taken into account?

APPENDIX 10B

CAPITAL BUDGETING WITH SPREADSHEETS

Spreadsheets are almost essential for constructing a capital budgeting framework or for using pro forma financial statements. Table 10B.2 is an example of a capital budgeting framework, using the data from the Majestic Mulch and Compost Company. The framework is completely integrated, changing one of the input variables at the top reformulates the whole problem. This is useful for sensitivity calculations as it would be tedious to recalculate each column in the framework by hand.

The highlighted cells exhibit the more complicated procedures in the framework. The first, E16, is the CCA calculation. The IF statement is used to decide what year it is, to take into consideration the half-year effect. The second, G32, calculates the changes in net working capital. It is computed as 15 percent of the current year's sales less 15 percent of the previous year's sales. In Year 1, however, the intial net working capital is subtracted instead. The last cell, L53, simply discounts the future cash flows back to Year 0 dollars.

A well-designed capital budgeting framework allows most inputs to be easily changed, simplifying sensitivity calculations. We now turn our attention to a simple sensitivity calculation, to explain the usefulness of spreadsheets.

Table 10B.1 shows two sensitivity tables: One varies the initial investment and the other varies the discount rate. Notice in the first that if the initial investment runs over budget by as little as $25,000, it makes the whole project unprofitable. The second sensitivity analysis demonstrates that the project is even more sensitive to discount rate fluctuations.

Spreadsheets are invaluable in problems such as these; they decrease the number of silly errors and make all values easier to check. They also allow for what-if analyses such as these.

Recall that many problems in each chapter are labelled, with an icon, as Spreadsheet Problems. For some good practice at capital budgeting on a spreadsheet, we suggest that you consider completing Problem 50 in particular.

TABLE 10B.1

	Initial Investment	NPV	Discount Rate	NPV
Sensitivity analysis	Base case	$ 4,604	15.0%	$ 4,604
	$750,000	44,626	10.0	177,240
	775,000	24,615	12.5	84,796
	800,000	4,604	15.0	4,604
	825,000	−15,407	17.5	−65,319
	850,000	−35,418	20.0	−126,589

TABLE 10B.2

Capital budgeting framework

	A	B	C	D	E	F	G	H	I	J	K	L
1	The Majestic Mulch and Compost Company											
2												
3	Input variables:											
4	Tax rate		40.0%		Discount rate		15.0%					
5	CCA rate		20.0%		NWC as a % of sale		15.0%					
6	Initial investment		$800,000									
7												
8												
9	Statements of comprehensive income											
10	Year				1	2	3	4	5	6	7	8
11	Unit price (Table 10.5)				$ 120	$ 120	$ 120	$ 110	$ 110	$ 110	$ 110	$ 110
12	Unit sales (Table 10.5)				3,000	5,000	6,000	6,500	6,000	5,000	4,000	3,000
13	Revenues (Unit price × Unit sales)				$360,000	$600,000	$720,000	$715,000	$660,000	$550,000	$440,000	$330,000
14	Variable costs ($60 × Unit sales)				180,000	300,000	360,000	390,000	360,000	300,000	240,000	180,000
15	Fixed costs				25,000	25,000	25,000	25,000	25,000	25,000	25,000	25,000
16	CCA				80,000	144,000	115,200	92,160	73,728	58,982	47,186	37,749
17	EBIT (Revenues − (Costs + CCA))				$ 75,000	$131,000	$219,800	$207,840	$201,272	$166,018	$127,814	$ 87,251
18	Taxes (EBIT × 40%)				30,000	52,400	87,920	83,136	80,509	66,407	51,126	34,901
19	Net income (EBIT-taxes)				$ 45,000	$ 78,600	$131,880	$124,704	$120,763	$ 99,611	$ 76,688	$ 52,351
20												
21												
22	Projected cash flows											
23	Year			0	1	2	3	4	5	6	7	8
24	Operating cash flows											
25	EBIT				$ 75,000	$131,000	$219,800	$207,840	$201,272	$166,018	$127,814	$ 87,251
26	CCA				80,000	144,000	115,200	92,160	73,728	58,982	47,186	37,749
27	Taxes				30,000	52,400	87,920	83,136	80,509	66,407	51,126	34,901
28	Op. cash flow (tax shield approach)				$125,000	$222,600	$247,080	$216,864	$194,491	$158,593	$123,874	$ 90,099
29												
30	Net working capital											
31	Initial NWC			$ 20,000								
32	NWC Increases				$ 34,000	36,000	$ 18,000	$ (750)	$ (8,250)	$ (16,500)	$ (16,500)	$ (16,500)
33	NWC recovery											$ (49,500)
34	Add'ns to NWC			$ 20,000	$ 34,000	$ 36,000	$ 18,000	$ (750)	$ (8,250)	$ (16,500)	$ (16,500)	$ (66,000)
35												
36												
37												
38												
39												
40	Capital Spending (Table 10.8)											
41	Initial inv.			$800,000								
42	After-tax salvage											$(150,000)
43	Net cap. spending			$800,000	$ -	$ -	$ -	$ -	$ -	$ -	$ -	$(150,000)
44												
45				0	1	2	3	4	5	6	7	8
46	Total project cash flow (OCF − Capital spending − Addn's to NWC)											
47				$(820,000)	$ 91,000	$186,600	$229,080	$217,614	$202,741	$175,093	$140,374	$306,099
48												
49	Cumulative cash flow											
50				$(820,000)	$(729,000)	$(542,400)	$(313,320)	$ (95,706)	$107,035	$282,128	$422,503	$728,602
51												
52	Discounted cash flow (@15%)											
53				$(820,000)	$ 79,130	$141,096	$150,624	$124,422	$100,798	$ 75,698	$ 52,772	$100,064
54												
55	NPV			$ 4,604								
56												
57	IRR			15.15%	Cash flows		Cell formulas					
58					$(820,000)		E16: =IF(E10=1,$C$6/2*$C$5,($C$6−SUM(D16:$E$16))*$C$5)					
59					$ 91,000		G32: =(G13*$G$5)−(F13*$G$5)					
60					$ 186,600		L53: −L47/((1+$G$4)^L45)					
61					$ 229,080							
62					$ 217,614							
63					$ 202,741							
64					$ 175,093							
65					$ 140,374							
66					$ 306,099							

PROJECT ANALYSIS AND EVALUATION

In March 2011, the movie *Mars Needs Moms*, an animated science fiction film, was released to negative reviews from both critics and general audiences. One critic wrote "the film looks neither fully real nor fully imagined." Others were even harsher, saying "Mars may need moms, but Earth needs good movies, and this isn't one of them" and "*Mars Needs Moms* isn't much of a movie, but it's a great teaching tool for how not to make an animated film."

Looking at the numbers, Walt Disney Pictures spent close to $150 million making the movie, plus millions more for marketing and distribution. Unfortunately for Walt Disney, *Mars Needs Moms* crashed and burned, pulling in only $40 million worldwide.

In fact, about 4 of 10 movies lose money at the box office, though DVD sales often help the final tally. Of course, there are movies that do quite well. Also in 2011, the Warner Brothers movie *Harry Potter and the Deathly Hallows: Part II* raked in about $1.3 billion worldwide at a production cost of $125 million.

Obviously, Walt Disney didn't plan to lose $110 million or so on *Mars Needs Moms*, but it happened. As the box office spinout of *Mars Needs Moms* shows, projects don't always go as companies think they will. This chapter explores how this can happen, and what companies can do to analyze and possibly avoid these situations.

Learning Objectives ▶

After studying this chapter, you should understand:

LO1 How to perform and interpret a sensitivity analysis for a proposed investment.

LO2 How to perform and interpret a scenario analysis for a proposed investment.

LO3 How to determine and interpret cash, accounting, and financial break-even points.

LO4 How the degree of operating leverage can affect the cash flows of a project.

LO5 How managerial options affect net present value.

In our previous chapter, we discussed how to identify and organize the relevant cash flows for capital investment decisions. Our primary interest there was in coming up with a preliminary estimate of the net present value for a proposed project. In this chapter, we focus on assessing the reliability of such an estimate and avoiding forecasting risk, the possibility that errors in projected cash flow may lead to incorrect decisions.

We begin by discussing the need for an evaluation of cash flow and NPV estimates. We go on to develop some tools that are useful for doing so. We also examine complications and concerns that can arise in project evaluation.

11.1 | Evaluating NPV Estimates

As we discussed in Chapter 9, an investment has a positive net present value if its market value exceeds its cost. Such an investment is desirable because it creates value for its owner. The primary problem in identifying such opportunities is that most of the time we can't actually observe the relevant market value. Instead, we estimate it. Having done so, it is only natural to wonder whether our estimates are at least close to the true values or whether we have fallen prey to forecasting risk. We consider this question next.

The Basic Problem

Suppose we are working on a preliminary DCF analysis along the lines we described in the previous chapter. We carefully identify the relevant cash flows, avoiding such things as sunk costs, and we remember to consider working capital requirements. We add back any depreciation; we account for possible erosion; and we pay attention to opportunity costs. Finally, we double-check our calculations, and, when all is said and done, the bottom line is that the estimated NPV is positive.

Now what? Do we stop here and move on to the next proposal? Probably not. The fact that the estimated NPV is positive is definitely a good sign, but, more than anything, this tells us we need to take a closer look.

If you think about it, there are two circumstances under which a discounted cash flow analysis could lead us to conclude that a project has a positive NPV. The first possibility is that the project really does have a positive NPV. That's the good news. The bad news is the second possibility: A project may appear to have a positive NPV because our estimate is inaccurate.

Notice that we could also err in the opposite way. If we conclude that a project has a negative NPV when the true NPV is positive, we lose a valuable opportunity.

Projected versus Actual Cash Flows

There is a somewhat subtle point we need to make here. When we say something like: "The projected cash flow in Year 4 is $700," what exactly do we mean? Does this mean we think the cash flow will actually be $700? Not really. It could happen, of course, but we would be surprised to see it turn out exactly that way. The reason is that the $700 projection is based only on what we know today. Almost anything could happen between now and then to change that cash flow.

Loosely speaking, we really mean that, if we took all the possible cash flows that could occur in four years and averaged them, the result would be $700. In other words, $700 is the expected cash flow. So, we don't really expect a projected cash flow to be exactly right in any one case. What we do expect is that, if we evaluate a large number of projects, our projections are right on the average.

Forecasting Risk

The key inputs into a DCF analysis are expected future cash flows. If these projections are seriously in error, we have a classic GIGO (garbage-in, garbage-out) system. In this case, no matter how carefully we arrange the numbers and manipulate them, the resulting answer can still be grossly misleading. This is the danger in using a relatively sophisticated technique like DCF. It is sometimes easy to get caught up in number crunching and forget the underlying nuts-and-bolts economic reality.

forecasting risk
The possibility that errors in projected cash flows lead to incorrect decisions.

As stated above, the possibility that we can make a bad decision because of errors in the projected cash flows is called **forecasting risk** (or estimation risk). Because of forecasting risk, there is the danger that we think a project has a positive NPV when it really does not. How is this possible? It happens if we are overly optimistic about the future and, as a result, our projected cash flows don't realistically reflect the possible future cash flows.

So far, we have not explicitly considered what to do about the possibility of errors in our forecasts, so one of our goals in this chapter is to develop some tools that are useful in identifying areas where potential errors exist and where they might be especially damaging. In one form or another, we try to assess the economic reasonableness of our estimates. We also consider how much damage can be done by errors in those estimates.

Sources of Value

The first line of defence against forecasting risk is simply to ask: What is it about this investment that leads to a positive NPV? We should be able to point to something specific as the source of value. For example, if the proposal under consideration involved a new product, we might ask questions such as: Are we certain that our new product is significantly better than that of the competition? Can we truly manufacture at lower cost, or distribute more effectively, or identify undeveloped market niches, or gain control of a market?

These are just a few of the potential sources of value. There are many others. For example, in 2010, Amazon.com, which had built its online empire by selling books, DVDs, and electronics, opened its online grocery store service. Why? The answer is that Amazon would be able to leverage its existing distribution network to provide groceries at lower price for the customers with zero delivery charges. A key factor to keep in mind is the degree of competition in the market. It is a basic principle of economics that positive NPV investments are rare in a highly competitive environment. Therefore, proposals that appear to show significant value in the face of stiff competition are particularly troublesome, and the likely reaction of the competition to any innovations must be closely examined.

Similarly, beware of forecasts that simply extrapolate past trends without taking into account changes in technology or human behaviour. Forecasts similar to the following fall prey to the forecaster's trap:

In 1860, several forecasters were secured from the financial community by the city of New York to forecast the future level of pollution caused by the use of chewing tobacco and horses.... In 1850, the spit level in the gutter and manure level in the middle of the road had both averaged half an inch (approximately 1 cm). By 1860, each had doubled to a level of one inch. Using this historical growth rate, the forecasters projected levels of two inches by 1870, four inches by 1880 and 1,024 inches (22.5 metres) by 1960![1]

To avoid the forecaster's trap, the point to remember is that positive NPV investments are probably not all that common, and the number of positive NPV projects is almost certainly limited for any given firm. If we can't articulate some sound economic basis for thinking ahead of time that we have found something special, the conclusion that our project has a positive NPV should be viewed with some suspicion.

Concept Questions

1. What is forecasting risk? Why is it a concern for the financial manager?
2. What are some potential sources of value in a new project?

11.2 | Scenario and Other What-If Analyses

Our basic approach to evaluating cash flow and NPV estimates involves asking what-if questions. Accordingly, we discuss some organized ways of going about a what-if analysis. Our goal in doing so is to assess the degree of forecasting risk and to identify those components most critical to the success or failure of an investment.

Getting Started

We are investigating a new project. Naturally, we begin by estimating NPV based on our projected cash flows. We call this the *base case*. Now, however, we recognize the possibility of error in those cash flow projections. After completing the base case, we wish to investigate the impact of different assumptions about the future on our estimates.

One way to organize this investigation is to put an upper and lower bound on the various components of the project. For example, suppose we forecast sales at 100 units per year. We know this estimate may be high or low, but we are relatively certain that it is not off by more than 10 units in either direction. We would thus pick a lower bound of 90 and an upper bound of 110. We go on to assign such bounds to any other cash flow components that we are unsure about.

When we pick these upper and lower bounds, we are not ruling out the possibility that the actual values could be outside this range. What we are saying, again loosely speaking, is that it is unlikely that the true average (as opposed to our estimated average) of the possible values is outside this range.

---

[1] This apocryphal example comes from L. Kryzanowski, T. Minh-Chau, and R. Seguin, *Business Solvency Risk Analysis* (Montreal: Institute of Canadian Bankers, 1990), chap. 5, p. 10.

An example is useful to illustrate the idea here. The project under consideration costs $200,000, has a five-year life, and no salvage value. Depreciation is straight-line to keep our example simpler.[2] The required return is 12 percent, and the tax rate is 34 percent. In addition, we have compiled the following information:

	Base Case	Lower Bound	Upper Bound
Unit sales	6000	5500	6500
Price per unit	$80	$75	$85
Variable costs per unit	60	58	62
Fixed costs per year	50,000	45,000	55,000

With this information, we can calculate the base case NPV by first calculating net income:

Sales	$480,000
Variable costs	360,000
Fixed costs	50,000
Depreciation	40,000
EBIT	$ 30,000
Taxes (34%)	10,200
Net income	$ 19,800

Cash flow is thus $30,000 + 40,000 − 10,200 = $59,800 per year. At 12 percent, the five-year annuity factor is 3.6048, so the base case NPV is:

$$\text{Base case NPV} = -\$200,000 + (59,800 \times 3.6048)$$
$$= \$15,567$$

Thus, the project looks good so far.

What we are going to do next is recalculate NPV varying some key inputs such as unit sales, price per unit, variable costs per unit, and fixed costs. With the base case calculations completed, you can see why we assumed straight-line depreciation. It allows us to focus on key variables without the complications of calculating net income separately for each year or using the PVCCATS formula. Of course, for full accuracy you should employ the CCA rules.

Scenario Analysis

scenario analysis
The determination of what happens to NPV estimates when we ask what-if questions.

The basic form of what-if analysis is called **scenario analysis**. What we do is investigate the changes in our NPV estimates that result from asking questions such as: What if unit sales realistically should be projected at 5500 units instead of 6000?

Once we start looking at alternative scenarios, we might find that most of the plausible ones result in positive NPVs. This gives us some confidence in proceeding with the project. If a substantial percentage of the scenarios looks bad, the degree of forecasting risk is high and further investigation is in order.

There are a number of possible scenarios we could consider. A good place to start is the worst-case scenario. This tells us the minimum NPV of the project. If this were positive, we would be in good shape. While we are at it, we also determine the other extreme, the best case. This puts an upper bound on our NPV.

To get the worst case, we assign the least favourable value to each item. This means low values for items such as units sold and price per unit and high values for costs. We do the reverse for the best case. For our project, these values would be:

	Worst Case	Best Case
Unit sales	5500	6500
Price per unit	$75	$85
Variable costs per unit	62	58
Fixed costs	55,000	45,000

With this information, we can calculate the net income and cash flows under each scenario (check these for yourself):

---

[2] We discuss how to change this later.

Scenario	Net Income	Cash Flow	Net Present Value	IRR
Base case	$19,800	$59,800	$ 15,567	15.1%
Worst case*	−15,510	24,490	−111,719	−14.4
Best case	59,730	99,730	159,504	40.9

*We assume a tax credit is created in our worst-case scenario.

What we learn is that under the worst scenario, the cash flow is still positive at $24,490. That's good news. The bad news is that the return is −14.4 percent in this case, and the NPV is −$111,719. Since the project costs $200,000, we stand to lose a little more than half of the original investment under the worst possible scenario. The best case offers an attractive 41 percent return.

The terms *best case* and *worst case* are very commonly used, and we will stick with them, but we should note they are somewhat misleading. The absolutely best thing that could happen would be something absurdly unlikely, such as launching a new diet soda and subsequently learning that our (patented) formulation also just happens to cure the common cold. Similarly, the true worst case would involve some incredibly remote possibility of total disaster. We're not claiming that these things don't happen; once in a while they do. Some products, such as personal computers, succeed beyond the wildest of expectations, and some, turn out to be absolute catastrophes nonetheless. For example, in April 2010, British Petroleum's Gulf of Mexico oil rig *Deepwater Horizon* caught fire and sank following an explosion, leading to a massive oil spill. The leak was finally stopped in July after releasing over 200 million gallons of crude oil into the Gulf. BP's costs associated with the disaster are expected to exceed $40 billion, perhaps by a wide margin. Instead, our point is that in assessing the reasonableness of an NPV estimate, we need to stick to cases that are reasonably likely to occur.

Instead of *best* and *worst*, then, it is probably more accurate to use the words *optimistic* and *pessimistic*. In broad terms, if we were thinking about a reasonable range for, say, unit sales, then what we call the best case would correspond to something near the upper end of that range. The worst case would simply correspond to the lower end.

Not all companies complete (or at least publish) all three estimates. For example, Almaden Minerals Ltd., a Vancouver-based exploration company specializing in the generation of new mineral prospects, made a press release with information concerning its Elk Gold Project in British Columbia. Table 11.1 shows the possible outcomes given by the company.

As you can see, the NPV is projected at $28.7 million in the base case and $67.9 million in the best case. Unfortunately, Almaden did not release a worst-case analysis, but we hope the company also examined this possibility.

As we have mentioned, we could examine an unlimited number of different scenarios. At a minimum, we might want to investigate two intermediate cases by going halfway between the base amounts and the extreme amounts. This would give us five scenarios in all, including the base case.

Beyond this point, it is hard to know when to stop. As we generate more and more possibilities, we run the risk of paralysis by analysis. The difficulty is that no matter how many scenarios we run on our spreadsheet, all we can learn are possibilities, some good and some bad. Beyond that, we don't get any guidance as to what to do. Scenario analysis is thus useful in telling us what can happen and in helping us gauge the potential for disaster, but it does not tell us whether to take the project.

Unfortunately, in practice, even the worst-case scenarios may not be low enough. A recent example is the stress test designed by the European Banking Authority and applied to a wide sample of European banks (representing 60% of the total EU banking assets). The worst-case assumption was based on a long-term interest rate of 3.45% in the Euro area in 2011. However, in 2011 the Euro area long-term interest rate was 4.06%. Besides, the stress test also assumed a worst-case scenario unemployment rate of 10.3% in 2011, but the unemployment rate was 10.4% at the end of 2011.

TABLE 11.1

Project Assumptions and Results for Base and US$1,200 Cases

Project summary	Base Case	$1,200 Case	Unit
Assumed gold price	1000	1200	$US/tr. oz
Tonnes per day treated	500	1000	tpd
Life	7	9	years
Total tonnes treated	1.1	2.6	MT
Grade	4.14	3.89	g/t
Waste: Ore ratio	16.4	30.1	
Plant recovery	92	92	%
Ounces Au produced	139,198	297,239	Tr.oz
Initial capital expense	9.91	17.50	$CADM
Working and preproduction capital	2.27	9.60	$CADM
Waste mining	2.42	1.90	$CAD/tonne waste
Ore mining	8.38	5.87	$CAD/tonne ore
Processing	20.68	14.74	$CAD/tonne ore
Administration and overheads	2.07	1.27	$CAD/tonne ore
Total operating cost	70.30	78.91	$CAD/tonne ore
Pre-tax NPV @ 8%	28.7	67.9	$CADM
Pre-tax IRR	51%	39%	
Max Exposure	13.66	33.53	$CADM
Payback, years from start production	1.85	3.30	years
ratio, gross earnings: max exposure	5.02	6.00	
ratio, NPV: max exposure	2.10	2.03	

Source: www.almadenminerals.com/News%20Releases/2011/jan24-11.html

Sensitivity Analysis

Sensitivity analysis is a variation on scenario analysis that is useful in pinpointing the areas where forecasting risk is especially severe. The basic idea with a sensitivity analysis is to freeze all the variables except one and see how sensitive our estimate of NPV is to changes in that one variable. The logic is exactly the same as for *ceteris paribus* analysis in economics.

If our NPV estimate turns out to be very sensitive to relatively small changes in the projected value of some component of projected cash flow, the forecasting risk associated with that variable is high. To put it another way, NPV depends critically on the assumptions we made about this variable.

Sensitivity analysis is a very commonly used tool. For example, in 2011, Seabridge Gold announced that it had completed a preliminary economic assessment to spend $1.26 billion in start-up costs building a gold-mining operation in Courageous Lake, Northwest Territories. The company reported that the project would have a life of 16 years and an IRR of 9.3 percent assuming a gold price of USD1089 per ounce. However, Seabridge further estimated that, at a price of USD1527 per ounce, the IRR would double to 18.1 percent. Thus, Seabridge focused on the sensitivity of the project's IRR to the price of gold. As of May 2012, Seabridge has been very fortunate with gold prices well above the best-case scenario. Since Seabridge conducted its analysis in 2010, gold prices have soared from $1,121 per ounce to $1,659 per ounce in May 2012.

To illustrate how sensitivity analysis works, we go back to our base case for every item except unit sales. We can then calculate cash flow and NPV using the largest and smallest unit sales figures. This is very easy to do on a spreadsheet program.

Scenario	Unit Sales	Cash Flow	Net Present Value	IRR
Base case	6000	$59,800	$15,567	15.1%
Worst case	5500	53,200	−8,226	10.3
Best case	6500	66,400	39,357	19.7

By way of comparison, we now freeze everything except fixed costs and repeat the analysis:

Scenario	Fixed Income	Cash Flow	Net Present Value	IRR
Base case	$50,000	$59,800	$15,567	15.1%
Worst case	55,000	56,500	3,670	12.7
Best case	45,000	63,100	27,461	17.4

What we see here is that, given our ranges, the estimated NPV of this project is more sensitive to projected unit sales than it is to projected fixed costs. In fact, under the worst case for fixed costs, the NPV is still positive.

The results of our sensitivity analysis for unit sales can be illustrated graphically as in Figure 11.1. Here we place NPV on the vertical axis and unit sales on the horizontal axis. When we plot the combinations of unit sales versus NPV, we see that all possible combinations fall on a straight line. The steeper the resulting line is, the greater the sensitivity of the estimated NPV to the projected value of the variable being investigated.

FIGURE 11.1

Sensitivity analysis for unit sales

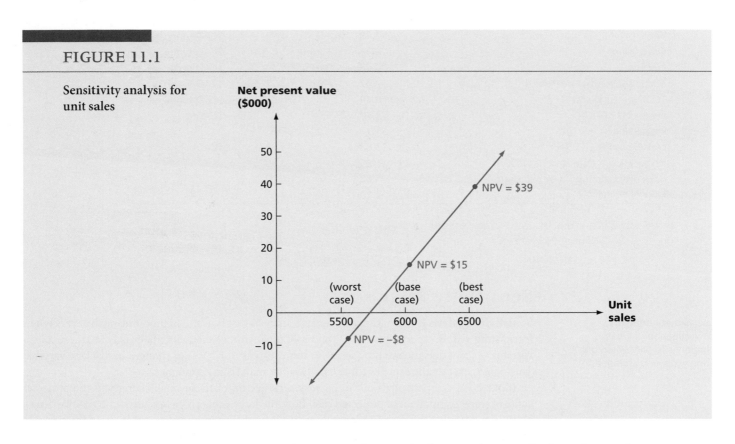

Sensitivity analysis can produce results that vary dramatically depending on the assumptions. For example, in early 2011, Bard Ventures, a Vancouver-based junior mining and exploration company with mineral interests in British Columbia and Ontario, announced its projections for a molybdenum mine in British Columbia. At a cost of capital of 10 percent and average molybdenum price of $19 per ton, the NPV of the new mine would be $112 million with an IRR of 12.4 percent. At a high price of $30 a ton, the NPV would be $1.15 billion, and the IRR would be 32 percent.

As we have illustrated, sensitivity analysis is useful in pinpointing those variables that deserve the most attention. If we find that our estimated NPV is especially sensitive to a variable that is difficult to forecast (such as unit sales), the degree of forecasting risk is high. We might decide that further market research would be a good idea in this case.

Because sensitivity analysis is a form of scenario analysis, it suffers from the same drawbacks. Sensitivity analysis is useful for pointing out where forecasting errors could do the most damage, but it does not tell us what to do about possible errors. Management experience and judgement must still come into play.

Simulation Analysis

simulation analysis
A combination of scenario and sensitivity analyses.

Scenario analysis and sensitivity analysis are widely used in part because they are easily executed on spreadsheets. With scenario analysis, we let all the different variables change, but we let them take on only a small number of values. With sensitivity analysis, we let only one variable change, but we let it take on a large number of values. If we combine the two approaches, the result is a crude form of **simulation analysis**.

Simulation analysis is potentially useful to measure risk in a complex system of variables. The technique is sometimes called *Monte Carlo simulation* and has been used successfully to test gambling strategies.

For example, researchers believed that casino gamblers could shift the odds in their favour in blackjack by varying their bets during the game. In blackjack, you play against the dealer and win if the dealer "goes bust" drawing cards that add to more than 21. The dealer must always take another card if his or her cards add to 16 or less. The probability of the dealer going bust increases as there are more face cards (worth 10) in the deck. To make the strategy work, players count all the cards as they are played and increase their bets when a high number of 10s remain in the deck.

Clearly, it would have been very expensive to test this strategy in a casino using real money. Researchers developed a computer simulation of blackjack and measured hypothetical winnings. They found that the strategy worked but required a substantial stake because it often took considerable time for the winnings to occur.[3]

As our blackjack example illustrates, simulation analysis allows all variables to vary at the same time. If we want to do this, we have to consider a very large number of scenarios, and computer assistance is almost certainly needed. In the simplest case, we start with unit sales and assume that any value in our 5500 to 6500 range is equally likely. We start by randomly picking one value (or by instructing a computer to do so).[4] We then randomly pick a price, a variable cost, and so on.

Once we have values for all the relevant components, we calculate an NPV. Since we won't know the project's risk until the simulation is finished, we avoid prejudging risk by discounting the cash flows at a riskless rate.[5] We repeat this sequence as much as we desire, probably several thousand times. The result is a large number of NPV estimates that we summarize by calculating the average value and some measure of how spread out the different possibilities are. For example, it would be of some interest to know what percentage of the possible scenarios result in negative estimated NPVs.

Because simulation is an extended form of scenario analysis, it has the same problems. Once we have the results, there is no simple decision rule that tells us what to do. Also, we have described a relatively simple form of simulation. To really do it right, we would have to consider the interrelationships between the different cash flow components. For example, oil sands production uses natural gas as input to heat bitumen in extracting oil. As a result, profit is enhanced by higher oil prices but reduced when the gas price goes up. It follows that the historical correlation between oil and natural gas prices is a key input to simulation of an oil sands investment project. However, the recent decoupling of oil and natural gas prices would have led to incorrect forecasts based on such a model. This shows how difficult it is to specify the interrelationships among the variables. Furthermore, we assumed that the possible values were equally likely to occur. It is probably more realistic to assume that values near the base case are more likely than extreme values, but coming up with the probabilities is difficult, to say the least.

For these reasons, the use of simulation is somewhat limited in practice. A recent survey found that about 40 percent of large corporations use sensitivity and scenario analyses as compared to around 20 percent using simulation. However, recent advances in computer software and hardware (and user sophistication) lead us to believe that simulation may become more common in the future, particularly for large-scale projects.

---

[3] To learn more about simulation, blackjack, and what happened when the strategy was implemented in Las Vegas, read *Beat the Dealer* by Edward O. Thorp (New York: Random House, 1962).

[4] Two popular software packages for simulation analysis are Crystal Ball (oracle.com/crystalball/index.html) and @Risk (palisade.com/risk/default.asp).

[5] The rate on Government of Canada Treasury bills is a common example of a riskless rate.

11.3 | Break-Even Analysis

It frequently turns out that the crucial variable for a project is sales volume. If we are thinking of a new product or entering a new market, for example, the hardest thing to forecast accurately is how much we can sell. For this reason, in order to control forecasting risk, sales volume is usually analyzed more closely than other variables.

Break-even analysis is a popular and commonly used tool for analyzing the relationships between sales volume and profitability. There are a variety of different break-even measures, and we have already seen several types. All break-even measures have a similar goal. Loosely speaking, we are always asking: How bad do sales have to get before we actually begin to lose money? Implicitly, we are also asking: Is it likely that things will get that bad? To get started on this subject, we discuss fixed and variable costs.

Fixed and Variable Costs

In discussing break-even, the difference between fixed and variable costs becomes very important. As a result, we need to be a little more explicit about the difference than we have been so far.

variable costs
Costs that change when the quantity of output changes.

VARIABLE COSTS   By definition, **variable costs** change as the quantity of output changes, and they are zero when production is zero. For example, direct labour costs and raw material costs are usually considered variable. This makes sense because, if we shut down operations tomorrow, there will be no future costs for labour or raw materials.

We assume that variable costs are a constant amount per unit of output. This simply means that total variable cost is equal to the cost per unit multiplied by the number of units. In other words, the relationship between total variable cost (VC), cost per unit of output (v), and total quantity of output (Q) can be written simply as:

$$\text{Variable cost} = \text{Total quantity of output} \times \text{Cost per unit of output}$$
$$VC = Q \times v$$

For example, suppose that v is $2 per unit. If Q is 1000 units, what will V_C be?

$$VC = Q \times v$$
$$= \$1,000 \times \$2$$
$$= \$2,000$$

Similarly, if Q is 5000 units, then V_C is $5000 \times \$2 = \$10,000$. Figure 11.2 illustrates the relationship between output level and variable costs in this case. In Figure 11.2, notice that increasing output by one unit results in variable costs rising by $2, so the "rise over the run" (the slope of the line) is given by $2/1 = \$2$.

fixed costs
Costs that do not change when the quantity of output changes during a particular time period.

FIXED COSTS   By definition, **fixed costs** do not change during a specified time period. So, unlike variable costs, they do not depend on the amount of goods or services produced during a period (at least within some range of production). For example, the lease payment on a production facility and the company president's salary are fixed costs, at least over some period.

Naturally, fixed costs are not fixed forever. They are fixed only during some particular time, say a quarter or a year. Beyond that time, leases can be terminated and executives retired. More to the point, any fixed cost can be modified or eliminated given enough time; so, in the long run, all costs are variable.

Notice that during the time that a cost is fixed, that cost is effectively a sunk cost because we are going to have to pay it no matter what.

TOTAL COSTS   Total costs (TC) for a given level of output are the sum of variable costs (VC) and fixed costs (FC):

$$TC = VC + FC$$
$$TC = v \times Q + FC$$

So, for example, if we have a variable cost of $3 per unit and fixed costs of $8,000 per year, our total cost is:

$$TC = \$3 \times Q + \$8,000$$

FIGURE 11.2

Output level and total costs

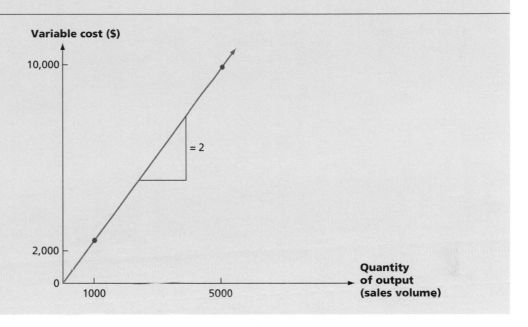

If we produce 6000 units, our total production cost would be $3 \times 6000 + \$8,000 = \$26,000$. At other production levels, we have:

Quantity Produced	Total Variable Cost	Fixed Costs	Total Costs
0	$ 0	$8,000	$ 8,000
1000	3,000	8,000	11,000
5000	15,000	8,000	23,000
10,000	30,000	8,000	38,000

marginal cost or incremental cost
The change in costs that occurs when there is a small change in output.

By plotting these points in Figure 11.3, we see that the relationship between quantity produced and total cost is given by a straight line. In Figure 11.3, notice that total costs are equal to fixed costs when sales are zero. Beyond that point, every one-unit increase in production leads to a $3 increase in total costs, so the slope of the line is 3. In other words, the **marginal cost** or **incremental cost** of producing one more unit is $3.

Accounting Break-Even

accounting break-even
The sales level that results in zero project net income.

The most widely used measure of break-even is **accounting break-even**. The accounting break-even point is simply the sales level that results in a zero project net income.

To determine a project's accounting break-even, we start with some common sense. Suppose we retail one-terabyte Blu-ray discs for $5 a piece. We can buy Blu-ray discs from a wholesale supplier for $3 a piece. We have accounting expenses of $600 in fixed costs and $300 in depreciation. How many Blu-ray discs do we have to sell to break even, that is, for net income to be zero?

For every Blu-ray disc we sell, we pick up $5 − 3 = $2 toward covering our other expenses. We have to cover a total of $600 + 300 = $900 in accounting expenses, so we obviously need to sell $900/$2 = 450 Blu-ray discs. We can check this by noting that, at a sales level of 450 units, our revenues are $5 × 450 = $2,250 and our variable costs are $3 × 450 = $1,350. The income statement is thus:

Sales	$2,250
Variable costs	1,350
Fixed costs	600
Depreciation	300
EBIT	$ 0
Taxes	$ 0
Net income	$ 0

FIGURE 11.3

Output level and
variable costs

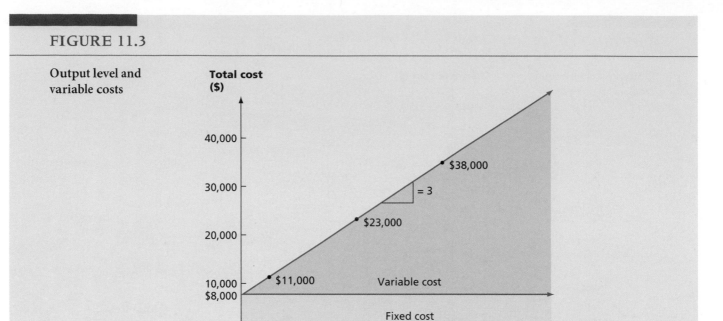

Remember, since we are discussing a proposed new project, we do not consider any interest expense in calculating net income or cash flow from the project. Also, notice that we include depreciation in calculating expenses here, even though depreciation is not a cash outflow. That is why we call it accounting break-even. Finally, notice that when net income is zero, so are pretax income and, of course, taxes. In accounting terms, our revenues are equal to our costs, so there is no profit to tax.

Figure 11.4 is another way to see what is happening. This figure looks like Figure 11.3 except that we add a line for revenues. As indicated, total revenues are zero when output is zero. Beyond that, each unit sold brings in another $5, so the slope of the revenue line is 5.

FIGURE 11.4

Accounting break-even

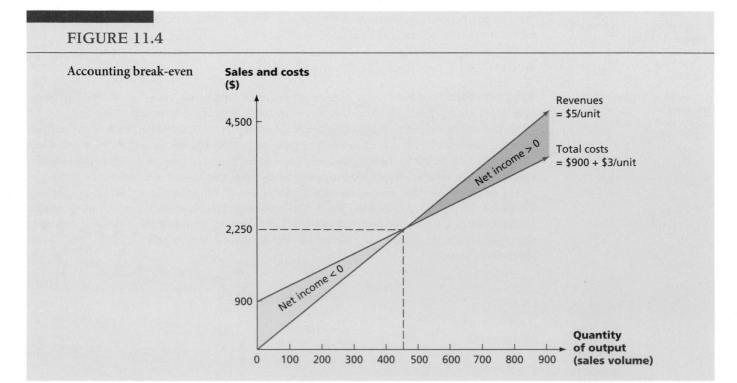

From our preceding discussion, we break even when revenues are equal to total costs. The line for revenues and the line for total cost cross right where output is 450 units. As illustrated, at any level below 450, our accounting profit is negative and, at any level above 450, we have a positive net income.

Accounting Break-Even: A Closer Look

In our numerical example, notice that the break-even level is equal to the sum of fixed costs and depreciation divided by price per unit less variable costs per unit. This is always true. To see why, we recall the following set of abbreviations for the different variables:

$$P = \text{Selling price per unit}$$
$$v = \text{Variable cost per unit}$$
$$Q = \text{Total units sold}$$
$$FC = \text{Fixed costs}$$
$$D = \text{Depreciation}$$
$$t = \text{Tax rate}$$
$$VC = \text{Variable cost in dollars}$$

Project net income is given by:

$$\text{Net income} = (\text{Sales} - \text{Variable costs} - \text{Fixed costs} - \text{Depreciation}) \times (1 - t)$$
$$= (S - VC - FC - D) \times (1 - t)$$

From here, it is not difficult to calculate the break-even point. If we set this net income equal to zero, we get:

$$\text{Net income} = 0 = (S - VC - FC - D) \times (1 - t)$$

Divide both sides by $(1 - t)$ to get:

$$S - VC - FC - D = 0$$

As we have seen, this says, when net income is zero, so is pretax income. If we recall that $S = P \times Q$ and $VC = v \times Q$, we can rearrange this to solve for the break-even level:

$$S - VC = FC + D$$
$$P \times Q - v \times Q = FC + D$$
$$(P - v) \times Q = FC + D \qquad [11.1]$$
$$Q = (FC + D)/(P - v)$$

This is the same result we described earlier.

Uses for the Accounting Break-Even

Why would anyone be interested in knowing the accounting break-even point? To illustrate how it can be useful, suppose we are a small specialty ice cream manufacturer in Vancouver with a strictly local distribution. We are thinking about expanding into new markets. Based on the estimated cash flow, we find that the expansion has a positive NPV.

Going back to our discussion of forecasting risk, it is likely that what makes or breaks our expansion is sales volume. The reason is that, in this case at least, we probably have a fairly good idea of what we can charge for the ice cream. Further, we know relevant production and distribution costs with a fair degree of accuracy because we are already in the business. What we do not know with any real precision is how much ice cream we can sell.

Given the costs and selling price, however, we can immediately calculate the break-even point. Once we have done so, we might find that we need to get 30 percent of the market just to break even. If we think that this is unlikely to occur because, for example, we only have 10 percent of our current market, we know that our forecast is questionable and there is a real possibility that the true NPV is negative.

On the other hand, we might find that we already have firm commitments from buyers for about the break-even amount, so we are almost certain that we can sell more. Because the forecasting risk is much lower, we have greater confidence in our estimates. If we need outside financing for our expansion, this break-even analysis would be useful in presenting our proposal to our banker.

COMPLICATIONS IN APPLYING BREAK-EVEN ANALYSIS   Our discussion ignored several complications you may encounter in applying this useful tool. To begin, it is only in the short run that revenues and variable costs fall along straight lines. For large increases in sales, price may decrease with volume discounts while variable costs increase as production runs up against capacity limits. If you have sufficient data, you can redraw cost and revenue as curves. Otherwise, remember that the analysis is most accurate in the short run.

Further, while our examples classified costs as fixed or variable, in practice some costs are semivariable (i.e., partly fixed and partly variable). A common example is telephone expense, which breaks down into a fixed charge plus a variable cost depending on the volume of calls. In applying break-even analysis, you have to make judgements on the breakdown.

Concept Questions

1. How are fixed costs similar to sunk costs?
2. What is net income at the accounting break-even point? What about taxes?
3. Why might a financial manager be interested in the accounting break-even point?

11.4 | Operating Cash Flow, Sales Volume, and Break-Even

Accounting break-even is one tool that is useful for project analysis. Ultimately, however, we are more interested in cash flow than accounting income. So, for example, if sales volume is the critical variable in avoiding forecasting risk, we need to know more about the relationship between sales volume and cash flow than just the accounting break-even.

Our goal in this section is to illustrate the relationship between operating cash flow and sales volume. We also discuss some other break-even measures. To simplify matters somewhat, we ignore the effect of taxes.[6] We start by looking at the relationship between accounting break-even and cash flow.

Accounting Break-Even and Cash Flow

Now that we know how to find the accounting break-even, it is natural to wonder what happens with cash flow. To illustrate, suppose that Victoria Sailboats Limited is considering whether to launch its new Mona-class sailboat. The selling price would be $40,000 per boat. The variable costs would be about half that, or $20,000 per boat, and fixed costs will be $500,000 per year.

THE BASE CASE   The total investment needed to undertake the project is $3.5 million for leasehold improvements to the company's factory. This amount will be depreciated straight-line to zero over the five-year life of the equipment. The salvage value is zero, and there are no working capital consequences. Victoria has a 20 percent required return on new projects.

Based on market surveys and historical experience, Victoria projects total sales for the five years at 425 boats, or about 85 boats per year. Should this project be launched?

To begin (ignoring taxes), the operating cash flow at 85 boats per year is:

$$
\begin{aligned}
\text{Operating cash flow} &= \text{EBIT} + \text{Depreciation} - \text{Taxes} \\
&= (S - VC - FC - D) + D - 0 \\
&= 85 \times (\$40{,}000 - 20{,}000) - \$500{,}000 \\
&= \$1{,}200{,}000 \text{ per year}
\end{aligned}
$$

At 20 percent, the five-year annuity factor is 2.9906, so the NPV is:

---

[6]This is a minor simplification because the firm pays no taxes when it just breaks even in the accounting sense. We also use straight-line depreciation, realistic in this case for leasehold improvements, for simplicity.

$$\begin{aligned} \text{NPV} &= -\$3,500,000 + 1,200,000 \times 2.9906 \\ &= -\$3,500,000 + 3,588,720 \\ &= \$88,720 \end{aligned}$$

In the absence of additional information, the project should be launched.

CALCULATING THE ACCOUNTING BREAK-EVEN LEVEL   To begin looking a little more closely at this project, you might ask a series of questions. For example, how many new boats does Victoria need to sell for the project to break even on an accounting basis? If Victoria does break even, what would be the annual cash flow from the project? What would be the return on the investment?

Before fixed costs and depreciation are considered, Victoria generates $40,000 - 20,000 = \$20,000$ per boat (this is revenue less variable cost). Depreciation is $3,500,000/5 = \$700,000$ per year. Fixed costs and depreciation together total $1.2 million, so Victoria needs to sell $(F_c + D)/(P - v) = \$1.2$ million$/\$20,000 = 60$ boats per year to break even on an accounting basis. This is 25 boats less than projected sales; so, assuming that Victoria is confident that its projection is accurate to within, say, 15 boats, it appears unlikely that the new investment will fail to at least break even on an accounting basis.

To calculate Victoria's cash flow, we note that if 60 boats are sold, net income is exactly zero. Recalling from our previous chapter that operating cash flow for a project can be written as net income plus depreciation (the bottom-up definition), the operating cash flow is obviously equal to the depreciation, or $700,000 in this case. The internal rate of return would be exactly zero (why?).

The bad news is that a project that just breaks even on an accounting basis has a negative NPV and a zero return. For our sailboat project, the fact that we would almost surely break even on an accounting basis is partially comforting since our downside risk (our potential loss) is limited, but we still don't know if the project is truly profitable. More work is needed.

SALES VOLUME AND OPERATING CASH FLOW   At this point, we can generalize our example and introduce some other break-even measures. As we just discussed, we know that, ignoring taxes, a project's operating cash flow (OCF) can be written simply as EBIT plus depreciation:[7]

$$\begin{aligned} \text{OCF} &= [(P - v) \times Q - FC - D] + D \\ &= (P - v) \times Q - FC \end{aligned} \qquad [11.2]$$

For the Victoria Sailboats project, the general relationship between operating cash flow and sales volume is thus:

$$\begin{aligned} \text{OCF} &= (P - v) \times Q - FC \\ &= (\$40,000 - 20,000) \times Q - \$500,000 \\ &= -\$500,000 + \$20,000 \times Q \end{aligned}$$

What this tells us is that the relationship between operating cash flow and sales volume is given by a straight line with a slope of $20,000 and a y-intercept of $-\$500,000$. If we calculate some different values, we get:

Quantity Sold	Operating Cash Flow (in dollars)
0	−500,000
15	−200,000
30	100,000
50	500,000
75	1,000,000

These points are plotted in Figure 11.5. In Figure 11.5, we have indicated three different break-even points. We already covered the accounting break-even. We discuss the other two next.

---

[7]With no taxes, depreciation drops out of cash flow because there is no tax shield.

FIGURE 11.5

Operating cash flow
and sales volume

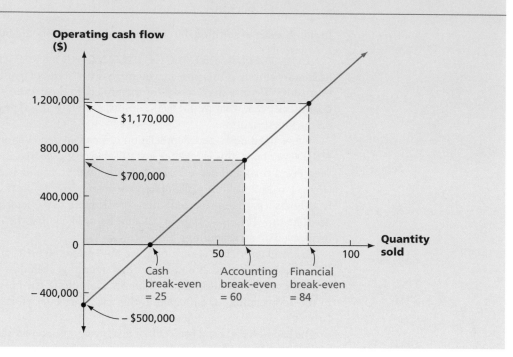

Cash Flow and Financial Break-Even Points

We know that the relationship between operating cash flow and sales volume (ignoring taxes) is:

$$OCF = (P - v) \times Q - FC$$

If we rearrange this and solve it for Q, we get:

$$Q = (FC + OCF)/(P - v) \qquad [11.3]$$

This tells us what sales volume (Q) is necessary to achieve any given OCF, so this result is more general than the accounting break-even. We use it to find the various break-even points in Figure 11.5.

CASH BREAK-EVEN   We have seen that our sailboat project that breaks even on an accounting basis has a net income of zero, but it still has a positive cash flow. At some sales level below the accounting break-even, the operating cash flow actually goes negative. This is a particularly unpleasant occurrence. If it happens, we actually have to supply additional cash to the project just to keep it afloat.

cash break-even
The sales level where operating cash flow is equal to zero.

To calculate the **cash break-even** (the point where operating cash flow is equal to zero), we put in a zero for OCF:

$$Q = (FC + 0)/(P - v)$$
$$= \$500,000/\$20,000$$
$$= 25$$

Victoria must therefore sell 25 boats to cover the $500,000 in fixed costs. As we show in Figure 11.5, this point occurs right where the operating cash flow line crosses the horizontal axis.

In this example, cash break-even is lower than accounting break-even. Equation 11.3 shows why; when we calculated accounting break-even we substituted depreciation of $700,000 for OCF. The formula for cash break-even sets OCF equal to zero. Figure 11.5 shows that accounting break-even is 60 boats and cash break-even, 25 boats. Accounting break-even is 35 boats higher. Since Victoria generates a $20,000 contribution per boat, the difference exactly covers the depreciation of $700,000 = 35 × $20,000.

This analysis also shows that cash break-even does not always have to be lower than accounting break-even. To see why, suppose Victoria had to make a cash outlay in Year 1 of $1 million for working capital. Accounting break-even remains at 60 boats. The new cash break-even is 75 boats:

$$Q = (FC + OCF)/(P - v)$$
$$= (\$500,000 + 1,000,000)/(\$20,000)$$
$$= 75$$

In general, retail firms and other companies that experience substantial needs for working capital relative to depreciation expenses have cash break-evens greater than accounting break-evens.

Regardless of whether the cash break-even point is more or less than the accounting break-even, a project that just breaks even on a cash flow basis can cover its own fixed operating costs, but that is all. It never pays back anything, so the original investment is a complete loss (the IRR is −100 percent).

financial break-even
The sales level that results in a zero NPV.

FINANCIAL BREAK-EVEN   The last case we consider is **financial break-even**, the sales level that results in a zero NPV. To the financial manager, this is the most interesting case. What we do is first determine what operating cash flow has to be for the NPV to be zero. We then use this amount to determine the sales volume.

To illustrate, recall that Victoria requires a 20 percent return on its $3,500,000 investment. How many sailboats does Victoria have to sell to break even once we account for the 20 percent per year opportunity cost?

The sailboat project has a five-year life. The project has a zero NPV when the present value of the operating cash flow equals the $3,500,000 investment. Since the cash flow is the same each year, we can solve for the unknown amount by viewing it as an ordinary annuity. The five-year annuity factor at 20 percent is 2.9906, and the OCF can be determined as follows:

$$\$3,500,000 = OCF \times 2.9906$$
$$OCF = \$3,500,000/2.9906$$
$$= \$1,170,334$$

Victoria thus needs an operating cash flow of $1,170,000 each year to break even. We can now plug this OCF into the equation for sales volume:

$$Q = (\$500,000 + \$1,170,334)/\$20,000$$
$$= 83.5$$

So Victoria needs to sell about 84 boats per year. This is not good news.

As indicated in Figure 11.5, the financial break-even is substantially higher than the accounting break-even point. This is often the case. Moreover, what we have discovered is that the sailboat project has a substantial degree of forecasting risk. We project sales of 85 boats per year, but it takes 84 just to earn our required return.

CONCLUSION   Overall, it seems unlikely that the Victoria Sailboats project would fail to break even on an accounting basis. However, there appears to be a very good chance that the true NPV is negative. This illustrates the danger in just looking at the accounting break-even.

Victoria can learn this lesson from the U.S. government. In the early 1970s, the U.S. Congress voted a guarantee for Lockheed Corporation, the airplane manufacturer, based on analysis that showed the L1011-TriStar would break even on an accounting basis. It subsequently turned out that the financial break-even point was much higher.

What should Victoria Sailboats do? Is the new project all wet? The decision at this point is essentially a managerial issue—a judgement call. The crucial questions are:

1. How much confidence do we have in our projections? Do we think that forecasting risk is too high?
2. How important is the project to the future of the company?
3. How badly will the company be hurt if sales do turn out low?

What options are available to the company?

We consider questions such as these in a later section. For future reference, our discussion of different break-even measures is summarized in Table 11.2.

Concept Questions

1. If a project breaks even on an accounting basis, what is its operating cash flow?
2. If a project breaks even on a cash basis, what is its operating cash flow?
3. If a project breaks even on a financial basis, what do you know about its discounted payback?

11.5 | Operating Leverage

We have discussed how to calculate and interpret various measures of break-even for a proposed project. What we have not explicitly discussed is what determines these points and how they might be changed. We now turn to this subject.

The Basic Idea

operating leverage
The degree to which a firm or project relies on fixed costs.

Operating leverage is the degree to which a project or firm is committed to fixed production costs. A firm with low operating leverage has low fixed costs (as a proportion of total costs) compared to a firm with high operating leverage. Generally, projects with a relatively heavy investment in plant and equipment have a relatively high degree of operating leverage. Such projects are said to be capital intensive. Airlines and hotels are two industries that have high operating leverage.

Any time we are thinking about a new venture, there are normally alternative ways of producing and delivering the product. For example, Victoria Sailboats can purchase the necessary equipment and build all the components for its sailboats in-house. Alternatively, some of the work could be farmed out to other firms. The first option involves a greater investment in plant and equipment, greater fixed costs and depreciation, and, as a result, a higher degree of operating leverage.

TABLE 11.2 Summary of break-even measures

The general expression.
Ignoring taxes, the relation between operating cash flow (OCF) and quantity of output or sales volume (Q) is

$$Q = \frac{FC + OCF}{P - v}$$

where
FC = Total fixed costs
P = Price per unit
v = Variable cost per unit
As shown next, this relation can be used to determine the accounting, cash, and financial break-even points.

The accounting break-even point.
Accounting break-even occurs when net income is zero. Operating cash flow (OCF) is equal to depreciation when net income is zero, so the accounting break-even point is:

$$Q = \frac{FC + D}{P - v}$$

A project that always just breaks even on an accounting basis has a payback exactly equal to its life, a negative NPV, and an IRR of zero.

The cash break-even point.
Cash break-even occurs when operating cash flow (OCF) is zero; the cash break-even point is thus:

$$Q = \frac{FC}{P - v}$$

A project that always just breaks even on a cash basis never pays back, its NPV is negative and equal to the initial outlay, and the IRR is −100%.

The financial break-even point.
Financial break-even occurs when the NPV of the project is zero. The financial break-even point is thus:

$$Q = \frac{FC + OCF^*}{P - v}$$

where OCF* is the level of OCF that results in a zero NPV. A project that breaks even on a financial basis has a discounted payback equal to its life, a zero NPV, and an IRR just equal to the required return.

Implications of Operating Leverage

Regardless of how it is measured, operating leverage has important implications for project evaluation. Fixed costs act like a lever in the sense that a small percentage change in operating revenue can be magnified into a large percentage change in operating cash flow and NPV. This explains why we call it operating leverage.

The higher the degree of operating leverage, the greater is the potential danger from forecasting risk. The reason is that relatively small errors in forecasting sales volume can get magnified or "levered up" into large errors in cash flow projections.

From a managerial perspective, one way of coping with highly uncertain projects is to keep the degree of operating leverage as low as possible.[8] This generally has the effect of keeping the break-even point (however measured) at its minimum level. We illustrate this point after discussing how to measure operating leverage.

Measuring Operating Leverage

degree of operating leverage (DOL)

The percentage change in operating cash flow relative to the percentage change in quantity sold.

One way of measuring operating leverage is to ask: If the quantity sold rises by 5 percent, what will be the percentage change in operating cash flow? In other words, the **degree of operating leverage (DOL)** is defined such that

Percentage change in OCF = DOL × Percentage change in Q

Based on the relationship between OCF and Q, DOL can be written as:[9]

$$DOL = 1 + FC/OCF$$

Also, based on our definition of OCF:

$$OCF + FC = (P - v) \times Q$$

Thus, DOL can be written as:

$$DOL = (OCF + FC)/OCF$$
$$= 1 + FC/OCF$$

The ratio FC/OCF simply measures fixed costs as a percentage of total operating cash flow. Notice that zero fixed costs would result in a DOL of 1, implying that changes in quantity sold would show up one for one in operating cash flow. In other words, no magnification or leverage effect would exist.

To illustrate this measure of operating leverage, we go back to the Victoria Sailboats project. Fixed costs were $500 and $(P - v)$ was $20, so OCF was:

$$OCF = -\$500 + 20 \times Q$$

Suppose Q is currently 50 boats. At this level of output, OCF is $-\$500 + 1,000 = \$500$.

If Q rises by 1 unit to 51, then the percentage change in Q is $(51 - 50)/50 = .02$, or 2%. OCF rises to $520, a change of $(P - v) = \$20$. The percentage change in OCF is $(\$520 - 500)/500 = .04$, or 4%. So a 2 percent increase in the number of boats sold leads to a 4 percent increase in operating cash flow. The degree of operating leverage must be exactly 2.00. We can check this by noting that:

$$DOL = 1 + FC/OCF$$
$$= 1 + \$500/\$500$$
$$= 2$$

This verifies our previous calculations.

---

[8] Another response is to keep the amount of debt low. We cover financial leverage in Chapter 16.

[9] To see this, note that, if Q goes up by 1 unit, OCF goes up by $(P - v)$. The percentage change in Q is $1/Q$, and the percentage change in OCF is $(P - v)/$OCF. Given this, we have:

Percentage of change in OCF = DOL × Percentage change in Q

$$(P - v)/OCF = DOL \times 1/Q$$
$$DOL = (P - v) \times Q/OCF$$

Our formulation of DOL depends on the current output level, Q. However, it can handle changes from the current level of any size, not just one unit. For example, suppose Q rises from 50 to 75, a 50 percent increase. With DOL equal to 2, operating cash flow should increase by 100 percent, or exactly double. Does it? The answer is yes, because, at a Q of 75, OCF is:

$$-\$500 + \$20 \times 75 = \$1,000$$

Notice that operating leverage declines as output (Q) rises. For example, at an output level of 75, we have:

$$
\begin{aligned}
\text{DOL} &= 1 + \$500/1,000 \\
&= 1.50
\end{aligned}
$$

The reason DOL declines is that fixed costs, considered as a percentage of operating cash flow, get smaller and smaller, so the leverage effect diminishes.[10]

What do you think DOL works out to at the cash break-even point, an output level of 25 boats? At the cash break-even point, OCF is zero. Since you cannot divide by zero, DOL is undefined.

EXAMPLE 11.1: Operating Leverage

The Huskies Corporation currently sells gourmet dog food for $1.20 per can. The variable cost is 80 cents per can, and the packaging and marketing operation has fixed costs of $360,000 per year. Depreciation is $60,000 per year. What is the accounting break-even? Ignoring taxes, what will be the increase in operating cash flow if the quantity sold rises to 10 percent more than the break-even point?

The accounting break-even is $420,000/.40 = 1,050,000 cans. As we know, the operating cash flow is equal to the $60,000 depreciation at this level of production, so the degree of operating leverage is:

$$
\begin{aligned}
\text{DOL} &= 1 + FC/OCF \\
&= 1 + \$360,000/\$60,000 \\
&= 7
\end{aligned}
$$

Given this, a 10 percent increase in the number of cans of dog food sold increases operating cash flow by a substantial 70 percent.

To check this answer, we note that if sales rise by 10 percent, the quantity sold rises to $1,050,000 \times 1.1 = 1,155,000$. Ignoring taxes, the operating cash flow is $1,155,000 \times .40 - \$360,000 = \$102,000$. Compared to the $60,000 cash flow we had, this is exactly 70 percent more: $102,000/60,000 = 1.70$.

Operating Leverage and Break-Even

We illustrate why operating leverage is an important consideration by examining the Victoria Sailboats project under an alternative scenario. At a Q of 85 boats, the degree of operating leverage for the sailboat project under the original scenario is:

$$
\begin{aligned}
\text{DOL} &= 1 + FC/\text{OCF} \\
&= 1 + \$500/1,200 \\
&= 1.42
\end{aligned}
$$

Also, recall that the NPV at a sales level of 85 boats was $88,720, and that the accounting break-even was 60 boats.

An option available to Victoria is to subcontract production of the boat hull assemblies. If it does, the necessary investment falls to $3.2 million, and the fixed operating costs fall to $180,000. However, variable costs rise to $25,000 per boat since subcontracting is more expensive than doing it in-house. Ignoring taxes, evaluate this option.

For practice, see if you don't agree with the following:

NPV at 20% (85 units) = $74,720

Accounting break-even = 55 boats

Degree of operating leverage = 1.16

---

[10] Students who have studied economics will recognize DOL as an elasticity. Recall that elasticities vary with quantity along demand and supply curves. For the same reason, DOL varies with unit sales, Q.

What has happened? This option results in slightly lower estimated net present value, and the accounting break-even point falls to 55 boats from 60 boats.

Given that this alternative has the lower NPV, is there any reason to consider it further? Maybe there is. The degree of operating leverage is substantially lower in the second case. If we are worried about the possibility of an overly optimistic projection, we might prefer to subcontract. There is another reason we might consider the second arrangement. If sales turned out better than expected, we always have the option of starting to produce in-house later. As a practical matter, it is much easier to increase operating leverage (by purchasing equipment) than to decrease it (by selling equipment).[11] As we discuss later, one of the drawbacks to discounted cash flow is that it is difficult to explicitly include options of this sort, even though they may be quite important.

Concept Questions

1. What is operating leverage?
2. How is operating leverage measured?
3. What are the implications of operating leverage for the financial manager?

11.6 | Managerial Options

In our capital budgeting analysis thus far, we have more or less ignored the possibility of future managerial actions. Implicitly, we assumed that once a project is launched, its basic features cannot be changed. For this reason, we say that our analysis is static (as opposed to dynamic).

managerial options or real options
Opportunities that managers can exploit if certain things happen in the future.

In reality, depending on what actually happens in the future, there are always ways to modify a project. We call these opportunities **managerial options or real options**. As we will see, in many cases managerial options can improve project cash flows, making the best case better while placing a floor under the worst case. As a result, ignoring such options would lead to forecasting risk in underestimating NPV. There are a great number of these options. The way a product is priced, manufactured, advertised, and produced can all be changed, and these are just a few of the possibilities.[12]

For example in February 2012, Stephen Harper, the prime minister of Canada, announced a 'panda diplomacy' agreement during his trip to China. Under the arrangement, two giant pandas will spend five years at the Toronto zoo and then move on to Calgary for another five years. The Toronto zoo, attracts around 1.3 million visitors each year but has suffered from a drop in attendance. Since 2008, the officials of the Toronto zoo were contemplating launching an ambitious project to revitalize the zoo.

The arrival of pandas will be costly for the Toronto zoo. The rent on the pandas is $1 million a year plus an extra $200,000 if a cub is born. Also, enormous amounts of bamboo must be shipped from the United States at an annual cost of $200,000 Is this a good managerial option for the Toronto zoo management?

In 1985, Toronto zoo experienced its highest annual attendance ever with 1.9 million visitors when it housed pandas for only three months The Toronto zoo management is confident that the zoo would break-even on this panda exhibit. The panda conservation program is a part of the zoo's 25 year master redevelopment plan. As this example suggests, the possibility of future actions is important. We discuss some of the most common types of managerial actions in the next few sections.[13]

CONTINGENCY PLANNING   The various what-if procedures, particularly the break-even measures, in this chapter have another use. We can also view them as primitive ways of exploring the dynamics of a project and investigating managerial options. What we think about are some of the possible futures that could come about and what actions we might take if they do.

---

[11] In the extreme case, if firms were able to readjust the ratio of variable and fixed costs continually, there would be no increased risk associated with greater operating leverage.

[12] We introduce managerial options here and return to the topic in more depth in Chapter 25.

[13] Sources for the panda option are cbc.ca/news/canada/toronto/story/2012/02/11/toronto-china-giant-pandas-zoo.html and ctv.ca/CTVNews/Canada/20120211/Chinese-pandas-expected-to-boost-Toronto-Zoo-attendance-120211/

contingency planning
Taking into account the managerial options that are implicit in a project.

For example, we might find that a project fails to break even when sales drop below 10,000 units. This is a fact that is interesting to know, but the more important thing is to go on and ask: What actions are we going to take if this actually occurs? This is called **contingency planning**, and it amounts to an investigation of some of the managerial options implicit in a project.

There is no limit to the number of possible futures or contingencies that we could investigate. However, there are some broad classes, and we consider these next.

THE OPTION TO EXPAND   One particularly important option that we have not explicitly addressed is the option to expand. If we truly find a positive NPV project, there is an obvious consideration. Can we expand the project or repeat it to get an even larger NPV? Our static analysis implicitly assumes that the scale of the project is fixed.

For example, if the sales demand for a particular product were to greatly exceed expectations, we might investigate increasing production. If this is not feasible for some reason, we could always increase cash flow by raising the price. Either way, the potential cash flow is higher than we have indicated because we have implicitly assumed that no expansion or price increase is possible. Overall, because we ignore the option to expand in our analysis, we underestimate NPV (all other things being equal).

THE OPTION TO ABANDON   At the other extreme, the option to scale back or even abandon a project is also quite valuable. For example, if a project does not break even on a cash flow basis, it can't even cover its own expenses. We would be better off if we just abandoned it. Our DCF analysis implicitly assumes that we would keep operating even in this case.

Sometimes the best thing to do is to reverse direction. For example, Merrill Lynch Canada has done this three times. First, it built up a retail brokerage operation in the 1980s and sold it to CIBC Wood Gundy in 1990. Later, in 1998, Merrill Lynch made headlines by paying $1.26 billion for Midland Walwyn, the last independently owned retail brokerage firm in Canada. The reason? Merrill Lynch wanted to continue its globalization drive and get back into the business it had earlier abandoned. However, in November 2001, Merrill Lynch Canada once again sold its retail brokerage and mutual fund and securities services businesses to CIBC Wood Gundy. This sale was part of an effort to cut back expenses on its international operations.

In reality, if sales demand were significantly below expectations, we might be able to sell some capacity or put it to another use. Maybe the product or service could be redesigned or otherwise improved. Regardless of the specifics, we once again underestimate NPV if we assume the project must last for some fixed number of years, no matter what happens in the future. For example, during the current economic crisis, GM and Chrysler had to shut down a number of plants in Canada and abandon some of their projects.

THE OPTION TO WAIT   Implicitly, we have treated proposed investments as if they were go or no-go decisions. Actually, there is a third possibility. The project can be postponed, perhaps in hope of more favourable conditions. We call this the option to wait.

For example, suppose an investment costs $120 and has a perpetual cash flow of $10 per year. If the discount rate is 10 percent, the NPV is $10/.10 − 120 = −$20, so the project should not be undertaken now. However, this does not mean we should forget about the project forever, because in the next period, the appropriate discount rate could be different. If it fell to, say, 5 percent, the NPV would be $10/.05 − 120 = $80, and we would take it.

More generally, as long as there is some possible future scenario under which a project has a positive NPV, the option to wait is valuable. Related to the option to wait is the option to suspend operations. For example, in 2012, Translink, the organization responsible for regional transportation around Vancouver, put its expansion plans on hold due to lack of cash. Of course, Translink could have raised money by increasing transit fares, but this action might have led to a decrease in ridership.

THE TAX OPTION   Investment decisions may trigger favourable or unfavourable tax treatment of existing assets. This can occur because, as you recall from Chapter 2, capital cost allowance calculations are usually based on assets in a pooled class. Tax liabilities for recaptured CCA and tax shelters from terminal losses occur only when an asset class is liquidated either by selling all the assets or writing the undepreciated capital cost below zero. As a result, management has a potentially valuable tax option.

For example, suppose your firm is planning to replace all its company delivery vans at the end of the year. Because of unfavourable conditions in the used vehicle market, prices are depressed and you expect to realize a loss. Since you are replacing the vehicles, as opposed to closing out the class, no immediate tax shelter results from the loss. If your company is profitable and the potential tax shelter sizable, you could exercise your tax option by closing out Class 12. To do this, you could lease the new vehicles or set up a separate firm to purchase the vehicles.

OPTIONS IN CAPITAL BUDGETING: AN EXAMPLE   Suppose we are examining a new project. To keep things relatively simple, we expect to sell 100 units per year at $1 net cash flow apiece into perpetuity. We thus expect the cash flow to be $100 per year.

In one year, we will know more about the project. In particular, we will have a better idea of whether it is successful or not. If it looks like a long-run success, the expected sales could be revised upward to 150 units per year. If it does not, the expected sales could be revised downward to 50 units per year.

Success and failure are equally likely. Notice that with an even chance of selling 50 or 150 units, the expected sales are still 100 units as we originally projected.

The cost is $550, and the discount rate is 20 percent. The project can be dismantled and sold in one year for $400, if we decide to abandon it. Should we take it?

A standard DCF analysis is not difficult. The expected cash flow is $100 per year forever and the discount rate is 20 percent. The PV of the cash flows is $100/.20 = $500, so the NPV is $500 − 550 = −$50. We shouldn't take it.

This analysis is static, however. In one year, we can sell out for $400. How can we account for this? What we have to do is to decide what we are going to do one year from now. In this simple case, there are only two contingencies that we need to evaluate, an upward revision and a downward revision, so the extra work is not great.

In one year, if the expected cash flows are revised to $50, the PV of the cash flows is revised downward to $50/.20 = $250. We get $400 by abandoning the project, so that is what we will do (the NPV of keeping the project in one year is $250 − 400 = $150).

If the demand is revised upward, the PV of the future cash flows at Year 1 is $150/.20 = $750. This exceeds the $400 abandonment value, so we would keep the project.

We now have a project that costs $550 today. In one year, we expect a cash flow of $100 from the project. In addition, this project would either be worth $400 (if we abandon it because it is a failure) or $750 (if we keep it because it succeeds). These outcomes are equally likely, so we expect it to be worth ($400 + 750)/2, or $575.

Summing up, in one year, we expect to have $100 in cash plus a project worth $575, or $675 total. At a 20 percent discount rate, this $675 is worth $562.50 today, so the NPV is $562.50 − 550 = $12.50. We should take it.

The NPV of our project has increased by $62.50. Where did this come from? Our original analysis implicitly assumed we would keep the project even if it was a failure. At Year 1, however, we saw that we were $150 better off ($400 versus $250) if we abandoned. There was a 50 percent chance of this happening, so the expected gain from abandoning is $75. The PV of the amount is the value of the option to abandon, $75/1.20 = $62.50.

STRATEGIC OPTIONS   Companies sometimes undertake new projects just to explore possibilities and evaluate potential future business strategies. This is a little like testing the water by sticking a toe in before diving. When Microsoft decided to buy Skype for US$8.5 billion in 2011, strategic considerations likely dominated immediate cash flow analysis.

Such projects are difficult to analyze using conventional DCF because most of the benefits come in the form of **strategic options,** that is, options for future, related business moves. Projects that create such options may be very valuable, but that value is difficult to measure. Research and development, for example, is an important and valuable activity for many firms precisely because it creates options for new products and procedures.

To give another example, a large manufacturer might decide to open a retail outlet as a pilot study. The primary goal is to gain some market insight. Because of the high start-up costs, this one operation won't break even. However, based on the sales experience from the pilot, we can then evaluate whether or not to open more outlets, to change the product mix, to enter new markets, and so on. The information gained and the resulting options for actions are all valuable, but coming up with a reliable dollar figure is probably not feasible.

strategic options
Options for future, related business products or strategies.

Strategic options can also include political issues. For example, in 2010, the government of Canada blocked BHP Billiton's proposed acquisition of Potash Corp. of Saskatchewan for $40 billion because the deal was not proven to be beneficial for Canada.

CONCLUSION   We have seen that incorporating options into capital budgeting analysis is not easy. What can we do about them in practice? The answer is that we can only keep them in the back of our minds as we work with the projected cash flows. We tend to underestimate NPV by ignoring options. The damage might be small for a highly structured, very specific proposal, but it might be great for an exploratory one such as a gold mine. The value of a gold mine depends on management's ability to shut it down if the price of gold falls below a certain point, and the ability to reopen it subsequently if conditions are right.[14] The most commonly used real options in Canada are the option to expand and the option to wait. Managers also report that a lack of expertise prevents them from realizing the full potential of real options.[15]

11.7 | Capital Rationing

Our final topic in this chapter is capital rationing. While not strictly related to forecasting risk, the theme of this chapter, capital rationing also represents a complication in capital budgeting, so we discuss it here. **Capital rationing** is said to exist when we have profitable (positive NPV) investments available but we can't get the needed funds to undertake them. For example, as division managers for a large corporation, we might identify $5 million in excellent projects, but find that, for whatever reason, we can spend only $2 million. Now what? Unfortunately, for reasons we discuss next there may be no truly satisfactory answer.

capital rationing
The situation that exists if a firm has positive NPV projects but cannot find the necessary financing.

SOFT RATIONING   The situation we have just described is **soft rationing**. This occurs when, for example, different units in a business are allocated some fixed amount of money each year for capital spending. Such an allocation is primarily a means of controlling and keeping track of overall spending. The important thing about soft rationing is that the corporation as a whole isn't short of capital; more can be raised on ordinary terms if management so desires.

soft rationing
The situation that occurs when units in a business are allocated a certain amount of financing for capital budgeting.

If we face soft rationing, the first thing to do is try to get a larger allocation. Failing that, then one common suggestion is to generate as large a net present value as possible within the existing budget. This amounts to choosing those projects with the largest benefit/cost ratio (profitability index).

Strictly speaking, this is the correct thing to do only if the soft rationing is a one-time event; that is, it won't exist next year. If the soft rationing is a chronic problem, something is amiss. The reason goes all the way back to Chapter 1. Ongoing soft rationing means we are constantly bypassing positive NPV investments. This contradicts our goal of the firm. When we are not trying to maximize value, the question of which projects to take becomes ambiguous because we no longer have an objective goal in the first place.

hard rationing
The situation that occurs when a business cannot raise financing for a project under any circumstances.

HARD RATIONING   With **hard rationing**, a business cannot raise capital for a project under any circumstances. For large, healthy corporations, this situation probably does not occur very often. This is fortunate because with hard rationing our DCF analysis breaks down, and the best course of action is ambiguous.

The reason that DCF analysis breaks down has to do with the required return. Suppose we say our required return is 20 percent. Implicitly, we are saying we will take a project with a return that exceeds this. However, if we face hard rationing, we are not going to take a new project no matter what the return on that project is, so the whole concept of a required return is ambiguous. About the only interpretation we can give this situation is that the required return is so large that no project has a positive NPV in the first place.

Hard rationing can occur when a company experiences financial distress, meaning that bankruptcy is a possibility. Also, a firm may not be able to raise capital without violating a pre-existing contractual agreement. We discuss these situations in greater detail in a later chapter.

---

[14] M. J. Brennan and E. S. Schwartz, "A New Approach to Evaluating Natural Resource Investments," *Midland Corporate Financial Journal* 3 (Spring 1985).

[15] Baker, H.K., Dutta, S., and Saadi, S. (2011), "Management Views on Real Options in Capital Budgeting?" Journal of Applied Finance, 21(1), pp. 18–29.

11.8 | SUMMARY AND CONCLUSIONS

In this chapter, we looked at some ways of evaluating the results of a discounted cash flow analysis. We also touched on some problems that can come up in practice. We saw that:

1. Net present value estimates depend on projected future cash flows. If there are errors in those projections, our estimated NPVs can be misleading. We called this forecasting risk.

2. Scenario and sensitivity analyses are useful tools for identifying which variables are critical to a project and where forecasting problems can do the most damage.

3. Break-even analysis in its various forms is a particularly common type of scenario analysis that is useful for identifying critical levels of sales.

4. Operating leverage is a key determinant of break-even levels. It reflects the degree to which a project or a firm is committed to fixed costs. The degree of operating leverage tells us the sensitivity of operating cash flow to changes in sales volume.

5. Projects usually have future managerial options associated with them. These options may be very important, but standard discounted cash flow analysis tends to ignore them.

6. Capital rationing occurs when apparently profitable projects cannot be funded. Standard discounted cash flow analysis is troublesome in this case because NPV is not necessarily the appropriate criterion anymore.

The most important thing to carry away from reading this chapter is that estimated NPVs or returns should not be taken at face value. They depend critically on projected cash flows. If there is room for significant disagreement about those projected cash flows, the results from the analysis have to be taken with a grain of salt.

Despite the problems we have discussed, discounted cash flow is still the way of attacking problems, because it forces us to ask the right questions. What we learn in this chapter is that knowing the questions to ask does not guarantee that we get all the answers.

Key Terms

accounting break-even (page 297)
capital rationing (page 310)
cash break-even (page 302)
contingency planning (page 308)
degree of operating leverage (page 305)
financial break-even (page 303)
fixed costs (page 296)
forecasting risk (page 289)
hard rationing (page 310)

managerial options or real options (page 307)
marginal cost or incremental cost (page 297)
operating leverage (page 304)
scenario analysis (page 291)
sensitivity analysis (page 293)
simulation analysis (page 295)
soft rationing (page 310)
strategic options (page 309)
variable costs (page 296)

Chapter Review Problems and Self-Test

Use the following base-case information to work the self-test problems.

A project under consideration costs $750,000, has a five-year life, and has no salvage value. Depreciation is straight-line to zero. The required return is 17 percent, and the tax rate is 34 percent. Sales are projected at 500 units per year. Price per unit is $2,500, variable cost per unit is $1,500, and fixed costs are $200,000 per year.

11.1   Scenario Analysis Suppose you think that the unit sales, price, variable cost, and fixed cost projections given here are accurate to within 5 percent. What are the upper and lower bounds for these projections? What is the base-case NPV? What are the best- and worst-case scenario NPVs?

11.2   Break-Even Analysis Given the base-case projections in the previous problem, what are the cash, accounting, and financial break-even sales levels for this project? Ignore taxes in answering.

Answers to Self-Test Problems

11.1   We can summarize the relevant information as follows:

	Base Case	Lower Bound	Upper Bound
Unit sales	500	475	525
Price per unit	$ 2,500	$ 2,375	$ 2,625
Variable cost per unit	$ 1,500	$ 1,425	$ 1,575
Fixed cost per year	$200,000	$190,000	$210,000

Depreciation is $150,000 per year; knowing this, we can calculate the cash flows under each scenario. Remember that we assign high costs and low prices and volume for the worst-case and just the opposite for the best-case scenario.

Scenario	Unit Sales	Unit Price	Unit Variable Cost	Fixed Costs	Cash Flow
Base case	500	$2,500	$1,500	$200,000	$249,000
Best case	525	2,625	1,425	190,000	341,400
Worst case	475	2,375	1,575	210,000	163,200

At 17 percent, the five-year annuity factor is 3.19935, so the NPVs are:

Base-case NPV $= -\$750,000 + 3.19935 \times \$249,000$

$\qquad\qquad = \$46,638$

Best-case NPV $= -\$750,000 + 3.19935 \times \$341,400$

$\qquad\qquad = \$342,258$

Worst-case NPV $= -\$750,000 + 3.19935 \times \$163,200$

$\qquad\qquad = -\$227,866$

11.2   In this case, we have $200,000 in cash fixed costs to cover. Each unit contributes $2,500 − 1,500 = $1,000 towards covering fixed costs. The cash break-even is thus $200,000/$1,000 = 200 units. We have another $150,000 in depreciation, so the accounting break-even is ($200,000 + 150,000)/$1,000 = 350 units.

To get the financial break-even, we need to find the OCF such that the project has a zero NPV. As we have seen, the five-year annuity factor is 3.19935 and the project costs $750,000, so the OCF must be such that:

$\qquad$ $750,000 = OCF \times 3.19935$

So, for the project to break even on a financial basis, the project's cash flow must be $750,000/3.19935, or $234,423 per year. If we add this to the $200,000 in cash fixed costs, we get a total of $434,423 that we have to cover. At $1,000 per unit, we need to sell $434,423/$1,000 = 435 units.

Concepts Review and Critical Thinking Questions

1. **(LO1)** What is forecasting risk? In general, would the degree of forecasting risk be greater for a new product or a cost-cutting proposal? Why?

2. **(LO2)** What is the essential difference between sensitivity analysis and scenario analysis?

3. **(LO3)** If you were to include the effect of taxes in break-even analysis, what do you think would happen to the cash, accounting, and financial break-even points?

4. **(LO3)** A co-worker claims that looking at all this marginal this and incremental that is just a bunch of nonsense, and states, "Listen, if our average revenue doesn't exceed our average cost, then we will have a negative cash flow, and we will go broke!" How do you respond?

5. **(LO5)** What is the option to abandon? Explain why we underestimate NPV if we ignore this option.

6. **(LO5)** In our previous chapter, we discussed Air Canada's launch of Tango. Suppose Tango ticket sales had gone extremely well and Air Canada was forced to expand capacity to meet demand. Air Canada's action in this case would be an example of exploiting what kind of option?

7. **(LO4)** At one time at least, many Japanese companies had a "no layoff" policy (for that matter, so did IBM). What are the implications of such a policy for the degree of operating leverage a company faces?

8. **(LO4)** Airlines offer an example of an industry in which the degree of operating leverage is fairly high. Why?

9.   **(LO5)** Natural resource extraction facilities (e.g., oil wells or gold mines) provide a good example of the value of the option to suspend operations. Why?

10.   **(LO1, 2)** In looking at Euro Disney, and its "Mickey Mouse" financial performance early on, note that the subsequent ac-

tions taken amount to a product reformulation. Is this a marketing issue, a finance issue, or both? What does Euro Disney's experience suggest about the importance of coordination between marketing and finance?

Questions and Problems

Basic
(Questions 1–15)

1.   **Calculating Costs and Break-Even (LO3)** Thunder Bay Inc. (TBI) manufactures biotech sunglasses. The variable materials cost is $10.48 per unit, and the variable labour cost is $6.89 per unit.

  a.   What is the variable cost per unit?

  b.   Suppose TBI incurs fixed costs of $870,000 during a year in which total production is 280,000 units. What are the total costs for the year?

  c.   If the selling price is $49.99 per unit, does TBI break even on a cash basis? If depreciation is $490,000 per year, what is the accounting break-even point?

2.   **Computing Average Cost (LO3)** Vickers Everwear Corporation can manufacture mountain climbing shoes for $31.85 per pair in variable raw material costs and $22.80 per pair in variable labour expense. The shoes sell for $145 per pair. Last year, production was 120,000 pairs. Fixed costs were $1,750,000. What were total production costs? What is the marginal cost per pair? What is the average cost? If the company is considering a one-time order for an extra 5000 pairs, what is the minimum acceptable total revenue from the order? Explain.

3.   **Scenario Analysis (LO2)** Whitewater Transmissions Inc. has the following estimates for its new gear assembly project: price = $1,400 per unit; variable costs = $220 per unit; fixed costs = $3.9 million; quantity = 85,000 units. Suppose the company believes all of its estimates are accurate only to within ±15 percent. What values should the company use for the four variables given here when it performs its best-case scenario analysis? What about the worst-case scenario?

4.   **Sensitivity Analysis (LO1)** For the company in the previous problem, suppose management is most concerned about the impact of its price estimate on the project's profitability. How could you address this concern? Describe how you would calculate your answer. What values would you use for the other forecast variables?

5.   **Sensitivity Analysis and Break-Even (LO1, 3)** We are evaluating a project that costs $924,000, has an eight-year life, and has no salvage value. Assume that depreciation is straight-line to zero over the life of the project. Sales are projected at 75,000 units per year. Price per unit is $46, variable cost per unit is $31, and fixed costs are $825,000 per year. The tax rate is 35 percent, and we require a 15 percent return on this project.

  a.   Calculate the accounting break-even point. What is the degree of operating leverage at the accounting break-even point?

  b.   Calculate the base-case cash flow and NPV. What is the sensitivity of NPV to changes in the sales figure? Explain what your answer tells you about a 500-unit decrease in projected sales.

  c.   What is the sensitivity of OCF to changes in the variable cost figure? Explain what your answer tells you about a $1 decrease in estimated variable costs.

6.   **Scenario Analysis (LO2)** In the previous problem, suppose the projections given for price, quantity, variable costs, and fixed costs are all accurate to within ±10 percent. Calculate the best-case and worst-case NPV figures.

7.   **Calculating Break-Even (LO3)** In each of the following cases, calculate the accounting break-even and the cash break-even points. Ignore any tax effects in calculating the cash break-even.

Unit Price	Unit Variable Cost	Fixed Costs	Depreciation
$3,020	$2,275	$9,000,000	$3,100,000
46	41	73,000	150,000
11	4	1,700	930

8.   **Calculating Break-Even (LO3)** In each of the following cases, find the unknown variable:

Accounting Break-Even	Unit Price	Unit Variable Cost	Fixed Costs	Depreciation
112,800	$39	$30	$ 820,000	?
165,000	?	27	3,200,000	$1,150,000
4,385	92	?	160,000	105,000

9.   **Calculating Break-Even (LO3)** A project has the following estimated data: price = $62 per unit; variable costs = $41 per unit; fixed costs = $15,500; required return = 12 percent; initial investment = $24,000; life = four years. Ignoring the effect of taxes, what is the accounting break-even quantity? The cash break-even quantity? The financial break-even quantity? What is the degree of operating leverage at the financial break-even level of output?

10.   **Using Break-Even Analysis (LO3)** Consider a project with the following data: accounting break-even quantity = 13,400 units; cash break-even quantity = 10,600 units; life = five years; fixed costs = $150,000; variable costs = $24 per unit; required return = 12 percent. Ignoring the effect of taxes, find the financial break-even quantity.

11. **Calculating Operating Leverage (LO4)** At an output level of 73,000 units, you calculate that the degree of operating leverage is 2.90. If output rises to 78,000 units, what will the percentage change in operating cash flow be? Will the new level of operating leverage be higher or lower? Explain.

12. **Leverage (LO4)** In the previous problem, suppose fixed costs are $150,000. What is the operating cash flow at 67,000 units? The degree of operating leverage?

13. **Operating Cash Flow and Leverage (LO4)** A proposed project has fixed costs of $84,000 per year. The operating cash flow at 7,500 units is $93,200. Ignoring the effect of taxes, what is the degree of operating leverage? If units sold rise from 7,500 to 8,000, what will be the increase in operating cash flow? What is the new degree of operating leverage?

14. **Cash Flow and Leverage (LO4)** At an output level of 15,000 units, you have calculated that the degree of operating leverage is 2.61. The operating cash flow is $57,000 in this case. Ignoring the effect of taxes, what are fixed costs? What will the operating cash flow be if output rises to 16,000 units? If output falls to 14,000 units?

15. **Leverage (LO4)** In the previous problem, what will be the new degree of operating leverage in each case?

Intermediate
(Questions
16–27) 16. **Break-Even Intuition (LO3)** Consider a project with a required return of $R\%$ that costs $\$I$ and will last for N years. The project uses straight-line depreciation to zero over the N-year life; there is no salvage value or net working capital requirements.

    a. At the accounting break-even level of output, what is the IRR of this project? The payback period? The NPV?

    b. At the cash break-even level of output, what is the IRR of this project? The payback period? The NPV?

    c. At the financial break-even level of output, what is the IRR of this project? The payback period? The NPV?

17. **Sensitivity Analysis (LO1)** Consider a four-year project with the following information: initial fixed asset investment = $420,000; straight-line depreciation to zero over the four-year life; zero salvage value; price = $25; variable costs = $16; fixed costs = $180,000; quantity sold = 75,000 units; tax rate = 34 percent. How sensitive is OCF to changes in quantity sold?

18. **Operating Leverage (LO4)** In the previous problem, what is the degree of operating leverage at the given level of output? What is the degree of operating leverage at the accounting break-even level of output?

19. **Project Analysis (LO1, 2, 3, 4)** You are considering a new product launch. The project will cost $1,400,000, have a four-year life, and have no salvage value; depreciation is straight-line to zero. Sales are projected at 180 units per year; price per unit will be $16,000, variable cost per unit will be $9,800, and fixed costs will be $430,000 per year. The required return on the project is 12 percent, and the relevant tax rate is 35 percent.

    a. Based on your experience, you think the unit sales, variable cost, and fixed cost projections given here are probably accurate to within ±10 percent. What are the upper and lower bounds for these projections? What is the base-case NPV? What are the best-case and worst-case scenarios?

    b. Evaluate the sensitivity of your base-case NPV to changes in fixed costs.

    c. What is the cash break-even level of output for this project (ignoring taxes)?

    d. What is the accounting break-even level of output for this project? What is the degree of operating leverage at the accounting break-even point? How do you interpret this number?

20. **Abandonment Value (LO5)** We are examining a new project. We expect to sell 8,750 units per year at $189 net cash flow apiece (including CCA) for the next 16 years. In other words, the annual operating cash flow is projected to be $189 × 8,750 = $1,653,750. The relevant discount rate is 14 percent, and the initial investment required is $5,500,000.

    a. What is the base-case NPV?

    b. After the first year, the project can be dismantled and sold for $2,800,000. If expected sales are revised based on the first year's performance, when would it make sense to abandon the investment? In other words, at what level of expected sales would it make sense to abandon the project?

    c. Explain how the $2,800,000 abandonment value can be viewed as the opportunity cost of keeping the project one year.

21. **Abandonment (LO5)** In the previous problem, suppose you think it is likely that expected sales will be revised upwards to 9500 units if the first year is a success and revised downwards to 4300 units if the first year is not a success.

    a. If success and failure are equally likely, what is the NPV of the project? Consider the possibility of abandonment in answering.

    b. What is the value of the option to abandon?

22. **Abandonment and Expansion (LO5)** In the previous problem, supposed the scale of the project can be doubled in one year in the sense that twice as many units can be produced and sold. Naturally, expansion would only be desirable if the project is a success. This implies that if the project is a success, projected sales after expansion will be 17,600. Again, assuming that success and failure are equally likely, what is the NPV of the project? Note that abandonment is still an option if the project is a failure. What is the value of the option to expand?

23. **Project Analysis (LO1, 2)** Baird Golf has decided to sell a new line of golf clubs. The clubs will sell for $825 per set and have a variable cost of $395 per set. The company has spent $150,000 for a marketing study that determined the company will sell 55,000 sets per year for seven years. The marketing study also determined that the company will lose sales of 10,000 sets of its high-priced clubs. The high-priced clubs sell at $1,100 and have variable costs of $650. The company will also increase sales of its cheap clubs by 12,000 sets. The cheap clubs sell for $410 and have variable costs of $185 per set. The fixed costs each year will be $9,200,000. The company has also spent $1,000,000 on research and development for the new clubs. The plant and equipment required will cost $29,400,000 and will be depreciated on a straight-line basis. The new clubs will also require an increase in net

working capital of $1,400,000 that will be returned at the end of the project. The tax rate is 40 percent, and the cost of capital is 10 percent. Calculate the payback period, the NPV, and the IRR.

24. **Scenario Analysis (LO2)** In the previous problem, you feel that the values are accurate to within only ±10 percent. What are the best-case and worst-case NPVs? (*Hint:* The price and variable costs for the two existing sets of clubs are known with certainty; only the sales gained or lost are uncertain.)

25. **Sensitivity Analysis (LO1)** Baird Golf would like to know the sensitivity of NPV to changes in the price of the new clubs and the quantity of new clubs sold. What is the sensitivity of the NPV to each of these variables?

26. **Break-Even Analysis (LO3)** Hybrid cars are touted as a "green" alternative; however, the financial aspects of hybrid ownership are not as clear. Consider a 2010 Lexus RX 450h, which had a list price of $5,565 (-including tax consequences) more than a Lexus RX 350. Additionally, the annual ownership costs (other than fuel) for the hybrid were expected to be $300 more than the traditional sedan. The mileage estimate was 5 litre/100 km for the hybrid and 6.7 for the traditional sedan.

    a. Assume that gasoline costs $1.35 per litre and you plan to keep either car for six years. How many kilometres per year would you need to drive to make the decision to buy the hybrid worthwhile, ignoring the time value of money?

    b. If you drive 15,000 km per year and keep either car for six years, what price per litre would make the decision to buy the hybrid worthwhile, ignoring the time value of money?

    c. Rework parts (a) and (b) assuming the appropriate interest rate is 10 percent and all cash flows occur at the end of the year.

    d. What assumption did the analysis in the previous parts make about the resale value of each car?

27. **Break-Even Analysis (LO3)** In an effort to capture the large jet market, Airbus invested $13 billion developing its A380, which is capable of carrying 800 passengers. The plane has a list price of $280 million. In discussing the plane, Airbus stated that the company would break even when 249 A380s were sold.

    a. Assuming the break-even sales figure given is the cash flow break-even, what is the cash flow per plane?

    b. Airbus promised its shareholders a 20 percent rate of return on the investment. If sales of the plane continue in perpetuity, how many planes must the company sell per year to deliver on this promise?

    c. Suppose instead that the sales of the A380 last for only 10 years. How many planes must Airbus sell per year to deliver the same rate of return?

Challenge 28. **Break-Even and Taxes (LO3)** This problem concerns the effect of taxes on the various break-even measures.
(Questions
28–33)
    a. Show that, when we consider taxes, the general relationship between operating cash flow, OCF, and sales volume, Q, can be written as:

$$Q = \frac{FC + \dfrac{OCF - T \times D}{1 - T}}{P - v}$$

    b. Use the expression in part (a) to find the cash, accounting, and financial break-even points for the Victoria sailboats example in the chapter. Assume a 38 percent tax rate.

    c. In part (b), the accounting break-even should be the same as before. Why? Verify this algebraically.

29. **Operating Leverage and Taxes (LO4)** Show that if we consider the effect of taxes, the degree of operating leverage can be written as:

$$DOL = 1 + [FC \times (1 - T) - T \times D]/OCF$$

Notice that this reduces to our previous result if $T = 0$. Can you interpret this in words?

30. **Scenario Analysis (LO2)** Consider a project to supply Thunder Bay with 25,000 tons of machine screws annually for automobile production. You will need an initial $3,600,000 investment in threading equipment to get the project started; the project will last for five years. The accounting department estimates that annual fixed costs will be $850,000 and that variable costs should be $185 per ton; the CCA rate for threading equipment is 20 percent. It also estimates a salvage value of $500,000 after dismantling costs. The marketing department estimates that the automakers will let the contract at a selling price of $280 per ton. The engineering department estimates you will need an initial net working capital investment of $360,000. You require a 13 percent return and face a marginal tax rate of 40 percent on this project.

    a. What is the estimated OCF for this project? The NPV? Should you pursue this project?

    b. Suppose you believe that the accounting department's initial cost and salvage value projections are accurate only to within ±15 percent; the marketing department's price estimate is accurate only within ±10 percent; and the engineering department's net working capital estimate is accurate only to within ±5 percent. What is your worst-case scenario for this project? Your best-case scenario? Do you still want to pursue the project?

31. **Sensitivity Analysis (LO1)** In Problem 30, suppose you're confident about your own projections, but you're a little unsure about Thunder Bay's actual machine screw requirement. What is the sensitivity of the project OCF to changes in the quantity supplied? What about the sensitivity of NPV to changes in quantity supplied? Given the sensitivity number you calculated, is there some minimum level of output below which you wouldn't want to operate? Why?

32. **Break-Even Analysis (LO3)** Use the results of Problem 28 to find the accounting, cash, and financial break-even quantities for the company in Problem 30.

33. **Operating Leverage (LO4)** Use the results of Problem 29 to find the degree of operating leverage for the company in Problem 30 at the base-case output level of 25,000 units. How does this number compare to the sensitivity figure you found in Problem 31? Verify that either approach will give you the same OCF figure at any new quantity level.

MINI CASE

As a financial analyst at Glencolin International (GI) you have been asked to revisit your analysis of the two capital investment alternatives submitted by the production department of the firm. (Detailed discussion of these alternatives is in the Mini Case at the end of Chapter 10.) The CFO is concerned that the analysis to date has not really addressed the risk in this project. Your task is to employ scenario and sensitivity analysis to explore how your original recommendation might change when subjected to a number of "what-ifs."

In your discussions with the CFO, the CIO and the head of the production department, you have pinpointed two key inputs to the capital budgeting decision: initial software development costs and expected savings in production costs (before tax). By properly designing the contract for software development, you are confident that initial software costs for each alternative can be kept in a range of plus or minus 15 percent of the original estimates. Savings in production costs are less certain because the software will involve new technology that has not been implemented before. An appropriate range for these costs is plus or minus 40 percent of the original estimates.

As the capital budgeting analyst, you are required to answer the following in your memo to the CFO:

a) Conduct sensitivity analysis to determine which of the two inputs has a greater input on the choice between the two projects.

b) Conduct scenario analysis to assess the risks of each alternative in turn. What are your conclusions?

c) Explain what your sensitivity and scenario analyses tell you about your original recommendations.

---

* We recommend using a spreadsheet in analyzing this Mini Case.

Internet Application Questions

1. The following website allows you to download a cash flow sensitivity analysis spreadsheet: bizfilings.com/toolkit/tools-forms/finance/business-finances/cash-flow-budget-worksheet.aspx. You are faced with two technologies, one with a higher cash flow but greater risk, and the second with a lower cash flow and less risk. How would you use the cash flow sensitivity spreadsheet to pick the right technology? What factors would you consider in the analysis?

2. Suncor Energy Inc. is an integrated oil company based in Calgary. The company's website, suncor.com, describes its businesses many of which involve real options. Go to the website and make a list of the real options of Suncor. Identify those which you think are most valuable today and explain why.

C H A P T E R   1 2

LESSONS FROM CAPITAL MARKET HISTORY

With the worldwide financial crisis and economic slowdown, the annual return for the S&P/TSX Composite in 2008 was −33.00 percent, the index's worst return in decades. In the recovery period, the S&P/TSX posted impressive returns of 34.35 percent in 2009 and 17.25 percent in 2011. U.S. stocks measured by the S&P 500 showed more modest returns of 9.26 percent and 8.10 percent for these respective years measured in Canadian dollars.

The superior performance of the Canadian index can be attributed to the stability of the financial services sector and the growth of the natural resources industry in Canada. In 2011 and early 2012, the S&P/TSX showed negative returns due to the slowdown in China and the European debt crisis. Five countries— Greece, Portugal, Italy, Spain, and Ireland, were particularly weak. In March 2012, the EU leaders signed off a bailout package for Greece worth €130 billion.

Learning Objectives ▶

After studying this chapter, you should understand:

LO1 How to calculate the return on an investment.

LO2 The historical returns on various important types of investments.

LO3 The historical risks on various important types of investments.

LO4 The implications of market efficiency.

Thus far, we haven't had much to say about what determines the required return on an investment. In one sense, the answer is very simple: The required return depends on the risk of the investment. The greater the risk is, the greater is the required return.

Having said this, we are left with a somewhat more difficult problem. How can we measure the amount of risk present in an investment? Put another way, what does it mean to say that one investment is riskier than another? Obviously, we need to define what we mean by risk if we are going to answer these questions. This is our task in the next two chapters.

From the last several chapters, we know that one of the responsibilities of the financial manager is to assess the value of proposed real asset investments. In doing this, it is important to know what financial investments have to offer. Going further, we saw in Chapter 2 that the cash flow of a firm equals the cash flow to creditors and shareholders. So the returns and risks of financial investments provide information on the real investments firms undertake.

Our goal in this chapter is to provide a perspective on what capital market history can tell us about risk and return. The most important thing to get out of this chapter is a feel for the numbers. What is a high return? What is a low one? More generally, what returns should we expect from financial assets and what are the risks from such investments? This perspective is essential for understanding how to analyze and value risky investment projects.

We start our discussion on risk and return by describing the historical experience of investors in Canadian financial markets. In 1931, for example, the stock market lost about 33 percent of its value. Just two years later, the stock market gained 51 percent. In more recent memory, the U.S. market lost about 21 percent of its value in 2008, while the Canadian market lost about 33 percent and gained around 34 percent in 2009. What lessons, if any, can financial managers learn from such shifts in the stock market? We explore the last half-century of market history to find out.

Not everyone agrees on the value of studying history. On the one hand, there is philosopher George Santayana's famous comment, "Those who cannot remember the past are condemned to repeat it." On the other hand, there is industrialist Henry Ford's equally famous comment, "History is more or less bunk." Nonetheless, based on recent events, perhaps everyone would agree with Mark Twain when he observed, "October. This is one of the peculiarly dangerous months to speculate in stocks in. The others are July, January, September, April, November, May, March, June, December, August, and February."

Two central lessons emerge from our study of market history: First, there is a reward for bearing risk. Second, the greater the risk, the greater the potential reward. To understand these facts about market returns, we devote much of this chapter to reporting the statistics and numbers that make up modern capital market history in Canada. Canadians also invest in the United States so we include some discussion of U.S. markets. In the next chapter, these facts provide the foundation for our study of how financial markets put a price on risk.

12.1 | Returns

We wish to discuss historical returns on different types of financial assets. We do this after briefly discussing how to calculate the return from investing.

Dollar Returns

If you buy an asset of any sort, your gain (or loss) from that investment is called the return on your investment. This return usually has two components: First, you may receive some cash directly while you own the investment. This is called the income component of your return. Second, the value of the asset you purchase often changes. In this case, you have a capital gain or capital loss on your investment.[1]

To illustrate, suppose Canadian Atlantic Enterprises has several thousand shares of stock outstanding. You purchased some of these shares at the beginning of the year. It is now year-end, and you want to find out how well you have done on your investment.

Over the year, a company may pay cash dividends to its shareholders. As a shareholder in Canadian Atlantic Enterprises, you are a part owner of the company. If the company is profitable, it may choose to distribute some of its profits to shareholders (we discuss the details of dividend policy in Chapter 17). So, as the owner of some stock, you receive some cash. This cash is the income component from owning the stock.

In addition to the dividend, the other part of your return is the capital gain or capital loss on the stock. This part arises from changes in the value of your investment. For example, consider the cash flows illustrated in Figure 12.1. The stock is selling for $37 per share. If you buy 100 shares, you have a total outlay of $3,700. Suppose that, over the year, the stock paid a dividend of $1.85 per share. By the end of the year, then, you would have received income of:

$$\text{Dividend} = \$1.85 \times 100 = \$185$$

Also, the value of the stock rises to $40.33 per share by the end of the year. Your 100 shares are worth $4,033, so you have a capital gain of:

$$\text{Capital gain} = (\$40.33 - \$37) \times 100 = \$333$$

On the other hand, if the price had dropped to, say, $34.78, you would have a capital loss of:

$$\text{Capital loss} = (\$34.78 - \$37) \times 100 = -\$222$$

Notice that a capital loss is the same thing as a negative capital gain.

The total dollar return on your investment is the sum of the dividend and the capital gain:

$$\text{Total dollar return} = \text{Dividend income} + \text{Capital gain (or loss)} \qquad [12.1]$$

---

[1] The after-tax dollar returns would be reduced by taxes levied differently for dividends and capital gains, as we discussed in Chapter 2.

FIGURE 12.1

Dollar returns

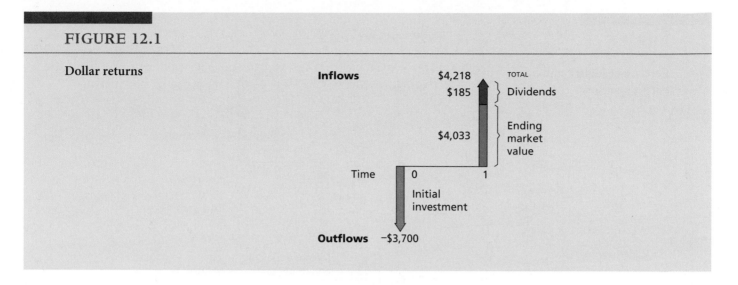

In our first example, the total dollar return is thus given by:

Total dollar return = $185 + 333 = $518

If you sold the stock at the end of the year, the total amount of cash you would have would be your initial investment plus the total return. In the preceding example, then:

$$\text{Total cash if stock is sold} = \text{Initial investment} + \text{Total return} \qquad [12.2]$$
$$= \$3,700 + 518$$
$$= \$4,218$$

As a check, notice that this is the same as the proceeds from the sale of the stock plus the dividends:

$$\text{Proceeds from stock sale} + \text{Dividends} = \$40.33 \times 100 + \$185$$
$$= \$4,033 + 185$$
$$= \$4,218$$

Suppose you hold on to your Canadian Atlantic stock and don't sell it at the end of the year. Should you still consider the capital gain as part of your return? Isn't this only a paper gain and not really a cash flow if you don't sell it?

The answer to the first question is a strong yes, and the answer to the second is an equally strong no. The capital gain is every bit as much a part of your return as the dividend, and you should certainly count it as part of your return. That you actually decided to keep the stock and not sell (you don't realize the gain) is irrelevant because you could have converted it to cash if you wanted to. Whether you choose to do so or not is up to you.

After all, if you insisted on converting your gain to cash, you could always sell the stock at year-end and immediately reinvest by buying the stock back. There is no net difference between doing this and just not selling (assuming there are no tax consequences from selling the stock). Again, the point is that whether you actually cash out or reinvest by not selling doesn't affect the return you earn.

Percentage Returns

It is usually more convenient to summarize information about returns in percentage terms, rather than dollar terms, because that way your return doesn't depend on how much you actually invest. The question we want to answer is: How much do we get for each dollar we invest?

To answer this question, let P_t be the price of the stock at the beginning of the year and let D_t be the dividend paid on the stock during the year. Consider the cash flows in Figure 12.2. These are the same as those in Figure 12.1, except we have now expressed everything on a per-share basis.

In our example, the price at the beginning of the year was $37 per share and the dividend paid during the year on each share was $1.85. As we discussed in Chapter 8, expressing the dividend as a percentage of the beginning stock price results in the dividend yield:

FIGURE 12.2

Percentage, dollar, and per-share returns

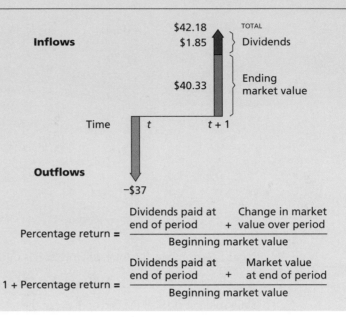

$$\text{Percentage return} = \frac{\text{Dividends paid at end of period} + \text{Change in market value over period}}{\text{Beginning market value}}$$

$$1 + \text{Percentage return} = \frac{\text{Dividends paid at end of period} + \text{Market value at end of period}}{\text{Beginning market value}}$$

$$\text{Dividend yield} = D_t/P_t$$
$$= \$1.85/\$37 = .05 = 5\%$$

This says that, for each dollar we invest, we get 5 cents in dividends.

The other component of our percentage return is the capital gains yield. This is calculated as the change in the price during the year (the capital gain) divided by the beginning price:

$$\text{Capital gains yield} = (P_{t+1} - P_t)/P_t$$
$$= (\$40.33 - 37)/\$37$$
$$= \$3.33/\$37$$
$$= 9\%$$

So, per dollar invested, you get 9 cents in capital gains.

Putting it together, per dollar invested, we get 5 cents in dividends and 9 cents in capital gains, a total of 14 cents. Our percentage return is 14 cents on the dollar, or 14 percent.

To check this, notice that you invested $3,700 and ended with $4,218. By what percentage did your $3,700 increase? As we saw, you picked up $4,218 − 3,700 = $518. This is a $518/$3,700 = 14% increase.

FIGURE 12.3

Cash flow—an investment example

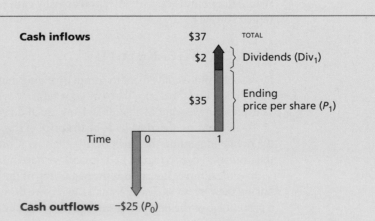

EXAMPLE 12.1: Calculating Returns

Suppose you buy some stock for $25 per share. At the end of the year, the price is $35 per share. During the year, you got a $2 dividend per share. This is the situation illustrated in Figure 12.3. What is the dividend yield? The capital gains yield? The percentage return? If your total investment was $1,000, how much do you have at the end of the year?

Your $2 dividend per share works out to a dividend yield of:

$$\text{Dividend yield} = D_t/P_t$$
$$= \$2/\$25 = .08 = 8\%$$

The per share capital gain is $10, so the capital gains yield is:

$$\text{Capital gains yield} = (P_{t+1} - P_t)/P_t$$
$$= (\$35 - 25)/\$25$$
$$= \$10/\$25$$
$$= 40\%$$

The total percentage return is thus 48 percent.

If you had invested $1,000, you would have $1,480 at the end of the year, a 48 percent increase. To check this, note that your $1,000 would have bought you $1,000/25 = 40 shares. Your 40 shares would then have paid you a total of 40 × $2 = $80 in cash dividends. Your $10 per share gain would give you a total capital gain of $10 × 40 = $400. Add these together, and you get the $480.

To give another example, stock in Apple Inc., began 2011 at $322.56 per share. Apple did not pay any dividends in 2011, and the stock price at the end of the year was $405. What was the return on Apple for the year? For practice, see if you agree that the answer is 25.56 percent. Of course, negative returns occur as well. For example, again in 2011, Research In Motion's stock price at the beginning of the year was $58.07 per share. No dividends were paid during the year and the stock ended the year at $14.80 per share. Verify that the loss was 74.51 percent for the year.

Concept Questions

1. What are the two parts of total return?
2. Why are unrealized capital gains or losses included in the calculation of returns?
3. What is the difference between a dollar return and a percentage return? Why are percentage returns more convenient?

12.2 | The Historical Record

Capital market history is of great interest to investment consultants who advise institutional investors on portfolio strategy. The data set we use is in Table 12.1. It is based on data originally assembled by Mercer Investment Consulting, drawing on two major studies. Roger Ibbotson and Rex Sinquefield conducted a famous set of studies dealing with rates of return in U.S. financial markets. James Hatch and Robert White examined Canadian returns.[2] Our data present year-to-year historical rates of return on six important types of financial investments. The returns can be interpreted as what you would have earned if you held portfolios of the following:

1. Canadian common stocks. The common stock portfolio is based on a sample of the largest companies (in total market value of outstanding stock) in Canada.[3]
2. U.S. common stocks. The U.S. common stock portfolio consists of 500 of the largest U.S. companies. The full historical series is given in U.S. dollars. A separate series presents U.S. stock returns in Canadian dollars adjusting for shifts in exchange rates.

[2]The two classic studies are R. G. Ibbotson and R. A. Sinquefield, *Stocks, Bonds, Bills, and Inflation* (Charlottesville, Va.: Financial Analysts Research Foundation, 1982), and J. Hatch and R. White, *Canadian Stocks, Bonds, Bills, and Inflation: 1950–1983* (Charlottesville, Va.: Financial Analysts Research Foundation, 1985). Additional sources used by Mercer Investment Consulting are Nesbitt Burns for small capitalization for small stocks, Scotia Capital Markets for Canada Treasury bills and long bonds, and Statistics Canada CANSIM for rates of exchange and inflation.

[3]From 1956 on, the S&P/TSX Composite is used. For earlier years, Mercer Investment Consulting used a sample provided by the TSX.

TABLE 12.1 Annual market index returns, 1948–2011

Year	Statistics Canada inflation	Canadian stocks S&P/ TSX Composite	DEX 91-day T-bill	Scotia Capital Markets long bonds	US stocks S&P 500 (Cdn. $)	Nesbitt Burns small stocks	S&P/TSX Venture Composite
1948	8.88	12.25	0.40	−0.80	5.50		
1949	1.09	23.85	0.45	5.18	22.15		
1950	5.91	51.69	0.51	1.74	39.18		
1951	10.66	25.44	0.71	−7.89	15.00		
1952	−1.38	0.01	0.95	5.01	13.68		
1953	0.00	2.56	1.54	5.00	−0.99		
1954	0.00	39.37	1.62	12.23	52.62		
1955	0.47	27.68	1.22	0.13	35.51		
1956	3.24	12.68	2.63	−8.87	2.35		
1957	1.79	−20.58	3.76	7.94	−8.51		
1958	2.64	31.25	2.27	1.92	40.49		
1959	1.29	4.59	4.39	−5.07	10.54		
1960	1.27	1.78	3.66	12.19	5.15		
1961	0.42	32.75	2.86	9.16	32.85		
1962	1.67	−7.09	3.81	5.03	−5.77		
1963	1.64	15.60	3.58	4.58	23.19		
1964	2.02	25.43	3.73	6.16	15.75		
1965	3.16	6.67	3.79	0.05	12.58		
1966	3.45	−7.07	4.89	−1.05	−9.33		
1967	4.07	18.09	4.38	−0.48	23.61		
1968	3.91	22.45	6.22	2.14	10.26		
1969	4.79	−0.81	6.83	−2.86	−8.50		
1970	1.31	−3.57	6.89	16.39	−1.96	−11.69	
1971	5.16	8.01	3.86	14.84	13.28	15.83	
1972	4.91	27.37	3.43	8.11	18.12	44.72	
1973	9.36	0.27	4.78	1.97	−14.58	−7.82	
1974	12.30	−25.93	7.68	−4.53	−26.87	−26.89	
1975	9.52	18.48	7.05	8.02	40.72	41.00	
1976	5.87	11.02	9.10	23.64	22.97	22.77	
1977	9.45	10.71	7.64	9.04	0.65	39.93	
1978	8.44	29.72	7.90	4.10	15.50	44.41	
1979	9.69	44.77	11.01	−2.83	16.52	46.04	
1980	11.20	30.13	12.23	2.18	35.51	42.86	
1981	12.20	−10.25	19.11	−2.09	−5.57	−15.10	
1982	9.23	5.54	15.27	45.82	25.84	4.55	
1983	4.51	35.49	9.39	9.61	24.07	44.30	
1984	3.77	−2.39	11.21	16.90	12.87	−2.33	
1985	4.38	25.07	9.70	26.68	39.82	38.98	
1986	4.19	8.95	9.34	17.21	16.96	12.33	
1987	4.12	5.88	8.20	1.77	−0.96	−5.47	
1988	3.96	11.08	8.94	11.30	7.21	5.46	
1989	5.17	21.37	11.95	15.17	27.74	10.66	
1990	5.00	−14.80	13.28	4.32	−3.06	−27.32	
1991	3.78	12.02	9.90	25.30	30.05	18.51	
1992	2.14	−1.43	6.65	11.57	18.42	13.01	
1993	1.70	32.55	5.63	22.09	14.40	52.26	
1994	0.23	−0.18	4.76	−7.39	7.48	−9.21	
1995	1.75	14.53	7.39	26.34	33.68	13.88	
1996	2.17	28.35	5.02	14.18	23.62	28.66	
1997	0.73	14.98	3.20	18.46	39.18	6.97	
1998	1.02	−1.58	4.74	12.85	37.71	−17.90	
1999	2.58	31.59	4.66	−5.98	14.14	20.29	
2000	3.23	7.41	5.49	12.97	−5.67	−4.29	
2001	0.60	−12.60	4.70	8.10	−6.50	0.70	
2002	4.30	−12.40	2.50	8.70	−22.70	−0.90	3.66
2003	1.60	26.70	2.90	6.70	5.30	42.70	63.24
2004	2.40	14.50	2.30	7.20	3.30	14.10	4.40
2005	2.00	23.29	2.58	6.46	3.80	13.70	22.62
2006	1.60	17.30	4.00	4.10	15.70	20.83	33.59
2007	2.10	9.80	4.40	3.70	−10.50	−11.38	−4.94
2008	1.20	−33.00	3.30	2.70	−21.20	−46.60	−71.93
2009	1.30	34.35	0.60	5.31	9.26	86.80	90.80
2010	2.40	17.27	0.50	12.10	8.10	36.10	50.45
2011	2.30	−8.57	1.00	17.72	4.39	−19.50	−35.07

Source: Mercer Investment Consulting, Bloomberg Financial Services, iShares, Cumis

3. TSX Venture stock. The TSX Venture stock portfolio consists of small and emerging companies that do not yet meet listing requirements for the S&P/TSX Composite Index.

4. Small stocks. The small stock portfolio is composed of the small capitalization Canadian stocks as compiled by BMO Nesbitt Burns.

5. Long bonds. The long bond portfolio has high-quality, long-term corporate, provincial, and Government of Canada bonds.

6. Canada Treasury bills. The T-bill portfolio has Treasury bills with a three-month maturity.

These returns are not adjusted for inflation or taxes; thus, they are nominal, pre-tax returns.

In addition to the year-to-year returns on these financial instruments, the year-to-year percentage change in the Statistics Canada Consumer Price Index (CPI) is also computed. This is a commonly used measure of inflation, so we can calculate real returns using this as the inflation rate.

The six asset classes included in Table 12.1 cover a broad range of investments popular with Canadian individuals and financial institutions. We include U.S. stocks since Canadian investors often invest abroad—particularly in the United States.[4]

A First Look

Before looking closely at the different portfolio returns, we take a look at the "big picture." Figure 12.4 shows what happened to $1 invested in three of these different portfolios at the beginning of 1957. We work with a sample period of 1957–2011 for two reasons: the years immediately after the Second World War do not reflect trends today and the TSE 300 (predecessor of the TSX) was introduced in 1956, making 1957 the first really comparable year. This decision is somewhat controversial and we return to it later as we draw lessons from our data. The growth in value for each of the different portfolios over the 55-year period ending in 2011 is given separately. Notice that, to get everything on a single graph, some modification in scaling is used. As is commonly done with financial series, the vertical axis is on a logarithmic scale such that equal distances measure equal percentage changes (as opposed to equal dollar changes) in value.

Looking at Figure 12.4, we see that the common stock investments did the best overall. Every dollar invested in Canadian stocks grew to $120.09 over the 55 years.

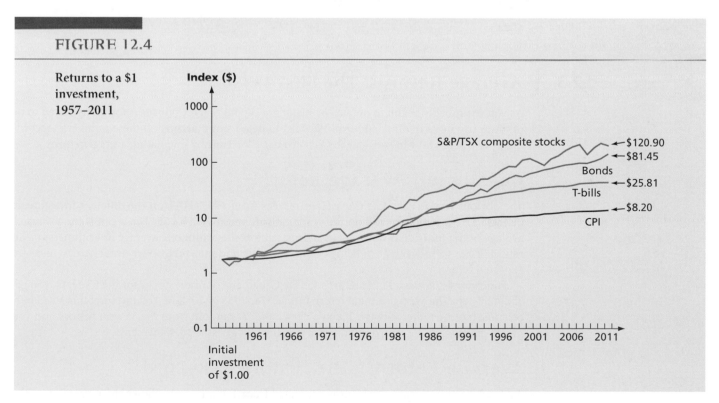

FIGURE 12.4

Returns to a $1 investment, 1957–2011

---

[4]Chapter 21 discusses exchange rate risk and other risks of foreign investments.

At the other end, the T-bill portfolio grew to only $25.81. Long bonds did better with an ending value of $81.45. These values are less impressive when we consider inflation over this period. As illustrated, the price level climbed such that $8.20 is needed just to replace the original $1.

Given the historical record as discussed so far, why would any investor hold any asset class other than common stocks? A close look at Figure 12.4 provides an answer. The T-bill portfolio and the long-term bond portfolio grew more slowly than did the stock portfolio, but they also grew much more steadily. The common stocks ended up on top, but as you can see, they grew erratically at times. For example, comparing Canadian stocks with T-bills, the stocks had a smaller return in 21 years during this 55-year period as you can see in Table 12.1.

A Closer Look

To illustrate the variability of the different investments, we look at a few selected years in Table 12.1. For example, looking at long-term bonds, we see the largest historical return (45.82 percent) occurred in 1982. This was a good year for bonds. The largest single-year return in the table is a very healthy 90.80 percent for the S&P/TSX Venture Composite in 2009. In the same year, T-bills returned only 0.60 percent. In contrast, the largest Treasury bill return was 19.11 percent (in 1981).

Concept Questions

1. With 20-20 hindsight, what was the best investment for the period 1981–82?
2. Why doesn't everyone just buy common stocks as investments?
3. What was the smallest return observed over the 52 years for each of these investments? When did it occur?
4. How many times did large Canadian stocks (common stocks) return more than 30 percent? How many times did they return less than 20 percent?
5. What was the longest winning streak (years without a negative return) for large Canadian stocks? For long-term bonds?
6. How often did the T-bill portfolio have a negative return?
7. How have Canadian stocks compared with U.S. stocks over the last 10 years?

12.3 | Average Returns: The First Lesson

As you've probably begun to notice, the history of capital market returns is too complicated to be of much use in its undigested form. We need to begin summarizing all these numbers. Accordingly, we discuss how to consider the detailed data. We start by calculating average returns.

Calculating Average Returns

The obvious way to calculate the average returns from 1957–2011 on the different investments in Table 12.1 is simply to add up the yearly returns and divide by 55. The result is the historical average of the individual values. Statisticians call this the arithmetic average or arithmetic mean return. It has the advantage of being easy to calculate and interpret, so we use it here to measure expected return.

For example, if you add the returns for the Canadian common stocks for the 55 years, you get about 574.86. The average annual return is thus 574.86/55 = 10.45%. You interpret this 10.45 percent just like any other average. If you picked a year at random from the 55-year history and you had to guess what the return in that year was, the best guess is 10.45 percent.

Average Returns: The Historical Record

Table 12.2 shows the average returns computed from Table 12.1. As shown, in a typical year, the small stocks increased in value by 13.71 percent. Notice also how much larger the stock returns are than the bond returns.

TABLE 12.2

Average annual returns, 1957–2011

Investment	Arithmetic Average Return (%)
Canadian common stocks	10.45
U.S. common stocks (Cdn $)	11.07
Long bonds	8.74
Small stocks	13.71
TSX Venture stocks	15.68
Inflation	3.95
Treasury bills	6.15

Average returns on small stocks and TSX Venture stocks are based on data from 1970–2011 and 2002–2011 respectively.

These averages are, of course, nominal since we haven't worried about inflation. Notice that the average inflation rate was 3.95 percent per year over this 55-year span. The nominal return on Canada Treasury bills was 6.15 percent per year. The average real return on Treasury bills was thus approximately 2.20 percent per year; so the real return on T-bills has been quite low historically.

At the other extreme, Canadian common stocks had an average real return of about 10.45% − 3.95% = 6.5%, which is relatively large. If you remember the Rule of 72 (Chapter 5), then a quick "back of the envelope" calculation tells us that 6 percent real growth doubles your buying power about every 12 years.

The TSX Venture stocks show an average return of 15.68 percent, which is higher than the return on T-bills.[5] Since venture stocks fluctuate greatly (as seen in Table 12.1) averages taken over short periods are considered extremely unreliable.

Risk Premiums

Now that we have computed some average returns, it seems logical to see how they compare with each other. Based on our discussion so far, one such comparison involves government-issued securities. These are free of much of the variability we see in, for example, the stock market.

The Government of Canada borrows money by issuing debt securities in different forms. The ones we focus on are Treasury bills. These have the shortest time to maturity of the different government securities. Because the government can always raise taxes to pay its bills, this debt is virtually free of any default risk over its short life. Thus, we call the rate on such debt the risk-free return, and we use it as a kind of benchmark.

A particularly interesting comparison involves the virtually risk-free return on T-bills and the very risky return on common stocks. The difference between these two returns can be interpreted as a measure of the excess return on the average risky asset (assuming that the stock of a large Canadian corporation has about average risk compared to all risky assets).

We call this the excess return because it is the additional return we earn by moving from a relatively risk-free investment to a risky one. Because it can be interpreted as a reward for bearing risk, we call it a **risk premium**.

risk premium
The excess return required from an investment in a risky asset over a risk-free investment.

From Table 12.2, we can calculate the risk premiums for the different investments. We report only the nominal risk premium in Table 12.3 because there is only a slight difference between the historical nominal and real risk premiums. The risk premium on T-bills is shown as zero in the table because we have assumed that they are riskless.

The First Lesson

Looking at Table 12.3, we see that the average risk premium earned by a typical Canadian common stock is 4.3 percent: 10.45 − 6.15 = 4.30. This is a significant reward. The fact that it exists historically is an important observation, and it is the basis for our first lesson: Risky assets, on average, earn a risk premium. Put another way, there is a reward for bearing risk.

[5] The S&P/TSX Venture Composite was preceded by the Canadian Venture Exchange (CDNX), which was created in November 1999. In 2001, the TSX Group purchased the CDNX and renamed it.

Why is this so? Why, for example, is the risk premium for common stocks larger than the risk premium for long bonds? More generally, what determines the relative sizes of the risk premiums for the different assets? The answers to these questions are at the heart of modern finance, and the next chapter is devoted to them. For now, part of the answer can be found by looking at the historical variability of the returns on these different investments. So, to get started, we now turn our attention to measuring variability in returns.

TABLE 12.3

Average annual returns and risk premiums, 1957–2011

Investment	Arithmetic Average return (%)	Risk Premium (%)
Canadian common stocks	10.45	4.30
U.S. common stocks (Cdn $)	11.07	4.92
Long bonds	8.74	2.58
Small stocks	13.71	7.56
TSX Venture stocks	15.68	9.53
Inflation	3.95	−2.21
Treasury bills	6.15	0.00

Average returns on small stocks and TSX Venture stocks are based on data from 1970–2011 and 2002–2011 respectively.

Concept Questions

1. What do we mean by excess return and risk premium?
2. What was the nominal risk premium on long bonds? The real risk premium?
3. What is the first lesson from capital market history?

12.4 | The Variability of Returns: The Second Lesson

We have already seen that the year-to-year returns on common stocks tend to be more volatile than the returns on, say, long-term bonds. Next we discuss measuring this variability so we can begin examining the subject of risk.

Frequency Distributions and Variability

To get started, we can draw a frequency distribution for the common Canadian stock returns similar to the one in Figure 12.5. What we have done here is to count the number of times the annual return on the common stock portfolio falls within each 5 percent range. For example, in Figure 12.5, the height of 1 in the range −30 percent to −25 percent means that 1 of the 55 annual returns was in that range.

Now we need to measure the spread in returns. We know, for example, that the return on Canadian common stocks in a typical year was 10.45 percent. We now want to know how far the actual return deviates from this average in a typical year. In other words, we need a measure of how volatile the return is. The **variance** and its square root, the **standard deviation**, are the most commonly used measures of volatility. We describe how to calculate them next.

variance
The average squared deviation between the actual return and the average return.

standard deviation
The positive square root of the variance.

The Historical Variance and Standard Deviation

The variance essentially measures the average squared difference between the actual returns and the average return. The bigger this number is, the more the actual returns tend to differ from the average return. Also, the larger the variance or standard deviation is, the more spread out the returns are.

FIGURE 12.5

Frequency distribution of returns on Canadian common stocks

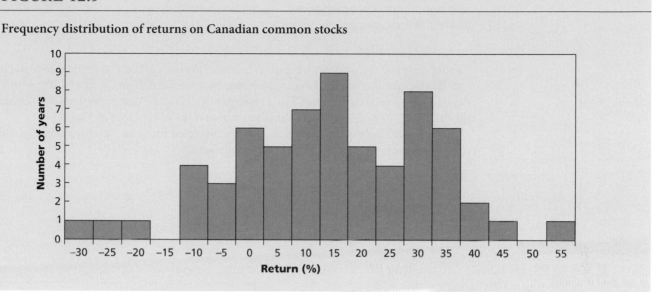

The way we calculate the variance and standard deviation depends on the situation. In this chapter, we are looking at historical returns; so the procedure we describe here is the correct one for calculating the historical variance and standard deviation. If we were examining projected future returns, the procedure would be different. We describe this procedure in the next chapter.

To illustrate how we calculate the historical variance, suppose a particular investment had returns of 10 percent, 12 percent, 3 percent, and −9 percent over the last four years. The average return is $(.10 + .12 + .03 − .09)/4 = 4\%$. Notice that the return is never actually equal to 4 percent. Instead, the first return deviates from the average by $.10 − .04 = .06$, the second return deviates from the average by $.12 − .04 = .08$, and so on. To compute the variance, we square each of these deviations, add them up, and divide the result by the number of returns less one, or three in this case. This information is summarized in the following table:

	(1) Actual Returns	(2) Average Return	(3) Deviation (1)−(2)	(4) Squared Deviation
	.10	.04	.06	.0036
	.12	.04	.08	.0064
	.03	.04	−.01	.0001
	−.09	.04	−.13	.0169
Totals	.16		.00	.0270

In the first column, we write down the four actual returns. In the third column, we calculate the difference between the actual returns and the average by subtracting out 4 percent. Finally, in the fourth column, we square the numbers in column 3 to get the squared deviations from the average.

The variance can now be calculated by dividing .0270, the sum of the squared deviations, by the number of returns less one. Let Var(R) or σ^2 (read this as sigma squared) stand for the variance of the return:

$$\text{Var}(R) = \sigma^2 = .027/(4 − 1) = .009$$

The standard deviation is the square root of the variance. So, if SD(R) or σ stands for the standard deviation of return:

$$\text{SD}(R) = \sigma = \sqrt{0.009} = .09487$$

The square root of the variance is used because the variance is measured in squared percentages and, thus, is hard to interpret. The standard deviation is an ordinary percentage, so the answer here could be written as 9.487 percent.

In the preceding table, notice that the sum of the deviations is equal to zero. This is always the case, and it provides a good way to check your work. In general, if we have T historical returns, where T is some number, we can write the historical variance as:

$$\text{Var}(R) = (1/(T-1))\left[\left(R_1 - \overline{R}\right)^2 + \ldots + \left(R_T - \overline{R}\right)^2\right] \qquad [12.3]$$

This formula tells us to do just what we did above: Take each of the T individual returns $(R_1, R_2, \ldots)$ and subtract the average return, $\overline{R}$; square the result, and add them up; finally, divide this total by the number of returns less one $(T-1)$ because our 55 years' data represents only a sample, not the full population. The standard deviation is always the square root of $\text{Var}(R)$.

Each of the above calculations can also be completed using an Excel spreadsheet. Once your data are entered, you can use the following functions:

Average = AVERAGE( )
Variance = VAR( )
Standard Deviation = STDEV( )

EXAMPLE 12.2: Calculating the Variance and Standard Deviation

Suppose Northern Radio Comm and the Canadian Empire Bank have experienced the following returns in the last four years:

Year	Northern Radio Comm Returns	Canadian Empire Bank Returns
2009	−.20	.05
2010	.50	.09
2011	.30	−.12
2012	.10	.20

What are the average returns? The variances? The standard deviations? Which investment was more volatile?

To calculate the average returns, we add the returns and divide by four. The results are:

Northern Radio Comm average return = $\overline{R}$ = (−0.20 + 0.50 + 0.30 + 0.10)/4 = .70/4 = .175
Canadian Empire Bank average return = $\overline{R}$ = (0.05 + 0.09 − 0.12 + 0.20)/4 = .22/4 = .055

To calculate the variance for Northern Radio Comm, we can summarize the relevant calculations as follows:

Year	(1) Actual Returns	(2) Average Returns	(3) Deviation (1) − (2)	(4) Squared Deviation
2010	−.20	.175	−.375	.140625
2011	.50	.175	.325	.105625
2012	.30	.175	.125	.015625
2013	.10	.175	−.075	.005625
Totals	.70		.000	.267500

Since there are four years of returns, we calculate the variances by dividing .2675 by (4 − 1) = 3:

	Northern Radio Comm	Canadian Empire Bank
Variance (σ^2)	.2675/3 = .0892	.0529/3 = .0176
Standard deviation (σ)	$\sqrt{.0892}$ = .2987	$\sqrt{.0176}$ = .1327

For practice, check that you get the same answer as we do for Canadian Empire Bank. Notice that the standard deviation for Northern Radio Comm, 29.87 percent, is a little more than twice Canadian Empire's 13.27 percent; Northern Radio Comm is thus the more volatile investment.[6]

The Historical Record

Table 12.4 summarizes much of our discussion of capital market history so far. It displays average returns and standard deviations of annual returns. We used spreadsheet software to calculate these standard deviations. For example, in Excel it is STDEV. In Table 12.4, notice, for example, that the standard deviation for the Canadian common stock portfolio (16.93 percent per year) is about four times as large as the T-bill portfolio's standard deviation (3.75 percent per year). We return to these figures momentarily.

---

[6]Since our two stocks have different average returns, it may be useful to look at their risks in comparison to the average returns. The coefficient of variation shows this. It equals (Standard deviation)/(Average return).

CALCULATOR HINTS	**Finding Standard Deviation (s) and Mean (x)**

(Using Texas Instruments BA II Plus Financial Calculator)

You can solve Example 12.2 using a financial calculator by doing the following:

Clear any previous data:

Action	Keystrokes
Select the data entry function of the calculator.	**2nd** [DATA]
Clear any pre-existing data from the worksheet.	**2nd** [CLR WORK]

Enter the data into the calculator.

Keystrokes			Calculator Display
−0.20	**ENTER**	↓	X01 = −0.20
		↓	Y01 = 1.00
0.50	**ENTER**	↓	X02 = 0.50
		↓	Y02 = 1.00
0.30	**ENTER**	↓	X03 = 0.30
		↓	Y03 = 1.00
0.10	**ENTER**	↓	X04 = 0.10
		↓	Y04 = 1.00

Before calculating the statistics:

Action	Keystroke	Calculator Display
Select the statistics calculation function of the calculator.	**2nd** [STAT]	Will display any pre-existing data from prior use
Clear any pre-existing data from the worksheet.	**2nd** [CLR WORK]	LIN
Set the calculator to 1-variable calculation mode.	**2nd** [SET]	
	Repeatedly tap the [SET] key to toggle the different options.	1-V

To view statistics of data set:

Action	Keystroke	Calculator Display
To view mean (x), toggle downward	↓	x = 0.1750
To view sample standard deviation (s), toggle downward	↓	Sx = 0.2986

Normal Distribution

normal distribution
A symmetric, bell-shaped frequency distribution that can be defined by its mean and standard deviation.

For many different random events in nature, a particular frequency distribution, the **normal distribution** (or bell curve), is useful for describing the probability of ending up in a given range. For example, the idea behind grading on a curve comes from the fact that exam scores often resemble a bell curve.

Figure 12.6 illustrates a normal distribution and its distinctive bell shape. As you can see, this distribution has a much cleaner appearance than the actual return distributions illustrated in Figure 12.5. Even so, like the normal distribution, the actual distributions do appear to be at least roughly mound-shaped and symmetrical. When this is true, the normal distribution is often a very good approximation.[7]

---

[7] It is debatable whether such a smooth picture would necessarily always be a normal distribution. But we assume it would be normal to make the statistical discussion as simple as possible.

TABLE 12.4

Historical returns and standard deviations, 1957–2011

Investment	Arithmetic Average return (%)	Standard Deviation (%)
Canadian common stocks	10.45	16.93
U.S. common stocks (Cdn $)	11.07	16.95
Long bonds	8.74	9.75
Small stocks	13.71	26.65
TSX Venture stocks	15.68	47.65
Inflation	3.95	3.13
Treasury bills	6.15	3.75

Average returns on small stocks and TSX Venture stocks are based on data from 1970–2011 and 2002–2011 respectively.

FIGURE 12.6

The normal distribution. Illustrated returns are based on the historical return and standard deviation for a portfolio of large common stocks.

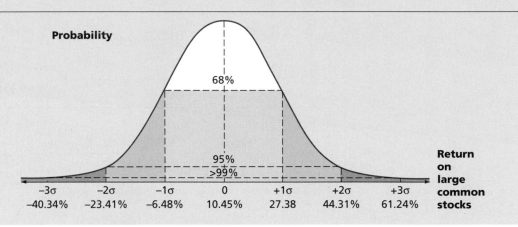

Also, keep in mind that the distributions in Figure 12.5 are based on only 55 yearly observations while Figure 12.6 is, in principle, based on an infinite number. So, if we had been able to observe returns for, say, 1,000 years, we might have filled in a lot of the irregularities and ended up with a much smoother picture. For our purposes, it is enough to observe that the returns are at least roughly normally distributed.

The usefulness of the normal distribution stems from the fact that it is completely described by the average and standard deviation. If you have these two numbers, there is nothing else to know. For example, with a normal distribution, the probability that we end up within one standard deviation of the average is about two-thirds. The probability that we end up within two standard deviations is about 95 percent. Finally, the probability of being more than three standard deviations away from the average is less than 1 percent. These ranges and the probabilities are illustrated in Figure 12.6.

To see why this is useful, recall from Table 12.4 that the standard deviation of returns on Canadian common stocks is 16.93 percent. The average return is 10.45 percent. So, assuming that the frequency distribution is at least approximately normal, the probability that the return in a given year is in the range −6.48 percent to 27.38 percent (10.45 percent plus or minus one standard deviation, 16.93 percent) is about two-thirds. This range is illustrated in Figure 12.6. In other words, there is about one chance in three that the return is outside the range. This literally tells you that, if you buy stocks in larger companies, you should expect to be outside this range in one year out of every three. This reinforces our earlier observations about stock market volatility. However, there is only a 5 percent chance (approximately) that we would end up outside the range −23.41 percent to 44.31 percent (10.45 percent plus or minus 2 × 16.93 percent). These points are also illustrated in Figure 12.6.

Value at Risk

We can take this one step further to create a measure of risk that is widely used. Suppose you are a risk management executive at a bank that has $100 million invested in stocks. You want to know how much you can lose in any one year. We just showed that based on historical data you would be outside the range of 23.41 percent to 44.31 percent only 5 percent of the time. Because we based this on a normal distribution, you know that the distribution is symmetric. In other words, the 5 percent chance of being outside the range breaks down into a 2.5 percent probability of a return above 44.31 percent and an equal 2.5 percent chance of a return below −23.41 percent. You want to find out how much you can lose, so you can safely ignore the chance of a return above 44.31 percent. Instead you focus on the 2.5 percent probability of a loss of more than 23.41 percent of the portfolio.

value at risk (VaR)
Statistical measure of maximum loss used by banks and other financial institutions to manage risk exposures.

What you have discovered is that 97.5 percent of the time, your loss will not exceed this level. On a portfolio of $100 million, this means that your maximum loss estimate is $100 million × (−23.41%) = −$23.41 million. This number is called **value at risk** (**VaR**). You can find examples of VaR in the annual report of Bank of Montreal and all other Canadian banks. Since VaR is a measure of possible loss, financial institutions use it in determining adequate capital levels. Financial institutions recognize that VaR likely underestimates the amount of capital needed because it is based on assuming a normal distribution of returns.

The Second Lesson

Our observations concerning the year-to-year variability in returns are the basis for our second lesson from capital market history. On average, bearing risk is handsomely rewarded, but in a given year, there is a significant chance of a dramatic change in value. Thus, our second lesson is: The greater the potential reward, the greater is the risk.

TSX Venture Stocks in Table 12.4 illustrate the second lesson over again, as this investment has both the highest average return and the largest standard deviation of any Canadian investment. On the contrary, Small stocks have the second-largest standard deviation, but also the second-smallest average return.

2008 The Bear Growled and Investors Howled

To reinforce our point concerning stock market volatility, consider that just a few short years ago, 2008, entered the record books as one of the worst years for stock market investors in Canadian and global history. How bad was it? As shown in Table 12.1, the widely followed S&P/TSX Composite plunged 33 percent.

Over the period, 1948–2011, 2008 was the worst year, although 1974 came close with a loss of 25.93 percent. Making matters worse, the downdraft continued with a further decline of 17 percent in early 2009. In all, from August of 2008 (when the decline began in Canada) through March of 2009 (when it ended), the S&P/TSX lost 50 percent of its value.

The drop in stock prices was a global phenomenon with the U.S. S&P 500 also falling by a similar percent in U.S. dollar terms. Many of the world's major markets were off by much more. China, India, and Russia, for example, all experienced declines of more than 50 percent. Iceland saw share prices drop by more than 90 percent in 2008. Trading on the Icelandic exchange was temporarily suspended on October 9, 2008. In what has to be a modern record for a single day, stocks fell by 76 percent when trading resumed on October 14.

Were there any bright spots in the financial crisis? The answer is yes because as stocks tanked, bonds did well with returns in Canada of 2.70 percent in 2008 and 5.31 percent in 2009. These returns were especially impressive considering that the rate of inflation was just over 1 percent.

Of course, stock prices can be volatile in both directions. Starting in March 2009, stock prices climbed for an overall return of 34.35 percent in 2009 and a further 17.27 percent in 2010. So what lessons should investors take away from this very recent, and very turbulent, bit of capital market history? First, and most obviously, stocks have significant risk! But there is a second, equally important lesson. Depending on the mix, a diversified portfolio of stocks and bonds might have suffered in 2008, but the losses would have been much smaller than those experienced by an all-stock portfolio. In other words, diversification matters, a point we will examine in detail in our next chapter.

Using Capital Market History

Based on the discussion in this section, you should begin to have an idea of the risks and rewards from investing. For example, suppose Canada Treasury bills are paying about 5 percent. Suppose further we have an investment that we think has about the same risk as a portfolio of large-firm Canadian common stocks. At a minimum, what return would this investment have to offer to catch our interest?

From Table 12.3, the risk premium on Canadian common stocks has been 4.30 percent historically, so a reasonable estimate of our required return would be this premium plus the T-bill rate, 5.0% + 4.30% = 9.30%. This may strike you as low, as during the 1990s, as well as in the years immediately after World War II, double-digit returns on Canadian and U.S. stocks were common, as Table 12.1 shows. Currently most financial executives and professional investment managers expect lower returns and smaller risk premiums in the future.[8]

We agree with their expectation and this relates to our earlier discussion of which data to use to calculate the market risk premium. In Table 12.1 we display returns data back to 1948 but only go back to 1957 when we calculate risk premiums in Table 12.3. This drops off the high returns experienced in many of the post-war years. If we recalculate the returns and risk premiums in Table 12.3 going all the way back to 1948, we arrive at a market risk premium of 6.59 percent. We think this is too high looking to the future but we have to recognize that this is a controversial point over which experts disagree.

We discuss the relationship between risk and required return in more detail in the next chapter.

EXAMPLE 12.3: Investing in Growth Stocks

The phrase *growth stock* is frequently a euphemism for *small-company stock*. Are such investments suitable for elderly, conservative investors? Before answering, you should consider the historical volatility. For example, from the historical record, what is the approximate probability that you could actually lose 10 percent or more of your money in a single year if you buy a portfolio of such companies?

Looking back at Table 12.4, the average return on small stocks is 13.71 percent and the standard deviation is 26.65 percent. Assuming the returns are approximately normal,

there is about a one-third probability that you could experience a return outside the range −12.94 percent to 40.36 percent (13.71 plus or minus 26.65 percent).

Because the normal distribution is symmetric, the odds of being above or below this range are equal. There is thus a one-sixth chance (half of one-third) that you could lose more than 12.94 percent. So you should expect this to happen once in every six years, on average. Such investments can thus be very volatile, and they are not well suited for those who cannot afford the risk.[9]

Concept Questions

1. In words, how do we calculate a variance? A standard deviation?
2. With a normal distribution, what is the probability of ending up more than one standard deviation below the average?
3. Assuming that long-term bonds have an approximately normal distribution, what is the approximate probability of earning 17 percent or more in a given year? With T-bills, what is this probability?
4. What is the first lesson from capital market history? The second?

---

[8] A survey of academic views on the market risk premium is in I. Welch, "Views of Financial Economists on the Equity Risk Premium and Other Issues," *Journal of Business* 73 (October 2000), pp. 501–537. Mercer Investment Consulting surveys professional investment managers in its annual *Fearless Forecast* available in the Knowledge Center at mercer.com/ic.

[9] Some researchers advise investors to "pensionize their nest eggs" using the new technique of product allocation to include life annuities in their portfolios: Moshe A. Milevsky; Alexandra C. Macqueen. (2010). Step 7: Use Product Allocation to Pensionize Your Nest Egg. In Pensionize Your Nest Egg (pp199–200). Hoboken, NJ: Wiley.

12.5 | More on Average Returns

Thus far in this chapter, we have looked closely at simple average returns. But there is another way of computing an average return. The fact that average returns are calculated two different ways leads to some confusion, so our goal in this section is to explain the two approaches and also the circumstances under which each is appropriate.

Arithmetic versus Geometric Averages

Let's start with a simple example. Suppose you buy a particular stock for $200. Unfortunately, the first year you own it, it falls to $100. The second year you own it, it rises back to $200, leaving you where you started (no dividends were paid).

What was your average return on this investment? Common sense seems to say that your average return must be exactly zero since you started with $200 and ended with $200. But if we calculate the returns year-by-year, we see that you lost 50 percent the first year (you lost half of your money). The second year, you made 100 percent (you doubled your money). Your average return over the two years was thus $(-50\% + 100\%)/2 = 25\%$!

So which is correct, 0 percent or 25 percent? The answer is that both are correct: They just answer different questions. The 0 percent is called the **geometric average return**. The 25 percent is called the **arithmetic average return**. The geometric average return answers the question *"What was your average compound return per year over a particular period?"* The arithmetic average return answers the question *"What was your return in an average year over a particular period?"*

Notice that, in previous sections, the average returns we calculated were all arithmetic averages, so we already know how to calculate them. What we need to do now is (1) learn how to calculate geometric averages and (2) learn the circumstances under which one average is more meaningful than the other.

geometric average return
The average compound return earned per year over a multi-year period.

arithmetic average return
The return earned in an average year over a multi-year period.

Calculating Geometric Average Returns

First, to illustrate how we calculate a geometric average return, suppose a particular investment had annual returns of 10 percent, 12 percent, 3 percent, and −9 percent over the last four years. The geometric average return over this four-year period is calculated as

$$(1.10 \times 1.12 \times 1.03 \times .91)^{1/4} - 1 = 3.66\%.$$

In contrast, the average arithmetic return we have been calculating is

$$(.10 + .12 + .03 - .09)/4 = 4.0\%.$$

In general, if we have T years of returns, the geometric average return over these T years is calculated using this formula:

$$\text{Geometric average return} = [(1 + R_1) \times (1 + R_2) \times \ldots \times (1 + R_T)]^{1/T} - 1 \qquad [12.4]$$

This formula tells us that four steps are required:

1. Take each of the T annual returns $R_1, R_2, \ldots, R_T$ and add a one to each (after converting them to decimals!).
2. Multiply all the numbers from step 1 together.
3. Take the result from step 2 and raise it to the power of $1/T$.
4. Finally, subtract one from the result of step 3. The result is the geometric average return.

EXAMPLE 12.4: Calculating the Geometric Average Return

Calculate the geometric average return for S&P 500 large-cap stocks for the first five years in Table 12.1, 1948–1952.

First, convert percentages to decimal returns, add one, and then calculate their product:

S&P 500 Returns	Product
5.50	1.055
22.15	×1.2215
39.18	×1.3918
15.00	×1.15
13.68	×1.1368
	2.3448

Notice that the number 2.3448 is what our investment is worth after five years if we started with a one dollar investment. The geometric average return is then calculated as

$$\text{Geometric average return} = 2.3448^{1/5} - 1 = 0.1858, \text{ or } 18.58\%$$

Thus the geometric average return is about 18.58 percent in this example. Here is a tip: If you are using a financial calculator, you can put $1 in as the present value, $2.3448 as the future value, and 5 as the number of periods. Then, solve for the unknown rate. You should get the same answer we did.

One thing you may have noticed in our examples thus far is that the geometric average returns seem to be smaller. It turns out that this will always be true (as long as the returns are not all identical, in which case the two "averages" would be the same).

As shown in Table 12.5, the geometric averages are all smaller, but the magnitude of the difference varies quite a bit. The reason is that the difference is greater for more volatile investments. In fact, there is useful approximation. Assuming all the numbers are expressed in decimals (as opposed to percentages), the geometric average return is approximately equal to the arithmetic average return minus half the variance. For example, looking at the Canadian stocks, the arithmetic average is .1045 and the standard deviation is .1693, implying that the variance is .0288. The approximate geometric average is thus .1045 − .0288/2 = .0901, which is quite close to the actual value.

TABLE 12.5

Geometric versus arithmetic average returns, 1957–2011

Investment	Average Return		
	Arithmetic (%)	Geometric (%)	Standard deviation (%)
Canadian common stocks	10.45	9.10	16.93
U.S. common stocks (Cdn $)	11.07	9.76	16.95
Long bonds	8.74	8.33	9.75
Small stocks	13.71	10.55	26.65
TSX Venture stocks	15.68	3.71	47.65
Inflation	3.95	3.90	3.13
Treasury bills	6.15	6.09	3.75

Average returns on small stocks and TSX Venture stocks are based on data from 1970–2011 and 2002–2011 respectively.

EXAMPLE 12.5: More Geometric Averages

Take a look back at Figure 12.4. There, we showed the value of a $1 investment after 55 years. Use the value for the S&P/TSX Composite stocks to check the geometric average in Table 12.5.

In Figure 12.4, the S&P/TSX Composite stocks grew to $120.09 over 55 years. The geometric average return is thus:

$$\text{Geometric average return} = \$120.09^{1/55} - 1$$
$$= 0.0910 \text{ or } 9.10\%$$

This 9.10% is the value shown in Table 12.5. For practice, check some of the other numbers in Table 12.5 the same way.

Arithmetic Average Return or Geometric Average Return?

When we look at historical returns, the difference between the geometric and arithmetic average returns isn't too hard to understand. To put it slightly differently, the geometric average tells you what you actually earned per year on average, compounded annually. The arithmetic average tells you what you earned in a typical year. You should use whichever one answers the question you want answered.

A somewhat trickier question concerns which average return to use when forecasting future wealth levels, and there's a lot of confusion on this point among analysts and financial planners. First, let's get one thing straight: If you *know* the true arithmetic average return, then this is what you should use in your forecast. So, for example, if you know the arithmetic return is 10 percent, then your best guess of the value of a $1,000 investment in 10 years is the future value of $1,000 at 10 percent for 10 years, or $2,593.74.

The problem we face, however, is that we usually only have *estimates* of the arithmetic and geometric returns, and estimates have errors. In this case, the arithmetic average return is probably too high for longer periods and the geometric average is probably too low for shorter periods. So, you should regard long-run projected wealth levels calculated using arithmetic averages as optimistic. Short-run projected wealth levels calculated using geometric averages are probably pessimistic.

As a practical matter, if you are using averages calculated over a long period of time (such as the 55 years we use) to forecast, then you should just split the difference between the arithmetic and geometric average returns. What this means is calculating the geometric mean market risk premium from Table 12.5: 9.10% − 6.09% = 3.01%. Our revised estimate of the market risk premium then becomes the average of this number and the arithmetic mean risk premium on Canadian common stocks of 4.30 percent from Table 12.3: (3.01% + 4.30%)/2 = 3.66%.[10]

This concludes our discussion of geometric versus arithmetic averages. One last note: In the future, when we say "average return," we mean arithmetic unless we explicitly say otherwise.

Concept Questions

1. If you wanted to forecast what the stock market is going to do over the next year, should you use an arithmetic or geometric average?
2. If you wanted to forecast what the stock market is going to do over the next century, should you use an arithmetic or geometric average?

12.6 | Capital Market Efficiency

Capital market history suggests that the market values of stocks and bonds can fluctuate widely from year to year. Why does this occur? At least part of the answer is that prices change because new information arrives, and investors reassess asset values based on that information.

The behaviour of market prices has been extensively studied. A question that has received particular attention is whether prices adjust quickly and correctly when new information arrives. A market is said to be efficient if this is the case. To be more precise, in an **efficient capital market**, current market prices fully reflect available information. By this we simply mean that, based on available information, there is no reason to believe the current price is too low or too high.

The concept of market efficiency is a rich one, and much has been written about it. A full discussion of the subject goes beyond the scope of our study of corporate finance. However, because the concept figures so prominently in studies of market history, we briefly describe the key points here.

efficient capital market
Market in which security prices reflect available information.

---

[10] Our approach here is adapted from M.E. Blume, "Unbiased Estimators of Long-Run Expected Rates of Return," *Journal of the American Statistical Association* 69:347 (September 1974), pp. 634–638.

Price Behaviour in an Efficient Market

To illustrate how prices behave in an efficient market, suppose the 3 Dee TV Corporation (3DT) has, through years of secret research and development, developed a television that projects TV programs into three-dimensional field that does not require an individual to wear 3D glasses. 3DT's capital budgeting analysis suggests that launching the new 3D television is a highly profitable move; in other words, the NPV appears to be positive and substantial. The key assumption thus far is that 3DT has not released any information about the new system, so the fact of its existence is only inside information.

Now consider a share of stock in 3DT. In an efficient market, its price reflects what is known about 3DT's current operations and profitability, and it reflects market opinion about 3DT's potential for future growth and profits. The value of the new 3D television is not reflected, however, because the market is unaware of its existence.

If the market agrees with 3DT's assessment of the value of the new project, 3DT's stock price rises when the decision to launch is made public. For example, assume the announcement is made in a press release on Wednesday morning. In an efficient market, the price of shares in 3DT adjusts quickly to this new information. Investors should not be able to buy the stock on Wednesday afternoon and make a profit on Thursday. This would imply that it took the stock market a full day to realize the implication of the 3DT press release. If the market is efficient, on Wednesday afternoon the price of 3DT shares already reflects the information contained in that morning's press release.

Figure 12.7 presents three possible stock price adjustments for 3DT. In Figure 12.7, Day 0 represents the announcement day. As illustrated, before the announcement, 3DT's stock sells for $140 per share. The NPV per share of the new system is, say, $40, so the new price would be $180 once the value of the new project is fully reflected.

FIGURE 12.7

Reaction of stock price to new information in efficient and inefficient markets

Efficient market reaction: The price instantaneously adjusts to and fully reflects new information; there is no tendency for subsequent increases and decreases.

Delayed reaction: The price partially adjusts to the new information; 10 days elapse before the price completely reflects the new information.

Overreaction: The price over adjusts to the new information; it "overshoots" the new price and subsequently corrects.

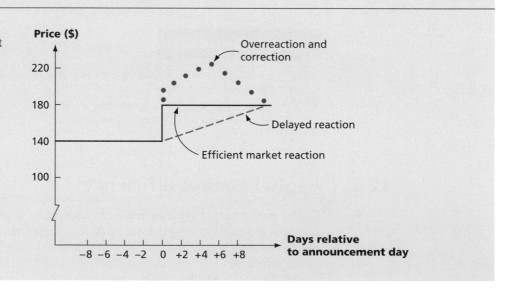

The solid line in Figure 12.7 represents the path taken by the stock price in an efficient market. In this case, the price adjusts immediately to the new information and no further changes in the price of the stock occur. The broken line in Figure 12.7 depicts a delayed reaction. Here it takes the market eight days or so to fully absorb the information. Finally, the dotted line illustrates an overreaction and subsequent adjustments to the correct price.

The broken line and the dotted line in Figure 12.7 illustrate paths that the stock price might take in an inefficient market. If, for example stock prices don't adjust immediately to new information (the broken line), buying stock immediately following the release of new information and then selling it several days later would be a positive NPV activity because the price is too low for several days after the announcement.

The Efficient Markets Hypothesis

efficient markets hypothesis (EMH)
The hypothesis is that actual capital markets, such as the TSX, are efficient.

The **efficient markets hypothesis (EMH)** asserts that well-organized capital markets such as the TSX and the NYSE are efficient markets, at least as a practical matter. In other words, an advocate of the EMH might argue that while inefficiencies may exist, they are relatively small and not common.

When a market is efficient, there is a very important implication for market participants: All investments in an efficient market are zero NPV investments. The reason is not complicated. If prices are neither too low nor too high, the difference between the market value of an investment and its cost is zero; hence, the NPV is zero. As a result, in an efficient market, investors get exactly what they pay for when they buy securities, and firms receive exactly what their stocks and bonds are worth when they sell them.

What makes a market efficient is competition among investors. Many individuals spend their lives trying to find mispriced stocks. For any given stock, they study what has happened in the past to the stock price and its dividends. They learn, to the extent possible, what a company's earnings have been, how much it owes to creditors, what taxes it pays, what businesses it is in, what new investments are planned, how sensitive it is to changes in the economy, and so on.

Not only is there a great deal to know about any particular company, but there is also a powerful incentive for knowing it; namely, the profit motive. If you know more about some company than other investors in the marketplace, you can profit from that knowledge by investing in the company's stock if you have good news and selling it if you have bad news.

The logical consequence of all this information being gathered and analyzed is that mispriced stocks will become fewer and fewer. In other words, because of competition among investors, the market is becoming increasingly efficient. A kind of equilibrium comes into being where there is just enough mispricing around for those who are best at identifying it to make a living at it. For most other investors, the activity of information gathering and analysis does not pay. We can use Microsoft to illustrate the competition for information. A survey found that there are 60 analysts on Wall Street, Bay Street, and around the world assigned to following this stock. As a result, the chances are very low that one analyst will discover some information or insight into the company that is unknown to the other 59.

No idea in finance has attracted as much attention as that of efficient markets, and not all the attention has been flattering. Rather than rehash the arguments here, we are content to observe that some markets are more efficient than others. For example, financial markets on the whole are probably much more efficient than real asset markets.

Efficiency does imply that the price a firm obtains when it sells a share of its stock is a fair price in the sense that it reflects the value of that stock given the information available about it. Shareholders do not have to worry that they are paying too much for a stock with a low dividend or some other sort of characteristic because the market has already incorporated that characteristic into the price. We sometimes say that the information has been "priced out."

The concept of efficient markets can be explained further by replying to a frequent objection. It is sometimes argued that the market cannot be efficient because stock prices fluctuate from day to day. If the prices are right, the argument goes, then why do they change so much and so often? From our prior discussion, these price movements are in no way inconsistent with efficiency. Investors are bombarded with information every day. The fact that prices fluctuate is, at least in part, a reflection of that information flow. The Canadian government's announcement on October 31st, 2006, to impose a new tax on income trusts came as a shock for the industry, and the S&P/TSX Composite Index immediately plummeted by 294 points as a reaction to this news.[11] This suggests the evidence that the markets are "informationally efficient." In fact, the absence of price movements in a world that changes as rapidly as ours would suggest inefficiency.[12]

---

[11] Two Canadian studies documents how this reaction reflected market efficiency: I.A. Glew and L.D. Johnson, "Consequences of the Halloween Nightmare: Analysis of Investors' Response to an Overnight Tax Legislation Change in the Canadian Income Trust Sector," *Canadian Journal of Administrative Sciences*, 2011, Vol. 28, Number 1, pp.53-69 and B. Amoako-Adu and B.F. Smith, "Valuation Effects of Recent Corporate Dividend and Income Trust Distribution Tax Changes," *Canadian Journal of Administrative Sciences*, 2008, Vol.25, Number 1, pp. 55-66.

[12] For a Canadian study showing the impact of some of this daily information flow related to business relocation announcements, see, H. Bhabra, U. Lel, and D. Tirtiroglu, "Stock Market's Reaction to Business Relocations: Canadian Evidence," *Canadian Journal of Administrative Sciences*, December 2002, Vol. 19, Number 4, pp. 346–358.

Jeremy Siegel on Efficient Market Theory and the Crisis

Financial journalist and best-selling author Roger Lowenstein didn't mince words in a piece for the *Washington Post* this summer: "The upside of the current Great Recession is that it could drive a stake through the heart of the academic nostrum known as the efficient-market hypothesis." In a similar vein, the highly respected money manager and financial analyst Jeremy Grantham wrote in his quarterly letter last January: "The incredibly inaccurate efficient market theory [caused] a lethally dangerous combination of asset bubbles, lax controls, pernicious incentives and wickedly complicated instruments [that] led to our current plight."

But is the Efficient Market Hypothesis (EMH) really responsible for the current crisis? The answer is no. The EMH, originally put forth by Eugene Fama of the University of Chicago in the 1960s, states that the prices of securities reflect all known information that impacts their value. The hypothesis does not claim that the market price is always right. On the contrary, it implies that the prices in the market are mostly wrong, but at any given moment it is not at all easy to say whether they are too high or too low. The fact that the best and brightest on Wall Street made so many mistakes shows how hard it is to beat the market.

This does not mean the EMH can be used as an excuse by the CEOs of the failed financial firms or by the regulators who did not see the risks that subprime mortgage-backed securities posed to the financial stability of the economy. Regulators wrongly believed that financial firms were offsetting their credit risks, while the banks and credit rating agencies were fooled by faulty models that underestimated the risk in real estate.

After the 1982 recession, the U.S. and world economies entered into a long period where the fluctuations in variables such as gross domestic product, industrial production, and employment were significantly lower than they had been since World War II. Economists called this period the "Great Moderation" and attributed the increased stability to better monetary policy, a larger service sector and better inventory control, among other factors.

The economic response to the Great Moderation was predictable: risk premiums shrank and individuals and firms took on more leverage. Housing prices were boosted by historically low nominal and real interest rates and the development of the securitized subprime lending market.

According to data collected by Prof. Robert Shiller of Yale University, in the 61 years from 1945 through 2006, the maximum cumulative decline in the average price of homes was 2.84% in 1991. If this low volatility of home prices persisted into the future, a mortgage security composed of a nationally diversified portfolio of loans comprising the first 80% of a home's value would have never come close to defaulting. The credit quality of home buyers was secondary because it was thought that underlying collateral—the home—could always cover the principal in the event the homeowner defaulted. These models led credit agencies to rate these subprime mortgages as "investment grade."

But this assessment was faulty. From 2000 through 2006, national home prices rose by 88.7%, far more than the 17.5% gain in the consumer price index or the paltry 1% rise in median household income. Never before have home prices jumped that far ahead of prices and incomes.

This should have sent up red flags and cast doubts on using models that looked only at historical declines to judge future risk. But these flags were ignored as Wall Street was reaping large profits bundling and selling the securities while Congress was happy that more Americans could enjoy the "American Dream" of home ownership. Indeed, through government-sponsored enterprises such as Fannie Mae and Freddie Mac, Washington helped fuel the subprime boom.

Neither the rating agencies' mistakes nor the overleveraging by the financial firms in the subprime securities is the fault of the Efficient Market Hypothesis. The fact that the yields on these mortgages were high despite their investment-grade rating indicated that the market was rightly suspicious of the quality of the securities, and this should have served as a warning to prospective buyers.

With few exceptions (Goldman Sachs being one), financial firms ignored these warnings. CEOs failed to exercise their authority to monitor overall risk of the firm and instead put their faith in technicians whose narrow models could not capture the big picture. One can only wonder if the large investment banks would have taken on such risks when they were all partnerships and the lead partner had all his wealth in the firm, as they were just a few decades ago.

The misreading of these economic trends did not just reside within the private sector. Former Fed Chairman Alan Greenspan stated before congressional committees last December that he was "shocked" that the top executives of the financial firms exposed their stockholders to such risk. But had he looked at their balance sheets, he would have realized that not only did they put their own shareholders at risk, but their leveraged positions threatened the viability of the entire financial system.

As home prices continued to climb and subprime mortgages proliferated, Mr. Greenspan and current Fed Chairman Ben Bernanke were perhaps the only ones influential enough to sound an alarm and soften the oncoming crisis. But they did not. For all the deserved kudos that the central bank received for their management of the crisis after the Lehman bankruptcy, the failure to see these problems building will stand as a permanent blot on the Fed's record.

Our crisis wasn't due to blind faith in the Efficient Market Hypothesis. The fact that risk premiums were low does not mean they were nonexistent and that market prices were right. Despite the recent recession, the Great Moderation is real and our economy is inherently more stable.

But this does not mean that risks have disappeared. To use an analogy, the fact that automobiles today are safer than they were years ago does not mean that you can drive at 120 mph.

A small bump on the road, perhaps insignificant at lower speeds, will easily flip the best-engineered car. Our financial firms drove too fast, our central bank failed to stop them, and the housing deflation crashed the banks and the economy.

Jeremy J. Siegel, Russell E. Palmer Professor of Finance at the University of Pennsylvania's Wharton School, is the author of "Stocks for the Long Run," now in its 5th edition from McGraw-Hill.

Market Efficiency—Forms and Evidence

It is common to distinguish among three forms of market efficiency. Depending on the degree of efficiency, we say that markets are either weak form efficient, semistrong form efficient, or strong form efficient. The difference between these forms relates to what information is reflected in prices.

We start with the extreme case. If the market is strong form efficient, then all information of every kind is reflected in stock prices. In such a market, there is no such thing as inside information. Thus, in our previous 3D1 example, we apparently were assuming the market was not strong form efficient.

Casual observation, particularly in recent years, suggests that inside information exists and it can be valuable to possess. Whether it is lawful or ethical to use that information is another issue. In any event, we conclude that private information about a particular stock may exist that is not currently reflected in the price of the stock. For example, prior knowledge of a takeover attempt can be very valuable as illustrated by the case of Raj Rajaratnam who was sentenced to 11 years in prison for illegal insider trading in New York in 2011. The prosecution proved that his Galleon Management fund earned $72 million U.S. based on illegal tips from corporate insiders.[13] The OSC is responsible for enforcement of insider trading rule is Canada. The accompanying box discusses one case of insider trading.

The second form of efficiency, semistrong efficiency, is the most controversial. In a market that is semistrong form efficient, all public information is reflected in the stock price. The reason this form is controversial is that it implies that a security analyst who tries to identify mispriced stocks using, for example, financial statement information is wasting time because that information is already reflected in the current price.

Studies of semistrong form efficiency include event studies that measure whether prices adjust rapidly to new information following the efficient markets pattern in Figure 12.7. Announcements of mergers, dividends, earnings, capital expenditures, and new issues of securities are a few examples. Although there are exceptions, event study tests for major exchanges including the TSX, NYSE, and Nasdaq generally support the view that these markets are semistrong efficient with respect to the arrival of new information. In fact, the tests suggest these markets are gifted with a certain amount of foresight. By this, we mean that news tends to leak out and be reflected in stock prices even before the official release of the information.

Referring back to Figure 12.7, what this means is that for stocks listed on major exchanges, the stock price reaction to new information is typically the one shown for an efficient market. In some cases, the price follows the pattern shown for overreaction and correction. For example, a classic study found that stocks recommended in *The Financial Post* "Hot Stock" column experienced price increases followed by declines.[14] Our conclusion here is that the market is mainly efficient

---

[13] The film *Wall Street*, Twentieth Century Fox, 1987, realistically illustrates how valuable the information can be. More on the Galleon story may be found at washingtonpost.com/business/economy/hedge-fund-billionaire-gets-11-year-sentence-in-fraud case/2011/10/13/gIQAa0PZhL print.html. The trading activities of company insiders in Canada can now be tracked on the System for Electronic Disclosure by Insiders at sedi.ca. To know more about the securities law and enforcements, visit osc.gov.on.ca/

[14] For more details see V. Mehrotra, W.W. Yu, and C. Zhang, "Market Reactions to *The Financial Post's* 'Hot Stock' Column," *Canadian Journal of Administrative Sciences* 16, June 1999, pp. 118–131.

but that there are some exceptions.

If the market is efficient in the semistrong form, no matter what publicly available information mutual fund managers rely on to pick stocks, their average returns should be the same as those of the average investor in the market as a whole. Researchers have tested mutual fund performance against a market index and found that, on average, fund managers have no special ability to beat the market.[15] This supports semistrong form efficiency. An important practical result of such studies is the growth of index funds that follow a passive investment strategy of investing in the market index. For example, TD Waterhouse Canadian Index Fund invests in the S&P/TSX Composite and its performance tracks that of the index. The fund has lower expenses than an actively managed fund because it does not employ analysts to pick stocks. Investors who believe in market efficiency prefer index investing because market efficiency means that the analysts will not beat the market consistently.

The third form of efficiency, weak form efficiency, suggests that, at a minimum, the current price of a stock reflects its own past prices. In other words, studying past prices in an attempt to identify mispriced securities is futile if the market is weak form efficient. Research supporting weak form efficiency suggests that successive price changes are generally consistent with a random walk where deviations from expected return are random. Tests on both the TSX and NYSE support weak form efficiency, although the results are more conclusive for the NYSE.[16] This form of efficiency might seem rather mild; however, it implies that searching for patterns in historical prices that identify mispriced stocks does not work in general. An exception to this statement occurred in the hot high tech market of the late 1990s. Some investors were able to achieve superior returns following momentum strategies based on the idea that stocks that went up yesterday are likely also to go up today. Day trading became very popular in this "momentum market."[17]

Although the bulk of the evidence supports the view that major markets such as the TSX, NYSE, and Nasdaq are reasonably efficient, we would not be fair if we did not note the existence of selected contrary results often termed anomalies.[18] These anomalies include crashes like those in 2008 and 1987 and seasonal movements in markets that have no rational explanation. We discuss these in detail in Chapter 26.

In summary, what does research on capital market history say about market efficiency? At risk of going out on a limb, the evidence does seem to tell us three things: First, prices do appear to respond very rapidly to new information, and the response is at least not grossly different from what we would expect in an efficient market. Second, the future of market prices, particularly in the short run, is very difficult to predict based on publicly available information. Third, if mispriced stocks do exist, there is no obvious means of identifying them. Put another way, simpleminded schemes based on public information will probably not be successful.[19]

---

[15] Two Canadian studies are M. A. Ayadi and L. Kryzanowski, "Portfolio Performance Measurement Using APM-free Kernel Models," *Journal of Banking and Finance*, 2005, Vol. 29, pp. 623–659 and G. Athanassakos, P. Carayannopoulos, and M. Racine, "Mutual Fund Performance: The Canadian Experience Between 1985 and 1996," *Canadian Journal of Financial Planning of the CAFP*, June 2000, Vol. 1, Issue 2, pp. 5–9. Chapter 26 discusses more of the evidence.

[16] A recent study supporting weak form efficiency for the TSX is V. Alexeev and F. Tapon, " Testing Weak Form Efficiency on the Toronto Stock Exchange", *Journal of Empirical Finance*, 2011, Vol. 18, pp. 661–691.

[17] Three Canadian studies on momentum are R. Deaves and P. Miu, " Refining Momentum Strategies by Conditioning on Prior Long-term Returns: Canadian Evidence", *Canadian Journal of Administrative Sciences*, 2007, Vol. 24, pp. 135–145; M. Cao and J. Wei, "Uncovering Sector Momentums", *Canadian Investment Review*, Winter 2002, pages 14–22 and M. Inglis and S. Cleary, "Momentum in Canadian Stock Returns," *Canadian Journal of Administrative Sciences*, September 1998, pp. 279–291.

[18] The effect is international and has been documented in most stock exchanges around the world occurring immediately after the close of the tax year. See V. Jog, "Stock Pricing Anomalies Revisited," *Canadian Investment Review*, Winter 1998, pp. 28–33 and S. Elfakhani, L.J. Lockwood, and R.S. Zaher, "Small Firm and Value Effects in the Canadian Stock Market," *Journal of Financial Research* 21, Fall 1998, pp. 277–291.

[19] The suggested readings for this chapter give references to the large body of U.S. and Canadian research on efficient markets. We return to the topic of market efficiency and behavioural finance in Chapter 26.

IN THEIR OWN WORDS...

A Case of Insider Trading in Canada

Andrew Rankin on Thursday confirmed for the first time that he is at fault for letting details of secret merger and takeover deals fall into the hands of a longtime friend, who used the information to make $4.5 million through insider trading.

The one-time star Bay Street investment banker, who was fired from his job almost seven years ago, made the surprise admission as part of a settlement agreement with the Ontario Securities Commission, which requires the market regulator to drop 10 counts of insider tipping against him.

The deal comes less than a week before the start of Rankin's second criminal trial. (His 2005 conviction was overturned on appeal.)

Rankin's "negligence" made Daniel Duic's insider trading possible, the agreement says, noting that Rankin gave his friend unsupervised access to his Toronto home, where secret documents were left out in the open.

Rankin, who declined to speak with reporters, also acknowledged that he discussed sensitive transaction details with Duic, but denied that he knew his former private-school classmate planned to use the information to make illegal trades. As part of Thursday's deal, the former Bay Street whiz kid must pay $250,000 toward the regulator's costs. He is also permanently banned from the securities industry and barred from trading for 10 years. Rankin was fired from his job as a managing director at RBC Dominion Securities in 2001. Criminal charges were later laid and he was convicted of insider tipping in July 2005.

Source: canada.com/topics/news/story.html?id=b8c871b8-ed83-43f7-b6cb-0b824bd0a6dc&k=54846. Used with permission.

Concept Questions

1. What is an efficient market?
2. What are the forms of market efficiency?
3. What evidence exists that major stock markets are efficient?
4. Explain anomalies in the efficient market hypothesis.

12.7 | SUMMARY AND CONCLUSIONS

This chapter explores the subject of capital market history. Such history is useful because it tells us what to expect in the way of returns from risky assets. We summed up our study of market history with two key lessons:

1. Risky assets, on average, earn a risk premium. There is a reward for bearing risk.
2. The greater the risk from a risky investment, the greater is the required reward.

These lessons have significant implications for financial managers. We consider these implications in the chapters ahead.

We also discussed the concept of market efficiency. In an efficient market, prices adjust quickly and correctly to new information. Consequently, asset prices in efficient markets are rarely too high or too low. How efficient capital markets (such as the TSX and NYSE) are is a matter of debate, but, at a minimum, they are probably much more efficient than most real asset markets.

Key Terms

arithmetic average return (page 333)
efficient capital market (page 335)
efficient markets hypothesis (EMH) (page 337)
geometric average return (page 333)
normal distribution (page 329)

risk premium (page 325)
standard deviation (page 326)
value at risk (VaR) (page 331)
variance (page 326)

Chapter Review Problems and Self-Test

12.1 **Recent Return History** Use Table 12.1 to calculate the average return over the five years 2007–2011 for Canadian common stocks, small stocks, and Treasury bills.

12.2 **More Recent Return History** Calculate the standard deviations using information from Problem 12.1. Which of the investments was the most volatile over this period?

Answers to Self-Test Problems

12.1 We calculate the averages as follows:

Year	TSX	Small	T-bills
2007	0.0980	−0.11380	0.0440
2008	−0.3300	−0.46600	0.0330
2008	0.3435	0.86800	0.0060
2010	0.1727	0.36100	0.0050
2011	−0.0857	−0.19500	0.0100
Average	0.0397	0.09084	0.0196

12.2 We first need to calculate the deviations from the average returns. Using the averages from Problem 12.1, we get:

Year	TSX	Small	T-bills
2007	0.0583	−0.2046	0.0244
2008	−0.3697	−0.5568	0.0134
2009	0.3038	0.7772	−0.0136
2010	0.1330	0.2702	−0.0146
2011	−0.1254	−0.2858	−0.0096

We square the deviations and calculate the variances and standard deviations:

Year	TSX	Small	T-bills
2007	0.003399	0.041878	0.000595
2008	0.136678	0.310071	0.000180
2009	0.092294	0.603978	0.000185
2010	0.017689	0.072986	0.000213
2011	0.015725	0.081705	0.000092
Variance	0.066446	0.277654	0.000316
Standard deviation	0.257772	0.526929	0.017785

To calculate the variances, we added the squared deviations and divided by four, the number of returns less one. Notice that the small stocks had substantially greater volatility with a higher average return. Once again, such investments are risky, particularly over short periods.

Concepts Review and Critical Thinking Questions

1. **(LO4)** Given that Nortel was up by more than 300 percent in the 12 months ending in July 2000, why didn't all investors hold Nortel?

2. **(LO4)** Given that Hayes was down by 98 percent for 1998, why did some investors hold the stock? Why didn't they sell out before the price declined so sharply?

3. **(LO2, 3)** We have seen that, over long periods of time, stock investments have tended to substantially outperform bond investments. However, it is not at all uncommon to observe investors with long horizons holding entirely bonds. Are such investors irrational?

4. **(LO4)** Explain why a characteristic of an efficient market is that investments in that market have zero NPVs.

5. **(LO4)** A stock market analyst is able to identify mispriced stocks by comparing the average price for the last 10 days to the average price for the last 60 days. If this is true, what do you know about the market?

6. **(LO4)** If a market is semistrong form efficient, is it also weak form efficient? Explain.

7. **(LO4)** What are the implications of the efficient markets hypothesis for investors who buy and sell stocks in an attempt to "beat the market"?

8. **(LO4)** Critically evaluate the following statement: Playing the stock market is like gambling. Such speculative investing has no social value, other than the pleasure people get from this form of gambling.

9. **(LO4)** There are several celebrated investors and stock pickers frequently mentioned in the financial press who have recorded huge returns on their investments over the past two decades. Is the success of these particular investors an invalidation of the EMH? Explain.

10. **(LO4)** For each of the following scenarios, discuss whether profit opportunities exist from trading in the stock of the firm under the conditions that (1) the market is not weak form efficient, (2) the market is weak form but not semistrong form

efficient, (3) the market is semistrong form but not strong form efficient, and (4) the market is strong form efficient.

a.   The stock price has risen steadily each day for the past 30 days.

b.   The financial statements for a company were released three days ago, and you believe you've uncovered some anomalies in the company's inventory and cost control reporting techniques that are causing the firm's true liquidity strength to be understated.

c.   You observe that the senior management of a company has been buying a lot of the company's stock on the open market over the past week.

Questions and Problems

Basic
(Questions 1–12)

1.   **Calculating Returns (LO1)** Suppose a stock had an initial price of $91 per share, paid a dividend of $2.40 per share during the year, and had an ending share price of $102. Compute the percentage total return.

2.   **Calculating Yields (LO1)** In Problem 1, what was the dividend yield? The capital gains yield?

3.   **Return Calculations (LO1)** Rework Problems 1 and 2 assuming the ending share price is $83.

4.   **Calculating Returns (LO1)** Suppose you bought a 7 percent coupon bond one year ago for $1,040. The bond sells for $1,070 today.

a.   Assuming a $1,000 face value, what was your total dollar return on this investment over the past year?

b.   What was your total nominal rate of return on this investment over the past year?

c.   If the inflation rate last year was 4 percent, what was your total real rate of return on this investment?

5.   **Nominal versus Real Returns (LO2)** What was the average annual return on Canadian stock from 1957 through 2011:

a.   In nominal terms?

b.   In real terms?

6.   **Bond Returns (LO2)** What is the historical real return on Scotia Capital Markets long bonds?

 7.   **Calculating Returns and Variability (LO1)** Using the following returns, calculate the arithmetic average returns, the variances, and the standard deviations for X and Y.

	Returns	
Year	X	Y
1	8%	16%
2	21	38
3	17	14
4	−16	−22
5	9	26

8.   **Risk Premiums (LO2, 3)** Refer to Table 12.1 in the text and look at the period from 1970 through 1975.

a.   Calculate the arithmetic average returns for large-company stocks and T-bills over this period.

b.   Calculate the standard deviation of the returns for large-company stocks and T-bills over this period.

c.   Calculate the observed risk premium in each year for the large-company stocks versus the T-bills. What was the average risk premium over this period? What was the standard deviation of the risk premium over this period?

d.   Is it possible for the risk premium to be negative before an investment is undertaken? Can the risk premium be negative after the fact? Explain.

9.   **Calculating Returns and Variability (LO1)** You've observed the following returns on Regina Computer's stock over the past five years: 7 percent, −12 percent, 11 percent, 38 percent, and 14 percent.

a.   What was the arithmetic average return on Regina's stock over this five-year period?

b.   What was the variance of Regina's returns over this period? The standard deviation?

10. **Calculating Real Returns and Risk Premiums (LO1)** For Problem 9, suppose the average inflation rate over this period was 3.5 percent and the average T-bill rate over the period was 4.2 percent.

a.   What was the average real return on Regina's stock?

b.   What was the average nominal risk premium on Regina's stock?

11. **Calculating Real Rates (LO1)** Given the information in Problems 9 and 10, what was the average real risk-free rate over this time period? What was the average real risk premium?

12. **Effects of Inflation (LO2)** Look at Table 12.1 and Figure 12.4 in the text. When were T-bill rates at their highest over the period from 1957 through 2011? Why do you think they were so high during this period? What relationship underlies your answer?

Intermediate
(Questions 13–20)

13. **Calculating Investment Returns (LO1)** You bought one of Glenelm Co.'s 8 percent coupon bonds one year ago for $1,030. These bonds make annual payments and mature six years from now. Suppose you decide to sell your bonds today, when the required return on the bonds is 7 percent. If the inflation rate was 4.2 percent over the past year, what was your total real return on investment?

14. **Calculating Returns and Variability (LO1)** You find a certain stock that had returns of 7 percent, −12 percent, 18 percent, and 19 percent for four of the last five years. If the average return of the stock over this period was 10.5 percent, what was the stock's return for the missing year? What is the standard deviation of the stock's return? Assume the face value of the bond is $1,000.

15. **Arithmetic and Geometric Returns (LO1)** A stock has had returns of 3 percent, 38 percent, 21 percent, −15 percent, 29 percent, and −13 percent over the last six years. What are the arithmetic and geometric returns for the stock?

16. **Arithmetic and Geometric Returns (LO1)** A stock has had the following year-end prices and dividends:

Year	Price	Dividend
1	$60.18	—
2	73.66	$0.60
3	94.18	0.64
4	89.35	0.72
5	78.49	0.80
6	95.05	1.20

    What are the arithmetic and geometric returns for the stock?

17. **Using Return Distributions (LO3)** Suppose the returns on long-term corporate bonds are normally distributed. Based on the historical record, what is the approximate probability that your return on these bonds will be less than −2.2 percent in a given year? What range of returns would you expect to see 95 percent of the time? What range would you expect to see 99 percent of the time?

18. **Using Return Distributions (LO3)** Assuming that the returns from holding small-company stocks are normally distributed, what is the approximate probability that your money will double in value in a single year? What about triple in value?

19. **Distributions (LO3)** In Problem 18, what is the probability that the return is less than −100 percent (think)? What are the implications for the distribution of returns?

20. **Calculating Returns (LO2, 3)** Refer to Table 12.1 in the text and look at the period from 1973 through 1980:

    a.   Calculate the average return for Treasury bills and the average annual inflation rate (consumer price index) for this period.

    b.   Calculate the standard deviation of Treasury bill returns and inflation over this period.

    c.   Calculate the real return for each year. What is the average real return for Treasury bills?

    d.   Many people consider Treasury bills risk-free. What do these calculations tell you about the potential risks of Treasury bills?

Challenge 21. Using Probability Distributions (LO3) Suppose the returns on Canadian stocks are normally distributed. Based on the
(Questions   historical record, use a cumulative normal probability table (rounded to the nearest table value) to determine the probability that
21–22)   in any given year you will lose money by investing in common stock.[20]

22. **Using Probability Distributions (LO3)** Suppose the returns on Scotia Capital Markets long bonds and T-bills are normally distributed. Based on the historical record, use a cumulative normal probability table (rounded to the nearest table value) to answer the following questions:

    a.   What is the probability that in any given year, the return on long-term corporate bonds will be greater than 10 percent? Less than 0 percent?

    b.   What is the probability that in any given year, the return on T-bills will be greater than 10 percent? Less than 0 percent?

    c.   In 1981, the return on Scotia Capital Markets long bonds was −2.09 percent. How likely is it that such a low return will recur at some point in the future? T-bills had a return of 19.11 percent in this same year. How likely is it that such a high return on T-bills will recur at some point in the future?

---

[20] The table can be found at the link: miha.ef.uni-lj.si/_dokumenti3plus2/195166/norm-tables.pdf

MINI CASE

A Job at Hillsdale Inc.

You recently graduated from university, and your job search led you to Hillsdale Inc. Because you felt the company's business was taking off, you accepted a job offer. The first day on the job, while you are finishing your employment paperwork, Shane Shillingford, who works in Finance, stops by to inform you about the company's defined contribution (DC) pension plan.

A DC pension plan is a retirement plan offered by many companies. Such plans are tax-deferred savings vehicles, meaning that any deposits you make into the plan are deducted from your current pre-tax income, so no current taxes are paid on the money. For example, assume your salary will be $80,000 per year. If you contribute $4,000 to the DC pension plan, you will pay taxes on only $76,000 in income. There are also no taxes paid on any capital gains or income while you are invested in the plan, but you do pay taxes when you withdraw money at retirement. As is fairly common, the company also has a 5 percent match. This means that the company will match your contribution up to 5 percent of your salary, but you must contribute to get the match.

The DC pension plan has several options for investments, most of which are mutual funds. A mutual fund is a portfolio of assets. When you purchase shares in a mutual fund, you are actually purchasing partial ownership of the fund's assets. The return of the fund is the weighted average of the return of the assets owned by the fund, minus any expenses. The largest expense is typically the management fee, paid to the fund manager. The management fee is compensation for the manager, who makes all of the investment decisions for the fund.

Hillsdale Inc. uses TD Canada Trust as its DC pension plan administrator. Here are the investment options offered for employees:

Company Stock One option in the DC pension plan is stock in Hillsdale Inc. The company is currently privately held. However, when you interviewed with the owner, Kevin Cooper, he informed you the company stock was expected to go public in the next three to four years. Until then, a company stock price is simply set each year by the board of directors.

TD Canadian Index Fund This mutual fund tracks the S&P/TSX Composite. Stocks in the fund are weighted exactly the same as the S&P/TSX Composite. This means the fund return is approximately the return on the S&P/TSX Composite, minus expenses. Because an index fund purchases assets based on the composition of the index it is following, the fund manager is not required to research stocks and make investment decisions. The result is that the fund expenses are usually low. The TD Canadian Index Fund charges expenses of 0.84 percent of assets per year.

TD Canadian Small-Cap Equity Fund This fund primarily invests in small-capitalization stocks. As such, the returns of the fund are more volatile. The fund can also invest 10 percent of its assets in companies based outside Canada. This fund charges 2.42 percent in expenses.

TD Canadian Blue Chip Equity Fund This fund invests primarily in large-capitalization stocks of companies based in Canada. The fund is managed by Margot Richie and has outperformed the market in six of the last eight years. The fund charges 2.23 percent in expenses.

TD Canadian Bond Fund This fund invests in long-term corporate bonds issued by Canada-domiciled companies. The fund is restricted to investments in bonds with an investment-grade credit rating. This fund charges 1.05 percent in expenses.

TD Canadian Money Market Fund This fund invests in short-term, high credit-quality debt instruments, which include Treasury bills. As such, the return on the money market fund is only slightly higher than the return on Treasury bills. Because of the credit quality and short-term nature of the investments, there is only a very slight risk of negative return. The fund charges 0.92 percent in expenses.

QUESTIONS

1. What advantages do the mutual funds offer compared to the company stock?

2. Assume that you invest 5 percent of your salary and receive the full 5 percent match from Hillsdale Inc. What EAR do you earn from the match? What conclusions do you draw about matching plans?

3. Assume you decide you should invest at least part of your money in large-capitalization stocks of companies based in Canada. What are the advantages and disadvantages of choosing the TD Canadian Blue Chip Equity Fund compared to the TD Canadian Index Fund?

4. The returns on the TD Canadian Small-Cap Equity Fund are the most volatile of all the mutual funds offered in the DC pension plan. Why would you ever want to invest in this fund? When you examine the expenses of the mutual funds, you will notice that this fund also has the highest expenses. Does this affect your decision to invest in this fund?

5. A measure of risk-adjusted performance that is often used is the Sharpe ratio. The Sharpe ratio is calculated as the risk premium of an asset divided by its standard deviation. The standard deviation and return of the funds over the past 10 years are listed in the following table. Calculate the Sharpe ratio for each of these funds. Assume that the expected return and standard deviation of the company stock will be 18 percent and 70 percent, respectively. Calculate the Sharpe ratio for the company stock. How appropriate is the Sharpe ratio for these assets? When would you use the Sharpe ratio?

Fund	10-Year Annual return (%)	Standard deviation (%)
TD Canadian Index	6.42	13.75
TD Canadian Small-Cap Equity	5.44	17.05
TD Canadian Blue Chip Equity	4.33	11.55
TD Canadian Bond	6.17	3.03

Source: theglobeandmail.com/globe-investor/funds-and-etfs/funds/

6. What portfolio allocation would you choose? Why? Explain your thinking carefully.

CHAPTER 13

RETURN, RISK, AND THE SECURITY MARKET LINE

Ⅲ Manulife Mutual Funds | For your future™

As of March 31, 2012, Manulife Dividend Fund generated a 5 year average return of 0.62 percent, underperforming the S&P/TSX Composite index, which in the same period gave an average return of 1.66 percent. In hindsight, investment in S&P/TSX Composite index looks to be a better investment than in the Manulife Dividend Fund. But can we judge an investment only on the basis of return? Over the last year the Manulife fund had a loss of 6.82%, which was better than the performance of the S&P/TSX Composite, which lost 9.76%. One cannot talk about returns in isolation because investment decisions always involve a trade-off between risk and return. This chapter explores the relationship between risk and return and also introduces the important concept of diversification and asset pricing.

Learning Objectives ▶

After studying this chapter, you should understand:

LO1 The calculation for expected returns and standard deviations for individual securities and portfolios.

LO2 The principle of diversification and the role of correlation.

LO3 Systematic and unsystematic risk.

LO4 Beta as a measure of risk and the security market line.

manulifemutualfunds.ca/

In our last chapter, we learned some important lessons from capital market history. Most importantly, there is a reward, on average, for bearing risk. We called this reward a *risk premium*. The second lesson is that this risk premium is larger for riskier investments. The principle that higher returns can be earned only by taking greater risks appeals to our moral sense that we cannot have something for nothing. This chapter explores the economic and managerial implications of this basic idea.

Thus far, we have concentrated mainly on the return behaviour of a few large portfolios. We need to expand our consideration to include individual assets and mutual funds. Accordingly, the purpose of this chapter is to provide the background necessary for learning how the risk premium is determined for such assets.

When we examine the risks associated with individual assets, we find two types of risk: systematic and unsystematic. This distinction is crucial because, as we see, systematic risks affect almost all assets in the economy, at least to some degree, while a particular unsystematic risk affects at most a small number of assets. We then develop the principle of diversification, which shows that highly diversified portfolios tend to have almost no unsystematic risk.

The principle of diversification has an important implication: To a diversified investor, only systematic risk matters. It follows that in deciding whether to buy a particular individual asset, a diversified investor is concerned only with that asset's systematic risk. This is a key observation, and it allows us to say a great deal about the risks and returns on individual assets. In particular, it is the basis for a famous relationship between risk and return called the security market line, or SML. To develop the SML, we introduce the equally famous beta coefficient, one of the centrepieces of modern finance. Beta and the SML are key concepts because they supply us with at least part of the answer to the question of how to determine the required return on an investment.

13.1 | Expected Returns and Variances

In our previous chapter, we discussed how to calculate average returns and variances using historical data. We now begin to discuss how to analyze returns and variances when the information we have concerns future possible returns and their possibilities.

Expected Return

We start with a straightforward case. Consider a single period of time, say, a year. We have two stocks, L and U, with the following characteristics: Stock L is expected to have a return of 25 percent in the coming year. Stock U is expected to have a return of 20 percent for the same period.[1]

In a situation like this, if all investors agreed on the expected returns, why would anyone want to hold Stock U? After all, why invest in one stock when the expectation is that another will do better? Clearly, the answer must depend on the risk of the two investments. The return on Stock L, although it is expected to be 25 percent, could actually be higher or lower.

For example, suppose the economy booms. In this case, we think Stock L would have a 70 percent return. If the economy enters a recession, we think the return would be −20 percent. Thus, we say there are two *states of the economy*, meaning that these are the only two possible situations. This setup is oversimplified, of course, but it allows us to illustrate some key ideas without a lot of computation.

Suppose we think a boom and a recession are equally likely to happen, a 50-50 chance of each. Table 13.1 illustrates the basic information we have described and some additional information about Stock U. Notice that Stock U earns 30 percent if there is a recession and 10 percent if there is a boom.

TABLE 13.1

States of the economy and stock returns	State of the Economy	Probability of State of the Economy	Security returns if state occurs	
			L	U
	Recession	0.5	−20%	30%
	Boom	0.5	70	10
		1.0		

Obviously, if you buy one of these stocks, say Stock U, what you earn in any particular year depends on what the economy does during that year. However, suppose the probabilities stay the same through time. If you hold U for a number of years, you'll earn 30 percent about half the time and 10 percent the other half. In this case, we say that your **expected return** on Stock U, $E(R_U)$, is 20 percent:

$$E(R_U) = .50 \times 30\% + .50 \times 10\% = 20\%$$

expected return
Return on a risky asset expected in the future.

In other words, you should expect to earn 20 percent from this stock, on average.

For Stock L, the probabilities are the same, but the possible returns are different. Here we lose 20 percent half the time, and we gain 70 percent the other half. The expected return on L, $E(R_L)$, is thus 25 percent:

---

[1]This is a good point to clarify the difference between expected return and required return. While the expected return reflects how investors think the stock will actually perform over a future period, the required return is the amount that investors must receive to compensate them for the risk they are accepting on any given investment.

$$E(R_L) = .50 \times -20\% + .50 \times 70\% = 25\%$$

Table 13.2 illustrates these calculations.

TABLE 13.2

Calculation of expected return

(1) State of Economy	(2) Probability of State of Economy	Stock L		Stock U	
		(3) Rate of Return if State Occurs	(4) Product (2) × (3)	(5) Rate of Return if State Occurs	(6) Product (2) × (5)
Recession	0.5	−.20	−.10	.30	.15
Boom	0.5	.70	.35	.10	.05
	1.0		$E(R_L) = 25\%$		$E(R_U) = 20\%$

In our previous chapter, we defined the risk premium as the difference between the return on a risky investment and a risk-free investment, and we calculated the historical risk premiums on some different investments. Using our projected returns, we can calculate the *projected or expected risk premium* as the difference between the expected return on a risky investment and the certain return on a risk-free investment.

For example, suppose risk-free investments are currently offering 8 percent. We say the risk-free rate (which we label as R_f) is 8 percent. Given this, what is the projected risk premium on Stock U? On Stock L? Since the expected return on Stock U, $E(R_U)$, is 20 percent, the projected risk premium is:

$$
\begin{aligned}
\text{Risk premium} &= \text{Expected return} - \text{Risk-free rate} \\
&= E(R_U) - R_f \\
&= 20\% - 8\% = 12\%
\end{aligned}
\tag{13.1}
$$

Similarly, the risk premium on Stock L is 25% − 8% = 17%.

In general, the expected return on a security or other asset is simply equal to the sum of the possible returns multiplied by their probabilities. So, if we have 100 possible returns, we would multiply each one by its probability and add the results. The result would be the expected return. The risk premium would be the difference between this expected return and the risk-free rate.

A useful generalized equation for expected return is:

$$E(R) = \sum_j R_j \times P_j \tag{13.2}$$

where

R_j = value of the *j*th outcome

P_j = associated probability of occurrence

$\sum_j$ = the sum over all *j*

EXAMPLE 13.1: Unequal Probabilities

Look back at Tables 13.1 and 13.2. Suppose you thought that a boom would only occur 20 percent of the time instead of 50 percent. What are the expected returns on Stocks U and L in this case? If the risk-free rate is 10 percent, what are the risk premiums?

The first thing to notice is that a recession must occur 80 percent of the time (1 − .20 = .80) because there are only two possibilities. With this in mind, Stock U has a 30 percent return in 80 percent of the years and a 10 percent return in 20 percent of the years. To calculate the expected

return, we again just multiply the possibilities by the probabilities and add up the results:

$$E(R_U) = .80 \times 30\% + .20 \times 10\% = 26\%$$

Table 13.3 summarizes the calculations for both stocks. Notice that the expected return on L is −2 percent.

The risk premium for Stock U is 26% − 10% = 16% in this case. The risk premium for Stock L is negative: −2% − 10% = −12%. This is a little odd, but, for reasons we discuss later, it is not impossible.

TABLE 13.3

(1) State of Economy	(2) Probability of State of Economy	Stock L		Stock U	
		(3) Rate of Return if State Occurs	(4) Product (2) × (3)	(5) Rate of Return if State Occurs	(6) Product (2) × (5)
Recession	.80	−.20	−.16	.30	.24
Boom	.20	.70	.14	.10	.02
	1.0		$E(R_L) = -2\%$		$E(R_U) = 26\%$

Calculating the Variance

To calculate the variances of the returns on our two stocks, we determine the squared deviations from the expected return. We then multiply each possible squared deviation by its probability. We add these, and the result is the variance. The standard deviation, as always, is the square root of the variance. It is important to note that later on in the chapter another alternative to calculating variance will be introduced, using the correlation coefficient.

Generalized equations for variance and standard deviation are

$$\sigma^2 = \Sigma_j[R_j - E(R)]^2 \times P_j$$
$$\sigma = \sqrt{\sigma^2}$$

[13.3]

To illustrate, Stock U has an expected return of $E(R_U) = 20\%$. In a given year, it could actually return either 30 percent or 10 percent. The possible deviations are thus 30% − 20% = 10% or 10% − 20% = −10%. In this case, the variance is:

$$\text{Variance} = \sigma^2 = .50 \times (10\%)^2 + .50 \times (-10\%)^2 = .01$$

The standard deviation is the square root of this: = .10 = 10%

$$\text{Standard deviation} = \sigma = \sqrt{.01} = .10 = 10\%$$

Table 13.4 summarizes these calculations for both stocks. Notice that Stock L has a much larger variance.

TABLE 13.4

Calculation of variance

(1) State of Economy	(2) Probability of State of Economy	(3) Return Deviation from Expected Return	(4) Squared Return Deviation from Expected Return	(5) Product (2) × (4)
Stock L				
Recession	0.5	−.20 − .25 = −.45	$(-.45)^2 = .2025$	.10125
Boom	0.5	.70 − .25 = .45	$(.45)^2 = .2025$	.10125
				$\sigma^2_L = .2025$
Stock U				
Recession	0.5	.30 − .20 = .10	$(.10)^2 = .01$	.005
Boom	0.5	.10 − .20 = −.10	$(-.10)^2 = .01$	.005
				$\sigma^2_U = .010$

When we put the expected return and variability information for our two stocks together, we have:

	Stock L	Stock U
Expected return, $E(R)$	25%	20%
Variance, σ^2	.2025	.0100
Standard deviation, σ	45%	10%

Stock L has a higher expected return, but U has less risk. You could get a 70 percent return on your investment in L, but you could also lose 20 percent. Notice that an investment in U always pays at least 10 percent.

Which of these two stocks should you buy? We can't really say; it depends on your personal preferences. We can be reasonably sure that some investors would prefer L to U and some would prefer U to L.

You've probably noticed that the way we calculated expected returns and variances here is somewhat different from the way we did it in the last chapter. The reason is that, in Chapter 12, we were examining actual historical returns, so we estimated the average return and the variance based on some actual events. Here, we have projected future returns and their associated probabilities, so this is the information with which we must work.

EXAMPLE 13.2: More Unequal Probabilities

Going back to Example 13.1, what are the variances on the two stocks once we have unequal probabilities? The standard deviations? We can summarize the needed calculations as follows:

(1) State of Economy	(2) Probability of State of Economy	(3) Return Deviation from Expected Return	(4) Squared Return Deviation from Expected Return	(5) Product (2) × (4)
Stock L				
Recession	.80	$-.20 - (-.02) = -.18$	.0324	.02592
Boom	.20	$.70 - (-.02) = .72$	.5184	.10368
				$\sigma^2_L = .12960$
Stock U				
Recession	.80	$.30 - .26 = .04$	.0016	.00128
Boom	.20	$.10 - .26 = -.16$	.0256	.00512
				$\sigma^2_U = .00640$

Based on these calculations, the standard deviation for L is $\sigma_L = \sqrt{.1296} = 36$ percent. The standard deviation for U is much smaller, $\sigma_U = \sqrt{.0064} = .08$ or 8 percent.

Concept Questions

1. How do we calculate the expected return on a security?
2. In words, how do we calculate the variance of the expected return?

13.2 | Portfolios

portfolio
Group of assets such as stocks and bonds held by an investor.

Thus far in this chapter, we have concentrated on individual assets considered separately. However, most investors actually hold a **portfolio** of assets. All we mean by this is that investors tend to own more than just a single stock, bond, or other asset. Given that this is so, portfolio return and portfolio risk are of obvious relevance. Accordingly, we now discuss portfolio expected returns and variances.

Portfolio Weights

There are many equivalent ways of describing a portfolio. The most convenient approach is to list the percentages of the total portfolio's value that are invested in each portfolio asset. We call these percentages the **portfolio weights**.

portfolio weights
Percentage of a portfolio's total value in a particular asset.

For example, if we have $50 in one asset and $150 in another, our total portfolio is worth $200. The percentage of our portfolio in the first asset is $50/$200 = 25 percent (0.25). The percentage of our portfolio in the second asset is $150/$200, or 75 percent (0.75). Our portfolio weights are thus .25 and .75. Notice that the weights have to add up to 1.00 since all of our money is invested somewhere.[2]

Portfolio Expected Returns

Let's go back to Stocks L and U. You put half your money in each. The portfolio weights are obviously .50 and .50. What is the pattern of returns on this portfolio? The expected return?

To answer these questions, suppose the economy actually enters a recession. In this case, half your money (the half in L) loses 20 percent. The other half (the half in U) gains 30 percent. Your portfolio return, R_p, in a recession is thus:

$$R_p = .50 \times (-20\%) + .50 \times 30\% = 5\%$$

Table 13.5 summarizes the remaining calculations. Notice that when a boom occurs, your portfolio would return 40 percent:

$$R_p = .50 \times 70\% + .50 \times 10\% = 40\%$$

As indicated in Table 13.5, the expected return on your portfolio, $E(R_p)$, is 22.5 percent.

We can save ourselves some work by calculating the expected return more directly. Given these portfolio weights, we could have reasoned that we expect half of our money to earn 25 percent (the half in L) and half of our money to earn 20 percent (the half in U). Our portfolio expected return is thus:

$$E(R_p) = .50 \times E(R_L) + .50 \times E(R_U)$$
$$= .50 \times 25\% + .50 \times 20\%$$
$$= 22.5\%$$

This is the same portfolio expected return we had before.

TABLE 13.5

Expected return on an equally weighted portfolio of Stock L and Stock U

(1) State of Economy	(2) Probability of State of Economy	(3) Portfolio Return if State Occurs	(4) Product (2) ×(3)
Recession	.50	1/2 × (−20%) + 1/2 × (30%) = 5%	2.5%
Boom	.50	1/2 × (70%) + 1/2 × (10%) = 40%	20.0
			$E(R_p)$ = 22.5%

---

[2] Some of it could be in cash, of course, but we would just consider the cash to be one of the portfolio assets.

This method of calculating the expected return on a portfolio works no matter how many assets are in the portfolio. Suppose we had n assets in our portfolio, where n is any number. If we let x_i stand for the percentage of our money in asset i, the expected return is:

$$E(R_p) = x_1 \times E(R_1) + x_2 \times E(R_2) + \ldots + x_n \times E(R_n) \qquad [13.4]$$

This says that the expected return on a portfolio is a straightforward combination of the expected returns on the assets in that portfolio. This seems somewhat obvious, but, as we examine next, the obvious approach is not always the right one.

EXAMPLE 13.3: Portfolio Expected Returns

Suppose we have the following projections on three stocks:

State of Economy	Probability of State	Stock A	Stock B	Stock C
		Returns		
Boom	.40	10%	15%	20%
Bust	.60	8%	4%	0%

What would be the expected return on a portfolio with equal amounts invested in each of the three stocks? What would the expected return be if half the portfolio were in A, with the remainder equally divided between B and C? From our earlier discussions, the expected returns on the individual stocks are (check these for practice):

$E(R_A) = 8.8\%$
$E(R_B) = 8.4\%$
$E(R_C) = 8.0\%$

If a portfolio has equal investments in each asset, the portfolio weights are all the same. Such a portfolio is said to be equally weighted. Since there are three stocks, the weights are all equal to 1/3. The portfolio expected return is thus:

$E(R_p) = (1/3) \times 8.8\% + (1/3) \times 8.4\% + (1/3) \times 8.0\%$
$= 8.4\%$

In the second case, check that the portfolio expected return is 8.5 percent.

Portfolio Variance

From our previous discussion, the expected return on a portfolio that contains equal investment in Stocks U and L is 22.5 percent. What is the standard deviation of return on this portfolio? Simple intuition might suggest that half the money has a standard deviation of 45 percent and the other half has a standard deviation of 10 percent, so the portfolio's standard deviation might be calculated as:

$$\sigma_p = .50 \times 45\% + .50 \times 10\% = 27.5\%$$

Unfortunately, this approach is incorrect.

Let's see what the standard deviation really is. Table 13.6 summarizes the relevant calculations. As we see, the portfolio's variance is about .031, and its standard deviation is less than we thought—it's only 17.5 percent. What is illustrated here is that the variance on a portfolio is not generally a simple combination of the variances of the assets in the portfolio.

We can illustrate this point a little more dramatically by considering a slightly different set of portfolio weights. Suppose we put 2/11 (about 18 percent) in L and the other 9/11 (about 82 percent) in U. If a recession occurs, this portfolio would have a return of:

$$R_p = \left(\frac{2}{11}\right) \times (-20\%) + \left(\frac{9}{11}\right) \times (30\%) = 20.91\%$$

If a boom occurs, this portfolio would have a return of:

$$R_p = \left(\frac{2}{11}\right) \times (70\%) + \left(\frac{9}{11}\right) \times (10\%) = 20.91\%$$

Notice that the return is the same no matter what happens. No further calculations are needed. This portfolio has a zero variance. Apparently, combining assets into portfolios can substantially alter the risks faced by the investor. This is a crucial observation, and we explore its implications in the next section.

TABLE 13.6

Variance on an equally weighted portfolio of Stock L and Stock U

(1) State of Economy	(2) Probability of State of Economy	(3) Portfolio Return if State Occurs	(4) Squared Deviation from Expected Return	(5) Product (2) × (4)
Recession	.50	5%	$(.05 - .225)^2 = .030625$	.0153125
Boom	.50	40%	$(.40 - .225)^2 = .030625$	.0153125
			$\sigma_P = \sqrt{.030625} = 17.5\%$	$\sigma^2_P = .030625$

EXAMPLE 13.4: Portfolio Variance and Standard Deviation

In Example 13.3, what are the standard deviations on the two portfolios? To answer, we first have to calculate the portfolio returns in the two states. We will work with the second portfolio, which has 50 percent in Stock A and 25 percent in each of Stocks B and C. The relevant calculations can be summarized as follows:

		Returns			
State of Economy	Probability of State	Stock A	Stock B	Stock C	Portfolio
Boom	.40	10%	15%	20%	13.75%
Bust	.60	8%	4%	0%	5.00%

The portfolio return when the economy booms is calculated as:

$$.50 \times 10\% + .25 \times 15\% + .25 \times 20\% = 13.75\%$$

The return when the economy goes bust is calculated the same way. The expected return on the portfolio is 8.5 percent. The variance is thus:

$$\sigma^2 = .40 \times (.1375 - .085)^2 + .60 \times (.05 - .085)^2 = .0018375$$

The standard deviation is thus about 4.3 percent. For our equally weighted portfolio, check to see that the standard deviation is about 5.4 percent.

Portfolio Standard Deviation and Diversification

How diversification reduces portfolio risk as measured by the portfolio standard deviation is worth exploring in some detail.[3] The key concept is *correlation*, which provides a reading on the extent to which the returns on two assets move together. If correlation is positive, we say that Assets A and B are positively correlated; if it is negative, we say they are negatively correlated; and if it is zero, the two assets are uncorrelated.

Figure 13.1 shows these three benchmark cases for two assets, A and B. The graphs on the left side plot the separate returns on the two securities through time. Each point on the graphs on the right side represents the returns for both A and B over a particular time interval. The figure shows examples of different values for the correlation coefficient, CORR (*Ra*, *Rb*), that range from −1.0 to 1.0.

To show how the graphs are constructed, we need to look at points 1 and 2 (on the upper left graph) and relate them to point 3 (on the upper right graph). Point 1 is a return on Company B and point 2 is a return on Company A. They both occur over the same time period, say, for example, the month of June. Both returns are above average. Point 3 represents the returns on both stocks in June. Other dots in the upper right graph represent the returns on both stocks in other months.

Because the returns on Security B have bigger swings than the returns on Security A, the slope of the line in the upper right graph is greater than one. Perfect positive correlation does not imply

---

[3] The ideas in this section were first developed systematically in an article written in 1952 by Harry Markowitz, "Portfolio Selection," *Journal of Finance* 7 (March 1952), pp. 77–91. His work laid the foundation for the development of the capital asset pricing model, principally by William F. Sharpe, "Capital Asset Prices: A Theory of Market Equilibrium under Conditions of Risk," *Journal of Finance* 19 (1964), pp. 425–42. These pioneers of modern portfolio theory were awarded the Nobel Prize in Economics in 1991.

that the slope is one. Rather, it implies that all points lie exactly on the line. Less-than-perfect positive correlation implies a positive slope, but the points do not lie exactly on the line. An example of less-than-perfect positive correlation is provided in the left side of Figure 13.2. As before, each point in the graph represents the returns on both securities in the same month. In a graph like this, the closer the points lie to the line, the closer the correlation is to one. In other words, a high correlation between the two returns implies that the graph has a tight fit.[4]

Less-than-perfect negative correlation implies a negative slope, but the points do not lie exactly on the line, as shown on the right side of Figure 13.2.

FIGURE 13.1

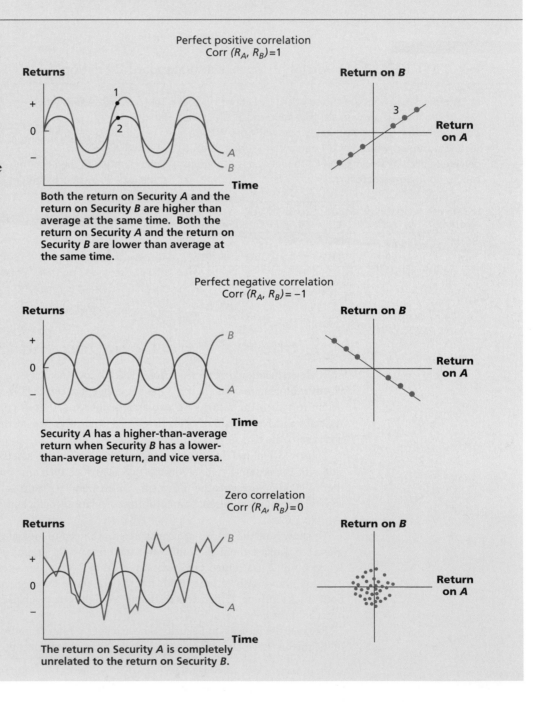

Examples of different correlation coefficients

The graphs on the left-hand side of the figure plot the separate returns on the two securities through time. Each point on the graphs on the right-hand side represents the returns for both A and B over a particular time period.

Perfect positive correlation
Corr $(R_A, R_B) = 1$

Both the return on Security *A* and the return on Security *B* are higher than average at the same time. Both the return on Security *A* and the return on Security *B* are lower than average at the same time.

Perfect negative correlation
Corr $(R_A, R_B) = -1$

Security *A* has a higher-than-average return when Security *B* has a lower-than-average return, and vice versa.

Zero correlation
Corr $(R_A, R_B) = 0$

The return on Security *A* is completely unrelated to the return on Security *B*.

---

[4] If we measure the correlation by regression analysis, the *correlation coefficient* is the square root of R squared, the regression coefficient of determination. For a perfect fit, R squared is one and the correlation coefficient is also one.

FIGURE 13.2

Graphs of possible relationships between two stocks

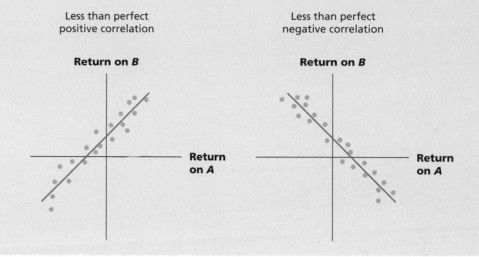

EXAMPLE 13.5: Correlation between Stocks U and L

What is the correlation between Stocks U and L from our earlier example if we assume the two states of the economy are equally probable? Table 13.2 shows the returns on each stock in recession and boom states.

	Stock L	Stock U
Recession	−.20	.30
Boom	.70	.10

Figure 13.3 plots the line exactly the same way as we plotted the graphs on the right sides of Figures 13.1 and 13.2. You can see from the figure that the line has a negative slope and all the points lie exactly on the line. (Since we only have two outcomes for each stock, the points must plot exactly on a straight line.) You can conclude that the correlation between Stocks U and L is equal to −1.0.

Our discussion of correlation provides us with a key building block of a formula for portfolio standard variance and its square root, portfolio standard deviation.

$$\sigma^2_P = x^2_L\sigma^2_L + x^2_U\sigma^2_U + 2x_Lx_U\text{CORR}_{L,U}\sigma_L\sigma_U \qquad [13.5]$$
$$\sigma_P = \sqrt{\sigma^2_P}$$

Recall that x_L and x_U are, respectively, the portfolio weights for Stocks U and L. $\text{CORR}_{L,U}$ is the correlation of the two stocks.

We can use the formula to check our previous calculation of portfolio standard deviation for a portfolio invested 50 percent in each stock.

$$= (.5)^2 \times (.45)^2 + (.5)^2 \times (.10)^2 + (2) \times (.5) \times (.5)$$
$$\times (-1.0) \times (.45) \times (.10)$$
$$= .030625$$
$$= \sqrt{.030625} = 17.5\%$$

These are the same results we got in Table 13.6.

The Efficient Set

Suppose U and L actually have a correlation of about +0.70. The opportunity set is graphed in Figure 13.4. In Figure 13.5, we have marked the minimum variance portfolio, MV. No risk-averse investor would hold any portfolio with expected return below MV. For example, no such investor would invest 100 percent in Stock U because such a portfolio has lower expected return and higher standard deviation than the minimum variance portfolio. We say that portfolios such as U are dominated by the minimum variance portfolio. (Since standard deviation is the square root of variance, the minimum variance portfolios also have minimum standard deviations as shown in Figures 13.4 and 13.5.) Though the entire curve from U to L is called the *feasible set*, investors only consider the curve from MV to L. This part of the curve is called the *efficient set*.

FIGURE 13.3

Correlation between
Stocks U and L

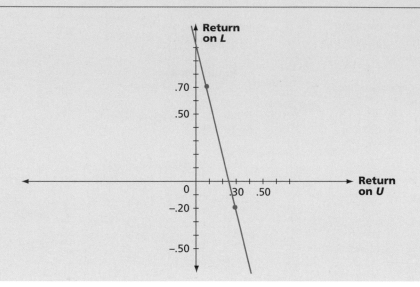

EXAMPLE 13.6: The Zero-Variance Portfolio

Can you find a portfolio of Stocks U and L with zero variance? Earlier, we showed that investing 2/11 (about 18 percent) of the portfolio in L and the other 9/11 (about 82 percent) in U gives the same expected portfolio return in either recession or boom. As a result, the portfolio variance and standard deviation should both be zero. We can check this with the formula for portfolio variance.

$$\sigma^2_p = \left(\frac{2}{11}\right)^2 \times (.45)^2 + \left(\frac{9}{11}\right)^2 \times (.10)^2 + 2 \times \left(\frac{2}{11}\right)$$
$$\times \left(\frac{9}{11}\right) \times (-1.0) \times (.45) \times (.10)$$
$$= .006694 + .006694 - .013388$$
$$= 0$$

You can see that the portfolio variance (and standard deviation) are zero because the weights were chosen to make the negative third term exactly offset the first two positive terms. This third term is called the *covariance term* because the product of the correlation times the two security standard deviations is the covariance of U and L.[5]

To explore how the portfolio standard deviation depends on correlation, Table 13.7 recalculates the portfolio standard deviation, changing the correlation between U and L, yet keeping the portfolio weights and all the other input data unchanged. When the correlation is perfectly negative, $CORR_{U,L} = -1.0$, the portfolio standard deviation is 0 as we just calculated. If the two stocks were uncorrelated ($CORR_{L,U} = 0$), the portfolio standard deviation becomes 11.5708 percent. And, with perfect positive correlation ($CORR_{L,U} = +1.0$) the portfolio standard deviation is 16.3636 percent.

When the returns on the two assets are perfectly correlated, the portfolio standard deviation is simply the weighted average of the individual standard deviations. In this special case:

$$16.3636 = \left(\frac{2}{11}\right) \times 45\% + \left(\frac{9}{11}\right) \times 10\%$$

With perfect correlation, all possible portfolios lie on a straight line between U and L in expected return/standard deviation space as shown in Figure 13.4. In this polar case, there is no benefit from diversification. But, as soon as correlation is less than perfectly positive, $CORR_{L,U} = +1.0$, diversification reduces risk.

As long as CORR is less than +1.0, the standard deviation of a portfolio of two securities is less than the weighted average of the standard deviations of the individual securities.

Figure 13.4 shows this important result by graphing all possible portfolios of U and L for the three cases for $CORR_{L,U}$ given in Table 13.7. The portfolios marked 1, 2, and 3 in Figure 13.4 all have an expected return of 20.91 percent as calculated in Table 13.7. Their standard deviations also come from Table 13.7. The other points on the respective lines or curves are derived by varying the portfolio weights for each value of $CORR_{L,U}$. Each line or curve represents all the possible portfolios of U and L for a given correlation. Each is called an *opportunity set* or *feasible set*. The lowest opportunity set representing $CORR_{L,U} = 1.0$ always has the largest standard deviation for any return level. Once again, this shows how diversification reduces risk as long as correlation is less than perfectly positive.

---

[5] As the number of stocks in the portfolio increases beyond the two in our example, the number of covariance terms increases geometrically. In general, for a portfolio of N securities, the number of covariance terms is $(N^2 - N)/2$. For example, a 10-stock portfolio has 45 covariance terms.

TABLE 13.7

Portfolio standard deviation and correlation

Stock L	$x_L = {}^2/_{11}$	$\sigma_L = 45\%$	$E(R_L) = 25\%$
Stock U	$x_U = {}^9/_{11}$	$\sigma_U = 10\%$	$E(R_U) = 20\%$

$E(R_P) = ({}^2/_{11}) \times 25\% + {}^9/_{11} \times 20\% = 20.91\%$

$CORR_{L,U}$ Portfolio	Standard Deviation of Portfolio s_P
1. −1.0	0.0000%
2. 0.0	11.5708%
3. +1.0	16.3636%

EXAMPLE 13.7: Benefits of Foreign Investment

What percentage of their equity portfolios should Canadian investors place outside of Canada? To come up with an answer we need to extend our discussion of historical average returns and risks in Chapter 12 to include foreign investment portfolios. It turns out that the feasible set looks like Figure 13.5 where points like U and L represent portfolios instead of individual stocks. Portfolio U represents 100 percent investment in Canadian equities and Portfolio L represents 100 percent in foreign equities. The domestic stock portfolio is less risky than the foreign portfolio. Does this mean Canadian portfolio managers should invest entirely in Canada?

The answer is no because the minimum variance portfolio with approximately 20 percent foreign content dominates portfolio U, the 100 percent domestic portfolio. Going from 0 percent to around 20 percent foreign content actually reduces portfolio standard deviation due to the diversification effect. Increasing the foreign content beyond around 20 percent increases portfolio risk but also raises expected return. At the time of writing in May 2012, professional investment managers held 30 to 50 percent of their portfolios outside of Canada.

Correlations in the Financial Crisis of 2007–2009

During the financial crisis, investors sought safety and liquidity causing equity markets to fall in all countries. The resulting increase in the correlation of returns across countries led some investors to doubt the benefits of international diversification. While higher correlations reduce its advantages, doubts about diversification were overstated for two reasons. First, although correlations undoubtedly increased during the crisis, they later returned to more normal levels. Second, even with relatively high positive correlation between assets, diversification still reduces risk as long as the correlation coefficient is less than 1.0 (perfect positive correlation).[6]

Concept Questions

1. What is a portfolio weight?
2. How do we calculate the expected return on a portfolio?
3. Is there a simple relationship between the standard deviation on a portfolio and the standard deviation of the assets in the portfolio?

---

[6] The discussion here draws on Z. Bodie, A. Kane, A.J. Marcus, S. Perrakis and P.J. Ryan, Investments, Seventh Canadian Edition, McGraw-Hill Ryerson, 2011, Chapter 23 and V., de Martel, V., "Is diversification dead?" Catalyst, 2009, 1(2), Retrieved from www2.blackrock.com/webcore/litService/search/getDocument.seam?venue=PUB_INS&source=CONTENT&ServiceName=PublicServiceView&ContentID=1111101021

FIGURE 13.4

Opportunity sets composed of holdings in Stock L and Stock U

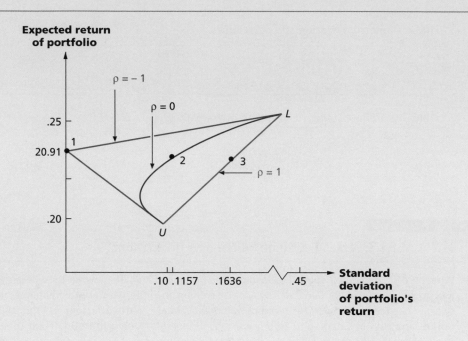

FIGURE 13.5

Efficient frontier

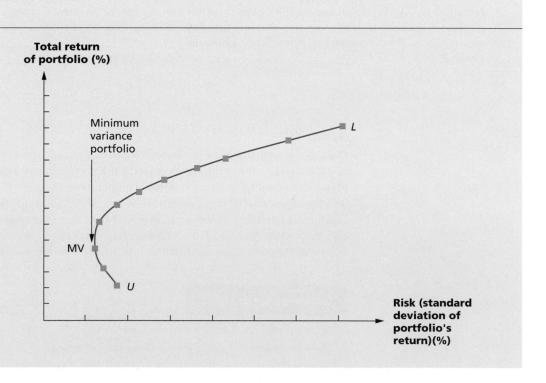

13.3 | Announcements, Surprises, and Expected Returns

Now that we know how to construct portfolios and evaluate their returns, we begin to describe more carefully the risks and returns associated with individual securities. Thus far, we have measured volatility by looking at the differences between the actual returns on an asset or portfolio, R, and the expected return, $E(R)$. We now look at why those deviations exist.

Expected and Unexpected Returns

To begin, for concreteness, we consider the return on the stock of TransCanada Industries. What will determine this stock's return in, say, the coming year? The return on any stock traded in a financial market is composed of two parts: First, the normal or expected return from the stock is the part of the return that shareholders in the market predict or expect. This return depends on the information shareholders have that bears on the stock, and it is based on the market's understanding today of the important factors that influence the stock in the coming year.

The second part of the return on the stock is the uncertain or risky part. This is the portion that comes from unexpected information that is revealed within the year. A list of all possible sources of such information is endless, but here are a few examples:

News about TransCanada's research.

Government figures released on gross national product (GNP).

The imminent bankruptcy of an important competitor.

The news that TransCanada's sales figures are higher than expected.

A sudden, unexpected drop in interest rates.

Based on this discussion, one way to write the return on TransCanada's stock in the coming year would be:

$$\text{Total return} = \text{Expected return} + \text{Unexpected return} \qquad [13.6]$$
$$R = E(R) + U$$

where R stands for the actual total return in the year, $E(R)$ stands for the expected part of the return, and U stands for the unexpected part of the return. What this says is that the actual return, R, differs from the expected return, $E(R)$, because of surprises that occur during the day.

Announcements and News

We need to be careful when we talk about the effect of news items on the return. For example, suppose that TransCanada Industries' business is such that the company prospers when GNP grows at a relatively high rate and suffers when GNP is relatively stagnant. In deciding what return to expect this year from owning stock in TransCanada, shareholders either implicitly or explicitly must think about what the GNP is likely to be for the year.

When the government actually announces GNP figures for the year, what will happen to the value of TransCanada Industries stock? Obviously, the answer depends on what figure is released. More to the point, however, the impact depends on how much of that figure is new information.

At the beginning of the year, market participants have some idea or forecast of what the yearly GNP will be. To the extent that shareholders had predicted the GNP, that prediction is already factored into the expected part of the return on the stock, $E(R)$. On the other hand, if the announced GNP is a surprise, the effect is part of U, the unanticipated portion of the return. As an example, suppose shareholders in the market had forecast that the GNP increase this year would be 0.5 percent. If the actual announcement this year is exactly 0.5 percent, the same as the forecast, the shareholders didn't really learn anything, and the announcement isn't news. There would be no impact on the stock price as a result. This is like receiving confirmation of something that you suspected all along; it doesn't reveal anything new.

To give a more concrete example, on October 5, 2011, the co-founder and former Chief Executive Officer of Apple Inc., Steve Jobs, passed away. This seems like it would have been disastrous news for Apple, but Apple's stock price dropped by only 0.2 percent on the announcement. Why? Because, years of declining health and resignation from the post of CEO, gave the market participants time to re-price Apple shares without his leadership. Since then up to the time of writing,

apple.com/ca/

the shares of Apple Inc. have gained more than 50%.

A common way of saying that an announcement isn't news is to say that the market has already "discounted" the announcement. The use of the word *discount* here is different from the use of the term in computing present values, but the spirit is the same. When we discount a dollar in the future, we say it is worth less to us because of the time value of money. When we discount an announcement or a news item, we mean it has less of an impact on the market because the market already knew much of it.

For example, going back to TransCanada Industries, suppose the government announced that the actual GNP increase during the year was 1.5 percent. Now shareholders have learned something, namely, that the increase is 1 percentage point higher than they had forecast. This difference between the actual result and the forecast, 1 percentage point in this example, is sometimes called the *innovation* or the *surprise*.

An announcement, then, can be broken into two parts, the anticipated or expected part and the surprise or innovation:

$$\text{Announcement} = \text{Expected part} + \text{Surprise} \qquad [13.7]$$

The expected part of any announcement is the part of the information that the market uses to form the expectation $E(R)$, of the return on the stock. The surprise is the news that influences the unanticipated return on the stock, U.

Our discussion of market efficiency in the previous chapter bears on this discussion. We are assuming that relevant information that is known today is already reflected in the expected return. This is identical to saying that the current price reflects relevant publicly available information. We are thus implicitly assuming that markets are at least reasonably efficient in the semistrong form sense.

Henceforth, when we speak of news, we mean the surprise part of an announcement and not the portion that the market has expected and, therefore, already discounted.

Concept Questions

1. What are the two basic parts of a return?
2. Under what conditions does an announcement have no effect on common stock prices?

13.4 | Risk: Systematic and Unsystematic

The unanticipated part of the return, that portion resulting from surprises, is the true risk of any investment. After all, if we always receive exactly what we expect, the investment is perfectly predictable and, by definition, risk-free. In other words, the risk of owning an asset comes from surprises—unanticipated events.

There are important differences, though, among various sources of risk. Look back at our previous list of news stories. Some of these stories are directed specifically at TransCanada Industries, and some are more general. Which of the news items are of specific importance to TransCanada Industries?

Announcements about interest rates or GNP are clearly important for nearly all companies, whereas the news about TransCanada Industries' president, its research, or its sales are of specific interest to TransCanada Industries. We distinguish between these two types of events however because, as we shall see, they have very different implications.

Systematic and Unsystematic Risk

systematic risk
A risk that influences a large number of assets. Also called market risk.

unsystematic risk
A risk that affects at most a small number of assets. Also called unique or asset-specific risks.

The first surprise, the one that affects a large number of assets, we label **systematic risk**. A systematic risk is one that influences a large number of assets, each to a greater or lesser extent. Because systematic risks are market-wide effects, they are sometimes called *market risks*.

The second type of surprise we call **unsystematic risk**. An unsystematic risk is one that affects a single asset or a small group of assets. Because these risks are unique to individual companies or assets, they are sometimes called *unique* or *asset-specific risks*. We use these terms interchangeably.

As we have seen, uncertainties about general economic conditions, such as GNP, interest rates, or inflation, are examples of systematic risks. These conditions affect nearly all companies to some degree. An unanticipated increase or surprise in inflation, for example, affects wages and the costs of the supplies that companies buy; it affects the value of the assets that companies own; and it affects the prices at which companies sell their products. Forces such as these, to which all companies are susceptible, are the essence of systematic risk.

In contrast, the announcement of an oil strike by a company primarily affects that company and, perhaps, a few others (such as primary competitors and suppliers). It is unlikely to have much of an effect on the world oil market, however, or on the affairs of companies not in the oil business.

Systematic and Unsystematic Components of Return

The distinction between a systematic risk and an unsystematic risk is never really as exact as we make it out to be. Even the most narrow and peculiar bits of news about a company ripple through the economy. This is true because every enterprise, no matter how tiny, is a part of the economy. It's like the tale of a kingdom that was lost because one horse lost a shoe. This is mostly hairsplitting, however. Some risks are clearly much more general than others. We'll see some evidence on this point in just a moment.

The distinction between the types of risk allows us to break down the surprise portion, U, of the return on TransCanada Industries stock into two parts. As before, we break the actual return down into its expected and surprise components:

$$R = E(R) + U$$

We now recognize that the total surprise for TransCanada Industries, U, has a systematic and an unsystematic component, so:

$$R = E(R) + \text{Systematic portion} + \text{Unsystematic portion} \qquad [13.8]$$

Because it is traditional, we use the Greek letter epsilon, ε, to stand for the unsystematic portion. Since systematic risks are often called market risks, we use the letter m to stand for the systematic part of the surprise. With these symbols, we can rewrite the total return:

$$R = E(R) + U$$
$$= E(R) + m + \varepsilon$$

The important thing about the way we have broken down the total surprise, U, is that the unsystematic portion, ε, is more or less unique to TransCanada Industries. For this reason, it is unrelated to the unsystematic portion of return on most other assets. To see why this is important, we need to return to the subject of portfolio risk.

Concept Questions

1. What are the two basic types of risk?
2. What is the distinction between the two types of risk?

13.5 | Diversification and Portfolio Risk

We've seen earlier that portfolio risks can, in principle, be quite different from the risks of the assets that make up the portfolio. We now look more closely at the riskiness of an individual asset versus the risk of a portfolio of many different assets. We once again examine some market history to get an idea of what happens with actual investments in capital markets.

The Effect of Diversification: Another Lesson from Market History

nyse.com
tmx.com

In our previous chapter, we saw that the standard deviation of the annual return on a portfolio of several hundred large common stocks has historically been about 17 percent per year for both the Toronto Stock Exchange and the New York Stock Exchange (see Table 12.4, for example). Does this mean the standard deviation of the annual return on a typical stock is about 17 percent? As you might suspect by now, the answer is no. This is an extremely important observation.

To examine the relationship between portfolio size and portfolio risk, Table 13.8 illustrates typical average annual standard deviations for equally weighted portfolios that contain different numbers of randomly selected NYSE securities.[7]

In Column 2 of Table 13.8, we see that the standard deviation for a "portfolio" of one security is about 49 percent. What this means is that, if you randomly selected a single NYSE stock and put all your money into it, your standard deviation of return would typically have been a substantial 49 percent per year. If you were to randomly select two stocks and invest half your money in each, your standard deviation would have been about 37 percent on average, and so on.

TABLE 13.8

Standard deviations of annual portfolio returns

(1) Number of Stocks in Portfolio	(2) Average Standard Deviation of Annual Portfolio Returns	(3) Ratio of Portfolio Standard Deviation to Standard Deviation of a Single Stock
1	49.24%	1.00
2	37.36	0.76
4	29.69	0.60
6	26.64	0.54
8	24.98	0.51
10	23.93	0.49
20	21.68	0.44
30	20.87	0.42
40	20.46	0.42
50	20.20	0.41
100	19.69	0.40
200	19.42	0.39
300	19.34	0.39
400	19.29	0.39
500	19.27	0.39
1,000	19.21	0.39

The important thing to notice in Table 13.8 is that the standard deviation declines as the number of securities is increased. By the time we have 30 randomly chosen stocks, the portfolio's standard deviation has declined by about 60 percent, from 49 to about 20 percent. With 500 securities, the standard deviation is 19.27 percent, similar to the 21 percent we saw in our previous chapter for the large common stock portfolio. The small difference exists because the portfolio securities and time periods examined are not identical.

---

[7] These figures are from Table 1 in a classic paper by Meir Statman, "How Many Stocks Make a Diversified Portfolio?" *Journal of Financial and Quantitative Analysis* 22 (September 1987), pp. 353–64. They were derived from E. J. Elton and M. J. Gruber, "Risk Reduction and Portfolio Size: An Analytic Solution," *Journal of Business* 50 (October 1977), pp. 415–37.

The Principle of Diversification

Figure 13.6 illustrates the point we've been discussing. What we have plotted is the standard deviation of return versus the number of stocks in the portfolio. Notice in Figure 13.6 that the benefit in risk reduction from adding securities drops as we add more and more. By the time we have 10 securities, the portfolio standard deviation has dropped from 49.2 to 23.9 percent, most of the effect is already realized, and by the time we get to 30 or so, there is very little remaining benefit. The data in Table 13.8 and Figure 13.6 are from the NYSE but a Canadian study documented the same effect. However, the Canadian researchers found that Canadian investors need to hold a larger number of stocks to achieve diversification. This is likely due to Canadian stocks being more concentrated in a few industries than in the U.S.[8]

FIGURE 13.6

Portfolio
diversification

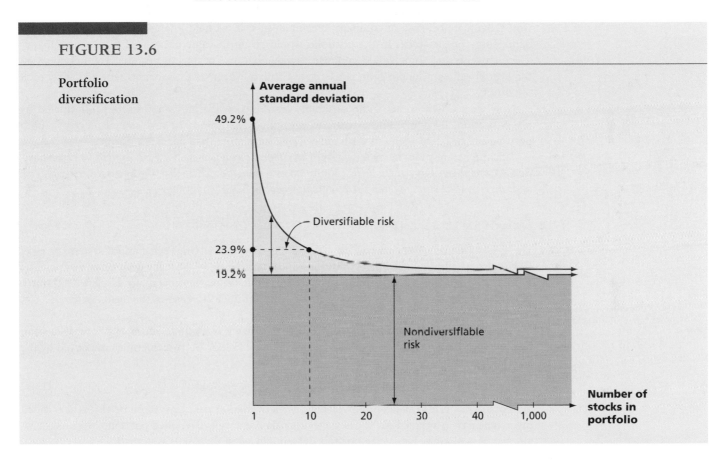

principle of diversification
Principle stating that spreading an investment across a number of assets eliminates some, but not all, of the risk.

Figure 13.6 illustrates two key points: First, the **principle of diversification** (discussed earlier) tells us that spreading an investment across many assets eliminates some of the risk. The shaded area in Figure 13.6, labelled diversifiable risk, is the part that can be eliminated by diversification.

The second point is equally important. A minimum level of risk cannot be eliminated simply by diversifying. This minimum level is labelled nondiversifiable risk in Figure 13.6. Taken together, these two points are another important lesson from capital market history: Diversification reduces risk, but only up to a point. Put another way, some risk is diversifiable and some is not.

To give a recent example of the impact of diversification, the S&P TSX Composite Index, which is a widely followed stock market index of large Canadian stocks, was down by 8.6% for the year 2011. As we saw in our previous chapter, this loss represents a bad year for a portfolio of large-cap stocks. Some of the biggest individual winners of the year were Westport Innovations (up a whopping 84 percent) and Dollarama (up 55 percent). But not all stocks were up: The losers included Yellow Media Inc. (down 91 percent) and Perpetual Energy Inc. (down 63 percent). Again, the lesson is clear: Diversification reduces exposure to extreme outcomes, both good and bad.

---

[8] For more on the Canadian study, see S. Cleary and D. Copp, "Diversification with Canadian stocks: How much is enough?" *Canadian Investment Review* 12, Fall 1999, pp. 21–25.

Diversification and Unsystematic Risk

From our discussion of portfolio risk, we know that some of the risk associated with individual assets can be diversified away and some cannot. We are left with an obvious question: Why is this so? It turns out that the answer hinges on the distinction we made earlier between systematic and unsystematic risk.

By definition, an unsystematic risk is one that is particular to a single asset or, at most, a small group. For example, if the asset under consideration is stock in a single company, the discovery of positive NPV projects such as successful new products and innovative cost savings tend to increase the value of the stock. Unanticipated lawsuits, industrial accidents, strikes, and similar events tend to decrease future cash flows and thereby reduce share values.

Here is the important observation: If we only held a single stock, the value of our investment would fluctuate because of company-specific events. If we held a large portfolio, on the other hand, some of the stocks in the portfolio would go up in value because of positive company-specific events and some would go down in value because of negative events. The net effect on the overall value of the portfolio is relatively small, however, as these effects tend to cancel each other out.

Now we see why some of the variability associated with individual assets is eliminated by diversification. By combining assets into portfolios, the unique or unsystematic events—both positive and negative—tend to wash out once we have more than just a few assets.

This important point bears repeating: *Unsystematic risk is essentially eliminated by diversification, so a relatively large portfolio has almost no unsystematic risk. In fact, the terms diversifiable risk and unsystematic risk are often used interchangeably.*

Diversification and Systematic Risk

We've seen that unsystematic risk can be eliminated by diversifying. What about systematic risk? Can it also be eliminated by diversification? The answer is no because, by definition, a systematic risk affects almost all assets to some degree. As a result, no matter how many assets we put into a portfolio, the systematic risk doesn't go away. Thus, for obvious reasons, the terms *systematic risk* and *nondiversifiable risk* are used interchangeably.

Because we have introduced so many different terms, it is useful to summarize our discussion before moving on. What we have seen is that the total risk of an investment, as measured by the standard deviation of its return, can be written as:

$$\text{Total risk} = \text{Systematic risk} + \text{Unsystematic risk} \qquad [13.9]$$

Systematic risk is also called nondiversifiable risk or market risk. Unsystematic risk is also called diversifiable risk, unique risk, or asset-specific risk. For a well-diversified portfolio, the unsystematic risk is negligible. For such a portfolio, essentially all of the risk is systematic.

Risk and the Sensible Investor

Having gone to all this trouble to show that unsystematic risk disappears in a well-diversified portfolio, how do we know that investors even want such portfolios? Suppose they like risk and don't want it to disappear?

We must admit that, theoretically at least, this is possible, but we argue that it does not describe what we think of as the typical investor. Our typical investor is *risk averse*. Risk-averse behaviour can be defined in many ways, but we prefer the following example: A fair gamble is one with zero expected return; a risk-averse investor would prefer to avoid fair gambles.

Why do investors choose well-diversified portfolios? Our answer is that they are risk averse, and risk-averse people avoid unnecessary risk, such as the unsystematic risk on a stock. If you do not think this is much of an answer to why investors choose well-diversified portfolios and avoid unsystematic risk, consider whether you would take on such a risk. For example, suppose you had worked all summer and had saved $5,000, which you intended to use for your university expenses. Now, suppose someone came up to you and offered to flip a coin for the money: heads, you would double your money, and tails, you would lose it all.

Would you take such a bet? Perhaps you would, but most people would not. Leaving aside any moral question that might surround gambling and recognizing that some people would take such a bet, it's our view that the average investor would not.

To induce the typical risk-averse investor to take a fair gamble, you must sweeten the pot. For example, you might need to raise the odds of winning from 50-50 to 70-30 or higher. The risk-averse investor can be induced to take fair gambles only if they are sweetened so that they become unfair to the investor's advantage.

TABLE 13.9

Average returns and standard deviations for two Canadian mutual funds and S&P/TSX Composite, 2010–2012

Fund	Annual return (%)	Standard deviation (%)
S&P/TSX Composite	15.59	13.79
CIBC Canadian Equity	12.73	13.87
CIBC Precious Metals	13.40	30.94

Source: theglobeandmail.com/globe-investor/funds-and-etfs/funds/

EXAMPLE 13.8: Risk of Canadian Mutual Funds

Table 13.9 shows the returns and standard deviations for two Canadian mutual funds over the three-year period ending March 31, 2012. The table also shows comparable statistics for the S&P/TSX Composite. As you would expect, the TSX portfolio is the most widely diversified of the three portfolios and has the lowest unsystematic risk. For this reason, it has the lowest portfolio standard deviation. The next lowest standard deviation is the CIBC Canadian Equity fund, which invests in equities across different Canadian industries.

The CIBC Precious Metals fund focuses on one sector of the economy. For example, its top three holdings at the end of March 2012 were Goldcorp Inc., Silver Wheaton, and B2Gold. The narrower focus of this fund makes it less diversified, with higher standard deviations.

What does this example tell us about how good these funds were as investments? To answer this question, we have to investigate asset pricing, our next topic.

Concept Questions

1. What happens to the standard deviation of return for a portfolio if we increase the number of securities in the portfolio?
2. What is the principle of diversification?
3. Why is some risk diversifiable? Why is some risk not diversifiable?
4. Why can't systematic risk be diversified away?
5. Explain the concept of risk aversion.

13.6 | Systematic Risk and Beta

The question that we now begin to address is: What determines the size of the risk premium on a risky asset? Put another way, why do some assets have a larger risk premium than other assets? The answer to these questions, as we discuss next, is also based on the distinction between systematic and unsystematic risk.

The Systematic Risk Principle

Thus far, we've seen that the total risk associated with an asset can be decomposed into two components: systematic and unsystematic risk. We have also seen that unsystematic risk can be essentially eliminated by diversification. The systematic risk present in an asset, on the other hand, cannot be eliminated by diversification.

systematic risk principle
Principle stating that the expected return on a risky asset depends only on that asset's systematic risk.

Based on our study of capital market history, we know that there is a reward, on average, for bearing risk. However, we now need to be more precise about what we mean by risk. The **systematic risk principle** states that the reward for bearing risk depends only on the systematic risk of an investment. The underlying rationale for this principle is straightforward: Because unsystematic risk can be eliminated at virtually no cost (by diversifying), there is no reward for bearing it. Put another way, the market does not reward risks that are born unnecessarily.

The systematic risk principle has a remarkable and very important implication: *The expected return on an asset depends only on that asset's systematic risk.* There is an obvious corollary to this principle: No matter how much total risk an asset has, only the systematic portion is relevant in determining the expected return (and the risk premium) on that asset.

Measuring Systematic Risk

Since systematic risk is the crucial determinant of an asset's expected return, we need some way of measuring the level of systematic risk for different investments. The specific measure that we use is called the **beta coefficient**, for which we will use the Greek symbol β. A beta coefficient, or beta for short, tells us how much systematic risk a particular asset has relative to an average asset representing the market portfolio. By definition, an average asset has a beta of 1.0 relative to itself. An asset with a beta of .50, therefore, has half as much systematic risk as an average asset; an asset with a beta of 2.0 has twice as much. These different levels of beta are illustrated in Figure 13.7. You can see that high beta assets display greater volatility over time.

beta coefficient
Amount of systematic risk present in a particular risky asset relative to an average risky asset.

FIGURE 13.7

Volatility: High and low betas

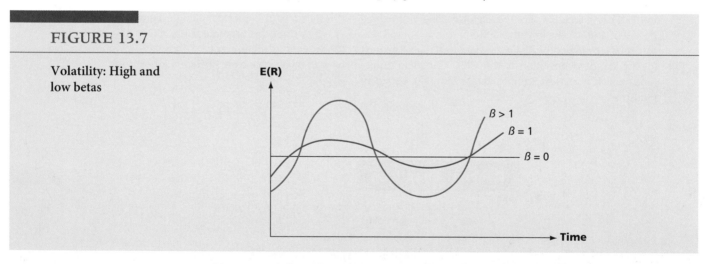

Table 13.10 contains the estimated beta coefficients for the stocks of some well-known companies ranging from 0.51 to 3.31.

TABLE 13.10

Beta coefficients for selected companies

Companies	Beta coefficient
Bank of Nova Scotia	0.78
Investors Group	0.76
Talisman Energy	1.43
Manulife Financial Corp.	1.39
Rogers Communications	0.51
Teck Resources Ltd.	3.31

Source: Financial Post Advisor, 2012

EXAMPLE 13.9: Total Risk versus Beta

Consider the following information on two securities. Which has greater total risk? Which has greater systematic risk? Greater unsystematic risk? Which asset has a higher risk premium?

	Standard Deviation	Beta
Security A	40%	.50
Security B	20	1.50

From our discussion in this section, Security A has greater total risk, but it has substantially less systematic risk. Since total risk is the sum of systematic and unsystematic risk, Security A must have greater unsystematic risk. Finally, from the systematic risk principle, Security B has a higher risk premium and a greater expected return, despite the fact that it has less total risk.

Remember that the expected return, and thus the risk premium, on an asset depends only on its systematic risk. Because assets with larger betas have greater systematic risks, they have greater expected returns. Thus, in Table 13.10, an investor who buys stock in Bank of Nova Scotia with a beta of 0.78, should expect to earn less, on average, than an investor who buys stock in Teck Resources Limited, with a beta of 3.31.

Portfolio Betas

Earlier, we saw that the riskiness of a portfolio does not have any simple relationship to the risks of the assets in the portfolio. A portfolio beta, however, can be calculated just like a portfolio expected return. For example, looking at Table 13.10, suppose you put half of your money in Bank of Nova Scotia and half in Teck Resources Limited. What would the beta of this combination be? Since Bank of Nova Scotia (BNS) has a beta of 0.78 and Teck Resources Ltd. (TRL) has a beta of 3.31, the portfolio's beta, β_P, would be:

scotiabank.ca

$$\beta_P = .50 \times \beta_{BNS} + .50 \times \beta_{TRL}$$
$$= .50 \times 0.78 + .50 \times 3.31$$
$$= 2.05$$

In general, if we had a large number of assets in a portfolio, we would multiply each asset's beta by its portfolio weight and then add the results to get the portfolio's beta.

EXAMPLE 13.10: Portfolio Betas

Suppose we had the following investments:

Security	Amount Invested	Expected Return	Beta
Stock A	$1,000	8%	.80
Stock B	2,000	12	.95
Stock C	3,000	15	1.10
Stock D	4,000	18	1.40

What is the expected return on this portfolio? What is the beta of this portfolio? Does this portfolio have more or less systematic risk than an average asset?

To answer, we first have to calculate the portfolio weights. Notice that the total amount invested is $10,000. Of this, $1,000/$10,000 = 10% is invested in Stock A. Similarly, 20 percent is invested in Stock B, 30 percent is in-

vested in Stock C, and 40 percent is invested in Stock D. The expected return, $E(R_P)$, is thus:

$$E(R_P) = .10 \times E(R_A) + .20 \times E(R_B) + .30 \times E(R_C) + .40 \times E(R_D)$$
$$= .10 \times 8\% + .20 \times 12\% + .30 \times 15\% + .40 \times 18\%$$
$$= 14.9\%$$

Similarly, the portfolio beta, β_P, is:

$$\beta_P = .10 \times \beta_A + .20 \times \beta_B + .30 \times \beta_C + .40 \times \beta_D$$
$$= .10 \times .80 + .20 \times .95 + .30 \times 1.10 + .40 \times 1.40$$
$$= 1.16$$

This portfolio thus has an expected return of 14.9 percent and a beta of 1.16. Since the beta is larger than 1.0, this portfolio has greater systematic risk than an average asset.

1. What is the systematic risk principle?
2. What does a beta coefficient measure?
3. How do you calculate a portfolio beta?
4. Does the expected return on a risky asset depend on that asset's total risk? Explain.

13.7 | The Security Market Line

We're now in a position to see how risk is rewarded in the marketplace. To begin, suppose Asset A has an expected return of $E(R_A) = 20\%$ and a beta of $\beta_A = 1.6$. Furthermore, the risk-free rate is $R_f = 8\%$, the return on 3-month Treasury bills. We choose this measure because it matches the investor's horizon for measuring performance. Notice that a risk-free asset, by definition, has no systematic risk (or unsystematic risk), so a risk-free asset has a beta of 0.

Beta and the Risk Premium

Consider a portfolio made up of Asset A and a risk-free asset. We can calculate some different possible portfolio expected returns and betas by varying the percentages invested in these two assets. For example, if 25 percent of the portfolio is invested in Asset A, the expected return is:

$$E(R_p) = .25 \times E(R_A) + (1 - .25) \times R_f$$
$$= .25 \times 20\% + .75 \times 8\%$$
$$= 11.0\%$$

Similarly, the beta on the portfolio, β_p, would be:

$$\beta_p = .25 \times \beta_A + (1 - .25) \times 0$$
$$= .25 \times 1.6$$
$$= .40$$

Notice that, since the weights have to add up to 1, the percentage invested in the risk-free asset is equal to 1 minus the percentage invested in Asset A.

One thing that you might wonder about is whether it is possible for the percentage invested in Asset A to exceed 100 percent. The answer is yes. This can happen if the investor borrows at the risk-free rate. For example, suppose an investor has $100 and borrows an additional $50 at 8 percent, the risk-free rate. The total investment in Asset A would be $150, or 150 percent of the investor's wealth. The expected return in this case would be:

$$E(R_p) = 1.50 \times E(R_A) + (1 - 1.50) \times R_f$$
$$= 1.50 \times 20\% - .50 \times 8\%$$
$$= 26\%$$

The beta on the portfolio would be:

$$\beta_p = 1.50 \times \beta_A + (1 - 1.50) \times 0$$
$$= 1.50 \times 1.6$$
$$= 2.4$$

We can calculate some other possibilities as follows:

Percentage of Portfolio in Asset A	Portfolio Expected Return	Portfolio Beta
0%	8%	0.0
25	11	0.4
50	14	0.8
75	17	1.2
100	20	1.6
125	23	2.0
150	26	2.4

In Figure 13.8A, these portfolio expected returns are plotted against the portfolio betas. Notice that all the combinations fall on a straight line.

FIGURE 13.8A

Portfolio expected returns and betas for Asset A

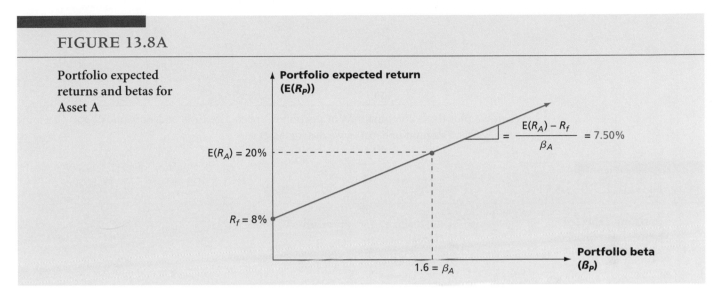

THE REWARD-TO-RISK RATIO What is the slope of the straight line in Figure 13.8A? As always, the slope of a straight line is equal to the "rise over the run." As we move out of the risk-free asset into Asset A, the beta increases from zero to 1.6 (a "run" of 1.6). At the same time, the expected return goes from 8 to 20 percent, a "rise" of 12 percent. The slope of the line is thus 12%/1.6 = 7.50%.

Notice that the slope of our line is just the risk premium on Asset A, $E(R_A) - R_f$, divided by Asset A's beta, β_A:

$$\text{Slope} = \frac{[E(R_A) - R_f]}{\beta_A}$$

$$= \frac{[20\% - 8\%]}{1.6} = 7.50\%$$

What this tells us is that Asset A offers a reward-to-risk ratio of 7.50 percent.[9] In other words, Asset A has a risk premium of 7.50 percent per unit of systematic risk.

THE BASIC ARGUMENT Now suppose we consider a second asset, Asset B. This asset has a beta of 1.2 and an expected return of 16 percent. Which investment is better, Asset A or Asset B? You might think that, once again, we really cannot say. Some investors might prefer A; some investors might prefer B. Actually, however, we can say: A is better because, as we demonstrate, B offers inadequate compensation for its level of systematic risk, at least relative to A.

To begin, we calculate different combinations of expected returns and betas for portfolios of Asset B and a risk-free asset just as we did for Asset A. For example, if we put 25 percent in Asset B and the remaining 75 percent in the risk-free asset, the portfolio's expected return would be:

$$E(R_P) = .25 \times E(R_B) + (1 - .25) \times R_f$$
$$= .25 \times 16\% + .75 \times 8\%$$
$$= 10\%$$

Similarly, the beta on the portfolio, βP, would be:

$$\beta_P = .25 \times \beta_B + (1 - .25) \times 0$$
$$= .25 \times 1.2$$
$$= .30$$

Some other possibilities are as follows:

---

[9]This ratio is sometimes called the Treynor index, after one of its originators.

Percentage of Portfolio in Asset B	Portfolio Expected Return	Portfolio Beta
0%	8%	0.0
25	10	0.3
50	12	0.6
75	14	0.9
100	16	1.2
125	18	1.5
150	20	1.8

When we plot these combinations of portfolio expected returns and portfolios betas in Figure 13.8B, we get a straight line just as we did for Asset A.

FIGURE 13.8B

Portfolio expected returns and betas for Asset B

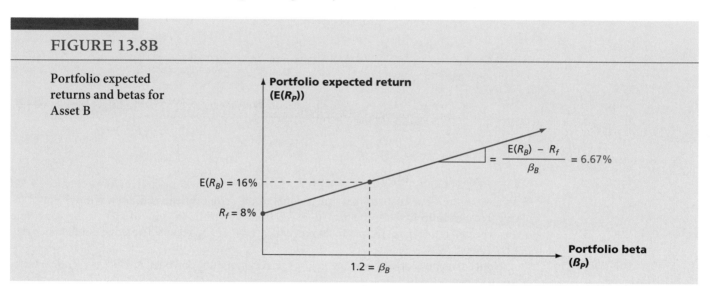

The key thing to notice is that when we compare the results for Assets A and B, as in Figure 13.8C, the line describing the combinations of expected returns and betas for Asset A is higher than the one for Asset B. This tells us that for any given level of systematic risk (as measured by β), some combination of Asset A and the risk-free asset always offers a larger return. This is why we were able to state that Asset A is a better investment than Asset B.

Another way of seeing that A offers a superior return for its level of risk is to note that the slope of our line for Asset B is:

$$\text{Slope} = \frac{[E(R_B) - R_f]}{\beta_B}$$

$$= \frac{[16\% - 8\%]}{1.2} = 6.67\%$$

Thus, Asset B has a reward-to-risk ratio of 6.67 percent, which is less than the 7.5 percent offered by Asset A.

THE FUNDAMENTAL RESULT   The situation we have described for Assets A and B cannot persist in a well-organized, active market, because investors would be attracted to Asset A and away from Asset B. As a result, Asset A's price would rise and Asset B's price would fall. Since prices and returns move in opposite directions, the result is that A's expected return would decline and B's would rise.

This buying and selling would continue until the two assets plotted on exactly the same line, which means they offer the same reward for bearing risk. In other words, in an active, competitive market, we must have:

$$\frac{[E(R_A) - R_f]}{\beta_A} = \frac{[E(R_B) - R_f]}{\beta_B}$$

This is the fundamental relationship between risk and return.

Our basic argument can be extended to more than just two assets. In fact, no matter how many assets we had, we would always reach the same conclusion:

The reward-to-risk ratio must be the same for all the assets in the market.

This result is really not so surprising. What it says, for example, is that, if one asset has twice as much systematic risk as another asset, its risk premium is simply twice as large.

Since all the assets in the market must have the same reward-to-risk ratio, they all must plot on the same line in market equilibrium. This argument is illustrated in Figure 13.9. As shown, Assets A and B plot directly on the line and thus have the same reward-to-risk ratio. If an asset plotted above the line, such as C in Figure 13.9, its price would rise, and its expected return would fall until it plotted exactly on the line. Similarly, if an asset plotted below the line, such as D in Figure 13.9, its expected return would rise until it too plotted directly on the line.

The arguments we have presented apply to active, competitive, well-functioning markets. The financial markets, such as the TSX, NYSE, and Nasdaq, best meet these criteria. Other markets, such as real asset markets, may or may not. For this reason, these concepts are most useful in examining financial markets. We thus focus on such markets here. However, as we discuss in a later section, the information about risk and return gleaned from financial markets is crucial in evaluating the investments that a corporation makes in real assets.

nasdaq.com

FIGURE 13.8C

Portfolio expected returns and betas for both assets

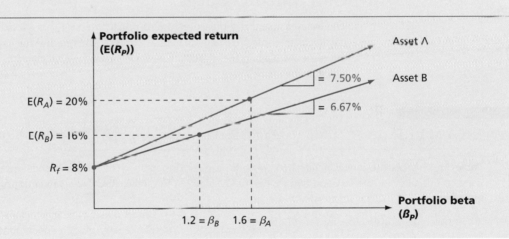

FIGURE 13.9

Expected returns and systematic risk

The fundamental relationship between beta and expected return is that all assets must have the same reward-to-risk ratio $[E(R_i) - R_f]/\beta_i$. This means they would all plot on the same straight line. Assets A and B are examples of this behaviour. Asset C's expected return is too high; Asset D's is too low.

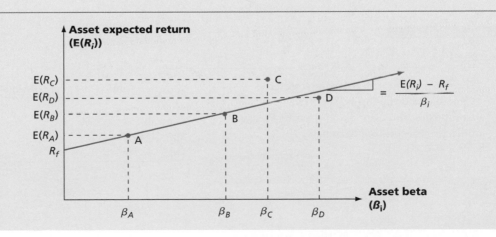

EXAMPLE 13.11: Beta and Stock Valuation

An asset is said to be overvalued if its price is too high given its expected return and risk. Suppose you observe the following situation:

Security	Beta	Expected Return
SWMS Company	1.3	14%
Insec Company	.8	10

The risk-free rate is currently 6 percent. Is one of the two preceding securities overvalued relative to the other?

To answer, we compute the reward-to-risk ratio for both. For SWMS, this ratio is (14% − 6%)/1.3 = 6.15%. For Insec, this ratio is 5 percent. What we conclude is that Insec offers an insufficient expected return for its level of risk, at least relative to SWMS. Since its expected return is too low, its price is too high. To see why this is true, recall

that the dividend valuation model presented in Chapter 8 treats price as the present value of future dividends.

$$P_0 = \frac{D_1}{(r - g)}$$

Projecting the dividend stream gives us D_1 and g. If the required rate of return is too low, the stock price will be too high. For example, suppose D_1 = $2.00 and g = 7 percent. If the expected rate of return on the stock is wrongly underestimated at 10 percent, the stock price estimate is $66.67. This price is too high if the true expected rate of return is 14 percent. At this higher rate of return, the stock price should fall to $28.57. In other words, Insec is overvalued relative to SWMS, and we would expect to see its price fall relative to SWMS's. Notice that we could also say that SWMS is undervalued relative to Insec.

Calculating Beta

The beta of a security measures the responsiveness of that security's return to the return on the market as a whole. To calculate beta, we draw a line relating the expected return on the security to different returns on the market. This line, called the *characteristic line* of the security, has a slope equal to the stock's beta.

EXAMPLE 13.12: Mutual Fund Performance

Table 13.11 gives the inputs needed to compute the reward-to-risk ratios for the TSX and two mutual funds. Starting with the TSX, the reward-to-risk ratio was:

(Average return − Riskless rate)/Beta
(7.37 − 3.07)/1.00 = 4.3%

You can verify that the reward-to-risk ratio for RBC Canadian Equity was 3.69 percent and the ratio for BMO Dividend was 8.49 percent. BMO Dividend fund beat the

market by earning a higher reward-to-risk ratio than the TSX, while RBC Canadian Equity fund underperformed over this period.

Unfortunately, in an efficient market, while past performance may guide expectations of future returns, these expectations may not be realized in actual returns. So, we would not expect that BMO Dividend fund would beat the market consistently over time.

TABLE 13.11

Average returns and betas for selected Canadian mutual funds, S&P/TSX Composite, and Canadian 3-month Treasury bills, 15 years ending March 31, 2012	Fund	Annual return (%)	Beta
	S&P/TSX Composite	7.37	1
	3-month Treasury bills	3.07	0
	RBC Canadian Equity	6.80	1.01
	BMO Dividend fund	9.35	0.74

Source: theglobeandmail.com/globe-investor/funds-and-etfs/funds/

Consider Figure 13.10, which displays returns for both a hypothetical company and the market as a whole.[10] Each point represents a pair of returns over a particular month. The vertical dimension measures the return on the stock over the month and the horizontal dimension that of the S&P/TSX Composite. (The S&P/TSX Composite is considered a reasonable proxy for the general market.)

FIGURE 13.10

Graphic representation of beta

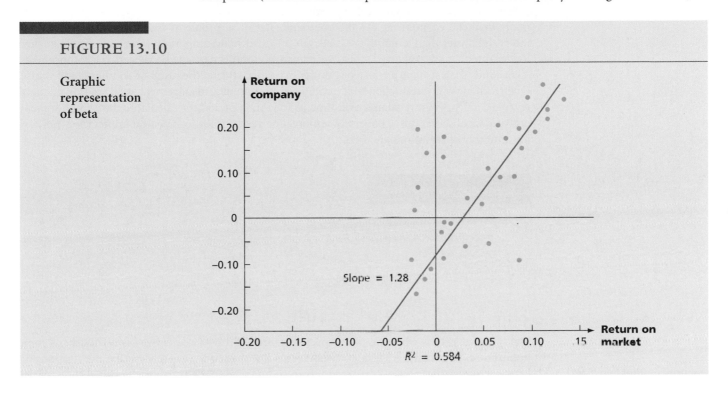

Figure 13.10 also shows the line of *best fit* superimposed on these points. In practical applications, this line is calculated from regression analysis. As one can see from the graph, the slope is 1.28. Because the average beta is 1, this indicates the stock's beta of 1.28 is higher than that for the average stock.

The goal of a financial analyst is to determine the beta that a stock will have in the future, because this is when the proceeds of an investment are received. Of course, past data must be used in regression analysis. Thus, it is incorrect to think of 1.28 as the beta of our example company. Rather it is our estimate of the firm's beta from past data.

The bottom of Figure 13.10 indicates that the company's R_2 over the time period is 0.584. What does this mean? R_2 measures how close the points in the figure are to the characteristic line. The highest value for R_2 is 1, a situation that would occur if all points lay exactly on the characteristic line. This would be the case where the security's return is determined only by the market's return without the security having any independent variation. The R_2 is likely to approach one for a large portfolio of securities. For example, many widely diversified mutual funds have R_2s of 0.80 or more. The lowest possible R_2 is zero, a situation occurring when two variables are entirely unrelated to each other. Those companies whose returns are pretty much independent of returns on the stock market would have R_2s near zero.

The risk of any security can be broken down into unsystematic and systematic risk. Whereas beta measures the amount of systematic risk, R_2 measures the *proportion* of total risk that is systematic. Thus, a low R_2 indicates that most of the risk of a firm is unsystematic.[11]

The mechanics for calculating betas are quite simple. People in business frequently estimate beta by using commercially available computer programs. Certain handheld calculators are also

---

[10] As we mentioned in Chapter 12, the return on a security includes both the dividend and the capital gain (or loss).

[11] Standard computer packages generally provide confidence intervals (error ranges) for beta estimates. One has greater confidence in beta estimates where the confidence interval is small. While stocks with high R^2s generally have small confidence intervals, it is the size of the confidence interval, not the R^2 itself, that is relevant here. Because expected return is related to systematic risk, the R^2 of a firm is of no concern to us once we know the firm's beta. This often surprises students trained in statistics, because R^2 is an important concept for many other purposes.

able to perform the calculation. In addition, a large number of services sell or even give away estimates of beta for different firms. For example, Table 13.10 presents a set of betas calculated by *Financial Post Advisor* in May 2012.

In calculating betas, analysts make a number of assumptions consistent with Canadian research on the capital asset pricing model.[12] First, they generally choose monthly data, as do many financial economists. On the one hand, statistical problems frequently arise when time intervals shorter than a month are used. On the other hand, important information is lost when longer intervals are employed. Thus, the choice of monthly data can be viewed as a compromise.

Second, analysts typically use just under five years of data, the result of another compromise. Due to changes in production mix, production techniques, management style, and/or financial leverage, a firm's nature adjusts over time. A long time period for calculating beta implies many out-of-date observations. Conversely, a short time period leads to statistical imprecision, because few monthly observations are used.

Concept Questions

1. What is the statistical procedure employed for calculating beta?
2. Why do financial analysts use monthly data when calculating beta?
3. What is R^2?

The Security Market Line

The line that results when we plot expected returns and beta coefficients is obviously of some importance, so it's time we gave it a name. This line, which we use to describe the relationship between systematic risk and expected return in financial markets, is usually called the **security market line (SML)**. After NPV, the SML is arguably the most important concept in modern finance.

security market line (SML)
Positively sloped straight line displaying the relationship between expected return and beta.

MARKET PORTFOLIOS   It will be very useful to know the equation of the SML. There are many different ways that we could write it, but one way is particularly common. Suppose we were to consider a portfolio made up of all of the assets in the market. Such a portfolio is called a *market portfolio*, and we write the expected return on this market portfolio as $E(R_M)$.

Since all the assets in the market must plot on the SML, so must a market portfolio made of those assets. To determine where it plots on the SML, we need to know the beta of the market portfolio, β_M. Because this portfolio is representative of all the assets in the market, it must have average systematic risk. In other words, it has a beta of one. We could therefore write the slope of the SML as:

$$\text{SML slope} = \frac{[E(R_M) - R_f]}{\beta_M} = \frac{[E(R_M) - R_f]}{1} = E(R_M) - R_f$$

market risk premium
Slope of the SML, the difference between the expected return on a market portfolio and the risk-free rate.

The term $E(R_M) - R_f$ is often called the **market risk premium** since it is the risk premium on a market portfolio.

THE CAPITAL ASSET PRICING MODEL   To finish up, if we let $E(R_i)$ and β_i stand for the expected return and beta, respectively, on any asset in the market, we know it must plot on the SML. As a result, we know that its reward-to-risk ratio is the same as the overall market's:

$$\frac{[E(R_i) - R_f]}{\beta_i} = E(R_M) - R_f$$

If we rearrange this, we can write the equation for the SML as:

$$E(R_i) = R_f + [E(R_M) - R_f] \times \beta_i \tag{13.10}$$

---

[12]See Z. Bodie, A. Kane, A. J. Marcus, S. Perrakis and P. J. Ryan, *Investments*, 7th Canadian ed. (Whitby, Ontario: McGraw-Hill Ryerson, 2011).

capital asset pricing model (CAPM)
Equation of the SML showing the relationship between expected return and beta.

This result is identical to the famous **capital asset pricing model (CAPM)**.[13]

What the CAPM shows is that the expected return for a particular asset depends on three things:

1. *The pure time value of money.* As measured by the risk-free rate, R_f, this is the reward for merely waiting for your money, without taking any risk.

2. *The reward for bearing systematic risk.* As measured by the market risk premium $[E(R_M) - R_f]$, this component is the reward the market offers for bearing an average amount of systematic risk in addition to waiting.

3. *The amount of systematic risk.* As measured by β_i, this is the amount of systematic risk present in a particular asset, relative to an average asset.

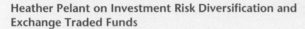

IN THEIR OWN WORDS...

Heather Pelant on Investment Risk Diversification and Exchange Traded Funds

Investors have been advised repeatedly to diversify their investment portfolios, but Canadians still have the bulk of their money invested in the Canadian market. That adds a new layer of risk to their investments, according to Heather Pelant, head of business development at Barclays Global Investors Canada.

"There's an opportunity to do a strategic rebalance right now," Pelant said in an interview. "The market has led Canadians to be overweight in Canadian equities... to me we have some embedded risks in those portfolios."

According to July 2007 statistics from the Investment Funds Institute of Canada, almost 27 percent of investments in the country are in Canadian equity funds, 22 percent are in domestic balanced mutual funds, 16 percent are in global and international equities and 13.3 percent are in global balanced funds.

According to a TD Economics report, investors who put most of their money in the Canadian market expose their portfolios to geographic risk from a potential downturn in the Canadian economy.

Not only is Canada a tiny part of the global market, representing roughly 3.5 percent of the world's equities, the TSX is dominated by energy, mining and financial company's. That heavy sectoral weighting results in investors having too few funds in high-tech, pharmaceuticals and other sectors prospering elsewhere around the world. Pelant said Canadians can easily realign their portfolios by investing in international exchange traded funds (ETFs), which track the performance of stock indexes from around the world and provide investors with a diversified index fund.

You can think about it in three ways. You can be broad or you can go country specific or you can go with global investors. You can add one or two ETFs to your portfolio and take a lot of risk off the table.

Pelant said ETFs have lower management expense ratios than mutual funds and are aimed at providing the same rate of return as the market, which has historically been better than what most mutual fund managers have achieved.

At a recent Barclays iShares adviser forum in Vancouver, Pelant said people think that, because mutual funds are actively managed, they're less affected by market volatility. Yet the opposite tends to be true.

In her presentation, she showed how fund managers add volatility, because they're trying to beat the market. "That comes with some risk," Pelant said.

She noted that finding a fund manager that does consistently well is difficult because he or she might do well in one period, but poorly in the next.

But Pelant added that if investors are comfortable with the risk and want to invest with a mutual fund in a sector or region, adding an ETF to the same asset class can cut the volatility of returns in half.

"Sometimes the index outperforms and sometimes the active manager underperforms, but combine the two [and] you end up with a better portfolio."

And if investors need to diversify their asset mix by adding more fixed income or by entering emerging markets, ETFs now cover those areas.

Investing in ETFs that match the market in the long run might sound attractive, but they're not without risk, and investors need to be comfortable with market volatility. And with the number of ETFs available in Canada today, it's important to know which one best suits your own investment goals. With sector specific ETFs like those for gold, silver or financial services, it's important to know the fund's inherent risk level, because some ETFs will be more riskier than others.

Heather Pelant is the Managing Director at BlackRock Hong Kong. Her comments are excerpted with permission from "To hedge investment risks, diversify and go global," by Richard Chu, *Business in Vancouver*, October 16–22, 2007.

---

[13] Our discussion leading up to the CAPM is actually much more closely related to a more recently developed theory, known as the arbitrage pricing theory (APT). The theory underlying the CAPM is a great deal more complex than we have indicated here, and the CAPM has a number of other implications that go beyond the scope of this discussion. As we present here, the CAPM and the APT have essentially identical implications, so we don't distinguish between them. Appendix 13A presents another way to develop the CAPM.

By the way, the CAPM works for portfolios of assets just as it does for individual assets. In an earlier section, we saw how to calculate a portfolio's β. To find the expected return on a portfolio, we simply use this β in the CAPM equation.

Figure 13.11 summarizes our discussion of the SML and the CAPM. As before, we plot the expected return against beta. Now we recognize that, based on the CAPM, the slope of the SML is equal to the market risk premium $[E(R_M) - R_f]$. This concludes our presentation of concepts related to the risk-return trade-off. For future reference, Table 13.12 summarizes the various concepts in the order we discussed them in.

FIGURE 13.11

The security market line (SML)

The slope of the security market line is equal to the market risk premium; i.e., the reward for bearing an average amount of systematic risk. The equation describing the SML can be written:
$E(R_i) = R_f + \beta_i \times [E(RM) - R_f]$
which is the capital asset pricing model (CAPM).

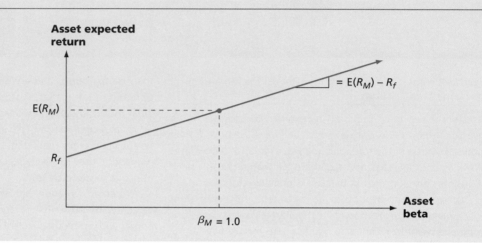

TABLE 13.12 Summary of risk and return

Total risk.
The *total risk* of an investment is measured by the variance or, more commonly, the standard deviation of its return.

Total return.
The *total return* on an investment has two components: the expected return and the unexpected return. The unexpected return comes about because of unanticipated events. The risk from investing stems from the possibility of unanticipated events.

Systematic and unsystematic risks.
Systematic risks (also called market risks) are unanticipated events that affect almost all assets to some degree because they are economy wide. Unsystematic risks are unanticipated events that affect single assets or small groups of assets. Unsystematic risks are also called *unique* or *asset-specific risks*.

The effect of diversification.
Some, but not all, of the risk associated with a risky investment can be eliminated by diversification. The reason is that unsystematic risks, which are unique to individual assets, tend to wash out in a large portfolio; systematic risks, which affect all of the assets in a portfolio to some extent, do not.

The systematic risk principle and beta.
Because unsystematic risk can be freely eliminated by diversification, the *systematic risk principle* states that the reward for bearing risk depends only on the level of systematic risk. The level of systematic risk in a particular asset, relative to average, is given by the beta of that asset.

The reward-to-risk ratio and the security market line.
The reward-to-risk ratio for asset i is the ratio of its risk premium $E(R_i) - R_f$ to its beta, β_i:
$$\frac{E(R_i) - R_f}{\beta_i}$$
In a well-functioning market, this ratio is the same for every asset. As a result, when asset expected returns are plotted against asset betas, all assets plot on the same straight line, called the *security market line* (SML).

The capital asset pricing model.
From the SML, the expected return on asset i can be written:
$E(R_i) = R_f + [E(R_M) - R_f] \times \beta_i$
This is the *capital asset pricing model* (CAPM). The expected return on a risky asset thus has three components: The first is the pure time value of money (R_f), the second is the market risk premium $[E(R_M) - R_f]$, and the third is the beta for that asset, β_i.

EXAMPLE 13.13: Risk and Return

Suppose the risk-free rate is 4 percent, the market risk premium is 8.6 percent, and a particular stock has a beta of 1.3. Based on the CAPM, what is the expected return on this stock? What would the expected return be if the beta were to double?

With a beta of 1.3, the risk premium for the stock would be 1.3 × 8.6%, or 11.18 percent. The risk-free rate is 4 percent, so the expected return is 15.18 percent. If the beta doubles to 2.6, the risk premium would double to 22.36 percent, so the expected return would be 26.36 percent.

Concept Questions

1. What is the fundamental relationship between risk and return in well-functioning markets?
2. What is the security market line? Why must all assets plot directly on it in a well-functioning market?
3. What is the capital asset pricing model (CAPM)? What does it tell us about the required return on a risky investment?

13.8 | Arbitrage Pricing Theory And Empirical Models

arbitrage pricing theory (APT)
An equilibrium asset pricing theory that is derived from a factor model by using diversification and arbitrage. It shows that the expected return on any risky asset is a linear combination of various factors.

The CAPM and the **arbitrage pricing theory (APT)** are alternative models of risk and return. One advantage of the APT is that it can handle multiple factors that the CAPM ignores. Although the bulk of our presentation in this chapter focused on the one-factor model, a multifactor model is probably more reflective of reality.

The APT assumes that stock returns are generated according to factor models. For example, we have described a stock's return as

Total return = Expected return + Unexpected return
$$R = E(R) + U$$

In APT, the unexpected return is related to several market factors. Suppose there are three such factors: unanticipated changes in inflation, GNP, and interest rates. The total return can be expanded as

$$R = E(R) + \beta_I F_I + \beta_{GNP} F_{GNP} + \beta_r F_r + \varepsilon \qquad [13.11]$$

The three factors F_I, F_{GNP}, and F_r represent systematic risk because these factors affect many securities. The term ε is considered unsystematic risk because it is unique to each individual security. Under this multifactor APT, we can generalize from three to K factors to express the relationship between risk and return as:

$$E(R) = R_F + E[(R_1) - R_F]\beta_1 + E[(R_2) - R_F]\beta_2 + E[(R_3) - R_F]\beta_3 + \ldots + E[(R_K) - R_F]\beta_K \quad [13.12]$$

In this equation, β_1 stands for the security's beta with respect to the first factor, β_2 stands for the security's beta with respect to the second factor, and so on. For example, if the first factor is inflation, β_1 is the security's inflation beta. The term $E(R_1)$ is the expected return on a security (or portfolio) whose beta with respect to the first factor is one and whose beta with respect to all other factors is zero. Because the market compensates for risk, $E((R_1) - R_F)$ is positive in the normal case.[14] (An analogous interpretation can be given to $E(R_2)$, $E(R_3)$, and so on.)

The equation states that the security's expected return is related to its factor betas. The argument is that each factor represents risk that cannot be diversified away. The higher a security's beta with regard to a particular factor, the higher the risk that security bears. In a rational world, the expected return on the security should compensate for this risk. The preceding equation states that the expected return is a summation of the risk-free rate plus the compensation for each type of risk the security bears.

---

[14] Actually $(R_i - R_F)$ could be negative in the case where factor i is perceived as a hedge of some sort.

As an example, consider a Canadian study where the factors were

1. The rate of growth in industrial production (INDUS).
2. The changes in the slope of the term structure of interest rates (the difference between the yield on long-term and short-term Canada bonds) (TERMS).
3. The default risk premium for bonds (measured as the difference between the yield on long-term Canada bonds and the yield on the ScotiaMcLeod corporate bond index) (RISKPREM).
4. The inflation (measured as the growth of the consumer price index) (INFL).
5. The value-weighted return on the market portfolio (S&P/TSX Composite) (MKRET).[15]

Using the period 1970–84, the empirical results of the study indicated that expected monthly returns on a sample of 100 TSX stocks could be described as a function of the risk premiums associated with these five factors.

Because many factors appear on the right side of the APT equation, the APT formulation explained expected returns in this Canadian sample more accurately than did the CAPM. However, as we mentioned earlier, one cannot easily determine which are the appropriate factors. The factors in this study were included for reasons of both common sense and convenience. They were not derived from theory and the choice of factors varies from study to study. A more recent Canadian study, for example, includes changes in a U.S. stock index and in exchange rates as factors.[16]

The CAPM and the APT by no means exhaust the models and techniques used in practice to measure the expected return on risky assets. Both the CAPM and the APT are *risk based*. They each measure the risk of a security by its beta(s) on some systematic factor(s), and they each argue that the expected excess return must be proportional to the beta(s). As we have seen, this is intuitively appealing and has a strong basis in theory, but there are alternative approaches.

One popular alternative is a multifactor empirical model developed by Fama and French and based less on a theory of how financial markets work and more on simply looking for regularities and relations in the past history of market data. In such an approach, the researcher specifies some parameters or attributes associated with the securities in question and then examines the data directly for a relation between these attributes and expected returns. Fama and French examine whether the expected return on a firm is related to its size and market to book ratio in addition to its beta. Is it true that small firms have higher average returns than large firms? Do growth companies with high market to book ratios have higher average returns than value companies with low market to book ratios?[17] A well-known extension of the Fama-French model includes a fourth, momentum factor measured by last year's stock return.[18]

Although multifactor models are commonly used in investment performance analysis they have not become standard practice in estimating the cost of capital. Surveys of corporate executives show that only 1 in 3 employ multifactor models for this purpose while over 70 percent rely on the CAPM.[19]

Concept Questions

1. What is the main advantage of the APT over the CAPM?

---

[15] E. Otuteye, "How Economic Forces Explain Canadian Stock Returns," *Canadian Investment Review*, Spring 1991, pp. 93–99.

[16] L. Kryzanowski, S. Lalancette, and M.C. To, "Performance Attribution using an APT with Prespecified Macro-factors and Time-Varying Risk Premia and Betas," *Journal of Financial and Quantitative Analysis 32* (June 1997), pp. 205–224. A further Canadian study is: B.F. Smith, "A Study of the Arbitrage Pricing Theory Using Daily Returns of Canadian Stocks," in M.J. Robinson and B.F. Smith, eds., *Canadian Capital Markets, London*, Ont., Ivey Business School, 1993.

[17] E.F. Fama and K.R. French, "Common Risk Factors in the Returns on Stocks and Bonds," *Journal of Financial Economics* 33 (1) (February 1993) and "Multifactor Explanations of Asset Pricing Anomalies," *Journal of Finance*, March 1996, 51:1, pp. 55–84.

[18] M. Carhart, "On Persistence in Mutual Fund Performance," *Journal of Finance* 52 (1997), pp. 57–82.

[19] J.R. Graham and C. R. Harvey, "The Theory and Practice of Corporate Finance: Evidence from the Field", *Journal of Financial Economics*, 2001, Vol. 60, pp. 187–243.

13.9 | SUMMARY AND CONCLUSIONS

This chapter covered the essentials of risk. Along the way, we introduced a number of definitions and concepts. The most important of these is the security market line, or SML. The SML is important because it tells us the reward offered in financial markets for bearing risk. Once we know this, we have a benchmark against which to compare the returns expected from real asset investments and to determine if they are desirable.

Because we covered quite a bit of ground, it's useful to summarize the basic economic logic underlying the SML as follows:

1. Based on capital market history, there is a reward for bearing risk. This reward is the risk premium on an asset.

2. The total risk associated with an asset has two parts: systematic risk and unsystematic risk. Unsystematic risk can be freely eliminated by diversification (this is the principle of diversification), so only systematic risk is rewarded. As a result, the risk premium on an asset is determined by its systematic risk. This is the systematic risk principle.

3. An asset's systematic risk, relative to average, can be measured by its beta coefficient, β_i. The risk premium on an asset is then given by its beta coefficient multiplied by the market risk premium $[E(R_M) - R_f] \times \beta_i$.

4. The expected return on an asset, $E(R_i)$, is equal to the risk-free rate, R_f, plus the risk premium.

$$E(R_i) = R_f + [E(R_M) - R_f] \times \beta_i$$

This is the equation of the SML, and it is often called the capital asset pricing model (CAPM).

This chapter completes our discussion of risk and return and concludes Part 5 of our book. Now that we have a better understanding of what determines a firm's cost of capital for an investment, the next several chapters examine more closely how firms raise the long-term capital needed for investment.

Key Terms

arbitrage pricing theory (APT) (page 377)
beta coefficient (page 366)
capital asset pricing model (CAPM) (page 375)
expected return (page 347)
market risk premium (page 374)
portfolio (page 351)

portfolio weights (page 351)
principle of diversification (page 363)
security market line (SML) (page 374)
systematic risk (page 360)
systematic risk principle (page 366)
unsystematic risk (page 360)

Chapter Review Problems and Self-Test

13.1 **Expected Return and Standard Deviation** This problem gives you some practice calculating measures of prospective portfolio performance. There are two assets and three states of the economy:

	Probability of	Rate of Return if State Occurs	
State of Economy	State of Economy	Stock A	Stock B
Recession	.20	−.15	.20
Normal	.50	.20	.30
Boom	.30	.60	.40

What are the expected returns and standard deviations for these two stocks?

13.2 **Portfolio Risk and Return** Using the information in the previous problem, suppose you have $20,000 total. If you put $15,000 in Stock A and the remainder in Stock B, what will be the expected return and standard deviation on your portfolio?

13.3 **Risk and Return** Suppose you observe the following situation:

Security	Beta	Expected Return
Cooley Inc.	1.8	22.00%
Moyer Company	1.6	20.44

If the risk-free rate is 7 percent, are these securities correctly priced? What would the risk-free rate have to be if they are correctly priced?

13.4 **CAPM** Suppose the risk-free rate is 8 percent. The expected return on the market is 16 percent. If a particular stock has a beta of .7, what is its expected return based on the CAPM? If another stock has an expected return of 24 percent, what must its beta be?

Answers to Self-Test Problems

13.1   The expected returns are just the possible returns multiplied by the associated probabilities:

$$E(R_A) = (.20 \times -.15) + (.50 \times .20) + (.30 \times .60) = 25\%$$
$$E(R_B) = (.20 \times .20) + (.50 \times .30) + (.30 \times .40) = 31\%$$

The variances are given by the sums of the squared deviations from the expected returns multiplied by their probabilities:

$$\sigma^2_A = .20 \times (-.15 - .25)^2 + .50 \times (.20 - .25)^2 + .30 \times (.60 - .25)^2$$
$$= (.20 \times -.40^2) + (.50 \times -.05^2) + (.30 \times .35^2)$$
$$= (.20 \times .16) + (.50 \times .0025) + (.30 \times .1225)$$
$$= .0700$$

$$\sigma^2_B = .20 \times (.20 - .31)^2 + .50 \times (.30 - .31)^2 + .30 \times (.40 - .31)^2$$
$$= (.20 \times -.11^2) + (.50 \times -.01^2) + (.30 \times .09^2)$$
$$= (.20 \times .0121) + (.50 \times .0001) + (.30 \times .0081)$$
$$= .0049$$

The standard deviations are thus:

$$\sigma_A = \sqrt{.0700} = 26.46\%$$
$$\sigma_B = \sqrt{.0049} = 7\%$$

13.2   The portfolio weights are $15,000/20,000 = .75$ and $5,000/20,000 = .25$. The expected return is thus:

$$E(R_P) = .75 \times E(R_A) + .25 \times E(R_B)$$
$$= (.75 \times 25\%) + (.25 \times 31\%)$$
$$= 26.5\%$$

Alternatively, we could calculate the portfolio's return in each of the states:

State of Economy	Probability of State of Economy	Portfolio Return if State Occurs
Recession	.20	$(.75 \times -.15) + (.25 \times .20) = -.0625$
Normal	.50	$(.75 \times .20) + (.25 \times .30) = .2250$
Boom	.30	$(.75 \times .60) + (.25 \times .40) = .5500$

The portfolio's expected return is:

$$E(R_P) = (.20 \times -.0625) + (.50 \times .2250) + (.30 \times .5500) = 26.5\%$$

This is the same as we had before.

The portfolio's variance is:

$$\sigma^2_P = .20 \times (-.0625 - .265)^2 + .50 \times (.225 - .265)^2 + .30 \times (.55 - .265)^2$$
$$= .0466$$

So the standard deviation is $\sqrt{.0466} = 21.59\%$.

13.3   If we compute the reward-to-risk ratios, we get $(22\% - 7\%)/1.8 = 8.33\%$ for Cooley versus 8.4% for Moyer. Relative to that of Cooley, Moyer's expected return is too high, so its price is too low.

If they are correctly priced, they must offer the same reward-to-risk ratio. The risk-free rate would have to be such that:

$$(22\% - R_f)/1.8 = (20.44\% - R_f)/1.6$$

With a little algebra, we find that the risk-free rate must be 8 percent:

$$22\% - R_f = (20.44\% - R_f)(1.8/1.6)$$
$$22\% - 20.44\% \times 1.125 = R_f - R_f \times 1.125$$
$$R_f = 8\%$$

13.4   Because the expected return on the market is 16 percent, the market risk premium is $16\% - 8\% = 8\%$. (the risk-free rate is 8 percent). The first stock has a beta of .7, so its expected return is $8\% + .7 \times 8\% = 13.6\%$.

For the second stock, notice that the risk premium is $24\% - 8\% = 16\%$. Because this is twice as large as the market risk premium, the beta must be exactly equal to 2. We can verify this using the CAPM:

$$E(R_i) = R_f + [E(R_M) - R_f] \times \beta_i$$
$$24\% = 8\% + (16\% - 8\%) \times \beta_i$$
$$\beta_i = 16\%/8\%$$
$$= 2.0$$

Concepts Review and Critical Thinking Questions

1.   (LO3) In broad terms, why is some risk diversifiable? Why are some risks nondiversifiable? Does it follow that an investor can control the level of unsystematic risk in a portfolio, but not the level of systematic risk?

2.   (LO3) Suppose the government announces that, based on a just-completed survey, the growth rate in the economy is likely to be 2 percent in the coming year, as compared to 5 percent for the year just completed. Will security prices in-

crease, decrease, or stay the same following this announcement? Does it make any difference whether or not the 2 percent figure was anticipated by the market? Explain.

3. **(LO3)** Classify the following events as mostly systematic or mostly unsystematic. Is the distinction clear in every case?

   a. Short-term interest rates increase unexpectedly.

   b. The interest rate a company pays on its short-term debt borrowing is increased by its bank.

   c. Oil prices unexpectedly decline.

   d. An oil tanker ruptures, creating a large oil spill.

   e. A manufacturer loses a multimillion-dollar product liability suit.

   f. A Supreme Court of Canada decision substantially broadens producer liability for injuries suffered by product users.

4. **(LO3)** Indicate whether the following events might cause stocks in general to change price, and whether they might cause Big Widget Corp.'s stock to change price.

   a. The government announces that inflation unexpectedly jumped by 2 percent last month.

   b. Big Widget's quarterly earnings report, just issued, generally fell in line with analysts' expectations.

   c. The government reports that economic growth last year was at 3 percent, which generally agreed with most economists' forecasts.

   d. The directors of Big Widget die in a plane crash.

   e. The Government of Canada approves changes to the tax code that will increase the top marginal corporate tax rate. The legislation had been debated for the previous six months.

5. **(LO1)** If a portfolio has a positive investment in every asset,

can the expected return on the portfolio be greater than that on every asset in the portfolio? Can it be less than that on every asset in the portfolio? If you answer yes to one or both of these questions, give an example to support your answer.

6. **(LO2)** True or false: The most important characteristic in determining the expected return of a well-diversified portfolio is the variances of the individual assets in the portfolio. Explain.

7. **(LO2)** If a portfolio has a positive investment in every asset, can the standard deviation on the portfolio be less than that on every asset in the portfolio? What about the portfolio beta?

8. **(LO4)** Is it possible that a risky asset could have a beta of zero? Explain. Based on the CAPM, what is the expected return on such an asset? Is it possible that a risky asset could have a negative beta? What does the CAPM predict about the expected return on such an asset? Can you give an explanation for your answer?

9. **(LO1)** In recent years, it has been common for companies to experience significant stock price changes in reaction to announcements of massive layoffs. Critics charge that such events encourage companies to fire long-time employees and that Bay Street is cheering them on. Do you agree or disagree?

10. **(LO1)** As indicated by a number of examples in this chapter, earnings announcements by companies are closely followed by, and frequently result in, share price revisions. Two issues should come to mind. First, earnings announcements concern past periods. If the market values stocks based on expectations of the future, why are numbers summarizing past performance relevant? Second, these announcements concern accounting earnings. Going back to Chapter 2, such earnings may have little to do with cash flow, so, again, why are they relevant?

Questions and Problems

Basic
(Questions 1–20)

1. **Determining Portfolio Weights (LO1)** What are the portfolio weights for a portfolio that has 145 shares of Stock A that sell for $45 per share and 110 shares of Stock B that sell for $27 per share?

2. **Portfolio Expected Return (LO1)** You own a portfolio that has $2,950 invested in Stock A and $3,700 invested in Stock B. If the expected returns on these stocks are 8 percent and 11 percent, respectively, what is the expected return on the portfolio?

3. **Portfolio Expected Return (LO1)** You own a portfolio that is 35 percent invested in Stock X, 20 percent in Stock Y, and 45 percent in Stock Z. The expected returns on these three stocks are 9 percent, 17 percent, and 13 percent, respectively. What is the expected return on the portfolio?

4. **Portfolio Expected Return (LO1)** You have $10,000 to invest in a stock portfolio. Your choices are Stock X with an expected return of 12 percent and Stock Y with an expected return of 9.5 percent. If your goal is to create a portfolio with an expected return of 11.1 percent, how much money will you invest in Stock X? In Stock Y?

5. **Calculating Expected Return (LO1)** Based on the following information, calculate the expected return:

State of Economy	Probability of State of Economy	Portfolio Return if State Occurs
Recession	.30	−.14
Boom	.70	.22

6. **Calculating Expected Return (LO1)** Based on the following information, calculate the expected return:

State of Economy	Probability of State of Economy	Portfolio Return if State Occurs
Recession	.20	−.18
Normal	.50	.11
Boom	.30	.29

7. **Calculating Returns and Standard Deviations (LO1)** Based on the following information, calculate the expected return and standard deviation for the two stocks:

State of Economy	Probability of State of Economy	Rate of Return if State Occurs	
		Stock A	Stock B
Recession	.20	.05	−.17
Normal	.55	.08	.12
Boom	.25	.13	.29

8. **Calculating Expected Returns (LO1)** A portfolio is invested 15 percent in Stock G, 55 percent in Stock J, and 30 percent in Stock K. The expected returns on these stocks are 8 percent, 14 percent, and 18 percent, respectively. What is the portfolio's expected return? How do you interpret your answer?

9. **Returns and Variances (LO1, 2)** Consider the following information:

State of Economy	Probability of State of Economy	Rate of Return if State Occurs		
		Stock A	Stock B	Stock C
Boom	.65	.07	.15	.33
Bust	.35	.13	.03	−.06

  a. What is the expected return on an equally weighted portfolio of these three stocks?

  b. What is the variance of a portfolio invested 20 percent each in A and B and 60 percent in C?

10. **Returns and Standard Deviations (LO1, 2)** Consider the following information:

State of Economy	Probability of State of Economy	Rate of Return if State Occurs		
		Stock A	Stock B	Stock C
Boom	.15	.35	.45	.27
Good	.55	.16	.10	.08
Poor	.25	−.01	−.06	−.04
Bust	.05	−.12	−.12	−.09

  a. Your portfolio is invested 30 percent each in A and C, and 40 percent in B. What is the expected return of the portfolio?

  b. What is the variance of this portfolio? The standard deviation?

11. **Calculating Portfolio Betas (LO4)** You own a stock portfolio invested 35 percent in Stock Q, 25 percent in Stock R, 30 percent in Stock S, and 10 percent in Stock T. The betas for these four stocks are .84, 1.17, 1.11, and 1.36, respectively. What is the portfolio beta?

12. **Calculating Portfolio Betas (LO4)** You own a portfolio equally invested in a risk-free asset and two stocks. If one of the stocks has a beta of 1.27 and the total portfolio is equally as risky as the market, what must the beta be for the other stock in your portfolio?

13. **Using CAPM (LO1, 4)** A stock has a beta of 1.05, the expected return on the market is 10 percent, and the risk-free rate is 3.8 percent. What must the expected return on this stock be?

14. **Using CAPM (LO1, 4)** A stock has an expected return of 10.2 percent, the risk-free rate is 4.5 percent, and the market risk premium is 7.5 percent. What must the beta of this stock be?

15. **Using CAPM (LO1, 4)** A stock has an expected return of 12.4 percent, its beta is 1.17, and the risk-free rate is 4.2 percent. What must the expected return on the market be?

16. **Using CAPM (LO4)** A stock has an expected return of 13.3 percent, its beta is 1.45, and the expected return on the market is 10.5 percent. What must the risk-free rate be?

17. **Using CAPM (LO1, 4)** A stock has a beta of 1.25 and an expected return of 14 percent. A risk-free asset currently earns 2.1 percent.

  a. What is the expected return on a portfolio that is equally invested in the two assets?

  b. If a portfolio of the two assets has a beta of .93, what are the portfolio weights?

  c. If a portfolio of the two assets has an expected return of 9 percent, what is its beta?

  d. If a portfolio of the two assets has a beta of 2.50, what are the portfolio weights? How do you interpret the weights for the two assets in this case? Explain.

18. **Using the SML (LO1, 4)** Asset W has an expected return of 12.8 percent and a beta of 1.25. If the risk-free rate is 4.1 percent, complete the following table for portfolios of Asset W and a risk-free asset. Illustrate the relationship between portfolio expected return and portfolio beta by plotting the expected returns against the betas. What is the slope of the line that results?

Percentage of Portfolio in Asset W	Portfolio Expected Return	Portfolio Beta
0%		
25		
50		
75		
100		
125		
150		

19. **Reward-to-Risk Ratios (LO4)** Stock Y has a beta of 1.3 and an expected return of 15.3 percent. Stock Z has a beta of .70 and an expected return of 9.3 percent. If the risk-free rate is 5.5 percent and the market risk premium is 6.8 percent, are these stocks correctly priced?

20. **Reward-to-Risk Ratios (LO4)** In the previous problem, what would the risk-free rate have to be for the two stocks to be correctly priced?

Intermediate 21. **Portfolio Returns (LO1, 2)** Using Table 12.4 from the previous chapter on capital market history, determine the return on a
(Questions portfolio that is equally invested in large-company stocks and long-term government bonds. What is the return on a portfolio
21–24) that is equally invested in small-company stocks and Treasury bills?

22. **CAPM (LO4)** Using the CAPM, show that the ratio of the risk premiums on two assets is equal to the ratio of their betas.

23. **Portfolio Returns and Deviations (LO1, 2)** Consider the following information about three stocks:

State of Economy	Probability of State of Economy	Rate of Return if State Occurs		
		Stock A	Stock B	Stock C
Boom	.20	.24	.36	.55
Normal	.55	.17	.13	.09
Bust	.25	.00	-.28	-.45

a. If your portfolio is invested 40 percent each in A and B and 20 percent in C, what is the portfolio expected return? The variance? The standard deviation?

b. If the expected T-bill rate is 3.80 percent, what is the expected risk premium on the portfolio?

c. If the expected inflation rate is 3.50 percent, what are the approximate and exact expected real returns on the portfolio? What are the approximate and exact expected real risk premiums on the portfolio?

24. **Analyzing a Portfolio (LO2)** You want to create a portfolio equally as risky as the market, and you have $1,000,000 to invest. Given this information, fill in the rest of the following table:

Asset	Investment	Beta
Stock A	$195,000	.95
Stock B	$340,000	1.15
Stock C		1.29
Risk-free asset		

Challenge 25. **Analyzing a Portfolio (LO2, 4)** You have $100,000 to invest in a portfolio containing Stock X and Stock Y. Your goal is to create
(Questions a portfolio that has an expected return of 17 percent. If Stock X has an expected return of 14.8 percent and a beta of 1.35, and
25–26) Stock Y has an expected return of 11.2 percent and a beta of .90, how much money will you invest in stock Y? How do you interpret your answer? What is the beta of your portfolio?

26. **Systematic versus Unsystematic Risk (LO3)** Consider the following information about Stocks I and II:

State of Economy	Probability of State of Economy	Rate of Return if State Occurs	
		Stock I	Stock II
Recession	.25	.02	−.25
Normal	.50	.21	.09
Irrational exuberance	.25	.06	.44

The market risk premium is 8 percent, and the risk-free rate is 4 percent. Which stock has the most systematic risk? Which one has the most unsystematic risk? Which stock is "riskier"? Explain.

27. **SML (LO4)** Suppose you observe the following situation:

Security	Beta	Expected Return
Pete Corp.	1.15	.129
Repete Co.	.84	.102

Assume these securities are correctly priced. Based on the CAPM, what is the expected return on the market? What is the risk-free rate?

28. **SML (LO1, 4)** Suppose you observe the following situation:

State of Economy	Probability of State	Return if State Occurs	
		Stock A	Stock B
Recession	.25	−.08	−.05
Normal	.60	.13	.14
Irrational exuberance	.15	.48	.29

a. Calculate the expected return on each stock.

b. Assuming the capital asset pricing model holds and stock A's beta is greater than stock B's beta by .25, what is the expected market risk premium?

Internet Application Questions

1. You have decided to invest in an equally weighted portfolio consisting of Petro-Canada, Royal Bank of Canada, Canadian Tire, and WestJet Airlines and need to find the beta of your portfolio. Go to finance.yahoo.com and follow the "Global Symbol Lookup" link to find the ticker symbols for each of these companies. Next, go back to finance.yahoo.com, enter one of the ticker symbols and get a stock quote. Follow the "Profile" link to find the beta for this company. You will then need to find the beta for each of the companies. What is the beta for your portfolio?

2. Go to money.msn.com and search for Reitmans Canada. Follow the "Quote" link to get the beta for the company. Go to bankofcanada.ca/rates/interest-rates/, and find the current interest rate for three-month treasury bills. Using this information, calculate the expected return on the market using the reward-to-risk ratio. What would be the expected stock price one year from now?

3. Recall that the site theglobeandmail.com/globe-investor/funds-and-etfs/funds/ contains considerable information on Canadian mutual funds. Visit the site and update the calculations in Example 13.12 to reflect the most recent three-year period.

4. You want to find the expected return for Bank of Montreal using the CAPM. First you need the market risk premium. Go to bmonesbittburns.com/economics/, and find "Daily Economic Update" under 'Publications'. Find the current interest rate for three-month Treasury bills. Use the average Canadian common stock return in Table 12.3 to calculate the market risk premium. If the beta for Bank of Montreal is 1.01, what is the expected return using CAPM?[20] What assumptions have you made to arrive at this number? As you may recall from Chapter 8, stock growth is often assumed to be equal to earnings growth. Compare your answer above with an EPS growth estimate from theglobeandmail.com/globe-investor/. What does this tell you about analyst estimates?

5. You have decided to invest in an equally weighted portfolio consisting of Rogers Communications, Bank of Montreal, and Goldcorp Inc. and need to find the beta of your portfolio. Go to finance.yahoo.com and follow the "Symbol Lookup" link to find the ticker symbols for each of these companies. Next, go back to finance.yahoo.com, enter one of the ticker symbols and get a stock quote. Follow the "Profile" link to find the beta for this company. You will then need to find the beta for each of the companies. What is the beta for your portfolio? (Note that this beta will compare the stock to the NYSE.)

6. Go to finance.yahoo.com and enter the ticker symbol RCI for Rogers Communication Inc. Follow the "Profile" link to get the beta for the company. Next, follow the "Research" link to find the estimated price in 12 months according to market analysts. Using the current share price and the mean target price, compute the expected return for this stock. Don't forget to include the expected dividend payments over the next year. Now go to money.cnn.com and find the current interest rate for three-month Treasury bills. Using this information, calculate the expected return on the market using the reward-to-risk ratio. Does this number make sense? Why or why not? (Note that the beta value you locate will compare Rogers Communication to the NYSE volatility. You should analyze this question from a U.S. perspective.)

APPENDIX 13A

DERIVATION OF THE CAPITAL ASSET PRICING MODEL

Up to this point, we have assumed that all assets on the efficient frontier are risky. Alternatively, an investor could easily combine a risky investment with an investment in a riskless or risk-free security, such as a Canada Treasury bill. Using the equation for portfolio variance (Equation 13A.1) we can find the variance of a portfolio with one risky and one risk-free asset:

$$\sigma^2_P = x^2_L \sigma^2_L + x^2_U \sigma^2_U + 2x_L x_U CORR_{L,U} \sigma_L \sigma_U \qquad [13A.1]$$

However, by definition, the risk-free asset (say, L in this example) has no variability so the equation for portfolio standard deviation reduces to:

$$\sigma^2_P = x^2_U \sigma^2_U$$
$$\sigma_P = \sqrt{\sigma^2_P} = x_U \sigma_U$$

The relationship between risk and return for one risky and one riskless asset is represented on a straight line between the risk-free rate and a pure investment in the risky asset as shown in Figure 13A.1. The line extends to the right of the point representing the risky asset when we assume the investor can borrow at the risk-free rate to take a leveraged position of more than 100 percent in the risky asset.

To form an optimal portfolio, an investor is likely to combine an investment in the riskless asset with a portfolio of risky assets. Figure 13A.1 illustrates our discussion by showing a risk-free asset and four risky assets: A, X, Q, and Y. If there is no riskless asset, the efficient set is the curve from X to Y. With a risk-free asset, it is possible to form portfolios like 1, 2, and 3 combining Q with the risk-free asset. Portfolios 4 and 5 combine the riskless asset with A.

---

[20] Note that if you have access to investment research services like those offered by TD Waterhouse or ScotiaMcLeod you could update the beta value by accessing their stock research section.

FIGURE 13A.1

Relationship between expected return and standard deviation for an investment in a combination of risky securities and the riskless asset

Portfolio Q is composed of
30 percent BCE
45 percent Bank of Montreal
25 percent Telus

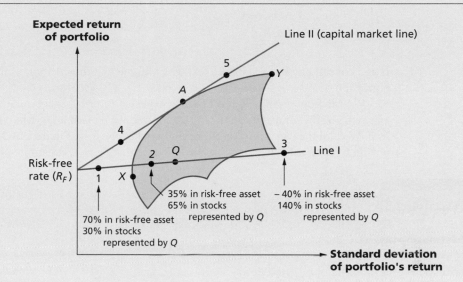

The graph illustrates an important point. With riskless borrowing and lending, the portfolio of risky assets held by any investor would always be point A. Regardless of the investor's tolerance for risk, he or she would never choose any other point on the efficient set of risky assets. Rather, an investor with a high aversion to risk would combine the securities of A with riskless assets. The investor would borrow at the risk-free rate to invest more funds in A had he or she low aversion to risk. In other words, all investors would choose portfolios along Line II, called the *capital market line*.

To move from our description of a single investor to market equilibrium, financial economists imagine a world where all investors possess the same estimates of expected returns, variance, and correlations. This assumption is called *homogeneous expectations*.

If all investors have homogeneous expectations, Figure 13A.1 becomes the same for all individuals. All investors sketch out the same efficient set of risky assets because they are working with the same inputs. This efficient set of risky assets is represented by the curve *XAY*. Because the same risk-free rate applies to everyone, all investors view point A as the portfolio of risky assets to be held. In a world with homogeneous expectations, all investors would hold the portfolio of risky assets represented by point A.

If all investors choose the same portfolio of risky assets, A, then A must be the market portfolio.[21] This is because, in our simplified world of homogeneous expectations, no asset would be demanded (and priced) if it were not in portfolio A. Since all assets have some demand and non-zero price, A has to be the market portfolio including all assets.

The variance of the market portfolio can be represented as:

$$\sigma^2_P \sum_{i=1}^{N} \sum_{j=1}^{N} x_j \sigma_{ij} \qquad [13A.2]$$

where we define σ_{ij} as the covariance of i with j if $i \neq j$ and σ_{ij} is the variance or σ^2_i if $i = j$.

$$\sigma_{ij} = CORR_{ij} \sigma_i \sigma_j$$

Using a little elementary calculus, we can represent a security's systematic risk (the contribution of security i to the risk of the market portfolio) by taking the partial derivative of the portfolio risk with respect to a change in the weight of the security. This measures the change in the portfolio variance when the weight of the security is increased slightly. For security 2,

$$\frac{\delta \sigma^2_P}{\delta x_2} = 2 \sum_{j=1}^{N} x_j \sigma_{i2} = 2 \left[x_1 COV(R_1, R_2) + x_2 \sigma^2_2 + x_3 COV(R_3, R_2) + \dots + x_N COV(R_N, R_2) \right] \qquad [13A.3]$$

---

[21] A market portfolio is a theoretical portfolio that includes every available type of asset at a level proportional to its market value.

The term within brackets in (Equation 13A.3) is $COV(R_2,R_M)$. This shows that systematic risk is proportional to a security's covariance with the market portfolio.

The final step is to standardize systematic risk by dividing by the variance of the market portfolio. The result is β_2 as presented in the text.

$$\beta_2 = \frac{COV(R_2,R_M)}{\sigma^2(R_M)} \qquad [13A.4]$$

If you consult any basic statistics text, you will see that this formula is identical to the β_2 obtained from a regression of R_2 on R_M.

We can now redraw Figure 13A.1 in expected return-β space, as shown in Figure 13A.2. The vertical axis remains the same, but on the horizontal axis we replace total risk (σ) with systematic risk as measured by β. We plot the two points on the capital market line from Figure 13A.1: R_F with $\beta = 0$ and M (the market portfolio represented by A) with a $\beta = 1$. To see that $\beta_M = 1$, substitute portfolio M for i in Equation 13A.4.

FIGURE 13A.2

Relationship between expected return on an individual security and beta of the security

R_F is the risk-free rate.
$\overline{R}_M$ is the expected return on the market portfolio.

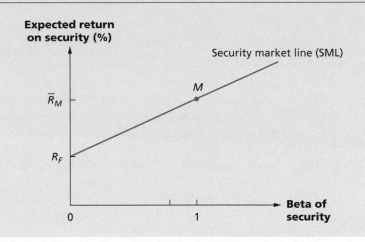

$$\beta_M = \frac{COV(R_M, R_M)}{\sigma^2(R_M)}$$
$$= \frac{CORR_{M,M}\sigma_M\sigma_M}{\sigma^2(R_M)}$$
$$= \frac{1.0 \times \sigma2_M}{\sigma^2(R_M)}$$
$$\beta_M = 1.0$$

The result is the security market line shown in Figure 13A.2. We can use the slope-intercept method to find that the intercept of the SML is R_F and the slope is $(R_M - R_F)$. The equation for the SML is:

$$E(R) = R_F + \beta(R_M - R_F)$$

And this completes the derivation of the capital asset pricing model.

Appendix Questions and Problems

A.1 A mutual fund A has a standard deviation of 13 percent (assume this fund to be on the efficient frontier; i.e., the fund plots on the capital market line). The risk-free rate is 3 percent. The standard deviation of the market's return is 18 percent, and the expected return on the market is 15 percent. What is the expected return on the mutual fund A?

PART 6

CHAPTER 14

COST OF CAPITAL

Resolute Forest Products Inc., formerly known as AbitibiBowater Inc., is a global leader in the forest products industry with a diverse range of products, including newsprint, commercial printing paper, market pulp, and wood products. 2010 proved to be a pivotal year for Resolute, as the Montreal-based firm successfully completed its restructuring plan. The objective of the restructuring plan was to focus on top-performing facilities by closing or idling 3.4 million tonnes of paper capacity and to capitalize on export market opportunities and promising growth markets for paper used in catalogues, magazine inserts, direct mail, inkjet paper, and paper packaging. In order to evaluate expansion opportunities, Resolute needs to know the cost of capital.

A lower cost of capital helps firms to compete effectively and move towards the goal of wealth maximization for the shareholders. In this chapter, we learn how to compute a firm's cost of capital and find out what it means to a firm and its investors.

Learning Objectives ▶

After studying this chapter, you should understand:

LO1 How to determine a firm's cost of equity capital.

LO2 How to determine a firm's cost of debt.

LO3 How to determine a firm's overall cost of capital.

LO4 How to correctly include flotation costs in capital budgeting projects.

LO5 Some of the pitfalls associated with a firm's overall cost of capital and what to do about them.

Suppose you have just become the president of a large company and the first decision you face is whether to go ahead with a plan to renovate the company's warehouse distribution system. The plan will cost the company $50 million, and it is expected to save $12 million per year after taxes over the next six years.

This is a familiar problem in capital budgeting. To address it, you would determine the relevant cash flows, discount them, and, if the net present value (NPV) is positive, take on the project; if the NPV is negative, you would scrap it. So far so good, but what should you use as the discount rate?

From our discussion of risk and return, you know that the correct discount rate depends on the riskiness of the warehouse distribution system. In particular, the new project would have a positive NPV only if its return exceeds what the financial markets offer on investments of similar risks. We called this minimum required return the cost of capital associated with the project.

Thus, to make the right decision as president, you must examine the returns that investors expect to earn on the securities represented in the pool of funds that would finance the project. You then use this information to arrive at an estimate of the project's cost of capital. Our primary purpose in this chapter is to describe how to do this. There are a variety of approaches to this task, and a number of conceptual and practical issues arise.

One of the most important concepts we develop is the weighted average cost of capital (WACC). This is the cost of capital for the firm as a whole, and it can be interpreted as the required return on the overall firm. In discussing the WACC, we recognize the fact that a firm normally raises capital in a variety of forms and that these different forms of capital may have different costs associated with them.

We also recognize in this chapter that taxes are an important consideration in determining the required return on an investment, because we are always interested in valuing the after-tax cash flows from a project. We therefore discuss how to incorporate taxes explicitly into our estimates of the cost of capital.

14.1 | The Cost of Capital: Some Preliminaries

In Chapter 13, we developed the security market line (SML) and used it to explore the relationship between the expected return on a security and its systematic risk. We concentrated on how the risky returns from buying securities looked from the viewpoint of, for example, a shareholder in the firm. This helped us understand more about the alternatives available to an investor in the capital markets.

In this chapter, we turn things around and look more closely at the other side of the problem, which is how these returns and securities look from the viewpoint of the companies that issue them. Note that the return an investor in a security receives is the cost of that security to the company that issued it.

Required Return versus Cost of Capital

When we say that the required return on an investment is, say, 10 percent, we usually mean the investment has a positive NPV only if its return exceeds 10 percent. Another way of interpreting the required return is to observe that the firm must earn 10 percent on the investment just to compensate its investors for the use of the capital needed to finance the project. This is why we could also say that 10 percent is the cost of capital associated with the investment.

To illustrate the point further, imagine that we were evaluating a risk-free project. In this case, how to determine the required return is obvious: We look at the capital markets and observe the current rate offered by risk-free investments, and we use this rate to discount the project's cash flows. Thus, the cost of capital for a risk-free investment is the risk-free rate.

If this project were risky, then, assuming that all the other information is unchanged, the required return is obviously higher. In other words, the cost of capital for this project, if it is risky, is greater than the risk-free rate, and the appropriate discount rate would exceed the risk-free rate.

We henceforth use the terms *required return*, *appropriate discount rate*, and *cost of capital* more or less interchangeably because, as the discussion in this section suggests, they all mean essentially the same thing. The key fact to grasp is that the cost of capital associated with an investment depends on the risk of that investment. This is one of the most important lessons in corporate finance, so it bears repeating: *The cost of capital depends primarily on the use of the funds, not the source. The use of the funds refers to risk associated with the investment.*

It is a common error to forget this crucial point and fall into the trap of thinking that the cost of capital for an investment depends primarily on how and where the capital is raised.

Financial Policy and Cost of Capital

We know that the particular mixture of debt and equity that a firm chooses to employ—its capital structure—is a managerial variable. In this chapter, we take the firm's financial policy as given. In particular, we assume the firm has a fixed debt/equity ratio that it maintains. This *D/E* ratio reflects the firm's target capital structure. How a firm might choose that ratio is the subject of Chapter 16.

From our discussion, we know that a firm's overall cost of capital reflects the required return on the firm's assets as a whole. Given that a firm uses both debt and equity capital, this overall cost of capital is a mixture of the returns needed to compensate its creditors and its shareholders. In other words, a firm's cost of capital reflects both its cost of debt capital and its cost of equity capital. We discuss these costs separately in the following sections.

14.2 | The Cost of Equity

cost of equity
The return that equity investors require on their investment in the firm.

We begin with the most difficult question on the subject of cost of capital: What is the firm's overall **cost of equity**? The reason this is a difficult question is that there is no way of directly observing the return that the firm's equity investors require on their investment. Instead, we must somehow estimate it. This section discusses two approaches to determining the cost of equity: the dividend growth model approach and the security market line (SML) approach.

The Dividend Growth Model Approach

The easiest way to estimate the cost of equity capital is to use the dividend growth model that we developed in Chapter 8. Recall that, under the assumption that the firm's dividend will grow at a constant rate, g, the price per share of the stock, P_0, can be written as:

$$P_0 = \frac{D_0 \times (1 + g)}{[R_E - g]} = \frac{D_1}{[R_E - g]}$$

where D_0 is the dividend just paid, and D_1 is the next period's projected dividend. Notice that we have used the symbol R_E (the E stands for equity) for the required return on the stock.

As we discussed in Chapter 8, we can arrange this to solve for R_E as follows:

$$R_E = (D_1/P_0) + g \qquad [14.1]$$

Since R_E is the return that the shareholders require on the stock, it can be interpreted as the firm's cost of equity capital.

IMPLEMENTING THE APPROACH   To estimate R_E using the dividend growth model approach, we obviously need three pieces of information: P_0, D_0, and g.[1] Of these, for a publicly traded, dividend-paying company, the first two can be observed directly, so they are easily obtainable. Only the third component, the expected growth rate in dividends, must be estimated.

For example, suppose Provincial Power Company, a large public utility, paid a dividend of $4 per share last year. The stock currently sells for $60 per share. You estimate the dividend will grow steadily at 6 percent per year into the indefinite future. What is the cost of equity capital for Provincial Power? Using the dividend growth model, the expected dividend for the coming year, D_1 is:

$$\begin{aligned}
D_1 &= D_0 \times (1 + g) \\
&= \$4 \times (1.06) \\
&= \$4.24
\end{aligned}$$

Given this, the cost of equity, R_E, is:

$$\begin{aligned}
R_E &= D_1/P_0 + g \\
&= \$4.24/\$60 + .06 \\
&= 13.07\%
\end{aligned}$$

The cost of equity is thus 13.07 percent.

ESTIMATING g To use the dividend growth model, we must come up with an estimate for g, the growth rate. There are essentially two ways of doing this: (1) use historical growth rates, or (2) use analysts' forecasts of future growth rates. Analysts' forecasts are available from the re-

---

[1] Notice that if we have D_0 and g, we can simply calculate D_1 by multiplying D_0 by $(1 + g)$.

search departments of investment dealers. Naturally, different sources have different estimates, so one approach might be to obtain multiple estimates and then average them.

Alternatively, we might observe dividends for the previous, say, five years, and calculate the compound growth rate. For example, suppose we observe the following for the James Bay Company:

Year	Dividend
2008	$1.10
2009	1.20
2010	1.35
2011	1.40
2012	1.55

The compound growth rate, g, is the rate at which $1.10 grew to $1.55 during four periods of growth.

$$\$1.10 \, (1 + g)^4 = \$1.55$$
$$(1 + g)^4 = \$1.55/\$1.10 = 1.4090$$
$$1 + g = (1.4090)^{0.25} = 1.0895$$
$$g = 0.0895 = 8.95\%$$

If historical growth has been volatile, the compound growth rate would be sensitive to our choice of beginning and ending years. In this case, it is better to calculate the year-to-year growth rates and average them.

Year	Dividend	Dollar Change	Percentage Change
2008	$1.10	—	—
2009	1.20	$.10	9.09%
2010	1.35	.15	12.50
2011	1.40	.05	3.70
2012	1.55	.15	10.71

Notice that we calculated the change in the dividend on a year-to-year basis and then expressed the change as a percentage. Thus, in 2009 for example, the dividend rose from $1.10 to $1.20, an increase of $.10. This represents a $.10/1.10 = 9.09% increase.

If we average the four growth rates, the result is (9.09 + 12.50 + 3.70 + 10.71)/4 = 9%, so we could use this as an estimate for the expected growth rate, g. In this case, averaging annual growth rates gives about the same answer as the compound growth rate. Other more sophisticated statistical techniques could be used, but they all amount to using past dividend growth to predict future dividend growth.[2]

AN ALTERNATIVE APPROACH   Another way to find g starts with earnings retention. Consider a business whose earnings next year are expected to be the same as earnings this year unless a net investment is made. The net investment will be positive only if some earnings are not paid out as dividends, that is, only if some earnings are retained. This leads to the following equation:

Earnings next year = Earnings this year + Retained earnings this year
× Return on retained earnings

The increase in earnings is a function of both the retained earnings and the return on retained earnings.

We now divide both sides of the equation by earnings this year yielding

$$\frac{\text{Earnings next year}}{\text{Earnings this year}}$$
$$= \frac{\text{Earnings this year}}{\text{Earnings this year}} + \frac{\text{Retained earnings this year}}{\text{Earnings this year}} \times \text{Return on retained earnings}$$

---

[2] Statistical techniques for calculating g include linear regression, geometric averaging, and exponential smoothing.

retention ratio
Retained earnings divided by
net income.

The left side of the last equation is simply one plus the growth rate in earnings, which we write as $1 + g$.[3] The ratio of retained earnings to earnings is called the **retention ratio**. Thus we can write:

$$1 + g = 1 + \text{Retention ratio} \times \text{Return on retained earnings}$$

return on equity (ROE)
Net income after interest and
taxes divided by average
common shareholders'
equity.

It is difficult for a financial analyst to determine the return to be expected on currently retained earnings, because the details on forthcoming projects are not generally public information. However, it is frequently assumed that the projects selected in the current year have the same risk and therefore the same anticipated return as projects in other years. Here, we can estimate the anticipated return on current retained earnings by the historical **return on equity (ROE)**. After all, ROE is simply the return on the firm's entire equity, which is the return on the accumulation of all the firm's past projects.

We now have a simple way to estimate growth:

$$g = \text{Retention ratio} \times \text{ROE}$$

ADVANTAGES AND DISADVANTAGES OF THE APPROACH Whichever way we estimate g, the primary advantage of the dividend growth model approach is its simplicity. It is both easy to understand and easy to use. There are a number of associated practical problems and disadvantages.

First and foremost, the dividend growth model is most applicable to companies that pay dividends. For companies that do not pay dividends, we can use the model and estimate g from growth in earnings. This is equivalent to assuming that one day dividends will be paid. Either way, the key underlying assumption is that the dividend grows at a constant rate. As our previous example illustrates, this will never be exactly the case. More generally, the model is really only applicable to cases where reasonably steady growth is likely to occur.

A second problem is that the estimated cost of equity is very sensitive to the estimated growth rate. An upward revision of g by just 1 percentage point, for example, increases the estimated cost of equity by at least a full percentage point. Since D_1 would probably be revised upwards as well, the increase would actually be somewhat larger than that.

Finally, this approach really does not explicitly consider risk. Unlike the SML approach (which we consider next), there is no direct adjustment for the riskiness of the investment. For example, there is no allowance for the degree of certainty or uncertainty surrounding the estimated growth rate in dividends. As a result, it is difficult to say whether or not the estimated return is commensurate with the level of risk.[4]

The SML Approach

In Chapter 13, we discussed the security market line (SML). Our primary conclusion was that the required or expected return on a risky investment depends on three things:

1. The risk-free rate, R_f.
2. The market risk premium, $E(R_M) - R_f$.
3. The systematic risk of the asset relative to average, which we called its beta coefficient, β.

Using the SML, the expected return on the company's equity, $E(R_E)$, can be written as:

$$E(R_E) = R_f + \beta_E \times [E(R_M) - R_f]$$

where β_E is the estimated beta for the equity. For the SML approach to be consistent with the dividend growth model, we drop the expectation sign, E, and henceforth write the required return from the SML, R_E, as:

$$R_E = R_f + \beta_E \times [R_M - R_f] \tag{14.2}$$

---

[3] Previously g referred to growth in dividends. However, the growth in earnings is equal to the growth rate in dividends in this context, because we assume the ratio of dividends to earnings is held constant.

[4] There is an implicit adjustment for risk because the current stock price is used. All other things being equal, the higher the risk, the lower the stock price. Further, the lower the stock price, the greater the cost of equity, again assuming all the other information is the same.

IMPLEMENTING THE APPROACH   To use the SML approach, we need a risk-free rate, R_f, an estimate of the market risk premium, $R_M - R_f$, and an estimate of the relevant beta, β_E. In Chapter 12 (Table 12.3), we saw that one estimate of the market risk premium (based on large capitalization Canadian common stocks) is around 4.30 percent. To reflect the long-term horizon over which we will apply the cost of equity, we measure the risk-free rate as the yield on 30-year Canada bonds around 5 percent.[5] Beta coefficients for publicly traded companies are widely available. Chapter 13 showed how to calculate betas from historical returns.

To illustrate, in Chapter 13 we saw that Investors Group had an estimated beta of 0.76 (Table 13.10). We could thus estimate Investors Group's cost of equity as:

$$R_{CU} = R_f + \beta \times [R_M - R_f]$$
$$= 5.0\% + 0.76 \times (4.30\%)$$
$$= 8.27\%$$

Thus, using the SML approach, Investors Group's cost of equity is about 8.27 percent.

ADVANTAGES AND DISADVANTAGES OF THE APPROACH   The SML approach has two primary advantages: First, it explicitly adjusts for risk. Second, it is applicable to companies other than those with steady dividend growth. Thus, it may be useful in a wider variety of circumstances.

There are drawbacks, of course. The SML approach requires that two things be estimated, the market risk premium and the beta coefficient. To the extent that our estimates are poor, the resulting cost of equity is inaccurate. For example, our estimate of the market risk premium, 4.30 percent, is based on about 50 years of returns on a particular portfolio of stocks. Using different time periods or different stocks could result in very different estimates.

Finally, as with the dividend growth model, we essentially rely on the past to predict the future when we use the SML approach. Economic conditions can change very quickly, so, as always, the past may not be a good guide to the future. On balance, the SML approach is considered to be "best practice" and is used most widely according to a survey of CFOs.[6] The dividend valuation model may be used as a check on the reasonableness of the SML result. We might also wish to compare the results to those for other, similar companies as a reality check.

For example, the SML approach provides useful estimates of the cost of equity for banks in different countries. On a global scale, the cost of equity estimates declined steadily from 1999 to 2005 and then increased from 2006 onward.[7]

The Cost of Equity in Rate Hearings

Suppose that Provincial Power, a regulated utility, has just applied for increases in the rates charged some of its customers. One test that regulators apply is called the "fair rate of return" rule. This means that they determine the fair rate of return on capital for the company and allow an increase in rates only if the company can show that revenues are insufficient to achieve this fair rate. For example, suppose a company had capital in the form of equity of $100 and net income of $8 providing a return of 8 percent. If the fair rate of return were 9 percent, the company would be allowed a rate increase sufficient to generate one additional dollar of net income.

Regulatory authorities determine the fair rate of return after hearing presentations by the company and by consumer groups. Since a higher fair rate of return helps make the case for rate increases, it is no surprise to find that consultants engaged by the company argue for a higher fair rate and consultants representing consumer groups argue for a lower fair rate. Because the fair rate of return depends on capital market conditions, consultants use the dividend growth approach and the SML approach, along with other techniques.

Suppose that Provincial Power has presented the regulators with a cost of equity of 11 percent. You are a consultant for a consumer group. What flaws would you look for?

---

[5] At the time of writing in May 2012, the 30-year Canada rate was 2.55 percent. Because many analysts believed that this rate was artificially low due to the relaxed monetary policy of the Bank of Canada, we use 5 percent.

[6] J.R. Graham and C.R. Harvey, "Theory and practice for corporate finance: evidence from the field," *Journal of Financial Economics* 60 (2001), pp. 187–243.

[7] Michael R King, 2009. "The cost of equity for global banks: a CAPM perspective from 1990 to 2009," *BIS Quarterly Review, Bank for International Settlements*, September.

If you think that the cost of equity is too high, you should challenge the assumed growth rate in dividends. Also, the market risk premium used in the SML may be too high.[8] If you are clever at working with these models and can remain unruffled when testifying, you may have career potential as a financial expert witness.

EXAMPLE 14.1: The Cost of Equity

At the time of writing, stock in Sun Life Financial Inc. was trading on the TSX at $22.34. Sun Life had a 120-month beta of 0.78. The market risk premium historically has been around 4.30 percent and our estimate of the risk-free rate in 2012 was 5.00 percent. Sun Life's last dividend was $1.44 and some analysts expected that the dividends would grow at 8 percent indefinitely. What is Sun Life's cost of equity?

$$R_E = R_f + \beta_E \times [R_M - R_f]$$
$$= 5.00\% + 0.78 \times 4.30\%$$
$$= 8.35\%$$

This suggests that 8.35 percent is Sun Life's cost of equity. We next use the dividend growth model as a check. The projected dividend is $D_0 \times (1 + g) = \$1.44 \times (1.08) = \$1.56$, so the expected return using this approach is:

$$R_E = D_1/P_0 + g$$
$$= \$1.56/\$22.34 + 0.08$$
$$= 14.98\%$$

Our two estimates differ significantly, so we will use the one in which we have the greater confidence—the SML. If the inputs are fairly reliable for the SML, it is preferred over the growth model, which may not apply in all companies. One key reason for this preference is that the SML considers risk (as measured by beta), while the growth model does not. We should also note that in our example the 8 percent indefinite growth rate seems quite high, so the dividend growth model may be overestimating the cost of equity. In this case, this gives us a cost of equity for Sun Life Financial Inc. of 8.35 percent.

Concept Questions

1. What do we mean when we say that a corporation's cost of equity capital is 16 percent?
2. What are two approaches to estimating the cost of equity capital?

14.3 | The Costs of Debt and Preferred Stock

In addition to ordinary equity, firms use debt and, to a lesser extent, preferred stock to finance their investments. As we discuss next, determining the costs of capital associated with these sources of financing is much easier than determining the cost of equity.

The Cost of Debt

cost of debt
The return that lenders require on the firm's debt.

The **cost of debt** is the return that the firm's long-term creditors demand on new borrowing. In principle, we could determine the beta for the firm's debt and then use the SML to estimate the required return on debt just as we estimate the required return on equity. This isn't really necessary, however.

Unlike a firm's cost of equity, its cost of debt can normally be observed either directly or indirectly, because the cost of debt is simply the interest rate the firm must pay on new borrowing, and we can observe interest rates in the financial markets. For example, if the firm already has bonds outstanding, then the yield to maturity on those bonds is the market-required rate on the firm's debt.

Alternatively, if we knew that the firm's bonds were rated, say, A, we can simply find out what the interest rate on newly issued A-rated bonds is. Either way, there is no need to actually estimate a beta for the debt since we can directly observe the rate we want to know.

---

[8] If you were the consultant for the company, you should counter that, at the time of writing, long-term bonds issued by Canadian utilities were yielding around 6.6 percent. Since equity is riskier than bonds, the cost of equity should be higher than 6.6 percent.

There is one thing to be careful about, though. The coupon rate on the firm's outstanding debt is irrelevant here. That just tells us roughly what the firm's cost of debt was back when the bonds were issued, not what the cost of debt is today.[9] This is why we have to look at the yield on the debt in today's marketplace. For consistency with our other notation, we use the symbol R_D for the cost of debt.

EXAMPLE 14.2: The Cost of Debt

At the time of writing, Encana Corporation had a bond outstanding with approximately 6 years to maturity (12 semi-annual coupons) and a coupon rate of 5.80 percent. The bond was currently selling for $112.22. What is Encana's cost of debt?

To answer this question, we need to solve the bond pricing formula for R, the yield to maturity:

$$\$112.22 = \sum_{t=1}^{12} \$2.9/\left(1 + \frac{R}{2}\right)^t + 100/\left(1 + \frac{R}{2}\right)^{12}$$

Using a spreadsheet or a financial calculator, we find that R is 3.52 percent. Encana's cost of debt is thus 3.52 percent.

The Cost of Preferred Stock

Determining the cost of fixed rate preferred stock is quite straightforward. As we discussed in Chapters 7 and 8, this type of preferred stock has a fixed dividend paid every period forever, so a share of preferred stock is essentially a perpetuity. The cost of preferred stock, R_P, is thus:

$$R_P = D/P_0 \qquad [14.3]$$

where D is the fixed dividend and P_0 is the current price per share of the preferred stock. Notice that the cost of preferred stock is simply equal to the dividend yield on the preferred stock. Alternatively, preferred stocks are rated in much the same way as bonds, so the cost of preferred stock can be estimated by observing the required returns on other, similarly rated shares of preferred stock.

EXAMPLE 14.3: Aimia's Cost of Preferred Stock

On May 09, 2012, Aimia Inc.'s preferred stock (AIM.PR.A) traded on the TSX with a dividend of $1.63 annually and a price of $26.00. What is Aimia's cost of preferred stock?

The cost of preferred stock is:

$$R_P = D/P_0$$
$$= \$1.63/\$26$$
$$= 6.3\%$$

So Aimia's cost of preferred stock is 6.3%.

Concept Questions

1. How can the cost of debt be calculated?
2. How can the cost of preferred stock be calculated?
3. Why is the coupon rate a bad estimate of a firm's cost of debt?

14.4 | The Weighted Average Cost of Capital

Now that we have the costs associated with the main sources of capital that the firm employs, we need to worry about the specific mix. As we mentioned earlier, we take this mix (the firm's capital structure) as given for now.

One of the implications of using WACC for a project is that we are assuming that money is

---

[9] The firm's cost of debt based on its historic borrowing is sometimes called the *embedded debt cost*.

raised in the optimal proportions. For instance, if the optimal weight for debt is 25 percent, raising $100 million means that $25 million will come from new debt and $75 million from common and preferred shares. Practically speaking, the firm would not raise these sums simultaneously by issuing both debt and equity. Instead, the firm may issue just debt, or just equity, which, at that point, has the effect of upsetting the optimal debt ratio. Issuing just one type of security and temporarily upsetting the optimal weights presents no problem as long as a subsequent issue takes the firm back to the optimal ratio for which it is striving. The point is that the firm's capital structure weights may fluctuate within some range in the short term, but the target weights should always be used in computing WACC.

In Chapter 3, we mentioned that financial analysts frequently focus on a firm's total capitalization, which is the sum of its long-term debt and equity. This is particularly true in determining the cost of capital; short-term liabilities are often ignored in the process. Some short-term liabilities such as accounts payable and accrued wages rise automatically with sales increases and have already been incorporated into cash flow estimates. We ignore them in calculating the cost of capital to avoid the error of double counting. Other current liabilities, short-term bank borrowing for example, are excluded because they support seasonal needs and are not part of the permanent capital structure.[10]

The Capital Structure Weights

We use the symbol E (for equity) to stand for the market value of the firm's equity. We calculate this by taking the number of shares outstanding and multiplying it by the price per share. Similarly, we use the symbol D_m (for debt) to stand for the market value of the firm's debt. For long-term debt, we calculate this by multiplying the market price of a single bond by the number of bonds outstanding.

For multiple bond issues (as there normally would be), we repeat this calculation for each and then add the results. If there is debt that is not publicly traded (because it was privately placed with a life insurance company, for example), we must observe the yields on similar, publicly traded debt and estimate the market value of the privately held debt using this yield as the discount rate.

Finally, we use the symbol V (for value) to stand for the combined market value of the debt and equity:

$$V = E + D_m \qquad\qquad [14.4]$$

If we divide both sides by V, we can calculate the percentages of the total capital represented by the debt and equity:

$$100\% = E/V + D_m/V \qquad\qquad [14.5]$$

These percentages can be interpreted just like portfolio weights, and they are often called the capital structure weights.

For example, if the total market value of a company's stock were calculated as $200 million and the total market value of the company's debt were calculated as $50 million, the combined value would be $250 million. Of this total, $E/V = \$200/250 = 80\%$, so 80 percent of the firm's financing is equity and the remaining 20 percent is debt.

We emphasize here that the correct way to proceed is to use the market values of the debt and equity. The reason is that, as we discussed in Chapters 1 and 2, market values measure management's success in achieving its goal: maximizing shareholder wealth. Under certain circumstances, such as a privately owned company, it may not be possible to get reliable estimates of these quantities. Even for publicly traded firms, market value weights present some difficulties. If there is a major shift in stock or bond prices, market value weights may fluctuate significantly so that the **weighted average cost of capital (WACC)** is quite another number by the time a weekend is over. In fact, because practitioners encounter some of these difficulties in computing WACC using market value weights, book values are usually the better alternative when market values are not readily available.

weighted average cost of capital (WACC)
The weighted average of the costs of debt and equity.

---

[10] If a firm used short-term bank loans as part of its permanent financing, we would include their cost as part of the cost of debt.

Taxes and the Weighted Average Cost of Capital

There is one final issue associated with the WACC. We called the preceding result the unadjusted WACC because we haven't considered taxes. Recall that we are always concerned with after-tax cash flows. If we are determining the discount rate appropriate to those cash flows, the discount rate also needs to be expressed on an after-tax basis.

As we discussed previously in various places in this book (and as we discuss later), the interest paid by a corporation is deductible for tax purposes. Payments to shareholders, such as dividends, are not. What this means, effectively, is that the government pays some of the interest provided the firm expects to have positive taxable income. Thus, in determining an after-tax discount rate, we need to distinguish between the pre-tax and the after-tax cost of debt.

To illustrate, suppose a firm borrows $1 million at 9 percent interest. The corporate tax rate is 40 percent. What is the after-tax interest rate on this loan? The total interest bill would be $90,000 per year. This amount is tax deductible, however, so the $90,000 interest reduces our tax bill by .40 × $90,000 = $36,000. The after-tax interest bill is thus $90,000 − 36,000 = $54,000. The after-tax interest rate is $54,000/$1 million = 5.4%.

Notice that, in general, the after-tax interest rate is simply equal to the pre-tax rate multiplied by one minus the tax rate. For example, using the preceding numbers, we find that the after-tax interest rate is 9% × (1 − .40) = 5.4%.

If we use the symbol T_C to stand for the corporate tax rate, the after-tax rate that we use in our WACC calculation can be written as $R_D \times (1 - T_C)$. Thus, once we consider the effect of taxes, the WACC is:

$$\text{WACC} = (E/V) \times R_E + (P/V) \times R_P + (D_m/V) \times R_D \times (1 - T_C) \qquad [14.6]$$

From now on, when we speak of the WACC, this is the number we have in mind.

This WACC has a very straightforward interpretation. It is the overall return that the firm must earn on its existing assets to maintain the value of its stock. It is also the required return on any investments by the firm that have essentially the same risks as existing operations. So, if we were evaluating the cash flows from a proposed expansion of our existing operations, this is the discount rate we would use.

EXAMPLE 14.4: Calculating the WACC

The B. B. Lean Company has 1.4 million shares of stock outstanding. The stock currently sells for $20 per share. The firm's debt is publicly traded and was recently quoted at 93 percent of face value. It has a total face value of $5 million, and it is currently priced to yield 11 percent. The risk-free rate is 8 percent, and the market risk premium is 3.4 percent. You've estimated that Lean has a beta of .74. If the corporate tax rate is 40 percent, what is the WACC of Lean Co.?

We can first determine the cost of equity and the cost of debt. From the SML, the cost of equity is 8% + .74 × 3.4% = 10.52%. The total value of the equity is 1.4 million × $20 = $28 million. The pre-tax cost of debt is the current yield to maturity on the outstanding debt, 11 percent. The debt sells for 93 percent of its face value, so its current mar-

ket value is .93 × $5 million = $4.65 million. The total market value of the equity and debt together is $28 + 4.65 = $32.65 million.

From here, we can calculate the WACC easily enough. The percentage of equity used by Lean to finance its operations is $28/$32.65 = 85.76%. Because the weights have to add up to 1, the percentage of debt is 1 − .8576 = 14.24%. The WACC is thus:

$$\begin{aligned} \text{WACC} &= (E/V) \times R_E + (D_m/V) \times R_D \times (1 - T_C) \\ &= .8576 \times 10.52\% + .1424 \times 11\% \times (1 - .40) \\ &= 9.96\% \end{aligned}$$

B. B. Lean thus has an overall weighted average cost of capital of 9.96 percent.

Solving the Warehouse Problem and Similar Capital Budgeting Problems

Now we can use the WACC to solve the warehouse problem that we posed at the beginning of the chapter. However, before we rush to discount the cash flows at the WACC to estimate NPV, we need to make sure we are doing the right thing.

Going back to first principles, we must find an alternative in the financial markets that is comparable to the warehouse renovation. To be comparable, an alternative must be of the same risk as the warehouse project. Projects that have the same risk are said to be in the same risk class.

The WACC for a firm reflects the risk and the target capital structure of the firm's existing assets as a whole. As a result, strictly speaking, the firm's WACC is the appropriate discount rate only if the proposed investment is a replica of the firm's existing operating activities.

In broader terms, whether or not we can use the firm's WACC to value the warehouse project depends on whether the warehouse project is in the same risk class as the firm. We assume that this project is an integral part of the overall business of the firm. In such cases, it is natural to think that the cost savings are as risky as the general cash flows of the firm, and the project is thus in the same risk class as the overall firm. More generally, projects like the warehouse renovation that are intimately related to the firm's existing operations are often viewed as being in the same risk class as the overall firm.

We can now see what the president should do. Suppose the firm has a target debt/equity ratio of 1/3. In this case, E/V is .75 and D_m/V is .25. The cost of debt is 10 percent, and the cost of equity is 20 percent. Assuming a 40 percent tax rate, the WACC is:

$$
\begin{aligned}
\text{WACC} &= (E/V) \times R_E + (D_m/V) \times (R_D \times (1 - T_C)) \\
&= .75 \times 20\% + .25 \times 10\% \times (1 - .40) \\
&= 16.5\%
\end{aligned}
$$

Recall that the warehouse project had a cost of $50 million and expected after-tax cash flows (the cost savings) of $12 million per year for six years. The NPV is thus:

$$
\text{NPV} = -\$50 + \$12/(1 + \text{WACC})^1 + \dots + \$12/(1 + \text{WACC})^6
$$

Since the cash flows are in the form of an ordinary annuity, we can calculate this NPV using 16.5 percent (the WACC) as the discount rate as follows:

$$
\begin{aligned}
\text{NPV} &= -\$50 + \$12 \times [1 - (1/(1 + 0.165)^6)]/0.165 \\
&= -\$50 + \$12 \times 3.6365 \\
&= -\$6.36
\end{aligned}
$$

Should the firm take on the warehouse renovation? The project has a negative NPV using the firm's WACC. This means the financial markets offer superior projects in the same risk class (namely, the firm itself). The answer is clear: The project should be rejected.

EXAMPLE 14.5: Using the WACC

A firm is considering a project that will result in initial cash savings of $5 million at the end of the first year and for an infinite period. These savings will grow at the rate of 5 percent per year. The firm has a debt/equity ratio of 0.5, a cost of equity of 29.2 percent, and a cost of debt of 10 percent. The cost-saving proposal is closely related to the firm's core business, so it is viewed as having the same risks as the overall firm. Should the firm take on the project?

Assuming a 40 percent tax rate, the firm should take on this project if it costs less than $30.36 million. To see this, first note that the PV is:

$$
\text{PV} = \$5 \text{ million}/[\text{WACC} - 0.05]
$$

This is an example of a growing perpetuity as discussed in Chapter 8. The WACC is:

$$
\begin{aligned}
\text{WACC} &= (E/V) \times R_E + (D_m/V) \times R_D \times (1 - T_C) \\
&= 2/3 \times 29.2\% + 1/3 \times 10\% \times (1 - .40) \\
&= 21.47\%
\end{aligned}
$$

The PV is thus:

$$
\text{PV} = \$5 \text{ million}/[.2147 - .05] = \$30.36 \text{ million}
$$

The NPV is positive only if the cost is less than $30.36 million.

For future reference, Table 14.1 summarizes our discussion of the WACC.

TABLE 14.1   Summary of capital cost calculations

The Cost of Equity, R_E

▶   SML approach (from Chapter 13—best practice):

$R_E = R_f + (R_M - R_f) \times \beta_E,$

where R_f is the risk-free rate, R_M is the expected return on the overall market, and β_E is the systematic risk of the equity.

▶   Dividend growth model approach (from Chapter 8 used as a check):

$R_E = D_1/P_0 + g,$

where D_1 is the expected dividend in one period, g is the dividend growth rate, and P_0 is the current stock price.

The Cost of Debt, R_D

▶   For a firm with publicly held debt, the cost of debt can be measured as the yield to maturity on the outstanding debt. The coupon rate is irrelevant. Yield to maturity is covered in Chapter 7.

▶   If the firm has no publicly traded debt, the cost of debt can be measured as the yield to maturity on similarly rated bonds (bond ratings are discussed in Chapter 7).

The Weighted Average Cost of Capital, WACC

▶   The firm's WACC is the overall required return on the firm as a whole. It is the appropriate discount rate to use for cash flows similar in risk to the overall firm.

▶   The WACC is calculated as

$WACC = E/V \times R_E + D_m/V \times R_D \times (1 - T_C),$

where T_C is the corporate tax rate, E is the market value of the firm's equity, D_m is the market value of the firm's debt, and $V = E + D_m$. Note that E/V is the percentage of the firm's financing (in market value terms) that is equity, and D_m/V is the percentage that is debt.

Concept Questions

1. How is the WACC calculated?
2. Why do we multiply the cost of debt by $(1 - T_C)$ when we compute the WACC?
3. Under what conditions is it correct to use the WACC to determine NPV?

Performance Evaluation: Another Use of the WACC

economic value added (EVA)
Performance measure based on WACC.

WACCs can also be used for performance evaluation purposes. Probably the best-known approach in this area is the **economic value added (EVA)** (also called economic value contribution (EVC)) method developed by Stern Stewart and Co. and implemented in Canada by the Corporate Renaissance Group. Companies such as Cogeco, Domtar, and Grand & Toy are among the Canadian firms that have been using EVA as a means of evaluating corporate performance. In Canada, a CICA survey showed that 45 percent of public companies and 27 percent of private firms are using some type of EVA analysis. Several studies found evidence that Canadian companies with higher economic value added enjoy larger shareholder returns.[11]

Although the details differ, the basic idea behind EVA and similar strategies is straightforward. Suppose we have $100 million in capital (debt and equity) tied up in our firm and our overall WACC is 12 percent. If we multiply these together, we get $12 million. Referring back to Chapter 2, if our cash flow from assets is less than this, we are, on an overall basis, destroying value. If cash flow from assets exceeds $12 million, we are creating value. In practice, strategies such as these suffer to a certain extent from problems with implementation. For example, it appears that the Corporate Renaissance Group makes extensive use of book values for debt and equity in computing cost of capital. Evidence is mixed on the track record of EVA in identifying undervalued

---

[11] Our comments on EVAs in Canada draw on S. Northfield, "A New Way to Measure Wealth," *The Globe and Mail*, June 13, 1998, B22; V. Jog, "Value and Wealth Creation in Canada," *Canadian Investment Review*, Winter 2003, pp. 45–50; S. Lieff and V. Jog, "Value Creation and Long-run Shareholder Returns: A Canadian Perspective", Sprott School of Business, Carleton University, Working Paper, 2005 and John M. Griffith, "The True Value of EVA," *Journal of Applied Finance*, Fall/Winter 2004, Vol. 14, No. 2, pp. 25–29. Appendix 14B discusses EVA in more detail.

securities. Even so, by focusing on value creation, WACC-based evaluation procedures force employees and management to pay attention to the real bottom line: increasing share prices.

IN THEIR OWN WORDS...

Bennett Stewart on EVA

A firm's weighted average cost of capital has important applications other than the discount rate in capital project evaluations. For instance, it is a key ingredient to measure a firm's true economic profit, or what I like to call EVA, standing for economic value added. Accounting rules dictate that the interest expense a company incurs on its debt financing be deducted from its reported profit, but those same rules ironically forbid deducting a charge for the shareholders' funds a firm uses. In economic terms, equity capital is in fact a very costly financing source; because shareholders bear the risk of being paid last, after all other stakeholders and investors are paid first. But according to accountants, shareholders' equity is free.

This egregious oversight has dire practical consequences. For one thing, it means that the profit figure accountants certify to be correct is inherently at odds with the net present value decision rule. For instance, it is a simple matter for management to inflate its reported earnings and earnings-per-share in ways that actually harm the shareholders by investing capital in projects that earn less than the overall cost of capital but more than the after-tax cost of borrowing money, which amounts to a trivial hurdle in most cases, a couple percentage points at most. In effect, EPS requires management to vault a mere three foot hurdle when to satisfy shareholders managers must jump a ten foot hurdle that includes the cost of equity. A prime example of the way accounting profit leads smart managers to do dumb things was Enron, where former top executives Ken Lay and Jeff Skilling boldly declared in the firm's 2000 annual report that they were "laser-focused on earnings per share,"

and so they were. Bonuses were funded out of book profit, and project developers were paid for signing up new deals and not generating a decent return on investment. Consequently, Enron's EPS was on the rise while its true economic profit—its EVA—measured after deducting the full cost of capital, was plummeting in the years leading up to the firm's demise—the result of massive misallocations of capital to ill-advised energy and new economy projects. The point is, EVA measures economic profit, the profit that actually discounts to net present value, and the maximization of which is every company's most important financial goal; yet for all its popularity EPS is just an accounting contrivance that is wholly unrelated to the maximization of shareholder wealth or sending the right decision signals to management.

Starting in the early 1990s firms around the world—ranging from Coca-Cola, to Briggs & Stratton, Herman Miller, and Eli Lilly in America, Siemens in Germany, Tata Consulting and the Godrej Group out of India, Brahma Beer in Brazil, and many, many more—began to turn to EVA as a new and better way to measure performance and set goals, make decisions and determine bonuses, and to communicate with investors and to teach business and finance basics to managers and employees. Properly tailored and implemented, EVA is a natural way to bring the cost of capital to life, and to turn everyone in a company into a capital conscientious, owner-entrepreneur.

Bennett Stewart is a co-founder of Stern Stewart & Co. and also the CEO of EVA Dimensions, a firm providing EVA data, valuation modelling, and hedge fund management. Stewart pioneered the practical development of EVA as chronicled in his book, *The Quest for Value*.

14.5 | Divisional and Project Costs of Capital

As we have seen, using the WACC as the discount rate for future cash flows is only appropriate when the proposed investment is similar to the firm's existing activities. This is not as restrictive as it sounds. If we were in the pizza business, for example, and we were thinking of opening a new location, the WACC is the discount rate to use. The same is true of a retailer thinking of opening a new store, a manufacturer thinking of expanding production, or a consumer products company thinking of expanding its markets.

Nonetheless, despite the usefulness of the WACC as a benchmark, there are clearly situations where the cash flows under consideration have risks distinctly different from those of the overall firm. We consider how to cope with this problem next.

The SML and the WACC

When we are evaluating investments with risks substantially different from the overall firm, the use of the WACC can potentially lead to poor decisions. Figure 14.1 illustrates why.

FIGURE 14.1

The security market
line (SML) and the
weighted average cost
of capital (WACC)

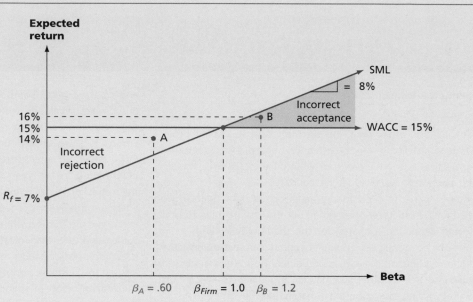

If a firm uses its WACC to make accept/reject decisions for all types of projects, it will have a tendency toward incorrectly accepting risky projects and incorrectly rejecting less risky projects.

In Figure 14.1, we have plotted an SML corresponding to a risk-free rate of 7 percent and a market risk premium of 8 percent. To keep things simple, we consider an all-equity company with a beta of 1. As we have indicated, the WACC and the cost of equity are exactly equal to 15 percent for this company, since there is no debt.

Suppose our firm uses its WACC to evaluate all investments. This means any investment with a return of greater than 15 percent is accepted and any investment with a return of less than 15 percent is rejected. We know from our study of risk and return, however, that a desirable investment is one that plots above the SML. As Figure 14.1 illustrates, using the WACC for all types of projects can result in the firm incorrectly accepting relatively risky projects and incorrectly rejecting relatively safe ones.

For example, consider point A. This project has a beta of .6 compared to the firm's beta of 1.0. It has an expected return of 14 percent. Is this a desirable investment? The answer is yes, because its required return is only:

$$\text{Required return} = R_f + \beta \times (R_M - R_f)$$
$$= 7\% + .60 \times 8\%$$
$$= 11.8\%$$

However, if we use the WACC as a cutoff, this project would be rejected because its return is less than 15 percent. This example illustrates that a firm using its WACC as a cutoff tends to reject profitable projects with risks less than those of the overall firm.

At the other extreme, consider point B. This project offers a 16 percent return, which exceeds the firm's cost of capital. This is not a good investment, however, because its return is inadequate, given its level of systematic risk. Nonetheless, if we use the WACC to evaluate it, it appears to be attractive. So the second error that arises if we use the WACC as a cutoff is that we tend to make unprofitable investments with risks greater than the overall firm. As a consequence, through time, a firm that uses its WACC to evaluate all projects has a tendency to both accept unprofitable investments and become increasingly risky.

Divisional Cost of Capital

The same type of problem with the WACC can arise in a corporation with more than one line of business. Imagine, for example, a corporation that has two divisions, a regulated telephone company and a high-tech communications company. The first of these (the telephone company) has relatively low risk; the second has relatively high risk. Companies like this spanning several industries are very common in Canada.

In this case, the firm's overall cost of capital is really a mixture of two different costs of capital, one for each division. If the two divisions were competing for resources, and the firm used a single WACC as a cutoff, which division would tend to be awarded greater funds for investment?

The answer is that the riskier division would tend to have greater returns (ignoring the greater risk), so it would tend to be the winner. The less glamorous operation might have great profit potential that ends up being ignored. Large corporations in Canada and the United States are aware of this problem and many work to develop separate divisional costs of capital.

The Pure Play Approach

We've seen that using the firm's WACC inappropriately can lead to problems. How can we come up with the appropriate discount rates in such circumstances? Because we cannot observe the returns on these investments, there generally is no direct way of coming up with a beta, for example. Instead, what we must do is examine other investments outside the firm that are in the same risk class as the one we are considering and use the market-required returns on these investments as the discount rate. In other words, we determine what the cost of capital is for such investments by locating some similar investments in the marketplace.

For example, going back to our telephone division, suppose we wanted to come up with a discount rate to use for that division. What we can do is to identify several other phone companies that have publicly traded securities. We might find that a typical phone company stock has a beta of .40, AA-rated debt, and a capital structure that is about 50 percent debt and 50 percent equity. Using this information, we could develop a WACC for a typical phone company and use this as our discount rate.

Alternatively, if we are thinking of entering a new line of business, we would try to develop the appropriate cost of capital by looking at the market-required returns on companies already in that business. In the language of Bay Street, a company that focuses only on a single line of business is called a **pure play**. For example, if you wanted to bet on the price of crude oil by purchasing common stocks, you would try to identify companies that dealt exclusively with this product because they would be the most affected by changes in the price of crude oil. Such companies would be called pure plays on the price of crude oil.

What we try to do here is to find companies that focus as exclusively as possible on the type of project in which we are interested. Our approach, therefore, is called the **pure play approach** to estimating the required return on an investment.

The pure play approach is also useful in finding the fair rate of return for utility companies. Going back to our earlier example, we use the pure play approach if Provincial Power is not a public company. Because a number of electric utilities in Canada are crown corporations, consultants for the two sides use publicly traded Canadian and U.S. utilities for comparison.

In Chapter 3, we discussed the subject of identifying similar companies for comparison purposes. The same problems that we described there come up here. The most obvious one is that we may not be able to find any suitable companies. In this case, how to determine a discount rate objectively becomes a very difficult question. Alternatively, a comparable company may be found but the comparison complicated by a different capital structure. In this case, we have to adjust the beta for the effect of leverage. Appendix 14A on adjusted present value (APV) explains how to do this.[12] The important thing is to be aware of the issue so we at least reduce the possibility of the kinds of mistakes that can arise when the WACC is used as a cutoff on all investments.

pure play approach
Use of a WACC that is unique to a particular project.

---

[12] Another approach is to develop an accounting beta using a formula that makes beta a function of the firm's financial ratios.

The Subjective Approach

Because of the difficulties that exist in objectively establishing discount rates for individual projects, firms often adopt an approach that involves making subjective adjustments to the overall WACC. To illustrate, suppose a firm has an overall WACC of 14 percent. It places all proposed projects into four categories as follows:

Category	Examples	Adjustment Factor	Discount Rate
High risk	New products	+6%	20%
Moderate risk	Cost savings, expansion of existing lines	+0	14
Low risk	Replacement of existing equipment	−4	10
Mandatory	Pollution control equipment	n.a.*	n.a.

*n.a. = Not applicable

The effect of this crude partitioning is to assume that all projects either fall into one of three risk classes or else they are mandatory. In this last case, the cost of capital is irrelevant since the project must be taken. Examples are safety and pollution control projects. With the subjective approach, the firm's WACC may change through time as economic conditions change. As this happens, the discount rates for the different types of projects also change.

Within each risk class, some projects presumably have more risk than others, and the danger of incorrect decisions still exists. Figure 14.2 illustrates this point. Comparing Figures 14.1 and 14.2, we see that similar problems exist, but the magnitude of the potential error is less with the subjective approach. For example, the project labelled A would be accepted if the WACC were used, but it is rejected once it is classified as a high-risk investment. What this illustrates is that some risk adjustment, even if it is subjective, is probably better than no risk adjustment.

It would be better, in principle, to determine the required return objectively for each project separately. However, as a practical matter, it may not be possible to go much beyond subjective adjustments because either the necessary information is unavailable or else the cost and effort required are simply not worthwhile.

FIGURE 14.2

The security market line (SML) and the subjective approach

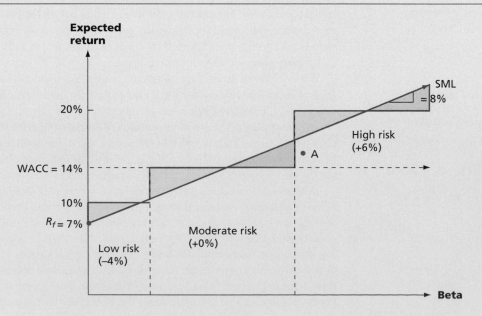

With the subjective approach, the firm places projects into one of several risk classes. The discount rate used to value the project is then determined by adding (for high risk) or subtracting (for low risk) an adjustment factor to or from the firm's WACC.

Concept Questions

1. What are the likely consequences if a firm uses its WACC to evaluate all proposed investments?
2. What is the pure play approach to determining the appropriate discount rate? When might it be used?

14.6 | Flotation Costs and the Weighted Average Cost of Capital

flotation costs
The costs associated with the issuance of new securities.

So far, we have not included **flotation costs** in our discussion of the weighted average cost of capital. If a company accepts a new project, it may be required to issue or float new bonds and stocks. This means the firm incurs flotation costs.

Sometimes it is suggested that the firm's WACC should be adjusted upward to reflect flotation costs. This is really not the best approach because, once again, the required return on an investment depends on the risk of the investment, not the source of the funds. This is not to say that flotation costs should be ignored; since these costs arise as a consequence of the decision to undertake a project, they are relevant cash flows. We therefore briefly discuss how to include them in a project analysis.

The Basic Approach

We start with a simple case. The Spatt Company, an all-equity firm, has a cost of equity of 20 percent. Since this firm is 100 percent equity, its WACC and its cost of equity are the same. Spatt is contemplating a large-scale $100 million expansion of its existing operations. The expansion would be funded by selling new stock.

Based on conversations with its investment dealer, Spatt believes its flotation costs would run 10 percent of the amount issued. This means that Spatt's proceeds from the equity sale would be only 90 percent of the amount sold. When flotation costs are considered, what is the cost of the expansion?

As we discuss in Chapter 15, Spatt needs to sell enough equity to raise $100 million after covering the flotation costs. In other words:

$100 million = (1 − .10) × Amount raised

Amount raised = $100/.90 = $111.11 million

Spatt's flotation costs are thus $11.11 million, and the true cost of the expansion is $111.11 million once we include flotation costs.

Things are only slightly more complicated if the firm uses both debt and equity. For example, suppose Spatt's target capital structure is 60 percent equity, 40 percent debt. The flotation costs associated with equity are still 10 percent, but the flotation costs for debt are less, say 5 percent.

Earlier, when we had different capital costs for debt and equity, we calculated a weighted average cost of capital using the target capital structure weights. Here, we do much the same thing. We can calculate a weighted average flotation cost, f_A, by multiplying the equity flotation cost, f_E, by the percentage of equity (E/V) and the debt flotation cost, f_D, by the percentage of debt (D_m/V) and then adding the two together:

$$f_A = (E/V) \times f_E + (D_m/V) \times f_D \qquad [14.7]$$
$$= 60\% \times .10 + 40\% \times .05$$
$$= 8\%$$

The weighted average flotation cost is thus 8 percent. What this tells us is that for every dollar in outside financing needed for new projects, the firm must actually raise $1/(1 − .08) = $1.087. In our previous example, the project cost is $100 million when we ignore flotation costs. If we include them, the true cost is $100/(1 − f_A) = $100/.92 = $108.7 million.

In taking issue costs into account, the firm must be careful not to use the wrong weights. The firm should use the target weights, even if it can finance the entire cost of the project with either debt or equity. The fact that a firm can finance a specific project with debt or equity is not directly relevant. If a firm has a target debt/equity ratio of 1, for example, but chooses to finance a particular project with all debt, it has to raise additional equity later to maintain its target debt/equity ratio. To take this into account, the firm should always use the target weights in calculating the flotation cost.[13]

EXAMPLE 14.6: Calculating the Weighted Average Flotation Cost

The Weinstein Corporation has a target capital structure that is 80 percent equity, 20 percent debt. The flotation costs for equity issues are 20 percent of the amount raised; the flotation costs for debt issues are 6 percent. If Weinstein needs $65 million for a new manufacturing facility, what is the true cost once flotation costs are considered?

We first calculate the weighted average flotation cost, f_A:

$$f_A = (E/V) \times f_E + (D_m/V) \times f_D$$
$$= 80\% \times .20 + 20\% \times .06$$
$$= 17.2\%$$

The weighted average flotation cost is thus 17.2 percent. The project cost is $65 million when we ignore flotation costs. If we include them, the true cost is $65/(1 - f_A) = $65/.828 = $78.5 million, again illustrating that flotation costs can be a considerable expense.

Flotation Costs and NPV

To illustrate how flotation costs can be included in an NPV analysis, suppose the Tripleday Printing Company is currently at its target debt/equity ratio of 100 percent. It is considering building a new $500,000 printing plant. This new plant is expected to generate after-tax cash flows of $73,150 per year forever. There are two financing options:

1. A $500,000 new issue of common stock. The issuance costs of the new common stock would be about 10 percent of the amount raised. The required return on the company's new equity is 20 percent.
2. A $500,000 issue of 30-year bonds. The issuance costs of the new debt would be 2 percent of the proceeds. The company can raise new debt at 10 percent. The company faces a 40-percent combined federal/provincial tax rate.

What is the NPV of the new printing plant?

To begin, since printing is the company's main line of business, we use the company's weighted average cost of capital to value the new printing plant:

$$\text{WACC} = (E/V) \times R_E + (D_m/V) \times R_D \times (1 - T_C)$$
$$= .50 \times 20\% + .50 \times 10\% \times (1 - .40)$$
$$= 13.0\%$$

Since the cash flows are $73,150 per year forever, the PV of the cash flows at 13.0 percent per year is:

$$\text{PV} = \$73,150/.13 = \$562,692$$

If we ignore flotation costs, the NPV is:

$$\text{NPV} = \$562,692 - 500,000 = \$62,692$$

The project generates an NPV greater than zero, so it should be accepted.

What about financing arrangements and issue costs? From the information just given, we know that the flotation costs are 2 percent for debt and 10 percent for equity. Since Tripleday uses equal amounts of debt and equity, the weighted average flotation cost, f_A, is:

---

[13] Since flotation costs may be amortized for tax purposes, there is a tax adjustment as explained in Appendix 14A.

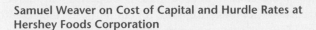

$$f_A = (E/V) \times f_E + (D_m/V) \times f_D$$
$$= .50 \times 10\% + .50 \times 2\%$$
$$= 6\%$$

Remember that the fact that Tripleday can finance the project with all debt or equity is irrelevant. Because Tripleday needs $500,000 to fund the new plant, the true cost, once we include flotation costs, is $500,000/(1 − f_A) = $500,000/.94 = $531,915. Since the PV of the cash flows is $562,692, the plant has an NPV of $562,692 − 531,915 = $30,777, so it is still a good investment. However, its return is lower than we initially might have thought.[14]

IN THEIR OWN WORDS...

Samuel Weaver on Cost of Capital and Hurdle Rates at Hershey Foods Corporation

At Hershey, we re-evaluate our cost of capital annually or as market conditions warrant. The calculation of the cost of capital essentially involves three different issues, each with a few alternatives:

- *Capital weights*
  Book value or market value weights
  Current or target capital structure

- *Cost of debt*
  Historical (coupon) interest rates
  Market based interest rates

- *Cost of equity*
  Dividend growth model
  Capital asset pricing model, or CAPM

At Hershey, we calculate our cost of capital officially based upon the projected "target" capital structure at the end of our three-year intermediate planning horizon. This allows management to see the immediate impact of strategic decisions related to the planned composition of Hershey's capital pool. The cost of debt is calculated as the anticipated weighted average after-tax cost of debt in that final plan year based upon the coupon rates attached to that debt. The cost of equity is computed via the dividend growth model.

We recently conducted a survey of the 10 food processing companies that we consider our industry group competitors. The result of this survey indicated that the cost of capital for most of these companies was in the 7 to 10 percent range. Furthermore, without exception, all 10 of these companies employed the CAPM when calculating their cost of equity.

Our experience has been that the dividend growth model works better for Hershey. We do pay dividends, and we do experience steady, stable growth in our dividends. This growth is also projected within our strategic plan. Consequently, the dividend growth model is technically applicable and appealing to management since it reflects their best estimate of the future long-term growth rate.

In addition to the calculation already described, the other possible combinations and permutations are calculated as barometers. Unofficially, the cost of capital is calculated using market weights, current marginal interest rates, and the CAPM cost of equity. For the most part, and due to rounding the cost of capital to the nearest whole percentage point, these alternative calculations yield approximately the same results.

From the cost of capital, individual project hurdle rates are developed using a subjectively determined risk premium based on the characteristics of the project. Projects are grouped into separate project categories, such as cost savings, capacity expansion, product line extension, and new products. For example, in general, a new product is more risky than a cost savings project. Consequently, each project category's hurdle rate reflects the level of risk and commensurate required return as perceived by senior management. As a result, capital project hurdle rates range from a slight premium over the cost of capital to the highest hurdle rate of approximately double the cost of capital.

Samuel Weaver, Ph.D., was formerly director, financial planning and analysis, for Hershey. He is a certified management accountant and certified financial manager. His position combined the theoretical with the pragmatic and involved the analysis of many different facets of finance in addition to capital expenditure analysis.

Concept Questions

1. What are flotation costs?
2. How are flotation costs included in an NPV analysis?

---

[14]Our example abstracts from the tax deductibility of some parts of flotation costs.

14.7 | Calculating WACC for Loblaw

We illustrate the practical application of the weighted average cost of capital by calculating it for a prominent Canadian company. Loblaw is a large food distribution company with operations across Canada. The company operates grocery stores under various banners. Loblaw's revenue for the year ending December 2011 was about $31.25 billion, with net earnings of $769 million.

As we pointed out, WACC calculations depend on market values as observed on a particular date. In this application, market values for Loblaw were observed on May 10, 2012.[15] Other information comes from annual statements at Loblaw's year-end on December 31, 2011.

Estimating Financing Proportions

Table 14.3 shows an abbreviated statement of financial position for Loblaw. Recall from our earlier discussion that when calculating the cost of capital, it is common to ignore short-term financing, such as payables and accruals. We also ignore short-term debt unless it is a permanent source of financing. As both current assets and current liabilities are ignored for our purposes, increases (or decreases) in current liabilities are netted against changes in current assets. Leases are included in long-term debt for the purposes of this analysis.

TABLE 14.3

Book value statement of financial positionon December 31, 2011 ($ millions)

Obtained from loblaw.ca. Author's calculation.

Assets		Liabilities and Equity	
Current	$6,462	Current	$ 4,718
		Deferred taxes and other	938
Long-term	10,966	Long-term debt	5,765
		Equity	
		Common equity	6,007
Total	$17,428	Total	$17,428

Ideally, we should calculate the market value of all sources of financing and determine the relative weights of each source. Sometimes, difficulties arise in finding the market value of non-traded bonds. This would require us to use book values for debt. This is not a problem for Loblaw as the company does not have any non-traded bonds. It is much more important to use the market value for calculation of equity weights than for debt, as the market value of common equity differs markedly from the book value.

Market Value Weights for Loblaw

To find the market value weights of debt and common stock we find the total market value of each. The market values are calculated as the number of shares times the share price. The figures for Loblaw, as of December 31, 2011, were 281,385,318 common shares and 9,000,000 preferred shares outstanding. Multiplying each by its price gives:

Security	Book Value ($ millions)	Market Price	Market Value ($ millions)
Interest-bearing debt	$5,765	—	$ 4,393.1*
Preferred Shares	225	27.57	248.1
	6,007	$38.48	10,828

Proportions	Dollars	Market Value Weights
Debt	$4,393.1	28.40%
Preferred Shares	248.1	1.60%
Common stock	10,828	70.00%
	$15,469.2	100.00%

*We calculate market value of interest-bearing debt below.

---

[15] Obtained from loblaw.ca. Used with permission.

As you can see from the market value weights, Loblaw capital structure contains common equity, debt and preferred stock.

Cost of Debt

Loblaw has 18 relatively long-term bond issues that account for virtually all of its long-term debt. To calculate the cost of debt, we combine these 18 issues and compute a weighted average. We use Bloomberg Financial Services to find quotes on the bonds. We should note here that finding the yield to maturity for all of a company's outstanding bond issues on a single day is unusual. If you remember our previous discussion on bonds, the bond market is not as liquid as the stock market, and on many days individual bond issues may not trade. To find the book value of the bonds, we also used Bloomberg Financial Services. The basic information is as follows:

Coupon Rate (%)	Maturity Date	Book Value (Face value, in $ millions)	Price (% of par)	Yield to Maturity
5.4000	20-Nov-13	200	105.2	1.906
6.0000	3-Mar-14	100	107.1	1.975
4.8500	8-May-14	350	105.43	2.043
7.1000	1-Jun-16	300	117.37	2.556
5.2200	18-Jun-20	350	113.28	3.335
6.6500	8-Nov-27	100	119.51	4.844
6.4500	9-Feb-28	200	116.76	4.908
6.5000	22-Jan-29	175	117.35	4.959
11.4000	23-May-31	200	176.99	5.053
6.8500	1-Mar-32	200	121.19	5.132
6.5400	17-Feb-33	200	118.09	5.114
8.7500	23-Nov-33	200	147.38	5.099
6.0500	9-Jun-34	200	112.1	5.127
6.1500	29-Jan-35	200	113.88	5.11
5.9000	18-Jan-36	300	110.63	5.12
6.4500	1-Mar-39	200	119.34	5.116
7.0000	7-Jun-40	150	126.19	5.204
5.8600	18-Jun-43	55	109.93	5.211

To calculate the total average cost of debt, we take the percentage of the total debt represented by each issue and multiply by the yield on the issue. We then add to get the overall weighted average debt cost. We use both book values and market values here for comparison. The results of the calculations are as follows:

Coupon Rate (%)	Book Value (Face value, in $ millions)	Percent age of Total	Price (Percentage of par)	Market Value (in $ millions)	Percentage of Total	Yield to Maturity	Book Values	Market Values
5.4000	200	5.43%	105.2%	210.40	4.79%	1.906%	0.104%	0.091%
6.0000	100	2.72%	107.1%	107.10	2.44%	1.975%	0.054%	0.048%
4.8500	350	9.51%	105.43%	369.01	8.40%	2.043%	0.194%	0.172%
7.1000	300	8.15%	117.37%	352.11	8.02%	2.556%	0.208%	0.205%
5.2200	350	9.51%	113.28%	396.48	9.03%	3.335%	0.317%	0.301%
6.6500	100	2.72%	119.51%	119.51	2.72%	4.844%	0.132%	0.132%
6.4500	200	5.43%	116.76%	233.52	5.32%	4.908%	0.267%	0.261%
6.5000	175	4.76%	117.35%	205.36	4.67%	4.959%	0.236%	0.232%
11.4000	200	5.43%	176.99%	353.98	8.06%	5.053%	0.275%	0.407%
6.8500	200	5.43%	121.19%	242.38	5.52%	5.132%	0.279%	0.283%
6.5400	200	5.43%	118.09%	236.18	5.38%	5.114%	0.278%	0.275%
8.7500	200	5.43%	147.38%	294.76	6.71%	5.099%	0.277%	0.342%
6.0500	200	5.43%	112.1%	224.20	5.10%	5.127%	0.279%	0.262%
6.1500	200	5.43%	113.88%	227.76	5.18%	5.11%	0.278%	0.265%
5.9000	300	8.15%	110.63%	331.89	7.55%	5.12%	0.417%	0.387%
6.4500	200	5.43%	119.34%	238.68	5.43%	5.116%	0.278%	0.278%
7.0000	150	4.08%	126.19%	189.29	4.31%	5.204%	0.212%	0.224%
5.8600	55	1.49%	109.93%	60.46	1.38%	5.211%	0.078%	0.072%
Total	$3,680	100%		$4,393.06			4.162%	4.236%

As these calculations show, Loblaw's cost of debt is 4.162% on a book value basis and 4.236% on a market value basis. They are very similar. Thus, for Loblaw, whether market values are used or book values are used makes only a small difference. The reason is simply that the market values and book values are similar. This will often be the case and explains why companies frequently use book values for debt in WACC calculations.

The last step that needs to be done is to convert the before-tax cost of debt to an after-tax cost. To do this, we use the average tax rate for Loblaw during 2011: 27.2 percent.

$$R_D(1 - T_C) = \text{Cost of Debt (Market Value)} \times (1 - T_C) = 4.236\% (1 - 0.272) = 3.08\%$$

Cost of Preferred Shares

The cost of preferred shares is obtained from Bloomberg Financial Services and its value is 5.597%. If a yield of a preferred share is not available online, it can also be obtained from yields of corporate preferred shares of similar rating.

Cost of Common Stock

To determine the cost of common stock for Loblaw, we begin with the CAPM and use the dividend valuation model as a reality check.

CAPM

$$\beta = 0.30$$
$$\text{Market risk premium} = 4.30\%[16]$$
$$\text{Risk-free rate} = 5\%$$

$$R_E = R_f + \beta(\text{Market risk premium})[17]$$
$$= 5.0\% + 0.30(4.30\%)$$
$$= 6.29\%$$

To calculate the cost of equity using the dividend valuation model, we need a growth rate for Loblaw. A geometric regression would be the most accurate; however, a geometric average is simpler and nearly as accurate. We use the EPS figures to determine the growth rate for Loblaw.

Year	EPS
2011	2.73
2010	2.45
2009	2.39
2008	1.99
2007	1.20
2006	−0.80
2005	2.72
2004	3.53
2003	3.07
2002	2.64
2001	2.04
2000	1.71
1999	1.37
1998	1.06
1997	0.88

Source: FP Advisor.

[16] We use the 60-month beta calculated by FP Advisor and the arithmetic mean market risk premium from Chapter 12 for the period 1957–2011. A further refinement would compute the market risk premium as the average of the arithmetic and geometric mean values.

[17] We consider Loblaw a going concern, so we use the risk-free rate on a long-term government bond estimated evaluation of 5%.

Dividend Valuation Model Growth Rate

$$(1 + g)^{14} = (\$2.73/0.88)$$
$$g = (3.10)^{1/14} - 1$$
$$g = 8.42\%$$

The geometric growth rate in EPS over the period 1997−2011 was 8.42 percent.[18]

$$\text{Dividend valuation model} = D_1/P_0 + g$$

To get next year's dividend, D_1, we adjust the current dividend of $0.84 for projected growth:

$$D_1 = D_0 (1 + g) = \$0.84(1.0842) = \$0.9107$$
$$P_0 = \$38.48$$
$$R_E = D_1/P_0 + g$$
$$= \$0.9107/\$38.48 + 0.0842$$
$$= 10.79\%$$

Notice that the estimates for the cost of equity are quite different. Remember that each method of estimating the cost of equity relies on different assumptions, so different estimates of the cost of equity should not surprise us. Recall that earlier we argued that the CAPM estimate follows best practices and that the Dividend Growth Model can be used as a reality check. In this case the CAPM estimate seems rather low. One reasonable approach would be to make a subjective adjustment to the CAPM estimate increasing it by half a percentage point to 6.8 percent.[19]

Since this seems like a reasonable number, we will use it in calculating the cost of equity in this example.

Loblaw's WACC

To find the weighted average cost of capital, we weight the cost of each source by the weights:

$$WACC = (E/V) R_E + (P/V) R_P + (D_m/V) R_D (1 - T_C)$$
$$= 0.70(6.80\%) + 0.0160(5.597\%) + 0.2840(3.08\%)$$
$$= 5.72\%$$

Our analysis shows that in May 2012 Loblaw's weighted average cost of capital was 5.72 percent.

14.8 | SUMMARY AND CONCLUSIONS

This chapter discussed cost of capital. The most important concept is the weighted average cost of capital (WACC) that we interpreted as the required rate of return on the overall firm. It is also the discount rate appropriate for cash flows that are similar in risk to the overall firm. We described how the WACC can be calculated as the weighted average of different sources of financing. We also illustrated how it can be used in certain types of analyses.

In addition, we pointed out situations in which it is inappropriate to use the WACC as the discount rate. To handle such cases, we described some alternative approaches to developing discount rates such as the pure play approach. We also discussed how the flotation costs associated with raising new capital can be included in an NPV analysis.

---

[18] Strictly speaking, the two growth rates will diverge unless the payout ratio is constant.

[19] This may be due to the influence of the market meltdown of 2008 and the European government debt crisis on the risk premium and risk-free rate as explained earlier.

Key Terms

adjusted present value (APV) (page 414)
cost of debt (page 393)
cost of equity (page 389)
economic value added (EVA) (page 398)
flotation costs (page 403)

pure play approach (page 401)
retention ratio (page 391)
return on equity (ROE) (page 391)
weighted average cost of capital (WACC) (page 395)

Chapter Review Problems and Self-Test

14.1 **Calculating the Cost of Equity** Suppose that stock in Boone Corporation has a beta of .90. The market risk premium is 7 percent, and the risk-free rate is 8 percent. Boone's last dividend was $1.80 per share, and the dividend is expected to grow at 7 percent indefinitely. The stock currently sells for $25. What is Boone's cost of equity capital?

14.2 **Calculating the WACC** In addition to the information in the previous problem, suppose Boone has a target debt/equity ratio of 50 percent. Its cost of debt is 8 percent, before taxes. If the tax rate is 40 percent, what is the WACC?

14.3 **Flotation Costs** Suppose that in the previous question Boone is seeking $40 million for a new project. The necessary funds have to be raised externally.

Boone's flotation costs for selling debt and equity are 3 percent and 12 percent, respectively. If flotation costs are considered, what is the true cost of the new project?

Answers to Self-Test Problems

14.1 We start with the SML approach. Based on the information given, the expected return on Boone's common stock is:

$$R_E = R_f + \beta_E \times [R_M - R_f]$$
$$= 8\% + .9 \times 7\%$$
$$= 14.3\%$$

We now use the dividend growth model. The projected dividend is $D_0 \times (1 + g) = \$1.80 \times (1.07) = \$1.926$, so the expected return using this approach is:

$$R_E = D_1/P_0 + g$$
$$= \$1.926/25 + .07$$
$$= 14.704\%$$

Since these two estimates, 14.3 percent and 14.7 percent, are fairly close, we average them. Boone's cost of equity is approximately 14.5 percent.

14.2 Since the target debt/equity ratio is .50, Boone uses $.50 in debt for every $1.00 in equity. In other words, Boone's target capital structure is 1/3 debt and 2/3 equity. The WACC is thus:

$$WACC = (E/V) \times R_E + (D_m/V) \times R_D \times (1 - T_C)$$
$$= 2/3 \times 14.5\% + 1/3 \times 8\% \times (1 - .40)$$
$$= 11.267\%$$

14.3 Since Boone uses both debt and equity to finance its operations, we first need the weighted average flotation cost. As in the previous problem, the percentage of equity financing is 2/3, so the weighted average cost is:

$$f_A = (E/V) \times f_E + (D_m/V) \times f_D$$
$$= 2/3 \times 12\% + 1/3 \times 3\%$$
$$= 9\%$$

If Boone needs $40 million after flotation costs, the true cost of the project is $\$40/(1 - f_A) = \$40/.91 = \$43.96$ million.

Concepts Review and Critical Thinking Questions

1. **(LO3)** On the most basic level, if a firm's WACC is 12 percent, what does this mean?

2. **(LO3)** In calculating the WACC, if you had to use book values for either debt or equity, which would you choose? Why?

3. **(LO5)** If you can borrow all the money you need for a project at 6 percent, doesn't it follow that 6 percent is your cost of capital for the project?

4. **(LO3)** Why do we use an after-tax figure for cost of debt but not for cost of equity?

5. **(LO1)** What are the advantages of using the DCF model for determining the cost of equity capital? What are the disadvantages? What specific piece of information do you need to find the cost of equity using this model? What are some of the

ways in which you could get this estimate?

6. **(LO1)** What are the advantages of using the SML approach to finding the cost of equity capital? What are the disadvantages? What are the specific pieces of information needed to use this method? Are all of these variables observable, or do they need to be estimated? What are some of the ways you could get these estimates?

7. **(LO2)** How do you determine the appropriate cost of debt for a company? Does it make a difference if the company's debt is privately placed as opposed to being publicly traded? How would you estimate the cost of debt for a firm whose only debt issues are privately held by institutional investors?

8. **(LO5)** Suppose Tom O'Bedlam, president of Bedlam Products Inc. has hired you to determine the firm's cost of debt and cost of equity capital.

    a. The stock currently sells for $50 per share, and the dividend per share will probably be about $5. Tom argues, "It will cost us $5 per share to use the stockholders' money this year, so the cost of equity is equal to 10 percent ($5/50)." What's wrong with this conclusion?

    b. Based on the most recent financial statements, Bedlam Products' total liabilities are $8 million. Total interest expense for the coming year will be about $1 million. Tom therefore reasons, "We owe $8 million, and we will pay $1 million interest. Therefore, our cost of debt is obviously $1 million/8 million = 12.5%." What's wrong with this conclusion?

    c. Based on his own analysis, Tom is recommending that the company increase its use of equity financing, because "debt costs 12.5 percent, but equity only costs 10 percent; thus equity is cheaper." Ignoring all the other issues, what do you think about the conclusion that the cost of equity is less than the cost of debt?

9. **(LO5)** Both Enbridge Inc., a large natural gas user, and Canadian Natural Resources Ltd., a major natural gas producer, are thinking of investing in natural gas wells near Edmonton. Both are all-equity-financed companies. Enbridge Inc. and Canadian Natural Resources Ltd. are looking at identical projects. They've analyzed their respective investments, which would involve a negative cash flow now and positive expected cash flows in the future. These cash flows would be the same for both firms. No debt would be used to finance the projects. Both companies estimate that their project would have a net present value of $1 million at an 18 percent discount rate and a −$1.1 million NPV at a 22 percent discount rate. Enbridge Inc. has a beta of 1.25, whereas Canadian Natural Resources Ltd. has a beta of .75. The expected risk premium on the market is 8 percent, and risk-free bonds are yielding 12 percent. Should either company proceed? Should both? Explain.

10. **(LO5)** Under what circumstances would it be appropriate for a firm to use different costs of capital for its different operating divisions? If the overall firm WACC were used as the hurdle rate for all divisions, would the riskier divisions or the more conservative divisions tend to get most of the investment projects? Why? If you were to try to estimate the appropriate cost of capital for different divisions, what problems might you encounter? What are two techniques you could use to develop a rough estimate for each division's cost of capital?

Questions and Problems

Basic
(Questions 1–19)

1. **Calculating Cost of Equity (LO1)** The Rollag Co. just issued a dividend of $2.75 per share on its common stock. The company is expected to maintain a constant 5.8 percent growth rate in its dividends indefinitely. If the stock sells for $59 a share, what is the company's cost of equity?

2. **Calculating Cost of Equity (LO1)** The Lenzie Corporation's common stock has a beta of 1.2. If the risk-free rate is 4.8 percent and the expected return on the market is 11 percent, what is the company's cost of equity capital?

3. **Calculating Cost of Equity (LO1)** Stock in Coalhurst Industries has a beta of 1.1. The market risk premium is 7 percent, and T-bills are currently yielding 4.5 percent. The company's most recent dividend was $1.70 per share, and dividends are expected to grow at a 6 percent annual rate indefinitely. If the stock sells for $39 per share, what is your best estimate of the company's cost of equity?

4. **Estimating the DCF Growth Rate (LO1)** Suppose Whitney Ltd. just issued a dividend of $1.69 per share on its common stock. The company paid dividends of $1.35, $1.43, $1.50, and $1.61 per share in the last four years. If the stock currently sells for $50, what is your best estimate of the company's cost of equity capital using the arithmetic average growth rate in dividends? What if you use the geometric average growth rate?

5. **Calculating Cost of Preferred Stock (LO1)** Coaldale Bank has an issue of preferred stock with a $4.25 stated dividend that just sold for $92 per share. What is the bank's cost of preferred stock?

6. **Calculating Cost of Debt (LO2)** Nobleford Inc. is trying to determine its cost of debt. The firm has a debt issue outstanding with 18 years to maturity that is quoted at 107 percent of face value. The issue makes semiannual payments and has an embedded cost of 6 percent annually. Assume the par value of the bond is $1,000. What is the company's pre-tax cost of debt? If the tax rate is 35 percent, what is the after-tax cost of debt?

7. **Calculating Cost of Debt (LO2)** Pearce's Cricket Farm issued a 30-year, 8 percent semiannual bond 3 years ago. The bond currently sells for 93 percent of its face value. The company's tax rate is 35 percent. Assume the par value of the bond is $1,000.

    a. What is the pre-tax cost of debt?

    b. What is the after-tax cost of debt?

    c. Which is more relevant, the pre-tax or the after-tax cost of debt? Why?

8. **Calculating Cost of Debt (LO2)** For the firm in Problem 7, suppose the book value of the debt issue is $60 million. In addition, the company has a second debt issue on the market, a zero coupon bond with 10 years left to maturity; the book value of this issue is $35 million and the bonds sell for 57 percent of par. What is the company's total book value of debt? The total market value? What is your best estimate of the after-tax cost of debt now?

9. **Calculating WACC (LO3)** Peacock Corporation has a target capital structure of 60 percent common stock, 5 percent preferred stock, and 35 percent debt. Its cost of equity is 12 percent, the cost of preferred stock is 5 percent, and the cost of debt is 7 percent. The relevant tax rate is 35 percent.

    a. What is Peacock's WACC?

   b. The company president has approached you about Peacock's capital structure. He wants to know why the company doesn't use more preferred stock financing because it costs less than debt. What would you tell the president?

10. **Taxes and WACC (LO3)** Iron Springs Manufacturing has a target debt-equity ratio of .45. Its cost of equity is 13 percent and its cost of debt is 6 percent. If the tax rate is 35 percent, what is the company's WACC?

11. **Finding the Target Capital Structure (LO3)** Turin Corp. has a weighted average cost of capital of 9.6 percent. The company's cost of equity is 12 percent and its pre-tax cost of debt is 7.9 percent. The tax rate is 35 percent. What is the company's target debt-equity ratio?

12. **Book Value versus Market Value (LO3)** Tempest Manufacturing has 8 million shares of common stock outstanding. The current share price is $73, and the book value per share is $7. Tempest Manufacturing also has two bond issues outstanding. The first bond issue has a face value of $70 million, an 7 percent coupon, and sells for 97 percent of par. The second issue has a face value of $50 million, has an 8 percent coupon, and sells for 108 percent of par. The first issue matures in 21 years, the second in 6 years.

   a. What are Tempest's capital structure weights on a book value basis?

   b. What are Tempest's capital structure weights on a market value basis?

   c. Which are more relevant, the book or market value weights? Why?

13. **Calculating the WACC (LO3)** In Problem 12, suppose the most recent dividend was $4.10 and the dividend growth rate is 6 percent. Assume that the overall cost of debt is the weighted average of that implied by the two outstanding debt issues. Assume the par value of each bond is $1,000. Both bonds make semiannual payments. The tax rate is 35 percent. What is the company's WACC?

14. **WACC (LO3)** Welling Inc. has a target debt-equity ratio of 1.25. Its WACC is 9.2 percent, and the tax rate is 35 percent.

   a. If Welling's cost of equity is 14 percent, what is its pre-tax cost of debt?

   b. If instead you know that the after-tax cost of debt is 6.8 percent, what is the cost of equity?

15. **Finding the WACC (LO3)** Given the following information for Magrath Power Co., find the WACC. Assume the company's tax rate is 35 percent.

Debt: 8,000 6.5 percent coupon bonds outstanding, $1,000 par value, 25 years to maturity, selling for 106 percent of par; the bonds make semiannual payments.

Common stock: 310,000 shares outstanding, selling for $57 per share; the beta is 1.05.

Preferred stock: 15,000 shares of 4 percent preferred stock outstanding, currently selling for $72 per share.

Market: 7 percent market risk premium and 4.5 percent risk-free rate.

16. **Finding the WACC (LO3)** Raymond Mining Corporation has 8.5 million shares of common stock outstanding, 250,000 shares of 5 percent preferred stock outstanding, and 135,000 7.5 percent semiannual bonds outstanding, par value $1,000 each. The common stock currently sells for $34 per share and has a beta of 1.25, the preferred stock currently sells for $91 per share, and the bonds have 15 years to maturity and sell for 114 percent of par. The market risk premium is 7.5 percent, T-bills are yielding 4 percent, and Adex Mining's tax rate is 35 percent.

   a. What is the firm's market value capital structure?

   b. If Raymond Mining is evaluating a new investment project that has the same risk as the firm's typical project, what rate should the firm use to discount the project's cash flows?

17. **SML and WACC (LO1)** An all-equity firm is considering the following projects:

Project	Beta	Expected Return
W	.60	8.8%
X	.85	9.5
Y	1.15	11.9
Z	1.45	15.0

The T-bill rate is 4 percent, and the expected return on the market is 11 percent.

   a. Which projects have a higher expected return than the firm's 11 percent cost of capital?

   b. Which projects should be accepted?

   c. Which projects would be incorrectly accepted or rejected if the firm's overall cost of capital were used as a hurdle rate?

18. **Calculating Flotation Costs (LO4)** Suppose your company needs $15 million to build a new assembly line. Your target debt-equity ratio is .60. The flotation cost for new equity is 8 percent, but the flotation cost for debt is only 5 percent. Your boss has decided to fund the project by borrowing money, because the flotation costs are lower and the needed funds are relatively small.

   a. What do you think about the rationale behind borrowing the entire amount?

   b. What is your company's weighted average flotation cost, assuming all equity is raised externally?

   c. What is the true cost of building the new assembly line after taking flotation costs into account? Does it matter in this case that the entire amount is being raised from debt?

19. **Calculating Flotation Costs (LO4)** Craddock Company needs to raise $55 million to start a new project and will raise the money by selling new bonds. The company will generate no internal equity for the foreseeable future. The company has a target

capital structure of 70 percent common stock, 5 percent preferred stock, and 25 percent debt. Flotation costs for issuing new common stock are 9 percent, for new preferred stock, 6 percent, and for new debt, 3 percent. What is the true initial cost figure Craddock should use when evaluating its project?

Intermediate 20. **WACC and NPV (LO3, 5)** Taber Inc. is considering a project that will result in initial after-tax cash savings of $1.8 million at
(Questions the end of the first year, and these savings will grow at a rate of 2 percent per year indefinitely. The firm has a target debt-equity
20–23) ratio of .80, a cost of equity of 12 percent, and an after-tax cost of debt of 4.8 percent. The cost-saving proposal is somewhat riskier than the usual project the firm undertakes; management uses the subjective approach and applies an adjustment factor of +2 percent to the cost of capital for such risky projects. Under what circumstances should the company take on the project?

21. **Flotation Costs (LO4)** Judson Inc. recently issued new securities to finance a new TV show. The project cost $14 million, and the company paid $725,000 in flotation costs. In addition, the equity issued had a flotation cost of 7 percent of the amount raised, whereas the debt issued had a flotation cost of 3 percent of the amount raised. If Judson issued new securities in the same proportion as its target capital structure, what is the company's target debt-equity ratio?

22. **Divisional Cost of Capital (LO3)** Wrentham Inc. has two divisions of equal size. Division A has a beta of 0.93, while Division B has a beta of 1.57. Wrentham has no debt, and is completely equity-financed. The real risk-free rate is 6.5 percent, and the market risk premium is 5.3 percent. The cost of capital for Wrentham is 16 percent. The projects in division A are discounted at A's required return, and division B's projects are discounted at B's required return. Which of the two divisions has a lower cost of capital than the overall cost of capital for the firm?

23. **Risk Adjusted WACC (LO3, 5)** Conrad Mining Inc. uses a cost of capital of 11 percent to evaluate average risk project and it adds or subtracts 3 percent to adjust for risk. Currently the firm has two mutually exclusive projects under consideration. Both the projects have an initial cost of $100,000 and will last four years.

Project A, riskier than average, will produce an annual cash flow of $72,164 at the end of each year.

Project B, of less than average risk will produce cash flows of $145,340 at the end of Years 3 and 4 only.

Which investment should firm chose and why?

Challenge 24. **Flotation Costs and NPV (LO3, 4)** Retlaw Corporation (RC) manufactures time series photographic equipment. It is currently
(Question at its target debt equity ratio of .80. It's considering building a new $50 million manufacturing facility. This new plant is expected
24) to generate after-tax cash flows of $6.2 million in perpetuity. The company raises all equity from outside financing. There are three financing options:

1. *A new issue of common stock:* The flotation costs of the new common stock would be 8 percent of the amount raised. The required return on the company's new equity is 14 percent.

2. *A new issue of 20-year bonds:* The flotation costs of the new bonds would be 4 percent of the proceeds. If the company issues these new bonds at an annual coupon rate of 8 percent, they will sell at par.

3. *Increased use of accounts payable financing:* Because this financing is part of the company's ongoing daily business, it has no flotation costs, and the company assigns it a cost that is the same as the overall firm WACC. Management has a target ratio of accounts payable to long-term debt of .15. (Assume there is no difference between the pre-tax and after-tax accounts payable cost.)

What is the NPV of the new plant? Assume that RC has a 35 percent tax rate.

Internet Application Questions

The following problems are interrelated and involve the steps necessary to calculate the WACC for Telus Corporation.

1. Most publicly traded companies in the United States are required to submit quarterly (10Q) and annual (10K) reports to the SEC detailing the financial operations of the company over the past quarter or year, respectively. These corporate filings are available on the SEC website at sec.gov. In Canada, companies make filings with the local regulatory body such as the Ontario Securities Commission, and the filings can be found at sedar.com. Go to the website and search for the most recent filings made by Telus Corporation. Locate the book value of debt, the book value of equity, and information breaking down the company's long-term debt.

2. You wish to calculate the cost of equity for Telus. Go to finance.yahoo.com and enter the ticker symbol "T.TO" to locate information on the firm's stock, listed on the TSX. Locate the most recent price for Telus, the market capitalization, the number of shares outstanding, the beta, and the most recent annual dividend. Can you use the dividend discount model in this case? Go to bankofcanada.ca and follow the "Interest Rates" link to locate the yield on the three-month Treasury bills. Assuming a 4 percent market risk premium, what is the cost of equity for Telus using CAPM?

3. You now need to calculate the cost of debt for Telus. Go to pfin.ca/canadianfixedincome/Default.aspx and, under Corporates section, search for yield to maturity data for some of Telus's bonds. What is the weighted average cost of debt for Telus using the book value weights and the market value weights? Does it make a difference if you use book value weights or market value weights?

4. Now you can calculate the weighted average cost of capital for Telus, using book value weights and market value weights, assuming Telus has a 35 percent marginal tax rate. Which number is more relevant?

MINI CASE

Cost of Capital for Lethbridge Computer Inc.

You have recently been hired by Lethbridge Computer Inc. (LCI), in its relatively new treasury management department. LCI was founded eight years ago by Geoff Boycott and currently operates 74 stores in Alberta. The company is privately owned by Geoff and his family, and it had sales of $115 million last year.

LCI primarily sells to customers who shop in the stores. Customers come to the store and talk with a sales representative. The sales representative assists the customer in determining the type of computer and peripherals that are necessary for the individual customer's computing needs. After the order is taken, the customer pays for the order immediately, and the computer is made to fill the order. Delivery of the computer averages 15 days, and it is guaranteed in 30 days.

LCI's growth to date has come from its profits. When the company had sufficient capital, it would open a new store. Other than scouting locations, relatively little formal analysis has been used in its capital budgeting process. Geoff has just read about capital budgeting techniques and has come to you for help. For starters, the company has never attempted to determine its cost of capital, and Geoff would like you to perform the analysis. Because the company is privately owned, it is difficult to determine the cost of equity for the company. Geoff wants you to use the pure play approach to estimate the cost of capital for LCI, On investigation, Geoff found that Dell USA's business model closely resembles that of LCI, and therefore chose Dell as the representative company for estimating LCI's cost of capital. The following questions will lead you through the steps to calculate this estimate:

Questions

1. Most publicly traded corporations are required to submit quarterly (10Q) and annual reports (10K) to the SEC detailing the financial operations of the company over the past quarter or year, respectively. These corporate filings are available on the SEC website at sec.gov. Go to the SEC website; follow the "Search for Company Filings" link and the "Companies & Other Filers" link; enter "Dell Inc."; and search for SEC filings made by Dell. Find the most recent 10Q or 10K, and download the form. Look on the balance sheet to find the book value of debt and the book value of equity. If you look further down the report, you should find a section titled "Long-term Debt and Interest Rate Risk Management" that will provide a breakdown of Dell's long-term debt.

2. To estimate the cost of equity for Dell, go to finance.yahoo.com and enter the ticker symbol DELL. Follow the links to answer the following questions: What is the most recent stock price listed for Dell? What is the market value of equity, or market capitalization? How many shares of stock does Dell have outstanding? What is the most recent annual dividend? Can you use the dividend discount model in this case? What is the beta for Dell? Now go back to finance.yahoo.com and follow the "bonds" link. What is the yield on 30-year Treasury Bonds? Using the historical market risk premium, what is the cost of equity for Dell using CAPM?

3. You now need to calculate the cost of debt for Dell. Go to finra.org/marketdata, enter Dell as the company, and find the yield to maturity for each of Dell's bonds. What is the weighted average cost of debt for Dell using the book value weights and using the market value weights? Does it make a difference in this case if you use book value weights or market value weights?

4. You now have all the necessary information to calculate the weighted average cost of capital for Dell. Calculate this using book value weights and market value weights, assuming Dell has a 35 percent marginal tax rate. Which number is more relevant?

5. You used Dell as a pure play company to estimate the cost of capital for LCI. Are there any potential problems with this approach in this situation?

APPENDIX 14A

ADJUSTED PRESENT VALUE

adjusted present value (APV)
Base case net present value of a project's operating cash flows plus present value of any financing benefits.

Adjusted present value (APV) is an alternative to WACC in analyzing capital budgeting proposals. Under APV, we first analyze a project under all-equity financing and then add the additional effects of debt. This can be written as

$$\text{Adjusted present value} = \text{All-equity value} + \text{Additional effects of debt}$$

In May 2009, Canadian General Tower (CGT) sought debt financing of $7.5 million from EDC to emerge from the auto sector turmoil. APV is preferable from a financial manager's perspective as it shows directly the sources of value created by a project.

We illustrate the APV methodology with a simple example.[20] Suppose BDE is considering a $10 million project that will last five years. Projected operating cash flows are $3 million annually. The risk-free rate is

---

[20] To make it easier to illustrate what is new in APV, we simplify the project details by assuming the operating cash flows are an annuity. Most Canadian projects generate variable cash flows due to the CCA rules. This is handled within APV by finding the present value of each source of cash flow separately exactly, as presented in Chapter 10.

10 percent and the cost of equity is 20 percent. This is often called the cost of unlevered equity because we assume initially that the firm has no debt.

All-Equity Value

Assuming that the project is financed with all equity, its value is

$$-\$10,000,000 + \$3,000,000 \times [1 - 1/(1.20)^5]/.20 = -\$1,028,164$$

An all-equity firm would clearly reject this project because the NPV is negative. And equity flotation costs (not considered yet) would only make the NPV more negative. However, debt financing may add enough value to the project to justify acceptance. We consider the effects of debt next.

Additional Effects of Debt

BDE can obtain a five-year, balloon payment loan for $7.5 million after flotation costs. The interest rate is the risk-free cost of debt of 10 percent. The flotation costs are 1 percent of the amount raised. The amount of the loan is determined using the firm's target capital structure. In this case, debt represents 75 percent of firm value so the loan for the $10 million project is $7.5 million. If the firm borrowed only $5 million, the difference of $2.5 million would remain as unused debt capacity for another project. This unused debt capacity would be a benefit of the current project. For this reason, we would still use $7.5 million in calculating the additional effects of debt for the current project.[21] We look at three ways in which debt financing alters the NPV of the project.

Flotation Costs

The formula introduced in the chapter gives us the flotation costs.

$$\$7,500,000 - (1 - .01) \times \text{Amount raised}$$
$$\text{Amount raised} = \$7,500,000/.99 = \$7,575,758$$

So flotation costs are $75,758 and in the text we added these to the initial outlay reducing NPV.

The APV method refines the estimate of flotation costs by recognizing that they generate a tax shield. Flotation costs are paid immediately but are deducted from taxes by amortizing over the life of the loan. In this example, the annual tax deduction for flotation costs is $75,758/5 years = $15,152. At a tax rate of 40 percent, the annual tax shield is $15,152 × .40 = $6,061.

To find the net flotation costs of the loan, add the present value of the tax shield to the flotation costs.

$$\text{Net flotation costs} = -\$75,758 + \$6,061 \times [1 - 1/(1.10)^5]/.10$$
$$= -\$75,758 + \$22,976 = -\$52,782$$

The net present value of the project after debt flotation costs but before the benefits of debt is

$$-\$1,028,164 - \$52,782 = -\$1,080,946$$

Tax Subsidy

The loan of $7.5 million is received at Date 0. Annual interest is $750,000 ($7,500,000 × .10). The interest cost after tax is $450,000 ($750,000 × (1 − .40)). The loan has a balloon payment of the full $7.5 million at the end of five years. The loan gives rise to three sets of cash flows—the loan received, the annual interest cost after taxes, and the repayment of principal. The net present value of the loan is simply the sum of three present values.

$$\begin{aligned}\text{NPV (Loan)} =\ &\text{Amount borrowed}\\ &- \text{Present value of after-tax interest payments}\\ &- \text{Present value of loan repayments}\\ =\ &\$7,500,000 - \$450,000 \times [1 - 1/(1.10)^5]/.10 - \$7,500,000/(1.10)^5\\ =\ &\$7,500,000 - \$1,705,854 - \$4,656,910\\ =\ &\$1,137,236\end{aligned}$$

The NPV of the loan is positive, reflecting the interest tax shield.[22]

---

[21] We base this explanation on teaching materials kindly provided by Alan Marshall.

[22] The NPV (Loan) must be zero in a no-tax world, because interest provides no tax shield there. To check this intuition, we calculate $0 = +\$7,500,000 - \$750,000[1 - 1/(1.10)^5]/.10 - \$7,500,000/(1.10)^5$

The adjusted present value of the project with this financing is:

$$APV = \text{All-equity value} - \text{Flotation costs of debt} + NPV \text{ (Loan)}$$
$$\$56,290 = -\$1,028,164 - \$52,782 + \$1,137,236$$

Though we previously saw that an all-equity firm would reject the project, a firm would accept the project if a \$7.5 million loan could be obtained.

Because this loan discussed was at the market rate of 10 percent, we have considered only two of the three additional effects of debt (flotation costs and tax subsidy) so far. We now examine another loan where the third effect arises.

Non-Market Rate Financing

In Canada a number of companies are fortunate enough to obtain subsidized financing from a governmental authority. Suppose the project of BDE is deemed socially beneficial and a federal governmental agency grants the firm a \$7.5 million loan at 8 percent interest. In addition, the agency absorbs all flotation costs. Clearly, the company would choose this loan over the one we previously calculated. At 8 percent interest, the annual interest payments are $\$7,500,000 \times .08 = \$600,000$. The after-tax payments are $\$360,000 = \$600,000 \times (1 - .40)$. Using the equation we developed,

$$
\begin{aligned}
NPV \text{ (Loan)} = & \text{ Amount borrowed} \\
& - \text{ Present value of after-tax interest payments} \\
& - \text{ Present value of loan repayments} \\
= & \ \$7,500,000 - \$360,000 \times [1 - 1/(1.10)^5]/.10 - \$7,500,000/(1.10)^5 \\
= & \ \$7,500,000 - \$1,364,683 - \$4,656,910 \\
= & \ \$1,478,407
\end{aligned}
$$

Notice that we still discount the cash flows at 10 percent when the firm is borrowing at 8 percent. This is done because 10 percent is the fair, market-wide rate. That is, 10 percent is the rate at which one could borrow without benefit of subsidization. The net present value of the subsidized loan is larger than the net present value of the earlier loan because the firm is now borrowing at the below-market rate of 8 percent. Note that the NPV (Loan) calculation captures both the tax effect and the non-market rate effect.

The net present value of the project with subsidized debt financing is:

$$APV = \text{All-equity value} - \text{Flotation costs of debt} + NPV \text{ (Loan)}$$
$$\$450,243 = -\$1,028,164 - 0 + \$1,478,407$$

Subsidized financing has enhanced the NPV substantially. The result is that the government debt subsidy program will likely achieve its result—encouraging the firm to invest in the kind of project the government agency wishes to encourage.

This example illustrates the adjusted present value (APV) approach. The approach begins with the present value of a project for the all-equity firm. Next, the effects of debt are added in. The approach has much to recommend it. It is intuitively appealing because individual components are calculated separately and added together in a simple way. And, if the debt from the project can be specified precisely, the present value of the debt can be calculated precisely.

APV and Beta

The APV approach discounts cash flows from a scale-enhancing project at the cost of unlevered equity, which is also the cost of capital for the all-equity firm. Because in this chapter we are considering firms that have debt, this unlevered equity does not exist. One must somehow use the beta of the levered equity (which really exists) to calculate the beta for the hypothetical unlevered firm. Then the SML line can be employed to determine the cost of equity capital for the unlevered firm.

We now show how to compute the unlevered firm's beta from the levered equity's beta. To begin, we treat the case of no corporate taxes to explain the intuition behind our results. However, corporate taxes must be included to achieve real-world applicability. We therefore consider taxes in the second case.

No Taxes

In the previous two chapters, we defined the value of the firm to be equal to the value of the firm's debt plus the value of its equity. For a levered firm, this can be represented as $V_L = B + S$. Imagine an individual who owns all the firm's debt and all its equity. In other words, this individual owns the entire firm. What is the beta of his or her portfolio of the firm's debt and equity?

As with any portfolio, the beta of this portfolio is a weighted average of the betas of the individual items in the portfolio. Hence, we have

$$\beta_{Portfolio} = \beta_{Levered\ firm} = \frac{Debt}{Debt + Equity} \times \beta_{Debt} + \frac{Equity}{Debt + Equity} \times \beta_{Equity}$$ [14A.1]

where β_{Equity} is the beta of the equity of the *levered* firm. Notice that the beta of debt is multiplied by Debt/(Debt + Equity), the percentage of debt in the capital structure. Similarly, the beta of equity is multiplied by the percentage of equity in the capital structure. Because the portfolio is the levered firm, the beta of the portfolio is equal to the beta of the levered firm.

The previous equation relates the betas of the financial instruments (debt and equity) to the beta of the levered firm. We need an extra step, however, because we want to relate the betas of the financial instruments to the beta of the firm had it been *unlevered*. Only in this way can we apply APV, because APV begins by discounting the project's cash flows for an all-equity firm.

Ignoring taxes, the cash flows to both the debt holders and the equity holders of a levered firm are equal to the cash flows to the equity holders of an otherwise identical unlevered firm. Because the cash flows are identical for the two firms, the betas of the two firms must be equal as well.

Because the beta of the unlevered firm is equal to Equation 14A.1, we have

$$\beta_{Unlevered\ firm} = \frac{Debt}{Debt + Equity} \times \beta_{Debt} + \frac{Equity}{Debt + Equity} \times \beta_{Equity}$$

The beta of debt is very low in practice. If we make the common assumption that the beta of debt is zero, we have the no-tax case:

$$\beta_{Unlevered\ firm} = \frac{Equity}{Debt + Equity} \times \beta_{Equity}$$ [14A.2]

Because Equity/(Debt + Equity) must be below 1 for a levered firm, it follows that $\beta_{Unlevered\ firm} < \beta_{Equity}$. In words, the beta of the unlevered firm must be less than the beta of the equity in an otherwise identical levered firm. This is consistent with our work on capital structure. We showed there that leverage increases the risk of equity. Because beta is a measure of risk, it is sensible that leverage increases the beta of equity.

Real-world corporations pay taxes, whereas the above results are for no taxes. Thus, although the previous discussion presents the intuition behind an important relationship, it does not help apply the APV method in practice. We examine the tax case next.

Corporate Taxes

It can be shown that the relationship between the beta of the unlevered firm and the beta of the levered equity in the corporate-tax case is:[23]

---

[23] This result holds if the beta of debt equals zero. To see this, note that

$$V_U + T_C B = V_L = B + S \quad (a)$$

where

V_U = value of unlevered firm B = value of debt in a levered firm
V_L = value of levered firm S = value of equity in a levered firm

The formula for V_L and V_U is discussed in Chapter 16.

As we stated in the text, the beta of the levered firm is a weighted average of the debt beta and the equity beta:

$$\frac{B}{B + S} \times \beta_B + \frac{S}{B + S} \times \beta_S$$

where β_B and β_S are the betas of the debt and the equity of the levered firm, respectively. Because $V_L = B + S$, we have

$$\frac{B}{V_L} \times \beta_B + \frac{S}{V_L} \times \beta_S \quad (b)$$

The beta of the leveraged firm can also be expressed as a weighted average of the beta of the unlevered firm and the beta of the tax shield:

$$\frac{V_U}{V_U + T_C B} \times \beta_U + \frac{T_C B}{V_U + T_C B} \times \beta_B$$

where β_U is the beta of the unlevered firm. This follows from Equation (a). Because $V_L = V_U + T_C B$, we have

$$\frac{V_U}{V_L} \times \beta_U + \frac{T_C B}{V_L} \times \beta_B \quad (c)$$

We can equate (b) and (c) because both represent the beta of a levered firm. Equation (a) tells us that $V_U = S + (1 - T_C) \times B$. Under the assumption that $\beta_B = 0$, equating (b) and (c) and using Equation (a) yields Equation 14A.3.

$$\beta_{\text{Unlevered firm}} = \frac{\text{Equity}}{\text{Equity} + (1 - T_C) \times \text{Debt}} \times \beta_{\text{Equity}} \qquad\qquad [14A.3]$$

Equation 14A.3 holds when (1) the corporation is taxed at the rate of T_C and (2) the debt has a zero beta.

Because Equity/(Equity $+ (1 - T_C) \times$ Debt) must be less than 1 for a levered firm, it follows that $\beta_{\text{Unlevered firm}} < \beta_{\text{Equity}}$. The corporate-tax case of (Equation 14A.3) is quite similar to the no-tax case of (Equation 14A.2), because the beta of levered equity must be greater than the beta of the unlevered firm in either case. The intuition that leverage increases the risk of equity applies in both cases.

However, notice that the two equations are not equal. It can be shown that leverage increases the equity beta less rapidly under corporate taxes. This occurs because, under taxes, leverage creates a riskless tax shield, thereby lowering the risk of the entire firm.

EXAMPLE 14A.1: Applying APV

Trans Canada Industries is considering a scale-enhancing project. The market value of the firm's debt is $100 million, and the market value of the firm's equity is $200 million. The debt is considered riskless. The corporate tax rate is 34 percent. Regression analysis indicates that the beta of the firm's equity is 2. The risk-free rate is 10 percent, and the expected market premium is 8.5 percent. What is the project's discount rate in the hypothetical case that Trans Canada is all equity?

We can answer this question in two steps.

1. Determining beta of hypothetical all-equity firm. Using Equation 14A.3, we have:

Unlevered beta:
[$200 million/$200 million + (1 − 0.34) × $100 million] × 2 = 1.50

2. Determining discount rate. We calculate the discount rate from the SML as:

Discount rate: $R_S = R_f + \beta \times [E(R_M) - R_f]$
22.75% = 10% + 1.50 × 8.5%

Thus, the APV method says that the project's NPV should be calculated by discounting the cash flows at the all equity rate of 22.75 percent. As we discussed earlier in this chapter, the tax shield should then be added to the NPV of the cash flows, yielding APV.

The Project Is Not Scale-Enhancing

This example assumed that the project is scale-enhancing, doing what the firm does already on a larger scale. So, we began with the beta of the firm's equity. If the project is not scale-enhancing, one could begin with the equity betas of firms in the industry of the project. For each firm, the hypothetical beta of the unlevered equity could be calculated by Equation 14A.3. The SML could then be used to determine the project's discount rate from the average of these betas.

Comparison of WACC and APV

In Chapter 14 we provided two approaches to capital budgeting for firms that use debt financing. Both WACC and APV attempt the same task: to value projects when debt financing is allowed. However, as we have shown, the approaches are markedly different in technique. Because of this, it is worthwhile to compare the two approaches.[24]

WACC is an older approach that has been used extensively in business. APV is a newer approach that, while attracting a large following in academic circles, is used less commonly in business. Over the years, we have met with many executives in firms using both approaches. They have frequently pointed out to us that the cost of equity, the cost of debt, and the proportions of debt and equity can easily be calculated for a firm as a whole.

Some projects are scale-enhancing with the same risk as the whole firm. An example is a fast-food chain adding more company-owned outlets. In this case, it is straightforward to calculate the project's NPV with WACC. However, both the proportions and the costs of debt and equity are different for the project than for the firm as a whole if the project is not scale-enhancing. WACC is more difficult to use in that case.

As a result, firms may switch between approaches using WACC for scale-enhancing projects and APV for special situations. For example, an acquisition of a firm in a completely different industry is clearly not scale-enhancing. So when Campeau Corporation, originally a real estate firm, acquired Federated Depart-

---

[24] In some circumstances faced by multinational firms, APV breaks down. See L. Booth, "Capital Budgeting Frameworks for the Multinational Corporation," *Journal of International Business Studies*, Fall 1982, pp. 113–23.

ment Stores, APV analysis would have been appropriate because Federated was in a different industry. Also, the acquisition was through a leveraged buyout involving a large (with hindsight, too large) amount of debt and the APV approach values the NPV of the loan.

1. What are the steps in using adjusted present value (APV) to value a project?
2. Compare APV with WACC. In what situations is each best applied?

Appendix Questions and Problems

A.1 APV Problem A mining company has discovered a small silver deposit neighbouring its existing mine site. It has been estimated that there is a 10-year supply of silver in the deposit that would return $13.5 million annually to the firm. The estimated cost of developing the site is $63.6 million and could be financed by the issuance of shares. The firm has experienced significant growth, and this is reflected in a cost of equity of 21.6 percent. After analyzing the returns to the project, the firm's chief financial officer (CFO) recommends to the board not to continue with it as it is not profitable to the firm. However, in speaking with an investment dealer the following week, the CFO is told that it would be possible to float bonds for up to $42 million carrying a coupon of 12 percent. The flotation costs for debt and equity are both 1.2 percent and the marginal tax rate for the firm is 40 percent. Is it profitable for the firm to continue with the project now?

A.2 APV Problem What would be the marginal benefit to the mining company if it could obtain a government loan for $42 million at 8.4 percent that has a balloon payment for the full amount at the end of 10 years? Assume there are no flotation costs for this loan.

A.3 APV Problem A firm is considering a project that will last five years and will generate an annual cash flow of $9 million. The project requires an initial investment of $28 million. Assume that the cost of equity for the project is 20 percent, if the project is 100 percent equity financed. The firm can obtain a loan for $22.5 million to start the project, at a rate of 10 percent ($2.25 million in interest paid each year, with principal paid in a lump sum at the end of the loan). However, the lender will only extend the loan for three years. The firm's tax rate is 30 percent. Calculate the APV of the project. Is this investment worthwhile for the firm?

APPENDIX 14B

ECONOMIC VALUE ADDED AND THE MEASUREMENT OF FINANCIAL PERFORMANCE

Chapter 13 shows how to calculate the appropriate discount rate for capital budgeting and other valuation problems. We now consider the measurement of financial performance. We introduce the concept of economic value added, which uses the same discount rate developed for capital budgeting. We begin with a simple example.

Calculating Economic Value Added

Many years ago, Henry Bodenheimer started Bodie's Blimps, one of the largest high-speed blimp manufacturers. Because growth was so rapid, Henry put most of his effort into capital budgeting. His approach to capital budgeting paralleled that of Chapter 13. He forecasted cash flows for various projects and discounted them at the cost of capital appropriate to the beta of the blimp business. However, these projects have grown rapidly, in some cases becoming whole divisions. He now needs to evaluate the performance of these divisions in order to reward his division managers. How does he perform the appropriate analysis?

Henry is aware that capital budgeting and performance measurement are essentially mirror images of each other. Capital budgeting is forward-looking by nature because one must estimate future cash flows to value a project. By contrast, performance measurement is backward-looking. As Henry stated to a group of his executives, "Capital budgeting is like looking through the windshield while driving a car. You need to know what lies further down the road to calculate a net present value. Performance measurement is like looking into the rearview mirror. You find out where you have been."

Henry first measured the performance of his various divisions by return on assets (ROA), an approach, which we treated in the appendix to Chapter 3. For example, if a division had earnings after tax of $1,000 and had assets of $10,000, the ROA would be[25]

$$\frac{\$1,000}{\$10,000} = 10\%$$

He calculated the ROA ratio for each of his divisions, paying a bonus to each of his division managers based on the size of that division's ROA. However, while ROA was generally effective in motivating his managers, there were a number of situations where it appeared that ROA was counterproductive.

For example, Henry always believed that Sharon Smith, head of the supersonic division, was his best manager. The ROA of Smith's division was generally in the high double digits, but the best estimate of the weighted average cost of capital for the division was only 20 percent. Furthermore, the division had been growing rapidly. However, as soon as Henry paid bonuses based on ROA, the division stopped growing. At that time, Smith's division had after-tax earnings of $2,000,000 on an asset base of $2,000,000, for an ROA of 100 percent ($2 million/$2 million).

Henry found out why the growth stopped when he suggested a project to Smith that would earn $1,000,000 per year on an investment of $2,000,000. This was clearly an attractive project with an ROA of 50 percent ($1 million/$2 million). He thought that Smith would jump at the chance to place his project into her division, because the ROA of the project was much higher than the cost of capital of 20 percent. However, Smith did everything she could to kill the project. And, as Henry later figured out, Smith was rational to do so. Smith must have realized that if the project were accepted, the division's ROA would become

$$\frac{\$2,000,000 + \$1,000,000}{\$2,000,000 + \$2,000,000} = 75\%$$

Thus, the ROA of Smith's division would fall from 100 percent to 75 percent if the project were accepted, with Smith's bonus falling in tandem.

Henry was later exposed to the economic-value-added (EVA) approach,[26] which seems to solve this particular problem. The formula for EVA is

[ROA − Weighted average cost of capital] × Total capital

Without the new project, the EVA of Smith's division would be:

[100% − 20%] × $2,000,000 = $1,600,000

This is an annual number. That is, the division would bring in $1.6 million above and beyond the cost of capital to the firm each year.

With the new project included, the EVA jumps to

[75% − 20%] × $4,000,000 = $2,200,000

If Sharon Smith knew that her bonus was based on EVA, she would now have an incentive to accept, not reject, the project. Although ROA appears in the EVA formula, EVA differs substantially from ROA. The big difference is that ROA is a percentage number and EVA is a dollar value. In the preceding example, EVA increased when the new project was added even though the ROA actually decreased. In this situation, EVA correctly incorporates the fact that a high return on a large division may be better than a very high return on a smaller division.

Further understanding of EVA can be achieved by rewriting the EVA formula. Because ROA × total capital is equal to earnings after tax, we can write the EVA formula as:

Earnings after tax − Weighted average cost of capital × Total capital

Thus, EVA can simply be viewed as earnings after capital costs. Although accountants subtract many costs (including depreciation) to get the earnings number shown in financial reports, they do not subtract out

---

[25] Earnings after tax is EBIT $(1 - T_C)$ where EBIT is earnings before interest and taxes and T_C is the tax rate. Stern Stewart and other EVA users refer to EBIT $(1 - T_C)$ as net operating profit after tax.

[26] Stern Stewart & Company have a copyright on the terms *economic value added* and EVA. Details on the Stern Stewart & Company EVA can be found in J. M. Stern, G. B. Stewart, and D. A. Chew, "The EVA Financial Management System," *Journal of Applied Corporate Finance* (Summer 1999).

capital costs. One can see the logic of accountants, because the cost of capital is very subjective. By contrast, costs such as COGS (cost of goods sold), SG&A (Selling, General and Administrative Expesnses), and even depreciation can be measured more objectively.[27] However, even if the cost of capital is difficult to estimate, it is hard to justify ignoring it completely. After all, this textbook argues that the cost of capital is a necessary input to capital budgeting. Shouldn't it also be a necessary input to performance measurement?

This example argues that EVA can increase investment for those firms that are currently underinvesting. However, there are many firms in the reverse situation; the managers are so focused on increasing earnings that they take on projects for which the profits do not justify the capital outlays. These managers either are unaware of capital costs or, knowing these costs, choose to ignore them. Because the cost of capital is right in the middle of the EVA formula, managers will not easily ignore these costs when evaluated on an EVA system.

One other advantage of EVA is that the number is either positive or it is negative. Plenty of divisions have negative EVAs for a number of years. Because these divisions are destroying more value than they are creating, a strong point can be made for liquidating these divisions. Although managers are generally emotionally opposed to this type of action, EVA analysis makes liquidation harder to ignore.

EXAMPLE 14B.1

Assume the following figures for the International Trade Corporation

$$\text{EBIT} = \$2.5 \text{ billion}$$
$$T_C = 0.4$$
$$r_{wacc} = 11\%$$

$$\text{Total capital contributed} = \text{Total debt} + \text{Equity}$$
$$= \$10 \text{ billion} + \$10 \text{ billion}$$
$$= \$20 \text{ billion}$$

Now we can calculate International Trade's EVA:

$$\text{EVA} = \text{EBIT} (1 - T_C) - r_{wacc} \times \text{Total capital}$$
$$= (\$2.5 \text{ billion} \times 0.6) - (0.11 \times \$20 \text{ billion})$$
$$= \$1.5 \text{ billion} - \$2.2 \text{ billion}$$
$$= -\$700 \text{ million}$$

In this example, International Trade Corporation has a negative EVA—it is destroying shareholder value.

Some Caveats on EVA

The preceding discussion puts EVA in a very positive light. However, one can certainly find much to criticize with EVA as well. We now focus on two well-known problems with EVA. First, the preceding example uses EVA for performance measurement, where we believe it properly belongs. To us, EVA seems a clear improvement over ROA and other financial ratios. However, EVA has little to offer for capital budgeting because EVA focuses only on current earnings. By contrast, net-present-value analysis uses projections of all future cash flows, where the cash flows will generally differ from year to year. Although supporters may argue that EVA correctly incorporates the weighted average cost of capital, one must remember that the discount rate in NPV analysis is the same weighted average cost of capital. That is, both approaches take the cost of equity capital based on beta and combine it with the cost of debt to get an estimate of this weighted average.

A second problem with EVA is that it may increase the shortsightedness of managers. Under EVA, a manager will be well rewarded today if earnings are high today. Future losses may not harm the manager, because there is a good chance that she will be promoted or have left the firm by then. Thus, the manager has an incentive to run a division with more regard for short-term than long-term value. By raising prices or cutting quality, the manager may increase current profits (and, therefore, current EVA). However, to the extent that customer satisfaction is reduced, future profits (and therefore future EVA) are likely to fall. However, one should not be too harsh with EVA here, because the same problem occurs with ROA. A manager who raises prices or cuts quality will increase current ROA at the expense of future ROA. The problem, then, is not EVA per se but with the use of accounting numbers in general. Because shareholders want the discounted present value of all cash flows to be maximized, managers with bonuses based on some function of current profits or current cash flows are likely to behave in a shortsighted way.

---

[27] Some EVA users add back depreciation and other non-cash items. A Canadian example is: B.A. Schofield, "Evaluating Stocks," *Canadian Investment Review* (Spring 2000).

Despite these shortcomings EVA or something similar is used widely by corporations in Canada and the U.S. Table 14B.1 lists some examples.

TABLE 14B.1

Selected economic value added users

United States	Canada
Bausch & Lomb	Alcan Aluminum
Briggs and Stratton Crop.	Cogeco Inc.
Coca-Cola Company	Domtar Inc.
Dun & Bradstreet Corp.	Grand & Toy
Eli Lilly & Co.	Long Manufacturing
JC Penney	Robin Hood Multifoods
Monsanto	
Rubbermaid Inc.	
Print	
Toys R Us	
U.S. Postal Service	
Whirlpool	

Source: Adapted from sternstewart.com.

Concept Questions

1. Why is capital budgeting important to a firm?
2. What is the major difference between EVA and ROA?
3. What are the advantages of using EVA?
4. What are the well-known problems of EVA?

Appendix Questions and Problems

B.1 As a new financial analyst at ABC Co., your manager has decided to give you two projects to evaluate for the company. Prior to undertaking either of these projects, the company has an ROA of 37 percent on total assets of $12 million. Project A would involve an investment of $5.5 million, and would derive after-tax earnings of $1.3 million. Project B would involve an investment of $3 million, but would only produce after-tax earnings of $450,000. The cost of capital for the firm is 17.5 percent. You have been asked to undertake an EVA analysis to determine which of these projects should be selected (if any).

B.2 You are the manager of a department that recently launched a new product line for High Flyer Incorporated. High Flyer invested $3.8 million of equity and $2.2 million of debt in the project, and the project has earned the company earnings before taxes of $1.25 million in 2006. The firm's capital structure has a market value of $110 million for debt and $185 million of equity. The cost of debt is 6.8 percent, and the cost of equity is currently 11.3 percent. If the firm pays taxes at a rate of 36 percent, what is the EVA of the project your department launched?

CHAPTER 15

RAISING CAPITAL

The Canadian Press/
Craig Ruttle

In an eagerly awaited initial public offering, the social networking giant Facebook went public on May 18, 2012. Assisted by leading underwriters such as Morgan Stanley and Goldman Sachs, Facebook sold around 420 million shares at U.S. $38 per share. While the shares of the company soared more than 10 percent at the start of trading on the NASDAQ it ended the day at its opening price. Obviously, this came as a disappointment to Facebook executives including Mark Zuckerberg, the CEO of the company.

According to a PwC review of IPO activity, the Canadian market for IPOs struggled to hit $2 billion in 2011. The European debt crises, the natural disaster in Japan, the political upheaval in the Middle East, and concerns over slowing growth in China created a weaker market for Canadian IPOs in 2011. In this chapter, we will examine the process by which companies such as Facebook sell stock to the public, the costs of doing so, and the role of investment banks in the process.

Learning Objectives ▶

After studying this chapter, you should understand:

LO1 The venture capital market and its role in the financing of new, high-risk ventures.

LO2 How securities are sold to the public and the role of investment banks in the process.

LO3 Initial public offerings and some of the costs of going public.

LO4 How rights are issued to existing shareholders and how to value those rights.

All firms must, at varying times, obtain capital. To do so, a firm must either borrow the money (debt financing), sell a portion of the firm (equity financing), or both. How a firm raises capital depends a great deal on the size of the firm, its life cycle stage, and its growth prospects.

In this chapter, we examine some of the ways in which firms actually raise capital. We begin by looking at companies in the early stages of their lives and the importance of venture capital for such firms. We then look at the process of going public and the role of investment banks. Along the way, we discuss many of the issues associated with selling securities to the public and their implications for all types of firms. We close the chapter with a discussion of sources of debt capital.

15.1 | The Financing Life Cycle of a Firm: Early-Stage Financing and Venture Capital

One day, you and a friend have a great idea for a new GPS device that drives a car automatically without manual intervention. Filled with entrepreneurial zeal, you christen the product 'Hands-Free Drive' and set about bringing it to market.

Working nights and weekends, you are able to create a prototype of your product. It doesn't actually work, but at least you can show it around to illustrate your idea. To develop the product, you need to hire programmers, buy a GPS device, hire automobile expert, and so on. Unfortunately, because you are both university students, your combined assets are not sufficient to cover a start-up company. You need what is often referred to as OPM—other people's money.

Your first thought might be to approach a bank for a loan. You would probably discover, however, that banks are generally not interested in making loans to start-up companies with no assets (other than an idea) run by fledgling entrepreneurs with no track record. Instead, your search for capital would very likely lead you to use your own wealth (mortgaging the home) as well as borrowing from relatives and wealthy friends. If more capital needs to be raised, the next step would lead you to the venture capital market.

Venture Capital

The term **venture capital** does not have a precise meaning, but it generally refers to financing for new, often high-risk, ventures. For example, before they went public, Research in Motion (RIM) and Apple were financed by venture capital. Individual venture capitalists invest their own money; so-called angels are usually individual investors, but they tend to specialize in smaller deals.[1] Venture capital firms specialize in pooling funds from various sources and investing them. The underlying sources of funds for such firms include individuals, pension funds, insurance companies, large corporations, and even university endowment funds. The broad term *private equity* is often used to label the rapidly growing area of equity financing for nonpublic companies.[2]

Venture capitalists and venture capital firms recognize that many or even most new ventures will not fly, but the occasional one will. The potential profits are enormous in such cases. To limit their risk, venture capitalists generally provide financing in stages. At each stage, enough money is invested to reach the next milestone or planning stage. For example, the *first-stage financing* might be enough to get a prototype built and a manufacturing plan completed. Based on the results, the *second-stage financing* might be a major investment needed to begin manufacturing, marketing, and distribution. There might be many such stages, each of which represents a key step in the process of growing the company.

Venture capital firms often specialize in different stages. Some specialize in very early "seed money," or ground floor, financing. In contrast, financing in the later stages might come from venture capitalists specializing in so-called mezzanine level financing, where *mezzanine level* refers to the level just above the ground floor.

The fact that financing is available in stages and is contingent on specified goals being met is a powerful motivating force for the firm's founders. Often, the founders receive relatively little in the way of salary and have substantial portions of their personal assets tied up in the business. At each stage of financing, the value of the founder's stake grows and the probability of success rises.

In addition to providing financing, venture capitalists often actively participate in running the firm, providing the benefit of experience with previous start-ups as well as general business expertise. This is especially true when the firm's founders have little or no hands-on experience in running a company.

Some Venture Capital Realities

Although there is a large venture capital market, the truth is that access to venture capital is really very limited. Venture capital companies receive huge numbers of unsolicited proposals, the vast majority of which end up in the circular file unread. Venture capitalists rely heavily on informal networks of lawyers, accountants, bankers, and other venture capitalists to help identify potential investments. As a result, personal contacts are important in gaining access to the venture capital market; it is very much an "introduction" market.

Another simple fact about venture capital is that it is incredibly expensive, a fact that is inevitable given the high risk involved in such firms. In a typical deal, the venture capitalist will demand (and get) 40 percent or more of the equity in the company. Venture capitalists will frequently hold voting preferred stock, giving them various priorities in the event that the company is sold or liquidated. The venture capitalist will typically demand (and get) several seats on the company's board of directors and may even appoint one or more members of senior management.

Choosing a Venture Capitalist

Some start-up companies, particularly those headed by experienced, previously successful entrepreneurs, will be in such demand that they will have the luxury of looking beyond the money in

---

[1] For discussion of this topic in Canada see A. Riding, "Roundtable on Angel Investment in Canada," *Canadian Investment Review,* Fall 2000; and Joseph Lo, "Note on Venture Capital," Richard Ivey School of Business, 9B04N005, 2004.

[2] So-called vulture capitalists specialize in high-risk investments in established, but financially distressed, firms.

choosing a venture capitalist. There are some key considerations in such a case, some of which can be summarized as follows:

1. Financial strength is important. The venture capitalist needs to have the resources and financial reserves for additional financing stages should they become necessary. This does not mean that bigger is necessarily better, however, because of our next consideration.

2. Style is important. Some venture capitalists will wish to be very much involved in day-to-day operations and decision making, whereas others will be content with monthly reports. Which are better depends on the firm and also on the venture capitalists' business skills. In addition, a large venture capital firm may be less flexible and more bureaucratic than a smaller "boutique" firm.

3. References are important. Has the venture capitalist been successful with similar firms? Of equal importance, how has the venture capitalist dealt with situations that didn't work out?

4. Contacts are important. A venture capitalist may be able to help the business in ways other than helping with financing and management by providing introductions to potentially important customers, suppliers, and other industry contacts. Venture capitalist firms frequently specialize in a few particular industries, and such specialization could prove quite valuable.

5. Exit strategy is important. Venture capitalists are generally not long-term investors. How and under what circumstances the venture capitalist will "cash out" of the business should be carefully evaluated.

Conclusion

If a start-up succeeds, the big payoff frequently comes when the company is sold to another company or goes public. The IPO process has created many "dot-com" millionaires. Either way, investment bankers are often involved in the process. We discuss the process of selling securities to the public in the next several sections, paying particular attention to the process of going public.

Concept Questions

1. What is venture capital?
2. Why is venture capital often provided in stages?

15.2 | The Public Issue

public issue
The creation and sale of securities on public markets.

As the term implies, a **public issue** refers to the creation and sale of securities, which are intended to be traded on the public markets. A firm issuing securities must satisfy a number of requirements set out by provincial regulations and statutes and enforced by provincial securities commissions. Regulation of the securities market in Canada is carried out by provincial commissions and through provincial securities acts. Each province and territory has its own securities commission. This is in contrast to the United States, where regulation is handled by a federal body, the Securities and Exchange Commission (SEC). The goal of the regulators is to promote the efficient flow of information about securities and the smooth functioning of securities markets.

All companies listed on the Toronto Stock Exchange come under the jurisdiction of the Ontario Securities Commission (OSC). The *Securities* Act sets forth the provincial regulations for all new securities issues involving the province of Ontario and the Toronto Stock Exchange. The OSC administers the act. Other provinces have similar legislation and regulating bodies; however, the OSC is the most noteworthy because of the scope of the TSX.[3] The Canadian Securities Administration (CSA) coordinates across provinces. One of the most recent efforts by the CSA has been to

---

[3] The TSX is Canada's largest exchange and its dollar trading ranked 8th in the world behind the NYSE Euronext (US) (number 1) and NASDAQ OMX (US) (number 2) in 2011. Chapter 8 discusses equity markets in more detail.

streamline Canadian securities regulations by establishing guidelines for uniform securities laws to be applied in Canada's 13 securities jurisdictions. In general terms, OSC rules seek to ensure that investors receive all material information on new issues in the form of a registration statement and prospectus.

The OSC's responsibilities for efficient information flow go beyond new issues. It continues to regulate the trading of securities after they have been issued to ensure adequate disclosure of information. For example, in April 2011 the OSC accused the former executives of Coventree Inc. of failing to disclose bad news to investors about the material changes in its asset-backed commercial paper (ABCP).

Another role of the OSC is gathering and publishing *insider reports* filed by major shareholders, officers, and directors of TSX-listed firms. To ensure efficient functioning of markets, the OSC oversees the training and supervision that investment dealers provide for their personnel. It also works with the Investment Industry Regulatory Organization of Canada (IIROC) to monitor investment dealers' capital positions. Increasing market volatility and the popularity of bought deals where the dealer assumes all the price risk make capital adequacy important.

15.3 | The Basic Procedure for a New Issue

There is a series of steps involved in issuing securities to the public. In general terms, the basic procedure is as follows:

1. Management's first step in issuing any securities to the public is to obtain approval from the board of directors. In some cases, the number of authorized shares of common stock must be increased. This requires a vote of the shareholders.

2. The firm must prepare and distribute copies of a preliminary **prospectus** to the OSC and to potential investors. The preliminary prospectus contains some of the financial information that will be contained in the final prospectus; it does not contain the price at which the security will be offered. The preliminary prospectus is sometimes called a **red herring**, in part because bold red letters are printed on the cover warning that the OSC has neither approved nor disapproved of the securities. The OSC studies the preliminary prospectus and notifies the company of any changes required. This process is usually completed within about two weeks.

3. Once the revised, final prospectus meets with the OSC's approval, a price is determined, and a full-fledged selling effort gets under way. A final prospectus must accompany the delivery of securities or confirmation of sale, whichever comes first. You can find current examples of Canadian prospectuses at the website of the System for Electronic Documents and Retrieval (SEDAR).

Tombstone advertisements are placed during and after the waiting period. The tombstone contains the name of the company whose securities are involved. It provides some information about the issue, and it lists the investment dealers (the underwriters) who are involved with selling the issue. We discuss the role of the investment dealers in selling securities more fully later.

The investment dealers are divided into groups called *brackets* on the tombstone and prospectus, and the names of the dealers are listed alphabetically within each bracket. The brackets are a kind of pecking order. In general, the higher the bracket, the greater the underwriter's prestige. In recent years, the use of printed tombstones has declined, in part as a cost-saving measure.

While an underwriter's prestige is important for a **seasoned new issue** by a well-known company already traded on the TSX, it is even more critical for the first public equity issue referred to as an **initial public offering (IPO)**, or an unseasoned new issue. An IPO occurs when a company decides to go public. Researchers have found that IPOs with prestigious underwriters perform better. This is likely because investors believe that prestigious underwriters, jealous of their reputations, shun questionable IPOs.[4]

prospectus
Legal document describing details of the issuing corporation and the proposed offering to potential investors.

red herring
A preliminary prospectus distributed to prospective investors in a new issue of securities.

seasoned new issue
A new issue of securities by a firm that has already issued securities in the past.

initial public offering (IPO)
A company's first equity issue made available to the public. Also an unseasoned new issue.

---

[4] Richard Carter and Steven Manaster, "Initial Public Offerings and Underwriter Reputation," *Journal of Finance* 1990, 45(4), 1045–1067.

Securities Registration

The SEC employs a shelf registration system designed to reduce repetitive filing requirements for large companies. The OSC's SFPD (short form prospectus distribution) system has a similar goal. The provincial securities commissions all have compatible legislation allowing certain securities issuers prompt access to capital markets without preparing a full preliminary and final prospectus before a distribution.

The SFPD system, accessible only by large companies, lets issuers file annual and interim financial statements regardless of whether they issue securities in a given year. To use the POP (Prompt Offering Prospectus) system, issuers must have not only reported for 36 months but also complied with the continuous disclosure requirements. Because the OSC has an extensive file of information on these companies, only a short prospectus is required when securities are issued.

In the early 1990s, securities regulators in Canada and the SEC in the United States introduced a Multi-Jurisdictional Disclosure System (MJDS). Under MJDS, large issuers in the two countries are allowed to issue securities in both countries under disclosure documents satisfactory to regulators in the home country. In its day, this was an important simplification of filing requirements for certain large Canadian companies. While MJDS is based on a model of companies issuing securities simultaneously at home and in foreign markets, many Canadian companies are cross-listed on the NYSE or Nasdaq. Cross-listing refers to the practice of listing a firm's shares for trading on other exchanges, usually in foreign countries. For Canadian firms, cross-listing opens up the alternative of issuing in larger U.S. stock markets. Possible advantages of U.S. listing include greater liquidity, lower trading costs, greater visibility, and greater investor protection under more stringent U.S. securities laws such as *Sarbanes-Oxley* on corporate governance. U.S. listing also brings possible disadvantages in the form of higher accounting and compliance costs. On balance, it remains undecided whether U.S. listing adds shareholder value.

Alternative Issue Methods

general cash offer
An issue of securities offered for sale to the general public on a cash basis.

rights offer
A public issue of securities in which securities are first offered to existing shareholders. Also called a rights offering.

For equity sales, there are two kinds of public issues: a **general cash offer** and a **rights offer** (or *rights offering*). With a cash offer, securities are offered to the general public. With a rights offer, securities are initially offered only to existing owners. Rights offers are fairly common in other countries, but they are relatively rare in Canada (and the United States), particularly in recent years. We therefore focus primarily on cash offers in this chapter.

The first public equity issue that is made by a company is referred to as an initial public offering, IPO, or an *unseasoned new issue*. This issue occurs when a company decides to go public. Obviously, all initial public offerings are cash offers. If the firm's existing shareholders wanted to buy the shares, the firm wouldn't have to sell them publicly in the first place.

seasoned equity offering (SEO)
A new equity issue of securities by a company that has previously issued securities to the public.

A **seasoned equity offering (SEO)** is a new issue for a company with securities that have been previously issued. A seasoned equity offering of common stock can be made by using a cash offer or a rights offer.

These methods of issuing new securities are shown in Table 15.1. They are discussed in Sections 15.4 through 15.8.

15.4 | The Cash Offer

If the public issue of securities is a cash offer, underwriters are usually involved. Underwriters perform the following services for corporate issuers:

- Formulating the method used to issue the securities.
- Pricing the new securities.
- Selling the new securities.

Typically, the underwriter buys the securities for less than the offering price and accepts the risk of not being able to sell them. Because underwriting involves risk, underwriters combine to form an underwriting group called a **syndicate** or a *banking group* to share the risk and help to sell the issue.

syndicate
A group of underwriters formed to reduce the risk and help to sell an issue.

In a syndicate, one or more managers arrange or co-manage the offering. This manager is designated as the lead manager and typically has the responsibility for packaging and executing the deal. The other underwriters in the syndicate serve primarily to distribute the issue.

TABLE 15.1

Methods of issuing new securities

Method	Type	Definition
Public Traditional negotiated cash offer	Firm commitment cash offer	Company negotiates an agreement with an investment banker to underwrite and distribute the new shares. A specified number of shares are bought by underwriters and sold at a higher price.
	Best efforts cash offer	Company has investment bankers sell as many of the new shares as possible at the agreed-upon price. There is no guarantee concerning how much cash will be raised.
	Dutch auction cash offer	Company has investment bankers auction shares to determine the highest offer price obtainable for a given number of shares to be sold.
Privileged subscription	Direct rights offer	Company offers the new stock directly to its existing shareholders.
	Standby rights offer	Like the direct rights offer, this contains a privileged subscription arrangement with existing shareholders. The net proceeds are guaranteed by the underwriters.
Nontraditional cash offer	Shelf cash offer	Qualifying companies can authorize all shares they expect to sell over a two-year period and sell them when needed.
	Competitive firm cash offer	Company can elect to award the underwriting contract through a public auction instead of negotiation.
Private	Direct placement	Securities are sold directly to the purchaser, who, at least until recently, generally could not resell securities for 4 months.

spread
Compensation to the underwriter, determined by the difference between the underwriter's buying price and offering price.

bought deal
One underwriter buys securities from an issuing firm and sells them directly to a small number of investors.

regular underwriting
The purchase of securities from the issuing company by an investment banker for resale to the public.

firm commitment underwriting
Underwriter buys the entire issue, assuming full financial responsibility for any unsold shares.

best efforts underwriting
Underwriter sells as much of the issue as possible, but can return any unsold shares to the issuer without financial responsibility.

The difference between the underwriter's buying and the offering price is called the **spread** or *discount*. It is the basic compensation received by the underwriter.

In Canada, firms often establish long-term relationships with their underwriters. With the growth in popularity of **bought deals**, competition among underwriters has increased. At the same time, mergers among investment dealers have reduced the number of underwriters. For example, RBC Dominion Securities grew through merger with six other investment dealers and a major capital injection by the Royal Bank.

Types of Underwriting

Two basic types of underwriting are possible in a cash offer: regular underwriting and a bought deal.

With **regular underwriting** the banking group of underwriters buys the securities from the issuing firm and resells them to the public for the purchase price plus an underwriting spread. Regular underwriting includes a market out clause that gives the banking group the option to decline the issue if the price drops dramatically. In this case, the deal is usually withdrawn. The issue might be repriced and/or reoffered at a later date. **Firm commitment underwriting** is like regular underwriting without the market out clause.

A close counterpart to regular underwriting is called **best efforts underwriting**. The underwriter is legally bound to use its best efforts to sell the securities at the agreed-on offering price. Beyond this, the underwriter does not guarantee any particular amount of money to the issuer. This form of underwriting is more common with initial public offerings (IPOs), and with smaller, less well-known companies.

Bought Deal

In a bought deal, the issuer sells the entire issue to one investment dealer or to a group that attempts to resell it. As in firm commitment underwriting, the investment dealer assumes all the price risk. The dealer usually markets the prospective issue to a few large, institutional investors. Issuers in bought deals are large, well-known firms qualifying for the use of SPDF to speed up OSC filings. For these reasons, bought deals are usually executed swiftly. Bought deals are the most popular form of underwriting in Canada today. Bought deals have smaller offer price discounts and smaller underwriting fees, implying superior pricing and thus, higher quality offerings.[5] For example in June 2012, Fortis Inc., a St. John's, Newfoundland and Labrador based international diversified electric utility holding company, closed its $601 million bought-deal offering of subscription receipts underwritten by a syndicate of underwriters led by CIBC World Markets Inc., Scotia Capital Inc., and TD Securities Inc.

Dutch Auction Underwriting

Dutch auction underwriting

The type of underwriting in which the offer price is set based on competitive bidding by investors. Also known as a *uniform price auction.*

google.com/about/company/

wrhambrecht.com

With **Dutch auction underwriting**, the underwriter does not set a fixed price for the shares to be sold. Instead, the underwriter conducts an auction in which investors bid for shares. The offer price is determined based on the submitted bids. A Dutch auction is also known by the more descriptive name *uniform price auction.* This approach to selling securities to the public was used by Google. It is still relatively new in the IPO market and has not been widely used there, but it is very common in the bond markets. For example, it is the sole procedure used by the U.S. Treasury to sell enormous quantities of notes, bonds, and bills to the public. Also, in June 2012, AOL Inc., an internet-based American giant, started a "Dutch auction" tender offer to buy back up to $400 million of its common stock. Earlier, the company sold more than 800 patents and related patent applications to Microsoft and used the sale proceeds to buy back the shares.

The best way to understand a Dutch or uniform price auction is to consider a simple example. Suppose the Rial Company wants to sell 400 shares to the public. The company receives five bids as follows:

Bidder	Quantity	Price
A	100 shares	$16
B	100 shares	14
C	200 shares	12
D	200 shares	12
E	200 shares	10

Thus, bidder A is willing to buy 100 shares at $16 each, bidder B is willing to buy 100 shares at $14, and so on. The Rial Company examines the bids to determine the highest price that will result in all 400 shares being sold. So, for example, at $14, A and B would buy only 200 shares, so that price is too high. Working our way down, all 400 shares won't be sold until we hit a price of $12, so $12 will be the offer price in the IPO. Bidders A through D will receive shares; bidder E will not.

There are two additional important points to observe in our example: First, all the winning bidders will pay $12, even bidders A and B, who actually bid a higher price. The fact that all successful bidders pay the same price is the reason for the name "uniform price auction." The idea in such an auction is to encourage bidders to bid aggressively by providing some protection against bidding a price that is too high.

Second, notice that at the $12 offer price, there are actually bids for 600 shares, which exceeds the 400 shares Rial wants to sell. Thus, there has to be some sort of allocation. How this is done varies a bit, but, in the IPO market, the approach has been to simply compute the ratio of shares offered to shares bid at the offer price or better, which, in our example, is 400/600 = 0.67, and allocate bidders that percentage of their bids. In other words, bidders A through D would each receive 67 percent of the shares they bid for at a price of $12 per share.

The Selling Period

While the issue is being sold to the public, the underwriting group agrees not to sell securities for less than the offering price until the syndicate dissolves. The principal underwriter is permitted to buy shares if the market price falls below the offering price. The purpose would be to support the market and stabilize the price from temporary downward pressure. If this issue remains unsold after a time (for example, 30 days), members can leave the group and sell their shares at whatever price the market allows.

---

[5] Pandes, J. Ari, Bought Deals: The Value of Underwriter Certification in Seasoned Equity Offerings (March 3, 2010). *Journal of Banking and Finance,* Vol. 34, No. 7, 2010.

The Overallotment Option

overallotment option
An underwriting provision that permits syndicate members to purchase additional shares at the original offering price.

Many underwriting contracts contain an **overallotment option** or *Green Shoe provision* that gives the members of the underwriting group the option to purchase additional shares at the offering price less fees and commissions.[6] The stated reason for the overallotment option is to cover excess demand and oversubscriptions. The option has a short maturity, around 30 days, and is limited to about 15 percent of the original number of shares issued.

The overallotment option is a benefit to the underwriting syndicate and a cost to the issuer. If the market price of the new issue rises immediately, the overallotment option allows the underwriters to buy additional shares from the issuer and immediately resell them to the public.

In the Facebook IPO introduced in the chapter opener, the underwriters had an option to exercise the Green Shoe provision and raise another $18.4 billion. When the IPO was priced and allocated, the underwriters sold at least 15% more shares than their initial allocation. That left them 'short' around 63 million shares. If there had been an increase in the share price, the underwriters would have exercised the *Green Shoe* option to go back to Facebook and buy those 63 million shares at $38, in order to cover their short position. As it turned out, the share price fell and the *Green Shoe* option was not taken up. The underwriters still needed to cover their short position which they did by buying those 63 million shares in the aftermarket at or around the issue price of $38 to stabilize the IPO price.

Lockup Agreements

lockup agreement
The part of the underwriting contract that specifies how long insiders must wait after an IPO before they can sell stock.

Although they are not required by law, almost all underwriting contracts contain so-called **lockup agreements**. Such agreements specify how long insiders must wait after an IPO before they can sell some or all of their stock. Lockup periods have become fairly standardized in recent years at 180 days. Thus, following an IPO, insiders can't cash out until six months have gone by, which ensures that they maintain a significant economic interest in the company going public.

Lockup periods are also important because it is not unusual for the number of locked-up shares to exceed the number of shares held by the public, sometimes by a substantial multiple. On the day the lockup period expires, there is the possibility that a large number of shares will hit the market on the same day and thereby depress values. The evidence suggests that, on average, companies backed by venture capital are particularly likely to experience a loss in value on the lockup expiration day.

The Quiet Period

For 40 calendar days following an IPO, both the OSC and the SEC require that a firm and its managing underwriters observe a "quiet period." This means that all communications with the public must be limited to ordinary announcements and other purely factual matters. The OSC's logic is that all relevant information should be contained in the prospectus. An important result of this requirement is that the underwriter's analysts are prohibited from making recommendations to investors. As soon as the quiet period ends, however, the managing underwriters typically publish research reports, usually accompanied by a favourable "buy" recommendation.

In 2004, Google experienced notable quiet period-related problems. Just before the IPO, an interview with Google co-founders Sergy Brin and Larry Page appeared in *Playboy*. The interview almost caused a postponement of the IPO, but Google was able to amend its prospectus in time.

The Investment Dealers

Investment dealers are at the heart of new security issues. They provide advice, market the securities (after investigating the market's receptiveness to the issue), and provide a guarantee of the amount an issue will raise (with a bought deal). To determine the offering price, the underwriter will meet with potential buyers, typically large institutional buyers such as mutual funds. Often, the underwriter and company management will do presentations in multiple cities, pitching the stock in what is known as a 'road show'. Potential buyers provide information on the price they would be willing to pay and the number of shares they would purchase at a particular price. This

---

[6]The term *Green Shoe provision* sounds quite exotic, but the origin is relatively mundane. It comes from the Green Shoe Company, which once granted such an option.

process of soliciting information about buyers and the prices and quantities they would demand is known as bookbuilding. As we will see, despite the bookbuilding process, underwriters frequently get the price wrong, or so it seems.

Table 15.2 lists the top underwriters of equity issuances in Canada for 2011. The table shows that TD Securities Inc. was the leading underwriter.

TABLE 15.2

Canada's top equity underwriters, 2011; ranked by total amount raised	1	TD Securities Inc.
	2	RBC Capital Markets
	3	BMO Capital Markets
	4	CIBC World Markets Inc.
	5	Scotiabank–Bank of Nova Scotia
	6	National Bank Financial Inc.
	7	Canaccord Capital Corp
	8	GMP Capital Corp
	9	Cormark Securities Inc.
	10	Peters & Co. Limited

Source: Material reprinted with the express permission of National Post, a division of Postmedia Network Inc.

Concept Questions

1. What are the basic procedures in selling a new issue?
2. What is a preliminary prospectus?
3. What is the POP system and what advantages does it offer?
4. What is the difference between a rights offer and a cash offer?
5. Why is an initial public offering necessarily a cash offer?

15.5 | IPOs and Underpricing

Determining the correct offering price is the most difficult thing an underwriter must do for an initial public offering. The issuing firm faces a potential cost if the offering price is set too high or too low. If the issue is priced too high, it may be unsuccessful and have to be withdrawn. If the issue is priced below the true market value, the issuer's existing shareholders will experience an opportunity loss when they sell their shares for less than they are worth.

Underpricing is fairly common. It obviously helps new shareholders earn a higher return on the shares they buy. However, the existing shareholders of the issuing firm are not helped by underpricing. To them, it is an indirect cost of issuing new securities. For example, on April 14, 2011, ZipCar Inc., the car sharing service company, went public on the Nasdaq, selling 38.6 million shares at a price of US $18, thereby raising $694.8 million. At the end of the first day of trading, the stock sold for US $28.00, up about 55 percent for the day. Based on these numbers, ZipCar's shares were apparently underpriced by US $10 each, which means that the company missed out on an additional US $386 million. On a much smaller scale, Middlefield Income Plus II Corp. began trading on the TSX at $11.65 per unit on March 20, 2012. The unit price jumped approximately 1.3 percent within the first two days of trading. The initial public offering was for 5,000,000 units, thus the money "left on the table" was over $750,000. A classic example of money "left on the table" is that of eToys, whose 8.2-million-share 1999 IPO was underpriced by $57 per share, or almost half a billion dollars in all! eToys could have used the money; it was bankrupt within two years.

IPO Underpricing: The 1999–2000 Experience

Figure 15.1 shows that 1999 and 2000 were extraordinary years in the IPO market. Almost 900 companies went public, and the average first-day return across the two years was about 65 percent.

During this time, 194 IPOs doubled, or more than doubled, in value on the first day. In contrast, only 39 percent did so in the preceding 24 years combined. One company, VA Linux, shot up 698 percent!

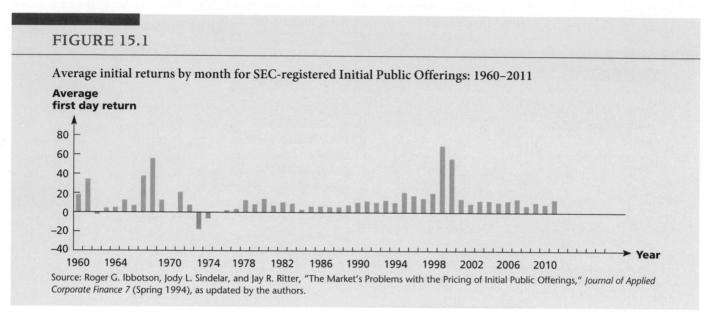

FIGURE 15.1

Average initial returns by month for SEC-registered Initial Public Offerings: 1960–2011

Source: Roger G. Ibbotson, Jody L. Sindelar, and Jay R. Ritter, "The Market's Problems with the Pricing of Initial Public Offerings," *Journal of Applied Corporate Finance 7* (Spring 1994), as updated by the authors.

The dollar amount raised in 2000, $66 billion, was a record, followed closely by 1999 at $65 billion. The underpricing was so severe in 1999 that companies left another $36 billion on the table, which was substantially more than 1990–1998 combined, and, in 2000, the amount was at least $27 billion. In other words, over the two-year period, companies missed out on $63 billion because of underpricing.

October 19, 1999, was one of the more memorable days during this time. The World Wrestling Federation (WWF) (now known as World Wrestling Entertainment, or WWE) and Martha Stewart Omnimedia both went public, so it was Martha Stewart versus "Stone Cold" Steve Austin in a Wall Street version of MTV's *Celebrity Deathmatch*. When the closing bell rang, it was a clear smackdown as Martha Stewart gained 98 percent on the first day compared to 48 percent for the WWF.

Evidence on Underpricing

Figure 15.1 provides a more general illustration of the underpricing phenomenon. What is shown is the year-by-year history of underpricing for SEC-registered IPOs.[7] The period covered is 1960 through 2011. Figure 15.2 presents the number of offerings in each year for the same period.

Figure 15.1 shows that underpricing can be quite dramatic, exceeding 60 percent in some years. In some cases, IPOs more than doubled in value, sometimes in a matter of hours. Also, the degree of underpricing varies through time, and periods of severe underpricing ("hot issue" markets) are followed by periods of little underpricing ("cold issue" markets). For example, in the 1960s, the average U.S. IPO was underpriced by 21.2 percent. In the 1970s, the average underpricing was much smaller (7.1 percent), and the amount of underpricing was actually very small or even negative for much of that time. Underpricing in the 1980s ran about 6.8 percent. For 1990–99, U.S. IPOs were underpriced by 21.0 percent on average, and they were underpriced by 22.8 percent in 2000–11.

From Figure 15.2, it is apparent that the number of IPOs is also highly variable through time. Further, there are pronounced cycles in both the degree of underpricing and the number of IPOs. Comparing Figures 15.1 and 15.2, we see that increases in the number of new offerings tend to follow periods of significant underpricing by roughly six months. This probably occurs because companies decide to go public when they perceive that the market is highly receptive to new issues.

---

[7]The discussion in this section draws on Roger G. Ibbotson, Jody L. Sindelar, and Jay R. Ritter, "The Market's Problems with the Pricing of Initial Public Offerings," *Journal of Applied Corporate Finance* 7 (Spring 1994).

IN THEIR OWN WORDS...

Jay Ritter on IPO Underpricing around the World

The United States is not the only country in which initial public offerings (IPOs) of common stock are underpriced. The phenomenon exists in every country with a stock market, although the extent of underpricing varies from country to country.

In general, countries with developed capital markets have more moderate underpricing than in emerging markets. During the Internet bubble of 1999–2000, however, underpricing in the developed capital markets increased dramatically. In the United States, for example, the average first-day return during 1999–2000 was 65 percent. The underpricing of Chinese IPOs used to be extreme, but in recent years it has moderated. In the 1990s, Chinese government regulations required that the offer price could not be more than 15 times earnings, even when comparable stocks had a price/earnings ratio of 45. In 2010, the average first day return was 40%, and there were more IPOs in China, raising more money, than any other country. After the bursting of the Internet bubble in mid-2000, the level of underpricing in the United States, Germany, and other developed capital markets has returned to more traditional levels.

The table below gives a summary of the average first-day returns on IPOs in a number of countries around the world, with the figures collected from a number of studies by various authors.

Jay R. Ritter is Cordell Professor of Finance at the University of Florida. An outstanding scholar, he is well known for his insightful analyses of new issues and going public.

Country	Sample Size	Time Period	Avg. Initial Return (%)	Country	Sample Size	Time Period	Avg. Initial Return (%)
Argentina	20	1991–1994	4.40	Jordan	53	1999–2008	149.00
Australia	1,103	1976–2006	19.80	Korea	1,521	1980–2009	63.50
Austria	96	1971–2006	6.50	Malaysia	350	1980–2006	69.60
Belgium	114	1984–2006	13.50	Mexico	88	1987–1994	15.90
Brazil	264	1979–2010	34.40	Netherlands	181	1982–2006	10.20
Bulgaria	9	2004–2007	36.50	New Zealand	214	1979–2006	20.30
Canada	635	1971–2006	7.10	Nigeria	114	1989–2006	12.70
Chile	65	1982–2006	8.40	Norway	153	1984–2006	9.60
China	2,102	1990–2010	137.40	Philippines	123	1987–2006	21.20
Cyprus	51	1999–2002	23.70	Poland	224	1991–2006	22.90
Denmark	145	1984–2006	8.10	Portugal	28	1992–2006	11.60
Egypt	53	1990–2000	8.40	Russia	40	1999–2006	4.20
Finland	162	1971–2006	17.20	Singapore	519	1973–2008	27.40
France	686	1983–2009	10.60	South Africa	285	1980–2007	18.00
Germany	704	1978–2009	25.20	Spain	128	1986–2006	10.90
Greece	373	1976–2009	50.80	Sri Lanka	105	1987–2008	33.50
Hong Kong	1,259	1980–2010	15.40	Sweden	406	1980–2006	27.30
India	2,811	1990–2007	92.70	Switzerland	159	1983–2008	28.00
Indonesia	361	1990–2010	26.30	Taiwan	1,312	1980–2006	37.20
Iran	279	1991–2004	22.40	Thailand	459	1987–2007	36.60
Ireland	31	1999–2006	23.70	Turkey	315	1990–2008	10.60
Israel	348	1990–2006	13.80	United Kingdom	4,205	1959–2009	16.30
Italy	273	1985–2009	16.40	United States	12,165	1960–2010	16.80
Japan	3,078	1970–2009	40.50				

Table 15.3 contains a year-by-year summary of underpricing for the years 1960–2011. As indicated, a grand total of 12,297 companies were included in this analysis. The degree of underpricing averaged 16.8 percent overall for the 52 years examined. Securities were overpriced on average in only 5 of the 52 years;. At the other extreme, in 1999, the 486 issues were underpriced, on average, by a remarkable 69.7 percent. Since the tech boom at the turn of the century, IPO volumes have stayed relatively high, mainly due to the popularity of income trust IPOs, but underpricing has declined because income trusts represent more mature, more easily valued businesses. In the recent financial crisis of 2007–2008, market conditions made it challenging for issuers seeking financing in the capital markets. The Canadian IPO market was relatively poor in the first quarter of 2012 with $20 million raised from 13 new issues. It was the third lowest total amount raised for any quarter in the past decade. Only the fourth quarter of 2008 ($2 million) and the first quarter of 2009 ($2.5 million) had lesser proceeds.

TABLE 15.3   Number of offerings, average first-day return, and gross proceeds of initial U.S. Public Offerings: 1960–2011

Year	Number of Offerings*	Average First-Day Return, %†	Gross Proceeds, $ Millions‡
1960	269	17.8	553
1961	435	34.1	1,243
1962	298	−1.6	431
1963	83	3.9	246
1964	97	5.3	380
1965	146	12.7	409
1966	85	7.1	275
1967	100	37.7	641
1968	368	55.9	1,205
1969	780	12.5	2,605
1970	358	−0.7	780
1971	391	21.2	1,655
1972	562	7.5	2,724
1973	105	−17.8	330
1974	9	−7.0	51
1975	12	−0.2	261
1976	26	1.9	214
1977	15	3.6	128
1978	19	12.6	207
1979	39	8.5	313
1980	75	13.9	934
1981	197	6.2	2,367
1982	81	10.7	1,016
1983	522	9.0	11,234
1984	222	2.5	2,841
1985	214	6.2	5,125
1986	479	6.0	15,697
1987	336	5.7	12,418
1988	130	5.4	4,141
1989	121	7.9	5,303
1990	115	10.5	4,325
1991	295	11.7	16,602
1992	416	10.2	22,678
1993	527	12.7	31,599
1994	411	9.8	17,544
1995	460	21.1	28,947
1996	688	17.2	42,425
1997	485	14.0	33,383
1998	318	20.2	34,614
1999	486	69.7	64,927
2000	381	56.3	64,844
2001	79	14.2	34,241
2002	70	8.6	22,136
2003	67	12.3	10,068
2004	184	12.2	32,269
2005	168	10.1	28,593
2006	162	11.9	30,648
2007	162	13.8	35,762
2008	21	6.4	22,762
2009	43	10.6	13,307
2010	103	8.8	31,068
2011	82	13.2	27,750
1960–69	2,661	21.2	7,988
1970–79	1,536	7.1	6,663
1980–89	2,377	6.8	61,076
1990–99	4,201	21.0	297,044
2000–11	1,522	22.8	353,448
1960–2011	12,297	16.8	726,219

*Beginning in 1975, the number of offerings excludes IPOs with an offer price of less than $5.00, ADRs, best efforts, units, and Regulation A offers (small issues, raising less than $1.5 million during the 1980s), real estate investment trusts (REITs), partnerships, and closed-end funds. Banks and S&Ls and non-CRSP-listed IPOs are included (unlike most other tables).

†First-day returns are computed as the percentage return from the offering price to the first closing market price.

‡Gross proceeds data are from Securities Data Co., and exclude overallotment options but include the international tranche, if any. No adjustments for inflation have been made.

Source: Professor Jay R. Ritter, University of Florida.

FIGURE 15.2

Number of offerings by month for SEC-registered Initial Public Offerings: 1960–2011

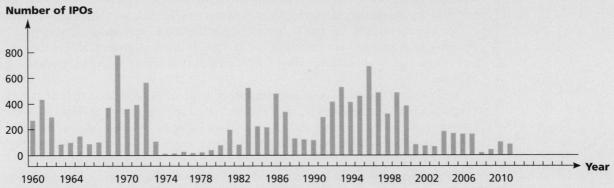

Source: Roger G. Ibbotson, Jody L. Sindelar, and Jay R. Ritter, "The Market's Problems with the Pricing of Initial Public Offerings," *Journal of Applied Corporate Finance 7* (Spring 1994), as updated by the authors.

TABLE 15.4

Average first-day returns, categorized by sales, for U.S. IPOs: 1980–2010*

	1980–89		1990–98		1999–2000		2001–2010	
Annual Sales of Issuing Firms	Number of Firms	First-Day Average Return	Number of Firms	First-Day Average Return	Number of Firms	First-Day Average Return	Number of Firms	First-Day Average Return
$0 ≤ Sales < $10m	424	10.4%	744	17.4%	334	68.8%	149	5.5%
$10m ≤ Sales < $20m	255	8.5	392	18.4	138	80.7	43	7.9
$20m ≤ Sales < $50m	495	7.7	792	18.7	154	75.7	143	13.5
$50m ≤ Sales < $100m	353	6.6	585	12.9	87	60.4	161	16.3
$100m ≤ Sales < $200m	238	4.8	451	11.9	58	39.1	144	14.4
$200m ≤ Sales	288	3.4	641	8.6	87	22.6	376	10.6
All	2,053	7.2	3,605	14.8	858	64.4	1,016	11.6

*Sales, measured in millions, are for the last 12 months prior to going public. All sales have been converted into dollars of 2003 purchasing power, using the Consumer Price Index. There are 7,532 IPOs, after excluding IPOs with an offer price of less than $5.00 per share, units, REITs, ADRs, closed-end funds, banks and S&Ls, firms not listed on CRSP within six months of the offer date, and 20 firms with missing sales. The average first day return is 18.0 percent.

Source: Professor Jay R. Ritter, University of Florida.

Why Does Underpricing Exist?

Based on the evidence we've examined, an obvious question is, why does underpricing continue to exist? As we discuss, there are various explanations, but, to date, there is a lack of complete agreement among researchers as to which is correct.

We present some pieces of the underpricing puzzle by stressing two important caveats to our preceding discussion. First, the average figures we have examined tend to obscure the fact that much of the apparent underpricing is attributable to the smaller, more highly speculative issues. This point is illustrated in Table 15.4, which shows the extent of underpricing for IPOs over the period from 1980 through 2010. Here, the firms are grouped based on their total sales in the 12 months prior to the IPO.

As illustrated in Table 15.4, the underpricing tends to be higher for firms with little to no sales in the previous year. These firms tend to be young firms, and such young firms can be very risky investments. Arguably, they must be significantly underpriced, on average, just to attract investors, and this is one explanation for the underpricing phenomenon.

The second caveat is that relatively few IPO buyers will actually get the initial high average returns observed in IPOs, and many will actually lose money. Although it is true that, on average, IPOs have positive initial returns, a significant fraction of them have price drops. Furthermore, when the price is too low, the issue is often "oversubscribed." This means investors will not be able to buy all the shares they want, and the underwriters will allocate the shares among investors.

The average investor will find it difficult to get shares in a "successful" offering (one in which the price increases) because there will not be enough shares to go around. On the other hand, an investor blindly submitting orders for IPOs tends to get more shares in issues that go down in price.

To illustrate, consider this tale of two investors. Smith knows very accurately what the Bonanza Corporation is worth when its shares are offered. She is confident that the shares are underpriced. Jones knows only that prices usually rise one month after an IPO. Armed with this information, Jones decides to buy 1000 shares of every IPO. Does he actually earn an abnormally high return on the initial offering?

The answer is no, and at least one reason is Smith. Knowing about the Bonanza Corporation, Smith invests all her money in its IPO. When the issue is oversubscribed, the underwriters have to somehow allocate the shares between Smith and Jones. The net result is that when an issue is underpriced, Jones doesn't get to buy as much of it as he wanted.

Smith also knows that the Blue Sky Corporation IPO is overpriced. In this case, she avoids its IPO altogether, and Jones ends up with a full 1000 shares. To summarize this tale, Jones gets fewer shares when more knowledgeable investors swarm to buy an underpriced issue and gets all he wants when the smart money avoids the issue.

This is an example of a "winner's curse," and it is thought to be another reason why IPOs have such a large average return. When the average investor "wins" and gets the entire allocation, it may be because those who knew better avoided the issue. The only way underwriters can counteract the winner's curse and attract the average investor is to underprice new issues (on average) so that the average investor still makes a profit.

Another reason for underpricing is that the underpricing is a kind of insurance for the investment banks. Conceivably, an investment bank could be sued successfully by angry customers if it consistently overpriced securities. Underpricing guarantees that, at least on average, customers will come out ahead.

A final reason for underpricing is that before the offer price is established, investment banks talk to big institutional investors to gauge the level of interest in the stock and to gather opinions about a suitable price. Underpricing is a way that the bank can reward these investors for truthfully revealing what they think the stock is worth and the number of shares they would like to buy.

Concept Questions

1. Why is underpricing a cost to the issuing firm?
2. Suppose a stockbroker calls you up out of the blue and offers to sell you "all the shares you want" of a new issue. Do you think the issue will be more or less underpriced than average?

15.6 | New Equity Sales and the Value of the Firm

It seems reasonable to believe that new long-term financing is arranged by firms after positive net present value projects are put together. As a consequence, when the announcement of external financing is made, the firm's market value should go up. Interestingly, this is not what happens. Stock prices tend to decline following the announcement of a new equity issue, and they tend to rise following a debt announcement. A number of researchers have studied this issue. Plausible reasons for this strange result include:

1. *Managerial information.* If management has superior information about the market value of the firm, it may know when the firm is overvalued. If it does, it attempts to issue new shares

of stock when the market value exceeds the correct value. This benefits existing shareholders. However, the potential new shareholders are not stupid, and they anticipate this superior information and discount it in lower market prices at the new issue date.

2. Debt usage. Issuing new equity may reveal that the company has too much debt or too little liquidity. One version of this argument is that the equity issue is a bad signal to the market. After all, if the new projects are favourable ones, why should the firm let new shareholders in on them? As you read earlier, in IPOs it is regarded as a positive signal when the original owners keep larger amounts of stock for themselves. Taking this argument to the limit, the firm could just issue debt and let the existing shareholders have all the gain.

3. *Issue costs.* As we discuss next, there are substantial costs associated with selling securities.

Concept Questions

1. What are some possible reasons that the price of stock drops on the announcement of a new equity issue?
2. Explain why we might expect a firm with a positive NPV investment to finance it with debt instead of equity.

15.7 | The Cost of Issuing Securities

Issuing securities to the public isn't free, and the costs of different methods are important determinants of which method is used. These costs associated with *floating* a new issue are generically called *flotation* costs. In this section, we take a closer look at the flotation costs associated with equity sales to the public.

The costs of selling stock fall into six categories: (1) the spread, (2) other direct expenses, (3) indirect expenses, (4) abnormal returns (discussed earlier), (5) underpricing, and (6) the overallotment option. We look at these costs first for United States and then for Canadian equity sales.

The Costs of Issuing Securities

Spread	The spread consists of direct fees paid by the issuer to the underwriting syndicate—the difference between the price the issuer receives and the offer price.
Other direct expenses	These are direct costs, incurred by the issuer, that are not part of the compensation to underwriters. These costs include filing fees, legal fees, and taxes—all reported on the prospectus.
Indirect expenses	These costs are not reported on the prospectus and include the costs of management time spent working on the new issue.
Abnormal returns	In a seasoned issue of stock, the price drops on average by 3 percent on the announcement of the issue.
Underpricing	For initial public offerings, losses arise from selling the stock below the correct value.
Overallotment (Green Shoe) option	The Green Shoe option gives the underwriters the right to buy additional shares at the offer price to cover overallotments.

Table 15.5 reports direct costs as a percentage of the gross amount raised for IPOs, SEOs, straight (ordinary) bonds, and convertible bonds sold by U.S. companies over the 19-year period from 1990 through 2008. These are direct costs only. Not included are indirect expenses, the cost of the overallotment option, underpricing (for IPOs), and abnormal returns (for SEOs).

As Table 15.5 shows, the direct costs alone can be very large, particularly for smaller issues (less than $10 million). On a smaller IPO, for example, the total direct costs amount to 25.22 percent of the amount raised. This means that if a company sells $10 million in stock, it will only net about $7.5 million; the other $2.5 million goes to cover the underwriter spread and other direct expenses. Typical underwriter spreads on an IPO range from about 5 percent up to 10 percent or so, but, for well over half of the IPOs in Table 15.5, the spread is exactly 7 percent, so this is, by far, the most common spread.

TABLE 15.5

Direct costs as a percentage of gross proceeds for equity (IPOs and SEOs) and straight and convertible bonds offered by U.S. operating companies: 1990–2008

| | Equity | | | | | | | | Bonds | | | | | | | |
| | IPOs | | | | SEOs | | | | Convertible Bonds | | | | Straight Bonds | | | |
Proceeds ($ in millions)	Number of Issues	Gross Spread	Other Direct Expense	Total Direct Cost	Number of Issues	Gross Spread	Other Direct Expense	Total Direct Cost	Number of Issues	Gross Spread	Other Direct Expense	Total Direct Cost	Number of Issues	Gross Spread	Other Direct Expense	Total Direct Cost
2–9.99	1,007	9.40%	15.82%	25.22%	515	8.11%	26.99%	35.11%	14	6.39%	3.43%	9.82%	3,962	1.64%	2.40%	4.03%
10–19.99	810	7.39	7.30	14.69	726	6.11	7.76	13.86	23	5.52	3.09	8.61	3,400	1.50	1.71	3.20
20–39.99	1,442	6.96	7.06	14.03	1,393	5.44	4.10	9.54	30	4.63	1.67	6.30	2,690	1.25	0.92	2.17
40–59.99	880	6.89	2.87	9.77	1,129	5.03	8.93	13.96	35	3.49	1.04	4.54	3,345	0.81	0.79	1.59
60–79.99	522	6.79	2.16	8.94	841	4.88	1.98	6.85	60	2.79	0.62	3.41	891	1.65	0.80	2.44
80–99.99	327	6.71	1.84	8.55	536	4.67	2.05	6.72	16	2.30	0.62	2.92	465	1.41	0.57	1.98
100–199.99	702	6.39	1.57	7.96	1,372	4.34	0.89	5.23	82	2.66	0.42	3.08	4,949	1.61	0.52	2.14
200–499.99	440	5.81	1.03	6.84	811	3.72	1.22	4.94	46	2.65	0.33	2.99	3,305	1.38	0.33	1.71
500 and up	155	5.01	0.49	5.50	264	3.10	0.27	3.37	7	2.16	0.13	2.29	1,261	0.61	0.15	0.76
Total	6,285	7.19	3.18	10.37	7,587	5.02	2.68	7.69	313	3.07	0.85	3.92	24,268	1.38	0.61	2.00

Source: Inmoo Lee, Scott Lochhead, Jay Ritter, and Quanshui Zhao, "The Costs of Raising Capital," *Journal of Financial Research* 19 (Spring 1996), updated by the authors.

Overall, four clear patterns emerge from Table 15.5. First of all, with the possible exception of straight debt offerings (about which we will have more to say later), there are substantial economies of scale. The underwriter spreads are smaller on larger issues, and the other direct costs fall sharply as a percentage of the amount raised, a reflection of the mostly fixed nature of such costs. Second, the costs associated with selling debt are substantially less than the costs of selling equity. Third, IPOs have higher expenses than SEOs, but the difference is not as great as might originally be guessed. Finally, straight bonds are cheaper to float than convertible bonds.

Table 15.5 tells only part of the story. For IPOs, the effective costs can be much greater because of the indirect costs. Table 15.6 reports both the direct costs of going public in Canada as of 2011. These figures understate the total cost because the study did not consider indirect expenses or the overallotment option. Once again we see that the costs of issuing securities can be considerable.

TABLE 15.6

Costs of going public in Canada: 2011		Toronto Stock Exchange	TSX Venture Exchange
	Listing Fees	$10,000–$200,000	$7,500–$40,000
	Accounting and Auditing Fees	$75,000–$100,000	$25,000–$100,000
	Legal Fees	$400,000–$750,000	Above $75,000
Source: TMX Group	Underwriters' Commission	4–6%	Up to 12%

Overall, three conclusions emerge from our discussion of underwriting:

1. Substantial economies of size are evident. Larger firms can raise equity more easily.
2. The cost associated with underpricing can be substantial and can exceed the direct costs.
3. The issue costs are higher for an initial public offering than for a seasoned offering.

IPOs in Practice: The Case of Athabasca Oil Sands

In March 2010, Athabasca Oil Sands Corp., began trading on the Toronto Stock Exchange. Athabasca, an Alberta based company, is focused on the sustainable development of oil sands in the Athabasca region in northeastern Alberta and light oil resources in northwestern Alberta.

Athabasca sold 75 million shares at $18 each generating $1.35 billion after flotation costs. The proceeds of the issue were used to extract tar-like bitumen from the ground using steam-assisted gravity drainage techniques. Morgan Stanley Canada Ltd. and GMP Securities Ltd. were the leading underwriters used in this offering. The underwriters had an overallotment option to purchase up to an additional 11.25 million shares of common stock "at the initial public offering price" that would increase the value of the deal to $1.55 billion.

The Athabasca IPO had a poor debut—shares plummeted[8] to $16.90 on the Toronto Stock Exchange, nearly a 6% drop from the IPO price of $18. The shares were apparently overpriced by $1.10, which means that the company cashed in on an additional $82.5 million. The shares fell an additional 33% during the first month of trading, making Athabasca one of the worst Canadian IPOs.[9] The drop in the share price can be attributed to the decrease in the crude oil prices, the European debt crises and concerns over increasing interest rates. The decrease in crude oil price would exacerbate Athabasca's prospects as it is costly to dig bitumen out of the ground and refine it into usable petroleum products.

15.8 | Rights

When new shares of common stock are sold to the general public, the proportional ownership of existing shareholders is likely reduced. However, if a preemptive right is contained in the firm's articles of incorporation, the firm must first offer any new issue of common stock to existing shareholders. If the articles of incorporation do not include a preemptive right, the firm has a choice of offering the issue of common stock directly to existing shareholders or to the public. In some industries, regulatory authorities set rules concerning rights. For example, before the *Bank Act* of 1980, chartered banks were required to raise equity exclusively through rights offerings.

An issue of common stock offered to existing shareholders is called a *rights offering*. In a rights offering, each shareholder is issued one right for every share owned. The rights give the shareholder an option to buy a specified number of new shares from the firm at a specified price within a specified time, after which time the rights are said to expire.

The terms of the rights offering are evidenced by certificates known as rights. Such rights are often traded on securities exchanges or over the counter.

The Mechanics of a Rights Offering

To illustrate the various considerations a financial manager has in a rights offering, we examine the situation faced by the National Power Company, whose abbreviated initial financial statements are given in Table 15.7.

As indicated in Table 15.7, National Power earns $2 million after taxes and has 1 million shares outstanding. Earnings per share are thus $2, and the stock sells for $20, or 10 times earnings (that is, the price-earnings ratio is 10). To fund a planned expansion, the company intends to raise $5 million of new equity funds by a rights offering.

---

[8] Source: divestor.com/2010/04/09/athabasca-oil-sands-ipo-first-day-of-trading/

[9] Source: bloomberg.com/news/2010-05-12/athabasca-oil-largest-canadian-ipo-since-1999-performs-worst-since-2007.html

TABLE 15.7

National Power Company financial statements before rights offering

Statement of Financial Position

Assets		Shareholders' Equity	
		Common stock	$ 5,000,000
		Retained earnings	10,000,000
Total	$15,000,000	Total	$15,000,000

Statement of Comprehensive Income

Earnings before taxes	$ 3,333,333
Taxes (40%)	1,333,333
Net income	2,000,000
Earnings per share	2
Shares outstanding	1,000,000
Market price per share	20
Total market value	$ 20,000,000

To execute a rights offering, the financial management of National Power has to answer the following questions:

1. What should the price per share be for the new stock?
2. How many shares will have to be sold?
3. How many shares will each shareholder be allowed to buy?

Also, management would probably want to ask:

4. What is the likely effect of the rights offering on the per share value of the existing stock?

It turns out that the answers to these questions are highly interrelated. We get to them in a moment. The early stages of a rights offering are the same as for the general cash offer. The difference between a rights offering and a general cash offer lies in how the shares are sold. As we discussed earlier, in a cash offer, shares are sold to retail and institutional investors through investment dealers. With a rights offer, National Power's existing shareholders are informed that they own one right for each share of stock they own. National Power then specifies how many rights a shareholder needs to buy one additional share at a specified price.

To take advantage of the rights offering, shareholders have to exercise the rights by filling out a subscription form and sending it, along with payment, to the firm's subscription agent. Shareholders of National Power actually have several choices: (1) exercise and subscribe to the entitled shares, (2) sell the rights, or (3) do nothing and let the rights expire. This third action is inadvisable, as long as the rights have value.

Number of Rights Needed to Purchase a Share

National Power wants to raise $5 million in new equity. Suppose the subscription price is set at $10 per share. How National Power arrived at that price is something we discuss later, but notice that the subscription price is substantially less than the current $20 per share market price.

At $10 per share, National Power will have to issue 500,000 new shares. This can be determined by dividing the total amount of funds to be raised by the subscription price:

$$\text{Number of new shares} = \text{Funds to be raised/Subscription price} \qquad [15.1]$$
$$= \$5,000,000/\$10 = 500,000 \text{ shares}$$

Because shareholders always get one right for each share of stock they own, 1 million rights would be issued by National Power. To determine how many rights are needed to buy one new share of stock, we can divide the number of existing outstanding shares of stock by the number of new shares:

$$\text{Number of rights needed to buy a share of stock} = \text{Old shares/New shares} \quad [15.2]$$
$$= 1,000,000/500,000 = 2 \text{ rights}$$

Thus, a shareholder needs to give up two rights plus $10 to receive a share of new stock. If all the shareholders do this, National Power could raise the required $5 million.

It should be clear that the subscription price, the number of new shares, and the number of rights needed to buy a new share of stock are interrelated. For example, National Power can lower the subscription price. If so, more new shares will have to be issued to raise $5 million in new equity. Several alternatives are worked out here:

Subscription Price	New Shares	Rights Needed to Buy a Share of Stock
$20	250,000	4
10	500,000	2
5	1,000,000	1

The Value of a Right

Rights clearly have value. In the case of National Power, the right to buy a share of stock worth $20 for $10 is definitely worth something. In fact, if you think about it, a right is essentially a call option. A call option gives the holder of the option the ability to buy a particular asset, in this case a stock, at a fixed price for a particular period of time. The most important difference between a right and an ordinary call option is that rights are issued by the firm, so they closely resemble warrants. In general, the valuation of options, rights, and warrants can be fairly complex, so we defer discussion of this to a later chapter. However, we can discuss the value of a right just prior to expiration in order to illustrate some important points.

Suppose a shareholder of National Power owns two shares of stock just before the rights offering. This situation is depicted in Table 15.8. Initially, the price of National Power is $20 per share, so the shareholder's total holding is worth $2 \times \$20 = \$40$. The National Power rights offer gives shareholders with two rights the opportunity to purchase one additional share for $10. The additional share does not carry a right.

TABLE 15.8

The value of rights: the individual shareholder

Initial Position	
Number of shares	2
Share price	$20
Value of holding	$40
Terms of Offer	
Subscription price	$10
Number of rights issued	2
Number of rights for a new share	2
After Offer	
Number of shares	3
Value of holdings	$50
Share price	$16.67
Value of a right	
Old price − New price	$20 − 16.67 = $3.33

The shareholder who has two shares receives two rights. The holding of the shareholder who exercises these rights and buys the new share would increase to three shares. The total investment would be $40 + 10 = $50 (the $40 initial value plus the $10 paid to the company).

The shareholder now holds three shares, all of which are identical because the new share does not have a right and the rights attached to the old shares have been exercised. Since the total cost of buying these three shares is $40 + 10 = $50, the price per share must end up at $50/3 = $16.67 (rounded to two decimal places).

Table 15.9 summarizes what happens to National Power's stock price. If all shareholders exercise their rights, the number of shares increases to 1 million + .5 million = 1.5 million. The value of the firm increases to $20 million + 5 million = $25 million. The value of each share thus drops to $25 million/1.5 million = $16.67 after the rights offering.

TABLE 15.9

National Power Company rights offering

Initial Position	
Number of shares	1 million
Share price	$20
Value of firm	$20 million
Terms of Offer	
Subscription price	$10
Number of rights issued	1 million
Number of rights for a share	2
After Offer	
Number of shares	1.5 million
Share price	$16.67
Value of firm	$25 million
Value of one right $20 − 16.67 = $3.33	

The difference between the old share price of $20 and the new share price of $16.67 reflects the fact that the old shares carried rights to subscribe to the new issue. The difference must be equal to the value of one right, that is, $20 − 16.67 = $3.33.

Although holding no shares of outstanding National Power stock, an investor who wants to subscribe to the new issue can do so by buying some rights. Suppose an outside investor buys two rights. This costs $3.33 × 2 = $6.67 (to account for previous rounding). If the investor exercises the rights at a subscription price of $10, the total cost would be $10 + 6.67 = $16.67. In return for this expenditure, the investor receives a share of the new stock, which, as we have seen, is worth $16.67.

EXAMPLE 15.1: Exercising Your Rights: Part I

In the National Power example, suppose the subscription price was set at $8. How many shares have to be sold? How many rights would you need to buy a new share? What is the value of a right? What will the price per share be after the rights offer?

To raise $5 million, $5 million/$8 = 625,000 shares need to be sold. There are 1 million shares outstanding, so

it will take 1 million/625,000 = 8/5 = 1.6 rights to buy a new share of stock (you can buy five new shares for every eight you own). After the rights offer, there will be 1.625 million shares, worth $25 million all together, so the per share value is $25/1.625 = $15.38 each. The value of a right is the $20 original price less the $15.38 ending price, or $4.62.

Theoretical Value of a Right

We can summarize the discussion with an equation for the theoretical value of a right during the rights-on period:

$$R_o = (M_o − S)/(N + 1)$$

[15.3]

where

M_o = common share price during the rights-on period
S = subscription price
N = number of rights required to buy one new share

We can illustrate the use of Equation 15.3 by checking our answer for the value of one right in Example 15.1.

$$R_o = (\$20 - 8)/(1.6 + 1) = \$4.62$$

This is the same answer we got in Example 15.1.

EXAMPLE 15.2: Exercising Your Rights: Part II

The Lagrange Point Company has proposed a rights offering. The stock currently sells for $40 per share. Under the terms of the offer, shareholders are allowed to buy one new share for every five that they own at a price of $25 per share. What is the value of a right? What is the ex-rights price?

You can buy five rights on shares for 5 × $40 = $200 and then exercise the rights for another $25. Your total investment is $225, and you end up with six ex-rights shares. The ex-rights price per share is $225/6 = $37.50 per share. The rights are thus worth $40 − 37.50 = $2.50 apiece.

Using Equation 15.3 we have:

$$R_0 = (\$40 - 25)/(5 + 1) = \$2.50$$

Ex Rights

ex rights
Period when stock is selling without a recently declared right, normally beginning two business days before the holder-of-record date.

holder-of-record date
The date on which existing shareholders on company records are designated as the recipients of stock rights. Also the date of record.

National Power's rights have substantial value. In addition, the rights offering would have a large impact on the market price of National Power's stock price. It would drop by $3.33 on the day when the shares trade **ex rights**.

The standard procedure for issuing rights involves the firm's setting a **holder-of-record date**. Following stock exchange rules, the stock typically goes ex-rights two trading days before the holder-of-record date. If the stock is sold before the ex-rights date—rights-on, with rights, or cum rights—the new owner receives the rights. After the ex-rights date, an investor who purchases the shares will not receive the rights. This is depicted for National Power in Figure 15.3

FIGURE 15.3

Ex-rights stock prices: the effect of rights on stock prices

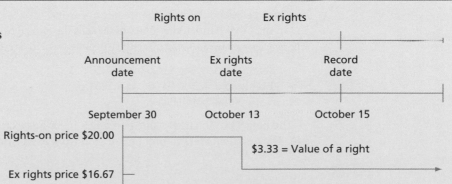

In a rights offering, there is a date of record, which is the last day that a shareholder can establish legal ownership. However, stocks are sold ex rights two business days before the record date. Before the ex rights day, the stock sells rights on, which means the purchaser receives the rights.

As illustrated, on September 30, National Power announced the terms of the rights offering, stating that the rights would be mailed on, say, November 1 to shareholders of record as of October 15. Since October 13 is the ex-rights date, only those shareholders who own the stock on or before October 12 receive the rights.

Value of Rights after Ex-Rights Date

When the stock goes ex rights, we saw that its price drops by the value of one right. Until the rights expire, holders can buy one share at the subscription price by exercising N rights. In equation form:[10]

$$M_e = M_o - R_o \qquad\qquad [15.4]$$

$$R_e = (M_e - S)/N \qquad\qquad [15.5]$$

where M_e = common share price during the ex-rights period and
M_o = rights-on common share price.

Checking the formula using Example 15.2 gives

$$M_e = \$40 - 2.50 = \$37.50$$
$$R_e = (\$37.50 - 25)/5 = \$2.50$$

The Underwriting Arrangements

Rights offerings are typically arranged using **standby underwriting**. In standby underwriting, the issuer makes a rights offering, and the underwriter makes a firm commitment to "take up" (that is, purchase) the unsubscribed portion of the issue. The underwriter usually gets a **standby fee** and additional amounts based on the securities taken up.

Standby underwriting protects the firm against undersubscription. This can occur if investors throw away rights or if bad news causes the market price of the stock to fall to less than the subscription price.

In practice, a small percentage (less than 10 percent) of shareholders fail to exercise valuable rights. This can probably be attributed to ignorance or vacations. Furthermore, shareholders are usually given an **oversubscription privilege** enabling them to purchase unsubscribed shares at the subscription price. The oversubscription privilege makes it unlikely that the corporate issuer would have to turn to its underwriter for help.

Effects on Shareholders

Shareholders can exercise their rights or sell them. In either case, the shareholder does not win or lose by the rights offering. The hypothetical holder of two shares of National Power has a portfolio worth $40. If the shareholder exercises the rights, he or she ends up with three shares worth a total of $50. In other words, by spending $10, the investor's holding increases in value by $10, which means the shareholder is neither better nor worse off.

On the other hand, if the shareholder sells the two rights for $3.33 each, he or she would obtain $3.33 × 2 = $6.67 and end up with two shares worth $16.67 and the cash from selling the right:

$$\text{Shares held} = 2 \times \$16.67 = \$33.33$$
$$\text{Rights sold} = 2 \times \$3.33\ = \$\ 6.67$$
$$\text{Total} = \$40.00$$

The new $33.33 market value plus $6.67 in cash is exactly the same as the original holding of $40. Thus, shareholders cannot lose or gain from exercising or selling rights.

---

[10] During the ex-rights period, a right represents a short-lived option to buy the stock. Equation 15.5 gives the minimum value of this option. The market value of rights is generally higher, as explained in our discussion of options in Chapter 25.

It is obvious that after the rights offering, the new market price of the firm's stock would be lower than it was before the rights offering. As we have seen, however, shareholders have suffered no loss because of the rights offering. Thus, the stock price decline is very much like a stock split, a device that is described in Chapter 17. The lower the subscription price, the greater is the price decline of a rights offering. It is important to emphasize that because shareholders receive rights equal in value to the price drop, the rights offering does not hurt shareholders.

There is one last issue. How do we set the subscription price in a rights offering? If you think about it, in theory, the subscription price really does not matter. It has to be less than the market price of the stock for the rights to have value, but, beyond this, the price is arbitrary. In principle, it could be as low as we cared to make it as long as it is not zero.

In practice, however, the subscription price is typically 20 to 25 percent less than the prevailing stock price. Once we recognize market inefficiencies and frictions, a subscription price too close to the share price may result in undersubscription due simply to market imperfections.

Cost of Rights Offerings

Until the early 1980s, rights offerings were the most popular method of raising new equity in Canada for seasoned issuers. (Obviously, you cannot use rights offerings for IPOs.) The reason was lower flotation costs from the simpler underwriting arrangements. Even though rights offerings lost some popularity with the advent of POP, they still are widely used by companies to raise capital. For example, in February 2011, Ivanhoe Mines completed one of the largest rights offerings in Canadian history, raising gross proceeds of US$1.18 billion. The proceeds of the rights offering were used to advance construction and development of Ivanhoe Mines' Oyu Tolgoi Copper and Gold Project in southern Mongolia.

Concept Questions

1. How does a rights offering work?
2. What are the questions that financial management must answer in a rights offering?
3. How is the value of a right determined?
4. When does a rights offering affect the value of a company's shares?
5. Does a rights offer cause a share price decrease? How are existing shareholders affected by a rights offer?

EXAMPLE 15.3: Right on or Rights-On?

In Example 15.2, suppose you could buy the rights for only $0.25 instead of the $2.50 we calculated. What could you do?

You can get rich quick, because you have found a money machine. Here's the recipe: Buy five rights for $1.25. Exercise them and pay $25 to get a new share. Your total investment to get one ex rights share is 5 × $0.25 + $25 = $26.25. Sell the share for $37.50 and pocket the $11.25 difference. Repeat as desired.

A variation on this theme actually occurred in the course of a rights offering by a major Canadian chartered bank in the mid-1980s. The bank's employee stock ownership plan had promoted share ownership by tellers and clerical staff who were unfamiliar with the workings of rights offerings. When they received notification of the rights offering, many employees did not bother to respond until they were personally solicited by other, more sophisticated employees who bought the rights for a fraction of their value. We do not endorse the ethics behind such transactions. But the incident does show why it pays for everyone who owns shares to understand the workings of rights offers.

15.9 | Dilution

dilution
Loss in existing shareholders' value, in terms of either ownership, market value, book value, or EPS.

A subject that comes up quite a bit in discussions involving the selling of securities is **dilution**. Dilution refers to a loss in existing shareholders' value. There are several kinds:

1. Dilution of percentage ownership.
2. Dilution of market value.
3. Dilution of book value and earnings per share.

The difference between these three types can be a little confusing and there are some common misconceptions about dilution, so we discuss it in this section.

Dilution of Proportionate Ownership

The first type of dilution can arise whenever a firm sells shares to the general public. For example, Joe Smith owns 5000 shares of Merit Shoe Company. Merit Shoe currently has 50,000 shares of stock outstanding; each share gets one vote. Smith thus controls 10 percent (5000/50,000) of the votes and gets 10 percent of the dividends.

If Merit Shoe issues 50,000 new shares of common stock to the public via a general cash offer, Smith's ownership in Merit Shoe may be diluted. If Smith does not participate in the new issue, his ownership drops to 5 percent (5000/100,000). Notice that the value of Smith's shares is unaffected; he just owns a smaller percentage of the firm.

Because a rights offering would ensure Joe Smith an opportunity to maintain his proportionate 10 percent share, dilution of the ownership of existing shareholders can be avoided by using a rights offering.

Dilution of Value: Book versus Market Values

We now examine dilution of value by looking at some accounting numbers. We do this to illustrate a fallacy concerning dilution; we do not mean to suggest that accounting dilution is more important than market value dilution. As we illustrate, quite the reverse is true.

Suppose Provincial Telephone Company (PTC) wants to build a new switching facility to meet future anticipated demands. PTC currently has 1 million shares outstanding and no debt. Each share is selling for $5, and the company has a $5 million market value. PTC's book value is $10 million total, or $10 per share.

PTC has experienced a variety of difficulties in the past, including cost overruns, regulatory delays, and below normal profits. These difficulties are reflected in the fact that PTC's market-to-book ratio is $5/$10 = .50 (successful firms rarely have market prices less than book values).

Net income for PTC is currently $1 million. With 1 million shares, earnings per share (EPS) are $1, and the return on equity (ROE) is $1/$10 = 10%.[11] PTC thus sells for five times earnings (the price/earnings ratio is five). PTC has 200 shareholders, each of whom holds 5000 shares each. The new plant will cost $2 million, so PTC has to issue 400,000 new shares ($5 × 400,000 = $2,000,000). There will thus be 1.4 million shares outstanding after the issue.

The ROE on the new plant is expected to be the same as for the company as a whole. In other words, net income is expected to go up by .10 × $2 million = $200,000. Total net income will thus be $1.2 million. The following things would occur:

1. With 1.4 million shares outstanding, EPS would be $1.2/1.4 = $.857 per share, down from $1.

2. The proportionate ownership of each old shareholder drops to 5000/1.4 million = .36 percent from .50 percent.

3. If the stock continues to sell for five times earnings, the value would drop to 5 × .857 = $4.29, a loss of $.71 per share.

---

[11] Return on equity (ROE) is equal to earnings per share divided by book value per share or, equivalently, net income divided by common equity. We discuss this and other financial ratios in some detail in Chapter 3.

4. The total book value is the old $10 million plus the new $2 million for a total of $12 million. Book value per share falls to $12 million/1.4 million = $8.57 per share.

If we take this example at face value, dilution of proportionate ownership, accounting dilution, and market value dilution all occur. PTC's stockholders appear to suffer significant losses.

A MISCONCEPTION   Our example appears to show that selling stock when the market-to-book ratio is less than 1 is detrimental to the shareholders. Some managers claim that this dilution occurs because EPS goes down whenever shares are issued where the market value is less than the book value.

When the market-to-book ratio is less than 1, increasing the number of shares does cause EPS to go down. Such a decline in EPS is accounting dilution, and accounting dilution always occurs under these circumstances.

Is it furthermore true that market value dilution will also necessarily occur? The answer is no. There is nothing incorrect about our example, but why the market value has decreased is not obvious. We discuss this next.

THE CORRECT ARGUMENTS   In this example, the market price falls from $5 per share to $4.29. This is true dilution, but why does it occur? The answer has to do with the new project. PTC is going to spend $2 million on the new switching facility. However, as shown in Table 15.10, the total market value of the company is going to rise from $5 million to $6 million, an increase of only $1 million. This simply means that the NPV of the new project is −$1 million. With 1.4 million shares, the loss per share is $1/1.4 = .71, as we calculated before.

TABLE 15.10

New issues and dilution: the case of Provincial Telephone Company

	(1) Initial	(2) Dilution	(3) No Dilution
Number of shares	1,000,000	1,400,000	1,400,000
Book value (B)	$10,000,000	$12,000,000	$12,000,000
Book value per share	$10	$8.57	$8.57
Market value	$5,000,000	$6,000,000	$8,000,000
Market price (P)	$5	$4.29	$5.71
Net income	$1,000,000	$1,200,000	$1,600,000
Return on equity (ROE)	0.10	0.10	0.13
Earnings per share (EPS)	$1	$0.86	$1.14
EPS/P	0.20	0.20	0.20
P/EPS	5	5	5
P/B	0.5	0.5	0.67
PROJECT			
Cost $2,000,000		NPV = −$1,000,000	NPV = $1,000,000

So, true dilution takes place for the shareholders of PTC because the NPV of the project is negative and the market knows it, not because the market-to-book ratio is less than 1. This negative NPV causes the market price to drop, and the accounting dilution has nothing to do with it.

Suppose that the new project had a positive NPV of $1 million. The total market value would rise by $2 + 1 = $3 million. As shown in Table 15.10 (third column), the price per share rises to $5.71. Notice that accounting dilution still occurs because the book value per share still falls, but there is no economic consequence to that fact. The market value of the stock rises.

The $.71 increase in share value comes about because of the $1 million NPV, which amounts to an increase in value of about $.71 per share. Also, as shown, if the ratio of price to EPS remains at 5, EPS must rise to $5.71/5 = $1.14. Total earnings (net income) rises to $1.14 per share × 1.4 million shares = $1.6 million. Finally, ROE would rise to $1.6 million/$12 million = 13.33%.

Concept Questions

1. What are the different kinds of dilution?

2. Is dilution important?

15.10 | Issuing Long-term Debt

The general procedures followed in a public issue of bonds are the same as those for stocks. The issue must be registered with the OSC and any other relevant provincial securities commissions, there must be a prospectus, and so on. The registration statement for a public issue of bonds, however, is different from the one for common stock. For bonds, the registration statement must indicate an indenture.

Another important difference is that debt is more likely to be issued privately. There are two basic forms of direct private long-term financing: term loans and private placement.

term loans
Direct business loans of, typically, one to five years.

Term loans are direct business loans. These loans have maturities of between one and five years. Most term loans are repayable during the life of the loan. The lenders include chartered banks, insurance companies, trust companies, and other lenders that specialize in corporate finance. The interest rate on a term loan may be either a fixed or floating rate.

syndicated loans
Loans made by a group of banks or other institutions.

Syndicated loans are loans made by a group (or syndicate) of banks and other institutional investors. They are used because large banks such as Citigroup and Royal Bank of Canada typically have a larger demand for loans than they can supply, and small regional banks frequently have more funds on hand than they can profitably lend to existing customers. As a result, a very large bank may arrange a loan with a firm or country and then sell portions of it to a syndicate of other banks. With a syndicated loan, each bank has a separate loan agreement with the borrowers.

A syndicated loan may be publicly traded. It may be a line of credit and be "undrawn" or it may be drawn and be used by a firm. Syndicated loans are always rated investment grade. However, a *leveraged* syndicated loan is rated speculative grade (i.e., it is "junk"). Every week, the *Wall Street Journal* reports on a number of syndicated loan deals, credit costs, and yields. In addition, syndicated loan prices are reported for a group of publicly traded loans. Research finds slightly higher default rates for syndicated loans when compared to corporate bonds.[12]

While there is no market for the public trading of syndicated loans, commercial and investment banks in the U.S. have created loan trading desks and a secondary loan market for syndicated loans. Further, the Loan Syndications and Trading Association was formed to help develop regulations and practices for this market. There is currently no similar market in Canada.[13]

private placements
Loans, usually long term in nature, provided directly by a limited number of investors.

Private placements are very similar to term loans except that the maturity is longer. Unlike term loans, privately placed debt usually employs an investment dealer. The dealer facilitates the process but does not underwrite the issue. A private placement does not require a full prospectus. Instead, the firm and its investment dealer only need to draw up an offering memorandum briefly describing the issuer and the issue. Most privately placed debt is sold to exempt purchasers. These are large insurance companies, pension funds, and other institutions, which, as sophisticated market participants, do not require the protection provided by studying a full prospectus.

The important differences between direct private long-term financing—term loans and private debt placements—and public issues of debt are:

1. Registration costs are lower for direct financing. A term loan avoids the cost of OSC registration. Private debt placements require an offering memorandum, but this is cheaper than preparing a full prospectus.

2. Direct placement is likely to have more restrictive covenants.

---

[12] Edward I. Altman and Heather J. Suggitt, "Default Rates in the Syndicated Bank Loan Market: A Longitudinal Analysis," *Journal of Banking and Finance*, vol. 24, 2000.

[13] This discussion of the secondary syndicated loan market is largely based upon the following Bank of Canada paper available at bankofcanada.ca: Jim Armstrong (2011), "The Syndicated Loan Market: Developments in the North American Context," Bank of Canada *Financial System Review*, 69–73.

3. It is easier to renegotiate a term loan or a private placement in the event of a default. It is harder to renegotiate a public issue because hundreds of holders are usually involved.

4. Life insurance companies and pension funds dominate the private-placement segment of the bond market. Chartered banks are significant participants in the term loan market.

5. The costs of distributing bonds are lower in the private market because fewer buyers are involved and the issue is not underwritten.

The interest rates on term loans and private placements are usually higher than those on an equivalent public issue. This reflects the trade-off between a higher interest rate and more flexible arrangements in the event of financial distress, as well as the lower costs associated with private placements.

An additional, and very important, consideration is that the flotation costs associated with selling debt are much less than the costs associated with selling equity.

Concept Questions

1. What is the difference between private and public bond issues?

2. A private placement is likely to have a higher interest rate than a public issue. Why?

15.11 | SUMMARY AND CONCLUSIONS

This chapter looks at how corporate securities are issued. The following are the main points:

1. The costs of issuing securities can be quite large. They are much lower (as a percentage) for larger issues.

2. The bought deal type of underwriting is far more prevalent for large issues than regular underwriting. This is probably connected to the savings available through Prompt Offering Prospectuses and concentrated selling efforts.

3. The direct and indirect costs of going public can be substantial. However, once a firm is public it can raise additional capital with much greater ease.

4. Rights offerings are cheaper than general cash offers. Even so, most new equity issues in the United States are underwritten general cash offers. In Canada, the bought deal is cheaper and dominates the new issue market.

Key Terms

best efforts underwriting (page 428)
bought deal (page 428)
dilution (page 446)
Dutch auction underwriting (page 429)
ex rights (page 443)
firm commitment underwriting (page 428)
general cash offer (page 427)
holder-of-record date (page 443)
initial public offering (IPO) (page 426)
lockup agreement (page 430)
overallotment option (page 430)
oversubscription privilege (page 444)
private placements (page 448)
prospectus (page 426)

public issue (page 425)
red herring (page 426)
regular underwriting (page 428)
rights offer (page 427)
seasoned equity offering (SEO) (page 427)
seasoned new issue (page 426)
spread (page 428)
standby fee (page 444)
standby underwriting (page 444)
syndicate (page 427)
syndicated loans (page 448)
term loans (page 448)
venture capital (page 424)

Chapter Review Problems and Self-Test

15.1 **Flotation Costs** The L5 Corporation is considering an equity issue to finance a new space station. A total of $10 million in new equity is needed. If the direct costs are estimated at 6 percent of the amount raised, how large does the issue need to be? What is the dollar amount of the flotation cost?

15.2 **Rights Offerings** The Hadron Corporation currently has 4 million shares outstanding. The stock sells for $50 per share. To raise $30 million for a new particle accelerator, the firm is considering a rights offering at $20 per share. What is the value of a right in this case? The ex-rights price?

Answers to Self-Test Problems

15.1 The firm needs to net $10 million after paying the 6 percent flotation costs. So the amount raised is given by:

Amount raised $\times$ (1 − .06) = $10 million
Amount raised = $10/.94 = $10.638 million

The total flotation cost is thus $638,000.

15.2 To raise $30 million at $20 per share, $30 million/$20 = 1.5 million shares will have to be sold. Before the offering, the firm is worth 4 million $\times$ $50 = $200 million. The issue raised $30 million and there will be 5.5 million shares outstanding. The value of an ex-rights share will therefore be $230/5.5 = $41.82. The value of a right is thus $50 − 41.82 = $8.18.

Concepts Review and Critical Thinking Questions

1. **(LO2)** In the aggregate, debt offerings are much more common than equity offerings and typically much larger as well. Why?

2. **(LO2)** Why are the costs of selling equity so much larger than the costs of selling debt?

3. **(LO2)** Why do noninvestment-grade bonds have much higher direct costs than investment-grade issues?

4. **(LO2)** Why is underpricing not a great concern with bond offerings?

Use the following information in answering the next three questions: ZipCar, the car sharing company, went public in April 2011. Assisted by the investment bank, The Goldman Sachs Group, Inc., ZipCar sold 9.68 million shares at $18 each, thereby raising a total of $174.28 million. At the end of the first day of trading, the stock sold for $28 per share, down from a high of $31.50 reached earlier in the day in frenzied trading. Based on the end-of-day numbers, ZipCar's shares were apparently underpriced by about $10 each, meaning that the company missed out on an additional $96.8 million.

5. **(LO3)** The Zipcar IPO was severely underpriced by about 56 percent. Should Zipcar be upset at Goldman over the underpricing?

6. **(LO3)** In the previous question, would it affect your thinking to know that, at the time of the IPO, Zipcar was only 10 years old, had only $186 million in revenues in 2010, and had never earned a profit? Additionally, the viability of the company's business model was still unproven.

7. **(LO3)** In the previous two questions, how would it affect your thinking to know that in addition to the 9.68 million shares offered in the IPO, Zipcar had an additional 30 million shares outstanding? Of those 30 million shares, 14.1 million shares were owned by four venture capital firms, and 15.5 million shares were owned by the 12 directors and executive officers.

8. **(LO4)** Ren-Stimpy International is planning to raise fresh equity capital by selling a large new issue of common stock. Ren-Stimpy is currently a publicly traded corporation, and it is trying to choose between an underwritten cash offer and a rights offering (not underwritten) to current shareholders. Ren-Stimpy management is interested in minimizing the selling costs and has asked you for advice on the choice of issue methods. What is your recommendation and why?

9. **(LO3)** In 1999, a certain assistant professor of finance bought 12 initial public offerings of common stock. He held each of these for approximately one month and then sold. The investment rule he followed was to submit a purchase order for every initial public offering of Internet companies. There were 22 of these offerings, and he submitted a purchase order for approximately $1,000 in stock for each of the companies. With 10 of these, no shares were allocated to this assistant professor. With 5 of the 12 offerings that were purchased, fewer than the requested number of shares were allocated.

   The year 1999 was very good for Internet company owners: on average, for the 22 companies that went public, the stocks were selling for 80 percent above the offering price a month after the initial offering date. The assistant professor looked at his performance record and found that the $8,400 invested in the 12 companies had grown to $10,000, representing a return of only about 20 percent (commissions were negligible). Did he have bad luck, or should he have expected to do worse than the average initial public offering investor? Explain.

Questions and Problems

Basic
(Questions
1–8)

1. Rights Offerings (LO4) Berczy Inc. is proposing a rights offering. Presently there are 400,000 shares outstanding at $73 each. There will be 50,000 new shares offered at $65 each.

    a.   What is the new market value of the company?

    b.   How many rights are associated with one of the new shares?

    c.   What is the ex-rights price?

    d.   What is the value of a right?

    e.   Why might a company have a rights offering rather than a general cash offer?

2. Rights Offerings (LO4) The Greensborough Corporation has announced a rights offer to raise $30 million for a new journal, the *Journal of Financial Excess*. This journal will review potential articles after the author pays a nonrefundable reviewing fee of $5,000 per page. The stock currently sells for $48 per share, and there are 3.9 million shares outstanding.

    a.   What is the maximum possible subscription price? What is the minimum?

    b.   If the subscription price is set at $43 per share, how many shares must be sold? How many rights will it take to buy one share?

    c.   What is the ex-rights price? What is the value of a right?

    d.   Show how a shareholder with 1000 shares before the offering and no desire (or money) to buy additional shares is not harmed by the rights offer.

3. Rights (LO4) Milliken Co. has concluded that additional equity financing will be needed to expand operations and that the needed funds will be best obtained through a rights offering. It has correctly determined that as a result of the rights offering, the share price will fall from $65 to $63.20 ($65 is the rights-on price; $63.20 is the ex-rights price, also known as the *when-issued* price). The company is seeking $17 million in additional funds with a per-share subscription price equal to $35. How many shares are there currently, before the offering? (Assume that the increment to the market value of the equity equals the gross proceeds from the offering.)

4. IPO Underpricing (LO3) The Markville Co. and the Unionville Co. have both announced IPOs at $40 per share. One of these is undervalued by $9, and the other is overvalued by $4, but you have no way of knowing which is which. You plan to buy 1000 shares of each issue. If an issue is underpriced, it will be rationed, and only half your order will be filled. If you *could* get 1000 shares in Markville and 1000 shares in Unionville, what would your profit be? What profit do you actually expect? What principle have you illustrated?

5. Calculating Flotation Costs (LO3) The Cresthaven Horses Corporation needs to raise $85 million to finance its expansion into new markets. The company will sell new shares of equity via a general cash offering to raise the needed funds. If the offer price is $16 per share and the company's underwriters charge an 8 percent spread, how many shares need to be sold?

6. Calculating Flotation Costs (LO3) In the previous problem, if the OSC filing fee and associated administrative expenses of the offering are $900,000, how many shares need to be sold?

7. Calculating Flotation Costs (LO3) The Rouge Co. has just gone public. Under a firm commitment agreement, Rouge received $17.67 for each of the 15 million shares sold. The initial offering price was $19 per share, and the stock rose to $23.18 per share in the first few minutes of trading. Rouge paid $900,000 in direct legal and other costs, and $320,000 in indirect costs. What was the flotation cost as a percentage of funds raised?

8. Price Dilution (LO3) Reesor Inc. has 175,000 shares of stock outstanding. Each share is worth $68, so the company's market value of equity is $11,900,000. Suppose the firm issues 30,000 new shares at the following prices: $68, $65, and $60. What will the effect be of each of these alternative offering prices on the existing price per share?

Intermediate
(Questions
9–15)

9. Dilution (LO3) Chancery Inc. wishes to expand its facilities. The company currently has 5 million shares outstanding and no debt. The stock sells for $31 per share, but the book value per share is $7. Net income is currently $3.2 million. The new facility will cost $45 million, and it will increase net income by $900,000.

    a.   Assuming a constant price–earnings ratio, what will the effect be of issuing new equity to finance the investment? To answer, calculate the new book value per share, the new total earnings, the new EPS, the new stock price, and the new market-to-book ratio. What is going on here?

    b.   What would the new net income for the company have to be for the stock price to remain unchanged?

10. Dilution (LO3) The Hagerman Heavy Metal Mining (H2M2) Corporation wants to diversify its operations. Some recent financial information for the company is shown here:

Stock price	$ 76
Number of shares	40,000
Total assets	$7,500,000
Total liabilities	$3,100,000
Net income	$ 850,000

H2M2 is considering an investment that has the same PE ratio as the firm. The cost of the investment is $800,000, and it will be financed with a new equity issue. The return on the investment will equal H2M2's current ROE. What will happen to the book value per share, the market value per share, and the EPS? What is the NPV of this investment? Does dilution take place?

11. **Dilution (LO3)** In the previous problem, what would the ROE on the investment have to be if we wanted the price after the offering to be $76 per share? (Assume the PE ratio remains constant.) What is the NPV of this investment? Does any dilution take place?

12. **Rights (LO4)** Milne Mfg. is considering a rights offer. The company has determined that the ex-rights price would be $83. The current price is $89 per share, and there are 24 million shares outstanding. The rights offer would raise a total of $50 million. What is the subscription price?

13. **Value of a Right (LO4)** Show that the value of a right just prior to expiration can be written as:

$$\text{Value of a right} = P_{RO} - P_X = (P_{RO} - P_S)/(N + 1)$$

where P_{RO}, P_S, and P_X stand for the rights-on price, the subscription price, and the ex-rights price, respectively, and N is the number of rights needed to buy one new share at the subscription price.

14. **Selling Rights (LO4)** Belford Corp. wants to raise $4.5 million via a rights offering. The company currently has 580,000 shares of common stock outstanding that sell for $45 per share. Its underwriter has set a subscription price of $20 per share and will charge the company a spread of 6 percent. If you currently own 5000 shares of stock in the company and decide not to participate in the rights offering, how much money can you get by selling your rights?

15. **Valuing a Right (LO4)** Cherrywood Inventory Systems Inc. has announced a rights offer. The company has announced that it will take four rights to buy a new share in the offering at a subscription price of $31. At the close of business the day before the ex-rights day, the company's stock sells for $56 per share. The next morning, you notice that the stock sells for $49 per share and the rights sell for $3 each. Are the stock and the rights correctly priced on the ex-rights day? Describe a transaction in which you could use these prices to create an immediate profit.

Internet Application Questions

1. What is the Investment Industry Regulatory Organization of Canada (iiroc.ca)? Describe its mandate, with particular attention on how the IIROC protects the investors' funds (cipf.ca).

2. What comprises the Canadian regulatory landscape (iiroc.ca/industry/industrycompliance/Pages/default.aspx) for securities trading? Also go to the website for the newest stock exchange in Canada, the TSX Venture Exchange. Describe the role played by the capital pool program (142.201.0.1/en/pdf/CPCBrochure.pdf) at the Venture Exchange.

3. What is the most recent Canadian IPO? Go to ipo.investcom.com and search under the "Date of Filing" link. What is the company? What exchange trades the stock? What was the IPO price? Is the company currently trading? If so, find the current price and calculate the return since inception.

4. What were the biggest first day returns in the latest quarter for IPOs in the U.S. markets? Go to hoovers.com, follow the "IPO Central" link, then the "IPO Scorecard" link.

5. You want to look at the most recent initial public offering filings on SEDAR. Go to ipo.investcom.com and locate the most recent company making a filing (note the name and ticker symbol of the company). Then go to sedar.com and search for the company. What is the name of the document filed with SEDAR for the IPO? What does this company do? What purpose does the company propose for the funds raised by the IPO?

6. Go to ipo.investcom.com and locate the largest Canadian offering listed. What is the name of the company? What industry is it in? What is the final offering price per share? How much does the company expect to raise in the offering? Who is (are) the lead underwriter(s)?

7. Go to hoovers.com; follow the "IPO Central" link, then the "IPO Scorecard" link. What companies are currently in the list for "Money Left on the Table," (capital that could have been raised had the stock been offered at a higher price)? Calculate the money on the table as a percentage of the value of the company at the offer price for all the companies on the list? Which company is the most underpriced?

8. Go to finance.yahoo.com and find the current share price of Facebook Inc.? Why was the Facebook IPO overpriced? Comment on the efficiency of NASDAQ in bringing shares to the market.

MINI CASE

The following material represents the cover page and summary of the prospectus for the initial public offering of the Markham Pest Control Corporation (MPCC), which is going public tomorrow with a firm commitment initial public offering managed by the investment banking firm of Drape and Grape. Answer the following questions:

a) Assume that you know nothing about MPCC other than the information contained in the prospectus. Based on your knowledge of finance, what is your prediction for the price of MPCC tomorrow? Provide a short explanation of why you think this will occur.

b) Assume that you have several thousand dollars to invest. When you get home from class tonight, you find that your stockbroker, whom you have not talked to for weeks, has called. She has left a message that MPCC is going public tomorrow and that she can get you several hundred shares at the offering price if you call her back first thing in the morning. Discuss the merits of this opportunity.

Prospectus   MPCC

Markham Pest Control Corporation

Of the shares being offered hereby, all 400,000 are being sold by the Markham Pest Control Corporation Inc. ("the Company"). Before the offering there has been no public market for the shares of MPCC, and no guarantee can be given that any such market will develop.

These securities have not been approved or disapproved by the OSC, nor has the commission passed upon the accuracy or adequacy of this prospectus. Any representation to the contrary is a criminal offence.

	Price to Public	Underwriting Discount	Proceeds to Company*
Per share	$12.00	$1.00	$11.00
Total	$4,000,000	$400,000	$3,600,000

*Before deducting expenses estimated at $27,000 and payable by the Company.

This is an initial public offering. The common shares are being offered, subject to prior sale, when, as, and if delivered to and accepted by the Underwriters and subject to approval of certain legal matters by their Counsel and by Counsel for the Company. The Underwriters reserve the right to withdraw, cancel, or modify such offer and to reject offers in whole or in part.

Drape and Grape, Investment Bankers
May 3, 2012
Prospectus Summary

The Company	The Markham Pest Control Corporation (MPCC) breeds and markets toads and tree frogs as ecologically safe insect-control mechanisms.
The Offering	400,000 shares of common stock, no par value.
Listing	The Company will seek listing on the TSX.
Shares Outstanding	As of December 31, 2011, 500,000 shares of common stock were outstanding. After the offering, 900,000 shares of common stock will be outstanding.
Use of Proceeds	To finance expansion of inventory and receivables and general working capital, and to pay for country club memberships for certain finance professors.

Selected Financial Information
(amounts in thousands except per share data)
Fiscal Year Ended December 31

	2009	2010	2011
Revenues	$65.00	$130.00	$260.00
Net earnings	4.50	17.00	30.00
Earnings per share	0.011	0.043	0.075

As of December 31, 2011

	Actual	As Adjusted for This Offering
Working capital	$10.00	$2,200
Total assets	$550	$2,856
Shareholders' equity	$460	$2,712

CHAPTER 16

FINANCIAL LEVERAGE AND CAPITAL STRUCTURE POLICY

In late 2009, Canwest Global Communications Corporation, then the largest media company in Canada, filed for bankruptcy as it had amassed a debt of $4 billion. The Winnipeg-based company owned a range of broadcasting and printing businesses, including the *National Post* newspaper. As a part of the bankruptcy process, Canwest's newspaper arm was sold to a group of creditors led by *National Post* CEO Paul Godfrey, through a newly formed company, Postmedia Network. Canwest's broadcasting arm was sold to Shaw Communications.

A firm's choice of how much debt it should have relative to equity is known as a capital structure decision. Such a choice has many implications for a firm and is far from being a settled issue in theory or practice. In this chapter, we discuss the basic ideas underlying capital structures and how firms choose them.

A firm's capital structure is really just a reflection of its borrowing policy. Should we borrow a lot of money, or just a little? At first glance, it probably seems that debt is something to be avoided. After all, the more debt a firm has, the greater is the risk of bankruptcy. What we learn is that debt is really a double-edged sword, and, properly used, debt can be enormously beneficial to a firm.

A good understanding of the effects of debt financing is important simply because the role of debt is so misunderstood, and many firms (and individuals) are too far conservative in their use of debt. Having said this, we can also say that firms sometimes err in the opposite direction, becoming too much heavily indebted, with bankruptcy as the unfortunate consequence. Striking the right balance is what the capital structure issue is all about.

Learning Objectives ▶

After studying this chapter, you should understand:

LO1   The effect of financial leverage on firm value and cost of capital.

LO2   The impact of taxes and bankruptcy on capital structure choice.

LO3   The essentials of the bankruptcy process.

Thus far, we have taken the firm's capital structure as given. Debt/equity ratios don't just drop on firms from the sky, of course, so now it's time to wonder where they do come from. Going back to Chapter 1, we call decisions about a firm's debt/equity ratio capital structure decisions.[1]

For the most part, a firm can choose any capital structure it wants. If management so desired, a firm could issue some bonds and use the proceeds to buy back some stock, thereby increasing the debt/equity ratio. Alternatively, it can issue stock and use the money to pay off some debt, thereby reducing the debt/equity ratio. These activities that alter the firm's existing capital structure are called capital *restructurings*. In general, such restructurings occur whenever the firm substitutes one capital structure for another while leaving the firm's assets unchanged.

Since the assets of a firm are not directly affected by a capital restructuring, we can examine the firm's capital structure decision separately from its other activities. This means a firm can consider capital restructuring decisions in isolation from its investment decisions. In this chapter then, we

---

[1] It is conventional to refer to decisions regarding debt and equity as capital structure decisions. However, the term *financial structure* would be more accurate, and we use the terms interchangeably.

ignore investment decisions and focus on the long-term financing, or capital structure, question. We consider only long-term financing because, as we explained in Chapter 14, short-term sources of financing are excluded in calculating capital structure weights.

What we see in this chapter is that capital structure decisions can have important implications for the value of the firm and its cost of capital. We also find that important elements of the capital structure decision are easy to identify, but precise measures of these elements are generally not obtainable. As a result, we are able to give only an incomplete answer to the question of what the best capital structure might be for a particular firm at a particular time.

16.1 | The Capital Structure Question

How should a firm choose its debt/equity ratio? Here, as always, we assume that the guiding principle is to choose the action that maximizes the value of a share of stock. As we discuss next, however, when it comes to capital structure decisions, this is essentially the same thing as maximizing the value of the firm, and, for convenience, we frame our discussion in terms of firm value.

Firm Value and Stock Value: An Example

The following example illustrates that the capital structure that maximizes the value of the firm is the one that financial managers should choose for the shareholders, so there is no conflict in our goals. To begin, suppose the market value of the J. J. Sprint Company is $1,000. The company currently has no debt, and J. J. Sprint's 100 shares sell for $10 each. Further suppose that J. J. Sprint restructures itself by borrowing $500 and then paying out the proceeds to shareholders as an extra dividend of $500/100 = $5 per share.

This restructuring changes the capital structure of the firm with no direct effect on the firm's assets. The immediate effect is to increase debt and decrease equity. However, what would be the final impact of the restructuring? Table 16.1 illustrates three possible outcomes in addition to the original no-debt case. Notice that in scenario II the value of the firm is unchanged at $1,000. In scenario I, firm value rises by $250; it falls by $250 in scenario III. We haven't yet said what might lead to these changes. For now, we just take them as possible outcomes to illustrate a point.

Since our goal is to benefit the shareholders, we next examine, in Table 16.2, the net payoffs to the shareholders in these scenarios. For now we ignore the impact of taxes on dividends, capital gains and losses. We see that, if the value of the firm stays the same, then shareholders experience a capital loss that exactly offsets the extra dividend. This is outcome II. In outcome I, the value of the firm increases to $1,250 and the shareholders come out ahead by $250. In other words, the restructuring has an NPV of $250 in this scenario. The NPV in scenario III is −$250.

TABLE 16.1

Possible firm values: No debt versus debt plus dividend

	No Debt	Debt plus Dividend		
	No Debt	I	II	III
Debt	$ 0	$ 500	$ 500	$500
Equity	1,000	750	500	250
Firm value	$1,000	$1,250	$1,000	$750

TABLE 16.2

Possible payoffs to shareholders: Debt plus dividend

	Debt plus Dividend		
	I	II	III
Equity value reduction	−$250	−$500	−$750
Dividends	500	500	500
Net effect	+$250	$ 0	−$250

The key observation to make here is that the change in the value of the firm is the same as the net effect on the shareholders. Financial managers can therefore try to find the capital structure that maximizes the value of the firm. Put another way, the NPV rule applies to capital structure decisions, and the change in the value of the overall firm is the NPV of a restructuring. Thus, J.J. Sprint should borrow $500 if it expects outcome I. The crucial question in determining a firm's capital structure is, of course, which scenario is likely to occur.

Capital Structure and the Cost of Capital

In Chapter 14, we discussed the concept of the firm's weighted average cost of capital (WACC). Recall that the WACC tells us that the firm's overall cost of capital is a weighted average of the costs of the various components of the firm's capital structure. When we described the WACC, we took the firm's capital structure as given. Thus, one important issue that we want to explore in this chapter is what happens to the cost of capital when we vary the amount of debt financing or the debt/equity ratio.[2]

A primary reason for studying the WACC is that the value of the firm is maximized when the WACC is minimized. To see this, recall that the WACC is the discount rate that is appropriate for the firm's overall cash flows. Because values and discount rates move in opposite directions, minimizing the WACC maximizes the value of the firm's cash flows.

Thus, we want to choose the firm's capital structure so that the WACC is minimized. For this reason, we say that one capital structure is better than another if it results in a lower weighted average cost of capital. Further, we say that a particular debt/equity ratio represents the *optimal capital structure* if it results in the lowest possible WACC. This is sometimes called the firm's target capital structure as well.

Concept Questions

1. Why should financial managers choose the capital structure that maximizes the value of the firm?
2. What is the relationship between the WACC and the value of the firm?
3. What is an optimal capital structure?

16.2 | The Effect of Financial Leverage

The previous section describes why the capital structure that produces the highest firm value (or the lowest cost of capital) is the one most beneficial to shareholders. In this section, we examine the impact of financial leverage on the payoffs to shareholders. As you may recall, financial leverage refers to the extent to which a firm relies on debt. The more debt financing a firm uses in its capital structure, the more financial leverage it employs.

As we describe, financial leverage can dramatically alter the payoffs to shareholders in the firm. Remarkably, however, financial leverage may not affect the overall cost of capital. If this is true, then a firm's capital structure is irrelevant because changes in capital structure won't affect the value of the firm. We return to this issue a little later.

The Basics of Financial Leverage

We start by illustrating how financial leverage works. For now, we ignore the impact of taxes. Also, for ease of presentation, we describe the impact of leverage in its effects on earnings per share (EPS) and return on equity (ROE). These are, of course, accounting numbers, and, as such, are not our primary concern. Using cash flows instead of these accounting numbers would lead to precisely the same conclusions, but a little more work would be needed. We discuss the impact on market values in a subsequent section.

---

[2]Note that when we looked at WACC, we considered the cost of debt to be related to bond issues. This cost could also be a bank debt financing rate if the firm predominantly uses that form of debt.

FINANCIAL LEVERAGE, EPS, AND ROE: AN EXAMPLE   The Trans North Corporation currently has no debt in its capital structure. The CFO, Kim Morris, is considering a restructuring that would involve issuing debt and using the proceeds to buy back some of the outstanding equity. Table 16.3 presents both the current and proposed capital structures. As shown, the firm's assets have a value of $8 million, and there are 400,000 shares outstanding. Because Trans North is an all-equity firm, the price per share is $20.

TABLE 16.3

Current and proposed capital structures for the Trans North Corporation

	Current	Proposed
Assets	$8,000,000	$8,000,000
Debt	0	4,000,000
Equity	8,000,000	4,000,000
Debt/equity ratio	0	1
Share price	$ 20	$ 20
Shares outstanding	400,000	200,000
Interest rate	10%	10%

The proposed debt issue would raise $4 million; the bonds would be issued at par with a coupon rate of 10 percent for a required return on debt of 10 percent. Since the stock sells for $20 per share, the $4 million in new debt would be used to purchase $4 million/$20 = 200,000 shares, leaving 200,000. After the restructuring, Trans North would have a capital structure that was 50 percent debt, so the debt/equity ratio would be 1. Notice that, for now, we assume the stock price remains at $20.

To investigate the impact of the proposed restructuring, Morris has prepared Table 16.4, that compares the firm's current capital structure to the proposed capital structure under three scenarios. The scenarios reflect different assumptions about the firm's EBIT. Under the expected scenario, the EBIT is $1 million. In the recession scenario, EBIT falls to $500,000. In the expansion scenario, it rises to $1.5 million.

TABLE 16.4

Capital structure scenarios for the Trans North Corporation

	Recession	Expected	Expansion
Current Capital Structure: No Debt			
EBIT	$500,000	$1,000,000	$1,500,000
Interest	0	0	0
Net income	$500,000	$1,000,000	$1,500,000
ROE	6.25%	12.50%	18.75%
EPS	$ 1.25	$ 2.50	$ 3.75
Proposed Capital Structure: Debt = $4 million			
EBIT	$500,000	$1,000,000	$1,500,000
Interest	400,000	400,000	400,000
Net income	$100,000	$ 600,000	$1,100,000
ROE	2.50%	15.00%	27.50%
EPS	$ .50	$ 3.00	$ 5.50

To illustrate some of the calculations in Table 16.4, consider the expansion case. EBIT is $1.5 million. With no debt (the current capital structure) and no taxes, net income is also $1.5 million. In this case, there are 400,000 shares worth $8 million total. EPS is therefore $1.5 million/400,000 = $3.75 per share. Also, since accounting return on equity (ROE) is net income divided by total equity, ROE is $1.5 million/$8 million = 18.75%.[3]

---

[3] ROE is discussed in some detail in Chapter 3.

With $4 million in debt (the proposed capital structure), things are somewhat different. Since the interest rate is 10 percent, the interest bill is $400,000. With EBIT of $1.5 million, interest of $400,000, and no taxes, net income is $1.1 million. Now there are only 200,000 shares worth $4 million total. EPS is therefore $1.1 million/200,000 = $5.50 per share versus the $3.75 per share that we calculated earlier. Furthermore, ROE is $1.1 million/$4 million = 27.5 percent. This is well above the 18.75 percent we calculated for the current capital structure. So our example in Table 16.4 shows how increased debt can magnify ROE when profitability is good.

Greater use of debt also magnifies ROE in the other direction. To see this, look at the recession case in Table 16.4. Under the current capital structure, EPS falls to $1.25 in a recession bringing ROE down to 6.25 percent. With more debt under the proposed capital structure, EPS is only $.50 and ROE drops to 2.50 percent. In brief, Table 16.4 shows that using more debt makes EPS and ROE more risky.

DEGREE OF FINANCIAL LEVERAGE   As our example shows, financial leverage measures how much earnings per share (and ROE) respond to changes in EBIT. It is the financial counterpart to operating leverage that we discussed in Chapter 11. We can generalize our discussion of financial leverage by introducing a formula for the degree of financial leverage:

$$\text{Degree of financial leverage} = \frac{\text{Percentage change in EPS}}{\text{Percentage change in EBIT}} \qquad [16.1]$$

Like the degree of operating leverage, DFL varies for different ranges of EPS and EBIT. To illustrate the formula, we calculate DFL for Trans North for an EBIT of $1 million. There are two calculations, one for the current and one for the proposed capital structure. Starting with the current capital structure:

$$\text{DFL} = \frac{(\$3.75 - 2.50)/2.50}{(\$1,500,000 - 1,000,000)/1,000,000}$$

$$\text{DFL} = \frac{.50}{.50}$$

$$\text{DFL} = 1.0$$

So for the existing capital structure, the degree of financial leverage is 1.0. For the proposed capital structure:

$$\text{DFL} = \frac{(\$5.50 - 3.00)/3.00}{(\$1,500,000 - 1,000,000)/1,000,000}$$

$$\text{DFL} = \frac{.83}{.50}$$

$$\text{DFL} = 1.67$$

The proposed capital structure includes debt and this increases the degree of financial leverage. Calculating DFL adds precision to our earlier observation that increasing financial leverage magnifies the gains and losses to shareholders. We can now say that EPS increases or decreases by a factor of 1.67 times the percentage increase or decrease in EBIT.

Many analysts use a convenient alternative formula for DFL:

$$\text{DFL} = \frac{\text{EBIT}}{\text{EBIT} - \text{Interest}} \qquad [16.2]$$

We recalculate DFL for the proposed capital structure at EBIT of $1 million to show that the new formula gives the same answer.

$$\text{DFL} = \frac{\$1,000,000}{\$1,000,000 - 400,000}$$

$$\text{DFL} = \frac{\$1,000,000}{\$600,000}$$

$$\text{DFL} = 1.67$$

EPS VERSUS EBIT   The impact of leverage is evident when the effect of the restructuring on EPS and ROE is examined. In particular, the variability in both EPS and ROE is much larger under the proposed capital structure. This illustrates how financial leverage acts to magnify gains and losses to shareholders.

In Figure 16.1, we take a closer look at the effect of the proposed restructuring. This figure plots earnings per share (EPS) against earnings before interest and taxes (EBIT) for the current and proposed capital structures. The first line, labelled "No debt," represents the case of no leverage. This line begins at the origin, indicating that EPS would be zero if EBIT were zero. From there, every $400,000 increase in EBIT increases EPS by $1 (because there are 400,000 shares outstanding).

The second line represents the proposed capital structure. Here, EPS is negative if EBIT is zero. This follows because $400,000 of interest must be paid regardless of the firm's profits. Since there are 200,000 shares in this case, the EPS is −$2 per share as shown. Similarly, if EBIT were $400,000, EPS would be exactly zero.

The important thing to notice in Figure 16.1 is that the slope of the line in this second case is steeper. In fact, for every $400,000 increase in EBIT, EPS rises by $2, so the line is twice as steep. This tells us that EPS is twice as sensitive to changes in EBIT because of the financial leverage employed.

Another observation to make in Figure 16.1 is that the lines intersect. At that point, EPS is exactly the same for both capital structures. To find this point, note that EPS is equal to EBIT/400,000 in the no-debt case. In the with-debt case, EPS is (EBIT − $400,000)/200,000. If we set these equal to each other, EBIT is:

$$\text{EBIT}/400{,}000 = (\text{EBIT} - 400{,}000)/200{,}000$$
$$\text{EBIT} = 2 \times (\text{EBIT} - \$400{,}000)$$
$$\text{EBIT} = \$800{,}000$$

FIGURE 16.1

Financial leverage, EPS, and EBIT for the Trans North Corporation

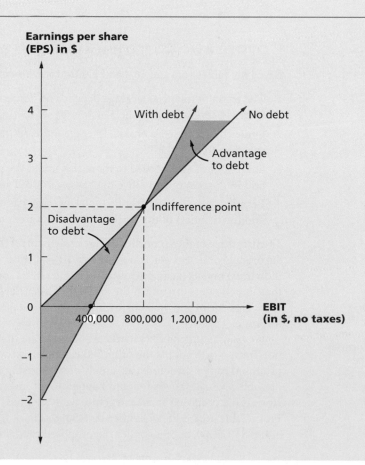

When EBIT is $800,000, EPS is $2 per share under either capital structure. This is labelled as the *indifference point* in Figure 16.1. If EBIT is above this level, leverage is beneficial; if it is below this point, it is not.

There is another, more intuitive way of seeing why the indifferent point is $800,000. Notice that, if the firm has no debt and its EBIT is $800,000, its net income is also $800,000. In this case, the ROE is 10 percent. This is precisely the same as the interest rate on the debt, so the firm earns a return that is just sufficient to pay the interest.

EXAMPLE 16.1: Indifference EBIT

The MPD Corporation has decided in favour of a capital restructuring. Currently, MPD uses no debt financing. Following the restructuring, however, debt would be $1 million. The interest rate on the debt would be 9 percent. MPD currently has 200,000 shares outstanding, and the price per share is $20. If the restructuring is expected to increase EPS, what is the minimum level for EBIT that MPD's management must be expecting? Ignore taxes in answering.[4]

To answer, we calculate EBIT at the indifferent point. At any EBIT above this, the increased financial leverage increases EPS, so this tells us the minimum level for EBIT. Under the old capital structure, EPS is simply EBIT/200,000. Under the new capital structure, the interest expense is $1 million × .09 = $90,000. Furthermore, with the $1 million

proceeds, MPD could repurchase $1 million/$20 = 50,000 shares of stock, leaving 150,000 outstanding. EPS is thus (EBIT − $90,000)/150,000.

Now that we know how to calculate EPS under both scenarios, we set them equal to each other and solve for the indifference point EBIT:

$$EBIT/200{,}000 = (EBIT - \$90{,}000)/150{,}000$$
$$EBIT = (4/3) \times (EBIT - \$90{,}000)$$
$$EBIT = \$360{,}000$$

Check that, in either case, EPS is $1.80 when EBIT is $360,000. Management at MPD is apparently of the opinion that EPS will exceed $1.80.

Corporate Borrowing and Homemade Leverage

Based on Tables 16.3 and 16.4 and Figure 16.1, Morris draws the following conclusions:

1. The effect of financial leverage depends on Trans North's EBIT. When EBIT is expected to increase, leverage is beneficial.
2. Under the expected scenario, leverage increases the returns to shareholders, both as measured by ROE and EPS.
3. Shareholders are exposed to more risk under the proposed capital structure since the EPS and ROE are more sensitive to changes in EBIT in this case.
4. Because of the impact that financial leverage has on both the expected return to shareholders and the riskiness of the stock, capital structure is an important consideration.

The first three of these conclusions are clearly correct. Does the last conclusion necessarily follow? Surprisingly, the answer is not necessarily—at least in a world of perfect capital markets where individual investors can borrow at the same rate as corporations. As we discuss next, the reason is that shareholders can adjust the amount of financial leverage by borrowing and lending on their own. This use of personal borrowing to alter the degree of financial leverage is called **homemade leverage**.

homemade leverage
The use of personal borrowing to change the overall amount of financial leverage to which the individual is exposed.

We now assume perfect markets and illustrate that it actually makes no difference whether or not Trans North adopts the proposed capital structure, because any shareholder who prefers the proposed capital structure can simply create it using homemade leverage. To begin, the first part of Table 16.5 shows what would happen to an investor who buys $2,000 worth of Trans North stock if the proposed capital structure were adopted. This investor purchases 100 shares of stock. From Table 16.4, EPS will either be $.50, $3.00, or $5.50, so the total earnings for 100 shares is either $50, $300, or $550 under the proposed capital structure.

---

[4]Note that at the break-even point, taxes are irrelevant.

TABLE 16.5

Proposed capital structure versus original capital structure with homemade leverage

	Recession	Expected	Expansion
Proposed Capital Structure			
EPS	$ .50	$ 3.00	$ 5.50
Earnings for 100 shares	50.00	300.00	550.00
Net cost = 100 shares at $20 = $2,000			
Original Capital Structure and Homemade Leverage			
EPS	$ 1.25	$ 2.50	$ 3.75
Earnings for 200 shares	250.00	500.00	750.00
Less: Interest on $2,000 at 10%	200.00	200.00	200.00
Net earnings	$ 50.00	$300.00	$550.00
Net cost = 200 shares at $20/share − Amount borrowed = $4,000 − 2,000 = $2,000			

Now, suppose that Trans North does not adopt the proposed capital structure. In this case, EPS is $1.25, $2.50, or $3.75. The second part of Table 16.5 demonstrates how a shareholder who preferred the payoffs under the proposed structure can create them using personal borrowing. To do this, the shareholder borrows $2,000 at 10 percent on his or her own. Our investor uses this amount, along with the original $2,000, to buy 200 shares of stock. As shown, the net payoffs are exactly the same as those for the proposed capital structure.

How did we know to borrow $2,000 to create the right payoffs? We are trying to replicate Trans North's proposed capital structure at the personal level. The proposed capital structure results in a debt/equity ratio of 1. To replicate it at the personal level, the shareholder must borrow enough to create this same debt/equity ratio. Since the shareholder has $2,000 in equity invested, borrowing another $2,000 creates a personal debt/equity ratio of 1.

This example demonstrates that investors can always increase financial leverage themselves to create a different pattern of payoffs. It thus makes no difference whether or not Trans North chooses the proposed capital structure.

EXAMPLE 16.2: Unlevering the Stock

In our Trans North example, suppose management adopts the proposed capital structure. Further suppose that an investor who owned 100 shares preferred the original capital structure. Show how this investor could "unlever" the stock to re-create the original payoffs.

	Recession	Expected	Expansion
EPS (proposed structure)	$ .50	$ 3.00	$ 5.50
Earnings for 50 shares	25.00	150.00	275.00
Plus: Interest on $1,000	100.00	100.00	100.00
Total payoff	$125.00	$250.00	$375.00

To create leverage, investors borrow on their own. To undo leverage, investors must lend money. For Trans North, the corporation borrowed an amount equal to half its value. The investor can unlever the stock by simply lending money in the same proportion. In this case, the investor sells 50 shares for $1,000 total and then lends out the $1,000 at 10 percent. The payoffs are calculated in the accompanying table. These are precisely the payoffs the investor would have experienced under the original capital structure.

Concept Questions

1. What is the impact of financial leverage on shareholders?
2. What is homemade leverage?
3. Why is Trans North's capital structure irrelevant?

16.3 | Capital Structure and the Cost of Equity Capital

We have seen that there is nothing special about corporate borrowing because investors can borrow or lend on their own. As a result, whichever capital structure Trans North chooses, the stock price is the same. Trans North's capital structure is thus irrelevant, at least in the simple world we examined.

M&M Proposition I
The value of the firm is independent of its capital structure.

Our Trans North example is based on a famous argument advanced by two Nobel laureates, Franco Modigliani and Merton Miller, whom we henceforth call M&M. What we illustrated for the Trans North Company is a special case of **M&M Proposition I**. M&M Proposition I states that it is completely irrelevant how a firm chooses to arrange its finances.

M&M Proposition I: The Pie Model

One way to illustrate M&M Proposition I is to imagine two firms that are identical on the left side of the statement of financial position. Their assets and operations are exactly the same. Each firm earns $EBIT every year indefinitely. No EBIT growth is projected. The right sides are different because the two firms finance their operations differently. We can view the capital structure question as a pie model. Why we chose this name is apparent in Figure 16.2. Figure 16.2 gives two possible ways of cutting up this pie between the equity slice, E, and the debt slice, D: 40–60 percent and 60–40 percent. However, the size of the pie in Figure 16.2 is the same for both firms because the value of the assets is the same. This is precisely what M&M Proposition I states: The size of the pie does not depend on how it is sliced.

FIGURE 16.2

Two pie models of capital structure

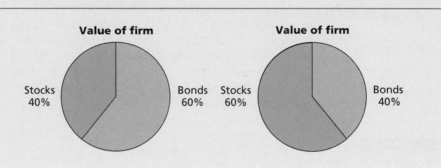

Proposition I is expressed in the following formula:

$$V_u = EBIT/R_E^u = V_L = E_L + D_L \qquad [16.3]$$

where

$$
\begin{aligned}
V_u &= \text{Value of the unlevered firm} \\
V_L &= \text{Value of the levered firm} \\
EBIT &= \text{Perpetual operating income} \\
R_E^u &= \text{Equity required return for the unlevered firm} \\
E_L &= \text{Market value of equity} \\
D_L &= \text{Market value of debt}
\end{aligned}
$$

The Cost of Equity and Financial Leverage: M&M Proposition II

Although changing the capital structure of the firm may not change the firm's total value, it does cause important changes in the firm's debt and equity. We now examine what happens to a firm financed with debt and equity when the debt/equity ratio is changed. To simplify our analysis, we continue to ignore taxes.

M&M PROPOSITION II   In Chapter 14, we saw that if we ignore taxes the weighted average cost of capital, WACC, is:

$$WACC = (E/V) \times R_E + (D/V) \times R_D$$

where $V = E + D$. We also saw that one way of interpreting the WACC is that it is the required return on the firm's overall assets. To remind us of this, we use the symbol R_A to stand for the WACC and write:

$$R_A = (E/V) \times R_E + (D/V) \times R_D$$

If we rearrange this to solve for the cost of equity capital, we see that:[5]

$$R_E = R_A + (R_A - R_D) \times (D/E) \qquad [16.4]$$

M&M Proposition II
A firm's cost of equity capital is a positive linear function of its capital structure.

This is the famous **M&M Proposition II**, which tells us that the cost of equity depends on three things: the required rate of return on the firm's assets, R_A; the firm's cost of debt, R_D; and the firm's debt/equity ratio, D/E.

Figure 16.3 summarizes our discussion thus far by plotting the cost of equity capital, R_E, against the debt/equity ratio. As shown, M&M Proposition II indicates that the cost of equity, R_E, is given by a straight line with a slope of $(R_A - R_D)$. The y-intercept corresponds to a firm with a debt/equity ratio of zero, so $R_A = R_E$ in that case. Figure 16.3 shows that, as the firm raises its debt/equity ratio, the increase in leverage raises the risk of the equity and, therefore, the required return or cost of equity (R_E).

FIGURE 16.3

The cost of equity and the WACC; M&M Propositions I and II with no taxes

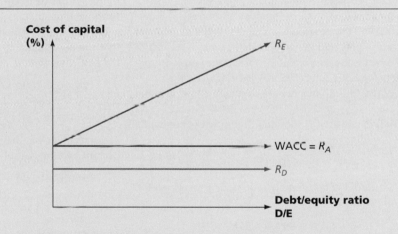

$R_E = R_A + (R_A - R_D) \times (D/E)$ by Proposition II

$WACC = \left(\frac{E}{V}\right)R_E + \left(\frac{D}{V}\right)R_D$

$V = D + E$

Notice in Figure 16.3 that the WACC doesn't depend on the debt/equity ratio; it's the same no matter what the debt/equity ratio is. This is another way of stating M&M Proposition I: The firm's overall cost of capital is unaffected by its capital structure. As illustrated, the fact that the cost of debt is lower than the cost of equity is exactly offset by the increase in the cost of equity from borrowing. In other words, the change in the capital structure weights (E/V and D/V) is exactly offset by the change in the cost of equity (R_E), so the WACC stays the same.

Business and Financial Risk

In our previous chapter, we discussed the use of the security market line (SML) to estimate the cost of equity capital. If we now combine the SML and M&M Proposition II, we can develop a

---

[5] Appendix 16B gives the full derivation.

particularly valuable insight into the cost of equity. Using the SML, we can write the required return on the firm's assets as:

$$R_A = R_f + (R_M - R_f) \times \beta_A$$

The beta coefficient in this case, β_A, is called the firm's asset beta, and it is a measure of the systematic risk of the firm's assets. It is also called the unlevered beta because it is the beta that the stock would have if the firm had no debt.

The cost of equity from the SML is:

$$R_E = R_f + (R_M - R_f) \times \beta_E$$

When this is combined with M&M Proposition II, it is straightforward to show the relationship between the equity beta, β_E, and the asset beta, β_A, is:[6]

$$\beta_E = \beta_A \times (1 + D/E) \qquad [16.5]$$

The term $(1 + D/E)$ here is the same as the equity multiplier described in Chapter 3, except here it is measured in market values instead of book values. In fact, from the Du Pont identity, we saw that the firm's return on assets (ROA) was equal to its return on equity (ROE) multiplied by the equity multiplier. Here we see a very similar result: The risk premium on the firm's equity is equal to the risk premium on the firm's assets multiplied by the equity multiplier.

EXAMPLE 16.3: The Cost of Equity Capital

The Ricardo Corporation has a weighted average cost of capital (unadjusted) of 12 percent. It can borrow at 8 percent. Assuming that Ricardo has a target capital structure of 80 percent equity and 20 percent debt, what is its cost of equity? What is the cost of equity if the target capital structure is 50 percent equity (D/E of 1.0)? Calculate the unadjusted WACC using your answers to verify that it is the same.

According to M&M Proposition II, the cost of equity, R_E, is:

$$R_E = R_A + (R_A - R_D) \times (D/E)$$

In the first case, the debt/equity ratio is .2/.8 = .25, so the cost of the equity is:

$$R_E = 12\% + (12\% - 8\%) \times (.25)$$
$$= 13\%$$

In the second case, check that the debt/equity ratio is 1.0, so the cost of equity is 16 percent.

We can now calculate the unadjusted WACC assuming that the percentage of equity financing is 80 percent and the cost of equity is 13 percent:

$$\text{WACC} = (E/V) \times R_E + (D/V) \times R_D$$
$$= .80 \times 13\% + .20 \times 8\%$$
$$= 12\%$$

In the second case, the percentage of equity financing is 50 percent and the cost of equity is 16 percent. The WACC is:

$$\text{WACC} = (E/V) \times R_E + (D/V) \times R_D$$
$$= .50 \times 16\% + .50 \times 8\%$$
$$= 12\%$$

As we calculated, the WACC is 12 percent in both cases.

We are now in a position to examine directly the impact of financial leverage on the firm's cost of equity. Rewriting things a bit, we see the equity beta has two components:

$$\beta_E = \beta_A + \beta_A \times (D/E)$$

The first component, β_A, is a measure of the riskiness of the firm's assets. Since this is determined primarily by the nature of the firm's operations, we say it measures the **business risk** of the equity. The second component, $\beta_A \times (D/E)$, depends on the firm's financial policy. We therefore say it measures the **financial risk** of the equity.

business risk
The equity risk that comes from the nature of the firm's operating activities.

financial risk
The equity risk that comes from the financial policy (i.e., capital structure) of the firm.

---

[6]To see this, assume the firm's debt has a beta of zero. This means that $R_D = R_f$. If we substitute for R_A and R_D in M&M Proposition II, we see that:

$$R_E = R_A + (R_A - R_D) \times (D/E)$$
$$= [R_f + \beta_A \times (R_M - R_f)] + ([R_f + \beta_A \times (R_M - R_f)] - R_f) \times (D/E)$$
$$= R_f + (R_M - R_f) \times \beta_A \times (1 + D/E)$$

Thus, the equity beta, β_E, equals the asset beta, β_A, multiplied by the equity multiplier, $(1 + D/E)$.

The total systematic risk of the firm's equity thus has two parts: business risk and financial risk. As we have illustrated, the firm's cost of equity rises when it increases its use of financial leverage because the financial risk of the stock increases. Shareholders require compensation in the form of a larger risk premium, thereby increasing the firm's cost of equity capital.

Concept Questions

1. What does M&M Proposition I state?
2. What are the two determinants of a firm's cost of equity?

IN THEIR OWN WORDS...

Merton H. Miller on Capital Structure—M&M 30 Years Later

How difficult it is to summarize briefly the contribution of these papers was brought home to me very clearly after Franco Modigliani was awarded the Nobel Prize in Economics, in part—but, of course, only in part—for the work in finance. The television camera crews from our local stations in Chicago immediately descended upon me. "We understand," they said, "that you worked with Modigliani some years back in developing these M&M theorems, and we wonder if you could explain them briefly to our television viewers." "How briefly?" I asked. "Oh, take 10 seconds," was the reply.

Ten seconds to explain the work of a lifetime! Ten seconds to describe two carefully reasoned articles, each running to more than 30 printed pages and each with 60 or so long footnotes! When they saw the look of dismay on my face, they said: "You don't have to go into details. Just give us the main points in simple, commonsense terms."

The main point of the cost-of-capital article was, in principle at least, simple enough to make. It said that in an economist's ideal world, the total market value of all the securities issued by a firm would be governed by the earning power and risk of its underlying real assets and would be independent of how the mix of securities issued to finance it was divided between debt instruments and equity capital. Some corporate treasurers might well think that they could enhance total value by increasing the proportion of debt instruments because yields on debt instruments, given their lower risk, are, by and large, substantially below those on equity capital. But, under the ideal conditions assumed, the added risk to the shareholders from issuing more debt will raise required yields on the equity by just enough to offset the seeming gain from use of low cost debt.

Such a summary would not only have been too long, but it relied on shorthand terms and concepts that are rich in connotations to economists, but hardly so to the general public. I thought, instead, of an analogy that we ourselves had invoked in the original paper. "Think of the firm," I said, "as a gigantic tub of whole milk. The farmer can sell the whole milk as is. Or he can separate out the cream and sell it at a considerably higher price than the whole milk would bring. (Selling cream is the

analog of a firm selling low-yield and hence high-priced debt securities.) But, of course, what the farmer would have left would be skim milk, with low butter-fat content and that would sell for much less than whole milk. Skim milk corresponds to the levered equity. The M&M proposition says that if there were no costs of separation (and, of course,

no government dairy support programs), the cream plus the skim milk would bring the same price as the whole milk."

The television people conferred among themselves for a while. They informed me that it was still too long, too complicated, and too academic. "Have you anything simpler?" they asked. I thought for another way that the M&M proposition is presented which stresses the role of securities as devices for "partitioning" a firm's payoffs among the group of its capital suppliers. "Think of the firm," I said, "as a gigantic pizza, divided into quarters. If now, you cut each quarter in half into eighths, the M&M proposition says that you will have more pieces, but not more pizza."

Once again widespread conversation. This time, they shut the lights off. They folded up their equipment. They thanked me for my cooperation. They said they would get back to me. But I knew that I had somehow lost my chance to start a new career as a packager of economic wisdom for TV viewers in convenient 10-second sound bites. Some have the talent for it; and some just don't.

The late Merton H. Miller was Robert R. McCormick Distinguished Service Professor at the University of Chicago Graduate School of Business. He was famous for his path-breaking work with Franco Modigliani on corporate capital structure, cost of capital, and dividend policy. He received the Nobel Prize in Economics for his contributions in 1990 shortly after this essay was prepared.

16.4 | M&M Propositions I and II with Corporate Taxes

Debt has two distinguishing features that we have not taken into proper account: First, as we have mentioned in a number of places, interest paid on debt is tax deductible. This is good for the firm, and it may be an added benefit to debt financing. Second, failure to meet debt obligations can result in bankruptcy. This is not good for the firm, and it may be an added cost of debt financing. Since we haven't explicitly considered either of these two features of debt, we may get a different answer about capital structure once we do. Accordingly, we consider taxes in this section and bankruptcy in the next one.

We can start by considering what happens to M&M Propositions I and II when we look at the effect of corporate taxes. To do this, we examine two firms, Firm U (unlevered) and Firm L (levered). These two firms are identical on the left side of the balance sheet, so their assets and operations are the same.

We assume EBIT is expected to be $1,000 every year forever for both firms. The difference between them is that Firm L has issued $1,000 worth of perpetual bonds on which it pays 8 percent interest every year. The interest bill is thus $.08 \times \$1,000 = \$80$ every year forever. Also, we assume the corporate tax rate is 30 percent.

For our two firms, U and L, we can now calculate the following:

	Firm U	Firm L
EBIT	$1,000	$1,000
Interest	0	80
Taxable income	$1,000	$ 920
Taxes (30%)	300	276
Net income	$ 700	$ 644

The Interest Tax Shield

To simplify things, we assume depreciation is equal to zero. We also assume capital spending is zero and there are no additions to NWC. In this case, the cash flow from assets is simply equal to EBIT − Taxes. For firms U and L we thus have:

Cash Flow from Assets	Firm U	Firm L
EBIT	$1,000	$1,000
−Taxes	300	276
Total	$ 700	$ 724

We immediately see that capital structure is now having some effect because the cash flows from U and L are not the same even though the two firms have identical assets.

To see what's going on, we can compute the cash flow to shareholders and bondholders.

Cash Flow	Firm U	Firm L
To shareholders	$ 700	$ 644
To bondholders	0	80
Total	$ 700	$ 724

What we are seeing is that the total cash flow to L is $24 more. This occurs because L's tax bill (which is a cash outflow) is $24 less. The fact that interest is deductible for tax purposes has generated a tax saving equal to the interest payment ($80) multiplied by the corporate tax rate (30 percent): $80 \times .30 = \$24$. We call this tax saving the **interest tax shield**.

interest tax shield
The tax saving attained by a firm from interest expense.

Taxes and M&M Proposition I

Since the debt is perpetual, the same $24 shield would be generated every year forever. The after-tax cash flow to L would thus be the same $700 that U earns plus the $24 tax shield. Since L's cash flow is always $24 greater, Firm L is worth more than Firm U by the value of this perpetuity.

Because the tax shield is generated by paying interest, it has the same risk as the debt, and 8 percent (the cost of debt) is therefore the appropriate discount rate. The value of the tax shield is thus:

$$PV = \$24/.08 = .30 \times 1,000 \times .08/.08 = .30(1,000) = \$300$$

As our example illustrates, the value of the tax shield can be written as:

$$\text{Value of the interest tax shield} = (T_C \times R_D \times D)/R_D \qquad [16.6]$$
$$= T_C \times D$$

We have now come up with another famous result, M&M Proposition I with corporate taxes. We have seen that the value of Firm L, V_L, exceeds the value of Firm U, V_U, by the present value of the interest tax shield, $T_C \times D$. M&M Proposition I with taxes therefore states that:

$$V_L = V_U + T_C \times D \qquad [16.7]$$

The effect of borrowing is illustrated in Figure 16.4. We have plotted the value of the levered firm, V_L, against the amount of debt, D. M&M Proposition I with corporate taxes implies that the relationship is given by a straight line with a slope of T_C and a y-intercept of V_U.

FIGURE 16.4

M&M Proposition I with taxes

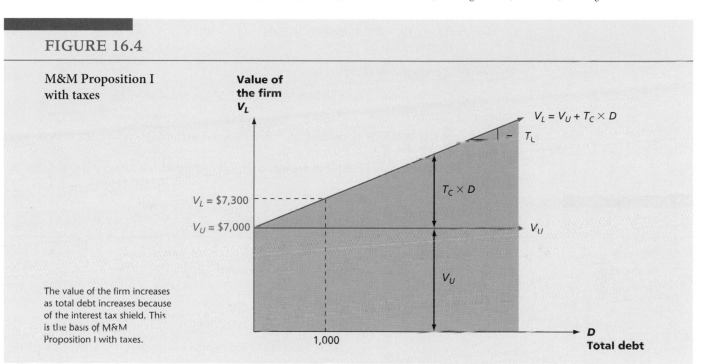

The value of the firm increases as total debt increases because of the interest tax shield. This is the basis of M&M Proposition I with taxes.

In Figure 16.4, we have also drawn a horizontal line representing V_U. As indicated, the distance between the two lines is $T_C \times D$, the present value of the tax shield.

Suppose the cost of capital for Firm U is 10 percent. We call this the **unlevered cost of capital**, (R_U). We can think of R_U as the cost of the capital the firm would have if it had no debt. Firm U's cash flow is $700 every year forever, and since U has no debt, the appropriate discount rate is $R_U = 10\%$. The value of the unlevered firm, V_U, is simply:

$$V_U = \text{EBIT} \times (1 - T_C)/R_U$$
$$= 700/.10$$
$$= \$7,000$$

The value of the levered firm, V_L, is:

$$V_L = V_U + T_C \times D$$
$$= \$7,000 + .30 \times \$1,000$$
$$= \$7,300$$

As Figure 16.4 indicates, the value of the firm goes up by $.30 for every $1 in debt. In other words, the NPV per dollar in debt is $.30. It is difficult to imagine why any corporation would not borrow to the absolute maximum under these circumstances.

The result of our analysis in this section is that, once we include taxes, capital structure definitely matters. However, we immediately reach the illogical conclusion that the optimal capital structure is 100 percent debt.

unlevered cost of capital (R_u)
The cost of capital of a firm that has no debt.

Taxes, the WACC, and Proposition II

The conclusion that the best capital structure is 100 percent debt also can be seen by examining the weighted average cost of capital. From our previous chapter, we know that, once we consider the effect of taxes, the WACC is:

$$\text{WACC} = (E/V) \times R_E + (D/V) \times R_D \times (1 - T_C)$$

To calculate this WACC, we need to know the cost of equity. M&M Proposition II with corporate taxes states that the cost of equity is:

$$R_E = R_U + (R_U - R_D) \times (D/E) \times (1 - T_C) \qquad [16.8]$$

To illustrate, we saw a moment ago that Firm L is worth $7,300 total. Since the debt is worth $1,000, the equity must be worth $7,300 - 1,000 = $6,300. For Firm L, the cost of equity is thus:

$$R_E = .10 + (.10 - .08) \times (\$1,000/\$6,300) \times (1 - .30)$$
$$= 10.22\%$$

The weighted average cost of capital is:

$$\text{WACC} = \$6,300/\$7,300 \times 10.22\% + \$1,000/\$7,300 \times 8\% \times (1 - .30)$$
$$= 9.6\%$$

Without debt, the WACC is 10 percent; with debt, it is 9.6 percent. Therefore, the firm is better off with debt.

This is a comprehensive example that illustrates most of the points we have discussed thus far.

EXAMPLE 16.4: The Cost of Equity and the Value of the Firm

You are given the following information for the Format Company:

$$\text{EBIT} = \$166.67$$
$$T_C = .40$$
$$D = \$500$$
$$R_U = .20$$

The cost of debt capital is 10 percent. What is the value of Format's equity? What is the cost of equity capital for Format? What is the WACC?

This one's easier than it looks. Remember that all the cash flows are perpetuities. The value of the firm if it had no debt, V_U, is:

$$V_U = \text{EBIT} \times (1 - T_C)/R_U$$
$$= 100/.20$$
$$= \$500$$

From M&M Proposition I with taxes, we know that the value of the firm with debt is:

$$V_L = V_U + T_C \times D$$
$$= \$500 + .40 \times \$500$$
$$= \$700$$

Since the firm is worth $700 total and the debt is worth $500, the equity is worth $200.

$$E = V_L - D$$
$$= \$700 - 500$$
$$= \$200$$

Thus, from M&M Proposition II with taxes, the cost of equity is:

$$R_E = R_U + (R_U - R_D) \times (D/E) \times (1 - T_C)$$
$$= .20 + (.20 - .10) \times (\$500/200) \times (1 - .40)$$
$$= 35\%$$

Finally, the WACC is:

$$\text{WACC} = (\$200/700) \times 35\% + (\$500/700) \times 10\%$$
$$\times (1 - .40)$$
$$= 14.29\%$$

Notice that this is substantially lower than the cost of capital for the firm with no debt ($R_U = 20\%$), so debt financing is highly advantageous.

Figure 16.5 summarizes our discussion concerning the relationship between the cost of equity, the after-tax cost of debt, and the weighted average cost of capital. For reference, we have included R_U, the unlevered cost of capital. In Figure 16.5, we have the debt/equity ratio on the horizontal axis. Notice how the WACC declines as the debt/equity ratio grows. This illustrates again that the more debt the firm uses, the lower is its WACC. Table 16.6 summarizes the key results for future reference.

FIGURE 16.5

The cost of equity and the WACC; M&M Propositions I and II with taxes

$R_E = R_U + (R_U - R_D) \times (D/E) \times (1 - T_C)$
by Proposition II with taxes

$\text{WACC} = \left(\frac{E}{V}\right) \times R_E + \left(\frac{D}{V}\right) \times R_D \times (1 - T_C)$

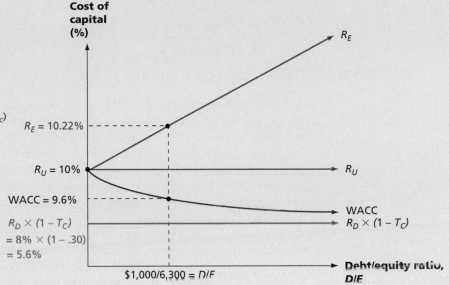

Cost of capital (%)

$R_E = 10.22\%$

$R_U = 10\%$

$\text{WACC} = 9.6\%$

$R_D \times (1 - T_C)$
$= 8\% \times (1 - .30)$
$= 5.6\%$

R_E

R_U

WACC
$R_D \times (1 - T_C)$

Debt/equity ratio, D/E

$\$1,000/6,300 = D/E$

TABLE 16.6   Modigliani and Miller summary

The no tax case

▶ *Proposition I:*
The value of the firm leveraged (V_L) is equal to the value of the firm unleveraged (V_U):
$V_L = V_U$
Implications of Proposition I:
1. A firm's capital structure is irrelevant.
2. A firm's weighted average cost of capital (WACC) is the same no matter what mixture of debt and equity is used to finance the firm.

▶ *Proposition II:*
The cost of equity, R_E, is
$R_E = R_A + (R_A - R_D) \times D/E$,
where R_A is the WACC, R_D is the cost of debt, and D/E is the debt/equity ratio.
Implications of Proposition II:
1. The cost of equity rises as the firm increases its use of debt financing.
2. The risk of the equity depends on two things, the riskiness of the firm's operations (business risk) and the degree of financial leverage (*financial risk*).

With taxes

▶ *Proposition I with taxes:*
The value of the firm leveraged (V_L) is equal to the value of the firm unleveraged (V_U) plus the present value of the interest tax shield:
$V_L = V_U + T_C \times D$
where T_C is the corporate tax rate and D is the amount of debt.
Implications of Proposition I:
1. Debt financing is highly advantageous, and, in the extreme, a firm's optimal capital structure is 100 percent debt.
2. A firm's weighted average cost of capital (WACC) decreases as the firm relies on debt financing.

▶ *Proposition II with taxes:*
The cost of equity, R_E, is
$R_E = R_U + (R_U - R_D) \times (D/E) \times (1 - T_C)$,
where R_U is the unleveraged cost of capital, that is, the cost of capital for the firm if it had no debt. Unlike Proposition I, the general implications of Proposition II are the same whether there are taxes or not.

> **Concept Questions**
>
> 1. What is the relationship between the value of an unlevered firm and the value of a levered firm once we consider the effect of corporate taxes?
> 2. If we only consider the effect of taxes, what is the optimum capital structure?

16.5 | Bankruptcy Costs

One limit to the amount of debt a firm might use comes in the form of *bankruptcy costs*. Bankruptcy costs are a form of the agency costs of debt introduced in Chapter 1. As the debt/equity ratio rises, so too does the probability that the firm could be unable to pay its bondholders what was promised to them. When this happens, ownership of the firm's assets is ultimately transferred from the shareholders to the bondholders. The credit crisis and recession starting at the end of 2007 brought an increase in large bankruptcies including Lehman Brothers, Washington Mutual and General Motors in the U.S. and Nortel and AbitibiBowater in Canada. All of these companies had taken on excessive leverage.

In principle, a firm is bankrupt when the value of its assets equals the value of the debt. When this occurs, the value of equity is zero and the shareholders turn over control of the firm to the bondholders. When this takes place, the bondholders hold assets whose value is exactly equal to what is owed on the debt. In a perfect world, there are no costs associated with this transfer of ownership, and the bondholders don't lose anything.

This idealized view of bankruptcy is not, of course, what happens in the real world. Ironically, it is expensive to go bankrupt. As we discuss, the costs associated with bankruptcy may eventually offset the tax-related gains from leverage.

Direct Bankruptcy Costs

When the value of a firm's assets equals the value of its debt, the firm is economically bankrupt in the sense that the equity has no value. However, the formal means of turning over the assets to the bondholders is a legal process, not an economic one. There are legal and administrative costs to bankruptcy, and it has been remarked that bankruptcies are to lawyers what blood is to sharks.

For example, in April 2009, Montreal based paper and pulp manufacturer, AbitibiBowater Inc., filed for bankruptcy in the U.S and Canada. Over the next one year, the company went through the bankruptcy process, finally emerging in December 2010 as Resolute Forest Products. The direct bankruptcy costs were staggering: Resolute spent over $250 million on lawyers, accountants, consultants, and examiners.

direct bankruptcy costs
The costs that are directly associated with bankruptcy, such as legal and administrative expenses.

Because of the expenses associated with bankruptcy, bondholders won't get all that they are owed. Some fraction of the firm's assets disappear in the legal process of going bankrupt. These are the legal and administrative expenses associated with the bankruptcy proceeding. We call these costs **direct bankruptcy costs**.

These direct bankruptcy costs are a disincentive to debt financing. When a firm goes bankrupt, suddenly, a piece of the firm disappears. This amounts to a bankruptcy tax. So a firm faces a trade-off: Borrowing saves a firm money on its corporate taxes, but the more a firm borrows, the more likely it is that the firm becomes bankrupt and has to pay the bankruptcy tax.

Indirect Bankruptcy Costs

indirect bankruptcy costs
The difficulties of running a business that is experiencing financial distress.

financial distress costs
The direct and indirect costs associated with going bankrupt or experiencing financial distress.

Because it is expensive to go bankrupt, a firm spends resources to avoid doing so. When a firm is having significant problems in meeting its debt obligations, we say it is experiencing financial distress. Some financially distressed firms ultimately file for bankruptcy, but most do not because they are able to recover or otherwise survive.

The costs of avoiding a bankruptcy filing by a financially distressed firm are one example of **indirect bankruptcy costs**. We use the term **financial distress costs** to refer generically to the direct and indirect costs associated with going bankrupt and/or avoiding a bankruptcy filing.

The problems that come up in financial distress are particularly severe, and the financial distress costs are thus larger, when the shareholders and the bondholders are different groups. Until the firm is legally bankrupt, the shareholders control it. They, of course, take actions in their own economic interests. Since the shareholders can be wiped out in a legal bankruptcy, they have a very strong incentive to avoid a bankruptcy filing.

The bondholders, on the other hand, are primarily concerned with protecting the value of the firm's assets and try to take control away from shareholders. They have a strong incentive to seek bankruptcy to protect their interests and keep shareholders from further dissipating the assets of the firm. The net effect of all this fighting is that a long, drawn-out, and potentially quite expensive, legal battle gets started.

Long before the wheels of justice begin to turn, the assets of the firm lose value because management is busy trying to avoid bankruptcy instead of running the business. Further, as they get desperate, managers may adopt go-for-broke strategies that increase the risk of the firm. A good example of this occurred in the failure of two banks in Western Canada in 1985. Because they were allowed to stay in business although they were economically insolvent, the banks had nothing to lose by taking great risks. Solvent banks had to pay increased deposit insurance premiums to shore up the resources of the Canada Deposit Insurance Corporation.

When firms are on the brink of bankruptcy, normal operations are disrupted, and sales are lost. Valuable employees leave, potentially fruitful programs are dropped to preserve cash, and otherwise profitable investments are not taken. For example, in 2009 General Motors and Chrysler after experiencing significant financial difficulty, filed for bankruptcy in the U.S. As a result of the bad news surrounding the companies, there was a loss of confidence in their automobiles. A survey showed that many people would not purchase an automobile from a bankrupt company because the company might not honour the warranty. This concern resulted in lost potential sales which only added to the companies' difficulties. In 2009, the Obama administration announced a program under which the U.S. Treasury would back the warranties of GM and Chrysler.

These are all indirect bankruptcy costs, or costs of financial distress. Whether or not the firm ultimately goes bankrupt, the net effect is a loss of value because the firm chose to use too much debt in its capital structure. This possibility of loss limits the amount of debt a firm chooses to use.

Agency Costs of Equity

Bankruptcy costs are agency costs of debt that increase with the amount of debt a firm uses. Agency costs of equity can result from shirking by owner-managers and work in the opposite direction. The idea is that when a firm run by an owner-entrepreneur issues debt, the entrepreneur has an incentive to work harder because he or she retains the claim to all the payoffs beyond the fixed interest on the debt. If the firm issues equity instead, the owner-entrepreneur's stake is diluted. In this case, the entrepreneur has more incentive to work shorter hours and to consume more perquisites (a big office, a company car, more expense account meals) than if the firm issues debt. Adelphia and Hollinger are two famous examples of publicly traded companies where owner-entrepreneurs allegedly used company funds to finance all sorts of perquisites.

Agency costs of equity are likely to be more significant for smaller firms where the dilution of ownership by issuing equity is significant. Underpricing of new equity issues, especially IPOs, discussed in Chapter 15, is the market's response to the agency costs of equity. In effect, underpricing passes most of these agency costs back to owner-entrepreneurs. The final effect is that firms may use more debt than otherwise.

In the 1980s, it was argued that *leveraged buyouts (LBOs)* significantly reduced the agency costs of equity. In an LBO, a purchaser (usually a team of existing management) buys out the shareholders at a price above the current market. In other words, the company goes private since the stock is placed in the hands of only a few people. Because the managers now own a substantial chunk of the business, they are likely to work harder than when they were simply employees. The track record of LBOs is at best mixed, and we discuss them in detail in Chapter 23.

Concept Questions

1. What are direct bankruptcy costs?
2. What are indirect bankruptcy costs?
3. What are the agency costs of equity?

16.6 | Optimal Capital Structure

Our previous two sections have established the basis for an optimal capital structure. A firm borrows because the interest tax shield is valuable. At relatively low debt levels, the probability of bankruptcy and financial distress is low, and the benefit from debt outweighs the cost. At very high debt levels, the possibility of financial distress is a chronic, ongoing problem for the firm, so the benefit from debt financing may be more than offset by the financial distress costs. Based on our discussion, it would appear that an optimal capital structure exists somewhere between these extremes.

The Static Theory of Capital Structure

static theory of capital structure
Theory that a firm borrows up to the point where the tax benefit from an extra dollar in debt is exactly equal to the cost that comes from the increased probability of financial distress.

The theory of capital structure that we have outlined is called the **static theory of capital structure**. It says that firms borrow up to the point where the tax benefit from an extra dollar in debt is exactly equal to the cost that comes from the increased probability of financial distress. We call this the static theory because it assumes the firm's assets and operations are fixed and it only considers possible changes in the debt/equity ratio.

The static theory is illustrated in Figure 16.6, which plots the value of the firm, V_L, against the amount of debt, D. In Figure 16.6, we have drawn lines corresponding to three different stories. The first is M&M Proposition I with no taxes. This is the horizontal line extending from V_U, and it indicates that the value of the firm is unaffected by its capital structure. The second case, M&M Proposition I with corporate taxes, is given by the upward-sloping straight line. These two cases are exactly the same as the ones we previously illustrated in Figure 16.4.

The third case in Figure 16.6 illustrates our current discussion: The value of the firm rises to a maximum and then declines beyond that point. This is the picture that we get from our static theory. The maximum value of the firm, V_L^*, is reached at D^*, so this is the optimal amount of borrowing. Put another way, the firm's optimal capital structure is composed of D^*/V_L^* in debt and $(1 - D^*/V_L^*)$ in equity.

The final thing to notice in Figure 16.6 is that the difference between the value of the firm in our static theory and the M&M value of the firm with taxes is the loss in value from the possibility of financial distress. Also, the difference between the static theory value of the firm and the M&M value with taxes is the gain from leverage, net of distress costs.[7]

FIGURE 16.6

The static theory of capital structure. The optimal capital structure and the value of the firm.

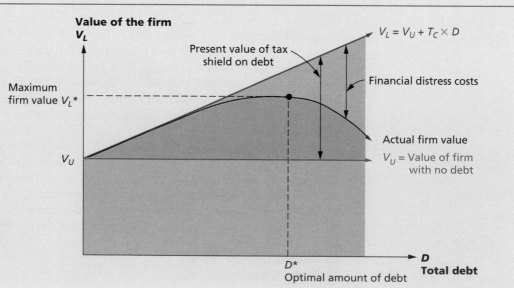

According to the static theory, the gain from the tax shield on debt is offset by financial distress costs. An optimal capital structure exists that just balances the additional gain from leverage against the added financial distress cost.

---

[7] Another way of arriving at Figure 16.6 is to introduce personal taxes on interest and equity disbursements. Interest is taxed more heavily than dividends and capital gains in Canada. This creates a tax disadvantage to leverage that partially offsets the corporate tax advantage to debt. This argument is developed in Appendix 16A.

Optimal Capital Structure and the Cost of Capital

As we discussed earlier, the capital structure that maximizes the value of the firm is also the one that minimizes the cost of capital. Figure 16.7 illustrates the static theory of capital structure in the weighted average cost of capital and the costs of debt and equity. Notice in Figure 16.7 that we have plotted the various capital costs against the debt/equity ratio, D/E.

Figure 16.7 is much the same as Figure 16.5 except that we have added a new line for the WACC. This line, which corresponds to the static theory, declines at first. This occurs because the after-tax cost of debt is cheaper than equity, at least initially, so the overall cost of capital declines.

At some point, the cost of debt begins to rise and the fact that debt is cheaper than equity is more than offset by the financial distress costs. At this point, further increases in debt actually increase the WACC. As illustrated, the minimum WACC occurs at the point D^*/E^*, just as we described earlier.

FIGURE 16.7

The static theory of capital structure. The optimal capital structure and the cost of capital.

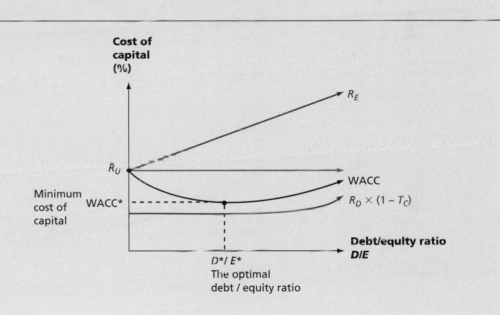

According to the static theory, the WACC falls initially because of the tax advantage to debt. Beyond the point D^*/E^*, it begins to rise because of financial distress costs.

Optimal Capital Structure: A Recap

With the help of Figure 16.8, we can recap (no pun intended) our discussion of capital structure and cost of capital. As we have noted, there are essentially three cases. We will use the simplest of the three cases as a starting point and then build up to the static theory of capital structure. Along the way, we will pay particular attention to the connection between capital structure, firm value, and cost of capital.

Figure 16.8 illustrates the original Modigliani and Miller (M&M) no-tax, no-bankruptcy argument in Case I. This is the most basic case. In the top part, we have plotted the value of the firm, V_L, against total debt, D. When there are no taxes, bankruptcy costs, or other real-world imperfections, we know that the total value of the firm is not affected by its debt policy, so V_L is simply constant. The bottom part of Figure 16.8 tells the same story in terms of the cost of capital. Here, the weighted average cost of capital, WACC, is plotted against the debt to equity ratio, D/E. As with total firm value, the overall cost of capital is not affected by debt policy in this basic case, so the WACC is constant.

FIGURE 16.8

The capital structure question

Case I
With no taxes or bankruptcy costs, the value of the firm and its weighted average cost of capital are not affected by capital structure.

Case II
With corporate taxes and no bankruptcy costs, the value of the firm increases and the weighted average cost of capital decreases as the amount of debt goes up.

Case III
With corporate taxes and bankruptcy costs, the value of the firm V_L^* reaches a maximum at D^*, the optimal amount of borrowing. At the same time, the weighted average cost of capital, WACC*, is minimized at D^*/E^*.

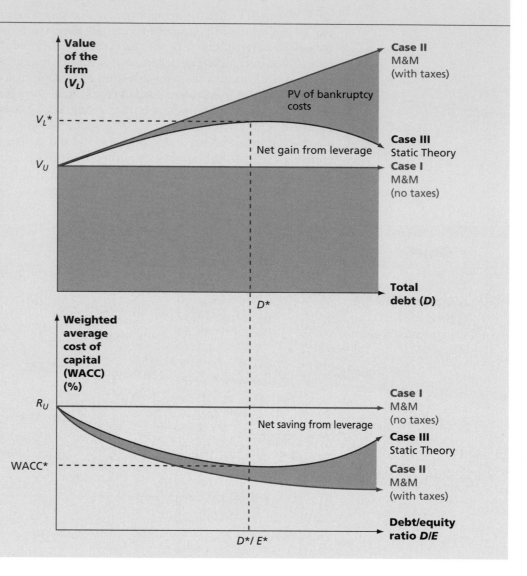

Next, we consider what happens to the original M&M arguments once taxes are introduced. As Case II illustrates, we now see that the firm's value critically depends on its debt policy. The more the firm borrows, the more it is worth. From our earlier discussion, we know this happens because interest payments are tax deductible, and the gain in firm value is just equal to the present value of the interest tax shield.

In the bottom part of Figure 16.8, notice how the WACC declines as the firm uses more and more debt financing. As the firm increases its financial leverage, the cost of equity does increase, but this increase is more than offset by the tax break associated with debt financing. As a result, the firm's overall cost of capital declines.

To finish our story, we include the impact of bankruptcy of financial distress costs to get Case III. As shown in the top part of Figure 16.8, the value of the firm will not be as large as we previously indicated. The reason is that the firm's value is reduced by the present value of the potential future bankruptcy costs. These costs grow as the firm borrows more and more, and they eventually overwhelm the tax advantage of debt financing. The optimal capital structure occurs at D^*, the point at which the tax saving from an additional dollar in debt financing is exactly balanced by the increased bankruptcy costs associated with the additional borrowing. This is the essence of the static theory of capital structure.

The bottom part of Figure 16.8 presents the optimal capital structure in terms of the cost of capital. Corresponding to D^*, the optimal debt level, is the optimal debt to equity ratio, D^*/E^*. At this level of debt financing, the lowest possible weighted average cost of capital, WACC*, occurs.

Capital Structure: Some Managerial Recommendations

The static model that we described is not capable of identifying a precise optimal capital structure, but it does point out two of the more relevant factors: taxes and financial distress. We can draw some limited conclusions concerning these.

TAXES   First, the tax benefit from leverage is obviously important only to firms that are in a tax-paying position. Firms with substantial accumulated losses get little value from the tax shield. Furthermore, firms that have substantial tax shields from other sources, such as depreciation, get less benefit from leverage.

Also, not all firms have the same tax rate. The higher the tax rate, the greater the incentive to borrow.

FINANCIAL DISTRESS   Firms with a greater risk of experiencing financial distress borrow less than firms with a lower risk of financial distress. For example, all other things being equal, the greater the volatility in EBIT, the less a firm should borrow.

In addition, financial distress is more costly for some firms than others. The costs of financial distress depend primarily on the firm's assets. In particular, financial distress costs are determined by how easily ownership of those assets can be transferred.

For example, a firm with mostly tangible assets that can be sold without great loss in value has an incentive to borrow more. If a firm has a large investment in land, buildings, and other tangible assets, it has lower financial costs than a firm with a large investment in research and development. Research and development typically has less resale value than land; thus, most of its value disappears in financial distress.

Timminco, a Canadian producer of silicon used for solar panels, provides an excellent example of the effects financial distress can have on a company. The firm faced considerable unexpected volatility in its earnings with reduced cash flow from silicon metal operations, slow growth in the solar market industry, and the restricted availability of funding. As a result, it appears to have relied too heavily on borrowing and was forced to enter into bankruptcy protection in January 2012. In April 2012, the company held an auction to sell off its business and assets.

Concept Questions

1. Describe the trade-off that defines the static theory of capital structure.
2. What are the important factors in making capital structure decisions?

16.7 | The Pie Again

Although it is comforting to know that the firm might have an optimal capital structure when we take account of such real-world matters as taxes and financial distress costs, it is disquieting to see the elegant, original M&M intuition (that is, the no-tax version) fall apart in the face of them.

Critics of the M&M theory often say it fails to hold as soon as we add in real-world issues and that the M&M theory is really just that, a theory that doesn't have much to say about the real world that we live in. In fact, they would argue that it is the M&M theory that is irrelevant, not capital structure. As we discuss next, however, taking that view blinds critics to the real value of the M&M theory.

The Extended Pie Model

To illustrate the value of the original M&M intuition, we briefly consider an expanded version of the pie model that we introduced earlier. In the extended pie model, taxes just represent another claim on the cash flows of the firm. Since taxes are reduced as leverage is increased, the value of the government's claim (G) on the firm's cash flows decreases with leverage.

Bankruptcy costs are also a claim on the cash flows. They come into play as the firm comes close to bankruptcy and has to alter its behaviour to attempt to stave off the event itself, and they become large when bankruptcy actually occurs. Thus, the value of the cash flows to this claim (B) rises with the debt/equity ratio.

The extended pie theory simply holds that all of these claims can be paid from only one source, the cash flows (CF) of the firm. Algebraically, we must have:

CF = Payments to shareholders + Payments to bondholders
     + Payments to the government
     + Payments to bankruptcy courts and lawyers
     + Payments to any and all other claimants to the cash flow of the firm

The extended pie model is illustrated in Figure 16.9. Notice that we have added a few slices for the other groups. Notice also the relative size of the slices as the firm's use of debt financing is increased.

With this list, we have not even begun to exhaust the potential claims to the firm's cash flows. To give an unusual example, everyone reading this book has an economic claim to the cash flows of General Motors Corporation (GM). After all, if you are injured in an accident involving a GM vehicle, you might sue GM, and, win or lose, GM expends some of its cash flow in dealing with the matter. For GM, or any other company, there should thus be a slice of the pie representing the potential lawsuits.

gm.com

This is the essence of the M&M intuition and theory: The value of the firm depends on the total cash flow of the firm. The firm's capital structure just cuts that cash flow up into slices without altering the total. What we recognize now is that the shareholders and the bondholders may not be the only ones who can claim a slice.

FIGURE 16.9

The extended pie model

In the extended pie model, the value of all the claims against the firm's cash flows is not affected by capital structure, but the relative value of claims changes as the amount of debt financing is increased.

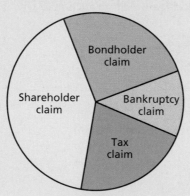

Lower financial leverage

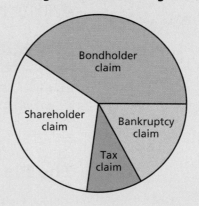

Higher financial leverage

Marketed Claims versus Non-Marketed Claims

With our extended pie model, there is an important distinction between claims such as those of shareholders and bondholders, on the one hand, and those of the government and potential litigants in lawsuits on the other. The first set of claims are *marketed claims*, and the second set are *non-marketed claims*. A key difference is that the marketed claims can be bought and sold in financial markets and the non-marketed claims cannot be.

When we speak of the value of the firm, we are generally referring just to the value of the marketed claims, V_M, and not the value of the non-marketed claims, V_N. If we write V_T for the total value of all the claims against a corporation's cash flows, then:

$$V_T = E + D + G + B + \ldots$$
$$= V_M + V_N$$

The essence of our extended pie model is that this total value, V_T, of all the claims to the firm's cash flows is unaltered by capital structure. However, the value of the marketed claims, V_M, may be affected by changes in the capital structure.

By the pie theory, any increase in V_M must imply an identical decrease in V_N. The optimal capital structure is thus the one that maximizes the value of the marketed claims, or, equivalently, minimizes the value of non-marketed claims such as taxes and bankruptcy costs.

Concept Questions

1. What are some of the claims to a firm's cash flows?
2. What is the difference between a marketed claim and a non-marketed claim?
3. What does the extended pie model say about the value of all the claims to a firm's cash flows?

16.8 | The Pecking-Order Theory

The static theory we have developed in this chapter has dominated thinking about capital structure for a long time, but it has some shortcomings. Perhaps the most obvious is that many large, financially sophisticated, and highly profitable firms use little debt. This is the opposite of what we would expect. Under the static theory, these are the firms that should use the *most* debt because there is little risk of bankruptcy and the value of the tax shield is substantial. Why do they use so little debt? The pecking-order theory, which we consider next, may be part of the answer.

Internal Financing and the Pecking Order

The pecking-order theory is an alternative to the static theory. A key element in the pecking-order theory is that firms prefer to use internal financing whenever possible. A simple reason is that selling securities to raise cash can be expensive, so it makes sense to avoid doing so if possible. If a firm is very profitable, it might never need external financing; so it would end up with little or no debt. For example, in December 2011, Google's balance sheet showed assets of $72.6 billion, of which almost $44.6 billion was classified as either cash or marketable securities. In fact, Google held so much of its assets in the form of securities that, at one point, it was in danger of being regulated as a mutual fund!

There is a more subtle reason that companies may prefer internal financing. Suppose you are the manager of a firm, and you need to raise external capital to fund a new venture. As an insider, you are privy to a lot of information that isn't known to the public. Based on your knowledge, the firm's future prospects are considerably brighter than outside investors realize. As a result, you think your stock is currently undervalued. Should you issue debt or equity to finance the new venture?

If you think about it, you definitely don't want to issue equity in this case. The reason is that your stock is undervalued, and you don't want to sell it too cheaply. So, you issue debt instead.

Would you ever want to issue equity? Suppose you thought your firm's stock was overvalued. It makes sense to raise money at inflated prices, but a problem crops up. If you try to sell equity, investors will realize that the shares are probably overvalued, and your stock price will take a hit. In other words, if you try to raise money by selling equity, you run the risk of signaling to investors that the price is too high. In fact, in the real world, companies rarely sell new equity, and the market reacts negatively to such sales when they occur.

So, we have a pecking order. Companies will use internal financing first. Then, they will issue debt if necessary. Equity will be sold pretty much as a last resort.

Implications of the Pecking Order

The pecking-order theory has several significant implications, a couple of which are at odds with our static trade-off theory:

1. *No target capital structure:* Under the pecking-order theory, there is no target or optimal debt–equity ratio. Instead, a firm's capital structure is determined by its need for external financing, which dictates the amount of debt the firm will have.

2. *Profitable firms use less debt:* Because profitable firms have greater internal cash flow, they will need less external financing and will therefore have less debt. As we mentioned earlier, this is a pattern that we seem to observe, at least for some companies.

3. *Companies will want financial slack:* To avoid selling new equity, companies will want to stockpile internally generated cash. Such a cash reserve is known as *financial slack*. It gives management the ability to finance projects as they appear and to move quickly if necessary.

Which theory, static trade-off or pecking order, is correct? Financial researchers have not reached a definitive conclusion on this issue, but we can make a few observations. The trade-off theory speaks more to long-run financial goals or strategies. The issues of tax shields and financial distress costs are plainly important in that context. The pecking-order theory is more concerned with the shorter-run, tactical issue of raising external funds to finance investments. So both theories are useful ways of understanding corporate use of debt. For example, it is probably the case that firms have long-run, target capital structures, but it is also probably true that they will deviate from those long-run targets as needed to avoid issuing new equity.

Concept Questions

1. Under the pecking-order theory, what is the order in which firms will obtain financing?
2. Why might firms prefer not to issue new equity?
3. What are some differences in implications of the static and pecking-order theories?

16.9 | Observed Capital Structures

No two firms have identical capital structures. Nonetheless, we see some regular elements when we start looking at actual capital structures. We discuss a few of these next.

A pattern is apparent when we compare capital structures across industries. Table 16.7 shows Canadian debt/equity ratios for selected industries measured at book values. You can see rather large differences in the use of debt among industries. Real estate developers and operators, for example, carry about three times as much debt as manufacturers. This is consistent with our discussion of the costs of financial distress. Real estate developers have large tangible assets while manufacturers carry significant intangible assets in the form of research and development.

Further, because different industries have different operating characteristics, for example, EBIT volatility and asset types, there does appear to be some connection between these characteristics and capital structure. Our story involving tax savings and financial distress costs is undoubtedly part of the reason, but, to date, there is no fully satisfactory theory that explains these regularities.

In practice, firms (and lenders) also look at the industry's debt/equity ratio as a guide. If the industry is sound, the industry average provides a useful benchmark. Of course, if the entire industry is in distress, the average leverage is likely too high. For example, in 2011, the average debt/equity ratio of the Arts, Entertainment and Recreation industry (2.868) was probably too high.

The leverage ratios in Table 16.7 are considerably higher than they were in the 1960s. Most of the increase in Canada came in the 1970s and early 1980s—periods of low interest rates and economic growth particularly in Western Canada. Significant corporate tax rates encouraged corporations to use debt financing. Table 16.7 shows that the construction industry had one of the highest uses of leverage in 2011 and this industry accounts for a major portion of the leverage increase for Canadian companies over the last 40 years. In the U.S., the increase in leverage was similar but occurred in the leveraged buyout period of the 1980s.[8]

---

[8] Our discussion of trends in leverage draws on M. Zyblock, "Corporate Financial Leverage: A Canada–U.S. Comparison, 1961–1996," *Statistics Canada*, Paper no. 111, December 1997 and P.M. Shum, "Taxes and Corporate Debt Policy in Canada: An Empirical Investigation," *Canadian Journal of Economics* 29, August 1996.

TABLE 16.7

Book value long-term debt/equity ratios for selected industries in Canada, 2011

Industry	Ratio
All industries	0.868
Non-financial	0.887
Agriculture, forestry, fishing, and hunting	1.097
Oil and gas extraction and support activities	0.593
Mining and quarrying (except oil and gas)	0.607
Utilities	1.228
Construction	1.444
Manufacturing	0.682
Wholesale trade	0.827
Retail trade	0.753
Transportation and warehousing	1.617
Information and cultural industries	1.302
Real estate and rental and leasing	1.504
Professional, scientific, and technical services	0.631
Administrative and support, waste management, and remediation services	0.791
Educational, healthcare, and social assistance services	0.715
Arts, entertainment and recreation	2.868
Accommodation and food services	2.180
Repair, maintenance, and personal services	0.871
Finance and insurance	0.815

Source: Statistics Canada "Quarterly financial statistics for enterprises," 61-008-XWE, Fourth Quarter, 2011, March 2012.

Concept Questions

1. Do Canadian corporations rely heavily on debt financing? What about U.S. corporations?
2. What regularities do we observe in capital structures?

16.10 | Long-Term Financing Under Financial Distress and Bankruptcy

One of the consequences of using debt is the possibility of financial distress, which can be defined in several ways:

1. *Business failure.* Although this term usually refers to a situation where a business has terminated with a loss to creditors, even an all-equity firm can fail.[9]
2. *Legal bankruptcy.* Firms bring petitions to a federal court for bankruptcy. **Bankruptcy** is a legal proceeding for liquidating or reorganizing a business.
3. *Technical insolvency.* Technical insolvency occurs when a firm defaults on a current legal obligation; for example, it does not pay a bill. Technical insolvency is a short-term condition that may be reversed to avoid bankruptcy.
4. *Accounting insolvency.* Firms with negative net worth are insolvent on the books. This happens when the total book liabilities exceed the book value of the total assets.

For future reference, we define bankruptcy as the transfer of some or all of the firm's assets to creditors. We now very briefly discuss what happens in financial distress and some of the relevant issues associated with bankruptcy.[10]

bankruptcy
A legal proceeding for liquidating or reorganizing a business. Also, the transfer of some or all of a firm's assets to its creditors.

---

[9] Dun & Bradstreet Canada Ltd. compiles failure statistics in "The Canadian Business Failure Record."

[10] Our discussion of bankruptcy procedures is based on the 2009 *Bankruptcy and Insolvency Act.*

Liquidation and Reorganization

liquidation
Termination of the firm as a going concern.

reorganization
Financial restructuring of a failing firm to attempt to continue operations as a going concern.

Firms that cannot or choose not to make contractually required payments to creditors have two basic options: liquidation or reorganization. Both of these options are covered under the *Bankruptcy and Insolvency Act (1992)*. **Liquidation** means termination of the firm as a going concern, and it involves selling the assets of the firm. The proceeds, net of selling costs, are distributed to creditors in order of established priority. **Reorganization** is the option of keeping the firm a going concern; it often involves issuing new securities to replace old securities. Liquidation or reorganization is the result of a bankruptcy proceeding, which occurs depends on whether the firm is worth more dead or alive.

Before the early 1990s, most legal bankruptcies in Canada ended with liquidation. More recently, more frequent cases of financial distress along with new bankruptcy laws are encouraging restructuring and reorganizations. For example, in 2003, Air Canada's cash flow was not enough to cover its operating expenses, including interest and principal payments on its $13 billion in debt. The company had experienced several unusual business circumstances including the terrorist attacks in 2001 and the SARS health crisis in Asia and Canada, and was said to be using up to $5 million a day in cash. The company decided to seek court protection to allow it to restructure its assets and avoid formal bankruptcy liquidation.

BANKRUPTCY LIQUIDATION   Liquidation occurs when the court directs sale of all assets of the firm. The following sequence of events is typical:

1. A petition is filed in a federal court. Corporations may file a voluntary petition, or involuntary petitions may be filed against the corporation by creditors.
2. A trustee-in-bankruptcy is elected by the creditors to take over the assets of the debtor corporation. The trustee attempts to liquidate the assets.
3. When the assets are liquidated, after the payment of the bankruptcy administration costs, the proceeds are distributed among the creditors.
4. If any assets remain, after expenses and payments to creditors, they are distributed to the shareholders.

The distribution of the proceeds of the liquidation occurs according to the following priority. The higher a claim is on the list, the more likely it is to be paid. In many of these categories, we omit various limitations and qualifications for the sake of brevity.

1. Administrative expenses associated with the bankruptcy.
2. Other expenses arising after the filing of an involuntary bankruptcy petition but before the appointment of a trustee.
3. Wages, salaries, and commissions.
4. Contributions to employee benefit plans.
5. Consumer claims.
6. Government tax claims.
7. Unsecured creditors.
8. Preferred shareholders.
9. Common shareholders.

Two qualifications to this list are in order: The first concerns secured creditors. Such creditors are entitled to the proceeds from the sale of the security and are outside this ordering. However, if the secured property is liquidated and provides cash insufficient to cover the amount owed, the secured creditors join with unsecured creditors in dividing the remaining liquidated value. In contrast, if the secured property is liquidated for proceeds greater than the secured claim, the net proceeds are used to pay unsecured creditors and others.

The second qualification is that, in reality, courts have a great deal of freedom in deciding what actually happens and who actually gets what in the event of bankruptcy; as a result, the priority just set out is not always followed.

The 1988 restructuring of Dome Petroleum is an example. Declining oil prices in 1986 found Dome already in difficulties after a series of earlier debt rescheduling. Dome's board believed that if the company went into bankruptcy, secured creditors could force disposal of assets at fire sale prices producing losses for unsecured creditors and shareholders. One estimate obtained at the time projected that unsecured creditors would receive at best 15 cents per dollar of debt under liquidation. As a result, the board sought and received court and regulatory approval for sale of the company as a going concern to Amoco Canada. Unsecured creditors eventually received 45 cents on the dollar.

BANKRUPTCY REORGANIZATION   The general objective of corporate reorganization is to plan to restructure the corporation with some provision for repayment of creditors. A typical sequence of events follows:

1. A voluntary petition can be filed by the corporation, or an involuntary petition can be filed by creditors.

2. A federal judge either approves or denies the petition. If the petition is approved, a time for filing proofs of claims is set. A stay of proceedings of 30 days is effected against all creditors.

3. In most cases, the corporation (the "debtor in possession") continues to run the business.

4. The corporation is required to submit a reorganization plan.

5. Creditors and shareholders are divided into classes. A class of creditors accepts the plan if a majority of the class (in dollars or in number) agrees to the plan. The secured creditors must vote before the unsecured creditors.

6. After acceptance by creditors, the plan is confirmed by the court.

7. Payments in cash, property, and securities are made to creditors and shareholders. The plan may provide for the issuance of new securities.

The corporation may wish to allow the old shareholders to retain some participation in the firm. Needless to say, this may involve some protest by the holders of unsecured debt.

So-called prepackaged bankruptcies are a relatively new phenomenon. What happens is that the corporation secures the necessary approval of a bankruptcy plan by a majority of its credi tors first, and then it files for bankruptcy. As a result, the company enters bankruptcy and reemerges almost immediately. In some cases, the bankruptcy procedure is needed to invoke the "cram down" power of the bankruptcy court. Under certain circumstances, a class of creditors can be forced to accept a bankruptcy plan even if they vote not to approve it, hence the remarkably descriptive phrase *cram down*.

Returning to our Air Canada example, the company underwent a major restructuring effort in June 2003. Air Canada sought court protection to reorganize, and reached agreements with all of its employee unions to workplace rule changes, job cuts, and wage reductions that would reduce operating expenses by approximately $1.1 billion per year. Creditors approved Air Canada's restructuring plan in August 2004. The plan called for creditors to receive a very small percentage of every dollar they were owed, but their approval of the plan opened up the option of picking up a 45.8 per cent interest in the parent company of Air Canada.

Air Canada has enjoyed mixed success since. The company recorded a $118 million net profit in the first quarter of 2006, compared to a $77 million net loss in the first quarter of 2005. The stock price was up to $33 a share in May 2006, compared to $1 a share in June 2003. However, at the time of writing in May 2012, the stock price was back down to $0.85 as the company faced lower demand and higher pension obligations resulting from the global recession.

Agreements to Avoid Bankruptcy

A firm can default on an obligation and still avoid bankruptcy. Because the legal process of bankruptcy can be lengthy and expensive, it is often in everyone's best interest to devise a "workout" that avoids a bankruptcy filing. Much of the time creditors can work with the management of a company that has defaulted on a loan contract. Voluntary arrangements to restructure the company's debt can be and often are made. This may involve *extension*, which postpones the date of payment, or *composition*, which involves a reduced payment.

Concept Questions

1. What is a bankruptcy?
2. What is the difference between liquidation and reorganization?

16.11 | Summary and Conclusions

The ideal mixture of debt and equity for a firm—its optimal capital structure—is the one that maximizes the value of the firm and minimizes the overall cost of capital. If we ignore taxes, financial distress costs, and any other imperfections, we find that there is no ideal mixture. Under these circumstances, the firm's capital structure is simply irrelevant, as we see in M&M Proposition I and II.

If we consider the effect of corporate taxes, we find that capital structure matters a great deal. This conclusion is based on the fact that interest is tax deductible and thus generates a valuable tax shield. Unfortunately, we also find that the optimal capital structure is 100 percent debt, which is not something we observe for healthy firms.

We next introduced costs associated with bankruptcy, or, more generally, financial distress. These costs reduce the attractiveness of debt financing. We concluded that an optimal capital structure exists when the net tax saving from an additional dollar in interest just equals the increase in expected financial distress costs. This is the essence of the static theory of capital structure.

When we examine actual capital structures, we find two regularities: First, firms in Canada typically do not use great amounts of debt, but they pay substantial taxes. This suggests there is a limit to the use of debt financing to generate tax shields. Second, firms in similar industries tend to have similar capital structures, suggesting that the nature of their assets and operations is an important determinant of capital structure.

Key Terms

bankruptcy (page 479)
business risk (page 464)
direct bankruptcy costs (page 470)
financial distress costs (page 470)
financial risk (page 464)
homemade leverage (page 460)
indirect bankruptcy costs (page 470)

interest tax shield (page 466)
liquidation (page 480)
M&M Proposition I (page 462)
M&M Proposition II (page 463)
reorganization (page 480)
static theory of capital structure (page 472)
unlevered cost of capital (R_U) (page 467)

Chapter Review Problems and Self-Test

16.1   EBIT and EPS Suppose the GNR Corporation has decided in favour of a capital restructuring that involves increasing its existing $5 million in debt to $25 million. The interest rate on the debt is 12 percent and is not expected to change. The firm currently has 1 million shares outstanding, and the price per share is $40. If the restructuring is expected to increase the ROE, what is the minimum level for EBIT that GNR's management must be expecting? Ignore taxes in your answer.

16.2   M&M Proposition II (no taxes) The Pro Bono Corporation has a WACC of 20 percent. Its cost of debt is 12 percent. If Pro Bono's debt/equity ratio is 2, what is its cost of equity capital?

If Pro Bono's equity beta is 1.5, what is its asset beta? Ignore taxes in your answer.

16.3   M&M Proposition I (with corporate taxes) The Deathstar Telecom Company (motto: "Reach out and clutch someone") expects an EBIT of $4,000 every year forever. Deathstar can borrow at 10 percent.

Suppose that Deathstar currently has no debt and its cost of equity is 14 percent. If the corporate tax rate is 30 percent, what is the value of the firm? What will the value be if Deathstar borrows $6,000 and uses the proceeds to buy up stock?

Answers to Self-Test Problems

16.1   To answer, we can calculate the break-even EBIT. At any EBIT more than this, the increased financial leverage increases EPS. Under the old capital structure, the interest bill is $5 million × .12 = $600,000. There are 1 million shares of stock, so, ignoring taxes, EPS is (EBIT − $600,000)/1 million.

Under the new capital structure, the interest expense is $25 million × .12 = $3 million. Furthermore, the debt rises by $20 million. This amount is sufficient to repurchase $20 million/$40 = 500,000 shares of stock, leaving 500,000 outstanding. EPS is thus (EBIT − $3 million)/500,000.

Now that we know how to calculate EPS under both scenarios, we set them equal to each other and solve for the break-even EBIT;

$$(EBIT − \$600,000)/1 \text{ million} = (EBIT − \$3 \text{ million})/500,000$$
$$(EBIT − \$600,000) = 2 × (EBIT − \$3 \text{ million})$$
$$EBIT = \$5,400,000$$

Check that, in either case, EPS is $4.80 when EBIT is $5.4 million.

16.2 According to M&M Proposition II (no taxes), the cost of equity is:

$$R_E = R_A + (R_A - R_D) \times (D/E)$$
$$= 20\% + (20\% - 12\%) \times 2$$
$$= 36\%$$

Also, we know that the equity beta is equal to the asset beta multiplied by the equity multiplier:

$$\beta_E = \beta_A \times (1 + D/E)$$

In this case, D/E is 2 and β_E is 1.5, so the asset beta is 1.5/3 = .50.

16.3 With no debt, Deathstar's WACC is 14 percent. This is also the unlevered cost of capital. The after-tax cash flow is $4,000 \times (1 - .30) = $2,800, so the value is just $V_U = $2,800/.14 = $20,000.

After the debt issue, Deathstar is worth the original $20,000 plus the present value of the tax shield. According to M&M Proposition I with taxes, the present value of the tax shield is $T_C \times D$, or .30 \times $6,000 = $1,800, so the firm is worth $20,000 + 1,800 = $21,800.

Concepts Review and Critical Thinking Questions

1. **(LO1)** Explain what is meant by business and financial risk. Suppose Firm A has greater business risk than Firm B. Is it true that Firm A also has a higher cost of equity capital? Explain.

2. **(LO1)** How would you answer in the following debate?

   Q: Isn't it true that the riskiness of a firm's equity will rise if the firm increases its use of debt financing?

   A: Yes, that's the essence of M&M Proposition II.

   Q: And isn't it true that, as a firm increases its use of borrowing, the likelihood of default increases, thereby increasing the risk of the firm's debt?

   A: Yes.

   Q: In other words, increased borrowing increases the risk of the equity and the debt?

   A: That's right.

   Q: Well, given that the firm uses only debt and equity financing, and given that the risks of both are increased by increased borrowing, does it not follow that increasing debt increases the overall risk of the firm and therefore decreases the value of the firm?

   A: ??

3. **(LO1)** Is there an easily identifiable debt-equity ratio that will maximize the value of a firm? Why or why not?

4. **(LO1)** Refer to the observed capital structures given in Table 16.7 of the text. What do you notice about the types of industries with respect to their average debt-equity ratios? Are certain types of industries more likely to be highly leveraged than others? What are some possible reasons for this observed segmentation? Do the operating results and tax history of the firms play a role? How about their future earnings prospects? Explain.

5. **(LO1)** Why is the use of debt financing referred to as financial "leverage"?

6. **(LO1)** What is homemade leverage?

7. **(LO3)** As mentioned in the text, some firms have filed for bankruptcy because of actual or likely litigation-related losses. Is this a proper use of the bankruptcy process?

8. **(LO3)** Firms sometimes use the threat of a bankruptcy filing to force creditors to renegotiate terms. Critics argue that in such cases, the firm is using bankruptcy laws "as a sword rather than a shield." Is this an ethical tactic?

9. **(LO1, 2)** In the context of the extended pie model, what is the basic goal of financial management with regard to capital structure?

10. **(LO3)** What basic options does a firm have if it cannot (or chooses not to) make a contractually required payment such as interest? Describe them.

11. **(LO3)** Absolute Priority Rule In the event of corporate liquidation proceedings, rank the following claimants of the firm from highest to lowest in order of their priority for being paid:

    a. Preferred shareholders.

    b. Canada Revenue Agency.

    c. Unsecured debt holders.

    d. The company pension plan.

    e. Common shareholders.

    f. Employee wages.

    g. The law firm representing the company in the bankruptcy proceedings.

Questions and Problems

Basic
(Questions 1–15)

1. **EBIT and Leverage (LO1)** Charny Inc. has no debt outstanding and a total market value of $180,000. Earnings before interest and taxes, EBIT, are projected to be $23,000 if economic conditions are normal. If there is strong expansion in the economy, then EBIT will be 20 percent higher. If there is a recession, then EBIT will be 30 percent lower. Charny is considering a $75,000 debt issue with a 7 percent interest rate. The proceeds will be used to repurchase shares of stock. There are currently 6,000 shares outstanding. Ignore taxes for this problem.

   a. Calculate earnings per share (EPS) under each of the three economic scenarios before any debt is issued. Also calculate the percentage changes in EPS when the economy expands or enters a recession.

   b. Repeat part (a) assuming that the company goes through with recapitalization. What do you observe?

2. **EBIT, Taxes, and Leverage (LO2)** Repeat parts (a) and (b) in Problem 1 assuming Charny has a tax rate of 35 percent.

3. **ROE and Leverage (LO1, 2)** Suppose the company in Problem 1 has a market-to-book ratio of 1.0.

   a. Calculate return on equity (ROE) under each of the three economic scenarios before any debt is issued. Also calculate the percentage changes in ROE for economic expansion and recession, assuming no taxes.

    b.   Repeat part (a) assuming the firm goes through with the proposed recapitalization.

    c.   Repeat parts (a) and (b) of this problem assuming the firm has a tax rate of 35 percent.

4.   **Break-Even EBIT (LO1)** Vanier Corporation is comparing two different capital structures: an all-equity plan (Plan I) and a levered plan (Plan II). Under Plan I, the company would have 210,000 shares of stock outstanding. Under Plan II, there would be 150,000 shares of stock outstanding and $2.28 million in debt outstanding. The interest rate on the debt is 8 percent, and there are no taxes.

    a.   If EBIT is $500,000, which plan will result in the higher EPS?

    b.   If EBIT is $750,000, which plan will result in the higher EPS?

    c.   What is the break-even EBIT?

5.   **M&M and Stock Value (LO1)** In Problem 4, use M&M Proposition I to find the price per share of equity under each of the two proposed plans. What is the value of the firm?

6.   **Break-Even EBIT and Leverage (LO1, 2)** Des Chatels Corp. is comparing two different capital structures. Plan I would result in 10,000 shares of stock and $90,000 in debt. Plan II would result in 7,600 shares of stock and $198,000 in debt. The interest rate on the debt is 10 percent.

    a.   Ignoring taxes, compare both of these plans to an all-equity plan assuming that EBIT will be $48,000. The all-equity plan would result in 12,000 shares of stock outstanding. Which of the three plans has the highest EPS? The lowest?

    b.   In part (a), what are the break-even levels of EBIT for each plan as compared to that for an all-equity plan? Is one higher than the other? Why?

    c.   Ignoring taxes, when will EPS be identical for Plans I and II?

    d.   Repeat parts (a), (b), and (c) assuming that the corporate tax rate is 40 percent. Are the break-even levels of EBIT different from before? Why or why not?

7.   **Leverage and Stock Value (LO1)** Ignoring taxes in Problem 6, what is the price per share of equity under Plan I? Plan II? What principle is illustrated by your answers?

8.   **Homemade Leverage (LO1)** Beauport Inc. a prominent consumer products firm, is debating whether to convert its all-equity capital structure to one that is 30 percent debt. Currently, there are 7,000 shares outstanding, and the price per share is $55. EBIT is expected to remain at $27,000 per year forever. The interest rate on new debt is 8 percent, and there are no taxes.

    a.   Denise, a shareholder of the firm, owns 100 shares of stock. What is her cash flow under the current capital structure, assuming the firm has a dividend payout rate of 100 percent?

    b.   What will Denise's cash flow be under the proposed capital structure of the firm? Assume she keeps all 100 of her shares.

    c.   Suppose the company does convert, but Denise prefers the current all-equity capital structure. Show how she could unlever her shares of stock to recreate the original capital structure.

    d.   Using your answer to part (c), explain why the company's choice of capital structure is irrelevant.

9.   **Homemade Leverage and WACC (LO1)** St. Louis Co. and St. Romuald Co. are identical firms in all respects except for their capital structure. St. Louis is all equity financed with $650,000 in stock. St. Romuald uses both stock and perpetual debt; its stock is worth $325,000 and the interest rate on its debt is 8 percent. Both firms expect EBIT to be $68,000. Ignore taxes.

    a.   Clifford owns $48,750 worth of St. Romuald's stock. What rate of return is he expecting?

    b.   Show how Clifford could generate exactly the same cash flows and rate of return by investing in St. Louis and using homemade leverage.

    c.   What is the cost of equity for St. Louis? What is it for St. Romuald?

    d.   What is the WACC for St. Louis? For St. Romuald? What principle have you illustrated?

10.   **M&M (LO1)** Limoilou Corp. uses no debt. The weighted average cost of capital is 8 percent. If the current market value of the equity is $18 million and there are no taxes, what is EBIT?

11.   **M&M and Taxes (LO2)** In the previous question, suppose the corporate tax rate is 35 percent. What is EBIT in this case? What is the WACC? Explain.

12.   **Calculating WACC (LO1)** Portneuf Industries has a debt–equity ratio of 1.5. Its WACC is 9 percent, and its cost of debt is 5.5 percent. The corporate tax rate is 35 percent.

    a.   What is the company's cost of equity capital?

    b.   What is the company's unlevered cost of equity capital?

    c.   What would the cost of equity be if the debt–equity ratio were 2? What if it were 1.0? What if it were zero?

13.   **Calculating WACC (LO1)** Laurier Corp. has no debt but can borrow at 6.1 percent. The firm's WACC is currently 9.5 percent, and the tax rate is 35 percent.

    a.   What is the company's cost of equity?

    b.   If the firm converts to 25 percent debt, what will its cost of equity be?

    c.   If the firm converts to 50 percent debt, what will its cost of equity be?

    d.   What is the company's WACC in part (b)? In part (c)?

14. **M&M and Taxes (LO2)** Elzear & Co. expects its EBIT to be $74,000 every year forever. The firm can borrow at 7 percent. Elzear currently has no debt, and its cost of equity is 12 percent. If the tax rate is 35 percent, what is the value of the firm? What will the value be if the company borrows $125,000 and uses the proceeds to repurchase shares?

15. **M&M and Taxes (LO2)** In Problem 14, what is the cost of equity after recapitalization? What is the WACC? What are the implications for the firm's capital structure decision?

Intermediate 16. **M&M (LO2)** Sillery Manufacturing has an expected EBIT of $73,000 in perpetuity and a tax rate of 35 percent. The firm has
(Questions $145,000 in outstanding debt at an interest rate of 7.25 percent, and its unlevered cost of capital is 11 percent. What is the value
16–18) of the firm according to M&M Proposition I with taxes? Should the company change its debt–equity ratio if the goal is to maximize the value of the firm? Explain.

17. **Firm Value (LO2)** Lazare Corporation expects an EBIT of $19,750 every year forever. Lazare currently has no debt, and its cost of equity is 15 percent. The firm can borrow at 10 percent. If the corporate tax rate is 35 percent, what is the value of the firm? What will the value be if the company converts to 50 percent debt? To 100 percent debt?

18. **Homemade Leverage (LO1)** The Montmagny Company and the Shawinigan Company are identical in every respect except that Montmagny is not levered. Financial information for the two firms appears in the following table. All earnings streams are perpetuities, and neither firm pays taxes. Both firms distribute all earnings available to common shareholders immediately.

	Montmagny	Shawinigan
Projected operating income	$ 500,000	$ 500,000
Year-end interest on debt	—	$ 78,000
Market value of stock	$3,100,000	$2,050,000
Market value of debt	—	$1,300,000

a. An investor who can borrow at 6 percent per year wishes to purchase 5 percent of Shawinigan's equity. Can he increase his dollar return by purchasing 5 percent of Montmagny's equity if he borrows so that the initial net costs of the strategies are the same?

b. Given the two investment strategies in (a), which will investors choose? When will this process cease?

Challenge 19. **Weighted Average Cost of Capital (LO1)** In a world of corporate taxes only, show that the WACC can be written as
(Questions $\text{WACC} = R_U \times [1 - T_C(D/V)]$.
19–24) 20. **Cost of Equity and Leverage (LO1)** Assuming a world of corporate taxes only, show that the cost of equity, RE, is as given in the chapter by M&M Proposition II with corporate taxes.

21. **Business and Financial Risk (LO1)** Assume a firm's debt is risk-free, so that the cost of debt equals the risk-free rate, R_f. Define β_A as the firm's *asset* beta—that is, the systematic risk of the firm's assets. Define β_E to be the beta of the firm's equity. Use the capital asset pricing model (CAPM) along with M&M Proposition II to show that $\beta_E = \beta_A \times (1 + D/E)$, where D/E is the debt–equity ratio. Assume the tax rate is zero.

22. **Shareholder Risk (LO1)** Suppose a firm's business operations are such that they mirror movements in the economy as a whole very closely; that is, the firm's asset beta is 1.0. Use the result of Problem 21 to find the equity beta for this firm for debt–equity ratios of 0, 1, 5, and 20. What does this tell you about the relationship between capital structure and shareholder risk? How is the shareholders' required return on equity affected? Explain.

23. **Bankruptcy (LO3)** A petition for the reorganization of the Boniface Company has been filed under the Insolvency Act. The trustees estimate the firm's liquidation value, after considering costs, is $102 million. Alternatively, the trustees, using the analysis of the Zulu Consulting firm, predict that the reorganized business will generate $18 million annual cash flows in perpetuity. The discount rate is 14 percent. Should Boniface be liquidated or reorganized? Why?

24. **Bankruptcy (LO3)** The Odanak Corporation (OC) has filed for bankruptcy. All of OC's assets would fetch $43 million on the open market today if put up for sale. The other alternative would be to reorganize the business. If this occurs, the company would generate $3.97 million cash flows in perpetuity. Since there are no competitors making products similar to OC, there is no company that can offer a comparable discount rate. Analysts estimate that the discount rate can be between 10 percent and 25 percent. If the company's discount rate is 10 percent, should the company be liquidated or reorganized? Is the answer the same for a 20 percent discount rate? What other factors may play a role in deciding whether to liquidate the company or reorganize it?

MINI CASE

Nicolet Real Estate Recapitalization

Nicolet Real Estate Company was founded 25 years ago by the current CEO, Steven Nicolet. The company purchases real estate, including land and buildings, and rents the property to tenants. The company has shown a profit every year for the past 18 years, and the shareholders are satisfied with the company's management. Prior to founding Nicolet Real Estate, Steven was the founder and CEO of a failed alpaca farming operation. The resulting bankruptcy made him extremely averse to debt financing. As a result, the company is entirely equity financed, with 12 million shares of common stock outstanding. The stock currently trades at $31.40 per share.

Nicolet is evaluating a plan to purchase a huge tract of land in the southeastern Canada for $80 million. The land will subsequently be leased to a developer who plans to build a gated community for the Canadian snowbird market. This purchase is expected to increase Nicolet's annual pre-tax earnings by $16 million in perpetuity. Scarlett Wright, the company's new CFO, has been put in charge of the project. Scarlett has determined that the company's current cost of capital is 10.2 percent. She feels that the company would be more valuable if it included debt in its capital structure, so she is evaluating whether the company should issue debt to entirely finance the project. Based on some conversations with investment banks, she thinks that the company can issue bonds at par value with an 6 percent coupon rate. From her analysis, she also believes that a capital structure in the range of 70 percent equity/30 percent debt would be optimal. If the company goes beyond 30 percent debt, its bonds would carry a lower rating and a much higher coupon because the possibility of financial distress and the associated costs would rise sharply. Nicholet has a 40 percent corporate tax rate (state and federal).

Questions

1. If Nicolet wishes to maximize its total market value, would you recommend that it issue debt or equity to finance the land purchase? Explain.

2. Construct Nicolet's market value statement of financial position before it announces the purchase.

3. Suppose Nicolet decides to issue equity to finance the purchase.
   a. What is the net present value of the project?
   b. Construct Nicolet's market value statement of financial position after it announces that the firm will finance the purchase using equity. What would be the new price per share of the firm's stock? How many shares will Nicolet need to issue to finance the purchase?
   c. Construct Nicolet's market value statement of financial position after the equity issue but before the purchase has been made. How many shares of common stock does Nicolet have outstanding? What is the price per share of the firm's stock?
   d. Construct Nicolet's market value statement of financial position after the purchase has been made.

4. Suppose Nicolet decides to issue debt to finance the purchase.
   a. What will the market value of the Nicolet company be if the purchase is financed with debt?
   b. Construct Nicolet's market value balance sheet after both the debt issue and the land purchase. What is the price per share of the firm's stock?

5. Which method of financing maximizes the per-share stock price of Nicolet's equity?

Internet Application Questions

1. Capital structure choice in textbooks usually revolves around debt versus equity. In reality, there are several shades of grey in between. For example, subordinated debt can often be a useful source of capital for many firms. The following website (bctechnology.com/connector/scripts/experts/subdebt.cfm) lists the benefits of including subordinated debt in a firm's capital structure. What types of firms would find this financing attractive?

2. Highly leveraged transactions called LBOs attempt to gain control of a firm through the use of borrowed funds, and their perpetrators hope to profit from de-leveraging the acquired assets in the future and doing a reverse LBO. Onex Corp. (onex.com) is an example of a Canadian company that specializes in doing LBO deals. Click on their website and explain the principles that underlie Onex's operating philosophy.

3. Go to ca.finance.yahoo.com/ and enter the ticker symbols for JDS Uniphase (JDSU), Suncor Energy (SU), and BCE Inc. (BCE). Click on "Key Statistics" link for each one. What are the long-term debt-to-equity and total debt-to-equity ratios for each of the companies? How do these values compare to the industry, sector, and S&P 500 for each company? Can you think of possible explanations for the differences among the three companies in terms of their financial structures?

4. A useful site for information on bankruptcy and reorganizations is found at abiworld.org. For the latest news, follow the "Bankruptcy Headlines" link on the site. How many companies filed for bankruptcy on this day? What conditions or issues caused these filings?

APPENDIX 16A

CAPITAL STRUCTURE AND PERSONAL TAXES

Up to this point, we considered corporate taxes only. Unfortunately, Canada Revenue Agency does not let us off that easily. As we saw in Chapter 2, income to individuals is taxed at different rates. For individuals in the top brackets, some kinds of personal income can be taxed more heavily than corporate income. Earlier, we showed that the value of a levered firm equals the value of an identical unlevered firm, V_U plus the present value of the interest tax shield $T_C \times D$.

$$V_L = V_U + T_C \times D$$

This approach considered only corporate taxes. In a classic paper, Miller derived another expression for the value of the levered firm taking into account personal taxes.[11] In Equation 16A.1, T_b is the personal tax rate on ordinary income, such as interest and T_S is the weighted average of the personal tax rate on equity distributions—dividends and capital gains.[12]

$$V_L = V_U + \left[1 - \frac{(1 - T_C) \times (1 - T_S)}{1 - T_b}\right] \times D \qquad [16A.1]$$

Value of the Firm with Personal and Corporate Taxes

If the personal tax rates on interest (T_b) and on equity distributions (T_S) happen to be the same, then our new, more complex expression (Equation 16A.1) simplifies to Equation 16.7, which is the result when there are no personal taxes. It follows that introducing personal taxes does not affect our valuation formula as long as equity distributions are taxed identically to interest at the personal level.

However, the gain from leverage is reduced when equity distributions are taxed more lightly than interest, that is when T_S is less than T_b. Here, more taxes are paid at the personal level for a levered firm than for an unlevered firm. In fact, imagine that $(1 - T_C) \times (1 - T_S) = 1 - T_b$. Formula 16A.1 tells us there is no gain from leverage at all! In other words, the value of the levered firm is equal to the value of the unlevered firm. The reason there is no gain from leverage is that the lower corporate taxes for a levered firm are exactly offset by higher personal taxes. These results are presented in Figure 16A.1.

---

[11] M. H. Miller, "Debt and Taxes," *Journal of Finance* 32 (May 1977), pp. 261–75.

[12] Shareholders receive

$$(EBIT - r_D D) \times (1 - T_C) \times (1 - T_S)$$

Bondholders receive

$$r_D D \times (1 - T_b)$$

Thus, the total cash flow to all stakeholders is

$$(EBIT - r_D D) \times (1 - T_C) \times (1 - T_S) + r_D D \times (1 - T_b)$$

which can be rewritten as

$$EBIT \times (1 - T_C) \times (1 - T_S) + r_D D \times (1 - T_b) \times \left[1 - \frac{(1 - T_C) \times (1 - T_S)}{1 - T_b}\right] \qquad (a)$$

The first term in Equation (a) is the cash flow from an unlevered firm after all taxes. The value of this stream must be V_U, the value of an unlevered firm. An individual buying a bond for B receives $r_D D \times (1 - T_b)$ after all taxes. Thus, the value of the second term in (a) must be

$$D \times \left[1 - \frac{(1 - T_C) \times (1 - T_S)}{1 - T_b}\right]$$

Therefore, the value of the stream in (a), which is the value of the levered firm, must be

$$V_U + \left[1 - \frac{(1 - T_C) \times (1 - T_S)}{1 - T_b}\right] \times D$$

FIGURE 16A.1

Gains from financial leverage with both corporate and personal taxes

T_C is the corporate tax rate.
T_b is the personal tax rate on interest.
T_s is the personal tax rate on dividends and other equity distributions.
Both personal taxes and corporate taxes are included. Bankruptcy costs and agency costs are ignored. The effect of debt on firm value depends on T_s, T_c, and T_b.

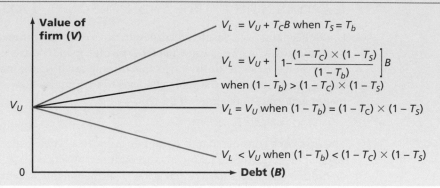

$V_L = V_U + T_C B$ when $T_s = T_b$

$V_L = V_U + \left[1 - \dfrac{(1 - T_C) \times (1 - T_S)}{(1 - T_b)} \right] B$
when $(1 - T_b) > (1 - T_C) \times (1 - T_S)$

$V_L = V_U$ when $(1 - T_b) = (1 - T_C) \times (1 - T_S)$

$V_L < V_U$ when $(1 - T_b) < (1 - T_C) \times (1 - T_S)$

EXAMPLE 16A.1: Financial Leverage with Personal Taxes

Acme Industries anticipates a perpetual pretax earning stream of $100,000 and faces a 36 percent corporate tax rate. Investors discount the earnings stream after corporate taxes at 15 percent. The personal tax rate on equity distributions is 20 percent and the personal tax rate on interest is 40 percent. Acme currently has an all-equity capital structure but is considering borrowing $120,000 at 10 percent. The value of the all-equity firm is:[13]

$$V_U = \frac{\$100,000 \times (1 - .36)}{0.15} = \$426,667$$

The value of the levered firm is

$$V_L = \$426,667 + \left[\frac{1 - (1 - .36) \times (1 - .20)}{(1 - .40)} \right] \times \$120,000$$
$$= \$444,267$$

The advantage to leverage here is $444,267 − $426,667 = $17,600. This is much smaller than the $43,200 = .36 × $120,000 = $T_C \times B$, which would have been the gain in a world with no personal taxes.

Acme had previously considered the choice years earlier when $T_B = 60$ percent, $T_C = 45$ percent and $T_S = 18$ percent. Here

$$V_L = \$366,667 + \left[\frac{1 - (1 - .45) \times (1 - .18)}{(1 - .60)} \right] \times \$120,000$$
$$= \$351,367$$

In this case, the value of the levered firm, V_L, is $351,367 which is less than the value of the unlevered firm, $V_U = $366,667. Hence, Acme was wise not to increase leverage years ago. Leverage causes a loss of value because the personal tax rate on interest is much higher than the personal tax rate on equity distributions. In other words, the reduc-

tion in corporate taxes from leverage is more than offset by the increase in taxes from leverage at the personal level.

Figure 16A.1 summarizes the different cases we considered. Which one is the most applicable to Canada? While the numbers are different for different firms in different provinces, Chapter 2 showed that interest income is taxed at the full marginal rate, around 40 percent for the top bracket. Equity distributions take the form of either dividends or capital gains and both are taxed more lightly than interest. As we showed in Chapter 2, dividend income is sheltered by the dividend tax credit.

While the exact numbers depend on the type of portfolio chosen, our first scenario for Acme is a reasonable tax scenario for Canadian investors and companies. In Canada, personal taxes reduce, but do not eliminate, the advantage to corporate leverage.

This result is still unrealistic. It suggests that firms should add debt, moving out on the second line from the top in Figure 16A.1, until 100 percent leverage is reached. Firms do not do this. One reason is that interest on debt is not the firm's only tax shield. Investment tax credits, capital cost allowance, and depletion allowances give rise to tax shields regardless of the firm's decision on leverage. Because these other tax shields exist, increased leverage brings with it a risk that income will not be high enough to utilize the debt tax shield fully. The result is that firms use a limited amount of debt.[14]

Of course, as we argued in the chapter, the costs of bankruptcy and financial distress are another reason healthy firms do not use 100 percent debt financing.

---

[13] Alternatively, we could have said that investors discount the earnings stream after both corporate and personal taxes at 12% = 15% (1 − .20):
$$V_U = \frac{\$100,000 \times (1 - .36) \times (1 - .20)}{.12} = \$426,667$$

[14] This argument was first advanced by H. DeAngelo and R. Masulis, "Optimal Capital Structure under Corporate and Personal Taxation," *Journal of Financial Economics,* March 1980, pp. 3–30 and is further discussed by Alfred H.R. Davis, "The Corporate Use of Debt Substitutes in Canada: A Test of Competing Versions of the Substitution Hypothesis," *Canadian Journal of Administrative Sciences,* March 1994, vol. 11, issue 1, p. 105.

Concept Questions

1. How does considering personal taxes on interest and equity distributions change the M&M conclusions on optimal debt?
2. Explain in words the logic behind Miller's theory of capital structure.
3. How does this theory apply in Canada?

Appendix Questions and Problems

A.1 Miller's model introduces personal taxes into the theory of capital structure. With both personal and corporate taxes, we got the same indifference result as with no taxes. Explain why.

A.2 This question is a follow-up to Question A.1 on Miller's model. In comparing this approach to M&M with corporate taxes, you can see that in one case both models imply that firms should use 100 percent debt financing. Explain how this conclusion occurs in each case. Why does it not occur in practice?

APPENDIX 16B

DERIVATION OF PROPOSITION II (EQUATION 16.4)

We use the symbol R_A to stand for WACC.

$$R_A = \text{WACC} = (E/V) \times R_E + (D/V) \times R_D$$

Multiplying both sides by V/E yields:

$$(D/E) R_D + R_E = (V/E) R_A$$

We can rewrite the right-hand side as:

$$(D/E) R_D + R_E = (D/E) R_A + R_A$$

Moving $(D/E) R_D$ to the right-hand side and rearranging gives:

$$R_E = R_A + (R_A - R_D) \times (D/E)$$

DIVIDENDS AND DIVIDEND POLICY

On May 2, 2012, Barrick Gold, the world's largest gold miner, headquartered in Toronto, reported a big first quarter profit of around US $1 billion. As a result, the company decided to hike its dividend by 33 percent to 20 cents US a share from 15 cents US. While other gold companies were known for paying low dividends, Barrick had increased its dividend by 260 percent in 5 years due to its superior earnings and operating cash flows. Explaining dividends and dividend policy is the focus of this chapter.

Learning Objectives ▶

After studying this chapter, you should understand:

LO1   Dividend types and how dividends are paid.

LO2   The issues surrounding dividend policy decisions.

LO3   The difference between cash and stock dividends.

LO4   Why share repurchases are an alternative to dividends.

Dividend policy is an important subject in corporate finance, and dividends are a major cash outlay for many corporations. At first glance, it may seem obvious that a firm would always want to give as much as possible back to its shareholders by paying dividends. It might seem equally obvious, however, that a firm can always invest the money for its shareholders instead of paying it out. The heart of the dividend policy question is just this: Should the firm pay out money to its shareholders, or should the firm take that money and invest it for its shareholders?

It may seem surprising, but much research and economic logic suggest that dividend policy doesn't matter. In fact, it turns out that the dividend policy issue is much like the capital structure question. The important elements are not difficult to identify, but the interactions between those elements are complex and no easy answer exists.

Dividend policy is controversial. Many implausible reasons are given for why dividend policy might be important, and many of the claims made about dividend policy are economically illogical. Even so, in the real world of corporate finance, determining the most appropriate dividend policy is considered an important issue. It could be that financial managers who worry about dividend policy are wasting time, but it could be true that we are missing something important in our discussions.

In part, all discussions of dividends are plagued by the "two-handed lawyer" problem. Former U.S. President Harry S. Truman, while discussing the legal implications of a possible presidential decision, asked his staff to set up a meeting with a lawyer. Supposedly, Truman said, "But I don't want one of those two-handed lawyers." When asked what a two-handed lawyer was, he replied, "You know, a lawyer who says, 'On the one hand I recommend you do so and so because of the following reasons, but on the other hand I recommend that you don't do it because of these other reasons.' "

Unfortunately, any sensible treatment of dividend policy appears to be written by a two-handed lawyer (or, in fairness, several two-handed financial economists). On the one hand, there are many good reasons for corporations to pay high dividends; on the other hand, there are also many good reasons to pay low dividends or no dividends.

We cover three broad topics that relate to dividends and dividend policy in this chapter. First, we describe the various kinds of dividends and how dividends are paid. Second, we consider an idealized case in which dividend policy doesn't matter. We then discuss the limitations of this case and present some practical arguments for both high- and low-dividend payouts. Finally, we conclude the chapter by looking at some strategies that corporations might employ to implement a dividend policy.

17.1 | Cash Dividends and Dividend Payment

dividend
Payment made out of a firm's earnings to its owners, either in the form of cash or stock.

distribution
Payment made by a firm to its owners from sources other than current or accumulated earnings.

The term **dividend** usually refers to cash paid out of earnings. If a payment is made from sources other than current or accumulated retained earnings, the term **distribution** rather than dividend is sometimes used. However, it is acceptable to refer to a distribution from earnings as a dividend and a distribution from capital as a liquidating dividend. More generally, any direct payment by the corporation to the shareholders may be considered a dividend or a part of dividend policy. Figure 17.1 shows how the dividend decision is part of distributing the firm's cash flow over different uses.

Dividends come in several different forms. The basic types of cash dividends are:

1. Regular cash dividends.
2. Extra dividends.
3. Special dividends.
4. Liquidating dividends.

Later in the chapter, we discuss dividends that are paid in stock instead of cash, and we also consider an alternative to cash dividends, stock repurchase.

Cash Dividends

regular cash dividend
Cash payment made by a firm to its owners in the normal course of business, usually made four times a year.

The most common type of dividend is a cash dividend. Commonly, public companies pay **regular cash dividends** four times a year. As the name suggests, these are cash payments made directly to shareholders, and they are made in the regular course of business. In other words, management sees nothing unusual about the dividend and no reason it won't be continued.

Sometimes firms pay a regular cash dividend and an extra cash dividend. By calling part of the payment extra, management is indicating it may or may not be repeated in the future. A *special dividend* is similar, but the name usually indicates that this dividend is viewed as a truly unusual or one-time event and won't be repeated. For example, in May 2010, Sears Canada paid a special dividend of $3.50 per share. The total payout of $368 million was the largest one-time corporate dividend in history. Finally, a *liquidating dividend* usually means that some or all of the business has been liquidated, that is, sold off. Debt covenants, discussed in Chapter 7, offer the firm's creditors protection against liquidating dividends that could violate their prior claim against assets and cash flows.

However it is labelled, a cash dividend payment reduces corporate cash and retained earnings, except in the case of a liquidating dividend (where capital may be reduced).

FIGURE 17.1

Distribution of corporate cash flow

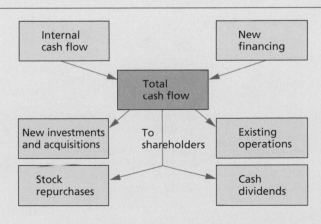

Standard Method of Cash Dividend Payment

The decision to pay a dividend rests in the hands of the board of directors of the corporation. When a dividend has been declared, it becomes a debt of the firm and cannot be rescinded easily. Sometime after it has been declared, a dividend is distributed to all shareholders as of some specific date.

Commonly, the amount of the cash dividend is expressed in dollars per share (*dividends per share*). As we have seen in other chapters, it is also expressed as a percentage of the market price (the *dividend yield*) or as a percentage of earnings per share (the *dividend payout*).

Dividend Payment: A Chronology

The mechanics of a dividend payment can be illustrated by the example in Figure 17.2 and the following description:

declaration date
Date on which the board of directors passes a resolution to pay a dividend.

ex-dividend date
Date two business days before the date of record, establishing those individuals entitled to a dividend.

date of record
Date on which holders of record are designated to receive a dividend.

date of payment
Date of the dividend payment.

1. **Declaration date**. On January 15, the board of directors passes a resolution to pay a dividend of $1 per share on February 16 to all holders of record as of January 30.

2. **Ex-dividend date**. To make sure that dividend cheques go to the right people, brokerage firms and stock exchanges establish an ex-dividend date. This date is two business days before the date of record (discussed next). If you buy the stock before this date, then you are entitled to the dividend. If you buy on this date or after, then the previous owner gets it.

   The ex-dividend date convention removes any ambiguity about who is entitled to the dividend. Since the dividend is valuable, the stock price is affected when it goes "ex." We examine this effect later.

   In Figure 17.2, Wednesday, January 28, is the ex-dividend date. Before this date, the stock is said to trade "with dividend" or "cum dividend." Afterwards the stock trades "ex dividend."

3. **Date of record**. Based on its records, the corporation prepares a list on January 30 of all individuals believed to be shareholders as of this date. These are the *holders of record* and January 30 is the *date of record*. The word believed is important here. If you buy the stock just before this date, the corporation's records may not reflect that fact. Without some modification, some of the dividend cheques would go to the wrong people. This is the reason for the ex-dividend day convention.

4. **Date of payment**. The dividends are paid on February 16.

More on the Ex-Dividend Date

The ex-dividend date is important and is a common source of confusion. We examine what happens to the stock when it goes ex, meaning that the ex-dividend date arrives. To illustrate, suppose we have a stock that sells for $10 per share. The board of directors declares a dividend of $1 per share, and the record date is Thursday, June 14. Based on our previous discussion, we know that the ex date will be two business (not calendar) days earlier on Tuesday, June 12.

FIGURE 17.2

Procedure for dividend payment

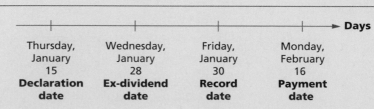

1. *Declaration date:* The board of directors declares a payment of dividends.
2. *Ex-dividend date:* A share of stock goes ex dividend on the date the seller is entitled to keep the dividend; under TSX rules, shares are traded ex dividend on and after the second business day before the record date.
3. *Record date:* The declared dividends are distributable to shareholders of record on a specific date.
4. *Payment date:* The dividend payment date.

FIGURE 17.3

Price behaviour around ex-dividend date for a $1 cash dividend

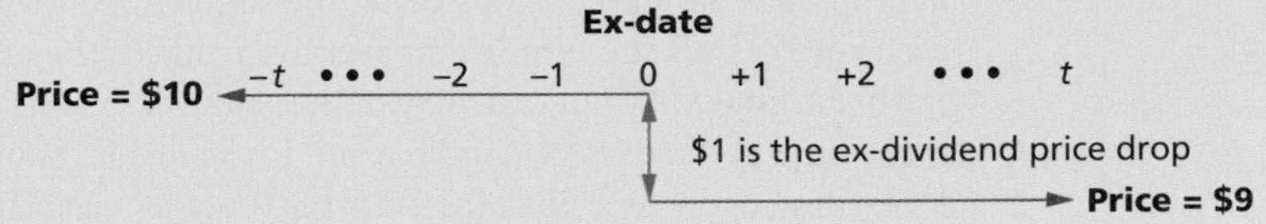

The stock price will fall by the amount of the dividend on the ex date (time 0). If the dividend is $1 per share, the price will be equal to $10 − $1 = $9 on the ex date:

Before ex date (−1) dividend = 0	Price = $10
Ex-date (0) dividend = $1	Price = $9

If you buy the stock on Monday, June 11, right as the market closes, you'll get the $1 dividend because the stock is trading cum dividend. If you wait and buy it right as the market opens on Tuesday, you won't get the $1 dividend. What will happen to the value of the stock overnight?

If you think about it, the stock is obviously worth about $1 less on Tuesday morning, so its price will drop by this amount between close of business on Monday and the Tuesday opening. In general, we expect the value of a share of stock to go down by about the dividend amount when the stock goes ex dividend. The key word here is *about*. Since dividends are taxed, the actual price drop might be closer to some measure of the after-tax value of the dividend. Determining this value is complicated because of the different tax rates and tax rules that apply for different buyers. The series of events described here is illustrated in Figure 17.3.

The amount of the price drop is a matter for empirical investigation. Researchers have argued that, due to personal taxes, the stock price should drop by less than the dividend.[1] For example, consider the case with no capital gains taxes. On the day before a stock goes ex dividend, shareholders must decide either to buy the stock immediately and pay tax on the forthcoming dividend, or to buy the stock tomorrow, thereby missing the dividend. If all investors are in a 30 percent bracket for dividends and the quarterly dividend is $1, the stock price should fall by $.70 on the ex-dividend date. If the stock price falls by this amount on the ex-dividend date, then purchasers receive the same return from either strategy.

EXAMPLE 17.1: "Ex" Marks the Day

The board of directors of Divided Airlines has declared a dividend of $2.50 per share payable on Tuesday, May 30, to shareholders of record as of Tuesday, May 9. Cal Icon buys 100 shares of Divided on Tuesday, May 2, for $150 per share. What is the ex date? Describe the events that will occur with regard to the cash dividend and the stock price.

The ex date is two business days before the date of record, Tuesday, May 9, so the stock will go ex on Friday, May 5. Cal buys the stock on Tuesday, May 2, so Cal has purchased the stock cum dividend. In other words, Cal gets $2.50 × 100 = $250 in dividends. The payment is made on Tuesday, May 30. When the stock does go ex on Friday, its value drops overnight by about $2.50 per share (or maybe a little less due to personal taxes).

Concept Questions

1. What are the different types of cash dividends?
2. What are the mechanics of the cash dividend payment?
3. How should the price of a stock change when it goes ex dividend?

[1] The original argument was advanced and tested for the United States by E. Elton and M. Gruber, "Marginal Stockholder Tax Rates and the Clientele Effect," *Review of Economics and Statistics* 52 (February 1970). Canadian evidence (discussed briefly later in this chapter) is from J. Lakonishok and T. Vermaelen, "Tax Reform and Ex-Dividend Day Behavior," *Journal of Finance* 38 (September 1983) pp. 1157–80, and L. D. Booth and D. J. Johnston, "The Ex-Dividend Day Behavior of Canadian Stock Prices: Tax Changes and Clientele Effects," *Journal of Finance* 39 (June 1984), pp. 457–76.

17.2 | Does Dividend Policy Matter?

To decide whether or not dividend policy matters, we first have to define what we mean by dividend policy. All other things being the same, of course dividends matter. Dividends are paid in cash, and cash is something that everybody likes. The question we are discussing here is whether the firm should pay out cash now or invest the cash and pay it out later. Dividend policy, therefore, is the time pattern of dividend payout. In particular, should the firm pay out a large percentage of its earnings now or a small (or even zero) percentage? This is the dividend policy question.

An Illustration of the Irrelevance of Dividend Policy

A powerful argument can be made that dividend policy does not matter. We illustrate this by considering the simple case of Wharton Corporation. Wharton is an all-equity firm that has existed for 10 years. The current financial managers plan to dissolve the firm in two years. The total cash flows that the firm will generate, including the proceeds from liquidation, are $10,000 in each of the next two years.

CURRENT POLICY: DIVIDENDS SET EQUAL TO CASH FLOW   At the present time, dividends at each date are set equal to the cash flow of $10,000. There are 100 shares outstanding, so the dividend per share will be $100. In Chapter 8, we stated that the value of the stock is equal to the present value of the future dividends. Assuming a 10 percent required return, the value of a share of stock today, P_0, is:

$$P_0 = D_1/(1 + R)^1 + D_2/(1 + R)^2$$
$$= \$100/1.10 + \$100/1.21 = \$173.55$$

The firm as a whole is thus worth $100 \times \$173.55 = \$17,355$.

Several members of the board of Wharton have expressed dissatisfaction with the current dividend policy and have asked you to analyze an alternative policy.

ALTERNATIVE POLICY: INITIAL DIVIDEND IS GREATER THAN CASH FLOW   Another policy is for the firm to pay a dividend of $110 per share on the first date, which is, of course, a total dividend of $11,000. Because the cash flow is only $10,000, an extra $1,000 must somehow be raised. One way to do it is to issue $1,000 of bonds or stock at Date 1. Assume that stock is issued. The new shareholders desire enough cash flow at Date 2 so that they earn the required 10 percent return on their Date 1 investment.[2]

What is the value of the firm with this new dividend policy? The new shareholders invest $1,000. They require a 10 percent return, so they demand $1,000 \times 1.10 = \$1,100$ of the Date 2 cash flow, leaving only $8,900 to the old shareholders. The dividends to the old shareholders would be:

	Date 1	Date 2
Aggregate dividends to old shareholders	$11,000	$8,900
Dividends per share	110	89

The present value of the dividends per share is therefore:

$$P_0 = \$110/1.10 + \$89/1.10^2 = \$173.55$$

This is the same present value as we had before.

The value of the stock is not affected by this switch in dividend policy even though we had to sell some new stock just to finance the dividend. In fact, no matter what pattern of dividend payout the firm chooses, the value of the stock is always the same in this example. In other words, for the Wharton Corporation, dividend policy makes no difference. The reason is simple: Any increase in a dividend at some point in time is exactly offset by a decrease somewhere else, so the net effect, once we account for time value, is zero.

HOMEMADE DIVIDENDS   There is an alternative and perhaps more intuitively appealing explanation about why dividend policy doesn't matter in our example. Suppose individual investor X prefers dividends per share of $100 at both Dates 1 and 2. Would he or she be disap-

---

[2]The same results would occur after an issue of bonds, though the arguments would be less easily presented.

pointed when informed that the firm's management is adopting the alternative dividend policy (dividends of $110 and $89 in the two dates, respectively)? Not necessarily, because the investor could easily reinvest the $10 of unneeded funds received on Date 1 by buying more Wharton stock. At 10 percent, this investment grows to $11 at Date 2. Thus, the investor would receive the desired net cash flow of $110 − 10 = $100 at Date 1 and $89 + 11 = $100 at Date 2.

Conversely, imagine Investor Z, preferring $110 of cash flow at Date 1 and $89 of cash flow at Date 2, finds that management pays dividends of $100 at both Dates 1 and 2. This investor can simply sell $10 worth of stock to boost his or her total cash at Date 1 to $110. Because this investment returns 10 percent, Investor Z gives up $11 at Date 2 ($10 × 1.1), leaving him with $100 − 11 = $89.

Our two investors are able to transform the corporation's dividend policy into a different policy by buying or selling on their own. The result is that investors are able to create **homemade dividends**. This means dissatisfied shareholders can alter the firm's dividend policy to suit themselves. As a result, there is no particular advantage to any one dividend policy that the firm might choose.

Many corporations actually assist their shareholders in creating homemade dividend policies by offering *automatic dividend reinvestment plans* (ADPs or DRIPs). As the name suggests, with such a plan, shareholders have the option of automatically reinvesting some or all of their cash dividends in shares of stock.

Under a new issue dividend reinvestment plan, investors buy new stock issued by the firm. They may receive a small discount on the stock, usually under 5 percent, or be able to buy without a broker's commission. This makes dividend reinvestment very attractive to investors who do not need cash flow from dividends. Since the discount or lower commission compares favourably with issue costs for new stock discussed in Chapter 15, dividend reinvestment plans are popular with large companies like BCE that periodically seek new common stock.[3]

Investment dealers also use financial engineering to create homemade dividends (or homemade capital gains). Called **stripped common shares**, these vehicles entitle holders to receive either all the dividends from one or a group of well-known companies or an installment receipt that packages any capital gain in the form of a call option. The option gives the investor the right to buy the underlying shares at a fixed price and so it is valuable if the shares appreciate beyond that price.

A TEST   Our discussion to this point can be summarized by considering the following true/false test questions:

1. True or false: Dividends are irrelevant.
2. True or false: Dividend policy is irrelevant.

The first statement is surely false, and the reason follows from common sense. Clearly, investors prefer higher dividends to lower dividends at any single date if the dividend level is held constant at every other date. To be more precise regarding the first question, if the dividend per share at a given date is raised while the dividend per share at each other date is held constant, the stock price rises. The reason is that the present value of the future dividends must go up if this occurs. This action can be accomplished by management decisions that improve productivity, increase tax savings, strengthen product marketing, or otherwise improve cash flow.

The second statement is true, at least in the simple case we have been examining. Dividend policy by itself cannot raise the dividend at one date while keeping it the same at all other dates. Rather, dividend policy merely establishes the trade-off between dividends at one date and dividends at another date. Once we allow for time value, the present value of the dividend stream is unchanged. Thus, in this simple world, dividend policy does not matter, because managers choosing either to raise or to lower the current dividend do not affect the current value of their firm. However, we have ignored several real-world factors that might lead us to change our minds; we pursue some of these in subsequent sections.

homemade dividends
Idea that individual investors can undo corporate dividend policy by reinvesting dividends or selling shares of stock.

stripped common shares
Common stock on which dividends and capital gains are repackaged and sold separately.

Concept Questions

1. How can an investor create a homemade dividend?
2. Are dividends irrelevant?

---

[3] Reinvested dividends are still taxable.

17.3 | Real-World Factors Favouring a Low Payout

The example we used to illustrate the irrelevance of dividend policy ignored taxes and flotation costs. In other words, we assumed perfect capital markets in which these and other imperfections did not exist. In this section, we see that these factors might lead us to prefer a low-dividend payout.

Taxes

The logic we used to establish that dividend policy does not affect firm value ignored the real-world complication of taxes. In Canada, both dividends and capital gains are taxed at effective rates less than the marginal tax rates.

For dividends, we showed in Chapter 2 that individual investors face a lower tax rate due to the dividend tax credit. Capital gains in the hands of individuals are taxed at 50 percent of the marginal tax rate. Since taxation only occurs when capital gains are realized, capital gains are very lightly taxed in Canada. On balance, capital gains are subject to lower taxes than dividends.

A firm that adopts a low-dividend payout reinvests the money instead of paying it out. This reinvestment increases the value of the firm and of the equity. All other things being equal, the net effect is that the capital gains portion of the return is higher in the future. So, the fact that capital gains are taxed favourably may lead us to prefer this approach.

This tax disadvantage of dividends doesn't necessarily lead to a policy of paying no dividends. Suppose a firm has some excess cash after selecting all positive NPV projects. The firm might consider the following alternatives to a dividend:

1. *Select additional capital budgeting projects.* Because the firm has taken all the available positive NPV projects already, it must invest its excess cash in negative NPV projects. This is clearly a policy at variance with the principles of corporate finance and represents an example of the agency costs of equity introduced in Chapter 1. Still, research suggests that some companies are guilty of doing this.[4] It is frequently argued that managers who adopt negative NPV projects are ripe for takeover, leveraged buyouts, and proxy fights.

2. *Repurchase shares.* A firm may rid itself of excess cash by repurchasing shares of stock. In both the United States and Canada, investors can treat profits on repurchased stock in public companies as capital gains and pay somewhat lower taxes than they would if the cash were distributed as a dividend.

3. *Acquire other companies.* To avoid the payment of dividends, a firm might use excess cash to acquire another company. This strategy has the advantage of acquiring profitable assets. However, a firm often incurs heavy costs when it embarks on an acquisition program. In addition, acquisitions are invariably made above the market price. Premiums of 20 to 80 percent are not uncommon. Because of this, a number of researchers have argued that mergers are not generally profitable to the acquiring company, even when firms are merged for a valid business purpose.[5] Therefore, a company making an acquisition merely to avoid a dividend is unlikely to succeed.

4. *Purchase financial assets.* The strategy of purchasing financial assets in lieu of a dividend payment can be illustrated with the following example.

Suppose the Regional Electric Company has $1,000 of extra cash. It can retain the cash and invest it in Treasury bills yielding 8 percent, or it can pay the cash to shareholders as a dividend. Shareholders can also invest in Treasury bills with the same yield. Suppose, realistically, that the tax rate is 44 percent on ordinary income like interest on Treasury bills for both the company and individual investors and the individual tax rate on dividends is 30 percent. What is the amount of cash that investors have after five years under each policy?

Dividends paid now:

If dividends are paid now, shareholders will receive $1,000 before taxes, or $1,000 \times (1 - .30) =$

---

[4]M. C. Jensen, "Agency Costs of Free Cash Flows, Corporate Finance and Takeovers," *American Economic Review*, May 1986, pp. 323–29.

[5]The original hypothesis comes from R. Roll, "The Hubris Hypothesis of Corporate Takeovers," *Journal of Business* (1986). Chapter 23 presents some Canadian examples.

$700 after taxes. This is the amount they invest. If the rate on T-bills is 8 percent, before taxes, then the after-tax return is 8% × (1 − .44) = 4.48% per year. Thus, in five years, the shareholders have:

$$\$700 \times (1 + 0.0448)^5 = \$871.49$$

Company retains cash:

If Regional Electric Company retains the cash, invests in Treasury bills, and pays out the proceeds five years from now, then $1,000 will be invested today. However, since the corporate tax rate is 44 percent, the after-tax return from the T-bills will be 8% × (1 − .44) = 4.48% per year. In five years, the investment will be worth:

$$\$1,000 \times (1 + 0.0448)^5 = \$1,244.99$$

If this amount is then paid out as a dividend, after taxes the shareholders receive:

$$\$1,244.99 \times (1 - .30) = \$871.49$$

In this case, dividends are the same after taxes whether the firm pays them now or later after investing in Treasury bills. The reason is that the firm invests exactly as profitably as the shareholders do on an after-tax basis.

This example shows that for a firm with extra cash, the dividend payout decision depends on personal and corporate tax rates. All other things the same, when personal tax rates are higher than corporate tax rates, a firm has an incentive to reduce dividend payouts. This would have occurred if we changed our example to have the firm invest in preferred stock instead of T-bills. (Recall from Chapter 8 that corporations enjoy a 100 percent exclusion of dividends from taxable income.) However, if personal tax rates on dividends are lower than corporate tax rates (for investors in lower tax brackets or tax-exempt investors), a firm has an incentive to pay out any excess cash in dividends.

These examples show that dividend policy is not always irrelevant when we consider personal and corporate taxes. To continue the discussion, we go back to the different tax treatment of dividends and capital gains.

EXPECTED RETURN, DIVIDENDS, AND PERSONAL TAXES   We illustrate the effect of personal taxes by considering a situation where dividends are taxed and capital gains are not taxed—a scenario that is not unrealistic for many Canadian individual investors. We show that a firm that provides more return in the form of dividends has a lower value (or a higher pre-tax required return) than one whose return is in the form of untaxed capital gains.

Suppose every shareholder is in the top tax bracket (tax rate on dividends of 30 percent) and is considering the stocks of Firm G and Firm D. Firm G pays no dividend, and Firm D pays a dividend. The current price of the stock of Firm G is $100, and next year's price is expected to be $120. The shareholder in Firm G thus expects a $20 capital gain. With no dividend, the return is $20/$100 = 20%. If capital gains are not taxed, the pre-tax and after-tax returns must be the same.[6]

Suppose the stock of Firm D is expected to pay a $20 dividend next year. If the stocks of Firm G and Firm D are equally risky, the market prices must be set so that their after-tax expected returns are equal. The after-tax return on Firm D thus has to be 20 percent.

What will be the price of stock in Firm D? The after-tax dividend is $20 × (1 − .30) = $14, so our investor has a total of $114 after taxes. At a 20 percent required rate of return (after taxes), the present value of this after-tax amount is:

$$\text{Present value} = \$114/1.20 = \$95.00$$

The market price of the stock in Firm D thus must be $95.00.

Some Evidence on Dividends and Taxes in Canada

Is our example showing higher pre-tax returns for stocks that pay dividends realistic for Canadian capital markets? Since tax laws change from budget to budget, we have to exercise caution in interpreting research results. Before 1972, capital gains were untaxed in Canada (as in our simplified

---

[6]Under current tax law, if the shareholder in Firm G does not sell the shares for a gain, it will be an unrealized capital gain, which is not taxed.

example). Research suggests stocks that paid dividends had higher pre-tax returns prior to 1972. From 1972 to 1977, the same study detected no difference in pre-tax returns.[7]

In 1985, the lifetime exemption on capital gains was introduced. Recent research found that investors anticipated this tax break for capital gains and bid up the prices of stocks with low dividend yields. Firms responded by lowering their dividend payouts. This all ended in 1994 when the federal budget ended the capital gains exemption.[8] In 2000, the federal budget lowered the taxable portion of capital gains from 75 to 50 percent. In November 2005, the government of Canada initiated changes with the goal of making dividend-paying stocks more attractive relative to income trusts by increasing the gross-up and the dividend tax credit.[9] We suspect that from the viewpoint of individual investors, higher dividends require larger pre-tax returns.

Another way of measuring the effective tax rates on dividends and capital gains in Canada is to look at ex-dividend day price drops. We showed earlier that, ignoring taxes, a stock price should drop by the amount of the dividend when it goes ex dividend. This is because the price drop offsets what investors lose by waiting to buy the stock until it goes ex dividend. If dividends are taxed and capital gains are tax free, the price drop should be lower, equal to the after-tax value of the dividend. However, if gains are taxed too, the price drop needs to be adjusted for the gains tax. An investor who waits for the stock to go ex dividend buys at a lower price and hence has a larger capital gain when the stock is sold later.

All this allowed researchers to infer tax rates from ex-dividend day behaviour. One study concludes that marginal investors who set prices are taxed more heavily on dividends than on capital gains.[10] This supports our argument: Individual investors likely look for higher pre-tax returns on dividend paying stocks.

Flotation Costs

In our example illustrating that dividend policy doesn't matter, we saw that the firm could sell some new stock if necessary to pay a dividend. As we mentioned in Chapter 15, selling new stock can be very expensive. If we include flotation costs in our argument, then we find that the value of the stock decreases if we sell new stock.

More generally, imagine two firms that are identical in every way except that one pays out a greater percentage of its cash flow in the form of dividends. Since the other firm plows back more, its equity grows faster. If these two firms are to remain identical, the one with the higher payout has to sell some stock periodically to catch up. Since this is expensive, a firm might be inclined to have a low payout.

Dividend Restrictions

In some cases, a corporation may face restrictions on its ability to pay dividends. For example, as we discussed in Chapter 7, a common feature of a bond indenture is a covenant prohibiting dividend payments above some level.

Concept Questions

1. What are the tax benefits of low dividends?
2. Why do flotation costs favour a low payout?

---

[7] I. G. Morgan, "Dividends and Stock Price Behaviour in Canada," *Journal of Business Administration* 12 (Fall 1989).

[8] B. Amoako-adu, M. Rashid, and M. Stebbins, "Capital Gains Tax and Equity Values: Empirical Test of Stock Price Reaction to the Introduction and Reduction of Capital Gains Tax Exemption, *Journal of Banking and Finance* 16 (1992), pp. 275–87; F. Adjaoud and D. Zeghal, "Taxation and Dividend Policy in Canada: New Evidence," *FINECO* (2nd Semester) 1993, pp. 141–54.

[9] We discuss these tax changes in detail in Chapter 2.

[10] L. Booth and D. Johnston, "Ex-Dividend Day Behavior." Their research also showed that interlisted stocks, traded on exchanges in both the United States and Canada, tended to be priced by U.S. investors and not be affected by Canadian tax changes. J. Lakonishok and T. Vermaelen, "Tax Reforms and Ex-Dividend Day Behavior," *Journal of Finance*, September 1983, pp. 1157–58, gives a competing explanation in terms of tax arbitrage by short-term traders.

17.4 | Real-World Factors Favouring a High Payout

In this section, we consider reasons a firm might pay its shareholders higher dividends even if it means the firm must issue more shares of stock to finance the dividend payments.

In a classic textbook, Benjamin Graham and David Dodd, have argued that firms should generally have high-dividend payouts because:

1. "The discounted value of near dividends is higher than the present worth of distant dividends."
2. Between "two companies with the same general earning power and same general position in an industry, the one paying the larger dividend will almost always sell at a higher price."[11]

Two factors favouring a high-dividend payout have been mentioned frequently by proponents of this view: the desire for current income and the resolution of uncertainty.

Desire for Current Income

It has been argued that many individuals desire current income. The classic example is the group of retired people and others living on fixed incomes, the proverbial "widows and orphans." It is argued that this group is willing to pay a premium to get a higher dividend yield. If this is true, it lends support to the second claim by Graham, Dodd, and Cottle.

It is easy to see, however, that this argument is not relevant in our simple case. An individual preferring high current cash flow but holding low-dividend securities could easily sell shares to provide the necessary funds. Similarly, an individual desiring a low current cash flow but holding high-dividend securities can just reinvest the dividend. This is just our homemade dividend argument again. Thus, in a world of no transaction costs, a high current dividend policy would be of no value to the shareholder.

The current income argument may have relevance in the real world. Here the sale of low-dividend stocks would involve brokerage fees and other transaction costs. Such a sale might also trigger capital gains taxes. These direct cash expenses could be avoided by an investment in high-dividend securities. In addition, the expenditure of the shareholder's own time when selling securities and the natural (but not necessarily rational) fear of consuming out of principal might further lead many investors to buy high-dividend securities.

Even so, to put this argument in perspective, remember that financial intermediaries such as mutual funds can (and do) perform these repackaging transactions for individuals at very low cost. Such intermediaries could buy low-dividend stocks, and, by a controlled policy of realizing gains, they could pay their investors at a higher rate.

Uncertainty Resolution

We have just pointed out that investors with substantial current consumption needs prefer high current dividends. In another classic treatment, the late Professor Myron Gordon argued that a high-dividend policy also benefits shareholders because it resolves uncertainty.[12]

According to Gordon, investors price a security by forecasting and discounting future dividends. Gordon then argues that forecasts of dividends to be received in the distant future have greater uncertainty than do forecasts of near-term dividends. Because investors dislike uncertainty, the stock price should be low for those companies that pay small dividends now in order to remit higher dividends later.

Gordon's argument is essentially a "bird-in-hand" story. A $1 dividend in a shareholder's pocket is somehow worth more than that same $1 in a bank account held by the corporation. By now, you should see the problem with this argument. A shareholder can create a bird in hand very easily just by selling some stock.

---

[11] Benjamin Graham & David Dodd (2008) Security Analysis: Sixth Edition, Foreword by Warren Buffett, McGraw-Hill Professional.

[12] M. Gordon, *The Investment, Financing and Valuation of the Corporation* (Homewood, IL: Richard D. Irwin, 1961).

Tax and Legal Benefits from High Dividends

Earlier, we saw that dividends were taxed more heavily than capital gains for individual investors. This fact is a powerful argument for a low payout. However, a number of other investors do not receive unfavourable tax treatment from holding high-dividend yield, rather than low-dividend yield, securities.

CORPORATE INVESTORS   A significant tax break on dividends occurs when a corporation owns stock in another corporation. A corporate shareholder receiving either common or preferred dividends is granted a 100 percent dividend exclusion.[13] Since the 100 percent exclusion does not apply to capital gains, this group is taxed unfavourably on capital gains.

As a result of the dividend exclusion, high-dividend, low capital gains stocks may be more appropriate for corporations to hold. As we discuss elsewhere, this is why corporations hold a substantial percentage of the outstanding preferred stock in the economy. This tax advantage of dividends also leads some corporations to hold high-yielding stocks instead of long-term bonds because there is no similar tax exclusion of interest payments to corporate bondholders.

TAX-EXEMPT INVESTORS   We have pointed out both the tax advantages and disadvantages of a low-dividend payout. Of course, this discussion is irrelevant to those in zero tax brackets. This group includes some of the largest investors in the economy, such as pension funds, endowment funds, and trust funds.

There are some legal reasons for large institutions to favour high-dividend yields: First, institutions such as pension funds and trust funds are often set up to manage money for the benefit of others. The managers of such institutions have a *fiduciary responsibility* to invest the money prudently. It has been considered imprudent in courts of law to buy stock in companies with no established dividend record.

Second, institutions such as university endowment funds and trust funds are frequently prohibited from spending any of the principal. Such institutions might, therefore, prefer high-dividend yield stocks so they have some ability to spend. Like widows and orphans, this group thus prefers current income. Unlike widows and orphans, in terms of the amount of stock owned, this group is very large and its market share is expanding rapidly.

Conclusion

Overall, individual investors (for whatever reason) may have a desire for current income and may thus be willing to pay the dividend tax. In addition, some very large investors such as corporations and tax-free institutions may have a very strong preference for high-dividend payouts.

Concept Questions

1. Why might some individual investors favour a high-dividend payout?
2. Why might some non-individual investors prefer a high-dividend payout?

17.5 | A Resolution of Real-World Factors?

In the previous sections, we presented some factors that favour a low-dividend policy and others that favour high dividends. In this section, we discuss two important concepts related to dividends and dividend policy: the information content of dividends and the clientele effect. The first topic illustrates both the importance of dividends in general and the importance of distinguishing between dividends and dividend policy. The second topic suggests that, despite the many real-world considerations we have discussed, the dividend payout ratio may not be as important as we originally imagined.

---

[13] For preferred stock, we assume the issuer has elected to pay the refundable withholding tax on preferred dividends.

Information Content of Dividends

To begin, we quickly review some of our earlier discussion. Previously, we examined three different positions on dividends:

1. Based on the homemade dividend argument, dividend policy is irrelevant.
2. Because of tax effects for individual investors and new issues costs, a low-dividend policy is the best.
3. Because of the desire for current income and related factors, a high-dividend policy is the best.

If you wanted to decide which of these positions is the right one, an obvious way to get started would be to look at what happens to stock prices when companies announce dividend changes. You would find with some consistency that stock prices rise when the current dividend is unexpectedly increased, and they generally fall when the dividend is unexpectedly decreased. What does this imply about any of the three positions just stated?

At first glance, the behaviour we describe seems consistent with the third position and inconsistent with the other two. In fact, many writers have argued this. If stock prices rise on dividend increases and fall on dividend decreases, isn't the market saying it approves of higher dividends?

Other authors have pointed out that this observation doesn't really tell us much about dividend policy. Everyone agrees that dividends are important, all other things being equal. Companies only cut dividends with great reluctance. Thus, a dividend cut is often a signal that the firm is in trouble.

More to the point, a dividend cut is usually not a voluntary, planned change in dividend policy. Instead, it usually signals that management does not think the current dividend policy can be maintained. As a result, expectations of future dividends should generally be revised downward. The present value of expected future dividends falls and so does the stock price.

In this case, the stock price declines following a dividend cut because future dividends are generally lower, not because the firm changes the percentage of its earnings it will pay out in the form of dividends.

Dividend Signalling in Practice

To give a particularly dramatic example, consider what happened to Perpetual Energy Inc., a natural gas-focused Canadian Corporation, on October 19, 2011. A dramatic decrease in natural gas prices made it difficult for the company to continue dividend payment. This was shocking news to the shareholders and the share price lost about one-third of its market value in a single day at the time of announcement. Of course, the phenomenon of a stock price decrease in the face of a dividend cut is not restricted to Canada. In February 2011, bookseller Barnes and Noble announced that it was suspending its $1 per share annual dividend in order to invest in digital products. In response, the stock price declined by around 14 percent.

In a similar vein, an unexpected increase in the dividend or dividend initiation signals good news. Management raises the dividend only when future earnings, cash flow, and general prospects are expected to rise enough so that the dividend does not have to be cut later. A dividend increase is management's signal to the market that the firm is expected to do well. The stock reacts favourably because expectations of future dividends are revised upward, not because the firm has increased its payout. Since the firm has to come up with cash to pay dividends, this kind of signal is more convincing than calling a press conference to announce good earnings prospects. For example, Apple Inc. announced that it was planning to resume the payment of dividends in 2012, which was a stellar year for the company.

Management behaviour is consistent with the notion of dividend signalling. In 1989, for example, the Bank of Montreal's earnings per share dropped from $4.89 the previous year to $.04 due to increased loan loss provisions for LDC debt. Yet the annual dividend was increased slightly from $2.00 to $2.12 per share. The payout ratio skyrocketed to 5300 percent ($2.12/$.04). Management signalled the market that earnings would recover in 1990, which they did. Investors turned to the idea of dividend signalling when evaluating bank stocks in the crash of 2008 and early 2009. Discounting the fear of bank dividend cuts, in February 2009, Sherry Cooper, Chief Economist,

BMO Capital Markets noted that "aside from the National Bank, none of the other five Canadian banks have cut their dividend since the Great Depression."[14]

Generally, the stock price reacts to the dividend change. The reaction can be attributed to changes in the amount of future dividends, not necessarily a change in dividend payout policy. This signal is called the **information content effect** of the dividend. The fact that dividend changes convey information about the firm to the market makes it difficult to interpret the effect of dividend policy of the firm.

information content effect
The market's reaction to a change in corporate dividend payout.

The Clientele Effect

In our earlier discussion, we saw that some groups (wealthy individuals, for example) have an incentive to pursue low-payout (or zero-payout) stocks. Other groups (corporations, for example) have an incentive to pursue high-payout stocks. Companies with high payouts thus attract one group and low-payout companies attract another.

Table 17.1 shows the dividends paid by the 15 largest Canadian companies in terms of market capitalization. In April 2012, mining stocks such as Potash Corp. and oil and gas stocks like Suncor Energy paid low dividends. Banks and utilities paid relatively high dividends.

clientele effect
Stocks attract particular groups based on dividend yield and the resulting tax effects.

Groups of investors attracted to different payouts are called *clienteles*, and what we have described is a **clientele effect**. The clientele effect argument states that different groups of investors desire different levels of dividends. When a firm chooses a particular dividend policy, the only effect is to attract a particular clientele. If a firm changes its dividend policy, it just attracts a different clientele.

What we are left with is a simple supply and demand argument. Suppose that 40 percent of all investors prefer high dividends, but only 20 percent of the firms pay high dividends. Here the high-dividend firms are in short supply; thus, their stock prices rise. Consequently, low-dividend firms would find it advantageous to switch policies until 40 percent of all firms have high payouts. At this point, the *dividend market* is in equilibrium. Further changes in dividend policy are pointless because all of the clienteles are satisfied. The dividend policy for any individual firm is now irrelevant.

TABLE 17.1

Largest TSX companies by market capitalization and dividends for April 13, 2012

Rank	Company	Market cap ($ billion)	Dividend Yield (%)
1	Royal Bank of Canada	80.6	4.1
2	Toronto-Dominion Bank	74.2	3.5
3	Bank of Nova Scotia	61.5	4.1
4	Suncor Energy	47.5	1.4
5	Barrick Gold Corp.	41.5	1.4
6	Imperial Oil Ltd.	37.0	1.1
7	Bank of Montreal	36.9	4.9
8	Potash Corp. of Saskatchewan Inc.	36.7	1.3
9	Canadian Natural Resources Ltd.	35.1	1.3
10	Canadian National Railway Co	34.6	1.9
11	GoldCorp Inc.	33.8	1.3
12	BCE Inc.	30.7	5.5
13	Enbridge Inc.	30.2	2.9
14	Canadian Imperial Bank of Commerce	30.0	4.8
15	TransCanada Corp.	29.9	4.1

Source: Drawn from *Canadian Business*, Investor 500, 2012.

[14]National Post, February 2, 2009

To see if you understand the clientele effect, consider the following statement: "In spite of the theoretical argument that dividend policy is irrelevant or that firms should not pay dividends, many investors like high dividends. Because of this fact, a firm can boost its share price by having a higher dividend payout ratio." True or false?

The answer is false if clienteles exist. As long as enough high-dividend firms satisfy the dividend-loving investors, a firm won't be able to boost its share price by paying high dividends.

Concept Questions

1. How does the market react to unexpected dividend changes? What does this tell us about dividends? About dividend policy?
2. What is a dividend clientele? All things considered, would you expect a risky firm with significant but highly uncertain growth prospects to have a low- or high-dividend payout?

17.6 | Establishing a Dividend Policy

How do firms actually determine the level of dividends that they pay at a particular time? As we have seen, there are good reasons for firms to pay high dividends and there are good reasons to pay low dividends.

We know some things about how dividends are paid in practice. Firms don't like to cut dividends. We saw this with Bank of Montreal earlier. As Table 17.2 shows, two chartered banks, Bank of Montreal and Bank of Nova Scotia, have been paying dividends for over 170 years.

TABLE 17.2

Paying dividends

Stock	Year Dividend Payments Began
Bank of Montreal	1829
Bank of Nova Scotia	1833
Royal Bank	1870

In the next section, we discuss a particular dividend policy strategy. In doing so, we emphasize the real-world features of dividend policy. We also analyze an alternative to cash dividends, a stock repurchase.

Residual Dividend Approach

Earlier, we noted that firms with higher dividend payouts have to sell stock more often. As we have seen, such sales are not very common and they can be very expensive. Consistent with this, we assume that the firm wishes to minimize the need to sell new equity. We also assume that the firm wishes to maintain its current capital structure.[15]

If a firm wishes to avoid new equity sales, then it has to rely on internally generated equity to finance new, positive NPV projects.[16] Dividends can only be paid out of what is left over. This leftover is called the *residual*, and such a dividend policy would be called a **residual dividend approach**.

residual dividend approach
Policy where a firm pays dividends only after meeting its investment needs while maintaining a desired debt-to-equity ratio.

With a residual dividend policy, the firm's objective is to meet its investment needs and maintain its desired debt/equity ratio before paying dividends. To illustrate, imagine that a firm has $1,000 in earnings and a debt/equity ratio of .50. Notice that, since the debt/equity ratio is .50,

---

[15] As in our discussion of the cost of capital in Chapter 14, the capital structure should be measured using market value weights.

[16] Our discussion of sustainable growth in Chapter 4 is relevant here. We assumed there that a firm has a fixed capital structure, profit margin, and capital intensity. If the firm raises no new equity and wishes to grow at some target rate, there is only one payout ratio consistent with these assumptions.

the firm has 50 cents in debt for every \$1.50 in value. The firm's capital structure is thus 1/3 debt and 2/3 equity.

The first step in implementing a residual dividend policy is to determine the amount of funds that can be generated without selling new equity. If the firm reinvests the entire \$1,000 and pays no dividend, equity increases by \$1,000. To keep the debt/equity ratio at .50, the firm must borrow an additional \$500. The total amount of funds that can be generated without selling new equity is thus \$1,000 + 500 = \$1,500.

The second step is to decide whether or not a dividend will be paid. To do this, we compare the total amount that can be generated without selling new equity (\$1,500 in this case) with planned capital spending. If funds needed exceed funds available, no dividend is paid. In addition, the firm will have to sell new equity to raise the needed finance or else (more likely) postpone some planned capital spending.

If funds needed are less than funds generated, a dividend will be paid. The amount of the dividend is the residual, that is, that portion of the earnings not needed to finance new projects. For example, suppose we have \$900 in planned capital spending. To maintain the firm's capital structure, this \$900 must be financed 2/3 equity and 1/3 debt. So, the firm actually borrows 1/3 × \$900 = \$300. The firm spends 2/3 × \$900 = \$600 of the \$1,000 in equity available. There is a \$1,000 − 600 = \$400 residual, so the dividend is \$400.

In sum, the firm has after-tax earnings of \$1,000. Dividends paid are \$400. Retained earnings are \$600, and new borrowing totals \$300. The firm's debt/equity ratio is unchanged at .50.

The relationship between physical investment and dividend payout is presented for six different levels of investment in Table 17.3 and illustrated in Figure 17.4. The first three rows of the table can be discussed together, because in each case no dividends are paid.

FIGURE 17.4

Relationship between dividends and investment in residual dividend policy

This figure illustrates that a firm with many investment opportunities will pay small amounts of dividends and a firm with few investment opportunities will pay relatively large amounts of dividends.

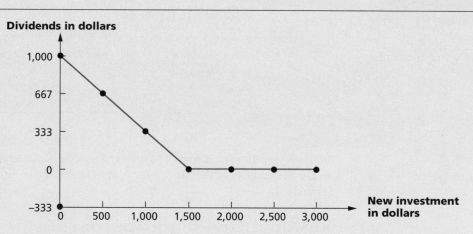

TABLE 17.3

Dividend policy under the residual approach

Row	(1) After tax Earnings	(2) New Investment	(3) Additional Debt	(4) Retained Earnings	(5) Additional Stock	(6) Dividends
1	\$1,000	\$3,000	\$1,000	\$1,000	\$1,000	\$0
2	1,000	2,000	667	1,000	333	0
3	1,000	1,500	500	1,000	0	0
4	1,000	1,000	333	667	0	333
5	1,000	500	167	333	0	667
6	1,000	0	0	0	0	1,000

In row 1, for example, note that new investment is $3,000. Additional debt of $1,000 and equity of $2,000 must be raised to keep the debt/equity ratio constant. Since this latter figure is greater than the $1,000 of earnings, all earnings are retained. Additional stock to be raised is also $1,000. In this example, since new stock is issued, dividends are not simultaneously paid out.

In rows 2 and 3, investment drops. Additional debt needed goes down as well since it is equal to 1/3 of investment. Because the amount of new equity needed is still greater than or equal to $1,000, all earnings are retained and no dividends are paid.

We finally find a situation in row 4 where a dividend is paid. Here, total investment is $1,000. To keep our debt/equity ratio constant, 1/3 of this investment, or $333, is financed by debt. The remaining 2/3 or $667, comes from internal funds, implying that the residual is $1,000 − 667 = $333. The dividend is equal to this $333 residual.

In this case, note that no additional stock is issued. Since the needed investment is even lower in rows 5 and 6, new debt is reduced further, retained earnings drop, and dividends increase. Again, no additional stock is issued.

Given our discussion, we expect those firms with many investment opportunities to pay a small percentage of their earnings as dividends and other firms with fewer opportunities to pay a high percentage of their earnings as dividends. Young, fast-growing firms commonly employ a low payout ratio, whereas older, slower-growing firms in more mature industries use a higher ratio. This pattern is consistent with firms' practice in the U.S. and Canada.[17]

We see this pattern somewhat in Table 17.4 where the Bank of Montreal is a slower-growing firm with a high payout; Canadian Tire is a faster-growing firm with a pattern of low payouts. Bank of Montreal had a steady payout in most of the years, but the payout increased to 91 percent on one occasion in 2009. This illustrates that firms will sometimes accept a significantly different payout ratio in order to avoid dividend cuts. In the case of Bank of Montreal, the change was driven by a drop in EPS in 2009 (due to the financial crisis in the U.S.).

TABLE 17.4

The stability of dividends

	Bank of Montreal				Canadian Tire		
	EPS	DPS	Payout		EPS	DPS	Payout
2000	3.30	1.00	30	2000	1.89	0.40	21
2001	2.72	1.12	41	2001	2.25	0.40	18
2002	2.73	1.20	44	2002	2.56	0.40	16
2003	3.51	1.34	38	2003	3.06	0.40	13
2004	4.53	1.59	35	2004	3.60	0.475	13
2005	4.74	1.85	39	2005	4.04	0.56	14
2006	5.25	2.26	43	2006	4.35	0.66	15
2007	4.18	2.71	65	2007	5.05	0.74	15
2008	3.79	2.80	74	2008	4.59	0.84	18
2009	3.09	2.80	91	2009	4.10	0.84	20
2010	4.78	2.80	59	2010	5.45	0.91	17
2011	5.28	2.80	53	2011	5.73	1.13	20

Source: Annual reports from sedar.com

Dividend Stability

The key point of the residual dividend approach is that dividends are paid only after all profitable investment opportunities are exhausted. Of course, a strict residual approach might lead to a very unstable dividend policy. If investment opportunities in one period are quite high, dividends would be low or zero. Conversely, dividends might be high in the next period if investment opportunities are considered less promising.

---

[17] Current research shows that in many other countries where shareholders have weaker legal rights, dividends are not linked to firm growth. Rather, they are seen as a way of prying wealth loose from the hands of controlling shareholders: R. LaPorta, F. Lopez-de-Silanes, A. Schleifer, and R.W. Vishny, "Agency Problems and Dividend Policies Around the World," *Journal of Finance* 2000.

Consider the case of Big Department Stores Inc., a retailer whose annual earnings are forecasted to be equal from year to year but whose quarterly earnings change throughout the year. They are low in each year's first quarter because of the post-Christmas business slump. Although earnings increase only slightly in the second and third quarters, they advance greatly in the fourth quarter as a result of the Christmas season. A graph of this firm's earnings is presented in Figure 17.5.

FIGURE 17.5

Earnings for Big Department Stores Inc.

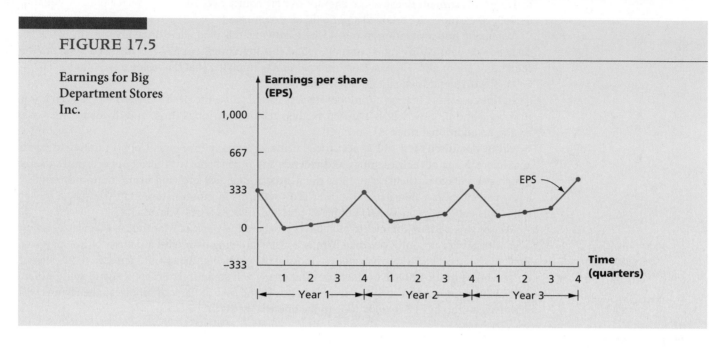

The firm can choose between at least two types of dividend policies. First, each quarter's dividend can be a fixed fraction of that quarter's earnings. Here, dividends vary throughout the year. This is a cyclical dividend policy. Second, each quarter's dividend can be a fixed fraction of yearly earnings, implying that all dividend payments would be equal. This is a stable dividend policy. These two types of dividend policies are displayed in Figure 17.6.

FIGURE 17.6

Alternative dividend policies for Big Department Stores Inc.

Cyclical dividend policy: Dividends are a constant proportion of earnings at each pay date. Stable dividend policy: Dividends are a constant proportion of earnings over an earnings cycle.

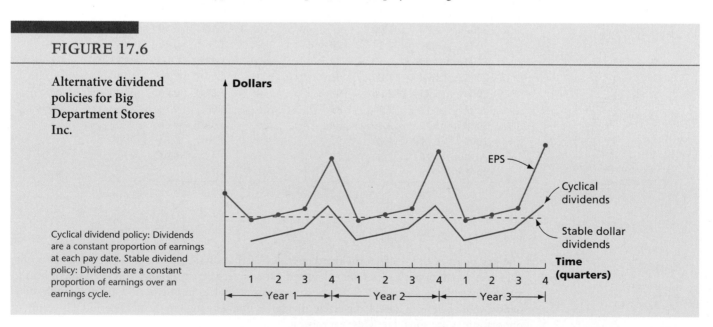

Corporate executives generally agree that a stable policy is in the interest of the firm and its shareholders. Dividend stability complements investor objectives of information content, income, and reduction in uncertainty. Institutional investors often follow "prudence" tests that restrict investment in firms that do not pay regular dividends. For all these reasons a stable dividend policy is common. For example, looking back at Table 17.4, the dividends paid by these large Canadian firms are much less volatile through time than their earnings.

The dividend policy might also depend on the class of shares. For example, in case of dual class shares the different classes of shareholders have different voting rights and dividend payments.

A Compromise Dividend Policy

In practice, many firms appear to follow what amounts to a compromise dividend policy. Such a policy is based on five main goals:

1. Avoid cutting back on positive NPV projects to pay a dividend.
2. Avoid dividend cuts.
3. Avoid the need to sell equity.
4. Maintain a target debt/equity ratio.
5. Maintain a target dividend payout ratio.

These goals are ranked more or less in order of their importance. In our strict residual approach, we assumed that the firm maintained a fixed debt/equity ratio. Under the compromise approach, that debt/equity ratio is viewed as a long-range goal. It is allowed to vary in the short run if necessary to avoid a dividend cut or the need to sell new equity.

target payout ratio
A firm's long-term desired dividend-to-earnings ratio.

In addition to a strong reluctance to cut dividends, financial managers tend to think of dividend payments in terms of a proportion of income, and they also tend to think investors are entitled to a "fair" share of corporate income. This share is the long-run **target payout ratio**, and it is the fraction of the earnings that the firm expects to pay as dividends under ordinary circumstances. Again, this is viewed as a long-range goal, so it might vary in the short run if needed. As a result, in the long run, earnings growth is followed by dividend increases, but only with a lag.

One can minimize the problems of dividend instability by creating two types of dividends: regular and extra. For companies using this approach, the regular dividend would likely be a relatively small fraction of permanent earnings, so that it could be sustained easily. Extra dividends would be granted when an increase in earnings was expected to be temporary.

Since investors look on an extra dividend as a bonus, there is relatively little disappointment when an extra dividend is not repeated.

Some Survey Evidence on Dividends

A recent study surveyed a large number of Canadian financial executives regarding dividend policy. Table 17.5 shows the top 5 factors influencing dividend policy.

As shown in Table 17.5, financial managers are highly disinclined to cut dividends. Moreover, they are very conscious of their previous dividends and desire to maintain a relatively steady dividend. In contrast, concerns about dividends affecting the firm's stock price are somewhat less important.

TABLE 17.5

Factors influencing dividend policy of Canadian financial firms

Factor	Moderate or High Level of Importance (%)
1. Stability of earnings	95.7
2. Pattern of past dividends	95.7
3. Level of current earnings	87.0
4. Level of expected future earnings	82.6
5. Concern about affecting the stock price	47.8

Source: Adapted from Table 2 of Baker, H.K., Dutta, S., And Saadi, S. (2008), "How Managers Of Financial Versus Non-Financial Firms View Dividends: The Canadian Evidence", *Global Finance Journal*, 19, pp. 171–186.

Table 17.6 is drawn from the same survey, but here the responses address the top five reasons for Canadian financial firms paying dividends Not surprisingly given the responses in Table 17.5 and our earlier discussion, the highest priority is maintaining a consistent dividend policy. The next several items are also consistent with our previous analysis. Financial managers are very concerned about earnings stability and future earnings levels in making dividend decisions, and they consider the availability of good investment opportunities. Survey respondents also believed that firm should disclose to investors its reasons for changing the cash dividend.

In contrast to our discussion in the earlier part of this chapter on taxes and flotation costs, the Canadian. financial managers in this survey did not think that personal taxes paid on dividends by shareholders are very important.

TABLE 17.6

Explanation for paying dividends: Canadian financial firms

Policy Statements	Percent Who Agree or Strongly Agree (%)
1. A firm should strive to maintain an uninterrupted record of dividend payments.	96.0
2. Investors generally regard dividend changes as signals about a firm's future prospects.	95.1
3. A firm should adequately disclose to investors its reasons for changing its cash dividend.	91.3
4. A firm's stock price generally falls when the firm unexpectedly decreases its dividend.	90.9
5. A firm's stock price generally rises when the firm unexpectedly increases its dividend.	87.0

Source: Adapted from Table 3 and Table 4 of Baker, H.K., Dutta, S., and Saadi, S. (2008), "How Managers of Financial versus Non-Financial Firms View Dividends: The Canadian Evidence", *Global Finance Journal*, 19, pp. 171–186.

Concept Questions

1. What is a residual dividend policy?
2. What is the chief drawback to a strict residual policy? What do many firms do in practice?

17.7 | Stock Repurchase: An Alternative to Cash Dividends

repurchase
Another method used to pay out a firm's earnings to its owners, which provides more preferable tax treatment than dividends.

When a firm wants to pay cash to its shareholders, it normally pays a cash dividend. Another way is to **repurchase** its own shares. Over recent years, share repurchase has grown in importance relative to dividends. Consider Figure 17.7, which shows the dividends and share repurchases for Canadian firms over the years from 1987 to 2008. As can be seen, the ratio of repurchases to earnings was far less than the ratio of dividends to earnings in the early years.

Following the market crash of 2008 and early 2009, the number of Canadian companies announcing share repurchases increased. For example, in February 2012, Tim Hortons announced a program to repurchase $200 million in shares. Also, in December 2011, Air Canada. announced a stock repurchase program, to increase the value of its shares, which were depressed due to ongoing labour talks, economic uncertainty, and dwindling growth prospects.

Cash Dividends versus Repurchase

Imagine an all-equity company with excess cash of $300,000. The firm pays no dividends, and its net income for the year just ended is $49,000. The market value statement of financial position at the end of the year is represented below.

Market Value Statement of Financial Position (before paying out excess cash)

Excess cash	$ 300,000	$ 0	Debt
Other assets	700,000	1,000,000	Equity
Total	$1,000,000	$1,000,000	

FIGURE 17.7

Dividends and Share
Repurchases of
Canadian firms:
1987–2008

Figure 5 of Mitchell, Chris,
"Essays on Capital Gains,
Household Consumption and
Corporate Payout Policy"
(2012). *Electronic Thesis and
Dissertation Repository*. Paper
687. ir.lib.uwo.ca/etd/687
Repurchase data covering the
years 1987–2000 provided by
McNally, William J. and Brian
F. Smith. "Long-Run Returns
Following Open Market Share
Repurchases." 2007. *Journal
of Banking and Finance*. Vol.
31, Issue 3, 703–717.

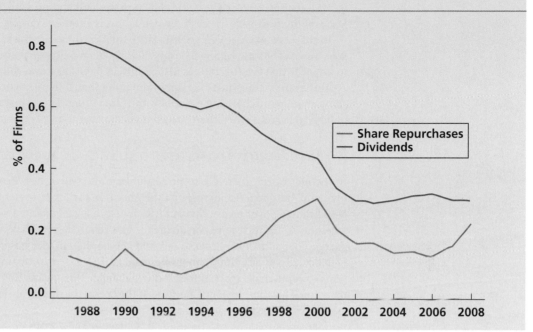

There are 100,000 shares outstanding. The total market value of the equity is $1 million, so the stock sells for $10 per share. Earnings per share (EPS) were $49,000/100,000 = $.49, and the price/earnings ratio (P/E) is $10/$.49 = 20.4.

One option the company is considering is a $300,000/100,000 = $3 per share extra cash dividend. Alternatively, the company is thinking of using the money to repurchase $300,000/$10 = 30,000 shares of stock.

If commissions, taxes, and other imperfections are ignored in our example, the shareholders shouldn't care which option is chosen. Does this seem surprising? It shouldn't, really. What is happening here is that the firm is paying out $300,000 in cash. The new statement of financial position is represented below.

Market Value Statement of Financial Position
(after paying out excess cash as dividends)

Excess cash	$ 0	$ 0	Debt
Other assets	700,000	700,000	Equity
Total	$ 700,000	$ 700,000	

If the cash is paid out as a dividend, there are still 100,000 shares outstanding, so each is worth $7.

The fact that the per-share value fell from $10 to $7 isn't a cause for concern. Consider a shareholder who owns 100 shares. At $10 per share before the dividend, the total value is $1,000.

After the $3 dividend, this same shareholder has 100 shares worth $7 each, for a total of $700, plus 100 × $3 = $300 in cash, for a combined total of $1,000. This just illustrates what we saw earlier: A cash dividend doesn't affect a shareholder's wealth if there are no imperfections. In this case, the stock price simply fell by $3 when the stock went ex dividend.

Also, since total earnings and the number of shares outstanding haven't changed, EPS is still 49 cents. The price/earnings ratio (P/E), however, falls to $7/.49 = 14.3. Why we are looking at accounting earnings and P/E ratios will be apparent just below.

Alternatively, if the company repurchases 30,000 shares, there will be 70,000 left outstanding. The statement of financial position looks the same.

Market Value Statement of Financial Position
(after paying out excess cash as stock repurchase)

Excess cash	$ 0	$ 0	Debt
Other assets	700,000	700,000	Equity
Total	$ 700,000	$ 700,000	

The company is worth $700,000 again, so each remaining share is worth $700,000/70,000 = $10 each. Our shareholder with 100 shares is obviously unaffected. For example, if the shareholder were so inclined, he or she could sell 30 shares and end up with $300 in cash and $700 in stock, just as if the firm pays the cash dividend. This is another example of a homemade dividend.

In this second case, EPS goes up since total earnings are the same while the number of shares goes down. The new EPS will be $49,000/70,000 = $.70 per share. However, the important thing to notice is that the P/E ratio is $10/$.70 = 14.3, just as it was following the dividend.

This example illustrates the important point that, if there are no imperfections, a cash dividend and a share repurchase are essentially the same thing. This is just another illustration of dividend policy irrelevance when there are no taxes or other imperfections.

Real-World Considerations in a Repurchase

In the real world, there are some accounting differences between a share repurchase and a cash dividend, but the most important difference is in the tax treatment. A repurchase has a significant tax advantage over a cash dividend. A dividend is taxed, and a shareholder has no choice about whether or not to receive the dividend. In a repurchase, a shareholder pays taxes only if (1) the shareholder actually chooses to sell, and (2) the shareholder has a taxable capital gain on the sale.

Normally, at any time, about one-third of TSX listed companies have announced their intentions to repurchase stock through the exchange. This means they plan to buy up to 5 percent of their stock for their treasury. Because of the favourable tax treatment of capital gains, a repurchase is a very sensible alternative to an extra dividend.

Share repurchases can be used to achieve other corporate goals such as altering the firm's capital structure or as a takeover defence. Many firms repurchase shares because management believes the stock is undervalued. This reason for repurchasing is controversial because it contradicts the efficient market hypothesis. However, there is considerable evidence that firms repurchasing shares do experience an increase in shareholder return.[18]

Share Repurchase and EPS

You may read in the popular financial press that a share repurchase is beneficial because earnings per share increase. As we have seen, this will happen. The reason is simply that a share repurchase reduces the number of outstanding shares, but it has no effect on total earnings. As a result, EPS rises.

However, the financial press may place undue emphasis on EPS figures in a repurchase agreement. In our example above, we saw that the value of the stock wasn't affected by the EPS change. In fact, the price/earnings ratio was exactly the same when we compared a cash dividend to a repurchase.

Since the increase in earnings per share is exactly tracked by the increase in the price per share, there is no net effect. Put another way, the increase in EPS is just an accounting adjustment that reflects (correctly) the change in the number of shares outstanding.

In the real world, to the extent that repurchases benefit the firm, we would argue that they do so primarily because of the tax considerations we discussed above.

Concept Questions

1. Why might a stock repurchase make more sense than an extra cash dividend?
2. Why don't all firms use stock repurchases instead of cash dividends?

17.8 | Stock Dividends and Stock Splits

stock dividend
Payment made by a firm to its owners in the form of stock, diluting the value of each share outstanding.

Another type of dividend is paid out in shares of stock. This type of dividend is called a **stock dividend**. A stock dividend is not a true dividend because it is not paid in cash. The effect of a stock

---

[18] This evidence is in: D. Ikenberry, J. Lakonishok, and T. Vermaelen, "Stock Repurchases in Canada: Performance and Strategic Trading," *Journal of Finance,* October 2000. For a contradictory view, see K. Li and W. McNally, "Information Signalling or Agency Conflicts: What Explains Canadian Open Market Share Repurchases?" *Working Paper,* Wilfrid Laurier University, March 2000.

dividend is to increase the number of shares that each owner holds. Since there are more shares outstanding, each is simply worth less.

A stock dividend is commonly expressed as a percentage; for example, a 20 percent stock dividend means that a shareholder receives one new share for every five currently owned (a 20 percent increase). Since every shareholder owns 20 percent more stock, the total number of shares outstanding rises by 20 percent. As we see in a moment, the result would be that each share of stock is worth about 20 percent less.

A **stock split** is essentially the same thing as a stock dividend, except that a split is expressed as a ratio instead of a percentage. When a split is declared, each share is split to create additional shares. For example, Coca-Cola stock split two-for-one in 2012 and each old share was split into two new shares.

stock split
An increase in a firm's shares outstanding without any change in owner's equity.

Some Details on Stock Splits and Stock Dividends

Stock splits and stock dividends have essentially the same impacts on the corporation: They increase the number of shares outstanding and reduce the value per share. Also, both options will have a similar impact on future cash dividends. When stocks split, the cash dividend per share is reduced accordingly. The accounting treatment is not the same, however. Under TSX rules, the maximum stock dividend is 25 percent, anything larger is considered a stock split. Further, stock dividends are taxable, but stock splits are not.

EXAMPLE OF A STOCK DIVIDEND   The Peterson Company, a consulting firm specializing in difficult accounting problems, has 10,000 shares of stock, each selling at $66. The total market value of the equity is $66 × 10,000 = $660,000. With a 10 percent stock dividend, each shareholder receives one additional share for each 10 presently owned, and the total number of shares outstanding after the dividend is 11,000.

Before the stock dividend, the equity portion of Peterson's statement of financial position might look like this:

Common stock (10,000 shares outstanding)	$210,000
Retained earnings	290,000
Total owners' equity	$500,000

The amount of the stock dividend is transferred from retained earnings to common stock. Since 1000 new shares are issued, the common stock account is increased by $66,000 (1000 shares at $66 each). Total owners' equity is unaffected by the stock dividend because no cash has come in or out, so retained earnings is reduced by the entire $66,000. The net effect of these machinations is that Peterson's equity accounts now look like this:

Common stock (11,000 shares outstanding)	$276,000
Retained earnings	224,000
Total owners' equity	$500,000

EXAMPLE OF A STOCK SPLIT   A stock split is conceptually similar to a stock dividend, but it is commonly expressed as a ratio. For example, in a three-for-two split, each shareholder receives one additional share of stock for each two held originally, so a three-for-two split amounts to a 50 percent stock dividend. Again, no cash is paid out, and the percentage of the entire firm that each shareholder owns is unaffected.

The accounting treatment of a stock split is a little different (and simpler) from that of a stock dividend. Suppose Peterson decides to declare a two-for-one stock split. The number of shares outstanding doubles to 20,000. The owner's equity after the split is the same as before the split except the new number of shares is noted.

Common stock (20,000 shares outstanding)	$210,000
Retained earnings	290,000
Total owners' equity	$500,000

Value of Stock Splits and Stock Dividends

The laws of logic tell us that stock splits and stock dividends can (1) leave the value of the firm unaffected, (2) increase its value, or (3) decrease its value. Unfortunately, the issues are complex enough that one cannot easily determine which of the three relationships holds.

THE BENCHMARK CASE   A strong case can be made that stock dividends and splits do not change either the wealth of any shareholder or the wealth of the firm as a whole. In our prior example, the equity was worth a total of $660,000. With the stock dividend, the number of shares increased to 11,000, so it seems that each would be worth $660,000/11,000 = $60.

For example, a shareholder who had 100 shares worth $66 each before the dividend would have 110 shares worth $60 each afterwards. The total value of the stock is $6,600 either way; so the stock dividend doesn't really have any economic affect.

With the stock split, there were 20,000 shares outstanding, so each should be worth $660,000/20,000 = $33. In other words, the number of shares doubles and the price halves. From these calculations, it appears that stock dividends and splits are just paper transactions.

Although these results are relatively obvious, there are reasons that are often given to suggest that there may be some benefits to these actions. The typical financial manager is aware of many real-world complexities, and, for that reason, the stock split or stock dividend decision is not treated lightly in practice.

trading range
Price range between highest and lowest prices at which a stock is traded.

TRADING RANGE   Proponents of stock dividends and stock splits frequently argue that a security has a proper **trading range**. When the security is priced above this level, many investors do not have the funds to buy the common trading unit called a *round lot* (*usually 100 shares*).

Although this argument is a popular one, its validity is questionable for a number of reasons. Mutual funds, pension funds, and other institutions have steadily increased their trading activity since World War II and now handle a sizeable percentage of total trading volume (over half of the trading volume on both the TSX and NYSE). Because these institutions buy and sell in huge amounts, the individual share price is of little concern. Furthermore, we sometimes observe share prices that are quite large without appearing to cause problems.

Finally, there is evidence that stock splits may actually decrease the liquidity of the company's shares. Following a two-for-one split, the number of shares traded should more than double if liquidity is increased by the split. This doesn't appear to happen, and the reverse is sometimes observed.

Regardless of the impact on liquidity, firms do split their stock. Some managers believe that keeping the share price within a range attractive to individual investors helps promote Canadian ownership.

Reverse Splits

reverse split
Procedure where a firm's number of shares outstanding is reduced.

A less frequently encountered financial maneuver is the **reverse split**. In a one-for-three reverse split, each investor exchanges three old shares for one new share. As mentioned previously with reference to stock splits and stock dividends, a case can be made that a reverse split changes nothing substantial about the company.

Given real-world imperfections, three related reasons are cited for reverse splits. First, transaction costs to shareholders may be less after the reverse split. Second, the liquidity and marketability of a company's stock might be improved when its price is raised to the popular trading range. Third, stocks selling below a certain level are not considered respectable, meaning that investors underestimate these firms' earnings, cash flow, growth, and stability. Some financial analysts argue that a reverse split can achieve instant respectability. As with stock splits, none of these reasons is particularly compelling, especially the third one.

There are two other reasons for reverse splits. First, stock exchanges have minimum price per share requirements. A reverse split may bring the stock price up to such a minimum. Second, companies sometimes perform reverse splits and, at the same time, buy out any shareholders who end up with less than a certain number of shares. This second tactic can be abusive if used to force out minority shareholders.

In the aftermath of the tech bubble, a number of technology firms made the decision to undertake reverse splits. More recently, in 2009, Domtar Corporation, the Montreal-based largest integrated producer of uncoated free sheet paper in North America, underwent a reverse stock split at a 1-for-12 ratio. Domtar management cited two reasons for undertaking a reverse split—to return the company's share price to a level similar to that of other widely owned companies and to attract a broader range of institutional investors.

17.9 | SUMMARY AND CONCLUSIONS

In this chapter, we discussed the types of dividends and how they are paid. We then defined dividend policy and examined whether or not dividend policy matters. Finally, we illustrated how a firm might establish a dividend policy and described an important alternative to cash dividends, a share repurchase.

In covering these subjects, we saw that:

1. Dividend policy is irrelevant when there are no taxes or other imperfections because shareholders can effectively undo the firm's dividend strategy. A shareholder who receives a dividend greater than desired can reinvest the excess. Conversely, the shareholder who receives a dividend that is smaller than desired can sell extra shares of stock.

2. Individual shareholder income taxes and new issue flotation costs are real-world considerations that favour a low-dividend payout. With taxes and new issue costs, the firm should pay out dividends only after all positive NPV projects have been fully financed.

3. There are groups in the economy that may favour a high payout. These include many large institutions such as pension plans. Recognizing that some groups prefer a high payout and some prefer a low payout, the clientele effect supports the idea that dividend policy responds to the needs of shareholders. For example, if 40 percent of the shareholders prefer low dividends and 60 percent of the shareholders prefer high dividends, approximately 40 percent of companies will have a low-dividend payout, while 60 percent will have a high payout. This sharply reduces the impact of any individual firm's dividend policy on its market price.

4. A firm wishing to pursue a strict residual dividend payout will have an unstable dividend. Dividend stability is usually viewed as highly desirable. We therefore discussed a compromise strategy that provides for a stable dividend and appears to be quite similar to the dividend policies many firms follow in practice.

5. A stock repurchase acts much like a cash dividend, but can have a significant tax advantage. Stock repurchases are therefore a very useful part of over-all dividend policy.

To close our discussion of dividends, we emphasize one last time the difference between dividends and dividend policy. Dividends are important, because the value of a share of stock is ultimately determined by the dividends that are paid. What is less clear is whether or not the time pattern of dividends (more now versus more later) matters. This is the dividend policy question, and it is not easy to give a definitive answer to it.

Key Terms

clientele effect (page 502)
date of payment (page 492)
date of record (page 492)
declaration date (page 492)
distribution (page 491)
dividend (page 491)
ex-dividend date (page 492)
homemade dividends (page 495)
information content effect (page 502)
regular cash dividend (page 491)

repurchase (page 508)
residual dividend approach (page 503)
reverse split (page 512)
stock dividend (page 510)
stock split (page 511)
stripped common shares (page 495)
target payout ratio (page 507)
trading range (page 512)

Chapter Review Problems and Self-Test

17.1   **Residual Dividend Policy** The Rapscallion Corporation practices a strict residual dividend policy and maintains a capital structure of 40 percent debt, 60 percent equity. Earnings for the year are $2,500. What is the maximum amount of capital spending possible without new equity? Suppose that planned investment outlays for the coming year are $3,000. Will Rapscallion be paying a dividend? If so, how much?

17.2   **Repurchase versus Cash Dividend** Trantor Corporation is deciding whether to pay out $300 in excess cash in the form of an extra dividend or a share repurchase. Current earnings are $1.50 per share and the stock sells for $15. The market value statement of financial position before paying out the $300 is as follows:

Statement of Financial Position (before paying out excess cash)			
Excess cash	$ 300	$ 400	Debt
Other assets	1,600	1,500	Equity
Total	$1,900	$1,900	

Evaluate the two alternatives for the effect on the price per share of the stock, the EPS, and the P/E ratio.

Answers to Self-Test Problems

17.1   Rapscallion has a debt/equity ratio of .40/.60 = 2/3. If the entire $2,500 in earnings were reinvested, $2,500 × 2/3 = $1,667 in new borrowing would be needed to keep the debt/equity unchanged. Total new financing possible without external equity is thus $2,500 + 1,667 = $4,167.

If planned outlays are $3,000, this amount can be financed 60 percent with equity. The needed equity is thus $3,000 × .60 = $1,800. This is less than the $2,500 in earnings, so a dividend of $2,500 − 1,800 = $700 would be paid.

17.2   The market value of the equity is $1,500. The price per share is $15, so there are 100 shares outstanding. The cash dividend would amount to $300/100 = $3 per share. When the stock goes ex dividend, the price drops by $3 per share to $12. Put another way, the total assets decrease by $300, so the equity value goes down by this amount to $1,200. With 100 shares, this is $12 per share. After the dividend, EPS is the same, $1.50, but the P/E ratio is $12/1.50 = 8 times.

With a repurchase, $300/15 = 20 shares would be bought up, leaving 80. The equity again is worth $1,200 total. With 80 shares, this is $1,200/80 = $15 per share, so the price doesn't change. Total earnings for Trantor must be $1.5 × 100 = $150. After the repurchase, EPS is higher at $150/80 = $1.875. The P/E ratio, however, is still $15/1.875 = 8 times.

Concepts Review and Critical Thinking Questions

1.   **(LO2)** How is it possible that dividends are so important, but, at the same time, dividend policy could be irrelevant?

2.   **(LO4)** What is the impact of a stock repurchase on a company's debt ratio? Does this suggest another use for excess cash?

3.   **(LO2)** What is the chief drawback to a strict residual dividend policy? Why is this a problem? How does a compromise policy work? How does it differ from a strict residual policy?

4.   **(LO1)** On Tuesday, December 8, Hometown Power Co.'s board of directors declares a dividend of 75 cents per share payable on Wednesday, January 17, to shareholders of record as of Wednesday, January 3. When is the ex-dividend date? If a shareholder buys stock before that date, who gets the dividends on those shares, the buyer or the seller?

5.   **(LO1)** Some corporations, like one British company that offers its large shareholders free crematorium use, pay dividends in kind (that is, offer their services to shareholders at below-market cost). Should mutual funds invest in stocks that pay these dividends in kind? (The fundholders do not receive these services.)

6.   **(LO2)** If increases in dividends tend to be followed by (immediate) increases in share prices, how can it be said that dividend policy is irrelevant?

7.   **(LO2)** Last month, East Coast Power Company, which had been having trouble with cost overruns on a nuclear power plant that it had been building, announced that it was "temporarily suspending payments due to the cash flow crunch associated with its investment program." The company's stock price dropped from $28.50 to $25 when this announcement was made. How would you interpret this change in the stock price (that is, what would you say caused it)?

8.   **(LO2)** The DRK Corporation has recently developed a dividend reinvestment plan, or DRIP. The plan allows investors to reinvest cash dividends automatically in DRK in exchange for new shares of stock. Over time, investors in DRK will be able to build their holdings by reinvesting dividends to purchase additional shares of the company.

Over 1000 companies offer dividend reinvestment plans. Most companies with DRIPs charge no brokerage or service fees. In fact, the shares of DRK will be purchased at a 10 percent discount from the market price. A consultant for DRK estimates that about 75 percent of DRK's shareholders will take part in this plan. This is somewhat higher than the average.

Evaluate DRK's dividend reinvestment plan. Will it increase shareholder wealth? Discuss the advantages and disadvantages involved here.

9.   **(LO2)** For initial public offerings of common stock, 1993 was a very big year, with over $43 billion raised by the process. Relatively few of the firms involved paid cash dividends. Why do you think that most chose not to pay cash dividends?

10.   **(LO2)** York University pays no taxes on its capital gains or on its dividend income and interest income. Would it be irrational to find low-dividend, high-growth stocks in its portfolio? Would it be irrational to find preferred shares in its portfolio? Explain.

Questions and Problems

Basic
(Questions
1–13)

1. Dividends and Taxes (LO2) Pandosy Inc. has declared a $5.10 per share dividend. Suppose capital gains are not taxed, but dividends are taxed at 15 percent. Pandosy sells for $93.85 per share, and the stock is about to go ex dividend. What do you think the ex-dividend price will be?

2. Stock Dividends (LO3) The owners' equity accounts for Okanagan International are shown here:

Common stock ($1 par value)	$ 20,000
Capital Surplus	285,000
Retained earnings	638,120
Total owners' equity	$943,120

a. If Okanagan stock currently sells for $30 per share and a 10 percent stock dividend is declared, how many new shares will be distributed? Show how the equity accounts would change.

b. If Okanagan declared a 25 percent stock dividend, how would the accounts change?

3. Stock Splits (LO3) For the company in Problem 2, show how the equity accounts will change if:

a. Okanagan declares a four-for-one stock split. How many shares are outstanding now?

b. Okanagan declares a one-for-five reverse stock split. How many shares are outstanding now?

4. Stock Splits and Stock Dividends (LO3) Mill Creek Corporation (MCC) currently has 425,000 shares of stock outstanding that sell for $80 per share. Assuming no market imperfections or tax effects exist, what will the share price be after:

a. MCC has a five-for-three stock split?

b. MCC has a 15 percent stock dividend?

c. MCC has a 42.5 percent stock dividend?

d. MCC has a four-for-seven reverse stock split?

Determine the new number of shares outstanding in parts (a) through (d).

5. Regular Dividends (LO1) The statement of financial position for Knox Corp. is shown here in market value terms. There are 9,000 shares of stock outstanding.

Market Value Statement of Financial Position

Cash	$ 43,700	Equity	$353,700
Fixed assets	310,000		
Total	$353,700	Total	$353,700

The company has declared a dividend of $1.40 per share. The stock goes ex dividend tomorrow. Ignoring any tax effects, what is the stock selling for today? What will it sell for tomorrow? What will the statement of financial position look like after the dividends are paid?

6. Share Repurchase (LO4) In the previous problem, suppose Knox has announced it is going to repurchase $12,600 worth of stock. What effect will this transaction have on the equity of the firm? How many shares will be outstanding? What will the price per share be after the repurchase? Ignoring tax effects, show how the share repurchase is effectively the same as a cash dividend.

7. Stock Dividends (LO3) The market value statement of financial position for McKinley Manufacturing is shown here. McKinley has declared a 25 percent stock dividend. The stock goes ex dividend tomorrow (the chronology for a stock dividend is similar to that for a cash dividend). There are 14,000 shares of stock outstanding. What will the ex-dividend price be?

Market Value Statement of Financial Position

Cash	$ 86,000	Debt	$145,000
Fixed assets	630,000	Equity	571,000
Total	$716,000	Total	$716,000

8. Stock Dividends (LO3) The company with the common equity accounts shown here has declared a 15 percent stock dividend when the market value of its stock is $43 per share. What effects on the equity accounts will the distribution of the stock dividend have?

Common stock ($1 par value)	$ 385,000
Capital surplus	846,000
Retained earnings	3,720,000
Total owners' equity	$4,951,000

9. Stock Splits (LO3) In the previous problem, suppose the company instead decides on a four-for-one stock split. The firm's 75-cent per share cash dividend on the new (post-split) shares represents an increase of 10 percent over last year's dividend on the presplit stock. What effect does this have on the equity accounts? What was last year's dividend per share?

10. Residual Dividend Policy (LO2) Crawford Inc., a litter recycling company, uses a residual dividend policy. A debt-equity ratio of 1.0 is considered optimal. Earnings for the period just ended were $1,400, and a dividend of $420 was declared. How much in new debt was borrowed? What were total capital outlays?

11. Residual Dividend Policy (LO2) Rutland Corporation has declared an annual dividend of $0.50 per share. For the year just ended, earnings were $8 per share.

    a. What is Rutland's payout ratio?

    b. Suppose Rutland has seven million shares outstanding. Borrowing for the coming year is planned at $14 million. What are planned investment outlays assuming a residual dividend policy? What target capital structure is implicit in these calculations?

12. Residual Dividend Policy (LO2) Summerland Corporation follows a strict residual dividend policy. Its debt-equity ratio is 1.5.

    a. If earnings for the year are $145,000, what is the maximum amount of capital spending possible with no new equity?

    b. If planned investment outlays for the coming year are $790,000, will Summerland pay a dividend? If so, how much?

    c. Does Summerland maintain a constant dividend payout? Why or why not?

13. Residual Dividend Policy (LO2) Penticton Rock (PR) Inc. predicts that earnings in the coming year will be $54 million. There are 19 million shares, and PR maintains a debt-equity ratio of 1.2.

    a. Calculate the maximum investment funds available without issuing new equity and the increase in borrowing that goes along with it.

    b. Suppose the firm uses a residual dividend policy. Planned capital expenditures total $74 million. Based on this information, what will the dividend per share be?

    c. In part (*b*), how much borrowing will take place? What is the addition to retained earnings?

    d. Suppose PR plans no capital outlays for the coming year. What will the dividend be under a residual policy? What will new borrowing be?

Intermediate **14. Homemade Dividends (LO2)** You own 1000 shares of stock in Armstrong Corporation. You will receive a $1.85 per share
(Questions dividend in one year. In two years, Armstrong will pay a liquidating dividend of $58 per share. The required return on
14–16) Armstrong stock is 15 percent. What is the current share price of your stock (ignoring taxes)? If you would rather have equal dividends in each of the next two years, show how you can accomplish this by creating homemade dividends. *Hint:* Dividends will be in the form of an annuity.

15. Homemade Dividends (LO2) In the previous problem, suppose you want only $750 total in dividends the first year. What will your homemade dividend be in two years?

 16. Stock Repurchase (LO4) Salmon Arm Corporation is evaluating an extra dividend versus a share repurchase. In either case, $11,000 would be spent. Current earnings are $1.40 per share, and the stock currently sells for $58 per share. There are 2,000 shares outstanding. Ignore taxes and other imperfections in answering the first two questions.

    a. Evaluate the two alternatives in terms of the effect on the price per share of the stock and shareholder wealth.

    b. What will be the effect on Salmon Arm's EPS and PE ratio under the two different scenarios?

    c. In the real world, which of these actions would you recommend? Why?

Challenge **17. Expected Return, Dividends, and Taxes (LO2)** The Sicamous Company and the Revelstoke Company are two firms whose
(Questions business risk is the same but that have different dividend policies. Sicamous pays no dividend, whereas Revelstoke has an
17–20) expected dividend yield of 4 percent. Suppose the capital gains tax rate is zero, whereas the income tax rate is 35 percent. Sicamous has an expected earnings growth rate of 15 percent annually, and its stock price is expected to grow at this same rate. If the after-tax expected returns on the two stocks are equal (because they are in the same risk class), what is the pre-tax required return on Revelstoke's stock?

18. Dividends and Taxes (LO2) As discussed in the text, in the absence of market imperfections and tax effects, we would expect the share price to decline by the amount of the dividend payment when the stock goes ex dividend. Once we consider the role of taxes, however, this is not necessarily true. One model has been proposed that incorporates tax effects into determining the ex-dividend price:[19]

$$(P_0 - P_X)/D = (1 - T_P)/(1 - T_G)$$

where P_0 is the price just before the stock goes ex, P_X is the ex-dividend share price, D is the amount of the dividend per share, T_P is the relevant marginal personal tax rate on dividends, and T_G is the effective marginal tax rate on capital gains.

    a. If $T_P = T_G = 0$, how much will the share price fall when the stock goes ex?

    b. If $T_P = 15$ percent and $T_G = 0$, how much will the share price fall?

    c. If $T_P = 15$ percent and $T_G = 30$ percent, how much will the share price fall?

    d. Suppose the only owners of stock are corporations. Recall that corporations get at least a 100 percent exemption from taxation on the dividend income they receive, but they do not get such an exemption on capital gains. If the corporation's income and capital gains tax rates are both 35 percent, what does this model predict the ex-dividend share price will be?

    e. What does this problem tell you about real-world tax considerations and the dividend policy of the firm?

---

[19] N. Elton and M. Gruber, "Marginal Stockholder Tax Rates and the Clientele Effect," *Review of Economics and Statistics* 52 (February 1970).

19. **Dividends versus Reinvestment (LO2)** Nelson Business Machine Co. (NBM) has $3 million of extra cash after taxes have been paid. NBM has two choices to make use of this cash. One alternative is to invest the cash in financial assets. The resulting investment income will be paid out as a special dividend at the end of three years. In this case, the firm can invest in Treasury bills yielding 3 percent or a 5 percent preferred stock. CRA regulations allow the company to exclude from taxable income 100 percent of the dividends received from investing in another company's stock. Another alternative is to pay out the cash now as dividends. This would allow the shareholders to invest on their own in Treasury bills with the same yield, or in preferred stock. The corporate tax rate is 40 percent. Assume the investor has a 40 percent personal income tax rate, which is applied to interest income. The personal dividend tax rate is 20 percent on common stock dividends after applying the dividend tax credit. Should the cash be paid today or in three years? Which of the two options generates the highest after-tax income for the shareholders?

20. **Dividends versus Reinvestment (LO2)** After completing its capital spending for the year, Banff Manufacturing has $1,000 extra cash. Banff's managers must choose between investing the cash in Canada bonds that yield 6 percent or paying the cash out to investors who would invest in the bonds themselves.

    a. If the corporate tax rate is 35 percent, what personal tax rate after applying the dividend tax credit would make the investors equally willing to receive the dividend or to let Banff invest the money?

    b. Is the answer to (a) reasonable? Why or why not?

    c. Suppose the only investment choice is a preferred stock that yields 9 percent. The corporate dividend exclusion of 100 percent applies. What personal tax rate will make the shareholders indifferent to the outcome of Banff's dividend decision?

    d. Is this a compelling argument for a low dividend-payout ratio? Why or why not?

MINI CASE

Kelowna Microchips Inc.

Kelowna Microchips Inc. (KMI) is a small company founded 15 years ago by electronics engineers Justin Langer and Suzanne Maher. KMI manufactures integrated circuits to capitalize on the complex mixed-signal design technology and has recently entered the market for frequency timing generators, or silicon timing devices, which provide the timing signals or "clocks" necessary to synchronize electronic systems. Its clock products originally were used in PC video graphics applications, but the market subsequently expanded to include motherboards, PC peripheral devices, and other digital consumer electronics, such as digital television boxes and game consoles. KMI also designs and markets custom application specific integrated circuits (ASICs) for industrial customers. The ASIC's design combines analog and digital, or mixed-signal, technology. In addition to Justin and Suzanne, Andrew Keegan, who provided capital for the company, is the third primary owner. Each owns 25 percent of the one million shares outstanding. The company has several other individuals, including current employees, who own the remaining shares.

Recently, the company designed a new computer motherboard. The company's design is both more efficient and less expensive to manufacture, and the KMI design is expected to become standard in many personal computers. After investigating the possibility of manufacturing the new motherboard, KMI determined that the costs involved in building a new plant would be prohibitive. The owners also decided that they were unwilling to bring in another large outside owner. Instead, KMI sold the design to an outside firm. The sale of the motherboard design was completed for an after-tax payment of $40 million.

QUESTIONS

1. Justin believes the company should use the extra cash to pay a special one-time dividend. How will this proposal affect the stock price? How will it affect the value of the company?

2. Suzanne believes the company should use the extra cash to pay off debt and upgrade and expand its existing manufacturing capability. How would Suzanne's proposals affect the company?

3. Andrew favors a share repurchase. He argues that a repurchase will increase the company's P/E ratio, return on assets, and return on equity. Are his arguments correct? How will a share repurchase affect the value of the company?

4. Another option discussed by Justin, Suzanne, and Andrew would be to begin a regular dividend payment to shareholders. How would you evaluate this proposal?

5. One way to value a share of stock is the dividend growth, or growing perpetuity, model. Consider the following: The dividend payout ratio is 1 minus b, where b is the "retention" or "plowback" ratio. So, the dividend next year will be the earnings next year, F_1, times 1 minus the retention ratio. The most commonly used equation to calculate the growth rate is the return on equity times the retention ratio. Substituting these relationships into the dividend growth model, we get the following equation to calculate the price of a share of stock today:

$$P_0 = \frac{E_1(1 - b)}{R_s - \text{ROE} \times b} \text{ where } R_s = \text{Expected rate of return}$$

What are the implications of this result in terms of whether the company should pay a dividend or upgrade and expand its manufacturing capability? Explain.

Internet Application Questions

1. Buying back a company's own shares is an alternative way of distributing corporate assets. Share buybacks involve both capital structure and dividend policy. In fact, share repurchases have overtaken dividends as the most popular means of cash payouts by corporations in the U.S. The following link explains the advantages of share repurchases, and also cautions against cases where repurchases have not or will not work.

   fool.com/EveningNews/FOTH/1998/foth981019.htm

   Discuss the following questions after reading the link above.

   a. Show that share repurchases and dividend payments are equivalent, in the sense that they do not affect relative corporate value.

   b. The link above argues that Circus Circus (NYSE: CIR) and Trump (NYSE: DJT) should have avoided buying back their shares. Do you agree with the admonition that highly leveraged firms should not use share buybacks? What are you assuming about dividend policy when you answer this question?

   c. The link also contends that share buybacks enhance shareholder value when done properly and cites three companies as virtuous examples: Coke (NYSE: KO), Intel (Nasdaq: INTC), and Chrysler (NYSE: C). Keeping in mind that the article was written in October 1998, what lessons do you draw from the successful repurchase strategies of these firms?

2. Dividend reinvestment plans (DRIPs) permit shareholders to automatically reinvest cash dividends in the company. To find out more about DRIPs go to fool.com/School/Drips.htm?ref=SchAg. What are the advantages that Motley Fool lists for DRIPs? What are the different types of DRIPs? What is a Direct Purchase Plan? How does a Direct Purchase Plan differ from a DRIP?

3. Information on recently announced dividends and stock splits for the U.S. markets can be found at earnings.com. How many companies went "ex" today? What is the largest declared dividend? Are there any reverse splits listed? What is the largest split in terms of the number of shares?

4. How many times has Royal Bank of Canada stock split? Go to the website rbc.com and visit the "Investor Relations" section. You will find share information, including dates of stock splits. Were there any splits accomplished in unique ways? When did the splits occur?

5. Go to canadiandividendstock.com/best-canadian-dividend-stocks/ and find the best Canadian dividend stocks for the most recent date. This website highlights some Canadian stocks which are high dividend achievers. To find the dividend history of Canadian stocks visit ca.dividendinvestor.com/

CHAPTER 18

SHORT-TERM FINANCE AND PLANNING

LCBO

During the fiscal year 2011–2012, Liquor Control Board of Ontario (LCBO), one of the world's largest single purchasers of beverage alcohol products, achieved record sales of $4.7 billion. It also transferred a record $1.63 billion to the Ontario government. These numbers were primarily due to operational efficiency achieved through excellent inventory management. The Board achieved record inventory turnover for its premium wine Vintages division as well as for sales of beers and spirits. Total inventory turnover for 2011–2012 was 7.6.

As this chapter will illustrate, choosing the best inventory levels and financing them appropriately are important elements of short-term financial management, and organizations like LCBO pay close attention to these decisions.

Learning Objectives ▶

After studying this chapter, you should understand:

LO1   The operating and cash cycles and why they are important.

LO2   The different types of short-term financial policy.

LO3   The essentials of short-term financial planning.

LO4   The sources and uses of cash on the statement of financial position.

LO5   The different types of short-term borrowing.

Interested in a career in short-term finance? Visit the Treasury Management Association of Canada at tmac-toronto.ca/

To this point, we have described many of the decisions of long-term finance, for example, capital budgeting, dividend policy, and financial structure. In this chapter, we begin to discuss short-term finance. Short-term finance is primarily concerned with the analysis of decisions that affect current assets and current liabilities.

Financial managers spend major blocks of time daily on short-term financial management. What types of questions fall under the general heading of short-term finance? To name just a very few:

1. What is a reasonable level of cash to keep on hand (in a bank) to pay bills?
2. How much should the firm borrow short-term?
3. How much credit should be extended to customers?
4. How much inventory should the firm carry?

Answering these questions is central to the financial manager's job. Short-term financial management is often an important part of entry-level jobs for new finance graduates.[1]

Frequently, the term *net working capital* is associated with short-term financial decision making. As we describe in Chapter 2 and elsewhere, net working capital is the difference between current assets and current liabilities. Often, short-term financial management is called *working capital management*. These terms mean the same thing.

There is no universally accepted definition of short-term finance. The most important difference between short-term and long-term finance is the timing of cash flows. Short-term financial decisions

---

[1] N. C. Hill and W. L. Sartoris, *Short-Term Financial Management* 2d ed., Prentice Hall College Division, 1995.

typically involve cash inflows and outflows that occur within a year or less. For example, short-term financial decisions are involved when a firm orders raw materials, pays in cash, and anticipates selling finished goods in one year for cash. In contrast, long-term financial decisions are involved when a firm purchases a special machine that reduces operating costs over, say, the next five years.

This chapter introduces the basic elements of short-term financial decisions. We begin by discussing the short-term operating activities of the firm. We then identify some alternative short-term financial policies. Finally, we outline the basic elements in a short-term financial plan and describe short-term financing instruments.

18.1 | Tracing Cash and Net Working Capital

In this section, we examine the components of cash and net working capital as they change from one year to the next. We have already discussed various aspects of this subject in Chapters 2, 3, and 4. We briefly review some of that discussion as it relates to short-term financing decisions. Our goal is to describe the short-term operating activities of the firm and their impact on cash and working capital.

To begin, recall that *current assets* are cash and other assets expected to convert to cash within the year. Current assets are presented in the statement of financial position in order of their accounting liquidity—the ease with which they can be converted to cash and the time it takes to do so. Four of the most important items found in the current asset section of a statement of financial position are cash, marketable securities (or cash equivalents), accounts receivable, and inventories.

Analogous to their investment in current assets, firms use several kinds of short-term debt, called *current liabilities*. Current liabilities are obligations expected to require cash payment within one year (or within the operating period if it is different from one year). The three major items found as current liabilities are accounts payable; expenses payable, including accrued wages and taxes; and notes payable.

Because we want to focus on changes in cash, we start by defining cash in terms of the other elements of the statement of financial position. This lets us isolate the cash account and explore the impact on cash from the firm's operating and financing decisions. The basic statement of financial position identity can be written as:

$$\text{Net working capital} + \text{Fixed assets} = \text{Long-term debt} + \text{Equity} \qquad [18.1]$$

Net working capital is cash plus other current assets less current liabilities; that is,

$$\text{Net working capital} = (\text{Cash} + \text{Other current assets}) - \text{Current liabilities} \qquad [18.2]$$

If we substitute this for net working capital in the basic statement of financial position identity and rearrange things a bit, cash is:

$$\text{Cash} = \text{Long-term debt} + \text{Equity} + \text{Current liabilities} - \text{Current assets (other than cash)} - \text{Fixed assets} \qquad [18.3]$$

This tells us in general terms that some activities naturally increase cash and some activities decrease it. We can list these along with an example of each as follows:

ACTIVITIES THAT INCREASE CASH
- Increasing long-term debt (borrowing long-term).
- Increasing equity (selling some stock).
- Increasing current liabilities (getting a 90-day loan).
- Decreasing current assets other than cash (selling some inventory for cash).
- Decreasing fixed assets (selling some property).

ACTIVITIES THAT DECREASE CASH
- Decreasing long-term debt (paying off a long-term debt).
- Decreasing equity (repurchasing some stock).
- Decreasing current liabilities (paying off a 90-day loan).
- Increasing current assets other than cash (buying some inventory for cash).
- Increasing fixed assets (buying some property).

Notice that our two lists are exact opposites. For example, floating a long-term bond issue increases cash (at least until the money is spent). Paying off a long-term bond issue decreases cash.

As we discussed in Chapter 3, those activities that increase cash are sources of cash. Those activities that decrease cash are uses of cash. Looking back at our list, sources of cash always involve increasing a liability (or equity) account or decreasing an asset account. This makes sense because increasing a liability means we have raised money by borrowing it or by selling an ownership interest in the firm. A decrease in an asset means we have sold or otherwise liquidated an asset. In either case, there is a cash inflow.

Uses of cash are just the reverse. A use of cash involves decreasing a liability by paying it off, perhaps, or an increase in assets from purchasing something. Both of these activities require that the firm spend some cash.

EXAMPLE 18.1 SOURCES AND USES

Here is a quick check of your understanding of sources and uses: If accounts payable goes up by $100, is this a source or use? If accounts receivable goes up by $100, is this a source or use?

Accounts payable are what we owe our suppliers. This is a short-term debt. If it rises by $100, we have effectively borrowed the money, so this is a source of cash. Receivables is what our customers owe to us, so an increase of $100 means that we loaned the money; this is a use of cash.

Concept Questions

1. What is the difference between net working capital and cash?
2. Will net working capital always increase when cash increases?
3. List five potential uses of cash.
4. List five potential sources of cash.

18.2 | The Operating Cycle and the Cash Cycle

The primary concern in short-term finance is the firm's short-run operating and financing activities. For a typical manufacturing firm, these short-run activities might consist of the following sequence of events and decisions:

Events	Decisions
1. Buying raw materials	1. How much inventory to order?
2. Paying cash	2. Borrow or draw down cash balance?
3. Manufacturing the product	3. What choice of production technology?
4. Selling the product	4. Should credit be extended to a particular customer?
5. Collecting cash	5. How to collect?

These activities create patterns of cash inflows and cash outflows. These cash flows are both unsynchronized and uncertain. They are unsynchronized because, for example, the payment of cash for raw materials does not happen at the same time as the receipt of cash from selling the product. They are uncertain because future sales and costs cannot be predicted precisely.

Small businesses in particular must pay attention to the timing of inflows and outflows. For example, Earthly Elements, a maker of dried floral gifts and accessories, was formed in March 2012. The owners of the firm rejoiced when they received a $10,000 order from a national home shopping service in November 2012. The order represented 20 percent of total orders for the year and was expected to give a big boost to the young company. Unfortunately, it cost Earthly Elements 25 percent more than expected to fill the order. Then, its customer was slow to pay. By the end of February 2013, the payment was 30 days late, and the company was running out of cash. By the time the payment was received in April, the firm had already closed its doors in March, a victim of the cash cycle.

Defining the Operating and Cash Cycles

We can start with a simple case. One day, call it Day 0, you purchase $1,000 worth of inventory on credit. You pay the bill 30 days later, and, after 30 more days, someone buys the $1,000 in inventory for $1,400. Your buyer does not actually pay for another 45 days. We can summarize these events chronologically as follows:

Day	Activity	Cash effect
0	Acquire inventory	none
30	Pay for inventory	−$1,000
60	Sell inventory on credit	none
105	Collect on sale	+$1,400

operating cycle
The time period between the acquisition of inventory and when cash is collected from receivables.

inventory period
The time it takes to acquire and sell inventory.

accounts receivable period
The time between sale of inventory and collection of the receivable.

THE OPERATING CYCLE   There are several things to notice in our example: First, the entire cycle, from the time we acquire some inventory to the time we collect the cash, takes 105 days. This is called the **operating cycle**.

As we illustrate, the operating cycle is the length of time it takes to acquire inventory, sell it, and collect for it. This cycle has two distinct components. The first part is the time it takes to acquire and sell the inventory. This 60-day span (in our example) is called the **inventory period**. The second part is the time it takes to collect on the sale, 45 days in our example. This is called the **accounts receivable period**.

Based on our definitions, the operating cycle is obviously just the sum of the inventory and receivables periods:

$$\text{Operating cycle} = \text{Inventory period} + \text{Accounts receivable period} \qquad [18.4]$$

$$105 \text{ days} = 60 \text{ days} + 45 \text{ days}$$

What the operating cycle describes is how a product moves through the current asset accounts. It begins life as inventory, it is converted to a receivable when it is sold, and it is finally converted to cash when we collect from the sale. Notice that, at each step, the asset is moving closer to cash.

accounts payable period
The time between receipt of inventory and payment for it.

cash cycle
The time between cash disbursement and cash collection.

THE CASH CYCLE   The second thing to notice is that the cash flows and other events that occur are not synchronized. For example, we didn't actually pay for the inventory until 30 days after we acquired it. This 30-day period is called the **accounts payable period**. Next, we spend cash on Day 30, but we don't collect until Day 105. Somehow or the other, we have to arrange to finance the $1,000 for $105 - 30 = 75$ days. This period is called the **cash cycle**.

The cash cycle, therefore, is the number of days that pass until we collect the cash from a sale, measured from when we actually pay for the inventory. Notice that, based on our definitions, the cash cycle is the difference between the operating cycle and the accounts payable period:

$$\text{Cash cycle} = \text{Operating cycle} - \text{Accounts payable period} \qquad [18.5]$$

$$75 \text{ days} = 105 \text{ days} - 30 \text{ days}$$

cash flow time line
Graphical representation of the operating cycle and the cash cycle.

Figure 18.1 depicts the short-term operating activities and cash flows for a typical manufacturing firm by looking at the cash flow time line. As shown, the **cash flow time line** is made up of the operating cycle and the cash cycle. In Figure 18.1, the need for short-term financial management is suggested by the gap between the cash inflows and cash outflows. This is related to the length of the operating cycle and accounts payable period.

The gap between short-term inflows and outflows can be filled either by borrowing or by holding a liquidity reserve in the form of cash or marketable securities. Alternatively, the gap can be shortened by changing the inventory, receivable, and payable periods. These are all managerial options that we discuss in this and subsequent chapters.

Internet-based bookseller and retailer Amazon.com provides an interesting example of the importance of managing the cash cycle. By mid-2012, the market value of Amazon.com was higher than (in fact more than 400 times as much as) that of Indigo Books & Music Inc., Canadian retail bookstore chain headquartered in Toronto, even though Amazon's sales were only 48 times greater.

How could Amazon.com be worth so much more? There are multiple reasons, but short-term management is one factor. During 2011, Amazon turned over its inventory about 9 times per year,

3 times faster than Indigo; so its inventory period was dramatically shorter. Even more strikingly, Amazon charges a customer's credit card when it ships a book, and it usually gets paid by the credit card firm within a day. This means Amazon has a negative cash cycle! In fact, during 2011, Amazon's cash cycle was a negative 38 days. Every sale therefore generates a cash inflow that can be put to work immediately.

THE OPERATING CYCLE AND THE FIRM'S ORGANIZATION CHART   Before we look at detailed examples of operating and cash cycles, realism dictates a look at the people involved in implementing a firm's policies. This is important because short-term financial management in a large corporation involves non-financial managers as well and there is potential for conflict as each manager looks at only part of the picture.[2] As you can see in Table 18.1, selling on credit involves the credit manager, the marketing manager, and the controller. Of these three, only two are responsible to the vice president of finance, as the marketing function has its own vice president in most large corporations. If the marketing function is trying to land a new account, it may seek more liberal credit terms as an inducement. Since this may increase the firm's investment in receivables or its exposure to the bad debt risk, conflict may result. To resolve such conflict, the firm must look beyond personalities to the ultimate impact on shareholder wealth.

FIGURE 18.1

Cash flow time line and the short-term operating activities of a typical manufacturing firm

The operating cycle is the time period from inventory purchase until the receipt of cash. (Sometimes the operating cycle includes the time from placement of the order until arrival of the stock.) The cash cycle is the time period from when cash is paid out to when cash is received.

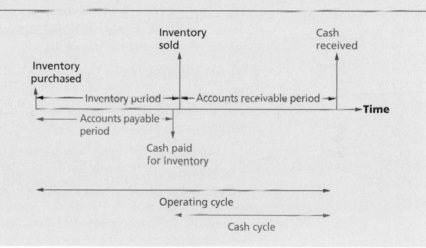

TABLE 18.1

Managers who deal with short-term financial problems

Title	Short-Term Financial Management Duties	Assets/Liabilities Influenced
Cash manager	Collection, concentration, disbursement; short-term investment; short-term borrowing; banking relations	Cash, marketable securities, short-term loans
Credit manager	Monitoring and control of accounts receivable; credit policy decisions	Accounts receivable
Marketing manager	Credit policy decisions	Accounts receivable
Purchasing manager	Decisions on purchase, suppliers; may negotiate payment terms	Inventory, accounts payable
Production manager	Setting of production schedules and materials requirements	Inventory, accounts payable
Payables manager	Decisions on payment policies and on whether to take discounts	Accounts payable
Controller	Accounting information on cash flows; reconciliation of accounts payable; application of payments to accounts receivable	Accounts receivable, accounts payable

Source: Ned C. Hill and William L. Sartoris, *Short-Term Financial Management,* 3rd ed. (Prentice Hall College Div., 1995)

---

[2]This discussion draws on N.C. Hill and W.L. Sartoris, *Short-Term Financial Management* 2d ed., Prentice Hall College Division, 1995.

Calculating the Operating and Cash Cycles

In our example, the lengths of time that made up the different periods were obvious. When all we have is financial statement information, however, we have to do a little more work. We illustrate these calculations next.

To begin, we need to determine various things like how long it takes, on average, to sell inventory and how long it takes, on average, to collect. We start by gathering some statement of financial position information such as the following (in $ thousands):

Item	Beginning	Ending	Average
Inventory	$2,000	$3,000	$2,500
Accounts receivable	1,600	2,000	1,800
Accounts payable	750	1,000	875

Also, from the most recent statement of comprehensive income, we might have the following figures (in $ thousands):

Net sales	$11,500
Cost of goods sold	8,200

We now need to calculate some financial ratios. We discussed these in some detail in Chapter 3; here we just define them and use them as needed.

THE OPERATING CYCLE   First, we need the inventory period. We spent $8.2 million on inventory (our cost of goods sold). Our average inventory was $2.5 million. We thus turned our inventory over 8.2/2.5 times during the year:[3]

$$\text{Inventory turnover} = \text{Cost of goods sold/Average inventory}$$
$$= \$8.2 \text{ million}/\$2.5 \text{ million} = 3.28 \text{ times}$$

Loosely speaking, this tells us that we bought and sold off our inventory 3.28 times during the year. This means that, on average, we held our inventory for:

$$\text{Inventory period} = 365 \text{ days/Inventory turnover}$$
$$= 365/3.28 = 111.3 \text{ days}$$

So the inventory period is about 111 days. On average, in other words, inventory sat for about 111 days before it was sold.

Similarly, receivables averaged $1.8 million, and sales were $11.5 million. Assuming that all sales were credit sales, the receivables turnover is:[4]

$$\text{Receivables turnover} = \text{Credit sales/Average accounts receivable}$$
$$= \$11.5 \text{ million}/\$1.8 \text{ million} = 6.4 \text{ times}$$

If we turn over our receivables 6.4 times, then the receivables period is:

$$\text{Receivables period} = 365 \text{ days/Receivables turnover}$$
$$= 365/6.4 = 57 \text{ days}$$

The receivables period is also called the *days' sales in receivables* or the *average collection period*. Whatever it is called, it tells us that our customers took an average of 57 days to pay.

The operating cycle is the sum of the inventory and receivables periods:

$$\text{Operating cycle} = \text{Inventory period} + \text{Accounts receivables period}$$
$$= 111 \text{ days} + 57 \text{ days} = 168 \text{ days}$$

This tells us that, on average, 168 days elapse between the time we acquire inventory, sell it, and collect for the sale.

---

[3] Notice that we have used the cost of goods sold in calculating inventory turnover. Sales is sometimes used instead. Also, rather than average inventory, ending inventory is often used. See Chapter 3 for some examples.

[4] If less than 100 percent of our sales are credit sales, we would just need a little more information, namely, credit sales for the year. See Chapter 3 for more discussion of this measure.

THE CASH CYCLE We now need the payables period. From the information just given, average payables were $875,000, and cost of goods sold was again $8.2 million. Our payables turnover is thus:

$$\text{Payables turnover} = \text{Cost of goods sold/Average payables}$$
$$= \$8.2 \text{ million/\$.875 million} = 9.4 \text{ times}$$

The payables period is:

$$\text{Payables period} = 365 \text{ days/Payables turnover}$$
$$= 365/9.4 = 39 \text{ days}$$

Thus, we took an average of 39 days to pay our bills.

Finally, the cash cycle is the difference between the operating cycle and the payables period:

$$\text{Cash cycle} = \text{Operating cycle} - \text{Accounts payables period}$$
$$= 168 \text{ days} - 39 \text{ days} = 129 \text{ days}$$

So, on average, there is a 129-day delay from the time we pay for merchandise and the time we collect on the sales.

Interpreting the Cash Cycle

Our examples show how the cash cycle depends on the inventory, receivables, and payables periods. Taken one at a time, the cash cycle increases as the inventory and receivables periods get longer. It decreases if the company is able to stall payment of payables, lengthening the payables period. Suppose a firm could purchase inventory, sell its product, collect receivables (perhaps selling for cash) and then pay suppliers all on the same day. This firm would have a cash cycle of zero days.

Some firms may meet this description but it is hard to think of many examples (gas retailing or dry cleaners might meet the description). Most firms have a positive cash cycle. Such firms require some additional financing for inventories and receivables. The longer the cash cycle, the more financing is required, other things being equal. You could also think of this concept in terms of liquidity. All firms need liquidity to operate. That means that a firm must create liquidity quickly (as in the case of a company with a short cash cycle), or it must invest in working capital on its statement of financial position. Since bankers are conservative and dislike surprises, they monitor the firm's cash cycle. A lengthening cycle may indicate obsolete, unsalable inventory or problems in collecting receivables. Unless these problems are detected and solved, the firm may require emergency financing or face insolvency.

EXAMPLE 18.2: The Operating and Cash Cycles

You have collected the following information for the Slowpay Company.

Item	Beginning	Ending
Inventory	$5,000	$7,000
Accounts receivable	1,600	2,400
Accounts payable	2,700	4,800

Sales for the year just ended were $50,000, and cost of goods sold was $30,000. How long does it take Slowpay to collect on its receivables? How long does merchandise stay around before it is sold? How long does Slowpay take to pay its bills?

We can first calculate the three turnover ratios:

Inventory turnover = $30,000/$6,000 = 5 times
Receivables turnover = $50,000/$2,000 = 25 times
Payables turnover = $30,000/$3,750 = 8 times

We use these to get the various periods:

Inventory period = 365/5 = 73 days
Receivables period = 365/25 = 14.6 days
Payables period = 365/8 = 45.6 days

All told, Slowpay collects on a sale in 14.6 days, inventory sits around for 73 days, and bills get paid after about 46 days. The operating cycle here is the sum of the inventory and receivables: 73 + 14.6 = 87.6 days. The cash cycle is the difference between the operating cycle and the payables period: 87.6 − 45.6 = 42 days.

Our calculations of the cash cycle used financial ratios introduced in Chapter 3. We can use some other ratio relationships from Chapter 3 to see how the cash cycle relates to profitability and sustainable growth. A good place to start is with the Du Pont equation for profitability as measured by return on assets (ROA):

$$ROA = \text{Profit margin} \times \text{Total asset turnover}$$
$$\text{Total asset turnover} = \text{Sales/Total assets}$$

Go back to the case of the firm with a lengthening cash cycle. Increased inventories and receivables that caused the cash cycle problem also reduce total asset turnover. The result is lower profitability. In other words, with more assets tied up over a longer cash cycle, the firm is less efficient and therefore less profitable. And, as if its troubles were not enough already, this firm suffers a drop in its sustainable growth rate.

Chapter 4 (in the discussion of Equation 4.5) showed that total asset turnover is directly linked to sustainable growth. Reducing total asset turnover lowers sustainable growth. This makes sense because our troubled firm must divert its financial resources into financing excess inventory and receivables.[5]

Concept Questions

1. What does it mean to say that a firm has an inventory turnover ratio of 4?
2. Describe the operating cycle and cash cycle. What are the differences?
3. Explain the connection between a firm's accounting-based profitability and its cash cycle.

18.3 | Some Aspects of Short-Term Financial Policy

The short-term financial policy that a firm adopts is reflected in at least two ways:

1. *The size of the firm's investment in current assets.* This is usually measured relative to the firm's level of total operating revenues. A *flexible* or accommodative short-term financial policy would maintain a relatively high ratio of current assets to sales. A *restrictive* short-term financial policy would entail a low ratio of current assets to sales.[6]
2. *The financing of current assets.* This is measured as the proportion of short-term debt (that is, current liabilities) and long-term debt used to finance current assets. A restrictive short-term financial policy means a high proportion of short-term debt relative to long-term financing, and a flexible policy means less short-term debt and more long-term debt.

If we take these two areas together, a firm with a flexible policy would have relatively large investment in current assets. It would finance this investment with relatively less in short-term debt. The net effect of a flexible policy is thus a relatively high level of net working capital. Put another way, with a flexible policy, the firm maintains a larger overall level of liquidity.

At the beginning of this chapter, we introduced the example of LCBO and its efforts to reduce inventory levels. We can now see that LCBO's working capital policy in relation to inventory management is moving from a more flexible to a more restrictive approach.

The Size of the Firm's Investment in Current Assets

Flexible short-term financial policies with regard to current assets include such actions as:

1. Keeping large balances of cash and marketable securities.
2. Making large investments in inventory.
3. Granting liberal credit terms, which result in a high level of accounts receivable.

[5] Further discussion of the cash cycle is in L. Kryzanowski, *Business Solvency Risk Analysis* (Montreal: Institute of Canadian Bankers, 1990), chap. 10.

[6] Some people use the term *conservative* in place of flexible and the term *aggressive* in place of restrictive.

Restrictive short-term financial policies would just be the opposite of these:

1. Keeping low cash balances and little investment in marketable securities.
2. Making small investments in inventory.
3. Allowing little or no credit sales, thereby minimizing accounts receivable.

Determining the optimal investment level in short-term assets requires an identification of the different costs of alternative short-term financing policies. The objective is to trade off the cost of a restrictive policy against the cost of a flexible one to arrive at the best compromise.

Current asset holdings are highest with a flexible short-term financial policy and lowest with a restrictive policy. So flexible short-term financial policies are costly in that they require a greater investment in cash and marketable securities, inventory, and accounts receivable. However, we expect future cash inflows to be higher with a flexible policy. For example, sales are stimulated by the use of a credit policy that provides liberal financing to customers. A large amount of finished inventory on hand ("on the shelf") provides a quick delivery service to customers and may increase sales. Similarly, a large inventory of raw materials may result in fewer production stoppages because of inventory shortages.[7]

A more restrictive short-term financial policy probably reduces future sales levels below those that would be achieved under flexible policies. It is also possible that higher prices can be charged to customers under flexible working capital policies. Customers may be willing to pay higher prices for the quick delivery service and more liberal credit terms implicit in flexible policies.

Managing current assets can be thought of as involving a trade-off between costs that rise and costs that fall with the level of investment. Costs that rise with increases in the level of investment in current assets are called **carrying costs**. The larger the investment a firm makes in its current assets, the higher its carrying costs are. Costs that fall with increases in the level of investment in current assets are called **shortage costs**.

In a general sense, carrying costs are the opportunity costs associated with current assets. The rate of return on current assets is very low when compared to other assets. For example, the rate of return on Treasury bills is usually considerably less than the rate of return firms would like to achieve overall. (Treasury bills are an important component of cash and marketable securities.)

Shortage costs are incurred when the investment in current assets is low. If a firm runs out of cash, it is forced to sell marketable securities. Of course, if a firm runs out of cash and marketable securities to sell, it may have to borrow, sell assets at fire-sale prices, or default on an obligation. This situation is called a cash out. A firm loses customers if it runs out of inventory (a stock out) or if it cannot extend credit to customers.

More generally, there are two kinds of shortage costs:

1. *Trading or order costs.* Order costs are the costs of placing an order for more cash (brokerage costs, for example) or more inventory (production set-up costs, for example).
2. *Costs related to lack of safety reserves.* These are costs of lost sales, lost customer goodwill, and disruption of production schedules.

The top part of Figure 18.2 illustrates the basic trade-off between carrying costs and shortage costs. On the vertical axis, we have costs measured in dollars and, on the horizontal axis, we have the amount of current assets. Carrying costs start at zero when current assets are zero and then climb steadily as current assets grow. Shortage costs start very high and then decline as we add current assets. The total cost of holding current assets is the sum of the two. Notice how the combined costs reach a minimum at CA*. This is the optimum level of current assets.

Current asset holdings are highest under a flexible policy. This is one in which the carrying costs are perceived to be low relative to shortage costs. This is Case A in Figure 18.2. In comparison, under restrictive current asset policies, carrying costs are perceived to be high relative to shortage costs. This is Case B in Figure 18.2.

---

carrying costs
Costs that rise with increases in the level of investment in current assets.

shortage costs
Costs that fall with increases in the level of investment in current assets.

---

[7] Many industries are reducing inventory through new technology. We discuss this approach, called just-in-time inventory (or production), in Chapter 20.

FIGURE 18.2

Carrying costs and shortage costs

Short-term financial policy: the optimal investment in current assets.
Carrying costs increase with the level of investment in current assets. They include the costs of maintaining economic value and opportunity costs. Shortage costs decrease with increases in the level of investment in current assets. They include trading costs and the costs related to being short of the current asset (for example, being short of cash). The firm's policy can be characterized as flexible or restrictive.

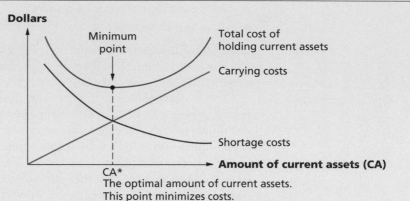

The optimal amount of current assets.
This point minimizes costs.

A flexible policy is most appropriate when carrying costs are low relative to shortage costs.

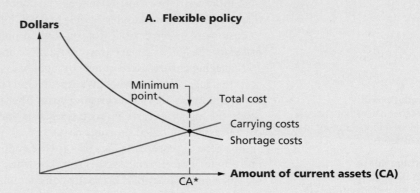

A restrictive policy is most appropriate when carrying costs are high relative to shortage costs.

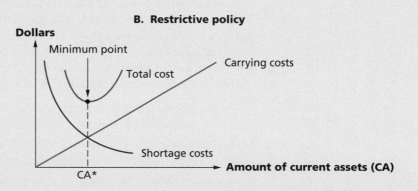

Alternative Financing Policies for Current Assets

In previous sections, we looked at the basic determinants of the level of investment in current assets, and we thus focused on the asset side of the statement of financial position. Now we turn to the financing side of the question. Here we are concerned with the relative amounts of short-term and long-term debt, assuming the investment in current assets is constant.

AN IDEAL CASE   We start with the simplest possible case: an ideal economy. In such an economy, short-term assets can always be financed with short-term debt, and long-term assets can be financed with long-term debt and equity. In this economy, net working capital is always zero.

Consider a simplified case for a grain elevator operator. Grain elevator operators buy crops after harvest, store them, and sell them during the year. They have high inventories of grain after the harvest and end up with low inventories just before the next harvest.

Bank loans with maturities of less than one year are used to finance the purchase of grain and the storage costs. These loans are paid off from the proceeds of the sale of grain.

The situation is shown in Figure 18.3. Long-term assets are assumed to grow over time, whereas current assets increase at the end of the harvest and then decline during the year. Short-term assets end up at zero just before the next harvest. Current (short-term) assets are financed by short-term debt, and long-term assets are financed with long-term debt and equity. Net working capital—current assets minus current liabilities—is always zero. Figure 18.3 displays a saw tooth pattern that we see again when we get to our discussion on cash management in the next chapter. For now, we need to discuss some alternative policies for financing current assets under less idealized conditions.

FIGURE 18.3

Financing policy for an ideal economy

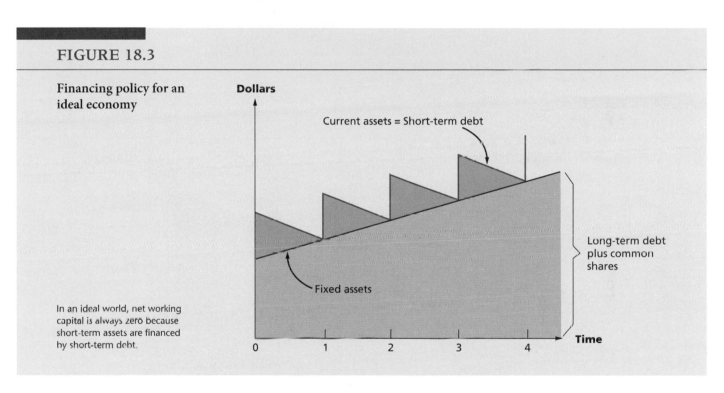

In an ideal world, net working capital is always zero because short-term assets are financed by short-term debt.

DIFFERENT POLICIES IN FINANCING CURRENT ASSETS   In the real world, it is not likely that current assets would ever drop to zero. For example, a long-term rising level of sales results in some permanent investment in current assets. Moreover, the firm's investments in long-term assets may show a great deal of variation.

A growing firm can be thought of as having a total asset requirement consisting of the current assets and long-term assets needed to run the business efficiently. The total asset requirement may exhibit change over time for many reasons, including (1) a general growth trend, (2) seasonal variation around the trend, and (3) unpredictable day-to-day and month-to-month fluctuations. This situation is depicted in Figure 18.4. (We have not tried to show the unpredictable day-to-day and month-to-month variations in the total asset requirement.)

The peaks and valleys in Figure 18.4 represent the firm's total asset needs through time. For example, for a lawn and garden supply firm, the peaks might represent inventory buildups prior to the spring selling season. The valleys would come about because of lower off-season inventories. There are two strategies such a firm might consider to meet its cyclical needs. First, the firm could keep a relatively large pool of marketable securities. As the need for inventory and other current assets began to rise, the firm would sell off marketable securities and use the cash to purchase whatever was needed. Once the inventory was sold and inventory holdings began to decline, the firm would reinvest in marketable securities. This approach is the flexible policy illustrated in Figure 18.5 as Policy F. Notice that the firm essentially uses a pool of marketable securities as a buffer against changing current asset needs.

FIGURE 18.4

The total asset
requirement over time

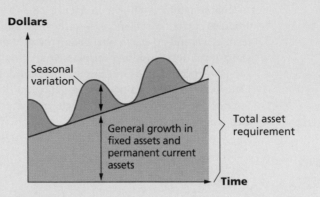

FIGURE 18.5

Alternative asset financing policies

Policy *F* always implies a short-term cash surplus
and a large investment in cash and marketable
securities.

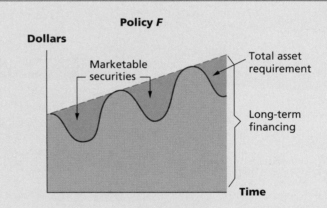

Policy *R* uses long-term financing for permanent
asset requirements only and short-term borrowing
for seasonal variations.

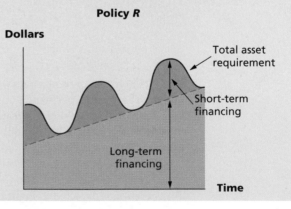

At the other extreme, the firm could keep relatively little in marketable securities. As the need for inventory and other assets began to rise, the firm would simply borrow the needed cash on a short-term basis. The firm would repay the loans as the need for assets cycled back down. This approach is the restrictive policy illustrated in Figure 18.5 as Policy *R*.

In comparing the two strategies illustrated in Figure 18.5, notice that the chief difference is the way in which the seasonal variation in asset needs is financed. In the flexible case, the firm finances internally, using its own cash and marketable securities. In the restrictive case, the firm finances the variation externally, borrowing the needed funds on a short-term basis. As we discussed previously, all else being the same, a firm with a flexible policy will have a greater investment in net working capital.

Which Financing Policy is Best?

What is the most appropriate amount of short-term borrowing? There is no definitive answer. Several considerations must be included in a proper analysis:

1. *Cash reserves.* The flexible financial policy implies surplus cash and little short-term borrowing. This policy reduces the probability that a firm would experience financial distress. Firms may not have to worry as much about meeting recurring, short-run obligations. However, this higher level of liquidity comes at a price. Investments in cash and marketable securities generally produce lower returns than investments in real assets. For example, suppose the firm invests any temporary excess liquidity in Treasury bills. The price of a Treasury bill is simply the present value of its future cash flow. It follows that, since present value and the cost of a Treasury bill are equal, Treasury bills are always zero net present value investments. If the firm followed another policy, the funds tied up in Treasury bills and other zero NPV short-term financial instruments could be invested to produce a positive NPV.

2. *Maturity hedging.* Most firms attempt to match the maturities of assets and liabilities. They finance inventories with short-term bank loans and fixed assets with long-term financing. Firms tend to avoid financing long-lived assets with short-term borrowing. This type of maturity mismatching is inherently more risky for two reasons: First, the cost of the financing is more uncertain because short-term interest rates are more volatile than longer rates. For example, in 1981, many short-term borrowers faced financial distress when short-term rates exceeded 20 percent.

   Second, maturity mismatching necessitates frequent refinancing and this produces roll-over risk, the risk that renewed short-term financing may not be available. A classic example is the financial distress faced in 1992 by Olympia & York (O&Y), a real estate development firm privately owned by the Reichmann family of Toronto. O&Y's main assets were office towers, including First Canadian Place in Toronto and Canary Wharf outside London, England. Financing for these long-term assets was short-term bank loans and commercial paper. In early 1992, investor fears about real estate prospects prevented O&Y from rolling over its commercial paper. To avoid default, the company turned to its bankers to negotiate emergency longer-term financing and, when that failed, had to file for bankruptcy protection.

3. *Relative interest rates.* Short-term interest rates are usually lower than long-term rates. This implies that it is, on the average, more costly to rely on long-term borrowing as compared to short-term borrowing. This is really a statement about the yield curve we introduced in Appendix 7B. What we are saying is that the yield curve is normally upward sloping.

Policies *F* and *R*, which are shown in Figure 18.5, are, of course, extreme cases. With *F*, the firm never does any short-term borrowing; with *R*, the firm never has a cash reserve (an investment in marketable securities). Figure 18.6 illustrates these two policies along with a compromise, Policy *C*.

With this compromise approach, the firm borrows short-term to cover peak financing needs, but it maintains a cash reserve in the form of marketable securities during slow periods. As current assets build up, the firm draws down this reserve before doing any short-term borrowing. This allows for some run-up in current assets before the firm has to resort to short-term borrowing.

Current Assets and Liabilities in Practice

candiantire.ca

Current assets made up around 56 percent of all assets for Canadian Tire in 2011. Short-term financial management deals with a significant portion of the statement of financial position for this large firm. For small firms, especially in the retailing and service sectors, current assets make up an even larger portion of total assets.

Over time, advances in technology are changing the way Canadian firms manage current assets. With new techniques such as just-in-time inventory and business-to-business e-business sales (B2B), firms are moving away from flexible policies and toward a more restrictive approach to current assets.

FIGURE 18.6
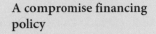

A compromise financing policy

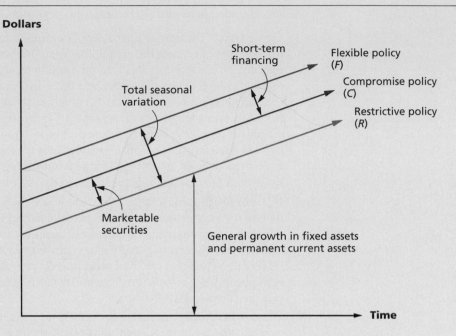

With a compromise policy, the firm keeps a reserve of liquidity, which it uses to initially finance seasonal variations in current asset needs. Short-term borrowing is used when the reserve is exhausted.

TABLE 18.2

Current assets and current liabilities as percentages of total current assets and total current liabilities for Canadian Tire 2010–2011

	2011	2010
Current assets		
Cash and cash equivalents	4.7%	8.7%
Short-term investments	2.8	3.0
Trade and other receivables	11.9	10.3
Loans receivable	58.7	61.9
Merchandise inventories	20.8	13.8
Income taxes recoverable	0.0	1.5
Prepaid expenses and deposits	0.6	0.6
Assets classified as held for sale	0.4	0.3
Total	100.0%	100.0%
Current liabilities		
Bank indebtedness	3.0%	3.6%
Deposits	28.5	18.9
Trade and other payables	39.5	36.3
Provisions	4.6	6.0
Short-term borrowings	8.5	3.1
Loans payable	15.1	21.1
Income taxes payable	0.1	0.0
Current portion of long-term debt	0.7	10.9
Total	100.0%	100.0%

Source: Drawn from the 2011 Canadian Tire Corporation Ltd. *Annual Report*.

Current liabilities are also declining as a percentage of total assets. Firms are practising maturity hedging as they match lower current liabilities with decreased current assets. In addition to these differences over time, there are differences between industries in policies on current assets and liabilities. Furthermore, firms responded to the recent economic downturn by relaxing their restrictive approach to current assets. Table 18.2 shows that Canadian Tire increased receivables and inventory as opposed to bank debt and payables.

The cash cycle is longer in some industries; various products and industry practices require different levels of inventory and receivables. This is why we saw in Chapter 3 that industry average ratios are not the same. Levels of current assets and liabilities differ across industries.[8] For example, the aircraft industry carries more than twice the amount of inventory of the other industries. Does this mean aircraft manufacturers are less efficient? Most likely, the higher inventory consists of airplanes under construction. Because building planes takes more time than most printing processes, it makes sense that aircraft manufacturers carry higher inventories than printing and publishing firms.

Concept Questions

1. What keeps the real world from being an ideal one where net working capital could always be zero?
2. What considerations determine the optimal size of the firm's investment in current assets?
3. What considerations determine the optimal compromise between flexible and restrictive net working capital policies?
4. How are industry differences reflected in working capital policies?

18.4 | The Cash Budget

cash budget
A forecast of cash receipts and disbursements for the next planning period.

The **cash budget** is a primary tool in short-run financial planning. It allows the financial manager to identify short-term financial needs and opportunities. Importantly, the cash budget helps the manager explore the need for short-term borrowing. The idea of the cash budget is simple: It records estimates of cash receipts (cash in) and disbursements (cash out). The result is an estimate of the cash surplus or deficit.

Sales and Cash Collections

We start with an example for the Fun Toys Corporation for which we prepare a quarterly cash budget. We could just as well use a monthly, weekly, or even daily basis. We choose quarters for convenience and also because a quarter is a common short-term business planning period.

All of Fun Toys' cash inflows come from the sale of toys. Cash budgeting for Fun Toys must therefore start with a sales forecast for the next year, by quarters:

	Q1	Q2	Q3	Q4
Sales (in $ millions)	$200	$300	$250	$400

Note that these are predicted sales, so there is forecasting risk here because actual sales could be more or less. Also, Fun Toys started the year with accounts receivable equal to $120.

Fun Toys has a 45-day receivables or average collection period. This means that half of the sales in a given quarter are collected the following quarter. This happens because sales made during the first 45 days of a quarter are collected in that quarter. Sales made in the second 45 days are collected in the next quarter. Note that we are assuming that each quarter has 90 days, so the 45-day collection period is the same as a half-quarter collection period.

Based on the sales forecasts, we now need to estimate Fun Toys' projected cash collections. First, any receivables that we have at the beginning of a quarter would be collected within 45 days, so all of them are collected sometime during the quarter. Second, as we discussed, any sales made in the first half of the quarter are collected, so total cash collections are:

---

[8] See N.G. Hill and W.L. Sartoris, *Short-Term Financial Management* 2d ed., Prentice Hall College Division, 1995.

$$\text{Cash collections} = \text{Beginning accounts receivable} + 1/2 \times \text{Sales} \qquad [18.6]$$

For example, in the first quarter, cash collections would be the beginning receivables of $120 plus half of sales, $1/2 \times \$200 = \$100$, for a total of $220.

Since beginning receivables are all collected along with half of sales, ending receivables for a particular quarter would be the other half of sales. First-quarter sales are projected at $200, so ending receivables are $100. This would be the beginning receivables in the second quarter. Cash collections in the second quarter are thus $100 plus half of the projected $300 in sales, or $250 total.

Continuing this process, we can summarize Fun Toys' projected cash collections as shown in Table 18.3. In this table, collections are shown as the only source of cash. Of course, this need not be the case. Other sources of cash could include asset sales, investment income, and receipts from planned long-term financing.

TABLE 18.3

Cash collections for Fun Toys (in $ millions)

Notes: Collections = Beginning receivables + 1/2 × Sales
Ending receivables = Beginning receivables + Sales − Collections
= 1/2 × Sales

	Q1	Q2	Q3	Q4
Beginning receivables	$120	$100	$150	$125
Sales	200	300	250	400
Cash collections	220	250	275	325
Ending receivables	100	150	125	200

Cash Outflows

Next, we consider the cash disbursements or payments. These come in four basic categories:

1. *Payments of accounts payable.* These are payments for goods or services rendered from suppliers, such as raw materials. Generally, these payments are made sometime after purchases.
2. *Wages, taxes, and other expenses.* This category includes all other regular costs of doing business that require actual expenditures. Depreciation, for example, is often thought of as a regular cost of business, but it requires no cash outflow, and is not included.
3. *Capital expenditures.* These are payments of cash for long-lived assets.
4. *Long-term financing expenses.* This category, for example, includes interest payments on long-term outstanding debt and dividend payments to shareholders.

Fun Toys' purchases from suppliers (in dollars) in a quarter are equal to 60 percent of next quarter's predicted sales. Fun Toys' payments to suppliers are equal to the previous quarter's purchases, so the accounts payable period is 90 days. For example, in the quarter just ended, Fun Toys ordered $.60 \times \$200 = \$120$ in supplies. This would actually be paid in the first quarter (Q1) of the coming year.

Wages, taxes, and other expenses are routinely 20 percent of sales; interest and dividends are currently $20 per quarter. In addition, Fun Toys plans a major plant expansion (a capital expenditure) of $100 in the second quarter. If we put all this information together, the cash outflows are as shown in Table 18.4.

The Cash Balance

The predicted net cash inflow is the difference between cash collections and cash disbursements. The net cash inflow for Fun Toys is shown in Table 18.5. What we see immediately is that there is a cash surplus in the first and third quarters and a cash deficit in the second and fourth.

We assume that Fun Toys starts the year with a $20 cash balance. Furthermore, Fun Toys maintains a $10 minimum cash balance to guard against unforeseen contingencies and forecasting errors. So we start the first quarter with $20 in cash. This increases by $40 during the quarter, and the ending balance is $60. Of this, $10 is reserved as a minimum, so we subtract it out and find that the first-quarter surplus is $60 − 10 = $50.

TABLE 18.4

Cash disbursements for Fun Toys (in $ millions)

	Q1	Q2	Q3	Q4
Payment of accounts (60% of sales)	$120	$180	$150	$240
Wages, taxes, other expenses	40	60	50	80
Capital expenditures	0	100	0	0
Long-term financing expenses (interest and dividends)	20	20	20	20
Total	$180	$360	$220	$340

TABLE 18.5

Net cash inflow for Fun Toys (in $ millions)

	Q1	Q2	Q3	Q4
Total cash collections	$220	$250	$275	$325
Total cash disbursements	180	360	220	340
Net cash inflow	$ 40	−$110	$ 55	$ 15

Fun Toys starts the second quarter with $60 in cash (the ending balance from the previous quarter). There is a net cash inflow of −$110, so the ending balance is $60 − 110 = −$50. We need another $10 as a buffer, so the total deficit is −$60. These calculations and those for the last two quarters are summarized in Table 18.6.

TABLE 18.6

Cash balance for Fun Toys (in $ millions)

	Q1	Q2	Q3	Q4
Beginning cash balance	$20	$60	−$50	$ 5
Net cash inflow	40	−110	55	−15
Ending cash balance	$60	−$50	$ 5	−$10
Minimum cash balance	−10	−10	−10	−10
Cumulative surplus (deficit)	$50	−$60	−$ 5	−$20

Beginning in the second quarter, Fun Toys has a cash shortfall of $60. This occurs because of the seasonal pattern of sales (higher toward the end of the second quarter), the delay in collections, and the planned capital expenditure.

The cash situation at Fun Toys is projected to improve to a $5 deficit in the third quarter, but, by year's end, Fun Toys still has a $20 deficit. Without some sort of financing, this deficit would carry over into the next year. We explore financing sources in the next section.
For now, we can make the following general comments on Fun Toys' cash needs:

1. Fun Toys' large outflow in the second quarter is not necessarily a sign of trouble. It results from delayed collections on sales and a planned capital expenditure (presumably a worthwhile one).

2. The figures in our example are based on a forecast. Sales could be much worse (or better) than the forecast.

Concept Questions

1. How would you do a sensitivity analysis (discussed in Chapter 11) for Fun Toys' net cash balance?

2. What could you learn from such an analysis?

18.5 | A Short-Term Financial Plan

To illustrate a completed short-term financial plan, we assume Fun Toys arranges to borrow any needed funds on a short-term basis. The interest rate is 20 percent APR, and it is compounded on a quarterly basis. From Chapter 6, we know that the rate is 20%/4 = 5% per quarter. We assume that Fun Toys starts the year with no short-term debt.

From Table 18.6, Fun Toys has a second-quarter deficit of $60 million. We have to borrow this amount. Net cash inflow in the following quarter is $55 million. We now have to pay $60 × .05 = $3 million in interest out of that, leaving $52 million to reduce the borrowing.

We still owe $60 − 52 = $8 million at the end of the third quarter. Interest in the last quarter is thus $8 × .05 = $.4 million. In addition, net inflows in the last quarter are −$15 million, so we have to borrow $15.4 million, bringing our total borrowing up to $15.4 + 8 = $23.4 million. Table 18.7 extends Table 18.6 to include these calculations.

TABLE 18.7

Short-term financial plan for Fun Toys (in $ millions)

	Q1	Q2	Q3	Q4
Beginning cash balance	$20	$ 60	$ 10	$10.0
Net cash inflow	40	−110	55	−15.0
New short-term borrowing	—	60	—	15.4
Interest on short-term borrowing	—	—	−3	−.4
Short-term borrowing repaid	—	—	−52	—
Ending cash balance	$60	$ 10	$ 10	$10.0
Minimum cash balance	−10	−10	−10	−10.0
Cumulative surplus (deficit)	$50	$ 0	$ 0	$ 0.0
Beginning short-term borrowing	0	0	60	8.0
Change in short-term debt	0	60	−52	15.4
Ending short-term debt	$ 0	$ 60	$ 8	$23.4

Notice that the ending short-term debt is just equal to the cumulative deficit for the entire year, $20, plus the interest paid during the year, $3 + .4 = $3.4, for a total of $23.4.

Our plan is very simple. For example, we ignored the fact that the interest paid on the short-term debt is tax deductible. We also ignored the fact that the cash surplus in the first quarter would earn some interest (which would be taxable). We could add on a number of refinements. Even so, our plan highlights the fact that in about 90 days, Fun Toys would need to borrow $60 million or so on a short-term basis. It's time to start lining up the source of the funds.

Our plan also illustrates that financing the firm's short-term needs costs more than $3 million in interest (before taxes) for the year. This is a starting point for Fun Toys to begin evaluating alternatives to reduce this expense. For example, can the $100 million planned expenditure be postponed or spread out? At 5 percent per quarter, short-term credit is expensive.

Also, if Fun Toys' sales are expected to keep growing, the $20 million plus deficit would probably also keep growing, and the need for additional financing is permanent. Fun Toys may wish to think about raising money on a long-term basis to cover this need.

As our example for Fun Toys illustrates, cash budgeting is a planning exercise because it forces the financial manager to think about future cash flows. This is important because, as we showed in Chapter 4, firms can "grow bankrupt" if there is no planning. This is why bankers, venture capitalists, and other financing sources stress the importance of management and planning.

Short-Term Planning and Risk

After it is revised, the short-term financial plan in Table 18.7 represents Fun Toys' best guess for the future. Large firms go beyond the best guess to ask what-if questions using scenario analysis, sensitivity analysis, and simulation. We introduced these techniques in Chapter 11's discussion of project analysis. They are tools for assessing the degree of forecasting risk and identifying those components most critical to the success or failure of a financial plan.

Recall that scenario analysis involves varying the base case plan to create several others—a best case, worst case, and so on. Each produces different financing needs to give the financial manager a first look at risk.

Sensitivity analysis is a variation on scenario analysis that is useful in pinpointing the areas where forecasting risk is especially severe. The basic idea of sensitivity analysis is to freeze all the variables except one and then see how sensitive our estimate of financing needs is to changes in that one variable. If our projected financing turns out to be very sensitive to, say, sales, then we know that extra effort in refining the sales forecast would pay off.

Since the original financial plan was almost surely developed on a computer spreadsheet, scenario and sensitivity analysis are quite straightforward and widely used.

Simulation analysis combines the features of scenario and sensitivity analysis varying all the variables over a range of outcomes simultaneously. The result of simulation analysis is a probability distribution of financing needs.

aircanada.ca

Air Canada uses simulation analysis in forecasting its cash needs. The simulation is useful in capturing the variability of cash flow components in the airline industry in Canada. Bad weather, for example, causes delays and cancelled flights, with unpredictable dislocation payments to travellers and crew overtime. This and other risks are reflected in a probability distribution of cash needs, giving the treasurer better information for planning borrowing needs. Beyond the weather, financial market turmoil can also create challenges for cash budgeting. The fallout of the credit crisis of 2007–2008 made it difficult for firms to raise capital as the lender base shrunk.

18.6 | Short-Term Borrowing

Fun Toys has a short-term financing problem. It cannot meet the forecasted cash outflows in the second quarter from internal sources. How it finances that shortfall depends on its financial policy. With a very flexible policy, Fun Toys might seek up to $60 million in long-term debt financing.

In addition, much of the cash deficit comes from the large capital expenditure. Arguably, this is a candidate for long-term financing. Examples discussed in Chapter 15 include issuing shares or bonds or taking a term loan from a chartered bank or other financial institution. If it chose equity financing through an initial public offering (IPO), Fun Toys would be following the example of Chapters Online. As the firm's Internet division, Chapters Online sells books, CD ROMs, DVDs and videos through its website. In September 1999, Chapters Online went public, raising equity at an offering price of $13.50 per share. A little under a year later, in August 2000, analysts calculated Chapters Online's "burn rate," the rate at which the firm was using cash, to determine its cash position. Given that the stock price had fallen from the offering price of $13.50 to $2.80 per share, a further equity offering seemed unlikely and the discussion of the firm's financial health focused on the availability of short-term borrowing.

Here we concentrate on two short-term borrowing alternatives: (1) unsecured borrowing and (2) secured borrowing.

Operating Loans

operating loan
Loan negotiated with banks for day-to-day operations.

The most common way to finance a temporary cash deficit is to arrange a short-term **operating loan** from a chartered bank. This is an agreement under which a firm is authorized to borrow up to a specified amount for a given period, usually one year (much like a credit card).[9] Operating loans can be either unsecured or secured by collateral. Large corporations with excellent credit ratings usually structure the facility as an unsecured line of credit. Because unsecured credit lines are backed only by projections of future cash flows, bankers offer this cash flow lending only to those with top-drawer credit.

Short-term lines of credit are classified as either *committed* or *noncommitted*. The latter is an informal arrangement. Committed lines of credit are more formal legal arrangements and usually involve a commitment fee paid by the firm to the bank (usually the fee is 0.25 percent of the total committed funds per year). A firm that pays a commitment fee for a committed line of credit is essentially buying insurance to guarantee that the bank can't back out of the agreement (absent some material change in the borrower's status).

COMPENSATING THE BANK   The interest rate on an operating loan is usually set equal to the bank's prime lending rate plus an additional percentage, and the rate usually floats. For example, suppose that the prime rate is 3 percent when the loan is initiated and the loan is at prime plus 1.5 percent. The original rate charged the borrower is 4.5 percent. If after, say, 125 days, prime increases to 3.5 percent, the company's borrowing rate goes up to 5 percent and interest charges are adjusted accordingly.

The premium charged over prime reflects the banker's assessment of the borrower's risk. Table 18.8 lists factors bankers use in assessing risk in loans to small business. Notice that risks related to management appear most often because poor management is considered the major risk with small business. There is a trend among bankers to look more closely at industry and economic risk factors. A similar set of risk factors applies to loans to large corporations.

TABLE 18.8

Factors mentioned in the credit files	Factor	Percent of Mentions (1,539 cases)
	1. **Economic environment** Opportunities and risks	6.1%
	2. **Industry environment** Competitive conditions, prospects, and risks	40.4
	3. **Client's marketing activities** Strategies, strengths, and weaknesses	30.8
	4. **Firm's operations management** Strengths and weaknesses	59.5
	5. **Client's financial resources, skills, and performance** Financial management expertise Historical or future profitability Future cash flows Future financing needs (beyond the current year)	44.9 84.8 41.6 20.5
	6. **Management capabilities and character** Strengths and weaknesses Length of ownership of the firm Past management experience relevant to the business	79.6 95.1 57.1
Source: Larry Wynant and James Hatch, *Banks and Small Business Borrowers* (London: University of Western Ontario, 1991), p. 136.	7. **Collateral security and the firm's net worth position**	97.7
	8. **Borrower's past relationship with bank**	65.3

---

[9]Descriptions of bank loans draw on L. Wynant and J. Hatch, *Banks and Small Business Borrowers* (London: University of Western Ontario, 1991).

Banks are in the business of lending mainly to low-risk borrowers. For this reason, bankers generally prefer to decline risky business loans that would require an interest rate more than prime plus 3 percent. Many of the loan requests that banks turn down are from small business, especially start-ups. Around 60 percent of these turn-downs find financing elsewhere. Alternative sources include venture capital financing discussed in Chapter 15 and federal and provincial government programs to assist small business.

In addition to charging interest, banks also levy fees for account activity and loan management. Small businesses may also pay application fees to cover the costs of processing loan applications. Fees are becoming increasingly important in bank compensation.[10] Fees and other details of any short-term business lending arrangements are highly negotiable. Banks generally work with firms to design a package of fees and interest.

Letters of Credit

letter of credit
A written statement by a bank that money will be paid, provided conditions specified in the letter are met.

A **letter of credit** is a common arrangement in international finance. With a letter of credit, the bank issuing the letter promises to make a loan if certain conditions are met. Typically, the letter guarantees payment on a shipment of goods provided that the goods arrive as promised. A letter of credit can be revocable (subject to cancellation) or irrevocable (not subject to cancellation if the specified conditions are met).

Secured Loans

Banks and other financial institutions often require security for an operating loan just as they do for a long-term loan. Table 18.8 shows that collateral security is a factor in virtually every small-business loan. Security for short-term loans usually consists of accounts receivable, inventories, or both because these are the assets most likely to retain value if the borrower goes bankrupt. Security is intended to reduce the lender's risk by providing a second "line of defence" behind the borrower's projected cash flows. To achieve this intention, the ideal collateral is Treasury bills or another asset whose value is independent of the borrower's business. We say this because, under the NPV principle, business assets derive their value from cash flow. When business is bad and cash flow low (or negative), the collateral value is greatly reduced. Several Canadian banks found this out in the early 1990s when they wrote off billions in real estate loans, and again in 2002 when the deteriorating financial health of several large telecom companies including Worldcom, Teleglobe, and Global Crossing resulted in significant loan write-downs.

covenants
A promise by the firm, included in the debt contract, to perform certain acts. A restrictive covenant imposes constraints on the firm to protect the interests of the debtholder.

In addition, banks routinely limit risk through loan conditions called **covenants**. Table 18.9 lists common covenants in Canadian small-business loans. You can see that bankers expect to have a detailed knowledge of their clients' businesses.

accounts receivable financing
A secured short-term loan that involves either the assignment or factoring of receivables.

Accounts receivable financing from chartered banks typically involves assigning receivables to the lender under a general assignment of book debts. Under assignment, the bank or other lender has the receivables as security, but the borrower is still responsible if a receivable can't be collected. The lending agreement establishes a margin usually 75 percent of current (under 90 days) receivables. As the firm makes sales, it submits its invoices to the bank and can borrow up to 75 percent of their value.

Inventory margins are set similarly to accounts receivable. Since inventory is often less liquid than receivables (bringing a lower percentage of book value in liquidations), inventory lending margins are lower, typically 50 percent.

Many small and medium-sized businesses secure their operating loans with both receivables and inventory. In this case, the lending limit fluctuates with both accounts according to the lending margins.

---

[10] U.S. banks sometimes require that the firm keep some account of money on deposit. This is called a compensating balance. A *compensating balance* is some of the firm's money kept by the bank in low-interest or non-interest-bearing accounts. By leaving these funds with the bank and receiving no interest, the firm further increases the effective interest rate earned by the bank on the line of credit, thereby compensating the bank.

TABLE 18.9

Loan conditions for approved bank credits in the credit file sample

Condition	Percent of Cases* (1,382 cases)
Postponement of shareholder claims	39.8%
Life insurance on key principals	39.4
Fire insurance on company premises	35.7
Accounts receivable and inventory reporting	27.8
Limits on withdrawals and dividends	11.9
Limits on capital expenditures	10.5
Maintenance of minimum working capital levels	2.9
Restrictions on further debt	2.5
Restrictions on disposal of company assets	1.7
Maintenance of minimum cash balances	0.9
Other conditions	6.2

*Adds up to more than 100 percent because of multiple responses.

Source: Larry Wynant and James Hatch, *Banks and Small Business Borrowers* (London: University of Western Ontario, 1991), p. 173.

EXAMPLE 18.3: Secured Borrowing for Fun Toys

Based on the cash budget we drew up earlier, the financial manager of Fun Toys has decided to seek a bank operating loan to cover the projected deficit of $60 million. The Royal Canadian National Bank has offered Fun Toys an operating loan at prime plus 1 percent to be secured by inventories. The lending officer has set a 75 percent margin on current receivables and 50 percent on inventory. Fun Toys has assured you that all its receivables are current and that two-thirds of payables were for inventory purchases. Can Fun Toys provide sufficient security for a $60 million operating loan?

Tables 18.3 and 18.4 show receivables and payables for Fun Toys for the next three quarters. Since the bank lends only against existing receivables and inventory, we use the Q1 beginning figures of $120 million for receivables and the same figure for payables. The full amount of the inventory is eligible for margining but only two-thirds of payables ($80) are inventory. We can calculate the amount that Fun Toys can secure as follows:

	Amount	× Margin	= Security
Receivables	$120	.75	$ 90
Inventory	80	.50	40
Total eligible security			$130

So Fun Toys could borrow up to $130 million under the margin formula and have no trouble securing a loan of $60 million

Factoring

In addition to bank borrowing, accounts receivable financing is also possible through factoring. A factor is an independent company that acts as "an outside credit department" for the client. It checks the credit of new customers, authorizes credit, handles collections and bookkeeping. If any accounts are late, the factor still pays the selling firm on an average maturity date determined in advance. The legal arrangement is that the factor purchases the accounts receivable from the firm. Thus, factoring provides insurance against bad debts because any defaults on bad accounts are the factor's problem. Companies such as Accord Financial Corp. in Canada, provide factoring services allowing client firms to shorten their collection cycles and expand sales. Accord purchases the client's receivables and provides up to 85% of the value of the approved invoices.[11]

Factoring in Canada is conducted by independent firms whose main customers are small businesses. Factoring is popular with manufacturers of retail goods, especially in the apparel business. The attraction of factoring to small businesses is that it allows outside professionals to handle the headaches of credit. To avoid magnifying those headaches, factors must offer cost savings and avoid alienating their clients' customers in the collection process.

[11] accordfinancial.com/financing-services/receivable-purchase-financing.html

maturity factoring
Short-term financing in which the factor purchases all of a firm's receivables and forwards the proceeds to the seller as soon as they are collected.

What we have described so far is **maturity factoring** and does not involve a formal financing arrangement. What factoring does is remove receivables from the statement of financial position and so, indirectly, it reduces the need for financing. It may also reduce the costs associated with granting credit. Because factors do business with many firms, they may be able to achieve scale economies, reduce risks through diversification, and carry more clout in collection.

Firms financing their receivables through a chartered bank may also use the services of a factor to improve the receivables' collateral value. In this case, the factor buys the receivables and assigns them to the bank. This is called *maturity factoring with assignment of equity*. Or the factor provides an advance on the receivables and charges interest at prime plus 2.5 to 3 percent. In advance factoring, the factor provides financing as well as other services.

EXAMPLE 18.4: Cost of Factoring

For the year just ended, LuLu's Fashions had $500,000 in credit sales monthly with an average maturity of receivables of 45 days. LuLu's uses a factor to obtain funds 15 days after the sale. This means the factor is advancing funds for $45 - 15 = 30$ days. The factor charges 10.5 percent interest (APR), 2.5 percent over the current prime rate of 8 percent. In addition, the factor charges a 1.5 percent fee for processing the receivables and assuming all credit risk. If LuLu's ran its own credit department, it would cost $2,000 per month in variable expenses and this is saved with factoring. What is the effective interest cost of factoring?

The costs are:

			Per Month
Interest = .105 × 30/365 × $500,000	=		$ 4,315
Factor's fee = .015 × $500,000	=		7,500
Variables expenses saved	=		−2,000
Total cost			$ 9,815

$9,815/$500,000 = 1.96 percent per month.

The effective annual rate (EAR) is $(1.0196)^{12} - 1 = 26.23$ percent.

Note that the factor takes on the risk of default by a buyer, thus providing insurance as well as immediate cash. More generally, the factor essentially takes over the firm's credit operations. This can result in a significant saving. The interest rate we calculated is therefore overstated, particularly if default is a significant possibility.

Securitized Receivables—A Financial Innovation

Financial engineers have come up with a new approach to receivables financing. When a large corporation such as Canadian Tire, securitized receivables, it sold them to Glacier Credit Card Trust, a wholly owned subsidiary. Glacier issued debentures and commercial paper backed by a diversified portfolio of receivables. Because receivables are liquid, Glacier debt is less risky than lending to Canadian Tire and the company hopes to benefit through interest savings. The growing market for asset-backed securities faced a major setback in the global credit crisis beginning in 2007. As a result, companies like Canadian Tire ensure that back-up financing from bank lines of credit and medium-term notes programs are in place.

Inventory Loans

inventory loan
A secured short-term loan to purchase inventory.

Inventory loans, or operating loans to finance inventory, feature assignment of inventory to the lender who then advances funds according to a predetermined margin as we discussed earlier. The specific legal arrangements depend on the type of inventory. The most sweeping form is the general security agreement that registers security over all a firm's assets. Inventory as a whole can be assigned under Section 178 of the *Bank Act*, or *Bill 97* in Quebec. If the inventory consists of equipment or large, movable assets, the appropriate legal form is a chattel mortgage (commercial pledge of equipment in Quebec).

trust receipt
An instrument acknowledging that the borrower holds certain goods in trust for the lender.

The legal form of the security arrangement can be tailored to the type of inventory. For example, with large, expensive items in inventory, the security agreement is often based on **trust receipts** listing the individual items by serial numbers. Trust receipts are used to support *floor plan financing* for automobile dealers and sellers of household appliances and other equipment. The advantage of floor plan financing is that it gives the lender a systematic way to monitor the inventory as it moves through the cash cycle. As the vehicles are sold, the dealer reports the sale to the lender and repays the financing.

IN THEIR OWN WORDS...

Ken Hitzig on Keeping Business Liquid through Factoring

Through subsidiaries in Canada and the United States, Accord Financial Corp. provides factoring services to small and medium-sized companies. Accord's customers are engaged in temporary staff placement, computer services, textiles, apparel, medical services, food distribution, sporting goods, leisure products, transportation, footwear, floor coverings, home furnishings, and industrial products.

Accord is engaged in the factoring business on both a recourse and non-recourse basis. Non-recourse factoring is a service provided to companies desiring to outsource their customer accounts receivable departments, including the risk of customer default. Almost all the work involving credit checking, recordkeeping, collections, and credit losses is effectively off-loaded on Accord for a predetermined fee. Financing is available, but few of Accord's clients avail themselves of this facility, preferring instead to fund their business through banks.

Accord's non-recourse service appeals to medium-sized companies (annual sales of $1–$10 million) which view the virtual elimination of customer credit risk as the single, most important benefit. Most of these clients are privately owned and the owners are very aware of preserving capital and avoiding unnecessary risk. The failure of a large customer could cause the bank to reduce or cancel the operating line of credit and jeopardize the owner's life savings. Non-recourse factoring with Accord solves the problem. As one client described it: "Accord's credit is best described in three words—Ship and Sleep."

Recourse factoring is similar to non-recourse but the customer credit risk remains with the client company. Accord purchases the invoices from the client for cash; however, in the event of customer default, Accord has the right to resell the account back to the client. Recourse factoring is attractive to small and medium-sized companies needing liquidity but unable to borrow from banks on the strength of their financial statements. These companies are usually thinly capitalized, going through a turnaround phase, growing rapidly or a combination of some or all of these traits. They usually have better-than-average quality customers, and by factoring their sales, they effectively exchange paper for cash.

Ken Hitzig is a Commerce graduate of McGill University and a Chartered Accountant. After an 18-year career at Aetna Factors Corp. Ltd., he left to start Accord Business Credit Inc. in 1978. Along with Montcap Financial Corp. in Canada and J.T.A. Factors, Inc. in South Carolina, Accord is now a subsidiary of Accord Financial Corp., a publicly held company listed on the Toronto Stock Exchange. Mr. Hitzig is Chairman, Board of Director of Accord Financial Corp.

Warehouse financing is a similar system in which the inventory that serves as security is identified and monitored. In this case, the inventory is segregated in a designated field or public warehouse run by a third party. The warehouse issues a *warehouse receipt* providing legal evidence of the existence of the security. Because the goods are segregated, warehouse financing is not suitable for work-in-progress inventory. On the other hand, this form of financing is ideally suited for inventories that improve with age such as whiskey or wine.

Trade Credit

When a firm purchases supplies on credit, the increase in accounts payable is a source of funds and automatic financing. As compared with bank financing, trade credit has the advantage of arising automatically from the firm's business. It does not require a formal financing agreement with covenants that may restrict the borrower's business activities. Suppliers offer credit to remain competitive; in many industries, the terms of credit include a cash discount for paying within a certain period. For example, suppose a supplier offers terms of 2/10, net 30.[12] If your firm makes a $1,000 purchase, you have a choice of paying after 10 days, taking the cash discount, or paying the full $1,000 after 30 days. Or you could stretch your payables by paying the $1,000 after, say, 45 days. The longer you wait, the longer the supplier is providing you with trade credit financing.

In making your decision, you should ask whether the cash discount provides a significant incentive for early payment. The answer is yes because the implicit interest rate is extremely high.

---

[12]Chapter 20 provides a full discussion of credit terms from the seller's viewpoint.

To see why the discount is important, we calculate the cost to the buyer of not paying early. To do this, we find the interest rate that the buyer is effectively paying for the trade credit. Suppose the order is for $1,000. The buyer can pay $980 in 10 days or wait another 20 days and pay $1,000. (For the moment, we ignore the possibility of stretching.) It's obvious that the buyer is effectively borrowing $980 for 20 days and that the buyer pays $20 in interest on the loan. What's the interest rate?

This interest is ordinary discount interest, which we discussed in Chapter 5. With $20 in interest on $980 borrowed, the rate is $20/$980 = 2.0408%. This is relatively low, but remember that this is the rate per 20-day period. There are 365/20 = 18.25 such periods in a year, so the buyer is paying an effective annual rate (EAR) of:

$$EAR = (1.020408)^{18.25} - 1 = 44.6\%$$

From the buyer's point of view, this is an expensive source of financing.

Now suppose the buyer decides to stretch its payables and pay in 45 days. What is the EAR now? The interest is still $20 on $980 borrowed so the rate is still 2.0408%. What stretching changes is the length of the loan period. Since we are paying on Day 45, the loan period is now $45 - 10 = 35$ days. There are 365/35 = 10.43 such periods in a year. The new EAR is:

$$EAR = (1.020408)^{10.43} - 1 = 23.5\%$$

So you can see that stretching reduces the EAR somewhat but this does not make it a recommended practice. Companies that habitually pay their suppliers late risk supplier ill will. This may impact unfavourably on delivery schedules and, in the extreme case, suppliers may cut off the firm or ship only terms of C.O.D. (cash on delivery). Late payment may also harm the firm's credit rating.

EXAMPLE 18.5: What's the Rate?

Ordinary tiles are often sold 3/30, net 60. What effective annual rate does a buyer pay by not taking the discount? What would the APR be if one were quoted?

Here we have 3 percent discount interest on $60 - 30 = 30$ days' credit. The rate per 30 days is .03/.97 = 3.093%. There are 365/30 = 12.17 such periods in a year, so the effective annual rate is:

$$EAR = (1.03093)^{12.17} - 1 = 44.9\%$$

The APR, as always, would be calculated by multiplying the rate per period by the number of periods:

$$APR = .03093 \times 12.17 = 37.6\%$$

An interest rate calculated like this APR is often quoted as the cost of the trade credit, and, as this example illustrates, the true cost can be seriously understated.

Money Market Financing

Large firms with excellent credit ratings can obtain financing directly from money markets. Two of the most important money market instruments for short-term financing are commercial paper and bankers acceptances.

Commercial paper consists of short-term notes issued by large and highly rated firms. Firms issuing commercial paper in Canada generally have borrowing needs over $20 million. Rating agencies, DBRS and Standard & Poor's (S&P) discussed in Chapter 7, rate commercial paper similarly to bonds. Typically, these notes are of short maturity, ranging from 30 to 90 days with some maturities up to 365 days. Commercial paper is offered in denominations of $100,000 and up. Because the firm issues paper directly and because it usually backs the issue with a special bank line of credit, the interest rate the firm obtains is less than the rate a bank would charge for a direct loan, usually by around 1 percent. Another advantage is that commercial paper offers the issuer flexibility in tailoring the maturity and size of the borrowing.

Bankers acceptances are a variant on commercial paper. When a bank accepts paper, it charges a stamping fee in return for a guarantee of the paper's principal and interest. Stamping fees vary from .20 percent to .75 percent. Bankers acceptances are more widely used than commercial paper in Canada because Canadian chartered banks enjoy stronger credit ratings than all but the largest corporations.[13] The main buyers of bankers acceptances and commercial paper are institutions, including mutual funds, insurance companies, and banks.

A disadvantage of borrowing through bankers acceptances or commercial paper is the risk that the market might temporarily dry up when it comes time to roll over the paper. Extendible commercial paper is an innovation designed to address the risk of market disruption. In the event that the issuer cannot obtain new financing through normal channels, the extension feature makes it possible to keep maturing paper in force beyond its stated maturity.

Figure 18.7 shows the short term financing market in Canada. Clearly, the Asset Backed Commercial Paper (ABCP) fell out of favour after the financial crises in 2008. However, Bankers Acceptances are steadily on the rise during the same period.

FIGURE 18.7

Short-term financing market in Canada

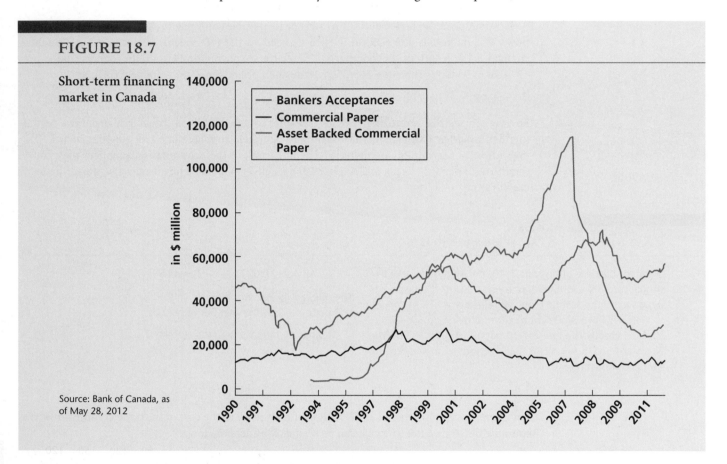

Source: Bank of Canada, as of May 28, 2012

Concept Questions

1. What are the two basic forms of short-term financing?
2. Describe two types of secured operating loans.
3. Describe factoring and the services it provides.
4. How does trade credit work? Should firms stretch their accounts payable?
5. Describe commercial paper and bankers acceptances. How do they differ?

---

[13] The reverse situation prevails in the United States, with commercial paper being more common.

18.7 | SUMMARY AND CONCLUSIONS

1. This chapter introduces the management of short-term finance. Short-term finance involves short-lived assets and liabilities. We trace and examine the short-term sources and uses of cash as they appear on the firm's financial statements. We see how current assets and current liabilities arise in the short-term operating activities and the cash cycle of the firm. This chapter shows why managing the cash cycle is critical to small businesses.

2. Managing short-term cash flows involves the minimizing of costs. The two major costs are carrying costs, the return forgone by keeping too much invested in short-term assets such as cash, and shortage costs, the cost of running out of short-term assets. The objective of managing short-term finance and doing short-term financial planning is to find the optimal trade-off between these two costs.

3. In an ideal economy, the firm could perfectly predict its short-term uses and sources of cash, and net working capital could be kept at zero. In the real world we live in, cash and net working capital provide a buffer that lets the firm meet its ongoing obligations. The financial manager seeks the optimal level of each of the current assets.

4. The financial manager can use the cash budget to identify short-term financial needs. The cash budget tells the manager what borrowing is required or what lending will be possible in the short run. The firm has available to it a number of possible ways of acquiring funds to meet short-term shortfalls, including unsecured and secured loans.

Key Terms

accounts payable period (page 522)
accounts receivable financing (page 539)
accounts receivable period (page 522)
carrying costs (page 527)
cash budget (page 533)
cash cycle (page 522)
cash flow time line (page 522)
covenants (page 539)

inventory loan (page 541)
inventory period (page 522)
letter of credit (page 539)
maturity factoring (page 541)
operating cycle (page 522)
operating loan (page 537)
shortage costs (page 537)
trust receipt (page 541)

Chapter Review Problems and Self-Test

18.1 **The Operating and Cash Cycles** Consider the following financial statement information for the Glory Road Company:

Item	Beginning	Ending
Inventory	$1,543	$1,669
Accounts receivable	4,418	3,952
Accounts payable	2,551	2,673
Net sales		$11,500
Cost of goods sold		8,200

Calculate the operating and cash cycles.

18.2 **Cash Balance for Masson Corporation** The Masson Corporation has a 60-day average collection period and wishes to maintain a $5 million minimum cash balance. Based on this and the following information, complete the cash budget. What conclusions do you draw?

MASSON CORPORATION
Cash Budget (in $ millions)

	Q1	Q2	Q3	Q4
Beginning receivables	$120			
Sales	90	120	150	120
Cash collections				
Ending receivables				
Total cash collections				
Total cash disbursements	80	160	180	160
Net cash inflow				
Beginning cash balance	$ 5			
Net cash inflow				
Ending cash balance				
Minimum cash balance				
Cumulative surplus (deficit)				

Answers to Self-Test Problems

18.1 We first need the turnover ratios. Note that we have used the average values for all statement of financial position items and that we have based the inventory and payables turnover measures on cost of goods sold.

Inventory turnover = $8,200/[(1,543 + 1,669)/2] = 5.11 times

Receivables turnover = $11,500/[(4,418 + 3,952)/2] = 2.75 times

Payables turnover = $8,200/[(2,551 + 2,673)/2] = 3.14 times

We can now calculate the various periods:

Inventory period = 365 days/5.11 times = 71.43 days
Receivables period = 365 days/2.75 times = 132.73 days
Payables period = 365 days/3.14 times = 116.24 days

So the time it takes to acquire inventory and sell it is about 71 days. Collection takes another 133 days, and the operating cycle is thus 71 + 133 = 204 days. The cash cycle is thus 204 days less the payables period, 204 − 116 = 88 days.

18.2   Since Masson has a 60-day collection period, only those sales made in the first 30 days of the quarter are collected in the same quarter. Total cash collections in the first quarter thus equal 30/90 = 1/3 of sales plus beginning receivables, or $120 + 1/3 × $90 = $150. Ending receivables for the first quarter (and the second quarter beginning receivables) are the other 2/3 of sales, or 2/3 × $90 = $60. The remaining calculations are straightforward, and the completed budget follows:

MASSON CORPORATION
Cash Budget (in $ millions)

	Q1	Q2	Q3	Q4
Beginning receivables	$120	$ 60	$ 80	$100
Sales	90	120	150	120
Cash collection	150	100	130	140
Ending receivables	$ 60	$ 80	$100	$ 80
Total cash collections	$150	$100	$130	$140
Total cash disbursements	80	160	180	160
Net cash inflow	$ 70	−$ 60	−$ 50	−$ 20
Beginning cash balance	$ 5	$ 75	$ 15	−$ 35
Net cash inflow	70	− 60	− 50	− 20
Ending cash balance	$ 75	$ 15	−$ 35	−$ 55
Minimum cash balance	−$ 5	−$ 5	−$ 5	−$ 5
Cumulative surplus (deficit)	$ 70	$ 10	−$ 40	−$ 60

The primary conclusion from this schedule is that beginning in the third quarter, Masson's cash surplus becomes a cash deficit. By the end of the year, Masson needs to arrange for $60 million in cash beyond what is available.

Concepts Review and Critical Thinking Questions

1. **Operating Cycle (LO1)** What are some of the characteristics of a firm with a long operating cycle?

2. **Cash Cycle (LO1)** What are some of the characteristics of a firm with a long cash cycle?

3. **Sources and Uses (LO4)** For the year just ended, you have gathered the following information about the Holly Corporation:
    a. A $200 dividend was paid.
    b. Accounts payable increased by $500.
    c. Fixed asset purchases were $900.
    d. Inventories increased by $625.
    e. Long-term debt decreased by $1,200.
    Label each as a source or use of cash and describe its effect on the firm's cash balance.

4. **Cost of Current Assets (LO2)** Loftis Manufacturing Inc. has recently installed a just-in-time (JIT) inventory system. Describe the effect this is likely to have on the company's carrying costs, shortage costs, and operating cycle.

5. **Operating and Cash Cycles (LO1)** Is it possible for a firm's cash cycle to be longer than its operating cycle? Explain why or why not.

Use the following information to answer Questions 6–10: Last month, BlueSky Airline announced that it would stretch out its bill payments to 45 days from 30 days. The reason given was that the company wanted to "control costs and optimize cash flow." The increased payables period will be in effect for all of the company's 4000 suppliers.

6. **Operating and Cash Cycles (LO1)** What impact did this change in payables policy have on BlueSky's operating cycle? Its cash cycle?

7. **Operating and Cash Cycles (LO1)** What impact did the announcement have on BlueSky's suppliers?

8. **Corporate Ethics (LO1)** Is it ethical for large firms to unilaterally lengthen their payables periods, particularly when dealing with smaller suppliers?

9. **Payables Period (LO1)** Why don't all firms simply increase their payables periods to shorten their cash cycles?

10. **Payables Period (LO1)** BlueSky lengthened its payables period to "control costs and optimize cash flow." Exactly what is the cash benefit to BlueSky from this change?

Questions and Problems

Basic
(Questions
1–12)

1. Changes in the Cash Account (LO4) Indicate the impact of the following corporate actions on cash, using the letter *I* for an increase, *D* for a decrease, or *N* when no change occurs:

a. A dividend is paid with funds received from a sale of debt.

b. Real estate is purchased and paid for with short-term debt.

c. Inventory is bought on credit.

d. A short-term bank loan is repaid.

e. Next year's taxes are prepaid.

f. Preferred stock is redeemed.

g. Sales are made on credit.

h. Interest on long-term debt is paid.

i. Payments for previous sales are collected.

j. The accounts payable balance is reduced.

k. A dividend is paid.

l. Production supplies are purchased and paid for with a short-term note.

m. Utility bills are paid.

n. Cash is paid for raw materials purchased for inventory.

o. Marketable securities are sold.

2. Cash Equation (LO3) Prince George Corp. has a book net worth of $13,205. Long-term debt is $8,200. Net working capital, other than cash, is $2,575. Fixed assets are $17,380. How much cash does the company have? If current liabilities are $1,630, what are current assets?

3. Changes in the Operating Cycle (LO1) Indicate the effect that the following will have on the operating cycle. Use the letter *I* to indicate an increase, the letter *D* for a decrease, and the letter *N* for no change:

a. Average receivables goes up.

b. Credit repayment times for customers are increased.

c. Inventory turnover goes from 3 times to 6 times.

d. Payables turnover goes from 6 times to 11 times.

e. Receivables turnover goes from 7 times to 9 times.

f. Payments to suppliers are accelerated.

4. Changes in Cycles (LO1) Indicate the impact of the following on the cash and operating cycles, respectively. Use the letter *I* to indicate an increase, the letter *D* for a decrease, and the letter *N* for no change:

a. The terms of cash discounts offered to customers are made less favourable.

b. The cash discounts offered by suppliers are decreased; thus, payments are made earlier.

c. An increased number of customers begin to pay in cash instead of with credit.

d. Fewer raw materials than usual are purchased.

e. A greater percentage of raw material purchases are paid for with credit.

f. More finished goods are produced for inventory instead of for order.

5. Calculating Cash Collections (LO3) The Charella Coffee Company has projected the following quarterly sales amounts for the coming year:

	Q1	Q2	Q3	Q4
Sales	$720	$750	$830	$910

a. Accounts receivable at the beginning of the year are $310. Charella has a 45-day collection period. Calculate cash collections in each of the four quarters by completing the following:

	Q1	Q2	Q3	Q4
Beginning receivables				
Sales				
Cash collections				
Ending receivables				

b. Rework (a) assuming a collection period of 60 days.

c. Rework (a) assuming a collection period of 30 days.

6. **Calculating Cycles (LO1)** Consider the following financial statement information for the Carlboo Corporation:

Item	Beginning	Ending
Inventory	$10,583	$12,142
Accounts receivable	5,130	5,340
Accounts payable	7,205	7,630
Credit sales		$97,381
Cost of goods sold		69,382

Calculate the operating and cash cycles. How do you interpret your answer? Assume 365 days in a year.

7. **Factoring Receivables (LO5)** Your firm has an average collection period of 29 days. Current practice is to factor all receivables immediately at a 1.25 percent discount. What is the effective cost of borrowing in this case? Assume that default is extremely unlikely. Assume 365 days in a year.

8. **Calculating Payments (LO3)** Ospika Products has projected the following sales for the coming year:

	Q1	Q2	Q3	Q4
Sales	$790	$870	$830	$930

Sales in the year following this one are projected to be 15 percent greater in each quarter.

a. Calculate payments to suppliers assuming that Ospika places orders during each quarter equal to 30 percent of projected sales for the next quarter. Assume that Ospika pays immediately. What is the payables period in this case?

	Q1	Q2	Q3	Q4
Payment of accounts	$	$	$	$

b. Rework (a) assuming a 90-day payables period.

c. Rework (a) assuming a 60-day payables period.

9. **Calculating Payments (LO3)** The Giscome Corporation's purchases from suppliers in a quarter are equal to 75 percent of the next quarter's forecast sales. The payables period is 60 days. Wages, taxes, and other expenses are 20 percent of sales, and interest and dividends are $90 per quarter. No capital expenditures are planned.

Projected quarterly sales are shown here:

	Q1	Q2	Q3	Q4
Sales	$1,930	$2,275	$1,810	$1,520

Sales for the first quarter of the following year are projected at $2,150. Calculate the company's cash outlays by completing the following:

	Q1	Q2	Q3	Q4
Payment of accounts				
Wages, taxes, other expenses				
Long-term financing expenses (interest and dividends)				
Total				

10. **Calculating Cash Collections (LO3)** The following is the sales budget for Yellowhead Inc. for the first quarter of 2013:

	January	February	March
Sales	$195,000	$215,000	$238,000

Credit sales are collected as follows:
65 percent in the month of the sale
20 percent in the month after the sale
15 percent in the second month after the sale

The accounts receivable balance at the end of the previous quarter was $86,000 ($59,000 of which was uncollected December sales).

a. Compute the sales for November.

b. Compute the sales for December.

c. Compute the cash collections from sales for each month from January through March.

11. **Calculating the Cash Budget (LO3)** Here are some important figures from the budget of Nechako Nougats Inc. for the second quarter of 2013:

	April	May	June
Credit sales	$312,000	$291,200	$350,400
Credit purchases	118,240	141,040	166,800
Cash disbursements			
Wages, taxes, and expenses	43,040	10,800	62,640
Interest	10,480	10,480	10,480
Equipment purchases	74,000	135,000	0

The company predicts that 5 percent of its credit sales will never be collected, 35 percent of its sales will be collected in the month of the sale, and the remaining 60 percent will be collected in the following month. Credit purchases will be paid in the month following the purchase.

In March 2013, credit sales were $196,000, and credit purchases were $134,000. Using this information, complete the following cash budget:

	April	May	June
Beginning cash balance	$112,000		
Cash receipts			
Cash collections from credit sales			
Total cash available			
Cash disbursements			
Purchases			
Wages, taxes, and expenses			
Interest			
Equipment purchases			
Total cash disbursements			
Ending cash balance			

12. **Sources and Uses (LO4)** Below are the most recent statements of financial position for Tabor Inc. Excluding accumulated depreciation, determine whether each item is a source or a use of cash, and the amount:

TABOR INC.
Statement of financial position
December 31, 2013

	2012	2013
Assets		
Cash	$ 30,400	$ 29,520
Accounts receivable	69,904	73,344
Inventories	60,800	63,736
Property, plant, and equipment	147,000	157,180
Less: Accumulated depreciation	45,730	52,280
Total assets	$262,374	$271,500
Liabilities and Equity		
Accounts payable	$ 44,994	$ 47,118
Accrued expenses	6,280	5,632
Long-term debt	25,600	28,000
Common stock	16,000	20,000
Accumulated retained earnings	169,500	170,750
Total liabilities and equity	$262,374	$271,500

Intermediate (Questions 13–16)

13. **Costs of Borrowing (LO3)** You've worked out a line of credit arrangement that allows you to borrow up to $50 million at any time. The interest rate is .53 percent per month. In addition, 5 percent of the amount that you borrow must be deposited in a non-interest-bearing account. Assume that your bank uses compound interest on its line of credit loans.
   a. What is the effective annual interest rate on this lending arrangement?
   b. Suppose you need $15 million today and you repay it in six months. How much interest will you pay?

14. **Costs of Borrowing (LO3)** A bank offers your firm a revolving credit arrangement for up to $70 million at an interest rate of 1.9 percent per quarter. The bank also requires you to maintain a compensating balance of 4 percent against the unused portion of the credit line, to be deposited in a non-interest-bearing account. Assume you have a short-term investment account at the bank that pays 1.05 percent per quarter, and assume that the bank uses compound interest on its revolving credit loans.
   a. What is your effective annual interest rate (an opportunity cost) on the revolving credit arrangement if your firm does not use it during the year?
   b. What is your effective annual interest rate on the lending arrangement if you borrow $45 million immediately and repay it in one year?
   c. What is your effective annual interest rate if you borrow $70 million immediately and repay it in one year?

15. **Calculating the Cash Budget (LO3)** Cottonwood Inc. has estimated sales (in millions) for the next four quarters as follows:

	Q1	Q2	Q3	Q4
Sales	$160	$175	$190	$215

Sales for the first quarter of the year after this one are projected at $170 million. Accounts receivable at the beginning of the year were $68 million. Cottonwood has a 45-day collection period.

Cottonwood's purchases from suppliers in a quarter are equal to 45 percent of the next quarter's forecast sales, and suppliers are normally paid in 36 days. Wages, taxes, and other expenses run about 25 percent of sales. Interest and dividends are $12 million per quarter.

Cottonwood plans a major capital outlay in the second quarter of $75 million. Finally, the company started the year with a $49 million cash balance and wishes to maintain a $30 million minimum balance.

a. Complete a cash budget for Cottonwood by filling in the following:

COTTONWOOD INC.
Cash Budget (in millions)

	Q1	Q2	Q3	Q4
Beginning cash balance	$49			
Net cash inflow				
Ending cash balance				
Minimum cash balance	30			
Cumulative surplus (deficit)				

b. Assume that Cottonwood can borrow any needed funds on a short-term basis at a rate of 3 percent per quarter and can invest any excess funds in short-term marketable securities at a rate of 2 percent per quarter. Prepare a short-term financial plan by filling in the following schedule. What is the net cash cost (total interest paid minus total investment income earned) for the year?

COTTONWOOD INC.
Short-Term Financial Plan (in millions)

	Q1	Q2	Q3	Q4
Beginning cash balance	$30			
Net cash inflow				
New short-term investments				
Income from short-term investments				
Short-term investments sold				
New short-term borrowing				
Interest on short-term borrowing				
Short-term borrowing repaid				
Ending cash balance				
Minimum cash balance				
Cumulative surplus (deficit)	30			
Beginning short-term investments				
Ending short-term investments				
Beginning short-term debt				
Ending short-term debt				

16. **Cash Management Policy (LO3)** Rework Problem 15 assuming:

   a. Cottonwood maintains a minimum cash balance of $40 million.

   b. Cottonwood maintains a minimum cash balance of $10 million.

   Based on your answers in (a) and (b), do you think the firm can boost its profit by changing its cash management policy? Are there other factors that must be considered as well? Explain.

Challenge 17.
(Question 17)
Costs of Borrowing (LO5) In exchange for a $400 million fixed commitment line of credit, your firm has agreed to do the following:

   1. Pay 2.1 percent per quarter on any funds actually borrowed.
   2. Maintain a 4 percent compensating balance on any funds actually borrowed.
   3. Pay an up-front commitment fee of .150 percent of the amount of the line.
      Based on this information, answer the following:

      a. Ignoring the commitment fee, what is the effective annual interest rate on this line of credit?

      b. Suppose your firm immediately uses $130 million of the line and pays it off in one year. What is the effective annual interest rate on this $130 million loan?

Internet Application Questions

1. Short-term financing is structured in many different ways. The following site from British Columbia describes different types of short-term credit.

   www.smallbusinessbc.ca

   What type of loan will suit the following companies' short-term financing needs?

   a.   Small garment store with seasonal sales.

   b.   Mid-sized pulp producer with level sales.

2. In many cases, a straight bank loan may not be the best source of funds. The following link describes a few of the alternative debt sources available to small businesses today.

   www.smallbusinessbc.ca

   Pick any three financing alternatives from the link above, and give an example of a business that would find the particular type of financing attractive.

CHAPTER 19

CASH AND LIQUIDITY MANAGEMENT

The Canadian Press/La Presse/Armand Trottier

Most often, when news breaks about a firm's cash position, it's because the firm is running low on cash. This happened to Air Canada as it faced a cash shortage resulting from reduced travel during the recession of 2009. The airline sought a loan of $600 million from Aeroplan, its parent company (ACE Aviation Holdings Inc.) and Export Development Canada. Air Canada was also short of cash in 2003, when it entered bankruptcy protection and had only $492 million in cash (falling considerably short of its obligations to creditors).[1] Around the same time, some firms had sizeable cash reserves. In 2004, Microsoft made the news regarding its cash position, but not because it was running low on cash. Cash reserves were at $76.6 billion until the company issued a special dividend of $3 a share, paying out a total of $30 billion to investors. In 2011, Microsoft had a cash reserve of around $53 billion. Why would firms such as these hold so much cash? We examine cash management in this chapter to explore this question and some related issues.

Learning Objectives ▶

After studying this chapter, you should understand:

LO1 The importance of float and how it affects the cash balances.

LO2 How firms manage their cash and some of the collection, concentration, and disbursement techniques used.

LO3 The advantages and disadvantages to holding cash and some of the ways to invest idle cash.

This chapter is about how firms manage cash. Cash management is not as complex and conceptually challenging as capital budgeting and asset pricing. Still this is a very important activity and financial managers in many companies, especially in the retail and services industries, spend a significant portion of their time on cash management.

The basic objective in cash management is to keep the investment in cash as low as possible while still keeping the firm operating efficiently and effectively. The goal usually reduces to the dictum, "Collect early and pay late." Accordingly, we discuss ways of accelerating collections and managing disbursements. Our examples feature large firms and how they use computer-based cash management services offered by banks.

In addition, firms must invest temporarily idle cash in short-term marketable securities. As we discuss in various places, these securities can be bought and sold in the financial markets. As a group, they have very little default risk, and most are highly marketable. There are different types of marketable securities and we discuss a few of the most important ones.

19.1 | Reasons for Holding Cash

John Maynard Keynes, in his great work, *The General Theory of Employment, Interest, and Money*, identified three reasons why liquidity is important: the precautionary motive, the speculative motive, and the transaction motive. We discuss these next.

---

[1] See Eric Reguly, "Gamble may pay off for Air Canada pilots," *The Globe and Mail*, May 31, 2003.

Speculative and Precautionary Motives

speculative motive
The need to hold cash to take advantage of additional investment opportunities, such as bargain purchases.

The **speculative motive** is the need to hold cash to be able to take advantage of, for example, bargain purchases that might arise, attractive interest rates, and (in the case of international firms) favourable exchange rate fluctuations.

For most firms, reserve borrowing ability and marketable securities can be used to satisfy speculative motives. Thus, for a modern firm, there might be a speculative motive for liquidity, but not necessarily for cash per se. Think of it this way: If you have a credit card with a very large credit limit, you can probably take advantage of any unusual bargains that come along without carrying any cash.

precautionary motive
The need to hold cash as a safety margin to act as a financial reserve.

This is also true, to a lesser extent, for precautionary motives. The **precautionary motive** is the need for a safety supply to act as a financial reserve. Once again, there probably is a precautionary motive for liquidity. However, given that the value of money market instruments is relatively certain and that instruments such as T-bills are extremely liquid, there is no real need to literally hold substantial amounts of cash for precautionary purposes.

Take the examples of Chrysler and Ford: both companies had argued during the late 1990s that they needed huge cash reserves to weather a downturn in the economy if one came. The automotive industry experiences large capital expenditures to engineer new models and update plant and equipment. Thus, the motive for these companies at the time was largely precautionary. The economic slowdown in 2001–2002 resulted in increased competition and larger sales incentives for these companies, and appeared to prove their arguments to be good ones. However, the cost of such reserves is high. If Ford could earn a 10 percent greater return by investing the money it has in reserves, the company would earn an additional $329,000 per day.

The Transaction Motive

transaction motive
The need to hold cash to satisfy normal disbursement and collection activities associated with a firm's ongoing operations.

Cash is needed to satisfy the **transaction motive**, the need to have cash on hand to pay bills. Transaction-related needs come from the normal disbursement and collection activities of the firm. The disbursement of cash includes the payment of wages and salaries, trade debts, taxes, and dividends.

Cash is collected from sales, the selling of assets, and new financing. The cash inflows (collections) and outflows (disbursements) are not perfectly synchronized, and some level of cash holdings is necessary to serve as a buffer. Perfect liquidity is the characteristic of cash that allows it to satisfy the transaction motive.

As electronic funds transfers and other high-speed, paperless payment mechanisms continue to develop, even the transaction demand for cash may all but disappear. Even if it does, however, there is still a demand for liquidity and a need to manage it efficiently.

Costs of Holding Cash

When a firm holds cash in excess of some necessary minimum, it incurs an opportunity cost. The opportunity cost of excess cash (held in currency or bank deposits) is the interest income that could be earned in the next best use, such as investment in marketable securities.

Given the opportunity cost of holding cash, why would a firm hold any cash? The answer is that a cash balance must be maintained to provide the liquidity necessary for transaction needs—paying bills. If the firm maintains too small a cash balance, it may run out of cash. When this happens, the firm may have to raise cash on a short-term basis. This could involve, for example, selling marketable securities or borrowing.

Activities such as selling marketable securities and borrowing involve various costs. As we've discussed, holding cash has an opportunity cost. To determine the target cash balance, the firm must weigh the benefits of holding cash against these costs. We discuss this subject in more detail in the next section.

Cash Management versus Liquidity Management

Before we move on, we should note that it is important to distinguish between true cash management and a more general subject, liquidity management. The distinction is a source of confusion because the word *cash* is used in practice in two different ways. First of all, it has its literal meaning, actual cash on hand. However, financial managers frequently use the word to describe a firm's holdings of cash along with its marketable securities, and marketable securities are sometimes called cash equivalents or near-cash. In the case of Ford's cash position, for example, what was actually being described was Ford's total cash and cash equivalents.

The distinction between liquidity management and cash management is straightforward. Liquidity management concerns the optimal quantity of liquid assets a firm should have on hand, and it is one particular aspect of the current asset management policies we discussed in our previous chapter. Cash management is much more closely related to optimizing mechanisms for collecting and disbursing cash, and it is this subject that we primarily focus on in this chapter.

> ### Concept Questions
>
> **1.** What is the transaction motive, and how does it lead firms to hold cash?
> **2.** What is the cost to the firm of holding excess cash?

19.2 | Determining the Target Cash Balance

target cash balance
A firm's desired cash level as determined by the trade-off between carrying costs and shortage costs.

adjustment costs
The costs associated with holding too little cash.

Based on our general discussion of current assets in the previous chapter, the **target cash balance** involves a trade-off between the opportunity costs of holding too much cash (the carrying costs) and the costs of holding too little (the shortage costs, also called **adjustment costs**). The nature of these costs depends on the firm's working capital policy.

If the firm has a flexible working capital policy, it probably maintains a marketable securities portfolio. As we showed earlier, large Canadian corporations carry portfolios of marketable securities. In this case, the adjustment or shortage costs are the trading costs associated with buying and selling securities. In addition to these costs, firms holding large amounts of cash may be too flexible. This can occur if management prefers the comfort of sitting on a large cash balance instead of investing in projects with positive net present values. If this happens, shareholders face an unwanted agency cost. In Chapter 23, we discuss how takeover bids can discipline such managers.[2]

If the firm has a restrictive working capital policy, it probably borrows short-term to meet cash shortages. The costs are the interest and other expenses associated with arranging a loan. The restrictive case is more realistic for small- and medium-sized companies.

In the following discussion, we assume the firm has a flexible policy. Its cash management consists of moving money in and out of marketable securities. This is a very traditional approach to the subject, and it is a nice way of illustrating the costs and benefits of holding cash. Keep in mind, however, that the distinction between cash and money market investments is becoming increasingly blurred as electronic technology allows easy and fast transfers.

The Basic Idea

Figure 19.1 presents the cash management problem for our flexible firm. If a firm tries to keep its cash holdings too low, it finds itself running out of cash more often than is desirable, and thus selling marketable securities (and perhaps later buying marketable securities to replace those sold) more frequently than it would if the cash balance were higher. Thus, trading costs are high when the size of the cash balance is low. These fall as the cash balance becomes larger.

In contrast, the opportunity costs of holding cash are very low if the firm holds very little cash. These costs increase as the cash holdings rise because the firm is giving up more and more in interest that could have been earned.

At point C^* in Figure 19.1, the sum of the costs is given by the total cost curve. As shown, the minimum total cost occurs where the two individual cost curves cross. At this point, the opportunity costs and the trading costs are equal. This is the target cash balance, and it is the point the firm should try to find.

---

[2] This argument was originated in M.C. Jensen, "Agency Costs of Free Cash Flow, Corporate Finance and Takeovers," *American Economic Review*, May 1986.

FIGURE 19.1

Costs of holding cash

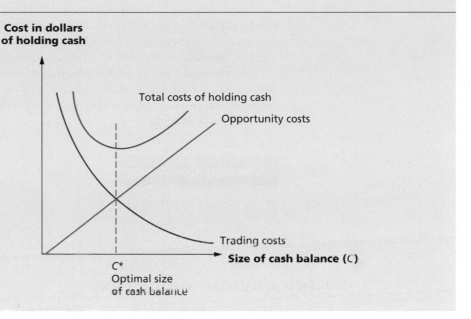

Trading costs are increased when the firm must sell securities to establish a cash balance. Opportunity costs are increased when there is a cash balance because there is no return to cash.

Figure 19.1 is essentially the same as one in the previous chapter. However, if we use real data on holding and opportunity costs, we can come up with a precise dollar optimum investment in cash. (Appendix 19A on Connect covers two models that do this in varying degrees of complexity.) Here, we focus only on their implications. All other things being equal:

1. The greater the interest rate, the lower is the target cash balance.

2. The greater the trading cost, the higher is the target balance.

These are both fairly obvious from looking at Figure 19.1, but they bring out an important point on the evolution of computerized cash management techniques. In the early 1980s, high interest rates (the prime rate was over 22 percent) caused the cost of idle cash to skyrocket. In response, large corporations and banks invested in applying computer and communications technologies to cash management. The result was lower trading costs. With systems in place, banks are now able to offer cash management services to smaller customers.

Going beyond the simple framework of Figure 19.1, the more advanced models also show that the target cash balance should be higher for firms facing greater uncertainty in forecasting their cash needs. This makes sense because such firms need a larger cash balance as a cushion against unexpected outflows. We cover cash management under uncertainty later in the chapter.

Other Factors Influencing the Target Cash Balance

Before moving on, we briefly discuss two additional considerations that affect the target cash balance.

First, in our discussion of cash management, we assume cash is invested in marketable securities such as Treasury bills. The firm obtains cash by selling these securities. Another alternative is to borrow cash. Borrowing introduces additional considerations to cash management:

1. Borrowing is likely to be more expensive than selling marketable securities because the interest rate is likely to be higher. For example, Figure 19.7 in a later section shows that the prime rate considerably exceeds all money market rates.

2. The need to borrow depends on management's desire to hold low cash balances. A firm is more likely to have to borrow to cover an unexpected cash outflow the greater its cash flow variability and the lower its investment in marketable securities.

Second, for large firms, the trading costs of buying and selling securities are very small when compared to the opportunity costs of holding cash. For example, in 2011, Microsoft had a cash reservoir of US$53 billion. If this cash won't be needed for 24 hours, should the firm invest the money or leave it sitting?

Suppose Microsoft can invest the money overnight at the call money rate. To do this, the treasurer arranges through a bank to lend funds for 24 hours to an investment dealer. According to Figure 19.7 in Section 19.4, this is an annualized rate of approximately 1 percent per year in Canada. The daily rate is about 0.27 basis points (.0027 percent).[3]

The daily return earned on $53 billion is thus $53b $\times$ 0.0027 $\div$ 100 = $1,431,000. The order cost would be much less than this. Following up on our earlier point about technology and cash management, large corporations buy and sell securities daily so they are unlikely to leave substantial amounts of cash idle.

> ### Concept Questions
>
> 1. What is a target cash balance?
> 2. How do changes in interest rates affect the target cash balance? Changes in trading costs?

19.3 | Understanding Float

float
The difference between book cash and bank cash, representing the net effect of cheques in the process of clearing.

As you no doubt know, the amount of money you have according to your cheque book can be very different from the amount of money that your bank thinks you have. The reason is that some of the cheques you have written haven't yet been presented to the bank for payment. The same thing is true for a business. The cash balance that a firm shows on its books is called the firm's *book* or *ledger balance*. The balance shown in its bank account is called its *available* or *collected balance*. The difference between the available balance and the ledger balance is called the **float**, and it represents the net effect of cheques in the process of clearing (moving through the banking system).

Disbursement Float

Cheques written by a firm generate disbursement float, causing a decrease in its book balance but no change in its available balance. For example, suppose General Mechanics Inc. (GMI) currently has $100,000 on deposit with its bank. On June 8, it buys some raw materials and puts a cheque in the mail for $100,000. The company's book balance is immediately reduced by $100,000 as a result.

GMI's bank, however, does not find out about this cheque until it is presented to GMI's bank for payment on, say, June 14. Until the cheque is presented, the firm's available balance is greater than its book balance by $100,000. In other words, before June 8, GMI has a zero float:

$$\text{Float} = \text{Firm's available balance} - \text{Firm's book balance}$$
$$= \$100,000 - \$100,000$$
$$= \$0$$

GMI's position from June 8 to June 14 is:

$$\text{Disbursement float} = \text{Firm's available balance} - \text{Firm's book balance}$$
$$= \$100,000 - \$0$$
$$= \$100,000$$

During this period while the cheque is clearing (moving through the mail and the banking system), GMI has a balance with the bank of $100,000. It can obtain the benefit of this cash while the cheque is clearing. For example, the available balance could be temporarily invested in marketable securities and thus earn more interest. We return to this subject a little later.

---

[3] A basis point is 1 percent of 1 percent. Also, the annual interest rate is calculated as $(1 + R)^{365} = 1.01$, implying a daily rate of .0027 percent.

Collection Float and Net Float

Cheques received by the firm create collection float. Collection float increases book balances but does not immediately change available balances. For example, suppose GMI receives a cheque from a customer for $100,000 on October 8. Assume, as before, that the company has $100,000 deposited at its bank and a zero float. It processes the cheque through the bookkeeping department and increases its book balance by $100,000 to $200,000. However, the additional cash is not available to GMI until the cheque is deposited in the firm's bank. This occurs on, say, October 9, the next day. In the meantime, the cash position at GMI reflects a collection float of $100,000. We can summarize these events. Before October 8, GMI's position is:

$$\text{Float} = \text{Firm's available balance} - \text{Firm's book balance}$$
$$= \$100,000 - \$100,000$$
$$= \$0$$

GMI's position from October 8 to October 9 is:

$$\text{Collection float} = \text{Firm's available balance} - \text{Firm's book balance}$$
$$= \$100,000 - \$200,000$$
$$= -\$100,000$$

In general, a firm's payment (disbursement) activities generate disbursement float, and its collection activities generate collection float. The net effect, that is, the sum of the total collection and disbursement floats, is the net float. The net float at a point in time is simply the overall difference between the firm's available balance and its book balance.

If the net float is positive, the firm's disbursement float exceeds its collection float and its available balance exceeds its book balance. In other words, the bank thinks the firm has more cash than it really does. This, of course, is desirable. If the available balance is less than the book balance, the firm has a net collection float. This is undesirable because we actually have more cash than the bank thinks we do, but we can't use it.

EXAMPLE 19.1: Staying Afloat

Suppose you have $5,000 on deposit. You write and mail a cheque for $1,000. You receive a cheque for $2,000 and put it in your wallet to deposit the next time you use a bank machine. What are your disbursement, collection, and net floats?

After you write the $1,000 cheque, you show a balance of $4,000 on your books, but the bank shows $5,000 while the cheque is moving through the mail and clearing. This is a disbursement float of $1,000.

After you receive the $2,000 cheque, you show a balance of $6,000. Your available balance doesn't rise until you deposit the cheque and it clears. This is a collection float of −$2,000. Your net float is the sum of the collection and disbursement floats, or −$1,000.

Overall, you show $6,000 on your books, but the bank only shows $5,000 cash. The discrepancy between your available balance and your book balance is the net float (−$1,000), and it is bad for you. If you write another cheque for $5,500, it might bounce even though it shouldn't. This is the reason the financial manager has to be more concerned with available balances than book balances.

Float Management

Float management involves controlling the collection and disbursement of cash. The objective in cash collection is to speed up collections and reduce the lag between the time customers pay their bills and the time the cheques are collected. The objective in cash disbursement is to control payments and minimize the firm's costs associated with making payments.

Float can be broken down into three parts: mail float, processing float, and availability float:

1. *Mail float* is the part of the collection and disbursement process where cheques are trapped in the postal system.
2. *Processing float* is the time it takes the receiver of a cheque to process the payment and deposit it in a bank.
3. *Availability float* refers to the time required to clear a cheque through the banking system. In the Canadian banking system, availability float does not exceed one day for creditworthy firms and is often zero, so this is the least important part.

Speeding collections involves reducing one or more of these float components. Slowing disbursements involves increasing one of them. Later, we describe some procedures for managing float times; before that, we need to discuss how float is measured.

MEASURING FLOAT   The size of the float depends on both the dollars and time delay involved. For example, suppose you receive a cheque for $500 from another province each month. It takes five days in the mail to reach you (the mail float) and one day for you to get over to the bank (the processing float). The bank gives you immediate availability (so there is no availability float). The total delay is $5 + 1 = 6$ days.

What is your average daily float? There are two equivalent ways of calculating the answer: First, you have a $500 float for six days, so we say the total float is $6 \times \$500 = \$3,000$. Assuming 30 days in the month, the average daily float is $\$3,000/30 = \$100$.

Second, your float is $500 for 6 days out of the month and zero the other 24 days (again assuming 30 days in a month). Your average daily float is thus:

$$
\begin{aligned}
\text{Average daily float} &= (6 \times \$500 + 24 \times 0)/30 \\
&= 6/30 \times \$500 + 24/30 \times 0 \\
&= \$3,000/30 \\
&= \$100
\end{aligned}
$$

This means that, on an average day, there is $100 that is not available to spend. In other words, on average, your book balance is $100 greater than your available balance, a $100 average collection float.

COST OF THE FLOAT   The basic cost to the firm of collection float is simply the opportunity cost from not being able to use the cash. At a minimum, the firm could earn interest on the cash if it were available for investing.

Suppose the Lambo Corporation has average daily receipts of $1,000 and a weighted average delay of three days. The average daily float is thus $3 \times \$1,000 = \$3,000$. This means that, on a typical day, there is $3,000 that is not earning interest. Suppose Lambo could eliminate the float entirely. What would be the benefit? If it costs $2,000 to eliminate the float, what is the NPV of doing it?

After the float is eliminated, daily receipts are still $1,000. We collect the same day since the float is eliminated, so daily collections are also still $1,000. The only change occurs the first day. On that day, we catch up and collect $1,000 from the sale made three days ago. Because the float is gone, we also collect on the sales made two days ago, one day ago, and today, for an additional $3,000. Total collections today are thus $4,000 instead of $1,000.

What we see is that Lambo generates an extra $3,000 today by eliminating the float. On every subsequent day, Lambo receives $1,000 in cash just as it did before the float was eliminated. If you recall our definition of relevant cash flow, the only change in the firm's cash flow from eliminating the float is this extra $3,000 that comes in immediately. No other cash flows are affected, so Lambo is $3,000 richer.

In other words, the PV of eliminating the float is simply equal to the total float. Lambo could pay this amount out as a dividend, invest it in interest-bearing assets, or do anything else with it. If it costs $2,000 to eliminate the float, the NPV is $\$3,000 - 2,000 = \$1,000$, so Lambo should do it.

SUMMARY OF FLOAT MEASURES
- Float = Firm's available balance − Firm's book balance
- Average daily float = Total float/Total days
- Average daily receipts = Total receipts/Total days
- Average daily float = Average daily receipts × Weighted average delay

ELECTRONIC DATA INTERCHANGE: THE END OF FLOAT?   *Electronic data interchange* (EDI) is a general term that refers to the growing practice of direct, electronic information exchange between all types of businesses. One important use of EDI, often called financial EDI, or FEDI, is to electronically transfer financial information and funds between parties, thereby eliminating paper invoices, paper cheques, mailing, and handling. For example, it is now possible to arrange to have your chequing account directly debited each month to pay many types of bills, and corporations now routinely directly deposit pay cheques into employee accounts. More generally, EDI allows a seller to send a bill electronically to a buyer, thereby avoiding the mail. The buyer can then authorize payment, which also occurs electronically. Its bank then transfers the funds to the seller's account at a different bank.

Major banks have implemented a financial EDI system for personal banking. Canadian banks have added personal banking services for clients using their Web-based systems whereby clients can pay bills online and can also receive their bills electronically instead of by mail. Partnering with Rogers Communications Inc. (discussed further in the accompanying box), CIBC is helping customers to transfer money easily using smartphones.

IN THEIR OWN WORDS...

'Mobile wallets' in Canada

A joint venture between Rogers Communications Inc. and the Canadian Imperial Bank of Commerce to turn smartphones into wallets capable of making day-to-day transactions with the swipe of a device represents the tip of the iceberg in a burgeoning mobile payments market, executives from both companies say. The country's fifth-largest bank and its biggest wireless carrier said Tuesday each is looking to partner with additional players in the nascent space. "It will scale from here," David Williamson, CIBC's senior vice-president of retail and business banking said in an interview following a press conference at the bank's Toronto headquarters. Importantly, the partnership hinges on a new standards framework the Canadian Bankers Association announced Monday that clears many of the security and logistical obstacles that have held back the deployment of a so-called "mobile wallet" for years.

With the concerns resolved, CIBC and Rogers—alongside credit-card issuers Mastercard and Visa Canada—will enable smartphone devices to act as a physical CIBC credit card and pay for groceries, gas, restaurant bills, and other small ticket items by the end of the year. Mr. Williamson said this is the first such deal to develop from the code, which had been in the works for months. While the bank is firmly focused on its partnership with Rogers, Mr. Williamson would not rule out working with competing mobile providers, such as BCE's Bell Mobility and Telus Corp. "At this time it would be fair to say we would like to bring this to others," the executive said. A spokeswoman for Telus, the country's third-largest carrier, said talks are taking place between it and financial institutions. "We are currently working with a number of banks to offer this service in the near future," spokeswoman Elisabeth Naplano said via email. The new opportunity for both financial institutions and wireless providers is based on near-field communications (NFC) technology, which sends data such as a person's card "credentials" over very short distances. In this instance, the data housed on a Rogers phone would be received by a small terminal near a traditional cash register. Credit card companies, which have been fast to roll out mobile payment solutions of their own using their own cards, are logical partners because of

their extensive "tap and go" networks already in place with merchants country wide, as well the loyalty and rewards programs they offer through their bank-sponsored cards, bank executives said.

Rogers will charge a flat-rate "rent" for a customer's CIBC credentials to be stored on their SIM card, the small, removable chip that acts as a digital repositories for wireless usage, numbers, contact information and other personal data. Rob Bruce, president of Rogers wireless and wireline operations, said roughly 300,000 customers have phones equipped with NFC technology in the market now, with the goal to have three-quarters of a million devices in use by the end of the year without specifying how many are CIBC credit-card holders and therefore eligible for the solution. In an interview, the executive said it was "premature" to speculate on what other financial institutions Rogers may partner with, but he said the company is working aggressively to broaden the program. "We're in very good shape," he said. While wireless credit and payment models have been in place for some time in emerging economies that lack large-scale banking infrastructure, there are only two other commercial NFC deployments like the one announced Tuesday in the world, Mr. Bruce said—underscoring the leap in innovation both CIBC and Rogers are taking. The first is from Telefónica SA of Spain while a second venture has been launched by a South Korean carrier. The sole handset partner supporting the CIBC-Rogers NFC solution to date is BlackBerry maker Research In Motion Ltd. Apple Inc.'s iPhone currently has no plans to bring on NFC technology, a blow to consumer adoption perhaps but boon to rival smartphone makers. Mr. Bruce said a "robust" roadmap is now in development for devices using Google's Android platform.

Source: *Financial Post*, May 15, 2012, By Jamie Sturgeon. Used with permission.

The net effect is that the length of time required to initiate and complete a business or personal transaction is shortened considerably, and much of what we normally think of as float is sharply reduced or eliminated. As the use of FEDI increases (which it will), float management will evolve to focus much more on issues surrounding computerized information exchange and funds transfers.

EXAMPLE 19.2: Reducing the Float

Instead of eliminating the float, suppose Lambo can reduce it to one day. What is the maximum Lambo should be willing to pay for this?

If Lambo can reduce the float from three days to one day, the amount of the float will fall from $3,000 to $1,000. We see immediately that the PV of doing this is just equal to the $2,000 float reduction. Lambo should thus be willing to pay up to $2,000.

Concept Questions

1. Would a firm be most interested in reducing a collection or disbursement float? Why?
2. How is daily average float calculated?
3. What is the benefit from reducing or eliminating float?

Accelerating Collections

Based on our discussion, we can depict the basic parts of the cash collection process in Figure 19.2. The total time in this process is made up of mailing time, cheque-processing time, and the bank's cheque-clearing time. The amount of time that cash spends in each part of the cash collection process depends on where the firm's customers are located and how efficient the firm is at collecting cash.

FIGURE 19.2

Float time line

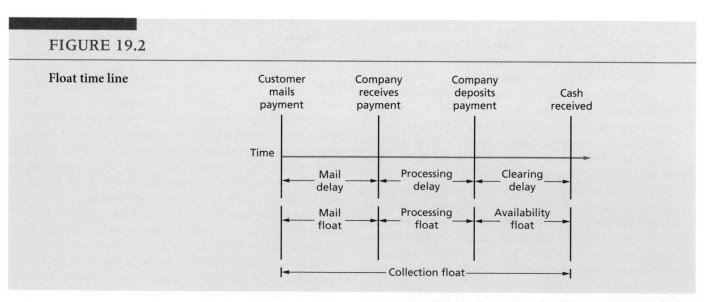

Coordinating the firm's efforts in all areas in Figure 19.2 is its cash flow information system. Tracking payments through the system and providing the cash manager with up-to-date daily cash balances and investment rates are its key tasks. Chartered banks offer cash information systems that all but put the bank on the manager's desk. Linking the manager's computer with the bank's system gives the manager access to account balances and transactions and information on money market rates. The system also allows the manager to transfer funds and make money market investments.

The cash management system has security features to prevent unauthorized use. Different passwords allow access to each level of authority. For example, you could give your receivables clerk access to deposit activity files but not to payroll. Some systems use **smart cards** for security. A smart card looks like a credit card but contains a computer chip that can be programmed to grant access to certain files only. The card must be inserted into an access device attached to a personal computer and provides another safeguard in addition to a password.

We next discuss several techniques used to accelerate collections and reduce collection time: systems to expedite mailing and cheque processing and concentration banking.

smart card
Much like an automated teller machine card; one use is within corporations to control access to information by employees.

Over-the-Counter Collections

In an over-the-counter system, customers pay in person at field offices or stores. Most large retailers, utilities, and many other firms receive some payments this way. Because the payments are made at a company location, there is no mail delay. The manager of the field location is responsible for ensuring that cheques and cash collected are deposited promptly and for reporting daily deposit amounts to the head office.

When payments are received by mail, a company may instruct customers to mail cheques to a collection point address on its invoices. By distributing the collection points locally throughout its market area, the company avoids the delays occurring when all payments are mailed to its head office. If the collection points are field offices, the next steps are the same as for over-the-counter collections. A popular alternative, lockboxes, contracts out the collection points to a bank.

LOCKBOXES   **Lockboxes** are special post office boxes set up to intercept accounts receivable payments. The collection process is started by business and retail customers mailing their cheques to a post office box instead of sending them to the firm. The lockbox is maintained at a local bank branch. Large corporations may maintain a number of lockboxes, one in each significant market area. The location depends on a trade-off between bank fees and savings on mailing time.

In the typical lockbox system, the local bank branch collects the lockbox cheques from the post office daily. The bank deposits the cheques directly to the firm's account. Details of the operation are recorded in some computer-usable form and sent to the firm.

A lockbox system reduces mailing time because cheques are received at a nearby post office instead of at corporate headquarters. Lockboxes also reduce the processing time because the corporation doesn't have to open the envelopes and deposit cheques for collection. In all, a bank lockbox should enable a firm to get its receipts processed, deposited, and cleared faster than if it were to receive cheques at its headquarters and deliver them itself to the bank for deposit and clearing.

lockboxes
Special post office boxes set up to intercept and speed up accounts receivable payments.

ELECTRONIC COLLECTION SYSTEMS   Over-the-counter and lockbox systems are standard ways to reduce mail and processing float time. They are used by almost all large Canadian firms that can benefit from them. Newer approaches focus on reducing float virtually to zero by replacing cheques with electronic fund transfers. Examples used in Canada include preauthorized payments, point-of-sale transfers, and electronic trade payables. We discuss the first two here and the third later when we look at disbursement systems.

Preauthorized payments are paperless transfers of contractual or installment payments from the customer's account directly to the firm's. Common applications are mortgage payments and installment payments for insurance, rent, cable TV, telephone, and so on. This system eliminates all invoice paperwork and the deposit and reconciliation of cheques. There is no mail or processing float.

Point-of-sale systems use **debit cards** to transfer funds directly from a customer's bank account to a retailer's. A debit card typically is a bank machine (ATM) card with a personal identification card (PIN) for security. Unlike a credit card, the funds are transferred immediately. Point-of-sale systems are common in Canada.

The next generation of cards for point-of-sale applications is the smart card mentioned earlier in its role of security for corporate cash management systems. Smart cards differ from debit cards in that they contain a chip that can hold a cash balance. Consumers can download small amounts of money (usually under $300) directly on the card and then spend it at point-of-sale terminals.

debit card
An automated teller machine card used at the point of purchase to avoid the use of cash. As this is not a credit card, money must be available in the user's bank account.

The advantage of smart cards is that, with the balance programmed on the card's chip, there is no need for the merchant to have technology that goes online to the customer's bank. Several Canadian banks have test marketed smart card technology in several Canadian communities.

CASH CONCENTRATION   Using lockboxes or other collection systems helps firms collect cheques from customers and get them deposited rapidly. But the job is not finished yet since these systems give the firm cash at a number of widely dispersed branches. Until it is concentrated in a central account, the cash is of little use to the firm for paying bills, reducing loans, or investing.

With a concentration banking system, sales receipts are processed at field sales offices and banks providing lockbox services and deposited locally. Surplus funds are transferred from the various local branches to a single, central concentration account. This process is illustrated in Figure 19.3, where concentration banks are combined with over-the-counter collection and lockboxes in a total cash management system.

FIGURE 19.3

Lockboxes and concentration banks in a cash management system

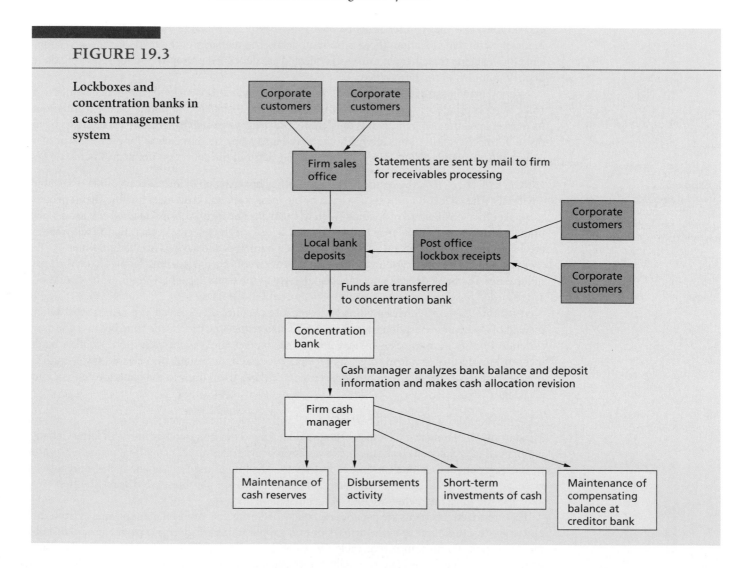

Large firms in Canada may manage collections through one chartered bank across the country. Chartered banks offer a concentrator account that automatically electronically transfers deposits at any branch in Canada to the firm's concentration account. These funds receive **same day value.** This means the firm has immediate use of the funds even though it takes 24 hours for a cheque to clear in Canada.[4] If the concentration involves branches of more than one bank, electronic transfers take place between banks.

same day value
Bank makes proceeds of cheques deposited available the same day before cheques clear.

---

[4]Since the bank is providing availability in advance of receiving funds, same day availability creates collection float for the bank. An interest charge on this float is usually included in the bank's fees.

Once the funds are in the concentration account, the bank can make automatic transfers to pay down the firm's credit line or, if there is a surplus, to an investment account. Transfers are made in units of minimum size agreed in advance. A common practice is in units of $5,000. Mid-sized firms lacking in money market expertise may invest in bank accounts at competitive interest rates. The largest firms have the capability to purchase money market instruments electronically.

Controlling Disbursements

Accelerating collections is one method of cash management; slowing disbursements is another. This can be a sensitive area and some practices exist that we do not recommend. For example, some small firms that are short of working capital make disbursements on the "squeaky wheel principle." Payables invoices are processed before their due dates and cheques printed. When the cheques are ready, the firm's controller puts them all in a desk drawer. As suppliers call and ask for their money, the cheques come out of the drawer and go into the mail! We do not recommend the desk drawer method because it is bad for supplier relations and borders on being unethical.

CONTROLLING DISBURSEMENTS IN PRACTICE   As we have seen, float in terms of slowing down payments comes from mail delivery, cheque-processing time, and collection of funds. In the United States, disbursement float can be increased by writing a cheque on a geographically distant bank. For example, a New York supplier might be paid with cheques drawn on a Los Angeles bank. This increases the time required for the cheques to clear through the banking system. Mailing cheques from remote post offices is another way firms slow disbursement. Because there are significant ethical (and legal) issues associated with deliberately delaying disbursements in these and similar ways, such strategies appear to be disappearing. In Canada, banks provide same day availability so the temptation is easy to resist.

For these reasons, the goal is to control rather than simply delay disbursements. A treasurer should try to pay payables on the last day appropriate for net terms or a discount.[5] The traditional way is to write a cheque and mail it timed to arrive on the due date. With the cash management system we described earlier, the payment can be programmed today for electronic transfer on the future due date. This eliminates paper along with guesswork about mail times.

The electronic payment is likely to come from a disbursement account, kept separate from the concentration account to ease accounting and control. Firms keep separate accounts for payroll, vendor disbursements, customer refunds, and so on. This makes it easy for the bank to provide each cost or profit centre with its own statement.

Firms use **zero-balance accounts** to avoid carrying extra balances in each disbursement account. With a zero-balance account, the firm, in cooperation with its bank, transfers in just enough funds to cover cheques presented that day. Figure 19.4 illustrates how such a system might work. In this case, the firm maintains two disbursement accounts, one for suppliers and one for payroll. As shown, when the firm does not use zero-balance accounts, each of these accounts must have a safety stock of cash to meet unanticipated demands. A firm that uses zero-balance accounts can keep one safety stock in a master account and transfer in the funds to the two subsidiary accounts as needed. The key is that the total amount of cash held as a buffer is smaller under the zero-balance arrangement, thereby freeing cash to be used elsewhere.

zero-balance account
A chequing account in which a zero balance is maintained by transfers of funds from a master account in an amount only large enough to cover cheques presented.

Concept Questions

1. What are collection and disbursement floats?
2. What are lockboxes? Concentration banking? Zero-balance accounts?
3. How do computer and communications technologies aid in cash management by large corporations?

---

[5] We discuss credit terms in depth in Chapter 20.

FIGURE 19.4

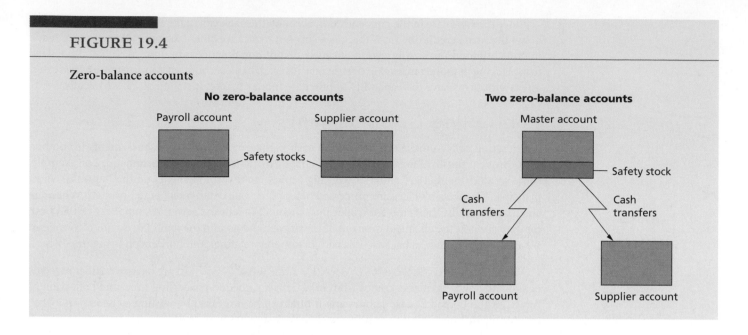

Zero-balance accounts

19.4 | Investing Idle Cash

If a firm has a temporary cash surplus, it can invest in short-term securities. As we have mentioned at various times, the market for short-term financial assets is called the money market. The maturity of short-term financial assets that trade in the money market is one year or less.

Most large firms manage their own short-term financial assets through transactions with banks and investment dealers. Some firms use money market funds that invest in short-term financial assets for a management fee. The management fee is compensation for the professional expertise and diversification provided by the fund manager.

Money market funds are becoming increasingly popular in Canada. Also, Canadian chartered banks offer arrangements in which the bank takes all excess available funds at the close of each business day and invests them for the firm.

Temporary Cash Surpluses

Firms have temporary cash surpluses for various reasons. Two of the most important are the financing of seasonal or cyclical activities and the financing of planned or possible expenditures.

SEASONAL OR CYCLICAL ACTIVITIES   Some firms have a predictable cash flow pattern. They have surplus cash flows during part of the year and deficit cash flows the rest of the year. For example, Toys "R" Us, a retail toy firm, has a seasonal cash flow pattern influenced by Christmas.

A firm such as Toys "R" Us may buy marketable securities when surplus cash flows occur and sell marketable securities when deficits occur. Of course, bank loans are another short-term financing device. The use of bank loans and marketable securities to meet temporary financing needs is illustrated in Figure 19.5. In this case, the firm is following a compromise working capital policy in the sense we discussed in the previous chapter.

PLANNED OR POSSIBLE EXPENDITURES   Firms frequently accumulate temporary investments in marketable securities to provide the cash for a plant construction program, dividend payment, and other large expenditures. Thus, firms may issue bonds and stocks before the cash is needed, investing the proceeds in short-term marketable securities, and then selling the securities to finance the expenditures. Also, firms may face the possibility of having to make a large cash outlay. An obvious example would be the possibility of losing a large lawsuit. Firms may build up cash surpluses against such a contingency.

FIGURE 19.5

Seasonal cash demands

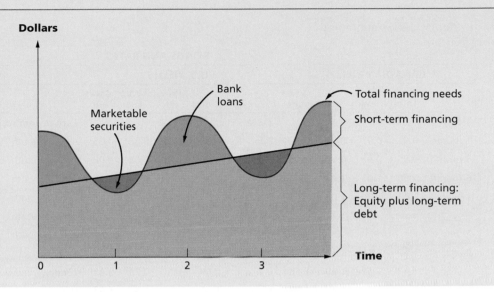

Time 1: A surplus cash flow exists. Seasonal demand for assets is low. The surplus cash flow is invested in short-term marketable securities.
Time 2: A deficit cash flow exists. Seasonal demand for assets is high. The financial deficit is financed by selling marketable securities and by bank borrowing.

Characteristics of Short-Term Securities

Given that a firm has some temporarily idle cash, there are a variety of short-term securities available for investing. The most important characteristics of these short-term marketable securities are their maturity, default risk, and marketability. Consistent with Chapter 12's discussion of risk and return, managers of marketable securities portfolios have an opportunity to increase expected returns in exchange for taking on higher risk. Marketable securities managers almost always resolve this trade-off in favour of low risk. Because this portfolio is a liquidity reserve, preservation of capital is generally the primary goal.

MATURITY   Maturity refers to the time period over which interest and principal payments are made. From Chapter 7, we know that for a given change in the level of interest rates, the prices of longer maturity securities change more than those of shorter maturity securities. As a consequence, firms that invest in long-term maturity securities are accepting greater risk than firms that invest in securities with short-term maturities.

We called this type of risk interest rate risk. Firms often limit their investments in marketable securities to those maturing in less than 90 days to avoid the risk of losses in value from changing interest rates. Of course, the expected return on securities with short-term maturities is usually (but not always) less than the expected return on securities with longer maturities.

For example, suppose you are the treasurer of a firm with $10 million needed to make a major capital investment after 90 days. You have decided to invest in obligations of the Government of Canada to eliminate all possible default risk. The newspaper (or your computer screen) provides you with the list of securities and rates in Figure 19.6. The safest investment is three-month Treasury bills yielding 0.95 percent. Because this matches the maturity of the investment with the planned holding period, there is no interest rate risk. After three months, the Treasury bills mature for a certain future cash flow of $10 million.[6]

If you invest instead in a 10-year Canada bond, the expected return is higher, 1.80 percent, but so is the risk. Again drawing on Chapter 7, if interest rates rise over the next three months, the bond drops in price. The resulting capital loss reduces the yield, possibly below the 0.95 percent on Treasury bills.

---

[6] Treasury bills are sold on a discount basis so the future cash flow includes principal and interest.

FIGURE 19.6

Money market quotations

BONDS AND RATES													
CANADIAN YIELDS					**U.S. YIELDS**					**INTERNATIONAL**			
	Latest	Prev. day	Wk ago	4 wks ago		Latest	Prev. day	Wk ago	4 wks ago		Latest	Prev. day	Wk ago	4 wks ago
T-Bills					*T-Bills*					*Euro-deposit rates (bid)*				
1-month	0.91	0.91	0.89	0.97	1-month	0.03	0.06	0.86	0.05	US$ 1-month	0.15	0.15	0.15	0.15
3-month	0.95	0.95	0.99	1.05	3-month	0.07	0.08	0.08	0.08	3-month	0.47	0.47	0.41	0.48
6-month	1.00	1.01	1.04	1.12	6-month	0.13	0.13	0.14	0.14	6-month	0.56	0.56	0.69	0.68
1-year	1.03	1.06	1.08	1.25						C$ 3-month	1.21	1.21	1.21	1.21
										euro 3-month	0.57	0.57	0.58	0.50
Bonds					*Bonds*					Yen 3-month	0.05	0.05	0.05	0.05
2-year	1.12	1.16	1.16	1.32	2-year	0.256	0.29	0.29	0.27	£ 3-month	0.90	0.90	0.90	0.91
5-year	1.32	1.39	1.40	1.58	5-year	0.69	0.77	0.73	0.83	*London interbank offer rate US$*				
10-year	1.80	1.87	1.88	2.02	10-year	1.61	1.74	1.73	1.93	US$ 1-month	0.24	0.24	0.24	0.24
30-year	2.33	2.39	2.40	2.59	30-year	2.70	2.85	2.82	3.12	3-month	0.47	0.47	0.47	0.47

Banker's acceptances (ask price)					*Commercial paper*					**BANK RATES**		
1-month	1.20	1.19	1.22	1.19	1-month	0.14	0.13	0.15	0.17	*Canada*		*United States*
3-month	1.23	1.22	1.29	1.11	3-month	0.21	0.20	0.20	0.19	Bank of Canada	1.25	Discount	0.75
6-month	1.32	1.32	1.32	1.38	6-month	0.36	0.33	0.32	0.31	Overnight Money	0.80	Prime	3.25
										Market Financing		
3-mth forward rate agreement					*3-mth forward rate agreement*					Prime	3.00	Federal Funds 0.16
3-month	1.22	1.26	1.27	1.41	3-month	0.52	0.52	053	0.47	Call Loan Average	1.00	
6-month	1.22	1.27	1.29	1.49	6-month	0.58	0.58	0.59	0.49	Supplied by Thomson Reuters.		
9-month	1.26	1.31	1.31	1.56	9-month	0.60	0.60	0.61	0.49	Indicative late afternoon rates.		

Source: The National Post, FP Investing, May 30, 2012, Used with permission. For current market quotations visit financialpost.com/markets/data/money-yields-can_us.html

DEFAULT RISK Default risk refers to the probability that interest and principal will not be paid in the promised amounts on the due dates (or not paid at all). In Chapter 7, we observed that various financial reporting agencies, such as DBRS and Standard and Poor's (S&P), compile and publish ratings of various corporate and public securities. These ratings are connected to default risk. Of course, some securities have negligible default risk, such as Canada Treasury bills. Given the purposes of investing idle corporate cash, firms typically avoid investing in marketable securities with significant default risk.

Small variations in default risk are reflected in the rates in Figure 19.6. For example, consider the rates on two alternative 90-day (three-month) Canadian investments on May 30 2012. Since the maturities are the same, they differ only in default risk. In increasing order of default risk, the securities are Treasury bills (0.95 percent yield) and banker's acceptances (1.23 percent yield). Treasury bills are backed by the credit of the Government of Canada. Banker's acceptances are generally a slightly less risky variation on commercial paper, as they are guaranteed by a chartered bank as well as by the issuing corporation.

MARKETABILITY   Marketability refers to how easy it is to convert an asset to cash; so marketability and liquidity mean much the same thing. Some money market instruments are much more marketable than others. At the top of the list are Treasury bills, which can be bought and sold very cheaply and very quickly in large amounts.

TAXES   Interest earned on money market securities is subject to federal and provincial corporate tax. Capital gains and dividends on common and preferred stock are taxed more lightly, but these long-term investments are subject to significant price fluctuations and most managers consider them too risky for the marketable securities portfolio. One exception is the strategy of **dividend capture.** Under this strategy portfolio managers purchase high-grade preferred stock or blue chip common stock just before a dividend payment. They hold the stock only long enough to receive the dividend. In this way, firms willing to tolerate price risk for a short period can benefit from the dividend exclusion that allows corporations to receive dividends tax free from other Canadian corporations.

dividend capture
A strategy in which an investor purchases securities to own them on the day of record and then quickly sells them; designed to attain dividends but avoid the risk of a lengthy hold.

Some Different Types of Money Market Securities

The money market securities listed in Figure 19.6 are generally highly marketable and short-term. They usually have low risk of default. They are issued by the federal government (for example, Treasury bills), domestic and foreign banks (certificates of deposit), and business corporations (commercial paper). Of the many types, we illustrate only a few of the most common here.

Treasury bills are obligations of the federal government that mature in 1, 2, 3, 6, or 12 months. They are sold at weekly auctions and traded actively over the counter by banks and investment dealers.

Commercial paper refers to short-term securities issued by finance companies, banks, and corporations. Typically, commercial paper is unsecured.[7] Maturities range from a few weeks to 270 days. There is no active secondary market in commercial paper. As a consequence, the marketability is low; however, firms that issue commercial paper often repurchase it directly before maturity. The default risk of commercial paper depends on the financial strength of the issuer. DBRS and S&P publish quality ratings for commercial paper. These ratings are similar to the bond ratings we discussed in Chapter 7.

As explained earlier, banker's acceptances are a form of corporate paper stamped by a chartered bank that adds its guarantee of principal and interest.

Certificates of deposit (CDs) are short-term loans to chartered banks. Rates quoted are for CDs in excess of $100,000. There are active markets in CDs of 3-month, 6-month, 9-month, and 12-month maturities, particularly in the United States.

Our brief look at money markets illustrates the challenges and opportunities for treasurers today. Securitization has produced dramatic growth in banker's acceptances and commercial paper.

Concept Questions

1. What are some reasons firms find themselves with idle cash?
2. What are some types of money market securities?
3. How does the design of money market securities reflect the trends of securitization, globalization, and financial engineering?

---

[7] Commercial paper and banker's acceptances are sources of short-term financing for their issuers. We discussed them in detail in Chapter 18.

19.5 | SUMMARY AND CONCLUSIONS

This chapter has described the computer-based cash management systems used by large corporations in Canada and worldwide. By moving cash efficiently and maximizing the amount available for short-term investment, the treasurer adds value to the firm. Our discussion made the following key points:

1. A firm holds cash to conduct transactions and to compensate banks for the various services they render.

2. The optimal amount of cash for a firm to hold depends on the opportunity cost of holding cash and the uncertainty of future cash inflows and outflows.

3. The difference between a firm's available balance and its book balance is the firm's net float. The float reflects the fact that some cheques have not cleared and are thus uncollected.

4. The firm can use a variety of procedures to manage the collection and disbursement of cash in such a way as to speed the collection of cash and control payments. Large firms use computerized cash management systems that include over-the-counter collections and lockboxes, concentration banking, and electronic disbursements through zero-balance accounts.

5. Because of seasonal and cyclical activities, to help finance planned expenditures, or as a contingency reserve, firms temporarily find themselves with a cash surplus. The money market offers a variety of possible vehicles for parking this idle cash.

Key Terms

adjustment costs (page 554)
debit card (page 561)
dividend capture (page 567)
float (page 556)
lockboxes (page 561)
precautionary motive (page 553)

same day value (page 562)
smart card (page 561)
speculative motive (page 553)
target cash balance (page 554)
transaction motive (page 553)
zero-balance account (page 563)

Chapter Review Problem and Self-Test

19.1 **Float Measurement** On a typical business day, a firm writes and mails cheques totalling $1,000. These cheques clear in six days on average. Simultaneously, the firm receives $1,300. The cash is available in one day on average. Calculate the disbursement float, the collection float, and the net float. How do you interpret the answer?

Answers to Self-Test Problem

19.1   The disbursement float is 6 days × $1,000 = $6,000. The collection float is 1 day × −$1,300 = −$1,300. The net float is $6,000 + (−$1,300) = $4,700. In other words, at any given time, the firm typically has uncashed cheques outstanding of $6,000. At the same time, it has uncollected receipts of $1,300. Thus, the firm's book balance is typically $4,700 less than its available balance, a positive $4,700 net float.

Concepts Review and Critical Thinking Questions

1. **(LO3)** Is it possible for a firm to have too much cash? Why would shareholders care if a firm accumulates large amounts of cash?

2. **(LO3)** What options are available to a firm if it believes it has too much cash? How about too little?

3. **(LO3)** Are shareholders and creditors likely to agree on how much cash a firm should keep on hand?

4. **(LO3)** In the discussion at the beginning of this chapter, do you think the motivations for holding cash are reasonable?

5. **(LO3)** What is the difference between cash management and liquidity management?

6. **(LO3)** Why is a preferred stock with a dividend tied to short-term interest rates an attractive short-term investment for corporations with excess cash?

7. **(LO2)** Which would a firm prefer: a net collection float or a net disbursement float? Why?

8. **(LO3)** For each of the short-term marketable securities given here, provide an example of the potential disadvantages the investment has for meeting a corporation's cash management goals.
   a. Treasury bills
   b. Ordinary preferred stock

c. Certificates of deposit (CDs)

d. Commercial paper

e. 10-year Canada bonds

9. **(LO3)** It is sometimes argued that excess cash held by a firm can aggravate agency problems (discussed in Chapter 1) and, more generally, reduce incentives for shareholder wealth maximization. How would you frame the issue here?

10. **(LO3)** One option a firm usually has with any excess cash is to pay its suppliers more quickly. What are the advantages and disadvantages of this use of excess cash?

11. **(LO3)** Another option usually available is to reduce the firm's outstanding debt. What are the advantages and disadvantages of this use of excess cash?

Questions and Problems

Basic
(Questions 1–10)

1. **Calculating Float (LO1)** In a typical month, the Saint John Corporation receives 80 cheques totalling $139,000. These are delayed four days on average. What is the average daily float? Assume 30 days in a month.

2. **Calculating Net Float (LO1)** Each business day, on average, a company writes cheques totalling $12,000 to pay its suppliers. The usual clearing time for the cheques is four days. Meanwhile, the company is receiving payments from its customers each day, in the form of cheques, totalling $23,000. The cash from the payments is available to the firm after two days.

   a. Calculate the company's disbursement float, collection float, and net float.

   b. How would your answer to part (a) change if the collected funds were available in one day instead of two?

3. **Costs of Float (LO1)** Lancaster Wine Inc. receives an average of $17,000 in cheques per day. The delay in clearing is typically three days. The current interest rate is .017 percent per day.

   a. What is the company's collection float?

   b. What is the most Lancaster should be willing to pay today to eliminate its float entirely?

   c. What is the highest daily fee the company should be willing to pay to eliminate its float entirely?

4. **Float and Weighted Average Delay (LO1)** Your neighbour goes to the post office once a month and picks up two cheques, one for $14,000 and one for $5,000. The larger cheque takes four days to clear after it is deposited; the smaller one takes 3 days. Assume 30 days in a month.

   a. What is the total float for the month?

   b. What is the average daily float?

   c. What are the average daily receipts and weighted average delay?

5. **NPV and Collection Time (LO2)** Your firm has an average receipt size of $125. A bank has approached you concerning a lockbox service that will decrease your total collection time by two days. You typically receive 6,400 cheques per day. The daily interest rate is .016 percent. If the bank charges a fee of $175 per day, should the lockbox project be accepted? What would the net annual savings be if the service were adopted?

6. **Using Weighted Average Delay (LO1)** A mail-order firm processes 5,300 cheques per month. Of these, 60 percent are for $43 and 40 percent are for $75. The $43 cheques are delayed two days on average; the $75 cheques are delayed three days on average. Assume 30 days in a month.

   a. What is the average daily collection float? How do you interpret your answer?

   b. What is the weighted average delay? Use the result to calculate the average daily float.

   c. How much should the firm be willing to pay to eliminate the float?

   d. If the interest rate is 7 percent per year, calculate the daily cost of the float. Assume 365 days per year.

   e. How much should the firm be willing to pay to reduce the weighted average float to 1.5 days?

7. **Value of Lockboxes (LO2)** Rothesay Submarine Manufacturing is investigating a lockbox system to reduce its collection time. It has determined the following:

Average number of payments per day	385
Average value of payment	$975
Variable lockbox fee (per transaction)	$.35
Daily interest rate on money market securities	.068%

   The total collection time will be reduced by three days if the lockbox system is adopted.

   a. What is the PV of adopting the system?

   b. What is the NPV of adopting the system?

   c. What is the net cash flow per day from adopting? Per cheque?

8. **Lockboxes and Collections (LO2)** It takes Quispamsis Modular Homes Inc. about six days to receive and deposit cheques from customers. Quispamsis's management is considering a lockbox system to reduce the firm's collection times. It is expected that the lockbox system will reduce receipt and deposit times to three days total. Average daily collections are $130,000, and the required rate of return is 9 percent per year. Assume 365 days per year.

   a. What is the reduction in outstanding cash balances as a result of implementing the lockbox system?

   b. What is the dollar return that could be earned on these savings?

c. What is the maximum monthly charge Quispamsis should pay for this lockbox system if the payment is due at the end of the month? What if the payment is due at the beginning of the month?

9. **Value of Delay (LO2)** Loch Alva Inc. disburses cheques every two weeks that average $86,000 and take seven days to clear. How much interest can the company earn annually if it delays transfer of funds from an interest-bearing account that pays .011 percent per day for these seven days? Ignore the effects of compounding interest.

10. **NPV and Reducing Float (LO2)** Lepreau Books Corporation has an agreement with Hampton Bank whereby the bank handles $5 million in collections a day and requires a $350,000 compensating balance. Lepreau Books is contemplating cancelling the agreement and dividing its eastern region so that two other banks will handle its business. Banks A and B will each handle $2.5 million of collections a day, and each requires a compensating balance of $200,000. Lepreau Books' financial management expects that collections will be accelerated by one day if the eastern region is divided. Should the company proceed with the new system? What will be the annual net savings? Assume that the T-bill rate is 2.5 percent annually.

Intermediate
(Questions
11–12)

11. **Lockboxes and Collection Time (LO2)** Norton Treehouses Inc., a Nova Scotia–based company, has determined that a majority of its customers are located in the Quebec area. It therefore is considering using a lockbox system offered by a bank located in Montreal. The bank has estimated that use of the system will reduce collection time by 1.5 days. Based on the following information, should the lockbox system be adopted?

Average number of payments per day	800
Average value of payment	$750
Variable lockbox fee (per transaction)	$.15
Annual interest rate on money market securities	5.5%

How would your answer change if there were a fixed charge of $6,000 per year in addition to the variable charge? Assume 365 days per year.

12. **Calculating Transactions Required (LO2)** Sussex Inc., a large fertilizer distributor based in Nova Scotia, is planning to use a lockbox system to speed up collections from its customers located on the West Coast. A Vancouver-area bank will provide this service for an annual fee of $10,000 plus 10 cents per transaction. The estimated reduction in collection and processing time is one day. If the average customer payment in this region is $5,700, how many customers each day, on average, are needed to make the system profitable for Sussex? Treasury bills are currently yielding 5 percent per year and assume 365 days per year.

MINI CASE

Cash Management at Donaghy Corporation

Donaghy Corporation was founded 20 years ago by its president, Jack Donaghy. The company originally began as a mail-order company, but has grown rapidly in recent years, in large part due to its website. Because of the wide geographical dispersion of the company's customers, it currently employs a lockbox system with collection centres in Vancouver, Calgary, Toronto, and Montreal.

Liz Lemon, the company's treasurer, has been examining the current cash collection policies. On average, each lockbox centre handles $175,000 in payments each day. The company's current policy is to invest these payments in short-term marketable securities daily at the collection centre banks. Every two weeks, the investment accounts are swept; the proceeds are wire-transferred to Donaghy's headquarters in Winnipeg to meet the company's payroll. The investment accounts each earn .012 percent per day, and the wire transfers cost .20 percent of the amount transferred.

Liz has been approached by the Royal Canadian Bank, about the possibility of setting up a concentration banking

system for Donaghy Corp. Royal Canadian will accept each of the lockbox centre's daily payments via automated clearinghouse (ACH) transfers in lieu of wire transfers. The ACH-transferred funds will not be available for use for one day. Once cleared, the funds will be deposited in a short-term account, which will also yield .012 percent per day. Each ACH transfer will cost $150. Jack has asked Liz to determine which cash management system will be the best for the company. As her assistant, Liz has asked you to answer the following questions:

Questions

1. What is Donaghy Corporation's total net cash flow available from the current lockbox system to meet payroll?

2. Under the terms outlined by the bank should the company proceed with the concentration banking system?

3. What cost of ACH transfers would make the company indifferent between the two systems?

Internet Application Questions

1. Cash management today involves integrating various functions such as invoicing and electronic deposits. For many mid-sized businesses, such tasks end up consuming valuable scarce resources if done in-house. SAP Canada (sap.com/canada/index.epx) provides consulting and implementation services in all cash and liquidity management. Search SAP's website and discuss what kinds of companies will find SAP Canada's services particularly useful.

2. ITG Canada (itg.com/our-locations/canada) provides equity trading research for institutions and brokers. Click on their website and explain what "soft dollar" arrangements are.

3. CIBC World Markets sells commercial paper in Canada and the U.S. to interested institutional investors. Go to the CIBC World Markets website at research.cibcwm.com and find out current information about the company's commercial paper. What is the credit rating for the paper in Canada and the U.S.? What firms provided the ratings? What is the minimum size CIBC World Markets will sell in Canada and the U.S.? For what duration?

4. What are the highest and lowest historical interest rates for commercial paper in Canada? Go to the Bank of Canada website at bankofcanada.ca and follow the link "Rates and Statistics," then "Canadian Interest Rates" and "Selected Historical Interest Rates." Find the highest and lowest interest rates for one-month and three-month prime corporate paper. What are they and when did they occur? What implications do these rates have for short-term financial planning and liquidity management?

CHAPTER 20

CREDIT AND INVENTORY MANAGEMENT

Courtesy of Toyota

I n May 2012, Toyota Canada Inc. posted an increase in sales of 65% over May 2011—a strong recovery from weak demand due to consumer uncertainty in 2011. In order to meet increased demand, Toyota Canada had to overcome supply and inventory problems arising from the tsunami in Japan and flooding in Thailand. This shows the importance of inventory management for companies such as Toyota Canada Inc. Proper management of inventory can have a significant impact on the profitability of a company and the value investors place on it. In this chapter, we discuss, among other things, how companies arrive at an optimal inventory level.

Learning Objectives ▶

After studying this chapter, you should understand:

LO1 **How firms manage their receivables and the basic components of a firm's credit policies.**

LO2 **The distinct elements of the terms of sale.**

LO3 **The factors that influence a firm's decision to grant credit.**

LO4 **How to evaluate credit policy.**

LO5 **The types of inventory and inventory management systems used by firms.**

LO6 **How to determine the costs of carrying inventory and the optimal inventory level.**

Most firms hold inventories to ensure that they have finished goods to meet sales demand and raw materials and work in process when they are needed in production. Deciding how much to hold is important to managers in production and marketing. Because inventories represent a significant investment with carrying costs, the financial manager is also involved in the decision. Our discussion of inventory looks at a traditional approach that focuses on the trade-off between carrying costs and shortage costs. We also present just-in-time inventory that offers an innovative solution.

This chapter also covers credit management. When a firm sells goods and services, it can demand cash on or before the delivery date, or it can extend credit to customers and allow some delay in payment. The next few sections provide an idea of what is involved in the firm's decision to grant credit to its customers. Granting credit is investing in a customer, an investment tied to the sale of a product or service.

Why do firms grant credit? Not all do, but the practice is extremely common. The obvious reason is that offering credit is a way of stimulating sales. The costs associated with granting credit are not trivial: First, there is the chance that the customer will not pay. Second, the firm has to bear the costs of carrying the receivables. The credit policy decision thus involves a trade-off between the benefits of increased sales and the costs of granting credit. We examine this trade-off in the next sections.

20.1 | Credit and Receivables

From an accounting perspective, when credit is granted, an account receivable is created. These receivables include credit to other firms, called *trade credit,* and credit granted to consumers, called *consumer credit.* About 10 percent of all the assets of Canadian industrial firms are in the form of accounts receivable. For retail firms, the figure is much higher. So receivables obviously represent a major investment of financial resources by Canadian businesses.

Furthermore, trade credit is a very important source of financing for corporations. Looking back at Table 18.2 in Chapter 18, Canadian Tire financed about 39.5 percent of total current liabilities through trade and other payable, more than any other single source of short-term financing. However we look at it, receivables and receivables management are key aspects of a firm's short-term financial policy.

Components of Credit Policy

If a firm decides to grant credit to its customers, it must establish procedures for extending credit and collecting. In particular, the firm has to deal with the following components of credit policy:

terms of sale
Conditions on which a firm sells its goods and services for cash or credit.

1. **Terms of sale**. The terms of sale establish how the firm proposes to sell its goods and services. A basic distinction is whether the firm requires cash or extends credit. If the firm does grant credit to a customer, the terms of sale specify (perhaps implicitly) the credit period, the cash discount and discount period, and the type of credit instrument.

credit analysis
The process of determining the probability that customers will or will not pay.

2. **Credit analysis**. In granting credit, a firm determines how much effort to expend trying to distinguish between customers who pay and customers who do not pay. Firms use a number of devices and procedures to determine the probability that customers will not pay, and put together, these are called *credit analysis*.

collection policy
Procedures followed by a firm in collecting accounts receivable.

3. **Collection policy**. After credit has been granted, the firm has the potential problem of collecting the cash when it becomes due, for which it must establish a collection policy.

In the next several sections, we discuss these components of credit policy that collectively make up the decision to grant credit.

The Cash Flows from Granting Credit

In a previous chapter, we described the accounts receivable period as the time it takes to collect on a sale. Several events occur during that period. These are the cash flows associated with granting credit, and they can be illustrated with a traditional cash flow diagram:

The cash flows of granting credit

As our time line indicates, the typical sequence of events when a firm grants credit is (1) the credit sale is made, (2) the customer sends a cheque to the firm, (3) the firm deposits the cheque, and (4) the firm's account is credited for the amount of the cheque.

Based on our discussion in the previous chapter, it is apparent that one of the factors influencing the receivables period is float. Thus, one way to reduce the receivables period is to speed up cheque mailing, processing, and clearing. Because we cover this subject elsewhere, we ignore float in our subsequent discussion and focus on what is likely to be the major determinant of the receivables period, credit policy. We come back to float at the end when we look at a computerized implementation of credit policy.

The Investment in Receivables

The investment in accounts receivable for any firm depends on the amount of credit sales and the average collection period. For example, if a firm's average collection period (ACP) is 30 days, at any given time there are 30 days' worth of sales outstanding. If sales run $1,000 per day, the firm's accounts receivable are equal to 30 days × $1,000 per day = $30,000.

As our example illustrates, a firm's receivables generally are equal to its average daily sales multiplied by its average collection period (ACP):

$$\text{Accounts receivable} = \text{Average daily sales} \times \text{ACP} \qquad [20.1]$$

Thus, a firm's investment in accounts receivable depends on factors that influence credit sales and collections.

We have seen the average collection period in various places, including Chapters 3 and 18. Recall that we use the terms *days' sales in receivables, receivables period,* and *average collection period* interchangeably to refer to the length of time it takes for the firm to collect on a sale.

Concept Questions

1. What are the basic components of credit policy?
2. What are the basic components of the terms of sale if a firm chooses to sell on credit?

20.2 | Terms of the Sale

As we just described, the terms of a sale are made up of three distinct elements:

1. The period for which credit is granted (the credit period).
2. The cash discount and the discount period.
3. The type of credit instrument.

Within a given industry, the terms of sales are usually fairly standard, but across industries these terms vary quite a bit. In many cases, the terms of sale are remarkably archaic and literally date to previous centuries. Organized systems of trade credit that resemble current practice can be easily traced to the great fairs of medieval Europe, and they almost surely existed long before then.

Why Trade Credit Exists

Set aside the venerable history of trade credit for a moment and ask yourself why it should exist.[1] After all, it is quite easy to imagine that all sales could be for cash. From the firm's viewpoint, this would get rid of receivables carrying costs and collection costs. Bad debts would be zero (assuming the firm was careful to accept no counterfeit money).

Imagine this cash-only economy in the context of perfectly competitive product and financial markets. Competition would force companies to lower their prices to pass the savings from immediate collections on to customers. Any company that chose to grant credit to its customers would have to raise its prices accordingly to survive. A purchaser who needed financing over the operating cycle could borrow from a bank or the money market. In this perfect market environment, it would make no difference to the seller or the buyer whether credit were granted.

In practice, firms spend significant resources setting credit policy and managing its implementation. So deviations from perfect markets—market imperfections—must explain why trade credit exists. We look briefly at several imperfections and how trade credit helps to overcome them.

In practice, both the buyer and seller have imperfect information. Buyers lack perfect information on the quality of the product. For this reason, the buyer may prefer credit terms that give time to return the product if it is defective or unsuitable. When the seller offers credit, it signals to potential customers that the product is of high quality and likely to provide satisfaction.[2]

In addition, in practice, any firm that grants credit or a loan lacks perfect information on the creditworthiness of the borrower. Although it is costly for a bank or other third-party lender to acquire this information, a seller that has been granting trade credit to a purchaser likely has it

---

[1] Our discussion draws on N. C. Hill and W. L. Sartoris, *Short-Term Financial Management*, 3rd ed. (Prentice Hall College Div., 1995), chap. 14.

[2] This use of signalling is very similar to dividend signalling discussed in Chapter 17. There corporations signalled the quality of projected cash flows by maintaining dividends even when earnings were down.

already. Further, the seller may have superior information on the resale value of the product serving as collateral. These information advantages may allow the seller to offer more attractive, more flexible credit terms and be more liberal in authorizing credit.[3]

Finally, perfect markets have zero transaction costs but, in reality, it is costly to set up a bank borrowing facility or to borrow in money markets. We discussed some of the costs in Chapter 18. It may be cheaper to utilize credit from the seller.

These reasons go a long way toward explaining the popularity of trade credit. Whatever the reasons, setting credit policy involves major decisions for the firm.

The Basic Form

The easiest way to understand the terms of sale is to consider an example. For bulk candy, terms of 2/10, net 60 are common. This means that customers have 60 days from the invoice date to pay the full amount. However, if payment is made within 10 days, a 2 percent cash discount can be taken.

Consider a buyer who places an order for $1,000, and assume that the terms of the sale are 2/10, net 60. The buyer has the option of paying $1,000 \times (1 - .02) = $980 in 10 days, or paying the full $1,000 in 60 days.

When the terms are stated as just net 30, then the customer has 30 days from the invoice date to pay the entire $1,000, and no discount is offered for early payment.

The Credit Period

credit period
The length of time that credit is granted.

The **credit period** is the basic length of time for which credit is granted. The credit period varies widely from industry to industry, but it is almost always between 30 and 120 days. When a cash discount is offered, the credit period has two components: the net credit period and the cash discount period. In most cases, the credit period and the cash discount conform to industry practice. Firms do not often deviate from the industry norm. For this reason, we focus on examples at the industry level.

The net credit period is the length of time the customer has to pay. The cash discount period, as the name suggests, is the time during which the discount is available. With 2/10, net 30, for example, the net credit period is 30 days and the cash discount period is 10 days.

invoice
Bill for goods or services provided by the seller to the purchaser.

THE INVOICE DATE   The invoice date is the beginning of the credit period. An **invoice** is a written account of merchandise shipped to the buyer. For individual items, by convention, the invoice date is usually the shipping date or the billing date, *not* the date the buyer receives the goods or the bill.

Many other arrangements exist. For example, the terms of sale might be ROG, for "receipt of goods." In this case, the credit starts when the customer receives the order. This might be used when the customer is in a remote location.

End-of-month (EOM) terms are fairly common. With EOM dating, all sales made during a particular month are assumed to be made at the end of that month. This is useful when a buyer makes purchases throughout the month, but the seller bills only once a month.

For example, terms of 2/10th EOM tell the buyer to take a 2 percent discount if payment is made by the 10th of the month, otherwise the full amount is due after that. Confusingly, the end of the month is sometimes taken to be the 25th day of the month. MOM, for middle of month, is another variation.

Seasonal dating is sometimes used to encourage sales of seasonal products during the off-season. A product that is sold primarily in the spring, such as bicycles or sporting goods, can be shipped in January with credit terms of 2/10, net 30. However, the invoice might be dated May 1, so the credit period actually begins at that time. This practice encourages buyers to order early.

LENGTH OF THE CREDIT PERIOD   A number of factors influence the length of the credit period. One of the most important is the *buyer's* inventory period and operating cycle. All other things being equal, the shorter these are, the shorter the credit period normally is.

---

[3]B. Biais and C. Gollier, "Trade Credit and Credit Rationing," *Review of Financial Studies*, January 1997, Volume 10, pp. 903–937.

Based on our discussion in Chapter 18, the operating cycle has two components: the inventory period and the receivables period. The inventory period is the time it takes the buyer to acquire inventory (from us), process it, and sell it. The receivables period is the time it then takes the buyer to collect on the sale. Note that the credit period that we offer is effectively the buyer's payables period.

By extending credit, we finance a portion of our buyer's operating cycle and thereby shorten the cash cycle. When our credit period exceeds the buyer's inventory period, we are financing not only the buyer's inventory purchases but also part of the buyer's receivables.

Furthermore, if our credit period exceeds our buyer's operating cycle, we are effectively providing financing for aspects of our customer's business beyond the immediate purchase and sale of our merchandise. The reason is that the buyer has a loan from us even after the merchandise is resold, and the buyer can use that credit for other purposes. For this reason, the length of the buyer's operating cycle is often cited as an appropriate upper limit to the credit period.

A number of other factors influence the credit period. Many of these also influence our customers' operating cycles; so, once again, these are related subjects. Among the most important are:

1. *Perishability and collateral value.* Perishable items have relatively rapid turnover and relatively low collateral value. Credit periods are thus shorter for such goods. For example, a food wholesaler selling fresh fruit and produce might use net seven terms. Alternatively, jewellery might be sold for 5/30, net four months.

2. *Consumer demand.* Products that are well established generally have more rapid turnover. Newer or slow-moving products often have longer credit periods to entice buyers. Also, as we have seen, sellers may choose to extend much longer credit periods for off-season sales (when customer demand is low).

3. *Cost, profitability, and standardization.* Relatively inexpensive goods tend to have shorter credit periods. The same is true for relatively standardized goods and raw materials. These all tend to have lower markups and higher turnover rates, both of which lead to shorter credit periods. There are exceptions. Auto dealers, for example, generally pay for cars as they are received.

4. *Credit risk.* The greater the credit risk of the buyer, the shorter the credit period is likely to be (assuming that credit is granted at all).

5. *The size of the account.* If the account is small, the credit period is shorter. Small accounts are more costly to manage, and the customers are less important.

6. *Competition.* When the seller is in a highly competitive market, longer credit periods may be offered as a way of attracting customers.

7. *Customer type.* A single seller might offer different credit terms to different buyers. A food wholesaler, for example, might supply grocers, bakeries, and restaurants. Each group would probably have different credit terms. More generally, sellers often have both wholesale and retail customers, and they frequently quote different terms to each.

Cash Discounts

cash discount
A discount given for a cash purchase.

As we have seen, **cash discounts** are often part of the terms of sale. The practice of granting discounts for cash purposes goes back more than 100 years and is widespread today. One reason discounts are offered is to speed the collection of receivables. This reduces the amount of credit being offered, and the firm must trade this off against the cost of the discount.

Notice that when a cash discount is offered, the credit is essentially free during the discount period. The buyer only pays for the credit after the discount expires. With 2/10, net 30, a rational buyer either pays in 10 days to make the greatest possible use of the free credit or pays in 30 days to get the longest possible use of the money in exchange for giving up the discount. So, by giving up the discount, the buyer effectively gets 30 − 10 = 20 days' credit.

Another reason for cash discounts is that they are a legal way of charging higher prices to customers that have had credit extended to them. In both Canada and the United States, the law prohibits discrimination in charging different prices to different buyers for the same product. In this sense, cash discounts are a convenient way of separately pricing the credit granted to customers.

ELECTRONIC CREDIT TERMS   In Chapter 19, we showed how electronic disbursements saved time and money. To induce buyers to pay electronically or to give discounts to large customers, some firms offer discounts of around 1 percent for electronic payment one day after the goods are delivered. If electronic disbursement is coupled with electronic data interchange, the buyer and seller negotiate the discount and the date for payment.

COST OF THE CREDIT   In our examples, it might seem that the discounts are rather small. With 2/10, net 30, for example, early payment gets the buyer only a 2 percent discount. Does this provide a significant incentive for early payment? The answer is yes because the implicit interest rate is extremely high.

To see why the discount is important, we will calculate the cost to the buyer of not paying early. To do this, we will find the interest rate the buyer is effectively paying for the trade credit. Suppose the order is for $1,000. The buyer can pay $980 in 10 days or wait another 20 days and pay $1,000. It's obvious that the buyer is effectively borrowing $980 for 20 days and that the buyer pays $20 in interest on the "loan." What's the interest rate?

This interest is ordinary discount interest, which we discussed in Chapter 5. With $20 in interest on $980 borrowed, the rate is $20/$980 = 2.0408%. This is relatively low, but remember that this is the rate per 20-day period. There are 365/20 = 18.25 such periods in a year, so, by not taking the discount, the buyer is paying an effective annual rate (EAR) of:

$$EAR = (1.020408)^{18.25} - 1 = 44.6\%$$

From the buyer's point of view, this is an expensive source of financing!

Given that the interest rate is so high here, it is unlikely that the seller benefits from early payment. Ignoring the possibility of default by the buyer, the decision by a customer to forgo the discount almost surely works to the seller's advantage.

TRADE DISCOUNTS   In some circumstances, the discount is not really an incentive for early payment but is instead a *trade discount*, a discount routinely given to some type of buyer. For example, with our 2/10th, EOM terms, the buyer takes a 2 percent discount if the invoice is paid by the 10th, but the bill is considered due on the 10th, and overdue after that. Thus, the credit period and the discount period are effectively the same, and there is no reward for paying before the due date.

EXAMPLE 20.1: What's the Rate?

Ordinary tiles are often sold 3/30, net 60. What effective annual rate does a buyer pay by not taking the discount? What would the APR be if one were quoted?

Here we have 3 percent discount interest on 60 − 30 = 30 days' credit. The rate per 30 days is .03/.97 = 3.093%. There are 365/30 = 12.17 such periods in a year, so the effective annual rate is:

$$EAR = (1.03093)^{12.17} - 1 = 44.9\%$$

The APR, as always, would be calculated by multiplying the rate per period by the number of periods:

$$APR = .03093 \times 12.17 = 37.6\%$$

An interest rate calculated like this APR is often quoted as the cost of the trade credit, and, as this example illustrates, can seriously understate the true cost.

THE CASH DISCOUNT AND THE ACP   To the extent that a cash discount encourages customers to pay early, it shortens the receivables period and, all other things being equal, reduces the firm's investment in receivables.

For example, suppose a firm currently has terms of net 30 and an ACP of 30 days. If it offers terms of 2/10, net 30, perhaps 50 percent of its customers (in terms of volume of purchases) would pay in 10 days. The remaining customers would still take an average of 30 days to pay. What would the new average collection period (ACP) be? If the firm's annual sales are $15 million (before discounts), what happens to the investment in receivables?

If half of the customers take 10 days to pay and half take 30, the new average collection period is:

New ACP = .50 × 10 days + .50 × 30 days = 20 days

The ACP thus falls from 30 days to 20 days. Average daily sales are $15 million/365 = $41,096 per day. Receivables thus fall by $41,096 × 10 = $410,960.

Credit Instruments

credit instrument
The evidence of indebtedness.

The **credit instrument** is the basic evidence of indebtedness. Most trade credit is offered on *open account*. This means the only formal instrument of credit is the invoice that is sent with the shipment of goods and that the customer signs as evidence the goods have been received. Afterward, the firm and its customers record the exchange on their books of account.

At times, the firm may require the customer to sign a *promissory note*. This is a basic IOU and might be used when the order is large, when there is no cash discount involved, and when the firm anticipates a problem in collections. Promissory notes are not common, but they can eliminate controversies later about the existence of debt.

One problem with promissory notes is that they are signed after delivery of the goods. To obtain a credit commitment from a customer before the goods are delivered, a firm arranges a *commercial draft*. Typically, the firm draws up a commercial draft calling for the customer to pay a specific amount by a specified date. The draft is then sent to the customer's bank with the shipping invoices.

When immediate payment on the draft is required, it is called a *sight draft*. If immediate payment is not required, the draft is a *time draft*. When the draft is presented and the buyer accepts it—meaning the buyer promises to pay it in the future—it is called a *trade acceptance* and is sent back to the selling firm. The seller can keep the acceptance, in effect providing trade credit financing to the buyer, or sell it to someone else. The third party buying the acceptance is a money market investor. This investor is now financing the buyer and the seller receives immediate payment less discount interest.

To make the trade acceptance more salable, a chartered bank may stamp it, meaning the bank is guaranteeing payment. Then the draft becomes a *bankers acceptance*. This arrangement is common in international trade and widely used domestically. Bankers acceptances are actively traded in the money market as we discussed in Chapter 19.

A firm can also use a conditional sales contract as a credit instrument. This is an arrangement where the firm retains legal ownership of the goods until the customer has completed payment. Conditional sales contracts usually are paid in installments and have an interest cost built into them.

Concept Questions

1. What considerations enter into the determination of the terms of sale?
2. Explain what terms of "3/45, net 90" mean. What is the implicit interest rate?

20.3 | Analyzing Credit Policy

In this section, we take a closer look at the factors that influence the decision to grant credit. Granting credit makes sense only if the NPV from doing so is positive. We thus need to look at the NPV of the decision to grant credit.

Credit Policy Effects

In evaluating credit policy, there are five basic factors to consider:

1. *Revenue effects.* When the firm grants credit, there is a delay in revenue collections as some customers take advantage of the credit offered and pay later. However, the firm may be able to charge a higher price if it grants credit and it may be able to increase the quantity sold. Total revenues may thus increase.

2. *Cost effects.* Although the firm may experience delayed revenues if it grants credit, it still incurs the costs of sales immediately. Whether or not the firm sells for cash or credit, it still has to acquire or produce the merchandise (and pay for it).

3. *The cost of debt.* When the firm grants credit, it must arrange to finance the resulting receivables. As a result, the firm's cost of short-term borrowing is a factor in the decision to grant credit.[4]

4. *The probability of nonpayment.* If the firm grants credit, some percentage of the credit buyers do not pay. This can't happen, of course, if the firm sells for cash.

5. *The cash discount.* When the firm offers a cash discount as part of its credit terms, some customers choose to pay early to take advantage of the discount.

Evaluating a Proposed Credit Policy

To illustrate how credit policy can be analyzed, we start with a relatively simple case. Locust Software has been in existence for two years; it is one of several successful firms that develop computer programs. Currently, Locust sells for cash only.

Locust is evaluating a request from some major customers to change its current policy to net 30 days. To analyze this proposal, we define the following:

P = Price per unit
v = Variable cost per unit
Q = Current quantity sold per month
Q' = Quantity sold under new policy
R = Monthly required return

For now, we ignore discounts and the possibility of default. Also, we ignore taxes because they don't affect our conclusions.

NPV OF SWITCHING POLICIES To illustrate the NPV of switching credit policies, suppose we had the following for Locust:

$P = \$49$
$v = \$20$
$Q = 100$
$Q' = 110$

If the required return is 2 percent per month, should Locust make the switch?

Currently, Locust has monthly sales of $P \times Q = \$4,900$. Variable costs each month are $v \times Q = \$2,000$, so the monthly cash flow from this activity is:

$$\text{Cash flow (old policy)} = (P - v)Q \qquad [20.2]$$
$$= (\$49 - 20) \times 100$$
$$= \$2,900$$

This is not the total cash flow for Locust, of course, but it is all that we need to look at because fixed costs and other components of cash flow are the same whether or not the switch is made. If Locust does switch to net 30 days on sales, the quantity sold rises to $Q' = 110$. Monthly revenues increase to $P \times Q'$, and costs are $v \times Q'$. The monthly cash flow under the new policy is thus:

$$\text{Cash flow (new policy)} = (P - v)Q' \qquad [20.3]$$
$$= (\$49 - 20) \times 110$$
$$= \$3,190$$

Going back to Chapter 10, the relevant incremental cash flow is the difference between the new and old cash flows:

---

[4]The cost of short-term debt is not necessarily the required return on receivables, although it is commonly assumed to be. As always, the required return on an investment depends on the risk of the investment, not the source of the financing. The buyer's cost of short-term debt is closer in spirit to the correct rate. We maintain the implicit assumption that the seller and the buyer have the same short-term debt cost. In any case, the time periods in credit decisions are relatively short, so a relatively small error in the discount rate does not have a large effect on our estimated NPV.

$$\text{Incremental cash inflow} = (P - v)(Q' - Q)$$
$$= (\$49 - 20) \times (110 - 100)$$
$$= \$290$$

This says the benefit each month of changing policies is equal to the gross profit per unit sold $(P - v) = \$29$, multiplied by the increase in sales $(Q' - Q) = 10$. The present value of the future incremental cash flows is thus:

$$PV = [(P - v)(Q' - Q)]/R \qquad [20.4]$$

For Locust, this present value works out to be:

$$PV = (\$29 \times 10)/.02 = \$14,500$$

Notice that we have treated the monthly cash flow as a perpetuity since the same benefit would be realized each month forever.

Now that we know the benefit of switching, what's the cost? There are two components to consider: First, since the quantity sold rises from Q to Q', Locust has to produce $Q' - Q$ more units today at a cost of $v(Q' - Q) = \$20 \times (110 - 100) = \$200$. Second, the sales that would have been collected this month under the current policy ($P \times Q = \$4,900$) are not collected. This happens because the sales made this month won't be collected until 30 days later under the new policy. The cost of the switch is the sum of these two components:

$$\text{Cost of switching} = PQ + v(Q' - Q), \qquad [20.5]$$
where PQ = present value in perpetuity of a one-month delay in receiving
the monthly revenue of PQ.

For Locust, this cost would be $\$4,900 + 200 = \$5,100$.

Putting it all together, the NPV of the switch is:

$$\text{NPV of switching} = -[PQ + v(Q' - Q)] + (P - v)(Q' - Q)/R \qquad [20.6]$$

For Locust, the cost of switching is $\$5,100$. As we saw, the benefit is $\$290$ per month, forever. At 2 percent per month, the NPV is:

$$NPV = -\$5,100 + \$290/.02$$
$$= -\$5,100 + 14,500$$
$$= \$9,400$$

Therefore, the switch is very profitable.

EXAMPLE 20.2: We'd Rather Fight than Switch

Suppose a company is considering a switch from all cash to net 30, but the quantity sold is not expected to change. What is the NPV of the switch? Explain.

In this case, $Q' - Q$ is zero, so the NPV is just $-P \times Q$. What this says is that the effect of the switch is simply to postpone one month's collections forever, with no benefit from doing so.

A BREAK-EVEN APPLICATION   Based on our discussion thus far, the key variable for Locust is $Q' - Q$, the increase in unit sales. The projected increase of 10 units is only an estimate, so there is some forecasting risk. Under the circumstances, it's natural to wonder what increase in unit sales is necessary to break even.

Earlier, the NPV of the switch was defined as:

$$NPV = -[PQ + v(Q' - Q)] + (P - v)(Q' - Q)/R$$

We can calculate the break-even point explicitly by setting the NPV equal to zero and solving for $(Q' - Q)$:

$$NPV = 0 = -[PQ + v(Q' - Q)] + (P - v)(Q' - Q)/R \qquad [20.7]$$
$$Q' - Q = (PQ)/[(P - v)/R - v]$$

For Locust, the break-even sales increase is thus:

$$Q' - Q = \$4,900/[\$29/.02 - \$20]$$
$$= 3.43 \text{ units}$$

This tells us that the switch is a good idea as long as we are confident we can sell at least 3.43 more units.

Concept Questions

1. What are the important effects to consider in a decision to offer credit?
2. Explain how to estimate the NPV of a credit policy switch.

20.4 | Optimal Credit Policy

So far, we've discussed how to compute net present value for a switch in credit policy. We have not discussed the optimal amount of credit or the optimal credit policy. In principle, the optimal amount of credit is determined where the incremental cash flows from increased sales are exactly equal to the incremental costs of carrying the increased investment in accounts receivable.

The Total Credit Cost Curve

The trade-off between granting credit and not granting credit isn't hard to identify, but it is difficult to quantify precisely. As a result, we can only describe an optimal credit policy.

To begin, the carrying costs associated with granting credit come in three forms:

1. The required return on receivables.
2. The losses from bad debts.
3. The costs of managing credit and credit collections.

We have already discussed the first and second of these. Making up the third cost of managing credit are the expenses associated with running the credit department. Firms that don't grant credit have no such department and no such expense. These three costs all increase as credit policy is relaxed.

If a firm has a very restrictive credit policy, all the preceding costs are low. In this case, the firm has a shortage of credit, so there is an opportunity cost. This opportunity cost is the extra potential profit from credit sales that is lost because credit is refused. This forgone benefit comes from two sources, the increase in quantity sold, Q' versus Q, and, potentially, a higher price. These costs go down as credit policy is relaxed.

credit cost curve
Graphical representation of the sum of the carrying costs and the opportunity costs of a credit policy.

The sum of the carrying costs and the opportunity costs of a particular credit policy is called the total **credit cost curve**. We have drawn such a curve in Figure 20.1. As this figure illustrates, there is a point where the total credit cost is minimized. This point corresponds to the optimal amount of credit or, equivalently, the optimal investment in receivables.

If the firm extends more credit than this minimum, the additional net cash flow from new customers does not cover the carrying costs of the investment in receivables. If the level of receivables is less than this amount, the firm is forgoing valuable profit opportunities.

In general, the costs and benefits from extending credit depend on the characteristics of particular firms and industries. All other things being equal, for example, it is likely that firms with (1) excess capacity, (2) low variable operating costs, and (3) repeat customers extend credit more liberally than otherwise. See if you can explain why each of these contributes to a more liberal credit policy.

Organizing the Credit Function

captive finance company
Wholly owned subsidiary that handles credit extension and receivables financing through commercial paper.

As we stated earlier, firms selling only for cash save the expense of running a credit department. In practice, firms that do grant credit may achieve some of these savings by contracting out all or part of the credit function to a factor, an insurance company, or a **captive finance company**. Chapter 18 discussed factoring, an arrangement where the firm sells its receivables to a factor that takes on all responsibility for credit checking, authorization, and collection. The factor also guarantees payment, ruling out defaults. Factors often provide accounts receivable financing as well. Small firms may find factoring cheaper than an in-house credit department.

FIGURE 20.1

The costs of granting credit

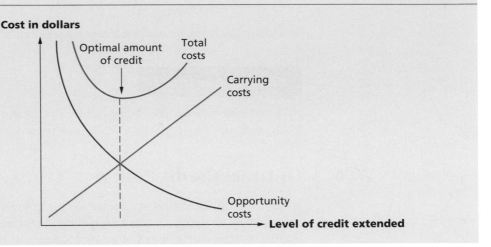

Carrying costs are the cash flows that must be incurred when credit is granted. They are positively related to the amount of credit extended. *Opportunity costs* are the lost sales from refusing credit. These costs go down when credit is granted.

Firms that run internal credit operations are self-insured against default risk. An alternative is to buy credit insurance through an insurance company. The insurance company offers coverage up to a preset dollar limit for accounts. As you would expect, accounts with a higher credit rating merit higher insurance limits.

Exporters may qualify for credit insurance through Export Development Canada (EDC), a Crown corporation of the federal government. For example, in May 2012, the EDC supported Vancouver-based North American Tungsten through its Accounts Receivable Insurance Program.[5]

Large corporations commonly extend credit through a subsidiary called a captive finance company, instead of a credit department. For example, before divesting it in 2008, General Motors Corporation financed its dealers and car buyers through its subsidiary, General Motors Acceptance Corporation (GMAC). Consumer and dealer receivables are the assets of GMAC and they are financed largely through commercial paper. Setting up the credit function as a separate legal entity has potential advantages in facilitating borrowing against receivables. Since they are segregated on the balance sheet of a captive, the receivables may make better collateral. As a result, the captive may be able to carry more debt and save on borrowing costs.[6]

A related issue in credit administration, whether through a finance captive or in-house, is the importance of having a set of written credit policies.[7] The policy covers credit terms, the information needed for credit analysis, collection procedures and the monitoring of receivables. Having the policy clearly stated helps control possible conflicts between the credit department and sales. For example, during the economic slowdown of 2008–2009, some Canadian companies tightened their credit granting rules to offset the higher probability of customer bankruptcy. Other companies eased credit to promote sales and to provide flexibility for regular customers. The decision depends on the considerations we analyzed earlier. Either way, sales and credit have to work together.

Concept Questions

1. What are the carrying costs of granting credit?
2. What are the opportunity costs of not granting credit?
3. Why do many large U.S. and Canadian corporations form captive finance subsidiaries?

---

[5] More information about EDC is at edc.ca

[6] The trend toward securitization of receivables through wholly owned subsidiaries discussed in Chapter 18 is supporting evidence. This somewhat controversial view of finance captives comes from G. S. Roberts and J. A. Viscione, "Captive Finance Subsidiaries and the M-Form Hypothesis," *Bell Journal of Economics,* Spring 1981, pp. 285–95.

[7] Our discussion draws on "A Written Credit Policy Can Overcome a Host of Potential Problems," Joint Venture Supplement, *The Financial Post,* June 20, 1991.

20.5 | Credit Analysis

Thus far, we have focused on establishing credit terms. Once a firm decides to grant credit to its customers, it must then establish guidelines for determining who is allowed to buy on credit as well as the credit limits to be set. Since the forces of competition often leave a firm little discretion in setting credit terms, credit managers focus on credit analysis, along with collection and receivables monitoring. Credit analysis refers to the process of deciding whether to extend credit to a particular customer. It usually involves two steps: gathering relevant information and determining creditworthiness.

Credit analysis is important simply because potential losses on receivables can be substantial. For example, at the end of 2010, IBM reported that $734 million of accounts receivable were doubtful, and GE reported a staggering $8.1 billion as allowance for losses.

When Should Credit Be Granted?

Imagine that a firm is trying to decide whether to grant credit to a customer. This decision can get complicated. For example, the answer depends on what happens if credit is refused. Will the customer simply pay cash or will the customer not make the purchase? To avoid this and other difficulties, we use some special cases to illustrate the key points.

A ONETIME SALE We start by considering the simplest case. A new customer wishes to buy one unit on credit at a price of P' per unit. If credit is refused, the customer would not make a purchase.

Furthermore, we assume that, if credit is granted, in one month, the customer either pays up or defaults. The probability of the second of these events is π. In this case, the probability (π) can be interpreted as the percentage of new customers who do not pay. Our business does not have repeat customers, so this is strictly a one-time sale. Finally, the required return on receivables is R per month and the variable cost is v per unit.

The analysis here is straightforward. If the firm refuses credit, the incremental cash flow is zero. If it grants credit, it spends v (the variable cost) this month and expects to collect $(1 - \pi)P'$ next month. The NPV of granting credit is:

$$NPV = -v + (1 - \pi)P'/(1 + R)$$ [20.8]

For example, for Locust Software, this NPV is:

$$NPV = -\$20 + (1 - \pi) \times \$49/(1.02)$$

With, say, a 20 percent rate of default, this works out to be:

$$NPV = -\$20 + .80 \times \$49/1.02 = \$18.43$$

Therefore, credit should be granted.

Our example illustrates an important point. In granting credit to a new customer, a firm risks its variable cost (v). It stands to gain the full price (P'). For a new customer, then, credit may be granted even if the default probability is high. For example, the break-even probability can be determined by setting the NPV equal to zero and solving for π:

$$NPV = 0 = -\$20 + (1 - \pi) \times \$49/(1.02)$$
$$(1 - \pi) = \$20/\$49 \times 1.02$$
$$\pi = 58.37\%$$

Locust should extend credit as long as there is at least a $1 - .583 = 41.7\%$ chance or better of collecting. This explains why firms with higher markups tend to have looser credit terms.

A common rule of thumb restates this information by asking, how many good accounts do we have to sell and collect to make up for the mistake of one write-off? Working with accounting numbers instead of NPVs, we can restate the break-even point as follows:

$$Profit = 0 = -variable\ cost \times probability\ of\ loss + profit\ margin \times probability\ of\ payment$$
$$0 = -v \times \pi + (P' - v)(1 - \pi)$$

In the Locust example, we have at the break-even point:

$$\text{Profit} = 0 = -\$20 \times \pi + (\$49 - \$20)(1 - \pi)$$

With a little algebra, we can solve for p = 60 percent, the same as we had earlier except for rounding error due to ignoring the present value. Notice that the break-even probability of default is simply the profit margin = $30/$49 = 61.2%. This makes sense since the seller breaks even if losses offset profits. Business people interpret this as saying that for every write-off we have to sell and collect around .61 good accounts.

Finally, notice that the break-even percentage of 61.2 percent is much higher than the break-even percentage of .04 percent we calculate in Appendix 20A (available on Connect), because that percentage is calculated assuming that $Q = Q'$, implying there are no new customers. The percentage calculated here applies to a potential new customer only.

The key difference between the analysis for a new customer versus an old one is what is at risk if we extend credit. For the new customer, there is no sale unless we extend credit so the amount at risk is the firm's variable cost. For the old customer, the answer is different. Because this customer has bought from us before with cash, if we grant credit we are risking the full price.

REPEAT BUSINESS   A second, very important factor to keep in mind is the possibility of repeat business. We can illustrate this by extending our onetime example. We make one important assumption: A new customer who does not default the first time remains a customer forever and never defaults. If the firm grants credit, it spends v this month. Next month, it either gets nothing if the customer defaults or it gets P if the customer pays. If the customer does pay, he or she buys another unit on credit and the firm spends v again. The net cash inflow for the month is thus $P - v$. In every subsequent month, this same $P - v$ occurs as the customer pays for the previous month's order and places a new one.

It follows from our discussion that, in one month, the firm has $0 with probability π. With probability $(1 - \pi)$, however, the firm has a new customer. The value of a new customer is equal to present value of $(P - v)$ every month forever:

$$PV = (P - v)/R$$

The NPV of extending credit is therefore:

$$NPV = -v + (1 - \pi)(P - v)/R \qquad [20.9]$$

For Locust, this is:

$$NPV = -\$20 + (1 - \pi) \times (\$49 - \$20)/.02$$
$$= -\$20 + (1 - \pi) \times \$1{,}450$$

Even if the probability of default is 90 percent, the NPV is:

$$NPV = -\$20 + .10 \times \$1{,}450 = \$125$$

Locust should extend credit unless default is a virtual certainty. The reason is that it costs only $20 to find out who is a good customer and who is not. A good customer is worth $1,450, however, so Locust can afford quite a few defaults.

Our repeat business example probably exaggerates the acceptable default probability, but it does illustrate that often the best way to do credit analysis is simply to extend credit to almost anyone. It also points out that the possibility of repeat business is a crucial consideration. In such cases, the important thing is to control the amount of credit initially offered so the possible loss is limited. The amount can be increased with time. Most often, the best predictor of whether customers will pay in the future is whether they have paid in the past.

Credit Information

If a firm does want credit information on customers, there are a number of sources. Information commonly used to assess creditworthiness includes the following:

1. *Financial statements.* A firm can ask a customer to supply financial statement information such as statements of financial position and statements of comprehensive income. Minimum standards and rules of thumb based on financial ratios like the ones we discussed in Chapter 3 can be used as a basis for extending or refusing credit.

2. *Credit reports on a customer's payment history with other firms.* Quite a few organizations sell information on the credit strength and credit history of business firms. Dun & Bradstreet Canada provides subscribers with a credit reference book and credit reports on individual firms. Ratings and information are available for a huge number of firms, including very small ones. Creditel of Canada also provides credit reporting.

Many firms have mechanized rules that allow for automatic approval of, say, all credit requests up to a preset dollar amount for firms with high ratings. Potential customers with ratings below some minimum are automatically rejected. All others are investigated further.

3. *Banks.* Banks may provide some assistance to their business customers in acquiring information on the creditworthiness of other firms.

4. *The customer's payment history with the firm.* The most obvious way to obtain information about the likelihood of a customer not paying is to examine whether the customer paid in the past and how much trouble collecting turned out to be.

Figure 20.2 illustrates just part of a Dun & Bradstreet credit report. As you can see, quite detailed information is available. Export Development Canada also provides credit profiles of U.S. and international companies.

EXAMPLE 20.3: Good and Bad Accounts at a Financial Institution

Suppose a lending officer at a chartered bank or other financial institution lends $1,000 to a customer who defaults completely. When this happens the lender has to write off the full $1,000. How many good $1,000 loans, paid in full and on time, does the lender have to make to offset the loss and break even on the lending portfolio?

To answer the question, we need to know the profit margin on loans. In banking this is called the **spread** between the lending rate and the cost of funds to the bank. The spread varies over the interest rate cycle but is usually around 2 or 3 percent. Supposing the spread is 2.5 percent, the bank makes $25 on every $1,000 loan. This means the lender must make $1,000/$25 = 40 good loans for every write-off. Our example illustrates one reason banks are conservative lenders. Low spreads leave little room for loan losses.

---

spread
The gap between the interest rate a bank pays on deposits and the rate it charges on loans.

five Cs of credit
The following five basic credit factors to be evaluated: character, capacity, capital, collateral, and conditions.

credit scoring
The process of quantifying the probability of default when granting consumer credit.

Credit Evaluation and Scoring

No magical formulas can assess the probability that a customer will not pay. In very general terms, the classic **five Cs of credit** are the basic factors to be evaluated:

1. *Character.* The customer's willingness to meet credit obligations.
2. *Capacity.* The customer's ability to meet credit obligations out of operating cash flows.
3. *Capital.* The customer's financial reserves.
4. *Collateral.* A pledged asset in the case of default.
5. *Conditions.* General economic conditions in the customer's line of business.

Credit scoring refers to the process of calculating a numerical rating for a customer based on information collected and then granting or refusing credit based on the result. For example, a firm might rate a customer on a scale of 1 (very poor) to 10 (very good) on each of the five Cs of credit using all the information available about the customer. A credit score could then be calculated based on the total. From experience, a firm might choose to grant credit only to customers with a score of more than, say, 30.

Firms such as credit card issuers have developed elaborate statistical models for credit scoring. This approach has the advantage of being objective as compared to scoring based on judgments on the five Cs. Usually, all the legally relevant and observable characteristics of a large pool of customers are studied to find their historic relation to default rates. Based on the results, it is possible to determine the variables that best predict whether or not a customer will pay and then calculate a credit score based on those variables.

FIGURE 20.2

A Dun & Bradstreet credit report

D&B Payment Analysis Report Sample

COPYRIGHT 2001 DUN & BRADSTREET INC. - PROVIDED UNDER CONTRACT
FOR THE EXCLUSIVE USE OF SUBSCRIBER XXX-XXXXXX.

ATTN: sample

BUSINESS SUMMARY
D-U-N-S: 80-473-5132
GORMAN MANUFACTURING COMPANY, INC

DATE PRINTED: January 18, 200-
SIC 27 52 COMMERCIAL PRINTING

SALES: ($)   17,685,297
HISTORY: CLEAR
CONTROL DATE: 1965
YEAR STARTED: MAY 21 1965
EMPLOYS: 105
EMPLOYS HERE: 100

492 KOLLER STREET
SAN FRANCISCO, CA 94110
TEL: 650 555-0000   LESLIE SMITH, PRES

Evidence of open Suit(s), Lien(s) and Judgment(s) in the D&B database
PAYDEX - Based on most recent 12 mos. trade   55 = 26 Days Beyond Terms
PAYDEX - Based on most recent 90 Days trade   48 = 36 Days Beyond Terms
Payments Within Terms (not dollar weighted)   47%

PAYMENT TRENDS
PAYDEX scores below are based on dollar weighted trade in most recent 12 mos.
        PRIOR 4 QTRS   CURRENT 12 MONTHS
        '''''''98 '''''''98   '''''''98 '''''''98 '''''''99 '''''''00
        MAR JUN SEP DEC   FEB MAR APR MAY JUN JUL AUG SEP OCT NOV DEC JAN

Firm   73 75 72 72   75 71 69 69 68 58 56 55 61 61 55 55
Industry
Quartiles
Upper   79 80 80 79   79   79   80   79
Median 75 75 76 75   75   75   75   75
Lower   66 66 67 67   67   66   67   66

Industry PAYDEX based on: KEY TO PAYDEX SCORES:
SIC: 2752   80 =   Within terms
1,286 Firms   75 = 8 Days Beyond Terms
                                     55 = 26 Days Beyond Terms
----
PUBLIC FILINGS SUMMARY
Currently, there is indication of open suit(s), lien(s), and/or judgment(s)
in D&B's Public Records database:
        Suit(s) 2   Lien(s) 2   Judgment(s) 1
The public record items contained in this report may have been paid,
terminated, vacated or released prior to the date this report was printed.

SPECIAL EVENTS
12/03/9-   On Mar 26, 199- the subject experienced a fire due to an earthquake.
              According to Leslie Smith, president, damages amounted to $35,000 which
              were fully covered by their insurance company. The business was closed
              for two days while employees settled personal matters.

SUMMARY OF PAYMENT HABITS
DOLLAR RANGE COMPARISONS
SUPPLIERS THAT   NUMBER OF   TOTAL   % OF DOLLAR AMOUNTS
EXTEND CREDIT OF...   EXPERIENCES   DOLLAR AMOUNT PAID WITHIN TERMS
                      # $ %
OVER $100,000   18   4,900,000   52
$50,000 - 99,999   15   955,000   78
$15,000 - 49,999   30   750,000   86
$ 5,000 - 14,999   46   330,000   77
$ 1,000 - 4,999   31   59,500   75
Under $1,000   14   5,600   48

OTHER PAYMENT CATEGORIES:
Cash Experiences   3   76,000   50,000
Paying Record Unknown 14   326,500   200,000
Unfavorable Comments   10   145,500   100,000
Placed For Collection:
   with D&B   0   0
   other   52   N/A
Highest Now Owing $1,000,000 Based on all trade
Highest Past Due $500,000   Based on all trade
Average High Credit $46,913   Based on industry trade

D&B
Dun & Bradstreet

multiple discriminant analysis (MDA)
Statistical technique for distinguishing between two samples on the basis of their observed characteristics.

One basic example of credit scoring employs a statistical technique called **multiple discriminant analysis (MDA)** to predict which customers will be good or bad accounts.[8] Similar to regression analysis, MDA chooses a set of variables that best discriminate between good and bad credits

[8] Our discussion of scoring models draws on Hill and Sartoris, *Short-Term Financial Management*, chap. 14; and L. Kryzanowski et al., *Business Solvency Risk Analysis* (Montreal: Institute of Canadian Bankers, 1990), chap. 6.

with hindsight in a sample for which the outcomes are known. The variables are then used to classify new applications that come in. For consumer credit, for example, these variables include length of time in current job, monthly income, whether the customer's home is owned or rented, other financial obligations, and so on. For business customers, ratios are the relevant variables.

To illustrate how MDA works without getting into the derivation, suppose only two ratios explain whether a business customer is creditworthy: sales/total assets and EBIT/total assets. What MDA does is draw a line to separate good (G) from bad (B) accounts as shown in Figure 20.3. The equation for the line is:

$$\text{Score} = Z = 0.4 \times [\text{Sales/Total assets}] + 3.0 \times \text{EBIT/Total assets} \qquad [20.10]$$

FIGURE 20.3

Credit scoring with multiple discriminant analysis

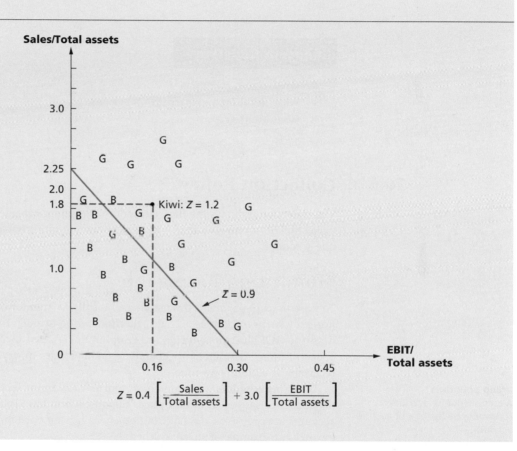

For example, suppose Locust Software has a credit application from Kiwi Computers. Kiwi's financial statements reveal sales/total assets of 1.8 and EBIT/total assets of .16. We can calculate Kiwi's score as:

$$Z = 0.4 \times 1.8 + 3.0 \times .16 = 1.2$$

The line in Figure 20.3 is drawn at a cutoff score of .90. Because Kiwi's score is higher, it lies above the line and the model predicts it will be a good account. The decision rule is to grant credit to all accounts with scores more than 0.9, that is to all accounts above the line.

To test the track record of scoring models, researchers have compared their predictions with actual outcomes. If the models were perfect, all good accounts would be above the line and all bad accounts below it. As you can see in Figure 20.3, the model does a reasonable job but there are some errors. For this reason, firms using scoring models assign scores near the line to a grey area for further investigation.

As you might expect, statistical scoring models work best when there is a large sample of similar credit applicants. Research on scoring models bears this out: the models are most useful in consumer credit.

Because credit-scoring models and procedures determine who is and is not creditworthy, it is not surprising that they have been the subject of government regulation. In particular, the kinds of background and demographic information that can be used in the credit decision are limited. For example, suppose a consumer applicant was formerly bankrupt but has discharged all obligations. After a waiting period that varies from province to province, this information cannot be used in the credit decision.

Credit scoring is used for business customers by Canadian chartered banks. Scoring for small business loans offers the advantages of objective analysis without taking more of the lending officer's time than could be justified for a small account.

Many Canadian banks have online information and application forms for small businesses. For example, visit the website of TD Canada Trust (tdcanadatrust.com/products-services/small-business/smallbusiness-index.jsp) or Royal Bank of Canada (rbcroyalbank.com/business/index.html).

Concept Questions

1. What is credit analysis?
2. What are the five Cs of credit?
3. What are credit scoring models and how are they used?

20.6 | Collection Policy

The collection policy is the final element management considers in establishing a credit policy. Collection policy involves monitoring receivables to spot trouble and obtaining payment on past-due accounts.

Monitoring Receivables

To keep track of payments by customers, most firms monitor outstanding accounts. First, a firm normally keeps track of its average collection period through time. If a firm is in a seasonal business, the ACP fluctuates during the year, but unexpected increases in the ACP are a cause for concern. Either customers in general are taking longer to pay, or some percentage of accounts receivable is seriously overdue.

aging schedule
A compilation of accounts receivable by the age of each account.

The **aging schedule** is a second basic tool for monitoring receivables. To prepare one, the credit department classifies accounts by age.[9] Suppose a firm has $100,000 in receivables. Some of these accounts are only a few days old, but others have been outstanding for quite some time. The following is an example of an aging schedule.

Aging Schedule

Age of Account	Amount	Percent of Total Value of Accounts Receivable
0–10 days	$ 50,000	50%
11–60 days	25,000	25
61–80 days	20,000	20
Over 80 days	5,000	5
	$100,000	100%

If this firm has a credit period of 60 days, 25 percent of its accounts are late. Whether or not this is serious depends on the nature of the firm's collection and customers. Often, accounts beyond a certain age are almost never collected. "The older the receivable, the less value it is to the business and the harder it is to collect."[10] Monitoring the age of accounts is very important in such cases.

---

[9] Aging schedules are used elsewhere in business. For example, aging schedules are often prepared for inventory items.

[10] The quotation is from S. Horvitch, "Debt Collection: When to Drop the Hammer on Delinquent Customers," *The Financial Post*, March 15, 1991, p. 39.

Firms with seasonal sales find the percentages on the aging schedule changing during the year. For example, if sales in the current month are very high, total receivables also increase sharply. This means the older accounts, as a percentage of total receivables, become smaller and might appear less important. Some firms have refined the aging schedule so that they have an idea of how it should change with peaks and valleys in their sales.

Collection Effort

A firm's credit policy should include the procedures to follow for customers who are overdue. A sample set of procedures is given in Table 20.1 for an account due in 30 days. The time line is an important part of the table since experienced credit managers stress the need for prompt action.

TABLE 20.1

Schedule of actions to follow up late payments (Stated terms: Net 30 days)	If Payment Is Not Made By:	Action
	40 days	Telephone call to customer's payables department
		Send duplicate invoice if needed
	50 days	Second telephone call to customer's payables department
	60 days	Warning letter (mild)
	73 days	Warning letter (strong)
	90 days	Telephone call to management level Notify that future deliveries will be made only on a COD basis until payment is made
	120 days	Stop further deliveries
		1. Initiate appropriate legal action if the account is large
		2. Turn over to a collection agency if the account is small

Source: Ned C. Hill and William L. Sartoris, *Short-Term Financial Management*, 3rd ed. (Prentice Hall College Div., 1995), p. 392.

The step at 90 days is severe: refusing to grant additional credit to the customer until arrearages are cleared up. This may antagonize a normally good customer, and it points to a potential conflict of interest between the collections department and the sales department.

After 120 days, the firm takes legal action only if the account is large. Legal action is expensive and, as we saw in Chapter 16, if the customer goes bankrupt as a result, there is usually little chance of recovering a significant portion of the credit extended. When this happens, the credit-granting firm is just another unsecured creditor. The firm can simply wait, or it can sell its receivable. For example, when book-seller Borders filed for bankruptcy in 2011, it owed US$178.8 million to its vendors and $18.6 million to its landlords. One of the largest vendors was publisher Penguin Putnam, which was owed $41.1 million. Of course, a firm can simply give up on its claim. Another publisher, Wiley, had already written off US $9 million in debt for books sold to Borders.

Credit Management in Practice

CO-OP Atlantic is a groceries and fuel distributor located in Moncton, New Brunswick. Its credit manager, Gary Steeves, is responsible for monitoring and collecting over $450 million in receivables annually. CO-OP's customers include large grocery stores with balances of more than $1 million as well as several thousand small accounts with balances around $1,000. By installing a computerized system, CO-OP has reduced its average collection period by two days with a savings (NPV) of millions. The system improved monitoring of receivables and credit granting analysis. It also saved on labour costs in processing receivables documentation.

To make monitoring easy, treasury credit staff call up customer information from a central database. For example, in the home fuel division, aging schedules are used to identify overdue accounts that require authorization by an analyst before further deliveries can be made. Under the old manual system, this information was not available. The system also provides collections staff with a daily list of accounts due for a telephone call together with a complete history of each.

Credit analysis centres around an early warning system that examines the solvency risk of existing and new commercial accounts. The software scores the accounts based on financial ratios. By mechanizing the analysis, CO-OP is now able to score all its large commercial accounts. Under the manual system, detailed financial analysis was done on an exception basis and often came too late.

CO-OP achieved these gains in monitoring and analysis without adding any staff in the credit department. The department has the same number of people as it did 10 years earlier when sales were half the present level. Gary Steeves estimates automation saved the company over $100,000 in additional wages.

Concept Questions

1. What tools can a manager use to monitor receivables?
2. What is an aging schedule?
3. Describe collection procedures and the reasons for them.
4. Describe the key features of a computerized credit system.

20.7 | Inventory Management

Like receivables, inventories represent a significant investment for many firms. For a typical Canadian manufacturing operation, inventories often exceed 20 percent of assets. For a retailer, inventories could represent more than 25 percent of assets. From our discussion in Chapter 18, we know that a firm's operating cycle is made up of its inventory period and its receivables period. This is one reason for discussing credit and inventory policy together. Beyond this, both credit policy and inventory policy are used to drive sales, and the two must be coordinated to ensure that the process of acquiring inventory, selling it, and collecting on the sale proceeds smoothly. For example, changes in credit policy designed to stimulate sales must be simultaneously accompanied by planning for adequate inventory.

The Financial Manager and Inventory Policy

Despite the size of an average firm's investment in inventories, the financial manager typically does not have primary control over inventory management. Instead, other functional areas such as purchasing, production, and marketing normally share decision-making authority. Inventory management has become an increasingly important specialty in its own right; often financial management has only input into the decision. For this reason, we only survey some basics of inventory and inventory policy in the sections ahead.

Inventory Types

For a manufacturer, inventory is normally classified into one of three categories: The first category is *raw material*. This is whatever the firm uses as a starting point in its production process. Raw materials might be something as basic as iron ore for a steel manufacturer or something as sophisticated as disk drives for a computer manufacturer.

The second type of inventory is *work-in-progress*, which is just what the name suggests, namely, unfinished product. How large this portion of inventory is depends on the length and organization of the production process. The third and final type of inventory is *finished goods*, that is, products ready to ship or sell. Merchandise inventory being held by retail and wholesale firms for sale could also be categorized as finished goods.

There are three things to keep in mind concerning inventory types. First, the names for the different types can be a little misleading because one company's raw materials could be another's finished goods. For example, going back to our steel manufacturer, iron ore would be a raw material, and steel would be the final product. An auto body panel stamping operation has steel as its raw material and auto body panels as its finished goods, and an automobile assembler has body panels as raw materials and automobiles as finished products.

The second thing to keep in mind is that the different types of inventory can be quite different in their liquidity. Raw materials that are commodity-like or relatively standardized can be easy to convert to cash. Work-in-progress, on the other hand, can be quite illiquid and have little more than scrap value. As always, the liquidity of finished goods depends on the nature of the product.

Finally, a very important distinction between finished goods and other types of inventories is the demand for an inventory item that becomes a part of another item is usually termed *derived* or *dependent* demand because a company's demand for the input item depends on its need for finished items. In contrast, the firm's demand for finished goods is not derived from demand for other inventory items, so it is sometimes said to be *independent*.

Inventory Costs

As we discussed in Chapter 18, two basic types of costs are associated with current assets in general and with inventory in particular. The first of these are *carrying costs*. Here, carrying costs represent all the direct and opportunity costs of keeping inventory on hand.

These include:

1. Storage and tracking costs.
2. Insurance and taxes.
3. Losses due to obsolescence, deterioration, or theft.
4. The opportunity cost of capital on the invested amount.

The sum of these costs can be substantial, roughly ranging from 20 to 40 percent of inventory value per year.

The other type of costs associated with inventory are *shortage costs*. These are costs associated with having inadequate inventory on hand. The two components are restocking costs and costs related to safety reserves. Depending on the firm's business, restocking or order costs are either the costs of placing an order with suppliers or the cost of setting up a production run. The costs related to safety reserves are opportunity losses such as lost sales and loss of customer goodwill that result from having inadequate inventory.

A basic trade-off in inventory management exists because carrying costs increase with inventory levels while shortage or restocking costs decline with inventory levels. The goal of inventory management is thus to minimize the sum of these two costs. We consider approaches to this goal in the next section.

Just to give you an idea of how important it is to balance carrying costs with shortage costs, consider the case of Kimberley-Clark, the well-known maker of Kleenex and Huggies. In the fourth quarter of 2010, the company cut production when compared to the same period the previous year. Unfortunately, the company underestimated demand and missed out an estimated $20 million in profit during the quarter.

Concept Questions

1. What are the different types of inventory?
2. What are three things to remember when examining inventory types?
3. What are the basic goals of inventory management?

20.8 | Inventory Management Techniques

As we described earlier, the goal of inventory management is usually framed as cost minimization. Three techniques are discussed in this section, ranging from the relatively simple to the very complex.

The ABC Approach

The ABC is a simple approach to inventory management where the basic idea is to divide inventory into three (or more) groups. The underlying rationale is that a small portion of inventory in terms of quantity might represent a large portion in terms of inventory value. For example, this situation would exist for a manufacturer that uses some relatively expensive, high-tech components and some relatively inexpensive basic materials in producing its products.

Figure 20.4 illustrates an ABC comparison of items by their percentage of inventory value and the percentage of items represented. As Figure 20.4 shows, the A Group constitutes only 10 percent of inventory by item count, but it represents over half the value of inventory. The A Group items are thus monitored closely, and inventory levels are kept relatively low. At the other end, basic inventory items, such as nuts and bolts, also exist; because these are crucial and inexpensive, large quantities are ordered and kept on hand. These would be C Group items. The B Group is made up of in-between items.

FIGURE 20.4

ABC inventory
analysis

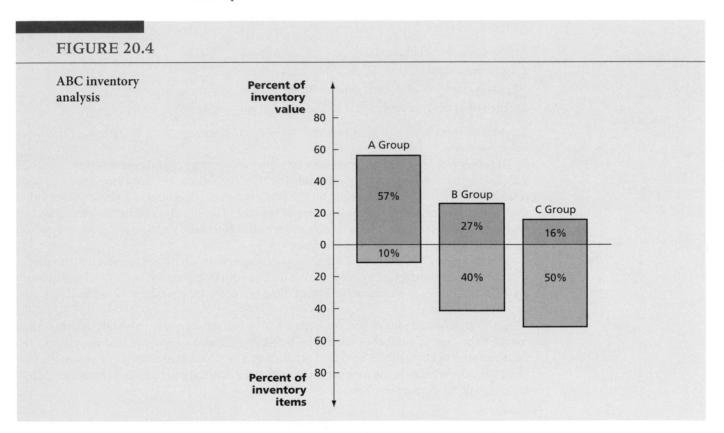

The Economic Order Quantity (EOQ) Model

The economic order quantity (EOQ) model is the best-known approach to explicitly establishing an optimum inventory level. The basic idea is illustrated in Figure 20.5, which plots the various costs associated with holding inventory (on the vertical axis) against inventory levels (on the horizontal axis). As shown, inventory carrying costs rise as inventory levels increase, while, at the same time, restocking costs decrease. From our general discussion in Chapter 18 and our discussion of the total credit cost curve in this chapter, the general shape of the total inventory cost curve is familiar. With the EOQ model, we attempt to specifically locate the minimum total cost point, Q^*.

In our following discussion, keep in mind that the actual cost of the inventory itself is not included. The reason is that the *total* amount of inventory the firm needs in a given year is dictated by sales. What we are analyzing here is how much the firm should have on hand at any particular time. More precisely, we are trying to determine what size order the firm should place when it restocks its inventory.

FIGURE 20.5

Costs of holding inventory

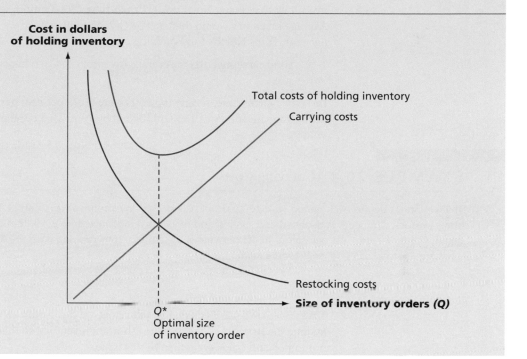

Restocking costs are increased when the firm holds a small quantity of inventory.
Carrying costs are increased when there is a large quantity of inventory on hand.
Total costs are the sum of the carrying and restocking costs.

INVENTORY DEPLETION   To develop the EOQ, we assume that the firm's inventory is sold at a steady rate until it hits zero. At that point, the firm restocks its inventory back to some optimal level. For example, suppose the Trans North Corporation starts out today with 3600 units of a particular item in inventory. Annual sales of this item are 46,800 units, which is about 900 per week. If Trans North sells 900 units in inventory each week, after four weeks, all the available inventory would be sold, and Trans North would restock by ordering (or manufacturing) another 3600 and start over. This selling and restocking process produces the saw tooth pattern for inventory holdings shown in Figure 20.6. As this figure illustrates, Trans North always starts with 3600 units in inventory and ends up at zero. On average, then, inventory is half of 3600, or 1800 units.

FIGURE 20.6

Inventory holdings for the Trans North Corporation

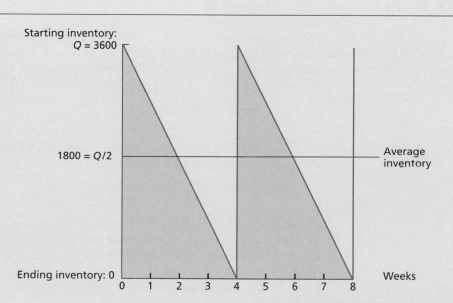

The Trans North Corporation starts with inventory of 3600 units. The quantity drops to zero by the fourth week. The average inventory is Q/2 = 3600/2 = 1800 over the period.

THE CARRYING COSTS Going back to Figure 20.5, we see that carrying costs are normally assumed to be directly proportional to inventory levels. Suppose we let Q be the quantity of inventory that Trans North orders each time (3600 units); we call this the restocking quantity. Average inventory would then just be $Q/2$, or 1800 units. If we let CC be the carrying cost per unit per year, Trans North's total carrying costs are as follows:

$$\text{Total carrying costs} = \text{Average inventory} \times \text{Carrying costs per unit} \qquad [20.11]$$
$$= (Q/2) \times CC$$

In Trans North's case, if carrying costs were $0.75 per unit per year, total carrying costs would be the average inventory of 1800 multiplied by $0.75, or $1,350 per year.

EXAMPLE 20.4: Carrying Costs

Thiewes Shoes begins each period with 100 pairs of hiking boots in stock. This stock is depleted each period and reordered. If the carrying cost per pair of boots per year is $3, what are the total carrying costs for the hiking boots?

Inventories always start at 100 items and end at zero, so average inventory is 50 items. At an annual cost of $3 per item, total carrying costs are $150.

THE SHORTAGE COSTS For now, we focus only on the restocking costs. In essence, we assume the firm never actually runs short on inventory, so that costs relating to safety reserves are not important. Later, we return to this issue.

Restocking costs are normally assumed to be fixed. In other words, every time we place an order, there are fixed costs associated with that order (remember the cost of the inventory itself is not considered here). Suppose we let T be the firm's total unit sales per year. If the firm orders Q units each time, it needs to place a total of T/Q orders. For Trans North, annual sales were 46,800, and the order size was 3600. Trans North thus places a total of $46,800/3600 = 13$ orders per year. If the fixed cost per order is F, the total restocking cost for the year would be:

$$\text{Total restocking cost} = \text{Fixed cost per order} \times \text{Number of orders} \qquad [20.12]$$
$$= F \times (T/Q)$$

For Trans North, order costs might be $50 per order, so the total restocking cost for 13 orders would be $50 \times 13 = $650 per year.

EXAMPLE 20.5: Restocking Costs

In our previous example, suppose Thiewes sells a total of 600 pairs of boots in a year. How many times per year does Thiewes restock? Suppose the restocking cost is $20 per order. What are total restocking costs?

Thiewes orders 100 items each time. Total sales are 600 items per year, so Thiewes restocks six times per year, or about every two months. The restocking costs would be 6 orders × $20 per order = $120.

THE TOTAL COSTS The total costs associated with holding inventory are the sum of the carrying costs and the restocking costs:

$$\text{Total costs} = \text{Carrying costs} + \text{Restocking costs} \qquad [20.13]$$
$$= (Q/2) \times CC + F \times (T/Q)$$

Our goal is to find the value of Q, the restocking quantity that minimizes this cost. To see how we might go about this, we can calculate total costs for some different values of Q. For the Trans North Corporation, we had carrying costs (CC) of $0.75 per unit per year, fixed costs per order (F) of $50 per order, and total unit sales (T) of 46,800 units. With these numbers, some possible total costs are (check some of these for practice):

Restocking Quantity (Q)	Carrying Costs (Q/2 × **CC**)	+	Restocking Costs (**F** × **T/Q**)	= Total Costs
500	$ 187.50		$4,680.00	$4,867.50
1000	375.00		2,340.00	2,715.00
1500	562.50		1,560.00	2,122.50
2000	750.00		1,170.00	1,920.00
2500	937.50		936.00	1,873.50
3000	1,125.00		780.00	1,905.00
3500	1,312.50		668.57	1,981.07

Inspecting the numbers, we see that total costs start at almost $5,000, and they decline to just under $1,900. The cost-minimizing quantity appears to be approximately 2500.

To find the precise cost-minimizing quantity, we can look back at Figure 20.5. What we notice is that the minimum point occurs right where the two lines cross. At this point, carrying costs and restocking costs are the same. For the particular types of costs we have assumed here, this is always true; so we can find the minimum point just by setting these costs equal to each other and solving for Q^*:

$$\text{Carrying costs} = \text{Restocking costs} \quad\quad [20.14]$$
$$(Q^*/2) \times CC = F \times (T/Q^*)$$

With a little algebra, we get that

$$Q^{*2} = \frac{2T \times F}{CC} \quad\quad [20.15]$$

To solve for Q^*, we take the square root of both sides to find that

$$Q^* = \sqrt{\frac{2T \times F}{CC}} \quad\quad [20.16]$$

This reorder quantity, which minimizes the total inventory cost, is called the economic order quantity (EOQ). For the Trans North Corporation, the EOQ is

$$Q^* = \sqrt{\frac{2T \times F}{CC}}$$
$$= \sqrt{\frac{(2 \times 46,800) \times \$50}{\$.75}}$$
$$= \sqrt{6,240,000}$$
$$= 2498 \text{ units}$$

Thus, for Trans North, the economic order quantity is actually 2498 units. At this level, check that the restocking costs and carrying costs are identical (they're both $936.75).[11]

Extensions to the EOQ Model

Thus far, we have assumed a company lets its inventory run down to zero and then reorders. In reality, a company reorders before its inventory goes to zero for two reasons: First, by always having at least some inventory on hand, the firm minimizes the risk of a stockout and the resulting losses of sales and customers. Second, when a firm does reorder, there is some time lag between placing the order and when the inventory arrives. Thus, to finish our discussion of the EOQ, we consider two extensions, safety stocks and reordering points.

---

[11] In general, EOQ is the minimum point on the total cost curve in Figure 20.5 where the derivative of total cost with respect to quantity is zero. From Equation 20.13:

$$\frac{d(\text{Total cost})}{dQ} = \frac{CC}{2} - \frac{T \times F}{Q^2} = 0$$

To find the optimal value of Q, we solve this equation for Q:

$$\frac{CC}{2} = \frac{T \times F}{Q^2}$$
$$Q^2 = \frac{2T \times F}{CC}$$
$$Q = \sqrt{\frac{2T \times F}{CC}}$$

EXAMPLE 20.6: The EOQ

Based on our previous two examples, what size orders should Thiewes place? How often will Thiewes restock? What are the carrying and restocking costs? The total costs?

We know that the total number of pairs of boots ordered for the year (*T*) is 600. The restocking cost (*F*) is $20 per order, and the carrying cost (*CC*) is $3. We can calculate the EOQ for Thiewes as shown to the right.

Since Thiewes sells 600 pairs per year, it restocks 600/89.44 = 6.71 times.[12] The total restocking costs are $20 × 6.71 = $134.16. Average inventory is 89.44/2 =

44.72 pairs of boots. The carrying costs will be $3 × 44.72 = $134.16, the same as the restocking costs. The total costs are thus $268.33.

$$EOQ^* = \sqrt{\frac{2T \times F}{CC}}$$
$$= \sqrt{\frac{(2 \times 600) \times \$20}{\$3}}$$
$$= \sqrt{8,000}$$
$$= 89.44 \text{ units}$$

SAFETY STOCKS   A safety stock refers to the minimum level of inventory that a firm keeps on hand. Inventories are reordered whenever the level of inventory falls to the safety stock level. The top of Figure 20.7 illustrates how a safety stock can be incorporated into our EOQ model. Notice that adding a safety stock simply means the firm does not run its inventory all the way down to zero. Other than this, the situation is identical to our earlier discussion of the EOQ.

REORDER POINTS   To allow for delivery time, a firm places orders before inventories reach a critical level. The reorder points are the times at which the firm actually places its inventory orders. These points are illustrated in the middle of Figure 20.7. As shown, the reorder points simply occur some fixed number of days (or weeks or months) before inventories are projected to reach zero.

One of the reasons a firm keeps a safety stock is to allow for uncertain delivery times. So we can combine our reorder point and safety stock discussions in the bottom part of Figure 20.7. The result is a generalized EOQ in which the firm orders in advance of anticipated needs and also keeps a safety stock of inventory to guard against unforeseen fluctuations in demand and delivery time.

Canadian Tire uses a modified EOQ approach to set target inventory levels for the thousands of items stocked in each store. Because the company markets its stores as providing one-stop shopping, it seeks a high service level with few stockouts. Safety stocks are set accordingly. An in-store computer, online with the cash registers, monitors sales and automatically sends an order to the warehouse computer when the stock level drops to the reorder point.

To implement reorder points successfully and minimize stockouts, it is important to have an accurate count of inventory. As we discussed at the beginning of this chapter, large retailers like Wal-Mart use radio frequency identification technology (RFID) to track inventory. Second-generation, matrix bar codes provide a cheaper alternative to RFIDs.

EXAMPLE 20.7: The Reorder Point for Hiking Boots

Suppose Thiewes Shoes wishes to hold a safety stock of hiking boots equal to six days' sales. If the store is open 300 days per year, what should be the safety stock? What is the reorder point for hiking boots?

The safety stock is 6/300 × 600 pairs = 12 pairs

The reorder point is when 12 pairs are on hand. If sales are evenly distributed, there will still be 6.71 orders per year.

Managing Derived-Demand Inventories

As we described previously, the demand for some inventory types is derived from, or dependent on, other inventory needs. A good example is an auto manufacturer where the demand for finished products depends on consumer demand, marketing programs, and other factors related to

---

[12] In practice, Thiewes would order 90 pairs of boots. It should also be pointed out that the EOQ model provides a guideline value, though there is some flexibility in the number chosen around this optimal point (without significantly increasing the total cost). For example, a convenient order size might be multiples of a dozen, so that 84 or 96 could be the number selected.

projected unit sales. The demand for inventory items such as tires, batteries, headlights, and other components is then completely determined by the number of autos planned.

Materials Requirements Planning (MRP)

Production and inventory specialists have developed computer-based systems for ordering and/ or scheduling production of demand-dependent inventories. These systems fall under the general heading of *materials requirements planning* (MRP). The basic idea behind MRP is that, once finished goods inventory levels are set, it is possible to back out what levels of work-in-progress inventories must exist to meet the need for finished goods. From there, it is possible to back out what raw materials inventories must be on hand. This ability to schedule backward from finished goods inventories stems from the dependent nature of work-in-progress and raw materials inventories. MRP is particularly important for complicated products where a variety of components are needed to create the finished product.

FIGURE 20.7

Safety stocks and reorder points

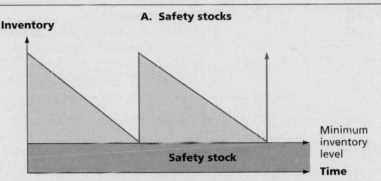

With a safety stock, the firm reorders when inventory reaches a minimum level.

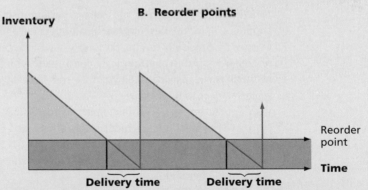

When there are lags in delivery or production times, the firm reorders when inventory reaches the reorder point.

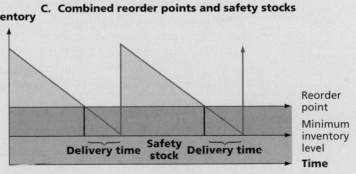

By combining safety stocks and reorder points, the firm maintains a buffer against unforeseen events.

Just-In-Time Inventory

just-in-time inventory (JIT)
Design for inventory in which parts, raw materials, and other work-in-process are delivered exactly as needed for production. Goal is to minimize inventory.

EOQ is a useful tool for many firms especially in the retail sector but the cutting edge of inventory management in manufacturing is a relatively new approach called **just-in-time inventory** or **just-in-time production**.[13] The basic idea is that raw materials, parts, and other work-in-process should be delivered at the exact time they are needed on the factory floor. Raw materials and work-in-process are no longer seen as a necessary buffer to decouple stages of production. Instead, all stages of production are recoupled and the goal is to reduce inventories of raw materials and work-in-process to zero.

At the heart of just-in-time inventory is a different approach to ordering or set-up costs. Under the traditional EOQ approach, these are considered fixed. As we saw, higher ordering costs translate into larger, less frequent orders. When producing for inventory, large set-up costs in switching production from one product to another mean longer production runs. Either way, the firm carries a large work-in-process inventory as the next stage of production gradually draws down the stock of work-in-process. If a manufacturer produces many different products, the burden of different work-in-process for each becomes excessive.

This was the problem faced by Toyota in Japan after World War II. To be competitive, the company needed to make a mix of vehicles, so no one model had a long production run. The solution was to attack set-up time and reduce it dramatically, by up to 75 percent. Thus, just-in-time inventory (production) was born.

Making just-in-time inventory work requires detailed materials requirements planning (MRP). As all stages of production are recoupled, careful coordination is needed. There are no longer inventory buffers to fall back on to cover planning errors or equipment downtime. This difference between the traditional approach and just-in-time inventory in resolving problems is captured in the following analogy drawn from a Japanese parable:

> The ship of enterprise floats on a lake of inventory. Problems can be thought of as rocks in the lake on which one is sailing a boat. The safety stock inventory approach is to raise the water level in the lake so that the rocks are not seen. The just-in-time approach is to chart carefully the location of the rocks and sail around them while keeping the water level at a minimum.[14]

When a manufacturer outsources parts and other work-in-process, planning must include suppliers. With the new approach, suppliers have to be capable of delivering smaller orders more often with precision timing. Suppliers need to receive high-quality information on the schedule of deliveries and to communicate continually with the buyer on the location of all shipments. So, in many ways, just-in-time inventory transfers the demands of inventory management from the manufacturer to its suppliers.

Manufacturers and suppliers use electronic data interchange (EDI) over integrated computer systems. The cash management system discussed in Chapter 19 is an example of EDI featuring communications between a firm and its bank. In implementing a just-in-time system, the firm and its supplier electronically exchange all information from the initial order to acknowledgment of the final payment.

On May 23, 2012, the workers of Canadian Pacific Railway walked off the job early to set off a strike that affected auto manufacturing plants, coal mines, farms as well as the retailer, Canadian Tire. Known for its just-in-time inventory system, Canadian Tire's normal operations were disrupted by the strike at CP. Further, in western Canada, Teck Resources Ltd., CP's largest customer, ships 650 rail cars of coal daily to the port in Vancouver from its mines in south-eastern British Columbia.[15] The strike also affected the just-in-time inventory systems of Teck Resources. This example shows the difficulties in implementing just-in-time inventory systems. Beyond information requirements, suppliers must meet very high quality standards. Manufacturers receive parts

---

[13] Our discussion of just-in-time inventory draws on J. Loring, "Inventory: Taking Stock," *Canadian Business*, April 1991; E. Corcoran, "Milliken & Co., Managing the Quality of a Textile Revolution," *Scientific American*, April 1990; and Hill and Sartoris, *Short-Term Financial Management*, chaps. 17 and 20. A good source of just-in-time production is J. D. Blackburn, ed., *Time-Based Competition: The Next Battleground in American Manufacturing* (Homewood, IL: Business One Irwin, 1991).

[14] Hill and Sartoris, *Short-Term Financial Management*, p. 457.

[15] cbc.ca/news/business/story/2012/05/23/f-canadian-pacific-railway-strike.html

and use them at once so there is no room for defects. Quality control and preventive maintenance become very important. The accompanying box shows the downside of Just-In-Time Inventory.

IN THEIR OWN WORDS...

The Downside of Just-in-Time Inventory

In a control center above a wide-body jet plant in Everett, Washington, a group of Boeing (BA) staffers is poring over data from suppliers in Japan—making sure the company has enough parts to build its 787 Dreamliner in the U.S.

It's a long list. Japanese manufacturers helped design and now produce 35 percent of the 787, 20 percent of the 777, and 15 percent of the 767. What they build can't be duplicated anywhere else, and Boeing can't call in a new supplier to make one piece if it runs short. So far, the jetmaker says it has enough inventory to keep running for a few weeks.

Thirty years ago, Japan taught U.S. companies to boost profit by keeping inventory lean. Now it's teaching them the risks. Mitsubishi Heavy Industries builds the 787's wing; no one else can do that job. General Motors (GM) decided on Mar. 17 to close its Shreveport (La.) Chevrolet Colorado and GMC Canyon pickup plant for a week because it lacked components. Deere (DE) is delaying deliveries of excavators and mining equipment. And Honda Motor (HMC) suspended orders from U.S. dealers for Japan-built Honda and Acura models that would be sold in May.

"Instead of months' worth of inventory, there are now days and even hours of inventory," says Jim Lawton, head of supply management solutions at consultant Dun & Bradstreet (DNB) and a former procurement chief for Hewlett-Packard (HPQ). "If supply is disrupted as in this situation, there's nowhere to get product."

Beginning in the 1980s, to compete with Japanese manufacturers, U.S. companies became reliant on single suppliers for key parts. It was cheaper to buy in bulk from one outfit than to split orders. Now quake damage has interrupted 25 percent of the world's silicon production because of the shutdown of plants owned by Shin-Etsu Chemical and MEMC Electronic Materials, says IHS iSuppli (IHS), an El Segundo (Calif.)-based researcher. The earthquake forced more than 130 plants, mostly in auto and electronics, to close as of Mar. 22, according to data compiled by Bloomberg. Some of the affected factories make items sold directly to consumers; others are sold to manufacturers.

At Dell (DELL), the world's third-largest personal computer maker, managers are concerned that the supply of optical disk drives and batteries from Japan may be interrupted, according to a person familiar with the matter. Power failures at plants that make silicon wafers could also cause shortages in the computer-chip market in six to 10 weeks, said the source, who asked not to be identified discussing matters involving suppliers. In a statement, Dell said it doesn't "see any significant immediate supply-chain disruption."

From a command center in Boeing's Everett factory, engineers can see aircraft production from a window and a 40-foot screen that displays live video from supplier operations, weather reports, and global news. Translators are on hand around the clock. Chicago-based Boeing, which has bought parts from Japan since the end of World War II, found damage at several sites, according to Boeing Japan President Mike Denton, who is working with officials there to get them running. The leading edge of the 787's wings are built at Spirit AeroSystems Holdings (SPR) in Tulsa and shipped to Mitsubishi Heavy in Nagoya, where the full wings are assembled, then flown to Everett. Boeing and Mitsubishi Heavy use special autoclave ovens to bake composite-plastic sections of the plane and wing skins. Boeing is three years late and billions of dollars over budget on the 787.

Only about 10 percent of companies have detailed plans to deal with supply disruptions, says Lawton, who calls logistics the fastest-growing piece of Dun & Bradstreet's business. Shortages may crop up in other countries as companies seek alternative sources, he adds.

Despite the risks, companies won't abandon just-in-time inventory because the cost savings are too great, says James Womack, founder of the Lean Enterprise Institute in Cambridge, Mass. "Once they grasp the situation and they've got a plan, I would predict they are able to restore a remarkable amount of production very quickly," he says. "Never sell Japan short."

Susanna Ray is a reporter for Bloomberg News in Seattle. Thomas Black is a reporter for Bloomberg News. Source: businessweek.com/magazine/content/11_14/b4222017701856.htm. Used with permission.

Concept Questions

1. Why do firms hold inventories?
2. Explain the basic idea behind the EOQ solution for inventory management.
3. What is just-in-time inventory? How does it differ from the more traditional EOQ approach?

20.9 | SUMMARY AND CONCLUSIONS

This chapter covered the basics of credit policy and inventory management. The major topics we discussed include:

1. The components of credit policy. We discussed the terms of sale, credit analysis, and collection policy. Under the general subject of terms of sale, the credit period, the cash discount and discount period, and the credit instrument were described.

2. Credit policy analysis. We develop the cash flows from the decision to grant credit and show how the credit decision can be analyzed in an NPV setting. The NPV of granting credit depends on five factors: revenue effects, cost effects, the cost of debt, the probability of non-payment, and the cash discount.

3. Optimal credit policy. The optimal amount of credit the firm offers depends on the competitive conditions under which it operates. These conditions determine the carrying costs associated with granting credit and the opportunity costs of the lost sales from refusing to offer credit. The optimal credit policy minimizes the sum of these two costs.

4. Credit analysis. We looked at the decision to grant credit to a particular customer. We saw that two considerations are very important: the cost relative to the selling price and the possibility of repeat business.

5. Collection policy. Collection policy is the method of monitoring the age of accounts receivable and dealing with past-due accounts. We describe how an aging schedule can be prepared and the procedures a firm might use to collect on past-due accounts.

6. The economic order quantity (EOQ) model. This traditional approach to inventory sets the optimal order size and with it the average inventory, trading off ordering or set-up costs against carrying costs. The optimal inventory minimizes the sum of these costs.

7. Just-in-time inventory. A relatively new approach, JIT reduces inventory by scheduling production and deliveries of work-in-process to arrive just in time for the next stage of production. Implementation requires detailed planning with suppliers and advanced information and communications systems such as Electronic Data Interchange (EDI).

Key Terms

aging schedule (page 588)
captive finance company (page 581)
cash discount (page 576)
collection policy (page 573)
credit analysis (page 573)
credit cost curve (page 581)
credit instrument (page 578)
credit period (page 575)

credit scoring (page 585)
five Cs of credit (page 585)
invoice (page 575)
just-in-time inventory (JIT) (page 598)
multiple discriminant analysis (MDA) (page 586)
spread (page 585)
terms of sale (page 573)

Chapter Review Problems and Self-Test

20.1 **Credit Policy** The Cold Fusion Corporation (manufacturer of the Mr. Fusion home power plant) is considering a new credit policy. The current policy is cash only. The new policy would involve extending credit for one period. Based on the following information, determine if a switch is advisable. The interest rate is 2.0 percent per period.

	Current Policy	New Policy
Price per unit	$ 175	$ 175
Cost per unit	$ 130	$ 130
Sales per period in units	1000	1100

20.2 **Discounts and Default Risk** The ICU Binocular Corporation is considering a change in credit policy. The current policy is cash only, and sales per period are 5000 units at a price of $95. If credit is offered, the new price would be $100 per unit and the credit would be extended for one period. Unit sales are not expected to change, and all customers would take the credit. ICU anticipates that 2 percent of its customers will default. If the required return is 3 percent per period, is the change a good idea? What if only half the customers take the offered credit?

20.3 **Credit Where Credit Is Due** You are trying to decide whether or not to extend credit to a particular customer. Your variable cost is $10 per unit; the selling price is $14. This customer wants to buy 100 units today and pay in 60 days. You think there is a 10 percent chance of default. The required return is 3 percent per 60 days. Should you extend credit? Assume this is a onetime sale and the customer will not buy if credit is not extended.

20.4 **The EOQ** Heusen Computer Manufacturing starts each period with 4000 CPUs in stock. This stock is depleted each month and reordered. If the carrying cost per CPU is $1, and the fixed order cost is $10, is Heusen following an economically advisable strategy?

Answers to Self-Test Problems

20.1 If the switch is made, an extra 100 units per period would be sold at a gross profit of $175 − 130 = $45 each. The total benefit is thus $45 × 100 = $4,500 per period. At 2.0 percent per period forever, the PV is $4,500/.02 = $225,000.

The cost of the switch is equal to this period's revenue of $175 × 1000 units = $175,000 plus the cost of producing the extra 100 units, 100 × $130 = $13,000. The total cost is thus $188,000, and the NPV is $225,000 − 188,000 = $37,000. The switch should be made.

20.2 The costs per period are the same whether or not credit is offered; so we can ignore the production costs. The firm currently sells and collects $95 × 5000 = $475,000 per period. If credit is offered, sales rise to $100 × 5000 = $500,000.

Defaults will be 2 percent of sales, so the cash inflow under the new policy is .98 × $500,000 = $490,000. This amounts to an extra $15,000 every period. At 3 percent per period, the PV is $15,000/.03 = $500,000. If the switch is made, ICU would give up this month's revenues of $475,000; so the NPV of the switch is $25,000. If only half switch, then the NPV is half as large: $12,500.

20.3 If the customer pays in 60 days, then you collect $14 × 100 = $1,400. There's only a 90 percent chance of collecting this; so you expect to get $1,400 × .90 = $1,260 in 60 days. The present value of this is $1,260/1.03 = $1,223.3. Your cost is $10 × 100 = $1,000; so the NPV is $223.3. Credit should be extended.

20.4 We can answer by first calculating Heusen's carrying and restocking costs. The average inventory is 2000 CPUs, and, since the carrying costs are $1 per CPU, total carrying costs are $2,000. Heusen restocks every month at a fixed order cost of $10, so the total restocking costs are $120. What we see is that carrying costs are large relative to reorder costs, so Heusen is carrying too much inventory.

To determine the optimal inventory policy, we can use the EOQ model. Because Heusen orders 4000 CPUs 12 times per year, total needs (T) are 48,000 CPUs. The fixed order cost is $10, and the carrying cost per unit (CC) is $1. The EOQ is therefore:

$$EOQ = \sqrt{\frac{2T \times F}{CC}}$$
$$= \sqrt{\frac{(2 \times 48,000) \times \$10}{\$1}}$$
$$= \sqrt{960,000}$$
$$= 979.8 \text{ units}$$

We can check this by noting that the average inventory is about 490 CPUs, so the carrying cost is $490. Heusen would have to reorder 48,000/979.8 = 49 times. The fixed reorder cost is $10, so the total restocking cost is also $490.

Concepts Review and Critical Thinking Questions

1. **(LO1)** Describe each of the following:
   a. Sight draft
   b. Time draft
   c. Banker's acceptance
   d. Promissory note
   e. Trade acceptance
2. **(LO2)** In what form is trade credit most commonly offered? What is the credit instrument in this case?
3. **(LO2)** What are the costs associated with carrying receivables? What are the costs associated with not granting credit? What do we call the sum of the costs for different levels of receivables?
4. **(LO4)** What are the five Cs of credit? Explain why each is important.
5. **(LO2)** What are some of the factors that determine the length of the credit period? Why is the length of the buyer's operating cycle often considered an upper bound on the length of the credit period?

6. **(LO2)** In each of the following pairings, indicate which firm would probably have a longer credit period and explain your reasoning.
   a. Firm A sells a miracle cure for baldness; Firm B sells toupees.
   b. Firm A specializes in products for landlords; Firm B specializes in products for renters.
   c. Firm A sells to customers with an inventory turnover of 10 times; Firm B sells to customers with an inventory turnover of 20 times.
   d. Firm A sells fresh fruit; Firm B sells canned fruit.
   e. Firm A sells and installs carpeting; Firm B sells rugs.
7. **(LO5)** What are the different inventory types? How do the types differ? Why are some types said to have dependent demand whereas other types are said to have independent demand?

8. **(LO5)** If a company moves to a JIT inventory management system, what will happen to inventory turnover? What will happen to total asset turnover? What will happen to return on equity, ROE? (Hint: remember the Du Pont equation from Chapter 3.)

9. **(LO5)** If a company's inventory carrying costs are $5 million per year and its fixed order costs are $8 million per year, do you think the firm keeps too much inventory on hand or too little? Why?

10. **(LO5)** At least part of Dell's corporate profits can be traced to its inventory management. Using just-in-time inventory, Dell typically maintains an inventory of three to four days' sales. Competitors such as Hewlett-Packard and IBM have attempted to match Dell's inventory policies, but lag far behind. In an industry where the price of PC components continues to decline, Dell clearly has a competitive advantage. Why would you say that it is to Dell's advantage to have such a short inventory period? If doing this is valuable, why don't all other PC manufacturers switch to Dell's approach?

Questions and Problems

Basic
(Questions 1–12)

1. **Cash Discounts (LO2)** You place an order for 350 units of inventory at a unit price of $140. The supplier offers terms of 1/10, net 30.
   a. How long do you have to pay before the account is overdue? If you take the full period, how much should you remit?
   b. What is the discount being offered? How quickly must you pay to get the discount? If you do take the discount, how much should you remit?
   c. If you don't take the discount, how much interest are you paying implicitly? How many days' credit are you receiving?

2. **Size of Accounts Receivable (LO1)** The Moncton Corporation has annual sales of $38 million. The average collection period is 34 days. What is the average investment in accounts receivable as shown on the balance sheet? Assume 365 days per year

3. **ACP and Accounts Receivable (LO1)** Kyoto Joe Inc. sells earnings forecasts for Japanese securities. Its credit terms are 2/10, net 30. Based on experience, 65 percent of all customers will take the discount.
   a. What is the average collection period for Kyoto Joe?
   b. If Kyoto Joe sells 1300 forecasts every month at a price of $1,750 each, what is its average balance sheet amount in accounts receivable? Assume 365 days per year.

4. **Size of Accounts Receivable (LO1)** Melanson Inc. has weekly credit sales of $17,300, and the average collection period is 36 days. What is the average accounts receivable figure?

5. **Terms of Sale (LO2)** A firm offers terms of 1/10, net 30. What effective annual interest rate does the firm earn when a customer does not take the discount? Assume 365 days per year. Without doing any calculations, explain what will happen to this effective rate if:
   a. The discount is changed to 2 percent.
   b. The credit period is increased to 45 days.
   c. The discount period is increased to 15 days.

6. **ACP and Receivables Turnover (LO1)** Dieppe Inc. has an average collection period of 33 days. Its average daily investment in receivables is $42,300. What are annual credit sales? What is the receivables turnover? Assume 365 days per year.

7. **Size of Accounts Receivable (LO1)** Champlain Ltd. sells 8,200 units of its perfume collection each year at a price per unit of $430. All sales are on credit with terms of 1/10, net 40. The discount is taken by 60 percent of the customers. What is the amount of the company's accounts receivable? In reaction to sales by its main competitor, Hamlet, Champlain is considering a change in its credit policy to terms of 2/10, net 30 to preserve its market share. How will this change in policy affect accounts receivable? Assume 365 days per year.

8. **Size of Accounts Receivable (LO1)** The Thaddee Corporation sells on credit terms of net 30. Its accounts are, on average, 7 days past due. If annual credit sales are $9.3 million, what is the company's balance sheet amount in accounts receivable? Assume 365 days per year.

9. **Evaluating Credit Policy (LO4)** Barn Yard Inc. is a wholesaler that stocks engine components and tests equipment for the commercial aircraft industry. A new customer has placed an order for eight high-bypass turbine engines, which increase fuel economy. The variable cost is $1.9 million per unit, and the credit price is $2.015 million each. Credit is extended for one period, and based on historical experience, payment for about 1 out of every 200 such orders is never collected. The required return is 1.8 percent per period.
   a. Assuming that this is a one-time order, should it be filled? The customer will not buy if credit is not extended.
   b. What is the break-even probability of default in part (a)?
   c. Suppose that customers who don't default become repeat customers and place the same order every period forever. Further assume that repeat customers never default. Should the order be filled? What is the break-even probability of default?
   d. Describe in general terms why credit terms will be more liberal when repeat orders are a possibility.

10. **Credit Policy Evaluation (LO4)** Hildegarde Inc. is considering a change in its cash-only sales policy. The new terms of sale would be net one month. Based on the following information, determine if Hildegarde should proceed or not. Describe the buildup of receivables in this case. The required return is 0.95 percent per month.

	Current Policy	New Policy
Price per unit	$720	$720
Cost per unit	$525	$525
Unit sales per month	1,240	1,290

11. **EOQ (LO6)** Odium Manufacturing uses 2500 switch assemblies per week and then reorders another 2500. If the relevant carrying cost per switch assembly is $7.50, and the fixed order cost is $1,300, is Odium's inventory policy optimal? Why or why not?

12. **EOQ (LO6)** The Crandall store begins each week with 300 phasers in stock. This stock is depleted each week and reordered. If the carrying cost per phaser is $38 per year and the fixed order cost is $75, what is the total carrying cost? What is the restocking cost? Should Crandall increase or decrease its order size? Describe an optimal inventory policy for Crandall in terms of order size and order frequency.

Intermediate 13. **EOQ Derivation (LO6)** Prove that when carrying costs and restocking costs are as described in the chapter, the EOQ must
(Questions occur at the point where the carrying costs and restocking costs are equal.
13–16)
14. **Credit Policy Evaluation (LO4)** The Berry Corporation is considering a change in its cash-only policy. The new terms would be net one period. Based on the following information, determine if Berry should proceed or not. The required return is 2.5 percent per period.

	Current Policy	New Policy
Price per unit	$86	$88
Cost per unit	$47	$47
Unit sales per month	3,510	3,620

15. **Credit Policy Evaluation (LO4)** Codiac Corp. currently has an all-cash credit policy. It is considering making a change in the credit policy by going to terms of net 30 days. Based on the following information, what do you recommend? The required return is .95 percent per month.

	Current Policy	New Policy
Price per unit	$150	$154
Cost per unit	$130	$133
Unit sales per month	1,550	1,580

16. **Credit Policy (LO4)** The Salisbury Bicycle Shop has decided to offer credit to its customers during the spring selling season. Sales are expected to be 500 bicycles. The average cost to the shop of a bicycle is $390. The owner knows that only 96 percent of the customers will be able to make their payments. To identify the remaining 4 percent, the company is considering subscribing to a credit agency. The initial charge for this service is $750, with an additional charge of $6 per individual report. Should she subscribe to the agency?

Challenge 17. **Break-Even Quantity (LO3)** In Problem 14, what is the break-even quantity for the new credit policy?
(Questions 18. **Credit Markup (LO3)** In Problem 14, what is the break-even price per unit that should be charged under the new credit policy?
17–22) Assume that the sales figure under the new policy is 3,750 units and all other values remain the same.

19. **Credit Markup (LO3)** In Problem 15, what is the break-even price per unit under the new credit policy? Assume all other values remain the same.

20. **Safety Stocks and Order Points (LO6)** Humphrey Inc. expects to sell 700 of its designer suits every week. The store is open seven days a week and expects to sell the same number of suits every day. The company has an EOQ of 500 suits and a safety stock of 100 suits. Once an order is placed, it takes three days for Humphrey to get the suits in. How many orders does the company place per year? Assume that it is Monday morning before the store opens, and a shipment of suits has just arrived. When will Humphrey place its next order?

21. **Evaluating Credit Policy (LO2)** Engi Sola Corp. manufactures solar engines for tractor trailers. Given the fuel savings available, new orders for 125 units have been made by customers requesting credit. The variable cost is $11,400 per unit, and the credit price is $13,000 each. Credit is extended for one period. The required return is 1.9 percent per period. If Engi Sola extends credit, it expects that 30 percent of the customers will repeat customers and place the same order every period forever and the remaining customers will be one-time orders. Should credit be extended?

22. **Evaluating Credit Policy (LO2)** In the previous problem, assume that the probability of default is 15 percent. Should the orders be filled now? Assume the number of repeat customers is affected by the defaults. In other words, 30 percent of the customers who do not default are expected to be repeat customers?

MINI CASE

Piepkorn Manufacturing Working Capital Management

You have recently been hired by Piepkorn Manufacturing to work in the newly established treasury department. Piepkorn Manufacturing is a small company that produces cardboard boxes in a variety of sizes for different purchasers. Gary Piepkorn, the owner of the company, works primarily in the sales and production areas of the company. Currently, the company puts all receivables in one shoebox and all payables in another. Because of the disorganized system, the finance area needs work, and that's what you've been brought in to do.

The company currently has a cash balance of $240,000, and it plans to purchase new box-folding machinery in the fourth quarter at a cost of $445,000. The machinery will be purchased with cash because of a discount offered. The company's policy is to maintain a minimum cash balance of $125,000. All sales and purchases are made on credit.

Gary Piepkorn has projected the following gross sales for each of the next four quarters:

	Q1	Q2	Q3	Q4
Gross sales	$1,240,000	$1,310,000	$1,370,000	$1,450,000

Also, gross sales for the first quarter of next year are projected at $1,290,000. Piepkorn currently has an accounts receivable period of 53 days and an accounts receivable balance of $630,000. Twenty percent of the accounts receivable balance is from a company that has just entered bankruptcy, and it is likely this portion of the accounts receivable will never be collected.

Piepkorn typically orders 50 percent of next quarter's projected gross sales in the current quarter, and suppliers are typically paid in 42 days. Wages, taxes, and other costs run about 30 percent of gross sales. The company has a quarterly interest payment of $130,000 on its long-term debt.

The company uses a local bank for its short-term financial needs. It pays 1.5 percent per quarter in all short-term borrowing and maintains a money market account that pays 1 percent per quarter on all short-term deposits.

Gary has asked you to prepare a cash budget and short-term financial plan for the company under the current policies. He has also asked you to prepare additional plans based on changes in several inputs.

The following questions introduce refinements to the short-term financial plan reflecting changes in the minimum cash balance, credit policy, and credit terms from suppliers. For each question, rework the cash budget and determine the incremental cash generated or expended due to the change. Based on your incremental cash calculation, state your recommendation on whether the change should be implemented. In your analysis, assume that all the preceding changes are in place.

Questions

1. Use the numbers given to complete the cash budget and short-term financial plan.

2. Rework the cash budget and short-term financial plan assuming Piepkorn changes to a minimum balance of $130,000.

3. You have looked at the credit policy offered by your competitors and have determined that the industry standard credit policy is 1/10, net 40. The discount will begin to be offered on the first day of the first quarter. You want to examine how this credit policy would affect the cash budget and short-term financial plan. If this credit policy is implemented, you believe that 40 percent of all sales will take advantage of it, and the accounts receivable period will decline to 36 days. Rework the cash budget and short-term financial plan under the new credit policy and a minimum cash balance of $130,000. What interest rate are you effectively offering customers?

4. You have talked to the company's suppliers about the credit terms Piepkorn receives. Currently, the company receives terms of net 45. The suppliers have stated that they would offer new credit terms of 1.5/15, net 40. The discount would begin to be offered in the first day of the first quarter. What interest rate are the suppliers offering the company? Rework the cash budget and short-term financial plan assuming you take the credit terms on all orders and the minimum cash balance is $100,000. Also assume that Piepkorn offers the credit terms in the previous question.

PIEPKORN MANUFACTURING
Cash Budget

	Q1	Q2	Q3	Q4
Target cash balance				
Net cash inflow				
Ending cash balance				
Minimum cash balance				
Cumulative surplus (deficit)				

PIEPKORN MANUFACTURING
Short-Term Financial Plan

	Q1	Q2	Q3	Q4
Target cash balance				
Net cash inflow				
New short-term investments				
Income from short-term investments				
Short-term investments sold				
New short-term borrowing				
Interest on short-term borrowing				
Short-term borrowing repaid				
Ending cash balance				
Minimum cash balance				
Cumulative surplus (deficit)				
Beginning short-term investments				
Ending short-term investments				
Beginning short-term debt				
Ending short-term debt				

Internet Application Questions

1. Working capital financing is no longer an area limited to traditional banks. In fact, for some high-growth industries, institutions such as the Business Development Bank of Canada (BDC) step in and provide both advice and working capital loans, sometimes leading a syndicate. Click on the BDC link below and describe their working capital financing arrangement. bdc.ca

2. Export Development Canada (EDC) (edc.ca) provides trade finance and risk management services to Canadian exporters and investors in up to 200 markets. Founded in 1944, EDC is a Crown corporation that operates as a commercial financial institution. One of their products is Equity Investments (edc.ca/EN/Our-Solutions/Pages/supply-chain-financing.aspx). This product allows a Canadian exporter to improve its financial efficiency of supply chain. Describe the advantage of this product *vis-à-vis* a more traditional line of credit (edc.ca/en/our-solutions/financing/foreign-buyer-financing/pages/lines-of-credit.aspx).

3. How do you think banks make personal credit line decisions? As a student, you often face a banker who is trying to ascertain your "credit score." TransUnion Canada is one of Canada's three major credit-reporting agencies. Go to transunion.ca and view the sample credit profile. Based on the credit-scoring model provided, what are three of the most important items banks look at when making the personal credit decision?

4. Canada Business Network, the Government Services for Entrepreneurs in Canada, provides best practices on improving working capital and inventory management. To learn more about forecasting and benchmarking techniques visit canadabusiness.ca/eng/page/2636/

CHAPTER 21

INTERNATIONAL CORPORATE FINANCE

© Designpics/All Canada Photos

On June 6, 2012, the Canadian dollar closed at 97 cents U.S. A high Canadian dollar creates challenges for export-sensitive manufacturers who must contend with a rising loonie that makes their goods more expensive. As for consumers, the rise in the loonie will make the price of imported foods and goods cheaper. According to Peter Hall, Chief Economist, EDC, "As the U.S. and global economies improve, higher economic flows will draw liquidity back into normal channels, weakening commodity prices. Lower commodity prices will hold the loonie just below parity, helping Canadian exporters to cash in on the global recovery." In this chapter, we explore the role played by currencies and exchange rates, along with a number of other key topics in international finance.

Learning Objectives ▶

After studying this chapter, you should understand:

LO1 The different terminologies used in international finance.

LO2 How exchange rates are quoted, what they mean, and the difference between spot and forward exchange rates.

LO3 Purchasing power parity, interest rate parity, unbiased forward rates, uncovered interest rate parity, and the generalized Fisher effect and their implications for exchange rate changes.

LO4 How to estimate NPV using home and foreign currency approaches.

LO5 The different types of exchange rate risk and ways firms manage exchange rate risk.

LO6 The impact of political risk on international business investing.

riotintoalcan.com
mccain.ca

Corporations with significant foreign operations are often called *international corporations* or *multinationals*. Such corporations must consider many financial factors that do not directly affect purely domestic firms. These include foreign exchange rates, differing interest rates from country to country, complex accounting methods for foreign operations, foreign tax rates, and foreign government intervention.

Key topics of international financial management, foreign exchange rates, for example, are also of interest to many smaller Canadian businesses. Canada has an open economy linked very closely by a free-trade agreement to its largest trading partner, the United States. There are also very important economic and financial ties to Europe, the Pacific Rim, and other major economies worldwide. To illustrate, in the Atlantic Provinces, independent fish plants that supply the Boston market also wholesale lobster to Europe. These smaller corporations do not qualify as multinationals in the league of Rio Tinto Alcan or McCain, but their financial managers must know how to manage foreign exchange risk.

The basic principles of corporate finance still apply to international corporations; like domestic companies, they seek to invest in projects that create more value for the shareholders than they cost and to arrange financing that raises cash at the lowest possible cost. In other words, the net present value principle holds for both foreign and domestic operations, but it is usually more complicated to apply the NPV rule to foreign investments.

One of the most significant complications of international finance is foreign exchange. The foreign exchange markets provide important information and opportunities for an international corporation when it undertakes capital budgeting and financing decisions. As we discuss, international exchange rates, interest rates, and inflation rates are closely related. We spend much of this chapter exploring the connection between these financial variables.

We won't have much to say here about the role of cultural and social differences in international business. Also, we do not discuss the implications of differing political and economic systems. These factors are of great importance to international businesses, but it would take another book to do them justice. Consequently, we focus only on some purely financial considerations in international finance and some key aspects of foreign exchange markets.

21.1 | Terminology

Chapter 1 had a lot to say about trends in world financial markets, including globalization. The first step in learning about international finance is to conquer the new vocabulary. As with any specialty, international finance is rich in jargon. Accordingly, we get started on the subject with a highly eclectic vocabulary exercise.

The terms that follow are presented alphabetically, and they are not of equal importance. We chose these particular ones because they appear frequently in the financial press or because they illustrate some of the colourful language of international finance.

1. The **cross-rate** is the implicit exchange rate between two currencies when both are quoted in some third currency. Usually the third currency is the U.S. dollar.

2. A **Eurobond** is a bond issued in multiple countries, but denominated in a single currency, usually the issuer's home currency. Such bonds have become an important way to raise capital for many international companies and governments. Eurobonds are issued outside the restrictions that apply to domestic offerings and are syndicated and traded mostly from London. Trading can and does occur anywhere there is a buyer and a seller.

3. **Eurocurrency** is money deposited in a financial centre outside of the country whose currency is involved. For instance, Eurodollars—the most widely used Eurocurrency—are U.S. dollars deposited in banks outside the U.S. banking system. EuroCanadian are Canadian dollar bank deposits outside Canada.

4. **Export Development Canada (EDC)** is a federal Crown corporation with a mandate to promote Canadian exports. EDC provides financing for foreign companies that purchase Canadian exports. EDC also insures exporters' receivables and provides coverage against loss of assets due to political risks in foreign markets. Most of EDC's customers are small businesses.[1]

5. **Foreign bonds**, unlike Eurobonds, are issued in a single country and are usually denominated in that country's currency. Often, the country in which these bonds are issued draws distinctions between them and bonds issued by domestic issuers, including different tax laws, restrictions on the amount issued, or tougher disclosure rules.

   Foreign bonds often are nicknamed for the country where they are issued: Yankee bonds (United States), Samurai bonds (Japan), Rembrandt bonds (the Netherlands), and Bulldog bonds (Britain). Partly because of tougher regulations and disclosure requirements, the foreign-bond market hasn't grown in past years with the vigor of the Eurobond market. A substantial portion of all foreign bonds is issued in Switzerland.

6. **Gilts**, technically, are British and Irish government securities, although the term also includes issues of local British authorities and some overseas public-sector offerings.

7. The **London Interbank Offer Rate (LIBOR)** is the rate that most international banks charge one another for loans of Eurodollars overnight in the London market. LIBOR is a cornerstone in the pricing of money market issues and other short-term debt issues by both government and corporate borrowers. Interest rates are frequently quoted as some spread over LIBOR, then they float with the LIBOR rate.[2]

---

cross-rate
The implicit exchange rate between two currencies (usually non-U.S.) quoted in some third currency (usually the U.S. dollar).

Eurobond
International bonds issued in multiple countries but denominated in a single currency (usually the issuer's currency).

Eurocurrency
Money deposited in a financial centre outside of the country whose currency is involved.

Export Development Canada (EDC)
Federal Crown corporation that promotes Canadian exports by making loans to foreign purchasers.

foreign bonds
International bonds issued in a single country, usually denominated in that country's currency.

gilts
British and Irish government securities, including issues of local British authorities and some overseas public-sector offerings.

London Interbank Offer Rate (LIBOR)
The rate most international banks charge one another for overnight Eurodollar loans.

---

[1] More information about EDC is available at its website: edc.ca

[2] For more on how LIBOR is calculated, see bbalibor.com/bbalibor-explained/the-basics

swaps
Agreements to exchange two securities or currencies.

8. There are two basic kinds of **swaps**: interest rate and currency. An *interest rate swap* occurs when two parties exchange a floating-rate payment for a fixed-rate payment or vice versa. *Currency swaps* are agreements to deliver one currency in exchange for another. Often both types of swaps are used in the same transaction when debt denominated in different currencies is swapped. Chartered banks make an active market in arranging swaps, and swap volumes have grown rapidly.

> ### Concept Questions
>
> **1.** What are the differences between a Eurobond and a foreign bond?
> **2.** What are Eurodollars?

21.2 | Foreign Exchange Markets and Exchange Rates

foreign exchange market
The market where one country's currency is traded for another's.

The **foreign exchange market**, also known as forex or FX market, is undoubtedly the world's largest financial market. It is the market where one country's currency is traded for another's. Most of the trading takes place in a few currencies: the U.S. dollar ($), the European Union Euro (EUR), the British pound sterling (£), the Japanese yen (¥), and the Swiss franc (CHF). Table 21.1 lists some of the more common currencies and their symbols.

The foreign exchange market is an over-the-counter market, so there is no single location where traders get together. Instead, market participants are located in the major banks around the world. They communicate using computers, telephones, and other telecommunications devices. For example, one communications network for foreign transactions is the Society for Worldwide Interbank Financial Telecommunications (SWIFT), a Belgian not-for-profit co-operative. Using data transmission lines, a bank in Toronto, the centre of Canada's foreign exchange trading, can send messages to a bank in London via SWIFT regional processing centres.

TABLE 21.1

International currency symbols (2012)

Country	Currency	Symbol	Country	Currency	Symbol
Australia	Australian Dollar	AUD	Japan	Yen	¥
Austria	Euro	EUR	Kuwait	Dinar	KWD
Belgium	Euro	EUR	Mexico	Peso	MXN
Canada	Canadian Dollar	CAD	Netherlands	Euro	EUR
China	Renminbi	RMB	Norway	Krone	NOK
Denmark	Krone	DKK	Saudi Arabia	Riyal	SAR
Finland	Euro	EUR	Singapore	Dollar	SGD
France	Euro	EUR	South Africa	Rand	R
Germany	Euro	EUR	Spain	Euro	EUR
Greece	Euro	EUR	Sweden	Krona	SEK
India	Rupee	₹	Switzerland	Franc	CHF
Iran	Rial	IRR	United Kingdom	Pound	£
Italy	Euro	EUR	United States	Dollar	$

The many different types of participants in the foreign exchange market include the following:

1. Importers who pay for goods involving foreign currencies by converting foreign exchange.
2. Exporters who receive foreign currency and may want to convert to the domestic currency.
3. Portfolio managers who buy or sell foreign stocks and bonds.
4. Foreign exchange brokers who match buy and sell orders.
5. Traders who "make a market" in foreign exchange.
6. Speculators who try to profit from changes in exchange rates.

Exchange Rates

exchange rate
The price of one country's currency expressed in another country's currency.

An **exchange rate** is simply the price of one country's currency expressed in another country's currency. In practice, almost all trading of currencies worldwide takes place in terms of the U.S. dollar.

EXCHANGE RATE QUOTATIONS Figure 21.1 reproduces exchange rate quotations as they appear in *The National Post* and *The Wall Street Journal*. Notice that the rates were supplied by Thomson Reuters. The bottom part of Figure 21.1 is the cross-rates of seven main currencies. Because of the heavy volume of transactions in U.S. dollars, U.S./Canada rates appear first. The first row at the top of Figure 21.1 (labelled "A US$ buys") gives the number of Canadian dollars it takes to buy one unit of foreign currency. For example, the U.S./Canada spot rate is quoted at 1.0279, which means you can buy one U.S. dollar today with 1.0279 Canadian dollars.[3]

For current exchange rates visit xe.com

The next section (labelled "A CAD buys") shows the indirect exchange rate. This is the amount of U.S. currency per Canadian dollar. The U.S./Canada spot rate is quoted here at 0.9729 U.S. dollars for one Canadian dollar. Naturally this second exchange rate is just the reciprocal of the first one, 1/0.9729 = 1.0279.

The rest of Figure 21.1 shows the exchange rates for other foreign currencies. Notice that the most important currencies are listed first: European euros, Japanese yen, and U.K. pounds. In this part of the figure, the table labelled "A CAD buys" gives the amount of foreign currency that one Canadian dollars is worth. For example, one Canadian dollar buys 0.6281 British pounds. The table labelled "A US$ buys" repeats the same information in U.S. dollars. With one U.S. dollar you can buy 0.6455 pounds.

CROSS-RATES AND TRIANGLE ARBITRAGE Using the U.S. dollar or the euro as the common denominator in quoting exchange rates greatly reduces the number of possible cross-currency quotes. For example, with five major currencies, there would potentially be 10 exchange rates instead of just 4.[4] Also, the fact that the dollar is used throughout cuts down on inconsistencies in the exchange rate quotations.

EXAMPLE 21.1: A yen for Fast Cars

Suppose you have CAD 1,000. Based on the rates in Figure 21.1, how many Japanese yen can you get? Alternatively, if a Porsche costs EUR 100,000, how many Canadian dollars will you need to buy it? (EUR is the abbreviation for euros.)

The exchange rate for yen is given in Canadian dollars per yen as 0.0130 (bottom section under yen). Your CAD 1,000 thus gets you:

$1,000/0.0130 dollars per yen = 76,923 yen

Since the exchange rate in dollars per euro is 1.2929, you need:

EUR 100,000 × 1.2929 CAD per EUR = CAD 129,290

---

[3] The spot rate is for immediate trading. Forward rates are for future transactions and are discussed in detail later.

[4] In discussing cross-rates, we follow Canadian practice of using the U.S. dollar. There are four exchange rates instead of five because one exchange rate would involve the exchange rate for a currency with itself. More generally, it might seem there should be 25 exchange rates with five currencies. There are 25 different combinations, but, of these, five involve the exchange rate of a currency for itself. Of the remaining 20, half of them are redundant because they are just the reciprocals of the exchange rate. Of the remaining 10, six can be eliminated by using a common denominator.

Earlier, we defined the cross-rate as the exchange rate for a non-U.S. currency expressed in another non-U.S. currency. For example, suppose we observed the following:

¥ per $1US = 100.00
AUD per $1US = 1.50

FIGURE 21.1 EXCHANGE RATE QUOTATIONS

FOREIGN EXCHANGE

A US$ buys:	Latest	Prev day	Day %ch	Wk %ch	4wk %ch	Inverse rate	A CAD$ buys:	Latest	Prev day	Day %ch	Wk %ch	4wk %ch	Inverse rate
Canada $	1.0279	1.0379	–1.0	–0.2	+2.6	0.9729	US$	0.9279	0.9635	+1.0	+0.2	–2.6	1.0279
euro	0.7955	0.8033	–1.0	–1.6	+2.9	1.2571	euro	0.774	0.7742	nil	–1.5	+0.3	1.292
Japan yen	79.23	78.76	+0.6	+0.2	–0.5	0.0126	Japan yen	77.05	75.85	+1.6	+0.4	–3.0	0.013
UK pound	0.6455	0.6503	–0.7	–0.1	+4.2	1.5492	UK pound	0.6281	0.6267	+0.2	+0.1	+1.5	1.5921
Swiss franc	0.9551	0.9647	–1.0	–1.6	+2.9	1.047	Swiss franc	0.9288	0.9289	nil	–1.5	+0.3	1.0767
Australia $	1.0082	1.0265	–1.8	–2.1	+1.4	0.9919	Australia $	0.9811	0.9894	–0.8	–2.0	–1.2	1.0193
Mexico peso	14.0278	14.2256	–1.4	–0.8	+3.9	0.0713	Mexico peso	13.6434	13.7029	–0.4	–0.6	+1.3	0.0733
Hong Kong	7.7582	7.7586	nil	–0.1	–0.1	0.1289	Hong Kong	7.5467	7.474	+1.0	+0.1	–2.6	0.1325
Singapore $	1.2748	1.2862	–0.9	–1.1	+1.8	0.7844	Singapore $	1.2399	1.2385	+0.1	–0.9	–0.8	0.8065
China renminbi	6.3637	6.367	–0.1	+0.1	+0.9	0.1571	China renminbi	6.191	6.1348	+0.9	+0.3	–1.7	0.1615
India rupee	55.27	55.55	–0.5	–1.5	+2.8	0.0181	India rupee	53.77	53.52	+0.5	–1.4	+0.2	0.0186
Russia rouble	32.3482	33.065	–2.2	–1.5	+6.5	0.0309	Russia rouble	31.4723	31.8576	–1.2	–1.3	+3.8	0.0318
Brazil real	2.03	2.0183	+0.6	+0.9	+3.1	0.4926	Brazil real	1.9751	1.9446	+1.6	+1.0	+0.5	0.5063
Israel shekel	3.8806	3.8979	–0.4	nil	+1.6	0.2577	Israel shekel	3.7756	3.7556	+0.5	+0.2	–1.1	0.2649

Supplied by Thomson Reuters.
Listings indicative of late afternoon rates.

FORWARD EXCHANGE

Per US$	1 mo	3 mo	6 mo	1 yr	2 yr	3 yr	4 yr	5 yr
C$	1.0285	1.0298	1.0316	1.0348	1.0413	1.0495	1.0544	1.0561
euro*	1.2572	1.2580	1.2594	1.2639	1.2731	1.2796	1.2871	1.2943
Yen	79.21	79.21	79.21	79.20	79.19	79.18	79.16	79.14
£*	1.5488	1.5484	1.5478	1.5469	1.5451	1.5437	1.5452	1.5478

Per CAD$	1 mo	3 mo	6 mo	1 yr	2 yr	3 yr	4 yr	5 yr
US$	0.9723	0.9711	0.9694	0.9663	0.9603	0.9528	0.9484	0.9469
euro*	1.2930	1.2955	1.2992	1.3079	1.3256	1.3429	1.3571	1.3669
Yen	76.98	76.82	76.57	75.95	74.42	72.49	70.48	68.41
£*	1.5928	1.5944	1.5965	1.6004	1.6082	1.6190	1.6279	1.6333

Source: *The National Post*, FP Investing, June 7, 2012. Used with permission. The most recent figures can be obtained from *The National Post* newspaper.

	Dollar	Euro	Pound	Franc	Peso	Yen	CAD
Canada	1.0276	1.2929	1.5924	1.0767	0.0733	0.0130	—
Japan	79.1899	99.6337	122.7173	82.9777	5.6455	—	77.0640
Mexico	14.0270	17.6482	21.7371	14.6979	—	0.1771	13.6504
Switzerland	0.9544	1.2007	1.4789	—	0.0680	0.0121	0.9287
U.K.	0.6453	0.8119	—	0.6762	0.0460	0.0081	0.6280
Euro	0.7948	—	1.2317	0.8328	0.0567	0.0100	0.7735
U.S.	—	1.2582	1.5497	1.0478	0.0713	0.0126	0.9732

Source: ICAP plc; historical data prior to 6/9/11: Thomson Reuters

Source: online.wsj.com/mdc/public/page/2_3023-keyrates.html

Suppose the cross-rate is quoted as:

¥ per AUD = 50.00

What do you think?

The cross-rate here is inconsistent with the exchange rates. To see this, suppose you have $100US. If you convert this to Australian dollars, you receive:

$100US × AUD 1.5 per $1 = AUD 150

If you convert this to yen at the cross-rate, you have:

AUD 150 × ¥50 per AUD 1 = ¥7,500

However, if you just convert your U.S. dollars to yen without going through Australian dollars, you have:

$100US × ¥100 per $1 = ¥10,000

What we see is that the yen has two prices, ¥100 per $1US and ¥75 per $1US, depending on how we get them.

To make money, we want to buy low, sell high. The important thing to note is that yen are cheaper if you buy them with U.S. dollars because you get 100 yen instead of just 75. You should proceed as follows:

1. Buy 10,000 yen for $100US.
2. Use the 10,000 yen to buy Australian dollars at the cross-rate. Since it takes 50 yen to buy an Australian dollar, you receive ¥10,000/50 = AUD 200.
3. Use the AUD 200 to buy U.S. dollars. Since the exchange rate is AUD 1.5 per dollar, you receive AUD 200/1.5 = $133.33, for a round-trip profit of $33.33.
4. Repeat steps 1 through 3.

This particular activity is called *triangle arbitrage* because the arbitrage involves moving through three different exchange rates.

$$¥100/1\$$$

$$AUD\ 1.5/1\$ = \$.67/AUD\ 1 \quad \leftarrow \quad AUD\ .02/¥1 = ¥50/AUD\ 1$$

To prevent such opportunities, it is not difficult to see that since a U.S. dollar buys you either 50 yen or 1.5 Australian dollars, the cross-rate must be:

(¥50/$1US)/(AUD 1.5/$1US) = ¥33.33/AUD 1

If it were anything else, there would be a triangle arbitrage opportunity.

Types of Transactions

There are two basic types of trades in the foreign exchange market: spot trades and forward trades. A **spot trade** is an agreement to exchange currency on the spot; this actually means the transaction is completed or settled within two business days. The exchange rate on a spot trade is called the **spot exchange rate**. Implicitly, all of the exchange rates and transactions we have discussed so far have referred to the spot market.

FORWARD EXCHANGE RATES A **forward trade** is an agreement to exchange currency at some time in the future. The exchange rate used is agreed on today and is called the **forward exchange rate**. A forward trade would normally be settled sometime in the next 12 months, but some forward rates are quoted for as far as 10 years into the future.

Look back at Figure 21.1 to see forward exchange rates quoted for some of the major currencies. For example, the spot exchange rate for the U.S. dollar is $1.0279. The six month forward exchange rate is U.S. $1 = 1.0316. This means you can buy one U.S. dollar today for $1.0279, or you can agree to take delivery of a U.S. dollar in six months and pay $1.0316 at that time.

Notice that the U.S. dollar is more expensive in the forward market ($1.0316 versus $1.0279). Since the U.S. dollar is more expensive in the future than it is today, it is said to be selling at a

spot trade
An agreement to trade currencies based on the exchange rate today for settlement in two days.

spot exchange rate
The exchange rate on a spot trade.

forward trade
Agreement to exchange currency at some time in the future.

forward exchange rate
The agreed-on exchange rate to be used in a forward trade.

premium relative to the Canadian dollar in the forward market. For the same reason, the Canadian dollar is said to be selling at a discount relative to the U.S. dollar. To see the discount, compare the spot and six-month forward rates in the "Per C$" section of Figure 21.1. The Canada/U.S. spot rate is 0.9729 and the six-month forward rate is 0.9694. The Canadian dollar is selling at a discount in the forward market since buyers with U.S. dollars will pay less for it six months from today.

EXAMPLE 21.2: Shedding Some Pounds

Suppose the exchange rates for the British pound and the euro are:

Pounds per $1US = 0.60
EUR per $1US = 0.90

The cross-rate is 1.6 euros per pound. Is this consistent? Explain how to go about making some money.

The cross-rate should be EUR 0.90/£ .60 = EUR 1.5 per pound. You can buy a pound for EUR 1.5 in one market,

and you can sell a pound for EUR 1.6 in another. So we want to first get some pounds, then use the pounds to buy some euros, and then sell the euros. Assuming you have $100US, you could:

1. Exchange U.S. dollars for pounds: $100US × 0.6 = £60.
2. Exchange pounds for euros: £60 × 1.6 = EUR 96.
3. Exchange euros for U.S. dollars: EUR 96/.90 = $106.67.

This would result in a $6.67 U.S. round-trip profit.

Why does the forward market exist? One answer is that it allows businesses and individuals to lock in a future exchange rate today, thereby eliminating any risk from unfavourable shifts in the exchange rate.

EXAMPLE 21.3

In Figure 21.1, the spot exchange rate and the six-month forward rate in Canadian dollars per pound are CAD 1.5921 = 1 pound and $1.5965 = 1 pound, respectively. If you expect 1 million pounds in six months, you will get 1 million pounds × $1.5965 per pound = $1.5965 million.

Since it is more expensive to buy a pound in the forward market than in the spot market ($1.5965 versus $1.5921), the Canadian dollar is selling at a discount relative to the pound.

EXAMPLE 21.4

From Figure 21.1, the spot and 12-month forward rates in yen per Canadian dollars are 77.05 yen = $1 and 75.95, respectively. You plan to convert ¥10 million in 12 months so you need to know the forward exchange rate in dollar per yen.

$1 = 75.95 yen
1 yen = 1/75.95 = $0.013166

So your ¥10 million converts to $131,666. The spot exchange rate in dollars per yen is 1/77.05 = $0.012979.

Either way you look at it, the yen is selling at a forward premium. One dollar will buy fewer yen 12 months from now than it does today. And if you converted your funds today, instead of waiting 12 months, you would get more yen.

Concept Questions

1. What is triangle arbitrage?
2. What do we mean by the six-month forward exchange rate?

21.3 | Purchasing Power Parity

purchasing power parity (PPP)
The idea that the exchange rate adjusts to keep purchasing power constant among currencies.

Now that we have discussed what exchange rate quotations mean, we can address an obvious question: What determines the level of the spot exchange rate? In addition, we know that exchange rates change through time. A related question is: What determines the rate of change in exchange rates? At least part of the answer in both cases goes by the name of **purchasing power parity** (**PPP**), the idea that the exchange rate adjusts to keep purchasing power constant among currencies. As we discuss next, there are two forms of PPP, absolute and relative.

Absolute Purchasing Power Parity

The basic idea behind *absolute purchasing power parity* is that a commodity costs the same regardless of what currency is used to purchase it or where it is selling. This is a very straight-forward concept. If a beer costs £2 in London, and the exchange rate is £.60 per Canadian dollar, then a beer costs £2/.60 = $3.33 in Montreal. In other words, absolute PPP says $5 will buy you the same number of, say, cheeseburgers anywhere in the world.

More formally, let S_0 be the spot exchange rate between the British pound and the Canadian dollar today (Time 0). Here we are quoting exchange rates as the amount of foreign currency per dollar. Let P_{CDN} and P_{UK} be the current Canadian and British prices, respectively, on a particular commodity, say, apples. Absolute PPP simply says that:

$$P_{UK} = S_0 \times P_{CDN}$$

This tells us that the British price for something is equal to the Canadian price for that same something, multiplied by the exchange rate.

The rationale behind PPP is similar to that behind triangle arbitrage. If PPP did not hold, arbitrage would be possible (in principle) by moving apples from one country to another. For example, suppose apples in Halifax are selling for $4 per bushel, while in London the price is £2.40 per bushel. Absolute PPP implies that:

$$P_{UK} = S_0 \times P_{CDN}$$
$$£2.40 = S_0 \times \$4$$
$$S_0 = £2.40/\$4 = £.60$$

That is, the implied spot exchange rate is £.60 per dollar. Equivalently, a pound is worth $1/£.60 = $1.67.

Suppose, instead, the actual exchange rate is £.50. Starting with $4, a trader could buy a bushel of apples in Halifax, ship it to London, and sell it there for £2.40. Our trader then converts the £2.40 into dollars at the prevailing exchange rate, $S_0 = £.50$, yielding a total of £2.40/.50 = $4.80. The round-trip gain is 80 cents.

Because of this profit potential, forces are set in motion to change the exchange rate and/or the price of apples. In our example, apples would begin moving from Halifax to London. The reduced supply of apples in Halifax would raise the price of apples there, and the increased supply in Britain would lower the price of apples in London.

In addition to moving apples around, apple traders would be busily converting pounds back into dollars to buy more apples. This activity increases the supply of pounds and simultaneously increases the demand for dollars. We would expect the value of a pound to fall. This means the dollar is getting more valuable, so it will take more pounds to buy one dollar. Since the exchange rate is quoted as pounds per dollar, we would expect the exchange rate to rise from £.50.

For absolute PPP to hold, several things must be true:

1. The transactions cost of trading apples—shipping, insurance, wastage, and so on—must be zero.
2. There are no barriers to trading apples, such as tariffs, taxes, or other political barriers such as voluntary restraint agreements.
3. Finally, an apple in Halifax must be identical to an apple in London. It won't do for you to send red apples to London if the English eat only green apples.

Given the fact that the transaction costs are not zero and that the other conditions are rarely exactly met, it is not surprising that absolute PPP is really applicable only to traded goods, and then only to very uniform ones.

For this reason, absolute PPP does not imply that a Mercedes costs the same as a Ford or that a nuclear power plant in France costs the same as one in Ontario. In the case of the cars, they are not identical. In the case of the power plants, even if they were identical, they are expensive and very difficult to ship. Still, we can observe major violations of PPP. For example, on a European trip in a recent summer, one of the authors noticed that a 500 mL bottle of Dutch beer cost 2 pounds (around $4.50 Canadian) in London but only 1.5 euros (around $2.40 Canadian) in Lisbon. This difference led thousands of students to plan vacations in Portugal instead of England. Despite the resulting increased demand for euros, the exchange rate has not adjusted to reflect PPP.

One interesting application of the theory behind purchasing power parity is the Big Mac Index updated and published regularly by *The Economist*.[5] The index calculates the exchange rate to the U.S. dollar that would result in McDonald's Big Mac burgers costing the same around the world (using the U.S. cost as a base). This calculated value is compared with the actual current exchange rate to determine if a currency is overvalued or undervalued. At the time of writing, the index supported the widespread belief that China was keeping its currency undervalued to promote its exports. On January 11, 2012, the Big Mac index showed that the Chinese renminbi was 42 percent undervalued against the U.S. dollar. A Big Mac in China cost US$2.44 while its average cost in the U.S. was US$4.20. To make the two prices equal would have required an exchange rate of RMB 3.67 to the U.S. dollar, compared with the actual rate of RMB 6.32.

Relative Purchasing Power Parity

As a practical matter, a relative version of purchasing power parity has evolved. *Relative purchasing power parity* does not tell us what determines the absolute level of the exchange rate. Instead, it tells what determines the change in the exchange rate over time.

THE BASIC IDEA   Suppose again that the British pound/Canadian dollar exchange rate is currently $S_0 = £.50$. Further suppose that the inflation rate in Britain is predicted to be 10 percent over the coming year and (for the moment) the inflation rate in Canada is predicted to be zero. What do you think the exchange rate will be in a year?

If you think about it, a dollar currently costs .50 pounds in Britain. With 10 percent inflation, we expect prices in Britain to generally rise by 10 percent. So we expect that the price of a dollar will go up by 10 percent and the exchange rate should rise to £.50 × 1.1 = £.55.

If the inflation rate in Canada is not zero, we need to worry about the relative inflation rates in the two countries. For example, suppose the Canadian inflation rate is predicted to be 4 percent. Relative to prices in Canada, prices in Britain are rising at a rate of 10% − 4% = 6% per year. So we expect the price of the dollar to rise by 6 percent, and the predicted exchange rate is £.50 × 1.06 = £.53.

THE RESULT   In general, relative PPP says that the change in the exchange rate is determined by the difference in the inflation rates between the two countries. To be more specific, we use the following notation:

$$S_0 = \text{Current (Time 0) spot exchange rate (foreign currency per dollar)}$$
$$E[S_t] = \text{Expected exchange rate in } t \text{ periods}$$
$$h_{CDN} = \text{Inflation rate in Canada}$$
$$h_{FC} = \text{Foreign country inflation rate}$$

Based on our discussion, relative PPP says the expected percentage change in the exchange rate over the next year, $(E[S_1] − S_0)/S_0$, is:

$$(E[S_1] − S_0)/S_0 = h_{FC} − h_{CDN} \qquad [21.1]$$

In words, relative PPP simply says that the expected percentage change in the exchange rate is equal to the difference in inflation rates. If we rearrange this slightly, we get:

$$E[S_1] = S_0 \times [1 + (h_{FC} − h_{CDN})] \qquad [21.2]$$

---

[5]This discussion is largely based on "McCurrencies," *The Economist*, April 24, 2003. For the latest on the index visit the website at economist.com/topics/big-mac-index.

This result makes a certain amount of sense, but care must be used in quoting the exchange rate. In our example involving Britain and Canada, relative PPP tells us the exchange rate rises by $h_{FC} - h_{CDN} = 10\% - 4\% = 6\%$ per year. Assuming the difference in inflation rates doesn't change, the expected exchange rate in two years, $E[S_2]$, is therefore:

$$E[S_2] = E[S_1] \times (1 + .06)$$
$$= .53 \times 1.06$$
$$= .562$$

Notice that we could have written this as:

$$E[S_2] = .53 \times 1.06$$
$$= (.50 \times 1.06) \times 1.06$$
$$= .50 \times 1.06^2$$

In general, relative PPP, says the expected exchange rate at sometime in the future, $E[S_t]$, is:

$$E[S_t] = S_0 \times [1 + (h_{FC} - h_{CDN})]^t \tag{21.3}$$

As we shall see, this is a very useful relationship.

Because we don't really expect absolute PPP to hold for most goods, we focus on relative PPP, or RPPP, in the following discussion.

EXAMPLE 21.5: It's All Relative

Suppose the Japanese exchange rate is currently 130 yen per dollar. The inflation rate in Japan over the next three years will run, say, 2 percent per year while the Canadian inflation rate will be 6 percent. Based on relative PPP, what would the exchange rate be in three years?

Since the Canadian inflation rate is higher, we expect a dollar to become less valuable. The exchange rate change would be 2% – 6% = –4% per year. Over three years, the exchange rate falls to:

$$E[S_3] = S_0 \times [1 + (h_{FC} - h_{CDN})]^3$$
$$= 130 \times [1 + (-.04)]^3$$
$$= 115.02$$

Currency Appreciation and Depreciation

We frequently hear these statements: The dollar strengthened (or weakened) in financial markets today or the dollar is expected to appreciate (or depreciate) relative to the pound. When we say the dollar strengthens or appreciates, we mean the value of a dollar rises, so it takes more foreign currency to buy a Canadian dollar.

What happens to the exchange rates as currencies fluctuate in value depends on how exchange rates are quoted. Since we are quoting them as units of foreign currency per dollar, the exchange rate moves in the same direction as the value of the dollar: It rises as the dollar strengthens, and it falls as the dollar weakens.

Relative PPP tells us the exchange rate rises if the Canadian inflation rate is lower than the foreign country's. This happens because the foreign currency depreciates in value and therefore weakens relative to the dollar.

Concept Questions

1. What does absolute PPP say? Why might it not hold for many goods?
2. According to relative PPP, what determines the change in exchange rates?

21.4 | Interest Rate Parity, Unbiased Forward Rates, and the Generalized Fisher Effect

The next issue we need to address is the relationship between the spot exchange rates, forward exchange rates, and interest rates. To get started, we need some additional notation:

$$F_t = \text{Forward exchange rate for settlement at time } t$$
$$R_{CDN} = \text{Canadian nominal risk-free interest rate}$$
$$R_{FC} = \text{Foreign country nominal risk-free interest rate}$$

As before, use S_0 to stand for the spot exchange rate. You can take the Canadian nominal risk-free rate, R_{CDN}, to be the T-bill rate.

Covered Interest Arbitrage

Suppose we observe the following information about Canada and the European Union (E.U.):

$$S_0 = \text{EUR } 0.65 \qquad R_{CDN} = 10\%$$
$$F_1 = \text{EUR } 0.60 \qquad R_G = 5\%$$

where R_G is the nominal risk-free rate in the E.U. The period is one year, so F_1 is the one-year forward rate.

Do you see an arbitrage opportunity here? There is one. Suppose you have $1 to invest, and you want a riskless investment. One option you have is to invest the $1 in a riskless Canadian investment such as a one-year T-bill. If you do this, in one period your $1 will be worth:

$$\$ \text{ value in 1 period} = \$1 \times (1 + R_{CDN})$$
$$= \$1.10$$

Alternatively, you can invest in the European risk-free investment. To do this, you need to convert your $1 to euros and simultaneously exercise a forward trade to convert euros back to dollars in one year. The necessary steps would be as follows:

1. Convert your $1 to $1 $\times S_0 =$ EUR 0.65.
2. At the same time, enter into a forward agreement to convert euros back to dollars in one year. Since the forward rate is EUR 0.60, you get $1 for every EUR 0.60 that you have in one year.
3. Invest your EUR 0.65 in Europe at R_G. In one year, you have:

$$\text{EUR value in 1 year} = \text{EUR } 0.65 \times (1 + R_G)$$
$$= \text{EUR } 0.65 \times 1.05$$
$$= \text{EUR } 0.6825$$

4. Convert your EUR 0.6825 back to dollars at the agreed-on rate of EUR 0.60 = $1. You end up with:

$$\$ \text{ value in 1 year} = \text{EUR } 0.6825/0.60$$
$$= \$1.1375$$

Notice that the value in one year from this strategy can be written as:

$$\$ \text{ value in 1 year} = \$1 \times S_0 \times (1 + R_G)/F_1$$
$$= \$1 \times 0.65 \times (1.05)/0.60$$
$$= \$1.1375$$

The return on this investment is apparently 13.75 percent. This is higher than the 10 percent we get from investing in Canada. Since both investments are risk-free, there is an arbitrage opportunity.

To exploit the difference in interest rates, you need to borrow, say, $5 million at the lower Canadian rate and invest it at the higher European rate. What is the round-trip profit from doing this? To find out, we can work through the preceding steps:

1. Convert the $5 million at EUR 0.65 = $1 to get EUR 3.25 million.
2. Agree to exchange euros for dollars in one year at EUR 0.60 to the dollar.

3. Invest the EUR 3.25 million for one year at $R_G = 5\%$. You end up with EUR 3.4125 million.

4. Convert the EUR 3.4125 million back to dollars to fulfill the forward contract. You receive EUR 3.4125 million/0.60 = \$5.6875 million.

5. Repay the loan with interest. You owe \$5 million plus 10 percent interest, for a total of \$5.5 million. You have \$5,687,500, so your round-trip profit is a risk-free \$187,500.

The activity that we have illustrated here goes by the name of *covered interest arbitrage*. The term *covered* refers to the fact that we are covered in the event of a change in the exchange rate because we lock in the forward exchange rate today.

Interest Rate Parity (IRP)

If we assume that significant covered interest arbitrage opportunities do not exist, there must be some relationship between spot exchange rates, forward exchange rates, and relative interest rates. To see what this relationship is, note that, in general, strategy 1—investing in a riskless Canadian investment—gives us $(1 + R_{CDN})$ for every dollar we invest. Strategy 2—investing in a foreign risk-free investment—gives us $S_0 \times (1 + R_{FC})/F_1$ for every dollar we invest. Since these have to be equal to prevent arbitrage, it must be the case that:

$$(1 + R_{CDN}) = S_0 \times (1 + R_{FC})/F_1$$

interest rate parity (IRP) The condition stating that the interest rate differential between two countries is equal to the difference between the forward exchange rate and the spot exchange rate.

Rearranging this a bit gets us the famous **interest rate parity (IRP)** condition:

$$F_1/S_0 = (1 + R_{FC})/(1 + R_{CDN}) \qquad [21.4]$$

A very useful approximation for IRP illustrates very clearly what is going on and is not difficult to remember. If we define the percentage forward premium or discount as $(F_1 - S_0)/S_0$, IRP says this percent premium or discount is approximately equal to the difference in interest rates:

$$(F_1 - S_0)/S_0 = R_{FC} - R_{CDN} \qquad [21.5]$$

Very loosely, what IRP says is that any difference in interest rates between two countries for some period is just offset by the change in the relative value of the currencies, thereby eliminating any arbitrage possibilities. Notice that we could also write:

$$F_1 = S_0 \times [1 + (R_{FC} - R_{CDN})] \qquad [21.6]$$

In general, if we have t periods instead of just one, the IRP approximation would be written as:

$$F_t = S_0 \times [1 + (R_{FC} - R_{CDN})]^t \qquad [21.7]$$

EXAMPLE 21.6: Parity Check

Suppose the exchange rate for Japanese yen, S_0, is currently ¥120 = \$1. If the interest rate in Canada is $R_{CDN} = 10\%$ and the interest rate in Japan is $R_J = 5\%$, what must the forward rate be to prevent covered interest arbitrage?

From IRP, we have:

$$\begin{aligned} F_1 &= S_0 \times [1 + (R_J - R_{CDN})] \\ &= ¥120 \times [1 + (.05 - .10)] \\ &= ¥120 \times .95 \\ &= ¥114 \end{aligned}$$

Notice that the yen sells at a premium relative to the dollar (why?).

Forward Rates and Future Spot Rates

unbiased forward rates (UFR) The condition stating that the current forward rate is an unbiased predictor of the future exchange rate.

In addition to PPP and IRP, there is one more basic relationship we need to discuss. What is the connection between the forward rate and the expected future spot rate? The **unbiased forward rates (UFR)** condition says the forward rate, F_1, is equal to the expected future spot rate, $E[S_1]$:

$$F_1 = E[S_1]$$

With t periods, UFR would be written as:

$$F_t = E[S_t]$$

Loosely, the UFR condition says that, on average, the forward exchange rate is equal to the future spot exchange rate.

If we ignore risk, the UFR condition should hold. Suppose the forward rate for the Japanese yen is consistently lower than the future spot rate by, say, 10 yen. This means that anyone who wanted to convert dollars to yen in the future would consistently get more yen by not agreeing to a forward exchange. The forward rate would have to rise to get anyone interested.

Similarly, if the forward rate were consistently higher than the future spot rate, anyone who wanted to convert yen to dollars would get more dollars per yen by not agreeing to a forward trade. The forward exchange rate would have to fall to attract such traders.

For these reasons, the forward and actual future spot rates should be equal to each other on average. What the future spot rate will actually be is uncertain, of course. The UFR condition may not hold if traders are willing to pay a premium to avoid this uncertainty. Recent research documents deviations from IRP during and after the financial crisis starting in 2007.[6] To the extent that the condition does hold, the six-month forward rate that we see today should be an unbiased predictor of what the exchange rate will actually be in six months.

Putting It All Together

We have developed three relationships, PPP, IRP, and UFR, that describe the relationships between key financial variables such as interest rates, exchange rates, and inflation rates. We now explore the implications of these relationships as a group.

UNCOVERED INTEREST PARITY To start, it is useful to collect our international financial market relationships in one place:

$$\text{RPPP: } E[S_1] = S_0 \times [1 + (h_{FC} - h_{CDN})]$$
$$\text{IRP: } F_1 = S_0 \times [1 + (R_{FC} - R_{CDN})]$$
$$\text{UFR: } F_1 = E[S_1]$$

We begin by combining UFR and IRP. Since $F_1 = E[S_1]$ from the UFR condition, we can substitute $E[S_1]$ for F_1 in IRP. The result is:

$$E[S_1] = S_0 \times [1 + (R_{FC} - R_{CDN})] \tag{21.8}$$

uncovered interest parity (UIP)
The condition stating that the expected percentage change in the exchange rate is equal to the difference in interest rates.

This important relationship is called **uncovered interest parity (UIP)**, and it plays a key role in our international capital budgeting discussion that follows. With t periods, UIP becomes:

$$E[S_t] = S_0 \times [1 + (R_{FC} - R_{CDN})]^t \tag{21.9}$$

THE GENERALIZED FISHER EFFECT Next, we compare RPPP and UIP. Both of them have $E[S_1]$ on the left side, so their right sides must be equal. We thus have that:

$$S_0 \times [1 + (h_{FC} - h_{CDN})] = S_0 \times [1 + (R_{FC} - R_{CDN})]$$
$$h_{FC} - h_{CDN} = R_{FC} - R_{CDN}$$

generalized Fisher effect (GFE)
The theory that real interest rates are equal across countries.

This tells us that the difference in risk-free returns between Canada and a foreign country is just equal to the difference in inflation rates. Rearranging this slightly gives us the **generalized Fisher effect (GFE)**:

$$R_{CDN} - h_{CDN} = R_{FC} - h_{FC} \tag{21.10}$$

The GFE says that real rates are equal across countries.[7]

The conclusion that real returns are equal across countries is really basic economics. If real returns were higher in, say, the United States than in Canada, money would flow out of Canadian financial markets and into U.S. markets. Asset prices in the United States would rise and their returns would fall. At the same time, asset prices in Canada would fall and their returns would rise. This process acts to equalize real returns.

---

[6] For more on deviations from IRP during the financial crisis see: R.M. Levich, "Evidence on Financial Globalization and Crises: Interest Rate Parity," G. Caprio, ed., *The Encyclopedia of Financial Globalization*, Elsevier, 2012.

[7] Notice that our result here is the approximate real rate, $R - h$ (see Chapter 7), because we used approximations for PPP and IRP.

Having said all this, we need to note several things: First, we really haven't explicitly dealt with risk in our discussion. We might reach a different conclusion about real returns once we do, particularly if people in different countries have different tastes and attitudes toward risk. Second, there are many barriers to the movement of money and capital around the world. Real returns might be different between two countries for long periods of time if money can't move freely between them.

Despite these problems, we expect capital markets to become increasingly internationalized. As this occurs, any differences in real rates that do exist will probably diminish. The laws of economics have very little respect for national boundaries.

Concept Questions

1. What is covered interest arbitrage?
2. What is the international Fisher effect?

EXAMPLE 21.7: Taking a High Toll

Suppose that in 2013 a federal authority starts constructing a Newfoundland-Labrador fixed link tunnel under the Strait of Belle Isle to connect Quebec and the island of Newfoundland. The tunnel will initially cost CAD100 million to build. Work will be complete in one year at which time the authority will pay off the present construction loan and replace it with long-term financing from capital markets. The loan will be paid off over 10 years with tolls collected from tunnel users.

In the meantime, it is time to renew the construction loan for one year. A group of Canadian banks has offered to lend $100 million for one year at 11 percent. A Japanese bank has offered a yen loan at 7 percent. Should the authority borrow in yen for one year to save 4 percent in interest—$4 million?

While you are considering, you come across the following information on exchange rates: the spot exchange rate is ¥110 per Canadian dollar ($0.009091 per ¥). The 12-month forward rate is ¥106 per dollar ($.0094340 per yen).

According to the UFR condition, the forward rate shows that the yen is expected to rise in value. It follows that the authority is naive if it expects to save $4 million by borrowing in Japan. The UIP condition tells us the yen should rise by just enough so that exchange losses on paying back the loan in more expensive yen exactly offset the lower interest rate. To prove this, we compare the balloon payments at the end of one year for borrowing in Canadian dollars and in yen. If the authority borrows in Canadian dollars at 11 percent, the principal and interest at the end of one year would be $111 million.

If the borrowing is in yen, the treasurer of the authority executes the following steps:

1. Borrow the equivalent of $100 million in yen. Converting at today's spot rate, this is $100 million × 110 = ¥11 billion.
2. At the end of 12 months, the authority owes ¥11 billion × (1.07) = ¥11.77 billion.
3. After 12 months, the authority purchases ¥11.77 billion in the spot market to repay the loan. The cost depends on the unknown future spot rate for the yen. By borrowing in Japan, the authority is gambling that the yen will not appreciate in value by enough to cancel the gains of the lower interest rate. In other words, the authority is betting that the future cost of buying ¥11.77 billion will not exceed $111 million. This gives us a break-even future spot rate:

$$¥11.77 \text{ billion} = \$111 \text{ million} \times F_1$$
$$F_1 = 11.77 \text{ billion}/111 \text{ million}$$
$$F_1 = 106.036$$

If the authority gambles, it could break even if the future spot rate is around 106 yen per dollar. This translates to 1/106 = $.009434 per yen. If the yen appreciates more, the authority loses. Suppose the yen goes up to $.01 or 100 yen to the dollar. Then the authority has to repay ¥11.77 billion × .01 = $118 million. This is equivalent to borrowing at 18 percent!

Our advice in this case is to borrow in Canada to eliminate foreign exchange risk. Or, if there is a good reason to borrow abroad, say better access to funds, the authority should hedge in the forward market.[8] Under this approach, steps 1 and 2 are the same. With a forward contract taken out when the borrowing is initiated, the future exchange rate is locked in at ¥106 to the dollar. Due to the IRP condition, it is no coincidence that this is the break-even rate.

---

[8] Currency futures or swaps offer another possible hedging vehicle. Chapter 24 discusses futures in more detail.

21.5 | International Capital Budgeting

Kihlstrom Equipment, a Canadian-based international company, is evaluating an overseas investment. Kihlstrom's exports of high-tech communications equipment have increased to such a degree that it is considering building a plant in France. The project would cost EUR 2.5 million to launch. The cash flows are expected to be EUR 1.1 million a year for the next three years.[9]

The current spot exchange rate for euros is EUR 0.65. Recall that this is euros per dollar, so a euro is worth $1/0.65 = $1.54. The risk-free rate in Canada is 5 percent, and the risk-free rate in France is 7 percent. Notice that the exchange rate and the two interest rates are observed in financial markets, not estimated.[10] Kihlstrom's required return on dollar investments of this sort is 10 percent.

Should Kihlstrom take this investment? As always, the answer depends on the NPV, but how do we calculate the net present value of this project in Canadian dollars? There are two basic ways to do this:

1. *The home currency approach.* Convert all the euro cash flows into dollars, and then discount at 10 percent to find the NPV in dollars. Notice that for this approach, we have to come up with the future exchange rates to convert the future projected euro cash flows into dollars.

2. *The foreign currency approach.* Determine the required return on euro investments, and discount the euro cash flows to find the NPV in euros. Then convert this euro NPV to a dollar NPV. This approach requires us to somehow convert the 10 percent dollar required return to the equivalent euro required return.

The difference between these two approaches is primarily a matter of when we convert from euros to dollars. In the first case, we convert before estimating the NPV. In the second case, we convert after estimating NPV.

It might appear that the second approach is superior because we only have to come up with one number, the euro discount rate. Furthermore, since the first approach requires us to forecast future exchange rates, it probably seems that there is greater room for error. As we illustrate next, however, based on our results the two approaches are really the same.

Method 1: The Home Currency Approach

To convert the project future cash flows into dollars, we invoke the uncovered interest parity (UIP) relation to come up with the project exchange rates. Based on our discussion, the expected exchange rate at time t, $E[S_t]$ is:

$$E[S_t] = S_0 \times [1 + (R_E - R_{CDN})]^t$$

where R_E stands for the nominal risk-free rate in France. Since R_E is 7 percent, R_{CDN} is 5 percent, and the current exchange rate (S_0) is EUR 0.65:

$$E[S_t] = 0.65 \times [1 + (.07 - .05)]^t$$
$$= 0.65 \times 1.02^t$$

The projected exchange rates for the communications equipment project are thus:

Year	Expected Exchange Rate
1	EUR 0.65 × 1.02¹ = EUR 0.663
2	EUR 0.65 × 1.02² = EUR 0.676
3	EUR 0.65 × 1.02³ = EUR 0.690

Using these exchange rates, along with the current exchange rate, we can convert all of the euro cash flows to dollars:

Year	(1) Cash Flow in EUR	(2) Expected Exchange Rate	(3) Cash Flow in $ (1)/(2)
0	−EUR 2.5	EUR 0.650	−$3.85
1	1.1	0.663	1.66
2	1.1	0.676	1.63
3	1.1	0.690	1.59

---

[9] In our discussion of Kihlstrom, all cash flows and interest rates are nominal unless we state otherwise.

[10] For example, the interest rates might be the short-term Eurodollar and euro deposit rates offered by large money centre banks.

To finish, we calculate the NPV in the ordinary way:

$$NPV = -\$3.85 + \$1.66/1.10 + \$1.63/1.10^2 + \$1.59/1.10^3$$
$$= \$.2 \text{ million}$$

So the project appears to be profitable.

Method 2: The Foreign Currency Approach

Kihlstrom requires a nominal return of 10 percent on the dollar-denominated cash flows. We need to convert this to a rate suitable for euro-denominated cash flows.

Based on the generalized Fisher effect, we know that the difference in the nominal rates is:

$$R_E - R_{CDN} = h_E - h_{CDN}$$
$$= 7\% - 5\% = 2\%$$

The appropriate discount rate for estimating the euro cash flows from the project is approximately equal to 10 percent plus an extra 2 percent to compensate for the greater euro inflation rate. If we calculate the NPV of the euro cash flows at this rate, we get:

$$NPV_E = -EUR\ 2.5 + EUR\ 1.1/1.12 + EUR\ 1.1/1.12^2 + EUR\ 1.1/1.12^3$$
$$= EUR\ 0.142 \text{ million}$$

The NPV of this project is EUR 0.142 million. Taking this project makes us EUR 0.142 million richer today. What is this in dollars? Since the exchange rate today is EUR 0.65, the dollar NPV of the project is:

$$NPV_\$ = NPV_E/S_0 = EUR\ 0.142/0.65 = \$.2 \text{ million}$$

This is the same dollar NPV as we previously calculated.

The important thing to recognize from our example is that the two capital budgeting procedures are actually the same and always give the same answer.[11] In this second approach, the fact that we are implicitly forecasting exchange rates is simply hidden. Even so, the foreign currency approach is computationally a little easier.

Unremitted Cash Flows

The previous example assumed that all after-tax cash flows from the foreign investment could be remitted to (paid out to) the parent firm. Actually, substantial differences can exist between the cash flows generated by a foreign project and the amount that can actually be remitted or repatriated to the parent firm.

A foreign subsidiary can remit funds to a parent in many ways, including the following:

1. Dividends.
2. Management fees for central services.
3. Royalties on the use of a trade name and patents.

However cash flows are repatriated, international firms must pay special attention to remittance because there may be current and future controls on remittances. Many governments are sensitive to the charge of being exploited by foreign national firms. In such cases, governments are tempted to limit the ability of international firms to remit cash flows. Funds that cannot currently be remitted are sometimes said to be blocked.

Concept Questions

1. What financial complications arise in international capital budgeting? Describe two procedures for estimating NPV in this case.
2. What are blocked funds?

---

[11] Actually, there will be a slight difference because we are using the approximate relationships. If we calculate the required return as $(1.10) \times (1 + .02) - 1 = 12.2\%$, we get exactly the same NPV. See the Mini Case at the end of the chapter for more detail.

21.6 | Financing International Projects

The Cost of Capital for International Firms

An important question for firms with international investments is whether the required return for international projects should be different from that of similar domestic projects. The answer to this question depends on:

1. Segmentation of the international financial market.
2. Foreign political risk of expropriation, foreign exchange controls, and taxes.

We save political risk for later discussion and focus here on the first point.

Suppose barriers prevented shareholders in Canada from holding foreign securities. If this were the case, the financial markets of different countries would be segmented. Further suppose that firms in Canada did not face the same barriers. In such a case, a firm engaging in international investing could provide indirect diversification for Canadian shareholders that they could not achieve by investing within Canada. This could lead to lowering of the risk premium on international projects.

On the other hand, if there were no barriers to international investing for shareholders, investors could get the benefit of international diversification for themselves by buying foreign securities. Then, the project cost of capital for Canadian firms would not depend on where the project was located.

To resolve this issue, researchers have compared the variance of purely domestic stock portfolios with international portfolios. The result is that international portfolios have lower variance. Because investors are not fully diversified internationally, firms can benefit from a lower cost of capital for international projects that provide diversification services for the firms' shareholders.[12]

International Diversification and Investors

As we just saw, there is evidence that international diversification by firms presently provides a service that investors cannot obtain themselves at reasonable cost. Holding foreign securities may subject investors to increased tax, trading, and information costs. Financial engineering is aiding investors in avoiding some of these costs. As a result, as investors diversify globally, the cost of capital advantage to firms is likely to decline.

standardandpoors.com

An *Index Participation* (IP) is a current example of a financially engineered vehicle for international diversification.[13] An IP on the Standard & Poor's 500 Stock Average, for example, gives an investor an asset that tracks this well-known U.S. market index. IPs are highly liquid, thus reducing trading costs. Information costs are also reduced since the holder need not research each of the 500 individual stocks that make up the index.

International diversification for Canadian investors is being made easier by the lowering of an important barrier. Effective 2001, the maximum allowable foreign holding for pension funds and Registered Retirement Savings Plans (RRSPs) increased to 30 percent. Increased demand is fuelled the development of new products to exploit this opportunity.

These and other financial engineering developments have helped to integrate the international financial market. Still, research suggests that local market effects influence prices of shares of firms with subsidiaries listed in different markets. For example, Royal Dutch Petroleum and Shell Transport are "twin" companies that merged in 1907. Each retains its own shares, Royal Dutch trading primarily in New York and Shell mainly trading in London. When the New York market goes up relative to London, researchers found that Royal Dutch shares rise relative to Shell even though there is no change in the companies' cash flows. All this means that, despite globalization of markets, some segmentation remains making international diversification worthwhile.[14]

---

[12] B. H. Solnik, "Why Not Diversify Internationally Rather than Domestically?" *Financial Analysts Journal*, July–August 1974.

[13] G. Axford and Y. Lin, "Surprise! Currency Risk Improves International Investment," *Canadian Treasury Management Review*, Royal Bank of Canada, March–April 1990.

[14] Our discussion is based on K.A. Froot and E.M.Dabora, "How are stock prices affected by the location of trade?" *Journal of Financial Economics 53*, August 1999, pp. 189–216. For more information on the effects of globalization on market correlation, see Dwarka Lakhan, "Increasing correlation reduces benefits of global diversification," *Canadian Treasurer*, August/September 2003 and G. Andrew Karolyi, "International stock market correlations," *Canadian Investment Review*, Summer 2001.

Sources of Short- and Intermediate-Term Financing

In raising short-term and medium-term cash, Canadian international firms have a choice between borrowing from a chartered bank at the Canadian rate or borrowing EuroCanadian (or other Eurocurrency) from a bank outside Canada through the Eurocurrency market.

Eurobanks
Banks that make loans and accept deposits in foreign currencies.

The Eurocurrency markets are the **Eurobanks** that make loans and accept deposits in foreign currencies. Most Eurocurrency trading involves the borrowing and lending of time deposits at Eurobanks. For example, suppose the Bank of Nova Scotia (BNS) receives a 30-day Eurodollar deposit from McCain in London. The BNS then makes a U.S. dollar-denominated loan to the Bank of Tokyo. Ultimately, the Bank of Tokyo makes a loan to a Japanese importer with invoices to pay in the United States. As our example shows, the Eurocurrency market is not a retail market. The customers are large corporations, banks, and governments.

scotiabank.com

One important characteristic of the Eurocurrency market is that loans are made on a floating rate basis. The interest rates are set at a fixed margin above the London Interbank Offered Rate (LIBOR) for the given period and currency involved. For example, if LIBOR is 1 percent and the margin is 0.5 percent for Eurodollar loans in a certain risk class, called a *tier*, the Eurodollar borrower pays an interest rate of 1.5 percent. Eurodollar loans have maturities ranging up to 10 years.

Securitization and globalization have produced alternatives to borrowing from a Eurobank.

Note Issuance Facility (NIF)
Large borrowers issue notes up to one year in maturity in the Euromarket. Banks underwrite or sell notes.

Under a **Note Issuance Facility (NIF)**, a large borrower issues short-term notes with maturities usually three to six months but ranging to one year.[15] Banks may underwrite NIFs or sell them to investors. In the latter case, where banks simply act as an agent, the Euronotes issued are called *Eurocommercial paper* (ECP). ECP is similar to domestic commercial paper but, because the Eurocredit market is not regulated, offers greater flexibility in available maturities and tax avoidance.

The drive to escape regulation (part of the regulatory dialectic introduced in Chapter 1) explains the attraction and growth of the Euromarkets. Eurocurrency markets developed to allow borrowers and banks to operate without regulation and taxes mainly in the United States. They offer borrowers an opportunity to tap large amounts of short-term funds quickly and at competitive rates. As banking regulations—for example capital rules—become tighter, alternatives to bank borrowing, such as NIFs, are growing and sharing the Euromarket with banks.

THE EUROBOND MARKET   Eurobonds are denominated in a particular currency and are issued simultaneously in the bond markets of several countries. The prefix *Euro* means the bonds are issued outside the countries in whose currencies they are denominated. For example, a French automobile firm issues 50,000 bonds with a face value of $1,000 (U.S.) each. When the bonds are issued, they are managed by London merchant bankers and listed on the London Stock Exchange.

Most Eurobonds are bearer bonds. The ownership of the bonds is established by possession of the bond. In contrast, foreign bonds (issued by foreign borrowers in a domestic capital market) are registered. This makes Eurobonds more attractive to Belgian dentists, investors who have a disdain for tax authorities.

Most issues of Eurobonds are arranged by underwriting. However, some Eurobonds are privately placed. Eurobonds appear as straight bonds, floating-rate notes, convertible bonds, zero coupon bonds, mortgage-backed bonds, and dual-currency bonds.

Concept Questions

1. Can firms reduce their risk and with it their costs of capital through diversifying with international projects?
2. What are the main sources of short and intermediate financing in Euro-markets?
3. Describe a Eurobond and its advantages over a foreign bond.

---

[15] Our discussion of NIFs draws on A. L. Melnik and S. E. Plaut, *The Short-Term Eurocredit Market* (New York: New York University Salomon Center, 1991), chap. 4.

21.7 | Exchange Rate Risk

exchange rate risk
The risk related to having international operations in a world where relative currency values vary.

Exchange rate risk is the natural consequence of international operations in a world where relative currency values move up and down. Managing exchange rate risk is an important part of international finance. As we discuss next, there are three different types of exchange rate risk or exposure: transaction exposure, economic exposure, and translation exposure.

Transaction Exposure

Transaction exposure is the day-to-day fluctuations in exchange rates that create short-run risks for international firms. Transaction exposure is also called short-run exposure. Most such firms have contractual agreements to buy and sell goods in the near future at set prices. When different currencies are involved, such transactions have an extra element of risk.

For example, imagine you are importing imitation pasta from Italy and reselling it in Canada under the Impasta brand name. Your largest customer has ordered 10,000 cases of Impasta. You place the order with your supplier today, but you won't pay until the goods arrive in 60 days. Your selling price is $6 per case. Your cost is 3.5 euros per case, and the exchange rate is currently EUR 0.65, so it takes 0.65 euros to buy $1.

At the current exchange rate, your cost in dollars from filling the order is EUR 3.5/0.65 = $5.38 per case, so your pre-tax profit on the order is 10,000 × ($6 − $5.38) = $6,200. However, the exchange rate in 60 days will probably be different, so your profit depends on what the future exchange rate turns out to be.

For example, if the rate goes to EUR 0.70, your cost is EUR 3.5/0.70 = $5 per case. Your profit goes to $10,000. If the exchange rate goes to, say, EUR 0.58, then your cost is EUR 3.5/0.58 = $6, and your profit is zero.

The short-run exposure in our example can be reduced or eliminated in several ways. The most obvious means of hedging is to enter into a forward exchange agreement to lock in an exchange rate. For example, suppose the 60-day forward rate is EUR 0.67. What is your profit if you hedge? What profit should you expect if you don't?

If you hedge, you lock in an exchange rate of EUR 0.67. Your cost in dollars is thus EUR 3.5/0.67 = $5.22 per case, so your profit is 10,000 × ($6 − $5.22) = $7,800. If you don't hedge, assuming that the forward rate is an unbiased predictor (in other words, assuming the UFR condition holds), you should expect the exchange rate to actually be EUR 0.67 in 60 days. You should expect to make $7,800.

Alternatively, if this is not feasible, you could simply borrow the dollars today, convert them into euros, and invest the euros for 60 days to earn some interest. From IRP, this amounts to entering into a forward contract.

Should the treasurer hedge or speculate? There are usually two reasons the treasurer should hedge:

1. In an efficient foreign exchange rate market, speculation is a zero NPV activity. Unless the treasurer has special information, nothing is gained from foreign exchange speculation.

2. The costs of hedging are not large. The treasurer can use forward contracts to hedge, and if the forward rate is equal to the expected spot, the costs of hedging are negligible.

MORE ADVANCED SHORT-TERM HEDGES   Of course, there are ways to hedge foreign exchange risk other than with forward contracts. Currency swaps, currency options, and other financially engineered products are taking considerable business away from the forward exchange market.[16] A currency swap is an arrangement between a borrower, a second borrower, called a **counterparty**, and a bank. The borrower and the counterparty each raise funds in a different currency and then swap liabilities. The bank guarantees the borrower's and counterparty's credit as in a bankers acceptance. The result is that the borrower obtains funds in the desired currency at a lower rate than for direct borrowing.

counterparty
Second borrower in currency swap. Counterparty borrows funds in currency desired by principal.

---

[16] Our discussion of currency swaps in practice draws on B. Critchley, "Explosion of New Products Cuts Foreign Currency Risk," *The Financial Post,* September 14, 1987. Further discussion of swaps is found in Chapter 24.

For example, in 1986 the federal government of Canada made an 80 billion yen bond issue and swapped part of it into U.S. dollars. The interest rate was six-month LIBOR and the ending liability was in U.S. dollars, not yen. The interest cost turned out to be 54 basis points below the cost of direct borrowing in the United States.

Currency options are similar to options on stock (discussed in Chapter 25) except the exercise price is an exchange rate.[17] They are exchange traded in the United States with exercise prices in various currencies including the Canadian dollar. Currency options can be exercised at any time before maturity. In the jargon of options, they are **American options**. A call option on the Canadian dollar gives the holder the right, but not the obligation, to buy CAD at a fixed exercise price in U.S.$. It increases in value as the CAD exchange rate in U.S.$ rises. A put option allows the holder to sell CAD at the exercise price. A put becomes more valuable when the CAD declines against the U.S.$.

The basic idea behind hedging with options is to take an options position opposite to the cash position. For this reason, hedge analysis starts by looking at the unhedged position of the business. For example, suppose an exporter expects to collect receivables totalling $1 million (U.S.) in 30 days. Suppose the present CAD exchange rate is $.96 (U.S.). If the rate remains at 96 cents, the exporter receives $1 million U.S./.96 = $1,041,667 (CAD) after 30 days. The exporter is at risk if the exchange rate rises so that the $1 million (U.S.) buys fewer Canadian dollars. For example, if the exchange rate rises to .98, the exporter receives only $1 million U.S./.98 = $1,020,408 (CAD). The loss of $21,258 comes out of profits.

Since the exporter loses if the exchange rate rises, buying call options is an appropriate hedge. Calls on the CAD increase in value if the exchange rate rises. The profit on the calls helps offset the loss on exchange. To implement this strategy, the exporter likely seeks expert advice on how many calls to buy and, more generally, the relative cost of hedging with options rather than with forwards.

Canadian sports teams like the Toronto Blue Jays and the Edmonton Oilers also face exchange rate risk. These organizations import talent, paying salaries in U.S. dollars while realizing most of their revenues from Canadian game attendance and television in Canadian dollars. The Jays estimate that a fluctuation of one cent in the Canadian dollar changes the profit for the franchise by about $700,000 over a year. The losses due to exchange rate differences are significant. Unlike the auto manufacturers discussed below, there is little a sports team can do to avoid this long-run exposure. In this case, hedging is likely the best policy.

Economic Exposure

Economic exposure is another term for long-run exposure. In the long run, the value of a foreign operation can fluctuate because of unanticipated changes in relative economic conditions. For example, imagine that we own a labour-intensive assembly operation located in another country to take advantage of lower wages. Through time, unexpected changes in economic conditions can raise the foreign wage levels to the point where the cost advantage is eliminated or even becomes negative.

Hedging long-run exposure is more difficult than hedging short-term risks. For one thing, organized forward markets don't exist for such long-term needs. Instead, the primary option that firms have is to try to match up foreign currency inflows and outflows. The same thing goes for matching foreign currency-denominated assets and liabilities. For example, a firm that sells in a foreign country might try to concentrate its raw material purchases and labour expense in that country. That way, the dollar values of its revenues and costs will move up and down together. Probably the best examples of this type of hedging are the so-called transplant auto manufacturers such as BMW, Honda, Mercedes, and Toyota, which now build locally a substantial portion of the cars they sell in the United States and Canada, thereby obtaining some degree of immunization against exchange rate movements. There can still be problems with this strategy. For example, many cars are built in Canada and exported to the United States.

Similarly, a firm can reduce its long-run exchange rate risk by borrowing in the foreign country. Fluctuations in the value of the foreign subsidiary's assets will then be at least partially offset by changes in the value of the liabilities.

American options
A call or put option that can be exercised on or before its expiration date.

oilers.nhl.com
bluejays.com

bmw.com
world.honda.com
mercedes-benz.com
toyota.com

---

[17] See Chapter 25 for a thorough introduction to options. Our discussion of currency options simplifies the description by discussing options on currency. In practice, options are written against currency futures contracts.

For example, the turmoil in the Asian currency markets in 1997 caught many companies napping, but not Avon. The U.S. cosmetics manufacturer had a significant exposure in Asia, with sales there comprising about 20 percent of the company's worldwide volume. To protect itself against currency fluctuations, Avon produced nearly all of its products in the country where they were sold, and purchased nearly all related raw materials in the same country as well. That way, their production costs and revenues were in the same currency. In addition, operating loans were denominated in the currency of the country where production was located to tie interest rates and payments to the local currency. All of this protects profits in the foreign market, but Avon still had the exposure related to translating profits back into dollars. To reduce that exposure, the company began having its foreign operating units remit earnings weekly rather than monthly to minimize "translation" risk, the subject of our next section.

Translation Exposure

When a Canadian company calculates its accounting net income and EPS for some period, it must translate everything into dollars. This can create some problems for the accounts when there are significant foreign operations. In particular, two issues arise:

1. What is the appropriate exchange rate to use for translating each statement of financial position account?
2. How should statement of financial position accounting gains and losses from foreign currency translation be handled?

To illustrate the accounting problem, suppose we started a small foreign subsidiary in Lilliputia a year ago. The local currency is the gulliver, abbreviated GL. At the beginning of the year, the exchange rate was GL 2 = CAD1, and the statement of financial position in gullivers looked like this:

Assets	GL 1,000	Liabilities	GL 500
		Equity	500

At 2 gullivers to the dollar, the beginning statement of financial position in dollars was:

Assets	$500	Liabilities	$250
		Equity	250

Lilliputia is a quiet place, and nothing at all actually happened during the year. As a result, net income was zero (before consideration of exchange rate changes). However, the exchange rate did change to 4 gullivers = $1 purely because the Lilliputian inflation rate is much higher than the Canadian inflation rate.

Since nothing happened, the accounting ending statement of financial position in gullivers is the same as the beginning one. However, if we convert it to dollars at the new exchange rate, we get:

Assets	$250	Liabilities	$125
		Equity	125

Notice that the value of the equity has gone down by $125, even though net income was zero. Despite the fact that absolutely nothing really happened, there is a $125 accounting loss. How to handle this $125 loss has been a controversial accounting question.

One obvious and consistent way to handle this loss is simply to report the loss on the parent's statement of comprehensive income. During periods of volatile exchange rates, this kind of treatment can dramatically impact an international company's reported EPS. This is purely an accounting phenomenon; even so, such fluctuations are disliked by financial managers.

The current compromise approach to translation gains and losses is based on rules set out in Canadian Institute of Chartered Accountants (CICA) S. 1651. The rules divide a firm's foreign subsidiaries into two categories: integrated and self-sustaining. For the most part, the rules require that all assets and liabilities must be translated from the subsidiary's currency into the parent's currency using the exchange rate that currently prevails.[18] Because Canadian accountants consolidate the financial statements of subsidiaries more than 50 percent owned by the parent firm, translation gains and losses are reflected on the statement of comprehensive income of the parent company.

For a self-sustaining subsidiary, any translation gains and losses that occur are accumulated in a special account within the shareholders' equity section of the parent company's statement of financial position. This account might be labelled something like "unrealized foreign exchange gains (losses)." These gains and losses are not reported on the statement of comprehensive income. As a result, the impact of translation gains and losses is not recognized explicitly in net income until the underlying assets and liabilities are sold or otherwise liquidated.

Managing Exchange Rate Risk

For a large multinational firm, the management of exchange rate risk is complicated by the fact that many different currencies may be involved in many different subsidiaries. It is very likely that a change in some exchange rate benefits some subsidiaries and hurts others. The net effect on the overall firm depends on its net exposure.

For example, suppose a firm has two divisions: Division A buys goods in Canada for dollars and sells them in Britain for pounds. Division B buys goods in Britain for pounds and sells them in Canada for dollars. If these two divisions are of roughly equal size in their inflows and outflows, the overall firm obviously has little exchange rate risk.

In our example, the firm's net position in pounds (the amount coming in less the amount going out) is small, so the exchange rate risk is small. However, if one division, acting on its own, were to start hedging its exchange rate risk, the overall firm's exchange risk would go up. The moral of the story is that multinational firms have to be conscious of the overall position that the firm has in a foreign currency. For this reason, exchange risk management is probably best handled on a centralized basis.

Concept Questions

1. What are the different types of exchange rate risk?
2. How can a firm hedge short-run exchange rate risk? Long-run exchange rate risk?

21.8 | Political and Governance Risks

political risk
Risk related to changes in value that arise because of political actions.

Political risk refers to changes in value that arise as a consequence of political actions. This is not purely a problem faced by international firms. For example, changes in Canadian or provincial tax laws and regulations may benefit some Canadian firms and hurt others, so political risk exists nationally as well as internationally. For example, the possibility of Quebec separation was seen by many as a political risk affecting firms located in the province. When firms announced plans to relocate to Toronto, stock market reaction was usually positive.[19]

Some countries do have more political risk than others, however. In such cases, the extra political risk may lead firms to require higher returns on overseas investments to compensate for the risk that funds will be blocked, critical operations interrupted, and contracts abrogated. For example, the rate of return required for an overseas investment made in "A" rated Chile would be less than the rate of return required for a foreign investment made in "B" rated Argentina. In the most extreme case, the possibility of outright confiscation may be a concern in countries with relatively unstable political environments.

---

[18] The rules also define the current exchange rate differently for the types of subsidiaries. An integrated subsidiary uses the exchange rate observed on the last day of its fiscal year. For a self-sustaining subsidiary, the exchange rate prescribed is the average rate over the year. For detailed discussion of CICA 1650, see A. Davis and G. Pinches, *Canadian Financial Management*, 4th ed. (Toronto, Ontario: Prentice-Hall, 2000).

[19] Our source here is: H. Bhabra, U. Lel, and D. Tirtiroglu, "Stock Market's Reaction to Business Relocations: Canadian Evidence," *Canadian Journal of Administrative Sciences*, December 2002, vol. 19, number 4, pp. 346–358.

Political risk also depends on the nature of the business; some businesses are less likely to be confiscated because they are not particularly valuable in the hands of a different owner. An assembly operation supplying subcomponents that only the parent company uses would not be an attractive takeover target, for example. Similarly, a manufacturing operation that requires the use of specialized components from the parent is of little value without the parent company's cooperation.

Natural resource developments, such as copper mining or oil drilling, are just the opposite. Once the operation is in place, much of the value is in the commodity. The political risk for such investments is much higher for this reason. Also, the issue of exploitation is more pronounced with such investments, again increasing the political risk.

Political risk can be hedged in several ways, particularly when confiscation or nationalization is a concern. As we stated earlier, insurance against political risk is available from Export Development Canada. Further, the use of local financing, perhaps from the government of the foreign country in question, reduces the possible loss because the company can refuse to pay on the debt in the event of unfavourable political activities. Based on our previous discussion, structuring the operation so that it requires significant parent company involvement to function is another way some firms try to reduce political risk.

At the other extreme, some companies avoid the implicit threats in the methods just discussed while trying to be good corporate citizens in the host country. This approach is an international application of the view of the corporation as responsible to shareholders and stakeholders that we presented in Chapter 1.

Corporate Governance Risk

With the internationalization of cross-border portfolios, and the global financial crisis, investors are looking more carefully at corporate governance of companies. For example, the rapid fall from grace of Satyam Computer Services—one of India's foremost IT outsourcing companies—has raised some important concerns around corporate governance for international investing in emerging markets. Rules-based governance systems promote greater transparency of information in markets and greater protection of shareholders. Good corporate governance can enhance the attractiveness of a country's financial markets relative to another. At the global level, initiatives such as the International Corporate Governance Network's code of practice in relation to investors' governance responsibilities are working towards strengthening corporate governance, improving transparency, and restoring investor confidence. For example, evidence also suggests that corporate governance plays an important role in shaping the market value of Korean public companies.[20]

Concept Questions

1. What is political risk?
2. What are some ways of hedging political risks?
3. Why is sound corporate governance important for companies?

---

[20] Kim, Woochan, Black, Bernard S., and Jang, Hasung, Does Corporate Governance Predict Firms' Market Values? Evidence from Korea (2006). Post-publication version, published in *Journal of Law, Economics, and Organization*, Vol. 22, No. 2, Fall 2006; ECGI—Finance Working Paper No. 86/2005; KDI School of Pub Policy & Management Paper No. 02-04; McCombs Research Paper Series No. 02-05; Stanford Law and Economics Olin Working Paper No. 237; U of Texas law, Law and Econ Research Paper No. 26. Available at SSRN: ssrn.com/abstract=311275

21.9 | SUMMARY AND CONCLUSIONS

The international firm has a more complicated life than the purely domestic firm. Management must understand the connection between interest rates, foreign currency exchange rates, and inflation. It must also become aware of a large number of different financial market regulations and tax systems. This chapter is intended to be a concise introduction to some of the financial issues that come up in international investing.

Our coverage was necessarily brief. The main topics we discussed include:

1. Some basic vocabulary. We briefly defined some exotic terms such as *LIBOR* and *Eurodollar*.

2. The basic mechanics of exchange rate quotations. We discussed the spot and forward markets and how exchange rates are interpreted.

3. The fundamental relationships between international financial variables:

   a. Absolute and relative purchasing power parity (PPP).

   b. Interest rate parity (IRP).

   c. Unbiased forward rates (UFR).

   Absolute purchasing power parity states that $1 should have the same purchasing power in each country. This means that an orange costs the same whether you buy it in Montreal or in Tokyo.

   Relative purchasing power parity means the expected percentage change in exchange rates between the currencies of two countries is equal to the difference in their inflation rates.

   Interest rate parity implies that the percentage difference between the forward exchange rate and the spot exchange rate is equal to the interest rate differential. We showed how covered interest arbitrage forces this relationship to hold.

   The unbiased forward rates condition indicates that the current forward rate is a good predictor of the future spot exchange rate.

4. International capital budgeting. We showed that the basic foreign exchange relationships imply two other conditions:

   a. Uncovered interest parity.

   b. Generalized Fisher effect.

   By invoking these two conditions, we learned how to estimate NPVs in foreign currencies and how to convert foreign currencies into dollars to estimate NPV in the usual way.

5. Exchange rate and political risk. We described the various types of exchange rate risk and discussed some commonly used approaches to managing the effect of fluctuating exchange rates on the cash flows and value of the international firm. We also discussed political risk and some ways of managing exposure to it.

Key Terms

American options (page 625)
counterparty (page 624)
cross-rate (page 607)
Eurobanks (page 623)
Eurobond (page 607)
Eurocurrency (page 607)
exchange rate (page 609)
exchange rate risk (page 624)
Export Development Canada (EDC) (page 607)
foreign bonds (page 607)
foreign exchange market (page 608)
forward exchange rate (page 611)
forward trade (page 611)

generalized Fisher effect (GFE) (page 618)
gilts (page 607)
interest rate parity (IRP) (page 617)
London Interbank Offer Rate (LIBOR) (page 607)
Note Issuance Facility (NIF) (page 623)
political risk (page 627)
purchasing power parity (PPP) (page 613)
spot exchange rate (page 611)
spot trade (page 611)
swaps (page 608)
unbiased forward rates (UFR) (page 617)
uncovered interest parity (UIP) (page 618)

Chapter Review Problems and Self-Test

21.1   Relative Purchasing Power Parity The inflation rate in Canada is projected at 6 percent per year for the next several years. The German inflation rate is projected to be 2 percent during that time. The exchange rate is currently EUR 0.6. Based on relative PPP, what is the expected exchange rate in two years?

21.2   Covered Interest Arbitrage The spot and 12-month forward rates on the Swiss franc are CHF 1.8 and CHF 1.7, respectively. The risk-free interest rate in Canada is 8 percent, and the risk-free rate in Switzerland is 5 percent. Is there an arbitrage opportunity here? How would you exploit it?

Answers to Self-Test Problems

21.1   From relative PPP, the expected exchange rate in two years, $E[S_2]$ is:

$$E[S_2] = S_0 \times [1 + (h_G - h_{CDN})]^2$$

where h_G is the European inflation rate. The current exchange rate is EUR 0.6, so the expected exchange rate is:

$$\begin{aligned} E[S_2] &= EUR\ 0.6 \times [1 + (.02 - .06)]^2 \\ &= EUR\ 0.6 \times .96^2 \\ &= EUR\ 0.55 \end{aligned}$$

21.2   From interest rate parity, the forward rate should be (approximately):

$$\begin{aligned} F_1 &= S_0 \times [1 + (R_{FC} - R_{CDN})] \\ &= 1.8 \times [1 + .05 - .08] \\ &= 1.75 \end{aligned}$$

Since the forward rate is actually CHF 1.7, there is an arbitrage opportunity.

To exploit the arbitrage, we first note that dollars are selling for CHF 1.7 each in the forward market. From IRP, this is too cheap because they should be selling for CHF 1.75. So we want to arrange to buy dollars with Swiss francs in the forward market. To do this, we can:

1. Today: Borrow, say, $10 million for 12 months. Convert it to CHF 18 million in the spot market, and forward contract at CHF 1.7 to convert it back to dollars in one year. Invest the CHF 18 million at 5 percent.

2. In one year: Your investment has grown to CHF 18 × 1.05 = CHF 18.9 million. Convert this to dollars at the rate of CHF 1.7 = $1. You have CHF 18.9 million/1.7 = $11,117,647. Pay off your loan with 8 percent interest at a cost of $10 million × 1.08 = $10,800,000 and pocket the difference of $317,647.

Concepts Review and Critical Thinking Questions

1.   **(LO2)** Suppose the exchange rate for the Swiss franc is quoted as CHF 1.50 in the spot market and CHF 1.53 in the 90-day forward market.

    a.   Is the dollar selling at a premium or a discount relative to the franc?

    b.   Does the financial market expect the franc to strengthen relative to the dollar? Explain.

    c.   What do you suspect is true about relative economic conditions in Canada and Switzerland?

2.   **(LO3)** Suppose the rate of inflation in the European Union will run about 3 percent higher than the Canadian inflation rate over the next several years. All other things being the same, what will happen to the euro versus dollar exchange rate? What relationship are you relying on in answering?

3.   **(LO2, 3)** The exchange rate for the Australian dollar is currently AUD1.15. This exchange rate is expected to rise by 10 percent over the next year.

    a.   Is the Australian dollar expected to get stronger or weaker?

    b.   What do you think about the relative inflation rates in Canada and Australia?

    c.   What do you think about the relative nominal interest rates in Canada and Australia? Relative real rates?

4.   **(LO1)** Which of the following most accurately describes a Yankee bond?

    a.   A bond issued by General Motors in Japan with the interest payable in U.S. dollars.

    b.   A bond issued by General Motors in Japan with the interest payable in yen.

    c.   A bond issued by Toyota in the United States with the interest payable in yen.

    d.   A bond issued by Toyota in the United States with the interest payable in dollars.

    e.   A bond issued by Toyota worldwide with the interest payable in dollars.

5.   **(LO2)** Are exchange rate changes necessarily good or bad for a particular company?

6.   **(LO5, 6)** Duracell International confirmed in October 1995 that it was planning to open battery-manufacturing plants in China and India. Manufacturing in these countries allows Duracell to avoid import duties of between 30 and 35 percent that have made alkaline batteries prohibitively expensive for some consumers. What additional advantages might Duracell see in this proposal? What are some of the risks to Duracell?

7.   **(LO3)** Given that many multinationals based in many countries have much greater sales outside their domestic markets than within them, what is the particular relevance of their domestic currency?

8.   **(LO3)** Are the following statements true or false? Explain why.

    a.   If the general price index in Great Britain rises faster than that in Canada, we would expect the pound to appreciate relative to the dollar.

    b.   Suppose you are a European machine tool exporter and you invoice all of your sales in foreign currency. Further suppose that the European Union monetary authorities begin to undertake an expansionary monetary policy. If it is certain that the easy money policy will result in higher inflation rates in the European Union relative to those in other countries, then you should use the forward markets to protect yourself against future losses resulting from the deterioration in the value of the euro.

c. If you could accurately estimate differences in the relative inflation rates of two countries over a long period of time, while other market participants were unable to do so, you could succesCHFully speculate in spot currency markets.

9. (LO5) Some countries encourage movements in their exchange rate relative to those of some other country as a short-term means of addressing foreign trade imbalances. For each of the following scenarios, evaluate the impact the announcement would have on a Canadian importer and a Canadian exporter doing business with the foreign country.

a. Officials in Ottawa announce that they are comfortable with a rising euro relative to the dollar.

b. British monetary authorities announce that they feel the pound has been driven too high by currency speculators relative to the U.S. dollar.

c. The Argentinian government announces that it will devalue the peso in an effort to improve its economy.

d. The Brazilian government announces that it will print billions of new reals and inject them into the economy, in an effort to reduce the country's 40 percent unemployment rate.

10. (LO3) We discussed five international capital market relationships: relative PPP, IRP, UFR, UIP, and the generalized Fisher effect. Which of these would you expect to hold most closely? Which do you think would be most likely to be violated?

Questions and Problems

Basic
(Questions 1–13)

1. **Using Exchange Rates (LO2)** Take a look back at Figure 21.1 to answer the following questions:
   a. If you have CAD100, how many euros can you get?
   b. How much is one euro worth?
   c. If you have 5 million euros, how many dollars do you have?
   d. Which is worth more, an Australian dollar or a Singapore dollar?
   e. Which is worth more, an Indian rupee or a Chinese renminbi?
   f. How many Canadian dollars can you get for a euro? What do you call this rate?
   g. Per unit, what is the most valuable currency of those listed? The least valuable?

2. **Using the Cross-Rate (LO2)** Use the information in Figure 21.1 to answer the following questions:
   a. Which would you rather have, $100 or £100? Why?
   b. Which would you rather have, 100 Swiss francs (CHF) or £100? Why?
   c. What is the cross-rate for Swiss francs in terms of British pounds? For British pounds in terms of Swiss francs?

3. **Forward Exchange Rates (LO2)** Use the information in Figure 21.1 to answer the following questions:
   a. What is the six-month forward rate for the Japanese yen in yen per Canadian dollar? Is the yen selling at a premium or a discount? Explain.
   b. What is the three-month forward rate for Canadian dollars in U.S. dollars per Canadian dollar? Is the dollar selling at a premium or a discount? Explain.
   c. What do you think will happen to the value of the Canadian dollar relative to the yen and the U.S. dollar, based on the information in the figure? Explain.

4. **Using Spot and Forward Exchange Rates (LO2)** Suppose the spot exchange rate for the Canadian dollar/US dollar is CAD1.05 and the six-month forward rate is CAD1.07.
   a. Which is worth more, a U.S. dollar or a Canadian dollar?
   b. Assuming absolute PPP holds, what is the cost in the United States of an Elkhead beer if the price in Canada is CAD2.50? Why might the beer actually sell at a different price in the United States?
   c. Is the U.S. dollar selling at a premium or a discount relative to the Canadian dollar?
   d. Which currency is expected to depreciate in value?
   e. Which country do you think has higher interest rates—the United States or Canada? Explain.

5. **Cross-Rates and Arbitrage (LO2)** Suppose the Japanese yen exchange rate is ¥80 = $1, and the British pound exchange rate is £1 = $1.58.
   a. What is the cross-rate in terms of yen per pound?
   b. Suppose the cross-rate is ¥129 = £1. Is there an arbitrage opportunity here? If there is, explain how to take advantage of the mispricing. What would your arbitrage profit be per dollar used?

6. **Interest Rate Parity (LO3)** Use Figure 21.1 to answer the following questions: Suppose interest rate parity holds, and the current six-month risk-free rate in Canada is 1.7 percent. What must the six-month risk-free rate be in Great Britain? In Japan? In European Union?

7. **Interest Rates and Arbitrage (LO3)** The treasurer of a major Canadian firm has $30 million to invest for three months. The interest rate in Canada is .24 percent per month. The interest rate in Great Britain is .29 percent per month. The spot exchange rate is £.631, and the three-month forward rate is £.633. Ignoring transaction costs, in which country would the treasurer want to invest the company's funds? Why?

8. **Inflation and Exchange Rates (LO3)** Suppose the current exchange rate for the Polish zloty is PLN2.86. The expected exchange rate in three years is PLN 2.94. What is the difference in the annual inflation rates for Canada and Poland over this period? Assume that the anticipated rate is constant for both countries. What relationship are you relying on in answering?

9. **Exchange Rate Risk (LO5)** Suppose your company imports computer motherboards from Singapore. The exchange rate is given in Figure 21.1. You have just placed an order for 30,000 motherboards at a cost to you of 233.5 Singapore dollars each. You will pay for the shipment when it arrives in 90 days. You can sell the motherboards for $195 each. Calculate your profit if the exchange rate goes up or down by 10 percent over the next 90 days. What is the break-even exchange rate? What percentage rise or fall does this represent in terms of the Singapore dollar versus the Canadian dollar?

10. **Exchange Rates and Arbitrage (LO3)** Suppose the spot and six-month forward rates on the Norwegian krone are NOK 5.78 and NOK 5.86, respectively. The annual risk-free rate in Canada is 3.8 percent, and the annual risk-free rate in Norway is 5.7 percent.

    a. Is there an arbitrage opportunity here? If so, how would you exploit it?

    b. What must the six-month forward rate be to prevent arbitrage?

11. **The Generalized Fisher Effect (LO3)** You observe that the inflation rate in Canada is 2.6 percent per year and that T-bills currently yield 3.4 percent annually. What do you estimate the inflation rate to be in:

    a. Australia, if short-term Australian government securities yield 4 percent per year?

    b. The United States, if short-term U.S. government securities yield 7 percent per year?

    c. Taiwan, if short-term Taiwanese government securities yield 9 percent per year?

12. **Spot versus Forward Rates (LO2)** Suppose the spot and three-month forward rates for the yen are ¥79.12 and ¥78.64, respectively.

    a. Is the yen expected to get stronger or weaker?

    b. What would you estimate is the difference between the annual inflation rates of Canada and Japan?

13. **Expected Spot Rates (LO2)** Suppose the spot exchange rate for the Hungarian forint is HUF 204.32. The inflation rate in Canada will be 1.9 percent per year. It will be 4.5 percent in Hungary. What do you predict the exchange rate will be in one year? In two years? In five years? What relationship are you using?

Intermediate (Questions 14–16)

14. **Capital Budgeting (LO4)** Gorbochevsky Equipment has an investment opportunity in Europe. The project costs EUR 12 million and is expected to produce cash flows of EUR 1.8 million in year 1, EUR 2.6 million in year 2, and EUR 3.5 million in year 3. The current spot exchange rate is $1.36/EUR; the current risk-free rate in Canada is 2.3 percent, compared to that in Europe of 1.8 percent. The appropriate discount rate for the project is estimated to be 13 percent, the Canadian cost of capital for the company. In addition, the subsidiary can be sold at the end of three years for an estimated EUR 8.9 million. What is the NPV of the project?

 15. **Capital Budgeting (LO4)** You are evaluating a proposed expansion of an existing subsidiary located in Switzerland. The cost of the expansion would be CHF 21 million. The cash flows from the project would be CHF 5.9 million per year for the next five years. The dollar required return is 12 percent per year, and the current exchange rate is CHF 1.09. The going rate on Eurodollars is 5 percent per year. It is 4 percent per year on Euroswiss.

    a. What do you project will happen to exchange rates over the next five years?

    b. Based on your answer in (a), convert the projected franc flows into dollar flows and calculate the NPV.

    c. What is the required return on franc cash flows? Based on your answer, calculate the NPV in francs and then convert to dollars.

16. **Translation Exposure (LO5)** Gumtako International has operations in Arrakis. The statement of financial position for this division in Arrakeen solaris shows assets of 27,000 solaris, debt in the amount of 11,000 solaris, and equity of 16,000 solaris.

    a. If the current exchange ratio is 1.50 solaris per dollar, what does the statement of financial position look like in dollars?

    b. Assume that one year from now the statement of financial position in solaris is exactly the same as at the beginning of the year. If the exchange rate is 1.60 solaris per dollar, what does the statement of financial position look like in dollars now?

    c. Rework part (b) assuming the exchange rate is 1.41 solaris per dollar.

Challenge (Questions 17–18)

17. **Translation Exposure (LO5)** In the previous problem, assume the equity increases by 1,250 solaris due to retained earnings. If the exchange rate at the end of the year is 1.54 solaris per dollar, what does the statement of financial position look like?

18. **Using the Generalized Fisher Effect (LO3, 4)** From our discussion of the Fisher effect in Chapter 7, we know that the actual relationship between a nominal rate, R, a real rate, r, and an inflation rate, h, can be written as:

$$1 + r = (1 + R)/(1 + h)$$

This is the *domestic* Fisher effect.

    a. What is the non-approximate form of the generalized Fisher effect?

    b. Based on your answer in (a), what is the exact form for UIP? (*Hint:* Recall the exact form of IRP and use UFR.)

    c. What is the exact form for relative PPP? (*Hint:* Combine your previous two answers.)

    d. Recalculate the NPV for the Kihlstrom drill bit project (discussed in Section 21.5) using the exact forms for UIP and the generalized Fisher effect. Verify that you get precisely the same answer either way.

MINI CASE

Tuxedo Air Goes International

Mark Taylor and Jack Rodwell, the owners of Tuxedo Air, have been in discussions with a light aircraft dealer in Italy about selling the company's planes in Europe. Tracy Jordon, the dealer, wants to add Tuxedo Air to his current retail line. Tracy has told Mark and Jack that he feels the retail sales will be approximately €5 million per month. All sales will be made in euros, and Tracy will retain 5 percent of retail sales as a commission, which will be paid in euros. Because the planes will be customized to order, the first sales will take place in one month. Tracy will pay Tuxedo Air for the order 90 days after it is filled. This payment schedule will continue for the length of the contract between the two companies.

Mark and Jack are confident the company can handle the extra volume with its existing facilities, but they are unsure about the potential financial risks of selling their planes in Europe. In their discussion with Tracy, they found that the current exchange rate is $1.35/EUR. At the current exchange rate, the company would spend 80 percent of the sales on production costs. This number does not reflect the sales commission paid to Tracy.

Mark and Jack have decided to ask Ed Cowan, the company's financial analyst, to prepare an analysis of the proposed international sales. Specifically, they ask Ed to answer the following questions:

Questions

1. What are the pros and cons of the international sales? What additional risks will the company face?

2. What happens to the company's profits if the dollar strengthens? What if the dollar weakens?

3. Ignoring taxes, what are Tuxedo Air's projected gains or losses from this proposed arrangement at the current exchange rate of $1.35/EUR? What happens to profits if the exchange rate changes to $1.25/EUR? At what exchange rate will the company break even?

4. How could the company hedge its exchange rate risk? What are the implications for this approach?

5. Taking all factors into account, should the company pursue the international sales further? Why or why not?

Internet Application Questions

The following web-links are related to equities that trade on foreign exchanges in the form of depository receipts. Trading on foreign exchanges allows the issuing firm to raise capital internationally, and benefit from increased scrutiny by foreign analysts.

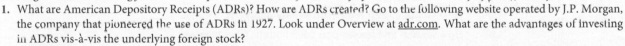

1. What are American Depository Receipts (ADRs)? How are ADRs created? Go to the following website operated by J.P. Morgan, the company that pioneered the use of ADRs in 1927. Look under Overview at adr.com. What are the advantages of investing in ADRs vis-à-vis the underlying foreign stock?

2. The Bank of New York Mellon is an important player in sponsoring ADRs. Go to its website at adrbnymellon.com and search for Hitachi (CUSIP: 433578507) ADR. What is the price of Hitachi ADR on the NYSE? Explain the meaning of RATIO on the ADR listings page. If 1 USD = ¥100, what do you think is the price of Hitachi's shares on the Tokyo Stock Exchange (in ¥)? You can find Hitachi's share prices on the TSE's website at tinx.com.

3. Go to the following website operated by Citibank, another big player in the ADR creation market: www.citiadr.idmanagedsolutions.com/www/front_page.idms. Explain how the dividend payment process works for ADRs. As a Canadian investor, do you face more foreign currency risk when you buy Hitachi's ADRs on the NYSE, or Hitachi's shares on the Tokyo Stock Exchange?

4. Go to marketvector.com and find the exchange rates section. Is the Canadian dollar expected to appreciate or depreciate compared to the U.S. dollar over the next six months? What is the difference in the annual inflation rates for the United States and Canada over this period? Assume that the anticipated rate is constant for both countries. What relationship are you relying on in your answers?

5. Go to the *Financial Times* site at ft.com, and find the currency section under the "Markets" link. Find the current exchange rate between the U.S. dollar and the euro. You can also locate interest rate information at this site. Find the Canadian dollar and euro interest rates. What must the one-year forward rate be to prevent arbitrage? What principle are you relying on in your answer?

6. Infosys Ltd., an Indian IT consulting and outsourcing services giant, has American Depository Receipts listed on the Nasdaq. Many ADRs listed on U.S. exchanges are for fractional shares. In the case of Infosys, one ADR is equal to one registered share. Find the information for Infosys by logging on to the Google Finance website (google.com/finance) and using the ticker symbol "INFY."

   a. Click on the "Historical Prices" link and find Infosys' closing price for May 2012. Assume the exchange rate on that day was $/₹53.73 and Infosys shares traded for ₹2,453. Is there an arbitrage opportunity available? If so, how would you take advantage of it?

   b. What exchange rate is necessary to eliminate the arbitrage opportunity available in part (a)?

LEASING

In March 2011, Bombardier Aerospace, the world's third largest civil aircraft manufacturer, headquartered in Montreal, signed an $8 billion aircraft-leasing agreement with ICBC Financial Leasing Company Limited. One of the largest leasing agreements Bombardier has ever signed, this deal was designed to support China's growing aviation market. As we will see in this chapter, leasing is just another form of financing for businesses and, for reasons we will discuss, the aircraft industry is particularly suited to leasing rather than buying.

Leasing is a way businesses finance plant, property, and equipment. Just about any asset that can be purchased can be leased, and there are many good reasons for leasing. For example, when we take vacations or business trips, renting a car for a few days is a convenient thing to do. After all, buying a car and selling it a week later would be a great nuisance. We discuss additional reasons for leasing in the sections that follow.

Learning Objectives ▶

After studying this chapter, you should understand:

LO1 The basics of a lease and the different types of leases.

LO2 How accounting rules and tax laws define financial leases.

LO3 The cash flows from leasing.

LO4 How to conduct a lease-versus-buy analysis.

LO5 How lessee and lessor can both benefit from leasing.

LO6 The difference between good and bad reasons for leasing.

aircanada.com
cfla-acfl.ca

Although corporations do both short-term leasing and long-term leasing, this chapter is primarily concerned with long-term leasing, where long-term typically means more than five years. As we discuss in greater detail shortly, leasing an asset on a long-term basis is much like borrowing the needed funds and simply buying the asset. Thus, long-term leasing is a form of financing much like long-term debt. When is leasing preferable to long-term borrowing? This is the question we seek to answer in this chapter.[1]

22.1 | Leases and Lease Types

lessee
The user of an asset in a leasing agreement. Lessee makes payments to lessor.

lessor
The owner of an asset in a leasing agreement. Lessor receives payments from the lessee.

A lease is a contractual agreement between two parties: the **lessee** and the **lessor**. The lessee is the user of the equipment; the lessor is the owner. Typically, a company first decides on the asset that it needs. Then it must decide how to finance the asset. If the firm decides to lease, it then negotiates a lease contract with a lessor for use of that asset. The lease agreement establishes that the lessee has the right to use the asset and, in return, must make periodic payments to the lessor, the owner of the asset. The lessor is usually either the asset's manufacturer or an independent leasing company. If the lessor is an independent leasing company, it must buy the asset from a

---

[1] Our discussion of lease valuation is drawn, in part, from Chapter 22 of S.A. Ross, R.W. Westerfield, J.F. Jaffe, and G.S. Roberts, *Corporate Finance*, 6th Canadian ed. (Whitby, Ontario: McGraw-Hill Ryerson, 2011), which contains a more comprehensive treatment and discusses some subtle, but important, issues not covered here.

manufacturer. The lessor then delivers the asset to the lessee, and the lease goes into effect. Some lessors play both roles. GE Capital, for example, leases GE's own products and also leases aircraft to Air Canada.

Leasing versus Buying

As far as the lessee is concerned, it is the use of the asset that is important, not necessarily who has title to it. One way to obtain the use of an asset is to lease it. Another way is obtain outside financing and buy it. Thus, the decision to lease or buy amounts to a comparison of alternative financing arrangements for the use of an asset.

You may think of leasing analysis as an extension of the capital budgeting decision. The lessee has already done capital budgeting analysis and found that buying the asset has a positive NPV. Leasing analysis investigates whether acquiring the use of the asset through leasing is better still.

Figure 22.1 compares leasing and buying. The lessee, Canadian Enterprises, might be a hospital, a law firm, or any other firm that uses computers. The lessor is an independent leasing company that purchased the computer from a manufacturer such as Hewlett-Packard Company (HP). Leases of this type, where the leasing company purchases the asset from the manufacturer, are called *direct leases*. Of course, HP might choose to lease its own computers, and many companies have set up wholly owned subsidiaries called *captive finance companies* to lease out their products.[2]

gecapital.ca
hp.com

FIGURE 22.1

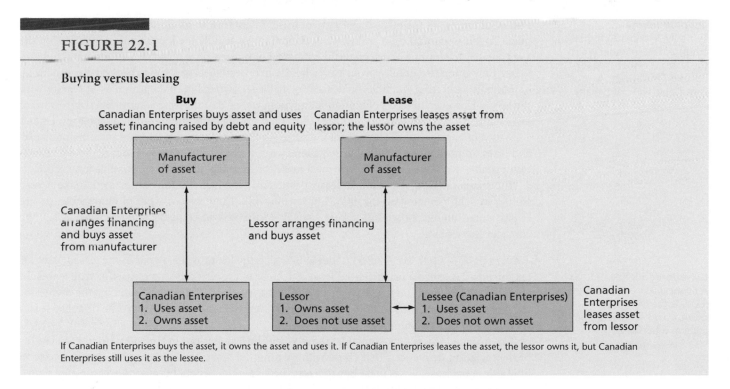

Buying versus leasing

If Canadian Enterprises buys the asset, it owns the asset and uses it. If Canadian Enterprises leases the asset, the lessor owns it, but Canadian Enterprises still uses it as the lessee.

As shown in Figure 22.1, Canadian Enterprises ends up using the asset either way. The key difference is that in the case of buying, Canadian Enterprises arranges the financing, purchases the asset, and holds title to the asset. In the case of leasing, the leasing company arranges the financing, purchases the asset, and holds title to it.

operating lease
Usually a shorter-term lease where the lessor is responsible for insurance, taxes, and upkeep. Often cancellable on short notice.

Operating Leases

Years ago, a lease where the lessee received an equipment operator along with the equipment was called an **operating lease.** Today, an operating lease (or service lease) is difficult to define precisely, but this form of leasing has several important characteristics.

---

[2] Captive finance companies (or subsidiaries) may do a number of other things, such as purchase the parent company's accounts receivable. Ford Credit and GE Capital are examples of captive finance companies. We discuss captive finance companies in Chapter 20.

First, with an operating lease, the payments received by the lessor are usually not enough to fully recover the cost of the asset. A primary reason is that operating leases are often relatively short-term. In such cases, the life of the lease can be much less than the economic life of the asset. For example, if you lease a car for two years, the car has a substantial residual value at the end of the lease, and the lease payments you make would pay off only a fraction of the original cost of the car.

A second characteristic is that an operating lease frequently requires that the lessor maintain the asset. The lessor is also responsible for any taxes or insurance. Of course, these costs would be passed on, at least in part to the lessee in the form of higher lease payments.

The third, and perhaps most interesting, feature of an operating lease is the cancellation option. This option gives the lessee the right to cancel the lease contract before the expiration date. If the option to cancel is exercised, the lessee returns the equipment to the lessor and ceases to make payments. The value of a cancellation clause depends on whether technological and/or economic conditions are likely to make the value of the asset to the lessee less than the value of the future lease payments under the lease. This was seen during the financial crisis of 2008, when the value of assets declined rapidly making the lease agreements less attractive.

To leasing practitioners, these three characteristics constitute an operating lease. However, as we see shortly, accountants use the term in a somewhat different way.

Financial Leases

financial leases
Typically, a longer-term, fully amortized lease under which the lessee is responsible for upkeep. Usually not cancellable without penalty.

Financial leases are the other major type of lease. In contrast to an operating lease, the payments made under a financial lease are usually sufficient to cover fully the lessor's cost of purchasing the asset and pay the lessor a return on the investment. For this reason, a financial lease is sometimes said to be a fully amortized or full-payout lease whereas an operating lease is said to be partially amortized.

For both operating and financial leases, formal legal ownership of the leased asset resides with the lessor. However, in terms of economic function, we see that the lessee enjoys the risk/reward of ownership in a financial lease. Operating leases, on the other hand, are more like a rental agreement.

With a financial lease, the lessee (not the lessor) is usually responsible for insurance, maintenance, and taxes. Importantly, a financial lease generally cannot be cancelled, at least not without a significant penalty. In other words, the lessee must make the lease payments or face possible legal action.

The characteristics of a financial lease, particularly the fact it is fully amortized, make it very similar to debt financing, so the name is a sensible one. Three special types of financial leases are of particular interest, *tax-oriented leases, sale and leaseback* agreements, and *leveraged leases*. We consider these next.

tax-oriented lease
A financial lease in which the lessor is the owner for tax purposes. Also called a true lease or a tax lease.

TAX-ORIENTED LEASES   A lease in which the lessor is the owner of the leased asset for tax purposes is called a **tax-oriented lease**. Such leases are also called tax leases or true leases. In contrast, a *conditional sales agreement lease* is not a true lease. Here, the "lessee" is the owner for tax purposes. Conditional sales agreement leases are really just secured loans. The financial leases we discuss in this chapter are all tax leases.

Tax-oriented leases make the most sense when the lessee is not in a position to use tax credits or depreciation deductions that come with owning the asset. By arranging for someone else to hold title, a tax lease passes these benefits on. The lessee can benefit because the lessor may return a portion of the tax benefits to the lessee in the form of lower lease costs.

SALE AND LEASEBACK AGREEMENTS   A sale and leaseback occurs when a company sells an asset it owns to another firm and immediately leases it back. In a sale and leaseback, two things happen:

1. The lessee receives cash from the sale of the asset.
2. The lessee continues to use the asset.

sale and leaseback
A financial lease in which the lessee sells an asset to the lessor and then leases it back.

An example of a **sale and leaseback** occurred in July 2009 when Air Canada arranged a sale and leaseback of three Boeing 777-300ER aircraft. The purchaser was GE Capital Aviation Centres institution and the transaction proceeds were $122 million providing Air Canada with immediate cash during the financial crises. Further examples include Canadian universities and hospitals that set up sale-leaseback deals for library books and medical equipment. With a sale and leaseback, the lessee may have the option of repurchasing the leased assets at the end of the lease. Tax changes have restricted sale-leasebacks in recent years.

leveraged lease
A financial lease where the lessor borrows a substantial fraction of the cost of the leased asset.

LEVERAGED LEASES   A **leveraged lease** is a tax-oriented lease involving three parties: a lessee, a lessor, and a lender. A typical arrangement might go as follows:

1. The lessee selects the asset, gets the value of using the asset, and makes the periodic lease payments.
2. The lessor usually puts up no more than 40 to 50 percent of the financing, is entitled to the lease payments, has title to the asset, and pays interest to the lenders.
3. The lenders supply the remaining financing and receive interest payments. Thus, the arrangement on the right side of Figure 22.1 would be a leveraged lease if the bulk of the financing were supplied by creditors.

The lenders in a leveraged lease typically use a non-recourse loan. This means the lender cannot turn to the lessor in case of a default. However, the lender is protected in two ways:

1. The lender has a first lien on the asset.
2. The lender may actually receive the lease payments from the lessee. The lender deducts the principal and interest due, and forwards whatever is left to the lessor.

> ### Concept Questions
>
> 1. What are the specific differences between an operating lease and a financial lease?
> 2. What is a tax-oriented lease?
> 3. What is a sale and leaseback agreement?

22.2 | Accounting and Leasing

Before current accounting rules were in place, leasing was frequently called *financing off the statement of financial position* (also referred to as off balance sheet financing). As the name implies, a firm could arrange to use an asset through a lease and not disclose the existence of the lease contract on the statement of financial position. Lessees only had to report information on leasing activity in the footnotes of their financial statements.

Of course, this meant firms could acquire the use of a substantial number of assets and incur a substantial long-term financial commitment through financial leases while not disclosing the impact of these arrangements in their financial statements. Operating leases, being cancellable at little or no penalty, do not involve a firm financial commitment. So operating leases did not generate much concern about complete disclosure. As a result, the accounting profession wanted to distinguish clearly between operating and financial leases to ensure that the impact of financial leases was included in the financial statements.

cica.ca

Under current Canadian Institute of Chartered Accountants rules for lease accounting, all financial leases (called *capital leases*) must be capitalized. These rules originated under Canadian GAAP and continue under IFRS. This requirement means that the present value of the lease payments must be calculated and reported along with debt and other liabilities on the right side of the lessee's statement of financial position.[3] The same amount must be shown as an asset on the statement of financial position. Operating leases are not disclosed on the statement of financial position. We discuss exactly what constitutes a financial or operating lease for accounting purposes next.

The accounting implications of current lease accounting rules are illustrated in Table 22.1. Imagine a firm that has $100,000 in assets and no debt, implying that the equity is also $100,000. The firm needs a truck that costs $100,000 (it's a big truck) that it can lease or buy. The top of the table shows the statement of financial position assuming that the firm borrows the money and buys the truck.

If the firm leases the truck, one of two things happen: If the lease is an operating lease, the statement of financial position looks like the one in the centre of the table. In this case, neither the asset (the truck) nor the liability (the lease payments) appear. If the lease is a capital (financial)

---

[3]The statement of comprehension income is also affected. The asset created is amortized over the lease life and reported income is adjusted downward. Current accounting rules are in CICA 3065.

lease, the statement of financial position would look like the one at the bottom of the table, where the truck is shown as an asset and the present value of the lease payments is shown as a liability.

As we discussed earlier, it is difficult, if not impossible, to give a precise definition of what constitutes a financial or operating lease. For accounting purposes under IFRS, a lease is declared to be a financial lease, and must therefore be disclosed, if at least one of the following criteria is met:

1. The lease transfers ownership of the property to the lessee by the end of the term of the lease.
2. The lessee has an option to purchase the asset at a price below fair market value (bargain purchase price option) when the lease expires.
3. The lease term is 75 percent or more of the estimated economic life of the asset.
4. The present value of the lease payments is at least 90 percent of the fair market value of the asset at the start of the lease.
5. The leased assets are of a specialised nature such that only the lessee can use them without major modifications being made.

If one or more of the five criteria is met, the lease is a capital lease; otherwise, it is an operating lease for accounting purposes.

A firm might be tempted to try and cook the books by taking advantage of the somewhat arbitrary distinction between operating leases and capital leases. Suppose a trucking firm wants to lease the $100,000 truck in our example in Table 22.1. The truck is expected to last for 15 years. A (perhaps unethical) financial manager could try to negotiate a lease contract for 10 years with lease payments having a present value of $89,000. These terms would get around criteria 3 and 4. If the other criteria are similarly circumvented, the arrangement will be an operating lease and will not show up on the statement of financial position.

TABLE 22.1

Leasing and the statement of financial position

1.	**Initial statement of financial position (the company buys a $100,000 truck with debt)**			
	Truck	$100,000	Debt	$100,000
	Other assets	100,000	Equity	100,000
	Total assets	$200,000	Total debt plus equity	$200,000
2.	**Operating lease (the company has an operating lease for the truck)**			
	Truck	$ 0	Debt	$ 0
	Other assets	100,000	Equity	100,000
	Total assets	$100,000	Total debt plus equity	$100,000
3.	**Capital (financial) lease (the company has a capital lease for the truck)**			
	Assets under capital lease	$100,000	Obligations under capital lease	$100,000
	Other assets	100,000		100,000
	Total assets	$200,000	Equity	$200,000
			Total debt plus equity	

In the first case, a $100,000 truck is purchased with debt. In the second case, an operating lease is used; no statement of financial position entries are created. In the third case, a capital (financial) lease is used; the lease payments are capitalized as a liability, and the leased truck appears as an asset.

There are several alleged benefits to hiding financial leases. One of the advantages to keeping leases off the statement of financial position has to do with fooling financial analysts, creditors, and investors. The idea is that if leases are not on the statement of financial position, they will not be noticed.

Financial managers who devote substantial effort to keeping leases off the statement of financial position are probably wasting time. Of course, if leases are not on the statement of financial position, traditional measures of financial leverage, such as the ratio of total debt to total assets, understate the true degree of financial leverage. As a consequence, the statement of financial position appears stronger than it really is, but it seems unlikely that this type of manipulation could mislead many people.

Nonetheless, firms do try to hide leases. For example, a controversial type of lease, known as a synthetic lease, has come to be widely used. The details are a little complex; in essence, a company arranges for a separate entity to purchase an asset (often a building) and then lease that asset back to the company. If the deal is properly structured, the company is considered the owner of the property for tax purposes, but for accounting purposes, the transaction is classified as an operating lease. Faced with investor criticism of this practice, some firms, such as Krispy Kreme Doughnuts, have announced that they will no longer engage in synthetic leasing.

Having said all of this, there are some reasons why a firm might reasonably try to come in under the radar of the accounting lease test. For example, if a firm's managers are told that capital spending is frozen, an operating lease may still be an option. Alternatively, a firm might face a restriction on additional borrowing (a loan covenant, perhaps). A financial lease counts as debt, but an operating lease does not.

Concept Questions

1. For accounting purposes, what constitutes a capital lease?
2. How are capital leases reported?

22.3 | Taxes, Canada Revenue Agency (CRA), and Leases

cra-arc.gc.ca

The lessee can deduct lease payments for income tax purposes if the lease is qualified by Canada Revenue Agency (CRA). The tax shields associated with lease payments are critical to the economic viability of a lease, so CRA guidelines are an important consideration. Tax rules on leasing have changed considerably in the last few years and further changes may occur. The discussion that follows gives you a good idea of rules in force at the time of writing.

Essentially, CRA requires that a lease be primarily for business purposes and not merely for tax avoidance. In particular, CRA is on the lookout for leases that are really conditional sales agreements in disguise. The reason is that, in a lease, the lessee gets a tax deduction on the full lease payment. In a conditional sales agreement, only the interest portion of the payment is deductible. When CRA detects one or more of the following, it disallows the lease:

1. The lessee automatically acquires title to the property after payment of a specified amount in the form of rentals.
2. The lessee is required to buy the property from the lessor during or at the termination of the lease.
3. The lessee has the right during or at the expiration of the lease to acquire the property at a price less than fair market value.

These rules also apply to sale-leaseback agreements. CRA auditors rule that a sale-leaseback is really a secured loan if they find one of the three terms in the sale-leaseback agreement.

Once leases are qualified for tax purposes, lessors still must be aware of further tax regulations limiting their use of CCA tax shields on leased assets. Current regulations allow lessors to deduct CCA from leasing income only. Any unused CCA tax shields cannot be passed along to other companies owned by the same parent holding company.

Concept Questions

1. Why is CRA concerned about leasing?
2. What are some of the standards CRA uses in evaluating a lease?

22.4 | The Cash Flows from Leasing

To begin our analysis of the leasing decision, we need to identify the relevant cash flows. The first part of this section illustrates how this is done. A key point, and one to watch for, is that taxes are a very important consideration in a lease analysis.

The Incremental Cash Flows

Consider the business decision facing TransCanada Distributors, a distribution firm that runs a fleet of company cars for its sales staff. Business has been expanding and the firm needs 50 additional cars to provide basic transportation in support of sales. The type of car required can be purchased wholesale for $10,000. TransCanada has determined that each car can be expected to generate an additional $6,000 per year in added sales for the next five years.

TransCanada has a corporate tax rate (combined federal and provincial) of 40 percent. The cars would qualify for a CCA rate of 40 percent (as rental cars) and, due to the hard-driving habits of TransCanada's sales staff, the cars would have no residual value after five years. Using all this information, a TransCanada financial analyst determines that acquiring the 50 cars is a capital budgeting decision with a positive NPV. At this point, TransCanada receives an offer from Financial Leasing Company to lease the cars to TransCanada for lease payments of $2,500 per year for each car over the five-year period. Lease payments are made at the beginning of the year. With the lease, TransCanada would remain responsible for maintenance, insurance, and operating expenses.

Susan Smart has been asked to compare the direct incremental cash flows from leasing the cars to the cash flows associated with buying them. The first thing she realizes is that, because TransCanada has the cars either way, the $6,000 saving is realized whether the cars are leased or purchased. Thus, this cost saving, and any other operating costs or revenues, can be ignored in the analysis because they are not incremental.

On reflection, Smart concludes that there are only three important cash flow differences between leasing and buying:[4]

1. If the cars are leased, TransCanada must make a lease payment of $2,500 each year. However, lease payments are fully tax deductible, so there is a tax shield of $1,000 on each lease payment. The after-tax lease payment is $2,500 − $1,000 = $1,500. This is a cost of leasing instead of buying.[5]

2. If the cars are leased, TransCanada does not have to spend $10,000 apiece today to buy them. This is a benefit to leasing.

3. If the cars are leased, TransCanada does not own them and cannot depreciate them for tax purposes.

TABLE 22.2

Tax shield on CCA for car	Year	UCC	CCA	Tax Shields
	0	$5,000	$2,000	$ 800
	1	8,000	3,200	1,280
	2	4,800	1,920	768
	3	2,880	1,152	461
	4	1,728	691	276
	5	1,037		415

Table 22.2 shows the CCA and UCC schedule for one car.[6] Notice that CRA's half-year rule means that the eligible UCC is only $5,000 when the car is put in use in Year 0. Table 22.2 also shows the tax shield on CCA for each year. For example, in Year 0, the tax shield is $2,000 × .40 = $800. The tax shields for Years 1–4 are calculated in the same way. In Year 5, the car is scrapped for a zero salvage value. We assume that the asset pool is closed at this time, so there is a tax shield on the

---

[4] There is a fourth consequence that we do not discuss here. If the car has a non-trivial salvage value and we lease, we give up that salvage value. This is another cost of leasing instead of buying that we consider later.

[5] Lease payments are made at the beginning of the year as shown in Table 22.3. Firms pay taxes later but our analysis ignores this difference for simplicity. Taxes paid later in the year should be discounted.

[6] To keep the lease and purchase alternatives comparable, we assume here that TransCanada buys the cars at the beginning of period 0.

terminal loss of $1,037 \times .40 = $415.[7] All these tax shields are lost to TransCanada if it leases, so they are a cost of leasing.

TABLE 22.3

Incremental cash flows for TransCanada from leasing one car instead of buying

	Year					
	0	1	2	3	4	5
Investment	$10,000					
Lease payment	−2,500	−$2,500	−$2,500	−$2,500	$2,500	
Payment shield	1,000	1,000	1,000	1,000	1,000	
Forgone tax shield	−800	−1,280	−768	−461	−276	−$415
Total cash flow	$ 7,700	−$2,780	−$2,268	−$1,961	−$1,776	−$415

The cash flows from leasing instead of buying are summarized in Table 22.3. Notice that the cost of the car shows up with a positive sign in Year 0. This is a reflection of the fact that TransCanada saves $10,000 by leasing instead of buying.

A NOTE ON TAXES   Susan Smart has assumed that TransCanada can use the tax benefits of the CCA allowances and the lease payments. This may not always be the case. If TransCanada were losing money, it would not pay taxes and the tax shelters would be worthless (unless they could be shifted to someone else). As we mentioned, this is one circumstance under which leasing may make a great deal of sense. If this were the case, the relevant lines in Table 22.3 would have to be changed to reflect a zero tax rate. We return to this point later.

Concept Questions

1. What are the cash flow consequences of leasing instead of buying?
2. Explain why the $10,000 in Table 22.3 is a positive number.

22.5 | Lease or Buy?

From our discussion thus far, Smart's analysis comes down to this: If TransCanada Distributors leases instead of buying, it saves $10,000 today because it avoids having to pay for the car, but it must give up the cash outflows detailed in Table 22.3 in exchange. We now must decide whether getting $10,000 today and then paying back these cash flows is a good idea.

A Preliminary Analysis

Suppose TransCanada were to borrow $10,000 today and promise to make after-tax payments of the cash flows shown in Table 22.3 over the next five years. This is essentially what the firm does when it leases instead of buying. What interest rate would TransCanada be paying on this "loan"? Going back to Chapter 9, we need to find the unknown rate that solves the following equation:

$$0 = 7,700 - \frac{2,780}{1+i} - \frac{2,268}{(1+i)^2} - \frac{1,961}{(1+i)^3} - \frac{1,776}{(1+i)^4} - \frac{415}{(1+i)^5}$$

The equation may be solved by trial and error using Microsoft Excel 2010 or any compatible spreadsheet to show that the discount rate is 7.8 percent after-tax.

The cash flows of our hypothetical loan are identical to the cash flows from leasing instead of borrowing, and what we have illustrated is that when TransCanada leases the car, it effectively arranges financing at an after-tax rate of 7.8 percent. Whether this is a good deal or not depends

---

[7] If the pool were continued, the remaining UCC of $1,037 would be depreciated to infinity as explained in Chapter 2. We consider this later.

on what rate TransCanada would pay if it simply borrowed the money. For example, suppose the firm can arrange a five-year loan with its bank at a rate of 11 percent. Should TransCanada sign the lease or should it go with the bank?

Because TransCanada is in a 40 percent tax bracket, the after-tax interest rate would be $11 \times (1 - .40) = 6.6$ percent. This is less than the 7.8 percent implicit after-tax rate on the lease. In this particular case, TransCanada is better off borrowing the money because it gets a better rate.

We have seen that TransCanada should buy instead of lease. The steps in our analysis can be summarized as follows:

1. Calculate the incremental after-tax cash flows from leasing instead of borrowing.
2. Use these cash flows to calculate the implicit after-tax interest rate on the lease.
3. Compare this rate to the company's after-tax borrowing cost and choose the cheaper source of financing.

The most important thing about our discussion thus far is that in evaluating a lease, the relevant rate for the comparison is the company's after-tax borrowing rate. The fundamental reason is that the alternative to leasing is long-term borrowing, so the after-tax borrowing rate on such borrowing is the relevant benchmark.

THREE POTENTIAL PITFALLS   There are three potential problems with the implicit rate on the lease that we calculated: First, this rate can be interpreted as the internal rate of return (IRR) on the decision to lease instead of buy, but doing so can be confusing. To see why, notice that the IRR from leasing is 7.8 percent, which is greater than TransCanada's after-tax borrowing cost of 6.6 percent. Normally, the higher the IRR the better, but we decided that leasing was a bad idea here. The reason is that the cash flows are not conventional; the first cash flow is positive and the rest are negative, which is just the opposite of the conventional case (see Chapter 9 for a discussion). With this cash flow pattern, the IRR represents the rate we pay, not the rate we earn, so the lower the IRR the better.

A second, and related, potential pitfall is that we calculated the advantage of leasing instead of borrowing. We could have done just the opposite and come up with the advantage to borrowing instead of leasing. If we did this, the cash flows would be the same, but the signs would be reversed. The IRR would be the same. Now, however, the cash flows are conventional, so we interpret the 7.8 percent IRR as saying that borrowing is better.

The third potential problem is that our implicit rate is based on the net cash flows of leasing instead of borrowing. There is another rate that is sometimes calculated that is just based on the lease payments. If we wanted to, we could note that the lease provides $10,000 in financing and requires five payments of $2,500 each. It is tempting to determine an implicit rate based on these numbers, but the resulting rate is not meaningful for making lease-versus-buy decisions because it ignores the CCA tax shields. It should not be confused with the implicit return on leasing instead of borrowing and buying.

Perhaps because of these potential confusions, the IRR approach we have outlined thus far is not as widely used as an NPV-based approach that we describe next.

NPV Analysis

Now that we know the relevant rate for evaluating a lease-versus-buy decision is the firm's after-tax borrowing cost, an NPV analysis is straightforward. We simply discount the cash flows in Table 22.3 back to the present at TransCanada's borrowing rate of 6.6 percent as follows:

$$NPV = \$7,700 - \frac{\$2,780}{(1.066)} - \frac{\$2,268}{(1.066)^2} - \frac{\$1,961}{(1.066)^3} - \frac{\$1,776}{(1.066)^4} - \frac{\$415}{(1.066)^5} = -\$199$$

net advantage to leasing (NAL)
The NPV of the decision to lease an asset instead of buying it.

The NPV from leasing instead of buying is −$199, verifying our earlier conclusion that leasing is a bad idea. Once again, notice the signs of the cash flows; the first is positive, the rest are negative. The NPV that we have computed here is often called the **net advantage to leasing** and abbreviated NAL. Surveys indicate that the NAL approach is the most popular means of lease analysis in the business world.

A Misconception

In our lease-versus-buy analysis, it looks as if we ignored the fact that if TransCanada borrows $10,000 to buy the car, it has to repay the money with interest. In fact, we reasoned that if TransCanada leased the car, it would be better off by $10,000 today because it wouldn't have to pay for the car. It is tempting to argue that if TransCanada borrowed the money, it wouldn't have to come up with the $10,000. Instead, the firm would make a series of principal and interest payments over the next five years. This observation is true, but not particularly relevant. The reason is that if Trans-Canada borrows $10,000 at an after-tax cost of 6.6 percent, the present value of the after-tax loan payments is simply $10,000, no matter what the repayment schedule is (assuming that the loan is fully amortized). Thus, we could write down the after-tax loan repayments and work with these, but it would just be extra work for no gain. (See Problem 11 at the end of the chapter for an example.)

EXAMPLE 22.1: Lease Evaluation

In our TransCanada example, suppose the firm is able to negotiate a lease payment of $2,000 per year. What would be the NPV of the lease in this case?

Table 22.4 shows the new cash flows. You can verify that the NPV of the lease (net advantage to leasing) at 6.6 percent is now a substantial $1,126.

TABLE 22.4

Revised NAL spreadsheet	Year					
	0	**1**	**2**	**3**	**4**	**5**
Investment	$10,000					
Lease payment	−2,000	−$2,000	−$2,000	−$2,000	−$2,000	
Payment shield	800	800	800	800	800	
Forgone tax shield	−800	−1,280	−768	161	−276	−$415
Total cash flow	$ 8,000	−$2,480	−$1,968	−$1,661	−$1,476	−$415
NAL	$ 1,126					

Asset Pool and Salvage Value

The TransCanada example where the asset pool is assumed to close and the salvage value of the vehicle is assumed to be zero at the end of four years is simplistic. In reality, this may occur in some circumstances but in most situations the asset pool will remain open and the car will have some resale value. To illustrate, we assume that the vehicle will have a $500 resale value.

Assuming that the asset pool will not close after the lease is complete, Table 22.5 shows the incremental cash flows for TransCanada leaving out the forgone tax shield.

TABLE 22.5

Incremental cash flows for TransCanada from leasing one car instead of buying	**0**	**1**	**2**	**3**	**4**
Investment	$10,000				
Lease payment	−2,500	−$2,500	−$2,500	−$2,500	−$2,500
Payment shield	1,000	1,000	1,000	1,000	1,000
Salvage value					−500
	$ 8,500	−$1,500	−$1,500	−$1,500	−$2,000

The present value of these payments, using the 6.6 percent discount rate calculated earlier is

$$PV = \$8,500 - \frac{\$1,500}{1.066} - \frac{\$1,500}{(1.066)^2} - \frac{\$1,500}{(1.066)^3} - \frac{\$2,000}{(1.066)^4} = \$2,986$$

Assuming that the salvage value for the vehicle is $500 at the end of four years, the present value of the CCA tax shield is[8]

$$
\begin{aligned}
PV &= \frac{[CdT_c]}{k+d} \times \frac{[1+0.5k]}{1+k} - \frac{SdT_c}{k+d} \times \frac{1}{(1+k)^n} \\
&= \frac{(\$10,000)(0.40)(0.40)}{0.066+0.40} \times \frac{[1+0.5(0.066)]}{1+0.066} - \frac{(\$500)(0.40)(0.40)}{0.066+0.40} \times \frac{1}{(1+0.066)^4} \\
&= \$3,194
\end{aligned}
$$

These revised calculations show that the net present value of leasing one car instead of buying amounts to $2,986 − $3,194 = −$208 when the vehicle has a salvage value of $500. Given that the NPV is negative, it would be better to buy the vehicle than to lease. The result is quite close to our previous answer where it was also better to buy than lease.

We can summarize our calculations in the following modified formula for the Net Advantage to Leasing (NAL):

$$NAL = Investment - PV \text{ (after-tax lease payments)} - PVCCATS - PV \text{ (Salvage)}$$

There is a risk associated with the estimation of salvage value and therefore a higher rate could be applied.

Concept Questions

1. What is the relevant discount rate for evaluating whether or not to lease an asset? Why?
2. Explain how to go about a lease-versus-buy analysis.

22.6 | A Leasing Paradox

We previously looked at the lease-versus-buy decision from the perspective of the potential lessee, TransCanada Distributors. We now turn things around and look at the lease from the perspective of the lessor, Financial Leasing Company. The cash flows associated with the lease from the lessor's perspective are shown in Table 22.6.[9] First, the lessor must buy each car for $10,000, so there is a $10,000 outflow today. Next, Financial Leasing depreciates the car at a CCA rate of 40 percent to obtain the CCA tax shields shown. Finally, the lessor receives a lease payment of $2,500 each year on which it pays taxes at a 40 percent tax rate. The after-tax lease payment received is $1,500.

TABLE 22.6

Cash flows to the lessor

	Year					
	0	**1**	**2**	**3**	**4**	**5**
Investment	−$10,000					
Lease payment	2,500	$2,500	$2,500	$2,500	$2,500	
Payment shield	−1,000	−1,000	−1,000	−1,000	−1,000	
Forgone tax shield	−800	1,280	768	461	276	$415
Total cash flow	−$ 7,700	$2,780	$2,268	$1,961	$1,776	$415
NAL	$ 199					

---

[8] Refer to Chapter 10 for the details on the formula.

[9] To keep things simple, we go back to our original case where salvage was zero and the asset pool closed.

What we see is that the cash flows to Financial Leasing (the lessor) are exactly the opposite of the cash flows to TransCanada Distributers (the lessee). This makes perfect sense because Financial Leasing and TransCanada are the only parties to the transaction, and the lease is a zero-sum game. In other words, if the lease has a positive NPV to one party, it must have a negative NPV to the other. Financial Leasing hopes that TransCanada will do the deal because the NPV would be +$199, just what TransCanada would lose.

We seem to have a paradox. In any leasing arrangement, one party must inevitably lose (or both parties exactly break even). Why would leasing occur? We know that leasing is very important in the business world, so the next section describes some factors that we have omitted thus far from our analysis. These factors can make a lease attractive to both parties.

EXAMPLE 22.2: It's the Lease We Can Do

In our TransCanada example, a lease payment of $2,500 makes the lease unattractive to TransCanada and a lease payment of $2,000 makes the lease very attractive. What payment would leave TransCanada indifferent to leasing or not leasing?

TransCanada is indifferent when the NPV from leasing is zero. For this to happen, the present value of the cash flows from leasing instead of buying would have to be −$10,000. From our previous efforts, we know the answer is to set the payments somewhere between $2,500 and $2,000. To find the exact payment, we use our spreadsheet as shown in Table 22.7. It turns out the NPV of leasing is zero for a payment of $2,425.

TABLE 22.7

Indifference lease payments	Year					
	0	**1**	**2**	**3**	**4**	**5**
Investment	$ 10,000					
Lease payment	−2,425	−$2,425	−$2,425	−$2,425	−$2,425	
Payment shield	970	970	970	970	970	
Forgone tax shield	800	−1,280	−768	−461	−276	−$415
Total cash flow	$ 7,745	−$2,735	−$2,223	−$1,916	−$1,731	−$415
NAL	$ 0					

Concept Questions

1. Why do we say that leasing is a zero-sum game?
2. What paradox does the first question create?

Resolving the Paradox

A lease contract is not a zero-sum game between the lessee and lessor when their effective tax rates differ. In this case, the lease can be structured so that both sides benefit. Any tax benefits from leasing can be split between the two firms by setting the lease payments at the appropriate level, and the shareholders of both firms benefit from this tax transfer arrangement. The loser is Canada Revenue Agency.

This works because a lease contract swaps two sets of tax shields. The lessor obtains the CCA tax shields due to ownership. The lessee receives the tax shield on lease payments made. In a full-payout lease, the total dollar amounts of the two sets of tax shields may be roughly the same, but the critical difference is the timing. CCA tax shields are accelerated deductions reducing the tax burden in early years. Lease payments, on the other hand, reduce taxes by the same amount in every year. As a result, the ownership tax shields often have a greater present value provided the firm is fully taxed.

The basic logic behind structuring a leasing deal makes a firm in a high tax bracket want to act as the lessor. Low tax (or untaxed) firms are lessees because they are not able to use the tax advantages of ownership, such as CCA and debt financing. These ownership tax shields are worth less to the lessee because the lessee faces a lower tax rate or may not have enough taxable income to absorb the accelerated tax shields in the early years.

Overall, less tax is paid by the lessee and lessor combined and this tax savings occurs sooner rather than later. The lessor gains on the tax side; the lessee may lose but the amount of any loss is less than the lessor gains. To make the lease attractive, the lessor must pass on some of the tax savings in the form of lower lease payments. In the end, the lessor gains by keeping part of the tax savings, the lessee gains through a lower lease payment, and CRA pays for both gains through a reduction in tax revenue.

To see how this would work in practice, recall the example of Section 22.4 and the situation of Financial Leasing. The value of the lease it proposed to TransCanada was $199. The value of the lease to TransCanada was exactly the opposite −$199. Since the lessor's gains came at the expense of the lessee, no deal could be arranged. However, if TransCanada pays no taxes and the lease payments are reduced to $2,437 from $2,500, both Financial Leasing and TransCanada find there is positive NPV in leasing.

To see this, we can rework Table 22.3 with a zero tax rate. This would be the case when Trans-Canada has enough alternate tax shields to reduce taxable income to zero for the foreseeable future.[10] In this case, notice that the cash flows from leasing are simply the lease payments of $2,437 because no CCA tax shield is lost and the lease payment is not tax deductible. The cash flows from leasing are thus:

	Year					
	0	1	2	3	4	5
Cost of car	$10,000					
Lease payment	−2,437	−$2,437	−$2,437	−$2,437	−$2,437	0
Cash flow	$ 7,563	−$2,437	−$2,437	−$2,437	−$2,437	0

The value of the lease for TransCanada is

$$\text{NAL} = \$7,563 - \$2,437 \times (1 - 1/1.11^4)/.11$$
$$= \$2.34$$

which is positive. Notice that the discount rate here is 11 percent because TransCanada pays no taxes; in other words, this is both the pre-tax and the after-tax rate.

From Table 22.8, the value of the lease to Financial Leasing can be worked out as +$36 using the after-tax discount rate of 6.6 percent.

TABLE 22.8

Revised cash flows to lessor

	Year					
	0	1	2	3	4	5
Investment	−$10,000					
Lease payment	2,437	$2,437	$2,437	$2,437	$2,437	
Payment shield	−974	−974	−974	−974	−974	
CCA tax shield	800	1,280	768	461	276	$415
Total cash flow	−$ 7,737	$2,743	$2,231	$1,924	$1,739	$415
NPV lessor	$ 36					

As a consequence of different tax rates, the lessee (TransCanada) gains $2.34, and the lessor (Financial Leasing) gains $36. CRA loses. What this example shows is that the lessor and the lessee can gain if their tax rates are different. The lease contract allows the lessor to take advantage

---

[10] Strictly speaking, the UCC of the cars would be carried on the books until the firm is able to claim CCA. However, the present value of the CCA tax shield would be low; so for the sake of simplicity, we ignore it here.

of the CCA and interest tax shields that cannot be used by the lessee. CRA experiences a net loss of tax revenue, and some of the tax gains to the lessor are passed on to the lessee in the form of lower lease payments.

Leasing and Capital Budgeting

Recall that we began the TransCanada car-leasing example by saying that the firm had already made a capital budgeting decision to acquire the 50 cars. Our analysis focused on whether to buy the cars or to lease them. For this reason we ignored the added sales generated by the car acquisition because they would be realized whether the cars were purchased or leased. We focused on what was incremental in developing the formula for the NPV of the decision to lease instead of buy. We called this the net advantage to leasing or NAL. NAL measures the value creation from leasing rather than buying the asset.

In our initial analysis, both TransCanada and the lessor, Financial Leasing, had the same tax rate and, as a result, NAL was −$199. This meant that if TransCanada leased the cars, the NPV of the capital budgeting decision would be $199 lower than if the firm bought the cars.

We then modified the example to recognize that, in practice, leasing deals are often designed to take benefit from a situation in which the lessor faces a higher tax rate than the lessee. In particular, we showed that when TransCanada pays no tax and Financial Leasing faces the same 40 percent tax rate as earlier, the NALs are positive to both parties. This occurs because the loser is CRA.

From a capital budgeting perspective, in this realistic case, the NAL to TransCanada of $2.34 tells us that the NPV of acquiring one car increases by this amount by using lease financing.

A major financial decision for many students is whether to buy or lease a car. We went to Industry Canada's Office of Consumer Affairs at ic.gc.ca/eic/site/oca-bc.nsf/eng/ca01851.html to find a lease-versus-buy calculator. We analyzed a new car purchase for $24,000 with a 60-month loan and no down payment. To lease the car for four years requires monthly taxes of $48.01 for an Ontario resident. The calculator assumes that a buyer would keep the car for eight years (the national average) and compares ownership to two four-year leases. According to Consumer Affairs buying the car is the better financial decision.[11]

EXAMPLE 22.3: Car Leasing

| CALCULATOR | TIPS | DEFINITIONS | APPLICATION NOTES |

Purchase

Province of Residence	Ontario (ON)
Purchase Price (excluding tax) [?]	$ 24,000
Freight and PDI? [?]	$ 1,000
Financing Rate [?]	6.25 %
Finance Term [?]	60 months
Tax Rate [?]	13 %
Amount To Be Financed [?]	$ 28,750
Trade-in Value of Current Vehicle [?]	$ 0.00
Down Payment [?]	$ 0.00
Monthly Payment [?]	$ 559.17
Total Interest Charges [?]	$ 4,799.88

(continued)

---

[11] For a general discussion of auto leasing that reaches the same conclusion see: J. Beltrame, "Leasing a car is the worst financial option for most," *Canadian Press*, March 2, 2012.

Compare With

Leasing Option 1 - Two Leases (8 years) ◉
Leasing Option 2 - Lease and Buy-Out ○

First Lease

Purchase Price (excluding tax) ?	$	24,000
Freight and PDI? ?	$	1,000
Financing Rate ?		6.25 %
Lease Term ?		48 months
Residual % ?		50 %
Residual Value ?	$	12,000
Trade-in Value of Current Vehicle ?	$	0
Down Payment (excluding tax) ?	$	0
Monthly Payment ?	$	369.3
Tax Rate ?		13 %
Monthly Taxes ?	$	48.01

Your Result

Purchase		**Lease**	
Monthly Payment	$549.44	Monthly Payments	
		1st lease	$417.31
		2nd lease	$417.31
Total Interest Charges	$4,716.50	1st lease	$4,726.29
		2nd lease	$4,726.29
		Total Interest Charges	$9,452.58
Total Outlay for Purchase	$32,966.40	Total Outlay over 8 years	$40,061.41
Approximate Maintenance Costs	$5,530.00	1st lease	$1,755.00
		2nd lease	$1,755.00
		Total Maintenance Costs	$3,510.00
Total Outlay including Maintenance Costs	$38,496.40	Total Outlay including Maintenance Costs	$43,571.41

Potential Saving*

Buying		**Leasing**	
Number of periods without payments	36 months	Number of periods without payments	0 months

* Does not take into account any spending on maintenance

Source: Industry Canada's Office of Consumer Affairs, ic.gc.ca/eic/site/oca-bc.nsf/eng/ca01851.html. Used with permission.

22.7 | Reasons for Leasing

Proponents of leasing make many claims about why firms should lease assets rather than buy them. Some of the reasons given to support leasing are good, while some are not. We discuss here the reasons for leasing we think are good and some that we think are not so good.

Good Reasons for Leasing

If leasing is a good choice, it is probably because one or more of the following is true:

1. Taxes may be reduced by leasing.
2. The lease contract may reduce certain types of uncertainty that might otherwise decrease the value of the firm.
3. Transaction costs can be lower for a lease contract than for buying the asset.

TAX ADVANTAGES   As we have hinted in various places, by far the most important reason for long-term leasing is tax avoidance. If the corporate income tax were repealed, long-term leasing would become much less important. The tax advantages of leasing exist because firms are in different tax brackets. A potential tax shield that cannot be used by one firm can be transferred to another by leasing. We saw this in our earlier discussion on resolving the paradox.

A REDUCTION OF UNCERTAINTY   We have noted that the lessee does not own the property when the lease expires. The value of the property at this time is called the *residual value* (or salvage value). At the time the lease contract is signed, there may be substantial uncertainty as to what the residual value of the asset is. A lease contract is a method that transfers this uncertainty from the lessee to the lessor.

Transferring the uncertainty about the residual value of an asset to the lessor makes sense when the lessor is better able to bear the risk. For example, if the lessor is the manufacturer, the lessor may be better able to assess and manage the risk associated with the residual value. The transfer of uncertainty to the lessor amounts to a form of insurance for the lessee. A lease, therefore, provides something besides long-term financing. Of course, the lessee pays for this insurance implicitly, but the lessee may view the insurance as a relative bargain.

LOWER TRANSACTION COSTS   The costs of changing ownership of an asset many times over its useful life are frequently greater than the costs of writing a lease agreement. Consider the choice that confronts a person who lives in Vancouver but must do business in Halifax for two days. It seems obvious that it will be cheaper to rent a hotel room for two nights than it would be to buy a condominium for two days and then to sell it. Thus, transactions costs may be the major reason for short-term leases (operating leases). However, they are probably not the major reason for long-term leases.

FEWER RESTRICTIONS AND SECURITY REQUIREMENTS   As we discussed in Chapter 7, with a secured loan, the borrower will generally agree to a set of restrictive covenants, spelled out in the indenture, or loan agreement. Such restrictions are not generally found in lease agreements. Also, with a secured loan, the borrower may have to pledge other assets as security. With a lease, only the leased asset is so encumbered.

Bad Reasons for Leasing

LEASING AND ACCOUNTING INCOME   Leasing can have a significant effect on the appearance of the firm's financial statements. If a firm is successful at keeping its leases off the books, the statement of financial position and statement of comprehension income can be made to look better. As a consequence, accounting-based performance measures such as return on assets (ROA) can appear to be higher.

For example, off-the-books leases (that is, operating leases) result in an expense, namely, the lease payment. However, in the early years of the lease, the expense is usually lower in accounting terms than if the asset were purchased. If an asset is purchased with debt financing, capital cost allowance and interest expenses are subtracted from revenues to determine accounting net income. With accelerated depreciation under the CCA rules, the total of the depreciation deduction and the interest expense almost always exceeds the lease payments. Thus, accounting net income is greater with leasing.

In addition, because an operating lease does not appear on the statement of financial position, total assets (and total liabilities) are lower than they would be if the firm borrowed the money and bought the asset. From Chapter 3, ROA is computed as net income divided by total assets. With an operating lease, the net income is bigger and total assets are smaller, so ROA is larger.

As we have discussed, however, the impact that leasing has on a firm's accounting statements is not likely to fool anyone. As always, what matters are the cash-flow consequences. Whether or not a lease has a positive NPV has little to do with its effect on a firm's financial statements.

100 PERCENT FINANCING   It is often claimed that an advantage to leasing is that it provides 100 percent financing, whereas secured equipment loans require an initial down payment. Of course, a firm can simply borrow the down payment from another source that provides unsecured credit. Moreover, leases do usually involve a down payment in the form of an advance lease payment (or security deposit). Even when they do not, leases may implicitly be secured by assets of the firm other than those being leased (leasing may give the appearance of 100 percent financing, but not the substance).

Having said this, we should add that it may be the case that a firm (particularly a small one) simply cannot obtain debt financing because, for example, additional debt would violate a loan agreement. Operating leases frequently do not count as debt, so they may be the only source of financing available. In such cases, it is not lease or buy—it is lease or die!

Other Reasons for Leasing

There are, of course, many special reasons for some companies to find advantages in leasing. For example, leasing may be used to circumvent capital expenditure control systems set up by bureaucratic firms. Government cutbacks have made leasing increasingly popular with municipalities, universities, school boards, and hospitals (the MUSH sector).

Leasing Decisions in Practice

The reduction-of-uncertainty motive for leasing is the one that is most often cited by corporations. For example, computers have a way of becoming technologically outdated very quickly, and computers are very commonly leased instead of purchased. In a recent U.S. survey, 82 percent of the responding firms cited the risk of obsolescence as an important reason for leasing, whereas only 57 percent cited the potential for cheaper financing.

Yet, cheaper financing based on shifting tax shields is an important motive for leasing. One piece of evidence is Canadian lessors' strong reaction to 1989 changes in tax laws restricting sale and leasebacks. Further evidence comes from a study analyzing decisions taken by Canadian railroads to lease rolling stock. The study examined 20 lease contracts and found that, in 17 cases, leasing provided cheaper financing than debt.[12] A third study confirmed the importance of taxes in leasing decisions. Looking at financial information for Canadian firms between 1985 and 1995, the research showed that firms with lower marginal tax rates tend to use more lease financing.

Concept Questions

1. Explain why differential tax rates may be a good reason for leasing.
2. If leasing is tax-motivated, who has the higher tax bracket, the lessee or lessor?

[12] T. K. Mukherjee, "A Survey of Corporate Leasing Analysis," *Financial Management* 20 (Autumn 1991), pp. 96–107; C. R. Dipchand, A. C. Gudikunst, and G. S. Roberts, "An Empirical Analysis of Canadian Railroad Leases," *Journal of Financial Research* 3 (Spring 1980), pp. 57–67; L. Shanker, "Tax Effects and the Leasing Decisions of Canadian Corporations," *Canadian Journal of Administrative Sciences* 14, June 1997, pp. 195–205.

22.8 | SUMMARY AND CONCLUSIONS

A large fraction of Canada's equipment is leased rather than purchased. This chapter describes different lease types, accounting and tax implications of leasing, and how to evaluate financial leases.

1. Leases can be separated into two types, financial and operating. Financial leases are generally longer-term, fully amortized, and not cancellable. In effect, the lessor obtains economic but not legal ownership. Operating leases are usually shorter-term, partially amortized, and cancellable; they can be likened to a rental agreement.

2. The distinction between financial and operating leases is important in financial accounting. Financial leases must be reported on a firm's statement of financial position; operating leases are not. We discussed the specific accounting criteria for classifying leases as financial or operating.

3. Taxes are an important consideration in leasing, and the Canada Revenue Agency has some specific rules about what constitutes a valid lease for tax purposes.

4. A long-term financial lease is a source of financing much like long-term borrowing. We showed how to go about an NPV analysis of the leasing decision to decide whether leasing is cheaper than borrowing. A key insight was that the appropriate discount rate is the firm's after-tax borrowing rate.

5. We saw that differential tax rates can make leasing an attractive proposition to all parties. We also mentioned that a lease decreases the uncertainty surrounding the residual value of the leased asset. This is a primary reason cited by corporations for leasing.

Key Terms

financial leases (page 636)
lessee (page 634)
lessor (page 634)
leveraged lease (page 637)

net advantage to leasing (NAL) (page 642)
operating lease (page 635)
sale and leaseback (page 636)
tax-oriented lease (page 636)

Chapter Review Problems and Self-Test

22.1 Your company wants to purchase a new network file server for its wide-area computer network. The server costs $24,000. It will be obsolete in three years. Your options are to borrow the money at 10 percent or lease the machine. If you lease it, the payments will be $9,000 per year, payable at the beginning of each year. If you buy the server, you can apply a CCA rate of 30 percent per year. The tax rate is 40 percent. Assuming the asset pool remains open, should you lease or buy?

22.2 In the previous question again assuming the asset pool remains open, what is the NPV of the lease to the lessor? At what lease payment do the lessee and the lessor both break even?

Answers to Self-Test Problems

22.1 Because the asset pool remains open after the useful life of the network file server, we can answer this question by using the net advantage to leasing (NAL) formula for this case shown in the text. This formula is:

NAL = Investment − PV (after-tax lease payments) − PVCCATS − PV (Salvage)

We are given all the information necessary to solve for NAL:

The investment necessary to purchase the asset = $24,000
The number of years, beginning at zero, that the new asset would be used = 3 (Year 0, Year 1, and Year 2)
The amount of money required to lease the asset for one year = $9,000
The applicable tax rate = 40%
The applicable after-tax interest rate = $10\%(1 - T)$
$$= 10\%(.6)$$
$$= 6\%$$
The applicable CCA rate = 30%
Salvage = $0

We then plug all of these numbers into the formula:

$$\text{NAL} = \$24{,}000 - \sum_{t=0}^{2} \frac{\$9{,}000(1 - .40)}{(1 + 0.06)^t} - \frac{0.40 \times 0.30 \times \$24{,}000}{0.06 + 0.30} \times \frac{1.03}{1.06}$$

$$\text{NAL} = \$24{,}000 - \$15{,}300 - \$7{,}774$$

$$\text{NAL} = \$926$$

Because the NAL formula gives a positive value of \$926, there is a net advantage to lease the file server.

22.2 The answer to the first part of the question is that the lessor has a NPV of −\$926. The lessor has lost what the lessee has gained. To solve the second question posed in 22.2 we can again refer to the NAL formula:

$$\text{NAL} = I - \sum_{t=0}^{2} \frac{L(1 - T)}{(1 + i)^t} - \frac{[TdI]}{i + d} \times \frac{[1 + 0.5i]}{1 + i}$$

We also use much of the information used to solve Problem 22.1. However, instead of using the value of \$9,000 for L, we make NAL $= 0$ and solve for L. We merely have to plug in the values for the information we know and rearrange the formula so that we may solve for L:

$$0 = 24{,}000 - \sum_{t=0}^{2} \frac{L(1 - .40)}{(1 + 0.06)^t} - \frac{0.40 \times 0.30 \times \$24{,}000}{0.06 + 0.30} \times \frac{1.03}{1.06}$$

$$0 = \$24{,}000 - \sum_{t=0}^{2} \frac{L(0.6)}{(1.06)^t} - \$7{,}774$$

$$\$16{,}226 = \sum_{t=0}^{2} \frac{L(0.6)}{(1.06)^t}$$

$$\$16{,}226 = \frac{L(0.6)}{(1.06)^0} + \frac{L(0.6)}{(1.06)^1} + \frac{L(0.6)}{(1.06)^2}$$

$$\$16{,}226 = .600L + .566L + .534L$$

$$\$16{,}226 = 1.7L$$

$$L = \$9{,}545$$

As we can now see, some of the tax advantages of the lessee have been transferred to the lessor and they are now in a break-even situation.

Concepts Review and Critical Thinking Questions

1. **(LO1)** What are the key differences between leasing and borrowing? Are they perfect substitutes?

2. **(LO2)** Taxes are an important consideration in the leasing decision. Who is more likely to lease, a profitable corporation in a high tax bracket or a less profitable one in a low tax bracket? Why?

3. **(LO4)** What are some of the potential problems with looking at IRRs in evaluating a leasing decision?

4. **(LO5)** Comment on the following remarks:
   a. Leasing reduces risk and can reduce a firm's cost of capital.
   b. Leasing provides 100 percent financing.
   c. If the tax advantages of leasing were eliminated, leasing would disappear.

5. **(LO2)** Discuss the accounting criteria for determining whether or not a lease must be reported on the statement of financial position. In each case, give a rationale for the criterion.

6. **(LO2)** Discuss CRA's criteria for determining whether or not a lease is valid. In each case, give a rationale for the criterion.

7. **(LO2)** What is meant by the term *financing off the statement of financial position*? When do leases provide such financing, and what are the accounting and economic consequences of such activity?

8. **(LO1, 6)** Why might a firm choose to engage in a sale and leaseback transaction? Give two reasons.

9. **(LO4)** Explain why the after-tax borrowing rate is the appropriate discount rate to use in lease evaluation.

Questions 10 and 11 refer to the Bombardier leasing example we used to open the chapter.

10. **(LO4)** Why would a leasing company be willing to buy planes from Bombardier and then lease them to the airline companies in China? How is this different from just loaning money to these companies to buy the planes?

11. **(LO4)** What do you suppose happens to the leased planes at the end of the lease period?

Questions and Problems

Basic **1.** **Lease or Buy (LO4)** Assuming the asset pool was closed when the network file server became obsolete, redo Self-Test Problem 22.1.
(Question 1)

Use the following information to work the next six problems.

You work for a nuclear research laboratory that is contemplating leasing a diagnostic scanner (leasing is a very common practice with expensive, high-tech equipment). The scanner costs \$6.3 million and it qualifies for a 30 percent CCA rate. Because of radiation contamination, it is valueless in four years. You can lease it for \$1.875 million per year for four years. Assume that assets pool remains open and payments are made at the end of the year.

Intermediate **2.** **Lease or Buy (LO4)** Assume the tax rate is 37 percent. You can borrow at 7.5 percent pre-tax. Should you lease or buy?
(Questions 2–10)

3. **Lessor View of Leasing (LO3)** What are the cash flows from the lease from the lessor's point of view? Assume a 37 percent tax bracket.

4. **Break-even Lease (LO4)** What would the lease payment have to be for both lessor and lessee to be indifferent to the lease?

5. **Tax Effects on Leasing (LO3)** Assume that your company does not contemplate paying taxes for the next several years. What are the cash flows from leasing?

6. **Leasing Profits (LO5)** In the previous equation, over what range of lease payments will the lease be profitable for both parties?

7. **Lease or Buy (LO4)** Rework Problem 2 assuming the scanner qualifies for a special CCA rate of 50 percent per year and that the asset pool remains open.

Use the following information to work Problems 8 through 10.

The Wildcat Oil Company is trying to decide whether to lease or buy a new computer-assisted drilling system for its oil exploration business. Management has already determined that acquisition of the system has a positive NPV. The system costs $9.4 million and qualifies for a 25 percent CCA rate. The equipment will have a $975,000 salvage value in 5 years. Wildcat's tax rate is 36 percent, and the firm can borrow at 9 percent. Southtown Leasing Company has offered to lease the drilling equipment to Wildcat for payments of $2.15 million per year. Southtown's policy is to require its lessees to make payments at the start of the year.

8. **Lease or Buy (LO4)** What is the NAL for Wildcat? What is the maximum lease payment that would be acceptable to the company?

 9. **Leasing and Salvage Value (LO4)** Suppose it is estimated that the equipment will have no salvage value at the end of the lease. What is the maximum lease payment acceptable to Wildcat now?

10. **Deposits in Leasing (LO4)** Many lessors require a security deposit in the form of a cash payment or other pledged collateral. Suppose Southtown requires Wildcat to pay a $750,000 security deposit at the inception of the lease. If the lease payment is still $2,150,000 a year, is it advantageous for Wildcat to lease the equipment now?

Challenge 11. **Lease versus Borrow (LO4)** Return to the case of the diagnostic scanner used in Problems 2 through 7. Suppose the entire
(Questions $6.3 million purchase price of the scanner is borrowed. The rate on the loan is 8 percent, and the loan will be repaid in equal
11–13) installments. Create a lease-versus-buy analysis that explicitly incorporates the loan payments. Show that the NPV of leasing instead of buying is not changed from what it was in Problem 2. Why is this so?

12. **Lease or Buy (LO4)** In the Self-Test Problem 21.1, suppose the server had a projected salvage value of $800. How would you conduct the lease-versus-buy analysis?

13. **Break-even Lease (LO4, 5)** An asset costs $675,000. The CCA rate for this asset is 25 percent. The asset's useful life is two years after which it will be worth $50,000. The corporate tax rate on ordinary income is 35 percent. The interest rate on risk-free cash flows is 10 percent.

   a. What set of lease payments will make the lessee and the lessor equally well off, assuming payments are made at the end of the year?

   b. Show the general condition that will make the value of a lease to the lessor the negative of the value to the lessee.

   c. Assume that the lessee pays no taxes and the lessor is in the 35 percent tax bracket. For what range of lease payments does the lease have a positive NPV for both parties?

Internet Application Questions

1. There are some very sensible reasons for leasing assets, and some that make you think more deeply. The following site argues mostly in favour of leasing. One of its arguments is that since lease payments are typically lower than loan payments on a purchase, the "savings" can be invested in higher yield instruments such as equity funds, and you therefore come out ahead at the end of the term. Is this a reasonable criticism of the borrow-and-buy alternative to leasing? leaseguide.com/lease03.htm

2. OK, are you ready for a test drive? CARS4U.COM provides a unique Internet-based car buying and leasing service where they will deliver the car of your choice to your doorstep (well, driveway). Look at the information for the VW Jetta below and decide whether the lease is preferable to financing and purchasing. To get the interest rate, add 1 percent to the current prime rate from Royal Bank (rbcroyalbank.com/rates/prime.html). Leasing and financing assumptions are provided below and in the link.

2013 Volkswagen Jetta 2.0L Sedan Comfortline

Term:	36 months	Rebate:	TBA
Cash down payment:	$2,500	Vehicle Type:	Sedan
Trade-in allowance:	$0	Engine:	2.0 litres, turbo charged 4 cylinder engine,
Interest rate:	Current market rate		115 horsepower and 4 valves per cylinder
Lease only:	50% Residual Value/Buyback		
MSRP:	$19,590	Fuel Economy:	City: 10 L/100 km Highway: 7 L/100 km
Est. Lease:	$360		
Cars4U.com Price:	$19,372		
Est. Financing:	$808		

3. The Equipment Lease Canada website provides completed information on equipment leasing in Canada. Visit equipmentleasecanada.com/ and click on 'Steps to Leasing' option under 'Equipment Leasing' menu. What are the steps to be taken by you for leasing your equipment?

MINI CASE

The Decision to Lease or Buy at Warf Computers

Warf Computers has decided to proceed with the manufacture and distribution of the virtual keyboard (VK) the company has developed. To undertake this venture, the company needs to obtain equipment for the production of the microphone for the keyboard. Because of the required sensitivity of the microphone and its small size, the company needs specialized equipment for production.

Nick Warf, the company president, has found a vendor for the equipment. Clapton Acoustical Equipment has offered to sell Warf Computers the necessary equipment at a price of $6.5 million. Because of the rapid development of new technology, the equipment falls in class 45 with a CCA rate of 45 percent. At the end of four years, the market value of the equipment is expected to be $780,000.

Alternatively, the company can lease the equipment from Hendrix Leasing. The lease contract calls for four annual payments of $1.69 million due at the beginning of the year. Additionally, Warf Computers must make a security deposit of $400,000 that will be returned when the lease expires. Warf Computers can issue bonds with a yield of 11 percent, and the company has a marginal tax rate of 35 percent.

Questions

1. Should Warf buy or lease the equipment?

2. Nick mentions to James Hendrix, the president of Hendrix Leasing, that although the company will need the equipment for four years, he would like a lease contract for two years instead. At the end of the two years, the lease could be renewed. Nick would also like to eliminate the security deposit, but he would be willing to increase the lease payments to $2.75 million for each of the two years. When the lease is renewed in two years, Hendrix would consider the increased lease payments in the first two years when calculating the terms of the renewal. The equipment is expected to have a market value of $1.9 million in two years. What is the NAL of the lease contract under these terms? Why might Nick prefer this lease? What are the potential ethical issues concerning the new lease terms?

3. In the leasing discussion, James informs Nick that the contract could include a purchase option for the equipment at the end of the lease. Hendrix Leasing offers three purchase options:

   a. An option to purchase the equipment at the fair market value.

   b. An option to purchase the equipment at a fixed price. The price will be negotiated before the lease is signed.

   c. An option to purchase the equipment at a price of $250,000.

   How would the inclusion of a purchase option affect the value of the lease?

4. James also informs Nick that the lease contract can include a cancellation option. The cancellation option would allow Warf Computers to cancel the lease on any anniversary date of the contract. To cancel the lease, Warf Computers would be required to give 30 days' notice prior to the anniversary date. How would the inclusion of a cancellation option affect the value of the lease?

MERGERS AND ACQUISITIONS

Bell

In March 2012, BCE Inc., Canada's largest telecommunications company, reached an agreement to buy Astral Media Inc. for $3.38 billion in cash and stock. Astral is Canada's largest radio broadcaster, owning 83 radio stations in 50 Canadian markets, as well as the largest pay and specialty TV broadcaster. The transaction provides Bell with Astral's slate of television stations that include HBO Canada, the Movie Network, and the Family Channel, as well as radio stations under brands like Virgin Radio and EZ Rock. However, the transaction was denied approval from the Canadian Radio-television and Telecommunications Commission and the Competition Bureau and was under review by the Federal cabinet at the time of writing. This chapter explores two basic issues: Why does a firm choose to merge with or acquire another firm, and how does it happen?

Learning Objectives ▶

After studying this chapter, you should understand:

LO1 The different types of mergers and acquisitions, why they should (or shouldn't) take place, and the terminology associated with them.

LO2 Taxable versus tax-free acquisitions.

LO3 How accountants construct the combined statement of financial position of a new company.

LO4 Some financial side effects of mergers and acquisitions.

LO5 Cash versus common stock financing in mergers and acquisitions.

LO6 How to estimate the NPV of a merger or an acquisition.

LO7 The gains from a merger or acquisition and how to value the transaction.

LO8 Divestitures involving equity carve-outs and spin-offs.

LO9 The use of different defensive tactics by the target firm's management.

There is no more dramatic or controversial activity in corporate finance than the acquisition of one firm by another or the merger of two firms. It is the stuff of headlines in the financial press, and occasionally it is an embarrassing source of scandal. And there are a lot of mergers. From 2001 to 2010, more than 10,000 mergers took place in Canada. This amounts to around 3 mergers per day, with a combined value of over $1.5 trillion.

The acquisition of one firm by another is, of course, an investment made under uncertainty, and the basic principles of valuation apply. Another firm should be acquired only if doing so generates a positive net present value to the shareholders of the acquiring firm. However, because the NPV of an acquisition candidate can be difficult to determine, mergers and acquisitions are interesting topics in their own right.

Some of the special problems that come up in this area of finance include:

1. The benefits from acquisitions can depend on such things as strategic fits. Strategic fits are difficult to define precisely, and it is not easy to estimate the value of strategic fits using discounted cash flow techniques.

2. There can be complex accounting, tax, and legal effects that must be considered when one firm is acquired by another.

3. Acquisitions are an important control device for shareholders. Some acquisitions are a consequence of an underlying conflict between the interests of existing managers and share-

td.com

holders. Agreeing to be acquired by another firm is one way that shareholders can remove existing managers.

4. Mergers and acquisitions sometimes involve "unfriendly" transactions. In such cases, when one firm attempts to acquire another, it does not always involve quiet negotiations. The sought-after firm often resists takeover and may resort to defensive tactics with exotic names such as poison pills or greenmail.

We discuss these and other issues associated with mergers in the next section. We begin by introducing the basic legal, accounting, and tax aspects of acquisitions.

23.1 | The Legal Forms of Acquisitions

There are three basic legal procedures that one firm can use to acquire another firm:

1. Merger or consolidation.
2. Acquisition of stock.
3. Acquisition of assets.

amalgamations
Combinations of firms that have been joined by merger, consolidation, or acquisition.

Although these forms are different from a legal standpoint, the financial press frequently does not distinguish between them. To make the terminology more confusing, both the Canadian and Ontario Business Corporation Acts refer to combinations of firms as **amalgamations**. In our discussion, we use the term *merger* regardless of the actual form of the acquisition.

In our discussion, we frequently refer to the acquiring firm as the *bidder*. This is the company that makes an offer to distribute cash or securities to obtain the stock or assets of another company. The firm that is sought (and perhaps acquired) is often called the *target firm*. The cash or securities offered to the target firm are the *consideration* in the acquisition.

Merger or Consolidation

merger
The complete absorption of one company by another, where the acquiring firm retains its identity and the acquired firm ceases to exist as a separate entity.

A **merger** refers to the complete absorption of one firm by another. The acquiring firm retains its name and its identity, and it acquires all the assets and liabilities of the acquired firm. After a merger, the acquired firm ceases to exist as a separate business entity.

consolidation
A merger in which a new firm is created and both the acquired and acquiring firm cease to exist.

A **consolidation** is the same as a merger except that a new firm is created. In a consolidation, both the acquiring firm and the acquired firm terminate their previous legal existence and become part of a new firm. For this reason, the distinction between the acquiring and the acquired firm is not as important in a consolidation as it is in a merger.

The rules for mergers and consolidations are basically the same. Acquisition by merger or consolidation results in a combination of the assets and liabilities of acquired and acquiring firms; the only difference is whether or not a new firm is created. We henceforth use the term *merger* to refer generically to both mergers and consolidations.

There are some advantages and some disadvantages to using a merger to acquire a firm:

1. A primary advantage is that a merger is legally simple and does not cost as much as other forms of acquisition. The reason is that the firms simply agree to combine their entire operations. Thus, for example, there is no need to transfer title to individual assets of the acquired firm to the acquiring firm.
2. A primary disadvantage is that a merger must be approved by a vote of the shareholders of each firm.[1] Typically, two-thirds (or even more) of the share votes are required for approval. Obtaining the necessary votes can be time consuming and difficult. Furthermore, as we later discuss in greater detail, the cooperation of the target firm's existing management is almost a necessity for a merger. This cooperation may not be easily or cheaply obtained.

---

[1] As we discuss later, obtaining majority assent is less of a problem in Canada than in the United States because fewer Canadian corporations are widely held.

Acquisition of Stock

tender offer
A public offer by one firm to directly buy the shares from another firm.

A second way to acquire another firm is to simply purchase the firm's voting stock in exchange for cash, shares of stock, or other securities. This process often starts as a private offer from the management of one firm to another. Regardless of how it starts, at some point the offer is taken directly to the target firm's shareholders. This can be accomplished by a **tender offer**. A tender offer is a public offer to buy shares. It is made by one firm directly to the shareholders of another firm.

If the shareholders choose to accept the offer, they tender their shares by exchanging them for cash or securities (or both), depending on the offer. A tender offer is frequently contingent on the bidder's obtaining some percentage of the total voting shares. If not enough shares are tendered, the offer might be withdrawn or reformulated.

circular bid
Corporate takeover bid communicated to the shareholders by direct mail.

stock exchange bid
Corporate takeover bid communicated to the shareholders through a stock exchange.

The takeover bid is communicated to the target firm's shareholders by public announcements such as newspaper advertisements. Takeover bids may be either by **circular bid** mailed directly to the target's shareholders or by **stock exchange bid** (through the facilities of the TSX or other exchange). In either case, Ontario securities law requires that the bidder mail a notice of the proposed share purchase to shareholders. Furthermore, the management of the target firm must also respond to the bid, including their recommendation to accept or to reject the bid. For a circular bid, the response must be mailed to shareholders. If the bid is made through a stock exchange, the response is through a press release.

The following factors are involved in choosing between an acquisition by stock and a merger:

1. In an acquisition by stock, no shareholder meetings have to be held and no vote is required. If the shareholders of the target firm don't like the offer, they are not required to accept it and need not tender their shares.

2. In an acquisition by stock, the bidding firm can deal directly with the shareholders of the target firm by using a tender offer. The target firm's management and board of directors can be bypassed.

3. Acquisition by stock is occasionally unfriendly. In such cases, a stock acquisition is used in an effort to circumvent the target firm's management, which is usually actively resisting acquisition. Resistance by the target firm's management often makes the cost of acquisition by stock higher than the cost of a merger.

4. Frequently, a significant minority of shareholders holds out in a tender offer. The target firm cannot be completely absorbed when this happens, and this may delay realization of the merger benefits or otherwise be costly.

5. Complete absorption of one firm by another requires a merger. Many acquisitions by stock end up with a formal merger later.

Acquisition of Assets

A firm can effectively acquire another firm by buying most or all of its assets. This accomplishes the same thing as buying the company. In this case, however, the target firm does not necessarily cease to exist, it just has its assets sold. The shell still exists unless its shareholders choose to dissolve it.

This type of acquisition requires a formal vote of the shareholders of the selling firm. One advantage to this approach is that there is no problem with minority shareholders holding out. However, acquisition of assets may involve transferring titles to individual assets. The legal process of transferring assets can be costly.

Acquisition Classifications

Financial analysts typically classify acquisitions into three types:

1. *Horizontal acquisition.* This is acquisition of a firm in the same industry as the bidder. The firms compete with each other in their product markets. A good example is the acquisition of Equinox Minerals by Barrick Gold Corp. for $7.3 billion in 2011.

barrick.com

2. *Vertical acquisition.* A vertical acquisition involves firms at different steps of the production process. For example, Google's purchase of Motorola Mobility for $12.5 billion in 2012 was a vertical merger. Google is a company providing Internet related products and services, while Motorola manufactures mobile phones.

3. *Conglomerate acquisition.* When the bidder and the target firm are not related to each other, the merger is called a conglomerate acquisition. In 2011, the acquisition of 75% stake in Maple Leaf Sports and Entertainment, owner of professional teams in Canada such as The Toronto Maple Leafs, Toronto Raptors, Toronto Marlies, and Toronto FC, by Bell Canada and Rogers Communications Inc., telecommunication companies, was considered a conglomerate acquisition.

A Note on Takeovers

Takeover is a general and imprecise term referring to the transfer of control of a firm from one group of shareholders to another. A takeover thus occurs whenever one group takes control from another.[2] This can occur in three ways: acquisitions, proxy contests, and going-private transactions. Thus, takeovers encompass a broader set of activities than just acquisitions. These activities can be depicted as follows:

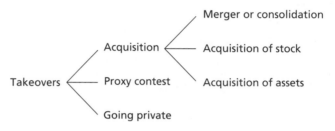

As we have mentioned, a takeover achieved by acquisition occurs by merger, tender offer, or purchase of assets. In mergers and tender offers, the bidder buys the voting common stock of the target firm.

Takeovers can also occur with **proxy contests**. Proxy contests occur when a group attempts to gain controlling seats on the board of directors by voting in new directors. A proxy is the right to cast someone else's votes. In a proxy contest, proxies are solicited by an unhappy group of shareholders from the rest of the shareholders.

In **going-private transactions**, all the equity shares of a public firm are purchased by a small group of investors. Usually, the group includes members of incumbent management and some outside investors. Such transactions have come to be known generically as **leveraged buyouts (LBOs)** because a large percentage of the money needed to buy the stock is usually borrowed. Such transactions are also termed *MBOs* (management buyouts) when existing management is heavily involved.[3] The shares of the firm are delisted from stock exchanges and no longer can be purchased in the open market. An example of an MBO was management's purchase of Sun Media Corp., publisher of *The Financial Post* and *Toronto Sun*, from Rogers Communications, in 1996. CIBC Wood Gundy also purchased some of the shares.

The role of private equity firms in mergers and acquisitions transactions has grown significantly in recent years. In Canada, $11.5 billion of private equity funds were raised in 2011. This represents a 69 percent increase over the previous year. The largest private equity deal in 2011 was the $2.1-billion acquisition of Husky International, an Ontario-based injection-molding company, by the OMERS pension fund and Berkshire Partners.[4]

In the wake of foreign takeovers, there have been conflicting views on the "hollowing out of the Canadian economy." On one hand the sell-off of icons such as Hudson Bay Company, Dofasco, Fairmont, and Domtar poses a risk of Canadian companies losing dominance to foreign players. On the other hand, these foreign acquisitions represent an opportunity for corporate Canada to increase its presence in the global economy.

There have been a large number of mergers and acquisitions in recent years many of them involving very familiar companies. Table 23.1 lists some of the largest mergers in Canada in recent years.

proxy contests
Attempts to gain control of a firm by soliciting a sufficient number of shareholder votes to replace existing management.

going-private transactions
All publicly owned stock in a firm is replaced with complete equity ownership by a private group.

leveraged buyouts (LBOs)
Going-private transactions in which a large percentage of the money used to buy the stock is borrowed. Often, incumbent management is involved.

---

[2] A takeover bid has a narrowed meaning as we explained earlier. *Control* may be defined as having a majority vote on the board of directors.

[3] LBOs and MBOs can involve proxy contests for control of the company.

[4] theglobeandmail.com/globe-investor/canadian-private-equity-deals-soar/article4171814/

Alternatives to Merger

strategic alliance
Agreement between firms to cooperate in pursuit of a joint goal.

joint venture
Typically an agreement between firms to create a separate, co-owned entity established to pursue a joint goal.

Firms don't have to merge to combine their efforts. At a minimum, two (or more) firms can simply agree to work together. They can sell each other's products, perhaps under different brand names, or jointly develop a new product or technology. Firms will frequently establish a **strategic alliance**, which is usually a formal agreement to cooperate in pursuit of a joint goal. An even more formal arrangement is a **joint venture**, which commonly involves two firms putting up the money to establish a new firm. For example, in May 2012, Rogers Communications Inc. and Canadian Imperial Bank of Commerce (CIBC) formed a joint venture to launch 'mobile wallets', smart phones with the capability of making day-to-day transactions.

TABLE 23.1

10 large mergers and acquisitions involving Canadian companies

Rank	Year	Value (Cdn $ billion)	Target Company	Acquiring Company
1	2007	$39.83	Alcan Inc.	Rio Tinto Group
2	2000	$39.72	The Seagram Company Ltd.	Vivendi S.A.
3	2009	$23.90	Petro-Canada	Suncor Energy Inc.
4	2006	$19.87	Inco Limited	Companhia Vale do Rio Doce
5	2006	$19.20	Falconbridge Limited	Xstrata plc
6	2007	$18.98	Reuters Group plc	The Thomson Corporation
7	1998	$15.37	PolyGram N.V.	The Seagram Company Ltd.
8	2003	$15.00	John Hancock Financial Services, Inc.	Manulife Financial Corporation
9	2008	$14.44	Fording Canadian Coal Trust	Teck Cominco Limited
10	2005	$11.88	Placer Dome Inc.	Barrick Gold Corporation

Source: FP *Infomart - as of May 31, 2012*

Concept Questions

1. What is a merger? How does a merger differ from other acquisition forms?
2. What is a takeover?

23.2 | Taxes and Acquisitions

If one firm buys another firm, the transaction may be taxable or tax free. In a *taxable acquisition*, the shareholders of the target firm are considered to have sold their shares, and they have capital gains or losses that are taxed. In a *tax-free acquisition*, since the acquisition is considered an exchange instead of a sale, no capital gain or loss occurs at that time.

Determinants of Tax Status

The general requirements for tax-free status are that the acquisition involves two Canadian corporations subject to corporate income tax and that there be a continuity of equity interest. In other words, the shareholders in the target firm must retain an equity interest in the bidder.

The specific requirements for a tax-free acquisition depend on the legal form of the acquisition; in general, if the buying firm offers the selling firm cash for its equity, it is a taxable acquisition. If shares of stock are offered, it is a tax-free acquisition.

In a tax-free acquisition, the selling shareholders are considered to have exchanged their old shares for new ones of equal value, and no capital gains or losses are experienced.

Taxable versus Tax-Free Acquisitions

There are two factors to consider when comparing a tax-free acquisition and a taxable acquisition: the capital gains effect and the write-up effect. The *capital gains effect* refers to the fact that the target firm's shareholders may have to pay capital gains taxes in a taxable acquisition. They may demand a higher price as compensation, thereby increasing the cost of the merger. This is a cost of taxable acquisition.

The tax status of an acquisition also affects the appraised value of the assets of the selling firm. In a taxable acquisition, the assets of the selling firm are revalued or "written up" from their historic book value to their estimated current market value. This is the *write-up effect*, and it is important because the depreciation expense on the acquired firm's assets can be increased in taxable acquisitions. Remember that an increase in depreciation is a non-cash expense, but it has the desirable effect of reducing taxes.

Concept Questions

1. What factors influence the choice between a taxable and a tax-free acquisition?

2. What is the write-up effect in a taxable acquisition?

23.3 | Accounting for Acquisitions

Firms keep two distinct sets of books: the shareholders' books and the tax books. In this section, we are considering the shareholders' books. When one firm buys another firm, the acquisition will be treated as a purchase on the shareholders' books.

The purchase accounting method of reporting acquisitions requires that the assets of the target firm be reported at their fair market value on the books of the bidder. This allows the bidder to establish a new cost basis for the acquired assets. With this method, an asset called *goodwill* is created for accounting purposes. Goodwill is the difference between the purchase price and the estimated fair value of the assets acquired.

To illustrate, suppose Firm A acquires Firm B, thereby creating a new firm, AB. The statements of financial position for the two firms on the date of the acquisition are shown in Table 23.2. Suppose Firm A pays $18 million in cash for Firm B. The money is raised by borrowing the full amount. The fixed assets in Firm B are appraised at $14 million fair market value. Since the working capital is $2 million, the statement of financial position assets are worth $16 million. Firm A thus pays $2 million in excess of the estimated market value of these assets. This amount is the goodwill.[5]

TABLE 23.2

Accounting for acquisitions: Purchase (in $ millions)

Firm A				Firm B			
Working capital	$ 4	Equity	$20	Working capital	$2	Equity	$10
Fixed assets	16			Fixed assets	8		
Total	$20		$20	Total	$10		$10

Firm AB			
Working capital	$ 6	Debt	$18
Fixed assets	30	Equity	20
Goodwill	2		
Total	$38		$38

The market value of the fixed assets of Firm B is $14 million. Firm A pays $18 million for Firm B by issuing debt.

---

[5] Remember, there are assets such as employee talents, good customers, growth opportunities, and other intangibles that don't show up on the statement of financial position. The $2 million excess pays for these.

The last statement of financial position in Table 23.2 shows what the new firm looks like under purchase accounting. Notice that:

1. The total assets of Firm AB increase to $38 million. The fixed assets increase to $30 million. This is the sum of the fixed assets of Firm A and the revalued fixed assets of Firm B ($16 million + 14 million = $30 million). Note that the tax effect of the write-up is ignored in this example.
2. The $2 million excess of the purchase price over the fair market value is reported as goodwill on the statement of financial position.[6]

Concept Questions

1. What is the role of goodwill in purchase accounting for mergers?

23.4 | Gains from Acquisition

To determine the gains from an acquisition, we need to first identify the relevant incremental cash flows, or, more generally, the source of value. In the broadest sense, acquiring another firm makes sense only if there is some concrete reason to believe that the target firm will somehow be worth more in our hands than it is worth now. As we will see, there are a number of reasons why this might be so.

Synergy

Suppose Firm A is contemplating acquiring Firm B. The acquisition will be beneficial if the combined firm will have value that is greater than the sum of the values of the separate firms. If we let V_{AB} stand for the value of the merged firm, then the merger makes sense only if:

$$V_{AB} > V_A + V_B$$

where V_A and V_B are the separate values. A successful merger thus requires that the value of the whole exceed the sum of the parts.

The difference between the value of the combined firm and the sum of the values of the firms as separate entities is the incremental net gain from the acquisition, ΔV:

$$\Delta V = V_{AB} - (V_A + V_B)$$

synergy
The positive incremental net gain associated with the combination of two firms through a merger or acquisition.

When ΔV is positive, the acquisition is said to generate **synergy**. For example, when Transcontinental Inc., bought Quad/Graphics Canada in 2012, it announced that the deal was expected to deliver more than $40 million in synergies.

If Firm A buys Firm B, it gets a company worth V_B plus the incremental gain, ΔV. The value of Firm B to Firm A (V_B^*) is thus:

$$\text{Value of Firm B to Firm A} = V_B^* = \Delta V + V_B$$

tctranscontinental.com

We place an $*$ on V_B^* to emphasize that we are referring to the value of Firm B to Firm A, not the value of Firm B as a separate entity.

V_B^* can be determined in two steps: (1) estimating V_B and (2) estimating ΔV. If B is a public company, then its market value as an independent firm under existing management (V_B) can be observed directly. If Firm B is not publicly owned, then its value will have to be estimated based on similar companies that are. Either way, the problem of determining a value for V_B^* requires determining a value for ΔV.

---

[6]You might wonder what would happen if the purchase price were less than the estimated fair market value. Amusingly, to be consistent, it seems that the accountants would need to create a liability called ill will! Instead, the fair market value is revised downward to equal the purchase price.

To determine the incremental value of an acquisition, we need to know the incremental cash flows. These are the cash flows for the combined firm less what A and B could generate separately. In other words, the incremental cash flow for evaluating a merger is the difference between the cash flow of the combined company and the sum of the cash flows for the two companies considered separately. We will label this incremental cash flow as ΔCF.

From our discussions in earlier chapters, we know that the incremental cash flow, ΔCF, can be broken down into four parts:

$$\Delta CF = \Delta EBIT + \Delta Depreciation - \Delta Tax - \Delta Capital\ requirements$$
$$= \Delta Revenue - \Delta Cost - \Delta Tax - \Delta Capital\ requirements$$

where $\Delta Revenue$ is the difference in revenues, $\Delta Cost$ is the difference in costs, ΔTax is the difference in taxes, and $\Delta Capital$ requirements is the change in new fixed assets and net working capital.

EXAMPLE 23.1: Synergy

Firms A and B are competitors with very similar assets and business risks. Both are all-equity firms with after-tax cash flows of $10 per year forever, and both have an overall cost of capital of 10 percent. Firm A is thinking of buying Firm B. The after-tax cash flow from the merged firm would be $21 per year. Does the merger generate synergy? What is V_B^*? What is ΔV?

The merger does generate synergy because the cash flow from the merged firm is $\Delta CF = \$1$ greater than the sum of the individual cash flows ($21 versus $20). Assuming that the risks stay the same, the value of the merged firm is $21/.10 = \$210$. Firms A and B are each worth $10/.10 = \$100$, for a total of $200. The incremental gain from the merger, ΔV, is thus $210 - 200 = \$10$. The total value of Firm B to Firm A, V_B^*, is $100 (the value of B as a separate company) plus $10 (the incremental gain), or $110.

Based on this breakdown, the merger will make sense only if one or more of these cash flow components are beneficially affected by the merger. The possible cash flow benefits of mergers and acquisitions thus fall into four basic categories: revenue enhancement, cost reductions, lower taxes, and reductions in capital needs.

Revenue Enhancement

One important reason for an acquisition is that the combined firm may generate greater revenues than two separate firms. Increases in revenue may come from marketing gains, strategic benefits, and increases in market power.

MARKETING GAINS   It is frequently claimed that mergers and acquisitions can produce greater operating revenues from improved marketing. For example, improvements might be made in the following areas:

1. Previously ineffective media programming and advertising efforts.
2. A weak existing distribution network.
3. An unbalanced product mix.

In 2011, when Canadian Tire acquired Forzani Group Limited, the company behind Sport Chek, Athlete's World, and Nevada Bob's Golf, Canadian Tire predicted that it would save $25 million annually, due to synergies in its supply chain, marketing, and international suppliers.

STRATEGIC BENEFITS   Some acquisitions promise a strategic advantage. This is an opportunity to take advantage of the competitive environment if certain things occur or, more generally, to enhance management flexibility with regard to the company's future operations. In this regard, a strategic benefit is more like an option than it is a standard investment opportunity.

For example, suppose a sewing machine firm can use its technology to enter other businesses. The small-motor technology from the original business can provide opportunities to begin manufacturing small appliances and electric typewriters. Similarly, electronics expertise gained in producing typewriters can be used to manufacture electronic printers.

The word *beachhead* describes the process of entering a new industry/market to exploit perceived opportunities. The beachhead is to spawn new opportunities based on intangible relationships. One example is Procter & Gamble's initial acquisition of the Charmin Paper Company as a beachhead that allowed Procter & Gamble to develop a highly interrelated cluster of paper products—disposable diapers, paper towels, feminine hygiene products, and bathroom tissue.[7]

pg.com

MARKET POWER   One firm may acquire another to increase its market share and market power. In such mergers, profits can be enhanced through higher prices and reduced competition for customers. In theory, such mergers are controlled by law. In practice, however, horizontal mergers are far more common in Canada than the United States due to weaker legal restrictions against combinations of competitors that might limit market competition.[8] In Canada, the Competition Bureau, an independent agency, is responsible for the administration and enforcement of the Competition Act, a law that prevents anti-competitive practices in the Canadian marketplace.

Cost Reductions

One of the most basic reasons to merge is that a combined firm may operate more efficiently than two separate firms. A firm can obtain greater operating efficiency in several different ways through a merger or an acquisition.

ECONOMIES OF SCALE   Economies of scale relate to the average cost per unit of producing goods and services. As Figure 23.1 shows, when the per-unit cost of production falls as the level of production increases, an economy of scale exists.

Frequently, the phrase *spreading overhead* is used in connection with economies of scale. This expression refers to the sharing of central facilities such as corporate headquarters, top management, and computer services.

FIGURE 23.1

Economies of scale

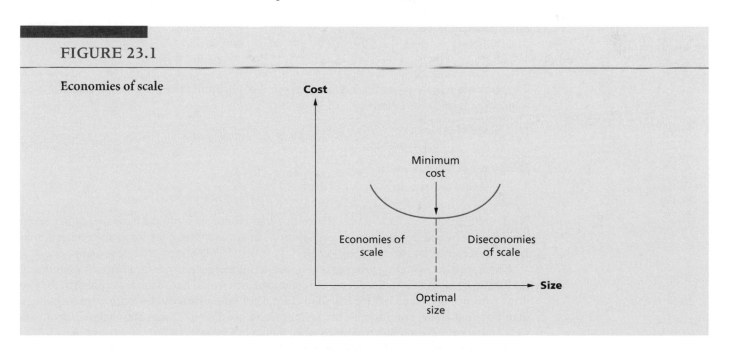

---

[7] This example comes from Michael Porter's *Competitive Advantage* (New York: Free Press, 1985).

[8] From the mid-1950s to the mid-1980s, only one merger in Canada was blocked under the *Combines Investigation Act.* In the same period, U.S. antitrust laws "prevented several hundred horizontal mergers" according to B. E. Eckbo, "Mergers and the Market for Corporate Control: the Canadian Evidence," *Canadian Journal of Economics*, May 1986, pp. 236–260.

gm.com

rogers.com

ECONOMIES OF VERTICAL INTEGRATION   Operating economies can be gained from vertical combinations as well as from horizontal combinations. The main purpose of vertical acquisitions is to make coordinating closely related operating activities easier. Benefits from vertical integration are probably the reason most forest product firms that cut timber also own sawmills and hauling equipment. Such economies may explain why some airline companies have purchased hotels and car rental companies.

Technology transfers are another reason for vertical integration. Consider the merger of General Motors Corporation and Hughes Aircraft in 1985. It seems natural that an automobile manufacturer might acquire an advanced electronics firm if the special technology of the electronics firm can be used to improve the quality of the automobile.

COMPLEMENTARY RESOURCES   Some firms acquire others to make better use of existing resources or to provide the missing ingredient for success. Think of a ski equipment store that could merge with a tennis equipment store to produce more even sales over both the winter and summer seasons, and thereby better use store capacity.

EVIDENCE ON REVENUE ENHANCEMENT AND COST REDUCTION   Most of the evidence on merger gains is measured in returns to shareholders. We discuss this later to see who gains in mergers. To attribute any gains from mergers to specific advantages like market share requires an industrial organization approach. A study of Canadian mergers in the 1970s finds that gains occurred in market share, productivity, or profitability. This suggests that revenue enhancement and cost reduction are valid reasons at least for some mergers. Inefficiencies in real goods markets explain why it is sometimes cheaper to acquire resources and strategic links through mergers. This was the main motive for widespread mergers in the Canadian oil and mining industries in recent years.

Scale economies and increasing market share are also important in current mergers. For example, when Rogers Wireless acquired Saskatchewan Communications Network in 2012, one of the main motives was to expand its national reach for Citytv content, allowing it to compete with other national broadcasters.

Tax Gains

Tax gains often are a powerful incentive for some acquisitions. The possible tax gains from an acquisition include the following:

1. The use of tax losses.
2. The use of unused debt capacity.
3. The use of surplus funds.
4. The ability to write up the value of depreciable assets.

NET OPERATING LOSSES   Firms that lose money on a pre-tax basis do not pay taxes. Such firms can end up with tax losses that they cannot use. These tax losses are referred to as NOL (an acronym for net operating losses).

A firm with net operating losses may be an attractive merger partner for a firm with significant tax liabilities. Absent any other effects, the combined firm would have a lower tax bill than the two firms considered separately. This is a good example of how a firm can be more valuable merged than standing alone. For example, tax savings made possible by Dome Petroleum's large losses were an important attraction to Amoco when it bought Dome in 1988.

There is an important qualification to our NOL discussion. Canadian tax laws permit firms that experience periods of profit and loss to even things out through loss carry-back and carry-forward provisions. A firm that has been profitable in the past but has a loss in the current year can get refunds of income taxes paid in the three previous years. After that, losses can be carried forward for up to seven years. Thus, a merger to exploit unused tax shields must offer tax savings over and above what can be accomplished by firms via carry-overs.

UNUSED DEBT CAPACITY   Some firms do not use as much debt as they are able. This makes them potential acquisition candidates. Adding debt can provide important tax savings, and many acquisitions are financed with debt. The acquiring company can deduct interest payments on the newly created debt and reduce taxes.[9]

SURPLUS FUNDS   Another quirk in the tax laws involves surplus funds. Consider a firm that has a free cash flow available after all taxes have been paid and after all positive net present value projects have been financed.

In this situation, aside from purchasing fixed income securities, the firm has several ways to spend the free cash flow, including:

1. Pay dividends.
2. Buy back its own shares.
3. Acquire shares in another firm.

We discussed the first two options in Chapter 17. We saw that an extra dividend increases the income tax paid by some investors. And, under Canada Revenue Agency regulations, share repurchase does not always reduce the taxes paid by shareholders when compared to paying dividends.

To avoid these problems, the firm can buy another firm. By doing this, the tax problem associated with paying a dividend is avoided.

ASSET WRITE-UPS   We have previously observed that, in a taxable acquisition, the assets of the acquired firm can be revalued. If the value of the assets is increased, tax deductions for depreciation are a gain.

Changing Capital Requirements

All firms must make investments in working capital and fixed assets to sustain an efficient level of operating activity. A merger may reduce the combined investments needed by the two firms. For example, Firm A may need to expand its manufacturing facilities while Firm B has significant excess capacity. It may be much cheaper for Firm A to buy Firm B than to build from scratch.

In addition, acquiring firms may see ways of more effectively managing existing assets. This can occur with a reduction in working capital by more efficient handling of cash, accounts receivable, and inventory. Finally, the acquiring firm may also sell certain assets that are not needed in the combined firm.

Avoiding Mistakes

Evaluating the benefit of a potential acquisition is more difficult than a standard capital budgeting analysis because so much of the value can come from intangible, or otherwise difficult to quantify, benefits. Consequently, there is a great deal of room for error. Here are some general rules to remember:

1. *Do not ignore market values.* There is no point and little gain to estimating the value of a publicly traded firm when that value can be directly observed. The current market value represents the consensus of investors concerning the firm's value (under existing management). Use this value as a starting point. If the firm is not publicly held, the place to start is with similar firms that are publicly held.
2. *Estimate only incremental cash flows.* It is important to estimate the cash flows that are incremental to the acquisition. Only incremental cash flows from an acquisition add value to the acquiring firm. Acquisition analysis should thus focus only on the newly created, incremental cash flows from the proposed acquisition.
3. *Use the correct discount rate.* The discount rate should be the required rate of return for the incremental cash flows associated with the acquisition. It should reflect the risk associated with the use of funds, not the source. In particular, if Firm A is acquiring Firm B, Firm A's cost of capital is not particularly relevant. Firm B's cost of capital is a much more appropriate discount rate because it reflects the risk of Firm B's cash flows.

---

[9] While unused debt capacity can be a valid reason for a merger, hindsight shows that many mergers in the 1980s overused debt financing. We discuss this in more detail later.

4. *Be aware of transaction costs.* An acquisition may involve substantial (and sometimes astounding) transaction costs. These include fees to investment bankers, legal fees, and disclosure requirements.

A Note on Inefficient Management and Opportunistic Takeover Offers

There are firms whose value could be increased with a change in management. These firms are poorly run or otherwise do not efficiently use their assets to create shareholder value. Mergers are a means of replacing management in such cases.[10]

Furthermore, the fact that a firm might benefit from a change in management does not necessarily mean that existing management is dishonest, incompetent, or negligent. Instead, just as some athletes are better than others, so might some management teams be better at running a business. This can be particularly true during times of technological change or other periods when innovations in business practice are occurring. In any case, to the extent that they can identify poorly run firms or firms that otherwise would benefit from a change in management, corporate raiders provide a valuable service to target firm shareholders and society in general.

The consumption of perks by top management is another inefficiency that may be eliminated by acquisition. For example, such perks as corporate jets, chauffer service, club memberships and spousal travel may reduce shareholder value if not linked to productivity gains.

On the other side of the ledger, bidders sometimes submit a "lowball" bid to try to gain control of a firm whose value is temporarily depressed due to market conditions outside the control of management. From the viewpoint of the target firm, such a bid is deemed opportunistic. Such bids were common at the time of the 2008 financial crises. More recently, at the time of writing, U.S. cosmetics producer, Avon Products, rejected a bid from rival Coty as opportunistic and undervaluing the company.

The Negative Side of Takeovers

While most financial analysts would likely agree that corporate raiders can deliver benefits to society, there is concern over whether the cost is too high. Critics of takeovers (and especially LBOs) are concerned that social costs are not counted when the post-takeover search for efficiency gains leads to plant closures and layoffs. When plants close or move, workers and equipment can be turned to other uses only at some cost to society. For example, taxpayers may need to subsidize retraining and relocation programs for workers or tax incentives for investment. For example, in the late 1990s larger companies bought two major financial institutions headquartered in London, Ontario: Canada Trust and London Life. In both cases, the head offices moved elsewhere, raising fears of lost jobs and economic dislocation.

Critics of takeovers argue that they reduce trust between management and labour thus reducing efficiency and increasing costs. They point to Japan, Germany, and Korea, where there are few takeovers, as examples of more efficient economies. They argue that, as an alternative to takeovers, a strong board of outside directors could maximize management's efficiency.[11]

Concept Questions

1. What are the relevant incremental cash flows for evaluating a merger candidate?
2. What are some different sources of gain from acquisition?
3. Are takeovers good for society? State the main arguments on both sides.

---

[10] Another alternative is for a firm to spin off or divest negative NPV divisions. See Chapter 11 for more discussion of the abandonment option.

[11] This section draws on C. Robinson's points in "C. Robinson versus W. Block, Are Corporate Takeovers Good or Bad? A Debate," *Canadian Investment Review*, Fall 1991, pp. 53–60; and on a piece by the late W. S. Allen, "Relegating Corporate Takeovers to the 'Campeaust' Heap: A Proposal," *Canadian Investment Review*, Spring 1990, pp. 71–76.

23.5 | Some Financial Side Effects of Acquisitions

In addition to the various possibilities we discussed, mergers can have some purely financial side effects; that is, things that occur regardless of whether the merger makes economic sense or not. Two such effects are particularly worth mentioning: EPS growth and diversification.

EPS Growth

earnings per share (EPS)
Net income minus any cash dividends on preferred stock, divided by the number of shares of common stock outstanding.

An acquisition can create the appearance of growth in **earnings per share (EPS)**. This may fool investors into thinking the firm is doing better than it really is. What happens is easiest to see with an example.

Suppose Global Resources Ltd. acquires Regional Enterprises. The financial positions of Global and Regional before the acquisition are shown in Table 23.3. Because the merger creates no additional value, the combined firm (Global Resources after acquiring Regional) has a value that is equal to the sum of the values of the two firms before the merger.

TABLE 23.3

Financial positions of Global Resources and Regional Enterprises

	Global Resources before Merger	Regional Enterprises before Merger	Global Resources after Merger	
			The Market is Smart	The Market is Fooled
Earnings per share	$ 1.00	$ 1.00	$ 1.43	$ 1.43
Price per share	$ 25.00	$ 10.00	$ 25.00	$ 35.71
Price/earnings ratio	25	10	17.5	25
Number of shares	100	100	140	140
Total earnings	$ 100	$ 100	$ 200	$ 200
Total value	$2,500	$1,000	$3,500	$5,000

Exchange ratio: 1 share in Global for 2.5 shares in Regional.

Both Global and Regional have 100 shares outstanding before the merger. However, Global sells for $25 per share versus $10 per share for Regional. Global therefore acquires Regional by exchanging 1 of its shares for every 2.5 Regional shares. Since there are 100 shares in Regional, it takes 100/2.5 = 40 shares in all.

After the merger, Global has 140 shares outstanding, and several things happen (see Column 3 of Table 23.3):

1. The market value of the combined firm is $3,500. This is equal to the sum of the values of the separate firms before the merger. If the market is smart, it realizes the combined firm is worth the sum of the values of the separate firms.

2. The earnings per share of the merged firm are $1.43. The acquisition enables Global to increase its earnings per share from $1 to $1.43, an increase of 43 percent.

3. Because the stock price of Global after the merger is the same as before the merger, the price/earnings ratio must fall. This is true as long as the market is smart and recognizes that the total market value has not been altered by the merger.

If the market is fooled, it might mistake the 43 percent increase in earnings per share for true growth. In this case, the price/earnings ratio of Global may not fall after the merger. Suppose the price/earnings ratio of Global remains equal to 25. Since the combined firm has earnings of $200, the total value of the combined firm increases to $5,000 (25 × $200). The per share value of Global increases to $35.71 ($5,000/140).

This is earnings growth magic. Like all good magic, it is just illusion. For it to work, the shareholders of Global and Regional must receive something for nothing. This, of course, is unlikely with so simple a trick.

Diversification

diversification
Investment in more than one asset; returns do not move proportionally in the same direction at the same time, thus reducing risk.

Diversification is commonly mentioned as a benefit to a merger. For example, U.S. Steel Corporation included diversification as a benefit in its acquisition of Marathon Oil Company in 1982, a merger that ranked in size just behind Campeau's purchase of Federated Department Stores. The problem is that diversification per se probably does not create value.

Going back to Chapter 13, diversification reduces unsystematic risk. We also saw that the value of an asset depends on its systematic risk and that diversification does not directly affect systematic risk. Since the unsystematic risk is not especially important, there is no particular benefit to reducing it.

An easy way to see why diversification isn't an important benefit to mergers is to consider someone who owned stock in U.S. Steel and Marathon Oil. Such a shareholder is already diversified between these two investments. The merger doesn't do anything that the shareholders can't do for themselves.

More generally, shareholders can get all the diversification they want by buying stock in different companies. As a result, they won't pay a premium for a merged company just for the benefit of diversification.

By the way, we are not saying that U.S. Steel (now USX Corporation) made a mistake. At the time of the merger, U.S. Steel was a cash-rich company (more than 20 percent of its assets were in the form of cash and marketable securities). It is not uncommon to see firms with surplus cash articulating a "need" for diversification.

Concept Questions

1. Why can a merger create the appearance of earnings growth?
2. Why is diversification by itself not a good reason for a merger?

23.6 | The Cost of an Acquisition

We've discussed some of the benefits of acquisition. We now need to discuss the cost of a merger.[12] We learned earlier that the net incremental gain to a merger is:

$$\Delta V = V_{AB} - (V_A + V_B)$$

Also, the total value of Firm B to Firm A, V_B^*, is:

$$V_B^* = V_B + \Delta V$$

The NPV of the merger is therefore:

$$\text{NPV} = V_B^* - \text{Cost to Firm A of the acquisition} \qquad [23.1]$$

To illustrate, suppose we have the following pre-merger information for Firm A and Firm B:

	Firm A	Firm B
Price per share	$ 20	$ 10
Number of shares	25	10
Total market value	$500	$100

Both of these firms are 100 percent equity. You estimate that the incremental value of the acquisition, ΔV, is $100.

The board of Firm B has indicated that it agrees to a sale if the price is $150, payable in cash or stock. This price for Firm B has two parts. Firm B is worth $100 as a stand-alone, so this is the minimum value that we could assign to Firm B. The second part, $50, is called the *merger premium*, and it represents the amount paid more than the stand-alone value.

---

[12] For a more complete discussion of the costs of a merger and the NPV approach, see S. C. Myers, "A Framework for Evaluating Mergers," in *Modern Developments in Financial Management*, ed. S. C. Myers (New York: Praeger Publishers, 1976).

Should Firm A acquire Firm B? Should it pay in cash or stock? To answer, we need to determine the NPV of the acquisition under both alternatives. We can start by noting that the value of Firm B to Firm A is:

$$V_B^* = \Delta V + V_B$$
$$= \$100 + 100 = \$200$$

The total value received by A from buying Firm B is thus $200. The question then is, how much does Firm A have to give up? The answer depends on whether cash or stock is used as the means of payment.

Case I: Cash Acquisition

The cost of an acquisition when cash is used is just the cash itself. So, if Firm A pays $150 in cash to purchase all the shares of Firm B, the cost of acquiring Firm B is $150. The NPV of a cash acquisition is:

$$NPV = V_B^* - Cost$$
$$= \$200 - 150 = \$50$$

The acquisition is, therefore, profitable.

After the merger, Firm AB still has 25 shares outstanding. The value of Firm A after the merger is:

$$V_{AB} = V_A + (V_B^* - Cost)$$
$$= \$500 + 200 - 150$$
$$= \$550$$

This is just the pre-merger value of $500 plus the $50 NPV. The price per share after the merger is $550/25 = $22, a gain of $2 per share.

Case II: Stock Acquisition

Things are somewhat more complicated when stock is the means of payment. In a cash merger, the shareholders in B receive cash for their stock, and, as in the previous U.S. Steel/Marathon Oil example, they no longer participate in the company. Thus, as we have seen, the cost of the acquisition is the amount of cash needed to pay off B's shareholders.

In a stock merger, no cash actually changes hands. Instead, the shareholders in B come in as new shareholders in the merged firm. The value of the merged firm is equal to the pre-merger values of Firms A and B plus the incremental gain from the merger, ΔV:

$$V_{AB} = V_A + V_B + \Delta V$$
$$= \$500 + 100 + 100$$
$$= \$700$$

To give $150 worth of stock for Firm B, Firm A has to give up $150/$20 = 7.5 shares. After the merger, there are thus 25 + 7.5 = 32.5 shares outstanding and the per-share value is $700/32.5 = $21.54.

Notice that the per-share price after the merger is lower under the stock purchase option. The reason has to do with the fact that B's shareholders own stock in the new firm.

It appears that Firm A paid $150 for Firm B. However, it actually paid more than that. When all is said and done, B's shareholders own 7.5 shares of stock in the merged firm. After the merger, each of these shares is worth $21.54. The total value of the consideration received by B's shareholders is thus 7.5 × $21.54 = $161.55.

This $161.55 is the true cost of the acquisition because it is what the sellers actually end up receiving. The NPV of the merger to Firm A is:

$$NPV = V_B^* - Cost$$
$$= \$200 - 161.55 = \$38.45$$

We can check this by noting that A started with 25 shares worth $20 each. The gain to A of $38.45 works out to be $38.45/25 = $1.54 per share. The value of the stock increases to $21.54 as we calculated.

When we compare the cash acquisition to the stock acquisition, we see that the cash acquisition is better in this case, because Firm A gets to keep all the NPV if it pays in cash. If it pays in stock, Firm B's shareholders share in the NPV by becoming new shareholders in A.

Cash versus Common Stock

The distinction between cash and common stock financing in a merger is an important one. If cash is used, the cost of an acquisition is not dependent on the acquisition gains. All other things being the same, if common stock is used, the cost is higher because Firm A's shareholders must share the acquisition gains with the shareholders of Firm B. However, if the NPV of the acquisition is negative, the loss is shared between the two firms.

Whether to finance an acquisition by cash or by shares of stock depends on several factors, including:[13]

1. *Sharing gains.* If cash is used to finance an acquisition, the selling firm's shareholders do not participate in the potential gains of the merger. Of course, if the acquisition is not a success, the losses are not shared, and shareholders of the acquiring firm are worse off than if stock were used.
2. *Taxes.* Acquisition by cash usually results in a taxable transaction. Acquisition by exchanging stock is generally tax free.
3. *Control.* Acquisition by cash does not affect the control of the acquiring firm. Acquisition with voting shares may have implications for control of the merged firm.

In 1999 and early 2000, high stock prices in the technology sector resulted in a number of acquisitions financed with shares as companies like JDS Uniphase and Nortel Networks expanded through acquisitions.

Concept Questions

1. Why does the true cost of a stock acquisition depend on the gain from the merger?
2. What are some important factors in deciding whether to use stock or cash in an acquisition?

23.7 | Defensive Tactics

Target firm managers frequently resist takeover attempts. Resistance usually starts with press releases and mailings to shareholders presenting management's viewpoint. It can eventually lead to legal action and solicitation of competing bids. Managerial action to defeat a takeover attempt may make target shareholders better off if it elicits a higher offer premium from the bidding firm or another firm.

Of course, management resistance may simply reflect pursuit of self-interest at the expense of shareholders. This is a controversial subject. At times, management resistance has greatly increased the amount ultimately received by shareholders. At other times, management resistance appears to have defeated all takeover attempts to the detriment of shareholders.

In this section, we describe various defensive tactics that have been used by target firms' managements to resist unfriendly attempts. The law surrounding these defences is not settled, and some of these manoeuvres may ultimately be deemed illegal or otherwise unsuitable. Our discussion of defensive tactics that may serve to entrench management at the expense of shareholders takes us into **corporate governance**. In addition to describing management's actions, we comment on how large pension funds and other institutional investors strive to reform the corporate governance practices of companies in which they invest.

corporate governance
Rules and practices relating to how corporations are governed by management, directors, and shareholders.

---

[13] In Canada, cash transactions for the deals mentioned in Table 23.1 ranged from 50 percent to 61 percent of annual transaction value.

The Control Block and the Corporate Charter

control block
An interest controlling 50 percent of outstanding votes plus one; thereby it may decide the fate of the firm.

If one individual or group owns 51 percent of a company's stock, this **control block** makes a hostile takeover virtually impossible. In the extreme, one interest may own all the stock. Examples are privately owned companies such as Olympia and York Developments Ltd. and Crown corporations such as Quebec Hydro. Many Canadian companies are subsidiaries of foreign corporations that own control blocks. Many domestically owned companies have controlling shareholders.[14]

As a result, control blocks are typical in Canada although they are the exception in the United States. Table 23.4 shows that around 55 percent of corporations in Canada are widely held versus 72 for the United States. One important implication is that minority shareholders need protection in Canada. One key group of minority shareholders are pension funds and other institutional investors. They are becoming increasingly vocal in opposing defensive tactics that are seen to be entrenching management at the expense of shareholders. We discuss several examples next.

For widely held companies, their corporate charters establish the conditions that allow for takeovers. The *corporate charter* refers to the articles of incorporation and corporate bylaws that establish the governance rules of the firm. Firms can amend their corporate charters to make acquisitions more difficult. For example, usually two-thirds of the shareholders of record must approve a merger. Firms can make it more difficult to be acquired by changing this to 80 percent or so. This is called a *supermajority amendment*.

Another device is to stagger the election of the board members. This makes it more difficult to elect a new board of directors quickly. We discuss staggered elections in Chapter 8.

TABLE 23.4

Comparison of Ownership and Control-Enhancing Mechanisms (in percentage)

	Canada	United States	Asia	Europe
Widely held	55.4	71.9	43.6	36.9
Controlled at 20% threshold	44.6	28.1	56.4	63.1
Of which: Family controlled	31.2	19.8	37.9	44.3
Widely-held financial	10.8	4.7	4.9	8.7
Widely-held corporation	2.6	2.4	9.0	2.0
State owned	0.0	0.0	4.6	4.1
Miscellaneous	0.0	1.2	0.0	3.4
Controlled by pyramiding or multiple-control chains	7.6	4.0	48.8	24.7
Controlled by dual-class shares	14.0	8.2	NA	19.9
Average ratio of cash flow to voting rights	89.2	94.0	74.6	87.0

Source: King, Michael R. & Santor, Eric, 2008. "Family values: Ownership structure, performance and capital structure of Canadian firms," *Journal of Banking & Finance*, Elsevier, vol. 32(11), pages 2423–2432, November.

Repurchase / Standstill Agreements

Managers of target firms may attempt to negotiate standstill agreements. Standstill agreements are contracts where the bidding firm agrees to limit its holdings in the target firm. These agreements usually lead to the end of takeover attempts.

In the U.S., standstill agreements often occur at the same time that a targeted repurchase is arranged. In a targeted repurchase, a firm buys a certain amount of its own stock from an individual investor, usually at a substantial premium. These premiums can be thought of as payments to potential bidders to eliminate unfriendly takeover attempts. Critics of such payments view them as bribes and label them **greenmail**. Paying greenmail may harm minority shareholders if it heads off a takeover that would raise the stock price.

greenmail
A targeted stock repurchase where payments are made to potential bidders to eliminate unfriendly takeover attempts.

Standstill agreements also occur in takeover attempts in Canada but without greenmail, which

---

[14]Important exceptions are chartered banks. As we showed in Chapter 1, at the time of writing, the *Bank Act* prohibited any one interest from owning more than 10 percent of the shares.

is ruled out by securities laws. For example, in December 2011, activist investor and a majority shareholder of Canadian Pacific Railway, Bill Ackman was offered a seat on the board of directors that was conditional on his signing a standstill agreement that would have stopped him from waging a proxy battle to replace most of the directors. The agreement would have also restricted his ability to buy a larger stake or to take any actions, such as proxy contests, that opposed CP's board. Critics of standstill agreements argue that in cases like this, such agreements often cause losses for minority shareholders by averting takeovers at a premium price.

Exclusionary Offers and Dual Class Stock

An exclusionary offer is the opposite of a targeted repurchase. Here the firm or an outside group makes an offer for a given amount of stock while excluding targeted shareholders, often holders of non-voting shares. This kind of an offer is made easier in Canada since dual-class, non-voting shares have historically been more prevalent than in the United States. Market regulators frown on such offers and an exclusionary offer for Canadian Tire voting shares was voided by the Ontario Securities Commission in 1986. Based on that precedent, it appears that any future exclusionary offers are likely to be viewed as an illegal form of discrimination against one group of shareholders.

In addition, corporate governance guidelines call for the removal of dual-class share structures although current academic research fails to find any harm to shareholders.[15] The percentage of dual-class shares in TSX reduced from 14% in 1993 to 6% in 2010.[16] For example, the Stronach family owned only 0.8 percent of the equity in the firm but controlled 66.2 percent of the votes at Magna International (the highest voting power to equity ownership ratio for a composite company). Magna, in turn, held voting control at Decoma and Tesma International (both also part of the S&P/TSX Composite) through use of dual-class share structures.[17] In August 2010, the company completed a $1.1 billion plan of arrangement to eliminate dual-class share structure.

Share Rights Plans

A **poison pill** is a tactic designed to repel would-be suitors. The term comes from the world of espionage. Agents are supposed to bite a pill of cyanide rather than permit capture. Presumably, this prevents enemy interrogators from learning important secrets.

In the equally colourful world of corporate finance, a poison pill is a financial device designed to make it impossible for a firm to be acquired without management's consent—unless the buyer is willing to commit financial suicide.

In recent years, many of the largest firms in the United States and Canada have adopted poison pill provisions of one form or another, often calling them **shareholder rights plans (SRPs)** or something similar. Inco introduced the first poison pill in Canada in 1988.

SRPs differ quite a bit in detail from company to company; we describe a kind of generic approach here. In general, when a company adopts an SRP, it distributes share rights to its existing shareholders.[18] These rights allow shareholders to buy shares of stock (or preferred stock) at some fixed price.

The rights issued with an SRP have a number of unusual features. First, the exercise or subscription price on the right is usually set high enough so the rights are well out of the money, meaning the purchase price is much higher than the current stock price. The rights are often good for 10 years, and the purchase or exercise price is usually a reasonable estimate of what the stock will be worth at that time.

Second, unlike ordinary stock rights, these rights can't be exercised immediately, and they can't be bought and sold separately from the stock. Also, they can essentially be cancelled by

Margin notes

magna.com

poison pill
A financial device designed to make unfriendly takeover attempts unappealing, if not impossible.

shareholder rights plan
Provisions allowing existing shareholders to purchase stock at some fixed price should an outside takeover bid take place, discouraging hostile takeover attempts.

---

[15] V. Jog, P. Zhu, and S. Dutta, "The Impact of Restricted Voting Share Structure on Firm Value and Performance," *Corporate Governance: An International Review*, 18, September 2010, pp. 415–437.

[16] Amoako-Adu, B., Baulkaran, V., & Smith, B. F. (2011). Unification of dual class shares in Canada with clinical case on Magna International. Financial Services Research Centre, School of Business and Economics, Wilfrid Laurier University.

[17] This discussion is drawn from S. Maich, "Stronach has most votes, least shares," *National Post*, June 11, 2003, IN1.

[18] We discuss ordinary share rights in Chapter 15.

management at any time; often, they can be redeemed (bought back) for a penny apiece, or some similarly trivial amount.

Things get interesting when, under certain circumstances, the rights are triggered. This means the rights become exercisable, they can be bought and sold separately from the stock, and they are not easily cancelled or redeemed. Typically, the rights are triggered when someone acquires 20 percent of the common stock or otherwise announces a tender offer.

When the rights are triggered, they can be exercised. Since they are out of the money, this fact is not especially important. Certain other features come into play, however. The most important is the flip-over provision.

The flip-over provision is the poison in the pill. In the event of a merger, the holder of a right can pay the exercise price and receive common stock in the merged firm worth twice the exercise price. In other words, holders of the right can buy stock in the merged firm at half price.[19]

The rights issued in connection with an SRP are poison pills because anyone trying to force a merger would trigger the rights. When this happens, all the target firm's shareholders can effectively buy stock in the merged firm at half price. This greatly increases the cost of the merger to the bidder because the target firm's shareholders end up with a much larger percentage of the merged firm.

Notice that the flip-over provision doesn't prevent someone from acquiring control of a firm by purchasing a majority interest. It just acts to prevent a complete merger of the two firms. Even so, this inability to combine can have serious tax and other implications for the buyer.

The intention of a poison pill is to force a bidder to negotiate with management. This can be bad news for shareholders of the target firm if it discourages takeovers and entrenches inefficient management. On the other hand, poison pills could be positive for the target's shareholders if they allow management time to find competing offers that maximize the selling price. For example, in 2012, Moneta Porcupine Mines Inc., a mining company headquartered in Timmins, Ontario, adopted a shareholder rights plan to protect against unwanted takeovers after it released a gold resource estimate for the Golden Highway project in Ontario.

In Canada, several arrangements exist that make poison pills more beneficial to target shareholders than in the U.S. First, the Ontario Securities Commission and its counterparts in other provinces, intervene in takeover bids to rule on the acceptability of poison pills. In many cases, the result has been to extend the waiting period and increase shareholder value.[20] Still, most large Canadian institutional investors like the Caisse de dépôt or Ontario Teachers' Pension Plan consider the introduction of poison pills to be a bad corporate governance practice.

Going Private and Leveraged Buyouts

As we have previously discussed, going private refers to what happens when the publicly owned stock in a firm is replaced with complete equity ownership by a private group, which may include elements of existing management. As a consequence, the firm's stock is taken off the market (if it is an exchange-traded stock, it is delisted) and is no longer traded.

One result of going private is that takeovers via tender offer can no longer occur since there are no publicly held shares. In this sense, an LBO (or, more specifically, a management buyout or MBO) can be a takeover defence. However, it's only a defence for management. From the stockholder's point of view, an LBO is a takeover because they are bought out.

In an LBO, the selling shareholders are invariably paid a premium more than the market price, just as they are in a merger.[21] As with a merger, the acquirer profits only if the synergy created is greater than the premium. Synergy is quite plausible in a merger of two firms, and we delineated a number of types of synergy earlier in the chapter. However, it is much more difficult to explain synergy in an LBO, because only one firm is involved.

---

[19] Some plans also contain flip-in provisions. These allow the holder to buy stock in the target company at half price when the target company is the surviving company in a merger. Simultaneously, the rights owned by the raider (the acquirer) are voided. A merger where the target is the surviving company is called a *reverse merger*.

[20] For a detailed discussion of poison pills in Canada, see P. Halpern, "Poison Pills: The Next Decade," *Canadian Investment Review* 11, Winter 1998, pp. 69–70.

[21] H. DeAngelo, L. DeAngelo, and E. M. Rice, "Going Private: Minority Freezeouts and Shareholder Wealth," *Journal of Law and Economics* 27 (1984). They show that the premiums paid to existing shareholders in U.S. LBOs and other going-private transactions are about the same as interfirm acquisitions.

There are generally two reasons given for the ability of an LBO to create value: First, the extra debt provides a tax deduction, which, as earlier chapters suggest, leads to an increase in firm value. Most LBOs are on firms with stable earnings and with low to moderate debt.[22] The LBO may simply increase the firm's debt to its optimum level.

Second, the LBO usually turns the previous managers into owners, thereby increasing their incentive to work hard. The increase in debt is a further incentive because the managers must earn more than the debt service to obtain any profit for themselves.

LBOs to Date: The Record

Since the mid-1980s, ongoing experience with LBOs has revealed some weaknesses both in the concept and the financing vehicle—junk bonds.

Problems facing LBOs in the early 1990s are exemplified in the trials of Robert Campeau whose real estate company took over Allied Stores in 1986 and then Federated Department Stores in 1988.

Campeau was correct; Federated Department Stores assets were undervalued at the pre-take-over share price of $33 but hindsight shows that the $73.50 per share takeover price was too high. Further, the deal was overleveraged with 97 percent debt financing. With either a lower purchase price, or lower leverage, the deal might have survived.[23]

Despite an injection of $300 million from Olympia & York Developments Ltd. (then owned by the Reichmann family of Toronto), Campeau Corporation had to default on its bank loans. As a result, the National Bank of Canada took over 35 percent of Campeau's voting stock in January 1990. Shortly after, Allied and Federated filed for bankruptcy protection in the United States. Over the next year, Campeau sold just under $2 billion in Canadian real estate to try to reduce its debt to manageable levels in order to survive.[24] In January 1991, Campeau Corporation's name was changed to Candev with a 65 percent control block in the hands of Olympia & York. Robert Campeau lost his seat on the board and all but 2 percent of the company's stock. LBO problems reflected on the high-yield or junk bonds used heavily to finance them. For example, when Allied and Federated sought bankruptcy protection in 1990, Campeau junk bonds that had a face value of $1,000 sold for $110.[25] In a more positive example, Kohlberg Kravis Roberts and Ontario Teachers' Pension Plan bought Yellow Pages from Bell Canada in a $3-billion LBO in 2002. In July 2003, they sold part of their holding for $1 billion in an income trust IPO.[26]

Other Defensive Devices

As corporate takeovers become more common, other colourful terms have become popular.

- *Golden parachutes.* Some target firms provide compensation to top-level management if a takeover occurs. This can be viewed as a payment to management to make it less concerned for its own welfare and more interested in shareholders when considering a takeover bid. Alternatively, the payment can be seen as an attempt to enrich management at the shareholders' expense. For example, in October 2010, the CEO of Potash Corp. of Saskatchewan Inc., Bill Doyle, was given a golden parachute as the company agreed to cover any penalty taxes he would incur if the U.S. deems his severance package excessive. This golden parachute can be viewed as the company's reaction to the proposed acquisition by BHP Billiton a few months earlier.
- *Crown jewels.* Firms often sell major assets—crown jewels—when faced with a takeover threat. This is sometimes referred to as the *scorched earth strategy*. For example, in 2012, when the market capitalization of Research in Motion Ltd. (RIM) was about 1% of that of

---

[22] T. Melman, "Leveraged Buyouts: How Everyone Can Win," *Canadian Investment Review*, Spring 1990, pp. 67–70, discusses LBOs from a management perspective.

[23] S. N. Kaplan, "Campeau's Acquisition of Federated, Value Destroyed or Value Added?" *Journal of Financial Economics*, December 1989, pp. 189–212.

[24] S. Horvitch, "Campeau 'Selling Itself' to Survive," *The Financial Post*, July 1, 1991, p. 22.

[25] See Edward Altman in Chapter 7 for more on problems with junk bonds in the United States.

[26] Our discussion draws on Laura Santini, "Deals & Dealmakers: Ontario Teachers' Makes Grade With Private-Equity Plays," *Wall Street Journal*, August 15, 2005, p. C1.

Apple Inc., there was speculation that RIM might avoid any acquisition by selling its crown jewels—patents and networks.

- *White knight.* Target firms sometimes seek a competing bid from a friendly bidder—a white knight—who promises to maintain the jobs of existing management and to refrain from selling the target's assets. For example in 2011, when Wi-LAN Inc., an Intellectual Property (IP) licensing company, made a hostile takeover bid to acquire Mosaid Technologies Inc., an Ottawa based patent enforcement firm, Mosaid obtained a white knight in the form of Sterling Partners, a leading private equity firm.

IN THEIR OWN WORDS...

Christine Dobby on Talent Acquisitions

THE BEST THING that can happen to a modern technological entrepreneur is to watch the object of their toil and anxiety evolve into a billion-dollar goliath. Running a close second is having that successful startup scooped up by a buyer with deep pockets for a big, fat payout. But with technology talent scarce in such places as Silicon Valley, buyers may come calling not for the business you've created with the sweat of your own brow, but rather the people you hired to help get it off the ground.

"One of the ways that's really emerged over the last little while for big companies like Google and Facebook and Twitter to get the best talent is to buy it," said Roger Chabra, a partner at Montreal-based venture capital firm Rho Canada Ventures. "It's certainly happening a lot more than it has, basically just because there's a talent war going on. Especially with big companies—particularly in environments like the Valley—there's real fighting in the trenches for great talent."

As more computer science graduates than ever go into business on their own, large, established Internet companies with vast demand for workers are struggling to hire. Small acquisitions can be a good way for them to address that problem, Mark MacLeod, general partner at Montreal based Real Ventures, a $50 million seed-stage fund, told a session on mergers and acquisitions at a PricewaterhouseCoopers LLP conference in Toronto last month. "If you have a really strong tech team, that commands valuations," he said. "A phenomenon we're seeing a lot more these days is kind of 'acqui-hires' or buying companies for talent." It's difficult to get a clear picture of just how prevalent the phenomenon is. From 2009 to 2011, 44% of Canadian technology companies that were acquired went to U.S. buyers, according to PwC. Mr. MacLeod pointed to Vancouver's Summify, a social media summary company that was snapped up by Twitter in January. Work on the Summify product was shut down and the team moved to San Francisco to work for the micro-blogging site.

Google Inc. has also grabbed some Canadian talent. In 2010, it acquired BumpTop, founded by Anand Agarawala, who developed the software product out of his University of Toronto master's degree research and now works as a product manager at the search engine giant. In some cases, Mr. Chabra said, a large company might acquire a startup solely for its team with the aim of absorbing the employees into its main operations,

often in California. Other times, the purchaser could be looking to expand its reach with new outposts and buying a ready-made team in a new city could be a convenient way to do that. The quick talent grab may be appealing to the buyer, but Mr. Chabra said some venture capital investors may try to block such sales because they get a portion of the purchase price but are cut out of bonuses given to individual team members for joining the acquirer.

Bonuses aside, acqui-hires may not sit well with those being acquired primarily for their brain power. "If you're working on something and the acquirer is really going to make this a big platform, and you're going to have a significant role in the company and budget to build a big team, then that's amazing," Mr. MacLeod said. "If you're just being acquired for talent and the product's going to be shelved, maybe that's not the best outcome."

Not every acquisition of a Canadian tech startup ends up in the shuttering of the product and transplant of the team south of the border. For example, California cloud-computing giant Salesforce.com Inc. has purchased Canadian companies, including Fredericton's Radian6 and Toronto's Rypple Inc., and kept the businesses and their workforces in place. London, Ont., resident Jaafer Haidar sold his own technology startup Carbyn Inc. to Buffalo, N.Y.-based Synacor Inc. this year. Other buyers were interested, including a large gaming outfit and a bigger Canadian company, Mr. Haidar said. But those two companies made it clear they were more intrigued by the Carbyn team's facility with HTML5 than its cloud-based product, which lets users log in and access their apps on any Internet-connected device.

"We enjoyed working together and working on this project. If [you are] acquired by a company that just wants the talent, then you become less of a team and more of an individual working on whatever the company wants you to work on," Mr. Haidar said, noting that his team has continued working together on the same product as a subsidiary of Synacor in Canada.

Christine Dobby writes for The Financial Post. Her comments are reproduced with permission from the July 3, 2012 edition.

Chapters, one of Canada's largest bookstore chains, was taken over for $121 million in February of 2001 by Trilogy Retail Enterprises, a firm headed by Indigo founder Heather Reisman and spouse Gerald Schwartz, of Onex Corp. The takeover was launched with the intention of merging Indigo and Chapters to create a Canadian bookstore super-chain.

Before giving in to Trilogy Retail Enterprises' final takeover bid of $121 million, Chapters' board of directors and management explored takeover defenses. Chapters had a poison pill in place to prevent a hostile takeover. When Trilogy made a partial bid which, if successful, would have given Trilogy 53 percent of Chapters, Chapters shareholders (other than the hostile bidder) had a right to purchase additional Chapters' shares at half the market price. As well, 51 days after Trilogy's initial bid, Chapters announced an offer from a white knight, Future Shop, which the Chapters' board recommended to the shareholders. Chapters entered into a support agreement with Future Shop which provided that the poison pill would only be waived for competing bids upon the take-up of Chapters' shares by Future Shop, and would remain in place to give Future Shop time to prepare and mail their offer. The poison pill was eventually removed because the OSC found that Future Shop had already had substantial time to prepare its bid. In the end, Future Shop's role as a white knight forced Trilogy to raise its bid to $121 million, finally resulting in the takeover after months of media-publicized drama.

Concept Questions

1. What can a firm do to make takeover less likely?
2. What is a share rights plan? Explain how the rights work.
3. What were the main problems faced by LBOs in the early 1990s?

23.8 | Some Evidence on Acquisitions

One of the most controversial issues surrounding our subject is whether mergers and acquisitions benefit shareholders. Quite a few studies have attempted to estimate the effect of mergers and takeovers on stock prices of the bidding and target firms. These are called *event studies* because they estimate abnormal stock-price changes on and around the offer-announcement date—the event. Abnormal returns are usually defined as the difference between actual stock returns and a market index, to take account of the influence of market-wide effects on the returns of individual securities.

Table 23.5 shows merger premiums in the Canada and the world in 2010 and 2011. The premium is the difference between the acquisition price per share and the previous share price of the target as a percentage of the previous price. For example, in the most recent period, bidders paid an average of 34.8 percent over the pre-merger price. This clearly shows that Canadian mergers benefit the target's shareholders. The average industry bid premiums in 2011 for Canada are marginally higher compared to the rest of the world.

Turning to Canadian research in Table 23.6 we find that targets do much better than bidders with an average return of 10 percent for mergers between 1994 and 2000. The other studies found that target firm shareholders in going-private transactions enjoyed an abnormal return of 25 percent.

These gains are a reflection of the merger premium that is typically paid by the acquiring firm. These gains are excess returns, that is, the returns over and above what the shareholders would normally have earned.

The shareholders of bidding firms do not fare as well. According to U.S. studies, bidders experience gains of 4 percent in tender offers, but this gain is about zero in mergers.[27] Canadian research places bidders' gains in a range from 0 to 11 percent. While some research suggests that bidding

---

[27] Loughran and Vijh find that bidders experience below-average returns for five years after acquisitions: T. Loughran and A. Vijh, "Do Long-Term Shareholders Benefit from Corporate Acquisitions," *Journal of Finance* (December 1997).

firms do poorly over a longer, three-year, period after the merger, the most recent findings show that losses to bidders' shareholders merely offset early gains with a net zero impact.[28]

What conclusions can be drawn from Tables 23.5 and our discussion? First, the evidence strongly suggests that the shareholders of successful target firms achieve substantial gains as a result of take-overs. In the U.S. the gains appear to be larger in tender offers than in mergers. This may reflect the fact that takeovers sometimes start with a friendly merger proposal from the bidder to the management of the target firm. If management rejects the offer, the bidding firm may take the offer directly to the shareholders with a tender offer. As a consequence, tender offers are frequently unfriendly.

Also, the target firm's management may actively oppose the offer with defensive tactics. This often has the result of raising the tender offer from the bidding firm; on average, friendly mergers may be arranged at lower premiums than unfriendly tender offers.

TABLE 23.5

Bid Premium: 2011 Average Premium to 4 week stock price

Sector	Canada		World	
	2011	2010	2011	2010
Consumer Products and Services	12.8	12.8	33.4	32.0
Consumer Staples	66.1	1.0	29.5	27.4
Energy and Power	37.4	35.1	30.8	24.4
Financials	31.2	28.4	29.9	30.4
Healthcare	40.5	30.1	35.8	35.1
High Technology	41.1	41.0	31.7	28.1
Industrials	69.0	31.9	31.2	24.2
Materials	31.1	34.9	29.4	30.6
Media and Entertainment	16.2	13.0	20.5	26.8
Real Estate	36.1	33.8	30.6	24.6
Retail	27.9	3.4	29.8	30.9
Telecommunications	53.1	53.1	32.2	26.3
Average Industry Total	34.8	34.1	30.5	28.8

Source: Thomson Reuters

TABLE 23.6

Abnormal returns in successful Canadian mergers

	Target	Bidder
1271 acquired, 242 targets, 1994–2000**	10%	1%
1930 mergers, 1964–1983*	9	3
119 mergers, 1963–1982†	23	11
173 going-private transactions, 1977–1989‡	25	NA
Minority buyouts	27	
Non-controlling bidder	24	
1300 acquisitions, 1993–2002#	NA	0%

*From B. Espen Eckbo, "Mergers and the Market for Corporate Control: The Canadian Evidence," *Canadian Journal of Economics*, May 1986, pp. 236–60. The test for bidders excluded firms involved in multiple mergers.
†From A. L. Calvet and J. Lefoll, "Information Asymmetry and Wealth Effect of Canadian Corporate Acquisitions," *Financial Review*, November 1987, pp. 415–431.
‡Modified from B. Amoako-Adu and B. Smith, "How Do Shareholders Fare in Minority Buyouts?" *Canadian Investment Review*, Fall 1991, pp. 79–88.
**From A. Yuce and A. Ng, "Effects of Private and Public Canadian Mergers," *Canadian Journal of Administrative Sciences*, June 2005, pp. 111–124.
#From S. Dutta and V. Jog, "The Long-term Performance of Acquiring Firms: A Re-examination of an Anomaly," *Journal of Banking and Finance* 33, 2009, pp. 1400–1412.

---

[28] P. André, M. Kooli, and J-F L'Her, "The Long-Run Performance of Mergers and Acquisitions: Evidence from the Canadian Stock Market," *Financial Management*, Winter 2004, pp. 27–43. and S. Dutta and V. Jog, "The Long-term Performance of Acquiring Firms: A Re-examination of an Anomaly," *Journal of Banking and Finance* 33, 2009, pp. 1400–1412.

The second conclusion we can draw is that the shareholders of bidding firms earn significantly less from takeovers. The balance is more even for Canadian mergers. This may be because there is less competition among bidders in Canada. Two reasons for this are that the Canadian capital market is smaller and that federal government agencies review foreign investments.[29]

In fact, studies have found that the acquiring firms in both countries actually lose value in many mergers.[30] These findings are a puzzle, and there are a variety of explanations:

1. Anticipated merger gains may not have been completely achieved, and shareholders thus experienced losses. This can happen if managers of bidding firms tend to overestimate the gains from acquisition, as we saw happened to Campeau Corporation.

2. The bidding firms are often much larger than the target firms. Thus, even though the dollar gains to the bidder may be similar to the dollar gains earned by shareholders of the target firm, the percentage gains are much lower.[31]

3. Another possible explanation for the low returns to the shareholders of bidding firms in takeovers is simply that management may not be acting in the interest of shareholders when it attempts to acquire other firms. Perhaps, it is attempting to increase the size of the firm, even if this reduces its value per share.

4. The market for takeovers may be sufficiently competitive that the NPV of acquiring is zero because the prices paid in acquisitions fully reflect the value of the acquired firms. In other words, the sellers capture all the gain.

5. The announcement of a takeover may not convey much new information to the market about the bidding firm. This can occur because firms frequently announce intentions to engage in merger programs long before they announce specific acquisitions. In this case, the stock price in the bidding firm may already reflect anticipated gains from mergers.

Concept Questions

1. What does the evidence say about the benefits of mergers and acquisitions to target company shareholders?
2. What does the evidence say about the benefits of mergers and acquisitions to acquiring company shareholders?
3. What is the evidence on whether minority shareholders are shortchanged in mergers?

23.9 | Divestitures and Restructurings

divestiture
The sale of assets, operations, divisions, and/or segments of a business to a third party.

In contrast to a merger or acquisition, a **divestiture** occurs when a firm sells assets, operations, divisions, and/or segments to a third party. Note that divestitures are an important part of M&A activity. After all, one company's acquisition is usually another's divestiture. Also, following a merger, it is very common for certain assets or divisions to be sold. Such sales may be required by antitrust regulations; they may be needed to raise cash to help pay for a deal; or the divested units may simply be unwanted by the acquirer.

Divestitures also occur when a company decides to sell off a part of itself for reasons unrelated to mergers and acquisitions. This can happen when a particular unit is unprofitable or not a good strategic fit. Or, a firm may decide to cash out of a very profitable operation. Finally, a cash-strapped firm may have to sell assets just to raise capital (this commonly occurs in bankruptcy).

A divestiture usually occurs like any other sale. A company lets it be known that it has assets for sale and seeks offers. If a suitable offer is forthcoming, a sale occurs.

In some cases, particularly when the desired divestiture is a relatively large operating unit,

---

[29] P. Halpern, "Poison Pills," p. 66; and A. L. Calvet and J. Lefoll, "Information Asymmetry," p. 432.

[30] S. Moeller, F. Schlingemann, and R. Stulz, "Wealth Destruction on a Massive Scale? A study of Acquiring Firm Returns in the Recent Merger Wave," *Journal of Finance* (April 2005).

[31] This factor cannot explain the imbalance in returns in the first Canadian study in Table 23.6. In this sample, bidder and target firms were about the same size.

equity carve-out
The sale of stock in a wholly owned subsidiary via an IPO.

companies will elect to do an **equity carve-out**. To do a carve-out, a parent company first creates a completely separate company of which the parent is the sole shareholder. Next, the parent company arranges an initial public offering (IPO) in which a fraction, perhaps 20 percent or so, of the parent's stock is sold to the public, thus creating a publicly held company. An example of an equity carve-out is Wendy's International selling a small portion of wholly-owned Tim Hortons via IPO in March 2006.

spin-off
The distribution of shares in a subsidiary to existing parent company shareholders.

Instead of a carve-out, a company can elect to do a **spin-off**. In a spin-off, the company simply distributes shares in the subsidiary to its existing shareholders on a pro rata basis. Shareholders can keep the shares or sell them as they see fit. Very commonly, a company will first do an equity carve-out to create an active market for the shares and then subsequently do a spin-off of the remaining shares at a later date. Many well-known companies were created by this route. For example, in May 2012, Sears Holdings Corp. planned to spin off a large part of its stake in Sears Canada Inc.

split-up
The splitting up of a company into two or more companies.

In a less common, but more drastic move, a company can elect to do (or be forced to do) a **split-up**. A split-up is just what the name suggests: A company splits itself into two or more new companies. Shareholders have their shares in the old company swapped for shares in the new companies. Probably the most famous split-up occurred in the United States in the 1980s. As a result of an antitrust suit brought by the Justice Department, AT&T was forced to split up through the creation of seven regional phone companies (the so-called Baby Bells). Today, the Baby Bells survive as companies such as BellSouth, SBC Communications, and Verizon.

Concept Questions

1. What is an equity carve-out? Why might a firm wish to do one?
2. What is a split-up? Why might a firm choose to do one?

23.10 | SUMMARY AND CONCLUSIONS

This chapter introduced you to the extensive literature on mergers and acquisitions. We touched on a number of issues, including:

1. Form of merger. One firm can acquire another in several different ways. The three legal forms of acquisition are merger and consolidation, acquisition of stock, and acquisition of assets.

2. Tax issues. Mergers and acquisitions can be taxable or tax-free transactions. The primary issue is whether the target firm's shareholders sell or exchange their shares. Generally, a cash purchase is a taxable merger, while a stock exchange is not taxable. In a taxable merger, there are capital gains effects and asset write-up effects to consider. In a stock exchange, the target firm's shareholders become shareholders in the merged firm.

3. Merger valuation. If Firm A is acquiring Firm B, the benefits (ΔV) from an acquisition are defined as the value of the combined firm (V_{AB}) less the value of the firms as separate entities (V_A and V_B), or:

$$\Delta V = V_{AB} - (V_A + V_B)$$

The gain to Firm A from acquiring Firm B is the increased value of the acquired firm (ΔV) plus the value of B as a separate firm. The total value of Firm B to Firm A, V_B^*, is thus:

$$V_B^* = \Delta V + V_B$$

An acquisition benefits the shareholders of the acquiring firm if this value is greater than the cost of the acquisition. The cost of an acquisition can be defined in general terms as the price paid to the shareholders of the acquired firm. The cost frequently includes a merger premium paid to the shareholders of the acquired firm. Moreover, the cost depends on the form of payment, that is, the choice between cash or common stock.

4. The possible benefits of an acquisition come from several possible sources, including the following:

   a. Revenue enhancement.

   b. Cost reduction.

   c. Lower taxes.

   d. Changing capital requirements.

5. Some of the most colourful language of finance comes from defensive tactics in acquisition battles. *Poison pills, golden parachutes,* and *greenmail* are terms that describe various anti-takeover tactics.

6. Mergers and acquisitions have been extensively studied. The basic conclusions are that, on average, the shareholders of target firms do very well, while the shareholders of bidding firms do not appear to gain anywhere near as much.

Key Terms

amalgamations (page 656)
circular bid (page 657)
consolidation (page 656)
control block (page 671)
corporate governance (page 670)
diversification (page 668)
divestiture (page 678)
earnings per share (EPS) (page 667)
equity carve-out (page 679)
going-private transactions (page 658)
greenmail (page 671)
joint venture (page 659)

leveraged buyouts (LBOs) (page 658)
merger (page 656)
poison pill (page 672)
proxy contests (page 658)
shareholder rights plan (page 672)
spin-off (page 679)
split-up (page 679)
stock exchange bid (page 657)
strategic alliance (page 659)
synergy (page 661)
tender offer (page 657)

Chapter Review Problems and Self-Test

23.1 Merger Value and Cost Consider the following information for two all-equity firms, A and B:

	Firm A	Firm B
Shares outstanding	100	50
Price per share	$50	$30

Firm A estimates that the value of the synergistic benefit from acquiring Firm B is $200. Firm B has indicated it would accept a cash purchase offer of $35 per share. Should Firm A proceed?

23.2 Stock Mergers and EPS Consider the following information for two all-equity firms, A and B:

	Firm A	Firm B
Total earnings	$1,000	$400
Shares outstanding	100	80
Price per share	$ 80	$ 30

Firm A is acquiring Firm B by exchanging 25 of its shares for all the shares in B. What is the cost of the merger if the merged firm is worth $11,000? What will happen to Firm A's EPS? Its P/E ratio?

Answers to Self-Test Problems

23.1 The total value of Firm B to Firm A is the pre-merger value of B plus the $200 gain from the merger. The pre-merger value of B is $30 × 50 = $1,500, so the total value is $1,700. At $35 per share, A is paying $35 × 50 = $1,750; the merger therefore has a negative NPV of −$50. At $35 per share, B is not an attractive merger partner.

23.2 After the merger, the firm would have 125 shares outstanding. Since the total value is $11,000, the price per share is $11,000/125 = $88, up from $80. Since Firm B's shareholders end up with 25 shares in the merged firm, the cost of the merger is 25 × $88 = $2,200, not 25 × 80 = $2,000. Also, the combined firm has $1,000 + 400 = $1,400 in earnings, so EPS will be $1,400/125 = $11.20, up from $1,000/100 = $10. The old P/E ratio was $80/$10 = 8. The new one is $88/11.20 = $7.86.

Concepts Review and Critical Thinking Questions

1. **(LO9)** Define each of the following terms:
   a. Greenmail
   b. White knight
   c. Golden parachute
   d. Crown jewels
   e. Corporate raider
   f. Poison pill
   g. Tender offer
   h. Leveraged buyout, or LBO

2. (LO4) Explain why diversification *per se* is probably not a good reason for merger.

3. (LO1) In January 1996, Dun and Bradstreet Corp. announced plans to split into three entities: an information services core to include Moody's credit-rating agencies, a company that would include the Nielsen media-rating business, and a third entity that would focus on tracking consumer packaged-goods purchases. D&B was not alone, because many companies voluntarily split up in the 1990s. Why might a firm do this? Is there a possibility of reverse synergy?

4. (LO9) Are poison pills good or bad for shareholders? How do you think acquiring firms are able to get around poison pills?

5. (LO2) Describe the advantages and disadvantages of a taxable merger as opposed to a tax-free exchange. What is the basic determinant of tax status in a merger? Would an LBO be taxable or non-taxable? Explain.

6. (LO7) What does it mean to say that a proposed merger will take advantage of available economies of scale? Suppose Eastern Power Co. and Western Power Co. are located in different time zones. Both of them operate at 60 percent of capacity except for peak periods, when they operate at 100 percent of ca-

pacity. The peak periods begin at 9:00 a.m. and 5:00 p.m. local time and last about 45 minutes. Explain why a merger between Eastern and Western might make sense.

7. (LO9) What types of actions might the management of a firm take to fight a hostile acquisition bid from an unwanted suitor? How do the target-firm shareholders benefit from the defensive tactics of their management team? How are the target-firm shareholders harmed by such actions? Explain.

8. (LO7) Suppose a company in which you own stock has attracted two takeover offers. Would it ever make sense for your company's management to favour the lower offer? Does the form of payment affect your answer at all?

9. (LO7) Acquiring-firm shareholders seem to benefit very little from takeovers. Why is this finding a puzzle? What are some of the reasons offered for it?

10. (LO8) What is the difference between an equity carve-out and a spin-off? Why would a corporation choose to do one over the other? Describe a situation where an equity carve-out would be more advantageous than a spin-off. Describe a situation where a spin-off would be more advantageous than an equity carve-out.

Questions and Problems

Basic 1. **Calculating Synergy (LO7)** Roseland Inc. has offered $417 million cash for all of the common stock in Forest Glade
(Questions Corporation. Based on recent market information, Forest Glade is worth $376 million as an independent operation. If the
1–10) merger makes economic sense for Roseland, what is the minimum estimated value of the synergistic benefits from the merger?

2. **Calculating synergy (LO7)** Tecumseh Inc. is analyzing the possible merger with Devonshire Inc. Savings from the merger are estimated to be a one-time after tax benefit of $120 million. Devonshire Inc. has 4 million shares outstanding at a current market price of $70 per share. What is the maximum cash price per share that could be paid for Devonshire Inc.?

3. **Statements of Financial Position for Mergers (LO3)** Consider the following pre-merger information about Firm X and Firm Y:

	Firm X	Firm Y
Total earnings	$91,000	$13,000
Shares outstanding	40,000	15,000
Per-share values:		
Market	$ 54	$ 17
Book	$ 14	$ 4

Assume that Firm X acquires Firm Y by paying cash for all the shares outstanding at a merger premium of $6 per share. Assuming that neither firm has any debt before or after the merger, construct the post-merger statement of financial position for Firm X assuming the use of the purchase accounting method.

4. **Statements of Financial Position for Mergers (LO3)** Assume that the following statements of financial position are stated and a book value. Construct a post-merger statement of financial position assuming that Amherst Co. purchases Essex Inc. and the pooling of interests method of accounting is used.

Amherst Co.

Current assets	$12,000	Current liabilities	$ 5,300
Net fixed assets	36,000	Long-term debt	9,800
		Equity	32,900
Total	$48,000	Total	$48,000

Essex Inc.

Current assets	$3,400	Current liabilities	$1,300
Net fixed assets	6,400	Long-term debt	1,900
		Equity	6,600
Total	$9,800	Total	$9,800

5. **Incorporating Goodwill (LO3)** In the previous problem, suppose the fair market value of Essex's fixed assets is $9,300 versus the $6,400 book value shown. Amherst pays $16,000 for Essex and raises the needed funds through an issue of long-term debt. Construct the post-merger statement of financial position now, assuming that the purchase method of accounting is used.

6. **Statements of Financial Position for Mergers (LO3)** Knapps Enterprises has acquired Leamington Corp. in a merger transaction. Construct the statement of financial position for the new corporation if the merger is treated as a pooling of interests for accounting purposes. The following statements of financial position represent the pre-merger book values for both firms:

Knapps Enterprises

Current assets	$ 4,800	Current liabilities	$ 2,800
Other assets	1,200	Long-term debt	7,500
Net fixed assets	15,300	Equity	11,000
Total	$21,300	Total	$21,300

Leamington Corp.

Current assets	$1,300	Current liabilities	$1,350
Other assets	510	Long-term debt	0
Net fixed assets	6,800	Equity	7,260
Total	$8,610	Total	$8,610

7. **Incorporating Goodwill (LO3)** In the previous problem, construct the statement of financial position for the new corporation assuming that the transaction is treated as a purchase for accounting purposes. The market value of Leamington's fixed assets is $8,700; the market values for current and other assets are the same as the book values. Assume that Knapps Enterprises issues $13,000 in new long-term debt to finance the acquisition.

8. **Cash versus Stock Payment (LO5)** Wheatley Corp. is analyzing the possible acquisition of Romney Company. Both firms have no debt. Wheatley believes the acquisition will increase its total after-tax annual cash flows by $2 million indefinitely. The current market value of Romney is $43 million, and that of Wheatley is $89 million. The appropriate discount rate for the incremental cash flows is 10 percent. Wheatley is trying to decide whether it should offer 40 percent of its stock or $61 million in cash to Romney's shareholders.

   a. What is the cost of each alternative?

   b. What is the NPV of each alternative?

   c. Which alternative should Wheatley choose?

9. **EPS, PE, and Mergers (LO1)** The shareholders of Tilbury Company have voted in favour of a buyout offer from Dover Corporation. Information about each firm is given here:

	Tilbury	Dover
Price-earnings ratio	13.5	21
Shares outstanding	90,000	210,000
Earnings	$180,000	$810,000

Tilbury's shareholders will receive one share of Dover stock for every three shares they hold in Tilbury.

   a. What will the EPS of Dover be after the merger? What will the PE ratio be if the NPV of the acquisition is zero?

   b. What must Dover feel is the value of the synergy between these two firms? Explain how your answer can be reconciled with the decision to go ahead with the takeover.

10. **Cash versus Stock as Payment (LO5)** Consider the following pre-merger information about a bidding firm (Firm B) and a target firm (Firm T). Assume that both firms have no debt outstanding.

	Firm B	Firm T
Shares outstanding	5,400	1,500
Price per share	$47	$19

Firm B has estimated that the value of the synergistic benefits from acquiring Firm T is $8,700.

   a. If Firm T is willing to be acquired for $21 per share in cash, what is the NPV of the merger?

   b. What will the price per share of the merged firm be, assuming the conditions in (a)?

   c. In part (a), what is the merger premium?

   d. Suppose Firm T is agreeable to a merger by an exchange of stock. If B offers one of its shares for every two of T's shares, what will the price per share of the merged firm be?

   e. What is the NPV of the merger assuming the conditions in (d)?

Intermediate
(Questions
11–16) 11. **Cash versus Stock as Payment (LO5)** In Problem 10, are the shareholders of Firm T better off with the cash offer or the stock offer? At what exchange ratio of B shares to T shares would the shareholders in T be indifferent between the two offers?

12. **Effects of a Stock Exchange (LO1)** Consider the following pre-merger information about Firm A and Firm B:

	Firm A	Firm B
Total earnings	$1,400	$600
Shares outstanding	1,000	200
Price per share	$ 43	$ 47

Assume that Firm A acquires Firm B via an exchange of stock at a price of $49 for each share of B's stock. Both A and B have no debt outstanding.

a.   What will the earnings per share (EPS) of Firm A be after the merger?

b.   What will firm A's price per share be after the merger if the market incorrectly analyzes this reported earnings growth (that is, the price-earnings ratio does not change)?

c.   What will the price-earnings ratio of the post-merger firm be if the market correctly analyzes the transaction?

d.   If there are no synergy gains, what will the share price of A be after the merger? What will the price-earnings ratio be? What does your answer for the share price tell you about the amount A bid for B? Was it too high? Too low? Explanation.

13.   **Merger NPV (LO6)** Show that the NPV of a merger can be expressed as the value of the synergistic benefits, ΔV, less the merger premium.

14.   **Merger NPV (LO6, 7)** Chatham Foods, which has 1 million shares outstanding, wishes to merge with Kent Drinks with 2.5 million shares outstanding. The market prices for Chatham Foods and Kent Drinks are $49 and $18 per share, respectively. The merger could create an estimated savings of $800,000 annually for the indefinite future. If Chatham Foods were willing to pay $25 per share for Kent Drinks, and the appropriate cost of capital is 14 percent, what would be the:

a.   Present value of the merger gain?

b.   Cost of the cash offer?

c.   NPV of the offer?

15.   **Merger NPV (LO6, 7)** Raleigh Couriers is analyzing the possible acquisition of Harwich Restaurants. Neither firm has debt. The forecasts of Raleigh show that the purchase would increase its annual after-tax cash flow by $350,000 indefinitely. The current market value of Harwich is $9 million. The current market value of Raleigh is $23 million. The appropriate discount rate for the incremental cash flows is 8 percent. Raleigh is trying to decide whether it should offer 25 percent of its stock or $12 million in cash to Harwich.

a.   What is the synergy from the merger?

b.   What is the value of Harwich to Raleigh?

c.   What is the cost to Raleigh of each alternative?

d.   What is the NPV to Raleigh of each alternative?

e.   Which alternative should Raleigh use?

16.   **Merger NPV (LO5, 7)** Blenheim PLC has a market value of $125 million and 5 million shares outstanding. Howard Department Store has a market value of $40 million and 2 million shares outstanding. Blenheim is contemplating acquiring Howard. Blenheim's CFO concludes that the combined firm with synergy will be worth $185 million, and Howard can be acquired at a premium of $10 million.

a.   If Blenheim offers 1.2 million shares of its stock in exchange for the 2 million shares of Howard, what will the stock price of Blenheim be after the acquisition?

b.   What exchange ration between the two stocks would make the value of a stock offer equivalent to a cash offer of $50 million?

Challenge 17.   **Calculating NPV (LO5, 6, 7)** Ridgetown News Inc. is considering making an offer to purchase Orford Publications. The vice
(Question   president of finance has collected the following information:
17)

	Ridgetown	Orford
Price–earnings ratio	14.5	9.2
Shares outstanding	1,300,000	175,000
Earnings	$3,900,000	$640,000
Dividends	950,000	310,000

Ridgetown also knows that securities analysts expect the earnings and dividends of Orford to grow at a constant rate of 5 percent each year. Ridgetown management believes that the acquisition of Orford will provide the firm with some economies of scale that will increase this growth rate to 7 percent per year.

a.   What is the value of Orford to Ridgetown?

b.   What would Ridgetown's gain be from this acquisition?

c.   If Ridgetown were to offer $38 in cash for each share of Orford, what would the NPV of the acquisition be?

d.   What's the most Ridgetown should be willing to pay in cash per share for the stock of Orford?

e.   If Ridgetown were to offer 100,000 of its shares in exchange for the outstanding stock of Orford, what would the NPV be?

f.   Should the acquisition be attempted? If so, should it be as in (c) or as in (e)?

g.   Ridgetown's outside financial consultants think that the 7 percent growth rate is too optimistic and a 6 percent rate is more realistic. How does this change your previous answers?

MINI CASE

The Elgin Golf–Dutton Golf Merger

Elgin Golf Inc. has been in merger talks with Dutton Golf Company for the past six months. After several rounds of negotiations, the offer under discussion is a cash offer of $550 million for Dutton Golf. Both companies have niche markets in the golf club industry, and both believe that a merger will result in synergies due to economies of scale in manufacturing and marketing, as well as significant savings in general and administrative expenses.

Bruce Wayne, the financial officer for Elgin, has been instrumental in the merger negotiations. Bruce has prepared the following pro forma financial statements for Dutton Golf assuming the merger takes place. The financial statements include all synergistic benefits from the merger.

If Elgin Golf buys Dutton Golf, an immediate dividend of $75 million would be paid from Dutton Golf to Elgin. Stock in Elgin Golf currently sells for $94 per share, and the company has 18 million shares of stock outstanding. Dutton Golf has 8 million shares of stock outstanding. Both companies can borrow at an 8 percent interest rate. Bruce believes the current cost of capital for Elgin Golf is 11 percent. The cost of capital for Dutton Golf is 12.4 percent, and the cost of equity is 16.9 percent. In five years, the value of Dutton Golf is expected to be $300 million.

Bruce has asked you to analyze the financial aspects of the potential merger. Specifically, he has asked you to answer the following questions:

1. Suppose Dutton shareholders will agree to a merger price of $43.75 per share. Should Elgin proceed with the merger?

2. What is the highest price per share that Elgin should be willing to pay for Dutton?

3. Suppose Elgin is unwilling to pay cash for the merger but will consider a stock exchange. What exchange rate would make the merger terms equivalent to the original merger price of $43.75 per share?

4. What is the highest exchange ratio Elgin should be willing to pay and still undertake the merger?

	2013	2014	2015	2016	2017
Sales	$400,000,000	$450,000,000	$500,000,000	$565,000,000	$625,000,000
Production costs	276,000,000	315,000,000	350,000,000	395,000,000	437,000,000
Depreciation	40,000,000	45,000,000	50,000,000	57,000,000	62,000,000
Other expenses	37,000,000	40,000,000	41,000,000	42,000,000	43,000,000
EBIT	$ 47,000,000	$ 50,000,000	$ 59,000,000	$ 71,000,000	$ 83,000,000
Interest	9,500,000	11,000,000	12,000,000	12,500,000	13,500,000
Taxable income	$ 37,500,000	$ 39,000,000	$ 47,000,000	$ 58,500,000	$ 69,500,000
Taxes (40%)	15,000,000	15,600,000	18,800,000	23,400,000	27,800,000
Net income	$ 22,500,000	$ 23,400,000	$ 28,200,000	$ 35,100,000	$ 41,700,000
Additions to retained earnings	0	$ 17,000,000	$ 13,000,000	$ 13,000,000	$ 12,000,000

Internet Application Questions

1. The Competition Bureau (competitionbureau.gc.ca) in Canada reviews all mergers for approval. Its main concern is whether a proposed merger is likely to reduce competition. In this regard, it has set guidelines that allow investors and firms to determine whether a proposed merger passes the Competition Bureau's test. These guidelines are explained in the link below.

laws.justice.gc.ca/eng/acts/C-34/index.html

Use the guidelines described above to make your own evaluation of the efficacy of the following mergers:

a. A vertical merger involving a timber mill and a pulp producer, and a conglomerate merger involving a liquor company and a film studio.

b. Rio Tinto's bid to acquire Alcan (riotintoalcan.com).

c. What is the Efficiency Exception principle in evaluating mergers?

CHAPTER 24

ENTERPRISE RISK MANAGEMENT

≥ TELUS

TELUS is a leading telecommunications company in Canada, with $10.4 billion of revenue and 12.73 million customer connections in 2011. The company provides a wide range of communication products and services. In its 2011 annual report, TELUS reported that it took positions in foreign currency forward contracts and currency options to lock in the exchange rates on U.S. dollar denominated transactions. TELUS also uses cross-currency interest rate swaps to hedge interest rate fluctuations and share-based compensation derivatives to hedge its price risk from cash-settled, share-based compensation. TELUS has various risk management financial instruments in place to manage its credit, liquidity, and market risks. As we will see in this chapter, these techniques are among the tools commonly used by firms to manage risk.

Learning Objectives ▶

After studying this chapter, you should understand:

LO1 The use of insurance as a risk-management tool.

LO2 The sources of financial risk.

LO3 How to identify specific financial risks faced by firms.

LO4 The basics of hedging with forward contracts and futures.

LO5 The basics of hedging with swaps and options.

telus.com

All businesses face risks of many types. Some, such as unexpected cost increases, may be obvious, while others, such as disasters caused by human error, are not. *Enterprise risk management (ERM)* is the process of identifying and assessing risks and, where financially sensible, seeking to mitigate potential damage. Companies have always taken steps to manage risks. The change in recent years has been more to view risk management as a holistic, integrated exercise rather than something to be done on a piecewise basis. There is much greater awareness of the variety, complexity, and interactions of risks at the company-wide level. In fact, as the benefits from ERM have become increasingly clear, many companies have created a new "c-level" executive position, the Chief Risk Officer (CRO).

Broadly speaking, risks fall into four types. First, hazard risks involve damage done by outside forces such as natural disasters, theft, and lawsuits. Second, financial risks arise from such things as adverse exchange rate changes, commodity price fluctuations, and interest rate movements. Third, operational risks encompass impairments or disruptions in operations from a wide variety of business-related sources including human resources; product development, distribution, and marketing; and supply chain management. Finally, strategic risks include large-scale issues such as competition, changing customer needs, social and demographic changes, regulatory and political trends, and technological innovation. Another important strategic risk is damage done to company reputation from product problems, fraud, or other unfavourable publicity.

One important aspect of ERM is to view risks in the context of the entire company. A risk that damages one division of a company might benefit another such that they more or less offset each other. In this case, mitigating the risk in one division makes the overall company worse off.

For example, consider a vertically integrated oil company in which one division drills for oil and another refines it. An increase in oil prices benefits the driller and harms the refiner, but taken together, there may be little or no overall impact on the company's cash flows. Similarly, for a multinational with operations in many countries, exchange rate fluctuations may have limited impact at the overall company level. Another thing to recognize is that not all the risks are worth eliminating. It is important to prioritize and identify risks that have the greatest potential for economic and social harm.

For all firms, risk management begins with prevention. Taking steps to promote things like product safety and accident avoidance are obviously very important, but they are likely to be very company-specific and thus hard to discuss in general terms. Prevention is also more of an operating activity than a financial activity. However, certain types of financial instruments are used by companies of all types to manage and mitigate risk, particularly financial and hazard risk, and these will be the primary focus of our chapter.

24.1 | Insurance

Insurance is the most widely used risk-management tool. It is generally employed to protect against hazard risks. Insurance can be used to provide protection against losses due to damage to a firm's property and any associated loss of income. It also protects against liabilities that may arise as a result of interactions with third parties. For example, like individuals, companies will usually carry property insurance to protect against large-scale losses due to hazards ranging from fire to storm damage. Other types of insurance commonly purchased include:

- *Commercial liability insurance* protects against costs that can occur because of damages to others caused by the company's products, operations, or employees.
- *Business interruption insurance* protects against the loss of earnings if business operations are interrupted by an insured event such as fire or natural disaster.
- *Key personnel insurance* protects against losses due to loss of critical employees.
- *Workers' compensation and employer's liability insurance* protects against costs a firm is required to pay in connection with work-related injuries sustained by its employees.

It is important that companies and their risk managers fully understand the policy limits, conditions, and perils covered by the insurance policies they purchase. For example, losses due to earthquakes, flooding, and terrorism are typically excluded from standard commercial property policies. Firms wishing coverage for these perils must make special arrangements with their insurers. Firms must also abide by policy conditions; for instance, policies often require the insurer to be notified of any loss in a timely manner. A risk manager does not want to become familiar with a firm's insurance policy exclusions after a loss occurs. Whether to purchase insurance is, at least in principle, a straightforward NPV question. The insurance premium is the cost. The benefit is the present value of the expected payout by the insurance company to the firm. For example, imagine a firm has a key production facility. There is a small chance, say 1-in-10,000 (or 0.01 percent) that the facility will be destroyed by fire or natural disaster in the next year. The cost to the firm to rebuild plus any lost profits would be $200 million if that occurs. Thus, the firm either loses $0 or $200 million. Its expected loss is:

$$\text{Expected loss} = 0.9999 \times \$0 + 0.0001 \times \$200 \text{ million} = \$20,000$$

Of course, if the firm could eliminate the possibility of loss for the present value of $20,000 (or less), it would do so. But assuming that the cost of completely eliminating the risk (if that is even technologically possible) is greater than the present value of $20,000, the firm can purchase insurance.

The firm's decision to purchase insurance or what types of insurance a firm decides to purchase depends on the nature of the firm's business, the size of the firm, the firm's risk aversion, as well as legal and third-party requirements that may demand proof of insurance. Large firms will often forego insurance against less costly events, opting to 'self-insure'. When looking across all of the smaller risks faced by a big firm, it can be less expensive to sustain a certain loss rate than to pay the insurance premium. Alternatively, firms may opt to purchase insurance with large deductibles, meaning the firm will cover losses up to some level before the insurance kicks in. This approach protects the firm from truly catastrophic losses.

1. What are some basic types of insurance purchased by companies?
2. What does it mean for a company to self-insure?

24.2 | Managing Financial Risk

hedging
Reducing a firm's exposure to price or rate fluctuations. Also, immunization.

derivative security
A financial asset that represents a claim to another financial asset.

Purchasing insurance is one way to manage risk, particularly hazard risk. Managing financial risk is often handled by firms without the assistance of insurance companies. In the remainder of this chapter, we discuss ways firms reduce their exposure to price and rate fluctuations, a process known as **hedging**. The term *immunization* is sometimes used as well. As we will discuss, there are many different types of hedging and many different techniques. Frequently, when a firm desires to hedge a particular risk, there will be no direct way of doing so. The financial manager's job in such cases is to create a way by using available financial instruments to create new ones. This process has come to be called *financial engineering*.

Financial risk management often involves the buying and selling of **derivative securities**. A derivative security is a financial asset that represents a claim to another financial asset. For example, a stock option gives the owner the right to buy or sell stock, a financial asset, so stock options are derivative securities. Financial engineering frequently involves creating new derivative securities, or else combining existing derivatives to accomplish specific hedging goals.

To effectively manage financial risk, financial managers need to identify the types of price fluctuations that have the greatest impact on the value of the firm. Sometimes these will be obvious, but sometimes they will not be. For example, consider a forest products company. If interest rates increase, then its borrowing costs will clearly rise. Beyond this, however, the demand for housing typically declines as interest rates rise. As housing demand falls, so does demand for lumber. An increase in interest rates thus leads to increased financing costs and, at the same time, decreased revenues.

The Impact of Financial Risk: The Credit Crisis of 2007–2009

The greatest credit crisis since the Great Depression of the 1930s started in the U.S. housing market and spread around the world. After recovering from the collapse of the dot-com bubble, the U.S. economy enjoyed a period of low interest rates and easy access to financing. Optimistic about growth and eager to obtain higher returns, investors and financial institutions took on increased credit and liquidity risks. Expansion of the U.S. mortgage market resulted.

Financial markets provided a favourable setting for financial engineering focused on credit risk in the form of structured securitization products. One example is the growth and seizure of the Canadian market for asset-backed commercial paper.

The confidence of investors in the U.S. and globally was also shaken by the collapse and rescue of several financial institutions in the U.K. and U.S. in early 2008. Panic resulted in the fall of 2008 when Lehman Brothers was allowed to fail. At the time of its collapse and bankruptcy filing, Lehman Brothers was the fourth-largest U.S. investment bank and largest bankruptcy filing to that point in time. Lehman's collapse greatly intensified the 2008 credit crisis and contributed to the evaporation of nearly US$10 trillion in market capitalization from global equity markets in October 2008.

The credit crisis led to a global recession and the implementation of bailout packages tallying in the billions. Governments around the world have since implemented an ambitious set of changes to financial institution regulation aimed at controlling excessive risk taking. At the time of writing in August 2012, the European financial crisis continues and it still remains to be seen how effective the new regulations will be.

The Risk Profile

risk profile
A plot showing how the value of the firm is affected by changes in prices or rates.

The basic tool for identifying and measuring a firm's exposure to financial risk is the **risk profile**. The risk profile is a plot showing the relationship between changes in the price of some good, service, or rate and changes in the value of the firm. Constructing a risk profile is conceptually very similar to performing a sensitivity analysis (described in Chapter 11).

To illustrate, consider an agricultural products company that has a large-scale wheat-farming operation. Because wheat prices can be very volatile, we might wish to investigate the firm's exposure to wheat price fluctuations, that is, its risk profile with regard to wheat prices. To do this, we plot changes in the value of the firm (ΔV) versus unexpected changes in wheat prices (ΔP_{wheat}). Figure 24.1 shows the result.

FIGURE 24.1

Risk profile for a wheat grower

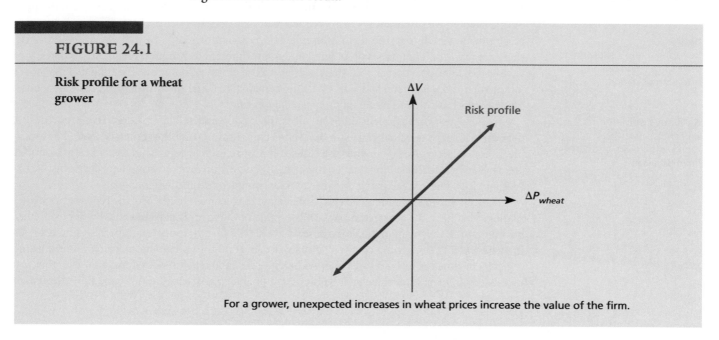

For a grower, unexpected increases in wheat prices increase the value of the firm.

The risk profile in Figure 24.1 tells us two things. First, because the line slopes up, increases in wheat prices will increase the value of the firm. Because wheat is an output, this comes as no surprise. Second, because the line has a fairly steep slope, this firm has a significant exposure to wheat price fluctuations, and it may wish to take steps to reduce that exposure.

Reducing Risk Exposure

Fluctuations in the price of any particular good or service can have very different effects on different types of firms. Going back to wheat prices, we now consider the case of a food processing operation. The food processor buys large quantities of wheat and has a risk profile like that illustrated in Figure 24.2. As with the agricultural products firm, the value of this firm is sensitive to wheat prices, but, because wheat is an input, increases in wheat prices lead to decreases in firm value.

Both the agricultural products firm and the food processor are exposed to wheat price fluctuations, but any fluctuations have opposite effects for the two firms. If these two firms get together, then much of the risk can be eliminated. The grower and the processor can simply agree that, at set dates in the future, the grower will deliver a certain quantity of wheat, and the processor will pay a set price. Once the agreement is signed, both firms will have locked in the price of wheat for as long as the contract is in effect, and both of their risk profiles with regard to wheat prices will be completely flat during that time.

FIGURE 24.2

Risk profile for a wheat buyer

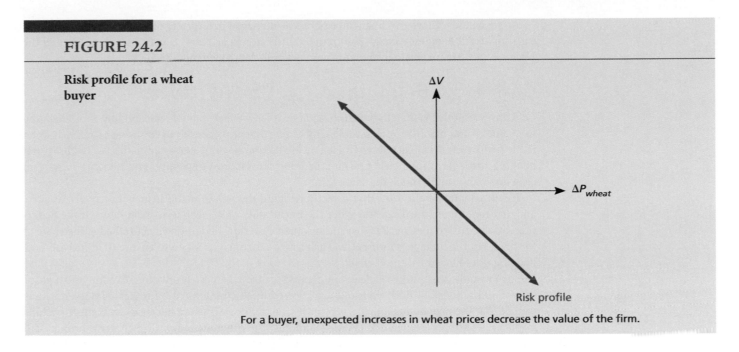

For a buyer, unexpected increases in wheat prices decrease the value of the firm.

We should note that, in reality, a firm that hedges financial risk usually wouldn't be able to create a completely flat risk profile. For example, our wheat grower doesn't actually know what the size of the crop will be ahead of time. If the crop is larger than expected, then some portion of the crop will be unhedged. If the crop is small, then the grower will have to buy more to fulfill the contract and will thereby be exposed to the risk of price changes. Either way, there is some exposure to wheat price fluctuations, but that exposure is sharply reduced by hedging.

There are a number of other reasons why perfect hedging is usually impossible, but this is not really a problem. With most financial risk management, the goal is to reduce the risk to more bearable levels and thereby flatten out the risk profile, not necessarily to eliminate the risk altogether.

In thinking about financial risk, there is an important distinction to be made. Price fluctuations have two components. Short-run, essentially temporary changes are the first component. The second component has to do with more long-run, essentially permanent changes. As we discuss next, these two types of changes have very different implications for the firm.

Hedging Short-Run Exposure

Short-run, temporary changes in prices result from unforeseen events or shocks. Some examples are sudden increases in orange juice prices because of a late Florida freeze, increases in oil prices because of political turmoil, and increases in lumber prices because available supplies are low following a hurricane. Price fluctuations of this sort are often called *transitory* changes.

Short-run price changes can drive a business into financial distress even though, in the long run, the business is fundamentally sound. This happens when a firm finds itself with sudden cost increases that it cannot pass on to its customers immediately. A negative cash flow position is created, and the firm may be unable to meet its financial obligations.

For example, wheat crops might be much larger than expected in a particular year because of unusually good growing conditions. At harvest time, wheat prices will be unexpectedly low. By that time, a wheat farmer will have already incurred most of the costs of production. If prices drop too low, revenues from the crop will be insufficient to cover the costs, and financial distress may result.

transactions exposure
Short-run financial risk arising from the need to buy or sell at uncertain prices or rates in the near future.

Short-run financial risk is often called **transactions exposure**. This name stems from the fact that short-term financial exposure typically arises because a firm must make transactions in the near future at uncertain prices or rates. With our wheat farmer, for example, the crop must be sold at the end of the harvest, but the wheat price is uncertain. Alternatively, a firm may have a bond issue that will mature next year that it will need to replace, but the interest rate that the firm will have to pay is not known.

As we will see, short-run financial risk can be managed in a variety of ways. The opportunities for short-term hedging have grown tremendously in recent years, and firms in Canada and the United States are increasingly hedging away transitory price changes.

Cash Flow Hedging: A Cautionary Note

One thing to notice is that, in our discussion thus far, we have talked conceptually about hedging the value of the firm. In our example concerning wheat prices, however, what is really hedged is the firm's near-term cash flow. In fact, at the risk of ignoring some subtleties, we will say that hedging short-term financial exposure, hedging transactions exposure, and hedging near-term cash flows amount to much the same thing.

It will usually be the case that directly hedging the value of the firm is not really feasible, and, instead, the firm will try to reduce the uncertainty of its near-term cash flows. If the firm is thereby able to avoid expensive disruptions, then cash flow hedging will act to hedge the value of the firm, but the linkage is indirect. In such cases, care must be taken to ensure that the cash flow hedging does have the desired effect.

For example, imagine a vertically integrated firm with an oil-producing division and a gasoline-retailing division. Both divisions are affected by fluctuations in oil prices. However, it may well be that the firm as a whole has very little transactions exposure because any transitory shifts in oil prices simply benefit one division and cost the other. The overall firm's risk profile with regard to oil prices is essentially flat. Put another way, the firm's *net* exposure is small. If one division, acting on its own, were to begin hedging its cash flows, then the firm as a whole would suddenly be exposed to financial risk. The point is that cash flow hedging should not be done in isolation. Instead, a firm needs to worry about its net exposure. As a result, any hedging activities should probably be done on a centralized, or at least cooperative, basis.

Hedging Long-Term Exposure

Price fluctuations can also be longer-run, more permanent changes. These result from fundamental shifts in the underlying economics of a business. If improvements in agricultural technology come about, for example, then wheat prices will permanently decline (in the absence of agricultural price subsidies!). If a firm is unable to adapt to the new technology, then it will not be economically viable over the long run.

economic exposure
Long-term financial risk arising from permanent changes in prices or other economic fundamentals.

A firm's exposure to long-run financial risks is often called its **economic exposure**. Because long-term exposure is rooted in fundamental economic forces, it is much more difficult, if not impossible, to hedge on a permanent basis. For example, is it possible that a wheat farmer and a food processor could permanently eliminate exposure to wheat price fluctuations by agreeing on a fixed price forever?

The answer is no, and, in fact, the effect of such an agreement might even be the opposite of the one desired. The reason is that if, over the long run, wheat prices were to change on a permanent basis, one party to this agreement would ultimately be unable to honour it. Either the buyer would be paying too much, or the seller would be receiving too little. In either case, the loser would become uncompetitive and be forced to take political and legal action to reopen the contract. This happened in Canada with the long-term agreement by the province of Newfoundland to sell power from Churchill Falls to Hydro Quebec. When prices rose in the 1990s, the contract was renegotiated.

Conclusion

In the long run, a business is either economically viable or it will fail. No amount of hedging can change this simple fact. Nonetheless, by hedging over the near term, a firm gives itself time to adjust its operations and thereby adapt to new conditions without expensive disruptions. So, drawing our discussion in this section together, we can say that, by managing financial risks, the firm can accomplish two important things. The first is that the firm insulates itself from otherwise troublesome transitory price fluctuations. The second is that the firm gives itself a little breathing room to adapt to fundamental changes in market conditions.

24.3 | Hedging with Forward Contracts

Forward contracts are among the oldest and most basic tools for managing financial risk. Our goal in this section is to describe forward contracts and discuss how they are used to hedge financial risk.

Forward Contracts: The Basics

forward contract
A legally binding agreement between two parties calling for the sale of an asset or product in the future at a price agreed upon today.

A **forward contract** is a legally binding agreement between two parties calling for the sale of an asset or product in the future at a price agreed upon today. Forward contracts are traded over the counter. The terms of the contract call for one party to deliver the goods to the other on a certain date in the future, called the *settlement date*. The other party pays the previously agreed-upon *forward price* and takes the goods. Looking back, note that the agreement we discussed between the wheat grower and the food processor was, in fact, a forward contract.

Forward contracts can be bought and sold. The *buyer* of a forward contract has the obligation to take delivery and pay for the goods; the *seller* has the obligation to make delivery and accept payment. The buyer of a forward contract benefits if prices increase because the buyer will have locked in a lower price. Similarly, the seller wins if prices fall because a higher selling price has been locked in. Note that one party to a forward contract can win only at the expense of the other, so a forward contract is a zero-sum game.

The Payoff Profile

payoff profile
A plot showing the gains and losses that will occur on a contract as the result of unexpected price changes.

The **payoff profile** is the key to understanding how forward contracts and other contracts that we discuss later are used to hedge financial risks. In general, a payoff profile is a plot showing the gains and losses on a contract that result from unexpected price changes. For example, suppose we were examining a forward contract on oil. Based on our discussion, the buyer of the forward contract is obligated to accept delivery of a specified quantity of oil at a future date and pay a set price. Part A of Figure 24.3 shows the resulting payoff profile on the forward contract from the buyer's perspective.

FIGURE 24.3

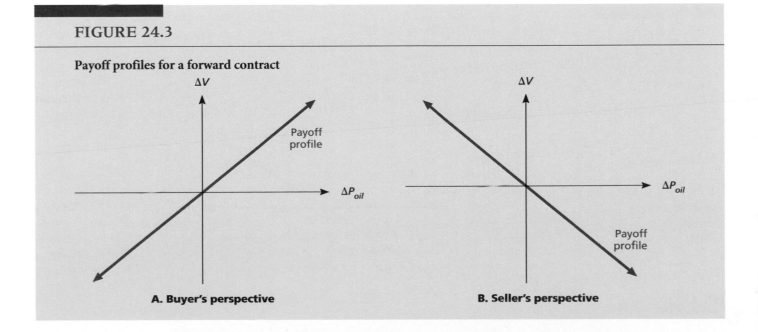

Payoff profiles for a forward contract

A. Buyer's perspective   B. Seller's perspective

Figure 24.3 shows that, as oil prices increase, the buyer of the forward contract benefits by having locked in a lower-than-market price. If oil prices decrease, then the buyer loses because that buyer ends up paying a higher-than-market price. For the seller of the forward contract, things are simply reversed. The payoff profile of the seller is illustrated in Part B of Figure 24.3.

Hedging with Forwards

To illustrate how forward contracts can be used to hedge, we consider the case of a utility that uses oil to generate power. The prices that our utility can charge are regulated and cannot be changed rapidly. As a result, sudden increases in oil prices are a source of financial risk. The utility's risk profile is illustrated in Figure 24.4.

FIGURE 24.4

Risk profile for an oil buyer

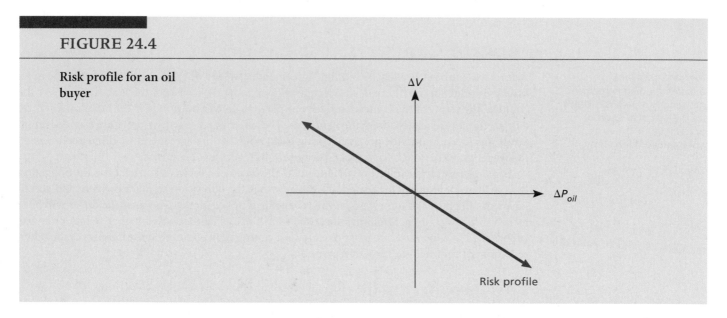

If we compare the risk profile in Figure 24.4 to the buyer's payoff profile on a forward contract shown in Figure 24.3, we see what the utility needs to do. The payoff profile for the buyer of a forward contract on oil is exactly the opposite of the utility's risk profile with respect to oil. If the utility buys a forward contract, its exposure to unexpected changes in oil prices will be eliminated. This result is shown in Figure 24.5.

FIGURE 24.5

Hedging with forward contracts

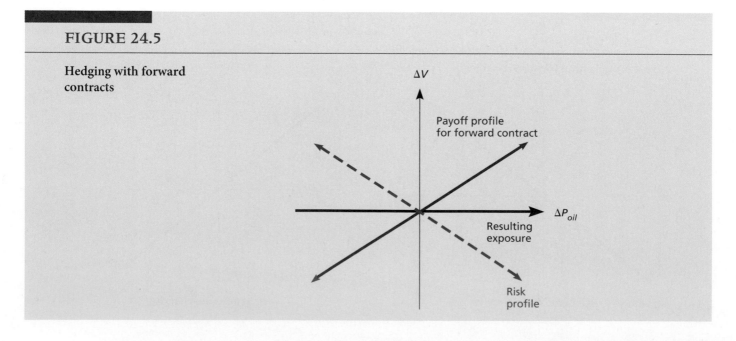

Our utility example illustrates the fundamental approach to managing financial risk. We first identify the firm's exposure to financial risk using a risk profile. We then try to find a financial arrangement, such as a forward contract, that has an offsetting payoff profile.

A CAVEAT   Figure 24.5 shows that the utility's net exposure to oil price fluctuations is zero. If oil prices rise, then the gains on the forward contract will offset the damage from increased costs. However, if oil prices decline, the benefit from lower costs will be offset by losses on the forward contract.

For example, in July 2010 Calgary based Encana Corp., one of North America's largest natural gas producers, suffered a US$505 million foreign exchange and hedging loss. Due to unexpected weakness in the price of natural gas, the price hedges of the company that covered around 60 percent of its production were set 50 percent higher than the benchmark natural gas prices resulting in a significant loss to Encana.

This example illustrates an important thing to remember about hedging with forward contracts. Price fluctuations can be good or bad, depending on which way they go. If we hedge with forward contracts, we do eliminate the risk associated with an adverse price change. However, we also eliminate the potential gain from a favourable move. You might wonder if we couldn't somehow just hedge against unfavourable moves. We can, and we describe how in a subsequent section.

CREDIT RISK   Another important thing to remember is that with a forward contract, no money changes hands when the contract is initiated. The contract is simply an agreement to transact in the future, so there is no up-front cost to the contract. However, because a forward contract is a financial obligation, there is credit risk. When the settlement date arrives, the party on the losing end of the contract has a significant incentive to default on the agreement. As we discuss in the next section, a variation on the forward contract exists that greatly diminishes this risk.

FORWARD CONTRACTS IN PRACTICE   Where are forward contracts commonly used to hedge? Because exchange rate fluctuations can have disastrous consequences for firms that have significant import or export operations, forward contracts are routinely used by such firms to hedge exchange rate risk. For example, Jaguar, the U.K. auto manufacturer, historically hedged the U.S. dollar–British pound exchange rate for six months into the future. (The subject of exchange rate hedging with forward contracts is discussed in greater detail in Chapter 21.)

jaguar.com

Another good example of hedging with forward contracts is the Forward Sales Program that Barrick Gold Corporation used to use. When the program was in full use, Barrick would commit to sell a fixed number of ounces of gold at a future date established by the company over a period of between 10 and 15 years. The contract provided for a premium above the current spot rates based on the difference between the market LIBOR rates and the gold lease rates.[1] Between 1991 and 2002, Barrick claimed to have secured additional revenue of $2.2 billion using the program. If gold prices rose above the contract price, Barrick would choose to sell into the spot market to maximize revenue. The long contract term and the flexibility in choosing a delivery date reduce the risks associated with forward contracts. Two problems can occur, however, that would negatively impact the returns associated with hedging. First, a situation of "backwardation" in which the gold lease rates are higher than short-term interest rates can occur. In this situation, forward prices under the program would be lower than spot prices, resulting in a negative premium. Second, gold prices could rise to the point where the contract expires and the gold must be delivered at a rate less than market prices. When this occurred in 2004 and 2005, pressure on management from shareholders led to a reduction in the use of the Forward Sales Program, and Barrick Gold pledged to eventually reduce the hedge book to zero.

Concept Questions

1. What is a forward contract? Describe the payoff profiles for the buyer and the seller of a forward contract.
2. Explain how a firm can alter its risk profile using forward contracts.

---

[1] The gold lease rate is the fee charged by a central bank to a gold bullion dealer that borrows gold from the central bank.

24.4 | Hedging with Futures Contracts

futures contract
A forward contract with the feature that gains and losses are realized each day rather than only on the settlement date.

A **futures contract** is exactly the same as a forward contract with one exception. With a forward contract, the buyer and seller realize gains or losses only on the settlement date. With a futures contract, gains and losses are realized on a daily basis. If we buy a futures contract on oil, then, if oil prices rise today, we have a profit and the seller of the contract has a loss. The seller pays up, and we start again tomorrow with neither party owing the other.

The daily settlement feature found in futures contracts is called *marking-to-market*. As we mentioned earlier, there is a significant risk of default with forward contracts. With daily marking-to-market, this risk is greatly reduced. This is probably why organized trading is much more common in futures contracts than in forward contracts (outside of international trade).

Trading in Futures

In Canada and elsewhere around the world, futures contracts for a remarkable variety of items are routinely bought and sold. The types of contracts available are traditionally divided into two groups, commodity futures and financial futures. With a financial future, the underlying goods are financial assets such as stocks, bonds, or currencies. With a commodity future, the underlying goods can be just about anything other than a financial asset.

There are commodity futures contracts on a wide variety of agricultural products such as canola, corn, orange juice, and, yes, pork bellies. There is even a contract on fertilizer. There are commodity contracts on precious metals such as gold and silver, and there are contracts on basic goods such as copper and lumber. There are contracts on various petroleum products such as crude oil, heating oil, and gasoline.

Wherever there is price volatility, there may be a demand for a futures contract, and new futures contracts are introduced on a fairly regular basis. For example, by some estimates, the potential value of wholesale trade in electricity in the United States is more than $100 billion a year, dwarfing the market for many other commodities such as gold, copper, wheat, and corn. Electricity producers, who own generating capacity, are "long" large quantities of the commodity. As the market develops, new futures contracts will allow energy producers and (large) consumers to hedge their transactions in electricity. Whether such contracts will be successful remains to be seen. Many new contracts don't pan out because there is not enough volume; such contracts are simply discontinued.

cmegroup.com
bombardier.com

It is even possible to have derivatives that are not linked to prices. The Chicago Mercantile Exchange has introduced weather futures for which the underlying is the number of snow days in a winter. Bombardier, the Canadian multinational manufacturer of Ski-Doo® snowmobiles, is using such snow derivatives to hedge its cash back promise to customers if there is no snow.[2] In 2012, The North American Derivatives Exchange sought to offer contracts tied to the results of the 2012 U.S. presidential elections and whether Democrats or Republicans would control the U.S. House, Senate, and White House. However, the Commodity Futures Trading Commission (CFTC) was quick in issuing an order to prohibit the North American Derivatives Exchange from introducing "political event contracts".

Futures Exchanges

There are a number of futures exchanges in the United States and elsewhere, and more are being established. The Chicago Board of Trade (CBT) is among the largest. Other notable exchanges include the Chicago Mercantile Exchange (CME), the International Money Market (IMM), the New York Futures Exchange (NYFE), a part of the NYSE, ICE Futures Canada, and the Montreal Exchange (ME).

Figure 24.6 gives a sample of selected futures contracts. Taking a look at the canola contracts, note that the contracts trade on ICE Futures Canada, one contract calls for the delivery of 20 metric tonnes of canola, and prices are quoted in Canadian dollars per metric tonne. The months in which the contracts mature are given in the first column.

---

[2]C. Smith, "Weather derivatives: An enormous potential," *Financial Times,* Derivatives Survey, June 28, 2000, p. vi.

FIGURE 24.6

Future prices (June 20, 2012)

Commodity Futures Price Quotes For Canadian Dollar (Globex)
(Price quotes for CME Canadian Dollar (Globex) delayed at least 10 minutes as per exchange requirements.)
Also available: pit. Session Quotes

| Click for Chart | Current Session | | | | | | | | Prior Day | | Opt's |
	Open	High	Low	Last	Time	Set	Chg	Vol	Set	Op Int	
Sep'12	0.98030	0.08240	0.97880	0.97950	09:04 Jun 20	-	−0.00100	28701	0.98050	88140	Call Put
Dec'12	0.97820	0.9800	0.97770	0.97810	09:04 Jun 20	-	−0.00070	16	0.97880	6378	Call Put
Mar'13	-	-	-	0.97750*	09:04 Jun 20	-		-	0.97700	1435	Call Put
Jun'13	0.97610	0.97610	0.97610	0.97610	09:00 Jun 20	-	0.00080	1	0.97530	311	Call Put
Sep'13	-	-	-	0.97350*	09:00 Jun 20	-	-	-	0.97350	44	Call Put

Times indicate exchange local time.
*An asterisk beside the last price indicates that the price is from a previous session.

Commodity Futures Price Quotes For Canola
(Price quotes for ICE (WCE) Canola delayed at least 10 minutes as per exchange requirements.)

| Click for Chart | Current Session | | | | | | | | Prior Day | | Opt's |
	Open	High	Low	Last	Time	Set	Chg	Vol	Set	Op Int	
Jul'12	621.40	623.90	615.70	619.00	08:57 Jun 20	-	−2.20	6807	621.20	27810	Call Put
Nov'12	580.50	584.40	576.10	579.70	08:57 Jun 20	-	−1.80	16426	581.50	142827	Call Put
Jan'13	583.90	587.40	580.60	582.30	08:57 Jun 20	-	−2.70	1416	585.00	23824	Call Put
Mar'13	587.80	590.40	582.40	586.00	08:57 Jun 20	-	−2.20	1984	588.20	11300	Call Put
May'13	588.00	591.00	582.60	587.70	09:04 Jun 20	-	−0.70	2983	588.40	8682	Call Put
Jul'13	591.70	592.10	586.70	589.10	09:04 Jun 20	-	−0.10	1065	589.20	2664	Call Put
Nov'13	-	-	-	550.00*	07:23 Jun 20	-	-	64	550.00	769	Call Put
Jan'14	-	-	-	550.00*	19:00 Jun 19	-	-	0	550.00	0	Call Put
Mar'14	-	-	-	550.00*	14:05 Jun 18	-	-	0	550.00	0	Call Put
May'14	-	-	-	550.00*	14:05 Jun 18	-	-	0	550.00	0	Call Put
Jul'14	-	-	-	550.00*	14:05 Jun 18	-	-	0	550.00	0	Call Put

Times indicate exchange local time.
*An asterisk beside the last price indicates that the price is from a previous session.

BAX — Three-Month Canadian Bankers' Acceptance Futures
Last Update: June 20, 2012, 10:05 Montréal time - (DATA 15 MINUTES DELAYED)

Month / Strike	Bid Price	Ask Price	Settl. Price	Net Change	Vol.
+ 12 JL	0.000	0.000	98.660	0.000	0
+ 12 AU	0.000	0.000	98.650	0.000	0
+ 12 SE	98.780	98.785	98.810	−0.025	5162
+ 12 DE	98.780	98.790	98.830	−0.040	10721
+ 13 MR	98.760	98.770	98.810	−0.040	8705
+ 13 JN	98.710	98.720	98.760	−0.050	3759
+ 13 SE	98.650	98.670	98.720	−0.060	2324
+ 13 DE	98.590	98.610	98.660	−0.060	1758
+ 14 MR	98.540	98.550	98.610	−0.070	609
+ 14 JN	98.480	98.490	98.550	−0.050	7
+ 14 SE	98.410	98.430	98.480	0.000	0
+ 12 DE	98.350	98.370	98.410	0.000	0
+ 15 MR	98.290	98.310	98.350	−0.040	50
+ 15 JN	98.210	98.240	98.260	0.000	0
Total					33095

Commodity Futures Price Quotes For Gold (Globex)
(Price quotes for COMEX Gold (Globex) delayed at least 10 minutes as per exchange requirements.)
Also available: pit. Session Quotes

Click for Chart	Current Session								Prior Day		Opt's
	Open	High	Low	Last	Time	Set	Chg	Vol	Set	Op Int	
Jun'12	1618.3	1618.3	1601.3	1601.3	10:11 Jun 20	-	−20.9	52	1622.2	688	Call Put
Jul'12	1618.1	1621.3	1594.5	1597.8	10:11 Jun 20	-	−24.5	343	1622.3	1272	Call Put
Aug'12	1619.3	1623.6	1595.1	1599.2	10:11 Jun 20	-	−24.0	71814	1623.2	223051	Call Put
Oct'12	1623.5	1623.8	1598.0	1598.0	10:11 Jun 20	-	−27.4	368	1625.4	19602	Call Put
Dec'12	1624.0	1627.8	1599.4	1603.0	10:11 Jun 20	-	−24.5	1249	1627.5	73480	Call Put
Feb'13	1630.1	1630.1	1605.9	1605.9	10:11 Jun 20	-	−23.7	108	1629.6	20757	Call Put
Apr'13	1616.0	1616.0	1616.0	1616.0	10:11 Jun 20	-	−15.6	182	1631.6	12841	Call Put
Jun'13	1620.0	1620.0	1620.0	1620.0	10:11 Jun 20	-	−13.6	433	1633.6	17187	Call Put
Aug'13	-	-	-	1594.7*	10:11 Jun 20	-	-	-	1635.8	1467	Call Put
Oct'13	-	-	-	1643.7*	10:11 Jun 20	-	-	-	1638.2	449	Call Put
Dec'13	-	-	-	1643.4*	10:11 Jun 20	-	-	-	1640.6	9340	Call Put
Feb'14	-	-	-	1672.1*	10:11 Jun 20	-	-	-	1643.2	6	Call Put
Apr'14	-	-	-	-	10:11 Jun 20	-	-	-	1645.9	1	Call Put
Jun'14	-	-	-	1619.3*	10:11 Jun 20	-	-	-	1648.6	7989	Call Put
Dec'14	-	-	-	1659.7*	10:11 Jun 20	-	-	-	1657.4	888	Call Put
Jun'15	-	-	-	1600.0*	10:11 Jun 20	-	-	-	1666.4	3309	Call Put
Dec'15	-	-	-	1620.5*	10:11 Jun 20	-	-	-	1678.1	12022	Call Put

Times indicate exchange local time.
*An asterisk beside the last price indicates that the price is from a previous session.

Light Crude Oil
(Price quotes for NYMEX Light Crude Oil delayed at least 10 minutes as per exchange requirements.)
Also available: pit. Session Quotes

Click for Chart	Current Session								Prior Day		Opt's
	Open	High	Low	Last	Time	Set	Chg	Vol	Set	Op Int	
Jul'12	84.04	84.34	82.79	83.04	10:15 Jun 20	-	−0.99	11245	84.03	24700	Call Put
Aug'12	84.36	84.72	83.09	83.38	10:15 Jun 20	-	−0.97	81421	84.35	292877	Call Put
Sep'12	84.67	85.05	83.45	83.73	10:15 Jun 20	-	−0.95	11236	84.68	129419	Call Put
Oct'12	84.87	85.33	83.81	84.08	10:15 Jun 20	-	−0.92	6325	85.00	73980	Call Put
Nov'12	85.23	85.69	84.21	84.47	10:15 Jun 20	-	−0.88	3570	85.35	67557	Call Put
Dec'12	85.57	86.06	84.58	84.83	10:15 Jun 20	-	−0.84	11387	85.67	169360	Call Put
Jan'13	85.80	86.37	85.00	85.15	10:15 Jun 20	-	−0.82	1000	85.97	56695	Call Put
Feb'13	86.61	86.61	85.39	85.39	10:15 Jun 20	-	−0.82	695	86.21	25375	Call Put
Mar'13	86.40	86.40	85.66	85.66	10:15 Jun 20	-	−0.74	2243	86.40	34662	Call Put
Apr'13	86.58	86.58	86.58	86.58	10:15 Jun 20	-	0.07	179	86.51	18073	Call Put
May'13	86.47	86.83	86.20	86.20	10:15 Jun 20	-	−0.40	223	86.60	17235	Call Put
Jun'13	86.33	86.93	86.18	86.23	10:15 Jun 20	-	−0.44	2803	86.67	75316	Call Put
Jul'13	-	-	-	86.45*	17:21 Jun 19	-	-	-	86.71	26958	Call Put
Aug'13	-	-	-	85.52*	17:21 Jun 19	-	-	-	86.68	13627	Call Put
Sep'13	-	-	-	85.57*	17:21 Jun 19	-	-	-	86.64	21367	Call Put
Oct'13	-	-	-	94.09*	17:21 Jun 19	-	-	-	86.61	12384	Call Put
Nov'13	-	-	-	86.50*	17:21 Jun 19	-	-	-	86.58	19224	Call Put
Dec'13	86.55	87.06	86.08	86.10	10:15 Jun 20	-	−0.44	4287	86.54	104890	Call Put
Jan'14	-	-	-	101.71*	17:21 Jun 19	-	-	-	86.38	18804	Call Put
Feb'14	-	-	-	102.73*	17:21 Jun 19	-	-	-	86.26	3661	Call Put
Mar'14	-	-	-	100.80*	17:21 Jun 19	-	-	-	86.12	7985	Call Put
Apr'14	-	-	-	85.45*	17:21 Jun 19	-	-	-	85.98	3595	Call Put
May'14	-	-	-	86.07*	17:21 Jun 19	-	-	-	85.85	3368	Call Put
Jun'14	85.95	86.00	85.95	86.00	10:15 Jun 20	-	0.28	51	85.72	38605	Call Put
Jul'14	-	-	-	101.00*	17:21 Jun 19	-	-	-	85.57	2163	Call Put
Aug'14				100.50*	17:21 Jun 19	-	-	-	85.43	1853	Call Put

Trading Unit: 1,000 U.S. barrels
Sources: futures.tradingcharts.com/marketquotes/CD.html, m-x.ca, cmegroup.com

For the canola contract with a July 2013 maturity, the number after the maturity month is the opening price ($591.70) followed by the highest price ($592.10) and the lowest price ($586.70) for the day. The *settlement price* is the next number ($589.10), and it is the closing price for the day. For purposes of marking-to-market, this is the figure used. The change (−0.10) listed is the movement in the settlement price since the previous trading session. Finally, the previous *open interest* (2,664), the number of contracts outstanding at the end of the previous trading session, is shown. The volume of trading is shown for the trading session (1,065).

To see how large futures trading can be, we take a look at the Chicago Mercantile Exchange (CME) Canadian dollar contracts (at the top of Figure 24.6). One contract is for $100,000. The previous day's total open interest for all months is 88,140 contracts. The total value outstanding is therefore C$8.8 billion for this one type of contract!

Hedging with Futures

Hedging with futures contracts is conceptually identical to hedging with forward contracts, and the payoff profile on a futures contract is drawn just like the profile for a forward contract. The only difference in hedging with futures is that the firm will have to maintain an account with an investment dealer so that gains and losses can be credited or debited each day as a part of the marking-to-market process.

Even though there is a large variety of futures contracts, it is unlikely that a particular firm will be able to find the precise hedging instrument it needs. For example, we might produce a particular grade or variety of oil, and find that no contract exists for exactly that grade. However, all oil prices tend to move together, so we could hedge our output using futures contracts on other grades of oil. Using a contract on a related, but not identical, asset as a means of hedging is called **cross-hedging**. In our example, the cross-hedger faces the risk that the futures price may not move closely with the price of the oil produced. The difference between the two prices is termed the **basis** and the risk faced by the cross hedger is **basis risk**.

When a firm does cross-hedge, it does not actually want to buy or sell the underlying asset. This presents no problem because the firm can reverse its futures position at some point before maturity. This simply means that if the firm sells a futures contract to hedge something, it will buy the same contract at a later date, thereby eliminating its futures position. In fact, futures contracts are very rarely held to maturity by anyone (despite horror stories of individuals waking up to find mountains of soybeans in their front yards), and, as a result, actual physical delivery very rarely takes place.

A related issue has to do with contract maturity. A firm might wish to hedge over a relatively long period of time, but the available contracts might have shorter maturities. A firm could therefore decide to roll over short-term contracts, but this entails some risks. For example, in stark contrast to Barrick's relative success with its Forward Sales Program, JP Morgan Chase & Co., the largest bank in the United States by assets and market capitalization, experienced considerable trouble in 2012 with its hedging program. In 2011, JP Morgan profited by making bearish bets on credit conditions. The European Central Bank's long-term loans to Euro zone banks spurred JP Morgan to make bullish bets in early 2012. The company suffered a heavy $2 billion loss when the prices moved against the bets starting April 2012. This came as a surprise to the U.S legislators when they were about to implement the Volcker Rule, a provision in the Dodd-Frank Wall Street Reform and Consumer Protection Act that restricts U.S. banks from making speculative investments that do not benefit the customers. As a result, JP Morgan CEO, Jamie Dimon came under heavy criticism when he appeared before a Congressional committee in June 2012.

cross-hedging
Hedging an asset with contracts written on a closely related, but not identical, asset.

basis risk
Risk that futures prices will not move directly with cash price hedged.

Concept Questions

1. What is a futures contract? How does it differ from a forward contract?
2. What is cross-hedging? Why is it important?

24.5 | Hedging with Swap Contracts

As the name suggests, a **swap contract** is an agreement by two parties to exchange, or swap, specified cash flows at specified intervals. Swaps are a recent innovation; they were first introduced to the public in 1981 when IBM and the World Bank entered into a swap agreement. The market for swaps has grown tremendously since that time.

A swap contract is really just a portfolio, or series, of forward contracts. Recall that with a forward contract, one party promises to exchange an asset (e.g., bushels of wheat) for another asset (cash) on a specific future date. With a swap, the only difference is that there are multiple exchanges instead of just one. In principle, a swap contract could be tailored to exchange just

swap contract
An agreement by two parties to exchange, or swap, specified cash flows at specified intervals in the future.

ibm.com
worldbank.com

about anything. In practice, most swap contracts fall into one of three basic categories: currency swaps, interest rate swaps, and commodity swaps. Other types will surely develop, but we will concentrate on just these three.

Currency Swaps

With a *currency swap*, two companies agree to exchange a specific amount of one currency for a specific amount of another at specific dates in the future. For example, suppose a Canadian firm has a German subsidiary and wishes to obtain debt financing for an expansion of the subsidiary's operations. Because most of the subsidiary's cash flows are in euros, the company would like the subsidiary to borrow and make payments in euros, thereby hedging against changes in the euros–dollar exchange rate. Unfortunately, the company has good access to Canadian debt markets, but not to German debt markets.

At the same time, a German firm would like to obtain Canadian dollar financing. It can borrow cheaply in euros, but not in dollars. Both firms face a similar problem. They can borrow at favourable rates, but not in the desired currency. A currency swap is a solution. These two firms simply agree to exchange dollars for euros at a fixed rate at specific future dates (the payment dates on the loans). Each firm thus obtains the best possible rate and then arranges to eliminate exposure to exchange rate changes by agreeing to exchange currencies, a neat solution. A further benefit is that the two firms can lower their transaction costs by working together in a swap.

Interest Rate Swaps

Imagine a firm that wishes to obtain a fixed-rate loan, but can only get a good deal on a floating-rate loan, that is, a loan for which the payments are adjusted periodically to reflect changes in interest rates. Another firm can obtain a fixed-rate loan, but wishes to obtain the lowest possible interest rate and is therefore willing to take a floating-rate loan. (Rates on floating-rate loans are generally lower than rates on fixed-rate loans; why?) Both firms could accomplish their objectives by agreeing to exchange loan payments; in other words, the two firms would make each other's loan payments. This is an example of an *interest rate swap*; what is really being exchanged is a floating interest rate for a fixed one.

Interest rate swaps and currency swaps are often combined. One firm obtains floating-rate financing in a particular currency and swaps it for fixed-rate financing in another currency. Also, note that payments on floating-rate loans are always based on some index, such as the one-year Treasury rate. An interest rate swap might involve exchanging one floating rate loan for another as a way of changing the underlying index. The most common interest rate swap is a "plain vanilla" swap. In a plain vanilla swap, a counterparty agrees to pay a sequence of fixed-rate interest payments on specific dates for a specific period of time and in turn receives a sequence of floating-rate interest payments. In a plain vanilla swap, the two cash flows are paid in the same currency.

Commodity Swaps

As the name suggests, a *commodity swap* is an agreement to exchange a fixed quantity of a commodity at fixed times in the future. Commodity swaps are the newest type of swap, and the market for them is small relative to that for other types. The potential for growth is enormous, however.

Swap contracts for oil have been engineered. For example, say that an oil user has a need for 20,000 barrels every quarter. The oil user could enter into a swap contract with an oil producer to supply the needed oil. What price would they agree on? As we mentioned previously, they can't fix a price forever. Instead, they could agree that the price would be equal to the *average* daily oil price from the previous 90 days. As a result of their using an average price, the impact of the relatively large daily price fluctuations in the oil market would be reduced, and both firms would benefit from a reduction in transactions exposure.

The Swap Dealer

Unlike futures contracts, swap contracts are not traded on organized exchanges. The main reason is that they are not sufficiently standardized. Instead, the *swap dealer* plays a key role in the swaps market. In the absence of a swap dealer, a firm that wished to enter into a swap would have to track down another firm that wanted the opposite end of the deal. This search would probably be expensive and time-consuming.

Instead, a firm wishing to enter into a swap agreement contacts a swap dealer, and the swap dealer takes the other side of the agreement. The swap dealer will then try to find an offsetting transaction with some other party or parties (perhaps another firm or another dealer). Failing this, a swap dealer will hedge its exposure using futures contracts.

Banks are the dominant swap dealers in Canada and the United States. As a large swap dealer, a bank would be involved in a variety of contracts. It would be swapping fixed-rate loans for floating-rate loans with some parties and doing just the opposite with other participants. The total collection of contracts in which a dealer is involved is called the *swap book*. The dealer will try to keep a balanced book to limit its net exposure. A balanced book is often called a *matched book*.

Interest Rate Swaps: An Example

To get a better understanding of swap contracts and the role of the swap dealer, we consider a floating-for-fixed interest rate swap. Suppose Company A can borrow at a floating rate equal to prime plus 1 percent or at a fixed rate of 10 percent. Company B can borrow at a floating rate of prime plus 2 percent or at a fixed rate of 9.5 percent. Company A desires a fixed-rate loan, whereas Company B desires a floating-rate loan. Clearly, a swap is in order.

Company A contacts a swap dealer, and a deal is struck. Company A borrows the money at a rate of prime plus 1 percent. The swap dealer agrees to cover the loan payments, and, in exchange, the company agrees to make fixed-rate payments to the swap dealer at a rate of, say, 9.75 percent. Notice that the swap dealer is making floating-rate payments and receiving fixed-rate payments. The company is making fixed-rate payments, so it has swapped a floating payment for a fixed one.

Company B also contacts a swap dealer. The deal here calls for Company B to borrow the money at a fixed rate of 9.5 percent. The swap dealer agrees to cover the fixed loan payments, and the company agrees to make floating-rate payments to the swap dealer at a rate of prime plus, say, 1.5 percent. In this second arrangement, the swap dealer is making fixed-rate payments and receiving floating-rate payments.

What's the net effect of these machinations? First, Company A gets a fixed-rate loan at a rate of 9.75 percent, which is cheaper than the 10 percent rate it can obtain on its own. Second, Company B gets a floating-rate loan at prime plus 1.5 instead of prime plus 2. The swap benefits both companies.

The swap dealer also wins. When all the dust settles, the swap dealer receives (from Company A) fixed-rate payments at a rate of 9.75 percent and makes fixed-rate payments (for Company B) at a rate of 9.5 percent. At the same time, it makes floating-rate payments (for Company A) at a rate of prime plus 1 percent and receives floating-rate payments at a rate of prime plus 1.5 percent (from Company B). Notice that the swap dealer's book is perfectly balanced, in terms of risk, and it has no exposure to interest rate volatility.

FIGURE 24.7

Illustration of an interest rate swap

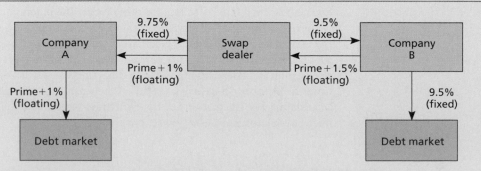

Company A borrows at prime plus 1% and swaps for a 9.75% fixed rate.
Company B borrows at 9.5% fixed and swaps for a prime plus 1.5% floating rate.

Figure 24.7 illustrates the transactions in our interest rate swap. Notice that the essence of the swap transactions is that one company swaps a fixed payment for a floating payment, while the other exchanges a floating payment for a fixed one. The swap dealer acts as an intermediary and profits from the spread between the rates it charges and the rates it receives.

Credit Default Swaps (CDS)

credit default swap
A contract that pays off when a credit event occurs, default by a particular company termed the reference entity, giving the buyer the right to sell corporate bonds issued by the reference entity at their face value.

Credit default swaps, along with other credit derivatives, make up one of the fastest growing markets in the financial world. A credit default swap (CDS) is a contract that pays off when a credit event occurs—default by a particular company, termed the reference entity. In this case, the buyer of the CDS has the right to sell corporate bonds issued by the reference entity to the CDS seller at their face value. Since bonds in default trade at a deep discount, the right to sell bonds at their face value becomes quite valuable when a default occurs.

Credit default swaps are an important risk management tool for financial institutions. By buying a CDS on a borrower, a bank sets up a payment in the event the borrower defaults on its loan. In effect, CDS is a form of insurance against credit losses.[3] The failure of the CDS market was one of the main triggers of the credit crisis of 2008. CDSs created a downward spiral in the capital markets bringing down major organizations such as AIG, Lehman Brothers, and Bear Stearns. Lehman Brothers declared bankruptcy, but the swift intervention of the U.S. government prevented AIG and Bear Stearns from following the same path. The market for credit default swaps grew from approximately US$900 billion in 2001 to around US$68 trillion in April 2008. A good part of this growth was due to investors misusing CDSs to implement "bets" on the credit default of issuers as opposed to hedging risk.[4]

Concept Questions

1. What is a swap contract? Describe three types.
2. Describe the role of the swap dealer.
3. Explain the cash flows in Figure 24.7.

24.6 | Hedging with Option Contracts

The contracts we have discussed thus far—forwards, futures, and swaps—are conceptually similar. In each case, two parties agree to transact on a future date or dates. The key is that both parties are obligated to complete the transaction.

option contract
An agreement that gives the owner the right, but not the obligation, to buy or sell a specific asset at a specific price for a set period of time.

In contrast, an **option contract** is an agreement that gives the owner the right, but not the obligation, to buy or sell (depending on the option type) some asset at a specified price for a specified time. Here we will quickly discuss some option basics and then focus on using options to hedge volatility in commodity prices, interest rates, and exchange rates. In doing so, we will sidestep a wealth of detail concerning option terminology, option trading strategies, and option valuation.

Option Terminology

call option
An option that gives the owner the right, but not the obligation, to buy an asset.

put option
An option that gives the owner the right, but not the obligation, to sell an asset.

Options come in two flavours, puts and calls. The owner of a **call option** has the right, but not the obligation, to buy an underlying asset at a fixed price, called the *strike price* or *exercise price*, for a specified time. The owner of a **put option** has the right, but not the obligation, to sell an underlying asset at a fixed price for a specified time.

The act of buying or selling the underlying asset using the option contract is called *exercising* the option. Some options ("American" options) can be exercised anytime up to and including the

---

[3] For more on credit default swaps, see J.C. Hull, *Fundamentals of Futures and Options Markets*, Seventh Edition, Pearson Prentice Hall, NJ, 2010, Chapter 23.

[4] "Credit default swaps and bank leverage," April 16, 2008 (available at: nakedcapitalism.com/2008/04/credit-default-swaps-and-bank-leverage.html).

expiration date (the last day); other options ("European" options) can only be exercised on the expiration date. Most options are American.

Because the buyer of a call option has the right to buy the underlying asset by paying the strike price, the seller of a call option is obligated to deliver the asset and accept the strike price if the option is exercised. Similarly, the buyer of the put option has the right to sell the underlying asset and receive the strike price. In this case, the seller of the put option must accept the asset and pay the strike price.

Options versus Forwards

There are two key differences between an option contract and a forward contract. The first is obvious. With a forward contract, both parties are obligated to transact; one party delivers the asset, and the other party pays for it. With an option, the transaction occurs only if the owner of the option chooses to exercise it.

The second difference between an option and a forward contract is that, whereas no money changes hands when a forward contract is created, the buyer of an option contract gains a valuable right and must pay the seller for that right. The price of the option is frequently called the *option premium*.

Option Payoff Profiles

Figure 24.8 shows the general payoff profile for a call option from the owner's viewpoint. The horizontal axis shows the difference between the asset's value and the strike price on the option. As illustrated, if the price of the underlying asset rises above the strike price, then the owner of the option will exercise the option and enjoy a profit. If the value of the asset falls below the strike price, the owner of the option will not exercise it. Notice that this payoff profile does not consider the premium that the buyer paid for the option.

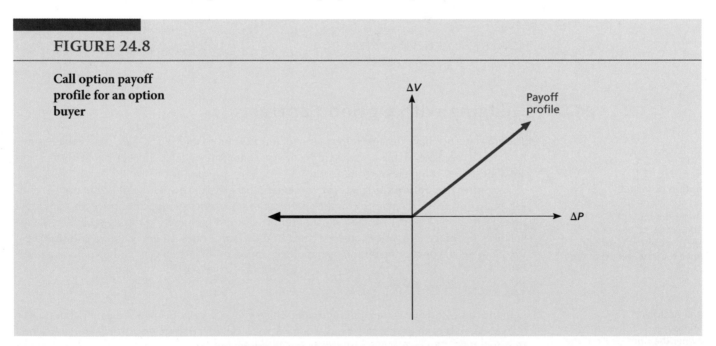

FIGURE 24.8

Call option payoff profile for an option buyer

The payoff profile that results from buying a call is repeated in Part A of Figure 24.9. Part B shows the payoff profile on a call option from the seller's side. A call option is a zero-sum game, so the seller's payoff profile is exactly the opposite of the buyer's.

Part C of Figure 24.9 shows the payoff profile for the buyer of a put option. In this case, if the asset's value falls below the strike price, then the buyer profits because the seller of the put must pay the strike price. Part D shows that the seller of the put option loses out when the price falls below the strike price.

FIGURE 24.9

Option payoff profiles

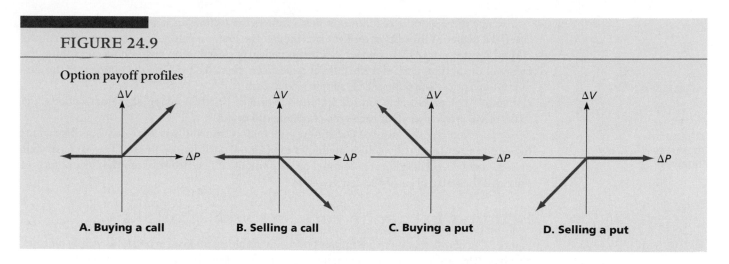

A. Buying a call   **B. Selling a call**   **C. Buying a put**   **D. Selling a put**

Option Hedging

Suppose a firm has a risk profile that looks like the one in Part A of Figure 24.10. If the firm wishes to hedge against adverse price movements using options, what should it do? Examining the different payoff profiles in Figure 24.9, we see that the one that has the desirable shape is C, buying a put. If the firm buys a put, then its net exposure is as illustrated in Part B of Figure 24.10.

FIGURE 24.10

Hedging with options

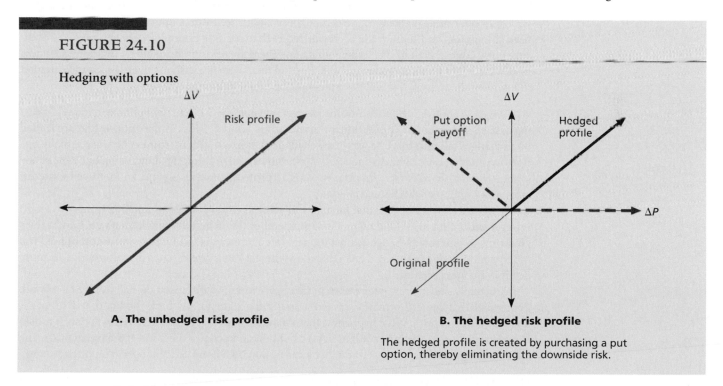

A. The unhedged risk profile   **B. The hedged risk profile**

The hedged profile is created by purchasing a put option, thereby eliminating the downside risk.

In this case, by buying a put option, the firm has eliminated the downside risk, that is, the risk of an adverse price movement. However, the firm has retained the upside potential. In other words, the put option acts as a kind of insurance policy. Remember that this desirable insurance is not free; the firm pays for it when it buys the put option.

Hedging Commodity Price Risk with Options

We saw earlier that there are futures contracts available for a variety of basic commodities. In addition, there are an increasing number of options available on these same commodities. In fact, the options that are typically traded on commodities are actually options on futures contracts, and, for this reason, they are called *futures options*.

The way these work is as follows: When a futures call option on, for example, wheat is exercised, the owner of the option receives two things. The first is a futures contract on wheat at the current futures price. This contract can be immediately closed at no cost. The second thing the owner of the option receives is the difference between the strike price on the option and the current futures price. The difference is simply paid in cash.

Figure 24.11 gives a few futures options quotations. Briefly, looking at the oat options, the strike prices are provided for each type of option: call or put.

cmegroup.com
cmegroup.com/company/
nymex.html

Suppose you buy the July 320 Oats futures call option. You will pay 2 2/8 cents per bushel for the option (they're actually sold in multiples of 5000 but we'll ignore this). If you exercise your option, you will receive a futures contract on oats and the difference between the current futures price and the strike price of 320 cents in cash.

Hedging Exchange Rate Risk with Options

Figure 24.11 shows that there are futures options available on *foreign currencies* as well as on commodities. These work in exactly the same way as commodities futures options. In addition, there are other traded options with which the underlying asset is just currency rather than a futures contract on a currency. Firms with significant exposure to exchange rate risk will frequently purchase put options to protect against adverse exchange rate changes.

Hedging Interest Rate Risk with Options

The use of options to hedge against interest rate risk is a very common practice, and there are a variety of options available to serve this purpose. Some are futures options like the ones we have been discussing, and these trade on organized exchanges. For example, we mentioned the Treasury bond contract in our discussion of futures. There are options available on this contract and a number of other financial futures as well. Beyond this, there is a thriving over-the-counter market in interest rate options. We will describe some of these options in this section.

A PRELIMINARY NOTE   Some interest rate options are actually options on interest-bearing assets such as bonds (or on futures contracts for bonds). Most of the options that are traded on exchanges fall into this category. As we will discuss in a moment, some others are actually options on interest rates. The distinction is important if we are thinking about using one type or the other to hedge. To illustrate, suppose we want to protect ourselves against an increase in interest rates using options; what should we do?

We need to buy an option that increases in value as interest rates go up. One thing we can do is buy a *put* option on a bond. Why a put? Remember that when interest rates go up, bond values go down, so one way to hedge against interest rate increases is to buy put options on bonds. The other way to hedge is to buy a *call* option on interest rates. We discuss this alternative in more detail in the next section.

We actually saw interest rate options in Chapter 7 when we discussed the call feature on a bond. Remember that the call provision gives the issuer the right to buy back the bond at a set price, known as the *call price*. What happens is that if interest rates fall, the bond's price will rise. If it rises above the call price, the buyer will exercise its option and acquire the bond at a bargain price. The call provision can thus be viewed as either a call option on a bond or a put option on interest rates.

INTEREST RATE CAPS   An *interest rate cap* is a call option on an interest rate. Suppose a firm has a floating-rate loan. It is concerned that interest rates will rise sharply and the firm will experience financial distress because of the increased loan payment. To guard against this, the firm can purchase an interest rate cap from a bank. What will happen is that if the loan payment ever rises above an agreed-upon limit (the "ceiling"), the bank will pay the difference between the actual payment and the ceiling to the firm in cash.

A *floor* is a put option on an interest rate. If a firm buys a cap and sells a floor, the result is a *collar*. By selling the put and buying the call, the firm protects itself against increases in interest rates beyond the ceiling by the cap. However, if interest rates drop below the floor, the put will be exercised against the firm. The result is that the rate the firm pays will not drop below the floor rate. In other words, the rate the firm pays will always be between the floor and the ceiling.

FIGURE 24.11

Future Options Prices: Wednesday, June 20, 2012

Oat Options (Expiring July 2012):

| | | CALLS | | | | | | | | PUTS | | | | | | |
Updated	Hi / Lo Limit	Volume	High	Low	Prior Settle	Change	Last	Strike Price	Last	Change	Prior Settle	Low	High	Volume	Hi / Lo Limit	Updated
7:04:16 PM CT 6/19/2012	31'4 No Limit	0			11'4			315	2'0 a	0'0	2'0	2'0 a			22'0 No Limit	9:31:37 AM CT 6/20/2012
10:54:38 AM CT 6/20/2012	27'4 No Limit	3	10'4	9'6 a	7'4	+2'2	9'6 a	320	2'2 a	-0'6	3'0	2'2 a	4'2	0	23'0 No Limit	9:31:39 AM CT 6/20/2012
10:50:47 AM CT 6/20/2012	25'4 No Limit	0	7'1 b		5'4	+0'7	6'3 a	325	4'2 a	-1'6	6'0	4'2 a		4	26'0 No Limit	11:25:24 AM CT 6/20/2012
10:50:49 AM CT 6/20/2012	22'7 No Limit	0	4'1 b	2'6 a	2'7	+1'0	3'7 a	330	5'2 a	-3.1	8'3	5'0	5'4	0	28'3 No Limit	10:38:40 AM CT 6/20/2012
10:33:51 AM CT 6/20/2012	22'1 No Limit	0	2'3 b		2'1	+0'2	2'3 b	335			12'5			3	32'5 No Limit	7:07:07 AM CT 6/20/2012

Silver Options (Expiring July 2012):

| | | CALLS | | | | | | | | PUTS | | | | | | |
Updated	Hi / Lo Limit	Volume	High	Low	Prior Settle	Change	Last	Strike Price	Last	Change	Prior Settle	Low	High	Volume	Hi / Lo Limit	Updated
9:01:05 AM CT 6/20/2012	No Limit 0.001	0	-	-	0.001	-	-	8500	-	-	56.632				No Limit 0.001	7:06:26 PM CT 6/19/2012
9:01:05 AM CT 6/20/2012	No Limit 0.001	0	-	-	0.001	-	-	8600	-	-	57.632				No Limit 0.001	7:07:00 PM CT 6/19/2012
9:01:05 AM CT 6/20/2012	No Limit 0.001	0	-	-	0.001	-	-	8700	-	-	58.632				No Limit 0.001	7:04:40 PM CT 6/19/2012
9:01:05 AM CT 6/20/2012	No Limit 0.001	0	-	-	0.001	-	-	9000	61.708a	+0.076	61.632		61.787 b		No Limit 0.001	10:27:04 PM CT 6/19/2012
9:01:05 AM CT 6/20/2012	No Limit 0.001	0	-	-	0.001	-	-	10000	-	-	71.632				No Limit 0.001	7:05:47 PM CT 6/19/2012

Light Sweet Crude Oil Options—1,000 U.S. barrels, cents per barrel (Expiring August 2012):

| | | CALLS | | | | | | | | PUTS | | | | | | |
Updated	Hi / Lo Limit	Volume	High	Low	Prior Settle	Change	Last	Strike Price	Last	Change	Prior Settle	Low	High	Volume	Hi / Lo Limit	Updated
11:40:22 AM CT 6/20/2012	No Limit 0.01	68	3.65 b	2.09 a	0.001	-1.51	12.09 a	8300	3.58 b	+1.33	2.25	2.06	3.58 b	179	No Limit 0.01	11:40:25 AM CT 6/20/2012
11:40:22 AM CT 6/20/2012	No Limit 0.01	87	3.33 b	1.87 a	0.001	-1.43	1.87 a	8350	3.86 b	+1.41	2.45	2.58	3.86 b	45	No Limit 0.01	11:40:25 AM CT 6/20/2012
11:40:25 AM CT 6/20/2012	No Limit 0.01	244	3.03 b	1.67 a	0.001	-1.34	1.67 a	8400	4.16 b	+1.50	2.66	2.47 a	4.16 b	53	No Limit 0.01	11:40:25 AM CT 6/20/2012
11:40:25 AM CT 6/20/2012	No Limit 0.01	115	2.83	1.48 a	0.001	-1.25	1.48 a	8450	4.47 b	+1.59	2.88	3.18	4.47 b	28	No Limit 0.01	11:40:25 AM CT 6/20/2012
11:40:22 AM CT 6/20/2012	No Limit 0.01	989	2.58	1.31 a	0.001	-1.18	1.31 a	8500	4.78 b	+1.66	3.12	2.91 a	4.78 b	59	No Limit 0.01	11:40:26 AM CT 6/20/2012

CAD/USD Options (Expiring September 2012):

| | CALLS | | | | | | | PUTS | | | | | | |
Updated	Volume	High	Low	Prior Settle	Change	Last	Strike Price	Last	Change	Prior Settle	Low	High	Volume	Updated
11:37:06 AM CT 6/20/2012	0	0.0222 b	0.0200 a	0.0221	-0.0021	0.0200 a	9700	0.0126 b	+0.0010	0.0116	0.0107	0.0126 b	11	11:37:21 AM CT 6/20/2012
11:37:26 AM CT 6/20/2012	0	0.0189 b	0.0168 a	0.0188	-0.0020	0.0168 a	9750	0.0146 b	+0.0013	0.0133	0.0130	0.0146 b	10	11:37:29 AM CT 6/20/2012
11:41:05 AM CT 6/20/2012	5	0.0160	0.0136 a	0.0158	-0.0022	0.0136 a	9800	0.0167 b	+0.0014	0.0153	0.0150 a	0.0167 b	0	11:37:13 AM CT 6/20/2012
11:38:58 AM CT 6/20/2012	0	0.0131 b	0.0111 a	0.0131	-0.0020	0.0111 a	9850	0.0192 b	+0.0016	0.0176	0.0174	0.0192 b	0	11:37:12 AM CT 6/20/2012
11:41:05 AM CT 6/20/2012	0	0.0107 b	0.0090 a	0.0107	-0.0017	0.0090 a	9900	0.0218 b	+0.0016	0.0202	0.0195 a	0.0218 b	0	11:37:06 AM CT 6/20/2012

Source: cmegroup.com

OTHER INTEREST RATE OPTIONS   We will close out our chapter by briefly mentioning two relatively new types of interest rate options. Suppose a firm has a floating-rate loan. The firm is comfortable with its floating-rate loan, but it would like to have the right to convert it to a fixed-rate loan in the future.

What can the firm do? What it wants is the right, but not the obligation, to swap its floating-rate loan for a fixed-rate loan. In other words, the firm needs to buy an option on a swap. Swap options exist, and they have the charming name *swaptions*.

We've seen that there are options on futures contracts and options on swap contracts, but what about options on options? Such options are called *compound* options. As we have just discussed, a cap is a call option on interest rates. Suppose a firm thinks that, depending on interest rates, it might like to buy a cap in the future. As you can probably guess, in this case, what the firm might want to do today is buy an option on a cap. Inevitably, it seems, an option on a cap is called a *caption*, and there is a growing market for these instruments.

Actual Use of Derivatives

Because derivatives do not usually appear in financial statements, it is much more difficult to observe the use of derivatives by firms compared to, say, bank debt. Much of our knowledge of corporate derivative use comes from academic surveys. Most surveys report that the use of derivatives appears to vary widely among large publicly traded firms. Large firms are far more likely to use derivatives than are small firms. Table 24.1 shows that for firms that use derivatives, foreign currency and interest rate derivatives are the most frequently used.

The prevailing view is that derivatives can be very helpful in reducing the variability of firm cash flows, which, in turn, reduces the various costs associated with financial distress. Therefore, it is somewhat puzzling that large firms use derivatives more often than small firms—because large firms tend to have less cash flow variability than small firms. Also, some surveys report that firms occasionally use derivatives when they want to speculate on future prices and not just to hedge risks.

TABLE 24.1

Derivatives Usage Survey Results

Percent of Companies Using Derivatives

2010	71%
2009	79%

In Which Asset Class Do You Use Derivatives?

	2010	2009
Interest rates	65%	68%
Currencies	62%	58%
Credit	13%	13%
Energy	19%	13%
Commodities	23%	22%
Equities	13%	9%

Source: Adapted from *Treasury & Risk Management* (March 2011 and March 2010).

Do You Expect Your Use of Derivatives to Change?

	2010		2009	
	Increase	Decrease	Increase	Decrease
Interest rates	19%	15%	13%	20%
Currencies	20%	8%	31%	6%
Credit	4%	4%	2%	13%
Energy	11%	7%	5%	9%
Commodities	16%	6%	12%	10%
Equities	6%	7%	7%	6%

Do You Use an Integrated Risk Management Strategy or Do You Hedge Transactions or Specific Currency Exposures?

	2010	2009
Hedge total risk	31.8%	21.1%
Hedge transactions	34.1%	47.4%
Hedge specific currency exposures	34.1%	31.6%

However, most of the evidence is consistent with the theory that derivatives are most frequently used by firms where financial distress costs are high and access to the capital markets is constrained.

Concept Questions

1. Suppose that the unhedged risk profile in Figure 24.10 sloped down instead of up. What option-based hedging strategy would be suitable in this case?
2. What is a futures option?
3. What is a caption? Who might want to buy one?

24.7 | SUMMARY AND CONCLUSIONS

This chapter has introduced some of the basic principles of financial risk management and financial engineering. The motivation for risk management and financial engineering stems from the fact that a firm will frequently have an undesirable exposure to some type of risk. This is particularly true today because of the increased volatility in key financial variables such as interest rates, exchange rates, and commodity prices.

We describe a firm's exposure to a particular risk with a risk profile. The goal of financial risk management is to alter the firm's risk profile through the buying and selling of derivative assets such as futures contracts, swap contracts, and options contracts. By finding instruments with appropriate payoff profiles, a firm can reduce or even eliminate its exposure to many types of risk.

Hedging cannot change the fundamental economic reality of a business. What it can do is allow a firm to avoid expensive and troublesome disruptions that might otherwise result from short-run, temporary price fluctuations. Hedging also gives a firm time to react and adapt to changing market conditions. Because of the price volatility and rapid economic change that characterize modern business, intelligently dealing with volatility has become an increasingly important task for financial managers.

There are many other option types available in addition to those we have discussed, and more are created every day. One very important aspect of financial risk management that we have not discussed is that options, forwards, futures, and swaps can be combined in a wide variety of ways to create new instruments. These basic contract types are really just the building blocks used by financial engineers to create new and innovative products for corporate risk management.

Key Terms

basis risk (page 698)
call option (page 701)
credit default swap (page 701)
cross-hedging (page 698)
derivative security (page 687)
economic exposure (page 690)
forward contract (page 691)
futures contract (page 694)

hedging (page 687)
option contract (page 701)
payoff profile (page 691)
put option (page 701)
risk profile (page 688)
swap contract (page 698)
transactions exposure (page 689)

Chapter Review Problems and Self-Test

24.1 **Futures Contracts** Suppose Golden Grain Farms (GGF) expects to harvest 50,000 bushels of wheat in September. GGF is concerned about the possibility of price fluctuations between now and September. The futures price for September wheat is $2 per bushel, and the relevant contract calls for 5000 bushels. What action should GGF take to lock in the $2 price? Suppose the price of wheat actually turns out to be $3. Evaluate GGF's gains and losses. Do the same for a price of $1. Ignore marking-to-market.

24.2 **Options Contracts** In the previous question, suppose that September futures put options with a strike price of $2 per bushel cost $.15 per bushel. Assuming that GGF hedges using put options, evaluate its gains and losses for wheat prices of $1, $2, and $3.

Answers to Self-Test Problems

24.1   GGF wants to deliver wheat and receive a fixed price, so it needs to *sell* futures contracts. Each contract calls for delivery of 5000 bushels, so GGF needs to sell 10 contracts. No money changes hands today.

If wheat prices actually turn out to be $3, then GGF will receive $150,000 for its crop, but it will have a loss of $50,000 on its futures position when it closes that position because the contracts require it to sell 50,000 bushels of wheat at $2, when the going price is $3. GGF thus nets $100,000 overall.

If wheat prices turn out to be $1 per bushel, then the crop will be worth only $50,000. However, GGF will have a profit of $50,000 on its futures position, so GGF again nets $100,000.

24.2   If GGF wants to insure against a price decline only, it can buy 10 put contracts. Each contract is for 5000 bushels, so the cost per contract is 5000 × $.15 = $750. For 10 contracts, the cost will be $7,500.

If wheat prices turn out to be $3, then GGF will not exercise the put options (why not?). Its crop is worth $150,000, but it is out the $7,500 cost of the options, so it nets $142,500.

If wheat prices fall to $1, the crop is worth $50,000. GGF will exercise its puts (why?) and thereby force the seller of the puts to pay $2 per bushel. GGF receives a total of $100,000. If we subtract the cost of the puts, we see that GGF's net is $92,500. In fact, verify that its net at any price of $2 or lower is $92,500.

Concepts Review and Critical Thinking Questions

1.   **(LO3)** If a firm is selling futures contracts on lumber as a hedging strategy, what must be true about the firm's exposure to lumber prices?

2.   **(LO3)** If a firm is buying call options on pork belly futures as a hedging strategy, what must be true about the firm's exposure to pork belly prices?

3.   **(LO4)** What is the difference between a forward contract and a futures contract? Why do you think that futures contracts are much more common? Are there any circumstances under which you might prefer to use forwards instead of futures? Explain.

4.   **(LO3)** Bubbling Crude Corporation, a large Alberta oil producer, would like to hedge against adverse movements in the price of oil, since this is the firm's primary source of revenue. What should the firm do? Provide at least two reasons why it probably will not be possible to achieve a completely flat risk profile with respect to oil prices.

5.   **(LO3)** A company produces an energy intensive product and uses natural gas as the energy source. The competition primarily uses oil. Explain why this company is exposed to fluctuations in both oil and natural gas prices.

6.   **(LO4, 5)** If a textile manufacturer wanted to hedge against adverse movements in cotton prices, it could buy cotton futures contracts or buy call options on cotton futures contracts. What would be the pros and cons of the two approaches?

7.   **(LO5)** Explain why a put option on a bond is conceptually the same as a call option on interest rates.

8.   **(LO3, 4, 5)** A company has a large bond issue maturing in one year. When it matures, the company will float a new issue. Current interest rates are attractive, and the company is concerned that rates next year will be higher. What are some hedging strategies that the company might use in this case?

9.   **(LO5)** Explain why a swap is effectively a series of forward contracts. Suppose a firm enters into a swap agreement with a swap dealer. Describe the nature of the default risk faced by both parties.

10.   **(LO5)** Suppose a firm enters into a fixed-for-floating interest rate swap with a swap dealer. Describe the cash flows that will occur as a result of the swap.

11.   **(LO3)** What is the difference between transactions and economic exposure? Which can be hedged more easily? Why?

12.   **(LO4)** Refer to Figure 24.6 in the text to answer this question. If a Canadian company exports its goods to the U.S., how would it use a U.S.-traded futures contract on Canadian dollars to hedge its exchange rate risk? Would it buy or sell Canadians futures? In answering, pay attention to how the exchange rate is quoted in the futures contract.

13.   **(LO4)** For the following scenarios, describe a hedging strategy using futures contracts that might be considered. If you think that a cross-hedge would be appropriate, discuss the reasons for your choice of contract.

   a.   A public utility is concerned about rising costs.

   b.   A candy manufacturer is concerned about rising costs.

   c.   A corn farmer fears that this year's harvest will be at record high levels across the country.

   d.   A manufacturer of photographic film is concerned about rising costs.

   e.   A natural gas producer believes there will be excess supply in the market this year.

   f.   A bank derives all its income from long-term, fixed-rate residential mortgages.

   g.   A stock mutual fund invests in large, blue-chip stocks and is concerned about a decline in the stock market.

   h.   A Canadian importer of Swiss army knives will pay for its order in six months in Swiss francs.

   i.   A Canadian exporter of construction equipment has agreed to sell some cranes to a German construction firm. The Canadian firm will be paid in euros in three months.

14.   **(LO5)** Looking back at the Telus example we used to open the chapter, why would you say Telus used swap cross-curreny agreements? In other words, why didn't Telus just go ahead and issue say, floating-rate bonds in Canada since the net effect of issuing fixed-rate U.S. bonds and then doing two swaps is to create a floating-rate Canadian dollar bond?

15.   **(LO2)** The sub-prime crisis demonstrated the enormous social costs arising from the misuse of financial engineering. What do you think caused this misuse? How can it be prevented in the future?

Questions and Problems

Basic
(Questions 1–4)

1. Futures Quotes (LO4) Refer to Figure 24.6 in the text to answer this question. Suppose you purchase a May 2013 canola futures contract on June 20, 2012. What will your profit or loss be if the canola prices turn out to be $537.25 per metric tonne at expiration?

2. Futures Quotes (LO4) Refer to Figure 24.6 in the text to answer this question. Supposed you sell June 2013 gold futures on June 20, 2012. What will your profit or loss be if gold prices turn out to be $1,590 per ounce at expiration? What if gold prices are $1,750 per ounce at expiration?

3. Futures Options Quotes (LO5) Refer to Figure 24.11 in the text to answer this question. Suppose you purchase an August 2012 call option on crude oil futures with a strike price of 8500 cents per barrel. How much does your option cost per barrel of oil? What is the total cost? Suppose the price of oil futures is 9000 cents per barrel at expiration of the options contract. What is your net profit or loss from this position? What if oil futures prices are 8000 cents per barrel at expiration?

4. Put and Call Payoffs (LO5) Suppose a financial manager buys call options on 50,000 barrels of oil with an exercise price of $83 per barrel. She simultaneously sells a put option on 50,000 barrels of oil with the same exercise price of $83 per barrel. Consider her gains and losses of oil prices are $75, $72, $80, $83, and $85. What if oil futures prices are $88.24 per barrel at expiration?

Intermediate
(Questions 5–7)

5. Hedging with Futures (LO4) Refer to Figure 24.6 in the text to answer this question. Suppose today is June 20, 2012, and your firm is a jewellery manufacturer that needs 1000 ounces of gold in October for the fall production run. You would like to lock in your costs today, because you're concerned that gold prices might go up between now and October.

a. How could you use gold futures contracts to hedge your risk exposure? What price would you be effectively locking in?

b. Suppose gold prices are $1,580 per ounce in October. What is the profit or loss on your futures position? Explain how your futures position has eliminated your exposure to price risk in the gold market.

6. Interest Rate Swaps (LO5) ABC Company and XYZ Company need to raise funds to pay for capital improvements at their manufacturing plants. ABC Company is a well-established firm with an excellent credit rating in the debt market; it can borrow funds either at 11 percent fixed rate or at LIBOR + 1 percent floating rate. XYZ Company is a fledgling start-up firm without a strong credit history. It can borrow funds either at 10 percent fixed rate or at LIBOR + 3 percent floating rate.

a. Is there an opportunity here for ABC and XYZ to benefit by means of an interest rate swap?

b. Suppose you've just been hired at a bank that acts as a dealer in the swaps market, and your boss has shown you the borrowing rate information for your clients ABC and XYZ. Describe how you could bring these two companies together in an interest rate swap that would make both firms better off, while netting your bank a 2.0 percent profit.

7. Insurance (LO1, 2) Suppose your company has a building worth $450 million. Because it is located in a high-risk area for natural disasters, the probability of a total loss in any particular year is 1.5 percent. What is your company's expected loss per year on this building?

Challenge
(Questions 8–10)

8. Financial Engineering (LO5) Suppose there were call options and forward contracts available on coal, but no put options. Show how a financial engineer could synthesize a put option using the available contracts. What does your answer tell you about the general relationship between puts, calls, and forwards?

9. Hedging (LO3, 4, 5) You are assigned to the risk management department of Torbram Wheels Inc., a Canadian chain of auto service shops with outlets in North America and internationally. Your office is located in Mississauga, Ontario, Canada and the earnings of Torbram are stated in Canadian dollars. Your responsibility is to manage the foreign exchange risk arising from operations in the European Community.

The current exchange rate is $1.29 U.S. per euro. Currently Torbram earns net profits from EC operations of 1.2 million euros per month, which are repatriated to the Canadian head office. The firm also has pension obligations to retired employees in the EC of 2 million euros per month. Pension funds for the entire company are managed in the Canadian head office and invested in Canadian assets. While the pension obligations are quite stable, monthly profits are subject to fluctuation with economic conditions and seasonality.

The CFO has identified one month as the appropriate planning horizon and foreign exchange forward contracts with a major bank, currency futures and currency futures options (puts and calls) as possible hedging vehicles. To complete your engagement, do the following:

a   Assess Torbram's exchange rate exposure.

b. Explain how Torbram could hedge with each of the possible vehicles. For each, state the appropriate position (buy or sell) and state your reasons briefly.

c. Suppose the CFO is committed to hedging all the foreign exchange risk from European operations. How would these considerations affect your recommendation on the best choice of hedging vehicle?

10. Insurance (LO1, 2) In calculating an insurance premium, the actuarially fair insurance premium is the premium that results in a zero NPV for both the insured and the insurer. As such, the present value of the expected loss is the actuarially fair insurance premium. Suppose your company wants to insure a building worth $380 million. The probability of loss is 1.25 percent in one year and the relevant discount rate is 4 percent.

a. What is the actuarially fair insurance premium?

b. Suppose that you can make modifications to the building that will reduce the probability of a loss to 0.90 percent. How much would you be willing to pay for these modifications?

MINI CASE

Johnson Mortgage Inc.

Danielle Johnson recently received her finance degree and has decided to enter the mortgage broker business. Rather than working for someone else, she will open her own shop. Her cousin Paul has approached her about a mortgage for a house he is building. The house will be completed in three months, and he will need the mortgage at that time. Paul wants a 25-year, fixed-rate mortgage in the amount of $500,000 with monthly payments.

Danielle has agreed to lend Paul the money in three months at the current market rate of 6 percent. Because Danielle is just starting out, she does not have $500,000 available for the loan; so she approaches William Wheaton, the president of IT Insurance Corporation, about purchasing the mortgage from her in three months. William has agreed to purchase the mortgage in three months, but he is unwilling to set a price on the mortgage. Instead, he has agreed in writing to purchase the mortgage at the market rate in three months. There are Government of Canada bond futures contracts available for delivery in three months. A Government of Canada bond contract is for $100,000 in face value of ten-year Government of Canada bonds.

Questions

1. What is the monthly mortgage payment on Paul's mortgage?

2. What is the most significant risk Danielle faces in this deal?

3. How can Danielle hedge this risk?

4. Suppose that in the next three months the market rate of interest rises to 7 percent.

   a. How much will William be willing to pay for the mortgage?

   b. What will happen to the value of Government of Canada bond futures contracts? Will the long or short position increase in value?

5. Suppose that in the next three months the market rate of interest falls to 5 percent.

   a. How much will William be willing to pay for the mortgage?

   b. What will happen to the value of Government of Canada bond futures contracts? Will the long or short position increase in value?

6. Are there any possible risks Danielle faces in using Government of Canada bond futures contracts to hedge her interest rate risk?

Internet Application Questions

1. Value at Risk is a powerful tool to analyze the risk of a portfolio. VaR attempts to estimate the dollar loss on a portfolio based on small probabilities. The following link explains all about VaR.

   gloriamundi.org

   Assuming that returns on a portfolio are normally distributed, reconcile the VaR measure to more traditional measures of risk such as the standard deviation of returns.

2. ICE Futures Canada provides several educational tools to help understand the world of futures trading. The following link explains the mechanics of futures trading and common futures jargon, and provides examples of hedging.

   theice.com/KnowledgeCenter.shtml

   Explain how a wheat farmer in Saskatchewan as well as a baker in Quebec can benefit from using futures.

3. Information on derivative instruments and markets can be found at numa.com. Among the references you can access is an "Options Strategy Guide." What technique(s) does the guide suggest if you are moderately bullish on the market? What about if you are neutral, expecting short-term weakness, and a longer term rally?

4. The Montreal Exchange is the main market for derivative products in Canada. The exchange provides an options calculator on its website at m-x.ca/accueil_en.php. Locate an option in the newspaper or on the exchange's website, and calculate its value using the online calculator.

5. National Futures Association (NFA) is the industry-wide, self-regulatory organization for the U.S. futures industry. Go to 'Video Library' section of NFA (www.nfa.futures.org/NFA-video-library/index.html) to look at the video tutorials on a variety of registration and compliance-related topics.

6. Chicago Board Options Exchange (CBOE) is the largest U.S. options exchange and creator of listed options. CBOE's educational initiatives come together in a comprehensive, online learning hub that offers option investors a foundation to build their knowledge and confidence when trading. Go to 'Learning Centre' of CBOE (www.cboe.com/LearnCenter/Default.aspx) and click on 'Online Tutorials' (www.cboe.com/LearnCenter/Tutorials.aspx). Read through the tutorials to understand the basics of Options.

CHAPTER 25

OPTIONS AND CORPORATE SECURITIES

IMAX®

On June 22, 2012, IMAX Corporation, one of the world's leading entertainment technology companies, headquartered in Mississauga, Ontario, had a call option trading on the Montreal Exchange with a $25 exercise price and an expiration date of July 12, 20 days away. On the same day, Cineplex Inc. had a call option with a similar exercise price of $25 and the same expiration date of July 12, 2012. Despite having the same exercise price and expiration date, the prices of the call option on these two stocks were different. The IMAX call option was selling at $0.52, and the Cineplex call option had a price of $4.20. In this chapter we will discuss the basics of options and also explore the factors affecting the price of options.

The IMAX® symbol is used with the permission of IMAX Corporation. IMAX® is a registered trademark of IMAX Corporation.

Learning Objectives ▶

After studying this chapter, you should understand:

LO1 The basics of call and put options and how to calculate their payoffs and profits.

LO2 The factors that affect option values and how to price call and put options using no arbitrage conditions.

LO3 The basics of employee stock options and their benefits and disadvantages.

LO4 How to value a firm's equity as an option on the firm's assets and use of option valuation to evaluate capital budgeting projects.

LO5 The basics of convertible bonds and warrants and how to value them.

Our previous chapter briefly examined options and their use in risk management. Options are a much broader topic, however, and there is much more to them than we have discussed so far. In fact, options are a part of everyday life. "Keep your options open" is sound business advice, and "We're out of options" is a sure sign of trouble. Options are obviously valuable, but actually putting a dollar value on one is not easy. How to value options is an important topic of research, and option pricing is one of the great success stories of modern finance.

option
A contract that gives its owner the right to buy or sell some asset at a fixed price on or before a given date.

In finance, an **option** is an arrangement that gives its owner the right to buy or sell an asset at a fixed price anytime on or before a given date. The most familiar options are stock options. These are options to buy and sell shares of common stock, and we discuss them in some detail. Almost all corporate securities have implicit or explicit option features. Furthermore, the use of such features is expanding with the growth of financial engineering. As a result, understanding securities that involve option features requires a general knowledge of the factors that determine an option's value.

This chapter starts with a description of different types of options. We identify and discuss the general factors that determine option values and show how ordinary debt and equity have option-like characteristics. We then illustrate how option features are incorporated into corporate securities by discussing warrants, convertible bonds, and other option-like securities.

25.1 | Options: The Basics

An option is a contract that gives its owner the right to buy or sell some asset at a fixed price on or before a given date. For example, an option on a building might give the holder of the option the right to buy the building for $1 million anytime on or before the Saturday before the third Wednesday in January 2016.

Options are a unique type of financial contract because they give the buyer the right, but not the obligation, to do something. The buyer uses the option only if it is profitable to do so; otherwise the option can be thrown away.

There is a special vocabulary associated with options. Here are some important definitions:

exercising the option
The act of buying or selling the underlying asset via the option contract.

1. **Exercising the option.** The act of buying or selling the underlying asset via the option contract is called exercising the option.

2. **Striking price or exercise price.** The fixed price specified in the option contract at which the holder can buy or sell the underlying asset is called the striking price or exercise price. The striking price is often just called the *strike price*.

striking price
The fixed price in the option contract at which the holder can buy or sell the underlying asset. Also the exercise price or strike price.

3. **Expiration date.** An option usually has a limited life. The option is said to expire at the end of its life. The last day on which the option can be exercised is called the expiration date.

4. **American options and European options.** An American option may be exercised anytime up to the expiration date. A European option can be exercised only on the expiration date.

expiration date
The last day on which an option can be exercised.

American option
An option that can be exercised at any time until its expiration date.

Puts and Calls

As we discussed in our previous chapter, options come in two basic types: puts and calls. Call options are the more common of the two and our discussion focuses mostly on calls. A **call option** gives the owner the right to buy an asset at a fixed price during a particular time period. It may help you to remember that a call option gives you the right to "call in" an asset.

European option
An option that can be exercised only on the expiration date.

A **put option** is essentially the opposite of a call option. Instead of giving the holder the right to buy some asset, it gives the holder the right to sell that asset for a fixed exercise price. If you buy a put option, you can force the seller to buy the asset from you for a fixed price and thereby "put it to him."

call option
The right to buy an asset at a fixed price during a particular period of time.

What about an investor who sells a call option? The seller receives money up front and has the obligation to sell the asset at the exercise price if the option holder wants it. Similarly, an investor who sells a put option receives cash up front and is then obligated to buy the asset at the exercise price if the option holder demands it.[1]

put option
The right to sell an asset at a fixed price during a particular period of time. The opposite of a call option.

The asset involved in an option could be anything. The options that are most widely bought and sold, however, are stock options. These are options to buy and sell shares of stock. Because these are the best-known options, we study them first. As we discuss stock options, keep in mind that the general principles apply to options involving any asset, not just shares of stock.

Stock Option Quotations

In the 1970s and 1980s, organized trading in options grew from literally zero into some of the world's largest markets. The tremendous growth in interest in derivative securities resulted from the greatly increased volatility in financial markets, which we discussed in Chapter 1.[2] Exchange trading in options began in 1973 on the Chicago Board Options Exchange (CBOE). The CBOE is still the largest organized options market; options are traded in a number of other places today, including Montreal, London, Paris, Tokyo, and Hong Kong.

cboe.com

Option trading in Canada began in 1975 on the Montreal Exchange. Today options are traded on the Montreal Exchange and are cleared through the Canadian Derivatives Clearing Corp. (CDCC). The CDCC stands between option buyers and option sellers, called writers. Put and call options involving stock in some of the best-known corporations in Canada are traded daily. Almost all such options are American (as opposed to European). Trading in Canadian options and other derivative securities has grown rapidly as banks, pension funds, and other financial institutions gain experience with hedging techniques using derivative securities.

To get started with option specifics, we look at a Montreal Exchange option quotation for a CDCC option:

---

[1] An investor who sells an option is often said to have "written" the option.

[2] Our discussion of the history of options trading draws on L. Gagnon, "Exchange-Traded Financial Derivatives in Canada: Finally Off the Launching Pad," *Canadian Investment Review*, Fall 1990, pp. 63–70, and J. Ilkiw, "From Suspicion to Optimism: The Story of Derivative Use by Pension Funds in Canada," *Canadian Investment Review*, Summer 1994, pp. 19–22.

BNS — Bank of Nova Scotia (Call Option):
Last Price: 53.110

Month / Strike	Bid Price	Ask Price	Last Price	Impl. Vol.	Vol.
+ 12 JL 50.000	3.100	3.200	3.100	18.27	35
+ 13 JA 42.000	11.150	11.350	11.000	31.70	10

scotiabank.com

The first thing listed here is the company identifier, BNS. This tells us these options involve the right to buy or sell shares of stock in Bank of Nova Scotia. To the right of the company identifier is the closing price of the stock. As of the close of business (in Montreal), Bank of Nova Scotia was selling for $53.11 per share.

Inside the table are the expiration date and strike price for the first call option. "12 JL" means the option expires in July 2012. All CDCC options expire after the close of trading on the third Friday of the expiration month. The first Bank of Nova Scotia option listed here has an exercise price of $50. The second option also has an exercise price of $42.

The first option listed would be described as the "BNS $50 call." The asking price for this option is $3.20. If you pay the $3.20, you have the right, between now and the third Friday in July, to buy one share of Bank of Nova Scotia stock for $50. Actually, trading occurs in round lots (multiples of 100 shares), so one option contract costs $3.20 × 100 = $320.

m-x.ca

Figure 25.1 contains a more detailed quote reproduced from the Montreal Exchange. (You can get option quotes online at the Montreal Exchange's website.) From our previous discussion, we know that these are Bank of Nova Scotia options and the Bank of Nova Scotia closed at $53.11 per share on the TSX. Notice that multiple striking prices ranging from $38 to $70 are available. Expiration dates range from July 2012 to January 2015.

To check your understanding of option quotes, suppose you wanted the right to buy 100 shares of Aurizon Mines Ltd. for $5 any time between now and the third Friday in August 2012. What should you order and how much will it cost you?

Since you want the right to buy the stock for $5, you need to buy a call option with a $5 exercise price. Place an order for one ARZ 2012 August $5 call. Since the August $5 call is quoted at $0.31 asking price, you have to pay $0.31 per share, or $31 in all (plus commission).

Option Payoffs

Looking at Figure 25.1, suppose you were to buy 50 BNS 2012 July $52 call contracts. The option is quoted at a $1.28 asking price, so the contracts cost $128 each. You would spend a total of 50 × $128 = $6,400. You wait a while and the expiration date rolls around. Now what? You have the right to buy Bank of Nova Scotia stock for $52 per share. If Bank of Nova Scotia is selling for less than $52 a share, this option isn't worth anything, and you throw it away. In this case, we say the option has finished "out of the money" since the exercise price exceeds the stock price. Suppose Bank of Nova Scotia rises to, say, $59 per share. Since you have the right to buy Bank of Nova Scotia at $52, you make a profit of $7 on each share on exercise. Each contract involves 100 shares, so you make $7 per share × 100 shares per contract = $700 per contract. Finally, you own 50 contracts, so the value of your options is a handsome $35,000. Notice that since you invested $6,400, your net profit is $28,600.

Ending Stock Price	Option Value (50 Contracts)	Net Profit (Loss)	Stock Value (121 shares)	Net Profit (Loss)
$45	$—	$ (6,400)	$5,445	$ (955)
50	$—	$ (6,400)	$6,050	$ (350)
55	$15,000	$ 8,600	$6,655	$ 255
60	$40,000	$33,600	$7,260	$ 860
65	$65,000	$58,600	$7,865	$1,465
70	$90,000	$83,600	$8,470	$2,070

As our example indicates, the gains and losses from buying call options can be quite large. To illustrate further, suppose you had simply purchased the stock with $6,400 at $53.11 each instead of buying call options. You would have about $6,400/53.11 = 120.50 shares (approximately 121 shares). We can now compare what you have when the options expire for different stock prices.

The option position clearly magnifies the gains and losses on the stock by a substantial amount. The reason is that payoff on your 50 option contracts is based on 50 × 100 = 5000 shares of stock instead of just 121.

FIGURE 25.1

Options quotations, June 22, 2012

BNS – Bank of Nova Scotia (The)
Last update: June 22, 2012, 13:44 Montréal time- (DATA 15 MINUTES DELAYED)   Refresh | Print
Last Price: 53.110   Net Change: 0.700 Bid Price: 53.110   Ask Price: 53.120   30-Day Historical Volatility: 19.14%

	Calls						Puts				
Month / Strike	Bid Price	Ask Price	Last Price	Impl. Vol.	Vol.	Month / Strike	Bid Price	Ask Price	Last Price	Impl. Vol.	Vol.
+ 12 JL 38.000	15.050	15.200	14.550	68.82	0	+ 12 JL 38.000	0.000	0.060	0.070	53.88	0
+ 12 JL 40.000	13.050	13.200	12.550	59.71	0	+ 12 JL 40.000	0.000	0.060	0.070	46.69	0
+ 12 JL 42.000	11.050	11.200	10.550	50.92	0	+ 12 JL 42.000	0.000	0.060	0.070	39.53	0
+ 12 JL 44.000	9.100	9.200	8.600	44.03	0	+ 12 JL 44.000	0.010	0.070	0.090	34.05	0
+ 12 JL 46.000	7.100	7.200	7.000	35.45	5	+ 12 JL 46.000	0.030	0.100	0.100	29.01	0
+ 12 JL 48.000	5.050	5.200	4.550	25.78	0	+ 12 JL 48.000	0.070	0.140	0.190	24.44	0
+ 12 JL 50.000	3.100	3.200	3.100	18.27	35	+ 12 JL 50.000	0.230	0.280	0.450	21.41	0
+ 12 JL 52.000	1.350	1.400	1.280	13.61	40	+ 12 JL 52.000	0.700	0.750	1.090	19.61	0
+ 12 JL 53.000	0.740	0.800	0.750	13.18	10	+ 12 JL 53.000	1.120	1.220	1.640	19.44	0
+ 12 JL 54.000	0.350	0.390	0.330	12.92	120	+ 12 JL 54.000	1.740	1.860	1.990	20.29	2
+ 12 JL 56.000	0.050	0.100	0.070	13.85	0	+ 12 JL 56.000	3.400	3.550	4.200	25.14	0
+ 12 JL 58.000	0.010	0.060	0.060	N/Av	0	+ 12 JL 58.000	5.350	5.500	6.150	32.58	0
+ 12 JL 60.000	0.010	0.060	0.060	N/Av	0	+ 12 JL 60.000	7.350	7.500	8.150	40.25	0
+ 12 JL 62.000	0.000	0.040	0.040	N/Av	0	+ 12 JL 62.000	9.350	9.500	10.150	47.27	0
+ 12 JL 64.000	0.000	0.040	0.040	N/Av	0	+ 12 JL 64.000	11.350	11.500	12.150	53.78	0
+ 12 JL 66.000	0.000	0.040	0.040	N/Av	0	+ 12 JL 66.000	13.350	13.500	14.150	59.91	0
+ 12 JL 68.000	0.000	0.040	0.040	N/Av	0	+ 12 JL 68.000	15.350	15.500	16.150	65.70	0
+ 12 JL 70.000	0.000	0.040	0.040	N/Av	0	+ 12 JL 70.000	17.350	17.500	18.150	71.20	0
+ 12 AU 42.000	11.050	11.200	10.600	41.83	0	+ 12 AU 42.000	0.060	0.140	0.150	33.71	0
+ 12 AU 44.000	9.050	9.200	8.600	35.04	0	+ 12 AU 44.000	0.100	0.150	0.210	29.26	0
+ 12 AU 46.000	7.000	7.200	6.600	28.36	0	+ 12 AU 46.000	0.180	0.220	0.320	26.20	0
+ 12 AU 48.000	5.100	5.200	4.650	22.32	0	+ 12 AU 48.000	0.330	0.380	0.450	23.41	10
+ 12 AU 50.000	3.300	3.400	3.200	18.56	10	+ 12 AU 50.000	0.620	0.710	0.900	21.24	0
+ 12 AU 52.000	1.800	1.850	1.600	16.87	0	+ 12 AU 52.000	1.190	1.290	1.280	19.55	229
+ 12 AU 54.000	0.790	0.850	0.820	15.66	395	+ 12 AU 54.000	2.170	2.270	2.220	18.68	44
+ 12 AU 56.000	0.250	0.290	0.230	14.92	0	+ 12 AU 56.000	3.600	3.700	4.300	18.97	0
+ 12 AU 58.000	0.050	0.100	0.100	14.72	0	+ 12 AU 58.000	5.400	5.550	6.150	21.38	0
+ 12 AU 60.000	0.000	0.060	0.060	N/Av	0	+ 12 AU 60.000	7.350	7.500	8.150	25.98	0
+ 12 AU 62.000	0.000	0.040	0.040	N/Av	0	+ 12 AU 62.000	9.350	9.500	10.150	30.70	0
+ 12 OC 40.000	13.050	13.200	12.600	40.10	0	+ 12 OC 40.000	0.240	0.270	0.300	32.06	34
+ 12 OC 42.000	11.050	11.200	10.600	35.02	0	+ 12 OC 42.000	0.330	0.380	0.480	29.97	0
+ 12 OC 44.000	9.100	9.200	8.700	29.58	0	+ 12 OC 44.000	0.480	0.530	0.700	27.92	0
+ 12 OC 46.000	7.200	7.350	6.900	25.97	0	+ 12 OC 46.000	0.700	0.760	0.930	26.05	0
+ 12 OC 48.000	5.500	5.600	5.200	23.28	0	+ 12 OC 48.000	1.030	1.100	1.340	24.46	0
+ 12 OC 50.000	3.950	4.000	4.000	21.24	22	+ 12 OC 50.000	1.530	1.610	1.900	22.82	0
+ 12 OC 52.000	2.610	2.680	2.500	19.70	4	+ 12 OC 52.000	2.250	2.330	2.710	21.56	0
+ 12 OC 54.000	1.540	1.600	1.460	18.20	95	+ 12 OC 54.000	3.200	3.350	3.800	20.71	0
+ 12 OC 56.000	0.780	0.820	0.780	16.86	106	+ 12 OC 56.000	4.500	4.650	5.150	20.21	0
+ 12 OC 58.000	0.330	0.370	0.320	15.93	0	+ 12 OC 58.000	6.050	6.200	6.800	20.32	0
+ 12 OC 60.000	0.120	0.160	0.150	15.22	0	+ 12 OC 60.000	7.850	8.000	8.600	21.80	0
+ 12 OC 62.000	0.040	0.120	0.120	N/Av	0	+ 12 OC 62.000	9.800	9.900	10.550	24.23	0
+ 12 OC 64.000	0.000	0.060	0.060	N/Av	0	+ 12 OC 64.000	11.750	11.900	12.500	26.62	0
+ 12 OC 66.000	0.000	0.040	0.040	N/Av	0	+ 12 OC 66.000	13.700	13.900	14.500	29.18	0
+ 12 OC 68.000	0.000	0.040	0.040	N/Av	0	+ 12 OC 68.000	15.700	15.850	16.500	32.03	0
+ 12 OC 70.000	0.000	0.040	0.040	N/Av	0	+ 12 OC 70.000	17.700	17.850	18.500	34.75	0
+ 13 JA 40.000	13.000	13.250	12.650	35.92	0	+ 13 JA 40.000	0.620	0.680	0.790	30.35	0
+ 13 JA 42.000	11.150	11.350	11.000	31.70	10	+ 13 JA 42.000	0.810	0.880	1.020	28.77	0
+ 13 JA 44.000	9.300	9.500	9.000	28.69	0	+ 13 JA 44.000	1.090	1.180	1.350	27.20	0
+ 13 JA 46.000	7.650	7.800	7.350	26.66	0	+ 13 JA 46.000	1.450	1.570	1.760	25.84	0
+ 13 JA 48.000	6.100	6.250	5.850	24.40	0	+ 13 JA 48.000	1.940	2.070	2.280	24.54	0
+ 13 JA 50.000	4.650	4.800	4.450	23.17	0	+ 13 JA 50.000	2.570	2.660	2.900	23.41	2
+ 13 JA 52.000	3.400	3.550	3.250	21.62	0	+ 13 JA 52.000	3.350	3.500	3.850	22.43	0
+ 13 JA 54.000	2.360	2.450	2.260	20.33	0	+ 13 JA 54.000	4.350	4.500	4.900	21.60	0

	Calls						Puts				
Month / Strike	Bid Price	Ask Price	Last Price	Impl. Vol.	Vol.	Month / Strike	Bid Price	Ask Price	Last Price	Impl. Vol.	Vol.
+ 13 JA 56.000	1.510	1.620	1.500	19.11	3	+ 13 JA 56.000	5.550	5.700	6.200	20.75	0
+ 13 JA 58.000	0.900	0.950	0.900	17.85	2	+ 13 JA 58.000	6.950	7.100	7.650	20.26	0
+ 13 JA 60.000	0.490	0.540	0.470	17.04	1	+ 13 JA 60.000	8.550	8.700	9.300	20.21	0
+ 13 JA 62.000	0.260	0.310	0.290	16.62	0	+ 13 JA 62.000	10.300	10.450	11.050	20.61	0
+ 13 JA 64.000	0.130	0.170	0.170	16.54	0	+ 13 JA 64.000	12.150	12.300	12.950	21.42	0
+ 14 JA 44.000	10.250	10.600	10.250	29.18	0	+ 14 JA 44.000	3.450	3.600	4.000	26.76	0
+ 14 JA 46.000	8.950	9.200	8.950	27.81	0	+ 14 JA 46.000	4.100	4.350	4.800	26.24	0
+ 14 JA 48.000	7.650	7.900	7.650	26.50	0	+ 14 JA 48.000	4.950	5.150	5.600	25.56	0
+ 14 JA 50.000	6.400	6.800	6.450	25.71	0	+ 14 JA 50.000	5.750	6.000	6.500	25.02	0
+ 14 JA 52.000	5.350	5.650	5.400	24.66	0	+ 14 JA 52.000	6.800	7.000	7.550	24.22	0
+ 14 JA 54.000	4.400	4.650	4.550	23.66	0	+ 14 JA 54.000	7.800	8.100	8.650	23.74	0
+ 14 JA 56.000	3.600	3.800	3.750	22.87	0	+ 14 JA 56.000	9.000	9.250	9.850	23.39	0
+ 14 JA 58.000	2.850	3.100	3.050	22.25	0	+ 14 JA 58.000	10.250	10.650	11.150	22.88	0
+ 14 JA 60.000	2.250	2.470	2.460	21.66	0	+ 14 JA 60.000	11.650	12.050	12.600	22.53	0
+ 14 JA 62.000	1.740	1.950	1.880	21.27	0	+ 14 JA 62.000	13.150	13.550	14.150	22.05	0
+ 14 JA 64.000	1.350	1.450	1.450	20.46	1	+ 14 JA 64.000	14.650	15.200	15.750	21.93	0
+ 15 JA 48.000	8.550	9.000	8.800	27.66	0	+ 15 JA 48.000	7.250	7.550	7.450	26.33	10
+ 15 JA 50.000	7.450	7.950	7.750	26.77	0	+ 15 JA 50.000	8.300	8.600	9.050	25.71	0
+ 15 JA 52.000	6.500	7.000	6.850	26.17	0	+ 15 JA 52.000	9.300	9.650	10.150	25.45	0
+ 15 JA 54.000	5.700	6.100	5.900	25.43	0	+ 15 JA 54.000	10.400	10.850	11.450	25.05	0
+ 15 JA 56.000	4.950	5.300	5.150	24.90	0	+ 15 JA 56.000	11.650	12.150	12.650	24.60	0
Total					859	Total					331

ARZ – Aurizon Mines Ltd.

Last update: June 22, 2012, 14:09 Montréal time- (DATA 15 MINUTES DELAYED)   Refresh | Print

Last Price: 4.680   Net Change: –0.040   Bid Price: 4.680   Ask Price: 4.690   30-Day Historical Volatility: 67.53%

	Calls						Puts				
Month / Strike	Bid Price	Ask Price	Last Price	Impl. Vol.	Vol.	Month / Strike	Bid Price	Ask Price	Last Price	Impl. Vol.	Vol.
+ 12 JL 2.500	2.170	2.210	2.230	110.90	0	+ 12 JL 2.500	0.000	0.070	0.080	145.23	0
+ 12 JL 3.000	1.670	1.720	1.730	88.59	0	+ 12 JL 3.000	0.000	0.070	0.080	108.87	0
+ 12 JL 4.000	0.710	0.780	0.790	58.75	0	+ 12 JL 4.000	0.040	0.100	0.090	61.27	0
+ 12 JL 5.000	0.120	0.180	0.190	52.50	0	+ 12 JL 5.000	0.420	0.490	0.510	50.07	0
+ 12 JL 6.000	0.010	0.050	0.060	62.06	0	+ 12 JL 6.000	1.300	1.360	1.350	N/Av	0
+ 12 JL 7.000	0.000	0.070	0.080	N/Av	0	+ 12 JL 7.000	2.290	2.340	2.340	N/Av	0
+ 12 JL 8.000	0.000	0.070	0.080	N/Av	0	+ 12 JL 8.000	3.250	3.350	3.350	N/Av	0
+ 12 AU 3.000	1.690	1.740	1.750	74.95	0	+ 12 AU 3.000	0.010	0.090	0.100	84.12	0
+ 12 AU 4.000	0.810	0.870	0.870	60.61	0	+ 12 AU 4.000	0.120	0.160	0.170	57.85	0
+ 12 AU 5.000	0.280	0.310	0.320	57.53	0	+ 12 AU 5.000	0.560	0.610	0.620	54.29	0
+ 12 AU 6.000	0.060	0.110	0.130	58.13	0	+ 12 AU 6.000	1.290	1.410	1.410	46.36	0
+ 12 AU 7.000	0.010	0.090	0.110	70.26	0	+ 12 AU 7.000	2.290	2.360	2.350	N/Av	0
+ 12 OC 2.500	2.200	2.260	2.270	73.81	0	+ 12 OC 2.500	0.020	0.140	0.120	86.62	0
+ 12 OC 3.000	1.750	1.810	1.820	68.47	0	+ 12 OC 3.000	0.050	0.110	0.100	65.88	0
+ 12 OC 4.000	0.960	1.010	1.030	58.48	0	+ 12 OC 4.000	0.260	0.300	0.300	56.99	0
+ 12 OC 5.000	0.440	0.490	0.500	55.23	0	+ 12 OC 5.000	0.730	0.780	0.790	53.83	0
+ 12 OC 6.000	0.180	0.220	0.240	54.45	0	+ 12 OC 6.000	1.460	1.520	1.530	53.08	0
+ 12 OC 7.000	0.070	0.120	0.150	56.52	0	+ 12 OC 7.000	2.350	2.430	2.420	55.87	0
+ 13 JA 2.500	2.250	2.320	2.330	67.78	0	+ 13 JA 2.500	0.060	0.110	0.110	66.54	0
+ 13 JA 3.000	1.820	1.900	1.910	62.95	0	+ 13 JA 3.000	0.120	0.160	0.170	59.63	0
+ 13 JA 4.000	1.110	1.180	1.190	57.13	0	+ 13 JA 4.000	0.400	0.450	0.450	55.69	0
+ 13 JA 5.000	0.620	0.680	0.700	54.30	0	+ 13 JA 5.000	0.890	0.960	0.970	53.14	0
+ 13 JA 6.000	0.330	0.390	0.410	53.59	0	+ 13 JA 6.000	1.600	1.670	1.670	52.78	0
+ 13 JA 7.000	0.180	0.230	0.240	54.10	0	+ 13 JA 7.000	2.440	2.520	2.520	53.64	0
Total					0	Total					0

Source: Montreal Exchange, June 22, 2012. Used with permission. (m-x.ca/nego_liste_en.php)

In our example, if the stock price changes by only a small amount, you lose all $6,400, with the option. With the stock, you still have about what you started with. Also notice that the option can never be worth less than zero because you can always just throw it away. As a result, you can never lose more than your original investment ($6,400 in our example).

Recognize that stock options are a zero-sum game. By this we mean that whatever the buyer of a stock option makes, the seller loses and vice versa. To illustrate, suppose that in our example you had sold 50 option contracts. You would receive $6,400 upfront, and you would be obligated to sell the stock for $52 if the buyer of the option wished to exercise it. In this situation, if the stock price ends up at or less than $52, you would be $6,400 ahead. If the stock price ends up more than $52, you have to sell something for less than it is worth, so you lose the difference. For example, if the stock price were $61, you would have to sell $50 \times 100 = 5000$ shares at $52 per share, so you would be out $61 - 52 = \$9$ per share, or $45,000. Because you received $6,400 up front, your net loss is $38,600. We can summarize some other possibilities as follows:

Ending Stock Price	Net Profit to Option Seller
$45	$6,400
50	6,400
55	(8,600)
60	(33,600)
65	(58,600)
70	(83,600)

Notice that the net profits to the option buyer (just calculated) are the opposites of these amounts.

Put Payoffs

Look at Figure 25.1. Suppose you buy 10 Aurizon 2012 October $5 put contracts. How much does this cost (ignoring commissions)? Just before the option expires, Aurizon is selling for $3 per share. Is this good news or bad news? What is your net profit?

The option is quoted at 0.79, so one contract costs $100 \times 0.79 = \$79$. Your 10 contracts total $790. You now have the right to sell 1000 shares of Aurizon for $5 per share—this is most definitely good news. You can buy 1000 shares at $3 and sell them for $5. Your puts are thus worth $2 \times 1000 = \$2,000$. Since you paid $790, your net profit is $2,000 - \$790 = \$1,210$.

Long-Term Options

Figure 25.1 also shows listings for Long-Term Options. In the United States, this is referred to as Long-Term Equity Anticipation Securities or LEAPS for short. These are long-term calls and puts that expire in January for terms of at least one year up to 2⅔ years. For example, Figure 25.1 lists call long-term options for Bank of Nova Scotia expiring in January 2013 and 2014—about 6 months and 1½ years respectively from the time of the price quotes.

Concept Questions

1. What is a call option? A put option?
2. If you thought a stock was going to drop sharply in value, how might you use stock options to profit from the decline?

25.2 | Fundamentals of Option Valuation

Now that we understand the basics of puts and calls, we can discuss what determines their values. We focus on call options in the following discussion, but the same type of analysis can be applied to put options.

Value of a Call Option at Expiration

We have already described the payoffs from call options for different stock prices. To continue this discussion, the following notation is useful:

S_1 = Stock price at expiration (in one period)
S_0 = Stock price today
C_1 = Value of the call option on the expiration date (in one period)
C_0 = Value of the call option today
E = Exercise price on the option

From our previous discussion, remember that if the stock price (S_1) is not more than the exercise price (E) on the expiration date, the call option (C_1) is worth zero. In other words:

$$C_1 = 0 \text{ if } S_1 \leq E$$

Or, equivalently:

$$C_1 = 0 \text{ if } (S_1 - E) \leq 0 \tag{25.1}$$

This is the case where the option is out of the money when it expires.

If the option finishes in the money, $S_1 > E$, the value of the option at expiration is equal to the difference:

$$C_1 = S_1 - E \text{ if } S_1 > E$$

Or, equivalently:

$$C_1 = S_1 - E \text{ if } (S_1 - E) > 0 \tag{25.2}$$

For example, suppose we have a call option with an exercise price of $10. The option is about to expire. If the stock is selling for $8, we have the right to pay $10 for something worth only $8. Our option is thus worth exactly zero because the stock price is less than the exercise price on the option ($S_1 \leq E$). If the stock is selling for $12, the option has value. Since we can buy the stock for $10, it is worth ($S_1 - E$) = $12 - $10 = $2.

Figure 25.2 plots the value of a call option at expiration against the stock price. The result looks something like a hockey stick. Notice that for every stock price less than E, the value of the option is zero. For every stock price greater than E, the value of the call option is ($S_1 - E$). Also, once the stock price exceeds the exercise price, the option's value goes up dollar for dollar with the stock price.

FIGURE 25.2

Value of a call option at expiration for different stock prices

As shown, the value of a call option at expiration is equal to zero if the stock price is less than or equal to the exercise price. The value of the call is equal to the stock price minus the exercise price ($S_1 - E$) if the stock price exceeds the exercise price. The resulting "hockey stick" shape is highlighted.

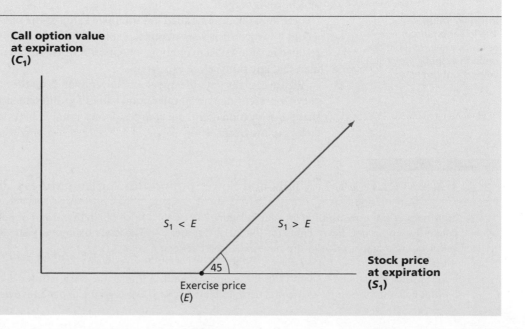

The Upper and Lower Bounds on a Call Option's Value

Now that we know how to determine C_1, the value of the call at expiration, we turn to a somewhat more challenging question: How can we determine C_0, the value sometime before expiration? We discuss this in the next several sections. For now, we establish the upper and lower bounds for the value of a call option.

THE UPPER BOUND   What is the most a call option could sell for? If you think about it, the answer is obvious. A call option gives you the right to buy a share of stock, so it can never be worth more than the stock itself. This tells us the upper bound on a call's value: A call option always sells for less than the underlying asset. So, in our notation, the upper bound is:

$$C_0 \le S_0 \tag{25.3}$$

THE LOWER BOUND   What is the least a call option could sell for? The answer here is a little less obvious. First, the call can't sell for less than zero, so $C_0 \ge 0$. Furthermore, if the stock price is greater than the exercise price, the call option is worth at least $S_0 - E$.

To see why, suppose we had a call option selling for $4. The stock price is $10, and the exercise price is $5. Is there a profit opportunity here? The answer is yes because you could buy the call for $4 and immediately exercise it by spending an additional $5. Your total cost of acquiring the stock is $4 + 5 = \$9$. If you turn around and immediately sell the stock for $10, you pocket a $1 certain profit.

Opportunities for riskless profits such as this one are called *arbitrages* or arbitrage opportunities. One who arbitrages is called an arbitrageur. The root for the term *arbitrage* is the same as the root for the word *arbitrate,* and an arbitrageur essentially arbitrates prices. In a well-organized market, significant arbitrages are, of course, rare.

In the case of a call option, to prevent arbitrage, the value of the call today must be greater than the stock price less the exercise price:

$$C_0 \ge S_0 - E$$

If we put our two conditions together, we have:

$$C_0 \ge 0 \text{ if } S_0 - E < 0 \tag{25.4}$$

$$C_0 \ge S_0 - E \text{ if } S_0 - E \ge 0$$

These conditions simply say that the lower bound on the call's value is either zero or $S_0 - E$, whichever is bigger.

intrinsic value
The lower bound of an option's value, or what the option would be worth if it were about to expire.

Our lower bound is called the **intrinsic value** of the option, and it is simply what the option would be worth if it were about to expire. With this definition, our discussion thus far can be restated as follows: At expiration, an option is worth its intrinsic value; it is generally worth more than that any time before expiration.

Figure 25.3 displays the upper and lower bounds on the value of a call option. Also plotted is a curve representing typical call option values for different stock prices before maturity. The exact shape and location of this curve depends on a number of factors. We begin our discussion of these factors in the next section.

EXAMPLE 25.1: Upper and Lower Bounds for Aurizon Mines Calls

Look back at the options listed for ARZ in Figure 25.1. Calculate the upper and lower limits for the 2012 October 3 call. Does the actual price in the newspaper fall between these limits?

ARZ stock closed at $4.68 and this is the upper bound. For this call, the stock price (S_0) is greater than the exercise price (E). In the jargon of options, this call is in the money. The lower bound call value is $1.68:

$$S_0 - E = \$4.68 - \$3 = \$1.68$$

The actual price of this call is $1.81 (Ask Price), which lies between the upper and lower bounds.

FIGURE 25.3

Value of a call option
before expiration for
different stock prices

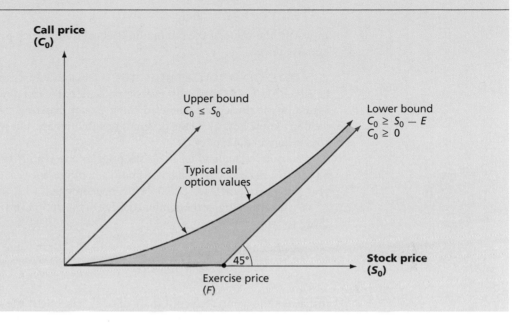

As shown, the upper bound
on a call's value is given by the
value of the stock ($C_0 \leq S_0$).
The lower bound is either
$S_0 - E$ or 0, whichever is
larger. The highlighted curve
illustrates the value of a call
option prior to maturity for
different stock prices.

A Simple Model: Part I

Option pricing can be a complex subject. Fortunately, as is often the case, many of the key insights can be illustrated with a simple example. Suppose we are looking at a call option with one year to expiration and an exercise price of $105. The stock currently sells for $100, and the risk-free rate, R_f, is 20 percent.

The value of the stock in one year is uncertain, of course. To keep things simple, suppose we know the stock price will either be $110 or $130. Importantly, we don't know the odds associated with these two prices. In other words, we know the possible values for the stock, but not the probabilities associated with those values.

Since the exercise price on the option is $105, we know the option will be worth either $110 − 105 = $5 or $130 − 105 = $25, but, once again, we don't know which. We do know one thing, however: Our call option is certain to finish in the money.

THE BASIC APPROACH   Here is the crucial observation: It is possible to duplicate exactly the payoffs on the stock using a combination of the option and the risk-free asset. How? Do the following: Buy one call option and invest $87.50 in a risk-free asset (such as a T-bill).

What will you have in a year? Your risk-free asset earns 20 percent, so it is worth $87.50 × 1.20 = $105. Your option is worth $5 or $25, so the total value is either $110 or $130, just like the stock:

Stock Value		Risk-Free Asset Value	+	Call Value	=	Total Value
$110	versus	$105	+	$ 5	=	$110
130	versus	105	+	25	=	130

As illustrated, these two strategies—buy a share of stock versus buy a call and invest in the risk-free asset—have exactly the same payoffs in the future.

Because these two strategies have the same future payoffs, they must have the same value today or else there would be an arbitrage opportunity. The stock sells for $100 today, so the value of the call option today, C_0, is:

$$\$100 = \$87.50 + C_0$$
$$C_0 = \$12.50$$

Where did we get the $87.50? This is just the present value of the exercise price on the option, calculated at the risk-free rate:

$$E/(1 + R_f) = \$105/1.20 = \$87.50$$

Thus, our example shows that the value of a call option in this simple case is given by:

$$S_0 = C_0 + E/(1 + R_f)$$
$$C_0 = S_0 - E/(1 + R_f)$$

[25.5]

In words, the value of the call option is equal to the stock price minus the present value of the exercise price.

A MORE COMPLICATED CASE   Obviously, our assumption that the stock price would be either $110 or $130 is a vast oversimplification. We can now develop a more realistic model by assuming the stock price can be anything greater than or equal to the exercise price. Once again, we don't know how likely the different possibilities are, but we are certain the option will finish somewhere in the money.

We again let S_1 stand for the stock price in one year. Now consider our strategy of investing $87.50 in a riskless asset and buying one call option. The riskless asset is again worth $105 in one year, and the option is worth $S_1 - \$105$, depending on what the stock price is.

When we investigate the combined value of the option and the riskless asset, we observe something very interesting:

$$\text{Combined value} = \text{Riskless asset value} + \text{Option value}$$
$$= \$105 + (S_1 - \$105)$$
$$= S_1$$

Just as we had before, buying a share of stock has exactly the same payoff as buying a call option and investing the present value of the exercise price in the riskless asset.

Once again, to prevent arbitrage, these two strategies must have the same cost, so the value of the call option is equal to the stock price less the present value of the exercise price:

$$C_0 = S_0 - E/(1 + R_f)$$

Our conclusion from this discussion is that determining the value of a call option is not difficult as long as we are certain the option will finish somewhere in the money.[3]

Four Factors Determining Option Values

If we continue to suppose that our option is certain to finish in the money, we can readily identify four factors that determine an option's value. There is a fifth factor that comes into play if the option can finish out of the money. We discuss this last factor in the next section.

For now, if we assume that the option expires in t periods, the present value of the exercise price is $E/(1 + R_f)^t$, and the value of the call is:

$$\text{Call option value} = \text{Stock value} - \text{Present value of the exercise price}$$

[25.6]

$$C_0 = S_0 - E/(1 + R_f)^t$$

If we look at this expression, the value of the call obviously depends on four things:

1. *The stock price.* The higher the stock price (S_0) is, the more the call is worth. This comes as no surprise because the option gives us the right to buy the stock at a fixed price.
2. *The exercise price.* The higher the exercise price (E) is, the less the call is worth. This is also not a surprise since the exercise price is what we have to pay to get the stock.
3. *The time to expiration.* The longer the time to expiration is (the bigger t is), the more the option is worth. Once again, this is obvious. Since the option gives us the right to buy for a fixed length of time, its value goes up as that length of time increases.

---

[3] You're probably wondering what would happen if the stock price were less than the present value of the exercise price, resulting in a negative value for the call option. This can't happen because we are certain the stock price will be at least E in one year since we know the stock will finish in the money. If the current price of the stock is less than $E/(1 + R_f)$, the return on the stock is certain to be greater than the risk-free rate, thereby creating an arbitrage opportunity. For example, if the stock were currently selling for $80, the minimum return would be ($105 − $80)/$80 = 31.25%. Since we can borrow at 20 percent, we can earn a certain minimum return of 11.25 percent per dollar borrowed. This, of course, is an arbitrage.

4. *The risk-free rate.* The higher the risk-free rate (R_f) is, the more the call is worth. This result is a little less obvious. Normally, we think of asset values going down as rates rise. In this case, the exercise price is a cash outflow, a liability. The current value of that liability goes down as the discount rate goes up.

25.3 | Valuing a Call Option

We now investigate the value of a call option when there is the possibility that the option will finish out of the money. We again examine the simple case of two possible future stock prices. This case lets us identify the remaining factor that determines an option's value.

A Simple Model: Part II

From our previous example, we have a stock that currently sells for $100. It will be worth either $110 or $130 in a year, and we don't know which. The risk-free rate is 20 percent. We are now looking at a different call option, however. This one has an exercise price of $120 instead of $105. What is the value of this call option?

This case is a little harder. If the stock ends up at $110, the option is out of the money and worth nothing. If the stock ends up at $130, the option is worth $130 − 120 = $10.

Our basic approach to determining the value of the call option is the same. We show once again that it is possible to combine the call option and a risk-free investment in a way that exactly duplicates the payoff from holding the stock. The only complication is that it's a little harder to determine how to do it.

For example, suppose we bought one call and invested the present value of the exercise price in a riskless asset as we did before. In one year, we would have $120 from the riskless investment plus an option worth either zero or $10. The total value is either $120 or $130. This is not the same as the value of the stock ($110 or $130), so the two strategies are not comparable.

Instead, consider investing the present value of $110 (the lower stock price) in a riskless asset. This guarantees us a $110 payoff. If the stock price is $110, any call options we own are worthless, and we have exactly $110 as desired.

When the stock is worth $130, the call option is worth $10. Our risk-free investment is worth $110, so we are $130 − 110 = $20 short. Since each call option is worth $10, we need to buy two of them to replicate the stock.

Thus, in this case, investing the present value of the lower stock price in a riskless asset and buying two call options exactly duplicates owning the stock. When the stock is worth $110, we have $110 from our risk-free investment. When the stock is worth $130, we have $110 from the risk-free investment plus two call options worth $10 each.

Because these two strategies have exactly the same value in the future, they must have the same value today or else arbitrage would be possible:

$$S_0 = \$100 = 2 \times C_0 + \$110/(1 + R_f)$$
$$2 \times C_0 = \$100 - \$110/1.20$$
$$C_0 = \$4.17$$

Each call option is thus worth $4.17.

EXAMPLE 25.2: Don't Call Us, We'll Call You

We are looking at two call options on the same stock, one with an exercise price of $20 and one with an exercise price of $30. The stock currently sells for $35. Its future price will either be $25 or $50. If the risk-free rate is 10 percent, what are the values of these call options?

The first case (the $20 exercise price) is not difficult since the option is sure to finish in the money. We know that the value is equal to the stock price less the present value of the exercise price:

$$C_0 = S_0 - E/(1 + R_f)$$
$$= \$35 - \$20/1.1$$
$$= \$16.82$$

In the second case, the exercise price is $30, so the option can finish out of the money. At expiration, the option is worth $0 if the stock is worth $25. The option is worth $50 - 30 = \$20 if it finishes in the money.

As before, we start by investing the present value of the lower stock price in the risk-free asset. This costs $25/1.1 = \$22.73. At expiration, we have $25 from this investment.

If the stock price is $50, we need an additional $25 to duplicate the stock payoff. Since each option is worth $20, we need $25/\$20 = 1.25 options. So, to prevent arbitrage, investing the present value of $25 in a risk-free asset and buying 1.25 call options has the same value as the stock:

$$S_0 = 1.25 \times C_0 + \$25/(1 + R_f)$$
$$\$35 = 1.25 \times C_0 + \$25/(1 + .10)$$
$$C_0 = \$9.82$$

Notice that this second option had to be worth less because it has the higher exercise price.

The Fifth Factor

We now illustrate the fifth (and last) factor that determines an option's value. Suppose that everything in our previous example is the same except the stock price can be $105 or $135 instead of $110 or $130. Notice that this change makes the stock's future price more volatile than before.

We investigate the same strategy that we used before: Invest the present value of the lower stock price ($105) in the risk-free asset and buy two call options. If the stock price is $105, as before, the call options have no value and we have $105 in all.

If the stock price is $135, each option is worth $S_1 - E = \$135 - 120 = \$15$. We have two calls, so our portfolio is worth $105 + 2 \times \$15 = \$135$. Once again, we have exactly replicated the value of the stock.

What has happened to the option's value? More to the point, the variance of the return on the stock has increased. Does the option's value go up or down? To find out, we need to solve for the value of the call just as we did before:

$$S_0 = \$100 = 2 \times C_0 + \$105/(1 + R_f)$$
$$2 \times C_0 = \$100 - \$105/1.20$$
$$C_0 = \$6.25$$

The value of the call option has gone up from $4.17 to $6.25.

Based on our example, the fifth and final factor that determines an option's value is the variance of the return on the underlying asset. Furthermore, the greater that variance is, the more the option is worth. This result appears a little odd at first, and it may be somewhat surprising to learn that increasing the risk (as measured by return variance) on the underlying asset increases the value of the option.

The reason that increasing the variance on the underlying asset increases the value of the option isn't hard to see in our example. Changing the lower stock price to $105 from $110 doesn't hurt a bit because the option is worth zero in either case. However, moving the upper possible price to $135 from $130 makes the option worth more when it is in the money.

More generally, increasing the variance of the possible future prices on the underlying asset doesn't affect the option's value when the option finishes out of the money. The value is always zero in this case. On the other hand, increasing that variance when the option is in the money only increases the possible payoffs, so the net effect is to increase the option's value. Put another way, since the downside risk is always limited, the only effect is to increase the upside potential.

In later discussion, we use the usual symbol, σ^2, to stand for the variance of the return on the underlying asset.

A Closer Look

Before moving on, it is useful to consider one last example. Suppose the stock price is $100 and it will either move up or down by 20 percent. The risk-free rate is 5 percent. What is the value of a call option with a $90 exercise price?

The stock price will either be $80 or $120. The option is worth zero when the stock is worth $80, and it's worth $120 − 90 = $30 when the stock is worth $120. We therefore invest the present value of $80 in the risk-free asset and buy some call options.

When the stock finishes at $120, our risk-free asset pays $80, leaving us $40 short. Each option is worth $30 in this case, so we need $40/$30 = 4/3 options to match the payoff on the stock. The option's value must thus be given by:

$$S_0 = 4/3 \times C_0 + \$80/1.05$$
$$C_0 = (3/4) \times (\$100 - \$76.19)$$
$$= \$17.86$$

option delta
The change in the stock price divided by the change in the call price.

To make our result a little bit more general, notice that the number of options you need to buy to replicate the stock is always equal to the change in stock price divided by the change in call price, where the change in stock price is the difference in the possible stock prices and the change in call price is the difference in the possible option values. The change in the stock price divided by the change in the call price is termed the **option delta**. In our current case, for example, the change in the stock price would be $120 − 80 = $40 and the change in the call price would be $30 − 0 = $30, so the change in the stock price divided by the change in the call price is $40/$30 = 4/3, as we calculated.

Notice also that when the stock is certain to finish in the money, the change in the stock price divided by the change in the call price is always exactly equal to one, so one call option is always needed. Otherwise, the change in the stock price divided by the change in the call price is greater than one, so more than one call option is needed.

This concludes our discussion of option valuation. The most important thing to remember is that the value of an option depends on five factors. Table 25.1 summarizes these factors and the direction of the influence for both puts and calls. In Table 25.1, the sign in parentheses indicates the direction of the influence.[4] In other words, the sign tells us whether the value of the option goes up or down when the value of a factor increases. For example, notice that increasing the exercise price reduces the value of a call option. Increasing any of the other four factors increases the value of the call. Notice also that the time to expiration and the variance act the same for puts and calls. The other three factors have opposite signs.

TABLE 25.1

Five factors that determine option values

Factor	Calls	Puts
Current value of the underlying asset	(+)	(−)
Exercise price on the option	(−)	(+)
Time to expiration on the option	(+)	(+)
Risk-free rate	(+)	(−)
Variance of return on underlying asset	(+)	(+)

We have not considered how to value a call option when the option can finish out of the money and the stock price can take on more than two values. A very famous result, the Black–Scholes option pricing model, is needed in this case. For developing this model, Myron Scholes and Robert Merton shared the 1997 Nobel Prize for economics. We cover this subject in the chapter appendix.

---

[4]The signs in Table 25.1 are for American options. For a European put option, the effect of increasing the time to expiration is ambiguous, and the direction of the influence can be positive or negative.

EXAMPLE 25.3: Option Prices and Time to Expiration and Variance

According to Table 25.1, when other things are held equal, increasing either time to expiration or stock price variance raises the prices of puts and calls. Is this theory consistent with the actual option prices in Figure 25.1?

We can look at time to expiration and pricing for BNS options. Starting with calls, all the other four factors are constant if we compare calls with the same exercise price but different expiration dates. There are six BNS calls with a $50 exercise price:

Call	Bid Price
July 12	3.10
Aug 12	3.30
Oct 12	3.95
Jan 13	4.65
Jan 14	6.4
Jan 15	7.45

As expected, the call prices increase with time to expiration.

Concept Questions

1. What are the five factors that determine an option's value?
2. What is the effect of an increase in each of the five factors on the value of a call option? Give an intuitive explanation for your answer.
3. What is the effect of an increase in each of the five factors on the value of a put option? Give an intuitive explanation for your answer.

25.4 | Employee Stock Options

employee stock option (ESO)
An option granted to an employee by a company giving the employee the right to buy shares of stock in the company at a fixed price for a fixed time.

Options are important in corporate finance in a lot of different ways. In this section, we begin to examine some of these by taking a look at **employee stock options**, or ESOs. An **ESO** is, in essence, a call option that a firm gives to employees giving them the right to buy shares of stock in the company. The practice of granting options to employees has become widespread. It is almost universal for upper management (see Figure 25.4), but some companies, like The Gap and Starbucks, grant options to almost every employee. Over 90 percent of firms listed on the Toronto Stock Exchange have a bonus plan and use stock options.[5] Thus, an understanding of ESOs is important. Why? Because you may very soon be an ESO holder!

FIGURE 25.4

Options Granted to the CEOs of Canada's Five Major Chartered Banks

Company	CEO	Number	Option Strike Price	Value reported in proxy circular	Price as of 4 Nov 2011	Value as of 4 Nov 2011
BMO	Bill Downe	219,749	34.13	$ 1,800,000	58.07	$ 5,260,791
Bank of Nova Scotia	Richard Waugh	444,084	33.89	3,010,000	52.24	8,148,941
CIBC	Gerald McCaughey	107,481	49.75	862,500	73.96	2,240,103
RBC	Gordon Nixon*	247,344	52.94	2,750,000	45.85	0
TD	Ed Clark	420,172	42.50	3,750,035	74.81	12,794,237
TOTAL				12,172,535		28,444,072

* Gordon Nixon chose to forego his variable income for 2009, which included options granted in December 2008; this table reflects options granted in December 2007 and reported in RBC's 2008 proxy circular.

Source: Canada's CEO Elite 100, Hugh Jackson, January 2012

---

[5] Zhou, Xianming, "CEO Pay, Firm Size, and Corporate Performance: Evidence From Canada." *Canadian Journal of Economics*, Vol. 33, Issue 1, February 2000.

ESO Features

Since ESOs are basically call options, we have already covered most of the important aspects. However, ESOs have a few features that make them different from regular stock options. The details differ from company to company, but a typical ESO has a 10-year life, which is much longer than most ordinary options. Unlike traded options, ESOs cannot be sold. They also have what is known as a "vesting" period. Often, for up to three years or so, an ESO cannot be exercised and also must be forfeited if an employee leaves the company. After this period, the options "vest," which means they can be exercised. Sometimes, employees who resign with vested options are given a limited time to exercise their options.

Why are ESOs granted? There are basically two reasons. First, going back to Chapter 1, the owners of a corporation (the shareholders) face the basic problem of aligning shareholder and management interests and also of providing incentives for employees to focus on corporate goals. ESOs are a powerful motivator because, as we have seen, the payoffs on options can be very large. High-level executives in particular stand to gain enormous wealth if they are successful in creating value for shareholders. Research studies in the U.S., Canada, and other countries find that, over the 1990s, the use of executive stock options served its goal of helping to tie executive compensation to company performance.[6] While such a link may be desirable in controlling agency problems, not all governance experts agree that ESOs are a good way to compensate executives. Opponents argue that share prices may go up or down due to external events that have little to do with executive performance.[7] For example, the decline of stock prices from 2001 to 2003, especially in the tech sector, had made options granted earlier almost worthless in motivating employees. For example, 750,000 options granted in 2000 to John Roth, then Nortel CEO, had an exercise price of $118.68. By 2009, Nortel was bankrupt.

See esopassociation.org for a site devoted to employee stock options.

The second reason some companies rely heavily on ESOs is that an ESO has no immediate, upfront, out-of-pocket cost to the corporation. In smaller, possibly cash-strapped, companies, ESOs are simply a substitute for ordinary wages. Employees are willing to accept them instead of cash, hoping for big payoffs in the future. In fact, ESOs are a major recruiting tool, allowing businesses to attract talent that they otherwise could not afford.

In 2003, Microsoft halted its stock options plan entirely, instead granting restricted Microsoft shares to a wide range of employees.[8] According to Microsoft CEO Steve Ballmer, the move towards granting restricted stock instead of ESOs would increase morale and retention. Another advantage that restricted stock offers is actual ownership of part of the company that links the personal objectives of the employee to the corporate objectives. Intel has since decided to scrap its own ESO plan in favour of restricted stock. This trend does not mean the end of ESOs. It only indicates that companies are becoming more conservative with their ESO plans and are looking to find the alternatives that best suit the company's corporate structure.

Publicly accountable enterprises in Canada are required to report under International Financial Reporting Standards (IFRS). Stock-based compensation will still need to be recorded based on the fair value of option grants. IFRS requires that companies measure the fair value of the employee stock options granted to employees at the date that they are granted. Companies should recognize the aggregate fair value of employee stock options based on their best estimate of the number of equity-settled options expected to vest.

ESO Repricing

ESOs are almost always "at the money" when they are issued, meaning that the stock price is equal to the strike price. Notice that, in this case, the intrinsic value is zero, so there is no value from immediate exercise. Of course, even though the intrinsic value is zero, an ESO is still quite valuable because of, among other things, its very long life.

If the stock falls significantly after an ESO is granted, then the option is said to be "underwater." On occasion, a company will decide to lower the strike price on underwater options. Such options are said to be "restruck" or "repriced."

---

[6] The most current study for Canada is by X. Zhou, referenced in footnote 5.

[7] Y. Allaire, "Pay for Value: Cutting the Gordian Knot of Executive Compensation", *Institute for Governance of Private and Public Organizations*, 2012.

[8] J. Nicholas Hoover. "The Options Mess," *InformationWeek*. Manhasset: July 10, 2006. Iss. 1097; p. 21.

For more information on ESOs, try the National Center for Employee Ownership at nceo.org.

The practice of repricing ESOs is very controversial. Companies that do it argue that once an ESO becomes deeply out of the money, it loses its incentive value because employees recognize there is only a small chance that the option will finish in the money. In fact, employees may leave and join other companies where they receive a fresh options grant.

Critics of repricing point out that a lowered strike price is, in essence, a reward for failing. They also point out that if employees know that options will be repriced, then much of the incentive effect is lost. Today, many companies award options on a regular basis, perhaps annually or even quarterly. That way, an employee will always have at least some options that are near the money even if others are underwater. Also, regular grants ensure that employees always have unvested options, which gives them an added incentive to stay with their current employer rather than forfeit the potentially valuable options.

> ### Concept Questions
>
> 1. What are the key differences between a traded stock option and an ESO?
> 2. What is ESO repricing? Why is it controversial?

25.5 | Equity as a Call Option on the Firm's Assets

Now that we understand the basic determinants of an option's value, we turn to examining some of the many ways that options appear in corporate finance. One of the most important insights we gain from studying options is that the common stock in a leveraged firm (one that has issued debt) is effectively a call option on the assets of the firm. This is a remarkable observation, and we explore it next.

An example is the easiest way to get started. Suppose a firm has a single debt issue outstanding. The face value is $1,000, and the debt is coming due in a year. There are no coupon payments between now and then, so the debt is effectively a pure discount bond. In addition, the current market value of the firm's assets is $950, and the risk-free rate is 12.5 percent.

In a year, the stockholders will have a choice. They can pay off the debt for $1,000 and thereby acquire the assets of the firm free and clear, or they can default on the debt. If they default, the bondholders will own the assets of the firm.

In this situation, the shareholders essentially have a call option on the assets of the firm with an exercise price of $1,000. They can exercise the option by paying the $1,000, or they cannot exercise the option by defaulting. Whether they choose to exercise obviously depends on the value of the firm's assets when the debt becomes due.

If the value of the firm's assets exceeds $1,000, the option is in the money, and the shareholders would exercise by paying off the debt. If the value of the firm's assets is less than $1,000, the option is out of the money, and the stockholders would optimally choose to default. What we now illustrate is that we can determine the values of the debt and equity using our option pricing results.

Case I: The Debt Is Risk-Free

Suppose that in one year the firm's assets will either be worth $1,100 or $1,200. What is the value today of the equity in the firm? The value of the debt? What is the interest rate on the debt?

To answer these questions, we recognize that the option (the equity in the firm) is certain to finish in the money because the value of the firm's assets ($1,100 or $1,200) always exceeds the face value of the debt. From our discussion in previous sections, we know that the option value is simply the difference between the value of the underlying asset and the present value of the exercise price (calculated at the risk-free rate). The present value of $1,000 in one year at 12.5 percent is $888.89. The current value of the firm is $950, so the option (the firm's equity) is worth $950 − 888.89 = $61.11.

What we see is that the equity, which is effectively an option to purchase the firm's assets, must be worth $61.11. The debt must therefore actually be worth $888.89. In fact, we really didn't need to know about options to handle this example, because the debt is risk free. The reason is that the bondholders are certain to receive $1,000. Since the debt is risk free, the appropriate discount rate (and the interest rate on the debt) is the risk-free rate. Therefore, we know immediately that the current value of the debt is $1,000/1.125 = $888.89. The equity is thus worth $950 − 888.89 = $61.11 as we calculated.

Case II: The Debt Is Risky

Suppose now that the value of the firm's assets in one year will be either $800 or $1,200. This case is a little more difficult because the debt is no longer risk free. If the value of the assets turns out to be $800, the shareholders will not exercise their option and thereby default. The stock is worth nothing in this case. If the assets are worth $1,200, the shareholders will exercise their option to pay off the debt and enjoy a profit of $1,200 − 1,000 = $200.

What we see is that the option (the equity in the firm) is worth either zero or $200. The assets are worth either $1,200 or $800. Based on our discussion in previous sections, a portfolio that has the present value of $800 invested in a risk-free asset and ($1,200 − $800)/($200 − $0) = 2 call options exactly replicates the assets of the firm.

The present value of $800 at the risk-free rate of 12.5 percent is $800/1.125 = $711.11. This amount, plus the value of the two call options, is equal to $950, the current value of the firm:

$$\$950 = 2 \times C_0 + \$711.11$$
$$C_0 = \$119.45$$

Because the call option is actually the firm's equity, the value of the equity is $119.45. The value of the debt is thus $950 − 119.45 = $830.55.

Finally, since the debt has a $1,000 face value and a current value of $830.55, the interest rate is $1,000/$830.55 − 1 = 20.40%. This exceeds the risk-free rate, of course, since the debt is now risky.

IN THEIR OWN WORDS...

Erik Lie on Option Backdating

Stock options can be granted to executive and other employees as an incentive device. They strengthen the relation between compensation and a firm's stock price performance, thus boosting effort and improving decision making within the firm. Further, to the extent that decision makers are risk averse (as most of us are), options induce more risk taking, which can benefit shareholders. However, options also have a dark side. They can be used to (i) conceal true compensation expenses in financial reports, (ii) evade corporate taxes, and (iii) siphon money from corporations to executives. One example that illustrates all three of these aspects is that of option backdating.

To understand the virtue of option backdating, it is first important to realize that for accounting, tax, and incentive reasons, most options are granted at-the-money, meaning that their exercise price equals the stock price on the grant date. Option backdating is the practice of selecting a past date (e.g., from the past month) when the stock price was particularly low to be the official grant date. This raises the value of the options, because they are effectively granted in-the-money. Unless this is properly disclosed and accounted for (which it rarely is), the practice of backdating can cause an array of problems. First, granting options that are effectively in-the-money violates many corporate option plans or other securities filings stating that the exercise price equals the fair market value on the grant day.

Second, camouflaging in-the-money options as at-the-money options understates compensation expenses in the financial statements. In fact, under the old accounting rule APB 25 that was phased out in 2005, companies could expense options according to their intrinsic value, such that at-the-money options were not expensed at all. Third, at-the-money option grants qualify for certain tax breaks that in-the-money option grants do not qualify for, such that backdating can result in underpaid taxes.

Empirical evidence shows that the practice of backdating was prevalent from the early 1990s to 2005, especially among tech firms. As this came to the attention of the media and regulators in 2006, a scandal erupted. More than 100 companies were investigated for manipulation of option grant dates. As a result, numerous executives were fired, old financial statements were restated, additional taxes became due, and countless lawsuits were filed against companies and their directors. With new disclosure rules, stricter enforcement of the requirement that took effect as part of the *Sarbanes-Oxley Act* in 2002 that grants have to be filed within two business days, and greater scrutiny by regulators and the investment community, we likely have put the practice of backdating options behind us.

Erik Lie is a Henry B. Tippie Research Professor of Finance at the University of Iowa. His research focuses on corporate financial policy, M&A, and executive compensation.

IN THEIR OWN WORDS...

Robert C. Merton on Applications of Options Analysis

Organized markets for trading options on stocks, fixed-income securities, currencies, financial futures, and a variety of commodities are among the most successful financial innovations of the past two decades.

Commercial success is not, however, the reason that option pricing analysis has become one of the cornerstones of finance theory. Instead, its central role derives from the fact that option-like structures permeate virtually every part of the field.

From the first observation more than 40 years ago that leveraged equity has the same payoff structure as a call option, option pricing theory has provided an integrated approach to the pricing of corporate liabilities, including all types of debt, preferred stocks, warrants, and rights. The same methodology has been applied to the pricing of pension fund insurance, deposit insurance, and other government loan guarantees. It has also been used to evaluate various labour contract provisions such as wage floors and guaranteed employment including tenure.

A significant and recent extension of options analysis has been to the evaluation of operating or "real" options in capital budgeting decisions. For example, a facility that can use various inputs to produce various outputs provides the firm with

operating options not available from a specialized facility that uses a fixed set of inputs to produce a single type of output. Similarly, choosing among technologies with different proportions of fixed and variable costs can be viewed as evaluating alternative options to change production levels, including abandonment of the project. Research and development projects are essentially options to either establish new markets, expand market share, or reduce production costs. As these examples suggest, options analysis is especially well suited to the task of evaluating the "flexibility" components of projects. These are precisely the components whose values are especially difficult to estimate by using traditional capital budgeting techniques.

Robert C. Merton is the School of Management Distinguished Professor of Finance at the MIT Sloan School of Management and the John and Natty McArthur University Professor emeritus at Harvard University. He received the 1997 Nobel Prize in Economics for his work on pricing options and other contingent claims and for this work on risk and uncertainty.

EXAMPLE 25.4: Equity as a Call Option

Swenson Software has a pure discount debt issue with a face value of $100. The issue is due in a year. At that time, the assets in the firm will be worth either $55 or $160, depending on the sales success of Swenson's latest product. The assets of the firm are currently worth $110. If the risk-free rate is 10 percent, what is the value of the equity in Swenson? The value of the debt? The interest rate on the debt?

To replicate the assets of the firm, we need to invest the present value of $55 in the risk-free asset. This costs $55/1.10 = $50. If the assets turn out to be worth $160,

the option is worth $160 − 100 = $60. Our risk-free asset would be worth $55, so we need ($160 − $55)/$60 = 1.75 call options. Since the firm is currently worth $110, we have:

$$\$110 = 1.75 \times C_0 + \$50$$
$$C_0 = \$34.29$$

The equity is thus worth $34.29; the debt is worth $110 − 34.29 = $75.71. The interest rate on the debt is about $100/$75.71 − 1 = 32.1%.

Concept Questions

1. Why do we say that the equity in a leveraged firm is effectively a call option on the firm's assets?
2. All other things being the same, would the stockholders of a firm prefer to increase or decrease the volatility of the firm's return on assets? Why? What about the bondholders? Give an intuitive explanation.

25.6 | Warrants

warrant
A security that gives the holder the right to purchase shares of stock at a fixed price over a given period of time.

A **warrant** is a corporate security that looks a lot like a call option. It gives the holder the right, but not the obligation, to buy shares of common stock directly from a company at a fixed price for a given time period. Each warrant specifies the number of shares of stock that the holder can buy, the exercise price, and the expiration date.[9]

The differences in contractual features between the call options that are traded on the Montreal Exchange and warrants are relatively minor. Warrants usually have much longer maturity periods, however. In fact, some warrants are actually perpetual and have no fixed expiration date.

sweeteners or equity kickers
A feature included in the terms of a new issue of debt or preferred shares to make the issue more attractive to initial investors.

Warrants are often called **sweeteners** or **equity kickers** because they are usually issued in combination with privately placed loans, bonds, or common or preferred shares. Throwing in some warrants is a way of making the deal a little more attractive to the lender, and it is very common. In fact, the use of warrants is becoming more popular judging by the increasing number listed on the TSX.

In most cases, warrants are attached to the bonds when issued. The loan agreement states whether the warrants are detachable from the bond. Usually, the warrant can be detached immediately and sold by the holder as a separate security.

For example, Air Canada traded at $0.92 per share on the TSX on June 1, 2012. Outstanding warrants allowed the holder to purchase one Air Canada share at $2.20, expiring on October 28, 2012. The warrants traded at $0.020 and were deep out of the money.

Just as we saw with call options, the lower limit on the value of a warrant is zero if Air Canada's stock price is less than $2.20 per share. If the price of Air Canada's common stock rises to more than $2.20 per share, the lower limit is the stock price minus $2.20. The upper limit is the price of Air Canada's common stock. A warrant to buy one share of common stock cannot sell at a price more than the price of the underlying common stock.

If, on the warrant expiration date, Air Canada stock traded for less than $2.20, the warrants would expire worthless.

With the growth of financial engineering, warrant issuers are creating new varieties. Some warrant issues give investors the right to buy the issuers' bonds instead of their stock. In addition, warrants are issued on their own instead of as sweeteners in a bond issue. In 1991, the Toronto-Dominion Bank combined these features in a $2.7 million stand-alone issue. The TD warrants gave the right to purchase debentures to be issued in the future.[10]

Echo Bay Mines Ltd. of Edmonton (a subsidiary of Kinross Gold Corp.) designed an innovative financing package including gold purchase warrants with a preferred share issue. The warrants gave the holder the right to buy gold at an exercise price of $595 (U.S.) per ounce. When the warrants were issued in 1981, gold was trading at $500 (U.S.) per ounce. A further condition restricted exercise of the warrants to cases where Echo Bay met certain production levels. As a result, how much these warrants were worth depended both on how well the company was doing and on gold prices.[11]

td.com
kinross.com

The Difference between Warrants and Call Options

As we have explained, from the holder's point of view, warrants are very similar to call options on common stock. A warrant, like a call option, gives its holder the right to buy common stock at a specified price. From the firm's point of view, however, a warrant is very different from a call option sold on the company's common stock.

The most important difference between call options and warrants is that call options are issued by individuals and warrants are issued by firms. When a call option is exercised, one investor buys stock from another investor. The company is not involved. When a warrant is exercised, the firm must issue new shares of stock. Each time a warrant is exercised, the firm receives some cash and the number of shares outstanding increases.

---

[9] Rights are another closely related corporate security. Their purpose, however, is to allow current shareholders to maintain proportionate ownership of the company when new shares are issued. The number of shares that can be purchased with each right will be calculated to maintain the proportionate ownership. We discuss rights in Chapter 15.

[10] B. Critchley, "The Top 10 Financings, Innovative Fund-Raising in Corporate Canada for '91," *Financial Post*, December 16, 1991, p. 15.

[11] P. P. Boyle and E. F. Kirzner, "Pricing Complex Options: Echo-Bay Ltd. Gold Purchase Warrants," *Canadian Journal of Administrative Sciences* 2, no. 12 (December 1985), pp. 294–306.

To illustrate, suppose the Endrun Company issues a warrant giving holders the right to buy one share of common stock at $25. Further suppose the warrant is exercised. Endrun must print one new stock certificate. In exchange for the stock certificate, it receives $25 from the holder.

In contrast, when a call option is exercised, there is no change in the number of shares outstanding. Suppose Bethany Enger purchases a call option on the common stock of the Endrun Company from Thomas Swift. The call option gives Enger the right to buy one share of common stock of the Endrun Company for $25.

If Enger chooses to exercise the call option, Swift is obligated to give her one share of Endrun's common stock in exchange for $25. If Swift does not already own a share, he must go into the stock market and buy one.

The call option amounts to a side bet between Enger and Swift on the value of the Endrun Company's common stock. When a call option is exercised, one investor gains and the other loses. The total number of outstanding Endrun shares remains constant, and no new funds are made available to the company.

Warrants and the Value of the Firm

Because the company is not involved in buying or selling options, puts and calls have no effect on the value of the firm. However, the firm is the original seller when warrants are involved, and warrants do affect the value of the firm. We compare the effect of call options and warrants in this section.

Imagine that Spencer Gould and Jennifer Rockefeller are two investors who together purchase six ounces of platinum at $500 per ounce. The total investment is 6 × $500 = $3,000, and each of the investors puts up half. They incorporate, print two stock certificates, and name the firm the GR Company. Each certificate represents a one-half claim to the platinum, and Gould and Rockefeller each own one certificate. The net effect of all of this is that Gould and Rockefeller have formed a company with platinum as its only asset.

THE EFFECT OF A CALL OPTION   Suppose Gould later decides to sell a call option to Francesca Fiske. The call option gives Fiske the right to buy Gould's share for $1,800 in one year.

At the end of the year, platinum is selling for $700 per ounce, so the value of the GR Company is 6 × $700 = $4,200. Each share is worth $4,200/2 = $2,100. Fiske exercises her option, and Gould must turn over his stock certificate and receive $1,800.

How would the firm be affected by the exercise? The number of shares won't be affected. There are still two of them, now owned by Rockefeller and Fiske. The shares are still worth $2,100. The only thing that happens is that, when Fiske exercises her option, she profits by $2,100 − 1,800 = $300. Gould loses by the same amount.

THE EFFECT OF A WARRANT   This story changes if a warrant is issued. Suppose Gould does not sell a call option to Fiske. Instead, Spencer Gould and Jennifer Rockefeller get together and decide to issue a warrant and sell it to Fiske. This means that, in effect, the GR Company decides to issue a warrant.

The warrant gives Fiske the right to receive a share of stock in the company at an exercise price of $1,800. If Fiske decides to exercise the warrant, the firm issues another stock certificate and gives it to Fiske in exchange for $1,800.

Suppose again that platinum rises to $700 an ounce. The firm is worth $4,200. Further suppose that Fiske exercises her warrant. Two things would occur:

1. Fiske would pay $1,800 to the firm.
2. The firm would print one stock certificate and give it to Fiske. The stock certificate represents a one-third claim on the platinum of the firm.

Fiske's one-third share seems to be worth only $4,200/3 = $1,400. This is not correct, because we have to add the $1,800 contributed to the firm by Fiske. The value of the firm increases by this amount, so:

$$\text{New value of firm} = \text{Value of platinum} + \text{Fiske's contribution to the firm}$$
$$= \$4,200 + 1,800$$
$$= \$6,000$$

Because Fiske has a one-third claim on the firm's value, her share is worth $6,000/3 = $2,000. By exercising the warrant, Fiske gains $2,000 − 1,800 = $200. This is illustrated in Table 25.2.

TABLE 25.2

Effect of a call option versus a warrant on the GR Company

	Value of Firm Based on Price of Platinum per Ounce	
	$700	$600
No Warrant or Call Option		
Gould's share	$2,100	$1,800
Rockefeller's share	2,100	1,800
Firm value	$4,200	$3,600
Call Option		
Gould's claim	$ 0	$1,800
Rockefeller's claim	2,100	1,800
Fiske's claim	2,100	0
Firm value	$4,200	$3,600
*Warrant**		
Gould's share	$2,000	$1,800
Rockefeller's share	2,000	1,800
Fiske's share	2,000	0
Firm value	$6,000	$3,600

* If the price of platinum is $700, the value of the firm is equal to the value of six ounces of platinum plus the excess dollars paid into the firm by Fiske. This amount is $4,200 + 1,800 = $6,000.

When the warrant is exercised, the exercise money goes to the firm. Since Fiske ends up owning one-third of the firm, she effectively gets back one-third of what she pays in. Because she really gives up only two-thirds of $1,800 to buy the stock, the effective exercise price is $2/3 \times \$1,800 = \$1,200$.

Fiske effectively pays out $1,200 to obtain a one-third interest in the assets of the firm (the platinum). This is worth $4,200/3 = $1,400. Fiske's gain, from this perspective, is $1,400 − 1,200 = $200 (exactly what we calculated earlier).

WARRANT VALUE AND STOCK VALUE   What is the value of the common stock of a firm that has issued warrants? Let's look at the market value of the GR Company just before and just after the exercise of Fiske's warrant. Just after exercise, the statement of financial position looks like this:

Cash	$1,800	Stock	$6,000
Platinum	4,200	(3 shares)	
Total	$6,000	Total	$6,000

As we saw, each share of stock is worth $6,000/3 = $2,000.

Whoever holds the warrant profits by $200 when the warrant is exercised; thus, the warrant is worth $200 just before expiration. The statement of financial position for the GR Company just before expiration is thus:

Platinum	$4,200	Warrant	$ 200
		Stock	4,000
		(2 shares)	
Total	$4,200	Total	$4,200

We calculate the value of the stock as the value of the assets ($4,200) less the value of the warrant ($200).

Notice that the value of each share just before expiration is $4,000/2 = $2,000 just as it is after expiration. The value of each share of stock is thus not changed by the exercise of the warrant. There is no dilution of share value from the exercise.

EARNINGS DILUTION   Warrants and convertible bonds frequently cause the number of shares to increase. This happens (1) when the warrants are exercised and (2) when the bonds are converted. As we have seen, this increase does not lower the per share value of the stock. However, it does cause the firm's net income to be spread over a larger number of shares; thus, earnings per share decrease.

Firms with significant amounts of warrants and convertible issues outstanding generally calculate and report earnings per share on a *fully diluted basis*. This means the calculation is based on the number of shares that would be outstanding if all the warrants were exercised and all the convertibles were converted. Since this increases the number of shares, the fully diluted EPS is lower than an EPS calculated only on the basis of shares actually outstanding.

> ### Concept Questions
>
> 1. What is a warrant?
> 2. Why are warrants different from call options?

25.7 | Convertible Bonds

convertible bond
A bond that can be exchanged for a fixed number of shares of stock for a specified amount of time.

A **convertible bond** is similar to a bond with warrants. The most important difference is that a bond with warrants can be separated into distinct securities (a bond and some warrants), but a convertible bond cannot be. A convertible bond gives the holder the right to exchange the bond for a fixed number of shares of stock anytime up to and including the maturity date of the bond.

Preferred shares can frequently be converted into common shares. A convertible preferred share is the same as a convertible bond except that it has an infinite maturity date.[12]

Features of a Convertible Bond

conversion price
The dollar amount of a bond's par value that is exchangeable for one share of stock.

conversion ratio
The number of shares per bond received for conversion into stock.

The basic features of a convertible bond can be illustrated by examining a particular issue. In June 2012, Discovery Air, a Canadian specialty aviation company founded in 2004, had a convertible bond outstanding, maturing after 12 years on June 30, 2016. The particular feature that makes the Discovery Air bonds interesting is that they are convertible into the common stock of Discovery Air anytime before maturity at a **conversion price** of $7.30 per share. Since each bond has a face value of $100, this means the holder of a Discovery Air convertible bond can exchange that bond for $100/$7.30 = 13.70 shares of Discovery Air stock. The number of shares received for each debenture is called the **conversion ratio**. On June 25, 2012, Discovery Air shares were trading at $3.30 on the TSX so the option to convert at $7.30 per share was out of the money.

On the same date, Algonquin Power & Utilities Corp., an Oakville, Ontario based company that owns power generation assets in Canada and the United States, had a convertible bond maturing on June 30, 2017 and trading at $119. The conversion ratio for the Algonquin convertible was 23.81 and the conversion price was $4.20. Since the stock was then trading at $6.39, the conversion option was in the money.

Value of a Convertible Bond

Even though the conversion feature of the convertible bond cannot be detached like a warrant, the value of the bond can still be decomposed into its bond value and the value of the conversion feature. We discuss how this is done next.

straight bond value
The value of a convertible bond if it could not be converted into common stock.

STRAIGHT BOND VALUE   The **straight bond value** is what the convertible bond would sell for if it could not be converted into common stock. This value depends on the general level of interest rates on debentures and on the default risk of the issuer.

Returning to our prior example, straight debentures issued by Discovery Air were yielding at 10.56 percent in June 2012. The straight bond value of Discovery Air convertible bonds can be determined by discounting the $8.38 annual coupon payment and maturity value at 10.56 percent, just as we did in Chapter 7. The Discovery Air convertible had 4 years to maturity in June 2012:[13]

---

[12] The dividends paid are, of course, not tax deductible for the corporation. Interest paid on a convertible bond is tax deductible.

[13] The latest data for convertible debentures can be obtained at financialpost.com/markets/data/bonds-debentures.html

$$\text{Straight bond value} = \$8.38 \times (1 - 1/1.1056^4)/.1056 + \$100/(1.1056)^4$$
$$= \$26.24 + 66.93$$
$$= \$93.17$$

The straight bond value of a convertible bond is a minimum value in the sense that the bond is always worth at least this amount. As we discuss, it is usually worth more.

conversion value
The value of a convertible bond if it was immediately converted into common stock.

CONVERSION VALUE   The **conversion value** of a convertible bond is what the bond would be worth if it were immediately converted into common stock. This value is computed by multiplying the current price of the stock by the number of shares received when the bond is converted.

For example, each Discovery Air convertible bond could be converted into 13.70 shares of common stock. Discovery Air common was selling for $3.30 at the time of writing in June 2012. Thus, the conversion value is $13.70 \times \$3.30 = \$45.21$.

A convertible cannot sell for less than its conversion value or an arbitrage exists. If Discovery Air's convertible sold for less than $45.21, investors would buy the bonds and convert them into common stock and sell the stock. The arbitrage profit would be the difference between the value of the stock and the bond's conversion value.

FLOOR VALUE   As we have seen, convertible bonds have two floor values: the straight bond value and the conversion value. The minimum value of a convertible bond is given by the greater of these two values. For the Discovery Air issue, the conversion value is $45.21, while the straight bond value is $93.17. At a minimum, this bond is thus worth $93.17.

Figure 25.5 plots the minimum value of a convertible bond against the value of the stock. The conversion value is determined by the value of the firm's underlying common stock. As the value of common stock rises and falls, the conversion value rises and falls with it. For example, if the value of Discovery Air's common stock increases by $1, the conversion value of its convertible bonds increases by $13.70.

In Figure 25.5, we have implicitly assumed that the convertible bond is default-free. In this case, the straight bond value does not depend on the stock price, so it is plotted as a horizontal line. Given the straight bond value, the minimum value of the convertible depends on the value of the stock. When this is low, the minimum value of a convertible is most significantly influenced by the underlying value as straight debt. This is the case for the Discovery Air convertible as the straight bond value, $93.17, far exceeds the conversion value of $45.21. However, when the value of the firm is very high, the value of a convertible bond is mostly determined by the underlying conversion value. This is also illustrated in Figure 25.5.

FIGURE 25.5

Minimum value of a convertible bond versus the value of the stock for a given interest rate

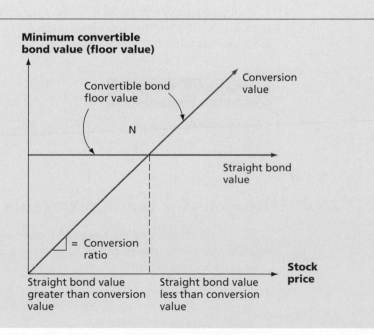

As shown, the minimum or "floor" value of a convertible bond is either its straight bond value or its conversion value, whichever is greater.

FIGURE 25.6

Value of a convertible bond versus value of the stock for a given interest rate

As shown, the value of a convertible bond is the sum of its floor value and its option value (highlighted region).

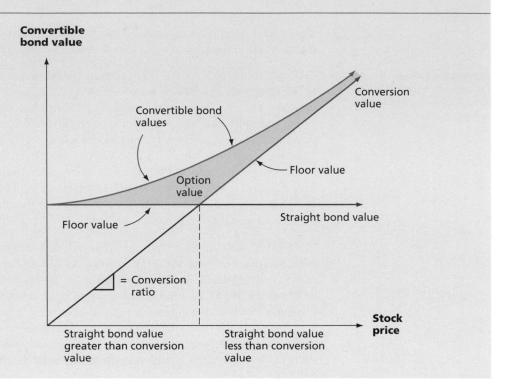

OPTION VALUE   The value of a convertible bond always exceeds the straight bond value and the conversion value unless the firm is in default or the bondholders are forced to convert. The reason is that holders of convertibles do not have to convert immediately. Instead, by waiting, they can take advantage of whichever is greater in the future, the straight bond value or the conversion value.

This option to wait has value, and it raises the value of the convertible bond over its floor value. The total value of the convertible is thus equal to the sum of the floor value and the option value. This is illustrated in Figure 25.6. Notice the similarity between this picture and the representation of the value of a call option in Figure 25.3.

Figure 25.6 can illustrate the Discovery Air convertible. Because the stock price, $3.30 at the time, was well below the conversion price of $7.30, the bond was trading based mainly on its straight bond value of $93.17. However, due to the option value, the actual price was higher.

Concept Questions

1. What are the conversion ratio, the conversion price, and the conversion premium?
2. What three elements make up the value of a convertible bond?

25.8 | Reasons for Issuing Warrants and Convertibles

Until recently, bonds with warrants and convertible bonds were not well understood. Surveys of financial executives have provided the most popular textbook reasons for warrants and convertibles. Here are two of them:

1. They allow companies to issue cheap bonds by attaching sweeteners to the bonds. Sweeteners allow the coupon rate on convertibles and bonds with warrants to be set at less than the market rates on straight bonds.

2. They give companies the chance to issue common stock at a premium more than current prices in the future. In this way, convertibles and bonds with warrants represent deferred sales of common stock at relatively high prices.

These justifications for convertibles and bonds with warrants are frequently mixed into free lunch explanations.

The Free Lunch Story

Suppose the RWJR Company can issue straight (non-convertible) subordinated debentures at 10 percent. It can also issue convertible bonds at 6 percent with a conversion value of $800. The conversion value means the holders can convert a convertible bond into 40 shares of common stock, which currently trades at $20.

A company treasurer who believes in free lunches might argue that convertible bonds should be issued because they represent a cheaper source of financing than either straight subordinated bonds or common stock. The treasurer points out that, if the company does poorly and the stock price does not rise to more than $20, the convertible bondholders do not convert the bonds into common stock. In this case, the company has obtained debt financing at below-market rates by attaching worthless equity kickers.

On the other hand, if the firm does well, the bondholders would convert. The company issues 40 shares. Because the company receives a bond with a face value of $1,000 in exchange for issuing 40 shares of common stock, the conversion price is $25.

Effectively, if the bondholders convert, the company has issued common stock at $25 per share. This is 20 percent more than the current common stock price of $20, so the company gets more money per share of stock. Thus, the treasurer happily points out, regardless of whether the company does well or poorly, convertible bonds are the cheapest form of financing. RWJR can't lose.

The problem with this story is that we can turn it around and create an argument showing that issuing warrants and convertibles is always a disaster. We call this the expensive lunch story.

The Expensive Lunch Story

Suppose we take a closer look at the RWJR Company and its proposal to sell convertible bonds. If the company performs badly and the stock price falls, bondholders do not exercise their conversion option. This suggests the RWJR Company should have issued common stock when prices were high. By issuing convertible bonds, the company lost a valuable opportunity.

On the other hand, if the company does well and the stock price rises, bondholders convert. Suppose the stock price rises to $40. The bondholders convert and the company is forced to sell stock worth $40 for an effective price of only $25. The new shareholders benefit. Put another way, if the company prospers, it would have been better to have issued straight debt so that the gains would not have to be shared.

Whether the convertible bonds are converted or not, the company has done worse than with straight bonds or new common stock. Issuing convertible bonds is a terrible idea.

Which is correct—the free lunch story or the expensive lunch story?

A Reconciliation

Reconciling our two stories requires only that we remember our central goal: Increase the wealth of the existing shareholders. Thus, with 20/20 hindsight, issuing convertible bonds turns out to be worse than issuing straight bonds and better than issuing common stock if the company prospers. The reason is that the prosperity has to be shared with bondholders after they convert.

In contrast, if a company does poorly, issuing convertible bonds turns out to be better than issuing straight bonds and worse than issuing common stock. The reason is that the firm benefited from the lower coupon payments on the convertible bond.

Both of our stories thus have a grain of truth; we just need to combine them. This is done in Table 25.3. Exactly the same arguments would be used in a comparison of a straight debt issue versus a bond/warrant package.

TABLE 25.3

The case for and against convertibles

	If Firm Does Poorly	If Firm Prospers
Convertible bonds *versus:*	Low stock price and no conversion	High stock price and conversion
Straight bonds	Cheap financing because coupon rate is lower (good outcome)	Expensive financing because bonds are converted, which dilutes existing equity (bad outcome)
Common stock	Expensive financing because the firm could have issued common stock at high prices (bad outcome)	Cheap financing because firm issues stock at high prices when bonds are converted (good outcome)

Concept Questions

1. What is wrong with the view that it is cheaper to issue a bond with a warrant or a convertible feature because the required coupon is lower?
2. What is wrong with the theory that says a convertible can be a good security to issue because it can be a way to sell stock at a price that is higher than the current stock price?

25.9 | Other Options

We've discussed two of the more common option-like securities, warrants, and convertibles. Options appear in many other places. We briefly describe a few such cases in this section.

The Call Provision on a Bond

As we discussed in Chapter 7, most corporate bonds are callable. A call provision allows a corporation to buy the bonds at a fixed price for a fixed time period. In other words, the corporation has a call option on the bonds. The cost of the call feature to the corporation is the cost of the option.

Convertible bonds are almost always callable. This means a convertible bond is really a package of three securities: a straight bond, a call option held by the bondholder (the conversion feature), and a call option held by the corporation (the call provision).

Put Bonds

The owner of a put bond has the right to force the issuer to repurchase the bond at a fixed price for a fixed period of time. Such a bond is a combination of a straight bond and a put option, hence the name.

For example, Canada Savings Bonds are put bonds since the holder can force the Government of Canada to repurchase them (through a financial institution acting as its agent) at 100 percent of the purchase price. The put option is exercisable at any time after the first two months of the bond's life. A more exotic, financially engineered example comes from Chapter 7 where we briefly discussed a LYON, a liquid yield option note. This is a callable, putable, convertible, pure discount bond. It is thus a package of a pure discount bond, two call options, and a put option. In 1991, Rogers Communication issued the first LYON in Canada.

The Overallotment Option

In Chapter 15, we mentioned that underwriters are frequently given the right to purchase additional shares of stock from a firm in an initial public offering (IPO). We called this the overallotment option. We now recognize that this provision is simply a call option (or, more accurately, a warrant) granted to the underwriter. The value of the option is an indirect form of compensation paid to the underwriter.

Insurance and Loan Guarantees

Insurance of one kind or another is a financial feature of everyday life. Most of the time, having insurance is like having a put option. For example, suppose you have $1 million in fire insurance on an office building. One night, your building burns down, reducing its value to nothing. In this case, you would effectively exercise your put option and force the insurer to pay you $1 million for something worth very little.

Loan guarantees are a form of insurance. If you lend money to a borrower who defaults, with a guaranteed loan you can collect from someone else, often the government. For example, when you lend money to a financial institution (by making a deposit), your loan is guaranteed (up to $100,000) by the federal government provided your institution is a member of the Canada Deposit Insurance Corporation (CDIC).

The federal government, with a loan guarantee, has provided a put option to the holders of risky debt. The value of the put option is the cost of the loan guarantee. Loan guarantees are not cost-free. This point was made absolutely clear to the CDIC when two banks collapsed in western Canada in 1985.

Because the put option allows a risky firm to borrow at subsidized rates, it is an asset to the shareholders. The riskier the firm, the greater the value of the guarantee and the more it is worth to the shareholders. Researchers modified the Black–Scholes model presented in this chapter's appendix to value the put option in CDIC deposit insurance for one of the Canadian banks that failed. They found that financial markets provided early warning of bank failures as the value of the put option increased significantly before the bank failed.[14]

U.S. taxpayers learned the same lesson about loan guarantees at far greater cost in the savings-and-loan collapse. The cost to U.S. taxpayers of making good on the guaranteed deposits in these institutions was a staggering amount.

One result of all this is that accountants in Canada, urged on by the auditor general, are forcing government agencies to report guarantees and other contingent liabilities in their financial statements. This may induce greater caution in extending guarantees in the first place.

Managerial Options

We introduced managerial options in our discussion of capital budgeting in Chapter 11. These options represent opportunities that managers can exploit if certain things happen in the future. Returning to such options, we now see that they represent **real options**—options with payoffs in real goods as opposed to asset prices. One example of a real option is production flexibility as we explain next.

real option
An option with payoffs in real goods.

The value of flexibility in production has long been recognized, but at what price? All other things being equal, a company would rather have production facilities that can quickly and cheaply adapt to changing circumstances than a plant that is limited in what and how much it can produce. Changing demand for products often necessitates changes in products and the changing costs of raw materials and other inputs can mean that the production process now in use may no longer be the cost-minimizing one.

However, a flexible production facility costs more than building one that is suited to one line of products or one pattern of inputs. In addition, a plant that is designed to be used with one product line and one pattern of inputs is usually optimized for those conditions. It is more efficient for that purpose than a flexible plant producing the same line of products and using the same inputs. A company building a production facility must trade off the advantages of flexibility against the additional costs.

AUTOMOBILE PRODUCTION   The market for automobiles is notoriously fickle. The hottest seller can be sports cars in one year and sport utility vehicles in the next. When you consider that it usually takes more than two years to design and bring a new model into production, the risks of the business become apparent.

world.honda.com

In an effort to cope with this ever-changing environment, Honda built a production facility in Canada that may be the ultimate in flexible production. According to popular accounts, this plant

---

[14] R. Giammarino, E. Schwartz, and J. Zechner, "Market Valuation of Bank Assets and Deposit Insurance in Canada," *Canadian Journal of Economics,* February 1989, pp. 109–27.

has the capacity to switch production from one car model to another in a matter of days! By contrast, it can take other manufacturers six months or longer to switch production from one model to another. In addition, a new model can require an entirely new set of assembly lines.

That is the good news. The bad news is that a flexible plant costs about $1.4 billion versus $1 billion for a typical automobile plant. The real question in building such a plant is whether the flexibility is worth the additional $400 million investment.

To find an answer to this question, we have to examine the value of having a flexible plant. Perhaps the most important variable determining which cars to produce is the changing demands and tastes for car models. For simplicity, let us assume that the flexible plant can produce either minivans or four-door sedans. Suppose, too, that it has a capacity of 300,000 vehicles a year and that it can produce either one type or the other, but not both at the same time. To illustrate our point, we will assume that the plant can be switched only once, three years from now, and that the lifetime of the plant is 10 years.

Currently there is a high demand for minivans, and the company forecasts that it will need to produce minivans at full capacity, 300,000 vehicles per year, for the next three years. Three years from now, though, there is a 50-percent chance that the public will prefer sedans rather than minivans and only 50,000 minivans per year could be produced and sold. Both the fixed plant and the flexible plant have a capacity of 300,000 vehicles per year. The profit for the flexible plant is $1,000 per vehicle on minivans and $1,100 per vehicle on sedans. A fixed plant dedicated to minivan production can only produce minivans, but it does so more efficiently. The cash flow from having the fixed plant produce minivans is $1,200 per minivan, rather than the $1,000 per minivan for the flexible plant.

The profits from a plant that is committed to producing minivans for the next 10 years will be $360 million per year for the first three years (300,000 × $1,200) and then will either continue at this rate for the next seven years or will drop to $60 million per year if demand switches to sedans (50,000 × $1,200). On the other hand, if demand switches to sedans, a flexible plant will be able to switch its production. Therefore, the profit from a flexible plant will stay at $300 million per year for the first three years (300,000 × $1,000) and then will either rise to $330 million if sedans come into favour (300,000 × $1,100) or stay at $300 million per year if it sticks to minivans. This demonstrates the smoothing of cash flows from having a flexible plant.

The company faces a seemingly simple choice now. It can either invest $1 billion in a committed plant to produce minivans for the next 10 years or it can invest $1.4 billion to give itself the option of switching from minivans to sedans in three years.

The possible results are illustrated in Figure 25.7.

Using a 15-percent discount rate, the present value of the cash flows generated by building a fixed plant dedicated to minivans is

$$\text{PV (Fixed Plant)} = \$360/1.15 + \$360/1.15^2 + \ldots + \$360/1.15^{10}$$
$$= \$1.807 \text{ billion}$$

if minivan production stays in demand. However, the present value will drop to

$$\text{PV (Fixed Plant)} = \$360/1.15 + \$360/1.15^2 + \$360/1.15^3 + \$60/1.15^4 + \ldots + \$60/1.15^{10}$$
$$= \$.986 \text{ billion}$$

if sedans come into favour.

If minivans stay in demand, the present value of the cash flows from a flexible plant will be

$$\text{PV (Flexible Plant)} = \$300/1.15 + \$300/1.15^2 + \ldots + \$300/1.15^{10}$$
$$= \$1.506 \text{ billion}$$

If sedans displace minivans in customers' affections, then

$$\text{PV (Flexible Plant)} = \$300/1.15 + \$300/1.15^2 + \$300/1.15^3 + \$330/1.15^4 + \ldots + \$330/1.15^{10}$$
$$= \$1.588 \text{ billion}$$

There is a 50-percent chance that minivans will stay in fashion and a 50-percent chance that they will not. If we assume that the firm is risk-neutral between these two possibilities, the expected present value is the average of the two. Of course, this may not be the case. It may be that a switch in tastes to sedans is correlated with changes in GNP or broad market movements, in which case

FIGURE 25.7

Yearly profits from a fixed plant and a flexible plant

Panel A: Fixed plant

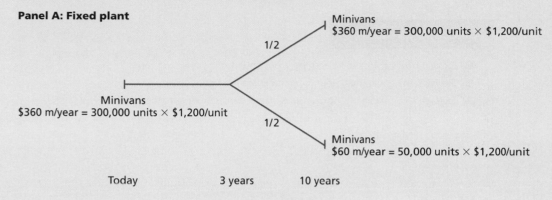

Panel B: Flexible plant

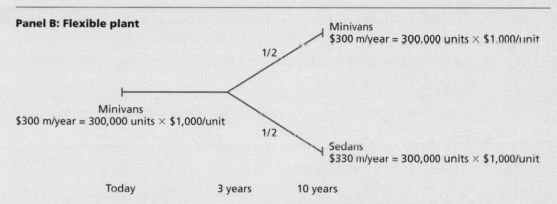

This graph shows the annual profits from a fixed plant and a flexible plant. A fixed plant can only produce minivans. Thus, if demand turns to sedans, the fixed plant will only sell 50,000 minivans. By contrast, the flexible plant can produce sedans if demand turns to that item. However, profit per unit is less in a flexible plant.

we would have to do a beta adjustment to compute the present value correctly. For now we will assume that this risk adjustment is already incorporated in the 15-percent discount rate and take the expected present value. While it is possible to develop a more accurate technique to solve such problems, our current assumption is quite reasonable as a practical matter. Thus,

$$\text{Expected PV (Fixed Plant)} = (1/2)\$1.807 \text{ billion} + (1/2)\$.986 \text{ billion}$$
$$= \$1.396 \text{ billion}$$

and

$$\text{Expected PV (Flexible Plant)} = (1/2)\$1.506 \text{ billion} + (1/2)\$1.588 \text{ billion}$$
$$= \$1.547 \text{ billion}$$

Comparing these calculations, we can see that the additional expected present value of having the flexibility to switch production is

$$\text{Expected PV (Flexible Plant)} - \text{Expected PV (Fixed Plant)}$$
$$= \$1.547 \text{ billion} - \$1.396 \text{ billion}$$
$$= \$151 \text{ million}$$

In other words, flexibility in this case is worth $151 million. Since the flexible plant costs $400 million more to build, the NPV of the flexible plant is less than that of the fixed plant. The price of flexibility is too high.

Research has shown that the decision to open or close gold mining operations could also be explained by the real options model.[15] The study found that mine closures are strongly influenced by factors like price and volatility of gold, the firm's operating costs, closing costs, and the size of gold reserves at the mine.

Concept Questions

1. Explain how car insurance acts like a put option.
2. Explain why government loan guarantees are not free.
3. Explain how managerial options can change capital budgeting decisions.

25.10 | SUMMARY AND CONCLUSIONS

This chapter described the basics of option valuation and discussed option-like corporate securities. In it, we saw that:

1. Options are contracts giving the right, but not the obligation, to buy and sell underlying assets at a fixed price during a specified time period.

    The most familiar options are puts and calls involving shares of stock. These options give the holder the right, but not the obligation, to sell (the put option) or buy (the call option) shares of common stock at a given price.

    As we discussed, the value of any option depends only on five factors:

    a. The price of the underlying asset.

    b. The exercise price.

    c. The expiration date.

    d. The interest rate on risk-free bonds.

    e. The volatility of the underlying asset's value.

2. A warrant gives the holder the right to buy shares of common stock directly from the company at a fixed exercise price for a given period of time. Typically, warrants are issued in a package with privately placed bonds. Often, they can be detached afterward and traded separately.

3. A convertible bond is a combination of a straight bond and a call option. The holder can give up the bond in exchange for a fixed number of shares of stock. The minimum value of a convertible bond is given by its straight bond value or its conversion value, whichever is greater.

4. Convertible bonds, warrants, and call options are similar, but important differences do exist:

    a. Warrants and convertible securities are issued by corporations. Call options are issued by and traded between individual investors.

    b. Warrants are usually issued privately and combined with a bond. In most cases, the warrants can be detached immediately after the issue. In some cases, warrants are issued with preferred stock, with common stock, or in publicly traded bond issues.

    c. Warrants and call options are exercised for cash. The holder of a warrant gives the company cash and receives new shares of the company's stock. The holder of a call option gives another individual cash in exchange for common stock. Convertible bonds are exercised by exchange; the individual gives the company back the bond in exchange for stock.

5. Many other corporate securities have option features. Bonds with call provisions, bonds with put provisions, and debt backed by a loan guarantee are just a few examples.

---

[15] A. Moel and P. Tufano, "When Are Real Options Exercised? An Empirical Study of Mine Closings," *The Review of Financial Studies,* Spring 2002.

Key Terms

Chapter Review Problems and Self-Test

25.1 **Value of a Call Option** Stock in the Barsoom Corporation is currently selling for $30 per share. In one year, the price would either be $30 or $40. T-bills with one year to maturity are paying 10 percent. What is the value of a call option with a $30 exercise price? A $34 exercise price?

25.2 **Convertible Bonds** The Kau Corporation, publisher of *Gourmand* magazine, has a convertible bond issue currently selling in the market for $900. Each bond can be exchanged for 100 shares of stock at the holder's option.

The bond has a 6 percent coupon, payable annually, and it matures in 12 years. Kau's debt is BBB-rated. Debt with this rating is priced to yield 12 percent. Stock in Kau is trading at $6 per share.

What is the conversion ratio on this bond? The conversion price? The conversion premium? What is the floor value of the bond? What is its option value?

Answers to Self-Test Problems

25.1 With a $30 exercise price, the option can't finish out of the money (it can finish "at the money" if the stock price is $30). We can replicate the stock by investing the present value of $30 in T-bills and buying one call option. Buying the T-bill would cost $30/1.1 = $27.27.

If the stock ends up at $30, the call option is worth zero and the T-bill pays $30. If the stock ends up at $40, the T-bill again pays $30, and the option is worth $40 − 30 = $10, so the package is worth $40. Since the T-bill/call option combination exactly duplicates the payoff on the stock, it has to be worth $30 or arbitrage is possible. Using the notation from the chapter, we can calculate the value of the call option:

$$S_0 = C_0 + E/(1 + R_f)$$
$$\$30 = C_0 + \$27.27$$
$$C_0 = \$2.73$$

With the $34 exercise price, we start by investing the present value of the lower stock price in T-bills. This guarantees us $30 when the stock price is $30. If the stock price is $40, the option is worth $40 − 34 = $6. We have $30 from our T-bill, so we need $10 from the options to match the stock. Since each option is worth $6, we need to buy $10/$6 = 1.67 call options. Notice that the difference in the possible stock prices is $10 ($\Delta S$) and the difference in the possible option prices is $6 ($\Delta C$), so $\Delta S/\Delta C = 1.67$.

To complete the calculation, the present value of the $30 plus 1.67 call options has to be worth $30 to prevent arbitrage, so:

$$\$30 = 1.67 \times C_0 + \$30/1.1$$
$$C_0 = \$2.73/1.67$$
$$= \$1.63$$

25.2 Since each bond can be exchanged for 100 shares, the conversion ratio is 100. The conversion price is the face value of the bond ($1,000) divided by the conversion ratio, $1,000/100 = $10. The conversion premium is the percentage difference between the current price and the conversion price, ($10 − $6)/$6 = 67%.

The floor value of the bond is the greater of its straight bond value and its conversion value. Its conversion value is what the bond is worth if it is immediately converted: $100 \times \$6 = \$600$. The straight bond value is what the bond would be worth if it were not convertible. The annual coupon is $60, and the bond matures in 12 years. At a 12 percent required return, the straight bond value is:

$$\text{Straight bond value} = \$60 \times (1 - 1/1.12^{12})/.12 + \$1,000/1.12^{12}$$
$$= \$371.66 + 256.68$$
$$= \$628.34$$

This exceeds the conversion value, so the floor value of the bond is $628.34. Finally, the option value is the value of the convertible in excess of its floor value. Since the bond is selling for $900, the option value is:

$$\text{Option value} = \$900 - 628.34$$
$$= \$271.66$$

Concepts Review and Critical Thinking Questions

1. **(LO1)** What is a call option? A put option? Under what circumstances might you want to buy each? Which one has greater *potential* profit? Why?

2. **(LO1)** Complete the following sentence for each of these investors:
   a. A buyer of call options
   b. A buyer of put options
   c. A seller (writer) of call options
   d. A seller (writer) of put options
   "The (buyer/seller) of a (put/call) option (pays/receives) money for the (right/obligation) to (buy/sell) a specified asset at a fixed price for a fixed length of time."

3. **(LO1)** What is the intrinsic value of a call option? How do we interpret this value?

4. **(LO1)** What is the value of a put option at maturity? Based on your answer, what is the intrinsic value of a put option?

5. **(LO2)** You notice that shares of stock in the Patel Corporation are going for $50 per share. Call options with an exercise price of $35 per share are selling for $10. What's wrong here? Describe how you can take advantage of this mispricing if the option expires today.

6. **(LO2)** If the risk of a stock increases, what is likely to happen to the price of call options on the stock? To the price of put options? Why?

7. **(LO2)** True or false: The unsystematic risk of a share of stock is irrelevant in valuing the stock because it can be diversified away; therefore, it is also irrelevant for valuing a call option on the stock. Explain.

8. **(LO1)** Suppose a certain stock currently sells for $30 per share. If a put option and a call option are available with $30 exercise prices, which do you think will sell for more, the put or the call? Explain.

9. **(LO2)** Suppose the interest rate on T-bills suddenly and unexpectedly rises. All other things being the same, what is the impact on call option values? On put option values?

10. **(LO1)** When you take out an ordinary student loan, it is usually the case that whoever holds that loan is given a guarantee by the federal government, meaning that the government will make up any payments you skip. This is just one example of the many loan guarantees made by the federal government. Such guarantees don't show up in calculations of government spending or in official deficit figures. Why not? Should they show up?

Questions and Problems

Basic
(Questions 1–13)

1. **Calculating Option Values (LO2)** T-bills currently yield 4.3 percent. Stock in Nina Manufacturing is currently selling for $67 per share. There is no possibility that the stock will be worth less than $50 per share in one year.
   a. What is the value of a call option with a $45 exercise price? What is the intrinsic value?
   b. What is the value of a call option with a $35 exercise price? What is the intrinsic value?
   c. What is the value of a put option with a $45 exercise price? What is the intrinsic value?

2. **Understanding Option Quotes (LO1)** Use the option quote information shown here to answer the questions that follow. The stock is currently selling for $84.

| Option and | | Strike | Calls | | Puts | |
TSX Close	Expiration	Price	Vol.	Last	Vol.	Last
RWJ	Mar	85	230	3.20	160	3.30
	Apr	85	170	9.05	127	8.05
	Jul	85	139	9.90	43	10.85
	Oct	85	60	10.80	11	10.45

   a. Are the call options in the money? What is the intrinsic value of an RWJ Corp. call option?
   b. Are the put options in the money? What is the intrinsic value of an RWJ Corp. put option?
   c. Two of the options are clearly mispriced. Which ones? At a minimum, what should the mispriced options sell for? Explain how you could profit from the mispricing in each case.

3. **Calculating Payoffs (LO1)** Use the option quote information shown here to answer the questions that follow. The stock is currently selling for $27.

| Option and | | Strike | Calls | | Puts | |
TSX Close	Expiration	Price	Vol.	Last	Vol.	Last
Macrosoft	Feb	28	85	0.23	40	1.23
	Mar	28	61	0.47	22	1.64
	May	28	22	0.75	11	2.06
	Aug	28	3	0.96	3	2.10

   a. Suppose you buy 10 contracts of the February 28 call option. How much will you pay, ignoring commissions?
   b. In part (a), suppose that Macrosoft stock is selling for $30 per share on the expiration date. How much is your options investment worth? What if the terminal stock price is $29? Explain.
   c. Suppose you buy 10 contracts of the August 28 put option. What is your maximum gain? On the expiration date, Macrosoft is selling for $23 per share. How much is your options investment worth? What is your net gain?
   d. In part (c), suppose you *sell* 10 of the August 28 put contracts. What is your net gain or loss if Macrosoft is selling for $25 at expiration? For $31? What is the break-even price, that is, the terminal stock price that results in a zero profit?

4. **Calculating Option Values (LO2)** The price of Newgen Corp. stock will be either $53 or $84 at the end of the year. Call options are available with one year to expiration. T-bills currently yield 6 percent.

   a. Suppose the current price of Newgen stock is $85. What is the value of the call option if the exercise price is $75 per share?

   b. Suppose the exercise price is $90 in part (a). What is the value of the call option now?

5. **Calculating Option Values (LO2)** The price of Tara Inc. stock will be either $64 or $86 at the end of the year. Call options are available with one year to expiration. T-bills currently yield 6 percent.

   a. Suppose the current price of Tara stock is $75. What is the value of the call option if the exercise price is $60 per share?

   b. Suppose the exercise price is $70 in part (a). What is the value of the call option now?

6. **Using the Pricing Equation (LO2)** A one-year call option *contract* on Cheesy Poofs Co. stock sells for $1,150. In one year, the stock will be worth $47 or $68 per share. The exercise price on the call option is $60. What is the current value of the stock if the risk-free rate is 3 percent?

7. **Equity as an Option (LO4)** Rackin Pinion Corporation's assets are currently worth $104. In one year, they will be worth either $100 or $129. The risk-free interest rate is 5 percent. Suppose Rackin Pinion has an outstanding debt issue with a face value of $100.

   a. What is the value of the equity?

   b. What is the value of the debt? The interest rate on the debt?

   c. Would the value of the equity go up or down if the risk-free rate were 20 percent? Why? What does your answer illustrate?

8. **Equity as an Option (LO4)** Buckeye Industries has a bond issue with a face value of $100 that is coming due in one year. The value of Buckeye's assets is currently $109. Jim Tressell, the CEO, believes that the assets in the firm will be worth either $92 or $138 in a year. The going rate on one-year T-bills is 6 percent.

   a. What is the value of Buckeye's equity? The value of the debt?

   b. Suppose Buckeye can reconfigure its existing assets in such a way that the value in a year will be $80 or $160. If the current value of the assets is unchanged, will the stockholders favour such a move? Why or why not?

9. **Calculating Conversion Value (LO5)** A $100 par convertible debenture has a conversion price for common stock of $28 per share. With the common stock selling at $37, what is the conversion value of the bond?

10. **Convertible Bonds (LO5)** The following facts apply to a convertible bond making semiannual payments:

Conversion price	$35/share
Coupon rate	5.4%
Par value	$100
Yield on nonconvertible debentures of same quality	7%
Maturity	30 years
Market price of stock	$34/share

   a. What is the minimum price at which the convertible should sell?

   b. What accounts for the premium of the market price of a convertible bond over the total market value of the common stock into which it can be converted?

11. **Calculating Values for Convertibles (LO5)** You have been hired to value a new 30-year callable, convertible bond. The bond has a 7.5 percent coupon, payable annually, and its face value is $100. The conversion price is $5.5 and the stock currently sells for $4.2.

   a. What is the minimum value of the bond? Comparable nonconvertible bonds are priced to yield 9 percent.

   b. What is the conversion premium for this bond?

12. **Calculating Warrant Values (LO5)** A bond with 20 detachable warrants has just been offered for sale at $100. The bond matures in 25 years and has an annual coupon of $5.5. Each warrant gives the owner the right to purchase two shares of stock in the company at $4.5 per share. Ordinary bonds (with no warrants) of similar quality are priced to yield 7 percent. What is the value of one warrant?

13. **Option to Wait (LO4)** Your company is deciding whether to invest in a new machine. The new machine will increase cash flow by $310,000 per year. You believe the technology used in the machine has a 10-year life; in other words, no matter when you purchase the machine, it will be obsolete 10 years from today. The machine is currently priced at $1,600,000. The cost of the machine will decline by $95,000 per year until it reaches $1,125,000, where it will remain. If your required return is 14 percent, should you purchase the machine? If so, when should you purchase it?

Intermediate
(Questions
14–19)
14. **Abandonment Value (LO4)** We are examining a new project. We expect to sell 6,500 units per year at $63 net cash flow apiece for the next 10 years. In other words, the annual operating cash flow is projected to be $63 × 6,500 = $409,500. The relevant discount rate is 14 percent, and the initial investment required is $1,600,000.

   a. What is the base-case NPV?

   b. After the first year, the project can be dismantled and sold for $1,200,000. If expected sales are revised based on the first year's performance, when would it make sense to abandon the investment? In other words, at what level of expected sales would it make sense to abandon the project?

   c. Explain how the $1,200,000 abandonment value can be viewed as the opportunity cost of keeping the project in one year.

15. **Abandonment (LO4)** In the previous problem, suppose you think it is likely that expected sales will be revised upwards to 9,000 units if the first year is a success and revised downwards to 3,500 units if the first year is not a success.

    a. If success and failure are equally likely, what is the NPV of the project? Consider the possibility of abandonment in answering.

    b. What is the value of the option to abandon?

16. **Abandonment and Expansion (LO4)** In the previous problem, suppose the scale of the project can be doubled in one year in the sense that twice as many units can be produced and sold. Naturally, expansion would only be desirable if the project is a success. This implies that if the project is a success, projected sales after expansion will be 18,000. Again assuming that success and failure are equally likely, what is the NPV of the project? Note that abandonment is still an option if the project is a failure. What is the value of the option to expand?

17. **Intuition and Option Value (LO2)** Suppose a share of stock sells for $54. The risk-free rate is 5 percent, and the stock price in one year will be either $60 or $70.

    a. What is the value of a call option with a $60 exercise price?

    b. What's wrong here? What would you do?

18. **Intuition and Convertibles (LO5)** Which of the following two sets of relationships, at time of issuance of convertible bonds, is more typical? Why?

	A	B
Offering price of bond	$ 80	$100
Bond value (straight debt)	80	95
Conversion value	100	90

19. **Convertible Calculations (LO5)** Alicia Inc. has a $100 face value convertible bond issue that is currently selling in the market for $96. Each bond is exchangeable at any time for 20 shares of the company's stock. The convertible bond has a 6.5 percent coupon, payable semiannually. Similar nonconvertible bonds are priced to yield 9 percent. The bond matures in 20 years. Stock in Alicia sells for $4.5 per share.

    a. What are the conversion ratio, conversion price, and conversion premium?

    b. What is the straight bond value? The conversion value?

    c. In part (b), what would the stock price have to be for the conversion value and the straight bond value to be equal?

    d. What is the option value of the bond?

20. **Abandonment Decisions (LO4)** Manga Products Inc. is considering a new product launch. The firm expects to have annual operating cash flow of $8 million for the next 8 years. Manga Products uses a discount rate of 11 percent for new product launches. The initial investment is $38 million. Assume that the project has no salvage value at the end of its economic life.

    a. What is the NPV of the new product?

    b. After the first year, the project can be dismantled and sold for $25 million. If estimates of remaining cash flows are revised based on the first year's experience, at what level of expected cash flows does it make sense to abandon the project?

Challenge (Questions 21–22)

21. **Pricing Convertibles (LO5)** You have been hired to value a new 25-year callable, convertible bond. The bond has a 4.8 percent coupon, payable annually. The conversion price is $9, and the stock currently sells for $3.21. The stock price is expected to grow at 11 percent per year. The bond is callable at $120, but, based on prior experience, it won't be called unless the conversion value is $130. The required return on this bond is 8 percent. What value would you assign? Par value of the bond is $100.

22. **Abandonment Decisions (LO4)** For some projects, it may be advantageous to terminate the project early. For example, if a project is losing money, you might be able to reduce your losses by scrapping out the assets and terminating the project, rather than continuing to lose money all the way through to the project's completion. Consider the following project of Hand Clapper Inc. The company is considering a four-year project to manufacture clap-command garage door openers. This project requires an initial investment of $15 million that will be depreciated straight-line to zero over the project's life. An initial investment in net working capital of $900,000 is required to support spare parts inventory; this cost is fully recoverable whenever the project ends. The company believes it can generate $10.9 million in pre-tax revenues with $4.1 million in total pre-tax operating costs. The tax rate is 38 percent and the discount rate is 13 percent. The market value of the equipment over the life of the project is as follows:

Year	Market Value (millions)
1	$13.00
2	10.00
3	7.50
4	0.85

    a. Assuming Hand Clapper operates this project for four years, what is the NPV?

    b. Now compute the project NPV assuming the project is abandoned after only one year, after two years, and after three years. What economic life for this project maximizes its value to the firm? What does this problem tell you about not considering abandonment possibilities when evaluating projects?

Internet Application Questions

1. The 1997 Nobel Prize for economics (nobelprize.org/nobel_prizes/economics/laureates/1997/index.html) was awarded to Robert C. Merton and Myron S. Scholes for their early pioneering work in options pricing. The following site contains the transcript of an interview conducted by the Public Broadcasting Service (pbs.org) of the U.S. and the two professors. The interview explains the principles behind options pricing, and the excitement the news of the Nobel Prize generated for the recipients. In two short sentences, can you paraphrase Scholes and Merton's explanation of the intuition behind their options pricing formula?

   pbs.org/newshour/bb/business/july-dec97/nobel_10-14.html

2. The Montreal Exchange (ME) (m-x.ca) is the premier venue for trading options in the Canada. The ME provides one of the best educational links to understand both the valuation of options, and the institutional details such as trading practices. Click on the ME link below to take a self-paced tutorial in options pricing and trading.

   m-x.ca/educ_oic_en.php

   When you are done with the tutorial, go back to the ME site and find and describe securities called Long Term Options (optionseducation.org/getting_started/options_overview/leaps.html?prt=mx). Note that the United States derivatives exchange, the counterpart of the ME, is the Chicago Board of Options Exchange (cboe.com).

3. Visit the website of the Montreal Exchange (m-x.ca). What are the three most active options on this trading day? What is the company, series, strike price, and volume of the three highest volume calls? Find the same information for puts?

4. The Montreal Exchange (m-x.ca) also provides information on expiration dates. Using the "Trading Calendar" tool (m-x.ca/nego_ca_en.php), on what day do equity options expire in the current month? On what day do they expire next month?

APPENDIX 25A

THE BLACK–SCHOLES OPTION PRICING MODEL

In our discussion of call options in this chapter, we did not discuss the general case where the stock can take on any value and the option can finish out of the money. The general approach to valuing a call option falls under the heading of the *Black–Scholes Option Pricing Model (OPM)*, a very famous result in finance. In addition to its theoretical importance, the OPM has great practical value. Many option traders carry handheld calculators or computing devices programmed with the Black–Scholes formula.

> There's a Black-Scholes calculator (and a lot more) at cboe.com

This appendix briefly discusses the Black–Scholes model. Because the underlying development is relatively complex, we present only the result and then focus on how to use it.

From our earlier discussion, when a *t*-period call option is certain to finish somewhere in the money, its value today, C_0, is equal to the value of the stock today, S_0, less the present value of the exercise price, $E/(1 + R_f)^t$:

$$C_0 = S_0 - E/(1 + R_f)^t$$

If the option can finish out of the money, this result needs modifying. Black and Scholes show that the value of a call option in this case is given by:

$$C_0 = S_0 \times N(d_1) - E/(1 + R_f)^t \times N(d_2) \qquad \text{[25A.1]}$$

where $N(d_1)$ and $N(d_2)$ are probabilities that must be calculated. This is the Black–Scholes OPM.[16]

In the Black–Scholes model, $N(d_1)$ is the probability that a standardized, normally distributed random variable (widely known as a *z* variable) is less than or equal to d_1, and $N(d_2)$ is the probability of a value that is less than or equal to d_2. Determining these probabilities requires a table such as Table 25A.1.

To illustrate, suppose we were given the following information:

$$S_0 = \$100$$
$$E = \$80$$
$$R_f = 1\% \text{ per month}$$
$$d_1 = 1.20$$
$$d_2 = .90$$
$$t = 9 \text{ months}$$

Based on this information, what is the value of the call option, C_0?

---

[16]Strictly speaking, the risk-free rate in the Black–Scholes model is the continuously compounded risk-free rate. Continuous compounding is discussed in Chapter 6.

To answer, we need to determine $N(d_1)$ and $N(d_2)$. In Table 25A.1, we first find the row corresponding to a d of 1.20. The corresponding probability, $N(d)$, is .8849, so this is $N(d_1)$. For d_2, the associated probability $N(d_2)$ is .8159. Using the Black–Scholes OPM, the value of the call option is thus:

$$\begin{aligned} C_0 &= S_0 \times N(d_1) - E/(1 + R_f)^t \times N(d_2) \\ &= \$100 \times .8849 - \$80/1.01^9 \times .8159 \\ &= \$88.49 - 59.68 \\ &= \$28.81 \end{aligned}$$

As this example illustrates, if we are given values for d_1 and d_2 (and the table), using the Black–Scholes model is not difficult. In general, however, we are not given the values of d_1 and d_2, and we must calculate them instead. This requires a little extra effort. The values for d_1 and d_2 for the Black–Scholes OPM are given by:

$$\begin{aligned} d_1 &= [ln(S_0/E) + (R_f + 1/2 \times \sigma^2) \times t]/[\sigma \times \sqrt{t}] \qquad \text{[25A.2]} \\ d_2 &= d_1 - \sigma \times \sqrt{t} \end{aligned}$$

In these expressions, σ is the standard deviation of the rate of return on the underlying asset. Also, $ln(S_0/E)$ is the natural logarithm of the current stock price divided by the exercise price (most calculators have a key labelled ln to perform this calculation).

The formula for d_1 looks intimidating, but using it is mostly a matter of "plug and chug" with a calculator. To illustrate, suppose we have the following:

$S_0 = \$70$
$E = \$80$
$R_f = 1\%$ per month
$\sigma = 2\%$ per month
$t = 9$ months

With these numbers, d_1 is:

$$\begin{aligned} d_1 &= [\ln(S_0/E) + (R_f + 1/2 \times \sigma^2) \times t]/[\sigma \times \sqrt{t}] \\ &= [\ln(.875) + (.01 + 1/2 \times .02^2) \times 9]/[.02 \times 3] \\ &= [-.1335 + .0918]/.06 \\ &\approx -.70 \end{aligned}$$

Given this result, d_2 is:

$$\begin{aligned} d_2 &= d_1 - \sigma \times \sqrt{t} \\ &= -.70 - .02 \times 3 \\ &= -.76 \end{aligned}$$

Referring to Table 25A.1, the values for $N(d_1)$ and $N(d_2)$ are .2420 and .2236, respectively. The value of the option is thus:

$$\begin{aligned} C_0 &= S_0 \times N(d_1) - E/(1 + R_f)^t \times N(d_2) \\ &= \$70 \times .2420 - \$80/1.01^9 \times .2236 \\ &= \$.58 \end{aligned}$$

This may seem a little small, but the stock price would have to rise by \$10 before the option would even be in the money.

Notice that we quoted the risk-free rate, the standard deviation, and the time to maturity in months in this example. We could have used days, weeks, or years as long as we are consistent in quoting all three of these using the same time units.

A question that sometimes comes up concerns the probabilities $N(d_1)$ and $N(d_2)$. Just what are they the probabilities of? In other words, how do we interpret them? The answer is that they don't really correspond to anything in the real world. We mention this because there is a common misconception about $N(d_2)$ in particular. It is frequently thought to be the probability that the stock price will exceed the strike price on the expiration day, which is also the probability that a call option will finish in the money. Unfortunately, that's not correct, at least not unless the expected return on the stock is equal to the risk-free rate.

TABLE 25A.1

Cumulative normal distribution

d	N(d)	d	N(d)	d	N(d)	d	N(d)	d	N(d)	d	N(d)
−3.00	.0013	−1.58	.0571	−0.76	.2236	0.06	.5239	0.86	.8051	1.66	.9515
−2.95	.0016	−1.56	.0594	−0.74	.2297	0.08	.5319	0.88	.8106	1.68	.9535
−2.90	.0019	−1.54	.0618	−0.72	.2358	0.10	.5398	0.90	.8159	1.70	.9554
−2.85	.0022	−1.52	.0643	−0.70	.2420	0.12	.5478	0.92	.8212	1.72	.9573
−2.80	.0026	−1.50	.0668	−0.68	.2483	0.14	.5557	0.94	.8264	1.74	.9591
−2.75	.0030	−1.48	.0694	−0.66	.2546	0.16	.5636	0.96	.8315	1.76	.9608
−2.70	.0035	−1.46	.0721	−0.64	.2611	0.18	.5714	0.98	.8365	1.78	.9625
−2.65	.0040	−1.44	.0749	−0.62	.2676	0.20	.5793	1.00	.8414	1.80	.9641
−2.60	.0047	−1.42	.0778	−0.60	.2743	0.22	.5871	1.02	.8461	1.82	.9656
−2.55	.0054	−1.40	.0808	−0.58	.2810	0.24	.5948	1.04	.8508	1.84	.9671
−2.50	.0062	−1.38	.0838	−0.56	.2877	0.26	.6026	1.06	.8554	1.86	.9686
−2.45	.0071	−1.36	.0869	−0.54	.2946	0.28	.6103	1.08	.8599	1.88	.9699
−2.40	.0082	−1.34	.0901	−0.52	.3015	0.30	.6179	1.10	.8643	1.90	.9713
−2.35	.0094	−1.32	.0934	−0.50	.3085	0.32	.6255	1.12	.8686	1.92	.9726
−2.30	.0107	−1.30	.0968	−0.48	.3156	0.34	.6331	1.14	.8729	1.94	.9738
−2.25	.0122	−1.28	.1003	−0.46	.3228	0.36	.6406	1.16	.8770	1.96	.9750
−2.20	.0139	−1.26	.1038	−0.44	.3300	0.38	.6480	1.18	.8810	1.98	.9761
−2.15	.0158	−1.24	.1075	−0.42	.3373	0.40	.6554	1.20	.8849	2.00	.9772
−2.10	.0179	−1.22	.1112	−0.40	.3446	0.42	.6628	1.22	.8888	2.05	.9798
2.05	.0202	−1.20	.1151	−0.38	.3520	0.44	.6700	1.24	.8925	2.10	.9821
−2.00	.0228	−1.18	.1190	−0.36	.3594	0.46	.6773	1.26	.8962	2.15	.9842
−1.98	.0239	−1.16	.1230	−0.34	.3669	0.48	.6844	1.28	.8997	2.20	.9861
−1.96	.0250	−1.14	.1271	−0.32	.3745	0.50	.6915	1.30	.9032	2.25	.9878
−1.94	.0262	−1.12	.1314	−0.30	.3821	0.52	.6985	1.32	.9066	2.30	.9893
−1.92	.0274	−1.10	.1357	−0.28	.3897	0.54	.7054	1.34	.9099	2.35	.9906
−1.90	.0287	−1.08	.1401	−0.26	.3974	0.56	.7123	1.36	.9131	2.40	.9918
−1.88	.0301	−1.06	.1446	**−0.24**	**.4052**	0.58	.7191	1.38	.9162	2.45	.9929
−1.86	.0314	−1.04	.1492	−0.22	.4129	0.60	.7258	1.40	.9192	2.50	.9938
−1.84	.0329	−1.02	.1539	−0.20	.4207	0.62	.7324	1.42	.9222	2.55	.9946
−1.82	.0344	−1.00	.1587	−0.18	.4286	0.64	.7389	1.44	.9251	2.60	.9953
−1.80	.0359	−0.98	.1635	−0.16	.4365	0.66	.7454	1.46	.9279	2.65	.9960
−1.78	.0375	−0.96	.1685	−0.14	.4443	0.68	.7518	1.48	.9306	2.70	.9965
−1.76	.0392	−0.94	.1736	−0.12	.4523	0.70	.7580	1.50	.9332	2.75	.9970
−1.74	.0409	−0.92	.1788	−0.10	.4602	0.72	.7642	1.52	.9357	2.80	.9974
−1.72	.0427	−0.90	.1841	−0.08	.4681	0.74	.7704	1.54	.9382	2.85	.9978
−1.70	.0446	−0.88	.1894	−0.06	.4761	0.76	.7764	1.56	.9406	2.90	.9981
−1.68	.0465	−0.86	.1949	−0.04	.4841	0.78	.7823	1.58	.9429	2.95	.9984
−1.66	.0485	−0.84	.2005	−0.02	.4920	0.80	.7882	1.60	.9452	3.00	.9986
−1.64	.0505	−0.82	.2061	0.00	.5000	0.82	.7939	1.62	.9474	3.05	.9989
−1.62	.0526	−0.80	.2119	0.02	.5080	0.84	.7996	1.64	.9495		
−1.60	.0548	−0.78	.2177	0.04	.5160						

This table shows the probability (N(d)) of observing a value less than or equal to d. For example, as illustrated, if d is −0.24, then N(d) is .4052.

SPREADSHEET STRATEGIES		

Black-Scholes Option Calculation

	A	B	C	D	E	F	G	H	I	J	K
1											
2		Using a spreadsheet to calculate Black-Scholes option prices									
3											
4	XYZ stock has a price of $65 and an annual return standard deviation of 50%. The riskless										
5	interest rate is 5%. Calculate call and put option prices with a strike of $60 and a 3-month										
6	time to expiration.										
7											
8		Stock =	65		d1 =	0.4952		N(d1) =	0.6898		
9		Strike =	60								
10		Sigma =	0.5		d2 =	0.2452		N(d2) =	0.5968		
11		Time =	0.25								
12		Rate =	0.05								
13											
14				Call = Stock x N(d1) – Strike x exp(– Rate x Time) x N(d2) =							$9.47
15											
16				Put = Strike x exp(– Rate x Time) + Call – Stock				=			$3.72
17											
18	Formula entered in E8 is =(LN(B8/B9)+(B12+0.5*B10^2)*B11)/(B10*SQRT(B11))										
19	Formula entered in E10 is =E8–B10*SQRT(B11)										
20	Formula entered in H8 is =NORMSDIST(E8)										
21	Formula entered in K10 is =NORMSDIST(E10)										
22	Formula entered in K14 is =B8*H8–B9*EXP(–B12*B11)*H10										
23	Formula entered in K16 is =B9*EXP(–B12*B11)+K14–B8										

Tables such as Table 25A.1 are the traditional means of looking up "z" values, but they have been mostly replaced by computers. They are not as accurate because of rounding, and they also have only a limited number of values. The *Spreadsheet Strategies* box shows how to calculate Black–Scholes call option prices using a spreadsheet.

Appendix Review Problems and Self-Test

A.1 Black–Scholes OPM: Part I Calculate the Black–Scholes price for a six-month option given the following:

$S_0 = \$80$
$E = \$70$
$R_f = 10\%$ per year
$d_1 = .82$
$d_2 = .74$

A.2 Black–Scholes OPM: Part II Calculate the Black–Scholes price for a nine-month option given the following:

$S_0 = \$80$
$E = \$70$
$\sigma = .30$ per year
$R_f = 10\%$ per year
$t = 9$ months

Answers to Appendix Self-Test Problems

A.1 $C_0 = 80 \times N(.82) - 70/(1.10)^{.5} \times N(.74)$

From Table 25A.1, the values for $N(.82)$ and $N(.74)$ are .7939 and .7704, respectively. The value of the option is about $12.10. Notice that since the interest rate (and standard deviation) is quoted on an annual basis, we used a t value of .50, representing a half year, in calculating the present value of the exercise price.

A.2 We first calculate d_1 and d_2:

$$d_1 = [\ln(S_0/E) + (R_f + 1/2 \times \sigma^2) \times t]/[\sigma \times \sqrt{t}]$$
$$= [\ln(80/70) + (.10 + 1/2 \times .30^2) \times (.75)]/[.30 \times \sqrt{.75}]$$
$$= .9325$$

$$d_2 = d_1 - \sigma \times \sqrt{t}$$
$$= .9325 - .30 \times \sqrt{.75}$$
$$= .6727$$

From Table 25A.1, $N(d_1)$ appears to be roughly .825, and $N(d_2)$ is about .75. Plugging these in, we determine that the option's value is $17.12. Notice again that we used an annual t value of $9/12 = .75$ in this case.

Appendix Questions and Problems

For Problems A.1 through A.3, round computed values for d_1 and d_2 to the nearest values in Table 25A.1 for determining $N(d_1)$ and $N(d_2)$, respectively.

Basic
(Questions
A.1–A.2)

A.1 Using the OPM Calculate the Black–Scholes option price in each of the cases that follow. The risk-free rate and standard deviation are quoted in annual terms. The last three cases may require some thought.

Stock Price	Exercise Price	Risk-Free Rate	Maturity	Standard Deviation	Call Price
$31	$37.50	07%	3 months	0.21	
40	29	03%	6 months	.15	
89	63	12%	9 months	0.24	
97	99	08%	12 months	.30	
0	35	05%	12 months	0.44	
125	17	04%	Forever	.35	
129	0	03%	6 months	0.21	
121	113	06%	6 months	.00	
50	74	13%	12 months	∞	

A.2 Equity as an Option and the OPM Childs Manufacturing has a discount bank loan that matures in one year and requires the firm to pay $2,950. The current market value of the firm's assets is $3,400. The annual *variance* for the firm's return on assets is 0.29, and the annual risk-free interest rate is 4.5 percent. Based on the Black–Scholes model, what is the market value of the firm's debt and equity?

Intermediate
(Question
A.3)

A.3 Changes in Variance and Equity Value Suppose that, in the previous problem, Childs is considering two mutually exclusive investments. Project A has an NPV of $135, and Project B has an NPV of $215. As a result of taking Project A, the variance of the firm's return on assets will increase to .39. If Project B is taken, the variance will fall to .22.

a.   What is the value of the firm's debt and equity if Project A is undertaken? If Project B is undertaken?

b.   Which project would the shareholders prefer? Can you reconcile your answer with the NPV rule?

c.   Suppose the shareholders and bondholders are in fact the same group of investors. Would this affect the answer to part (b)?

d.   What does this problem suggest to you about shareholder incentives?

CHAPTER 26

BEHAVIOURAL FINANCE: IMPLICATIONS FOR FINANCIAL MANAGEMENT

The NASDAQ stock market was raging in the late 1990s, gaining about 23 percent in 1996, 14 percent in 1997, 35 percent in 1998, and 62 percent in 1999. Of course, that spectacular run came to a jarring halt, and the NASDAQ lost about 40 percent in 2000, followed by another 30 percent in 2001. The ISDEX, an index of Internet-related stocks, rose from 100 in January 1996 to 1100 in February 2000, a gain of about 1000 percent! It then fell like a rock to 600 by May 2000.

The performance of the NASDAQ over this period, and particularly the rise and fall of Internet stocks, has been described by many as one of the greatest market "bubbles" in history. The argument is that prices were inflated to economically ridiculous levels before investors came to their senses, which then caused the bubble to pop and prices to plunge. Debate over whether the stock market of the late 1990s really was a bubble has generated much controversy.

The Canadian based network company, Nortel, was damaged when the Internet bubble burst. The S&P/TSX went up 30 percent in 1999 largely on the strength of Nortel, which rose to become around 40% of the index market capitalization, which was about $1 trillion. Questioning the value of this stock, a number of fund managers benchmarked their performance against a capped S&P/TSX index in which Nortel was limited to 10 percent. This judgment was confirmed when Nortel later went bankrupt in 2009.

In this chapter, we introduce the subject of behavioural finance, which deals with questions such as how bubbles can come to exist. Some of the issues we discuss are quite controversial and unsettled. We will describe competing ideas, present some evidence on both sides, and examine the implications for financial managers.

Learning Objectives ▶

After studying this chapter, you should understand:

LO1 How behaviours such as overconfidence, overoptimism, and confirmation bias can affect decision-making.

LO2 How framing effects can result in inconsistent and/or incorrect decisions.

LO3 How the use of heuristics can lead to suboptimal financial decisions.

LO4 The shortcomings and limitations to market efficiency from the behavioural finance view.

Be honest: Do you think of yourself as a better than average driver? If you do, you are not alone. About 80 percent of the people who are asked this question will say yes. Evidently, we tend to overestimate our abilities behind the wheel. Is the same true when it comes to making financial management decisions?

It will probably not surprise you when we say that human beings sometimes make errors in judgment. How these errors, and other aspects of human behaviour, affect financial managers falls under the general heading of "behavioural finance." In this chapter, our goal is to acquaint you with some common types of mistakes and their financial implications. As you will see, researchers have identified a wide variety of potentially damaging behaviours. By learning to recognize situations in which mistakes are common, you will become a better decision-maker, both in the context of financial management and elsewhere.

26.1 | Introduction to Behavioural Finance

Sooner or later, you are going to make a financial decision that winds up costing you (and possibly your employer and/or stockholders) a lot of money. Why is this going to happen? You already know the answer. Sometimes, you make sound decisions, but you get unlucky in the sense that something happens that you could not have reasonably anticipated. Other times (however painful to admit), you just make a bad decision, one that could have (and should have) been avoided. The beginning of business wisdom is to recognize the circumstances that lead to poor decisions and thereby cut down on the damage done by financial blunders.

As we have previously noted, the area of research known as **behavioural finance** attempts to understand and explain how reasoning errors influence financial decisions. Much of the research done in the behavioural finance area stems from work in cognitive psychology, which is the study of how people, including financial managers, think, reason, and make decisions. Errors in reasoning are often called cognitive errors. In the next several subsections, we will review three main categories of such errors: (1) biases, (2) framing effects, and (3) heuristics.[1]

behavioural finance
The area of finance dealing with the implications of reasoning errors on financial decisions.

26.2 | Biases

If your decisions exhibit systematic biases, then you will make systematic errors in judgment. The type of error depends on the type of bias. In this section, we discuss three particularly relevant biases: (1) overconfidence, (2) overoptimism, and (3) confirmation bias.

Overconfidence

Serious errors in judgment occur in the business world due to **overconfidence**. We are all overconfident about our abilities in at least some areas (recall our question about driving ability at the beginning of the chapter). Here is another example that we see a lot: Ask yourself what grade you will receive in this course (in spite of the arbitrary and capricious nature of the professor). In our experience, almost everyone will either say "A" or, at worst, "B." Sadly, when this happens, we are always confident (but not overconfident) that at least some of our students are going to be disappointed.

overconfidence
The belief that your abilities are better than they really are.

In general, you are overconfident when you overestimate your ability to make the correct choice or decision. For example, most business decisions require judgments about the unknown future. The belief that you can forecast the future with precision is a common form of overconfidence.

Another good example of overconfidence comes from studies of stock investors. Researchers have examined large numbers of actual brokerage accounts to see how investors fare when they choose stocks. Overconfidence by investors would cause them to overestimate their ability to pick the best stocks, leading to excessive trading. The evidence supports this view. First, investors hurt themselves by trading. The accounts that have the most trading significantly underperform the accounts with the least trading, primarily because of the costs associated with trades.

A second finding is equally interesting. Accounts registered to men underperform those registered to women. The reason is that men trade more on average. This extra trading is consistent with evidence from psychology that men have greater degrees of overconfidence than women.

Further, education does not necessarily control overconfidence. According to a Canadian study, more educated people exhibit greater overconfidence than do people with less education.[2]

Overoptimism

Overoptimism leads to overestimating the likelihood of a good outcome and underestimating the likelihood of a bad outcome. Overoptimism and overconfidence are related, but they are not the same thing. An overconfident individual could (overconfidently) forecast a bad outcome, for example.

overoptimism
Taking an overly optimistic view of potential outcomes.

Optimism is usually thought of as a good thing. Optimistic people have "upbeat personalities" and "sunny dispositions." However, excessive optimism leads to bad decisions. In a capital

---

[1] A highly readable book on behavioural finance is: L.F. Ackert and R. Deaves, *Behavioral Finance: Psychology, Decision-Making, and Markets*, South-Western Cengage Learning, 2010.

[2] G. Bhandari and R. Deaves, "The Demographics of Overconfidence," *Journal of Behavioral Finance* 7 (1), 2006, pages 5–11.

budgeting context, overly optimistic analysts will consistently overestimate cash flows and under-estimate the probability of failure. Doing so leads to upward-biased estimates of project NPVs, a common occurrence in the business world.

Optimism and its opposite, depression, are linked to seasonal cycles measured by the number of hours of daylight. Studies suggest that stock traders around the globe are more risk averse during the darker months.[3]

Confirmation Bias

When you are evaluating a decision, you collect information and opinions. A common bias in this regard is to focus more on information that agrees with your opinion and to downplay or ignore information that doesn't agree with or support your position. This phenomenon is known as **confirmation bias**, and people who suffer from it tend to spend too much time trying to prove themselves correct rather than searching for information that might prove them wrong.

Here is a classic example from psychology. Below are four cards. Notice that the cards are labelled *a*, *b*, 2, and 3. You are asked to evaluate the following statement: "Any card with a vowel on one side has an even number on the other." You are asked which of the four cards has to be turned over to decide if the statement is true or false. It costs $100 to turn over a card, so you want to be economical as possible. What do you do?

> **confirmation bias**
> Searching for (and giving more weight to) information and opinion that confirms what you believe rather than information and opinion to the contrary.

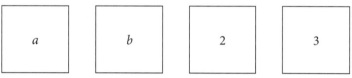

You would probably begin by turning over the card with an *a* on it, which is correct. If we find an odd number, then we are done because the statement is not correct.

Suppose we find an even number. What next? Most people will turn over the card with a 2. Is that the right choice? If we find a vowel, then we confirm the statement, but if we find a consonant, we don't learn anything. In other words, this card can't prove that the statement is wrong; it can only confirm it, so selecting this card is an example of confirmation bias.

Continuing, there is no point in turning over the card labelled "*b*" because the statement doesn't say anything about consonants, which leaves us with the last card. Do we have to turn it over? The answer is yes because it might have a vowel on the other side, which would disprove the statement, but most people will chose the 2 card over the 3 card.

Concept Questions

1. What is overconfidence? How is it likely to be costly?
2. What is overoptimism? How is it likely to be costly?
3. What is confirmation bias? How is it likely to be costly?

26.3 | Framing Effects

You are susceptible to framing effects if your decisions depend on how a problem or question is framed. Consider the following example: A disaster has occurred, 600 people are at risk, and you are in charge. You must choose between the two following rescue operations:

SCENARIO 1
Option A: Exactly 200 people will be saved.
Option B: There is a 1/3 chance that all 600 people will be saved and a 2/3 chance that no people will be saved.

---

[3] M.J. Kamstra, L.A. Kramer and M.D. Levi, "Winter Blues: Seasonal Affective Disorder (SAD) and Stock Market Returns," *American Economic Review*, 93 (1), 324–343, March 2003.

Which would you choose? There is no necessarily right answer, but most people will choose Option A. Now suppose your choices are as follows:

> SCENARIO 2
> Option C: Exactly 400 people will die.
> Option D: There is a 1/3 chance that nobody will die and a 2/3 chance that all 600 will die.

Now which do you pick? Again, there is no right answer, but most people will choose option D.

Although most people will choose options A and D in our hypothetical scenarios, you probably see that doing so is inconsistent because options A and C are identical, as are options B and D. Why do people make inconsistent choices? It's because the options are framed differently. The first scenario is positive because it emphasizes the number that will be saved. The second is negative because it focuses on losses, and people react differently to positive versus negative framing, which is a form of **frame dependence**.

frame dependence
The tendency of individuals to make different (and potentially inconsistent) decisions depending on how a question or problem is framed.

Loss Aversion

Here is another example that illustrates a particular type of frame dependence:

> SCENARIO 1: Suppose we give you $1,000. You have the following choices:
> Option A: You can receive another $500 for sure.
> Option B: You can flip a fair coin. If the coin flip comes up heads, you gain another $1,000, but if it comes up tails, you gain nothing.
>
> SCENARIO 2: Suppose we give you $2,000. You have the following choices:
> Option C: You can lose $500 for sure.
> Option D: You can flip a fair coin. If the coin flip comes up heads, you lose $1,000, but if it comes up tails, you lose nothing.

What were your answers? Did you choose option A in the first scenario and option D in the second? If that's what you did, you are guilty of just focusing on gains and losses, and not paying attention to what really matters, namely, the impact on your wealth. However, you are not alone. About 85 percent of the people who are presented with the first scenario choose option A, and about 70 percent of the people who are presented with the second scenario choose option D.

If you look closely at the two scenarios, you will see that they are actually identical. You end up with $1,500 for sure if you pick option A or C, or else you end up with a 50-50 chance of either $1,000 or $2,000 if you pick option B or D. So, you should pick the same option in both scenarios. Which option you prefer is up to you, but the point is that you should never pick option A in our first scenario and option D in our second one.

This example illustrates an important aspect of financial decision-making. Focusing on gains and losses instead of overall wealth is an example of narrow framing, and it leads to a phenomenon known as loss aversion. In fact, the reason that most people avoid option C in scenario 2 in our example is that it is expressed as a sure loss of $500. In general, researchers have found that individuals are reluctant to realize losses and will, for example, gamble at unfavorable odds to avoid doing so.

Loss aversion is also known as get-evenitis or the break-even effect because it frequently shows up as individuals and companies hang on to bad investments and projects (and perhaps even invest more) hoping that something will happen that will allow them to break even and thereby escape without a loss. For example, we discussed the irrelevance of sunk costs in the context of capital budgeting, and the idea of a sunk cost seems clear. Nonetheless, we constantly see companies (and individuals) throw good money after bad rather than just recognize a loss in the face of sunk costs.

How destructive is get-evenitis? Perhaps the most famous case occurred in 1995, when 28-year-old Nicholas Leeson caused the collapse of his employer, the 233-year-old Barings Bank. At the end of 1992, Mr. Leeson had lost about £2 million, which he hid in a secret account. By the end of 1993, his losses were about £23 million, and they mushroomed to £208 million at the end of 1994 (at the time, this was $512 million).

Instead of admitting to these losses, Mr. Leeson gambled more of the bank's money in an attempt to "double-up and catch-up." On February 23, 1995, Mr. Leeson's losses were about

£827 million ($1.3 billion), and his trading irregularities were uncovered. Although he attempted to flee from prosecution, he was caught, arrested, tried, convicted, and imprisoned. Also, his wife divorced him.

Do you suffer from get-evenitis? Maybe so. Consider the following scenario: You just lost $78 somehow. You can just live with the loss, or you can make a bet. If you make the bet, there is an 80 percent chance that your loss will grow to $100 (from $78) and a 20 percent chance that your loss will be nothing. Do you take the loss or take the bet? We bet you choose the bet. If you do, you have get-evenitis because the bet is a bad one. Instead of a sure loss of $78, your expected loss from the bet is $.80 \times \$100 + .20 \times \$0 = \$80$.

In corporate finance, loss aversion can be quite damaging. We already mentioned the pursuit of sunk costs. We also might see managers bypassing positive NPV projects because they have the possibility of large losses (perhaps with low probability). Another phenomenon that we see is debt avoidance. As we discuss in our coverage of capital structure, debt financing generates valuable tax shields for profitable companies. Even so, there are hundreds of profitable companies listed on major stock exchanges that completely (or almost completely) avoid debt financing. Because debt financing increases the likelihood of losses and even bankruptcy, this potentially costly behaviour could be due to loss aversion.

House Money

Las Vegas casinos know all about a concept called playing with house money. The casinos have found that gamblers are far more likely to take big risks with money that they have won from the casino (i.e., house money). Also casinos have found that gamblers are not as upset about losing house money as they are about losing the money they brought with them to gamble.

It may seem natural for you to feel that some money is precious because you earned it through hard work, sweat, and sacrifice, while other money is less precious because it came to you as a windfall. But these feelings are plainly irrational because any dollar you have buys the same amount of goods and services no matter how you obtained that dollar.

Let's consider another common situation to illustrate several of the ideas we have explored thus far. Consider the following two investments:

Investment 1: You bought 100 shares in Moore Enterprises for $35 per share. The shares immediately fell to $20 each.

Investment 2: At the same time, you bought 100 shares in Miller Co. for $5 per share. The shares immediately jumped to $20 each.

How would you feel about your investments?

You would probably feel pretty good about your Miller investment and be unhappy with your Moore investment. Here are some other things that might occur:

1. You might tell yourself that your Miller investment was a great idea on your part; you're a stock-picking genius. The drop in value on the Moore shares wasn't your fault—it was just bad luck. This is a form of *confirmation bias*, and it also illustrates *self-attribution bias*, which is taking credit for good outcomes that occur for reasons beyond your control, while attributing bad outcomes to bad luck or misfortune.

2. You might be unhappy that your big winner was essentially nullified by your loser, but notice in our example that your overall wealth did not change. Suppose instead that shares in both companies didn't change in price at all, so that your overall wealth was unchanged. Would you feel the same way?

3. You might be inclined to sell your Miller stock to "realize" the gain, but hold on to your Moore stock in hopes of avoiding the loss (which is, of course, loss aversion). The tendency to sell winners and hold losers is known as the *disposition effect*. Plainly, the rational thing to do is to decide if the stocks are attractive investments at their new prices and react accordingly.

Suppose you decide to keep both stocks a little longer. Once you do, both decline to $15. You might now feel very differently about the decline depending on which stock you looked at. With Moore, the decline makes a bad situation even worse. Now you are down $20 per share on your investment. On the other hand, with Miller you only "give back" some of your "paper profit." You are still way ahead. This kind of thinking is playing with house money. Whether you lose from your original investment or from your investment gains is irrelevant.

Our Moore and Miller example illustrates what can happen when you become emotionally invested in decisions such as stock purchases. When you add a new stock to your portfolio, it is human nature for you to associate the stock with its purchase price. As the price of the stock changes through time, you will have unrealized gains or losses when you compare the current price to the purchase price. Through time, you will mentally account for these gains and losses, and how you feel about the investment depends on whether you are ahead or behind. This behaviour is known as *mental accounting*.

When you engage in mental accounting, you unknowingly have a personal relationship with each of your stocks. As a result, it becomes harder to sell one of them. It is as if you have to "break up" with this stock or "fire" it from your portfolio. As with personal relationships, these stock relationships can be complicated and, believe it or not, make selling stocks difficult at times. What can you do about mental accounting? Legendary investor Warren Buffet offers the following advice: "The stock doesn't know you own it. You have feelings about it, but it has no feelings about you. The stock doesn't know what you paid. People shouldn't get emotionally involved with their stocks."

Loss aversion, mental accounting, and the house money effect are important examples of how narrow framing leads to poor decisions. Other, related types of judgment errors have been documented. Here are a few examples:

Myopic loss aversion: This behaviour is the tendency to focus on avoiding short term losses, even at the expense of long-term gains. For example, you might fail to invest in stocks for long-term retirement purposes because you have a fear of loss in the near term.

Regret aversion: This aversion is the tendency to avoid making a decision because you fear that, in hindsight, the decision would have been less than optimal. Regret aversion relates to myopic loss aversion.

Endowment effect: This effect is the tendency to consider something that you own to be worth more than it would be if you did not own it. Because of the endowment effect, people sometimes demand more money to give up something than they would be willing to pay to acquire it.

Money illusion: If you suffer from money illusion, you are confused between real buying power and nominal buying power (i.e., you do not account for the effects of inflation).

Concept Questions

1. What is frame dependence? How is it likely to be costly?
2. What is loss aversion? How is it likely to be costly?
3. What is the house money effect? Why is it irrational?

26.4 | Heuristics

heuristics
Shortcuts or rules of thumb used to make decisions.

Financial managers (and managers in general) often rely on rules of thumb, or **heuristics**, in making decisions. For example, a manager might decide that any project with a payback period less than two years is acceptable and therefore not bother with additional analysis. As a practical matter, this mental shortcut might be just fine for most circumstances, but we know that sooner or later, it will lead to the acceptance of a negative NPV project.

The Affect Heuristic

affect heuristic
The reliance on instinct instead of analysis in making decisions.

We frequently hear business and political leaders talk about following their gut instinct. In essence, such people are making decisions based on whether the chosen outcome or path feels "right" emotionally. Psychologists use the term affect (as in affection) to refer to emotional feelings, and the reliance on gut instinct is called the **affect heuristic**.

Reliance on instinct is closely related to reliance on intuition and/or experience. Both intuition and experience are important and, when used properly, help decision-makers identify potential risks and rewards. However, instinct, intuition, and experience should be viewed as complements to formal analysis, not substitutes. Overreliance on emotions in making decisions will almost surely lead (at least on occasion) to costly outcomes that could have been avoided with careful, structured thinking. An obvious example would be making capital budgeting decisions based on instinct rather than on market research and discounted cash flow analysis.

The Representativeness Heuristic

People often assume that a particular person, object, or outcome is broadly representative of a larger class. For example, suppose an employer hired a graduate of your high-quality educational institution and, in fact, is quite pleased with that person. The employer might be inclined to look to your school again for future employees because the students are so good. Of course, in doing so, the employer is assuming that the recent hire is representative of all the students, which is an example of the **representativeness heuristic**. A little more generally, the representativeness heuristic is the reliance on stereotypes, analogies, or limited samples to form opinions about an entire class.

representativeness heuristic
The reliance on stereotypes, analogies, or limited samples to form opinions about an entire class.

Representativeness and Randomness

Another implication of the representativeness heuristic has to do with perceiving patterns or causes where none exist. For example, basketball fans generally believe that success breeds success. Suppose we look at the recent performance of two basketball players named Bargnani and DeRozan. Both of these players make half of their shots. But, Bargnani has just made two shots in a row, while DeRozan has just missed two in a row. Researchers have found that if they ask 100 basketball fans which player has the better chance of making the next shot, 91 of them will say Bargnani, because he has a "hot hand." Further, 84 of these fans believe that it is important for teammates to pass the ball to Bargnani after he has made two or three shots in a row.

But, and the sports fans among you will have a hard time with this, researchers have found that the hot hand is an illusion. That is, players really do not deviate much from their long-run shooting averages—although fans, players, announcers, and coaches think they do. Cognitive psychologists actually studied the shooting percentage of one professional basketball team for a season. Here is what they found:

Shooting Percentages and the History of Previous Attempts

Shooting Percentage on Next Shot	History of Previous Attempts
46%	Has made 3 in a row
50%	Has made 2 in a row
51%	Has made 1 in a row
52%	First short of the game
54%	Has missed 1 in a row
53%	Has missed 2 in a row
56%	Has missed 3 in a row

Detailed analysis of shooting data failed to show that players make or miss shots more or less frequently than what would be expected by chance. That is, statistically speaking, all the shooting percentages listed here are the same.

From the shooting percentages, it may appear that teams will try harder to stop a shooter who has made the last two or three shots. To take this into account, researchers also studied free-throw percentages. Researchers told fans that a certain player was a 70 percent free-throw shooter and was shooting two foul shots. They asked fans to predict what would happen on the second shot if the player

1. Made the first free throw.
2. Missed the first free throw.

Fans thought that this 70 percent free-throw shooter would make 74 percent of the second free throws after making the first free throw but would only make 66 percent of the second free throws after missing the first free throw. Researchers studied free-throw data from a professional basketball team over two seasons. They found that the result of the first free throw does not matter when it comes to making or missing the second free throw. On average, the shooting percentage on the second free throw was 75 percent when the player made the first free throw. On average, the shooting percentage on the second free throw was also 75 percent when the player missed the first free throw.

It is true that basketball players shoot in streaks. But these streaks are within the bounds of long-run shooting percentages. So, it is an illusion that players are either "hot" or "cold." If you are a believer in the hot hand, however, you are likely to reject these facts because you "know better" from watching your favourite teams over the years. If you do, you are being fooled by randomness.

The *clustering illusion* is our human belief that random events that occur in clusters are not really random. For example, it strikes most people as very unusual if heads comes up four times in a row during a series of coin flips. However, if a fair coin is flipped 20 times, there is about a 50 percent chance of getting four heads in a row. Ask yourself, if you flip four heads in a row, do you think you have a "hot hand" at coin flipping?

The Gambler's Fallacy

People commit the gambler's fallacy when they assume that a departure from what occurs on average, or in the long run, will be corrected in the short run. Interestingly, some people suffer from both the hot-hand illusion (which predicts continuation in the short run) and the gambler's fallacy (which predicts reversal in the short run)! The idea is that because an event has not happened recently, it has become overdue and is more likely to occur. People sometimes refer (wrongly) to the law of averages in such cases.

Roulette is a random gambling game where gamblers can make various bets on the spin of the wheel. There are 38 numbers on a North American roulette table, 2 green (or white) ones, 18 red ones, and 18 black ones. One possible bet is to bet whether the spin will result in a red number or in a black number. Suppose a red number has appeared five times in a row. Gamblers will often become (over) confident that the next spin will be black, when the true chance remains at about 50 percent (of course, it is exactly 18 in 38).

The misconception arises from the human intuition that the overall odds of the wheel must be reflected in a small number of spins. That is, gamblers often become convinced that the wheel is "due" to hit a black number after a series of red numbers. Gamblers do know that the odds of a black number appearing are always unchanged: 18 in 38. But, gamblers cannot help but feel that after a long series of red numbers, a black one must appear to restore the balance between red and black numbers over time.

Of course, there are many other related errors and biases due to heuristics. Here is a partial list:

Law of small numbers: If you believe in the law of small numbers, you believe that a small sample of outcomes always resembles the long-run distribution of outcomes. If your investment guru has been right five out of seven times recently, you might believe that his long-run average of being correct is also five out of seven. The law of small numbers is related to recency bias (see our next item) and to the gambler's fallacy.

Recency bias: Humans tend to give recent events more importance than less recent events. For example, during the great bull market that occurred from 1995 to 1999, many investors thought the market would continue its big gains for a long time—forgetting that bear markets also occur (which happened from 2000 to 2002). Recency bias is related to the law of small numbers.

Anchoring and adjustment: People have an anchoring bias when they are unable to account for new information in a correct way. That is, they become "anchored" to a previous price or other value. If you have an anchoring bias, you will tend to be overly conservative in the face of fresh news.

Aversion to ambiguity: This bias results when people shy away from the unknown. For example, consider the following choice. You get $1,000 for sure, or you can draw a ball out of a big bin containing 100 balls. If the ball is blue, you win $2,000. If it is red, you win nothing. When people are told that there are 50 blue balls and 50 red balls in the bin, about 40 percent choose to draw a ball. When they are told nothing about how many balls in the bin are blue, most choose to take the $1,000—ignoring the possibility that the odds might really be in their favour. That is, there could be more than 50 blue balls in the bin.

False consensus: This is the tendency to think that other people are thinking the same thing you are thinking (with no real evidence). False consensus relates to overconfidence and confirmation bias.

Availability bias: You suffer from availability bias when you put too much weight on information that is easily available and place too little weight on information that is hard to obtain. Your financial decisions will suffer if you only consider information that is easy to obtain.

Concept Questions

1. What is the affect heuristic? How is it likely to be costly?
2. What is the representativeness heuristic? How is it likely to be costly?
3. What is the gambler's fallacy?

26.5 | Behavioural Finance and Market Efficiency

Our discussion thus far has focused on how cognitive errors by individuals can lead to poor business decisions. It seems both clear and noncontroversial that such errors are both real and financially important. We now venture into a much less clear area—the implications of behavioural finance for stock prices.

In Chapter 12, we introduced the notion of market efficiency. The key idea is that in an efficient market, prices fully reflect available information. Put differently, prices are correct in the sense that a stock purchase or sale is a zero NPV investment. In a well-organized, liquid market such as the NYSE or TSX, the argument is that competition among profit-motivated, economically rational traders ensures that prices can never drift far from their zero-NPV level.

In this chapter, we have already seen a few examples of how cognitive errors, such as overconfidence, can lead to damaging decisions in the context of stock ownership. If many traders behave in ways that are economically irrational, then is there still reason to think that markets are efficient?

First off, it is important to realize that the efficient markets hypothesis does not require every investor to be rational. Instead, all that is required for a market to be efficient is at least some smart and well-financed investors. These investors are prepared to buy and sell to take advantage of any mispricing in the marketplace. This activity is what keeps markets efficient. It is sometimes said that market efficiency doesn't require that *everyone* be rational, just that *someone* be.

Limits to Arbitrage

Investors who buy and sell to exploit mispricings are engaging in a form of *arbitrage* and are known as *arbitrageurs* (or just *arbs* for short). Sometimes, however, a problem arises in this context. The term limits to arbitrage refers to the notion that, under certain circumstances, it may not be possible for rational, well-capitalized traders to correct a mispricing, at least not quickly. The reason is that strategies designed to eliminate mispricings are often risky, costly, or somehow restricted. Three important such problems are:

1. **Firm-specific risk:** This issue is the most obvious risk facing a would-be arbitrageur. Suppose that you believe that the observed price on Research in Motion (RIM) stock is too low, so you purchase many, many shares. Then, there is some unanticipated negative news that drives the price of RIM stock even lower. Of course, you could try to hedge some of the firm-specific risk, but any hedge you create is likely to be either imperfect and/or costly.

noise trader
A trader whose trades are not based on information or meaningful financial analysis.

2. **Noise trader risk:** A **noise trader** is someone whose trades are not based on information or financially meaningful analysis. Noise traders could, in principle, act together to worsen a mispricing in the short run. Noise trader risk is important because the worsening of a mispricing could force the arbitrageur to liquidate early and sustain steep losses. As Keynes once famously observed, "Markets can remain irrational longer than you can remain solvent."[4]

---

[4] This remark is generally attributed to Keynes, but whether he actually said it is not known.

sentiment-based risk
A source of risk to investors above and beyond firm specific risk and overall market risk.

Noise trader risk is also called **sentiment-based risk**, meaning the risk that an asset's price is being influenced by sentiment (or irrational belief) rather than fact-based financial analysis. If sentiment-based risk exists, then it is another source of risk beyond the systematic and unsystematic risks we discussed in an earlier chapter.

3. **Implementation costs:** All trades cost money. In some cases, the cost of correcting a mispricing may exceed the potential gains. For example, suppose you believe a small, thinly-traded stock is significantly undervalued. You want to buy a large quantity. The problem is that as soon as you try to place a huge order, the price would jump because the stock isn't heavily traded.

When these or other risks and costs are present, a mispricing may persist because arbitrage is too risky or too costly. Collectively, these risks and costs create barriers or limits to arbitrage. How important these limits are is difficult to say, but we do know that mispricings occur, at least on occasion. To illustrate, we next consider two well-known examples.

THE 3COM/PALM MISPRICING   On March 2, 2000, 3Com, a profitable provider of computer networking products and services, sold 5 percent of its Palm subsidiary to the public via an initial public offering (IPO). 3Com planned to distribute the remaining Palm shares to 3Com shareholders at a later date.[5] Under the plan, if you owned one share of 3Com, you would receive 1.5 shares of Palm. So, after 3Com sold part of Palm via the IPO, investors could buy Palm shares directly, or they could buy them indirectly by purchasing shares of 3Com.

What makes this case interesting is what happened in the days that followed the Palm IPO. If you owned one 3Com share, you would be entitled, eventually, to 1.5 shares of Palm. Therefore, each 3Com share should be worth at least 1.5 times the value of each Palm share. We say at least because the other parts of 3Com were profitable. As a result, each 3Com share should have been worth much more than 1.5 times the value of one Palm share. But, as you might guess, things did not work out this way.

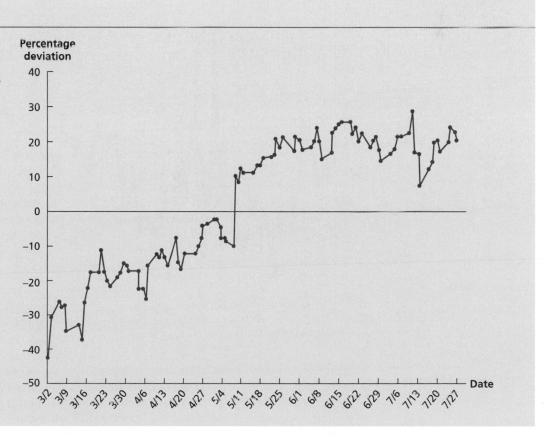

FIGURE 26.1

The Percentage Difference between 1 Share of 3Com and 1.5 Shares of Palm, March 2, 2000, to July 27, 2000

---

[5]In other words, as we discuss in our chapter on mergers and acquisitions, 3Com did an equity carve-out and planned to subsequently spin off the remaining shares.

The day before the Palm IPO, shares in 3Com sold for $104.13. After the first day of trading, Palm closed at $95.06 per share. Multiplying $95.06 by 1.5 results in $142.59, which is the minimum value one would expect to pay for 3Com. But the day Palm closed at $95.06, 3Com shares closed at $81.81, more than $60 lower than the price implied by Palm. It gets stranger.

A 3Com price of $81.81 when Palm is selling for $95.06 implies that the market values the rest of 3Com's businesses (per share) at: $81.81 − 142.59 = −$60.78. Given the number of 3Com shares outstanding at the time, this means the market placed a negative value of about −$22 billion for the rest of 3Com's businesses. Of course, a stock price cannot be negative. This means, then, that the price of Palm relative to 3Com was much too high, and investors should have bought and sold such that the negative value was instantly eliminated.

What happened? As you can see in Figure 26.1, the market valued 3Com and Palm shares in such a way that the non-Palm part of 3Com had a negative value for about two months, from March 2, 2000, until May 8, 2000. Even then, it took approval by the IRS for 3Com to proceed with the planned distribution of Palm shares before the non-Palm part of 3Com once again had a positive value.

THE ROYAL DUTCH/SHELL PRICE RATIO   Another fairly well known example of an apparent mispricing involves two large oil companies. In 1907, Royal Dutch of the Netherlands and Shell of the UK agreed to merge their business enterprises and split operating profits on a 60–40 basis. So, whenever the stock prices of Royal Dutch and Shell are not in a 60–40 ratio, there is a potential opportunity to make an arbitrage profit.

FIGURE 26.2

Royal Dutch and Shell 60–40 Price Ratio Deviations, 1962 to 2005

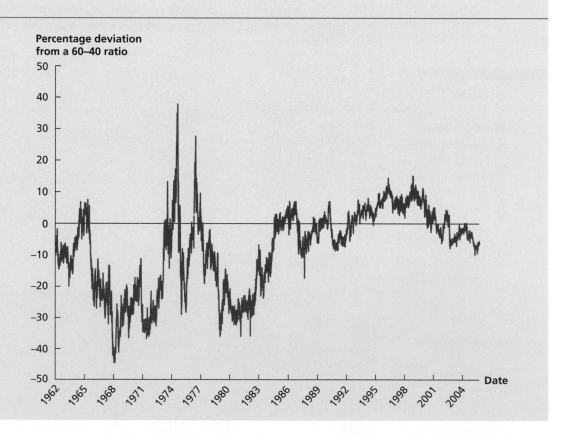

Figure 26.2 contains a plot of the daily deviations from the 60–40 ratio of the Royal Dutch price to the Shell price. If the prices of Royal Dutch and Shell are in a 60–40 ratio, there is a zero percentage deviation. If the price of Royal Dutch is too high compared to the Shell price, there is a positive deviation. If the price of Royal Dutch is too low compared to the price of Shell, there is a negative deviation. As you can see in Figure 26.2, there have been large and persistent deviations from the 60–40 ratio. In fact, the ratio is seldom at 60–40 for most of the time from 1962 through mid-2005 (when the companies merged).

Bubbles and Crashes

As the famous American band Blue Öyster Cult penned in its popular song 'Godzilla,' "History shows again and again, how nature points up the folly of men."[6] Nowhere is this statement seemingly more appropriate in finance than in a discussion of bubbles and crashes.

A **bubble** occurs when market prices soar far in excess of what normal and rational analysis would suggest. Investment bubbles eventually pop because they are not based on fundamental values. When a bubble does pop, investors find themselves holding assets with plummeting values.

A **crash** is a significant and sudden drop in market-wide values. Crashes are generally associated with a bubble. Typically, a bubble lasts much longer than a crash. A bubble can form over weeks, months, or even years. Crashes, on the other hand, are sudden, generally lasting less than a week. However, the disastrous financial aftermath of a crash can last for years.

THE CRASH OF 1929   During the Roaring Twenties, the stock market was supposed to be the place where everyone could get rich. The market was widely believed to be a no-risk situation. Many people invested their life savings without learning about the potential pitfalls of investing. At the time, investors could purchase stocks by putting up 10 percent of the purchase price and borrowing the remainder from a broker. This level of leverage was one factor that led to the sudden market downdraft in October 1929.

bubble
A situation where observed prices soar far higher than fundamentals and rational analysis would suggest.

crash
A situation where market prices collapse significantly and suddenly.

FIGURE 26.3

Dow Jones Industrial Average, October 21, 1929, to October 31, 1929

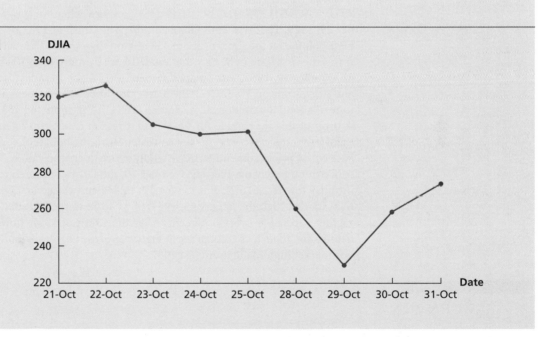

As you can see in Figure 26.3, on Friday, October 25, the Dow Jones Industrial Average closed up about a point, at 301.22. On Monday, October 28, it closed at 260.64, down 13.5 percent. On Tuesday, October 29, the Dow closed at 230.07, with an intraday low of 212.33, which was about 30 percent lower than the closing level on the previous Friday. On this day, known as "Black Tuesday," NYSE volume of 16.4 million shares was more than four times normal levels.

The crash of 1929 also had a huge impact on prices on the Montreal Exchange, Canada's major stock exchange at that time. Figure 26.4 shows the index value of a portfolio with equal weights in Canadian common stocks from 1922 to 1940. The roller coaster ride of prices was similar to the experience in the U.S.

---

[6]Lyrics from "Godzilla," by Donald "Buck Dharma" Roeser (as performed by Blue Öyster Cult).

FIGURE 26.4

Equally Weighted Bond and Stock Index 1922–1940*

Source: L. Kryzanowski and G.S. Roberts, "Capital Forbearance: Depression-era Experience of Canadian Life Insurance Companies," *Canadian Journal of Administrative Sciences,* March 1998, pages 1–16.

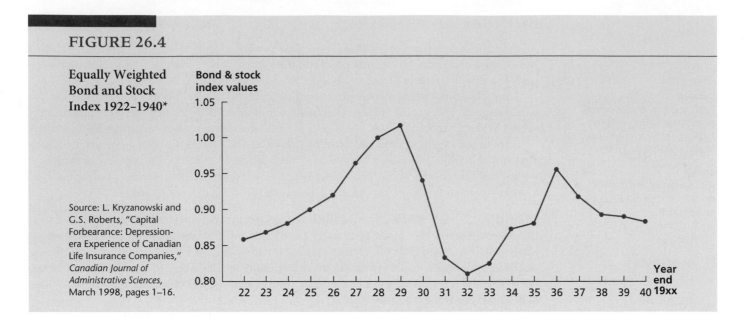

THE CRASH OF OCTOBER 1987   Once, when we spoke of the Crash, we meant October 29, 1929. That was until October 1987. The Crash of 1987 began on Friday, October 16. On huge volume (at the time) of about 338 million shares, the DJIA fell 108 points to close at 2,246.73. It was the first time in history that the DJIA fell by more than 100 points in one day.

October 19, 1987, now wears the mantle of "Black Monday," and this day was indeed a dark and stormy one on Wall Street; the market lost about 22.6 percent of its value on a new record volume of about 600 million shares traded. The DJIA plummeted 508.32 points to close at 1,738.74. A drop of this magnitude for no apparent reason is not consistent with market efficiency. One theory sees the crash as evidence consistent with the bubble theory of speculative markets. That is, security prices sometimes move wildly above their true values.

During the day on Tuesday, October 20, the DJIA continued to plunge in value, reaching an intraday low of 1,616.21. But the market rallied and closed at 1,841.01, up 102 points. From the then market high on August 25, 1987, of 2,746.65 to the intraday low on October 20, 1987, the market had fallen over 40 percent. After the Crash of 1987, however, there was no protracted depression. In fact, as you can see in Figure 26.5, the DJIA took only two years to surpass its previous market high made in August 1987.

FIGURE 26.5

Dow Jones Industrial Average, October 1986 to October 1990

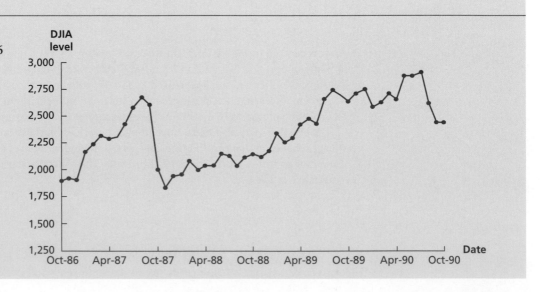

What happened? It's not exactly ancient history, but, here again, debate rages. One faction says that irrational investors had bid up stock prices to ridiculous levels until Black Monday, when the bubble burst, leading to panic selling as investors dumped their stocks. The other faction says that before Black Monday, markets were volatile, volume was heavy, and some ominous signs about the economy were filtering in. From the close on October 13 to the close on October 16, 1987, for example, the market fell by over 10 percent, the largest three-day drop since May 1940 (when German troops broke through French lines near the start of World War II). To top it all off, market values had risen sharply because of a dramatic increase in takeover activity, but the U.S. Congress was in session and was actively considering antitakeover legislation.

Another factor is that beginning a few years before the Crash of 1987, large investors had developed techniques known as program trading designed for very rapid selling of enormous quantities of shares of stock following a market decline. These techniques were still largely untested because the market had been strong for years. However, following the huge sell-off on October 16, 1987, sell orders came pouring in on Monday at a pace never before seen. In fact, these program trades were (and are) blamed by some for much of what happened.

One of the few things we know for certain about the Crash of 1987 is that the stock exchanges suffered a meltdown. The NYSE simply could not handle the volume. Posting of prices was delayed by hours, so investors had no idea what their positions were worth. The specialists couldn't handle the flow of orders, and some specialists actually began selling. NASDAQ went off-line when it became impossible to get through to market makers.

On the two days following the crash, prices *rose* by about 14 percent, one of the biggest short-term gains ever. Prices remained volatile for some time, but as antitakeover talk in Congress died down, the market recovered.

THE NIKKEI CRASH   The crash of the Nikkei Index, which began in 1990, lengthened into a particularly long bear market. It is quite like the Crash of 1929 in that respect.

The Asian crash started with a booming bull market in the 1980s. Japan and emerging Asian economies seemed to be forming a powerful economic force. The "Asian economy" became an investor outlet for those wary of the U.S. market after the Crash of 1987.

To give you some idea of the bubble that was forming in Japan between 1955 and 1989, real estate prices in Japan increased by 70 times, and stock prices increased 100 times over. In 1989, price-earnings ratios of Japanese stocks climbed to unheard of levels as the Nikkei Index soared past 39,000. In retrospect, there were numerous warning signals about the Japanese market. At the time, however, optimism about the continued growth in the Japanese market remained high. Crashes never seem to occur when the outlook is poor, so, as with other crashes, many people did not see the impending Nikkei crash.

FIGURE 26.6

Nikkei 225 Index, January 1984 to December 2007

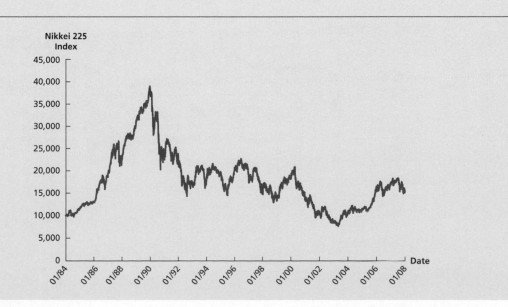

As you can see in Figure 26.6, in three years from December 1986 to the peak in December 1989, the Nikkei 225 Index rose 115 percent. Over the next three years, the index lost 57 percent of its value. In April 2003, the Nikkei Index stood at a level that was 80 percent off its peak in December 1989.

THE "DOT-COM" BUBBLE AND CRASH   How many Web sites do you think existed at the end of 1994? Would you believe only about 10,000? By the end of 1999, the number of active Web sites stood at about 9,500,000 and at the end of 2011, there were about 600,000,000 active Web sites.

By the mid-1990s, the rise in Internet use and its international growth potential fueled widespread excitement over the "new economy." Investors did not seem to care about solid business plans—only big ideas. Investor euphoria led to a surge in Internet IPOs, which were commonly referred to as "dot-coms" because so many of their names ended in ".com." Of course, the lack of solid business models doomed many of the newly formed companies. Many of them suffered huge losses and some folded relatively shortly after their IPOs.

The extent of the dot-com bubble and subsequent crash is presented in Table 26.1 and Figure 26.7, which compare the Amex Internet Index and the S&P 500 Index. As shown in Table 26.1, the Amex Internet Index soared from a level of 114.68 on October 1, 1998, to its peak of 688.52 in late March 2000, an increase of 500 percent. The Amex Internet Index then fell to a level of 58.59 in early October 2002, a drop of 91 percent. By contrast, the S&P 500 Index rallied about 31 percent in the same 1998–2000 time period and fell 40 percent during the 2000–2002 time period.

FIGURE 26.7

Values of the AMEX Internet Index and the S&P 500 Index, October 1995 through December 2007

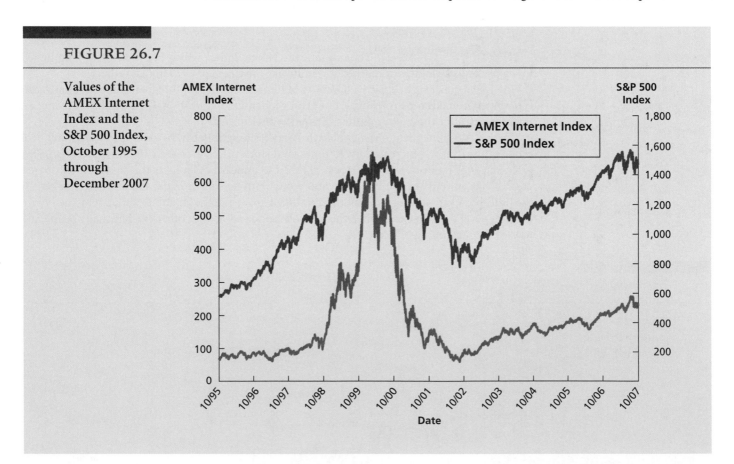

TABLE 26.1

Values of the Amex Internet Index and the S&P 500 Index

Date	Amex Internet Index Value	Gain to Peak from Oct. 1, 1998 (%)	Loss from Peak to Trough (%)	S&P 500 Index Value	Gain to Peak from Oct. 1, 1998 (%)	Loss from Peak to Trough (%)
October 1, 1998	114.68			986.39		
Later March 2000 (Internet index peak)	688.52	500		1,293.72	31	
Early October 2002 (Internet index trough)	58.59		−91	776.76		−40

Source: Author calculations.

CRASH OF 2008   The crash of 2008, also known as the financial crisis, was the worst crash in stock market history since 1929. We discussed the causes of the crisis in Chapter 1. To recap briefly, the United States Federal Reserve lowered interest rates aggressively in order to restore confidence in the economy after the Internet bubble burst in 2001. In the U.S., individuals with bad credit ratings, sub-prime borrowers, looked to banks to provide loans at historically low interest rates for home purchases. Investors also reacted to these low rates by seeking higher returns. The financial industry responded by manufacturing sub-prime mortgages and asset-backed securities. These securities had risks that were hard to assess. Once housing prices began to cool and interest rates rose, sub-prime borrowers started defaulting on their loans and the collapse of the sub-prime market ensued. With mortgages serving as the underlying asset supporting most of the financial instruments that investment banks, institutions, and retail buyers had acquired, these assets lost much of their value and hundreds of billions of dollars of write-downs followed. A major panic broke out with the failure of Lehman brothers on September 15, 2008. This resulted in huge losses and even bankruptcy for several banks in the United States and Europe, resulting in massive government financial assistance. Figure 26.8 shows the huge drop in Dow Jones Index during 2008.

FIGURE 26.8

Dow Jones Index, 2001 to 2012

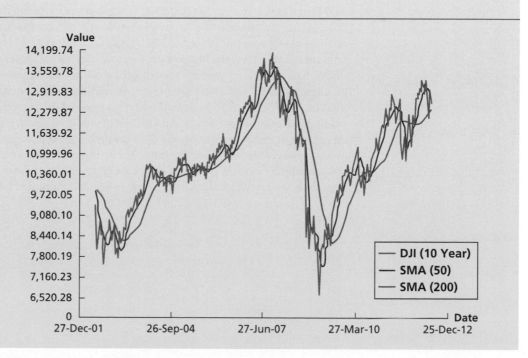

Source: Dow Jones Indexes (djindexes.com)

The financial crisis had a global impact. In Canada, the S&P/TSX index fell 33 percent in 2008. At the time of writing in November 2012, the aftermath of the financial crisis continues in the form of the European financial crisis as we discussed in Chapter 24.

By now, you're probably wondering how anyone could sensibly think that financial markets are in any way efficient. Before you make up your mind, be sure to read our next section carefully. As you will see, there is a powerful argument in favour of market efficiency.

26.6 | Market Efficiency and the Performance of Professional Money Managers

As we discussed in Chapter 1, a mutual fund pools money from many investors and pays a professional to manage the portfolio. We will focus here on equity funds that buy only stocks. There are hundreds of equity funds in Canada and thousands in the United States and globally, and the performance of these professionally managed funds has been extensively studied.[7]

Most equity funds are actively managed, meaning that the fund manager actively buys and sells stocks in an attempt to improve the fund's performance. However, one type of mutual fund, known as an index fund, is passively managed. Such funds just try to replicate the performance of stock market indexes, so there is no trading (unless the index changes, which happens from time to time). The most common type of index fund mimics the S&P/TSX 60 in Canada and the S&P 500 index in the U.S., both of which we studied in Chapter 12. The Vanguard 500 Index Fund is a well-known example. As of mid-2012, this fund was one of the largest mutual funds in the United States, with over $112 billion U.S. in assets.

If markets are not efficient because investors behave irrationally, then stock prices will deviate from their zero-NPV levels, and it should be possible to devise profitable trading strategies to take advantage of these mispricings. As a result, professional money managers in actively managed mutual funds should be able to systematically outperform index funds. In fact, that is what money managers are paid large sums to do.

The number of equity funds has grown substantially during the past 20 years. Figure 26.9 shows the growth in the number of such funds from 1986 through 2009 in the U.S. The green line shows the total number of funds that have existed for at least one year, while the purple line shows the number of funds that have existed for at least 10 years. From Figure 26.9, you can see that it is difficult for professional money managers to keep their funds in existence for 10 years (if it were easy, there would not be much difference between the green line and the purple line).

Figure 26.9 also shows the number of these funds that beat the performance of the Vanguard 500 Index Fund. You can see that there is much more variation in the orange line than in the blue line. What this means is that in any given year, it is hard to predict how many professional money managers will beat the Vanguard 500 Index Fund. But the low level and low variation of the blue line means that the percentage of professional money managers who can beat the Vanguard 500 Index Fund over a 10-year investment period is low and stable.

Figures 26.10 and 26.11 are bar charts that show the percentage of managed equity funds that beat the Vanguard 500 Index Fund. Figure 26.10 uses return data for the previous year only, while Figure 26.11 uses return data for the previous 10 years. As you can see from Figure 26.10, in only 12 of the 24 years spanning 1986 through 2009 did more than half the professional money managers beat the Vanguard 500 Index Fund. The performance is worse when it comes to 10-year investment periods. As shown in Figure 26.11, in only 4 of these 24 investment periods did more than half the professional money managers beat the Vanguard 500 Index Fund.

---

[7] Further discussion of the mutual fund industry is in Chapter 1.

FIGURE 26.9

The Growth of Actively Managed Equity Funds, 1986–2009

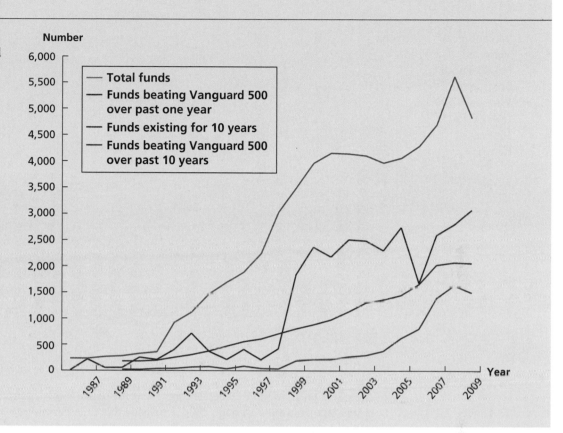

FIGURE 26.10

The Percentage of Managed Equity Funds Beating the Vanguard 500 Index Fund, One-Year Returns

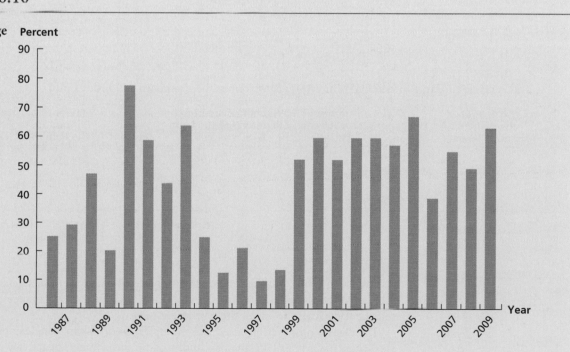

FIGURE 26.11

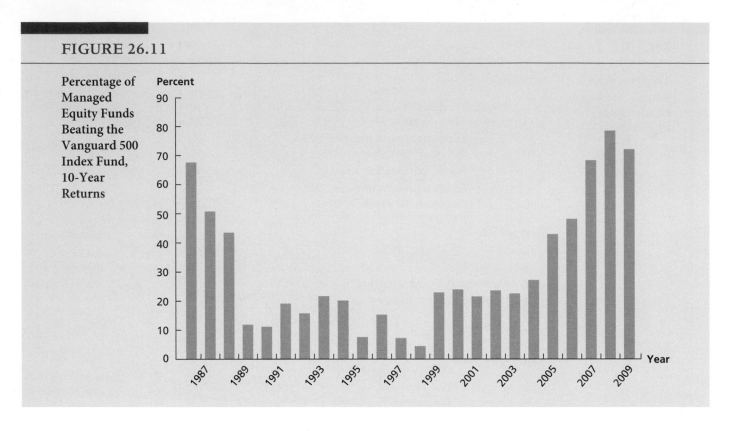

Percentage of Managed Equity Funds Beating the Vanguard 500 Index Fund, 10-Year Returns

Table 26.2 presents more evidence concerning the performance of professional money managers. Using data from 1980 through 2009, we divide this time period into 1-year investment periods, rolling 3-year investment periods, rolling 5-year investment periods, and rolling 10-year investment periods. Then, after we calculate the number of investment periods, we ask two questions: (1) What percentage of the time did half the professionally managed funds beat the Vanguard 500 Index Fund? and (2) What percentage of the time did three-fourths of the professionally managed funds beat the Vanguard 500 Index Fund?

TABLE 26.2

The Performance of Professional Money Managers versus the Vanguard 500 Index Fund

Length of Each Investment Period (Years)	span	Number of Investment Periods	Number of Investment Periods Half the Fund Beat Vanguard	Percent	Number of Investment Periods Three-Fourths of the Fund Beat Vanguard	Percent
1	1980–2009	30	14	46.7%	2	6.7%
3	1982–2009	28	11	39.3	0	0.0
5	1984–2009	26	9	34.6	0	0.0
10	1989–2009	21	3	14.3	1	4.8

Source: Author calculations.

As you see in Table 26.2, the performance of professional money managers is generally quite poor relative to the Vanguard 500 Index Fund. In addition, the performance of professional money managers declines the longer the investment period.

The discussion so far has used U.S. examples. Do the same conclusions hold for Canada? As we discuss in Chapter 12, Canadian studies of the performance of actively managed mutual funds also conclude that on average, mutual fund managers fail to outperform the market index.

Taken together with the U.S. evidence this raises some difficult and uncomfortable questions for security analysts and other investment professionals. If markets are inefficient, and tools like fundamental analysis are valuable, why don't mutual fund managers do better? Why can't mutual fund managers even beat a broad market index?

The performance of professional money managers is especially troublesome when we consider the enormous resources at their disposal and the substantial survivorship bias that exists. The survivorship bias comes into being because managers and funds that do especially poorly disappear. If beating the market were possible, then this Darwinian process of elimination should lead to a situation in which the survivors, as a group, are capable of doing so. The fact that professional money managers seem to lack the ability to outperform a broad market index is consistent with the notion that, overall, the equity market is efficient.

So where does our discussion of behavioural finance and market efficiency leave us? Are the major financial markets efficient? Based on the past 40 or so years of research, we can make an observation or two. We start by noting that the relevant question isn't "Are markets efficient?" Instead, it is "How efficient are markets?" It seems clear that markets are not perfectly efficient, and barriers to arbitrage do exist. On the other hand, the inability of professional money managers to outperform simple market indexes consistently strongly suggests that the major markets operate with a relatively high degree of efficiency.

IN THEIR OWN WORDS...

Hersh Shefrin on Behavioural Finance

Most of the chief financial officers (CFOs) I know admit that there is a gap between what they learned about corporate finance in business schools and what they put into practice as executives. A major reason for this gap is the material you are studying in this chapter.

It really is true that financial managers do not practice textbook corporate finance. In the 1990s, I became convinced that this was the case after I joined the organization Financial Executives International (FEI), which gave me an opportunity to meet many CFOs on a regular basis and discuss with them how they practice corporate finance. In doing so, I gained a great deal of information that led me to conclude that behavioural finance was highly applicable to corporate life.

Behavioural corporate finance is important for at least three reasons. First, being human, financial managers are susceptible to the behavioural phenomena you are reading about in this chapter. Textbook corporate finance offers many valuable concepts, tools, and techniques. My point is not the material in traditional corporate finance textbooks lacks value, but that psychological obstacles often stand in the way of this material being implemented correctly.

Second, the people with whom financial managers interact are also susceptible to mistakes. Expecting other people to be immune to mistakes is itself an error that can lead managers to make bad decisions.

Third, investors' mistakes can sometimes lead prices to be inefficient. In this respect, managers can make one of two different mistakes. They might believe that prices are efficient when they are actually inefficient. Or they might believe that prices are inefficient when they are actually efficient. Managers need to know how to think about the vulnerability to both types of errors, and how to deal with each.

The material in this chapter is a wonderful start to learning about behavioural finance. However, for this material to really make a difference, you need to integrate the material with what you are learning about traditional topics such as capital budgeting, capital structure, valuation, payout policy, market efficiency, corporate governance, and mergers and acquisition. You need to study behavioural cases about real people making real decisions and see how psychology impacts those decisions. You need to learn from their mistakes in an effort to make better decisions yourself. This is how behavioural corporate finance will generate value for you.

Hersh Shefrin holds the Mario L. Belotti Chair at the Leavey School of Business at Santa Clara University and is the author of *Behavioral Corporate Finance: Decisions that Create Value*.

26.7 | SUMMARY AND CONCLUSIONS

In this chapter, we examine some of the implications of research in cognitive psychology and behavioural finance. In the first part of the chapter, we learned that a key to becoming a better financial decision-maker is to be aware of, and avoid, certain types of behaviours. By studying behavioural finance, you can see the potential damage from errors due to biases, frame dependence, and heuristics.

Biases can lead to bad decisions because they lead to unnecessarily poor estimates of future outcomes. Overoptimism, for example, produces overly favourable estimates and opinions. Frame dependence results in narrow framing, which is focusing on the smaller picture instead of the bigger one. The use of heuristics as shortcuts ignores potentially valuable insights that more detailed analysis would reveal.

In the second part of the chapter, we turned to a much more difficult question and one where the evidence is not at all clear. Do errors in judgment by investors influence market prices and lead to market inefficiencies? This question is the subject of raging debate among researchers and practitioners, and we are not going to take sides. Instead, our goal is to introduce you to the ideas and issues.

We saw that market inefficiencies can be difficult for arbitrageurs to exploit because of firm-specific risk, noise trader (or sentiment-based) risk, and implementation costs. We called these difficulties *limits* (or *barriers*) *to arbitrage*, and the implication is that some inefficiencies may only gradually disappear, and smaller inefficiencies can persist if they cannot be profitably exploited.

Looking back at market history, we saw some examples of evident mispricing, such as the Palm IPO. We also saw that markets appear to be susceptible to bubbles and crashes, suggesting significant inefficiency. However, we closed the chapter by examining the performance of professional money managers. The evidence here is quite clear and striking. The pros cannot consistently outperform broad market indexes, which is strong evidence in favour of market efficiency.

Key Terms

affect heuristic (page 755)
behavioural finance (page 751)
bubble (page 761)
confirmation bias (page 752)
crash (page 761)
frame dependence (page 753)

heuristics (page 755)
noise trader (page 758)
overconfidence (page 751)
overoptimism (page 751)
representativeness heuristic (page 756)
sentiment-based risk (page 759)

Concepts Review and Critical Thinking Questions

1. **(LO4)** In the chapter, we discussed the 3Com/Palm and Royal Dutch/Shell mispricings. Which of the limits to arbitrage is least likely to be the main reason for these mispricings? Explain.

2. **(LO1)** How could overconfidence affect the financial manager of the firm and the firm's shareholders?

3. **(LO4)** How can frame dependence lead to irrational investment decisions?

4. **(LO4)** What is noise trader risk? How can noise trader risk lead to market inefficiencies?

5. **(LO3)** Suppose you are flipping a fair coin in a coin-flipping contest and have flipped eight heads in a row. What is the probability of flipping a head on your next coin flip? Suppose you flipped a head on your ninth toss. What is the probability of flipping a head on your tenth toss?

6. **(LO4)** In the mid- to late-1990s, the performance of the pros was unusually poor—on the order of 90 percent of all equity mutual funds underperformed a passively managed index fund. How does this fact bear on the issue of market efficiency?

7. **(LO4)** The efficient market hypothesis implies that all mutual funds should obtain the same expected risk-adjusted returns. Therefore, we can simply pick mutual funds at random. Is this statement true or false? Explain.

8. **(LO4)** Some people argue that the efficient market hypothesis cannot explain the 1987 market crash or the high price-to-earnings ratio of Internet stocks during the late 1990s. What alternative hypothesis is currently used for these two phenomena?

9. **(LO4)** Proponents of behavioural finance use three concepts to argue that markets are not efficient. What are these arguments?

10. **(LO2)** In the chapter, we presented an example where you had lost $78 and were given the opportunity to make a wager in which your loss would increase to $100 for 80 percent of the time decrease to $0 for 20 percent of the time. Using the stand-alone principal from capital budgeting, explain how your decision to accept or reject the proposal could have been affected by frame dependence. In other words, reframe the question in a way in which most people are likely to analyze the proposal correctly.

Questions and Problems

Basic
(Questions 1–9)

1. (LO1, 2, 3) John Cutter has owned a home in Toronto for the past 45 years. He is thinking of downsizing by selling his house and moving to a rental apartment for his retirement. John observes that housing prices in the city have grown at 7 percent annually over this period. Based on this information, he decides to stay in his house in order to enjoy future gains. What behavioural finance concept is John exhibiting and how is this influencing his decision-making?

2. (LO1, 2, 3) Pamela Landry, a novice investor from Montreal, bought 2,000 shares of Research In Motion (RIM) stock during August 2012. During this period, RIM reported a loss of $518 million in revenues from the previous year. The company required around $300 million in restructuring costs and laid off more than 3,000 employees. Explain the behavioural finance concept Pamela is exhibiting and how is this influencing her decision-making.

3. (LO1, 2, 3) Forest Gump, a hockey player from Edmonton, holds two types of accounts—a risky and a retirement account. He purchases Greek and Spanish bonds for his risky account and invests in Bank of Montreal and Royal Bank of Canada stocks, which are known for paying steady dividends, for his retirement account as he requires a steady source of income after he retires. Explain the behavioural finance concept Forest is exhibiting and how is this influencing his decision-making.

4. (LO1, 2, 3) Jack Sparrow, a Vancouver based techie, had a fascination for Facebook Inc. shares. He bought 200 shares of Facebook during the IPO for $38 on May 18, 2012. During August 2012, the share price fell below half its IPO price for the first time. Jack was not willing to sell the shares below the purchase price and he decided to wait for the price to climb up. Explain the behavioural finance concept Jack is exhibiting and how is this influencing his decision-making.

5. (LO1, 2, 3) Sharon Nicol, an employee of IMAX Corporation holds 800 shares of her company stock. She thinks the company had a huge growing potential and decides not to sell any of the IMAX shares in her portfolio. Explain the behavioural finance concept Sharon is exhibiting and how is this influencing her decision-making.

6. (LO1, 2, 3) Matthew and Stephen Fleming are experienced wealth managers in Manitoba. On August 20, 2012, Matthew and Stephen bought 200 shares of Steinbach Gold Inc. and Selkirk Technology Limited. On August 21, 2012, Steinbach put out a press release stating that the company found new gold reserves near the Atitaki Provincial Park. On the same day, Selkirk lost a patent lawsuit worth $1 billion. As a result of these news items, Steinbach's share price went up by 15 percent and Selkirk's share price dipped by 20 percent. Matthew considered himself as an ace stock picker while Stephen attributed the drop in shares of Selkirk to bad luck. Explain the behavioural finance concept Matthew and Stephen are exhibiting and how it is this influencing their decision-making.

7. (LO1, 2, 3) Lucy Smith was in a dilemma to choose between two stocks: Telus Communications (listed on the TSX) and Seair Inc. (listed on the TSX Venture Exchange). On the Internet, she was able to find a large amount of information about Telus and the Canadian telecom industry but was unable to find much about Seair. As a result, Lucy decided to invest in Telus rather than Seair. Explain the behavioural finance concept Lucy is exhibiting and how is this influencing her decision-making.

8. (LO1, 2, 3) Jenna Simpson, a retired investment advisor from Regina, conducted a research on Baux Inc., an aluminum mining company from Saskatchewan. She found out that the company's stock price would suffer in the short term due to fluctuation in aluminum prices even though the stock price was expected to increase in the next 10 years due to excess demand for aluminum. Hence, she decides not to invest in the company's stock fearing a loss in the short term. What behavioural finance concept is Jenna is exhibiting and how is this influencing her decision-making?

9. (LO4) Faced with new competition from Samsung Galaxy Tabs, Apple Inc. releases a new iPad, which has a faster processor and better features, on Monday at 11 am. What do you expect would happen to the stock price of Apple on NASDAQ? Is your answer consistent with the efficient market hypothesis?

Internet Application Questions

1. Visit <u>behaviouralfinance.net</u> and familiarize yourself with the list of behavioural finance terms that are not covered in this chapter.

2. The Allianz Global Investors Center for Behavioral Finance (<u>befi.allianzgi.com/en/Pages/default.aspx</u>) puts academic theory into action, turning behavioural insights into actionable ideas and practical tools for financial advisors, plan sponsors and investors. Professor Richard Thaler of the University of Chicago Booth School of Business describes behavioural finance using the NFL draft as an example (<u>befi.allianzgi.com/en/befi-tv/Pages/richard-thaler.aspx</u>). What are the behavioural principles that drive both money mistakes and comparable suboptimal behaviour in the domain of sports?

MINI CASE

Your Pension Account at Tuxedo Air

You have been at your job with Tuxedo Air for a week now and have decided you need to sign up for the company's defined contribution pension plan. Under the plan, pension contributions are invested according to your choice. Even after your discussion with Audrey Sanborn, the Bledsoe Financial Services representative, you are still unsure as to which investment option you should choose. Recall that the options available to you are stock in Tuxedo Air, the Bledsoe S&P/TSX 60 Index Fund, the Bledsoe Small-Cap Fund, the Bledsoe Canadian Large-Capitalization Stock Fund, the Bledsoe Bond Fund, and the Bledsoe Money Market Fund. You have decided that you should invest in a diversified portfolio, with 70 percent of your investment in equities, 25 percent in bonds, and 5 percent in the money market fund.

You have also decided to focus your equity investment on large-cap Canadian stocks, but you are debating whether to select the S&P/TSX 60 Index Fund or the Canadian Large-Capitalization Stock Fund. In thinking it over, you understand the basic difference between the two funds. One is a purely passive fund that replicates a widely followed Canadian large-cap index, the S&P/TSX 60, and has low fees. The other is actively managed with the intention that the skill of the portfolio manager will result in improved performance relative to an index. Fees are higher in the latter fund. You are just not certain which way to go, so you ask Ed Cowan, who works in the company's finance area, for advice.

After discussing your concerns, Ed gives you some information comparing the performance of equity mutual funds and the market index in the U.S. The Vanguard 500 is the world's largest equity index mutual fund. It replicates the S&P 500, and its return is only negligibly different from the S&P 500. Fees are very low. As a result, the Vanguard 500 is a U.S. counterpart to the Bledsoe S&P/TSX 60 Index Fund offered in the pension plan, but it has been in existence for much longer, so you can study its track record for over two decades. Ed tells you that Canadian research has produced results similar to those in Figure 26.11. He suggests that you study this figure and answer the following questions:

Questions

1. What implications do you draw from the graph for mutual fund investors?

2. Is the graph consistent or inconsistent with market efficiency? Explain carefully.

3. What investment decision would you make for the equity portion of your pension account? Why?

GLOSSARY

accounting break-even   The sales level that results in zero project net income. (p. 297)

accounts payable period   The time between receipt of inventory and payment for it. (p. 522)

accounts receivable financing   A secured short-term loan that involves either the assignment or factoring of receivables. (p. 539)

accounts receivable period   The time between sale of inventory and collection of the receivable. (p. 522)

adjusted present value (APV)   Base case net present value of a project's operating cash flows plus present value of any financing benefits. (p. 414)

adjustment costs   The costs associated with holding too little cash. Also called *shortage costs*. (p. 554)

affect heuristic   The reliance on instinct instead of analysis in making decisions. (p. 755)

agency problem   The possibility of conflicts of interest between the shareholders and management of a firm. (p. 10)

aggregation   The process by which smaller investment proposals of each of a firm's operational units are added up and treated as one big project. (p. 86)

aging schedule   A compilation of accounts receivable by the age of each account. (p. 588)

amalgamations   Combinations of firms that have been joined by merger, consolidation, or acquisition. (p. 656)

American option   A call or put option that can be exercised on or before its expiration date. (p. 625, p. 712)

annual percentage rate (APR)   The interest rate charged per period multiplied by the number of periods per year. (p. 148)

annuity   A level stream of cash flows for a fixed period of time. (p. 135)

annuity due   An annuity for which the cash flows occur at the beginning of the period. (p. 141)

arbitrage pricing theory (APT)   An equilibrium asset pricing theory that is derived from a factor model by using diversification and arbitrage. It shows that the expected return on any risky asset is a linear combination of various factors. (p. 377)

arithmetic average return   The return earned in an average year over a multiyear period. (p. 333)

average accounting return (AAR)   An investment's average net income divided by its average book value. (p. 228)

average tax rate   Total taxes paid divided by total taxable income. (p. 37)

balance sheet   See *statement of financial position*.

bankruptcy   A legal proceeding for liquidating or reorganizing a business. Also, the transfer of some or all of a firm's assets to its creditors. (p. 479)

basis risk   Risk that futures prices will not move directly with cash price hedged. (p. 698)

bearer form   Bond issued without record of the owner's name; payment is made to whoever holds the bond. (p. 175)

behavioural finance   The area of finance dealing with the implications of reasoning errors on financial decisions. (p. 751)

benefit/cost ratio   The profitability index of an investment project. (p. 238)

best efforts underwriting   Underwriter sells as much of the issue as possible, but can return any unsold shares to the issuer without financial responsibility. (p. 428)

beta coefficient   Amount of systematic risk present in a particular risky asset relative to an average risky asset. (p. 366)

bought deal   One underwriter buys securities from an issuing firm and sells them directly to a small number of investors. (p. 428)

bubble   A situation where observed prices soar far higher than fundamentals and rational analysis would suggest. (p. 761)

business risk   The equity risk that comes from the nature of the firm's operating activities. (p. 464)

call option   An option that gives the owner the right, but not the obligation, to buy an asset. (p. 701); The right to buy an asset at a fixed price during a particular period of time. (p. 712)

call premium   Amount by which the call price exceeds the par value of the bond. (p. 176)

call protected   Bond during period in which it cannot be redeemed by the issuer. (p. 176)

call provision   Agreement giving the corporation the option to repurchase the bond at a specified price before maturity. (p. 176)

Canada plus call   Call provision that compensates bond investors for interest differential, making it unattractive for an issuer to call a bond. (p. 176)

Canada yield curve   A plot of the yields on Government of Canada notes and bonds relative to maturity. (p. 188)

capital asset pricing model (CAPM)   Equation of the SML showing the relationship between expected return and beta. (p. 375)

capital budgeting   The process of planning and managing a firm's investment in long-term assets. (p. 2)

capital cost allowance (CCA)   Depreciation for tax purposes, not necessarily the same as depreciation under IFRS. (p. 42); Depreciation method under Canadian tax law allowing for the accelerated write-off of property under various classifications. (p. 254)

capital gains   The increase in value of an investment over its purchase price. (p. 39)

capital gains yield   The dividend growth rate or the rate at which the value of an investment grows. (p. 203)

capital intensity ratio   A firm's total assets divided by its sales, or the amount of assets needed to generate $1 in sales. (p. 91)

capital markets   Financial markets where long-term debt and equity securities are bought and sold. (p. 15)

capital rationing   The situation that exists if a firm has positive NPV projects but cannot find the necessary financing. (p. 310)

capital structure   The mix of debt and equity maintained by a firm. (p. 3)

captive finance company   Wholly owned subsidiary that handles credit extension and receivables financing through commercial paper. (p. 581)

carrying costs   Costs that rise with increases in the level of investment in current assets. (p. 527)

cash break-even   The sales level where operating cash flow is equal to zero. (p. 302)

cash budget   A forecast of cash receipts and disbursements for the next planning period. (p. 533)

cash cycle   The time between cash disbursement and cash collection. (p. 522)

cash discount   A discount given for a cash purchase. (p. 576)

cash flow from assets   The total of cash flow to bondholders and cash flow to shareholders, consisting of: operating cash flow, capital spending, and additions to net working capital. (p. 32)

cash flow time line   Graphical representation of the operating cycle and the cash cycle. (p. 522)

cash flow to creditors   A firm's interest payments to creditors less net new borrowings. (p. 34)

cash flow to shareholders   Dividends paid out by a firm less net new equity raised. (p. 34)

circular bid   Corporate takeover bid communicated to the shareholders by direct mail. (p. 657)

clean price   The price of a bond net of accrued interest; this is the price that is typically quoted. (p. 182)

clientele effect   Stocks attract particular groups based on dividend yield and the resulting tax effects. (p. 502)

collection policy   Procedures followed by a firm in collecting accounts receivable. (p. 573)

common-base-year statement   A standardized financial statement presenting all items relative to a certain base year amount. (p. 59)

common-size statement   A standardized financial statement presenting all items in percentage terms. Statements of financial position are shown as a percentage of assets and statements of consolidated income as a percentage of sales. (p. 57)

common stock   Equity without priority for dividends or in bankruptcy. (p. 205)

compounding   The process of accumulating interest in an investment over time to earn more interest. (p. 112)

compound interest   Interest earned on both the initial principal and the interest reinvested from prior periods. (p. 112)

confirmation bias   Searching for (and giving more weight to) information and opinion that confirms what you believe rather than information and opinion to the contrary. (p. 752)

consol   A type of perpetuity. (p. 142)

consolidation   A merger in which a new firm is created and both the acquired and acquiring firm cease to exist. (p. 656)

contingency planning   Taking into account the managerial options that are implicit in a project. (p. 308)

control block   An interest controlling 50 percent of outstanding votes plus one; thereby it may decide the fate of the firm. (p. 671)

conversion price   The dollar amount of a bond's par value that is exchangeable for one share of stock. (p. 732)

conversion ratio   The number of shares per bond received for conversion into stock. (p. 732)

conversion value   The value of a convertible bond if it was immediately converted into common stock. (p. 733)

convertible bond   A bond that can be exchanged for a fixed number of shares of stock for a specified amount of time. (p. 732)

corporate governance   Rules for corporate organization and conduct; practices relating to how corporations are governed by management, directors, and shareholders. (pp. 11, 670)

corporation   A business created as a distinct legal entity owned by one or more individuals or entities. (p. 5)

cost of debt   The return that lenders require on the firm's debt. (p. 393)

cost of equity   The return that equity investors require on their investment in the firm. (p. 389)

counterparty   Second borrower in currency swap. Counterparty borrows funds in currency desired by principal. (p. 624)

coupon   The stated interest payment made on a bond. (p. 165)

coupon rate   The annual coupon divided by the face value of a bond. (p. 166)

covenants   A promise by the firm, included in the debt contract, to perform certain acts. A restrictive covenant imposes constraints on the firm to protect the interests of the debt holder. (p. 539)

crash   A situation where market prices collapse significantly and suddenly. (p. 761)

credit analysis   The process of determining the probability that customers will or will not pay. (p. 573)

credit cost curve   Graphical representation of the sum of the carrying costs and the opportunity costs of a credit policy. (p. 581)

credit default swap   A contract that pays off when a credit event occurs, default by a particular company termed the reference entity, giving the buyer the right to sell corporate bonds issued by the reference entity at their face value. (p. 701)

credit instrument   The evidence of indebtedness. (p. 578)

credit period   The length of time that credit is granted. (p. 575)

credit scoring   The process of quantifying the probability of default when granting consumer credit. (p. 585)

cross-hedging   Hedging an asset with contracts written on a closely related, but not identical, asset. (p. 698)

cross-rate   The implicit exchange rate between two currencies (usually non-U.S.) quoted in some third currency (usually the U.S. dollar). (p. 607)

cumulative voting   Procedure where a shareholder may cast all votes for one member of the board of directors. (p. 218)

date of payment   Date of the dividend payment. (p. 492)

date of record   Date on which holders of record are designated to receive a dividend. (p. 492)

debenture   Unsecured debt, usually with a maturity of 10 years or more. (p. 175)

debit card   An automated teller machine card used at the point of purchase to avoid the use of cash. As this is not a credit card, money must be available in the user's bank account. (p. 561)

debt capacity   The ability to borrow to increase firm value. (p. 98)

declaration date   Date on which the board of directors passes a resolution to pay a dividend. (p. 492)

default risk premium   The portion of a nominal interest rate or bond yield that represents compensation for the possibility of default. (p. 189)

deferred call   Call provision prohibiting the company from redeeming the bond before a certain date. (p. 176)

degree of operating leverage (DOL)   The percentage change in operating cash flow relative to the percentage change in quantity sold. (p. 305)

depreciation (CCA) tax shield   Tax saving that results from the CCA deduction, calculated as depreciation multiplied by the corporate tax rate. (p. 264)

derivative securities   Options, futures, and other securities whose value derives from the price of another, underlying, asset. (p. 20); Financial assets that represent claims to another financial asset. (p. 687)

dilution   Loss in existing shareholders' value, in terms of either ownership, market value, book value, or EPS. (p. 446)

direct bankruptcy costs   The costs that are directly associated with bankruptcy, such as legal and administrative expenses. (p. 470)

dirty price   The price of a bond including accrued interest, also known as the *full* or *invoice price*. This is the price the buyer actually pays. (p. 182)

discount   To calculate the present value of some future amount. (p. 119)

discounted cash flow (DCF) valuation   The process of valuing an investment by discounting its future cash flows. (p. 222)

discounted payback period   The length of time required for an investment's discounted cash flows to equal its initial cost. (p. 227)

discount rate   The rate used to calculate the present value of future cash flows. (p. 120)

distribution   Payment made by a firm to its owners from sources other than current or accumulated earnings. (p. 491)

diversification   Investment in more than one asset; returns do not move proportionally in the same direction at the same time, thus reducing risk. (p. 668)

divestiture   The sale of assets, operations, divisions, and/or segments of a business to a third party. (p. 678)

dividend   Return on capital of corporation paid by company to shareholders in either cash or stock. (p. 206); Payment made out of a firm's earnings to its owners, either in cash or stock. (p. 491)

dividend capture   A strategy in which an investor purchases securities to own them on the day of record and then quickly sells them; designed to attain dividends but avoid the risk of a lengthy hold. (p. 567)

dividend growth model   A model that determines the current price of a stock as its dividend next period, divided by the discount rate less the dividend growth rate. (p. 199)

dividend payout ratio   Amount of cash paid out to shareholders divided by net income. (p. 90)

dividend tax credit   Tax formula that reduces the effective tax rate on dividends. (p. 39)

dividend yield   A stock's cash dividend divided by its current price. (p. 203)

Du Pont identity   Popular expression breaking ROE into three parts: profit margin, total asset turnover, and financial leverage. (p. 71)

Dutch auction underwriting   The type of underwriting in which the offer price is set based on competitive bidding by investors. Also known as a *uniform price auction*. (p. 429)

earnings per share (EPS)   Net income minus any cash dividends on preferred stock, divided by the number of shares of common stock outstanding. (p. 667)

economic exposure   Long-term financial risk arising from permanent changes in prices or other economic fundamentals. (p. 690)

economic value added (EVA)   Performance measure based on WACC. (p. 398)

effective annual rate (EAR)   The interest rate expressed as if it were compounded once per year. (p. 146)

efficient capital market   Market in which security prices reflect available information. (p. 335)

efficient markets hypothesis (EMH)   The hypothesis is that actual capital markets, such as the TSX, are efficient. (p. 337)

employee stock option (ESO)   An option granted to an employee by a company giving the employee the right to buy shares of stock in the company at a fixed price for a fixed time. (p. 724)

equity carve-out   The sale of stock in a wholly owned subsidiary via an IPO. (p. 679)

equivalent annual cost (EAC)   The present value of a project's costs calculated on an annual basis. (p. 273)

erosion   The portion of cash flows of a new project that come at the expense of a firm's existing operations. (p. 252)

Eurobanks   Banks that make loans and accept deposits in foreign currencies. (p. 623)

Eurobond   International bonds issued in multiple countries but denominated in a single currency (usually the issuer's currency). (p. 607)

Eurocurrency   Money deposited in a financial centre outside of the country whose currency is involved. (p. 607)

European option   An option that can be exercised only on the expiration date. (p. 712)

ex-dividend date   Date two business days before the date of record, establishing those individuals entitled to a dividend. (p. 492)

exchange rate   The price of one country's currency expressed in another country's currency. (p. 609)

exchange rate risk   The risk related to having international operations in a world where relative currency values vary. (p. 624)

exercising the option   The act of buying or selling the underlying asset via the option contract. (p. 712)

expected return   Return on a risky asset expected in the future. (p. 347)

expiration date   The last day on which an option can be exercised. (p. 712)

Export Development Canada (EDC)   Federal Crown corporation that promotes Canadian exports by making loans to foreign purchasers. (p. 607)

ex rights   Period when stock is selling without a recently declared right, normally beginning two business days before the holder-of-record date. (p. 443)

external financing needed (EFN)   The amount of financing required to balance both sides of the balance sheet or statement of financial position. (p. 92)

face value   The principal amount of a bond that is repaid at the end of the term. Also called par value. (p. 166)

financial break-even   The sales level that results in a zero NPV. (p. 303)

financial distress costs   The direct and indirect costs associated with going bankrupt or experiencing financial distress. (p. 470)

financial engineering   Creation of new securities or financial processes. (p. 20)

financial leases   Typically, a longer-term, fully amortized lease under which the lessee is responsible for upkeep. Usually not cancellable without penalty. (p. 636)

financial ratios   Relationships determined from a firm's financial information and used for comparison purposes. (p. 60)

financial risk   The equity risk that comes from the financial policy (i.e., capital structure) of the firm. (p. 464)

firm commitment underwriting   Underwriter buys the entire issue, assuming full financial responsibility for any unsold shares. (p. 428)

Fisher effect   The relationship between nominal returns, real returns, and inflation. (p. 185)

five Cs of credit   The following five basic credit factors to be evaluated: character, capacity, capital, collateral, and conditions. (p. 585)

fixed costs   Costs that do not change when the quantity of output changes during a particular time period. (p. 296)

float   The difference between book cash and bank cash, representing the net effect of cheques in the process of clearing. (p. 556)

flotation costs   The costs associated with the issuance of new securities. (p. 403)

forecasting risk   The possibility that errors in projected cash flows lead to incorrect decisions. (p. 289)

foreign bonds   International bonds issued in a single country, usually denominated in that country's currency. (p. 607)

foreign exchange market   The market where one country's currency is traded for another's. (p. 608)

forward contract   A legally binding agreement between two parties calling for the sale of an asset or product in the future at a price agreed upon today. (p. 691)

forward exchange rate   The agreed-on exchange rate to be used in a forward trade. (p. 611)

forward trade   Agreement to exchange currency at some time in the future. (p. 611)

frame dependence   The tendency of individuals to make different (and potentially inconsistent) decisions depending on how a question or problem is framed. (p. 753)

free cash flow   Another name for cash flow from assets. (p. 34)

futures contract   A forward contract with the feature that gains and losses are realized each day rather than only on the settlement date. (p. 694)

future value (FV)   The amount an investment is worth after one or more periods. Also known as *compound value*. (p. 112)

general cash offer   An issue of securities offered for sale to the general public on a cash basis. (p. 427)

generalized Fisher effect (GFE)   The theory that real interest rates are equal across countries. (p. 618)

geometric average return   The average compound return earned per year over a multiyear period. (p. 333)

gilts   British and Irish government securities, including issues of local British authorities and some overseas public-sector offerings. (p. 607)

going-private transactions   All publicly owned stock in a firm is replaced with complete equity ownership by a private group. (p. 658)

greenmail   A targeted stock repurchase where payments are made to potential bidders to eliminate unfriendly takeover attempts. (p. 671)

growing annuity   A finite number of growing annual cash flows. (p. 145)

growing perpetuity   A constant stream of cash flows without end that is expected to rise indefinitely. (p. 143)

half-year rule   CRA's requirement to figure CCA on only one-half of an asset's installed cost for its first year of use. (p. 42)

hard rationing   The situation that occurs when a business cannot raise financing for a project under any circumstances. (p. 310)

hedging   Reducing a firm's exposure to price or rate fluctuations. Also called *immunization*. (p. 687)

heuristics   Shortcuts or rules of thumb used to make decisions. (p. 755)

holder-of-record date   The date on which existing shareholders on company records are designated as the recipients of stock rights. Also called the *date of record*. (p. 443)

homemade dividends   Idea that individual investors can undo corporate dividend policy by reinvesting dividends or selling shares of stock. (p. 495)

homemade leverage   The use of personal borrowing to change the overall amount of financial leverage to which the individual is exposed. (p. 460)

income statement   See *statement of comprehensive income*.

incremental cash flows   The difference between a firm's future cash flows with a project and without the project. (p. 251)

indenture   Written agreement between the corporation and the lender detailing the terms of the debt issue. (p. 174)

indirect bankruptcy costs   The difficulties of running a business that is experiencing financial distress. (p. 470)

inflation premium   The portion of a nominal interest rate that represents compensation for expected future inflation. (p. 187)

information content effect The market's reaction to a change in corporate dividend payout. (p. 502)

initial public offering (IPO) A company's first equity issue made available to the public. Also called an *unseasoned new issue.* (p. 426)

interest on interest Interest earned on the reinvestment of previous interest payments. (p. 112)

interest rate parity (IRP) The condition stating that the interest rate differential between two countries is equal to the difference between the forward exchange rate and the spot exchange rate. (p. 617)

interest rate risk premium The compensation investors demand for bearing interest rate risk. (p. 187)

interest tax shield The tax saving attained by a firm from interest expense. (p. 466)

internal growth rate The growth rate a firm can maintain with only internal financing. (p. 97)

internal rate of return (IRR) The discount rate that makes the NPV of an investment zero. (p. 230)

intrinsic value The lower bound of an option's value, or what the option would be worth if it were about to expire. (p. 718)

inventory loan A secured short-term loan to purchase inventory. (p. 541)

inventory period The time it takes to acquire and sell inventory. (p. 522)

invoice Bill for goods or services provided by the seller to the purchaser. (p. 575)

joint venture Typically an agreement between firms to create a separate, co-owned entity established to pursue a joint goal. (p. 659)

just-in-time inventory (JIT) Design for inventory in which parts, raw materials, and other work-in-process is delivered exactly as needed for production. Goal is to minimize inventory. (p. 598)

lessee The user of an asset in a leasing agreement. Lessee makes payments to lessor. (p. 634)

lessor The owner of an asset in a leasing agreement. Lessor receives payments from the lessee. (p. 634)

letter of credit A written statement by a bank that money will be paid, provided conditions specified in the letter are met. (p. 539)

leveraged buyouts (LBOs) Going-private transactions in which a large percentage of the money used to buy the stock is borrowed. Often, incumbent management is involved. (p. 658)

leveraged lease A financial lease where the lessor borrows a substantial fraction of the cost of the leased asset. (p. 637)

liquidation Termination of the firm as a going concern. (p. 480)

liquidity premium The portion of a nominal interest rate or bond yield that represents compensation for lack of liquidity. (p. 189)

lockboxes Special post office boxes set up to intercept and speed up accounts receivable payments. (p. 561)

lockup agreement The part of the underwriting contract that specifies how long insiders must wait after an IPO before they can sell stock. (p. 430)

London Interbank Offer Rate (LIBOR) The rate most international banks charge one another for overnight Eurodollar loans. (p. 607)

loss carry-forward, carry-back Using a year's capital losses to offset capital gains in past or future years. (p. 40)

M&M Proposition I The value of the firm is independent of its capital structure. (p. 462)

M&M Proposition II A firm's cost of equity capital is a positive linear function of its capital structure. (p. 463)

managerial options Opportunities that managers can exploit if certain things happen in the future. Also known as *sell options.* (p. 307)

marginal cost or incremental cost The change in costs that occurs when there is a small change in output. (p. 297)

marginal tax rate Amount of tax payable on the next dollar earned. (p. 37)

market risk premium Slope of the SML, the difference between the expected return on a market portfolio and the risk-free rate. (p. 374)

maturity date Specified date at which the principal amount of a bond is paid. (p. 166)

maturity factoring Short-term financing in which the factor purchases all of a firm's receivables and forwards the proceeds to the seller as soon as they are collected. (p. 541)

merger The complete absorption of one company by another, where the acquiring firm retains its identity and the acquired firm ceases to exist as a separate entity. (p. 656)

money markets Financial markets where short-term debt securities are bought and sold. (p. 15)

multiple discriminant analysis (MDA) Statistical technique for distinguishing between two samples on the basis of their observed characteristics. (p. 586)

multiple rates of return One potential problem in using the IRR method if more than one discount rate makes the NPV of an investment zero. (p. 234)

mutually exclusive investment decisions One potential problem in using the IRR method is the acceptance of one project excludes that of another. (p. 234)

net acquisitions Total installed cost of capital acquisitions minus adjusted cost of any disposals within an asset pool. (p. 43)

net advantage to leasing (NAL) The net present value (NPV) of the decision to lease an asset instead of buying it. (p. 642)

net present value (NPV) The difference between an investment's market value and its cost. (p. 221)

net present value profile A graphical representation of the relationship between an investment's NPVs and various discount rates. (p. 232)

noise trader A trader whose trades are not based on information or meaningful financial analysis. (p. 758)

nominal rates Interest rates or rates of return that have not been adjusted for inflation. (p. 184)

non-cash items Expenses charged against revenues that do not directly affect cash flow, such as depreciation. (p. 31)

normal distribution A symmetric, bell-shaped frequency distribution that can be defined by its mean and standard deviation. (p. 329)

note Unsecured debt, usually with a maturity under 10 years. (p. 175)

Note Issuance Facility (NIF) Large borrowers issue notes up to one year in maturity in the Euromarket. Banks underwrite or sell notes. (p. 623)

operating cash flow Cash generated from a firm's normal business activities. (p. 32)

operating cycle The time period between the acquisition of inventory and when cash is collected from receivables. (p. 522)

operating lease Usually a shorter-term lease where the lessor is responsible for insurance, taxes, and upkeep. Often cancellable on short notice. (p. 635)

operating leverage The degree to which a firm or project relies on fixed costs. (p. 304)

operating loan Loan negotiated with banks for day-to-day operations. (p. 537)

opportunity cost The most valuable alternative that is given up if a particular investment is undertaken. (p. 252)

option A contract that gives its owner the right to buy or sell some asset at a fixed price on or before a given date. (p. 711)

option contract An agreement that gives the owner the right, but not the obligation, to buy or sell a specific asset at a specific price for a set period of time. (p. 701)

option delta The change in the stock price divided by the change in the call price. (p. 723)

overallotment option An underwriting provision that permits syndicate members to purchase additional shares at the original offering price. (p. 430)

overconfidence The belief that your abilities are better than they really are. (p. 751)

overoptimism Taking an overly optimistic view of potential outcomes. (p. 751)

oversubscription privilege Allows shareholders to purchase unsubscribed shares in a rights offering at the subscription price. (p. 444)

partnership A business formed by two or more co-owners. (p. 5)

payback period The amount of time required for an investment to generate cash flows to recover its initial cost. (p. 225)

payoff profile A plot showing the gains and losses that will occur on a contract as the result of unexpected price changes. (p. 691)

percentage of sales approach Financial planning method in which accounts are projected depending on a firm's predicted sales level. (p. 90)

perpetuity An annuity in which the cash flows continue forever. (p. 142)

planning horizon The long-range time period the financial planning process focuses on, usually the next two to five years. (p. 86)

poison pill A financial device designed to make unfriendly takeover attempts unappealing, if not impossible. (p. 672)

political risk Risk related to changes in value that arise because of political actions. (p. 627)

portfolio Group of assets such as stocks and bonds held by an investor. (p. 351)

portfolio weights Percentage of a portfolio's total value in a particular asset. (p. 351)

precautionary motive The need to hold cash as a safety margin to act as a financial reserve. (p. 553)

preferred stock Stock with dividend priority over common stock, normally with a fixed dividend rate, often without voting rights. (p. 207)

present value (PV) The current value of future cash flows discounted at the appropriate discount rate. (p. 119)

principle of diversification Principle stating that spreading an investment across a number of assets eliminates some, but not all, of the risk. (p. 363)

private placements Loans, usually long term in nature, provided directly by a limited number of investors. (p. 448)

profitability index (PI) The present value of an investment's future cash flows divided by its initial cost. Also known as *benefit/cost ratio*. (p. 238)

pro forma financial statements Financial statements projecting future years' operations. (p. 254)

prospectus Legal document describing details of the issuing corporation and the proposed offering to potential investors. (p. 426)

protective covenant Part of the indenture limiting certain transactions that can be taken during the term of the loan, usually to protect the lender's interest. (p. 176)

proxy Grant of authority by shareholder allowing for another individual to vote his or her shares. (p. 218)

proxy contests Attempts to gain control of a firm by soliciting a sufficient number of shareholder votes to replace existing management. (p. 658)

public issue The creation and sale of securities on public markets. (p. 425)

purchasing power parity (PPP) The idea that the exchange rate adjusts to keep purchasing power constant among currencies. (p. 613)

pure play approach Use of a WACC that is unique to a particular project. (p. 401)

put option An option that gives the owner the right, but not the obligation, to sell an asset. (p. 701); The right to sell an asset at a fixed price during a particular period of time. The opposite of a call option. (p. 712)

realized capital gains The increase in value of an investment, when converted to cash. (p. 39)

real option An option with payoffs in real goods. (p. 737)

real rates Interest rates or rates of return that have been adjusted for inflation. (p. 184)

recaptured depreciation The taxable difference between adjusted cost of disposal and UCC when UCC is smaller. (p. 44)

red herring A preliminary prospectus distributed to prospective investors in a new issue of securities. (p. 426)

registered form Registrar of company records ownership of each bond; payment is made directly to the owner of record. (p. 175)

regular cash dividend Cash payment made by a firm to its owners in the normal course of business, usually made four times a year. (p. 491)

regular underwriting The purchase of securities from the issuing company by an investment banker for resale to the public. (p. 428)

regulatory dialectic   The pressures financial institutions and regulatory bodies exert on each other. (p. 21)

reorganization   Financial restructuring of a failing firm to attempt to continue operations as a going concern. (p. 480)

representativeness heuristic   The reliance on stereotypes, analogies, or limited samples to form opinions about an entire class. (p. 756)

repurchase   Another method used to pay out a firm's earnings to its owners, which provides more preferable tax treatment than dividends. (p. 508)

residual dividend approach   Policy where a firm pays dividends only after meeting its investment needs while maintaining a desired debt-to-equity ratio. (p. 503)

retention ratio or plowback ratio   Retained earnings divided by net income. (pp. 91, 391)

retractable bond   Bond that may be sold back to the issuer at a prespecified price before maturity. (p. 181)

return on equity (ROE)   Net income after interest and taxes divided by average common shareholders' equity. (p. 391)

reverse split   Procedure where a firm's number of shares outstanding is reduced. (p. 512)

rights offer   A public issue of securities in which securities are first offered to existing shareholders. Also called a *rights offering*. (p. 427)

risk premium   The excess return required from an investment in a risky asset over a risk-free investment. (p. 325)

risk profile   A plot showing how the value of the firm is affected by changes in prices or rates. (p. 688)

sale and leaseback   A financial lease in which the lessee sells an asset to the lessor and then leases it back. (p. 636)

same day value   Bank makes proceeds of cheques deposited available the same day before cheques clear. (p. 562)

scenario analysis   The determination of what happens to NPV estimates when we ask what-if questions. (p. 291)

seasoned equity offering (SEO)   A new equity issue of securities by a company that has previously issued securities to the public. (p. 427)

seasoned new issue   A new issue of securities by a firm that has already issued securities in the past. (p. 426)

security market line (SML)   Positively sloped straight line displaying the relationship between expected return and beta. (p. 374)

sentiment-based risk   A source of risk to investors above and beyond firm specific risk and overall market risk. (p. 759)

sensitivity analysis   Investigation of what happens to NPV when only one variable is changed. (p. 293)

shareholder rights plan   Provisions allowing existing shareholders to purchase stock at some fixed price should an outside takeover bid take place, discouraging hostile takeover attempts. (p. 672)

shortage costs   Costs that fall with increases in the level of investment in current assets. (p. 527)

simple interest   Interest earned only on the original principal amount invested. (p. 112)

simulation analysis   A combination of scenario and sensitivity analyses. (p. 295)

sinking fund   Account managed by the bond trustee for early bond redemption. (p. 176)

smart card   Much like an automated teller machine card; one use is within corporations to control access to information by employees. (p. 561)

soft rationing   The situation that occurs when units in a business are allocated a certain amount of financing for capital budgeting. (p. 310)

sole proprietorship   A business owned by a single individual. (p. 4)

sources of cash   A firm's activities that generate cash. (p. 54)

speculative motive   The need to hold cash to take advantage of additional investment opportunities, such as bargain purchases. (p. 553)

spin-off   The distribution of shares in a subsidiary to existing parent company shareholders. (p. 679)

split-up   The splitting up of a company into two or more companies. (p. 679)

spot exchange rate   The exchange rate on a spot trade. (p. 611)

spot trade   An agreement to trade currencies based on the exchange rate today for settlement in two days. (p. 611)

spread   Compensation to the underwriter, determined by the difference between the underwriter's buying price and offering price. (p. 428); The gap between the interest rate a bank pays on deposits and the rate it charges on loans. (p. 585)

stakeholder   Anyone who potentially has a claim on a firm. (p. 12)

stand-alone principle   Evaluation of a project based on the project's incremental cash flows. (p. 251)

standard deviation   The positive square root of the variance. (p. 326)

standby fee   Amount paid to underwriter participating in standby underwriting agreement. (p. 444)

standby underwriting   Agreement where the underwriter agrees to purchase the unsubscribed portion of the issue. (p. 444)

stated interest rate   The interest rate expressed in terms of the interest payment made each period. Also known as *quoted interest rate*. (p. 146)

statement of cash flows   A firm's financial statement that summarizes its sources and uses of cash over a specified period. (p. 56)

statement of comprehensive income   Financial statement summarizing a firm's performance over a period of time. Formerly called an income statement. (p. 30)

statement of financial position   Financial statement showing a firm's accounting value on a particular date. Formerly called a balance sheet. (p. 25)

static theory of capital structure   Theory that a firm borrows up to the point where the tax benefit from an extra dollar in debt is exactly equal to the cost that comes from the increased probability of financial distress. (p. 472)

stock dividend   Payment made by a firm to its owners in the form of stock, diluting the value of each share outstanding. (p. 510)

stock exchange bid   Corporate takeover bid communicated to the shareholders through a stock exchange. (p. 657)

stock split   An increase in a firm's shares outstanding without any change in owner's equity. (p. 511)

straight bond value   The value of a convertible bond if it could not be converted into common stock. (p. 732)

straight voting   Procedure where a shareholder may cast all votes for each member of the board of directors. (p. 218)

strategic alliance   Agreement between firms to cooperate in pursuit of a joint goal. (p. 659)

strategic options   Options for future, related business products or strategies. (p. 309)

striking price   The fixed price in the option contract at which the holder can buy or sell the underlying asset. Also called the *exercise price or strike price*. (p. 712)

stripped bond/zero-coupon bond   A bond that makes no coupon payments, thus initially priced at a deep discount. (p. 179)

stripped common shares   Common stock on which dividends and capital gains are repackaged and sold separately. (p. 495)

sunk cost   A cost that has already been incurred and cannot be removed and therefore should not be considered in an investment decision. (p. 251)

sustainable growth rate (SGR)   The growth rate a firm can maintain given its debt capacity, ROE, and retention ratio. (p. 98)

swaps   Agreements to exchange two securities or currencies. (p. 608)

swap contract   An agreement by two parties to exchange, or swap, specified cash flows at specified intervals in the future. (p. 698)

sweeteners or equity kickers   A feature included in the terms of a new issue of debt or preferred shares to make the issue more attractive to initial investors. (p. 729)

syndicate   A group of underwriters formed to reduce the risk and help to sell an issue. (p. 427)

syndicated loans   Loans made by a group of banks or other institutions. (p. 448)

synergy   The positive incremental net gain associated with the combination of two firms through a merger or acquisition. (p. 661)

systematic risk   A risk that influences a large number of assets. Also called *market risk*. (p. 360)

systematic risk principle   Principle stating that the expected return on a risky asset depends only on that asset's systematic risk. (p. 366)

target cash balance   A firm's desired cash level as determined by the trade-off between carrying costs and shortage costs. (p. 554)

target payout ratio   A firm's long-term desired dividend-to-earnings ratio. (p. 507)

tax-oriented lease   A financial lease in which the lessor is the owner for tax purposes. Also called a *true lease* or a *tax lease*. (p. 636)

tender offer   A public offer by one firm to directly buy the shares from another firm. (p. 657)

terminal loss   The difference between UCC and adjusted cost of disposal when the UCC is greater. (p. 43)

term loans   Direct business loans of, typically, one to five years. (p. 448)

terms of sale   Conditions on which a firm sells its goods and services for cash or credit. (p. 573)

term structure of interest rates   The relationship between nominal interest rates on default-free, pure discount securities and time to maturity; that is, the pure time value of money. (p. 187)

trading range   Price range between highest and lowest prices at which a stock is traded. (p. 512)

transaction motive   The need to hold cash to satisfy normal disbursement and collection activities associated with a firm's ongoing operations. (p. 553)

transactions exposure   Short-run financial risk arising from the need to buy or sell at uncertain prices or rates in the near future. (p. 689)

trust receipt   An instrument acknowledging that the borrower holds certain goods in trust for the lender. (p. 541)

unbiased forward rates (UFR)   The condition stating that the current forward rate is an unbiased predictor of the future exchange rate. (p. 617)

uncovered interest parity (UIP)   The condition stating that the expected percentage change in the exchange rate is equal to the difference in interest rates. (p. 618)

unlevered cost of capital   The cost of capital of a firm that has no debt. (p. 467)

unsystematic risk   A risk that affects at most a small number of assets. Also called *unique* or *asset-specific risks*. (p. 360)

uses of cash   A firm's activities in which cash is spent. (p. 54)

value at risk (VaR)   Statistical measure of maximum loss used by banks and other financial institutions to manage risk exposures. (p. 331)

variable costs   Costs that change when the quantity of output changes. (p. 296)

variance   The average squared deviation between the actual return and the average return. (p. 326)

venture capital   Financing for new, often high-risk ventures. (p. 424)

warrant   A security that gives the holder the right to purchase shares of stock at a fixed price over a given period of time. (p. 729)

weighted average cost of capital (WACC)   The weighted average of the costs of debt and equity. (p. 395)

working capital management   Planning and managing the firm's current assets and liabilities. (p. 4)

yield to maturity (YTM)   The market interest rate that equates a bond's present value of interest payments and principal repayment with its price. (p. 166)

zero-balance account   A chequing account in which a zero balance is maintained by transfers of funds from a master account in an amount only large enough to cover cheques presented. (p. 563)

Name Index

EQUATION INDEX

Chapters	Selected Topics of Interest	Benefits to You
PART ONE OVERVIEW OF CORPORATE FINANCE		
Chapter 1 Introduction to Corporate Finance	• *New material:* Perspective on the financial crisis of 2007–2009 and its aftermath, in particular, the European government debt credit crisis	• Links to headlines on financial crisis.
	• Goal of the firm and agency problems	• Stresses value creation as the most fundamental aspect of management and describes agency issues that can arise.
	• Ethics, financial management, and executive compensation	• Brings in real-world issues concerning conflicts of interest and current controversies surrounding ethical conduct and management pay.
Chapter 2 Financial Statements, Cash Flow, and Taxes	• *New material:* Financial statements conforming to IFRS	• Links to current practice.
	• Cash flow vs. earnings	• Defines cash flow and the differences between cash flow and earnings.
	• Market values vs. book values	• Emphasizes the relevance of market values over book values.
PART TWO FINANCIAL STATEMENTS AND LONG-TERM FINANCIAL PLANNING		
Chapter 3 Working with Financial Statements	• Using financial statement information	• Discusses the advantages and disadvantages of using financial statements.
Chapter 4 Long-Term Financial Planning and Corporate Growth	• Explanation of alternative formulas for sustainable and internal growth rates	• Explanation of growth rate formulas clears up a common misunderstanding about these formulas and the circumstances under which alternative formulas are correct.
	• Thorough coverage of sustainable growth as a planning tool	• Provides a vehicle for examining the interrelationships among operations, financing, and growth.
PART THREE VALUATION OF FUTURE CASH FLOWS		
Chapter 5 Introduction to Valuation: The Time Value of Money	• First of two chapters on time value of money	• Relatively short chapter introduces the basic ideas on time value of money to get students started on this traditionally difficult topic.
Chapter 6 Discounted Cash Flow Valuation	• Second of two chapters on time value of money	• Covers more advanced time value topics with numerous examples, calculator tips, and Excel spreadsheet exhibits. Contains many real-world examples.
Chapter 7 Interest Rates and Bond Valuation	• *New material:* Discussion of bond fund strategies at time of European government debt crisis	• Links chapter material to current events.
	• "Clean" vs. "dirty" bond prices and accrued interest	• Clears up the pricing of bonds between coupon payment dates and also bond market quoting conventions.
	• Bond ratings	• Up-to-date discussion of bond rating agencies and ratings given to debt. Includes the latest descriptions of ratings used by DBRS.
Chapter 8 Stock Valuation	• *New material:* Stock valuation using multiples	• Broadens coverage of valuation techniques.
	• *New material:* Examples of shareholder activism at Canadian Pacific and Magna International	• Expands governance coverage and links chapter material to current events.
PART FOUR CAPITAL BUDGETING		
Chapter 9 Net Present Value and Other Investment Criteria	• *New material:* Enhanced discussion of multiple IRRs and modified IRR	• Clarifies properties of IRR.
	• *New material:* Practice of capital budgeting in Canada	• Current Canadian material demonstrates relevance of techniques presented.
	• First of three chapters on capital budgeting	• Relatively short chapter introduces key ideas on an intuitive level to help students with this traditionally difficult topic.
	• NPV, IRR, payback, discounted payback, and accounting rate of return	• Consistent, balanced examination of advantages and disadvantages of various criteria.

Chapters	Selected Topics of Interest	Benefits to You
Chapter 10 Making Capital Investment Decisions	• Project cash flow	• Thorough coverage of project cash flows and the relevant numbers for a project analysis.
	• Alternative cash flow definitions	• Emphasizes the equivalence of various formulas, thereby removing common misunderstandings.
	• Special cases of DCF analysis	• Considers important applications of chapter tools.
Chapter 11 Project Analysis and Evaluation	• *New material:* Detailed examples added of scenario analysis in gold mining and managerial options in zoo management	• Brings technique to life in real-world example.
	• Sources of value	• Stresses the need to understand the economic basis for value creation in a project.
	• Scenario and sensitivity "what-if" analyses	• Illustrates how to apply and interpret these tools in a project analysis.
	• Break-even analysis	• Covers cash, accounting, and financial break-even levels.

PART FIVE   RISK AND RETURN

Chapters	Selected Topics of Interest	Benefits to You
Chapter 12 Lessons from Capital Market History	• *New material:* Capital market history updated through 2011, new section on market volatility in 2008, In Their Own Words box on the crash of 2008 and the efficient markets hypothesis	• Extensively covers historical returns, volatilities, and risk premiums.
	• Geometric vs. arithmetic returns	• Discusses calculation and interpretation of geometric returns. Clarifies common misconceptions regarding appropriate use of arithmetic vs. geometric average returns.
	• Market efficiency	• Discusses efficient markets hypothesis along with common misconceptions.
Chapter 13 Return, Risk, and the Security Market Line	• *New material:* Correlations in the financial crisis	• Explains instability in correlations with a current example.
	• Diversification, systematic and unsystematic risk	• Illustrates basics of risk and return in straightforward fashion.
	• Beta and the security market line	• Develops the security market line with an intuitive approach that bypasses much of the usual portfolio theory and statistics.

PART SIX   COST OF CAPITAL AND LONG-TERM FINANCIAL POLICY

Chapters	Selected Topics of Interest	Benefits to You
Chapter 14 Cost of Capital	• Cost of capital estimation	• Contains a complete step-by-step illustration of cost of capital for publicly traded Loblaw Companies.
Chapter 15 Raising Capital	• Dutch auction IPOs	• Explains uniform price auctions using Google IPO as an example.
	• IPO "quiet periods"	• Explains the OSC's and SEC's quiet period rules.
	• Lockup agreements	• Briefly discusses the importance of lockup agreements.
	• IPOs in practice	• Takes in-depth look at IPOs of Facebook and Athabasca Oil Sands.
Chapter 16 Financial Leverage and Capital Structure Policy	• *New material:* Pecking order theory	• Expands coverage of capital structure.
	• Basics of financial leverage	• Illustrates the effect of leverage on risk and return.
	• Optimal capital structure	• Describes the basic trade-offs leading to an optimal capital structure.
	• Financial distress and bankruptcy	• Briefly surveys the bankruptcy process.
Chapter 17 Dividends and Dividend Policy	• *New material:* Recent Canadian survey evidence on dividend policy	• Survey results show the most important (and least important) factors that financial managers consider when setting dividend policy.
	• Dividends and dividend policy	• Describes dividend payments and the factors favouring higher and lower payout policies.